W9-AOG-479

WAR IN HUMAN CIVILIZATION

WAR
IN HUMAN
CIVILIZATION

AZAR GAT

OXFORD
UNIVERSITY PRESS

OXFORD
UNIVERSITY PRESS

Great Clarendon Street, Oxford OX2 6DP

Oxford University Press is a department of the University of Oxford.
It furthers the University's objective of excellence in research, scholarship,
and education by publishing worldwide in

Oxford New York

Auckland Cape Town Dar es Salaam Hong Kong Karachi
Kuala Lumpur Madrid Melbourne Mexico City Nairobi
New Delhi Shanghai Taipei Toronto

With offices in

Argentina Austria Brazil Chile Czech Republic France Greece
Guatemala Hungary Italy Japan Poland Portugal Singapore
South Korea Switzerland Thailand Turkey Ukraine Vietnam

Oxford is a registered trade mark of Oxford University Press
in the UK and in certain other countries

Published in the United States
by Oxford University Press Inc., New York

British Library Cataloguing in Publication Data
Data available

Library of Congress Cataloging in Publication Data
Gat, Azar.
  War in human civilization / Azar Gat.
      p. cm.
  Includes bibliographical references and index.
  ISBN–13: 978–0–19–926213–7 (alk. paper)
  ISBN–10: 0–19–926213–6 (alk. paper)
  1. War and society. 2. War and civilization. 3. War—History. I. Title.
  HM554. G37 2006
  303.6′6—dc22   2006017223

Typeset by RefineCatch Limited, Bungay, Suffolk
Printed in Great Britain by
Clays Ltd., St. Ives plc

ISBN 0–19–926213–6   978–0–19–926213–7

1

To my family

Contents

Contents

Preface: The Riddle of War

This is an ambitious book. It sets out to find the answers to the most fundamental questions relating to the 'riddle of war'. Why do people engage in the deadly and destructive activity of fighting? Is it rooted in human nature or is it a late cultural invention? Have people always engaged in fighting or did they start to do so only with the advent of agriculture, the state, and civilization? How were these, and later, major developments in human history affected by war and, in turn, how did they affect war? Under what conditions, if at all, can war be eliminated, and is it declining at present?

These questions are not new and have seemingly resisted conclusive answers to the point that both questions and answers appear almost as clichés. In reality, however, they have very rarely been subjected to rigorous comprehensive investigation and, indeed, have largely been regarded as being too 'big' for serious scholarly treatment. With war being connected to everything else and everything else being connected to war, explaining war and tracing its development in relation to human development in general almost amount to a theory and history of everything. As so much is relevant to the subject, one is required to read pretty much 'everything' and become sufficiently expert in many fields. These are the prerequisites that it has been necessary to meet to produce this book.

Indeed, in pursuing the subject of war the book draws on information and insights from a wide range of scholarly disciplines and branches of knowledge, most notably: animal behaviour (ethology), evolutionary theory, evolutionary psychology, anthropology, archaeology, history, historical sociology, and political science. Separated from each other by disciplinary walls, they all too often remain self-contained and oblivious of, if not down-right hostile to, the other's methods, perspectives, and bodies of knowledge. Each discipline has its particular subject matter, choice methods for studying it, a set of dominating research questions, and, not least, distinctive terminology, historical development, and fashionable concerns. Together, all these constitute a disciplinary 'culture' and set the criteria for each discipline's 'standard research'—assimilated through professional training—which defines what constitutes good questions, acceptable answers, and a

Preface

legitimate scholarly pursuit. In consequence, not unlike the different cultures, societies, and states dealt with in this book, different disciplines habitually find the others alien, their language quirky, and their scholarly agenda misconstrued. Even when dealing with related subjects, they find it difficult to communicate or to make the others' work relevant to their own interests. One might even say that, *particularly* when dealing with related subjects, mutual scepticism, disdain, and even derision often prevail between disciplines—some of which is justified, because disciplines tend to be stronger on their special pursuits and weaker on others. Thus scholars in the humanities and social sciences have long been trained to believe that biology and human biology are practically irrelevant to their subjects. Historians are typically horrified by social scientists' careless treatment of the particularities of each time and place and by their often crude modelling, whereas the latter, for their part, believe that historians are so immersed in reconstructing the minutiae of particular periods and societies as to be professionally incapable of seeing any broader and more general picture.

The broad interdisciplinary perspective that guides this book is intended to create a whole that is larger than the sum of its parts, because the book is not a survey of existing knowledge, or merely a synthesis, let alone a textbook, but is designed as a fully fledged research book throughout. As much as it builds on and enormously profits from the wealth of scholarly literature in the various disciplines, the book takes issue with many extant studies and theses on almost every point with which it deals. As with the proverbial forest and trees, a broad and interdisciplinary perspective has the potential to generate significant new insights that may all too often be missed by, and be of benefit to, specialized scholars working on their particular turfs. Obviously, for such an undertaking to be scholarly sound nor can the forest be substituted for the trees, and everything must be firmly grounded in existing research and fact. To ensure that the work offered here meets the most rigorous standards and that its fruit reaches the various scholarly communities concerned, I made a point of publishing themes from it in article form in scholarly journals of the relevant disciplines. For the errors that have inevitably still found their way into this book I hope to be excused.

It should be stressed, however, that even though this book is primarily a scholarly enterprise, it is written with an eye to the general reader. As much as possible, the more technical points, which are of greater interest to scholars, have been included in the endnotes, which the reader can choose

x

whether or not to follow. Most of all, the book is an invitation to participate in an intellectual adventure. Reading for and writing it were done with a consuming interest and were a source of immense pleasure for me. Hopefully, this will filter through to the reader.

This project is the culmination of a life-long passion for the study of war. One wonders how growing up in Israel aroused and nourished that passion. I turned eight in June 1967, the month of the Arab–Israeli Six Day War, when I was finishing the second grade and acquiring fluent reading. From about that time, the subject of war became the centre of my reading and thought. Eventually this led to a doctorate at Oxford, an academic career, and the writing of a series of books on modern European military thought. I reached the stage where I felt more prepared to get to grips with the phenomenon of war in a search for deeper understanding of what ultimately it was all about. Trained as a historian with a preference for painting on wide canvases and teaching in a political science department, I still had to familiarize myself with wholly new fields of knowledge—indeed, new worlds. At the personal level, if at no other, this has been the most rewarding experience.

The book has been nine years in the making, between 1996 and 2005. When I began working on it the Cold War had ended and a New World Order of peace had been proclaimed. I finish the book after the 11 September 2001 attacks in the USA, which foreshadow the possibility of unconventional terror and again make war a topical issue and the subject of wide public interest and concern. Although these events have inevitably left their mark on the book, particularly on its penultimate chapter, the motivation behind the book and its main arguments are independent of them. At the same time, aimed at a comprehensive understanding, this book will, it is hoped, be of some use to anybody whom world developments—past and present—have made to ponder the puzzle of war.

Tel Aviv
August 2005

Acknowledgements

During the years that this book was in the making, I incurred many pleasant debts to people and institutions that lent me their help and support. Friends and colleagues took the time to read and comment on various drafts, offering invaluable advice. At the top of the list stands Alexander Yakobson, the only person who read every chapter of the book as it was completed; I grew to rely on Alex's wisdom so much that I would not have it any other way. Parts of the typescript were read by Abraham Ben-Zvi, Eyal Chowers, Gil Friedman, Sir Michael Howard, Paul Kennedy, Robert Lieber, Zeev Maoz, John Mueller, Geoffrey Parker, Yossi Shain, and David Vital. I am deeply thankful to them all.

Annual visiting appointments, one at the Mershon Center of the Ohio State University, directed by R. Ned Lebow, and another as the Goldman Visiting Professor at Georgetown University, facilitated the writing of this book. Tel Aviv University granted me two sabbatical years. Expenses involved in producing the book were covered in part by the Ezer Weitzman Chair of National Security, of which I am the incumbent. I am grateful to the Weitzman family and to the donor Mr Edouard Seroussi for their support. I benefited from the opportunity to try out my ideas in three lectures that I gave at the Center for New Institutional Social Science, Washington University, St Louis, at the invitation of its Director Itai Sened. Among several other venues for such lectures was the conference on revolutionary war and total war, organized by Roger Chickering and Stig Foerster at the German Historical Institute in Washington, DC.

Finally, I am grateful to the *Journal of Anthropological Research*, *Anthropological Quarterly*, *Anthropos*, *Journal of Strategic Studies*, *Comparative Studies of Six City-State Cultures*, edited by Mogens H. Hansen, and *World Politics*, for allowing me to use material that previously appeared in them in article form.

List of Illustrations

List of Illustrations

List of Illustrations

Maps

Tables

Part 1

WARFARE IN THE FIRST TWO MILLION YEARS: ENVIRONMENT, GENES, AND CULTURE

1

Introduction:
The 'Human State of Nature'

Is war grounded, perhaps inescapably, in human nature? Does it have primordial roots in humans' innate violence and deadly aggressive behaviour against their own kind? This seems to be the first and most commonly asked question when people ponder the enigma of war.

But how do we observe 'human nature'? All animal species, except humans, have a more or less fixed way of life, which is predominantly determined by their genes, and which changes, if at all, only with the species itself in the relatively slow pace of biological evolution and can thus be meaningfully addressed as 'natural' for them. For this reason, animals have a zoology, an ethology (the science of animal behaviour), and, in geological time, an evolution, but they have no history. By contrast, humans evolved mammalian learning capacity to unprecedented heights and explosive potential. On top of their biological inheritance, they have evolved and pass on to their contemporaries and descendants the accumulated and ever more complex array of artefacts, techniques, modes of behaviour and communication, and belief systems known as culture. Vastly faster than biological evolution, cultural evolution has dramatically transformed and diversified the human way of life. It can be regarded as humanity's most distinctive trait.

Humans have lived in a myriad of cultures, which have been constantly in flux, substantially different from one another and all, in a way, 'artificial'. We have been carried to an almost incredible distance from our origins. As a result, extreme relativists, empiricists, and historicists have traditionally held that humans are almost infinitely elastic, questioning whether anything called 'human nature' exists in any meaningful sense. At most, it is agreed that nature and nurture, genes and the environment, biology and culture, 'hardware' and 'software' are closely interwoven and practically inseparable in the shaping of humans. Both components, and their wealth of inter-actions, have constantly to be kept in mind when one seeks to study the remarkable human evolution.

And yet, at the starting point of this interaction, there is still a very strong sense in which we can speak, for humans, about the 'state of nature' as something other than a seventeenth-century philosophical abstraction. During 99.5 per cent of the almost two million years of evolution of our genus *Homo*, all humans lived a fairly distinctive way of life, that of hunter–gatherers. Only 10,000 years ago in some areas, and even more recently in others—a brief moment in evolutionary terms—did humans turn to agri-culture and animal husbandry. This change, which is discussed later, was a cultural innovation, involving scarcely any significant biological change. Thus, modern humans evolved biologically over millions of years in adapt-ing to the selective pressures of hunter–gatherer existence. In the anthropo-logical literature, the concept of 'primitive war', which makes no distinction between hunter–gatherers and pre-state agriculturalists, is commonly used to describe 'original' warfare. Although this category has some value, it should be realized that in evolutionary terms it lumps together the abo-riginal condition of all humans with a quite recent cultural innovation. Agricultural society, even more recently topped by the growth of the state and of civilization, is the tip of the iceberg in human history, the vast depth of which in time is obscured in most people's minds by the scarcity of information.

To be sure, human hunter–gatherer existence was never quite uniform. It varied in adaptation to diverse ecological niches, and these adaptations themselves evolved with the accelerating evolution of the genus *Homo* itself over its long period of existence. As the revolutionary advances in the molecular study of DNA have revealed, all humans living today are closely related and belong to the species *Homo sapiens sapiens*, whose remains have been found in Africa from more than 100,000 years ago. The celebrated cave and rock art and other exquisite artefacts of *Homo sapiens sapiens*, which reached new heights during the period known as the Upper Palaeolithic, or Upper Old Stone Age, between 35,000 and 15,000 years ago, are cultural evidence—in addition to the anatomical one of skeletal remains—of a mind that is indistinguishable from ours in its capacity. Varieties of archaic *Homo sapiens* date back to up to half a million years ago. They were preceded from about two million years ago by *Homo erectus*, the first human species that led a hunter–gatherer existence throughout much of the Old World. In technical sophistication, tool refinement, use of fire, level of communication, and ability to plan ahead—to mention just some variables—later hunter–gatherers were more sophisticated and successful than their biologically more primitive predecessors in the genus *Homo*.[1] I touch on some of the differences in hunter–gatherers' existence that are relevant to the subject later. Still, there is also a great deal of similarity and continuity in the hunter–gatherer way of life, extending from the origins of the genus *Homo* to the present.

So, did humans, in their evolutionary natural environment and evolutionary natural way of life as hunter–gatherers, fight? Was fighting an intrinsic aspect of their particular mode of adaptation, moulded by selective pressures for millions of years? In other words, has their evolutionary path made warfare 'natural' to humans? Or, alternatively, did fighting come later, only after culture really took off, and is it therefore 'unnatural' to humans? The two antithetical classical answers to this question have been advanced in the seventeenth and eighteenth centuries—after the Europeans' great geographical voyages brought them into contact with a vast variety of aboriginal peoples—by Thomas Hobbes and Jean-Jacques Rousseau. For Hobbes, the human 'state of nature' was one of endemic 'warre', murderous feuds for gain, safety, and reputation, a war of every man against every man, which made life 'poore, nasty, brutish, and short' (*Leviathan*, 1651, 13). People were rescued and elevated from this condition only by the creation of the state, the coercive power of which enforced at least internal peace. By contrast, according to Rousseau's *Discourse on the Origins and Foundation of Inequality among Mankind* (1755), aboriginal humans lived sparsely and generally harmoniously in nature, peacefully exploiting her abundant resources. Only with the coming of agriculture, demographic growth, private property, division of class and state coercion, claimed Rousseau, did war, and all the other ills of civilization, spring up.

So suggestive and persuasive were both these views of the past that they have remained with us, with little variation, since their inception. During most of the nineteenth century, the period in which European supremacy and belief in 'progress' and in the gradual uplifting ascent of civilization were in their apogee, it was mainly the Hobbesian image of the 'brute' and the 'savage' that dominated, colouring ethnographic reports as westerners expanded their rule over the globe. Conversely, during the twentieth century, as disillusionment with 'progress' and civilization grew and European supremacy began to wane, it was the Rousseauite idyllic picture of the aboriginal that increasingly dominated anthropology.

The past decades have seen an explosion of field and theoretical work on themes related to this subject, which have greatly enhanced our knowledge and which call for a new comprehensive attempt at finally resolving the enigma. Three sources in particular have yielded a wealth of information and insights: first, broad empirical context for comparison and contrast is offered by the study of animal aggression and fighting; second, empirical evidence relating to the question of fighting among hunter–gatherers is provided by the study of hunter–gatherer populations that have survived to the present or were closely observed by westerners in the recent past; this evidence is supplemented by archaeological findings relating to prehistoric hunter–gatherers; and, third, a general explanatory perspective is suggested by evolutionary theory.

OF BEASTS AND MEN

During the 1960s, the question of why humans fought appeared to have become more perplexing than it had ever been before, as a number of separate and sometimes contradictory ideas from within and on the fringes of the scientific community regarding animal and human aggression struck public consciousness with tremendous effect.

One such idea was advanced by popular writer Robert Ardrey, in his *African Genesis* (1961) and other best-selling books. At that time, zoologists believed that our closest relatives, the chimpanzees, were vegetarian, non-violent, and non-territorial. It was an image that resonated well with the 1960s' creed of 'return to nature'. Ardrey claimed that it had been our ancestors' adoption of hunting and meat eating that had turned them into 'killer apes', predators who regularly turned their new skills and weapons against their own kind. The idea had been suggested to him by palaeontologist (researcher of fossilized bones) Raymond Dart, who had interpreted skull wounds in specimens of Australopithecus as weapon inflicted. Cerebrally ape-like, but erect and bi-pedal species, the Australopithecians are believed to have been the ancestors of the genus *Homo* and its link to the apes. The hominid line is estimated to have diverged from the chimpanzee some seven million years ago, and Australopithecians have been found to have lived until one million years ago. Dart's theory did not hold long, however. Since the 1960s palaeontology has advanced by leaps and bounds. We now know infinitely more about Australopithecians: they were predominantly vegetarians; no stone tools related to them have been found; and the celebrated skull wounds are believed to have been caused by a leopard. This, however, has not necessarily invalidated the claim about *humans* becoming killers with the adoption of hunting and meat eating. This idea was advanced by the anthropologist S. L. Washburn and popularized by the zoologist Desmond Morris in his best-selling book, *The Naked Ape* (1966).

Other extremely influential ideas about animal and human aggression were advanced by Nobel laureate and co-founder of ethology, Konrad Lorenz, in his *On Aggression* (1966; German original 1963). In response to Ardrey, Lorenz pointed out that, among animals, fighting—that is, violence within the species (intraspecific)—bore little relationship to predation. Contrary to popular ideas, herbivores fight among themselves no less, and sometimes more, viciously and frequently than carnivores. However, Lorenz claimed that animals very rarely fought members of their own species to death. In the hunter–prey relationship, killing is necessary because consumption of the prey is the rationale of the whole exercise. By contrast, intraspecific violent conflict is mostly about access to resources and females. If one adversary stops the fight by retreating or signalling submission, further violence becomes unnecessary. According to Lorenz, signals of surrender and submission serve as biological cues that turn off the victor's aggression. Furthermore, if the adversary's will, rather than life, is the target, demonstration—which has a smaller role in the hunter–prey relationship—is almost as important as brute force. The adversary can simply be intimidated by threatening displays of size, strength, and vigour.

Lorenz's expertise was the varieties of animal displays of strength and signals of submission. He termed the resulting form of animal intraspecific fighting 'ritualized'. The term is misleading. Ritual implies merely going through the motions. Here, however, was a high stakes–high risk–high gain–conflict, involving both display and actual force, and intended to deter or enforce. At any rate, whereas Ardrey drew a divide between humans and chimpanzees in respect of deadly fighting, Lorenz's claims drew an even sharper divide between humans—who regularly kill each other in fighting—and all other animal species. Human violence now appeared unique and, therefore, enigmatic, and called for some special explanation. Lorenz, for instance, suggested that in evolutionary terms human weapons, and hence lethality, developed too recently and too fast for the mechanisms of intraspecific restraint to catch up. In any case, the idea that 'we are the most ruthless species that has ever marched the earth' became widely accepted.[2]

As it happened, some of the most fundamental ideas that stood at the basis of the 1960s' influential theories have since been all but reversed by the scientific community. To begin with, field study—pioneered by Jane Goodall at Gombe, in Tanzania, from the mid-1960s, and joined by other researchers since—for the first time provided a close, sustained, and reliable scientific observation on the chimpanzees' way of life in their natural habitat. The findings have been revolutionary. For instance, it has been revealed that rather than being vegetarian, chimpanzees (and other primates) crave meat as a prime food. Primarily, although not exclusively, males, acting in co-operation, isolate, hunt, and avidly eat other animals, mostly monkeys and small mammals, but also straying, weak or infant alien chimpanzees. (Savannah baboons also hunt, if somewhat less successfully.) Furthermore, the chimpanzees' group—several dozen strong and consisting of males and females with their infants—has been found to be highly territorial. The males patrol the boundaries of the group's territory and fiercely attack any intruder, including foreign chimpanzees (but not lone females coming to join the group). They also aggressively raid foreign territories.

Goodall documented a conflict between two groups that lasted several years. The males of one of the groups invaded and gradually, one by one, isolated and killed first the males and then the other members of the other group, finally annexing its territory. Instances of murderous aggression, even by females, especially against infants that were not their own, have also been observed *within* the group. Finally, on occasion, chimpanzees would threaten with, beat with and throw sticks and stones.[3] From being humans' idyllic antithesis in the 1960s' culture, the friendly, playfully naughty, and intelligent, but also jealous, quarrelsome, killing, and even warring, chimpanzees now increasingly mirror what we have commonly thought about ourselves. There is nothing particularly exceptional about humans in this respect.

Not only the divide between humans and chimpanzees with respect to fighting and killing but also the much broader divide between humans and the rest of the animal kingdom has been erased. Rapidly expanding research has drastically altered scientific perceptions. In contrast to Lorenz's claim, intraspecific killing has been found to be the norm and one of the main causes of animal mortality. It is true that between mature males fighting for access to resources and females, the weaker or loser normally decides at some stage to cut its losses and break off the fight, either by displaying submission, if the fight takes place within a group of social animals, or by retreating. The same applies to intergroup fighting in social animals, such as lions, wolves, hyenas, baboons, and rats. Nevertheless, severe wounds inflicted during a fight are often a cause of mortality, either directly or by diminishing the animal's capacity to obtain food. In addition, beaten, deprived, and submissive animals have been found to be more susceptible to disease and to have considerably shorter life expectancy. Furthermore, by far the most vulnerable to intraspecific violence are infants. For example, a new leader of a lion pride will systematically kill all the cubs of the previous monarch, despite their mothers' desperate efforts to hide them. It does so in order to enable the lionesses to come into oestrus and have its own offspring, which is not possible as long as they raise other cubs.

Langur monkey and gorilla males have been observed to behave in a similar manner. Solitary animals, such as the rest of the big cats and bears, try to do the same against violent maternal resistance whenever they find the opportunity. Presumably for similar reasons, chimpanzee males have also been observed to kill infants that are not their own when the group is joined by a nursing mother. Even more widespread is the intraspecific elimination of alien infants, chicks, and eggs, carried out in order to get rid of actual or potential competition for resources or in cannibalism. This cause of mortality is particularly high among species with an extreme so-called 'r' strategy of reproduction, which maximizes the number of offspring rather than parental care of fewer offspring ('K' strategy). Finally, young siblings fiercely compete for nourishment. In some species, for instance among eagle chicks, but also among rabbits and other seemingly harmless creatures, this competition regularly results in merciless fighting in times of food shortage, when the strong might kill, and often cannibalize, the weaker siblings.[4] Nature documentaries have vividly brought all this home to millions of television viewers, completing the demise of the 1960s' perceptions.

Leading authorities have estimated that the rate of intraspecific killing among humans is similar and in some cases greatly inferior to that of other animal species. According to one of them, it is in fact many times inferior to that of any mammalian species studied.[5] In any case, the similarity is striking: most killing in the animal kingdom is carried out for prey, as it is with humans (animal hunting), but there is also substantial killing of conspecifics—one's own kind—in competition for the opportunity to prey and mate and for other vital activities, as it is with humans. Thus, in a few decades, the scholarly picture has changed drastically. At least in the *scale* of intraspecific killing, humans have lost their supposed uniqueness and are no longer regarded as an exception in killing their kind.

To be sure, the scale and form of killing in nature are not uniform among all species. They depend on each species' particular mode of adaptation, especially its forms of subsistence and mating, and of course they also vary between individuals within a species. For example, although the common chimpanzee (*Pan troglodytes*) has been found to resemble humans in its violent behaviour, the more recently discovered pygmy chimpanzee or bonobo (*Pan paniscus*) exhibits an almost idyllic life of free sex and little violence, much as in the 1960s' perceptions of the common chimpanzee.[6] Thus human fighting has to be examined in context and detail. Why and how did humans fight in the 'state of nature'? How did this stand in comparison with patterns prevailing in the animal kingdom? And even before that, did hunter–gatherers fight at all? Perhaps humans in the state of nature are exceptional, and closer to the bonobo, in their avoidance of fighting and killing—quite the opposite of the view that we have just discussed? Who was right after all—Hobbes or Rousseau? Surprisingly, despite the wealth of evidence, this last is a question about which anthropologists have failed to reach a definite conclusion. It must be settled first.

2

Peaceful or War-like: Did Hunter–Gatherers Fight?

It was the Rousseauite school that increasingly dominated anthropology during the twentieth century, allied as it was with the liberal critique of civilization's 'unnatural' and harmful traits. The school's view regarding human fighting was yet another idea that gained supremacy—capturing the public's attention—in the 1960s, and is still influential today. Its most famous representative was the anthropologist Margaret Mead. The title of her article, 'Warfare is only an invention—not a biological necessity' (1940), seems to epitomize the Rousseauite attitude. In actuality, the weight of Mead's article was more on the second half of the title. She rightly objected to biological determinism, pointing out that some societies fought whereas others did not. Her answer as to why this was so—fighting as a cultural invention in response to particular circumstances—was less than satisfactory, but she was well aware that even among peoples of the most basic social organization—hunter–gatherers—some, if not most, of them engaged in warfare.[1] It was not an awareness shared by all later anthropologists. Many of them have been impressed by the theories that denied intraspecific killing among animals and by the apparent absence of warfare among some extant hunter–gatherer peoples studied in the 1950s and 1960s, such as the !Kung Bushmen of the Kalahari Desert, the Hadza of east Africa, and the Pygmies of central Africa. These anthropologists have held that, because hunter–gatherers were thinly spread, supposedly untied to a territory, and held few possessions, they did not engage in fighting. Warfare has been assumed to have come later, with agriculture and the state. This view still lingers on, mostly but not solely among non-experts. It involves a curious selective blindness to whole aspects of the evidence that we possess about hunter–gatherers.[2]

A powerful attack on the dominant Rousseauite view in the anthropological study of 'primitive war' has been delivered in Lawrence Keeley's excellent *War before Civilization: The myth of the peaceful savage* (1996). Amassing overwhelming evidence, Keeley has all but demolished the doctrine that pre-state societies were peaceful and, hence, that warfare is a later cultural invention. All the same, his book has a major lacuna, with the result that the question is only pushed one stage back to its true Rousseauite focal point. An archaeologist of the Neolithic period, when people adopted agriculture and animal husbandry, Keeley has cited extensive evidence of warfare, predominantly derived from a great variety of primitive, pre-state, agricultural societies from around the globe and across time. However, as mentioned above, agriculture and animal husbandry are themselves relatively recent cultural inventions, taken up by human societies only during the past 10,000 years. Might it not then be possible that warfare emerged only with these major developments, when people began to possess valuable stored food and other property that was worth fighting for, as, indeed, was Rousseau's original claim? This would mean that human fighting began, not during the past five millennia, with the emergence of the state, but from ten millennia ago, with the transition to agriculture. Thus, the fundamental question remains open: were people peaceful before that point in time, during the over 100,000 years of existence of our species, *Homo sapiens sapiens*, and the two million years of existence of our genus, *Homo*—that is, during the human 'evolutionary state of nature'? Because during that vast timespan people lived as hunter–gatherers, the evidence of fighting from pre-state agricultural societies may not apply to them. Therefore, in order really to resolve the Hobbes–Rousseau debate, the concept of 'primitive warfare' that lumps together hunter–gatherers and pre-state agriculturalists must be disentangled, and attention fixed on hunter–gatherers alone in their relationship with each other.[3]

The scholarly study of hunter–gatherers is yet another field that has developed exponentially since the 1960s. It was inaugurated as a comparative field of research with an important conference and the ensuing volume *Man the Hunter* (1968), edited by Richard Lee and Irven DeVore. Many other excellent studies have followed since. The picture that has emerged from these studies is of neither a Hobbesian hell nor a Rousseauite paradise of pre-sin innocence, but a more mundane complex. In a Rousseauite vein, hunter–gatherers have been found to have laboured less, had more leisure, and been generally healthier than agriculturalists. 'The original affluent society' was the hyperbolic catchphrase coined in the 1960s to describe these findings. Still, periodic droughts, or any other adverse climatic condition affecting their subsistence, often decimated them. Also, on the bleak side, pressure on resources was avoided by widespread infanticide, especially of baby girls. Hobbes's image of an endemic state of 'warre' and lack of security in the absence of state authority has been found to be perhaps somewhat overdrawn, but not by that much. Quarrels were rife among hunter–gatherers as among the rest of humankind, resulting in very high homicide rates among most hunter–gatherer peoples, much higher than in any modern industrial society. And yes, intergroup fighting and killing were widespread among them.

Hunter–gatherers lived in extended family groups of several generations (clans or, in more recent anthropological parlance, local groups). As with the chimpanzees, these groups have been universally found to consist of between 20 and 70 members, most typically 25. As with the chimpanzees, they were mostly patrilineal—that is, it is more often the females who came from outside, whereas the males stayed in the group and were therefore closely related. Unlike the chimpanzees, several family (local) groups came together in a regional group. The regional group or a number of related regional groups often represented a 'dialect tribe' and had their own name and a distinct sense of self-identity as a 'people'. Depending on the resource richness of its environment, the regional group could live fairly concentrated together or assemble seasonally for festivals, in which common rituals were performed and marriages were agreed upon and took place.[4] Computer simulations have shown that the number 150–200 is the minimum required for the balance and stability of an endogamous marriage circle.[5] Indeed, regional group size has been found to vary from 175 up to 1,400 people in extreme cases, with 500 as a common average. Relationships with neighbouring regional groups included exchange, common ritual, alliances—and warfare.

Few hunter–gatherer peoples have survived in their original way of life

13

until close to the present, and they too have been fast transformed by contact with the modern world. These extant peoples are now recognized to have had special features that are not wholly representative of the full range of the prehistorical hunter–gatherer way of life. They were largely confined to poor environments, such as the Arctic and deserts, which were unsuitable for agriculture. In some cases they were pushed there by the pressure of more populous agricultural communities, on whose margins they held a sometimes tenuous and subservient existence. In consequence, because of the low productivity of the environments that most surviving hunter–gatherers inhabited, they had very low population densities: fewer than one person per square mile, often far fewer, was the norm. They moved a lot to subsist and had very few possessions. As a result, they were remarkably egalitarian. Their main division of labour and status was related to sex and age. This is the prevailing image of simple hunter–gatherers, but it is partly misleading. Before the advent of agriculture, hunter–gatherers inhabited the entire globe, including its richest ecological environments. In many places, they still did when contact with westerners was made in modern times. Under these conditions, hunter–gatherers' population densities, subsistence modes, mobility, and social order were considerably more varied than they are among more recent hunter–gatherer populations. All the same, fighting is recorded across the whole range of hunter–gatherer societies, from the simplest to the most complex.

Our knowledge of hunter–gatherer fighting during the Pleistocene, the period spanning most of human evolution from 2,000,000 to 10,000 years ago, is inherently inconclusive. The evidence from these distant times is extremely patchy, and that which might indicate warfare can also be interpreted differently. Stone axes, spearheads, and arrowheads have a dual purpose and could have been used only for hunting. Wooden shields, leather body armour, and tusk helmets—familiar from historical hunter–gatherers —do not preserve. In fossilized injured bones, hunting and daily-life accidents are difficult to distinguish from those caused by fighting.[6] Nevertheless, comprehensive examinations of large specimens of such bones have concluded that at least some of them were injured in combat. In some cases, arrow- and spearheads were found buried in the injured bones and skulls. A Neanderthal man from some 50,000 years ago, found with a stabbing wound in the chest from a right-handed opponent, is our earliest documented specimen. Later cases of interpersonal lethal injuries among

Neanderthal men have also been identified. The evidence becomes more plentiful as we move closer to the present; preservation is better not only for natural reasons but because people began to bury their dead. At Sandalja II in the former Yugoslavia a group of 29 people from the Upper Palaeolithic have been found with their skulls smashed. Violent injuries were also found to be very common in Upper Palaeolithic cemeteries in the former Czechoslovakia. In the Late Palaeolithic cemetery at Gebel Sahaba in Egyptian Nubia over 40 per cent of the men, women, and children buried there were victims of stone projectile injuries, some of them multiple.[7] Moreover, evidence of fighting among historically recorded hunter–gatherers, whose way of life was not very far from that of their Upper Palaeolithic ancestors, is abundant.

During the 1960s cases of hunter–gatherer peoples among whom group fighting appeared to be unknown attracted all the attention. The most prominent of those cases was that of the central Canadian Arctic Eskimos. This is hardly surprising. In the first place, they inhabited one of the harshest environments on earth and were very thinly spread. Second, the resources on which they depended were also diffuse and could not be monopolized. It is not that these Eskimos lacked violence. They had a very high rate of quarrels, blood feuds, and homicide. Moreover, as we see later, to both their east and west, in Greenland and coastal Alaska, where conditions were different, the Eskimos were both strongly territorial and war-like.[8] As mentioned earlier, the Kalahari Bushmen, east African Hadza, and central African Pygmies were also celebrated as entirely peaceful in 1960s' anthropology. Being among the last hunter–gatherer populations that could be observed in their traditional way of life, they achieved a sort of 'paradigmatic' status.[9] However, there is clear evidence that in the past they had been involved in fighting not only with their agricultural and pastoral neighbours, who had pressured them into their current isolated environment, but also among themselves even before contact with non-hunter–gatherers. Recent homicide rates among them were also very high, many times higher than in the modern United States of America, which registers the highest rates of homicide of all industrial societies. Only with the coming of state authority and state police in Canada and southern Africa did violence rates decline.[10]

For all that, the argument here is not that *all* hunter–gatherers invariably fight. Human societies—be they hunter–gatherer, agricultural or industrial—have lived in peace for longer or shorter periods. Why this is so is discussed later. Yet most societies observed to date have engaged in warfare from time to time, including the simplest hunter–gatherers. One comparative study of 99 hunter–gatherer bands belonging to 37 different cultures found that practically all of them engaged in warfare at the time of the study or had ceased to do so in the recent past. According to another study, in 90 per cent of hunter–gatherer societies there was violent conflict, and most of them engaged in intergroup warfare at least every two years, similar to or more than the rest of human societies. The author of yet other comprehensive cross-cultural studies similarly concluded that 'the greater the dependence upon hunting, the greater the frequency of warfare'.[11]

As already mentioned, simple hunter–gatherers, who were thinly dispersed and nomadic, and had no substantial possessions, are at the centre of the Rousseauite claim. Supposedly, they were peaceful because they had little to fight over and could always choose to go elsewhere rather than fight. Simple hunter–gatherers are particularly significant because, during most of the two million years of the Pleistocene and until about 35,000 years ago (the Upper Palaeolithic), *all* humans were apparently hunter–gatherers of the simple sort. Yet the evidence from historical simple hunter–gatherers is that they fought, and with substantial casualties. It is true that in many of the known cases the evidence can be disputed because of outside interference that might have distorted the original, 'pure' hunter–gatherer way of life. There is a paradox here that is very difficult to overcome. Hunter–gatherers have no written records. Thus the evidence about them must inevitably derive mainly from literate peoples who came into contact with them. Until such contact is made, there is a thick veil of darkness around them, pierced only by the tenuous light of archaeology. However, as with the elementary particles of physics, contact itself changes the observed. Most of the recent and historical hunter–gatherers interacted with agriculturalists and pastoralists, among other things coveting and stealing their products and livestock, which resulted in violence. Some have been profoundly affected by contact with westerners. All such cases constitute 'contaminated samples' for the purpose of testing the Rousseauite hypothesis.

An example is shown by the inhabitants of the Americas and Oceania (including hunter–gatherers) who were decimated by European epidemics to which they had practically no natural immunity. These epidemics quickly spread into regions that had not yet come into direct contact with the newcomers, affecting their demography and social patterns even before the white man arrived. For another example, the simple hunter–gatherers of the North American Great Plains acquired the horse and the gun from the Europeans from the middle of the seventeenth century, a change that revolutionized and greatly expanded the millennia-old bison- (buffalo-) hunting way of life. In addition, the Indians of the Great Plains began to trade furs and hides with the westerners. Both these factors contributed to the Plains Indians' famous bellicosity. Despite archaeological evidence to the contrary and the opinion of all scholars on the subject, the notion that these Indians had been peaceful before western contact took root during the high tide of Rousseauism.[12]

The problem, then, is how to observe as 'pure' examples of hunter–gatherers as possible, little affected by contact with agriculturalists and pastoralists, to see whether they fought among themselves.

SIMPLE HUNTER–GATHERERS: THE AUSTRALIAN 'LABORATORY'

Fortunately for our subject, we have one almost ideal large-scale 'laboratory' or 'conservation' of simple hunter–gatherer peoples in historical times, which is as clear as we can get of outside interference. This is the vast continent of Australia, which was exclusively inhabited by the Aboriginal hunter–gatherers. Surprisingly, the invaluable uniqueness of this 'laboratory' has not been sufficiently appreciated in recent anthropological literature, overshadowed as it has been by later field studies of the African Bushmen, whose scholarly value is much inferior to that of the Australians.[13] The Europeans arrived in Australia late in colonial terms, with settlement beginning in 1788, spreading slowly, and being even slower to affect remote areas of the interior and north. There had been no agriculturalists and pastoralists at all in Australia before the European arrival. The continent was the home of an estimated 300,000 hunter–gatherers, distributed among 400–700 regional groups, which averaged 500–600 people each. To be sure, here too no complete 'isolation' can be claimed: the natives of southern Australia were eliminated before they could be studied; European epidemics affected more remote parts, reducing the natives' numbers even before direct contact was made; in the north there had been some Aboriginal contact with the natives of Melanesia.[14] All the same, the Aborigines' hunter–gatherer way of life was of the simplest sort there is. As a result of their isolation, they did not even have the bow, invented in the rest of the world some 20,000 years ago and assumed by some scholars to have enhanced, or even inaugurated, warfare, by allowing people to fight from afar and, hence, from relative safety. Of truly long-range weapons, only the famous boomerang was used in Australia. Nevertheless, as Mead herself—although not some of her colleagues and disciples—was well aware, warfare, with spear, club, stone knife, and wooden shield (unlike the others, clearly a specialized fighting rather than a hunting device) had been widespread in Australia.[15] Indeed, fighting scenes with the whole range of armament are extensively depicted in Aboriginal rock art dating back at least 10,000 years.[16]

As some scholars have pointed out, even low-population densities and relative mobility over low-yield terrain do not necessarily mean lack of competition and territoriality. Low-yield environment simply requires larger territories for subsistence. Nor does wide spacing out mean that there are empty spaces to move to. As a rule, there are none, because species quickly fill up their particular habitat and soon push against its boundaries. Mobility and nomadic existence are practised *within* a circumscribed territory. Many animal species that also require very large territories for subsistence and are therefore widely spaced out—such as lion prides—hotly defend their territories against intruders that try to improve their lot. The same applies to humans. Contrary to a lingering popular impression from 1960s' anthropology, evidence of territoriality exists for most hunter–gatherer societies examined. Indeed, some territories are better, have richer wildlife, than others and are, therefore, much coveted. Access to scarce resources, such as water in arid or semi-arid areas, is the object of even greater competition.[17] Furthermore, as mentioned earlier, in the past simple hunter–gatherers inhabited not only isolated arid areas but also, indeed mainly, the world's most fertile environmental niches. These were usually to be found along rivers (especially river mouths), swamps, and seashores, which abounded in exploitable wildlife and were intensely competed for.

In Australia, as elsewhere, such lush environments had much denser populations than arid areas: up to two people per square kilometre or six people per kilometre of coastline—a high density for hunter–gatherers.[18] This resulted in much greater contact and much more competition with other groups. Again, such conditions were common enough among late Pleistocene hunter–gatherers. An anthropological model sensibly suggests that defended territoriality and violent competition will increase in ratio to the growing predictability and density of the resources, which make the effort to monopolize them worthwhile.[19] All the same, in Australia, even in the desert areas of the central regions, where population densities were often as low as one person per 50 square kilometres, or even lower, let alone in the resource-rich and more densely populated areas, group territories existed and their boundaries were well defined and normally kept. These boundaries criss-crossed the continent and by and large were apparently very old. There was no 'vast common land', as some 1960s' anthropologists believed. Rather than the free ranging of the Rousseauite anthropological imagination, the Aborigines (similar to the Greenland Eskimos, another good 'laboratory' of simple hunter–gatherers) were in fact 'restricted nomads' or 'centrally based wanderers', confined for life to their ancestral home territories. These territories were sanctioned by totem and myth, with trespass regarded as a grave crime. Strangers provoked alarm and as a rule kept off. Uninvited, they were likely to encounter aggressive demonstration and violence. Inter- and intragroup fighting were rife.[20]

The natives of Tasmania are a good starting point for our review, because they were the backwater of backwaters. There were an estimated 4,000 Tasmanians when the Europeans arrived. Their island had been isolated from mainland Australia for more than 10,000 years, and their technology and social organization were the most primitive ever recorded. They did not even possess the boomerang. Their population density was also among the lowest there is. Still, lethal raiding and counter-raiding took place among their groups. Territorial boundaries were kept and mutual apprehension was the rule.[21]

By the mid-nineteenth century, the Tasmanians were hunted into extinction by European settlers. But on the mainland, Aboriginal tribes survived. In a classic fieldwork, M. J. Meggitt studied the Walbiri tribe of the central Australian desert, whose population density was as low as one person per 90 square kilometres, among the lowest there is. He investigated the Walbiri relations with the other hunter–gatherer tribes in the surrounding

Australia's Aboriginals were pure, isolated hunter–gatherers, who possessed practically no property. They offer the best laboratory for the all-pervasiveness and intensity of fighting before agriculture and the state:

Beginning of a quarrel during a welcoming ceremony, Arunta tribe. Photos from the turn of the twentieth century, when state rule in the centre and north of the continent was still nominal

A raiding party is returning after killing. They are met by mourning women whose relative's death they avenged; Arunta tribe, Atninga

Aboriginal shields: unlike spears and boomerangs, their only possible purpose was fighting. Also note them in the previous photos

territories. With some of these neighbours relations were friendly, with others hostile. In the latter case, raids and counter-raids were common:

> The men's descriptions made it clear that the Warramunga (and Waringari) trespasses were not merely hunting forays impelled by food shortages in the invaders' own territory but rather were raids undertaken to combine hunting for sport and the abduction of women. Often, too, the raiders were simply spoiling for a fight. They were met with force, and deaths occurred on both sides. Walbiri war parties would then invade the Warramunga country in retaliation. If they were able to surprise the enemy camps and kill or drive off the men, they carried away any women they found.

On one recorded occasion around the beginning of the twentieth century, things came to a head on a wider scale and with a different motive:

> Until then, the Waringari had claimed the ownership of the few native wells at Tanami and the country surrounding them, but in a pitched battle for the possession of the water the Walbiri drove the Waringari from the area, which they incorporated into their own territory. By desert standards the engagement was spectacular, the dead on either side numbering a score or more.[22]

Gerald Wheeler specified the following motives for the frequent inter- and intragroup fighting: 'women, murder (most often supposed to be done by magic), and territorial trespass.'[23] He drew on anthropological accounts from all parts of Australia.

Indeed, tropical northern Australia was also barely affected by Europeans until the twentieth century. However, in comparison with the arid centre, population densities there were much higher, and contact among Aboriginal hunter–gatherers was much greater. In another classic case study of an Aboriginal tribe, conducted in Arnhem Land in the north during the late 1920s, W. Lloyd Warner wrote: 'Warfare is one of the most important social activities of the Murngin people and surrounding tribes.' According to Warner, most fighting took place to avenge the death of relatives, and the rest followed the stealing of women, accusations of death by sorcery and acts of sacrilege.[24] One major action in Arnhem Land, which occurred because of an accusation of sacrilege, is described by anthropologist T. G. H. Strehlow:

> To punish Ltjabakuka and his men meant the wiping out of the whole camp of people normally resident at Irbmankara, so that no witness should be left alive who could have revealed the names of the attackers. A large party of avengers drawn from the Matuntara area along the Palmer River, and from some Southern Aranda local groups, was accordingly assembled and led to Irbmankara by Tjinawariti, who was described to me as having been a Matuntara 'ceremonial chief' from the Palmer River whose prowess as a warrior had given him a great reputation. . . . Tjinawariti and his men fell upon Irbmankara one evening, after all the local folk, as they believed, had returned to their camps from their day's quests for food. Men, women and children were massacred indiscriminately, and the party turned back in the belief that they had not left behind any witness.

However, a few witnesses did survive to tell the story. Thus:

> it was possible for friendly Western Aranda groups to take revenge for the massacre of Irbmankara. A small band of experienced warriors, led by Nameia, went deep into the areas whence the killers had come. This party had to live off their enemy's lands and lie low, sometimes for weeks, between each kill; for they had to pick off their victims in singles or twos and threes whenever suitable occasions arose. But by patience and superb bushcraft they achieved their errand; and finally they managed to kill Tjinawariti as well.[25]

Anthropologist R. G. Kimber, drawing on a variety of studies and sources, summarizes as follows:

> One can infer from archaeological evidence that conflict has been an ancient problem, and many mythological accounts also suggest this. Small-scale conflict, with very occasional deaths, was no doubt the norm, but the 'payback law' could result in lengthy feuds. On other occasions major conflicts had dramatic demographic implications.

Kimber cites evidence of some such major conflicts, including the one described by Strehlow:

> In about 1840, at a locality called Nariwalpa, in response to insults, the

'Jandruwontas and Piliatapas killed so many Diari men, that the ground was covered with their dead bodies'. . . . Strehlow gives the most dramatic account of a major arid-country conflict. He estimates that 80–100 men, women and children were killed in one attack in 1875 at Running Waters, on the Finke River. In retaliation, all but one of the attacking party of 'perhaps fifty to sixty warriors' were killed over the next three years, as were some of their family members. This indicates that some 20% of two identifiable 'tribes' were killed in this exchange.

Long-distance expeditions to search for, and exchange, luxury, decorative, and prestige goods took place even in the simplest societies. They involved crossing group territories, normally, but not always, peacefully:

> The red ochre gathering expeditions . . . involved travel from the eastern portion of the study area to the Flinders Ranges. . . . These expeditions took place on a regular basis, were normally all-males parties, and although cordial relationships between groups were sought, fighting appears to have been a common hazard faced by travelling parties. One entire party, with the exception of one man, is recorded as having been ambushed and killed in about 1870, whilst in about 1874 all but one of a group of 30 men were 'entombed in the excavations'.

Kimber concludes:

> The evidence suggests that major conflict could be expected in the well-watered areas, where population density was at its greatest, or during regular 'trespasser travel' for high-prized products. Although exact figures will never be known, a low death rate of possibly 5% every generation can be suggested for the regions of least conflict, and a high death-rate of perhaps 20% every three generations elsewhere.[26]

More about the form, demography, and termination of armed conflict among the Tiwi of northern Australia is provided by anthropologist Arnold Pilling: 'The night raids were effectively terminated, about 1912, when Sir Baldwin Spencer was inadvertently injured by a Tiwi during a spear-throwing demonstration.' It was then made clear that fighting would no longer be tolerated by the Europeans:

> This Spencer incident was correlated with the end of night raiding and sneak attacks and it *appeared* to have stopped pitched battles producing death. But, in fact, as late as 1948 death-causing battles with clubs were occurring. . . . Under the old pattern, sneak attack was sufficiently common that informants spoke of special ecological adjustments to it . . . the threatened group A was likely to move to the mangroves, a very specialised and unpleasant ecological niche with, among other things, crocodiles and a sloshy mud floor.

Demographically:

> It is important to note the incidence of fatalities associated with the old pattern of attacks and the way of life with which it was correlated. In one decade (1893–1903), at least sixteen males in the 25-to-45 age group were killed in feuding; either during sneak attacks or in arranged pitch battles. Those killed represented over 10 per cent of all males in that age category, which was the age group of the young fathers.[27]

Obviously, estimates such as this and that by Kimber are highly tentative. Nevertheless, they are remarkably similar and also in general agreement with those suggested by Warner. Of a population of 3,000 in the tribes in his study area, Warner had record of 'about one hundred deaths in the last twenty years caused by war'. He doubled that number to fill up for the areas in his study area for which no accurate record was available, arriving at some 200 people killed altogether during 20 years.[28] As we shall see, all these figures tally with those of many other primitive societies. They represent very high rates of killing, higher than that of industrialized societies, which have supposedly been involved in massively lethal wars.

For some anthropologists even such unequivocal evidence is not enough. Although no expert on the Aborigines maintains that they had lacked fighting before European arrival, it has become the vogue in anthropology to claim that everything changed with, and little can be said about what preceded, contact. However, precisely in this connection we possess a truly remarkable testimony. In 1803, only 15 years after the European first arrived in Australia, a 13-year-old English boy named William Buckley (1790–1856) was brought to the new continent with the first convict ship arriving at the penal settlement at Port Philip (now Melbourne). He escaped shortly after, and for 32 years, until 1835, he lived with an Aboriginal tribe. During that time, he learnt to speak their language and participated in their daily activities. No anthropologist has ever achieved a similar familiarity and at such an early date. After returning to 'civilization', Buckley on several occasions related his experience. His account appears to be remarkably authentic with respect to everything that can be verified concerning the natives' life. Among other things, he describes about a dozen battle scenes, and many lethal feuds, raids, and ambushes, comprising an integral part of the native traditional way of life.[29] I return to his testimony in various contexts later.

Thus, as the layperson—but, curiously, not many anthropologists—would have naturally supposed, most hunter–gatherers, even of the most simple and diffuse sort, regularly engaged in fighting. Moreover, they lived under constant fear of violent conflict, which shaped their ordinary daily life. Death in fighting was among the principal causes of their mortality. The vast, continent-size, isolated Australian 'laboratory' is uniquely demonstrative in this respect, largely dispensing with the chronic doubts and inherently irrefutable objections—arising from the 'contact paradox'—about the 'purity' of the cases of hunter–gatherers' warfare recorded in other parts of the world. Inferring from this evidence and from the drastically reformed research about intraspecific deadly violence within animal species, fighting was probably an integral part of hunter–gatherers' existence throughout the genus *Homo*'s evolutionary history of millions of years.

WARFARE AMONG COMPLEX HUNTER–GATHERERS

Thus, contrary to the still widely held Rousseauite view, fighting was not a recent invention, associated with the emergence of sedentary settlement, food storage, property, high population densities, and social stratification. Still, even if these revolutionary changes in the human way of life did not bring warfare into being, how did they affect it?

In general, the above changes are related to the advent of agriculture from around 10,000 years ago. In some cases, however, they predate agriculture. Since the late Upper Palaeolithic, they emerged in some of the richest ecological niches of the world even in the absence of agricultural subsistence. As mentioned earlier, the richest wildlife niches were those located along particularly high-yield stretches of water, such as swamps, lakes, estuaries, river mouths, and seashores. In some of these niches so-called complex hunter–gatherer societies evolved. This meant that human population density was higher; that the extended family groups in the regional groups lived closely together in larger concentrations; that people were more sedentary, preserving food and stocking it where seasonality was involved—that is, they were 'collectors' rather than mere 'foragers'; that they engaged extensively in crafts and trade; and that they had considerable property, with the rich and strong monopolizing the stretches of land with the best access to the resources.[30] Regrettably, as always in these matters, good evidence about complex hunter–gatherer societies exists only in a very limited number of cases. And yet these cases also tell the story of life under the ever-present shadow of warfare.

Conditions of resource abundance were not the only prerequisite for complex hunter–gatherer societies to evolve. Presumably, biologically modern humans were also necessary. Only our species, *Homo sapiens sapiens*, was apparently able to exploit the resource-rich environments effectively enough to support permanent large concentrations of people. Aquarian resources in particular required efficient fishing techniques, not developed before the advent of *Homo sapiens sapiens*.[31] In addition, only biologically modern humans apparently possessed the sophisticated communication and social skills that made possible life in large-scale and complex societies. Indeed, complex hunter–gatherers are first documented in the late Upper Palaeolithic, some 20,000 years ago, in the Dordogne region in the south of France, the part of the world most extensively studied by palaeoanthropologists. During that period, conditions of profusion prevailed in the Dordogne, with the landscape dotted by lakes, streams, and forests. Complex hunter–gatherer societies of hunters, fishers, and collectors spread further into the south of France and north of Spain during the Mesolithic or Middle Stone Age, roughly between 11,000 and 7,000 years ago. Evidence of other complex hunter–gatherer populations during that period has been found in Ukraine, Japan, Denmark, and the Levant. The archaeological record in all these cases reveals high population densities, exquisite artefacts, often utilizing raw materials carried from afar and, hence, widespread exchange, and some magnificent graves, full of these artefacts—the archaeologists' standard indication of the existence of a wealthy elite and developed social ranking.

The trouble with prehistoric times is that they cannot speak. Artefacts alone are mute. In the absence of writing, there is no story to tell, no concrete record of deeds, thoughts, or social life. However, in southern France and northern Spain in the late Upper Palaeolithic, this veil of darkness has been partly pierced by what is, historically, second best to a human voice: among the modern humans who inhabited these regions the emergence and flourishing of human art are best documented. Undoubtedly the most famous aspect of this artistic outburst is the exquisite pictorial representations of Upper Palaeolithic 'cave art'. Unfortunately from the historical point of view, the drawings from the Upper Palaeolithic are mostly of animals, depicted in the liveliest manner. Humans comprise only three per cent of the images and, in contrast to the animals, their representations are very sketchy. There is only one human figure found that seems to be pierced with arrows.[32] However, in Mesolithic 'rock painting' in the Spanish Levant (about 10,000–5,000 BC), representations of humans rise to 40 per cent of the total.[33] These include several depictions of battle scenes, even though all sorts of alternative explanations, such as ritual and dance, were suggested by those who denied the existence of warfare among hunter–gatherers.

More recent research has brought to light the wealth of Australian Aboriginal 'rock art', which is as old as its European counterpart. According

Mesolithic rock paintings depicting fighting from the Spanish Levant:

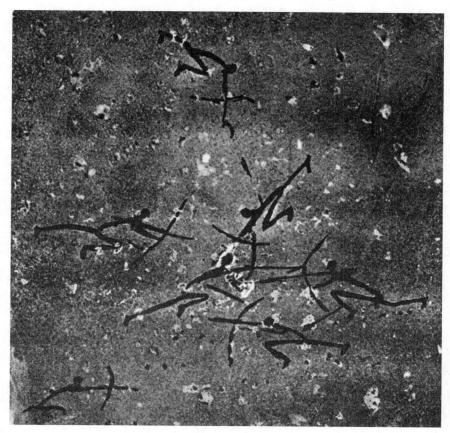

Archers fighting

27

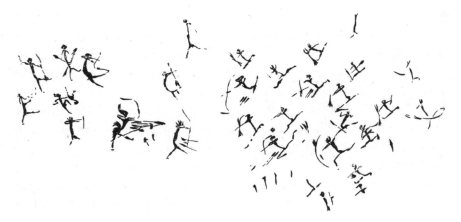

Battle scene

A warrior stricken by arrows

to one study of over 650 sites in Arnhem Land in northern Australia, the oldest depictions include large animals but not humans. There, as well, human images begin to figure prominently only from about 10,000 years ago, and include numerous battle scenes. At first, these representations show

'Execution'

mainly fighting among a few individuals or small groups, but from about 6,000 years ago there are also images of large-scale encounters: 111 figures participating in one battle scene, 68 and 52 in others. The authors of the study reasonably speculate that the larger fighting groups may reflect denser and more complex human concentrations that had evolved in Arnhem Land by that period.[34] In any case, as both the prehistoric rock art depictions of fighting and the recent evidence of warfare from the central Australian desert demonstrate, fighting took place in thinly as well as in densely populated areas. Depictions of battle scenes among the Bushmen in South Africa, apparently stretching back to the pre-Bantu (agricultural) period, corroborate this. The largest scene depicts 12 people on one side and 17 plus 11 'reserves' on the other.[35] Scenes of shield-bearing warriors similarly appear in the prehistoric rock art of the nomadic bison (buffalo) hunters and gatherers of the American Plains.[36]

Evidence of violent death from the European Mesolithic is also traceable in the archaeological record:

> One of the most gruesome instances is provided by Ofnet Cave in Germany, where two caches of 'trophy' skulls were found, arranged 'like eggs in a basket', comprising the disembodied heads of thirty-four men, women, and children, most with multiple holes knocked through their skulls by stone axes.[37]

Rousseauites have interpreted this artistic and archaeological evidence as proof that warfare emerged only with the competition that grew with greater population densities and more complex societies. Others have connected the battle scenes to the invention of the bow some 20,000 years ago, which they suggested inaugurated warfare by making possible killing from afar. However, as the rich and diverse Australian data demonstrate, both claims are incorrect. Seeing coins only where there is light from a lamppost is one of the most serious possible distortions. The fact that fighting is recorded by the newly evolving art (and specifically with the later diffusion of human representations) does not mean that it evolved at the same time. What actually makes the archaeological signs of warfare from the Mesolithic, and even Upper Palaeolithic, less open to dispute than those of earlier times is growing sedentism. It left evidence of fortifications, burnt settlements, large-scale communal cemeteries, and, indeed, art—the sort of evidence without which archaeology grapples in the dark but which is *necessarily* absent before sedentism.

All the same, for a better understanding of complex hunter–gatherer societies—and the question of warfare—we need yet better records than pictorial and archaeological ones: those of writing. And, inevitably, written records exist only where historically literate peoples encountered complex hunter–gatherers. This is not an easy requirement. By and large, by the time written civilization evolved, the world's lush ecological environments in which complex hunter–gatherer societies might develop had long been taken over by agriculturalists. For literate civilizations to be in touch with complex hunter–gatherers—as opposed to simple ones, which might survive in marginal, unproductive environments—a meeting of worlds or a journey in time was necessary. Such a meeting, or a whole series of meetings, in effect took place when the Europeans from the Old World arrived in the New. To set aside any popular misconception, most of the Americas had long been inhabited by agriculturalists. Still, we have records of a major region where complex hunter–gatherer populations flourished—the north-west coast of North America.

Extensively studied since the pioneering work carried out by the distinguished anthropologist Franz Boas in the late nineteenth century, the north-west coast cultures of the North American continent are a dream laboratory of complex hunter–gatherers, almost as good as the Australian continent is for simpler ones. Virtually isolated from contact with agriculturalists, and as western contact began only in the late eighteenth century, the north-west coast constitutes almost as 'pure' an object of study as Australia. Furthermore, as a conservation cosmos, it is no less vast and diverse, providing, similar to Australia, not merely one, possibly accidental, 'case study' but a whole multitude of them, which can therefore be taken as much more representative. In the coastal strip that stretches from the north-western states of the USA through Canada and Alaska, some 2,500 miles long, scores of linguistically different 'peoples' and hundreds of 'tribes' lived, mostly Indians but also Eskimos in coastal Alaska. Each of these peoples had a population in the hundreds and even thousands, with the regional groups sometimes linked in higher loose confederacies.

As in the lushest environments in Australia, population densities in some southern regions of the north-west coast were as high as eight (and, in places, even twenty) people per mile of coastline, or three to five people per square mile. Population at contact in mainland USA and the Canadian part alone is estimated at 150,000, and together with Alaska it easily rivalled that of the mostly arid Australian continent.[38] These large numbers and high population densities resulted from the extremely rich marine resources of the north-west coast, especially the salmon runs up the numerous rivers. Skilful canoeing made it possible for the inhabitants to engage in deep-sea fishing. Hunting of marine mammals was widespread. Abundant land game, mainly birds, and deer in the south and caribou in the north, augmented the population's subsistence base. Seasonal food was preserved and stocked. And yet, throughout the tremendous length of this seeming land of plenty, warfare was rife and bloody. As we saw with respect to Australia, its ever-present shadow affected people's entire way of life.

Various reasons were given by the participants and outside observers for the prominence of armed conflict along the north-west coast. To begin with, access to resources was hotly contested. Plenty is partly a misleading notion, because plenty is relative, first, to the number of mouths that have to be fed. The more resource rich a region, the more people it attracts from outside, and the more internal population growth will take place. As Thomas Malthus pointed out, a new equilibrium between resource volume and population numbers would eventually be reached, recreating the same tenuous ratio of subsistence that has been the fate of most pre-industrial societies throughout human history. Thus, both within and between the regional groups and peoples, those who succeeded in controlling the rich river mouths, for instance, were better off than those living along exposed seashores, upstream or, worst, inland. Within the groups, this was the source of developed social ranking between rich and poor, aristocratic and common, especially in the more affluent south. At the two extremes, slaves were owned by and worked for the very rich. Between both peoples and regional groups, the differences in access to resources were the cause of recurring warfare, resulting from migratory pressures into coveted territories and endemic border disputes. Territorial boundaries were well known and, at the peril of death, were normally not crossed. As a rule, people did not feel safe to go where they did not have relatives. Group territories were sanctioned by ceremony and ritual. The magnificent huge Indian totems for which the region is famous were among the marks of clan territories. Some trade routes were occasionally open for travel, depending on the specific conditions of the times, people, and goods concerned. Such crossing of boundaries followed traditional established customs and practices. Otherwise, strangers were assumed to be hostile, and trespassers would be attacked and killed, often after being tortured. Suspicion was well grounded. In addition to the quest for territorial gain, inevitable seasonal and other natural food supply shortages and 'stresses' were a common cause of alien attack. Particularly in times of famine, war parties raided the stored food of their more affluent neighbours. Slave raiding was another constant threat and source of warfare. Abduction of women was widespread.[39]

Indeed, want and hunger were not the only reasons for fighting. Plenty and scarcity are relative not only to the number of mouths to be fed but also to the potentially ever-expanding and insatiable range of human needs and desires. It is as if, paradoxically, human competition increases with abundance, as well as with deficiency, taking more complex forms and expressions, widening social gaps and enhancing stratification.[40] The wealthy can support and, therefore, have, more wives, as was the case, for example, among both the elders who dominated the Australian groups and the north-west coast 'big men'. Rivalry over women was a principal, sometimes the principal, cause of deadly violence. Furthermore, although the capacity to consume simple, subsistence products is inherently limited, that of more refined, lucrative ones is practically open ended. One can simply move up-market. So-called ostentatious consumption comes in, and complex hunter–gatherer societies were the first to experience it. One main avenue for such consumption is that of prestige decorative items. Beautifully crafted from scarce and exotic raw materials, often brought from afar, these were exchanged for food surpluses in developed trade networks. Both in Upper Palaeolithic Europe and in the north-west coast cultures, similar items are found in archaeological records. They include ivory, obsidian, shell, bone, and horn artefacts, such as jewellery, sculptures, and artfully carved and decorated practical tools. Exquisite featherwork and fine clothing are less preserved in the archaeological record but are also known to have been objects of desire. Finally, the north-west coast Indians are famous for a social institution known also from other 'primitive' and not so primitive societies—the potlatch or competitive feast. Vying for prestige, 'big men' held large social feasts in which they served vast quantities of food as well as literally destroying all sorts of their own valuable property as a mark of their wealth. Thus, to accumulate wealth—by gaining better access to resource-rich areas, by monopolizing trade and by the acquisition of slaves—armed force and warfare were often required.

As in *all* cases of hunter–gatherer, 'primitive' or, indeed, any other sort of warfare, people of the north-west coast also reported seemingly different and more varied motives than the material. In truth, they often placed these motives at the top of their list, mentioning retribution for insults and wrongs, blood revenge, pursuit of prestige, and the taking of heads as war trophies. I return to discuss the question of motives more systematically in later chapters. As with *all* other cases of hunter–gatherer and 'primitive' deadly conflict, fighting in the north-west coast ranged from small-scale incidents, carried out by few people and resulting in few casualties, to large-scale affairs involving hundreds of participants and on occasions ending with as many casualties. Canoe ocean war expeditions of hundreds of miles were recorded in this region. As a result of the constant threat of war, settlements were located in easily defensible sites and were regularly fortified by palisades and trenches. Elaborate features such as concealed exits, secret connecting and escape tunnels, hideaways, double-walled houses, slat protection, and spiked rolling logs were in use in these settlements.[41] I discuss the modes of warfare in greater detail in Chapter 6.

A new stage began in the north-west coast with the arrival of the white man. Regular contact with Russian navy ships, merchants, and trade posts began in the last years of the eighteenth century and rapidly intensified. Contact with US traders soon followed. The object of the trade was furs, exchanged for western goods, such as metal tools, clothing, glass beads, and firearms. The new source of wealth and competition may have accentuated both social stratification and warfare among the natives. Slave labour may have become more useful and widespread, with the wealthiest possessing as many as dozens of slaves. Tribes, local groups, and entrepreneurial 'big men' within them strove to get hold of and monopolize the lucrative trade. Warfare was constantly recorded by western observers during much of the nineteenth century, ceasing only with the establishment of firm western rule.

Some anthropologists, such as R. Brian Ferguson, have suggested that western goods had already begun to penetrate the region by indirect routes earlier in the eighteenth century, and that they had been partly responsible for growing competition and for the belligerency evident in the accounts of old native informers about that period. Still, the indirect penetration of western goods in a proto-contact phase could not have been very substantial. Furthermore, as these scholars themselves, in agreement with all other research, recognize, warfare in the north-west coast was anyway very old, predating 'proto-contact'—it is archaeologically recorded in the region, with little apparent variation, for no less than 4,000 years. Linguistic evidence shows that slavery, established through war, was also very old throughout the region.[42] Indeed, the natives' use of body armour made of several layers of hide or of wooden slat and rod—a specialized fighting device extensively reported by the first European explorers in the late eighteenth century and currently displayed in museums—actually seems to have declined after the white man's arrival. It was rendered useless by musket fire. A similar development took place with the Plains Indians' shields and skin armour, and for the same reason.[43]

Nevertheless, a broader debate followed. Expanding their argument to horticulturalists in Central and South America, Ferguson and others, invoking the 'contact paradox', have generally claimed that western arrival significantly altered native warfare in a so-called tribal zone. They had created a stir, which was, however, largely overblown. As most of these anthropologists were well aware of the evidence for extensive and brutal warfare before contact and took care to mention it, albeit very briefly, their point (or what remains of it) would have in effect been very narrow indeed.[44]

To summarize the findings from our two—Australian and north-west coast—hunter–gatherer 'dream laboratories', they clearly show, across a very large variety of native peoples living in their original settings, that hunter–gatherers, from the very simple to the more complex, fought among themselves. Deadly conflict, if not endemic, was ever to be expected. The fear of it restricted people to well-circumscribed home territories and necessitated constant precautions and special protective measures. Killing in fighting was among the main causes of mortality. Was fighting more frequent and intense among complex hunter–gatherers than among simpler ones? Higher population densities, more concentrated resources, and intensified competition for accumulated wealth and prestige suggest this in accepted anthropological models, but measurement seems practically impossible now. Deadly conflict among more numerous concentrations of people may *seem* to be more widespread, but was violence *per capita*, as measured in the percentage of killings in the general mortality, less among simple hunter–gatherers? Tenuous estimates, such as those by Kimber, cited above, suggest that it was, although not by a different order of magnitude. Simple hunter–gatherers also fought, with all the consequences that fighting entailed.[45] Thus the evidence suggests that hunter–gatherers in their evolutionary natural environment and evolutionary natural way of life, shaped in humankind's evolutionary history over millions of years, widely engaged in fighting among themselves. In this sense, rather than being a late cultural 'invention', fighting would seem to be, if not 'natural', then certainly not 'unnatural' to humans. But why is this so? What is the evolutionary rationale for this dangerous, deadly activity?

3

Why Fighting? The Evolutionary Perspective

INNATE BUT OPTIONAL TACTIC

If warfare was not a late cultural 'invention', is it then innate in human nature and, if so, in what way? The idea has a long pedigree, going back at least to the Hebrew Bible's dictum, incorporated into Christian doctrine, that 'the inclination of man's heart is evil from childhood' (*Genesis* 8.21). This idea has since taken many versions and forms. After the First World War, it was revived—for instance, by Sigmund Freud. Like many of his contemporaries, Freud was aghast at and perplexed by the seemingly frenzied blood letting and destruction of the First World War, and later by the gathering storm of the Second World War. In major new statements of psychoanalytic theory and then in two famous letters to Albert Einstein, he tried to explain how the magnificent edifice of nineteenth-century European civilization, which educated Europeans, including Freud himself, had regarded as the pinnacle of human development, had so easily succumbed. Freud had always believed that civilization was tenuously built on the shaky foundations of man's primordial drives. However, so senseless, irrational, and suicidal did the turmoil of the time appear, that he found it necessary to introduce a new element into his theory. He suggested that, side by side with the sexual life drive, man possessed a destructive, indeed, self-destructive, drive—a 'death instinct'. As with all instincts, although increasingly subdued by the advance of civilization, it was always liable to break through civilization's thin crust and was never likely to be totally suppressed. Freud did try to give biological and even evolutionary support to his claim, in order to explain *why* this was so. How did it come to be that man possessed such an improbable 'death wish', so detrimental to his survival and prosperity. Still, postulating the two antithetical drives, like two Manichaean idols with lives of their own, Freud himself felt, and apologized to Einstein, that all this may seem as a 'kind of mythology'.[1] His disciples within the psychoanalytic movement have also felt uneasy about this later change to his theory.

At least on the surface, other theorists were more careful to work within the logic of evolutionary theory. Distinguished ethologists Konrad Lorenz and Niko Tinbergen and psychiatrist Anthony Storr claimed that man possessed a basic aggression instinct or drive which had been evolutionarily useful to him in his savage past, even though it may have become harmful within the context of civilization. This was another idea that captured the headlines in the 1960s. Not unlike other drives, such as those for sex and food, claimed the proponents of that idea, the aggression drive built up in us until it reached such levels that it required release. If it could not be diverted to other channels, such as sport, it might overflow in various expressions of aggression and violence.[2]

The idea of a basic aggressive drive, almost blindly and automatically filling up from itself, was very attractive to the general public, because it appeared to explain seemingly senseless and irrational eruptions of violence and warfare. It came under heavy criticism, however, and was widely rejected by the scientific community. It was pointed out that aggression was a wholly different biological mechanism from the basic drives such as those for food or sex. Aggression does not accumulate in the body by a hormone loop mechanism, with a rising level that demands release. People have to feed regularly if they are to stay alive, and in the relevant ages they can normally avoid sexual activity altogether only by extraordinary restraint and at the cost of considerable distress. By contrast, people can live in peace for their entire lives, without suffering on that account, to put it mildly, from any particular distress. As we well know, whole societies can live in peace for generations. Indeed, there is miscomprehension here about the crucial difference that exists between the evolutionary *functions* of the activities in question. In the evolutionary calculus, nourishment and sex, for example, are primary biological ends, directly linked, the one to the organism's existence and the other to its reproduction. By contrast, aggression is a means, a tactic—and only one among many—for the achievement of the primary biological ends. As a means, its utilization depends on its usefulness.

It might be argued that communication, for example, is also a means, and yet humans can become deeply distressed if deprived of it. However, the functional need of communication is fairly unambiguous and straightforward, whereas aggression is in special need of always being assessed against alternative behaviour tactics, such as retreat, submission and co-operation, because aggression is a highly dangerous tactic. It might expose its user to serious bodily harm and even death, easily proving counterproductive. On average, 'trigger happy' individuals are likely to be of shorter life expectancy and, by diminishing their chances of survival and reproduction, would be selected against. Indeed, an illuminating application of game theory to biology has shown that a strategy of unrestricted offensive is evolutionarily untenable.[3] Thus, as research stresses, the use of aggression in both animals and humans depends in any given situation on a continuous intuitive assessment of the chances and risks, stakes and alternatives.[4] The higher the stakes and the less promising the alternatives, the more readily might aggression be used even with lower chances and higher risks. Each species, and individuals within a species, variably modulate their strategy to take account of their particular circumstances.

Hence the emotional mechanisms involved, for biological functions are regulated by sensual stimuli. Nourishment and reproduction, as vital primary needs, are stimulated by intense sensual desires and gratifications that are almost one directional. Of course, these do not operate without limits and constraints. They have levels of saturation and might lead to overindulgence—for instance, there is only a limited amount that one can eat at one time, which if exceeded is signalled by a feeling of nausea. Also, as we know only too well, in societies of plenty, such as our own, overeating can become detrimental. Still, for all living creatures, including the vast majority of people throughout human history, food has been in short supply, and it has generally been essential to have as much of it as it has been possible to obtain. Therefore, food has always been an object of sensual desire. Similarly, too much sex might become counterproductive, for example, if it distracts from other essential activities such as the search for food, leads to the neglect of existing offspring or causes trouble with dangerous sexual competitors. In addition, females are much more choosy than males in selecting sex partners because of the potentially smaller number of offspring that they are capable of having. In all these cases, sexual activity must be constrained if one is not to diminish rather than increase one's reproductive success. Within constraints such as these, more sexual activity is generally better for reproductive success, so throughout nature sex is generally much desired.

By comparison, as aggression is only one possible, and highly dangerous, tactic, rather than a primary need, the emotional mechanisms that regulate it are sharply antithetical, ready to turn it on and off. On the 'on' side, the primary motives and drives that trigger aggression are emotionally underpinned not merely by feelings such as fear and animosity; the fighting activity itself is stimulated by individual and communal thrill, enjoyment in the competitive exercise of spiritual and physical faculties, and even cruelty, blood lust, and killing ecstasy. These are all emotional mechanisms intended to fuel and sustain aggression. Equally, however, on the other, 'off', side, aggression is emotionally suppressed and deterred by fear, spiritual and physical fatigue, compassion, abhorrence of violence, and revulsion of bloodshed. It seems almost redundant to point out that there are also tremendous emotional stimuli for co-operation and peaceful behaviour. These antithetical emotional arrays, each triggered to support a conflicting stimulus, to and against aggression, are the reason why throughout the ages artists, thinkers, and ordinary folk of all sorts have claimed with conviction that people rejoice in war, whereas others have held with equal self-persuasion that people regard it as an unmitigated disaster. *Both* sentiments have been there, more or less active, depending on the circumstances. Singing the praises of war and decrying its horrors have both been common human responses.

Returning to our original question: is violent and deadly aggression, then, innate in human nature, is it 'in our genes', and, if so, in what way? The answer is that it is, but only as a skill, potential, propensity, or predisposition. This goes beyond the fact, endlessly stressed by scientists, that genes are more a general design plan, open to environmental influences, than a ready-made menu for action. It has all too often been assumed that aggression has to be either an 'invention'—that is, wholly learnt and optional—or innate like a primary drive that is fairly 'hard wired' and extremely difficult to suppress. In actuality, aggression, as a tactical skill—and a highly dangerous one—is *both* innate and optional. To be sure, it is a most basic and central skill, of regular usefulness in the struggle for existence. This is why it is innate in living creatures, including humans; strong selection pressures over many millions of years have made it so. Indeed, it must be stressed that, while being optional, aggression has always been a *major* option, and thus very close to the surface and easily triggered.[5] At the same time, however, when conditions that may trigger aggression are less prominent, or alternative means are available or can be construed, aggression levels can decline, sometimes even to the point where the whole behavioural pattern is barely activated. Violent aggression levels fluctuate in response to conditions.

Psychological theory has now come to the same view, maintaining that aggressive behaviour, although innate as a potential, develops by social learning.[6] This is supported by brain research, which tells us that brain design, particularly but not only in humans, is flexible, especially in the early stages of life. It extensively rearranges itself, creating new neuron circuits in response to changing environmental challenges. Thus, individuals, groups and societies (and research shows that animals as well) are conditioned to become more or less violent by the sort of environment to which they have been exposed. We intuitively know this to be true from daily life experience: young people growing in violent social circumstances becoming violent; beaten children becoming beating parents; and so on. History shows this, in that some societies famously became more bellicose, whereas others were more pacific. During the heyday of the Rousseauite school, anthropologists searched for hunter–gatherer and primitive agricultural societies that exhibited no war-like behaviour, to show that warfare was a 'cultural invention' rather than a 'biological necessity'. They were able to locate a few, mostly peaceful societies, generally small ones living in remote and isolated environments, having withdrawn from the world into 'refuge enclaves' after being driven away by stronger neighbours.[7] In truth, however, anthropologists need not have searched so far, as there are well-known examples of modern societies, such as the Swiss and the Swedish, that have not engaged in warfare for two centuries, after having earlier been, each in its turn, the most war-like in Europe. (The fact that they had fought before is insignificant for the 'biological drive' argument, because it cannot seriously be claimed that the forefathers' martial activities satisfy the needs of their present-day descendants.) All the same, 'peaceful societies' do not prove that warfare is an invention any more than bellicose societies and the general prevalence of warfare in history prove that it is a biological necessity. To repeat the point, deadly aggression is a major, evolution-shaped, innate potential that, given the right conditions, has always been easily triggered. However, its occurrence and prevalence are subject to wide fluctuations, depending on the prominence of these conditions.

THE EVOLUTIONARY CALCULUS

From its inception, Charles Darwin's theory of evolution was applied to the explanation of war, in passing by Darwin himself, and widely by both his scholarly and popular disciples. It was most notably used by Herbert Spencer and William Graham Sumner. Sumner's *War* in particular is a highly insightful work that retains much of its freshness.[8] Sumner influenced Maurice R. Davie's excellent *The Evolution of War* (1929). However, as with other fields of social study, some of the evolutionary literature on war was tinted by social Darwinism and, as the tide turned against the latter, the application of the evolutionary perspective to social questions, including that of war, was discredited for much of the twentieth century.

Two major developments reversed the trend again. The breaking of the DNA genetic code in the early 1950s, establishing the biochemical basis of Gregor Mendel's theory of inheritance, finally provided Darwin's theory of evolution with the exact biological mechanism of inheritance that it had earlier lacked. This discovery has opened the way for continuous revolutionary advances in genetics, giving new impetus to evolutionary theory. In addition, the previously dominant behaviouralist and liberal doctrines of humans as a *tabula rasa* had begun to recede in all fields of knowledge by the 1970s. The application of evolutionary theory to human affairs, known as 'sociobiology' or, better, evolutionary psychology, began its comeback, growing ever stronger. The intense opposition that it created, giving rise to the 'sociobiological debate' of the late 1970s, has considerably calmed down in professional circles. It lingers on, mainly as stereotypes, among historians, social scientists, and cultural students, many of whom have, regrettably, not bothered to familiarize themselves with the relevant literature.[9] I ask such readers to withhold their incredulity until I fully deploy my arguments. From Darwin's concluding passage to his *The Origin of Species*, only

41

the famous second part is usually quoted, although the first was as pro-grammatic: 'In the future I see open fields for more important researches. Psychology will be securely based on the foundation already well laid by Mr. Herbert Spencer, that of the necessary acquirement of each mental power and capacity by gradation. Much light will be thrown on the origin of man and his history.'[10] This was no social Darwinist's but Darwin's own research programme.

From the start, the theory of evolution redefined the question of war in more than one way. First and foremost, it provided a non-transcendent explanation to the age-old question of why the world was so constructed that competition and fighting formed an integral part of it. Darwin's evolutionary theory centres on the idea that organisms evolve blindly by natural selection, which takes place in their struggle for survival against environmental conditions and, because of their successful proliferation, also against each other for scarce resources. Those most able to survive and reproduce increase their numbers in the general population, together with the qualities that make them good at survival and reproduction. In turn, they increase the pressure on the resources and refuel the contest. This contest takes the form of either indirect competition or direct conflict. The distinction between the two was first elaborated systematically by the sociologist Georg Simmel, at the start of the twentieth century.[11] In a competition, the protagonists strive to outdo each other in order to achieve a desired good by employing whatever means is at their disposal except direct action against the other. A competition runs parallel. By contrast, in a conflict, direct action against the competitor is taken in order to eliminate it or lower its ability to engage in the competition. If physical injury is used, a conflict becomes a violent one.

There is no 'reason' for the existence of either competition or conflict, other than that they both proved successful techniques in the struggle for survival. 'Success' is not defined by any transcendent measurement but by the inherent logic of the evolutionary process. Thus, while making the order of life appear drastically more arbitrary than it had earlier been, evolutionary theory made the role of fighting in that order less so. In doing this it also presented the motives for fighting as less arbitrary. In the book of nature, the motives for fighting ultimately had to make sense in terms of the evolutionary rationale of survival and reproduction, because maladaptive behaviour was selected against. Thus evolutionary theory reconstrued the question of fighting in the following way: it suggested a deeper natural rationale for fighting and, by inference from that rationale, claimed, in a previously unnecessary way, that this tremendously deadly and wasteful behaviour was somehow carried out in a manner that promoted survival and reproductive success. But what manner, and whose survival?

Obviously, it was not survival for all but only for the winners in the contest for the limited resources that made survival and reproduction possible, for the 'fittest' in the never-ending game of survival and reproduction. This contest is both inter- and intraspecific—that is, taking place among both members of different species and members of the same species. In fact, as scientists have realized, reviving a point emphasized by Darwin himself, the contest is far more intense among members of the same species, because they live in the same ecological niches, consume the same sort of food, and vie for the same mates.[12] As we have seen, ethologists and biologists believed for a short while that animals did not kill members of their own species. Some of them claimed that this was so because intraspecific killing would have endangered the survival of the species. There were even some evolutionary theorists who thought this claim valid. However, it has been not only found empirically erroneous, but also (necessarily) theoretically rejected.[13] Intraspecific fighting and killing take place because the decisive factor in the evolutionary contest is individuals' efforts to pass on their *own* genes to the next generations by whatever cost-effective means, rather than those of strangers.

There are two reasons why there is no uninterrupted effort to eliminate conspecifics. In the special case of social animals, one's conspecifics within a group are important for one's own success, for example, in hunting and defence—more on that later. More generally, among all animals, the main factor is that other conspecifics are also strong, and the risks and costs of a systematic effort to eliminate them would be evolutionarily counterproductive. As between the great powers, a balance of power and mutual deterrence exists between individual conspecifics, motivated by concern not for the survival of the species but for their own survival.[14] For that reason, animals also try to avoid violent confrontations with strong rivals from *other* species, not only their own, a point curiously missed by Lorenz. Fighting and killing break out only from time to time when the stakes get higher and the odds more favourable.

To remove all too prevalent misunderstandings about the evolutionary rationale, even at the risk of restating the obvious, the argument, of course, is not that these behaviour patterns are a matter of conscious decision and complex calculation by flies, mice, lions, or even humans, but simply that those who have not so behaved have failed to be represented in the next generations, and their maladaptive genes, responsible for their maladaptive behaviour, have been selected out. The most complex structural engineering and behaviour patterns have thus evolved in, and program even the simplest organisms, including those lacking any consciousness. This underlying rationale of evolutionary theory should always be kept in mind.

One's genes are passed on to the next generations not only through one's own offspring but also through other close kin who share the same genes.[15] Siblings share, on average, 50 per cent of their genes, the same percentage as parents and offspring. Half-siblings share, on average, 25 per cent of their genes. Cousins share 12.5 per cent of their genes. This is the basis of the old idea that 'blood is thicker than water'. An individual's close kin constitute a reservoir of his or her own genes, and are, therefore, evolutionarily worth caring for and defending against all others, even at the risk to the individual's own survival, depending on the closeness of the relationship and the number of kin involved. Evolutionarily, it is even worthwhile for an individual to sacrifice itself if, by that act, it saves more than two brothers, four half-brothers, or eight cousins. Taking risks for them is worthwhile even at lower ratios. The evolutionary rationale thus favours not individual survival but 'kin selection' or 'inclusive fitness' of the same genes in oneself and in one's kin. In evolutionary terms, it is ultimately the survival and propagation of the *genes* that count.

Among social insects, the members of whole colonies, numbering in the hundreds and thousands, are on average three-quarter siblings or even clones. Individuals therefore readily sacrifice themselves in defence of their colony, which, as an enormous close family, represents a far larger concentration of their own genes than they themselves do. However, human family relations are not similarly structured, nor do they extend to the scale of large societies. Let us return to the 'human state of nature'—that is, the 99.5 per cent of their evolutionary history in which humans led a hunter–gatherer existence, which is responsible for their evolutionary inheritance. As we have seen, the basic social unit among hunter–gatherers is the extended family group (clan; local group) which numbers a few dozen close kin: elderly parents, siblings and their nuclear families. It is easy to see why the members of these groups co-operate, share, and take risks in defending each other. It is mostly with these primary groups that people's allegiance rests. Moreover, human local groups, similar to those of the chimpanzees, are predominantly patrilocal and patrilineal—that is, it is the females who leave their families on marriage, joining the males who stay with their original family groups. The local, family group is thus composed of brethren. As in nature the males, for reasons demonstrated later, are generally the more combative sex, the human local groups' cohesiveness in conflict is further strengthened.[16]

Hunter–gatherers also have a higher form of social grouping—the regional group and confederation of regional groups ('dialect tribes')— numbering hundreds and even more members. One of the main functions of the regional group is mutual co-operation in warfare. But why risk one's life for other members of these larger groups? Although the regional group is the main marriage circle, most of its members are only remotely related. They are different in this respect from the colony of social insects or the local family group. Still, the logic of kinship continues to exercise a strong influence. In the first place, although not every member of the regional group is a close kin of all the others, the regional group is a dense network of close kinship. When a daughter of one clan is given in marriage to another clan, this daughter and her children represent an evolutionary 'investment' 'deposited' by the wife's clan in the husband's. In caring for its investment, the wife's clan becomes interested in the survival of the 'bank' with which this investment is deposited—that is, predominantly the daughter's husband, but also his clan's members. They become important for the investment to thrive. Links such as these criss-cross the regional group, making clans ready to take risks in sup- port of each other against the environment, other animals or strangers, for the good of their shared investment. It is this evolutionary rationale that accounts for the well-recognized fact that kin relationships and marriage links consti- tute the primary social bonds in 'primitive' and not so primitive societies. As we have seen earlier, hunter–gatherers felt safe to go only where they had kin. Political treaties throughout the ages have been cemented by marriage.

Furthermore, the rationale of kinship does not terminate with close kin but extends further, although down a sharply declining curve. The same logic that makes it evolutionarily beneficial to sacrifice one's life in order to save more than two siblings or eight cousins, and take risks at even lower ratios, holds true for 32 second cousins, 128 third cousins, or 512 fourth cousins. This, in fact, is pretty much what a regional group is, and is the main

45

reason why members of the group will prefer the other members of the group to outsiders and even be willing to take some risk for them. As most marriages take place within the regional group, there is a wide gap between the 'us' of the tribe and outsiders.[17] However, as the rationale of kinship applies further—to 2,048 fifth cousins, 8,192 sixth cousins, 32,768 seventh cousins, to entire peoples, and even humanity as a whole—does this not amount to a doctrine of brotherly love, the same idea of 'species solidarity' rejected before? There is a pitfall here of ignoring the other side of the kinship equation.

The closer the kin, the greater the evolutionary reward for caring for them, but only as long as they do not threaten the prospects of even closer kin in the gene economy. For example, a sibling, who, on average, represents 50 per cent of one's own genes, is a highly valued genetic partner, and it is worthwhile paying a considerable price and taking substantial risks for its survival. However, one is genetically doubly closer to oneself than to a sibling, so in cases of severe competition between them, siblings' rivalry can become intense and even deadly. Such competition takes place, for instance, for vital parental care among infants, especially at times of acute scarcity. It can occur when the reproductive future of two siblings clashes—for example, over a prize mate or the prospects of their respective offspring. Here again, while nephews and nieces are evolutionary favoured by their uncle/aunt, these uncles/aunts doubly favour their own offspring. Hence the all too familiar jealousy, tensions, and antagonism between relatives. To sum up a complex subject, kinship ties are balanced by the competition that kin may pose to even closer kin, who represent greater genetic partnership, down to oneself and offspring.[18] People are thus evolutionarily inclined to support closer relatives against more distant ones (unless they themselves get into such a severe conflict with their close kin that they turn to seek allies outside, an eventuality that has been universally regarded as abnormal and morally problematic). A traditional Arab proverb expresses this evolutionary rationale: 'I against my brother; I and my brother against my cousin; I and my brother and my cousin against the world.'

This explains the familiar relationship structure among clan members, clans, and tribes, which, according to ethnographic reports, reveals deadly aggression incidents at *all* levels. Fighting and killing take place both within and between tribes. This is more complex than the simple ingroup co-operation/outgroup rivalry, suggested by Spencer and Sumner. Our distinction between 'blood feuds' and 'warfare', 'homicide' and 'war killing' is in fact largely arbitrary, reflecting our point of view as members of more or less orderly societies. Typically, as Franz Boas noted among the eastern, Great Plains, and north-west American Indians, 'the term "war" includes not only fights between tribes or clans but also deeds of individuals who set out to kill a member or members of another group'.[19] The phenomenon with which we are dealing is deadly aggression, explained by the same evolutionary rationale.

Tensions and rivalries among close kin are widespread. Inhibitions against violence among them are very strong, because it is evolutionarily highly damaging to oneself. Nevertheless, when one's own evolutionary prospects are seriously threatened, close kin hostility might escalate. The story of Cain and Abel demonstrates both the intense competition and the strong inhibitions involved in such occurrences. Intra-family (mostly, but not only, marital) violence, even deadly violence, takes place in all societies;[20] otherwise, whatever the internal tensions and rivalries among them, clan members would tend to support each other, among other things, in disputes and clashes with members of other clans, which sometimes may escalate to incidents of deadly aggression. In inter-clan rivalry, clans that have inter-married are likely to support each other against other clans. Finally, the clans of one regional group will normally support each other against other regional groups, with whom their genetic kin relationships are far more remote than they are within their own regional group. However, whereas the evolutionary penalty for killing a 'stranger' declines to insignificance, especially in comparison with the possible gains, the willingness to take risks in support of distant relatives within the regional group also declines sharply in comparison with the risks that might be taken to support close kin. The perception of who is 'us' is relative and can be greatly expanded, but, overall, only with diminishing returns and in subordination to a closer 'us'. Still, as we have seen, one would be evolutionarily willing to give one's life for more than 32 second cousins, 128 third cousins, or 512 fourth cousins—that is, roughly speaking, for one's regional group. This explains the cases of altruistic self-sacrifice to save one's people or a large number of them. However, it is not often the case that the fate of a whole tribe is in the hands of one individual, as it might be with smaller, close-kin groups. Therefore, the closer the kin the more would an individual be likely to risk itself, or even display self-sacrifice, for their survival.

How do we know who our kin are? In nature, from micro-organisms to humans, there are biological and social cues for recognizing close kin.[21] Humans grow up together with their close kin, remember marriages and births, and are informed about kin relationships. For more distant kin, however, people have rougher indications. Similar physical features (phenotype) are one such indication of genetic relatedness. Thus, different and unfamiliar racial groups are likely to appear more alien. Moreover, apart from biology, humans have culture and are differentiated by their cultures. As culture, particularly among hunter–gatherers, was local and thus strongly correlated with kinship, cultural identity became a strong predictor of kinship. Humans are, therefore, distinctively inclined to side with people who share the same culture against foreigners.[22] The more different another culture is, the 'stranger' and less part of 'us' would it be regarded. Indeed, even between relatively close culture groups people are acutely attuned to the subtlest of differences in dialect, accent, dressing style and behaviour, tending to give preference to their closest likes. This is the 'narcissism of minor differences' between close ethnicities that perplexed Freud.[23] Again, he tried to explain it as a bottled-up expression of an elementary aggressive drive, thus turning the matter on its head and denying it any logic, evolutionary or otherwise: why aggression should express itself in this particular domain remained wholly obscure. Indeed, Freud confessed his puzzlement over the reasons for group ties in general. In actuality, it is ethnic differences that may trigger aggression, rather than the other way around. The preference for one's closer cultural likes over those who are more remote expresses a deeply ingrained preference for one's closer kin.

LARGER GROUPS

Culture sharing, most notably that of language, is also crucial in another way. Not only is it in itself a strong predictor of kin relatedness in small human communities, but it is also a highly significant tool of human social co-operation, because, on top of kinship, humans developed additional mechanisms for social co-operation. In principle, there are strong advantages to co-operation. In warfare, for example, there is a strong advantage to group size; two people, or two clans, acting in co-operation are doubly stronger than one, and have, perhaps, four times the chances of gaining the upper hand.[24] The problem with co-operation is, however, that one has a clear incentive to reap its benefits while avoiding one's share in the costs. Rational choice theorists call this the problem of the 'free rider'. It is a problem that underlies much of social behaviour, as, for example, with tax paying. Where a central authority, such as the state, exists, it can compel 'free riders' to contribute their share to the common good. However, even when authority does not exist or is very weak, as is the case, for instance, among hunter–gatherers, there are still mechanisms that can sustain social co-operation in groups that are intimate enough to allow mutual surveillance and social accounting.[25] If detected, a 'free rider' faces the danger of being excluded, 'ostracized', from the system of co-operation which is on the whole beneficial to him. Not only do people keep a very watchful eye for 'cheaters' and 'defectors', but compared with other animal species they also have very long memories. They would help other people on the assumption that they would get similar help in return, either immediately or some time in the future, depending on the circumstances. If the expected return fails to arrive, people are likely to cease co-operating. This is the basis for the so-called reciprocal altruism in human relations, which explains most of human seeming altruism towards non-kin. It is the sort of 'goodwill accounting' that underlies daily life relationships.[26]

Thus, on top of the level of co-operation implicit in the kinship network, people in a regional group would take risks for each other in expectation of similar behaviour by others within a system of risk sharing which, on the whole, has great benefits for them all. To be sure, the temptation to 'defect' from contributing one's share is very strong and ever present, especially if defection can remain undetected and on issues of life and death. Co-operation is thus constantly threatened by subtle and not so subtle forms of 'defection' and 'cheating', which is the reason why people are highly sensitive to shades in others' behaviour that might indicate their trust-worthiness. A 'positive character' is rewarded because people infer, from observation of one's behaviour towards others, one's likely behaviour towards themselves. 'Reciprocal altruism' is thus extended into 'generalized' or 'indirect reciprocal altruism' in larger social groupings.[27] As our ordinary life experience teaches us, 'reciprocal altruism' and 'generalized' or 'indirect reciprocal altruism' are at once a fragile but fairly effective mechanism of social co-operation. In any case, the regional group is a large form of social organization small enough to be sustained by both motives for social co-operation specified by evolutionary theorists: 'genuine altruism' among close kin *and* 'reciprocal altruism' among those who are not. People are inclined to help those who share the same genes with them, and those who can help do so. The regional group is small enough to have dense kinship networks, as well as for all its members to know each other, to be in contact with them, and to hold them to account.

It is here that shared culture is significant. As with genes, culture changes over time, only much faster. Culture thus diversifies among human populations in inverse relation to the contact among them. In dispersed human populations, such as those of hunter–gatherers, cultural communities can be very small. Both among the Eskimos and among the Bushmen of South Africa more or less similar languages are shared across thousands of kilometres. But in Australia lingual diversity among the hundreds of regional groups or 'dialect tribes' was much greater. There were more than 200 different languages and even more dialects.[28] As mentioned earlier, shared culture is not only a strong indication of kinship in small communities (the Eskimos and Bushmen are genetically quite homogeneous whereas the Australian Aborigines are genetically diverse, apparently descending from several old waves of immigration);[29] shared culture is also a necessary tool of social co-operation. Co-operation is dramatically more effective when cultural codes, above all language, are shared. The regional groups, or 'dialect tribes', differing from their neighbours in their language and customs, are thus the most effective frameworks of social co-operation for their members. Outside them, people would find themselves at a great disadvantage, as any immigrant knows. Therefore, shared culture in a world of cultural diversity further increases the social stake of a regional group's members in their group's survival. The regional group is bound together by mutually reinforcing and overlapping ties of kinship, social co-operation, and cultural distinctiveness.

Hence the phenomenon of 'ethnocentrism', a universal feature of the regional group which would be expanded on to larger ethnic groupings later in history. Ethnocentrism is an innate predisposition to divide the world sharply between the superior ethnic 'us' and all 'others' (which may be allies, enemies, or simply aliens). Sumner, who coined the term, illustrated its various manifestations with illuminating examples.[30] The following are some more examples that have an all too familiar ring. The 'Eskimo' (a general Indian name for their Arctic zone neighbours) 'called themselves by a variety of words which usually meant "real people". Eskimos regarded themselves literally as real people, as a class apart from all other human beings.'[31] The Yanomamo hunters and horticulturalists from the Orinoco basin between Brazil and Venezuela:

> believe that they were the first, finest, and most refined form of man to inhabit the earth. All other people are inferior . . . explaining their strange customs and peculiar languages. Yanomamo in fact means 'humanity', or at least the most important segment of humanity. All other peoples are known by the term *naba*, a concept that implies an invidious distinction between 'true' man and 'sub-human' man. . . . A foreigner is usually tolerated if he is able to provide the Yanomamo with useful items . . . but apart from that he is usually held with some contempt.

Even within the Yanomamo themselves:

> any difference between adjacent groups is exaggerated and ridiculed. Language differences in particular are promptly noted and criticised by the Yanomamo. . . . The characteristic reaction of any group to a tape recording made in another area was this: 'They speak crooked; we speak straight, the right way!'[32]

The interrelationship of kinship, social co-operation, and culture in the regional group has bearing on two major debates about human evolution. The first of these relates to biological group selection. As we have seen, modern evolutionary theory centres on individual or gene survival, with co-operation explained by the principles of 'kin selection' and 'reciprocal altruism', and the latter expanding to 'indirect' or 'generalized' 'reciprocal altruism'. However, there is an older view—which was relegated to the margins by modern theorists but which has more recently been effecting a qualified comeback—suggesting that there also exists another mechanism of co-operation. According to this view, first raised as a possibility by Darwin himself, biological selection takes place not only at the individual or gene level but also among groups. A group that is biologically endowed with greater solidarity and with individual willingness to sacrifice for the group would defeat less cohesive groups. Thus genes for genuine ingroup altruism—in addition to kinship and the calculations of reciprocal altruism—would result in greater survival of the group's members.[33]

Older, expansive formulations of this argument have been rejected by modern evolutionary biologists, on the grounds that genes for self-sacrifice on behalf of the group would have the effect of annihilating those who possessed them much faster than aiding them through improved group survival, and that 'cheaters' would proliferate. However, as some scholars have noted, the whole debate has been somewhat misconstrued. It revolves around a supposed distinction between kin selection and group selection, an abstraction that ignores the actual evolutionary history of humans, whose chronology was unknown to Darwin. In reality, throughout the vast major-ity of human evolutionary history, groups were, anyhow, small kin groups.[34] Truly large societies of non- (or remote) kin emerged only very recently, with agriculture and civilization. In terms of biological evolution (to differ-entiate from cultural evolution), they are far too recent to have a significant effect on human biology. It is thus meaningless to speak of 'group selection' as opposed to kin selection in human biological evolution actually domi-nated by kin groups. Even the regional group is a relative latecomer, although not so late as to have no biological basis.

Indeed, the overlapping and close links of kinship, social co-operation, and cultural distinctiveness in the hunter–gatherers' regional group is per-haps less than accidental. We should ask ourselves since when did humans live in regional groups. It should be recalled that chimpanzees have no such large groupings, nor are there indications of their existence among *Homo erectus* or archaic varieties of *Homo sapiens* for most of the genus *Homo*'s evolutionary history. Apparently, regional groups appeared only with mod-ern man, *Homo sapiens sapiens*. It is also to our species that the evolution of advanced lingual skills is attributed (though the uniqueness of the species in this respect is a matter of controversy); and it is with *Homo sapiens sapiens* that the explosion of culture and cultural diversity in tool making, crafts, art, and ritual is for the first time extensively documented, reaching new heights during the Upper Palaeolithic, from some 35,000 years ago. All these new developments are interdependent and mutually reinforcing. They were obviously evolutionarily advantageous in many ways, some of which are, perhaps, clearer than others. The advantages of more sophisticated tools and better communication are the most obvious. However, on the assumption that advanced lingual skills and shared culture facilitated the evolution of the regional group, which encompassed hundreds, the regional group had several major evolutionary advantages. For one thing, there was an advantage to favouring one's medium-range kin (the regional group) over far more remote kin, known as 'strangers'. More importantly, perhaps, the regional group was a far stronger grouping than the extended family group. It was simply a larger aggregate of force. This would have given *Homo sapiens sapiens* a clear advantage in an armed conflict with rivals who did not live in regional groups. Even if we reject group selection—as distinct from kin selection—as a significant factor in human evolutionary history, broader kin solidarity within a larger kin grouping would have made a great difference.[35]

Herein may lie the decisive factor in explaining one of the big enigmas in human evolution. *Homo sapiens sapiens* is now known to have spread from Africa, displacing all archaic human species that had earlier inhabited the Old World. In the best-documented case, *Homo sapiens sapiens* displaced—that is, drove to extinction—Neanderthal man, who had prospered in Europe and the Middle East. How did this happen? Peaceful explanations for this displacement dominated during the heyday of Rousseauism, and still do. Prehistorians have pointed out that even a small advantage in subsistence or reproduction, easily achieved, for example, by better tools or better communication, was enough for a wide divergence in population size to open up over not so many generations. Still, as has been asked by Jared Diamond, is it reasonable to suppose that the Neanderthals simply watched their best hunting fields gradually be taken up by the alien *Homo sapiens sapiens*, with no resort to violence at all? The American Indians, for instance, did not just sit still when the white man killed the bison upon which their livelihood depended. If the process at the beginning of the Upper Palaeolithic was not entirely peaceful after all, was the Neanderthal not a formidable rival? He was more strongly built than *Homo sapiens sapiens*, quite intelligent and a proficient hunter of big game at close quarters.

Diamond has suggested a number of possible explanations for the Neanderthals' demise. As with the isolated populations of the Americas and Australasia at the time of western expansion, they may have lacked natural immunity to epidemics brought by the invaders. However, whether *Homo sapiens sapiens* had anything like the resistance developed by the sixteenth-century dwellers of the open and largely urban Eurasian land-mass is questionable. Diamond also suggested that the greatly superior lingual communication of *Homo sapiens sapiens*, and the resulting advantage in in-group co-operation, decided the issue in their favour.[36] This is plausible. However, better communication was probably one of the principal prerequisites of larger social groupings. If it is the case that *Homo sapiens sapiens* maintained regional (tribal) group ties, whereas the Neanderthals did not have or had much weaker ones, this would have been an overwhelming advantage. Co-operation among tribe members would have created a decisive numerical superiority over the far fewer members of the Neanderthal family groups, thus explaining the Neanderthal's mysterious disappearance. The same logic can help to explain the universal triumph of *Homo sapiens sapiens* after its spread from Africa some 80,000 years ago and the displacement of all archaic humans throughout the world, which otherwise remains quite mysterious.

I wrote a specialized article on this subject, to which interested readers are referred.[37] My hypothesis, of course, is very difficult to verify. The best argument in its favour is that the regional group indeed seems to have emerged, or at least become prominent, with fully modern *Homo sapiens sapiens*. It should not be regarded as one of the many cultural inventions of *Homo sapiens sapiens*. Instead, as with the very *potential* to create culture and complex language—that is, advanced symbolic networks—the capacity for regional group relationships, with which advanced symbolic capability is intimately linked, seems to have been a skill that *Homo sapiens sapiens* had evolved biologically. As with language, regional grouping, as a minimum, exists wherever *Homo sapiens sapiens* lives. Aristotle may have exaggerated only one step in defining the members of our species as political animals by nature.

Indeed, the evolutionary roles of some forms of cultural life, such as communal ritual and ceremonies, and even the communal aspects of art, which are otherwise quite mysterious, might at least be partly explained by the evolutionary advantages of large group co-operation. As with war, religion is a complex social phenomenon. It is probably the result of several different interacting factors. Thus it might be a byproduct of the much wider scope of the powers of imagination and comprehension of *Homo sapiens sapiens*, which made them ponder, fear, and attempt to come to terms with death and the cosmic forces of nature and the universe.[38] If this line of explanation, first articulated by Thomas Hobbes and developed by various modern anthropologists of religion, is valid, there remains, however, the question of whether this 'byproduct', which plays such a prominent role in human history, is evolutionarily beneficial or detrimental. There can be two opposite arguments here, or a mixture of the two. One would stress the terrific costs that people have always invested in religion and that would appear as a wholly senseless waste of often scarce resources, better spent on people's worldly needs. In modern evolutionary terms, aided by our recent experience with computers, religion would thus be regarded as a 'bug', 'parasite', or 'virus' on the advanced intellectual 'software' of *Homo sapiens sapiens*.[39] As we see later, such things are common in the evolutionary process. No design, including those of evolution, is free from handicaps, and the only comfort for those who are burdened by them is that their rivals and competitors are also burdened by similar or other handicaps.

Conversely, religion may have had in it, evolutionarily speaking, more than worthless expenditure of resources and time. For one thing, it can be regarded as part of the large 'defence costs', which, as we see, all animal species have to incur. From Emile Durkheim, whose book *The Elementary Forms of the Religious Life* (1915) concentrated on the Australian Aboriginal groups, functionalist theorists have argued that religion's main role was in fostering social cohesion. Machiavelli, Rousseau, and the nineteenth-century French positivists had held more or less the same view. As Richard Dawkins observes, discussing the same idea in evolutionary terms: 'What a weapon! Religious faith deserves a chapter to itself in the annals of war technology.'[40] We know this only too well from history. Addressing the supposed beginnings of religion, this may mean that in those new, larger, regional groupings in which common ritual and cult ceremonies were more intensive, social co-operation became more habitual and spiritually more strongly legitimized. This was probably translated into an advantage in warfare. Indeed, not only did communal ritual and ceremonies play a central role in the life of every regional group with which we are familiar; but ritual ties were also observed everywhere to have formed the principal basis for larger alliances and confederations between regional groups, the so-called Amphictionic alliances, after the ancient Greek example. And one of the primary roles of such alliances was war. The emerging manifestations of a greatly expanded symbolic capacity, such as language, religion, art, and regional grouping, may thus have reinforced each other to give *Homo sapiens sapiens* an advantage in warfare.[41]

To be sure, although regional groups had a clear advantage in fighting against people who had no regional grouping (presumably pre-*Homo sapiens sapiens* humans), they had no such decisive advantage when *all* people lived in regional groups. This, however, as we see later, is the nature of all 'arms races'.

4

Motivation: Food and Sex

W hat are the evolutionary rewards that can make the highly dangerous activity of fighting worthwhile? This question touches on the age-old philosophical and psychological enquiry into the nature of the basic human system of motivation, needs, and desires. Numerous lists of basic needs and desires have been put together over the centuries, more or less casually or convincingly. The most recent ones show little if any marked progress over the older, back to Thomas Hobbes's *Leviathan* (Chapter 6).[1] In the absence of an evolutionary perspective, these lists have always had something arbitrary and trivial about them. They lacked a unifying regulatory rationale that would suggest why the various needs and desires came to be, or how they related to each other. Indeed, when varying unitary 'principles' of human behaviour were put forward, it was mostly in this respect that they were lacking. The splits in the psychoanalytic movement are a good example of this. While Freud claimed that the basic human drive was sexuality, Alfred Adler, following Henri Bergson and Friedrich Nietzsche, argued that it was in fact the striving for superiority, and Karl Gustav Jung emphasized the quest for creativity and whole-being. There was no way of deciding, other than faith within what indeed became semi-religious orthodox sects, why it was that this drive rather than the other one was the 'truly' basic one, or why in fact there should be a unitary basic drive at all.

The human motivational system is, of course, not my topic. In this book it concerns us only in its relation to the subject of fighting. Again we start from the 'human state of nature', the 99.5 per cent of the genus *Homo*'s evolutionary history in which humans lived in small kin groups as hunter–gatherers, a timespan that is responsible for our biological inheritance. In this 'state of nature' people's behaviour patterns are generally to be considered as evolutionarily adaptive. Later in the book, we see how this evolutionary inheritance has interacted with, and been transformed by, the staggering and manifold human cultural development.

The causes of primitive warfare remain a puzzle in anthropology. In the past decades, the discussion has been largely dominated by what has been presented as a controversy between the evolutionist and an alternative, cultural–materialist theory. That the controversy has taken this form is a result of the historical development of anthropology. One of the principal theoretical approaches in anthropology, cultural materialism stresses people's desire to improve their material lot as the basis of human motivation. As there is a very substantial grain of truth in this idea, cultural materialism has had an obvious explanatory appeal. However, its limitations should have been equally clear, and they were revealed, for example, in the anthropological study of war during the 1970s. Rather than hunter–gatherers, it was primitive agriculturalists, horticulturalists, who stood at the centre of the debate. These were the Yanomamo, living in the rain forests of the Orinoco basin in the Brazil–Venezuela border region, and the highland peoples of New Guinea in today's Indonesia and Papua New Guinea. It was not clear why these horticulturalists fought among themselves (and they did), because there was no real sign that either the Yanomamo or some of the New Guinea highlanders experienced agricultural land shortage. The proponents of the materialist school thus suggested that they fought over highly valued animal protein. With the Yanomamo, this took the form of competition over hunting resources in the forests around their villages. In New Guinea, the competition was allegedly over grazing grounds in the forests for domesticated pigs. Although this interpretation had some plausibility, it did not sit quite comfortably with all the evidence.[2] Indeed, as we see later, the cultural materialists themselves began to look for complementary explanations.

At a more fundamental level, as with other theoretical 'systems' such as the psychoanalytic schools mentioned earlier, the cultural materialists never seriously explained, never felt that there was a need to explain, their central argument: why was it that the quest for material gains was the overriding motive of human action? This was simply postulated by them as a fact of life, the way things were, in the same way that anthropology as a discipline never asked itself what was the reason for kin solidarity (or for the incest taboo) that anthropologists everywhere observed as fundamental features of the societies that they studied. Furthermore, the predominance of the material- ist argument necessitated that all other possible motives would be somehow explained away as secondary, derivative, or disguises for the material motive. As with the Marxist perception of a materialistic 'infrastructure' versus ideo- logical 'superstructure', there was, again, some truth in this as well. Still, the materialist argument often called for elaborate intellectual acrobatics, which in extreme cases made cultural materialism famous for the most contrived explanatory stories.[3]

As modern evolutionary theory, which had been evolving since the 1960s, gathered momentum in the mid-1970s, it slowly began to win atten- tion among anthropologists. One of the first anthropologists influenced by it was Napoleon A. Chagnon, who had already been the best-known student of the Yanomamo. In one article (and a documentary film), he showed, for example, how in a quarrel in a Yanomamo village people were divided along kin lines, rushing to support their close kin in successively expanding kin circles, as the theory of kin selection would predict. In other articles, Chagnon argued that Yanomamo warfare, as well as their internal conflicts, were predominantly about reproductive opportunities. In inter-village war- fare, women were regularly raped or kidnapped for marriage, or both. Village headmen and distinguished warriors had many wives and children, many times more than ordinary people did. Violent feuds within the village were chiefly caused by adultery.[4]

As we see later, most of these ideas were true. Unfortunately, however, Chagnon—who in the 'protein controversy' wholly opposed the idea that Yanomamo warfare involved competition over hunting territories—gave the impression that evolutionary theory was about reproduction in the narrow (sexual) rather than the broadest sense (for example, feeding the offspring). His arguments have thus opened themselves to all sorts of criti- cisms; anthropologists have anyhow exhibited considerable resistance to the intrusion of evolutionary theory that called for a thorough re-evaluation of accepted anthropological interpretative traditions. Many of the criticisms levelled against Chagnon's position have been poorly informed about the fundamentals of evolutionary theory—for instance, one critic queried why, if fighting was beneficial for inclusive fitness, it was not continuous and ubiquitous.[5] Repeating an error that we have already discussed, he failed to realize that fighting, like any other behaviour, could be only one possible tactic for inclusive fitness, depending for its success, and activation, on the presence of specific conditions. Another cluster of often-voiced criticisms was that it was not true that people were motivated by the desire to maximize the number of their offspring, that the widespread occurrence of infanticide among primitive people was one example that belied this idea, and that women were sought for economic as well as sexual purposes, as a labour force.[6]

The flaws in these criticisms can be pointed out only briefly here. It is not that people consciously 'want' to maximize the number of their children. Although there is also some human desire for children and a great attachment to them once they exist, it is mainly the desire for sex—Thomas Malthus's 'passion'—that functions in nature as the powerful biological proximate (intermediate) mechanism for maximizing reproduction. As humans, and other living creatures, normally engage in sex throughout their fertile lives, they have a vast reproductive potential, which, before effective contraception, mainly depended for its realization on environmental conditions. Infanticide typically takes place when conditions of resource scarcity threaten the survival chances of the newborn's elder siblings, as, for example, of an elder nursing infant—inclusive fitness is not about maximizing offspring number but about maximizing the number of surviving offspring. The fact that women may sometimes also be valued for economic reasons is strictly in line with evolutionary theory—people must feed, find shelter, and protect themselves (somatic activities) in order to reproduce successfully.[7]

This brings us to the crux of the current anthropological controversy. Having initially emphasized only the reproductive implications of warfare, thus giving rise to the misguided notion among his critics that this was all that evolutionary theory was about, Chagnon has correctly begun to stress the complementary nature of the somatic and reproductive efforts within this theory.[8] Curiously, however, he has largely undermined his own position, and thus left the whole debate on the wrong track, by suggesting that in doing so he has been 'synthesizing' the insights of evolutionary theory with those of cultural materialism. There seemed to be a similar need for a synthesis from the other side. Chagnon's main protagonist in recent years, R. Brian Ferguson, has advanced a highly elaborate and increasingly one-dimensional materialistic interpretation of the causes of primitive war-fare. However, after exhausting all options for explaining away and playing down any non-material motive, he has had to admit that some such motives did in fact exist.[9] Offering, as he did, an increasingly narrow interpretation, he, too, has called for a broadening of approach to the study of the causes of war.[10] Seemingly shared by both sides, it has been a call that other anthropologists involved in the debate could only welcome.

However, the real meaning of Chagnon's argument was that evolutionary theory in fact encompassed the materialist interpretation, let alone its eco-logical counterpart—indeed, that it offered the broad explanatory rationale for principal materialist/ecological insights. What required synthesis were the somatic and reproductive elements in explaining war rather than the materialist and evolutionary theories, because evolutionary theory had always consisted of both elements. The false dichotomy of the reproductive versus materialist debate is demonstrated by some of the debate's strange twists and turns. As we see later, in looking for a complement to their game shortage hypothesis, materialists such as Marvin Harris came up with a reproductive interpretation. On the other side, even though Chagnon has acknowledged both the somatic and the reproductive elements of evo-lutionary theory, he has continued to claim that with primitive people—in general, not only with the Yanomamo—it was the reproductive rather than the somatic reasons that were chiefly responsible for warfare.

In fact, the 'human state of nature' was not that different from the general state of nature. Both somatic and reproductive struggles were an integral part of it. Cultural diversity in human societies is stressed by social scientists and historians for excellent reasons, but all too often to the point of losing sight of our easily observed large core of species specificity.[11] It has long been assumed by many in these disciplines that people may be moved to action—including fighting—for practically any reason. However, in reality, hunter–gatherers, and other primitive societies, manifested a remarkably similar set of reasons for fighting and remarkably similar warfare patterns, regularly observed by field anthropologists wherever they went. It is the intricate interactions and manifold refraction of these reasons in humans, exponen-tially multiplied by cultural development, that are responsible for the stag-gering wealth and complexity of our species' behaviour patterns, including that of fighting. As Sumner put it: the great motives that move people to social activity—including fighting—are hunger, love, vanity, and fear of superior powers.[12] Although I now go through the reasons for warfare among hunter–gatherers (as observed by anthropologists) seemingly one by one, it is not the intention here to provide yet another 'list' of separate elements. Instead, I seek to show how the various 'reasons' come together in an integrated motivational complex. This complex has been shaped by the logic of evolution and natural selection for billions of years, including the history of millions of years of our genus *Homo*, and of tens of thousands of years of our species, *Homo sapiens sapiens*.

SUBSISTENCE RESOURCES: HUNTING TERRITORIES, WATER, SHELTER, RAW MATERIALS

Resource competition is a prime cause of aggression, violence, and deadly violence in nature. The reason for this is that food, water, and, to a lesser degree, shelter against the elements are tremendous selection forces. As Darwin, following Malthus, explained, living organisms, including humans, tended to propagate rapidly. Their numbers are constrained and checked only by the limited resources of their particular ecological habitats and by all sorts of competitors, such as conspecifics, animals of other species that have similar consumption patterns, predators, parasites, and pathogens.[13]

Some anthropologists have disputed that this rationale applied to humans, pointing out that hunter–gatherers, both recent and during the Pleistocene, exhibited on average little if any demographic growth over long periods of time and constantly regulated their numbers through infanticide. However, as we have already seen, infanticide is generally used to maximize the number of surviving offspring precisely when people push against the resource walls of their particular environment. When these environments suddenly expand, an unusual event in nature, demographic growth is dramatic. In recorded history, we are familiar with many such instances. Perhaps the best known is the rapid proliferation of Old World wildlife into new territories in the wake of the European age of discovery. Mice, rats, and rabbits, for example, did spectacularly well in the Americas and Oceania, where their traditional competitors were absent or weak. Humans propagated equally dramatically in similar circumstances. More than a million and a half years ago, *Homo erectus* broke out of his original habitat in Africa and filled up large parts of the Old World. From about 80,000 years ago *Homo sapiens sapiens* repeated that process on an even wider scale. In the most famous examples, only in the last tens of thousands of years, small groups of our species crossed from Asia through the frozen Bering Straits into North America, previously uninhabited by humans. In a remarkably short time, these small groups propagated into hundreds of thousands and millions of people, even before the introduction of agriculture, filling up the Americas from the far north to the south. In the same way, the Pacific islands, widely separated by thousands of kilometres of ocean, were inhabited only during the last two millennia by small groups of east Asian people, who made the crossing with their canoes. Again, these first settlers, in most cases probably no more than a few dozen people on each island, rapidly filled up their new habitats, increasing in numbers to thousands and tens of thousands.

These dramatic cases only demonstrate once more that as a rule, and contrary to the Rousseauite belief, our Palaeolithic ancestors had no empty spaces to move to. The human—similar to the animal—tendency for maximizing reproduction was constantly checked by resource scarcity and competition, mostly by conspecifics. As mentioned, this competition was largely about nourishment, the basic and most critical somatic activity of all living creatures, which often causes dramatic fluctuations in their numbers. Resource competition, and conflict, are not, however, a given quantity but a highly modulated variable. Resource competition and conflict change over time and place in relation to the varying nature of the resources available and of human population patterns in diverse ecological habitats.[14] Human adaptations in different ecological environments are by far the most diverse in nature. The basic question, then, is: what are the factors that act as the main brakes on human populations in any particular habitat? What are the main scarcities, stresses and hence objects of human competition? Again, the answer to these questions is not fixed but varies considerably in relation to the conditions.

As we saw, in extreme cases such as the mid-Canadian Arctic, where resources were highly diffuse and human population density was very low, resource competition and conflict barely existed. In arid and semi-arid environments, such as those of central Australia, where human population density was also very low, water holes were often the main cause of resource competition and conflict. They were obviously critical in times of drought, when whole groups of Aborigines are recorded as having perished. For this reason, however, there was a tendency to control them even when stress was less pressing. Indeed, as we have seen with respect to the Walbiri and Waringari hunter–gatherers of the mid-Australian desert recorded by Meggitt, fighting, to the scale of 'pitched battles', could take place in order to 'occupy' and monopolize wells.[15] In well-watered environments, where there was no water shortage and hence no water competition, food often became the chief cause of resource competition and conflict, especially at times of stress, but also in expectation of and preparation for stress.[16] As Lourandos writes in respect of Aboriginal Australia: 'In south-western Victoria, competition between groups involved a wide range of natural resources, including territory, and is recorded by many early European observers throughout Victoria.' Despite his general abstention from the words conflict or fighting, Lourandos's next sentence shows that his 'competition' also includes 'combat'.[17] Resources meant above all food. The nature of the food in question obviously varied with the environment. Still, it seems safe to conclude that it was predominantly meat of all sorts— be it of land animals, birds, or fish—which was hotly contested among hunter–gatherers.

This fact, which is simply a consequence of nutritional value, is discernible throughout nature. Herbivores rarely fight over food, because the nutritional value of grass is too low for effective monopolization. To put it in terms of the anthropological model that relates defended territoriality and violent competition to resource density,[18] the nutritional value of grass is simply too 'diffuse' to make the effort to monopolize it cost-effective. Fruit, roots, seeds, and some plants are considerably more nutritious than grass and are often the object of competition and fighting, among both animals and humans. Meat, however, represents the most concentrated nutritional value in nature and is the object of the most intense competition. Animals may defend territories to monopolize mates or food, or both. The higher the nutritional value of their food, the more the food element of territorial behaviour would be present in addition to the reproductive element. At the top of the food chain, meat eaters would not only defend their hunting territories against conspecifics; whenever they had the opportunity, they would also act against predators from other species to weed out competitors. Lions, for example, have been observed to kill leopard and hyena cubs whenever they could find them. Game resources are the principal factor determining predators' spacing out in nature.

Indeed, before and during the 'protein controversy', game resources have been consistently shown in a series of studies to play a similar role across a whole range of primitive human societies examined. Chagnon was right that there were other, and perhaps even more important, (reproductive) reasons for Yanomamo warfare, but he was wrong in claiming that game competition was not a reason at all. As his protagonists reminded him, he himself had noted that 'game animals are not abundant, and an area is rapidly hunted out'. His protagonists accepted that the Yanomamo suffered from no 'protein deficiency', but they pointed out that the minimum levels of consumption achieved were secured only by a static population level, kept static by, among other things, the high mortality rates in fighting recorded among the Yanomamo, as well as among other primitive peoples. A rise in human population level would easily be translated into game depletion,[19] hence the inherent state of competition and conflict between the human hunters. Alien hunters would naturally be regarded as competitors and encounter animosity. Indeed, in environments where game were highly concentrated and unevenly spread, food competition and conflict would be the most intense. As we saw in both northern and southern Australia and in the American north-west, prime concentrations of fish, birds, and other wildlife, such as river mouths, were far superior to ordinary stretches of beach or river shore, let alone inland territories. Violent clashes, brought about by hunting forays and population movements, were commonplace, undoubtedly becoming more intense when hunger and starvation loomed. According to one comparative study, territory changed hands among hunter–gatherers up to a rate of five to ten per cent per generation.[20] Things were further complicated in instances where the vital concentrations of game were geographically mobile rather than more or less static. Migration routes of bison (buffalo) herds on the North American Great Plains were changing and difficult to predict. Hunting in other tribes' territories thus became necessary from time to time, often resulting in warfare.[21] Upper Palaeolithic hunters of large game in Europe, from France to Ukraine, may have exhibited similar patterns to the American Indian bison hunters.

The main point of all this is that resource competition and conflict existed in most hunter–gatherer societies. But how significant they were, how they ranked in comparison with other possible reasons for conflict, and what resource specifically was mostly in conflict depended on the particular conditions of the human and natural environment in question. Scarcities and stresses, and hence the causes and occurrence of conflict, varied. The concept of territoriality, which was brought to the fore in the 1960s by Ardrey, Lorenz, and Tinbergen, ought to be looked at in this light. Similar to aggression, territoriality is not a blind instinct. It is subservient to the evolutionary calculus, especially in humans, whose habitats are so diverse. Among hunter–gatherers, territories varied dramatically in size—territorial behaviour itself could gain or lose in significance—in direct relation to the resources and resource competition. The same applies to population density, another popular explanation in the 1960s for violence. In other than the most extreme cases, it is mainly in relation to resource scarcity, and hence as a factor in resource competition, that population density would function as a trigger for fighting. Otherwise, Tokyo and the Netherlands would have been among the most violent places on earth.[22]

In conclusion, let us understand more closely the evolutionary calculation that can make the highly dangerous activity of fighting over resources worthwhile. In our societies of plenty, it might be difficult to comprehend how precarious people's subsistence in pre-modern societies was (and still is). The spectre of hunger and starvation always loomed over their heads. Affecting both mortality and reproduction (the latter through human sexual appetite and women's fertility), it constantly, in varying degrees, trimmed down their numbers, acting in combination with disease. Thus, struggle over resources was very often evolutionarily cost-effective. The benefits of fighting must also be matched against possible alternatives (other than starvation). One of them was to break contact and move elsewhere. This, of course, often happened, especially if one's enemy was much stronger, but this strategy had clear limitations. As already noted, by and large, there were no 'empty spaces' for people to move to. In the first place, space is not even and the best, most productive, habitats were normally already taken. One could be forced out to less hospitable environments, which may also have been earlier populated by other less fortunate people. Indeed, finding empty niches required exploration, which again might involve violent encounters with other human groups. Furthermore, a move meant leaving the group's own habitat, with the resources and dangers of which the group's members were intimately familiar, and travelling into uncharted environments. For hunter–gatherers, such a change could involve heavy penalties. Moreover, giving in to pressure from outside might establish a pattern of victimization. Encouraged by their success, the alien group might repeat and even increase its pressure. A strategy of conflict, therefore, concerns not only the object currently in dispute but also the whole pattern of future relations. Standing up for one's own might in fact mean lessening the occurrence of conflict in the future. No less so, and perhaps more, than actual fighting, conflict is about deterrence. The spectacular nature of the activity of fighting had largely obscured this fact before the nuclear age.

Having discussed the possible benefits and alternatives of fighting, deterrence brings us to its costs. Conflict would become an evolutionarily more attractive strategy if those who resort to it lower their risk of serious bodily harm and death. Consequently, displays of strength and threats of aggressive behaviour are the most widely used weapons in conflict, among both animals and humans. It is the state of mutual apprehension and armed surveillance—more than the spates of active fighting which, of course, establish this pattern of relations—that is the norm among human groups. Furthermore, when humans, and animals, do resort to deadly violence, they mostly do so under conditions in which the odds are greatly tilted in their favour. As we see later, it is not the open pitched battle but the raid and ambush that characterize primitive warfare and constitute its most deadly forms. People, however, were at the receiving, as well as the inflicting, end of these asymmetrical forms of fighting. Thus mortality rates in hunter–gatherers' warfare were still very substantial, higher than in any modern society.

Animals are important not only for their meat but also as a source of hides and furs for clothing in cool climates, and of bone, horn, and other materials for tools. Other vital raw materials for making tools include flint and obsidian (volcanic glass). There are also luxury, prestige, and exotic goods such as pigments (ochre), ivory, and feathers, the evolutionary value of which is discussed later. In most cases, these raw materials may not in themselves be scarce among hunter–gatherers, in the sense that there may be enough of them in the environment for all. Nevertheless, as we saw in Australia, they may still lead to violent conflict. As at least some of these items might be unevenly spread, the nearby inhabitants often tried to monopolize them for trade purposes. Furthermore, crossing group boundaries to obtain raw materials might also carry the risk of violent confrontation because of the state of conflict and mutual apprehension over other things that might prevail among human groups. In the evolutionarily shaped motivational complex that may lead to conflict, the elements are mixed, intertwined, and mutually affected.

REPRODUCTION

The struggle for reproduction is about access to sexual partners of reproductive potential. There is a fundamental asymmetry here between males and females, which runs throughout nature. Females invest a great deal more in carrying and rearing the fertilized eggs, and often also the offspring that come out of them. Their reproductive potential is limited by this heavy logistical burden, because they can carry and rear only a limited number of fertilized eggs or offspring at one time and, hence, in a lifetime. In optimal natural conditions, human females, for instance, can give birth to more than 20 children, but more realistically to between a half and a quarter that number. Thus, although sufficient sexual activity is necessary for maximizing female conception, increasing the number of sex partners is not. At any time, a female can be fertilized only once. Consequently, evolutionarily speaking, she must take care to make the best of it. It is quality rather than quantity that she seeks. What she requires is that the male who fertilizes her should be the best that she can find. Hence, she must be choosy. She must select the male who looks the best equipped for survival and reproduction, so that he imparts his genes, and his qualities, to the offspring. In those species, similar to the human, where the male also contributes to the raising of the offspring, his skills as a provider and his loyalty are other crucial considerations.

In contrast to the female, a male has theoretically almost no limit to the number of offspring that he can have. He can fertilize an indefinite number of females, thus multiplying his own genes in the next generations. The male's reproductive capacity increases in direct relation to the number of his sex partners, whereas the female's does not. In real life, the sexually most successful human males, for example, can have, indeed often had, scores of children. The main brake on male sexual success is competition from other males.

All this, of course, is only an abstract. Around this rationale, sexual strategies in nature are highly diverse and have many nuances.[23] Some species are highly polygynous. In many social animals, the leading male monopolizes all the females in the group. Fighting among the males for control over the harem is most intense and for good reason: the evolutionary stakes are the highest. In many species, especially among herbivores, access to females is practically the only reason for intraspecific fighting. The more polygynous a species, the greater would be the size difference between males and females (sexual dimorphism), because males would be selected for size and ferocity. Among the apes, the highly polygynous gorilla is the best example of this. Males of many non-social species also fight among themselves for any sexually receptive female that they encounter. Not all species, however, are highly polygynous. Access to females can be more evenly spread, all the way down to pair monogamy. However, although monogamy reduces, it by no means terminates, male competition. In monogamous systems, the quality of the female partner also gains significance. If the male is restricted to one partner, it becomes highly important for him as well to choose the partner with the best reproductive qualities that he can get: young, healthy and optimally built for bearing offspring—that is, in sexual parlance, the most attractive female.

Where do humans stand on this scale? The need to take care of very slowly maturing offspring, which requires sustained investment by both parents, turns humans in the monogamous direction, to pair bonding. As we saw, this in itself significantly reduces male competition and violence, because reproductive opportunities are more equally spread. Competition over the best female partners remains, however. Furthermore, humans, and men in particular, are not strictly monogamous. In the first place, men would tend to have more than one wife when they can. Only a minority can, however. Although in most known human societies, including those of hunter–gatherers, polygyny was legitimate, only a few, select, well-to-do men in these societies were able to support, and thus have, the extra wives and children. Second, in addition to official or unofficial wives, men would tend to search for extramarital sexual liaisons with other women, married or unmarried. On the man's part, this infidelity is—evolutionarily speaking—a strategy intended to increase his reproductive success by gaining a chance to fertilize more women. On the 'other woman's' part, if she is unmarried, an affair might be her only chance of a sexual relationship, or an opportunity for a relationship with a successful man (attractive and supporting). For a married woman as well, an affair might be an opportunity for a relationship with a better-quality man than the one she has, promise extra care and support, or provide insurance against marriage failure.

Again, this is only an abstract, because the 'battle of the sexes' and sexual infidelity are not our subject. But, indeed, how does all this affect human violent conflict and fighting? The evidence across the range of hunter–gatherer peoples (and that of primitive agriculturalists) tells the same story. Within the tribe, women-related quarrels, violence, so-called blood feuds, and homicide were rife, often as the principal category of violence. Some incidents were caused by suitors' competition, some by women's abduction and forced sex, some by broken promises of marriage, and most, perhaps, by jealous husbands over suspicion of wives' infidelity. Between tribes, the picture is not very different, and is equally uniform. Warfare regularly involved stealing of women, who were then subjected to multiple rape, or taken for marriage, or both. Indeed, the story of Moses' command to the Children of Israel to kill all the Midianites except for the virgin women who could be taken (*Numbers* 31. 17–18) typifies victors' conduct through-out history: kill the men, rape the women, and take the most young and beautiful as war trophies. If women could not be taken because of the enemy's opposition, or because of domestic opposition at home, they would often be killed like the men and children, in order to decrease the numbers of the enemy.

So hunter–gatherers' warfare commonly involved the stealing and raping of women; but was it about women? Was the stealing and raping of women the cause or a side effect of hunter–gatherers' warfare? In recent anthropological literature, this question was posed by Ferguson in respect of Yanomamo warfare. Ferguson, who holds that warfare is caused by material reasons, has disputed Chagnon's claim that the Yanomamo fought primarily for women. Chagnon, for his part, dismissed the materialist position, enlist-ing the testimony of Yanomamo men who had told him, amused: 'Even though we like meat, we like women a whole lot more!' However, even Chagnon wavered on occasions about whether Yanomamo warfare was really about women.[24]

The Yanomamo are hunters and horticulturalists rather than pure hunter–gatherers. However, the fundamental question in dispute is relevant to pure hunter–gatherers as well. As indicated, I think that this question is in fact pointless and has repeatedly bemused scholars and led them to a dead end. It artificially takes out and isolates one element from the wholeness of the human motivational complex that may lead to warfare, losing sight of the overall rationale that underpins these elements. It is as though one were to ask what is 'really' the thing people are after in going to the supermarket: bread, meat, or cheese. In fact it is only in specific cases that the question of the more prominent motive becomes meaningful.[25] In the evolution-shaped 'human state of nature', the human motivational complex consists of varying mixtures of the particular scarcities for which people in any given society may resort to violent competition. Both somatic and reproductive elements may be present with humans; moreover, both these elements are interconnected and they give rise, in turn, to other elements, which are discussed later. Among hunter–gatherers, women were often a strong motive for warfare, frequently the main motive, but rarely the only one. Again, women are such a prominent motive because reproductive opportunities are a very strong selective force indeed.

The continent-size Australian laboratory of simple hunter–gatherers is, once more, an unmatched source of data, already cited in this connection as an example by Darwin (and in Chapter 3 above).[26] According to the Englishman William Buckley, who lived with the Aborigines from 1803 to 1835, most of the frequent fighting and killing among them:

> were occasioned by the women having been taken away from one tribe to another; which was of frequent occurrence. At other times they were caused by the women willingly leaving their husbands, and joining other men. . . . [T]hese dear creatures were at the bottom of every mischief.[27]

In the isolated Tasmania, the natives reported similar reasons for the endemic fighting, territorial segregation, and mutual apprehension that prevailed among their groups. Food could become scarce in the winters, but women were the main cause of feuding and fighting.[28]

Polygyny was a significant factor in many places. It was legitimate among all the Aborigine tribes of Australia and highly desired by the men. However, comparative studies among the tribes show that men with only one wife comprised the largest category among married men, often the majority. Men with two wives comprised the second largest category. The percentage of men with three or more wives fell sharply, to around 10–15 per cent of all married men, with the figures declining with every extra wife.[29] To how many wives could the most successful men aspire? There was a significant environmental variation here. In the arid central desert, four, five, or six wives were the top. Five or six was also the top figure mentioned by Buckley for the Aborigines living in the region of Port Philip (Melbourne) in the south-east in the early nineteenth century. However, in the richer and more productive parts of Arnhem Land and nearby islands in the north, a few men could have as many as 10–12 wives, and in some places, in the most extreme cases, even double that number. There was a direct correlation of resource density, resource accumulation and monopolization, social ranking, and polygyny.[30] Naturally, the increase in the number of a man's wives generally correlated with his reproduction rate (number of children). Statistics for the Aborigines are scarce.[31] However, among the Xavante horticulturalists of Brazil, for example, 16 of the 37 men in one village (74 of 184 according to a larger survey) had more than one wife. The chief had five, more than any other man. He fathered 23 surviving offspring who constituted 25 per cent of the surviving offspring in that generation. Shinbone, a most successful Yanomamo man, had 43 children. His brothers were also highly successful, so Shinbone's father had 14 children, 143 grandchildren, 335 great-grandchildren, and 401 great-great-grandchildren, at the time of the research.[32]

The same applied to hunter–gatherers. The leaders of the Aka Pygmies were found to be more than twice as polygynous as ordinary people, and to father more children.[33] As we saw, resource scarcity reduced social differentiation, including in marriage, but did not eliminate it. Among the !Kung of the arid Kalahari Desert, polygyny was much more limited, but five per cent of married men still had two wives.[34] Women-related feuds were the main cause of homicide among them. The natives of the American north-west coast and Arctic, our other great microcosm of hunter–gatherer peoples, demonstrate the same trend. In the extremely harsh conditions of the mid-Canadian Arctic, where resources were scarce and diffuse, fighting over resources barely existed. As a result of the resource scarcity, marriages among the native Eskimos were also predominantly monogamous. One study registered only 3 polygynies of 61 marriages. Still, wife stealing was widespread, and probably the main cause of homicide and 'blood feuds' among the Eskimos.[35] 'A stranger in the camp, particularly if he was travelling with his wife, could become easy prey to the local people. He might be killed by any camp fellow in need of a woman.' Among the Eskimos of the more densely populated Alaskan coast, abduction of women was a principal cause of warfare. Polygyny, too, was more common among

71

them, although restricted to the few.[36] Strong *Ingalik* ('big men') often had a second wife, and 'there was a fellow who had five wives at one time and seven at another. This man was a great fighter and had obtained his women by raiding'.[37]

As discussed in Chapter 3, the resource-rich environment of the north-west coast accentuated resource competition and social ranking. Conflict over resources was therefore intense. However, resource competition was not disassociated from reproduction, but constituted, in fact, an integral whole with it. Typically, women are not even mentioned in Ferguson's elaborate materialist study of north-west coast Indian warfare. Nevertheless, they were there. Most natives of the north-west coast were monogamous. However, the rich, strong, and powerful were mostly polygynous. The number of wives varied from tribe to tribe, but 'a number' or 'several' is normally quoted, and up to 20 wives are mentioned in one case. The household of such successful men is repeatedly described as having been very substantial and impressive indeed. Furthermore, as is universally the case, the mainly female slaves taken in the raids and working for their captors also shared their masters' bed.[38]

After all, what was the reason that more resources and more prestigious goods were desired and accumulated by the natives, most successfully by the chiefs and 'big men'? For somatic reasons, to be sure—that is, above all, in order to feed, clothe, and dwell as well as they could, but also to feed, clothe, and house larger families, with more wives and more children, and to demonstrate their ability to do so in advance, in order to rank as worthy of the extra wives. Competition over women can lead to warfare indirectly as well as directly. Conflict over resources was at least partly conflict over the ability to acquire and support women and children. Brian Hayden has advanced an anthropological model whereby simple resources in resource-rich societies are accumulated and converted to luxury items in an intensified competition for status, prestige, and power.[39] He could add women to the list of converted goods. Resources, reproduction, and, as we see later, status, are interconnected and interchangeable in the evolution-shaped complex that motivates people. Resources are convertible to more and 'better' women. In some fortunate cases—as with mass and energy in Einstein's equations—the opposite is also true, and women generate resources that are greater than those that they and the children require from the husband. With the Indians of the Great Plains, for instance, the many women of the chiefs and 'big men' produced decorated robes for the white man's trade.[40] Finally, both resources and women contributed to status, which in turn was likely to increase one's access to resources and matrimonial opportunities. The explanation for their wars that M. J. Meggitt recorded from the Mae Enga horticulturalists of New Guinea highlands ties all these elements together wonderfully:

> A clan that lacks sufficient land cannot produce enough of the crops and the pigs needed to obtain the wives who are to bear future warriors to guard its domains and daughters whose brideprice will secure mates for their 'brothers'. . . . And without wives, how can this clan tend its gardens and pigs? How can we contribute to exchange of pigs to attract military and economic support in times of trouble? Therefore, men say, a clan has no choice but to use all means at its command to acquire more land as quickly as possible, or it will have a short life.[41]

Polygyny among the Enga was 'the ideal', practised, according to one sample, by 17.2 per cent of the men. Among another highlands tribe, the Goilala, it amounted to 12 per cent of the men (16 per cent of the married men), with some men having as many as four wives. With them as well, marriages were an interrelated complex, comprising sexual, economic, and alliance aspects.[42]

As mentioned earlier, wealth, status, matrimonial success, and power were similarly interconnected among the 'big men' of northern Australia.[43] The same pattern applied to the 'big men' (umialik) of the Eskimo hunter–gatherers of the Alaskan coast:

> In case of a theft the umialik, as the man with the most material goods, was likely to have been the victim. If he had more than one wife, his ties of blood and marriage were greater than those of others, and he could depend on many persons for support. Furthermore, by being an umialik he was a person whose opinions the others respected.[44]

A positive feedback loop mechanism was in operation. Chagnon has shown one way in which this mechanism worked with the Yanomamo, and Ian Keen, an authority on Aborigines' marriage, has independently detected the same pattern among the Australian hunter–gatherers. Clan growth depended on reproductive success. Now, the largest clans in a tribe, those comprising more siblings and cousins, acted, as always, on the principle of kin solidarity vis-à-vis the rest of the tribe. They moved on to increase their advantage by controlling leadership positions, resources, and marriage opportunities at the expense of the others. As a result, large clans tended to dominate a tribe, politically and demographically, over time. The Yanomamo Shinbone family, mentioned above, grew into several villages within a few generations.[45] The notion that there is a self- and mutually reinforcing tendency that works in favour of the rich, mighty, and successful, facilitating their access to the 'good things of life', goes back a long way. The idea that 'the rich get richer' is valid in a much wider sense. To succeed, a man had to have as many as possible of the following qualifications: he had to be a good provider (hunter), strong, socially ('politically') astute, and come from a large ('good') family.

Polygyny greatly exacerbated women's scarcity and direct and indirect male competition and conflict over them. Indeed, a cross-cultural study has found polygyny to be one of the most distinctive correlates that there is of feuding and internal warfare.[46] There is another factor contributing to women's scarcity and male competition. In all hunter–gatherer (and agricultural) societies, female infanticide is regularly practised. Parents prefer boys who can hunt (or work in the fields) and protect. Infanticide is often covert and attributed to accidents, but census statistics of pre-industrial societies tell an unmistakable story. Although the number of male and female babies should be nearly equal at birth (105:100 in favour of boys), there are many more boys than girls in childhood. Surveys of hundreds of different communities from over 100 different cultures (of which about a fifth were hunter–gatherers) has shown that juvenile sex ratios averaged 127:100 in favour of boys, with an even higher rate in some societies. The Eskimos are one of the most extreme cases. Their harsh environment made them wholly dependent on male hunting, whereas female foraging played a greater economic role in milder climates. Thus, female infanticide was particularly widespread among them. They registered childhood sex ratios of 150:100 and even 200:100 in favour of boys. No wonder then that the Eskimos experienced such a high homicide rate over women, even though polygyny barely existed among them. Among Australian Aboriginal tribes childhood ratios of 125:100 and even 138:100 in favour of boys were recorded. The Orinoco and Amazonian basin hunters and horticulturalists have been closely studied. Their childhood boy ratio to every 100 girls is: Yanomamo 129 (140 for the first two years of life), Xavante 124, Peruvian Cashinahua 148. In Fiji the figure was 133. In tribal Montenegro it was estimated at 160. Although the evidence is naturally weaker, similar ratios in favour of males have been found among the skeletons of adult Middle and Upper Palaeolithic hunter–gatherers, indicating a similar practice of female infanticide that may go back hundreds of thousands of years.[47]

Polygyny and female infanticide thus created a scarcity of women and increased men's competition for them. How was this competition resolved? This was partly by peaceful, albeit still oppressive, means. Although a study of the Walbiri Aborigines shows that no men were excluded from marriage altogether,[48] things may have been different for a small minority of marginalized men in more ranked hunter–gatherer societies. Furthermore, in all primitive societies females were married at puberty, whereas most males married in their late 20s or even 30s. This 10- to 15-year difference in matrimonial age between men and women helped a great deal to offset the sex imbalance. In addition, males were victims of hunting accidents (and boys have always been and continue to be more prone to accidental death in risky games than girls), although this may have been partly offset by female deaths in giving birth. Finally, however, there was also open conflict: male death in feuding and warfare.

The correlation of male violent death and women's scarcity was first pointed out by Warner in his study of the north Australian Murngin, and later independently rediscovered and greatly elaborated by Divale and Harris.[49] Among the Yanomamo, for instance, and they can be regarded as representative in this respect: about 15 per cent of the adults die as a result of inter- and intragroup violence. The division of violent death between males and females is very uneven, however. The figure for the males is 24 per cent versus 7 per cent for the females.[50] The Plains Indians showed a deficit of 50 per cent for the adult males in the Blackfoot tribe in 1805 and 33 per cent in 1858, whereas during the reservation period the sex ratio rapidly approached 50:50.[51] Although the Yanomamo are dubbed the 'fierce people' and the Plains Indians held a similar reputation, much the same applies to the !Kung Bushmen of the Kalahari Desert, popularly regarded as a model 'peaceful' society. Anthropologist Richard Lee, who contributed to the creation of this popular impression, nevertheless reports that in his study area in the period 1963–9, there were 22 cases of homicide; 19 of the victims were males, as were all of the 25 killers.[52]

In this way, as statistical studies show, male and female numbers in primitive societies—highly tilted in favour of males in childhood—tend to level out in adulthood. Violent conflict is thus one of the principal means through which competition over women is both expressed and resolved. Furthermore, as Divale and Harris have shown, there is a vicious circle here: in societies that lived under the constant threat and eventuality of violence, families' preference for males who would protect them increased. Families' choices thus further reinforced the scarcity of women and male competition and violence connected with them, even though, from the social perspective, more females would have reduced both. Thus conflict and violence fed partly on themselves. As is often the case, the rational choice of each family when left to its own devices conflicted with the common good. The only solution to such 'prisoners' dilemmas', as they are called, is from above. Remarkably, it has been shown that in those primitive societies on which modern states enforced internal and external peace, female infanticide, as measured by juvenile sex ratios, declined substantially.[53] However, to take caution, there is another factor that was not noted by Divale and Harris: in all probability, the state's sanction itself may have deterred and decreased infanticide.

As mentioned earlier, among the victims of male competition for women are the young adult males, who are obliged to postpone marriage for quite a long time. This universal and probably very old trend among primitive human communities has some interesting evolutionary consequences. Men reach sexual maturity at an older age than women, which is quite the opposite from what we would expect in view of the fact that man's reproductive role and reproductive organs involve a much lighter physical burden than the woman's. The main reason for this later male maturation seems to be male competition. Men are given a few more years to grow up and gain strength before being exposed to potential violent conflict.[54] Another consequence of young adult males' sexual deprivation is their marked restlessness, risk-taking behaviour, and belligerency. This has been a highly observable feature in all societies. Young adult males are simply 'programmed' for greater risk taking, because their matrimonial status quo is evolutionarily highly unsatisfactory. They still have to conquer their place in life. They have thus always been the most natural recruits for violent action and war. Male murder rates peak in both London and Detroit (although 40 times higher in the latter) at the age of 25.[55] Indeed, more mature males, already in possession of women and children, are naturally 'programmed' to adopt more conservative, 'safer', behavioural strategies.

INTERLUDE: MAN THE BEAST?

It would appear that up till now I have been a little vague about something. I have generally discussed 'humans' and 'human warfare', where perhaps I should have more accurately referred to men. From earliest times and throughout history, fighting has been associated with men. Cross-cultural studies of male/female difference have found serious violence as the most distinctive sex difference that there is, except, of course, for child bearing itself. Is that a matter of education and social conventions, or are men naturally far more adapted to fighting than women? This question has much contemporary relevance and is at the centre of a heated public debate about women's equality in modern society: can and should women nowadays enlist in combat roles in the armed services?

The first obvious and generally controversy-free, fighting-related difference between men and women is that of physical strength. Men are considerably stronger than women, on average, of course, and all the following data are on average. To begin with, men are bigger than women. They are about nine per cent taller and proportionately heavier. Even these facts do not tell the whole story, because in muscle and bone mass men's advantage is bigger still. Relative to body weight, men are more muscular and bony, with the main difference concentrated in the arms, chest and shoulders. Fat comprises only 15 per cent of their body weight, compared with 27 per cent in women. As athletic results and repeated tests show, men's biggest physical advantage is in strength. Although they are less flexible than women, only about 10 per cent faster, and have a 4:3 advantage in aerobic capacity, they are doubly as strong as women (except for the legs, where the ratio is again 4:3 in favour of men).[56] As throughout human history fighting has been a trial of force, this sex difference has been crucial.

Anatomy is not everything, however. As mentioned, the quoted data are average. It in fact comprises a wide range within each sex, and there is obviously some overlap between the scales of the two sexes. Some women are stronger than or as strong as some men. There is, however, another sex difference to consider. Are men by nature mentally more aggressive than women, especially being more predisposed to violence and, even more, to serious violence? Are the minds as well as the bodies of males and females different? This is a highly charged topic in the contemporary debate. *Tabula rasa* liberals and feminists during the 1960s and early 1970s believed that, apart from obvious physical differences, men and women were the same. All other differences were attributed to education and social conventions.[57] Over time, however, as more and more women entered the 'man's world' in the workplace and all other walks of social life, many later-generation feminists have come to a different position. They have come to feel that the 'man's world' was exactly that—very much structured to fit the needs, aims, and norms that were peculiarly male. They have felt that mere equality of access to male-structured domains was unsatisfying for women.

Gender attitudes to sex are one of the most interesting cases in point. One of the greatest achievements of the sexual revolution of the 1960s was that women in the west have earned the right to much the same freedom in sexual relations as men had always enjoyed. Soon, however, women discovered that they did not want to exercise that freedom in quite the same way as men. Thus, although latter-day feminists have continued to seek equality and opportunity, many of them now feel that these mean freedom to behave in greater harmony with women's own particular needs and aims, and, wherever necessary, change the world in that direction. Interestingly, it has now been feminists, not only male chauvinists, who have stressed women's qualities versus men's. Indeed, feminists have charged that it was peculiarly male tendencies, such as overcompetitiveness, emotional coldness, faulty communication, and aggressiveness, that were responsible for many, if not most, of this world's ills, including war.[58]

Those feminists may claim some support from the scientific research of human biology, which earlier had all too often been somehow regarded impatiently as irrelevant to the debate. The whole trend of recent scientific research has stressed sex differences in the mind as well as the body. In this chapter, we have already referred to the biological explanation for the differing sexual attitudes of men and women, but scientists have discovered many more differences. Repeated cognitive studies have revealed, on average, male advantage in spatial orientation, which might also explain the persistently recorded male advantage in mathematics, especially at the very highest levels. Women have recorded better in spatial attention to detail and spatial memory, verbal skills, and judging other people's moods and complex human situations—the famous 'female intuition'. These differences have long been attributed solely to education and social expectations, but the great changes in social attitudes that have taken place in the last generation seem not to have altered them much. Indeed, one of the 'hardest' sciences of them all, brain research, has yielded significant sex differences. Cognitive studies, aided by brain scanning, have revealed that men and women in fact use different parts of their brains in coping with various cognitive tasks. Furthermore, whereas the right and left hemispheres of a man's brain are much more specialized, those of women operate in greater co-operation, and the corpus callosum connecting them is larger. Not only are the bodies of women and men structured somewhat differently but also that particular organ of their bodies, the brain, and hence their minds.

The architect of these different structures is our genes, and their agent is the sex hormones, particularly the famous male hormone, testosterone. Scientists have found that its presence begins to structure the male as different from the female right from the start, from the very beginning of the fetus's evolution in the uterus (biologically, the original form is the female). Male and female differences in identity are already largely shaped at birth, and behavioural differences between the sexes are recorded very early, before social conditioning can play an effective role. Crudely put, baby girls are more interested in people, whereas baby boys are more interested in things. Later on, despite the great changes that have taken place in educational patterns and the efforts of conscientious parents, boys and girls show differences in play preferences, with the boys much more inclined to competitive, rough and tumble, aggressive games and toys. Females also produce testosterone, only much less than males. In addition, some divergences from testosterone norms have occurred as a result of natural reasons (which produce identified medical syndromes) and owing to chemical influences caused, for example, by medication. It has been found that so-called tomboy behaviour in girls correlated closely with higher levels of testosterone. On the other side, low testosterone levels in males result in unassertive and 'feminine' behaviour, whereas the highest levels of testosterone to which men are exposed during adolescence result in extra aggressiveness.[59] Traditional human insight, embodied in such concepts as the Chinese yin and yang, has been found to be not that far off the mark.

Perpetration of serious violence and crime is in fact the most distinctive sex difference there is, cross-culturally. As mentioned earlier, among the !Kung Bushmen, all of the 22 killings registered in 1963–9 were committed by men. Of 34 cases of bodily assault, all but one were committed by men.[60] In the USA, males comprise 83 per cent of murderers, a similar share of those committing aggravated assault, 93 per cent of drunken drivers and about the same percentage of armed robbers. Even though murder rates diverge widely in other parts of the world, the woman/man split remains roughly the same in favour of men. Furthermore, even that sharp split does not tell the whole story.[61] The actual split is sharper still, because much of the serious female violence and murder comes in response to male violence or under male leadership. Thus, as a comprehensive survey reveals:

> Crime statistics from Australia, Botswana, Brazil, Canada, Denmark, England and Wales, Germany, Iceland, India, Kenya, Mexico, Nigeria, Scotland, Uganda, a dozen different locations in the United States, and Zaire, as well as from thirteenth- and fourteenth-century England and nineteenth-century America—from hunter–gatherer communities, tribal societies, and medieval and modern nation-states—all uncover the same fundamental pattern. In all these societies, with a single exception, the probability that the same-sex murder has been committed by a man, not a woman, ranges from 92 to 100 percent.[62]

This brings us to the nature of women's aggression and violence. Women can also be aggressive. However, their aggressiveness is much less channelled to physical violence than men's aggressiveness is, and even less to serious physical violence. Typically, women resort to serious violence in two cases: when the danger comes close to home—in desperate defence against an acute threat to themselves and their children; or to harm the 'other woman' in rivalry over a man. Furthermore, in comparison with men's violent aggression, that of women tends to be non-physical, indirect, and anonymous.[63]

What is the source of this most distinctive sex difference in serious violence? Again, the biological explanation is clear and was first elaborated by Darwin.[64] Both the bodies and minds of women and men have been subjected to somewhat different evolutionary pressures during the millions of years of human evolution. These pressures have been most different where sex specialization and diverging reproductive roles have been most involved. As scholars have pointed out, precisely because in humans both parents invest in child rearing, sex specialization/division of labour became more possible than in some other animal species, including our closest relatives, the chimpanzees. In evolutionary terms, women specialized in child bearing and rearing and in foraging close to the home base, whereas men specialized in long-distance hunting and in the struggle to acquire and defend women and children, specializations that required, among other things, force and ferocity. Indeed, the difference was more than occupational. Not only did men compete for women both inside and outside the group, but, in case of a threat to the children, the father, although also highly significant for the children's provision, was more expendable than the mother in this respect. For this reason as well, the men formed the group's main line of defence, while the women covered the children to the best of their abilities. Moreover, Palaeolithic men were of no use to the enemy. For them, the options were either running away or fighting to the finish. By contrast, women were themselves a resource in competition. They had better chances than the men did to survive the day by submitting, conforming, co-operating, and manipulating. Both the capabilities and evolutionary strategies of men and women, capabilities and strategies that were of course interconnected and mutually reinforcing, made men much more predisposed to fighting than women.

But do environmental influences, most notably education and social norms, not count at all? Do genes not always interact with culture? Obviously, environmental influences matter a great deal and are responsible for a wide diversity of cultural norms. However, contrary to the fashion in much of the gender studies, cultural norms are not infinitely flexible and wholly relative. As a rule, cultural norms play, and diverge, along a scale set by our inborn dispositions. (Needless to say, the subject is extremely complex and, as we see later, it becomes even more complex with the new opportunities, interactions, and tensions created by accelerated cultural evolution.) The fact remains that among hunter–gatherers, in the 'human state of nature', women's participation in warfare was extremely marginal. Even more than hunting, in which women also marginally engaged in a few societies, fighting was a male preserve and the most marked sex difference. Indeed, in this case, it can certainly be said that among hunter–gatherers social norms reinforced inborn dispositions. Even if some women were physically and mentally capable of participating in a warriors' group, this very rarely happened. The 'culture of war' and the 'bond of brotherhood' within the warriors' group were famously cultivated among the men. As mentioned earlier, the local groups in the human state of nature were literally composed of brethren. Furthermore, women were to be defended rather than interfere with the warriors' group cohesion by the powerful forces of sexual distraction.[65]

This does not mean that women had no role in warfare. In most cases they, too, had very high stakes in what the men were fighting for, or at the very least in their men themselves.[66] Thus women in primitive warfare often accompanied the men to battle and took part in it as cheerers and providers of auxiliary services, such as the gathering and re-supply of used arrows and spears. As mentioned earlier, only in very rare cases did they actively participate in the fight, mainly by shooting arrows, and if the danger reached the inner ring of women and children, women also desperately tried to contribute to the defence. The famous Amazons, of course, were, significantly, a myth, albeit, like many myths, not entirely devoid of some basis in reality. The Scythian and Sarmatian pastoralist horse archers of the Ukrainian steppe were described by the classical Greek authors as the 'neighbours' of the Amazons. Some of the warrior graves excavated in the region were those of women, buried with full military gear. In one Scythian royal *kurgan* (mound) four of fifty warrior graves belonged to females. In the supposed Sarmatian region, 20 per cent of the warrior graves excavated were those of women.[67] The bow made possible a marginally greater female participation in warfare.

Civilization created many new, 'artificial' conditions and relationships, making a far-reaching transformation in the human way of life possible. Nevertheless, throughout most of history, female participation in warfare barely changed at all from the patterns described above, which had been evolutionarily shaped by physical, mental, and social constraints. Apart from desperate home defence, women's participation in warfare was limited to auxiliary services to the male warriors as camp followers and prostitutes. To be sure, women were excluded from many activities and occupations in historical societies. Still, they were absent from the warriors' ranks to an ever-larger degree than from any other occupation in which they traditionally did not participate. But what about modern, industrialized, and especially advanced industrial societies? These have undergone tremendous, unprecedented changes, which, among other things, greatly transformed women's place in society. How do these changes affect, and how can they affect, women's participation in combat roles in the armed services?

The bottom line is that they do, although overall perhaps not by a very wide margin. Physically, fighting with guns and explosives has already made a change. For example, in eighteenth- and nineteenth-century Dahomey, the king's army included an elite bodyguard unit of women, which grew in number from hundreds to thousands. The women, armed with guns, as well as with bows and arrows, machetes and clubs, were reputedly ferocious warriors.[68] From the late nineteenth century, women began to participate actively in many revolutionary and guerrilla forces, which combined informal social structures and radical ideologies. Their participation in combat roles in the Soviet and Yugoslav armed forces during the Second World War and on the communist side in Vietnam is well known. However, even in these often-cited cases, where a radical social ideology prevailed, the home country was invaded and women were anyhow at grave risk, and an acute shortage of manpower existed, women's role in warfare was still limited. Most women took men's places in the factories and fields, or performed auxiliary services within the armed forces. Those who actually participated in combat roles amounted to no more than 8–12 per cent of the combat troops, not far from their estimated share in the famous Dahomey army or in those very few tribal societies that had allowed women to participate in battle, including the Scythian and Sarmatian 'Amazons'. Furthermore, in Soviet Russia, Yugoslavia, Vietnam, and other revolutionary countries, women were excluded from combat roles once the war was over.[69]

Why is this so, and how likely is this situation to persist in advanced industrial societies? After all, the modern mechanical and electronic battlefield has created numerous tasks that involve little if any physical force. Fighting is done with firepower, and the movement of people and loads is largely mechanical. Many women can drive or fire an armoured fighting vehicle as well as many men, or for that matter command the vehicle, an armoured battalion, or an armoured army. Some women are even strong enough to be able to serve in ordinary infantry units, which still rely heavily on physical force. However, Hollywood's *G. I. Jane* notwithstanding, women are rarely likely to be strong enough for elite infantry and commando units—no more in fact than they are likely to compete successfully in any serious men's football league, let alone boxing or weightlifting. Women flew as combat pilots in the Soviet air force during the Second World War. But how many of them can successfully compete for similar capacities in the much more competitive air forces of modern advanced powers has still to be ascertained. In any case, this leaves many active combat roles that women can perform.

The mental sex differences in respect of warfare have similarly narrowed but not closed. As much of today's fighting activity is done from afar and with little physical contact, it involves much less of the aggressive and violent attitude traditionally associated with men. Even if not wholly a matter of pushing buttons, modern fighting more than before bears the character of an occupation that requires more cool-headed professionalism and organizational discipline than aggressive predisposition. There can be little doubt that women could cope successfully with the mental task if they so wished. But would they so wish? The indications are that the number of those who would wish it is far smaller that that of men. Even if the physical aspect posed no problem, far fewer women than men are inclined to combat activity and combat careers. The reasons for this motivational difference again go back to fundamental sex-related predispositions. On average, men are more attracted to this type of competitive, high-risk, violent, machine-related activity. In the same way that the introduction of effective contraceptives, although greatly affecting women's sexual attitude, has not closed the gap between the sexual behaviour of men and women, far-reaching changes in social and family patterns do not wholly eradicate sex-related occupational preferences.

Throughout history women's overburden with child bearing and rearing was one of the factors that precluded their active participation in warfare. Indeed, significantly, the famous Dahomey women warriors unit was only possible because its members, officially married to the king, were forced to celibacy on penalty of death. The force may have evolved from the harem guard, to which no man was allowed access. Furthermore, the women may have customarily undergone excision at childhood.[70] Even though women in today's developed world give birth to only two children, on average, and household duties are far lighter than before and more equally divided between the sexes, the woman's share in raising the children still tends to be larger. (Despite the doctrine of equality, the law recognizes this by tending to prefer the woman for custody of the children in cases of divorce.) More than men, women would shrink from a highly risky career that involves long periods of absence from the husband and children. This sort of preference has long been attributed to lingering cultural inequalities in the way society is structured. Although these inequalities were indeed acute and still exist, it would now seem that their inborn element was too easily overlooked. Even if the greatest equality of access to the educational and labour markets were achieved, the sex differences would be such that the inclinations of men and women would, on average, be different in some important respects. Even in Scandinavia, where nearly 80 per cent of women are in the workforce, fewer than 10 per cent of the women work in occupations where the sex balance is roughly equal. Half of all workers are in jobs where their own sex accounts for 90 per cent of employees.[71] The choice of a combat career is a field in which the sex difference is particularly marked.

The Netherlands is a case in point, having the most egalitarian legislation and policy in the developed world. From the late 1970s the Dutch authorities granted women equal access to all military jobs and have acted intensively to encourage them to exercise this freedom of opportunity. Nevertheless, as the feminist authors of a study on the subject have written with dismay: 'The interest of women in the army seemed to diminish more than to increase. . . . The physical requirements remained a problem and so did the acceptance of women by their male colleagues. . . . The demands for combat jobs in the infantry, cavalry, artillery and the Royal Engineers are too high to be met by most women.' Female participation in the army, especially in combat roles, remained in the low percentage points. In Norway as well, another country with highly egalitarian legislation and policy, the picture is very similar, partly, although not solely, because of women's own lack of interest.[72]

But what about those women who do desire a combat role and a combat career? In the labour market as well, many occupations are unevenly divided between the sexes, but equality of access on merit has nevertheless been secured in the developed countries to any member of either sex who chooses any particular occupation. Are there any special arguments that might warrant an exceptional status to the occupation of fighting? More complex family arrangements, mentioned by reluctant armed services, have already been discussed. These may be overcome by a combination of female and military compromises. The prospect of possible captivity is a major consideration. As we have seen, women are far more exposed than men to sexual abuse, especially when out of the protection of the law and orderly society. This, too, however, is a risk that society might choose to leave to individual female choice. Finally, can men and women live close together for long periods of service in intimate combat groups without being distracted by sexual attraction that would disrupt their combat effectiveness? Does not the famous 'male bonding' in the combat group depend on the absence of women? Is not the 'culture of war' itself, those traditional qualities of warrior masculinity, best inculcated in an exclusive man's world?

Indeed, at this point some feminists form an awkward alliance with male sceptics, arguing that experience shows that participation in combat units makes women forfeit their own true nature and adopt male-type thinking and behaviour.

We lack sufficient experience to judge how significantly the dynamics created in modern mixed-sex fighting units would affect their combat effectiveness. In principle, fighting units need not, of course, necessarily be mixed for women to participate in them. Separate units for men and women are also possible. In summary, it would probably not be wild speculation to suggest that the forces that have opened the labour market for women are too irresistible for the armed services to withstand. Women are integrated in larger numbers, even in combat roles. On the other hand, women's participation in such roles will probably remain marginal compared with that of men. The evolution-shaped physical, mental, and social factors that have made fighting the most polarized sex-related activity are unlikely to disappear.[73]

5

Motivation: The Web of Desire

The interconnected competition over resources and reproduction is the *root* cause of conflict and fighting in humans, as in all other animal species. Other causes and expressions of fighting in nature, and the motivational and emotional mechanisms associated with them, are a derivative of, and subordinate to, these primary causes, and *originally* evolved this way in humans as well. This, of course, does not make them any less 'real' but only explains their function in the evolution-shaped motivational complex and, thus, how they came to be. It is to these 'second-level causes' and motivational mechanisms, directly linked to the first, that I now turn.

DOMINANCE: RANK, STATUS, PRESTIGE, HONOUR

Among social mammals and primates, higher rank in the group gives improved share in communal resources, such as hunting spoils, and better access to females. In some species, such as baboons and wolves, rank differences are sharp, with the so-called alpha males (and sometimes also females) reaping most of the advantages, relative to the other group members. Even in those social species, such as the chimpanzees, where group relations are more egalitarian, 'leadership' positions confer considerable somatic and reproductive advantages. For this reason, rank in the group is hotly contested among social mammals and social primates. Status rivalry is acute and never ending. It is the strong, fierce, and—among our sophisticated cousins, the chimpanzees—also the 'politically' astute that win status by the actual and implied use of force.[1] Rivalry for rank and domination in nature is, then, a proximate means in the competition for resources and reproduction. For reasons already discussed in Chapter 4, this rivalry is far stronger among males and closely correlates with testosterone levels.

Closer to the chimpanzees' pattern, human groups in the 'state of nature' were more egalitarian than those of some species but still displayed significant status differences. As we have seen, differences in strength, hunting skills, social astuteness, and clan size unfolded and accentuated in direct relation to the abundance of the resources available. The more resource rich the environment and the denser the human population, the further would societies develop, in anthropological terms, from egalitarian to ranked, and then to stratified.[2] However, even in those so-called egalitarian societies, which lived in the most inhospitable environments on earth, status mattered. Richard Lee, studying the !Kung Bushmen of the Kalahari Desert, one of the poorest, most dispersed, and most egalitarian hunter–gatherer societies, finally concedes this against his Marxist predilection and whole thesis in his revealingly entitled article 'Politics, sexual and non-sexual, in egalitarian society'.[3] In the first place, although leadership in such societies was weak and informal, standing at the centre of social networks conferred advantages. Furthermore, quite apart from leadership positions, social esteem mattered a great deal. For example, according to William Buckley, who lived with the Australian Aborigines for 32 years in the early nineteenth century:

> They acknowledged no particular chief as being superior to the rest; but he who is most skilful and useful to the general community, is looked upon with the greatest esteem, and is considered to be entitled to more wives than any of the others.[4]

In determining one's status, image and perception have always been as important as more tangible reality. Although obviously standing in more or less close relation to that reality, they could not be reduced to it. A reputation of being successful and successful qualities reinforced each other. Successful qualities had to be advertised. Thus, overt or subtler display of worth is a constant human activity, as it is with animals. It is limited by the balancing consideration of avoiding the provocation of a negative social response, because other people also jealously guard their honour in the social competition for esteem. In traditional societies, in particular, people were predisposed to go to great lengths in defence of their honour. The slightest offence could provoke violence. Where no strong centralized authority existed, one's honour was a social commodity of vital significance, affecting both somatic and reproductive chances.[5]

Does this mean that what people who strive for leadership or esteem 'really' want is sexual opportunity or resources? Not necessarily. Wanting is subjective, and mentally it can be genuinely disassociated from ultimate evolutionary aims. For instance, people widely desire love and sex for their own sake rather than for the offspring that can result from these activities, and whom they often positively, and even desperately, do not want. In the same way, the pursuit of rank and esteem in humans, as with animals, was closely associated with better somatic and reproductive prospects, and evolved as a proximate means for achieving them, even though the evolutionary aim can remain unconscious.[6] For this reason, humans were prepared to risk violence to gain and defend rank and esteem in the same way that they were prepared to do so for subsistence goods, women, or kin. In the final evolutionary analysis, it all came to the same thing.

Thus, as we have also seen with respect to competition for women, competition for rank and esteem could lead to violent conflict indirectly as well as directly. For instance, we have earlier noted that even in the simplest societies people desired ornamental, ostentatious, and prestige goods, with no apparent subsistence value. Although 'cultural materialists' lump these goods together with subsistence goods, their social function and significance are wholly different. Ornamentation of body and clothes by colours, shapes, or coloured and shaped objects is designed to enhance physically desirable features that function everywhere in nature as cues for health, vigour, youth, and fertility. Obviously, we can only hint at this subject that evolutionary theorists have begun to explore.[7] For example: in human females, but also in males, shining and clear eye, lip, hair, and skin colour functions as such a cue, which can be enhanced artificially; natural—and by extension, added—symmetrical, orderly, and refined features signal good genes, good nourishment, and high-quality physical design; tall and magnificent headgear enhances one's size; and so forth. We should bear in mind that it is precisely on these products of the illusions industry—cosmetics, fashion, and jewellery—that people everywhere spend so much. Furthermore, causes and effects refract and multiply in ever more complex interactions. Where some ornamentations are scarce and therefore precious, the very fact that one is able to afford them indicates wealth and success. Hence the source of what economist Thorstein Veblen, referring to early twentieth-century American society, called 'conspicuous consumption'. In Stone Age societies, luxury goods, as well as the ostentatious consumption of ordinary ones, became in themselves objects of desire as social symbols of status. For this reason, people may fight for them.

Direct and indirect competition for rank and esteem obviously takes numerous other forms. Some scholars have disputed that a reputation as a warrior contributed to one's reproductive success by enhancing one's status in the group. Such a reputation surely increases the social demand for the warrior in time of emergency and, in a society that is particularly prone to war, the warrior's status inevitably rises. A reputation as a warrior also increases one's deterrence in relation to other members of one's own group—again, an advantage in social bargaining. On the other hand, reputable warriors are arguably more vulnerable to early death and, hence, might be disadvantaged by a shorter reproductive trajectory and interrupted off-spring care.[8] All in all, a warrior's reputation, like pugnacity itself, thus seems to be a variable commodity, the value of which depends on the wider benefits connected with it under the particular circumstances of any given society. It would mean more in a society in which internal and external insecurity is more acute, and in which martial skills are closely linked to the ability to acquire material, and hence also social, benefits.

For this reason, marks of martial excellence are also advertised. The Plains Indians, for example, were famous for their elaborate system of distinctions for bravery in war, known as the *counting of coups*. As a principal determinant of social ranking, coups were hotly pursued. One of these coups was, of course, the famous scalping. Indeed, trophy heads of fallen enemies were widely taken in primitive societies. Signs of scalping have been found on fossilized human bones. The most gruesome prehistoric find is two 7,500-year-old caches of trophy heads from Ofnet Cave in Germany, arranged 'like eggs in a basket', comprising the mutilated skulls of 34 men, women, and children.[9] Trophy heads served much the same social purpose for primi-tive warriors as medals, decorations, or marks of fallen enemy aircraft do for modern ones. This explains why head hunting has been regularly observed by anthropologists as a frequent source of warfare among primitive people. This practice—which seemed to make no sense, evolutionary or other—was attributed by some early anthropologists to bare, instinctive, human pugnacity. In fact, when a basic state of competition and conflict (and, hence, suspicion and hostility) over resources or women prevails between two societies, harming the enemy becomes a positive thing and, in consequence, also carries social esteem. Under these circumstances, head hunting can be practised not only as a byproduct of warfare, that has other specific purposes, but also 'for itself', to harm the enemy and win prestige at home. That this activity further reinforces hostility and suspicion, refuelling the war complex, is beyond doubt. Hostility and war tend to escalate, thus, at least partly, although not wholly, feeding on themselves.

Again, it is this intermixing of mutually related motives that has repeatedly confounded scholars. This is most apparent, for example, in the debate over the Plains Indians, in which different scholars highlighted different motives to explain their warfare. Marian Smith, for instance, recognized that horse stealing and hunting privileges were apparent motives of Indian warfare. She also specified revenge, which I discuss later. Yet she believed that the pursuit of social esteem (*coups*) was the *real* cause, the 'one common element' of all the others.[10] Rightly reacting against such views, Bernard Mishkin stressed the economic motives of Plains Indian warfare. However, he nevertheless sensed that there might be a deeper connection involved. In his conclusion he came closer to an integrated approach to the problem:

> The relationship of the economic factor in war to the game element contains no contradiction. . . . Prestige status and property control are almost universally associated. . . . In the case of the Plains, rank distinctions similarly involve economic differentiation. Because war above all, yielded property returns, the men who achieved formal military status also accumulated wealth.[11]

Mishkin has separately also noted the women component associated with Indian ranking. He listed the '25 most famous men' among the Kiowa of Oklahoma. According to his findings: 'Polygamy in the general population never rose to more than 10 per cent; 50 per cent of the "25" are polygamous.' Although he never fully crossed the conceptual threshold, Mishkin was thus not very far away from a view that would dispose of hopeless dichotomies and connect the various elements of the Indian war complex together.[12]

Torture and humiliation of captured enemies were another widespread practice among the Indians, as elsewhere, cross-culturally. This behaviour can also be explained partly as an expression of the craving for domination and superiority. To be sure, as we shall see, torture and humiliation were sometimes administered in revenge, for their deterrence effect, or to extract information. However, in human societies characterized by a competition for higher status, they were also manifestations of an emotional desire— sometimes reaching the point of sadism—to extract responses of submission, helplessness, and begging from the 'other'. Indeed, the unfortunate captive was sometimes prepared to suffer more to deny this gratification to the enemy by maintaining unflinching dignity. Some societies even preferred such dignified behaviour from their tortured captives, because, in what appears to have been an interesting twist, such behaviour only testified to their captive's greater honour, thus magnifying the value of his capture and defeat. As we have already noted, motives are mixed, interacting, and widely refracted in myriad forms. Nevertheless, it is the purpose of this study to show that this seemingly immense complexity and inexhaustible diversity is traced back to a central core, shaped by the evolutionary rationale. Tracing complexity to its basic elements is far more applicable to the study of humans, and in a far more meaningful way, than most historians, anthropologists, and culture students have been trained to believe.

REVENGE: RETALIATION TO ELIMINATE AND DETER

Revenge has probably been the most regular and prominent cause of fighting cited in anthropological accounts of pre-state societies. Violence was activated to avenge injuries to honour, property, women, and kin. If life was taken, revenge reached its peak, often leading to a vicious circle of death and counter-death.

How is this most prevalent, risky, and often bloody behaviour pattern to be explained? From the evolutionary perspective, revenge is retaliation that is intended either to destroy an enemy or to foster deterrence against him, as well as against third parties. This, of course, applies to non-physical and non-violent, as well as to physical and violent, action. If one does not pay back on an injury, one may signal weakness and expose oneself to further injuries, not only from the original offender but also from others. A process of victimization might be created.[13] Of course, it is equally common for one to accept an injury from someone stronger silently and take the consequences of reduced status. Which of these two strategies to follow depends on one's overall assessment of the stakes and relative balance of power. This rationale applies wherever there is no higher authority that can be relied upon for protection—that is, in so-called anarchic systems, originally described by Thomas Hobbes. It thus applies in modern societies to the wide spheres of social relations in which the state or other authoritative bodies do not intervene. In pre-state societies, however, it applied far more widely to the basic protection of life, property, and the like, which the state later took under its authority. One could only rely on oneself and one's kin and allies to defend one's own. In case of an injury, retaliation—that is, 'revenge'—was the principal method either to annihilate the offender or to re-establish deterrence.

But is not this explanation for revenge too clinical or, worse, simplistic? Are not people moved to revenge by blind rage rather than by calculation? Also, is not revenge simply a primitive method of administering justice, and thus ought it to be considered within the realm of morality rather than within that of security and deterrence theory? I have raised these typical questions only in order to once more reiterate the point that is all too often misunderstood with respect to evolutionary theory. Basic emotions evolved, and are tuned the way they are, in response to very long periods of adaptive selective pressures. They are proximate mechanisms in the service of somatic and reproductive purposes. To work, they do not need to be conscious; perhaps it is even better for them not to be, and the vast majority of them indeed are not—in humans, let alone in animals. This is a vital clue for understanding the otherwise inexplicable, seemingly arbitrary, and even counterintuitive concept of unconscious motives, employed in many theories in psychology and the social sciences. Thus the instinctive desire to hit back is a basic emotional response that evolved precisely because those who hit back—of course, within the limits mentioned above—were generally more successful in protecting their own by destroying their enemies and/or by creating deterrence against them and vis-à-vis other people. Humans have far longer memories than do animals and, thus, revenge—the social settling of accounts with those who offended them—assumes a wholly new level with them.

The same applies to the notions of justice and morality. Their evolutionary foundation in humans—which has obviously undergone great cultural elaboration—is the principle of 'reciprocal altruism' and 'indirect' or 'generalized reciprocal altruism', intended to foster mutually beneficial cooperation by a system of benefits and sanctions. A famous computerized game in game theory has demonstrated 'tit for tat' to be the most effective strategy that a 'player' can adopt. He ought to reciprocate positive actions in the interest of mutually beneficial co-operation, and retaliate when his partner fails him in order to persuade this partner that he cannot get away with it.[14] Obviously, computerized games are simplistic. For this same reason, however, they can sometimes serve to illuminate basic, underlying patterns.

'Tit for tat' poses a problem. One's offender cannot always be eliminated. Furthermore, the offender has kin who would avenge him, and it is even more difficult to eliminate them as well. Optimally, no one is to escape, but, as we saw with the Aboriginal conflict described by Strehlow, and as Burch and Correll write about the Alaskan Eskimos, this could rarely be achieved:

> The objective of warfare in North Alaska was to annihilate the members of the enemy group, men, women, and children. . . . A fully successful war thus served to terminate inter-regional relations altogether through the elimination of the members of one entire group. The typical result, however, was only partial success, some members of both groups being killed, and others surviving. Thus warfare tended to perpetuate inter-regional hostilities since survivors were always morally obliged to seek revenge.[15]

Thus, in many cases, tit for tat becomes a negative loop of retaliation and counter-retaliation from which it is very hard to exit. One original offence may produce a pattern of prolonged hostility. 'Blood revenge' in particular, starting from a single incident, may take numerous lives over years and generations. Retaliation can thus produce escalation rather than annihilation or deterrence. Fighting seems to feed on, and perpetuate, itself, bearing a wholly disproportional relation to its 'original' cause. Similar to a Moloch, it seems to take on a life of its own. People are 'locked' into conflict against their wishes and, so it would seem, their best interests. How can it be beneficial to lose many kin in revenge and counter-revenge in order to avenge the original death of one? It is this factor that has always given warfare an irrational appearance, which seemed to defy a purely utilitarian explanation. As with the plague or famine, warfare often appeared as one of the great scourges of human life, but one that, paradoxically, was self-inflicted.

How to explain this puzzle? In the first place, it must again be stressed that both the original offence and retaliation arise from a fundamental state of inter-human competition, which also carries the potential of conflict and is consequently fraught with suspicion and insecurity. Without this basic state of somatic and reproductive competition and potential conflict, retaliation as a behaviour pattern would not have evolved. Indeed, sometimes revenge is merely a pretext for conflict over more fundamental reasons.[16] However, as we have seen, while explaining the root cause of retaliation, this does not in itself or in most cases account for retaliation's escalation into what often seems to be a self-defeating cycle. To account for this, additional explanations must be provided.

Again game theory proves helpful. A famous, perhaps the most famous, game in this branch of rationality research is known as the 'prisoner's dilemma'. It demonstrates how people under certain conditions are rationally pushed by these conditions to adopt strategies that are not in their best interest. Although by temperament and outlook I shrink from mathematics and modelling, I can only advise readers of similar inclinations that understanding the logic of the 'prisoner's dilemma' is worthwhile. The story goes as follows. Two prisoners are separately interrogated on a crime that they jointly committed. If one throws the blame on the other, the former goes free, whereas his friend, who keeps silent, gets a heavy sentence. If both tell on each other, they both get heavy sentences, although somewhat moderated by their willingness to co-operate with the authorities. If both keep silent, the authorities would have little evidence against them, and both of them would get a light sentence. Now, under these conditions, what would be the rational strategy for each of the isolated prisoners to adopt? Rationally, each must choose to 'defect', because, unable to secure co-operation with the other, this option is best *regardless* of the option that the other takes independently. However, as both prisoners are rationally obliged to defect, both get a heavy sentence, whereas if they could secure co-operation between them, both could have benefited. Their rational choice under conditions of isolation is thus inferior to their optimal choice had they been able to secure co-operation between themselves.

As with any game, the 'prisoner's dilemma' is predicated on its given assumptions. It has proved so fruitful because it has been found that many situations in real life have elements of the 'prisoner's dilemma'. As we saw earlier, it explains, for example, why people are rational in trying to evade paying taxes if they believe that they can get away with it, even though the existence of the tax system as a whole benefits them, or why they would bring their beasts on to an unregulated overgrazed common land, even though overgrazing would destroy it completely, to everybody's loss. Similarly, in the absence of an authority that can enforce mutually beneficial co-operation on people, or at least minimize their damages, the cycle of retaliation is often their only rational option. If they do not retaliate, they might invite new injuries. However, although it is their rational course of action, retaliation is often not their optimal one. It may expose them to very heavy costs. Nevertheless, it may go on, among other things, because a lack of, or bad, communication with the enemy—which is natural in view of the animosity and fear prevailing between the antagonists—can preclude, as in the 'prisoner's dilemma', a deal to terminate the cycle of retribution.

Indeed, if one side is not pushed to defeat, how does the cycle end? In all pre-state societies the same mechanisms are employed. Sooner or later, often with the help of a third party who acts as a go-between, thus bridging the communication problem, the bruised parties accept a truce or reconciliation, leaving their past injuries to rest. They either recognize the balance of retribution as even or specify some sort of compensation from one side to the other to make it even.[17] Obviously, the truce or reconciliation may not hold for long. Animosity and a cycle of violence may flare up again, because of either the old grudges or a fundamental state of competition, or because of a combination of the two. In turn, these factors generate, and are reinforced by, ever-present mutual suspicion.

Clearly, the 'prisoner's dilemma' is of great relevance to explaining the war complex as a whole: the cycle of animosity and war, and not just that of revenge and retribution. I return to this later on, but first a word of caution: not all violent conflicts or acts of revenge fall under the special terms of the 'prisoner's dilemma'. In the context of a fundamental resource scarcity, if one is able to eliminate, decisively weaken, or subdue the enemy, and consequently reap most of the advantages, then this outcome is better for one's interests than a compromise. It is only when such a decisive result cannot be achieved, or can be achieved only at a great cost, that the conditions specified by the 'prisoner's dilemma' come into play. Under these conditions, the rivals are locked into a struggle that is very costly for both, lacking the mechanisms to escape into a better solution.

POWER AND THE 'SECURITY DILEMMA'

Revenge or retaliation is an active reaction to an injury, arising from a competitive and, hence, potentially conflicting basic state of relations. As we have seen, a passive reaction in the form of some sort of submission is also possible, depending on the circumstances, and in reality both reactions take place and intermix. However, as Hobbes perceived brilliantly (*Leviathan*, 13), the basic condition of competition and potential conflict, which gives rise to endemic suspicion and insecurity, invites not only a reactive but also a pre-emptive response, which further magnifies mutual suspicion and insecurity. It must be stressed that the source of the potential conflict here is again of a 'second level'. It does not necessarily arise directly from an actual conflict over the somatic and reproductive resources themselves, but from the fear, suspicion, and insecurity created by the potential of those 'first-level' causes for conflict.[18] Potential conflict can thus breed conflict. When the 'other' must be regarded as a potential enemy, his very existence poses a threat, because he might suddenly attack one day. How can one know, for example, if a straying stranger is on a peaceful trade expedition or is out to steal a woman? John Ewers' description of this problem with respect to the Plains Indians is revealing, if only the 'first-' and 'second-level' causes that he mentions are understood in their causal connection rather than being regarded separately:

> The roots of intertribal warfare in this region can be found in the very nature of tribalism itself—in the common disposition of the members of each tribe to regard *their* tribe as 'the people' and to look upon outsiders with suspicion. This is not to deny that other and more specific causes for intertribal conflict existed—competition for choice hunting grounds, capture of women, or horse, or inanimate property, and individual desire for recognition and status through the winning of war honors. But in an atmosphere charged with intertribal distrust even an imagined slight by an outsider could lead to retaliation against other members of his tribe. . . . [I]t was much easier to start a war than it was to end one.[19]

In this fundamental state of insecurity, one must in the first place take precautions against possible attack and increase one's strength as much as possible—for instance, defend and conceal one's dwelling by natural and artificial means; keep at a safe distance from, and maintain lookouts for, the potential enemy; and form alliances to oppose him. The other side, however, faces a similar security problem and takes similar precautions. The fear, suspicion, and feeling of insecurity are mutual and natural, even in the absence of a concrete hostile intent on the part of the other, let alone if some such intent exists.

Things do not stop with precautionary and defensive measures. The reason for this is that such measures often inherently possess some offensive potential—indirectly or directly. For example, indirectly, a defended home base may have the effect of freeing one for offensive action with a reduced fear of a counter-strike. In other words, it reduces mutual deterrence. Directly, a defensive alliance, for example, may be translated into an offensive one, and this prospect is bound to be regarded with apprehension by the other side. Intensified training for war, occupation of some advanced posts, and the employment of reconnaissance parties, even if intended as defensive measures, can strengthen offensive capabilities, and are naturally viewed in that light by the other side. As a result of all this, measures that one takes to increase one's security in an insecure world often decrease the other's security, even if this was not intended, and vice versa. One's strength is the other's weakness.

What are the consequences of this so-called security dilemma?[20] In the first place, it tends to escalate 'arms races' further. Arms races between competitors take place throughout nature. They are one way of presenting the evolutionary process.[21] Through natural selection, they produce faster cheetahs and gazelles, more devious parasites or viruses and more immune 'hosts', deer with longer horns to fight one another, and so on. Many of these arms races involve very heavy costs to the organism, which would not have been necessary if it were not for the competition. This, for example, is the reason why trees have trunks. They only undertake the enormous expenditure involved in growing trunks because of their life-and-death struggle to outgrow other trees in reaching as high as possible to get sunlight. In an apparent paradox, as with humans, competition is most intense in environments of plenty, where more competitors can play and more resources be accumulated. This is why trees grow highest in the dense forests of the water-rich tropical and temperate climates.

Arms races often have truly paradoxical results. The continuous and escalating effort to get ahead of the competitor may prove successful, in which case the competitor is destroyed or severely weakened, and the victor reaps the benefits. However, in many cases, every step on one side is matched by a counter-step on the other. Consequently, even though each side invests increasing resources in the conflict, none gains an advantage. This is called, after one of Alice's puzzles in Lewis Carroll's *Through the Looking-Glass*, the 'Red Queen effect': both sides run faster and faster only to find themselves staying where they were. Arms races may thus become a 'prisoner's dilemma'. If the sides gave up the hope of outpacing each other and winning the contest, they could at least save themselves the heavy costs incurred, which anyway cancel each other out. However, they are often unable to stop the race, because of suspicion, faulty communication, and inability to verify what exactly the other side is doing. Arms races can be stopped, limited, or slowed down only if at least some of these preconditions can be overcome.

As mentioned earlier, arms races are in general the natural outcome of competition. The special feature of arm races created by the security dilemma is that their basic motivation on both sides is defensive. Each side fears the other, but every step that one side takes to strengthen security scares the other into similar steps, and vice versa, in an escalating spiral. It is once more a 'prisoner's dilemma' fuelled by mutual suspicion. Again, one way to stop the spiral is to find means to reduce mutual suspicion. Marriage ties used to be a classic measure for achieving this aim in all pre-modern societies. Fostering familiarity and demonstrating goodwill through mutual friendly visits and ceremonial feasts were another prominent universal measure. For all that, suspicion and insecurity are difficult to overcome for the reasons mentioned above. Indeed, as we see later, even ostensibly friendly feasts sometimes turned out to be treacherous. There is another way, however, to reduce the insecurity. Although both sides on the security dilemma may be motivated by defensive concerns, they may chose to pre-empt actively—that is, not only take defensive precautions but also attack the other side in order to eliminate or severely weaken them as a potential enemy. Indeed, this option in itself makes the other side even more insecure, rendering the security dilemma more acute. Warfare can thus become a self-fulfilling prophecy. The fear of war breeds war. As full security is difficult to achieve, constant warfare can be waged, conquest carried afar, and power accumulated, all truly motivated by security concerns—that is, 'for defence'. Of course, in reality motives are often mixed, with the security motive coexisting with others.

To conclude, as we saw with respect to 'honour' and 'revenge', the basic condition of inter-human competition and potential conflict creates 'second-level' causes for warfare, arising from the first. This does not mean that actual competition over somatic and reproductive resources has to exist on every particular occasion for the security dilemma to flare up. Still, it is the prospect of such competition that stands behind the mutual insecurity, and the stronger the competition and potential conflict, the more the security dilemma will grow. A conflictual condition may thus, at least partly, feed and grow on itself, leading through 'prisoners' dilemmas' to clashes that seem to be forced on the antagonists against their wishes and best interests, to costs that can be heavier than the rewards for which the sides ostensibly fight. The Yanomamo, among whom security was of course only one motive in their motivational war complex, expressed the dilemma beautifully when they complained: 'We are tired of fighting. We don't want to kill anymore. But the others are treacherous and cannot be trusted.'[22]

How is this paradoxical state of affairs possible? It is possible because natural selection operates on the principle of individual competition. There is no higher authority ('Nature') that regulates the competition and prevents 'prisoners' dilemmas' or 'market failures'. Organisms can co-operate, compete, or fight to maximize survival and reproduction. Sometimes, fighting is the most promising choice for at least one of the sides. At other times, however, fighting, although their rational choice, is not their optimal one. They may be forced into it because under conditions of information scarcity, faulty communication, and inability to make sure that the other side will abide by their word, a deal for mutually beneficial co-operation cannot be secured. In these cases, conflict seems to take life of its own. Similar to a Moloch, it consumes the warring parties caught up in its fire, irrespective of their true wishes or interests.[23]

WORLD-VIEW AND THE SUPERNATURAL

I have systematically surveyed the motives for hunter–gatherers' warfare regularly cited in the anthropological literature, attempting to show how these motives can all be traced back to somatic and reproductive conflict, either directly or indirectly, through 'first-' or 'second-level' evolution-shaped proximate mechanisms. But is this all? Does this interpretation not amount to 'crude materialism'? What about the world of culture that, after all, is our most distinctive mark as members of the species *Homo sapiens sapiens*? Do we not know from history that people kill and get killed for ideas and ideals? Indeed, anthropologists universally reported one 'spiritual' factor as being among the most prominent causes of warfare among hunter–gatherers, as well as among primitive agriculturalists. This was fears and accusations of sorcery. In communities in which spiritual life was permeated—as it invariably was—with supernatural beliefs, sacred cults and rituals, and the practice of magic, this was a potent force. All known hunter–gatherer societies—as with any other human society—exhibit the universal human quest for ordering and manipulating the cosmos.

I cannot presume here to do justice to a subject that is notoriously even more complex than warfare. Still, as I have already suggested, the human quest for ordering the cosmos is probably a product of *Homo sapiens sapiens'* vastly expanded intellectual and imaginative faculties. In order to cope with their environment, humans strive to identify, understand, and explain the forces operating within and behind it, so that they can at least predict and, if possible, also manipulate these forces and their effects to their advantage. They are *predisposed* to assume that such forces are there. With respect to both their natural and their human environment, humans achieved impressive successes in using these methods. The quest for an understanding thus evolved into a fundamental human trait. Humans must have answers as to the reasons and direction of the world around them. Stretching this faculty the furthest, humans have a deep emotional need for a comprehensive interpretative framework, or set of interpretative 'stories', that would explain, connect the various elements of, and give meaning to their world and their own existence within it. They need a cognitive map of, and a manipulative manual for, the universe, which by lessening the realm of the unknown would give them a sense of security and control, allay their fears, and alleviate their pain and distress. Where answers are beyond their scope, or beyond experience, they fill up the gaps by speculating or 'mythologizing'.[24]

I use the word 'mythologizing' somewhat reluctantly, because what forces and effects are real, what interpretations have validity, and what manipulative methods are effective are not always easy to determine. Theory and mythology, natural and supernatural, science and magic are dichotomies shaped by later human reasoning. In fact, all of them are rooted in the search for the underlying forces behind the phenomena and the quest to enlist them on one's side. In principle, what led from the 'theological' to the 'metaphysical' and to the 'scientific', in Auguste Comte's famous nineteenth-century formulation, was mainly a growing rejection of authoritative tradition and commitment to free thought, as well as an increasing adoption of a stricter discipline of procedures for verifying hypotheses by experience.[25] Having thus qualified my discussion, there remains within the human quest for ordering the cosmos a tension between the need for knowledge and manipulation, which lends itself more easily to test by trial and error, and the need for meaning, harmony, security, and consolation, which generally proves highly resistant to evidence—indeed, it often openly thrives on counter-experience and the improbable. It is this second element that forms the realm of the sacred. In this interpretation, *Homo sapiens sapiens*' vastly expanded intellectual faculties brought forth as a byproduct, as a 'bug' on its 'programme', some anxieties, intellectual concerns, and emotional needs that are highly susceptible to a certain sort of overarching, emotionally invested, almost 'addictive' ideas.

Hunter–gatherers speculated about the way their world was structured and developed techniques to control it. Sometimes the speculations were at least partly valid whereas the techniques were not, sometimes the opposite was true, sometimes both speculations and techniques had validity, and sometimes both had not. For survival, some ideas and practices were adaptive, whereas some were maladaptive, or made no adaptive difference. Adaptive value was often determined not only by the intended purpose but also by unintentional side effects or byproducts. Thus, as mentioned earlier, these byproducts or 'spandrels', in Gould's and Lewontin's term, could function either as a 'virus' that thrived independently at the expense of its 'host' or as a friendly 'bacterium' beneficially co-opted by the host, or both.[26] The question to ask, then, is in what way did hunter–gatherers' 'metaphysics' affect hunter–gatherers' warfare.

Earlier I mentioned one such possible effect. As Durkheim and his disciples have stressed, communal supernatural beliefs, myths, cults, and rituals probably strengthened group identity and, hence, cohesion.[27] Whatever their direct costs in time and resources, they can thus be regarded, among other things, as indirect, but highly adaptive, 'defence costs'. Furthermore, similar to language and other elements of culture—or the human 'symbolic universe'—beliefs, cults, and rituals, once internalized in early age by social learning, are very difficult to change. People are cognitively and emotionally heavily invested in them. Changing one's 'mental landscape', perhaps even more than changing the 'physical landscape', can be very costly, sometimes prohibitively so. This also increases one's stake in one's own group, while enhancing the 'otherness' of the 'other'.[28]

But how did hunter–gatherers' world-view and supernatural beliefs and practices affect not only social cohesion in the case of conflict and warfare, but also the reasons for conflict and warfare themselves, our subject in this chapter? I would like to argue that on the whole they added on, sometimes accentuating, reasons that I have already discussed. Let us return to the evidence of anthropological accounts, which tell a remarkably similar story across hunter–gatherers' cultures. The all-familiar glory of the gods, or the need to pacify them, let alone missionary reasons, never appear as reasons for hunter–gatherers' warfare. These come later and are discussed in due course. Religion, like warfare, is transformed by cultural evolution. In the hunter–gatherers' world of animistic spirits, totems, and shamanism, the supernatural reasons cited for warfare are different.

As mentioned earlier, the most regularly cited reason is fear and accusations of sorcery. It should be noted, however, that these did not appear randomly. They generally arose and were directed against people whom the victim of the alleged sorcery felt had reason to want to harm him. This, of course, does not necessarily mean that they really did. It certainly does not mean that these people actually did harm the victim by witchcraft. What it does mean is that competition, potential conflict, animosity, and suspicion were conducive to fears and accusations of sorcery. To clarify the point further, it is not that these 'imagined' fears and accusations do not add to the occurrence of deadly violence beyond the 'real' or potentially 'real' causes that underlie them. They certainly do. But, to a greater degree than with the security dilemma, the paranoia here reflects the running amok of real, or potentially real, fears and insecurity, thus further exacerbating and escalating the war complex. Chagnon's account nicely captures the manner in which mutual suspicion and insecurity were closely related to accusations of sorcery among the Yanomamo:

> The feast and alliance can and often do fail to establish stable, amicable relationships between sovereign villages. When this happens, the group may coexist for a period of time without any overt expressions of hostility. This, however, is an unstable situation, and no two villages that are within comfortable walking distance from each other can maintain such a relationship indefinitely: They must become allies, or hostility is likely to develop between

them. Indifference leads to ignorance or suspicion, and this soon gives way to accusations of sorcery. Once the relationship is of this sort, a death in one of the villages will be attributed to the malevolent *hekura* sent by shamans in the other village, and raids will eventually take place between them.[29]

Supernatural elements sometimes came into play in connection with motives for warfare other than fear and insecurity—for instance, as we have previously seen, trespassing was often regarded as an offence against a group's sanctified territory. In other cases, an act of sacrilege against the clan's totem was regarded as an insult to the clan itself. Durkheim stressed this sort of symbolic projection in his great study of religion based on the Australian Aborigines. In both these instances the supernatural element functioned as a sanctified sanction and symbol of less imagined goods: resources and honour. The totem was thus similar to an emblem or a flag. Of course, in some cases the supernatural motives were evoked as mere pretexts for other reasons. However, even where they were not, these motives added an extra dimension in the realm of the spiritual, sanctified, and legitimate to existing motives.

Thus, for example, the Dugum Dani of highland New Guinea, who fought for pigs, women, and land, saw 'ghostly revenge' as inseparable from their war complex. They had to placate their ghosts who became angry with them if a killing among the Dugum Dani was not avenged:

> When the enemy kills one of their own people, the ghostly threat rises; the greater the felt threat, the more the people strive to kill an enemy, which act alone will reduce the threat.[30]

Similarly, the Gebusi of lowland New Guinea had the highest homicide rates recorded anywhere. The reason given for the killings was retribution for sorcery, but, as the anthropologist Bruce Knauft (not a 'sociobiologist'), concludes, these

> were informed by a deeper causal mechanism: male dispute over women. . . . There remains a striking correlation in Gebusi society between homicidal sorcery attribution and lack of reciprocity in sister exchange marriage. . . . Gebusi sorcery attribution is about unresolved and even unacknowledged improprieties in the balance of marital exchange.[31]

Is not this interpretation of the role of the supernatural in hunter–gatherers' warfare 'reductionist'? Not as I understand it. In the first place, as I have noted, the supernatural, similar to the security dilemma, does seem to 'take a life of its own', escalating conflict and violence beyond their 'original' motives. More broadly, I suggest that a crude distinction between 'infrastructure' and 'superstructure' misses the point. Instead, all elements—'physical' and 'spiritual'—of hunter–gatherers' warfare in the evolution-shaped 'human state of nature' should be viewed as aspects of a comprehensive way of life, to which they were generally all tuned.

MIXED MOTIVES: CANNIBALISM

Cannibalism existed among many primitive societies—including hunter–gatherers—but is far more widely reported because it is one of those negative practices often attributed to aliens. As Meggitt, for example, writes, the Aboriginal hunter–gatherers of the central Australian desert were convinced (with little foundation, in his opinion) that alien tribes killed and ate strangers.[32] And such a belief was most common among tribal societies. Obviously, it grew largely from the vicious circle of fear, insecurity, and faulty information arising from and reinforcing basic human competition and rivalry. In this form, similar to accusations of sorcery, the fear of cannibalism had the effect of accentuating the security dilemma. So typically a figment of the frightened imagination was the charge of cannibalism in many reported cases that anthropologist William Arens, in *The Man Eating Myth* (1979), claimed that cannibalism never existed in any meaningful way as a social practice. However, as other anthropologists protested, cannibalism was not wholly imagined. Its existence is well documented in numerous cases throughout the tribal societies of the Americas, the Pacific, and, to a lesser degree, Africa, reached by the Europeans in modern times. Clear signs of it were also found in prehistoric sites, including those of the Neanderthals.[33] What propelled it?

Anthropologists have come to the conclusion that, as with any other complex human behaviour pattern—like warfare itself—cannibalism was caused by various, often mixed, motives.[34] However, as with warfare, although the phenomenon was complex, this complexity itself sprang from the interaction of simpler, more fundamental, human motives.[35] In some cases, in line with its popular image, cannibalism was practised for the meat, and captives were cooked and eaten. It is even reported that some tribal societies developed a taste for human flesh. In this form, cannibalism was a resource conflict in which other people were the prey—that is, the resource itself. The best recorded cases of this sort of cannibalism come from those large reserves of primitive peoples in northern South America and in the islands of south-east Asia and the Pacific: Papua New Guinea, Borneo, Sumatra, Java, and Fiji.

Still, in most cases, resource or 'culinary' cannibalism was not widespread. Why not? Here, again, let us look at other animal species. With them as well, cannibalism exists but proportionally stands in no comparison to normal preying. As seen earlier, the reason for this is that preying on one's conspecifics is dangerous, not for the species, but for oneself, because conspecifics are generally of the same order of strength as oneself—hence the 'inhibitions' against both fighting and cannibalism. Indeed, for the same reason, preying on other predators, or even on very strong herbivores such as elephants, rhinos, and hippopotami, which are also dangerously equipped, is highly irregular. Normal preying is regularly done on species that are overall weaker and less dangerous than one's own. (Contrary to appearance, this applies even to humans hunting elephants, not only to leopards hunting gazelles.) Conspecifics, and other predators, are scared off and sometimes fought in order to facilitate normal preying. Hunting is by far the more widespread activity, compared with which fighting is rare.

Indeed, 'culinary' cannibalism rarely if ever occurs alone, and nor does it account for most recorded cases of cannibalism. Anthropologists have observed that cannibalism is universally practised in conjunction with an elaborate ritualistic and shamanist activity, within the context of comprehensive symbolic and mythological systems. In fact, in most cases of cannibalism, only an (nutritionally) insignificant part of the victim is actually consumed. What is the purpose of this ritualistic cannibalism? William Buckley reports on the Aborigines with whom he lived for half of his life: 'I have seen them eat small portions of the flesh of their enemies slain in battle. They appear to do this, not for any particular liking for human flesh, but from the impression that, by eating their adversaries' flesh they themselves would become better warriors.' He also specified a variety of other motives for the practice.[36] Indeed, as anthropologists across primitive societies have recorded, eating from the enemy's flesh signified revenge and superiority over the defeated; it allowed people to inherit the victim's secret strength, his spirit, the famous *mana*, as it is called in Polynesia. It demonstrated manliness, ferocity, prowess, and transcendence of ordinary limits, thus functioning as a political gesture within the group. In sum, cannibalism, as a phenomenon and as a cause for war, has its roots in various mixes of the components already examined in the human motivational complex.

How mixed these motives are is most gruesomely demonstrated in the only known civilization that practised cannibalism to any significant degree: the Aztec empire. With the Aztecs, taking captives for the purpose of human sacrifice was one of the principal motives for warfare and assumed a grandiose scale. Aztec warriors were trained to take prisoners in preference to killing, and subjugated peoples were forced to deliver human beings in tribute. The victims in their thousands were sacrificed to the gods on the temples of Tenochtitlan, the Aztec capital, because the Aztec religion prescribed that human blood was necessary to keep the sun going and, thus, life on earth. However, only the victim's heart was sacrificed. Priests and warriors then ate from the victim's flesh in ceremonial feasts, which took place throughout the city. The cultural materialist anthropologists Marvin Harris and Michael Harner thus suggested that the real reason for the Aztec human sacrifices, and war complex, was lack of meat. Mesoamerica possessed no domesticated herbivores for meat supply. The valley of Mexico was densely populated. Thus, human flesh became an essential source of protein.[37] As with most cultural–materialist explanations, this interpretation may have some element of truth and is seductively simple, but it is also vastly overdrawn and one sided. There had been major civilizations in Mesoamerica, including large urban ones in the valley of Mexico, for 3,000 years before the Aztecs, and, although human sacrifice and some ritual cannibalism had been practised, none of these civilizations that we know of had engaged in these practices on such a grandiose scale. The Aztecs themselves have never been reported to have consumed human flesh out of the ritualistic context—on the battlefield, for example. If there was a nutritional element in the unique Aztec case, it amalgamated with the supernatural–ritualistic element in an integral cultural practice. Which element was the 'primary' one is impossible to tell and it seems almost meaningless to ask.

Equally, it would be a mistake to suppose that the motive for Aztec warfare was wholly or even mainly religious. As we see later, the Aztec rulers and people engaged in warfare for the variety of motives that always propelled states and empires to war, in Mesoamerica or elsewhere: resources, prestige, power, defence, as well as the supernatural and the rest of the motives already discussed.[38] Human sacrifice and some cannibalism were practices rooted in and interacting with the variety of motives in the human motivational complex.

The Aztec civilization represents an isolated foray from our current discussion of the 'human state of nature'. But, indeed, why did cannibalism—ritualistic or culinary—generally disappear with civilization? Materialists have reasonably suggested that enslavement replaced massacre and cannibalism as the most profitable use for captives.[39] However, it should be added that this development took place in conjunction with an evolutionarily engrained disinclination among all species—the roots of which we have already seen—to consume conspecifics as ordinary practice. Contrary to Harris, cannibalism was never regarded as ordinary meat consumption.[40]

PLAYFULNESS, ADVENTURISM, SADISM, ECSTASY

Finally, for all that we have said up till now about the evolution-shaped aims of warfare, do people not also fight for no particular purpose, just for the fun of it, as a sport-like activity, a game, an adventure, and outlet, in 'expressive warfare' arising from sheer 'pugnacity'?

As playing and sports are often regarded—indeed, defined—as 'purpose-less', 'expressive', 'pure fun' activities,[41] let us start with a few words about their nature. It should be remembered that playing is in no way unique to humans but is characteristic of all mammals. What is its evolutionary logic? After all, on the face of it, it is an activity that consumes a great deal of energy for no apparent gain. In fact, its purpose is physical exercise and behavioural training for the tasks of life, such as hunting, escaping predators and natural dangers, fighting, and nurturing, and social co-operation in all these. For this reason, in all mammalian species it is the young that exhibit the most active and enthusiastic play behaviour, compared with the more mature and experienced.[42] Sports are the same thing with the competitive element more strongly emphasized. In addition to training, it gives the more qualified an opportunity to demonstrate their superior abilities and, thus, win the esteem of their group members. Adventurism, too, has its evolutionary rationale; it is a high-risk/high-gain and explorative behaviour. Again, it is most prevalent among the young, who still need to find their place in life. As adaptive behaviours are normally encouraged by emotional gratifications, play, sports, and some adventure are generally enjoyable.[43]

So games and sports are, among other functions, preparation for fighting. In this light, fighting may even be perpetrated in rare cases as playful training for more serious fighting. However, the question under consideration is broader: is not fighting sometimes perpetrated not for any purpose but for evoking the sort of emotional gratifications associated with play or sport behaviour, as an adventure to dissipate boredom? Earlier we saw that emotional gratifications serve in nature as proximate, intermediate mechanisms for the attainment of evolutionary aims, and that this applied to the activity of fighting as well. However, we also noted that, being, as it is, a highly risky tactic, fighting evokes deeply negative as well as positive emotional responses to regulate and switch it on and off. As long as these responses are closely tied to calculations of evolutionary cost–benefit, as is normally the case, there is nothing particular to discuss. But do not emotional gratifications sometimes take on a life of their own in perpetrating fighting, as well as in other activities? I claim that they do, but as overextension rather than as negation of the evolutionary logic.

In the first place, it should be borne in mind that even wholly playful or 'expressive' fighting behaviour came to be only within a general evolutionary context in which conflict is normal and fighting a distinct possibility and, therefore, a deeply rooted behaviour pattern. In this respect, wholly 'purposeless' violence is a 'misplaced' or 'mis-activated' expression of a 'normal', evolutionarily shaped behaviour. I return to this in a moment. Second, as with accusations of sorcery, it should be noted that even seemingly 'purposeless' violence is not purely random. As in Meggitt's account of the clashes between the Walbiri and Warramunga in the central Australian desert, it is much more often directed against aliens or competitors than against perceived friends.[44] Thus, again, it is often an extension of, or 'overreaction' to, a state of competition and potential conflict.

Still, allowing that some 'purposeless', 'expressive' violence does exist, at least marginally, what does it mean to describe it as 'misplaced', 'mis-activated', or even 'deviant' or 'abnormal'? Surely this is not to express moral or any other sort of value judgement. Our only purpose is to understand this behaviour in the evolutionary context, which, as I have been claiming, shapes the behaviour of all creatures, including our own basic drives and emotional mechanisms. What does a 'misplaced' or 'mis-activated' behaviour mean in this context? It means a behaviour that, while having an evolutionary root, is expressed out of its evolutionarily 'designed' context, and thus normally also in a maladaptive manner. If violent aggression brings evolutionary benefits, it cannot truly be regarded as purposeless; on the other hand, truly purposeless aggression is most likely to be maladaptive because of the serious risks involved in violent activity. This raises another question: if a behaviour is activated out of its evolution-shaped context and is maladaptive, how does it survive rather than be selected against?

In reality, maladaptive traits are constantly selected against. For this reason, their prevalence remains marginal. Still, they do exist. As natural selection has been weeding them out for geological time, why do they still occur at all? There are several reasons for this. It is not only that natural selection is perpetual because of mutations, the unique gene recombination that occurs with every new individual, and changing environmental conditions; the main reason is that no mechanism, whether purposefully designed by humans or blindly by natural selection, is ever perfect, 100 per cent efficient, or fully tuned. As with any other design, the products of natural selection, for all their marvels, vary greatly in their level of sophistication, have limitations, flaws, and 'bugs', can operate only in a proximate manner, and are, thus, far from optimal and often make 'wrong' choices. The only requirement that they are bound to meet is that they be good enough to survive—so long as they survive—in a given environment and facing given competitive challenges.

Returning to our subject, the emotional mechanisms controlling violence have all the limitations mentioned above. Among other limitations, they can be triggered or 'mis-activated' into 'purposeless', 'expressive', 'spontaneous', or 'misdirected' violence—in some circumstances and some individuals more than in others. This certainly happens and should be taken into account. However, as with overeating or sleeplessness—to give more familiar examples—such behaviour should be understood as a range of deviation from an evolutionarily shaped norm. Purely 'expressive' or 'purposeless' violence occurs, but is on the whole marginal to and 'deviant' from evolutionarily shaped aggression mechanisms and behaviour.

110

Let us take sadism as an example. It can produce all sorts of behaviour—including fighting—that has no purpose other than sadistic emotional gratification. In such form, however, sadism is relatively rare and originates as a deviation from evolution-based emotions. In the first place, it deviates from 'normal' cruelty, the evolutionary rationale of which is clear: cruelty is the emotional stimulation to hurt one's adversary, a drive that, of course, is often tempered by, and takes a back seat to, other behavioural stimuli and considerations, within the overall behavioural calculus. Of course, let there be no misunderstanding: 'normal' cruelty expresses itself horrendously. The point is only that it is an evolution-shaped and potentially adaptive behaviour. In addition to cruelty, sadism often has other roots. As we have seen, it also derives, and deviates, from the evolution-shaped desire for superiority over others.

Ecstatic behaviour is another case in point. Ecstasy is a feeling of elation and transcendence produced by an increasing flow of hormones such as adrenaline, serotonin, and dopamine. It reduces body sensitivity to pain and fatigue, raises its energy to a high pitch, and lowers normal inhibitions. In nature, ecstatic behaviour can be produced during an outstanding bodily exertion, often associated with struggle and fighting. However, humans very early on found ways to arouse it 'artificially' for the feel-good effect itself—for instance, through rhythmic dance and singing or by the use of narcotic substances. Anthropologists have become increasingly aware of the widespread use of narcotics in prehistoric societies, including in warfare.[45] In some cases, narcotic substances were used before fighting and in preparation for it; a few shots of alcohol before an assault was ordinary practice in most armies until not very long ago. However, in other cases, the ecstatic condition itself can breed violence; again, drunkenness is a major reason for, or greatly contributes to, the occurrence of violence in many societies. Furthermore, in some cases, the sequence can be completely reversed, and fighting entered into in order to produce ecstatic sensations—for example, in addition to 'ordinary' reasons, such as money, females, social esteem, and so forth, which, as mentioned earlier, already promotes adventurism among the young, this motivation plays a prominent role—often in conjunction with alcohol—in perpetrating the 'purposeless' violence of youth gangs. Again, what we have in these last two categories is a mostly maladaptive outgrowth and deviation from an evolution-shaped behavioural pattern.

In summary, 'purposeless', 'expressive', 'playful' fighting exists in the motivational complex for war. However, it does not occur as an 'independent', 'exceptional' element that seemingly coexists with the evolutionary rationale, but is both relatively marginal to the norm of evolution-shaped behaviours and explained by them, even when it deviates from their adaptive logic.

CONCLUSION

There is a long tradition in anthropology that has failed to see an adaptive logic behind 'primitive warfare'. In a curious reversal of the evolutionary rationale, some anthropologists believe warfare to have been an essentially non-adaptive trait in the human state of nature, which has only begun to 'pay off' with the coming of agriculture and the state. One representative of this tradition, C. R. Hallpike, writes:

> Why, then, is primitive warfare so common if it is not adaptive? The answer is clearly that there are a number of very widespread factors that lead to it: the aggressive propensities of young males, lack of effective social control in acephalous societies, mutual suspicions between different groups, revenge, the self-maintaining properties of social system, problems in developing mediatory institutions, religious associations between success in warfare and vitality in general, and so on.[46]

But *why* is it that young men have such aggressive propensities? *Why* does a lack of social control and mediatory institutions lead to warfare if no underlying conflict exists? *Why* should there be any mutual suspicion at all under these circumstances? *What* triggers revenge in the first place? *Why* are religion and vitality associated with success in war? Finally, is the widespread occurrence of intraspecific fighting among animals also to be regarded as non-adaptive? These questions failed even to be asked, let alone answered. The untenable notion that, in the highly competitive evolutionary state of nature, fighting occurred 'just so' as a 'ritualistic' and 'expressive', purposeless activity, to satisfy 'psychological' needs with no basis in the practical conditions of life, has gained much currency.

One reason why Hallpike, like many others, has tied himself in these strange knots is his erroneous belief that not only was there little to fight about in primitive society, but also that fighting was in any case wholly ineffective as an expression of competition, because it did not lead to conquest and extermination.[47] Again, the concept of 'ritualistic fighting' has been mostly responsible for distorting perceptions on the subject. We see more about this as I turn to examine the patterns of fighting in the human evolutionary state of nature.

6

'Primitive Warfare': How Was It Done?

The decision whether or not to opt for fighting is based in nature on an evolution-shaped calculus of cost–benefit, on the assessment of risks versus potential gains. I have systematically covered the benefit side in humans, what people in the state of nature fight for, which, as in nature at large, boils down to somatic and reproductive motives, and the proximate and derivative motives built upon them. I now turn to the cost side, and here, as well, I claim that the 'human state of nature' is fundamentally not very different from the general state of nature.

With respect to both aboriginal humans and other animal species, a persistent illusion prevailed during the 1960s and early 1970s, fostered by Konrad Lorenz, that intraspecific fighting was 'ritualized'—that is, consisted mainly of display and, in any case, rarely involved killing. As mentioned before, with regard to both humans and animals, this illusion has been dispelled by later research that has found a great deal of intraspecific killing taking place in many species. The reason for the earlier error was that serious violence was initiated only under conditions that minimized a protagonist's prospects of being hurt itself. Hence the relative rarity of serious 'open battle'—our customary measure of fighting—among humans and animals in nature, as opposed to other, less conspicuous forms of intraspecific killing. Violence becomes a more attractive proposition the lower the risk of heavy costs to oneself. Thus, the principle of deadly violence in nature is fighting against weakness, only at highly favourable odds—asymmetrical fighting.[1]

Hence the pattern of violent conflict between two adult animals. Much of it consists of display, intended to impress the other with one's strength and ferocity in order to persuade it to give up the fight. Some serious fighting regularly takes place to prove the point if mere demonstration is not enough. In this fighting, severe and often lethal wounds can be inflicted. However, once one side recognizes defeat and withdraws, the winner in most (though not all) cases does not persist to finish off its adversary. The reason for this is not intraspecific benevolence, especially when the fight does not involve close kin or same-group members that benefit from mutual co-operation. Animals would normally avoid fights to the finish with competitors from *other* species as well. The reason is the risk of serious wounds to oneself from a continuation of a fight with a defeated but desperate and still heavily armed opponent. Such wounds not only may be dangerous in themselves, but can also reduce the winner's ability to obtain food and weaken it vis-à-vis other rivals, which might take advantage of its plight. As there is no social security in nature, any serious wound might mean starvation. Thus, once the object of the fight has been secured with the rival's defeat and withdrawal, the cost–benefit calculus changes in most cases against the continuation of the fight. Indeed, animals have no qualms about riskless killing of the much weaker and helpless of their kind, as well as of other competing species. As mentioned earlier, most intraspecific killing is done against defenceless cubs and chicks that are not one's own, either for reproductive reasons or to weed out future competitors for food.

In the 'human state of nature' as well, most serious attempts at killing and most killings are done when the victims of the attack can be caught helpless, relatively defenceless, and, above all, little capable of effectively harming the attackers. Hence the pattern of so-called primitive warfare, which is, again, remarkably uniform and manifests itself regularly with any society of hunter–gatherers and primitive agriculturalists studied. There is some tendency in anthropology for particular, mostly recently studied and well-publicized cases, to dominate scholarly attention at a given time. Consequently, the pattern of 'primitive warfare' has been 'rediscovered' independently with little if any variation, generation after generation, by various scholars observing different societies. The most notable examples are the North American Indians, the Alaskan Eskimos, the Australian

Aborigines, the highlanders of Papua New Guinea, and the Yanomamo. Indeed, even before anthropologists took over, this pattern had been widely discerned by Europeans during the period of western discovery and expansion. As Adam Ferguson wrote in his *An Essay on the History of Civil Society* (1767), referring to 'the rude nations of America':

> Their ordinary method of making war is by ambuscade; and they strive, by over-reaching and enemy, to commit the greatest slaughter, or to make the greatest number of prisoners, with the least hazard to themselves. They deem it a folly to expose their own persons in assaulting an enemy, and do not rejoice in victories which are stained in the blood of their own people. They do not value themselves, as in Europe, on defying their enemy upon equal terms.[2]

I now attempt to outline the pattern of 'primitive warfare'. As before, I give priority to the evidence from hunter–gatherers' warfare, which reflects the vast timespan of the evolution-shaped 'human state of nature'. Similar evidence from primitive agriculturalists will be cited only in support; in this respect in particular they show no significant change from hunter–gatherers.

BATTLE, AMBUSH, RAID

In 1930, W. Lloyd Warner, studying the Aboriginal Murngin hunter–gatherers of Arnhem Land in Australia's Northern Territories, fully laid out the pattern of 'primitive warfare'. Little of significance on the subject has since been added to his excellent account. Warner described a whole scale of violent conflicts, ranging from individual feuds to conflicts of small groups, a clan, and several clans (tribal). To summarize his findings, on all scales the pattern was the same: face-to-face confrontations were usually mostly demonstrative and low in casualties, but a great deal of killing was done by surprise, mostly during unilateral actions.

Let us start with face-to-face confrontations. Feuds by individuals, often aided by kin, were very frequent, resulting from reasons that have already been discussed, mostly relating to women. Both sides were armed, and strong words were often followed by blows with clubs and by spear throwing. However, both sides were held back by their kin and friends and prevented from getting to grips with or seriously hurting each other. In fact:

The contestants usually depend upon this, and talk much 'harder' (*dal*) to each other than they would if they knew they were going to be allowed to have a free play at each other. . . . They are able, by remonstrating with their friends and struggling to get free from them, to vent their outraged emotions and prove to the community that no one can impinge upon their rights without a valiant effort being made to prevent this from happening. Obviously there is a certain amount of bluff in the conduct of the contestants on some occasions . . . few killings ever result.[3]

Conflict between clans or tribes, too, could lead to face-to-face confrontations, or battles, the place and time of which were normally agreed upon in advance. Here, as well, the combatants hardly ever closed in on each other. The two opposing dispersed lines stood at a spear-throwing distance, about 50 feet, hurling spears at one another while dodging the enemy's spears. In some cases, such battles were intended in advance to put an end to a conflict and were thus truly 'ceremonial', with the spear throwing restrained and mixed with ceremonial dances. Once blood was spilt, or even before, the grievances were seen as settled, and the battle was terminated. However, sometimes even these ceremonial fights could escalate into real battles, in the heat of conflict, by accident, or by treachery. Furthermore, in many other cases, true battles were intended from the start. Still, as the opposing parties kept a safe distance from each other, casualties were normally low even in these real battles. An exception could occur when trickery was used, as, for example, when one party hid a group of warriors who then attacked the other party by ambush on the flank or rear. Then, heavy casualties could ensue.

However, the most lethal and common form of warfare was the raid, using surprise and taking place mostly at night. This could be carried out by individuals or small groups, who intended to kill a specific enemy, or members of a specific family, usually when their victims were asleep in camp. Although these raids were small-scale affairs, they often resulted in casualties. The raid could also be conducted on a large scale, by raiding parties coming from whole clans or tribes. In such cases, the camp of the attacked party could be surrounded, and its unprepared, often sleeping, dwellers massacred indiscriminately (except for women who could be abducted). By far the most killings in 'primitive warfare' were registered in these larger raids. In Warner's study, 35 people were killed in large-scale raids, 27 in small-scale raids, 29 in large battles in which ambushes were used, 3 in ordinary battles, and 2 in individual face-to-face encounters.[4] Both battles and raids were prepared for and ended with elaborate ritualistic and shamanist activity. People painted themselves in war colours, both as part of this activity and in order to terrify the enemy.

Although Warner's comprehensive study is singular in being specifically dedicated to warfare, the evidence from other studies of the Aborigines indicate that the pattern that he describes held true all over Australia, in both well-watered and arid environments.[5] For example, in addition to numerous raids, ambushes, and feuds, William Buckley describes some dozen major face-to-face encounters among the Aboriginal tribes with whom he lived in 1803–35. These were conducted mainly with throwing of spears and boomerangs and, although lasting for hours, they regularly resulted in only one to three people dead. Casualties in raids were similar, unless a whole camp was surprised:

> The contests between the Watouronga, of Geelong, and the Warrorongs, of the Yarra, were fierce and bloody. I have accompanied the former in their attacks on the latter. When coming suddenly upon them in the night, they have destroyed without mercy men, women and children.[6]

Although names obviously change, and anthropologists' descriptive categories can vary slightly (I have not stuck to Warner's original ones either), the pattern of 'primitive warfare' manifests itself independently everywhere. The main difference from Aboriginal Australia is that other parts of the world had the bow, the only effect of which was to increase the range of engagement even further. The other great 'pure' laboratory of hunter–gatherers, the American north-west coast, again serves as a prime example. Here the canoe played a major role as a means of movement, and villages were more permanent and fortified, but the overall pattern of warfare remained the same. The following are some select citations from otherwise fairly similar accounts of north-west coast warfare. The German geographers and ethnographers Aurel and Arthur Krause noted in 1878–9 'the almost endless enmities between individuals as well as tribes and clans'. They observed that 'the Tlingit does not have personal courage to face obvious danger'. Thus 'open warfare was usually avoided, but if one tribe made war on another, it was done mostly by setting up an ambush or attack by night'. 'Ceremonial' battles were sometimes agreed upon to bring a conflict to an end.[7] According to Franz Boas: 'The Indians avoided open warfare but endeavored to surprise the helpless or unsuspecting and unarmed victim. . . . Individuals also attacked their enemies, not in open battle, but from ambush.' The main form of warfare was the raid on the enemy's village, which was frequently devastating even though villages were often fortified:

> The enemy was attacked early in the morning, when it was still dark. . . . The attacking party rarely met with resistance, because they always tried to surprise the enemy while asleep. . . . When the men were killed, their heads were cut off with their war axes. They burned the village. Women who pleased the warriors, and children, were taken as slaves.[8]

Philip Drucker also noted that 'weapons, tactics, trophies, and other details were alike in feuds and wars'. 'The favorite tactics was the familiar American Indian night raid.' Frontal attacks were carried out only out of necessity, when a raiding party was itself surprised and came under devastating fire with the water to its back and little option of retreat:

> Other and more successful, tactics were variations on the encirclement theme. . . . Another sort of tactics was that of out-and-out treachery. . . . The technique usually consisted in offering peace, and suggesting a marriage be arranged to cement the new tranquillity. At some stage of the festivities, the plotters arranged to have their men distributed among the foe, each trying to maneuver himself into a place on the right of his intended victim so that he would be able to whip out a dagger or club to strike him down when the war chief gave a certain signal.

As Drucker concludes:

> If we evaluate Nootkan warfare on the basis of its effectiveness, we must grant it considerable efficiency. The Hisau'ishth and the Otsosat were exterminated within recent times; the groups inhabiting Muchalat Arm were reduced from several hundred to less than forty persons, and other groups are said to have been wiped out completely in ancient days, all by the type of warfare described.[9]

Eskimo warfare on the Alaskan coast followed a similar pattern. According to E. W. Nelson:

> Previous to the arrival of the Russians on the Alaskan shore of Bering sea the Eskimo waged an almost constant intertribal warfare; at the same time, along the line of contact with the Tinné tribes of the interior, a bitter feud was always in existence. The people of the coast . . . have many tales of villages destroyed by war parties of Tinné. . . . Several Tinné were killed by Malemut

while hunting reindeer on the strip of uninhabited tundra lying between the districts occupied by the two peoples.

. . . [A] favorite mode of carrying on their ancient warfare was to lie in ambush near a village until night and then to creep up and close the passage-way to the kashim, thus confining the men within, and afterwards shooting them with arrows through the smoke hole in the roof. Sometimes the women were put to death, at other times they were taken home by the victors; but the men and the boys were always killed.

Normally, the men 'would set out stealthily to surprise the enemy during the night. If they failed in this an open battle ensued'.[10]

Oswalt portrays a similar picture,[11] as does Burch,[12] who writes that 'the general pattern of warfare was the same throughout the Northwest Alaskan area'. Again, raiding was the principal method of warfare. Open face-to-face fighting was entered into only under conditions of clear superiority, or when the sides accidentally bumped into each other, mainly en route to a raid. Both Nelson and Burch agree that in such cases a fire-fight began: 'the early stages of these confrontations were rather ritualized affairs in which the men jumped about with stiff-legged movements and taunted one another, arrows nocked and poised for firing.'[13] This could go on for hours, with intervals for rest sometimes declared. According to Burch, the sides could then close on each other, although there seems to be some disagreement between him and his informers on how serious things really became at this stage. He specifically acknowledges that they told him that their ancestors had much preferred fire to shock tactics in these battles. Still, he speculates that the closing-in stage 'must have' involved close-quarters fighting with clubs and similar weapons, which led to serious killing. Nelson, for his part, writes about the battle almost exclusively in terms of arrow shooting. Although his description may sometimes also give the impression of substantial casualties, he never specifically says so. According to Robert Spencer: 'such "battles" seem always to have been indecisive.'[14]

The similar tactical methods of the Great Plains Indians, both before and after their adoption of the horse, are so extensively documented as to have become a world-famous folklore. According to Marian Smith: 'Whether a war party consisted of one warrior or a man and one or two of his most intimate friends, or of one to four hundred warriors, or even of the whole tribe the purpose and general form of its procedure did not change.' The night raid and dawn attack were the norm. 'The mortality in Plains fighting was highest when attack took the enemy unprepared. . . . In such cases the weaker groups were often completely annihilated. The mortality of pitched battles, which was of more frequent occurrence than is generally supposed, was considerably lower.' The reason for this was that 'Unnecessary endangering of lives was . . . avoided'.[15] According to Robert Mishkin: 'the form of warfare preferred on the Plains [was] the surprise attack. . . . Such surprise attacks . . . did not permit concerted defense. . . . One side attacked stealthily and the other side was more or less compelled to suffer the attack and to retaliate later, if possible, when the victors were themselves unprepared and unsuspecting.'[16] John Ewers, specifically documenting the historical and archaeological evidence for Plains Indian warfare before contact, writes:

> The greatest damage was done when a large war party surprised, attacked, and wiped out a small hunting camp . . . casualties were few in pitched battles between relatively equal numbers of warriors. There was no close contact in these large battles. The opposing forces formed lines facing each other, barely within arrow range. They protected themselves behind large rawhide shields, and shot arrows from their long bows. They also wore body armor of several thicknesses of rawhide. . . . Darkness generally brought an end to the battle.[17]

In an excellent study, Frank Secoy describes the same pattern of pre-horse–pre-gun fighting. There was the generally preferred destructive raid, and there was the battle, which was a two-stage affair. In the first stage, the sides confronted each other in two long lines for hours, shooting arrows while protecting themselves behind their shields. Next, they could close in. As in Burch's case, there is a disagreement between Secoy and his source as to what happened then. He suggests that usually a brief and bloody hand-to-hand struggle took place. However, according to his sole source, the famous testimony of the 75- to 80-year-old Blackfoot Saukamappee, given in 1787–8:

> On both sides several were wounded, but none lay on the ground; and night put an end to the battle, without a scalp being taken on either side, and in those days such was the result, unless one party was more numerous than the other. The great mischief of war then, was as now, by attacking and destroying small camps of ten to thirty tents.[18]

Napoleon Chagnon attracted great attention to the pattern of 'primitive warfare' with his classic study of the Yanomamo. The Yanomamo were hunters and primitive horticulturalists rather than pure hunter–gatherers, but their methods of warfare were not very different. In fact, although the Yanomamo were dubbed 'the fierce people' by Chagnon, lived constantly

The Yanomamo:

A club fight over infidelity. Wounds to the head and blood flows are evident

under the threat of warfare, and had very high rates of violent death, their patterns of warfare—at least as described by Chagnon for the time that he stayed with them—were even more small scale than elsewhere. Their rhetoric aside, the 'fierce people' were very reluctant to expose themselves to danger.[19] Face-to-face confrontations were strongly regulated, taking a tournament-like form, to avoid fatal injuries as much as possible. The antagonists in a conflict, either individuals or groups, faced each other, exchanging blows in turn. Depending on the gravity of the grievance that ignited the confrontation, the exchange of blows escalated in form. The mildest form, with bare hands, was chest pounding, which the antagonists inflicted in rotation on each other. Next came side slapping, also with bare hands. Then came the club fight, which obviously resulted in much more severe injuries but rarely in fatalities. Finally, formal, prearranged, spear-throwing battles were very rare, let alone those involving arrow shooting.

122

A raiding party is assembling. Note the war body paint, practically a universal feature in tribal society

Again, it is the fear of being killed rather than killing that restricted the Yanomamo in their face-to-face encounters. Killing was principally done by stealth. As Chagnon writes, the raid was 'warfare proper', carried out mostly at night and unleashed at dawn.[20] The large-scale raid to encircle and annihilate a camp or a village, which we saw elsewhere, does not figure in Chagnon's account. Instead, the Yanomamo experienced incessant raids and counter-raids, which, even if they involved a substantial numbers of warriors, usually ended in a hasty retreat after the raiding party succeeded in killing one or few individuals who strayed out of camp or by shooting arrows into it. However, if killings in each raid were few, they accumulated rapidly. As Chagnon writes, the village where he stayed 'was being raided actively by about a dozen different groups while I conducted my fieldwork, groups that raided it about 25 times in a period of 15 months'.[21] Sometimes, the pressure of war and casualties forced the inhabitants of a village to leave it and find shelter in other villages (obviously at a price). The enemy then destroyed

123

their dwellings and gardens. Finally, extensive killing could also take place in 'treacherous feasts' of the kind already seen.[22]

The world's largest and most isolated concentration of primitive agricul-turalists is to be found in the highlands of New Guinea. The native peoples had not been contacted by Europeans or any other outsiders until the mid-dle of the twentieth century and even later. For this reason, they attracted much anthropological attention. Living in clans that consisted of a few hundred people each and in clusters of clans that could reach thousands, the highlanders inhabited valley communities separated by rugged and forested mountains and spoke about 700 different languages (out of the world's roughly 5,000 extant languages). They constantly had to face the threat or the actuality of warfare, which was still taking place among them until contact. Indeed, it was the perpetual risk of warfare, more than its occasional occurrence, that created a permanent state of insecurity and preparedness among them. Here again, warfare took the form that we know only too well, described independently by anthropologists more or less contempor-aneously with Chagnon's study of the Yanomamo.[23]

The familiar, formal, prearranged battles between communities involved arrow shooting or spear throwing from afar, with the combatants taking cover behind large shields. Called 'small fights' or 'nothing fights' by the Maring, one of those highland peoples, these battles were noisy and could last days and even weeks, but they were much like 'tourneys' (tournaments), and 'deaths or serious injuries in them were rare'.[24] Sometimes, 'nothing fights' could escalate to 'true fights' involving close-quarter weapons such as spears and axes. Still, the combatants rarely closed in to come to grips with each other in a true mêlée. The battle remained static, with the sides exchanging blows behind their shields, while keeping back and taking care not to expose themselves or to be caught isolated. Thus warfare could proceed for weeks or even months without heavy casualties. Battles would be abandoned when it rained or when the combatants felt that they needed a rest. Often the battles were a vent for grievances and, through the verbal communication made possible by the concentration of the people on the battlefield, opened the way to an armistice. As seen in Australia, substantial casualties ensued only in those relatively rare cases in which the enemy was surprised from the back by an ambush or by approaching allies. In such cases, a 'rout' could occur, with the warriors and their families escaping their village, which was then destroyed by the victors.

Battle scenes from New Guinea. These most typical photos are possibly the only existing ones of a globally attested occurrence. They were taken in the early 1960s, when state rule in the region was still nominal. Casualties in such face-to-face confrontations were usually low because the sides kept their distance from each other. However, extensive killing took place in raids and ambushes

Watchtower overlooking in the direction of neighbouring groups. Since conflict and violent death were rife in pre-state societies, insecurity was the norm, affecting every aspect of daily life

But, again, the most lethal form of warfare in highland New Guinea was the raid. This could be carried out by individuals or small groups settling 'private affairs', or by whole clans. Conducted mostly at night and climaxing at dawn, the raiders strove to catch the enemy asleep and kill as many of them as possible, particularly the men but also women and children. In most cases, if the raiding party was not large enough, the raiders quickly withdrew before the enemy could regain its nerve and fight back. However, sometimes 'these tactics could annihilate the manpower of an enemy clan' in one stroke, and literally drive it to extinction.[25] As on the north-west coast of America, many villages in highland New Guinea were surrounded by palisades and obstacles for protection, and in some cases watchtowers were built. Sites that were difficult to access were favoured. Strangers were feared and suspected, and trespassing between communities carried the risk of death and was generally avoided. Treachery on visits also occurred and could result in many casualties. When a 'rout' or a devastating raid took place, the defeated side, which was driven out of its home village, could either recover after a while and return with the support of its allies, perhaps losing some land, or sometimes it was permanently vanquished, with its land annexed by the victors.

Studies of other 'tribal' societies, such as the Higi of the Nigerian–Cameroon border area and the Montenegrins, draw a remarkably similar picture.[26] In all the cases described and everywhere else, as with the Aboriginal Australians mentioned first, elaborate ritualistic activity took place before, after, and often during warfare—to enlist supernatural support, to let the dead know that they were being avenged, and to purify the warriors who had killed. People painted themselves for war and often wore a specially adorned war dress.

ASYMMETRICAL, FIRST-STRIKE KILLING

It has been demonstrated here that the pattern of fighting in the 'human state of nature' largely paralleled that of the state of nature in general. With both humans and animals, serious, deadly, face-to-face fighting was rare, not because of intraspecific benevolence but to avoid the risk to oneself and to one's close kin; it should be remembered that in calling for

127

a violent venture one predominantly relied on close kin to join. Considerable intraspecific killing did take place, but it was carried out against the weak and defenceless who could not fight back effectively. Thus deadly fighting was normally asymmetrical, with the casualties overwhelmingly concentrated on the receiving end. However, at this point, there was a difference between humans and other animal species. Among animals, it is mostly the young that stand at the receiving end of intraspecific killing, whereas adults—although sometimes fatally wounded in a fight—are relatively secure. By contrast, among humans, although women and children were often killed, it was mainly the men fighters themselves who suffered most of the casualties. With humans, too, deadly fighting was asymmetrical, in the sense that it was conducted under conditions in which the enemy were caught helpless and unable to fight back, mostly by surprise. However, among humans, the asymmetry regularly rotated, with the receiving and inflicting ends changing places: the helpless victim of today's raid was himself the raider tomorrow. Thus the adult fighters themselves bore the brunt of the casualties, although normally not simultaneously but each side in its turn. What is the source of this difference between humans and other animal species?

Mutual deterrence, which is generally effective among adult animals, fails in humans under certain conditions, specified above, because of that principal threat to deterrence: first-strike capability. Why do humans possess it to a much larger degree than other animal species? It is because of the most distinctive human capability: tool making. The more advanced the capability became, the more lethal humans became, while, at the same time, the more their physique became slender because tools replaced muscles, bones, and teeth; *Homo sapiens sapiens* is more slightly built than the Neanderthal and *Homo erectus*, who in turn were less muscled than the great apes. In short, the growth in human offensive capability was linked with a steady decrease in their natural defences.

Some scholars have already sought a connection between human intraspecific lethality and the unique human tool-making capability. Initially, however, this was done in the wrong way. Lorenz and Desmond Morris, for instance, suggested that the development of weapons in human evolution was so rapid that it overtook normal inhibitions against intraspecific killing.[27] However, in the first place, humans have been using tools as weapons for millions of years, more than ample time for any evolutionary adaptation to take place—we have changed dramatically over that time period. Second, no inhibitions against intraspecific killing, of the sort presumed by Lorenz and Morris, do in fact exist in nature. Third, despite their weapons, humans in the state of nature continued to avoid serious face-to-face encounters, as do animals. Thus it was also not the ability to fight from a safe distance that changed things, as some other scholars have suggested. In face-to-face fighting, mutual deterrence continued to work quite effectively, as it does with animals, with the increased distance that the fighters kept between themselves and the enemy ensuring their relative safety.

Where human special intraspecific vulnerability mostly revealed itself was when the attack came by surprise. This was very different from the conditions prevailing among animals. Not only is it more difficult among most animal species to get close to a rival without being noticed, because of more acute senses, but also it is above all more difficult to finish off a conspecific in one stroke even if surprise is achieved. As mentioned earlier, animals are more strongly built because their bodies are their weapons; furthermore, their weapons are 'on them' and, therefore, are constantly ready for use. By contrast, if humans can be caught unarmed, they are at a tremendous disadvantage and are extremely vulnerable. Humans thus became quintessential first-strike creatures. As with other animal species, they normally did not seriously fight conspecifics on the open battlefield for fear of being hurt themselves. However, unlike other animal species, they were able to kill adult conspecifics by surprise, when their adversaries were unarmed and vulnerable.[28]

And kill they did. As with other animal species, mortality from intraspecific violence was very substantial among humans in the state of nature, with the difference that the adult fighters themselves took much more of the punishment. Estimates of hunter–gatherers' mortality rates in fighting before the coming of state authority are inherently tenuous, yet they tally remarkably with one another, even though they were formed wholly independently from each other, a fact that greatly enhances their aggregate, cumulative validity. We have already encountered some of the relevant data here and there. For the Murngin of Arnhem Land during a period of 20 years, Warner estimated this rate at 200 men of a total population of 3,000 of both sexes, of whom approximately 700 were men. This amounts to about 30 per cent of the men. Violent mortality among the women and children is not mentioned. Pilling's estimate of at least 10 per cent killed among the

Tiwi men in one decade comes within the same range. Kimber's estimate, for a generation, of 5 per cent mortality in fighting in arid areas and about 6.5 per cent in well-watered ones refers to violent mortality in relation to the entire population's overall mortality rates. It also suggests a very high violent mortality rate.[29] The Plains Indians showed a deficit of 50 per cent for the men in the Blackfoot tribe in 1805 and a 33 per cent deficit in 1858.[30] Even among the Eskimos of the central Canadian Arctic, who lacked group warfare, violent death, in so-called blood feuds and homicide, was estimated by one authority at one per 1,000 per year, 10 times the US peak rate of 1990. As Jean Briggs has revealingly written: 'Readers of Canadian Inuit ethnography, my own *Never in Anger* (1970) in particular, have sometimes concluded that Inuit are always and everywhere pacific. Nothing could be farther from the truth.'[31] The rate for the !Kung Bushmen of the Kalahari, the famous 'harmless people', was 0.29 per 1,000 per year, and had been 0.42 before the coming of firm state authority.[32]

The somewhat better data that exist for primitive agriculturalists basically tell the same story as those for the hunter–gatherers. As mentioned earlier, among the Yanomamo about 15 per cent of the adults died as a result of inter- and intragroup violence: 24 per cent of the males and 7 per cent of the females.[33] The Waorani (Auca) of the Ecuadorian Amazon, who resemble the Yanomamo in their subsistence patterns and in the causes and style of fighting, hold the registered world record: more than 60 per cent of adult deaths over five generations were caused by feuding and warfare.[34] In highland Papua New Guinea independent estimates are again very similar: among the Dani, 28.5 per cent of the men and 2.4 per cent of the women have been reckoned to have died violently.[35] Among the Enga, 34.8 per cent of the men have been estimated to have met the same fate; Meggitt had records of 34 wars among them in 50 years;[36] among the Hewa, killing was estimated at 7.78 per 1,000 per year;[37] among the Goilala, whose total population was barely over 150, there were 29 (predominantly men) killed during a period of 35 years;[38] among the lowland Gebusi, 35.2 per cent of the men and 29.3 per cent of the women fell victim to homicide; the high rate for the women may be explained by the fact that killing was mainly related to failure to reciprocate in sister exchange marriage.[39] Violent death in tribal Montenegro at the beginning of the twentieth century was estimated at 25 per cent.[40] Archaeology unearths similar finds. In the late prehistoric Indian site of Madisonville, Ohio, 22 per cent of the adult male skulls had wounds and 8 per cent were fractured.[41] In a prehistoric cemetery site in Illinois, 16 per cent of the individuals buried there had met a violent death.[42]

All this suggests that average human violent mortality rates among adults in the state of nature may have been in the order of 15 per cent (25 per cent for the men); extremely sparse populations living in areas where resources were diffuse probably occupied the lower part of the scale, but not by a very wide margin. Furthermore, as Meggitt observes with respect to both the Australian Aborigines and New Guinea Enga highlanders, most of the men carried wound marks and scars, and regarded them as a matter of course.[43] Chagnon portrays the same picture for the Yanomamo. At least in this respect, Hobbes was closer to the truth than Rousseau about the human state of nature.

Did the emergence of the state reduce violent mortality rates? In contrast to the Rousseauite anthropological imagination, some scholars have claimed that modern wars, despite their massive death tolls, have a much less lethal demographic effect overall than did pre-state fighting.[44] State warfare altered the patterns of fighting in ways that I examine later, and at least by significantly reducing intragroup violence—that is, 'blood feuds' and 'homicide'—seems also to have reduced overall violent death rates. Statistical comparisons are again very tenuous. But the key factor seems to be the level of the population's exposure to war, either by direct (male) participation or through violence against non-combatants. Violent mortality has thus been a factor of warfare's totality. The more total the state warfare, the more its death rate has approached pre-state lethality.

In the Second Punic War (218–202 BC), ancient Rome's most devastating conflict, of which we have relatively good census and other demographic statistics, Rome (and Italy) lost, according to one minimalist estimate, at least 17 if not more than 20 per cent of its adult male population.[45] But a calamity of such magnitude was exceptional. Some parts of Germany are estimated to have suffered even greater demographic losses during the Thirty Years War (1618–48). In relation to the general mortality, death in war in France, one of the most war-like nations in Europe, is estimated by one source at 1.1 per cent in the seventeenth century, 2.7 per cent in the eighteenth century, 3 per cent in the nineteenth century, and 6.3 per cent in the first three decades of the twentieth century.[46] In the American Civil War 1.3 per cent of the population were either killed or wounded. In the First World War about 3 per cent of both the French and German populations died, representing roughly 15 per cent of the adult males. In the Second World War over 15 per cent of the Soviet Union's population perished, and around 5 per cent in Germany. However, when averaged over time, even the dreadful figures from these cataclysmic events fall short of those for primitive societies.

If, overall, state wars have indeed been less lethal than pre-state fighting, this may help to explain the observations by some leading authorities that human intraspecific killing is in fact much smaller than that of any mammalian species studied.[47] They referred to the violent mortality rates of modern societies. Tellingly, the gap between humans and other animal species closes when we go back to the 'human state of nature'. As with the state of nature in general, the 'human state of nature' was indeed, after all, highly insecure and fraught with violent death.

All the same, as we have seen, possessing a unique intraspecific first-strike capability (whose inherent instability has attracted so much attention in the nuclear age), the human adult fighters were rotationally on the receiving as well as on the inflicting end of nature's normal asymmetrical killing. They engaged in high-casualty stealth warfare, in which today's killer could be tomorrow's victim. True first-strike capability gives an enormous advantage to the side that strikes first, and thus, theoretically, almost forces one to pre-empt; because in the absence of a higher, regulating authority, or other security mechanisms, the protagonists are again locked in the 'security dilemma' variant of the 'prisoner's dilemma', where none of them can be guaranteed that the other would not strike first if one refrained from doing so. If annihilation or a major reduction of the enemy's strength is in fact achieved, so much the better. If not, then tit for tat might follow until mutual deterrence is re-established and killing is stopped by agreement. Such killing often appears senseless. But as we have seen, the conflict situation in itself regularly forces the antagonists to escalate beyond their original competitive motives.

7

Conclusion: Fighting in the Evolutionary State of Nature

The human state of nature, examined in this part, is crucially different from the concept of the seventeenth and eighteenth centuries. The old concept, which still underlies anthropological discussion of 'primitive warfare', refers to pre-state peoples, thereby lumping together hunter–gatherers and pre-state agriculturalists. However, for more than 100 years, palaeoanthropology, palaeoarchaeology, and evolutionary theory have been revealing that these two categories cannot be treated in such an indiscriminate manner. The hunter–gatherer way of life, while, of course, also evolving a great deal over the genus *Homo*'s two-million-year history, covers 99.5 per cent of that history. It encompasses more than 90 per cent of the history of the species *Homo sapiens sapiens*, depending on the particular timing of the adoption of agriculture by each group of our species, a development that in some of them, of course, never happened. Agriculture is a recent cultural invention, starting in the most pioneering groups of our species only some 10,000 years ago, and having little effect on human biology. Thus, in the light of modern scientific understanding, to speak in a meaningful manner about the human state of nature is to address human adaptations to the human natural habitats, which are responsible for the human biological inheritance. Our concept, therefore, is the *evolutionary* human state of nature. Primitive agriculturalists, particularly those who, similar to hunter–gatherers, lived in relatively small and dispersed groups, relied heavily on hunting for subsistence, and did not experience arable land shortage as a main somatic stress, may exhibit significant continuities with the hunter–gatherer way of life, which in many respects can make them useful for the study of the human state of nature. However, such an extension must be done with discrimination, and the similarity certainly cannot be assumed automatically.

The human state of nature is revealed to be fundamentally no different from the state of nature in general. However, what exactly either of them is has been a matter of considerable disputes. Regarding the state of nature in general, Konrad Lorenz claimed that intraspecific fighting was mostly demonstrative and stopped short of killing. He thought that this was a result of intraspecific inhibitions intended to preserve the species, and his view dominated during the 1960s and much of the 1970s. However, since then both zoological observations and evolutionary theory have turned against his thesis. It has been revealed that intraspecific killing is widespread in nature, but is mostly directed against the young who are too weak to fight back. Conspecifics are in fact each other's main competitors, vying as they are for the same mates and resources. However, adult conspecifics are also of roughly the same order of strength and are therefore particularly dangerous to each other. Fighting generally stops when one of the sides yields, because self-preservation imposes restraint on the victor. Killing in nature is normally done against the defenceless, when the odds are heavily tilted and little risk is involved.

The argument about the human state of nature is much older, formulated in the way that it is by Hobbes and Rousseau. Concentrating on two vast pure 'conservations' of recently extant hunter–gatherers—the Australian continent and the American north-west coast—in which the 'contact paradox' with agriculturalists, civilization, or westerners can be practically eliminated, we have found that Hobbes was closer to the truth. As with other animal species, humans regularly fought among themselves in the state of nature. Thus, it was not the advent of agriculture or civilization that inaugurated warfare. During the Palaeolithic period, hunter–gatherers inhabited the richest ecological niches of the world and were not as thinly dispersed to the point of minimizing contact among them, as some of today's marginalized hunter–gatherers are. They were never free-rangers in a vast 'common land', but were in fact 'restricted nomads' within their native and jealously guarded territories. They lived in small kin groups, starting from the extended family group to the larger regional one (tribe).

Kinship predominated in determining the direction of human aggression. As the principle of 'inclusive fitness' or 'kin selection' predicts, people would tend to side with their closer kin against more remote ones. They would be willing to risk their lives in direct relation to the closeness and number of their kin who are in danger. They recognize their kin by growing up with them, living with them, being told who they are, and by all sorts of physical and behavioural similarities that they share with them. Hence, the various activations of semi-kin–group solidarity, easily replicated when the right conditions are present. For example, the famous 'male bonding' created in small groups of warriors has long been identified as the mainstay of troops' cohesion and fighting spirit. Some scholars have rightly suggested that it was evolutionarily rooted in small-group solidarity, which had been necessary among Palaeolithic hunters. The only thing that must be added is that this Palaeolithic male group consisted of close kin; indeed the local group was literally composed of brethren. In sociological and anthropological parlance, they were 'fraternal interest groups'.[1] It is a sense of brotherhood of sorts that can be artificially recreated in small groups of non- (or remote) kin that intensively and comprehensively share their daily existence.

Indeed, the evolution-shaped mechanisms for identifying kin have been shown to be susceptible to misdirection under other 'artificial' circumstances as well. One illuminating example, often quoted in the anthropological literature, is same-group children in Israeli kibbutzim. In these communes, children used to be raised together from birth in communal nurseries rather than in their own families' homes. It has been found that, when these children grew up, they treated each other as siblings, at least in the sense that they hardly ever intermarried. Unexpectedly, in an environment that never wished them to do so, they instinctively applied the universal, biologically rooted, taboo against incest to their pseudo-kin.[2] There are other major manifestations of kin-solidarity transference. Sports teams, for example, generate intense emotions of identification, mimicking those created by the struggle of a group of one's own people against outsiders. The sports contest fundamentally functions as a mock battle.[3]

In the hunter–gatherer regional group of around 500, shared culture was a distinctive mark of kinship, as well as a strong basis for social co-operation.

This is the deeply engrained evolutionary root of ethnocentrism, xeno-phobia, patriotism, and nationalism.[4] With the coming of agriculture, civilization, and modernity, as shared-culture communities expanded a thousand- and even millionfold, the sentiment of kin solidarity expanded far beyond its original evolutionary setting and scope. One's people or nation—an extension of the original genetic cum cultural regional group—can evoke the greatest devotion, indeed, *fraternity* within a *motherland* or *fatherland* (the words are revealing), no matter how genetically related its members actually are (a feature that varies among modern peoples, albeit with surprising genes–culture congruity[5]). Individuals are genuinely prepared to risk and sacrifice themselves—not only under coercion but also voluntarily—for these large shared-culture, semi-, and sometimes pseudo- or 'imagined' kin groups. This is so even though the broader their concept of who their genetic cum symbolic folk are, the less can they actually influence this folk's survival by their own self-sacrifice. The evolutionary logic of kin selection in small groups has been inflated beyond its original applicability.

This is the 'atavistic' element that baffled modern observers often evoke vaguely in order to explain people's willingness to kill and get killed for seemingly remote causes. It provided an indispensable clue for understand-ing why, for instance, beyond all real utilitarian considerations, a Frenchman or a German was prepared to get killed for Alsace-Lorraine, the possession of which had no practical bearing on his daily life. In the great extension of culture groups and consciousness boundaries brought about by modern conditions, these provinces could be perceived by him as the close-by home territory of his immediate close-kin group. In the state of nature, this had meant possessions of essential value, evolutionarily worth risking one's life for.

This persistence and shift of evolution-shaped behaviours in radically altered cultural settings is at the core of human historical development. Consciousness of the fact that the original conditions no longer apply often has little effect on patterns of behaviour determined by deeply engrained, evolution-shaped, proximate stimuli. To give one more simple example: people continue to exhibit a strong preference for sweet foods, even though sweetness is now 'artificially' added and is harmful to us, rather than being indicative of maturity and prime nutrition in fruit, as it used to be in our original evolutionary setting. The relatively recent cultural take-off and accelerating pace of human development have left our biological inheritance very little time to catch up. This does not necessarily mean that war became maladaptive when taken out of its evolution-shaped context. As we see later, nature and culture have been mixed in complex interactions throughout human history. All the same, as humanity moved away from its evolutionary state of nature, all sorts of behaviour shaped in this state, including fighting, assumed new significance and new roles that have not been fully in line with their original, evolution-shaped rationale.

Conflict and fighting in the human state of nature, as in the state of nature in general, were fundamentally caused by competition. Although violence is evoked, and suppressed, by powerful emotional stimuli (which, like other stimuli, can sometimes take over), it is not a primary, 'irresistible' drive; it is highly tuned, both innate and optional, evolution-shaped tactics, turned on and off in response to changes in the calculus of survival and reproduction. The widespread notion that, in the extremely competitive evolutionary state of nature, fighting occurred 'just so' to satisfy 'psychological' needs— that it was essentially non-adaptive and only began to 'pay off' with the coming of agriculture and the state—constitutes such a curious reversal of the evolutionary rationale as to border on the absurd. As a result of organisms' tendency to propagate rapidly when resources are abundant, scarcity and competition are the norm in nature. Co-operation, peaceful competition, and violent conflict are variably used and intermixed—depending on the circumstances and the chances of success—to fulfil desires originally shaped by the struggle for 'inclusive fitness'. The answer to the often-voiced puzzle of why people fight is that they fight to gain the very same things that constitute the objects of human desire in general. And throughout nature, including the human state of nature, the objects of desire are in short supply, while being vital for survival. People risk their lives in fighting—again the subject of widespread puzzlement in our societies of plenty—simply because loss and gain of the tangible and intangible goods that determine survival and reproductive success for them and their kin can be greater than the risks of fighting.

Violent conflict can be activated by competition over scarce resources. What resources were scarce and were the cause of resource stress in any particular society varied, but mostly it had to do with highly nutritious meat. Deadly violence is also regularly activated in competition over women. Although human males are less polygynous than those of some other species, they still compete over the quality and number of women whom they can have. Abduction of women, rape, accusations of adultery, and broken promises of marriage are widespread direct causes of reproductive conflict, whereas resource competition in order to be able to afford more women and children is an indirect cause as well as a direct one. As W. D. Hamilton, the doyen of modern evolutionary theory, saw: for 'hunter–gatherers . . . to raise mean fitness in a group either new territory or outside mates have to be obtained somehow'.[6] Conflict sometimes resulted in significant net gains in women and/or subsistence resources. Moreover, and this point is often missed, for evolution to work, net gains in intergroup conflict characterized by very high mortality rates are not necessary, because intergroup conflict also results in intragroup selection, as some group members on both sides get killed, decreasing the internal pressure on the resources for those who survive.

From the primary somatic and reproductive aims, other, proximate and derivative, 'second-level', aims arise. It is not only the best providers who can subsist better and have more wives and children, but also the social arbiters within the group who can use their position to reap somatic and reproductive advantages. Hence the competition for esteem, prestige, power, and leadership, as proximate goods, which, like the primary competition itself, can also take the form of violent conflict. Again, this violence can be either direct or indirect, the latter being intended to achieve the symbolic or tangible goods that confer esteem, prestige, power, and leadership. There are highly complex interactions here, which are, however, underpinned in principle by a simple evolutionary rationale.

The fundamental state of competition and potential violent conflict produces additional causes for conflict. There is often retaliation for an offence or injury, lest it persist and become a pattern of victimization. Retaliation or 'revenge' is thus intended either to eliminate the rival or to re-establish deterrence against him and others by demonstrating that one is not powerless and has the means to strike back. Tit for tat may end when the balance is settled, but it may also escalate, leading to a self-perpetuating cycle of strikes and counter-strikes. Both sides then accumulate losses that are sometimes immeasurably greater than the original injuries that caused the conflict in the first place. Nevertheless, the antagonists are often locked into conflict because of all sorts of communication problems that make it difficult to reach a negotiated settlement, or because of inability to secure that the other side abides by it. In a sort of 'prisoner's dilemma', their rational option under such conditions is often much inferior to their optimal one.

Similarly, in a state of potential conflict, security precautions are called for, which may take defensive as well as offensive or pre-emptive character. This 'security dilemma' variant of the 'prisoner's dilemma' again means that the very ability of the other to attack, whether or not he actually wishes to do so, poses a threat that can force one into action. In the absence of a strong central authority, a lack of information about the other and an inability to guarantee an agreement of mutual security frequently breed suspicion, hostility, and conflict, seemingly 'imposed' on the sides 'against their wishes' and best interests. Arms races, brought about by each side's desire to get ahead or keep abreast of the other, may produce an advantage to one side but often merely produce a 'Red Queen effect', by which both sides escalate their resource investment only to find themselves in the same position vis-à-vis the other. As with trees growing trunks, massive investment is enforced on the competitors simply by the reality of an unregulated competition.

Thus, in principle, two major factors correlate closely with the likely occurrence of violent conflict. The first of these is scarcity. Somatic stresses and reproductive deprivation would give rise to a more desperate and risk-taking behaviour, including violence. This is the idea expressed in the proverb that hungry wolves would beat satiated dogs. Obviously, as we saw, scarcity is partly relative. Competition—and violent conflict—can intensify where opportunities and abundance increase. Hence the significance of the second factor: the existence of societal regulatory mechanisms that would keep competition within non-violent channels. As violent behaviour, while being an innate potential, is socially learnt, either pugnacity or pacificism can be habituated by experience. Anarchic systems—either inter- or intrasocial—would be more violence prone and more accustomed to the use of violence. It is again for this reason that wild wolves would beat domesticated dogs.

The effect of competition and potential conflict on the lives of people in the state of nature can now be more carefully defined. As we have seen, fighting broke out from time to time and was responsible for high rates of mortality, as high as 25–30 per cent of the adult males. This does not mean that all hunter–gatherer societies were equally war-like. There were differences among them as there would later be differences in this respect among states. Still, as with states in historical times, a fundamental condition of competition and plurality made fighting a norm that very few communities could escape or fail to be prepared for, no matter what their particular inclinations. Indeed, although the notions of 'incessant' or 'endemic' fighting are thereby justified, they can be partly misleading. Although actual, active fighting was in effect sparse, it is its danger that dominated people's lives. This idea, pointed out by Hobbes (*Leviathan*, 13), has also been sensed by modern anthropologists.[7] In an afterthought, 'Balancing the picture of fierceness', that Chagnon added to later editions of his *Yanomamo: The fierce people*, he wrote:

> First of all, the Yanomamo do not spend all or even a major fraction of their walking hours making wars on neighbors. . . . Second, warfare among the Yanomamo varies from region to region and from time to time: it is extremely intense in some areas at particular times, and almost non-existent in other areas. Even the most 'warlike' villages have long periods of relative peace during which time daily life is tranquil and happy. . . . On the other hand, even the least warlike villages suddenly find themselves embroiled in an active war, or the peace of the temporary tranquil is shattered by an unexpected raid.[8]

This is more or less the picture that we have encountered everywhere among hunger–gatherers, in the human state of nature. People sometimes live in peace with their neighbours, sometimes in conflict. Competition is widespread but varies considerably in its expression and intensity. Where it exists, it can lead to more or less amicable compromises, covertly or overtly based on mutual deterrence. Where compromise is less amicable or stable, or is not reached at all, violence can break out. Thus, no less than actual fighting, it is the threat of violent conflict that shapes people's lives in the state of nature. Fear, mutual deterrence, and insecurity bind them to their home territory and own people, and force them to adopt precautions and never to be completely off their guard. Both among other primates and among humans, field observations and laboratory tests have demonstrated that strangers trigger an initial response of high alarm, suspicion, insecurity, and aggression.[9] The stark stereotyping of aliens and, even more, enemies, painted in the darkest, most menacing shades, is an all too familiar basic human response. The worst intentions are assumed and a tremendous defensive emotional mobilization takes place. Under conditions of competition and potential conflict, the evolution-shaped response is 'better safe than sorry'. Naturally, as the other side tends to react similarly, worst-case analyses tend to be self-fulfilling. Alarm, suspicion, insecurity, and aggression decline after a while if the strangers are observed to be non-threatening, in the sense that they are non-aggressive, or make no large claim to sharing resources, or prove ready for low-cost compromise, coexistence, or even co-operation (exchange). However, a measure of alienation and xenophobia remains.

We have seen that the reality of competition and conflict breeds more competition and conflict. Competition and conflict grow from a funda-mental state of scarcity, but then, because of the suspicion, insecurity, and craving for power that they create, they also feed on themselves and take on a life of their own. A competition can be won by a more efficient utilization of resources, but, paradoxically, also by investing more of the resources in the competition itself. As with trunk-growing trees or with large and muscled bodies, the competition can consume much of the resources for which it is waged. At least partly, it can thereby increase the scarcity and further inten-sify itself. In a conflict in particular, most if not all of the so-called defence costs or conflict costs (except for some 'spin-off' effects) are in effect dis-bursed out of the time and resources that can be directly invested in pro-vision. As we see later, with agriculture and accumulated resources, conflict would also directly *diminish* resources as each side destroyed the other's property. However, even in the state of nature, if the antagonist is not beaten, a 'Red Queen effect' may be created, in which both sides may lose from the competition/conflict. Conflict cannot then even be regarded as a 'zero-sum game', a competition in which one's loss is the other's gain and vice versa. It is possible for both sides to lose; in evolutionary/reproductive terms this mainly means death of kin and decreased subsistence and reproduction for the living. However, give up the conflict unilaterally may mean even heavier losses, so both sides may be bound by the unregulated competitive/ conflictual situation to stick to their guns until agreement for a cessation of hostilities can be reached. As people have always vaguely sensed and puzzled, conflict has rarely been confined to or proportioned by the objectives that originally brought it into being.

Competition and conflict are thus 'real' in the sense that they arise from genuine scarcities among evolution-shaped, self-propagating organisms and can end in vital gains for one and losses for the other; at the same time, they are often also 'inflated', partly self-perpetuating, and mutually damaging, because of the logic imposed on the antagonists by the conflict itself in an anarchic, unregulated environment that provides no way out from 'prisoners' dilemmas' and 'market failures', and may mean net losses for both. In a way, this justifies both of the widely held polarized attitudes to war: the one that sees it as a serious business for serious aims and the other that is shocked by its absurdity.

Finally, a few concluding remarks on the evolutionary perspective that has underpinned our study of the human state of nature. I hope that I have been able to demonstrate that evolutionary theory, our major key for understanding nature, is vital for understanding the human state of nature, fighting in the state of nature, and human nature in general. I have no illusions, however, that I have succeeded in convincing the unconvinced. For various reasons, evolutionary theory has always stirred violent, and not always informed, opposition. Today, as it is affecting a great revival in the human sciences, evolutionary theory is often received as alien by people trained in other disciplines, some of which are academically and emotionally heavily invested in different and even contradictory ideas. Fanciful and sensational echoes of 'sociobiology' encountered in popular and journalistic sources often do not help its cause either.

As our only grand scientific theory for understanding nature, evolutionary theory does not 'compete' with scholarly constructs such as psychoanalytic theories, 'materialism', or 'functionalism'; in fact, it may encompass some of their main insights within a comprehensive interpretative framework.[10] For instance, we have seen how the differing elementary drives posited by Freud, Jung, and Adler, respectively, as the underlying regulating principle for understanding human behaviour—sex, creativeness and the quest for meaning, and the craving for superiority—all come together and interact within the framework of evolutionary theory, which also provides an explanation for their otherwise mysterious origin. Similarly, evolutionary theory explains why humans, and other organisms, are indeed motivated by a desire for material goods, but treats this motive in conjunction with, rather than in isolation from, other motives, shaped together by a comprehensive reproductive and somatic rationale. Evolutionary theory explains how long-cited motives for fighting—such as Sumner's hunger, love, vanity, and fear of superior powers—came to be and how they hang together and interconnect.

'Functionalism' used to be a popular approach in the social sciences, which has more recently come under criticism. It is motivated by much the same questions, and comes up with much the same answers, as evolutionary theory. It seeks to explain social phenomena as adaptive regulatory mechanisms intended to keep the system working. There is, however, a whole set of interrelated problems with this approach. Functionalism does not explain how these 'mechanisms' came to be, or evolved; they are simply postulated to be there. It evokes function for social phenomena without making clear who gave them this function: does it arise from a divine order, or is it embedded in other 'sky hooks', such as transcendent harmony supposedly existing in nature and even in society? Furthermore, why should the social system, social phenomena, and social function be permeated with a desire for equilibrium? Functionalism has difficulties with change and tends to have a static picture of reality. Thus functionalism stands things on their head or approaches them from the wrong direction. Rather than explain general social phenomena and relationships from the bottom up, by contextual interactions of living agents, it purports to explain individual action by social abstracts, particularly that of 'stability'.[11]

In our subject, a cultural materialist such as Marvin Harris and a cultural ecologist such as Andrew Vayda have suggested in a functionalist vein that fighting was a demographic mechanism triggered by pressure on the resources, as well as by a surplus of men in relation to women. As we have seen, both factors—the somatic and the reproductive—are indeed central to explaining fighting, so their interpretation is very much in the right direction. It is the *functionalist* reasoning, rather than answers, that is misconstrued. Fighting is not one of nature's or of society's regulating mechanisms for contending with overpopulation; rather, it is one of the strategies that *people*, and other organisms, employ to gain the upper hand in response to increased competition that may arise from demographic growth. The same, incidentally, applies to Malthus's other positive checks on over-population: famine and pestilence. These are not 'regulating mechanisms' embedded in nature's design. Instead, famine is actually what happens to a population that has outgrown its means of subsistence. Similarly, a denser population is simply more vulnerable to the propagation of parasites and pathogens. Obviously, if functionalist reasoning was merely *façon de parler* or accepted 'shorthand', in the same way that we speak of organisms 'wanting' to increase their numbers, there would have been no problem. However, for functionalists, function is regarded as a genuine explanation rather than *façon de parler*.[12]

143

Some readers may fail to see the advantage of the evolutionary over the functionalist interpretation of demographic pressure, or, indeed, wonder why evolutionary theory should be presented here as different from, and superior to, any other scholarly approach to the study of humans in the state of nature. Is it because it is the ruling theory in the study of nature? If so, is this not an argument from authority rather than from the theory's own merits? However, it is my claim that evolutionary theory has won its commanding position in the natural sciences precisely because it has been recognized to be nature's immanent principle rather than an artificial analytical construct. Indeed, from the nineteenth century, evolutionary theory has been perceived as the only non-transcendent mechanism for explaining life's complex design. To repeat, this mechanism is blind natural selection in which in every stage those who were endowed with the most suitable qualities for surviving and reproducing remained. There is no reason why they remained other than that they proved successful in the struggle for survival. Thus 'success' is not defined by any transcendent measurement but by the immanent logic of the evolutionary process.

This point needs emphasizing also in order to allay other often-voiced concerns with respect to the application of evolutionary theory to human affairs. The evolutionary logic in itself has no normative implications. It can inform us about human natural predispositions, the often ignored effects of which we would be wise to take into account but which are often variable and even contradictory. (Late nineteenth- and early twentieth-century social Darwinists, on the one hand, and *tabula rasa* liberals, on the other, erred here in two opposite directions.) We may choose to follow such predispositions or rebel against them. There is nothing sacred or morally compelling about maximizing survival for the fittest. This is merely the blind, algorithmic mechanism of natural 'design'. The human brain—itself a product of evolution and a powerful instrument of conscious, purposeful, and future oriented, rather than blind, design—may come up with more satisfactory arrangements.

This brings us to another widespread cause of resistance to 'sociobiology'. This is the belief that it upholds biological determinism in a subject that is distinctively determined by human culture—that it is precisely the non-biological element that makes humans and the human achievement what they are. Darwinism may thus be regarded as our key to understanding nature but as mostly irrelevant for understanding human society shaped by culture. In fact, historians and social scientists are much more prone to disregard the biological element in human culture than are proponents of evolutionary theory to neglect the cultural. The latter emphatically do not believe in biological determinism. While bringing to light our evolution-shaped innate genetic inheritance, they have come up with illuminating insights for explaining gene–culture interactions. For once humans had evolved agriculture, they set in train a continuous chain of developments that have taken them further and further away from their evolutionary natural way of life as hunter–gatherers. Human society has been radically transformed and staggeringly diversified. Original, evolution-shaped, innate human wants, desires, and proximate behavioural and emotional mechanisms now expressed themselves within radically altered, 'artificial' conditions, which were very different from those in which they had evolved. In the process, while never disappearing, they were greatly modified, assuming novel and widely varied appearances. These gene–culture interactions are the stuff from which human history is made, including the history of fighting. Indeed, it is to cultural evolution and the evolution of gene–culture interactions, as humans moved out of their evolutionary shaped state of nature, that I now turn.

Part 2

AGRICULTURE, CIVILIZATION, AND WAR

8

Introduction: Evolving Cultural Complexity

In Part 1 we saw that, contrary to the widely held Rousseauite belief, human fighting was not a recent 'cultural invention' that had truly begun or had become serious only with the advent of agriculture and, later, the state and civilization. Undoubtedly, however, these landmark cultural developments, which revolutionized the human way of life, profoundly affected warfare. I now proceed to examine the transformation of warfare in relation to the major developments of human cultural evolution. But, first, a few words about the concept of cultural evolution itself, and the manner in which it is used in this book.

Cultural evolution is an even older concept than biological evolution. It became prominent with the eighteenth-century idea of 'Progress' and with nineteenth-century Hegelian, Marxist, and positivist philosophies. It was influentially championed by the founding fathers of sociology and anthropology, such as Herbert Spencer, Edward Tylor, and Lewis Henry Morgan. Then a reaction set in. The great nineteenth-century evolutionary 'systems' were criticized for being abstract, insensitive to the actual 'untidiness' of historical reality, speculative, metaphysical, and teleological, postulating 'History' as the advance of 'Progress'. Even the concepts introduced by Adam Ferguson, and amplified by Morgan and Gordon Childe about humanity's transition from 'Savagery' through 'Barbarism' to 'Civilization', no longer sounded right. Franz Boas changed the direction of anthropological research by rejecting all speculations about unknown origins and evolution, concentrating instead on the empirical study of extant societies. Still, as archaeological research increasingly expanded our knowledge of the past, the evolutionary approach to human culture has continued to have its proponents among archaeologists and anthropologists, who at the same time have striven to avoid the non-empirical aspects that had marred their predecessors' work. In a Boasian vein, most cultural evolutionists in this tradition have also drawn a sharp divide between biological and cultural evolution, denying that the former had any but the most trivial significance in human affairs, which they have supposed to be almost infinitely malleable by culture.[1]

The first thing to clarify, then, is the relationship between the two types of evolution. The *analogies* between them have always been recognized. To begin with, both deal with the continuous, recursive reproduction of replicating forms—biological or cultural—the occasional variations of which are at least to some degree subject to all sorts of selective pressures. In biology, the replicators are the genes, stored and transmitted between generations in the cellular nuclei. In culture, the replicators are behaviours and ideas—'memes' in Richard Dawkins' inspired phrase—accumulated during life in brains and transmitted between them through learning. Hence one of the chief differences between biological and cultural evolution: the former involves 'inborn' replicators that can be passed on only to offspring; the latter is concerned with acquired traits that can be replicated 'horizontally', in principle to any brain. The inheritance of acquired traits is called Lamarckian, after the doctrine of Darwin's predecessor, which Darwin ruled out in biology. It makes the pace of cultural evolution infinitely faster. Still, in cultural evolution, too, the replicators are highly durable. Systems of symbols and practices, such as languages and customs, passed on and reproduced generation after generation, are particularly slow to change. But even they do—by random 'drift' and 'mutation', by purposeful adaptation, or by the influence of foreign 'memes'.[2]

Biological and cultural evolutions are, however, related by more than analogy. They represent a continuum, not just a break, in human evolution—indeed, in evolution in general. In the first place, the one originated from the other. Underlying the take-off of cultural evolution was the perfection of one of the latest tricks of *biological* evolution: a greatly enhanced ability to teach and learn. This ability did not begin with *Homo sapiens'* vastly improved cerebral capacity for manipulating and communicating symbols. A bigger and more flexible 'open' brain design, capable of being partly shaped during life by interaction with the environment through experience and learning, had been a device increasingly developed in later products of the evolutionary 'arms race' such as birds, big mammals, primates, apes, and archaic humans. However, with *Homo sapiens sapiens* this growing capacity had crossed a threshold. In response to outside stimuli, our genetically constructed 'hardware' is capable of considerable restructuring through life (especially at early ages) and of taking on an unprecedented diversity of 'software'. It can consequently generate a yet more staggering range of 'applications'. This is evident in the Upper Palaeolithic 'cultural explosion', and thereafter. Cultural evolution proved to be an explosive potential. Human evolution has since been overwhelmingly cultural rather than biological.[3]

Cultural evolution has not worked on a clean slate, however. Not only did it originate, as a capacity, from biological evolution; it has been working on a human physiological and psychological 'landscape' deeply grooved by long-evolved inborn predispositions. The staggering diversity of human cultural forms and the amazing trajectory of human cultural evolution have brought some historicist thinkers of the nineteenth and twentieth centuries to claims that humankind's peculiar quality is precisely that it lacks such a thing as 'nature'. Humans have been proclaimed to be 'all history'—that is, wholly culturally determined. Cultural evolutionists have tended to assume that, given the right socialization, humans were capable of embracing practically *any* behaviour. However, since the 1950s, Noam Chomsky's revolution in linguistics has presented the humanities and social sciences with an illuminating old–new model, which heralded the eclipse of the *tabula rasa* view of the human mind that had dominated the middle of the twentieth century. Chomsky and his disciples have argued that, although thousands of human languages are recognized today, and an unknown, far larger number were spoken in the past, all human languages share a common 'deep' set of syntax patterns. These patterns appear to reflect our innate language-handling mechanisms that make language use so easy and natural to us. Thus humans are in principle capable of generating any hypothetical language, but only as long as its 'meta-structure' complies with these deep common patterns.[4] This would give an infinite, but at the same time also highly constrained, variety.

As the quintessential culture form, language has proved to be an illuminating model for human mind structures in general. Most cultural evolutionists have erred in embracing one side of a false nature–nurture dichotomy. There is indeed a staggering diversity of cultural forms and great cultural 'elasticity', but not quite *any* form goes. Cultural choices and preferences did not simply 'take over' from biology. Instead, the rich diversity of cultural forms has been built on and around a fairly recognizable deep core of evolution-shaped, innate propensities, needs, and desires—ultimate ends, proximate mechanisms, and derivative byproducts—sometimes, to be sure, as we see later, in rebellion against them or as an expression of conflicts between them, but nevertheless in constant interaction with them. With cultural evolution all biological bets are not off; they are hedged. Biology and culture constitute an amalgamated compound that co-evolves in mutual interaction. The whole thing is better viewed as a marvellously complex but far from 'arbitrary' edifice. Our biological predispositions heavily bias our cultural choices; in turn, as some studies have demonstrated, our cultural choices can select for some biological traits. Cultural traits, too, are subject to selective pressures. Some cultural traits directly affect the survival and reproductive success of the populations with which they are associated. In other cases, they affect not the survivability of the human populations themselves but that of the 'population' of ideas and practices, as some 'memes' push out and replace others within the same human population. They do not necessarily have to have a better adaptive value. Some cultural traits are simply more 'addictive' in more or less specific biocultural settings, and may spread in the same way that a virus or a parasite spreads in a biological population. They may even be harmful to the survival and reproductive success of the population that they 'infect', but, because they spread fast enough to other populations, they avoid extinction. There is a 'long leash' connecting the elements of the biocultural compounds, but a leash nevertheless.[5] This persistence and variation of human motives and other predispositions under changing cultural conditions—in their relation to fighting—are one of my main concerns in the rest of this book.

Indeed, there is yet another element of continuity between biological and cultural evolution. Largely fuelled by selection in an ever-going evolutionary 'arms race', both forms of evolution tend over time to produce ever more complex 'designs'. As mentioned above, learning and the capacity to generate culture were themselves one of the latest 'innovations' of biological evolution. Cultural evolution has then continued biological evolution in creating greater complexity, simply by force of the competition that takes place among reproducing, propagating replicators of any sort. The whole race gets ever faster and more competitive, because the participants are continuously getting better, more 'professional' at it; they are getting better not only in adaptation but also in *adaptability*. It is for this reason that natural selection, starting from relatively simple bacteria nearly 4 billion years ago, took until roughly 1.5 billion years ago to evolve the first multicellular organisms. Increasingly larger multicellular organisms, which possessed increasingly diversified, mutually co-operating specialized organs, then followed at an ever-accelerating pace: vascular plants evolved around 400 million years ago; amphibians, reptiles, and mammals evolved from fish between 400 and 250 million years ago; the first birds followed about 135 million years ago. The land and then the air began to be colonized only in these relatively recent times.[6]

Complexity is defined by the number and diversity of different, specialized, and mutually dependent parts, integrated within functional hierarchical structures. Originally, it was Spencer, falling out of favour in the twentieth century, who described the work of evolution—biological and cultural—as a process of growing complexity from 'incoherent homogeneity to coherent heterogeneity, through successive differentiations and integrations'. But, indeed, does not our concept of growing complexity constitute a return to the nineteenth-century's teleological view of evolution as 'Progress'? This crucial point must be carefully understood. The process described is not 'Progressive' in any value sense, nor does it necessarily lead to 'growing happiness', 'well-being', or any other 'goal'. Where there is a strong element of inner propensity involved, and there is, it is to be understood only in terms of the non-transcendent, 'immanent' tendency of recursively reproducing and propagating replicators to evolve—through competition and selection—more sophisticated and complex designs for dealing with a competitive environment. (To be sure, greater efficiency sometimes involves simplification rather than growing complexity, but in most cases the opposite is correct.) This inherent tendency in evolution towards greater complexity does not confer 'inevitability' on the process. Evolutionary forms can remain little changed for a very long time. They can also regress or become extinct when evolving into a 'dead end' or when encountering a drastic—self-generated or extraneous—adverse change in their environment. We are familiar with several catastrophic mass extinctions in natural evolution, and one cosmic collision, for example, can in principle destroy all life on earth—indeed, Earth itself. The process is not 'preordained'. Still, wherever and so long as they exist, the inherent general dynamic over time of competing propagating replicators of any sort (biological and cultural ones being, as we now see, only specific instances) is to evolve into becoming better in the evolutionary contest. Evolutionary history thus forms more than a mere sequence. It is directional in the sense that it generally tends to evolve greater complexity. This is a gradual process, in which every step in growing complexity must build on a less complex stage as a necessary precondition.

The way in which ordered complexity, or self-organization, evolves 'spontaneously' from simple elements entering simple interactions is one of the hottest topics on the edge of current scientific research.[7] One of the interesting features of this process is, again, that it is not wholly 'arbitrary'— that is, it cannot produce *any* form. The emergence of complexity is constrained not only by the gradual nature of the process, but also by the propensities of the materials at hand in the 'design space'—physical, chemical, organic, or cultural. Thus, although many different worlds can evolve (and have evolved, in different times and places in Earth's natural and cultural history), similar 'constraints' have repeatedly led to the independent emergence of similar structures in different times and places. In natural evolution, for example, photosynthesis, the extraction of energy from sunlight, was invented several times over by many different bacteria. Winged flight evolved independently many times, with insects, pterodactyls, bats, birds, and various fish. Sexual reproduction also evolved independently several times.[8] Only then did each of these 'mechanisms' diffuse further from its independent loci of emergence. In cultural evolution as well, similar major structures emerged independently of each other in different times and places, when the right conditions were present. People brought about the evolution of agriculture in at least four independent major loci—possibly double that number. Later, the state and civilization emerged in a more or less similar number of independent loci, at different times. Only then have these culturally evolved structures diffused across the world from these original loci, owing to their strong selective advantages.[9]

The strategy that this book follows is to trace the development of war in relation to the relative chronology of these major transformations in the human way of life, rather than in relation to the customary fixed chronology, arbitrarily derived from the particular history of the west. Thus, for example, the civilizations of pre-Columbian Mesoamerica and Peru, magnificent and sophisticated in many ways as they were, are treated here as late Stone Age or Copper Age states and empires, most instructively viewed as the 'equivalent' of the Old-World early Mesopotamian and Egyptian civilizations, at the level the latter had achieved by the first half of the third millennium BC.[10] Here were separate, practically unconnected worlds that evolved independently in different absolute times. All the same, although these New- and Old-World civilizations obviously exhibited substantial local variations between them, as any different civilizations do, their late Stone Age and Copper Age infrastructure makes them sufficiently similar to be fruitfully studied together. As already noted, the 'science fiction' quality of the European discovery of the Americas is that it constituted not only a voyage in space but also in relative time.

In the same way, the European Middle Ages are not treated here, as their name implies, as an 'intermediate' phase in a linear development of the west, between antiquity and modern times. Their first part, the Dark Ages, is better viewed as a 'collapse' of civilization, as far as the classical Mediterranean world is concerned, and as a continuation of the Iron Age cultures of northern Europe in the history of the peoples that overtook the Roman world. This period involved a return to all the features of pre-civilization: the disappearance of literacy, cities, and large-scale economies. In relative time, the Dark Ages *preceded*, as it were, rather than followed, classical antiquity, and they are comparatively best studied in conjunction with other prehistoric Iron Age societies. The later part of the Middle Ages is best viewed in terms of a re-emergence of 'civilization', in its European or Christian variety, as urbanism, writing, and money economy revived. To be sure, this re-emergence did not occur on a clean slate but was strongly influenced over both time and space by the legacy of classical civilization and by cultural diffusion, mainly from the Moslem and Chinese civilizations.

This relative, comparative approach, and the examples cited, are commonplace among archaeologists but are unusual for historians, who are concerned with the specific 'earlier' and 'later' of particular societies. Historians are also justly suspicious of both the concept of cultural 'stages' and insensitive cross-cultural comparisons. It is therefore important to emphasize the flexible and non-dogmatic nature of the evolutionary and comparative framework that underlies this book. As a result of similar biocultural–environmental 'constraints', similar human culture forms have often evolved independently, along 'parallel' or 'converging' paths in different and unconnected societies. Cultural diffusion obviously reinforces similarities where societies touch. It is worthwhile to pursue such similarities as far as they go. However, ever different specific local conditions and sheer contingency, resulting in different developmental histories or 'multilinearity', also produce inexhaustible diversity of cultural forms. *Both* the major similarities and some of the salient varieties in human history are outlined here as the framework for our study of the development of human armed conflict. It is through the dual, complementary processes of generalization *and* differentiation that human understanding works.

The relative clock and flexible ruler used in this book measure *change*, over both time and space. Thus, the scope of the first part of this book was framed so wide as to address human fighting in the slowly evolving 'first two million years'. However, as human cultural evolution accelerates and diversifies through history, our 'epochs' will steadily contract, to thousands, and then hundreds of years. In this part, I successively examine the effect on warfare of the two major 'take-off' transitions in human cultural evolution: the emergence of agriculture and animal husbandry; and the growth of the state and of civilization. I start with a structural anthropological–sociological–historical account of these processes in their relation to fighting. In the concluding chapter, I more systematically attempt to tie together my findings in Part 2 with those of Part 1, bringing out the lines of continuity and change in the causes and form of violent conflict, as humans moved away from their 'evolutionary state of nature' and underwent the great transformations of cultural evolution.

9

Tribal Warfare in *Agraria* and *Pastoralia*

THE ADVENT AND SPREAD OF FARMING

About 10,000 years ago, some time before 8,000 BC, people in south-west Asia (the Near East) pioneered agriculture, followed some 1,000–1,500 years later by animal husbandry. They grew wheat, barley, and pulses, and later fruit and vegetables, and raised sheep and goats, and later pigs and cattle. Within 2,000–4,000 years after south-west Asia, similar developments independently took off in east Asia (millet, pigs, and chicken, and later rice, soya beans, and fruit), Mesoamerica (maize, beans, squash, peppers, avocados), and the Andes (beans, chilli, corn, manioc, peanuts, potatoes, cotton). Other, secondary, semi-independent centres of domestication followed in Melanesia, sub-equatorial Africa, and the eastern parts of North America.[1] From its centres of origin, farming spread to cover most the world's surface that was suitable for it. Its effects were profound. Most significantly perhaps, within 5,000 years after its inception—again with remarkable synchronicity—states and civilizations emerged independently in each and every one of the original centres of farming. I first attempt briefly to outline and explain the advent and spread of farming, and then to assess its impact on and relationship with warfare.

Why people adopted agriculture is not such an easy question to answer as it may appear at first sight. In the heyday of the idea of 'Progress' during

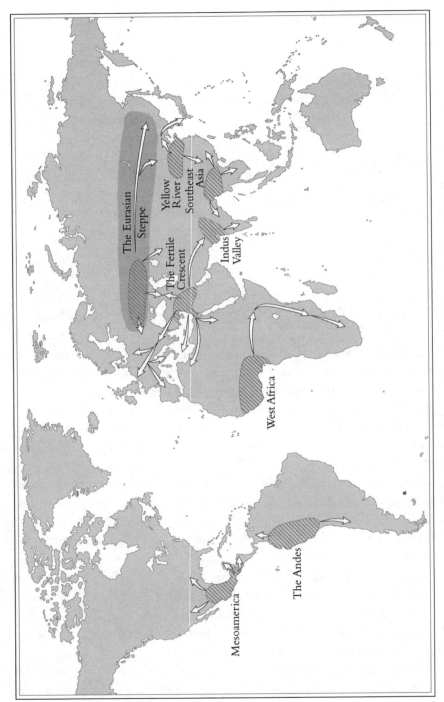

The Eurasian Steppe

Yellow River

Southeast Asia

The Fertile Crescent

Indus Valley

West Africa

Mesoamerica

The Andes

Origins and spread of agriculture and the state (major centres)

the eighteenth and nineteenth centuries, the answer seemed self-evident. Agriculture was assumed to be an obvious improvement to human diet, way of life, and control over nature. Thus, in humanity's continuous ascent, people were supposed to have taken it up simply when they had hit on the idea. By the twentieth century, however, not only has there been a general loss of confidence in the notion of 'Progress', but archaeology and anthropology have come up with finds that undermined the traditional view of agriculture as a desirable improvement. In the first place, anthropologists noted that hunter–gatherers worked much less and enjoyed much more leisure than agriculturalists. In switching to agriculture, people gradually took on a regime of hard toil, a transformation mythically echoed in the biblical curse of humanity banished from the Garden of Eden: 'In the sweat of thy face shalt thou eat bread' (*Genesis* 3.19). For this reason, historically observed hunter–gatherers were reluctant to take up agriculture even when they had farmers as their neighbours. The problem, then, was not ignorance of the idea. Pre-agriculture *Homo sapiens sapiens* people, living in nature, were not unaware of the *possibility* of active cultivation. For a long time, however, they chose not to pursue it. Archaeologists and anthropologists have further found that hunter–gatherers were overall healthier than agriculturalists. Many of our familiar infectious diseases, such as measles, smallpox, influenza, diphtheria, and tuberculosis, apparently came to humans from domesticated animals. Life in dense sedentary populations, in close proximity to human and animal excrement, vastly increased infection by pathogens and parasites. Finally, over time, dietary variety actually *decreased* with the transition to agriculture. Most people became dependent on an unbalanced diet based on a small variety of easily grown staples.[2]

So why did people in different parts of the world at roughly the same time suddenly take up plant cultivation and animal husbandry? Scholars still debate this question, and the following is my own preferred synthesis. The underlying dynamic was probably human demographic growth, which became particularly marked with the rise of *Homo sapiens sapiens* during the last 100,000 years. This demographic growth was both fuelled by and sustained through two mechanisms: emigration and technological innovation. *Homo sapiens sapiens* spread to cover all of the Old World, displacing more archaic human populations. Groups of *Homo sapiens sapiens* then discovered and rapidly populated the Americas (and Oceania), previously uninhabited by humans. Simultaneously, our species' increasingly more efficient hunting and fishing tools and techniques made possible increasingly denser populations during the Upper Palaeolithic. A resulting overkill of large game brought about diversification to a wider spectrum of wild food resources. Correspondingly, with no new major spaces to spread to, with more efficient subsistence techniques, and with denser populations, human groups in lush environments became more sedentary. In such environments they no longer needed to move around as much as previously, nor did they possess as large territories as before to be able to do so. As archaeology has been uncovering, sedentism was everywhere a prerequisite of pristine agriculture, rather than the other way around. Human settlement in many different parts of the globe had taken this more sedentary, resource-intensive form by the end of the Old Stone Age (European Palaeolithic), around 15,000 years ago, and during the Middle Stone Age (Mesolithic). It is the worldwide demographic growth of human population that accounts for the otherwise puzzling, almost simultaneous occurrence of parallel developments, such as greater population densities, growing sedentism, and the advent of agriculture, in different corners of the earth.

Skeletal remains show that people in those more sedentary and more densely populated areas where agriculture and animal husbandry began did not particularly suffer from resource stress. Demographic growth acted as a catalyst to the adoption of cultivation in a more subtle way. It was probably the reality of sedentism itself, once established, that made some cultivation a more natural option than it had been under a more nomadic way of life. Where seasonal changes affecting food availability were marked (as in semi-dry climates) and where a suitable wild variety of potential breeds existed, these factors acted as further catalysts for change.[3] A new process was set in train.

We now realize better how gradual the change was. The so-called Neolithic Revolution—and it was profoundly revolutionary—is currently more regularly referred to as a transition or transformation that took thousands of years to unravel. In the first place, the wild species took thousands of years of human selection to increase their susceptibility to human control and their productivity—that is, to become domesticated. Simultaneously, human care of favoured wild species evolved from protection, elimination of competitors, and assistance in distribution to direct, purposeful cultivation.[4] Cultivation techniques themselves then constantly improved in efficiency, from shifting, 'slash-and-burn' horticulture through more intensive forms of horticulture, including irrigation, to the plough and other forms of agriculture. Correspondingly, cultivation's share in providing human needs progressively expanded, whereas that of hunting and gathering, which for a long time went on side by side with horticulture, increasingly shrank.

This was a self-reinforcing process that constantly reproduced the preconditions for its further advance. It became a one-way road from which it was increasingly difficult to retract. The more productive cultivation grew the more worthwhile an activity it became. The more productive it grew the denser the human population it could support. The denser the human population and the more intensive the cultivation, the more the wildlife and, consequently, human foraging activity contracted. The denser the human population the more intensive cultivation had to become in order to extract food from smaller per-capita plots of land. Sedentary life made possible far more extensive material possessions and gradually laid the ground for tremendous economic, social, and cultural diversification and sophistication. Still, as the process of agricultural intensification ran its course by the eve of industrialization, some 80–90 per cent of the world's population consisted of hard toiling, disease-infested, malnourished peasants, suffering high mortality rates and struggling to extract meagre subsistence from small, intensively cultivated agricultural lots. How was this paradoxical result possible?

Again the main answer is demographic growth, and a spectacular one. The transition to farming seems to have increased the human mortality rate (and generally decreased human health), but it increased the human birth rate far more. Women's net fertility grew owing to a combination of factors, including: a permanent home base, shortened lactation periods (which acts in mammals as a natural anti-pregnancy means), increased calorific intake (mainly carbohydrates stored as body fat), and greater demand for working hands in the fields and at home. Birth rates nearly doubled between hunter–gatherers and agriculturalists, on average from about four to five births per woman to six to eight.[5] As plant and animal cultivation meant far greater food yield from a given space, these many more babies could be fed. The result was a continuous demographic explosion. Cultivation's far greater productivity translated into ever-larger numbers—necessitating ever-growing intensification—rather than into per capita growth in well-being. This was a runaway 'Red Queen' process.[6]

World population at the beginning of the Neolithic or New Stone Age, the era of agriculture some 10,000 years ago, can be only roughly estimated.

Based on the density of archaeological sites and the known density of recently extant hunter–gatherer populations, estimates range from 5 to 15 million people worldwide. Cultivation and husbandry brought an estimated tenfold increase in that number in the first five millennia after their advent, with an increase by perhaps as much as a factor of 100 by the eve of industrialization, another 5,000 years later. Once again this demographic growth depended on two factors: agricultural intensification of existing cultivated land, related to innovation in technology and method; and the availability of as yet uncultivated land that could be turned to cultivation. Both the intensification and expansion options took place in parallel over time. Whereas lush environments could support only a few hunter–gatherers per square kilometre, they could sustain dozens of farmers in the same space unit, and up to hundreds where intensive systems of irrigation had evolved. The numbers were smaller but the density ratios between hunter–gatherers and cultivators remain pretty much the same in less productive environments.[7] At the same time, cultivation and husbandry continuously spread out from their centres of origin. There were three ways by which this spread could take place: the original farmers themselves would spread out into uncultivated lands as their numbers incessantly grew, pushing out the local hunter–gatherers by sheer numbers or mixing with them to a greater or lesser degree; farming would be taken up by hunter–gatherer communities neighbouring on the farmers by way of cultural imitation—that is, farming rather than the farmers spread; or a combination of the two processes could occur. In (pre)historical reality, all three options apparently took place.

The scholarly debate on the subject seems to result in the following rule of thumb: cultivation spread by farmer colonists into areas previously populated sparsely by simple hunter–gatherers, who could offer little effective resistance; by contrast, farmer colonists were able to make little headway into areas populated by denser communities of more sedentary hunter–gatherers; the latter eventually themselves adopted agriculture through cultural imitation.[8] A striking instance of the first model, which took place relatively late in time to leave its particularly clear marks, is the expansion of the Bantu-speaking farmers. Spreading from west Africa from the first millennium BC, they took over 1,000 years gradually to colonize central and south-east Africa. In the process, they pushed out and greatly reduced the Khoisanid populations of hunter–gatherers (today's Bushmen and Khoikhoi

[Hottentots] of south-west Africa), who earlier appear to have inhabited the whole of east Africa from north to south. This shift, long attested to by the existence of the Bantu family of languages, has been documented by archaeology and, more recently, by the new methods of population genetics. In this case, the spread of farming meant the spread of the original farmers themselves, and their languages, replacing other, sparse populations of hunter–gatherers.

The spread of farming from its oldest and most influential centre in the Near East is of particular interest, although the evidence is buried much deeper in the past and is far more complex. Europe was one direction into which Near Eastern farming spread. It is archaeologically documented to have spread from Anatolia in a north-westerly direction at a mean rate of one kilometre per year, reaching the farthest, Atlantic end of the continent by the fifth millennium BC, with local variations, of course, affecting this 'wave of advance'. Most archaeologists agree that, at least in the Balkans and central Europe, farming was introduced by migrating colonists from the Near East. The beginning of agriculture in central Europe is associated with a uniform archaeological culture (LSB), which emerged fully out of no visible indigenous origins. The earlier, thinly spread population of simple hunter–gatherers was apparently more or less displaced and possibly partly assimilated by the newcomers. However, along the resource-rich north-western European seashore, from the Iberian Peninsula to the Baltic, denser, more populous Mesolithic societies of complex hunter–gatherers lived. The archaeological record suggests that these societies held their own. Here agriculture, as well as other elements of culture, may have diffused across the agricultural frontier with trade, intermarriage, and other forms of contact—including warfare—all documented by archaeology. As with the Bantu-speaking farmer colonizers in Africa, evidence in support of this prehistoric development comes from population genetics, which provides new deep insights into our 'fossilized' past. It turns out that the most significant genetic gradient on the population map of modern Europe goes from south-east to north-west, apparently recording the wave-like shape of the Neolithic farmers' colonizing advance.

Europe was only one direction that the Neolithic expansion of Near Eastern farming and farmers took. Through either colonization or diffusion, or through both, farming appears to have spread to the east, through the Iranian Plateau to the Indian subcontinent, as well as to the south-west, to

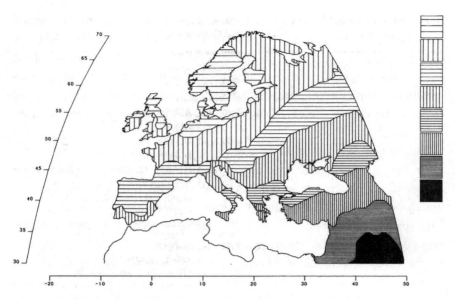

Genetic map of Europe (first principal component): the spread of Near East agriculturalists? (Source: L. L. Cavalli-Sforza, P. Menozzi, and A. Piazza, *The History and Geography of Human Genes*, Princeton, 1994; permission by Princeton University Press)

the Nile Valley and north Africa. These developments are attested to by the spread of the Neolithic sites and by the types of domesticated breeds found in them that derive from the Near East. Furthermore, as we saw with the Bantu-speakers' colonization in Africa, languages offer another means of piercing the past's thick veil of darkness and tracing the development and branching of ethnic communities. Some theories suggest that three of the world's largest language families originated from, and 'fossilize', the Near Eastern Neolithic colonization cum assimilation. In the eastern direction there is the Elamo–Dravidian family of languages, the earliest textually recorded representative of which, Elamite, from south-west Iran, is known from the third millennium BC; descendants of Dravidian are still spoken in south India, with some surviving relics in Pakistan. Later rolled back by the advance of Indo-European speakers, the Elamo–Dravidian family of languages is believed once to have stretched continuously from the Tigris to the Indian Ocean. The south-westerly direction of the Near Eastern Neolithic spread of farmers and farming is presumably reflected in the Afro-Asiatic (Hamito–Semitic) family of languages. Its oldest textually recorded representatives, ancient Egyptian and Akkadian, are known from the third millennium BC, and its many other members—Assyrian, Aramaic, Phoenician, Canaanite, Hebrew, Arabic, and all the way to the Amharic of Ethiopia and Berber of north Africa (to mention just a few)—are also well known from antiquity. Finally, archaeologist Colin Renfrew has controversially suggested that the European direction of the Neolithic colonization from Anatolia is the source of the Indo-European family of languages.[9] In other world centres of farming, a similar model has been advanced to explain the spread of the language families of east and south-east Asia: Sino-Tibetan, Tai-Austronesian(-)Austro-Asiatic—presumably carried in diverging directions by the original cultivators (millet in the north, rice in the south) from about 5000 BC.[10]

Obviously, all these large language families could not have come to be just by accident, without some mechanism of spread. As linguists are agreed, some processes of cultural unification, at least partly or wholly caused by population movements, must have brought them about. The known tempo of language mutation indicates that the processes that created these language families cannot be more than a number of thousands of years old, because otherwise the various languages in each family would have diverged from each other so much as to lose all recognizable resemblance. The spread of farming from 10,000 years ago is a prime possible mover of this sort of lingual/ethnic expansion. It is not the only possible one, however. As we see later, other prime movers of language unification existed down the road of history. To be sure, the processes at issue were historically complex, 'untidy', and multilayered, with their details largely irretrievable from prehistory and unsusceptible to full reconstruction. Their main interest to us is in so far as they can help to shed light on the interrelationship that existed between the spread of farming and warfare. In the first place, how violent was the process?

ARMED CONFLICT IN THE SPREAD OF FARMING

As already noted, despite archaeology's paramount role in unearthing the past, the light that it sheds on prehistory can only be dim. Events, ethnicity, and much of the non-material culture, including language, leave a particularly poor mark in the surviving record in the absence of a human voice. Historical language distribution and, more recently, genetic markers can offer further insight into prehistory: the former, because of the relatively rapid pace of lingual evolution (albeit the most slowly mutating form of culture)—only thousands of years back; the latter much, and potentially ever, deeper. However, as seen in Part 1, to breathe life into the bare bones of archaeological finds and infuse them with social detail, there is no substitute to carefully controlled analogies from the ethnography of prehistoric farming peoples who came into contact with, and were documented by, literate cultures. I attempt to draw from and combine both types of evidence—the archaeological and the ethnographic.

With respect to warfare, a fairly modulated relationship appears to have existed between hunter–gatherers and farmers. Farmers had the advantage of numbers, because their populations were denser and their social units larger. On the other hand, they were stationary, and their crops and farm animals were highly vulnerable to human predatory incursions, as well as to acts of vandalism.[11] The temptation for hunter–gatherers was strong, especially but not only in times of stress. As nomads who lacked significant property, they held the initiative, could choose the time of their raids, and were considerably less exposed to retaliatory counter-raids. Thus peaceful relations and exchange regularly rotated with raids and violence between these two population types, each regarding the other as particularly alien and inferior in their way of life. What counted most in the farmers' expansion into lands suitable for cultivation and inhabited by sparse hunter–gatherer populations was not direct armed confrontations, or even deterrence by superior numbers, but the settlement, demographic, and ecological facts that the colonizers created on the ground over generations and centuries. Rather than invasion, this was an inherently protracted process—barely if at all perceivable in the lifetimes of people—that occasional raiding for farm produce by hunter–gatherers, which undoubtedly took place, did not fundamentally change. The process ended only when the dwindling hunter–gatherer groups were gradually pushed out into regions unsuitable for cultivation, from which their members continued sporadically to raid their agricultural neighbours. Of course, as mentioned earlier, in some cases hunter–gatherers took up farming themselves, imitating and partly mixing with the colonizers. And farming also spread through cultural imitation into relatively dense communities of complex hunter–gatherers, into whose territories farmer colonizers were less able to make headway and whose raiding they had to endure.

Hunter–gatherers' raids on farmers were mostly hit and run, most probably being small-scale affairs of a theft and 'armed burglary' nature, especially where the farmers possessed domesticated animals. Where such farm animals existed, they were almost invariably the chief objective, a prime concentration of easily movable nutrients to be taken away from either their fields of pasture or their enclosures. Bantu archaeological sites, for example, show the animals penned at the centre of the settlements,[12] an obvious protective means—undoubtedly from preying animals, possibly from other farmers, but in all likelihood also from hunter–gatherers. In southern Africa, for example, as recorded by Europeans after contact and depicted in earlier rock paintings, the San Bushmen sporadically engaged in cattle raiding on their neighbouring Bantu farmers and Khoikhoi pastoralists, which occasionally resulted in warfare.[13] The frontier between the dense Mesolithic hunter–gatherers of the north-west European coast and the early Neolithic central European farmers of ostensible Near Eastern origin shows archaeological signs of violent friction: there was a no-man's-land between the two populations; walled enclosures in the farming settlements were presumably used for protecting the livestock; at least some of the settlements themselves were defended by stockades and ditches; and there were traces of settlement burning and of scalping. Evidence of fortified villages similarly appears shortly after the expansion of farming through the Mediterranean into Greece and Italy, probably also indicating raiding by local dense Mesolithic hunter–gatherers.[14]

Crops were another object of hunter–gatherer raiding on farmers, although these were far more difficult to obtain forcefully in bulk than livestock. Theft of produce from fields took place, but for logistic reasons could only be marginal. To be significant, the storage of harvested produce within the agricultural settlements had to be taken. Furthermore, unlike in livestock raiding—as large quantities of agricultural produce could not be moved away, certainly not in a rush—the farmers themselves would have had to be killed if the raiders were to avail themselves of their rich storage of food resources.

In historical times, the Apache and Navaho hunter–gatherers of the semi-arid regions of the Great Plains regularly raided their pueblo agriculturalist neighbours of the present south-west USA. Normally, these were small-scale affairs, carried out by individuals and small groups. Farm animals were the main goal, and villages were usually not taken, although houses were occasionally broken into.[15] However, by these recorded times, after contact, the hunter–gatherers of the Great Plains had obtained the horse from the Europeans, whereas the pueblo agriculturalists had obtained farm animals. These imports considerably changed both communities' earlier patterns of life. In contrast to the Old World, farm animals had barely existed at all in America before contact, partly because of a lack of suitable wild varieties for domestication, particularly bovines (cattle), caprines (goats and sheep), and equids (horses, donkeys). With the exception of dogs, and variably in some regions—turkeys, guinea pigs, and small dromedaries (llama, alpaca)—farming in America meant predominantly agriculture.[16] It should also be noted that the Na-Dene Athapaskan speakers, Apache and Navaho, may themselves have arrived in the region from the north only as late as AD 1500.

All the same, the pueblo agriculturalists had taken measures to defend their storage and dwellings from early in prehistory. As agriculture and sedentism took off in the region towards the middle of the first millennium AD (with the domesticated breeds originally diffusing from Mexico), evidence of a stockade surrounding a settlement was found: 'other sites may have had stockades too, but the excavators did not look for them.'[17] Mississippi–Missouri agriculturalists of roughly the same period similarly surrounded their settlements with palisades, moats, and ditches, evidently at least partly constructed against their Great Plains' nomadic hunter–gatherer neighbours. Returning to the south-west pueblos, the large settlements of the advanced Chaco Canyon culture around AD 1000—the centres for up to thousands of farmers, ritual, crafts, and trade—were famously built in a closed horseshoe pattern. Outwardly, the dwellings and storage rooms formed a closed wall, which in Pueblo Bonito, for example, rose as high as four to five stories. The slightly later, magnificent, Mesa Verde pueblos were built high up the canyon's side, sheltered by the cliffs. The houses were closely packed together, forming continuous walls that blocked access into the settlement. Towers in each settlement apparently served for observation and refuge.

These defensive measures may have been taken at least partly against other agricultural communities. As we see later, relations between the

'Cliff Palace', Mesa Verde. Flourishing in Colorado in the twelfth century AD, this pueblo settlement included over 200 rooms with an estimated population of over 400 people. Sheltered by the cliff, it presented a walled front of continuous dwellings, which blocked access when ladders were raised

agriculturalists themselves often saw the eruption of hostilities. Nevertheless, marauding hunter–gatherer groups must have constituted a threat, especially in such oasis communities on the verge of the semi-arid steppe. The earliest known pueblo-like settlement of clustered, impregnable houses (according to their excavator, clearly designed for defence), and one of the earliest known large agricultural, crafts, and trade settlements anywhere, was unearthed in the most ancient centre of agriculture, south-west Asia. This is Çatal-Hüyük in Anatolia from the mid-seventh millennium BC, far removed from the American pueblos in both time and space, but less in 'relative time', in the chronology and development of agricultural society.[18] Admittedly, the inhabitants of Çatal-Hüyük already possessed cattle. Thus the most striking evidence for a specific hunter–gatherers' threat to *crop-growing* farmers would appear to be yet older, indeed the oldest: Jericho.

Jericho, in the valley of the Jordan River, is among the very first known agricultural settlements in the pristine cradle of agriculture itself, dating from the late ninth millennium BC. By the eighth millennium,

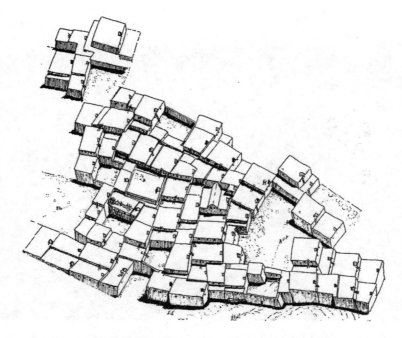

A reconstructed section of Çatal-Hüyük in Anatolia. Prospering in the mid-seventh millennium BC, it is one of the earliest known large settlements anywhere. In this pueblo-like settlement of clustered, impregnable houses, access was by ladders. Contrary to the Rousseauite belief, fortifications simply became possible with sedentism, rather than being made necessary by agriculture

even before the domestication of animals, early Neolithic (Pre-Pottery Neolithic A or PPNA) Jericho, a ten acre site with an estimated population of 2,000–3,000 (figures now tend to be revised downwards), was already surrounded by a free-standing stone wall, 600 metres long, perhaps 4 metres tall, and 1–2 metres wide. At the bottom of the wall, a large moat was cut in the rock bed, and behind the wall an 8.5 metre stone tower was found. Kathleen Kenyon, the site's excavator in the 1950s, believed that Jericho was not unique for its time and that other such large settlements would be found close to the region. She thus held that the fortifications had been erected against these other agricultural settlements rather than against marauding hunter–gatherers, and that the later (PPNB) walled settlement found at the site was indeed a sign of foreign occupation by another settled people. Other scholars speculated that Jericho may have been a major trading centre in Dead Sea minerals, making it a coveted prize.[19] However, after

Jericho, the earliest known walled settlement by far. A view of the free-standing stone wall and moat, dated to the eighth millennium BC

decades of archaeological research, it has become clear that no similar large settlement existed to rival early Neolithic Jericho—that it was indeed unique for its time. Furthermore, there was a clear time separation between the first and second layers at the site, practically ruling out a forceful occupation by another settled community. Evidence of either mineral processing and trade or the material wealth associated with it has not been found. Thus, as archaeologist James Mellaart concludes, an acute threat from marauding hunter–gatherer groups to their stored crops, lives, and, indeed, uniquely fertile land would seem to have been the main factor that propelled the inhabitants of this pristine agricultural oasis to cluster together and undertake the labour involved in the massive defensive construction.[20]

In summary, crops would appear to have been far more difficult and dangerous to obtain by force than livestock. Crop raiding required occupation of the settlement by the raiders, violent action to kill the inhabitants, and, hence, large-scale, co-ordinated action. It would seem to have been less frequent but more serious an undertaking than livestock raiding. However, when starvation loomed, it would have been highly tempting for the raiders, and, needless to say, the loss of their crops would have meant starvation for the farmers as well, who could not afford to run away. During raids on farming settlements, the Navaho and Apache, for example, also carried captured women away with them. When raiders were killed, vengeance raids followed, sometimes consisting of up to 200 participants, igniting a cycle of hostility and retribution. Scalps were taken by the warriors.[21]

In any event, over time, as hunter–gatherers were contracting in number worldwide, conflict took place mainly among the farmers themselves. The appearance of fortifications, so dramatically typified by Jericho's two firsts—agriculture and stone walls—has been taken by Rousseauites to indicate that violent conflict emerged, or truly took off, only with agriculture. After all, fortifications are the first unequivocal sign of warfare that can be detected by the tools at the disposal of archaeology. However, as already seen, the correlation is unwarranted, and it has been highly misleading. Fortifications were indeed a new phenomenon, but they were predominantly a function of sedentism rather than of violent conflict alone. As the American north-west coast demonstrates, sedentary hunter–gatherers in lush environments also protected their settlements with fortifications. If simpler hunter–gatherers did not, it was because they were nomadic, in the same way that later-day pastoralists would not erect fortifications, despite both group types' high exposure to violence and violent death.

Indeed, nor did even the advent of cultivation lead everywhere and immediately to fortifications, in the way that it did in Jericho. In the Near East from the eighth to the fifth millennia BC, after the advent of farming and before the onset of urbanization, indications of fortifications have been excavated in some settlements, although in most no signs of fortifications have been found, probably because in the majority none existed.[22] In many other regions of the world as well, it took a long time for fortifications to appear and proliferate. Some authors have interpreted this as an indication that during the spread of agriculture there was still an abundance of empty space and free land to move into and, hence, that violent conflict was less of a factor, if at all.[23] However, this argument has very limited, if any, validity. The objects of human fighting were far from being confined to arable land. As we have seen, there was everywhere strong competition for women (and raids for them), often flaring up into violent conflict. Hunting territories continued to be of the utmost importance, because for a very long time hunting supplemented horticulture and animal husbandry as a significant source of nutrients. Killings in turn led to continuing cycles of revenge and retribution. Furthermore, with farming there were now livestock and crops to be had. Everything we know ethnographically about historical horticulturalists suggests that the lives of their prehistorical predecessors were insecure and fraught with violent death.

So why did fortifications not emerge everywhere hand in hand with agriculture? A combination of factors accounts for this. In the first place, for a very long time farming meant shifting, highly extensive horticulture, with fields abandoned and settlements moved to new locations every few years, when the soil's fertility was exhausted. Both housing and defensive installations were rudimentary. Shifting horticulturalists were actually less sedentary than the intensive hunter–gatherer–fishers of the American north-west coast, for example. Furthermore, in many regions of the world, such as temperate central and northern Europe until late in prehistory, settlement took the form of family farms ('homesteads') and small hamlets, sparsely spread out in the fertile land. This was very different from the settlement pattern in the dry Near East, let alone a desert oasis such as Jericho, with its water source, naturally irrigated and naturally fertilized alluvial fan, warm, productive winter climate, and abundance of wildlife. All these were a magnet for a dense and truly sedentary farmer settlement from the start, making Jericho appear far ahead of its time and somewhat of a scholarly puzzle.[24] As mentioned earlier, signs of fortified village sites appear in Greece and Italy shortly after the start of farming, and later also become evident in central Europe.[25] However, no large villages existed in northern Europe until the first millennium BC, and even later in the far north. The people in the widely dispersed family farms and hamlets often did not have the means to erect significant defences and, more importantly, lacked the manpower to guard them continuously. (To draw a remote analogy, they were in no different position in this respect from the European 'homestead' settlers in the American 'Wild West'.) Violent conflict among simple agriculturalists was, anyway, largely between clans (that is, 'internal') and was mainly carried out on a small scale and by surprise. As one authority has put it: 'Ethnography suggests that warfare is likely to have been rife amongst many agricultural societies in prehistoric Europe before the prevalence of fortifications.'[26]

Indeed, the general picture drawn from such cases in which both archaeological and historical sources exist and can be brought to bear on each other is clear enough. For example, the Greeks of the Dark Ages between the twelfth and eighth centuries BC, the Celts of northern Italy during the fourth and third centuries BC, the Germans around the beginning of the Christian era, the Northmen of Norway and Sweden as late as the middle of the first millennium AD, and the highlander Scots until the late European Middle Ages, all lived in mostly unfortified family farms and small hamlets, while experiencing an insecure, often violent, and even bellicose existence. As Polybius writes, the Celts 'lived in unwalled villages . . . and were exclusively occupied with war and agriculture'.[27] More recently, the nineteenth century's Montenegrins, who had an estimated violent death rate among adult males of about 25 per cent, built houses with small windows and thick walls but no specialized communal fortifications. Violent conflict was one, but only one, among several factors that affected the clustering of farmers into villages, which could then be fortified. Uneven resource distribution in space (fertile land, water), increased agricultural intensification, denser population, scarcer land, and tighter social networks that led to larger-scale communal warfare were some of the other factors involved.

Ethnography has additional instructive cases to offer. As we have already seen, the Yanomamo horticulturalists and hunters, who experienced endemic, deadly, but particularly small-scale, hostilities, lived in small villages surrounded by the most rudimentary palisades. The more intensive horticulturalists of highland New Guinea—also experiencing incessant armed strife, including large-scale night raids—lived some in fortified settlements and some in dispersed farmsteads. The Mae Enga, for example, whose violent death rate for men was almost 35 per cent, lived in clan farmsteads—'defended, literally, to the last yard'—and lacked fortified villages.[28]

The multi-island societies of Polynesia are another highly diverse laboratory for pre-state agricultural communities, not yet examined in this book. From the time that they were reached by Europeans in the later part of the eighteenth century, the Pacific islands fired European imagination with the vision of pristine, innocent, happy, non-corrupt, pre-civilization, peaceful people enjoying natural plenty and free love, the epitome of the Rousseauite view. However, as far as violent conflict was concerned (and much else beside), nothing was further from the truth. The different island societies of this vastly dispersed archipelago were notoriously rife with violence. According to a major study of 18 of them—the smallest, reef atolls, containing no more than a couple of thousand inhabitants, the largest, a few hundred thousand strong—not one lacked endemic warfare. According to another leading authority: 'Warfare . . . was ubiquitous in Polynesia.' Nor was it a recent phenomenon there, because derivatives of the word *toa*, warrior, are shared by the various Polynesian languages, indicating that it goes back to well before their vast dispersal in ocean voyages thousands of years ago.[29] Fortifications, however, although conspicuous in many places, were far from being evident everywhere or from correlating with the intensity of warfare. For example: 'In striking contrast to New Zealand or Rapa, the Hawaiian Islands—despite the endemic warfare that characterized late prehistoric [that is, known—author's comment] Hawaiian culture— generally lack fortified sites.'[30]

To conclude, the ethnographic evidence of pre-state agricultural societies shows very high violence rates, which did not always manifest themselves in the construction of fortifications. Fortifications can thus serve as a mark of violent conflict only in a positive manner.[31]

It is time to move a step forward, to examine the nature of these simple farming societies and enquire into what sort of violent conflict they engaged in.

TRIBAL SOCIETIES

The ethnographic record brings out something that is barely detectable by archaeology: people—hunter–gatherers or simple agriculturalists—are not just spread out in household or village groups (or do not just share in wide archaeological tool 'cultures'). In every locality they participate in and are linked by social ties, in which kinship and culture play a determining role. Admittedly, from the 1960s anthropologists have become less confident than they used to be with the concept of the 'tribe', and more conscious of its fluidity and diversity. But the same reservations apply to any other perfectly meaningful concept, such as the state, society, or a people. Tribal networks and affiliations in simple, pre-urban and pre-state agricultural societies are often—almost inherently—loose, but they exist. Sceptic influential anthropologist Morton Fried has gone as far as suggesting that the tribe is a 'secondary phenomenon', created only under the impact of more complex social entities (states), primarily, perhaps, in the form of conflict.[32] However, *inter-tribal* conflict predated the state and served as a powerful formative force for the tribe.

Much greater productivity and, hence, much greater (and growing) population densities meant that agricultural tribes were larger than the hunter–gatherer tribe, or 'regional group'. This was predominantly a function of the fact that more people were in touch and interacting within contact distance. Wider kin groups now lived closer together. We have already seen this in the larger regional groups of the denser hunter–gatherers of the American north-west coast, which reached as many as 2,000 people, in comparison with the average 500 of simpler hunter–gatherers. However, although larger than hunter–gatherer groups, agricultural tribes were still relatively small-scale societies, normally consisting of anything between two and a few tens of thousands of people. Tribes were not necessarily of a different ethnic and language stock from their neighbours, although dialect differences were common. Separate tribes existed within larger, sometimes much larger, ethnic populations and subpopulations, with interactions among the tribes of the same ethnic population being either peaceful or hostile, mostly rotating between the two. These wider ethnic populations and subpopulations are often referred to as a 'people' or 'nation' but are better addressed as *ethnos* (Greek) or *ethnie* (French).[33] They shared ethnocultural features, but, unlike tribes, little or any ties that would make them a *social* entity.

Although demonstrating considerable cultural and ethnic persistence over time, *ethnies* and tribes were far from being 'primordial' or static. New *ethnies* and tribes branched out and evolved into separate existence as their original *ethnos* or tribe grew over a certain size and spread out over larger space and into new localities. Tribes also split because of internal strife, and could be dispersed, eliminated, or absorbed by foreign tribes and *ethnies*. Several tribes from a particular *ethnos* (occasionally including foreign tribal elements as well) sometimes came together in larger tribal confederacies, in response to various stimuli, again including armed conflict perhaps as the chief factor. For example, some of the tribes described in Tacitus's invaluable *Germania* in the first century AD—one of the fullest surveys of ancient tribal societies that we have—are not heard of later or during the Germanic migrations of the fifth century. On the other hand, two of the major latter-day Germanic tribal entities, the Franks and the Alamanni, appear as such only in the third century, presumably from processes of confederation and amalgamation involving earlier known tribes on the Roman frontier. The name Alamanni (meaning all men) hints at such processes.

Another celebrated case in point is the Iroquois of the American northeast, turned by Lewis Morgan into a paradigm for tribal society in general in his *Ancient Society* (1877), which was fully taken up by Friedrich Engels. The Iroquois League of five tribes that inhabited today's upstate New York—the Mohawks, Oneidas, Onondagas, Cayugas, and Senecas—became famous for fierceness and military prowess in the seventeenth-century colonial and native wars for power and trade. However, the League predated the arrival of the Dutch, French, and English in North America. The exact date of its foundation is unknown, but, based on the strong native traditions, scholars are agreed that it was probably created some time before or after 1500. Furthermore, it was founded as a League of Peace among its member tribes, which had earlier existed separately and in a state of endemic and vicious intra-warfare. Archaeology shows that the thinly dispersed farming sites in the region, which had been colonized a few centuries earlier, were clustering into large fortified villages after AD 1000. These fortified villages remained the typical settlement pattern in colonial times and were described in detail by the Europeans. It should be noted that the League did not encompass all the tribes of the Iroquois dialect speakers, with some of whom, such as the Huron Confederacy of five tribes to their north-west, the League was engaged in repeated wars that resulted in the displacement and partial extermination of the Hurons. Demographic calculations are tenuous, because European epidemics decimated the natives of North America. Still, although the Iroquois speakers as a whole are estimated at 90,000 people in the first half of the seventeenth century, the League of Five numbered 20,000–30,000. The individual member tribes ranged in size from 2,000 to 7,000, and were capable of fielding no more than a few hundred to 1,000–1,500 warriors each, at most.[34]

Again, comparative ethnographic data offer a clear picture of the typical size and composition of tribal societies. At contact, the Huron Confederacy consisted of an estimated 21,000 people, the Powhatan Confederacy in Virginia of 15,000–20,000, and the Cherokee of the south-east of around the same number.[35] The Creek Confederacy of the Mexican Gulf consisted of six tribes, and the Dakota (Sioux) 'nation' of a dozen. There were 27 tribes and tribal confederacies on the Great Plains. The four tribal confederacies that dominated the northern Plains (Dakota, Blackfoot, Cree, Mandan-Hidatsa) consisted each of an estimated 15,000–25,000 people. To their south, the Pawnee Confederacy numbered 7,000–10,000, divided into four tribal bands.[36] The Kiowa tribe of the southern Plains probably never numbered more than 2,000.[37] In Mesoamerica, the Aztecs were one among seven Nahuatl-speaking tribes who immigrated into the Valley of Mexico from the north. Their original tribal composition was still evident in the internal borough division of Tenochtitlan, the city that they built in the fourteenth and fifteenth centuries, as they grew into statehood and later into an imperial power.

During the Celtic invasions of the Mediterranean world in the fourth and third centuries BC—the Celts' first major appearance in written history—six named tribes (or parts of tribes) settled down in Italy and three in Asia Minor, the latter comprising together some 20,000 people.[38] In the middle of the first century BC, during his conquest of Gaul, part of the Celts' core homeland, Julius Caesar mentions about 100 larger Celtic tribal communities (*civitas* or *populus*), already undergoing the start of urbanization and in the process of transition from tribalism.[39] Over 30 main tribal groupings are identified in Britain during the Roman conquest of the first century AD.[40] Some 50 tribal entities are mentioned in Tacitus's *Germania* (who states that he names only the more significant ones), whereas 69 are recorded by the geographer Ptolemy in the second century AD.[41] One of the later Germanic confederacies, the Franks, was apparently formed from some eight Lower Rhine tribal groups.[42] Classical sources mention 50–100 Thracian tribes (roughly in today's Bulgaria).[43] Similar to the Aztec Tenochtitlan, Athens originated from a confederation of elements from the four Ionian tribes, Sparta from elements of the three Dorian tribes, and Rome from three Latin tribal entities. Indeed, as Morgan recognized— following in the footsteps of Adam Ferguson's *An Essay on the History of Civil Society* (1767) and himself adopted by Engels—there was a clear similarity between the tribal societies encountered by the modern Europeans during their 'Age of Discovery' and those with which they were familiar from their classical education: the early ancient Greeks and Romans and their later north European neighbours. This was a long journey in fixed chronology but a rather shorter one in relative time. Montenegro was probably the last tribal society in Europe, persisting into the age of the gun and still in evidence in the late nineteenth century. The 30-odd Montenegrin tribes, engulfed in endless inter-clan and inter-tribe violence, as well as in vicious struggles against Turkish occupation, numbered around 2,000 each.[44]

In Polynesia, a few thousand people to a tribe was the standard, although in Hawaii, Tonga, and Samoa, tribes were as much as a few tens of thousands strong.[45] In New Zealand, a total population of a few hundred thousand was divided among some 40, often warring, tribes.[46]

In Africa, studies of pre-state *ethnies* in the first half of the twentieth century registered the following results. The Dinka of southern Sudan numbered some 900,000, divided into 25 main tribal groups of widely diverging sizes, with the largest further divided into 'sub-tribes'. Their neighbours, the Nuer, totalled 300,000, with tribal size also varying considerably from a few thousand to 45,000. The Logoli and Vugusu Bantu of western Kenya comprised about 300,000, divided into some 20 tribes. The Konkomba in northern Togo comprised 45,000 people, divided into several tribes. The Lugbara of Uganda and Zaire numbered 250,000, divided into some 60 tribes averaging 4,000 people each. The Bwamba of the same region numbered roughly 30,000. The Tallensi of the Gold Coast totalled about 35,000 out of a larger lingual and ethnic stock of about 170,000. The Zulu 'nation' of a few hundred thousand people was united in the early nineteenth century from many previously independent tribes, each totalling a few thousand.[47]

All these small-scale societies were based on expanding and interlocking kinship circles, which, as we have seen in Part 1, correlated strongly with common locality and common culture. Nuclear families came together in extended ones, which were linked with other related families in clans. The principal body of social interaction in tribal societies, the clan, was actually or supposedly descended from a common founding father, who was generally believed to have had a supernatural and heroic origin. Related clans generally came together in phraeries, which constituted the highest subdivisions of the tribe. These successive subdivisions have different names in different anthropological studies, as well as, of course, in different societies, but the general structure was fairly similar. With kinship being the constituting element of society, ancestry and genealogy were orally recorded many generations back. Loyalty was extended above all to family and clan, with inter-clan violent conflict being at least as prevalent as larger-scale conflict; the term 'segmentary society' is often used to describe this social structure for a good reason. Clans and phraeries could come together in an armed alliance to counter external threats. The same applies to the co-operation of whole tribes in tribal confederacies. In all these cases, the language of kinship and ancestry was regularly invoked to enlist support. Ancestral, matrimonial, local, and lingual ties were reinforced by other common cultural traits, most importantly those of ritual networks and Amphictionic alliances.

Status differences were of the utmost importance in tribal societies. Some scholars have already noted that the term 'egalitarian society', commonly applied in anthropology to most hunter–gatherer and many horticultural societies, is a relative one. As we have seen, even where property was minimal, status and prestige mattered a great deal—for example, in marriage opportunities. Status and prestige varied between individuals and were jealously pursued and defended. Here, too, the term 'segmentary' has been suggested as better than 'egalitarian' to denote the loose and fragmented hierarchical structure of these societies.[48] The same was true in very simple horticultural societies (such as the Yanomamo), where property was similarly insignificant. However, skill- and kin-based differences in status and esteem were to grow steadily and to magnify vastly as property increasingly grew to dominate social relations. Relative aboriginal human equality was a function of aboriginal relative poverty, because hunter–gatherers possessed little that could encumber their nomadic way of life and as they subsisted directly from nature. From the start of sedentism and/or animal husbandry, property and, consequently, social power could be *accumulated*.

Livestock was the first and primary form of property accumulation in simple farming societies that still barely experienced arable land's shortage. Cattle (and sheep) were universally, and still are, the measure of wealth, indeed the primary form of currency, in all known simple farming societies that possessed them. For this reason, in Tacitus's *Germania* (5) as well as in twentieth-century Africa, people cared about the number of animals that they possessed more than about their quality. Pigs played the same role among the highlanders of New Guinea. Domesticated horses and camels would be added to the list later on, wherever and whenever they arrived. Livestock was the main bride price, again demonstrating the close inter-relationship between the various elements of the somatic–reproductive complex. In tribal African societies in particular, competition over women was heavily skewed along wealth and age lines, creating a true intergenerational conflict. In the same way that the elders in the Australian hunter–gatherer groups monopolized marriages among them at the young men's expense, the elders in many African tribal societies kept the control of the family and clan livestock tightly in their hands, continuing to marry polygynously into old age. Thus, although females were married at puberty, males were forced to postpone the start of family life until their 30s. Estimates suggest that in some regions as many as two-thirds of the women may have been in polygynous marriages, whereas up to half of the adult men may have been unmarried at any time. It is little wonder that the abduction of women, elopement, and violence were widespread among the young men.

The postponement of family life was largely responsible for the wide-spread African institution of age sets, in which the young adult male bachelors, unable to start families, lived together in warrior age groups. This restless element was universally the most war-like part of society. 'Young men might cultivate a distinct subculture stressing beauty, dress, ornament, virility, insolence, and aggression.'[49] According to Tacitus, the Germans 'are almost the only barbarians who are content with a wife apiece: *the very few exceptions*' are those of high birth. According to a modern study of early Germanic society: 'Polygamy is mentioned by a number of our sources in the version known as resource polygamy: those who could afford it could have more than one wife.' The same applied to the North-men of Scandinavia. In these relatively poor Germanic and North societies, also, cattle were the main measurement of wealth, and bride price was paid. Although not as deprived as their African counterparts, young male bachelors tended to flock around distinguished war leaders in search of their fortune.[50]

Livestock could also buy scarce utility and ornamental–prestige–exotic–luxury goods, which, in addition to those already mentioned in Part 1, soon included fine clothing and, later, copper, followed by silver and gold. All three metals—the first to be extracted by sedentary farming societies—were of almost purely ornamental–conspicuous value, publicly displaying wealth and social status. Accumulated copper in the form of body rings continued to serve as a mark of wealth and status in many recently extant simple farming societies around the world. Greek and Roman authors commented on the Celt fondness for what to classical taste seemed extravagant and boastful gold body adornment among the males. Finally, with population growth, arable land increasingly became an object of competition. Varying in fertility and accessibility from the start, it increasingly became a scarcer (and more intensely cultivated) resource.[51] Slaves to work in the fields and in the house were acquired by the rich, mostly obtained in raiding on foreign people and later also from the poor who had to sell themselves into bondage.

The growth of property differences and social stratification was a gradual process. Various factors interacted in each society in determining its form and pace, but, as a rule, its economic and social elements were intimately linked. Many tribal societies (especially the 'poorer' ones) were socially as well as economically 'egalitarian', again relatively speaking. The clans' elders carried particular weight, and collective decisions were reached by tribal assemblies of all free men. The classical authors' depictions of the Celts and Germans were remarkably paralleled throughout the tribal lands encountered by modern Europeans in America, the Pacific, and Africa. The clans were sometimes ranked genealogically, according to real or fictitious seniority in the main male line. Two types of distinctive status emerged in many, but not all, tribal societies. They have been labelled 'chief' and 'big man' in a paradigmatic study of Polynesia.[52]

In those tribal societies that had the 'office' of chief (and many did not), the chief mostly possessed very limited authority. He could be openly elected or, more commonly, the office was the preserve of a senior clan and inherited within it, although not necessarily from father to son and often through elections. The chief sometimes, but not always, was the leader in war. He co-ordinated social activities and served as an arbiter in social disputes. He also fulfilled ritualistic functions. In all these activities he wielded little coercive power. What authority he had rested on the legitimacy of office, seniority, persuasion, and consent. The 'big man', on the other hand, held no office. His status derived from his social astuteness and 'entrepreneurial' spirit, charisma, prowess, and skilful use of his property. He stood in intricate social relations with a group of followers from his own clan and often from others, to which he offered patronage and protection, economic assistance in times of stress, and benefits in general, where such were available for distribution. In return, of course, he received their subordination and support, which could then be used to enhance his status, property, and matrimonial success further. His social position rested on a two-way, but distinctively unequal, give-and-take relationship.[53]

Even where the economy was somewhat more advanced than that of Polynesia, the same pattern prevailed. According to Polybius (2:17), writing on the third- and second-century BC north Italian Celts: 'Their possessions consisted of cattle and gold . . . those among them being the most feared and the most powerful who were thought to have the largest number of attendants and associates.' In Africa, the ideal was 'women, cattle and command over men', 'embodied in the image of the Big Man wealthy in grain stores, cattle, gold, and above all people to provide labour, power, and security . . . surrounded by his wives, married and unmarried sons, younger brothers, poor relations, dependants, and swarming children'.[54]

It is these kin-based, loose social organizations and internal status competition under conditions of increasing material resources that underlay social activity in tribal societies, including that of warfare.

TRIBAL WARFARE

A study of early medieval Irish military history approached its subject in words that apply to all tribal societies: 'From a modern standpoint, there was little warfare but much violence.' There was little of the familiar state-organized, large-scale, centralized, soldier-executed warfare, but violent armed conflict, and the threat of it, were all pervasive. Our state-based distinction between external war and internal peace had scant validity.[55] The following synthesizes the remarkably similar record of violent conflict in tribal societies, taken independently around the world (noting some of the differences as well). Citation of the relevant particular studies will be necessarily sparing and only made in reference to specific facts.

At the bottom of the violence scale in tribal societies, there were frequent inter-clan 'feuds' over gardens, fields, livestock, women, status and honour, and accusations of sorcery, often escalating into vicious cycles of hostility and retribution. We have already seen this among the natives of New Guinea, and the same picture held true in other tribal societies. Social mediation could only partly compensate for the lack of a central authority in resolving such feuds, and yet fewer checks operated in conflict between larger social entities. Raids on other tribal territories and settlements were the most common form of warfare. These were little changed from what we have already seen in Part 1. They ranged in scale from affairs that involved few to dozens and hundreds of individuals. Participation was voluntary (if we disregard social pressure). The raids were initiated by chiefs, 'big men', or any distinguished warrior, who raised the matter before the men–warrior assemblies and led those who chose to join in, often mostly from his own and related clans. Military leadership was minimal, only in effect for the duration of the hostilities, had no disciplinary power, and exercised the most rudimentary tactical control.

People joined raids for all of the interconnected reasons already discussed, with the material element somewhat transformed in both nature and significance: from natural (mainly hunting) resources to cultivated, produced, and accumulated ones. Where livestock existed, it was almost invariably the main prize, as is well documented among the Greeks of the Dark Age, Celts, Germans, early medieval Irish, and highlander Scots up until the eighteenth century, and in tribal Africa even later. In tribal farming societies, livestock booty could significantly change one's material standing. Other nutritious produce could also be at stake; in the little Tongareva Atoll, for example, in Polynesia, wars were fought for coconut trees.[56] Raiding—and a warrior reputation—were a major avenue of social mobility for leaders and led alike. Head taking—a mark of warrior prowess—was reported by horrified classical Greeks and Romans with respect to their barbarian neighbours in central and northern Europe. In nineteenth-century Montenegro, enemy heads displayed in front of houses and settlements similarly shocked foreign observers, as they had in seventeenth-century Iroquois lands, and still would in twentieth-century Amazonia. Women were regularly raped and kidnapped. Adult male prisoners were rarely taken. When they were, horrific torture and sacrificial death, often including ritualistic cannibalism, were commonly inflicted. Some prisoners, especially from among the young, were taken as slaves. In other cases, as, for example, among the Iroquois, prisoners were forcibly adopted into Iroquois society (after being made to run the gauntlet), to fill up the dwindling ranks of this war-like people. Early Roman traditions also reveal an uncommon willingness to absorb foreign and defeated elements into the nascent Roman society to swell its ranks. Living in a highly insecure world, in which force and self-help were pretty much the law, warrior prestige a social advantage, honour a social currency to be jealously defended, and looting a key to wealth and status, many tribal societies tended to be warrior societies. Farm work fell largely on the women. Oral epics of warfare, heroes, and adventure (and the gods) were everywhere the staple literary form.

Still, being voluntary and kin based, raiding parties did the utmost to avoid casualties to themselves. Enemy settlements, including fortified villages, were stormed at dawn, when the inhabitants were asleep. The Iroquois' raids on Huron fortified villages and those by the Maori in New Zealand on each other's *pa* (fortified village) are among the best documented historically.[57] If surprise failed, the attackers normally withdrew. Sieges were extremely rare and ineffective. Treacherous feasts are also universally attested to. However, raids could lead into enemy ambushes or unintended head-on encounters en route (and result in counter-raids), in all of which the raiders could incur heavy casualties. Formal battles were largely demonstrative, often producing more noise than blood.[58] Dancing, chanting, loud music, derision of the enemy, and individual boasting and displays of bravado—reported, for example, by variably terrified, bemused, and amused Romans, who found them barbarous, childish, and grotesque—accounted for much of the noise. Leaders and distinguished warriors regularly vied for status by taking their group's cause in single combats with their counterparts on the opposite side, while both armed hosts observed the spectacle. With this custom being very familiar from early Greek and Roman epic traditions, some Roman magistrates still accepted and won encounters with Celtic chiefs in the fourth and third centuries BC. But the custom would appear increasingly primitive and outdated to later-day Romans.[59]

Armaments in tribal warfare were privately owned and generally poor. As already seen, in Stone Age societies they mainly consisted of spears (as well as axes, clubs, and knives), bows and arrows and other missiles, shields, occasional forms of leather armour, and, more rarely, tusk helmets. Metals brought about a change in the materials used and, of course, a vast improvement in effectiveness, but surprisingly little change in the *types* of weapons. The expensive and lucrative bronze, the first utility metal to be manufactured (in Eurasia but not in the Americas, Africa, or the Pacific), from the third but mostly in the second millennium BC, was used only by the elite, and possessed a prestige as well as military value. In the Iron Age as well, iron was mainly limited to spear-, axe-, and arrowheads. Metal-consuming and more expensive to produce helmets, armour, and even swords were uncommon until very late, and mainly possessed by the elite. Thus warriors often fought naked or half-naked in bravado (although leather body protection was also used). Body paint was universally applied. After the spread of the domesticated horse in Eurasia, the elite in some tribal farming societies fought mounted on chariots and later on horseback. However, the great majority of the warriors fought on foot.

In time, the set battle was growing in significance and was becoming bloodier than it had been in simpler tribal farming societies. Several factors account for this process. Gradually, farming intensification and population densities increased. Armed hosts raided deeper and for longer. The larger the forces involved, the greater the distances that they covered; and the more inhabited the country, the less were their chances of affecting surprise and operating by stealth. The richer and more vital the booty involved, the more were both sides prepared to risk life in open battle to secure it. When the land itself was at stake, the odds were perhaps the highest. Clearly the most critical cases were those involving population movements. In the 1960s, rightly reacting against an earlier, romantic view of history dominated by 'tribal invasions' and conquests, the so-called New Archaeology downplayed population movements in prehistory, emphasizing instead autochthonous, processual developments. In the meantime, however, the pendulum has swung back a great deal. Historically recorded tribal movements, as well as archaeological evidence for prehistorical ones, are overwhelming.[60] Tribal factions, tribes, and tribal confederacies—with families and possessions—were sometimes on the move into other territories. The reasons for these movements are only vaguely recorded, and included internal divisions, population pressure/land scarcity, land depletion, and natural disasters and stresses. In turn, such movements could produce a chain reaction or ripple effect throughout tribal land, as tribes that were pressurized and pushed from their own territory would exercise pressure on others. Not only the land, but every belonging and the families became exposed in these folk migrations and would be defended to the death on both sides.

The Celtic and Germanic worlds provide the best documented examples of such folk movements from the fourth century BC on, culminating in the great Germanic migrations of the fourth and fifth centuries AD, under the pressure of the Huns. But we know that such movements had also been taking place under much dimmer historical light within the Celtic and Germanic worlds. For example, the Celts' expansion from the fifth century BC from their original homeland between the Marne and Moselle rivers into central and western Europe is documented archaeologically (La Tène Culture) as well as linguistically. Similar movements are evident elsewhere in tribal societies. To be sure, when a tribal-civilized frontier was involved, as in the Mediterranean–north European case, the attraction of gold, fine manufactured goods, other luxuries (wine), and rich farming booty added a new incentive ('pull') to the folk movements. The need to engage the disciplined armies of the state-civilized world in set-piece battles grew correspondingly.

When things came to serious open battle, there was little to no disciplined formation or tactical control among the tribal hosts, except for the occasional use of ambushes and ruses. Leaders mainly led by example, in heroic fashion. The famous Germanic 'wedge' formation was probably an expression of this heroic-type leadership, with the war leader at the head, followed by his men. Otherwise, the clash of forces centred on individuals and small groups, engaged in a mêlée-style fighting across the front. A crude phalanx-like formation with locked shields is variably reported throughout northern Europe, but mostly in later times. The long sword, with which European tribal warriors were characteristically armed as their friction with the civilized peoples to their south intensified, typified the mêlée style of warfare. It contrasted with the short sword of the classical Mediterranean armies, intended for close-quarters fighting in dense formations. Against the Greeks and Romans, the Celts and Germans relied on the furious onslaught of vigorous and intimidating warriors, brought up in martial and bellicose societies (and superior in physique), which the classical armies found terrifying and difficult to withstand. In the battles against the Celts, from Allia in 387 BC to Telamon in 225, and against the Germans, from the Cimbri and

Teutoni invasions at the end of the second century BC to Adrianople and the Germanic migrations, Roman defeats were almost as frequent as Roman victories. However, if the initial barbarian onslaught was withstood, the state armies' disciplined and more cohesive formations, better tactical control, and superior weapons and armour for close-quarters fighting usually prevailed. In the eyes of the classical Greeks and Romans, their northern neighbours lacked stability and perseverance, and were quick to swing from exuberant ferocity to pitiful despair.

Furthermore, contrary to customary exaggerations by the ancient sources and subsequent modern images, the Celtic and Germanic hosts, even when they took the form of folk movements of tribes and tribal confederations with families, carts, livestock, and all, rarely numbered more than tens of thousands people, with up to 20,000 warriors at most. These were formidable numbers, no doubt, even by the scale of the classical Mediterranean polities. Still, the Romans could lose one battle after the other and re-enter the field with new armies drawn from their much greater manpower resources, already much greater than those of the barbarians in the third century BC, when Rome had dominated Italy. By contrast, the Celts and Germanic hosts could lose only once. Despite their terrifying marches in history, their tribal societies were by their very nature relatively small scale. The Roman Empire finally succumbed to the barbarian enemies that it had defeated for centuries, for a variety of related reasons: the Germanic folk movements of the late fourth and early fifth centuries AD across the Rhine and Danube frontiers—propelled by the Hunnic pressure—were more general geographically and demographically than the earlier, more isolated tribal forays; the Germanic tribal formations clustered into larger groupings, partly under the impact of contact with Rome; the Empire was torn in endemic civil wars between rival generals and emperors; these emperors and generals were tempted to enlist the tribal warriors into their service, first on an individual basis and, later and more dangerously, in their own tribal groupings, settled within the Empire (*foederati*). Still, even then, the Vandals, the Alans, and their allies, for example, totalled together around 80,000 people before crossing from Spain to Africa in 428, of whom probably 20,000 at most were capable of bearing arms. And the Visigoth and Ostrogoth heterogeneous tribal conglomerations are estimated to have each been only slightly larger.[61]

To be sure, civilized centralized states normally had a variety of other means at their disposal for manipulating tribal societies to their advantage and for rendering them less dangerous. Furthermore, tribal societies were themselves transformed by contact with states and civilizations, as well as by internal processes. However, before examining the transformation of these societies from their tribal form, I first turn to examine other newcomers of the Neolithic revolution, who made their appearance only slightly after the farmers: pastoral tribal societies.

PASTORAL TRIBAL WARFARE

The steady contraction of hunter–gatherers in the face of spreading agriculture entered a new phase whenever and wherever pastoralists took up those parts of the marginal land that were unsuitable for cultivation but could be used for husbandry. This first major economic diversification within the Neolithic—between agriculturalists and pastoralists—created a new type of mobile, semi-nomadic neighbours to the farming societies, which was much more significant in all respects, including the military, than the hunter–gatherers had been.

As already mentioned, animal husbandry evolved in close succession to agriculture in south-west Asia. From the seventh millennium BC, the early farming communities in this region engaged in mixed farming, involving both cultivation and husbandry. This form of farming spread into Europe, where it persisted for millennia. According to Caesar (*The Gallic War*, 4.1, 5.14, 6.21), the more primitive, and more war-like, north European tribesmen that he encountered—the inland Britons and Germans—relied more heavily on cattle husbandry than on agriculture. However, in south-west Asia (and north Africa), where the difference between fertile and semi-arid land was starker than in temperate Europe, a stronger process of diversification gradually took place. The same applied to the east European–west Asian steppe. Beginning from the fifth and fourth millennia, an increasingly pastoral way of life was forming on the marginal lands surrounding the farming societies, as groups moved to exploit this economic niche.[62] They raised sheep and goats, and in more lush steppes also cattle (and horses), subsisting primarily on the dairy products (and the blood of live animals) rather than on the meat. However, diversification between farmers and herders was not clear cut but graduated. Whereas the farmers continued to raise livestock, the herders did not give up farming altogether, supplementing their diet by planting seasonal crops and practising varying degrees of mobility. As we see later, pure nomadism emerged only with developed horseback riding in the first millennium BC, and even then only in some specialized environments.

Pastoralists also possessed tribal, kin-based networks.[63] Although their use of the land was highly extensive, it was far more efficient economically than that of the hunter–gatherers. Thus, although the herders' density and absolute numbers were much lower than those of the farmers,[64] their social groups—more widely dispersed than those of the farmers but keeping in touch by far greater mobility—were individually of roughly the same order of size as the farmers'. Again the ethnographic record testifies to that. In mid-twentieth-century east Africa, for example, the pastoral Datoga numbered 30,000, divided between several tribes or sub-tribes. The famous Maasai totalled close to 250,000, divided between 17 tribes, each numbering between a few thousand and a few tens of thousand.[65] The Dodoth numbered 20,000.[66] The Karimojong tribal community also comprised 20,000.[67] The Dinka and Nuer semi-pastoralists have already been mentioned. The Basseri tribe of southern Iran comprised an estimated 16,000 people, divided into 12 descent groups, which were further divided into large extended families. The total pastoral population in the region totalled hundreds of thousands.[68] The pastoral Bedouin tribes on the middle Euphrates in northern Syria in the early twentieth century numbered a few thousand 'tents' each, and up to 10,000 for tribal confederations.[69]

The excavated archives of the kingdom of Mari in that same region, relating to the nineteenth and eighteenth centuries BC, offer the most extensive picture that we possess of the pastoralist population in the ancient Fertile Crescent. Of the three major Amorite pastoral tribal confederations in the Mari domain, ten Hanean, five Benjaminite, and three Sutean tribes are mentioned by name. There were other, smaller tribal groups, and the tribes themselves were further divided along kin lines.[70] The ancient Israelites' presence in (pre- or proto-)history starts as they appear coalesced—in a process with origins that remain mostly obscure—into 12 tribes of various sizes, internal clan divisions, and closeness to each other. At least their core element was made up of herding tribal groups in a process of settling down, speaking similar dialects (which were also no different from those spoken by their other neighbours in Canaan and its vicinity), and coming together in a loose military–Amphictionic alliance. In the light of archaeological surveys, estimates of the early Israelite population are now sharply revised downward, to considerably fewer than 100,000 people.[71] According to Pliny (*Natural History*, 5.4.29–30), there were 516 *populi*, including 53 urban groups, in Roman north Africa, a major region of semi-nomadic tribal pastoralists. He named only 25 of these, whereas a modern catalogue of the ancient sources has been able to list fewer than 130.[72]

Pastoral tribes also centred on kin and clan. The position of chief (coming from a senior clan and mostly restricted in authority, as we have seen) existed in some but not in others. Material and social status could vary considerably among clans, families, and individuals, with livestock by far the prime possession. Although the average was a few dozen cattle or close to 100 small stock per family (tent), the rich possessed hundreds of animals.[73] Stock transactions and the ability to circulate it in support of others were central to social status. The chief transaction, of course, involved bride price, which often required substantial payment in stock. For example, one influential 'millionaire' among the Dodoth of east Africa possessed (and the word is apt) 10 women (8 of whom still lived), 15 sons, and 23 daughters, who had between them 10 sons-in-law, 9 daughters-in-law, and 25 grandchildren, at the time of the study. These folk in turn tended to the man's large stock and extensive seasonal gardens and supported him in social dealings, again demonstrating strikingly how somatic, reproductive, and status successes reinforced each other.[74] Similarly, rich Tutsi livestock owners in Rwanda had several wives, who in turn themselves 'were an economic asset' in supervising dispersed homesteads. There again 'children and cows' reinforced 'power and reputation', and vice versa: 'from the point of view of power, the significance of children was to provide cattle and connexions.'[75]

The monopolization of the women by the clans' and families' patriarchs in Africa, already mentioned earlier, was particularly noticeable among African pastoralists, where the elders controlled the livestock. The related institution of age sets of bachelor warriors was similarly particularly strong among the African pastoralists, and their young members were noted for their belligerency. Livestock raids on other tribes were endemic, often accompanied by the stealing of women, giving the African herders their special warrior reputation.[76] Inter-clan feuds were even more frequent. Cattle raiding targeted the animal enclosures near the settlements at night or the pastures in the day. The raiders then rapidly withdrew with their booty before the raided could get organized and pursue them in force.[77] Pasture-land was another major cause of violent conflict, as was water in more arid environments. At least as far as conflict was concerned, *pastoralia* was very far from its romantic image of blessed tranquillity.

If pastoralists were incessantly in conflict among themselves, they consti-tuted an even greater threat to farmers. Modern research of extant societies has shed light on the complex nature of herder–farmer interactions, which encompassed much more than hostility, mutual disdain, and conflict (all of them present). In response to changing opportunities, groups changed their position on a wide spectrum between the 'pure' forms, and the two subsist-ence modes were in any case symbiotic. Everywhere, the pastoralists traded with the farmers for crops, as well as a variety of craft goods, paying with animal meat, hides, wool, and dairy products. Still, violence remained an overwhelming temptation for the pastoralists. In the first place, the farmers themselves possessed livestock that could be raided. Second, their lands offered rich pasture and water, especially in semi-arid environments and in times of stress. Herders' trespassing of agricultural land was commonplace, and their concept of land tenure obviously differed from that of the agricul-turalists. Third, if agricultural produce could be stolen, won, or extorted rather than paid for, so much the better. And last but not least, in a conflict with farmers, the herders enjoyed significant advantages previously held by hunter–gatherers, while being far more numerous than the latter had been. Their mobility made them elusive, gave them the initiative, and partly secured them against counter-raids. The farmers, on the other hand, were sitting targets and highly vulnerable to acts of vandalism. Furthermore, life in the wild and on the move generally made the herders better warriors.[78]

The incursions of tribal pastoralists on farming societies have been widely noted by scholars as events of major historical significance. However, atten-tion has mainly focused on the cases that occurred after the domestication of the horse on the Eurasian steppe and its use first for drawing war chariots and, later, for military horseback riding. The domestication of the horse transformed and greatly boosted the pastoral–nomadic way of life, as well as greatly enhancing the pastoralists' power. Furthermore, much of this process occurred in historical times, at least in the sense that its effects were recorded by the literate states and civilizations that had developed by then and that had to contend with the pastoralists' enhanced, and sometimes devastating, threat. However, pastoralists existed before the domestication and extensive use of the horse—less than fully nomadic and less mobile, but still far more nomadic and mobile than the farmers. How did they fare in conflict with their neighbouring farming communities?

In attempting to answer this question we are fortunate in having different regions of the world that represent different 'modes' or 'stages' in the evolution of pastoral societies. Pastoralism started in south-west Asia; subsequently, the domestication of the horse was achieved by pastoralists on the east European–west Asian steppe, probably in Ukraine; the development of the wheel took place in either or in a combination of the above regions. All these developments occurred in Eurasia and spread throughout the landmass. However, because of geographical obstacles and ecological constraints, none of them spread into or emerged independently in either America or Oceania (raising of llama and alpaca in the Andes was restricted to the highlands and did not evolve into a pastoral way of life). Consequently, both regions gave rise to herder-less, horse-less, and wheel-less societies. The absence of pastoralists also accounts for the survival of significant hunter–gatherer populations in the marginal lands of the Americas. By comparison, sub-Saharan Africa, east Africa in particular, provides an 'intermediate' case, more closely akin to that of the early, pre-horse pastoralist societies of south-west Asia. Domesticated herd animals spread from the north very early in the Neolithic, even before the desiccation of the Sahara, and pastoralism has existed in the region for millennia. However, later newcomers such as the horse did not spread into west Africa across the Sahara until towards the middle of the second millennium AD, and into east Africa not until modernity. Substantial horse-less and wheel-less pastoral tribal societies existed in east Africa up until the twentieth century. The pattern of their relations with their agricultural neighbours—widely noted by the arriving Europeans—was marked by a predatory tendency on the part of the herders towards the farmers. Most notably, during the last millennium or so, pastoralist speakers of Nilotic languages continuously expanded from southern Sudan into south-west Ethiopia, Kenya, Tanzania, Uganda, and Rwanda–Burundi, harassing, sometimes displacing, and sometimes dominating the local Bantu-speaking farmers (and each other).

In some cases, this pattern became out-and-out political domination. The better-known instances took place in Ankole, Nyoro, Baganda, and Bunyoro in Uganda, and perhaps the most famous: Tutsi rule over the Hutu

in Rwanda and Burundi. The dominant pastoral elite in these various societies consisted of only about 10–15 per cent of the population. Some
scholars—in a 1960s' tradition—have mainly explained the pastoralists'
domination by their greater potential for economic growth and their hierarchical social structure.[79] Most, however, have little doubt that this domination was underpinned by the use and threat of force. Pastoralist domination
was expressed in preferential land exploitation, the exaction of agricultural
tribute from the farmers, and the constitution of the herders as a warrior-
ruling elite group. Relations of such elite groups with the farmer population
could involve various degrees of mutual assimilation and amalgamation,
although usually of an unequal nature, with a patron–client relationship and
occasionally even separate caste formation evolving. (Elsewhere, such a caste
formation is best known in the case of the Aryan-speaking pastoralist
invaders of India.) Over time, almost invariably, the intruding pastoralists
would themselves settle down on the fertile agricultural land into a more
mixed and sedentary form of subsistence, and be transformed in the process,
in Africa and elsewhere. Polities mixing conquering and conquered would
emerge. 'Political systems tended to become more centralized through the
domination of settled cultivators by more mobile and warlike pastoral
elites.'[80]

The east African ethnographic analogy can help to shed light on
pastoralist–farmer relationships in the late prehistoric and protohistoric
Near East, the cradle of pre-horse pastoralism. This subject, including its
violent aspects, has been the focus of scholarly attention and debate. By the
third millennium BC, petty-states, city-states, and states had evolved in the
farming communities of the Fertile Crescent. However, late in the millennium, crises befell the urban communities throughout the region. Written
records exist mainly for its eastern part, the Mesopotamian civilization.
There, in the twenty-fourth century BC, the Semitic Sargon of Akkad,
'whose fathers had lived in tents', rose to rule the old Sumerian domains.
The empire that he created was destroyed in the time of his successors by
the Gutian pastoralists. Furthermore, as the millennium drew to a close (and
the surviving written sources become better), Mesopotamian civilization
was subjected to continuous, wide-scale infiltration and harassment by
western Semitic tribal pastoralists from northern Syria, whom the locals
called Martu (in Sumerian) or Amurru (in Akkadian)—that is, 'westerners'—the Amorites of the Hebrew Bible. The kings of the Third

Dynasty of Ur, the dominant power at the time, carried out military expeditions against them. Furthermore, they built a 280 kilometre long wall joining the Tigris and the Euphrates to curtail their incursions—the first of such obstacles erected by state civilizations against their pastoral neighbours, and preceding the famous wall of China by nearly 2,000 years. As with later such works, the wall's effectiveness proved limited. The disintegration of the Ur III empire both facilitated and was precipitated by the Amorite incursions. In the mayhem that followed, Amorite tribal groups and Amorite leaders were actively involved as raiders, looters, invaders, mercenaries in the service of the city-states' rulers, and usurpers. By the beginning of the second millennium, Amorite-ruling dynasties and elites had established themselves throughout the region: in Larsa, Babylon (the famous Hammurabi), Marad, Sippar, Kish, Mari, and Assyria. These rulers, too, boasted that 'their fathers had lived in tents'.[81]

For the parallel events in the more western part of the Fertile Crescent, the Levant, especially its southern region, we mainly have to rely on archaeological finds, because written records are almost non-existent. From about 2350 down to 1950 BC, in later-day Syria, Israel, and Trans-Jordan, the massively fortified urban settlements of the Early Bronze Age (III) suddenly declined. Most were abandoned, although a few were destroyed or taken over by new ruling elites. The pioneers of archaeological and historical research in the region connected this upheaval to invasions by the Amorite pastoralists known from the Mesopotamian texts. In the Bible, too, during the Israelite settlement a millennium later, the Amorites are said to have occupied the marginal country of Trans-Jordan and the central hills of Canaan. However, more recent scholars have rejected the view that, in the Levant (as opposed to Mesopotamia), their original homeland, the Amorites (and the Aramaeans and Israelites of the late second millennium BC) constituted foreign and ethnically different invading tribal 'peoples'. From the study of extant societies these scholars learnt about the symbiotic and shifting relationships of pastoral and agricultural populations in the same region. In their reading of the ancient texts, the Amurru and their kind denoted marginal elements within the same 'social space', rather than truly foreign peoples. The image of military invasions has given way to that of 'processual' internal economic and social change within a 'dimorphic', pastoral–agrarian society. Other scholars have emphasized conflict between a ruling urban and state elite that attempted to dominate the countryside with its farmers

195

and herders alike, rather than conflict between the farmers and herders themselves. The urban centres of the Levant are supposed to have declined because of internal 'system collapse' relating to this tension, a decline in the international trade, Egyptian raids for which there is some but by no means extensive Egyptian typographical evidence, or another, yet unknown, reason.[82]

All these are highly significant points. And yet, here as well, the pendulum may have swung too far, and much of the debate seems to have become more apparent than real. The following synthesis can be suggested. It is now clear that the tribal pastoralists were not fully nomadic (and certainly were not horse nomads), nor did they come from the Syrian or Arab 'desert', as an earlier view, dating back to the nineteenth century, had it. Only from the middle of the first millennium BC on, when both the domestication of the horse on the Eurasian steppe and that of the camel in Arabia had evolved sufficiently, could pastoralism become fully nomadic in the former environment and taken up in the latter. The pre-horse and pre-camel tribal pastoralists lived on the outer and inner fringes of the farming communities, on the marginal land that was not conducive to cultivation because of low or irregular water supply (100–400 millimetres annual precipitation) or because of a rugged terrain. They practised varying degrees of nomadism, engaged at least in seasonal cereal crop raising, and extensively interacted with the farmers, with relations involving both exchange and conflict, the latter mostly in the form of raids. Although not fully nomadic, they were nevertheless far more mobile and opportunistically aggressive than the farmers.

The question of the pastoralists' ethnic and social relationship to the farmers is somewhat misleadingly drawn. Political, social, and ethnic boundaries were much too ambiguous and diffuse, and communities too small, kin based, and juxtaposed, in the Near East of the third and second millennia, to make the pastoral tribal elements living in the marginal lands on the borders of and among the farming communities either truly intrasocial or strictly foreign; the whole range of the spectrum was probably in evidence, depending on the circumstances.[83] In Mesopotamia, the pastoral Amorites clearly arrived from outside, spoke a different language, and were by all customary standards ethnically and socially different until they gradually assimilated. In the Levant, the geographical and ethnic differences between the pastoralists and agriculturalists may or may not have been less, and, indeed, things may not have been quite the same in the Amorite, Aramaean, and Israelite cases. It should be remembered that, even as late as the nineteenth- and twentieth-century Middle East, Bedouin pastoralist tribes and peasant (falahin) communities were ethnically distinct from and alien towards each other, even though they spoke related (Arabic) dialects. The categories of modern nationalism are misleading here, for example, as in the currently fashionable claim that the ancient Hebrews were actually Canaanites because they spoke dialects close to those of their neighbouring city dwellers and farmers of the plains.

More refined archaeological studies—for example, of the differences versus continuities during the urban decline in the Early Bronze Age III–IV transition—highly valuable as they are, cannot truly resolve the ethnic question one way or another so long as we do not possess better written records. Nor can they conclusively decide whether or not pastoralists—Amorite or others—were responsible for the decline. And yet the fact remains that although Egyptian raids are hypothesized as one possible reason for the urban decline in the Levant, Egypt herself, where, as in Mesopotamia, we possess some written records, experienced at that time Semitic pastoral infiltration from the east into the Delta. As elsewhere in the Fertile Crescent around the turn of the third to second millennia BC, this infiltration was associated with crisis. The intruders were apparently instrumental in bringing about the collapse of the Old Kingdom and the mayhem of the First Intermediate period. In Egypt, again, the newcomers were clearly foreigners.

On the other hand, the pastoralists' conduct mostly did not correspond to the old image of 'waves of invasion'. Again, one example is suggested by the Tutsi infiltration into the upland pastures between the much more populous Hutu farming tribal communities and polities inhabiting the lowland. From the upland the Tutsi proceeded to gain ascendancy over the Hutu and over the country. In some ways, this process tallies with the recent archaeological finds about the Israelites' settlement in the scarcely populated hill country of Canaan, from which they slowly expanded to dominate the densely inhabited plains. In the Israelite case, archaeology and written traditions can be brought to bear on each other. The protracted and piecemeal process revealed by archaeology, apparently involving fragmented and shifting tribal groupings, corresponds better to the early traditions preserved in the *Book of Judges* than to the *Book of Joshua*'s depiction of a unified invasion, expressing the later ideology of the state period.[84]

The east African analogy can help to dispel doubts expressed in the research of the ancient Near East whether horse-less (or pre-horse) pastoralists possessed any military advantage at all over farming communities (and petty-polities), as mounted pastoralists would in later times.[85] The clustering of settlements into walled cities in Mesopotamia during the fourth millennium BC probably was predominantly a result of conflict between large-scale, dense, and progressively centralized farming and trading communities. However, the population clustering and emergence of walled settlements in the socially and politically less advanced Early Bronze Age southern Levant during the first half of the third millennium may have been an indication of a growing pastoral threat to the countryside more than of conflict between settled farmer communities.[86] As the Mesopotamian record shows, more or less peaceful pastoralist infiltration into new regions went hand in hand with endemic raiding whenever the opportunity arose and weakness was detected. Vulnerability encouraged more ambitious takeovers. Urban and state organization provided the more powerful authorities of the region's sedentary communities with the means to try to control and dominate the tribal pastoralists.[87] It should be remembered that in the ancient Fertile Crescent we are not dealing solely with tribal–tribal relationships between farmers and herders, as in some other parts of the globe. All the same, the pastoral tribal elements could expand when the farming polities were declining, but could very well also bring about such decline themselves.

To gain the ascendancy, the pastoral tribes did not necessarily need to storm the fortified urban sites, which they undoubtedly found difficult to do. As in Mesopotamia, in some developed urban centres the transformation could sometimes be affected by leaders of mercenary tribal pastoralists, hired by the local rulers because of the pastoralists' reputation as warriors and taking over from their old masters. Such actions by hired ethnic warriors would become standard in history. This, however, was not the pastoralists' only possible route to dominance. By undermining the vulnerable agricultural hinterland upon which the cities' fragile economy was based, they could send the cities into fairly rapid decline and demise, thus providing the causal mechanism for the sort of 'system collapse' evoked by the 'processualists'. No other than a leading critic of the old view of foreign pastoral occupation has written: 'with tribesmen occupying large tracts of the countryside, with food supplies curtailed, and trade diminished, the cities would tend to shrink in upon themselves and lapse into sterile poverty'. In

Mesopotamia, writes another scholar: 'the Amorites took over the spaces outside the fortified cities, isolating them from one another. The fields were neglected and the price of barely skyrocketed, up to 60 times its normal price.'[88]

In reaction against earlier views, the trend in recent Levant archaeology has been to argue that the urban collapse did not necessarily mean serious depopulation, but that the rural and pastoral settlements are simply more elusive to archaeological detection. However, 'Dark Ages' appear universally to feature depopulation, because of the collapse of long-distance trade and the economy of scale, because of growing insecurity, and because pastoral subsistence is far more extensive than agriculture. Over time, the farming communities amalgamated in various forms with the pastoral elements, some of which themselves took up a more sedentary way of life, leaving the marginal lands open to new pastoral group formations. The Aramaeans and Israelites of the late second millennium BC may have constituted such later pastoral identity formations, after some of the Amorite pastoral elements of a millennium earlier had settled down.[89]

In east Africa, the ascendancy of the pastoralists led to a great expansion of the Nilotic languages. In the ancient Near East, too, it has been suggested that the spread of the Semitic languages was connected to the emergence and spread of the pastoralists through and from the 'inner flank' of the Fertile Crescent. This dual process allegedly took place from the fourth and third millennia on, and is attested to by Old Akkadian, Amorite, and other later known branches of Semitic languages.[90] It supposedly resulted in the displacement of the original languages of the farmer communities, as is documented, for example, in the cradle of civilization itself. Sumerian was practically displaced by Akkadian and only survived because it had already been literally recorded and had a liturgical function. Most place names in the ancient Levant are of non-Semitic etymology—a sure linguistic sign of the presence of earlier lingual strata in the region. The close similarity between the early Semitic languages, as they are known from the late third and second millennia BC, also suggests that their spread and diversification could not have begun much earlier. Lingual replacement of this sort does not mean population replacement, although various degrees of the latter may take place. The language change would mostly be affected by the dominant social position achieved by the pastoralists.

Although such a process is inevitably largely conjectural as far as Semitic languages are concerned, it is widely documented in later history in such cases as the spread of the Altaic languages by the Turks and Mongols throughout central and western Asia, the spread of Arabic throughout the Middle East and north Africa, and the Uralic Hungarian migration into central Europe. The first two of these cases involved vast expansions, and all of them were achieved within relatively short periods of time between the mid-first and mid-second millennia AD, by horse (and in the Arab case also camel) pastoralists. However, as the Nilotic and possibly also Semitic cases demonstrate, horse-less pastoralists, although less mobile than horse nomads, would have been able to effect similar if less spectacular processes. Traversing much greater distances than the land-bound farmers, opportunistically aggressive pastoral societies were ideal vehicles for linguistic spread by means of so-called elite dominance.

Indeed, pastoralism has been suggested as a second possible mover (in lieu of farming) responsible for the creation of some of the large language families of Eurasia. Pre-Colombian America, where domesticated animals played an insignificant role and no herding societies existed, was extremely fragmented linguistically, four times more so than Eurasia.[91] There were 23 language families and 375 different languages in North America alone (some 2,000 languages in all of the Americas). Mixed farming may have been more potent in spreading language, as is attested by the Bantu expansion in Africa, and possibly by the Neolithic farmer expansions in and from the Near East, mentioned earlier. All the same, several different languages groups—Hattic, Hurrian, Urartian, Sumerian—had survived to be recorded in writing across the northern rim of the ancient Near East before the Semitic and Indo-European language families displaced almost everything between them by the late second millennium BC. This may suggest a much greater earlier (Neolithic?) lingual heterogeneity in the ancient Near East. Thus pastoralism, even in a horse-less or pre-horse form, may have been an even more effective agent of lingual spread than mixed farming in a process involving large-scale expansion and military–political domination. To be sure, in the same way that in Norman England the local Germanic language was eventually adopted—somewhat changed—by the conquerors, in some cases it was the dominant pastoral elite who adopted the language of the local, and much larger, farmer population, rather than the other way around. In Uganda and Rwanda, for example, Bantu languages are spoken, and the Altaic Bulgarian horse pastoralists adopted the language of the Slav farmer communities whom they had conquered in the eighth century AD.

PROTO-HORSE PASTORALISTS

These pastoralist expansions bring us to yet another, larger, and the most widely discussed centre of pastoralism—the Neolithic and Early Bronze Age east European–west Asian steppe. Attention has focused on two highly publicized and arguably related issues: the domestication of the horse and its various applications, and the origin and spread of the Indo-European family of languages.

Wild horses survived at least until the late Neolithic throughout Europe, but it was on the steppe that they flourished in large herds. During the fourth millennium BC, they were extensively hunted, as well as being domesticated, by the local inhabitants. What uses did this humble, small (130–140 centimetres high), pony-like animal serve? This has become a hotly debated question. There is general agreement that initially, and for a very long time, its main use was for meat (and milk products); butchering marks and patterns testify to this. In this respect, the wild horse did not differ from the American bison in its economic function for the natives, whereas the domesticated breed was like any other flock animal—such as cattle, caprines, or, indeed, the reindeer in the north—around which herding societies in various ecological niches evolved. However, was the horse used for other purposes too—that is, for transportation—and since when? A few antler finds interpreted as cheek pieces, and, recently, signs of characteristic molar wear found on a single horse specimen (but not on others), may indicate the use of bits from as early as the fourth millennium BC on the Ukrainian steppe.[92] This means that the horse was apparently used as a pack animal, perhaps also for light traction (of sledges), and, indeed, for riding. In the Near East, other equids, such as the ass and, less successfully, the onager (or hybrid of the onager and ass), were similarly domesticated and used for such purposes during roughly the same period.

The reindeer in the north is perhaps the closest analogy: it was tamed as well as hunted; it was eaten; it served as a pack animal and for traction, as well as being partly ridden.[93] However, the discovery of horse bits has generated a trend among some scholars to regard full horseback pastoralism, familiar only from the first millennium BC, as dating back to the fourth and third millennia. Some popular writers have been quick to envisage early mounted pastoral–warrior hordes on the later model roaming through Eurasia.[94] This image has been associated with the theory that proto-Indo-European (PIE)—from which the whole language family branched out—was originally the language of the south-east European–west Asian steppe pastoralists and was spread through pastoral migratory–military expansions.[95]

There are fundamental flaws in this interpretation of early horseback riding. In the first place, archaeological representations show extensive and military use of horseback riding only from the first millennium BC, when it universally replaced the horse-drawn chariot that had dominated warfare throughout Eurasia during the second millennium.[96] This leads to other pertinent questions, which have surprisingly not been asked. If horseback riding was militarily more effective than the chariot warfare that it replaced, as it undoubtedly was, why was it the latter that ruled everywhere after the invention of the chariot at the beginning of the second millennium BC rather than the allegedly older horseback riding? To resolve this apparent puzzle, it has been widely argued that elite snobbery and social norms associated with the prestigious chariot were responsible for its dominance and persistence in the civilizations of the ancient Near East, the Aegean, and China.[97] However, this proposition rests on the unlikely assumption that, in the highly competitive world of the great powers' struggle, a more effective instrument such as the warhorse, supposedly already in existence, was everywhere suppressed for more than a millennium.

Even more inexplicable, why did the steppe pastoralists themselves, if they had been intimately familiar with a better option, ride horse-drawn war chariots in their first (proto)historically recorded expansions from the Iranian plateau into India and the northern part of the Fertile Crescent during the second millennium BC?[98] Furthermore, if the steppe pastoralists who had allegedly been responsible for the spread of the Indo-European languages into central Europe and Anatolia during the fourth and third millennia had done so with the advantage of the warhorse, why did they desert this superior weapon in Europe, as elsewhere, and use chariots during the second and early first millennia? Indeed, if hordes of horse pastoralists existed in the fourth and third millennia, why did they not make their presence felt on the civilizations of the Fertile Crescent in the way that the horse nomads would do from the first millennium BC on, with devastating effects, throughout the civilized world? Finally, why did the north African semi-nomadic pastoralists ride chariots rather than on horseback until the middle of the first millennium BC?[99]

No interpretation along lines of slow diffusion is convincing. We know that parallel contemporary inventions, such as the ox-drawn, disc-wheeled, heavy wagon and cart, invented in the late fourth millennium, and the horse-drawn, spoke-wheeled, light and swift chariot, invented in the late third millennium, spread explosively. They both took no more than 500 years to appear everywhere from the Atlantic to the Urals.[100] The latter took another 500 years only to arrive in China from the Eurasian steppe.[101] What made the warhorse, if indeed it went back to the fourth and third millennia, any different? After all, after the Europeans brought the horse to America, the Indians took no more than a century or so to evolve fully equestrian warrior societies that filled up the Great Plains.

An earlier generation of scholars more or less knew the answer. They believed that for a variety of possible reasons the early domesticated horse had not been suitable for effective riding and could only draw chariots when these had been developed. It was the discovery of archaeological signs that the horse had in fact been ridden as early as the fourth millennium that has confused the issue in recent years. Essential for the dissolution of the puzzle is the realization that horse riding is not an all-or-nothing proposition and that domestication is a protracted process rather than an event. As mentioned earlier with respect to agricultural and animal domestication in general, a millennia-long process of selective breeding was required gradually to increase the species' biological susceptibility to human needs. Correspondingly, cultural innovations in method and hardware over time made possible a more efficient use of the domesticated breeds. The problem then is not horseback riding, which apparently came very early, but *effective* horseback riding, and for military purposes. From this perspective, the evolution of the warhorse took several millennia and underwent several gradual stages.[102] One of the last major developments in this process—the invention and diffusion of the stirrups from the mid–first millennium AD—has been widely credited with the perfection of military horsemanship.[103] It is therefore curious that earlier, and generally known, developments have not always been fully recognized as pertinent to the question at hand.

Horses were apparently ridden in the fourth and third millennia BC, but so also were donkeys, and, in later periods, reindeer, which ancient rock paintings even show carrying mounted archers in a hunt. Nevertheless, donkeys and reindeer were never considered suitable for effective mounted warfare. Riding a 13 hand high horse is possible, but not for a sustained gallop. Riding the early horse may have been mainly possible from a hind position rather than from the back, as is the case with the donkey and as Babylonian, Egyptian, and Mycenaean representations of horse riding from the early to mid-second millennium BC widely suggest.[104] The idea that the civilizations of the ancient Near East, accustomed to the donkey, simply failed to comprehend for a millennium how to ride the horse properly does not make sense.[105] During most of the second millennium, these were horse-breeding polities (for chariots), whose elites were thoroughly and proudly equestrian, and intimately familiar with the horse. Furthermore, had they failed to discover the secrets of 'correct' riding themselves, the neighbouring nomads would have quickly taught them. Rather than by social convention, horse use was apparently constrained by biology and technology. Thus the horse's effective use for military purposes was made possible only by the year 2000 BC, with the invention of the light, spoke-wheeled chariot that a team of horses could draw swiftly for sustained periods. Only the breeding of larger and stronger 14 and 15 hand high animals, known from early first-millennium BC representations (today's medium-size horse), made effective mounted combat possible in terms of swift, controlled, and sustained gallop. Indeed, once horseback riding for military purposes began, it again took no more than 500 years to spread throughout Eurasia and north Africa. A series of subsequent successive innovations, such as the saddle, horseshoe, and stirrups, then built on that development during the ensuing millennium, further enhancing the effectiveness of combat horseback riding.

Does this pull the ground from underneath the theory of a fourth- and third-millennium BC pastoral–expansionist origin for PIE language spread, by dispelling the supposed existence of militarily superior horse pastoralists at that time?[106] Not necessarily. As we have seen, pastoralism and, within it, horse pastoralism were historically graduated phenomena, as were the farming societies themselves. The early south-east European steppe pastoralists represent one 'phase' in this development. They possessed ox-drawn wagons and carts that made their families and belongings more easily mobile than those of pedestrian pastoralists. Furthermore, if their horses were not effective for horseback fighting, they nevertheless may have been more effective in transporting the pastoralist warriors from one place to another—that is, in enhancing their '*strategic* mobility'. If, as we have seen in east Africa and in the ancient Near East, pedestrian pastoralists enjoyed a military advantage over the farmer communities and petty-polities, oxen wagon and proto-horse pastoralists may have possessed an even greater advantage in prehistoric Europe. In central Europe, unlike the ancient Near East, the tribal pastoralists faced tribal farmer communities, rather than states, and their possession of the horse—even if this did not imply full horseback combat riding—must have further enhanced their advantage. The trouble with such supposed migrations and expansions is that they took place in the thick darkness of prehistory that only lets through the faintest of echoes of even the most dramatic of events. Nevertheless, there is considerable agreement among archaeologists that the evidence does suggest an expansion of east European steppe pastoralists with their wagons, horses, and typical pit graves through the Danube corridor into central Europe, the Balkans, and Anatolia during the fourth and third millennia.[107] Settlement clustering and much increased fortifications are also detectable in these regions.

As stated in an in-depth study of the Hungarian plain, at the westernmost end of this initial expansion (and of all later pastoralist intrusions into Europe, from the Huns and Avars to the Magyars):

> [an] important development of this period was the appearance of a large number of tumuli. . . . Such burials have close analogies on the Pontic steppes, and other examples are known from the lower Danube. They have plausibly been interpreted as evidence for an intrusive steppe population, maintaining a cultural distinctiveness alongside native groups. . . . By 2800 BC these populations had fused. . . . Innovations at this time include . . . the advent of horse-breeding on a large scale. Trade in metal items, and also warfare, increased in significance. . . . Sites in this period . . . now had a forti-fied character . . . it is the advantage of height which is being sought. . . . It thus seems likely that small populations of eastern origin penetrated around and within established groups in the eastern Carpathian Basin: and this inter-pretation is strengthened by the spatial exclusiveness of these two distribu-tions. If this is so, then the tumulus-building groups seem to have sought relatively open terrain (presumably for stock-raising).[108]

According to a wider survey:

> During the fourth millennium, archaeologists perceive a structural reorgan-ization of society across much of Southeastern Europe. Evidence for this comes from the abandonment of the tell sites which had flourished for several

millennia; the displacement of previous cultures in almost every direction except eastwards; movement to marginal locations, such as islands and caves, or easily fortified hilltop sites. . . . This abandonment and movement, often propelling neighbouring cultures into one another, operated against the background not only of somewhat elusive traces of hybridization with the steppe cultures such as the Usatovo and Cernavoda I, but also with continuous incursions of mobile pastoralists. . . . Out of this period there later emerges a new cultural horizon that integrates cultures across Eastern Europe, including the northwest Pontic, and western Anatolia. . . . This consolidation in Southeast Europe was played out against a continuous background of further incursions from the steppe. What was sporadically attested prior to 3000 BC swelled during the third millennium to provide unequivocal evidence for movement of populations from the Pontic-Caspian steppe into the Balkans. . . . The evidence for a westward movement of Pontic-Caspian peoples is not limited to the Danube; kurgan burials now appear in Romania, Bulgaria, Yugoslavia and as far west as the Tisza river in Hungary.[109]

The genetic map of Europe, which, as mentioned earlier, shows the strongest gradient from south-east to north-west, presumably indicating the original migration into central Europe of Neolithic farmers from Anatolia, also reveals a distinctive gradient from east to west. This is interpreted as a residue of successive migrations by steppe pastoralists into Europe, some of whom are known from historical times, and some possibly prehistoric and related to the original spread of PIE speakers, who may have been the early Eurasian steppe pastoralists.[110]

The protracted and graduated nature of the domestication and use of the horse may also sit more comfortably with the time depth required for the vast territorial spread of the Indo-European languages, if the pastoralists were indeed the motive power behind it. The ox-wagon and proto-horse pastoralists may have started the expansion from the steppe into central Europe, the Balkans, and Anatolia in the fourth and third millennia. During the third millennium, groups of central European Indo-European speakers may have continued to expand northward, a move believed to be reflected in the spread of the largely pastoral warrior Corded Ware/Battle Axe cultures throughout northern Europe. Correspondingly, most scholars believe that the Indo-European-speaking ancestors of the Hittites and the Greeks were already more or less in their historically known locations by the third millennium BC. Their movements into these locations are associated with the collapse of some 100 Early Bronze Age II fortified sites in western Anatolia around 2700–2600 BC and the destruction of the Early Helladic II

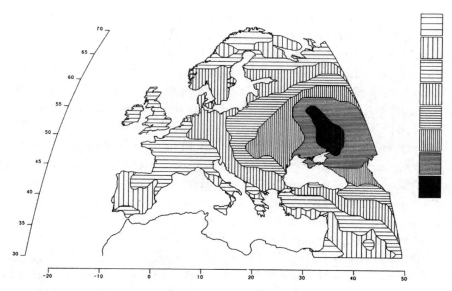

Genetic map of Europe (third principal component): invasions from the steppe? (Source: L. L. Cavalli-Sforza, P. Menozzi, and A. Piazza, *The History and Geography of Human Genes*, Princeton, 1994; permission by Princeton University Press)

culture in Greece around 2200. Both the Hittites and Greeks then adopted the chariot when it came along during the second millennium, as did the eastern, Indo-Iranian branch of the steppe pastoralists who went on to expand into the northern Fertile Crescent (Mitanni), the Iranian plateau, and down into India.[111] Similarly, the central and north European Indo-European speakers (now pressurized by chariot steppe pastoralists) may have used the chariot to expand further west and south, in steps that remain largely obscure, down to the spread of the Hallstatt and La Tène charioteer cultures in the first half of the first millennium BC. In protohistorical times, the Indo-European-speaking Celtiberians, for example, entered the Iberian Peninsula only in the mid-first millennium BC, partly displacing the local non-Indo European speakers of Iberian, Tartessian, and Basque.[112] As linguists have always pointed out, the expansion of the Indo-European languages must have been a multilayered and untidy process.

It should be re-emphasized that the spread of the Indo-European languages did not mean the displacement by a particular population or race of all others, as nineteenth- and early twentieth-century (often racist) theorists held. Although the original PIE speakers may have been an ethnos of sorts and although a certain amount of genetic flow was probably involved in all the subsequent stages of the protracted and multilayered spread of the Indo-European languages, much, probably most, of this spread was done through elite dominance over indigenous populations. The historically known speakers of the Indo-European languages constitute no genetic community, as nineteenth-century theorists were disappointed to discover in India, where they went in search of blond Aryans. Nor did the PIE speakers enjoy a particular 'genius' that would account for their spread, apart from a contingent military superiority derived from pastoralism, the horse, and the chariot. The same, of course, applies in the later and far better documented cases of the Turkish expansion in Anatolia and Arab expansion in the Middle East and north Africa, where very large indigenous populations changed language through the processes of elite dominance by relatively small groups of pastoralist horse nomads.

The coming of the horse did not work in favour of the pastoralists everywhere. In some regions, the horse was first adopted by the urban and farmer communities. In the late second millennium BC, it is clear from both the biblical and the archaeological evidence that the early Israelite tribal pastoralists did not yet possess the horse. The same apparently applies to the pastoralist Aramaean of north Syria, who during the twelfth to tenth centuries BC continually raided Assyria and Babylon. By that time, throughout the Fertile Crescent, the horse-drawn war chariot, introduced from the north, had become the weapon of the urban elite of the farming societies.[113] Consequently, the balance of power that existed between the pastoral and the settled was very different from what had prevailed during the earlier Amorite intrusions or that would prevail in east Africa. Indeed, the Israelites were long restricted to the hills, whereas the Canaanite city-states dominated the fertile plains. As we see later, in both Syria and Canaan, the late second-millennium pastoralists probably took advantage of the destruction of the city polities by a third party—the Sea Peoples.

This survey of horse-less and proto-horse pastoralists is an eminent reminder of the part played by contingency in human evolution. In localities, such as the Americas or Oceania, in which wild herd animals suitable for domestication did not exist or which were poorly connected with the Eurasian landmass where they did exist, pastoral tribal societies did not emerge.[114] Where the horse was absent for similar reasons but other domesticated herding animals were available, as in sub-Saharan Africa, pedestrian pastoralism has persisted to the present. The domestication of the horse itself—a paramount factor in human history—depended on the horse's biological potential for continued directed evolution through human breeding. Again this contingency and variations allow for some controlled comparisons. For instance, may the livestock of the farmers and pastoralists have been the real, 'serious' trigger for warfare? Where they existed, livestock were certainly a major cause, but in America and New Zealand (where the local Maori did not even possess the pigs that were present in the rest of south-east Asia and Oceania) people nevertheless fought viciously.

It may not be superfluous at this time to reiterate some comments by way of clarification. My discussion of human belligerency does not assume that all tribal societies, or all people, were equally war-like. There has always been a great variation between societies, arising from their specific and complex set of circumstances. Still, practically all societies, to a greater or lesser degree, had to contend with the possibility of violent conflict, prepare themselves for it, and occasionally engage in it. Although extreme bellicosity may have been a double-edged sword, leading some societies to expansion but others to destruction, it is clear that out-and-out pacifism in the 'tribal zone' was an assured ticket to subjugation and demise. In an unregulated world of absolute and relative scarcity, all human societies were more or less obliged to 'play the game'. It might also be necessary to mention that, although socialized in a regime of internal and external insecurity and potential and actual violence—a regime that was often conducive to the inculcation of warrior values—people in tribal societies were obviously not only threatening but capable of a whole range of behaviour and emotion. As Strabo (*Geography*, 4.4.2), writing about the dreaded Celtic warrior society, assured *his* civilized readership in the classical Mediterranean world: 'The whole race . . . is madly fond of war, high spirited and quick to battle, but otherwise straightforward and not of evil character.'[115]

This granted, pastoral societies in general, for reasons we have already seen, tended to be more menacing to the farmers than the other way around. The evolution of horseback pastoralism and horseback fighting would vastly increase the pastoral threat. However, by the time mounted herding societies had evolved, things had not stood still in *agraria* either, because tribes and petty-polities had been giving way to states and vast empires.

ARMED RETINUES: WEALTH AND FORCE IN THE TRANSITION FROM THE TRIBE

The production and accumulation of resources, which was progressively the outcome of the Neolithic revolution, did not inaugurate either social differentiation or violent conflict, but it enormously magnified the former and greatly affected the latter. Intergroup resource conflict no longer solely concerned access to the utilization of natural resources, even though arable and pasture land, water, and raw materials, for example, remained hotly contested; it also concerned the direct acquisition of resources produced by others, through looting and tribute, and sometimes the acquisition of the others themselves as slaves, who would produce the resources under their owners' direct control. Similarly, power became a major avenue to resource accumulation within societies. Wealth strengthened the hand of those who held it in social dealings and vice versa, in a positive loop feedback. Rousseau, who was the first to bring this process into focus, was on far firmer ground here than in his portrayal of aboriginal innocence. The more affluent a society was, the more power relations within it become skewed in favour of the rich and mighty and the more they could channel resources their way, while relentlessly vying among themselves—occasionally violently —for power, wealth, prestige, and all the other benefits that these entailed. A 'predatory' or 'parasitic' existence had now become an option in both inter- and intrasocial relations, not in any value sense but in that power, force, and coercion could now be directly utilized to appropriate products rather than merely to clear the ground of competitors for the exercise of production. Although coercive and productive relations were normally mixed, distinctively predatory specializations were now in evidence.

Wealth accumulation, social differentiation, and outside conflict were in many intricate ways interrelated and mutually affecting processes, through which chiefs and 'big men' grew in importance. Booty from raiding became a major avenue for 'primary' resource accumulation and social differentiation. A successful war leader now attracted followers not only on an *ad hoc* basis, for a specific raid called for in a tribal assembly, but on a more permanent footing. He could draw on his resources to feed and maintain them, with a view to generating even greater resources for himself and his men (the traditional principle of an equal distribution of booty was being eroded).

War had to pay for war. The whole system required permanent raiding if the host of warriors was to remain with the leader. Successful raiding further enhanced the wealth and power of the leaders in cattle, precious metals, slaves, fields, dependants, and armed men, which in turn magnified their social position. Communal tribal and clan possession of the land, periodically rotated between the clans—Marx's 'archaic communism'—increasingly gave way to forms of private property. Accumulated property 'objectified' status differences, turning 'ranked' societies into 'stratified' ones and chiefs and 'big men' into nascent aristocracy. No longer could any enterprising man or famous warrior become a 'big man' or a war leader; these positions increasingly presupposed a wide economic and social base to begin with, making leadership more firmly institutionalized with the elite. All the same, as the social prizes increased, so did the competition for them, with a successful warrior career being one of the chief avenues for social mobility. Young warriors joined famous war leaders in search of fortune. They formed 'retinues' or hosts of 'companion' warriors around them, making warfare their occupation, with predatory existence as its rationale. They lived and dined together—communal feasts and drink at their leader's table constituted a central part of their keep.

Wherever these processes took place, tribal society was transformed. Power and power relations were no longer grounded solely in kinship. A new element was introduced. Chiefs and 'big men' could now make use of armed retinues, dependants, and clients to throw their weight around in social dealings. These hosts largely came from their own and related clans, but also from other clans and even from outside the tribe altogether, and were bound to their patron by the supra-kin ties of economic and social benefits and obligations. Elite ties, too, cut across tribe and kin relations. Chiefs and 'big men' from different tribal communities not only raided one another but also exchanged prestige goods and cemented alliances and sacred friendships between them, both against a third party and in mutual support against competitors and rivals at home, often against 'tribal interests'. Mutual hospitality, gifts, and assistance in times of need among the elite were guaranteed by custom, honour, and self-interest.[116]

Julius Caesar's observations on the Celtic and Germanic societies, and those of Tacitus on *Germania* more than a century later, provide some of the earliest and clearest anthropological accounts of the transformation of tribal society. As already mentioned, earlier Celtic society of the third to mid-second centuries BC, as described by Polybius (*The Histories* 2.17), knew 'no pursuit other than war and agriculture'. The status of chiefs, war leaders, and 'big men' was largely determined by the size of their entourage of clients and 'companion' warriors. The companions feasted together, seated according to a fiercely competed warrior status rank. Potlatch feasts were occasions for lavish displays of wealth—consumed, given away in gifts, and destroyed by the chiefs and 'big men'.[117] In turn, this 'investment' in enhanced status was expected to bring the war leaders still greater resources in the warrior-raiding economy. Over time, Celtic society grew increasingly stratified. The Gaul that Caesar describes was already well advanced in the transition from tribalism to nascent states, a process partly generated by trade and other forms of intercourse with the Roman world. By the first century BC, urban centres or towns (*oppida*) had emerged in Gaul for the first time. Society had become highly stratified, with chiefs and 'big men' transformed into a powerful aristocracy.

Caesar's account is full of acute observations on the transformation of Celtic society (*The Gallic War*, especially 6.11–15). The old tribal assemblies had been reduced in significance, and ordinary men had all but lost their say. Many of the poor became clients of the aristocratic families, whereas young warriors joined their retinues and, according to Caesar, engaged in raids and counter-raids year by year. The number of one's retainers and clients was 'the one form of influence and power known to them'. Caesar writes, for example, of one of the most powerful among the Helvetii, who when called to trial on charge of conspiring to achieve absolute rule came with 'all his retainers, to the number of some ten thousand men, and also assembled there all his clients and debtors, of whom he had a great number, and through their means escaped from taking his trial' (1.4). He also writes that 'The more powerful chiefs, *and such as had the means to hire men*, commonly endeavoured to make themselves kings' (2.1; my italics).

This state of affairs was characteristic of a society already on the road away from its older tribal form, something of which Caesar was well aware. He contrasted Gaul with the Germans of his time, among whom ancient, more primitive, and more egalitarian tribal society was still the norm (6.21–6). However, by Tacitus's times, Germanic society had also changed considerably, again partly owing to contact with the expanding Roman world. It remained less developed than Gaul of the first century BC and more closely approximated the Celt society described by Polybius a century or two earlier; no urban settlement of any sort existed in *Germania*, nor would exist until late in the first millennium AD. However, whereas, in Caesar's times, Germanic war leaders were chosen *ad hoc* by the tribal assemblies for the duration of the military activity, chiefs and 'big men' now attracted retinues of young warriors, creating permanent supra-tribal foci of power around them. Tacitus's account of these retinues (*comitatus*) of 'companions' (*comites*), whose raison d'être was the spoils of war, is one of the most cited classical texts:

> There is great rivalry among the retainers to decide who shall have the first place with his chief, and among the chieftains as to who shall have the largest and keenest retinue. This means rank and strength. . . . Many high-born youth voluntarily seek those tribes which are at the time engaged in some war; for . . . they distinguish themselves more readily in the midst of uncertainties: besides, you cannot keep up a great retinue except by war and violence, for it is from their leader's bounty that they demand that glorious war-horse, and that murderous and masterful spear; banqueting and a certain rude but lavish outfit are equivalent to salary. . . . When they are not entering on war, they spend much time in . . . idleness—creatures who eat and sleep, the best and bravest warriors doing nothing, having handed over the charge of their home, hearth, and estate to the women and the old men and the weakest members of the family.[118]

The classical authors were regularly confounded as to how exactly to render tribal institutions and offices in terms that would correspond to those of their own civilizations (which of course they did not). This has created considerable difficulties for modern scholars as well, who have often sought guidance in an anthropologically informed comparative approach; for again, institutions and offices show remarkable similarity throughout tribal land. Caesar, who was the closest, keenest, and most authoritative observer imaginable, consistently referred to the Gallic chiefs and nascent aristocracy as *principes*, which was a reasonably good rendering (akin to the English derivative adjective/noun 'principal' or chief, rather than 'prince'). The lesser aristocracy and 'big men' he rendered as *equites*—cavalry—in correspondence to the name of a Roman estate, which like any other ancient social elite originally formed the mounted arm, but the traditional English translation of which as 'knights' is misleading.

Tacitus, too, called the Germanic powerful in possession of retinue *principes*. However, elsewhere (*Germania* 7), when describing the traditional tribal offices, he used the Latin designations kings (*rex, reges*) and war leaders (*dux, duces*)—the former appointed on account of high birth, the latter for valour. Although *dux* was a neutral rendering for a war leader (unlike the later European duke, it was not an official title in Tacitus's Rome), *rex* was a more problematic term. Tacitus made it very clear that both offices had very limited authority and even fewer disciplinary powers, and that they mainly led by reputation and example, as was regularly the case in tribal societies. Still, the confusion of tribal chiefs with state kings has been commonplace among people from state societies coming in touch with tribal ones. Very often the confusion went beyond the application of familiar vocabulary to alien institutions, with the observers and intruders from civilization attributing to the tribal chiefs power and authority that they did not possess. Indeed, as we see later, in many colonial situations, from Roman to modern times, the colonial power, preferring to work with a centralized client authority, actually turned chiefs into kings, investing in them the power and authority that they had previously lacked.

Interestingly, the difficulties of comprehension and terminology experienced by both the classical authors and the modern scholars are not only manifest with respect to the tribal lands of northern Europe, but they also extend to the Greeks' and Romans' own past in their own pre-state period, the memory of which only dimly survived into historic times in myth, epic, and tradition. This was because very little separated the early Greeks and Romans from their northern neighbours, except that the former were closer to the cradle of civilization in the ancient Near East and, therefore, were, each in turn, earlier to be affected by it. The Greeks must have been tribal people before the rise of the Mycenaean polities in the mid-second millennium BC, but no narrative record exists for this early period to fill in the archaeological evidence. However, as the crest of the elite Mycenaean civilization collapsed around 1200 BC, the Greeks reverted to tribal and kin-based existence in the turbulent and materially and culturally impoverished Dark Age, between the twelfth and eighth centuries BC, maintaining a mainly pastoral and rudimentary agricultural economy. Although the Dark Age is so called partly because writing had been lost and no literary records were produced during that period, historical echoes survived as oral traditions and were written down when writing and civilized life began to re-emerge in Greece around the middle of the eighth century BC. The paramount literary source for this past—for the ancient Greeks as well as for us—is of course the Homeric epics. The *Iliad* preserves a faint memory of the glory of the Mycenaean world, sung by bards through the centuries of the Dark Age and exposed by modern archaeology. However, scholars are agreed that much else in that epic and particularly in its twin, the world of Odysseus, in fact reflects social institutions and the conditions of life in the late Dark Age, not long before the Homeric epics were written down.[119]

We are conscious of the existence of the Dark Age Greek tribes, albeit vaguely, because they left traces in historical time and in the polis. In the 'world of Odysseus', tribal society was segmented, highly stratified, and dominated by the households of rich local chiefs and 'big men', with their retainers and clients. This was a very insecure world, in which the powerful made raiding their prime occupation and a way of life. As mentioned earlier, no walled sites existed to protect the widely dispersed population and farms until the ninth or even eighth centuries BC.[120] Again, cattle, precious metals, and slaves—mainly women and children—were the main prizes, whereas the adult males were massacred or driven away. As the epic tradition tells us, young beautiful captive women were most coveted for sharing their master's bed. In these heroic societies, too, retinues were kept on the spoils of war, a warrior ethos prevailed, and power and wealth were inseparable. The kin network was transformed to the extent that the powerful heads of the household estates (*oikos*) extended their clan (*genos*) names to encompass and subsume the clans of their clients and dependants. It was now only *their* clan names and *their* genealogy that counted, and only they claimed ancestry from gods and semi-legendary heroes.[121]

The title of these chiefly heads during the Dark Age, *basileus*, is better understood in terms of its meaning in the earlier, stately Mycenaean written records, when it denoted the relatively lowly office of a village head, than by the meaning that it was to assume during the transition from the Dark Age and in classical times—that of a king. When Homer refers to true kings, such as Priam of Troy or Zeus, he uses the term *anax*, the title of the Mycenaean kings as revealed in the excavated tablets (*wanax*). The *basileis* were powerful tribal and local chiefs and 'big men' with hereditary status derived from birth and wealth. They held military leadership, as well as communal ritualistic and judicial functions, in a segmented tribal and localized society.[122] As elsewhere, they were apparently elected from within a leading clan rather than the son simply inheriting the office from the father. While popular tribal assemblies declined in importance, the counsel and support of the main clans' elders were necessary for any general action, as opposed to 'private' ventures pursued by the 'big men' and their retinues alone. Our knowledge is appallingly limited, but as we see in other civilizations, it would seem that by protohistorical times, during the early evolution of the *polis*, some *basileis* would work to transform their limited chiefly status into more centralized authority ('chiefdom') and into true kingship. All the same, the highly circumscribed authority of the two, co-reigning Spartan kings in historical times seems to have been a residue of earlier tribal institutions rather than later constitutional constraints. As some scholars have noted, it was only the tyrants (a neutral word in early Greece) of the seventh and sixth centuries BC, during the rise of the polis, that for the first time exercised autocratic authority.

Morgan (followed by Engels) was the first to point all of this out in his pioneering study of tribal society with respect to both the Greek *basileus* and the early Roman *rex*. The office of the first semi-legendary Roman *reges*—traditionally dating from the eighth century BC—essentially meant confederate chiefs who acted as war leaders and high priests. It was the same chiefly title preserved in other early and necessarily pre-state Indo-European languages: Sanskrit *raj*, Gaulis *rix*, Old Irish *ri*, Tracian *Rhesos*, Greek *aregon/archon*, Gothic *reiks*.[123] It would seem that only later, under Etruscan domination, with the rise of statehood and the beginning of urbanization in the sixth century BC, did the last *reges* attempt to achieve what we now understand as true kingship. Consequently, the last, 'proud' *rex* was famously deported from Rome in 510–509 BC by the former tribal powerful, already turned into nascent aristocracy.

The later Romans' knowledge of these early and different times was dim in the extreme and shrouded in myths. Not even a Roman contemporary epic source such as the *Iliad* and *Odyssey* exists. Still, here too, down through history, these aristocratic families dominated society through their hosts of retainers, clients, and dependants, over whom their clan (*gens*) name was called. They claimed divine and heroic descent and vigorously vied with each other for dominance. The republic that they established after the abolition of kingship was a means through which they successfully strove to institutionalize their domination over the rest, while regulating the internal competition between them. Yet some surviving early Roman traditions kept the memory of how the rudimentary state period had actually been. For example, in 479 BC, one of the most powerful of the Roman clans, the Fabii, took it upon itself to carry out the war against the Etruscan city of

Veii, 'as if it were our own family feud'. According to the first-century BC historian Livy (2.48–9), 306 clan members, accompanied by a large host of kinsmen (*cognati*) and friends (*sodales*), participated in the affair. His contemporary, Dionysius of Halicarnassus, adds (9.15) that the entire host of kinsmen and clients (*pelatai*) numbered 4,000 men.

But let us return from the perspective of the historical–literate peoples observing their own distant and misty pre-state past to their observations on their contemporary tribesmen, with whom they traded and warred and by whom they were raided. It might be added at this point that tribesmen's raiding took place not only on land but also from the sea. Here, as well, chiefs and 'big men' played a prominent role in organizing raiding hosts from all those who wished to join them in search of fortune: in equipping the boats and ships; in leading the expeditions; and, in opportune circumstances, in settling down in foreign lands. Sea raiding of this sort was probably as old as seafaring itself (for example, the American north-west coast), extending back into the Neolithic. Raiding and piracy are known to have been well established on both sides of the Mediterranean, at least by the second millennium BC. They were an integral part of the 'world of Odysseus'.

Our sources are much better where the Roman Empire is concerned. Sea trading and raiding along the Atlantic coast and across the Channel had become well developed by Celtic times. Caesar (3.8 and 3.13–15) was impressed by the large and advanced Celt ships, well adapted to the waves and winds of the Atlantic. Furthermore, despite modern scholarship's appalling lack of information, it is more or less agreed that *someone* had to introduce the Celtic tongues into the British islands, a process that necessarily involved at least some migration from the Continent. According to Caesar (5.12), the coastal inhabitants whom he met in his expeditions to Britain shared the tribal names and general customs of tribes in Belgium, from where they had arrived 'to seek booty by invasion'.

Frisian and later also Frankish sea raids on Roman Gaul were a constant menace during the Empire. From the mid-third century AD, the easternmost Germanic people, the Goths, who had migrated from the Baltic to settle down on the shores of the Black Sea, raided the other side of the Empire by both sea and land. Sea expeditions by warrior hosts, organized and led by Gothic chiefs and war leaders, raided and looted the rich shore provinces of the Balkans and Asia Minor, and even penetrated into the

Mediterranean and threatened Constantinople itself.[124] On the Atlantic coast, by the mid-first millennium AD, the more northern Germanic peoples, the Angles, Saxons, and Jutes, became the chief sea raiders on both sides of the Channel. Famously, but in a process the exact details of which remain largely obscure in protohistory, chiefs and war leaders at the head of warrior hosts—intermittently playing the roles of raiders and mercenaries for the local rulers—took the opportunity gradually to settle down in Britain and expand inland, bringing their families from overseas.

We have somewhat better information about the most successful sea raiders, the yet more northerly, indeed the northernmost, branch of the Germanic peoples, in Scandinavia, known as Northmen or Vikings. Their maritime exploits are in many ways exceptional, but otherwise their case exhibits remarkably similar processes to those that we have seen recurring many times over. On account of their location, the Northmen were simply the last to be drawn into and react with the expanding orbit of civilization, as it moved north-west from the Mediterranean. At the time of their raids, in the ninth and tenth centuries AD, the Northmen were still in the process of transition to statehood—somewhat later than their more southern neighbours, who had mostly undergone that process in connection with their migrations into the Roman Empire. Many traditional features of the Old Norse society and tribal past were still evident. At the end of the first century AD, Tacitus referred in Scandinavia to tribal entities such as the Suiones (Svear or Swedes), already the most prominent power in what is today central Sweden—Ptolemy's 'island' Scandia, where he names some other tribes as well. More tribal designations are mentioned in Jordanes' sixth-century *Getica*, designations that are echoed in the old names of Scandinavian provinces, among them: in today's Sweden, the Hallin (Halland), Liothida (Lyuthgud, modern Luggude), Bergio (Bjäre), Gautigoths (Göta-land), and Suetidi/Swedes; in today's Norway, the Granni of Grenland, Augandzi of Agder, Harothi of Hordaland, and Rugi of Rogaland; and finally the Dani, who had moved into today's Denmark from the seashore islands after the southern migration of the earlier Germanic tribal inhabitants.[125] The Lapps and Finns in the north and east excepted, all these tribal formations were ethnically closely related and spoke Old Norse, which was just starting to differentiate from other north Germanic dialects to its south.

By the second half of the first millennium, Norse society was becoming increasingly stratified. In Denmark in particular, which was closer and better connected to the rest of Europe, towns were beginning to emerge. In societies still based on local kin networks, the local powerful were increasing in strength. Tribal assemblies and tribal militias of all free men still played a role, but chiefs and 'big men' (*godar, jarl* [earls], *hersar* [*herr* = war host], *hauldar* [holders], and a variety of other designations) now offered not only leadership in war but also local patronage and security. Here, too, they were rich in cattle and slaves, the former partly and the latter mostly acquired in raids. They also grew stronger in clients and dependants, competed vigorously and violently among themselves, claimed supernatural descent, and gathered retinues of young warriors around them in pursuit of power and booty.[126]

By the ninth century, as the Northmen started their raids on western Europe, two major developments had taken place. First, archaeology shows that they had acquired the sail from their southern neighbours, while earlier only possessing oared boats. Second, kingship had begun to evolve among them, gradually bringing the local powerful under central authority and forcibly turning them into a subordinate aristocracy. Knowledge, including chronology, of early Scandinavian kingship, is limited in the extreme, because paradoxically we know less about the Northmen at home than abroad, where they were chronicled by their victims. The main exception is the famous oral epic sagas, written down in Iceland much later, beginning from the twelfth century. It seems clear that, again, Denmark led the way in the evolution of kingship, some time after the middle of the first millennium, followed by Sweden. In Norway, kingship was the latest to evolve and expand. Thus Iceland, colonized by Norwegians from the late ninth century, best preserved the structure and institutions of Old Norse society, with its assemblies of free men and fiercely competing 'big men'. In any event, when Viking raiding began, it was still mostly 'big men's' organized hosts that carried out these ventures (most notably in the case of the Norwegian raids on the north of the British Isles). Indeed, in some cases, these 'big men' were fugitives from the transformations at home and from the expansion of kingly authority. Scandinavian kings became active in sea-borne expeditions against western Europe only later in the Viking era, Norwegian kings being the latest, not before the eleventh century.

Thus the raiding parties that terrorized the inhabitants of western Europe were relatively small ones, consisting of as few as several to a few dozen ships and a few hundred warriors, who joined a leader for the expedition.[127] Under this leader, whose authority was limited, these warrior bands were largely egalitarian, 'brotherhoods' of 'fellows'. The bands' strength came from their aquatic mobility on the seas and up the rivers, which made it possible for them to strike unexpectedly, by surprise, and with their victims almost incapable of assembling superior forces. Their mode of warfare was similarly based on stealth, relying on night attacks, ambushes, hiding in woods and marshes, ruses, and hasty retreats. They made skilful use of hastily erected field fortifications. Still, if things came to more serious fighting, these warrior groups, the product of a simple and unruly society, were superior to the more domesticated peoples in the lands to their south, unless larger forces were co-ordinated to pin them down. In this way, they looted, raped, burnt, killed, and extorted, driving the locals to find refuge in fortified settlements that were springing up throughout western Europe. Fragmented state power in western Europe attempted to organize naval and military resources and construct fortifications to oppose them, or else tried to bribe them away or buy peace by granting them provinces to settle in and rule. Normandy in France was the first such case of a major settlement, and Norwegian and Danish settlement took place all along the north and east coasts of the British Isles—no different in effect from the earlier Celt and Anglo-Saxon migratory waves. As Scandinavian kings, foremost Danish, entered the scene, gradually taking the place of 'big men' and their warrior bands, expeditions grew to hundreds of ships and thousands of warriors, and settlement and foreign domination intensified.

It is evident from all this how much our choice of cases depends on the contact of tribal societies with literate people who could document them. Even protohistorical and patchy narrative evidence, as most of our evidence inevitably is, is immeasurably superior to no narrative at all. For example, there may have been some similarity between the Vikings' exploits and those of the 'Sea Peoples', documented briefly but dramatically in surviving Egyptian, Hittite, and Ugaritic royal records of the thirteenth and early twelfth centuries BC. We know pathetically little about these peoples, the most famous of which are the biblical Philistines. Apparently, the Sea Peoples mostly came from the Aegean cultural sphere: the islands; the mainly Indo-European Luwian language-speaking Anatolian seashore provinces of Lycia, Caria, and Cilicia; and possibly also the Greek mainland. They may have variably consisted of tribal groups on the move (women and children on ox-drawn carts are depicted in Egyptian reliefs), chiefly war bands engaged in raiding, piracy, and mercenary service, and fugitives from invasions and rising state power. Their activity was somehow connected with a larger movement of peoples and a general upheaval in the eastern Mediterranean around 1200 BC that among other things caused the destruction of the Hittite Empire in Anatolia and possibly also of the Mycenaean civilization. The sea people's raids devastated Cyprus and the Levant coast, where many of the large cities, including the principal mercantile one of Ugarit, were sacked and destroyed, plunging the region, as in Greece, into a centuries-long Dark Age. On several occasions, their hosts invaded Egypt— on their own and as mercenaries in the service of others—only to be repulsed in great land and sea battles by the pharaohs Merneptah and Ramesses III. Some of them, including, most notably, the Philistines, were then settled by the Egyptians, and later ruled the southern coastal plain of Canaan.[128] This is more or less the most that can be inferred from our sources about the tribal and band background of at least some of the Sea Peoples. As with the Angles, Saxons, Jutes, Northmen, or any other tribal society mentioned here, their nascent polities are discussed further in the next chapter.

The Sea Peoples defeated in a naval battle by Ramesses III. Early twelfth century BC. Relief at Medinet Habu. (For the land battle see p. 353)

CHIEFDOMS

The road from tribal societies to polities was an evolutionary one. With wealth accumulation, growing social differentiation, and the rise of chiefly and 'big men's' retinues, there often arrived a point when chiefly power was no longer merely dominant within society but grew truly to dominate it. On the strength of their retinues, chiefs, or war leaders and 'big men' turned chiefs (violent usurpation within and between the chiefly clans was commonplace and murderous), were able to secure a type of authority and control that they had not possessed in simpler tribal societies.

Once more, power and wealth were closely intertwined in this process. As Tacitus writes about *Germania* (15), in one's own tribe people were made to understand that the chiefs and 'big men' would be pleased with 'complimentary contributions' in cattle or crops. Hesiod, too, around 700 BC writes about the 'gift-eating *basilees*' (*Works and Days* 37–9), mentioned in the context of their arbitration and judicial status. These contributions and gifts served for the keep of the armed retinues and fuelled their growth, in a spiral process that further enhanced chiefly power and wealth. Neighbouring communities were similarly encouraged to send 'gifts' to buy goodwill—a clear 'protection money'. Indeed, the traditional Mafia dons in Sicily were local powerful of a similar sort, flourishing in a society in which state authority was weak. Where chiefly power was centralized, even more formal systems of tribute and tax extraction were introduced. Henchmen were employed to supervise the countryside, and authority was exercised through minor, subordinate chiefs and formally institutionalized family and village heads. Although the semblance of kin and tribal fraternity was maintained, and much of old egalitarian customs, particularly within the companions in the armed retinue, was preserved, these centralized and multilayered, 'complex', chiefly entities, the so-called chiefdoms, were far more hierarchical and authoritative than ordinary tribal or chiefly societies. Social power was gravitating further away from kinship.[129]

One of the classic and best-documented examples of chiefdoms survived into modern Europe in the wild and unruly Scottish highlands and islands, a remnant of Celtic chiefdoms that had once prevailed all along the western rim of the British Isles. Until the crushing of the clan system by state power after the Battle of Culloden in AD 1746, the Scottish kings, followed by the British crown, found the expansion of state rule into this rugged and poor environment both difficult to achieve and of dubious value. The great local chiefs extended their clan's name—the Macleod, the Macdonald, the Clanranald, the Campbell, the MacGregor—over their people, ruling under the mantle of a close kin system, recorded in extensive genealogies and, where necessary, fictitiously expanded. With a sham-paternal ideology strongly entrenched and cultivated, the chief played the role of father and patron to his clan. Although the clansmen owed him tribute, mainly in the form of foodstuff, drink, and cloth, a fraction of their contribution was returned to them, as the chief—like the Mafia dons—demonstrated his generosity in helping out clients in need and during hard times. A household retinue of armed men and henchmen was kept on the tribute, dining on the chief's table in feasts that, on suitable occasions, when hosting other chiefs or dignitaries, turned into lavish displays of power and wealth. Personal ornaments, weapons, and other prestige goods were exchanged as gifts and commodities among chiefs, and between them and the outside world. Chiefs struck strategic alliances in the form of brotherly friendships, vowing loyalty to each other 'through disgrace and infamy'. Similar to elsewhere, many Scottish chiefs had 'two or three wives during their lifetime . . . siring many children', with marriages partly calculated to cement alliances. Feuding with and raiding on neighbouring clans were incessant, with cattle stolen and corn stores set on fire. As one 'settlement of feud' between chiefs in 1609 declared, it extended to all their 'awin kin, freyndis, tennentis, dependaris and aleyris to haif', and settled all past 'murthowris, heirshippes, spuilzeis of goodis, and raising of fyre commit by ather of thame agains utheris'.[130]

Religion also played a role in the consolidation of many a 'chiefdom', including, for example, the Celtic 'chiefdoms' of pre-Christian Ireland. Chiefs tended to expand and tighten their grip on the ritualistic functions that they had already possessed in many tribal societies, as well as to centralize and enhance communal liturgy to strengthen their ideological legitimacy and their chiefdom's cohesion. How dominant these ritualistic functions and liturgical authority were in the creation of chiefdoms is debatable. The trouble is that most of our evidence for the more prominent 'priestly' chiefdoms comes from the silent record of archaeology. However, where we do possess historically recorded observations (for example, again, early medieval Irish chiefdoms[131]), social, economic, 'military', and religious power—fostered through retinues and henchmen—seem to go hand in hand. A substantial modicum of coercion was essential for any serious process of power centralization in tribal societies.

The widely dispersed Polynesian island societies of diverse tribal systems, ranging from the relatively egalitarian to the distinctively hierarchical, offer the best ethnographic record of these interacting processes and mutually reinforcing factors. Among them, those of Tonga, Society Islands, Tahiti, and, most notably, Hawaii exhibited highly stratified societies, some of which consisted of tens of thousands of people, headed by several, pyramidal grades of chiefs, with a 'paramount' at the pinnacle. A wide gap separated chief from commoner. The most centralized and complex of these 'chiefdoms' were only a short step from states, with the main difference lying in their tribal form and scale. The chiefs were the custodians of the tribal cults and rituals. They not only levied tribute and marshalled corvée work, but also organized communal production on a grand scale. 'Functional' anthropologists of an earlier generation used to refer to a 'redistributive' chiefly economy, where production accumulating in the chief's central storage was supposed to have been rationed back to the people. It has since been recognized that the flow of products was distinctly unequal, lavishly maintaining the chiefly elite and their entourage.[132] Warring and raiding between the 'chiefdoms' were incessant, with warrior power as significant inwardly as outwardly. Thus, although the chief's person was sacred, often taboo, and celebrated in elaborate ritual, 'the usurpation of power, by prominent warriors and particularly by junior collaterals of a ruling chief, is a recurrent theme of Polynesian political traditions. . . . Hawaiians say, "Every king acts as a conqueror when he is installed", for if he has not actually sacrificed the late king, he is usually presumed to have poisoned him.' Overt and covert violence dominated foreign, social, and elite relationships in these ritualistic, economic, and military chiefdoms.[133]

Pre-colonial Africa offers another large variety of chiefdoms, existing side by side with 'egalitarian' and stratified tribal societies and with states, in diverse geographical and ecological regions. The pattern, however, is remarkably uniform. 'Aristocrats had a better diet than commoners. . . . They wore rare furs and abundant jewelry in copper and other materials. Rulers had much larger homes and their cattle were more beautiful and numerous. Because they had more cattle they had more wives and children. . . . Raiding was only one of the methods they employed.' They 'built up power in various ways: by attracting clients in time of famine or by controlling scarce resources . . . using various forms of sacred authority to enhance their power'.[134] In Mali of the fourteenth century, 'the underlying political units were local chiefdoms headed by descendants of pioneer colonists, military noblemen dominating commoners and slaves'. In the western savanna, 'the *fama* was both a master of the land and the political chief of a *kafu*'. This tiny polity was described by a nineteenth-century traveller: 'In the middle of the forest are immense clearings several kilometres in diameter. In the centre are grouped seven, eight, ten, often fifteen villages, individually fortified.'[135] Struggles for office within the chiefly families were as endemic and violent as intercommunal conflicts.

Finally, having reviewed quite a number of literary recorded tribal societies in the process of transformation into 'chiefdoms', we are better informed for a glance at the evidence for such prehistoric societies. Here we are entering a world with no individual or communal names, epic traditions, or narrative tales of any sort. There are two main indications in the archaeological record of the process discussed. The principal and universal one is chiefly graves: large burial sites, often very large, erected by communal labour, full of prestige items, including weapons, that testify to the dead person's wealth and status. Second, more ambiguously, fortified sites can sometimes be an indication of developed chiefly seats of centralized chiefdoms. As we have already seen, fortified sites are not always evident even where endemic violence is known to have existed. Where they are evident, they can represent fortified village sites and hilltop refuges of ordinary tribal societies (such as the Maori *pa* in New Zealand), wherein chiefly authority, if it existed at all, was distinctly limited. However, sometimes the excavated site's layout may reveal sharp social differentiation, in chiefly housing, for example, and especially, again, if lavish chiefly burials are unearthed. Such fortified chiefly seats would appear to have been solely associated with chiefdoms—which commanded the authority for their construction—rather than with 'ordinary' tribal chiefs, who did not.

As mentioned earlier, in prehistoric Europe fortified sites appear in the Mediterranean countries and the Balkans since the Neolithic. From the late Bronze Age and particularly the Iron Age, they dot the landscape of western and central Europe. Surprisingly for the world's most excavated continent, the enclosed space of many of these sites has not been seriously dug. It remains unclear in such cases whether they served as fortified villages,

A reconstructed stockade around an early Iron Age settlement at Biskupin, Poland. Lausitz culture. As locally plentiful materials were utilized, wood, earth, clay-mud, and stone were variably used by pre-state societies in different environments around the world

refuge sites for scattered tribal communities, or fortified centres of chiefly leaders and their retinues. In some cases, however, particularly during the late Iron Age, there is evidence of hierarchical spacing out of hilltop forts of various size categories around a central site, as well as of very large and rich chiefly warrior burial mounds and of monopolization of the production and trade of prestige goods. All these testify to the existence of centralized and even complex 'chiefdoms', with paramount chiefs dominating the country-side through subordinate subchiefs and local chiefs.[136] In the south-east European steppe as well, fortified centres and lavish chiefly warrior burials suggest the existence of a strong elite—with at least the occasional ' chief-dom'—among the semi-nomadic 'proto-horse' and chariot Bronze Age pastoralists.[137]

Both in late Neolithic England (the 'age of Stonehenge') and in the North American midwest woodland (Adena and Hopewell cultures), 'religious', 'priestly' chiefdoms are assumed by archaeologists on the basis of

Maiden Castle, near Dorchester, England. Although the multiple earth fortifications in this Iron Age site are enormous, a similar pattern is found in many sites worldwide. The elaborate gate fortifications are more specialized, made necessary by the need to allow in the locals' wheeled vehicles, including chariots

the excavated communities' monumental mounds, which are cult mortuary rather than 'military' constructions. As the communities in question are prehistoric and as the evidence is purely archaeological, it is impossible to determine whether and to what degree a violent aspect was involved in these chiefdoms' make-up. As already seen, in the historically known Hawaiian chiefdoms, for example, shrines and other sacred sites rather than fortifications were built, even though violent conflict was endemic. There are possible indications of warfare and of fortifications in some late Hopewell sites (for example, Fort Hill and Fort Ancient, Ohio), and extensive

227

traces of full-scale intercommunal violence in the later and more complex Mississippian culture, where the large ceremonial mound sites, as well as the villages, were surrounded by palisades. As a recent dedicated survey has concluded: 'hostilities clearly forced people in some places to protect themselves by enclosing their settlements within walls. Despite the strangely persistent image of harmony in prehistory, warfare requiring people to take special measures to protect themselves was commonplace long before Europeans arrived in force in eastern North America.'[138] Similar religious–economic–military 'chiefdoms' existed throughout Central America, some of them giving rise to the Maya polities.[139]

On the whole, it would seem that economic, religious, and military aspects were usually intertwined and often inseparable in the formation of chiefdoms, although figuring variably in different societies and different circumstances.[140] In the ancient Near East, for example, some fortified sites in Anatolia and northern Syria of the fifth millennium BC (for example, Mersin) are interpreted as seats of chiefdom/petty-state heads and their warrior hosts. On the other hand, the Sumerian urban sites are widely believed to have evolved from fifth millennium religious–economic chief–priestly centres (Ubaid). Only with population clustering and the appearance of cities and city walls are warrior leaders supposed to have risen to dominate the Sumerian polities, as they did in historical times.[141] All the same, the limitations of the archaeological evidence and the ethnographic record suggest that the initial concentration of power in prehistoric Sumer is unlikely to have rested on religious–economic factors alone.

How large were the chiefly and 'big men's' retinues of armed men that were instrumental in the transformation of tribal-kin society? Good data are scarce, but wherever figures are available it would appear that even the largest of these armed retinues consisted of no more than a few hundred men, with about 200 as a recurring figure.[142] Smaller retinues were made up of dozens of armed men. It should be remembered, however, that these seemingly modest numbers were not modest at all in the context of tribal society and, indeed, that they could have a snowball effect. As in business, those who have money have the means to make more of it. In a society that had no centralized authority and no centralized standing armed force, armed retinues of 'professional' warriors who owed allegiance to a single man could not be effectively contested by anything other than another armed retinue at the disposal of some other chief or 'big man'. In consequence, as we have seen, the local powerful were able to grow further in power, wealth, and number of clients. Their armed force assumed an onion-like structure. Its inner, standing, and readily usable core was made up of their armed retinue of up to a few hundred 'professional' warriors. But, in time of need, one's clients could be called for assistance, and being powerful meant that one had not only powerful enemies but also powerful friends and allies. As we have seen with the early Roman Fabii and in Caesar's Gaul, all these could bring the number of one's armed supporters to thousands. Furthermore, wherever chiefly heads used their armed retinues to secure more centralized and monopolistic control over tribal society, creating 'chiefdoms', the manpower of the entire tribe, formerly freely participating in armed ventures announced in tribal assemblies, could be called up to participate. To at least some degree, coercive and disciplinary means could now be applied to marshal the men in these tribal and local 'militias'. Again, the Scottish 'clan' chiefdoms and those of Hawaii offer examples of these mandatory military call-ups of the tribal men by their chiefs. Alternatively, successful war leaders conducting large-scale raiding and even occupying land, whose retinues swelled into hosts of thousands by the influx of aspiring warriors from far afield, could turn these hosts into the nucleus of new and independent tribal groupings under their domination.

Correspondingly, a qualitative differentiation took place among the warriors of the transforming tribal society. The standing retinues of young warriors who made warfare their occupation were elite forces. Growing social stratification affected the famously free farmer–warriors who had constituted the backbone of traditional tribal society—indeed, in many ways, *had been* tribal society. (The very word for a people in many languages originally often had at least the connotation of an armed host—Old German *heri, folk, liuti*; early Greek *laos*.[143]) The more well-to-do 'free holders' more or less retained their military role. But of those who increasingly lost their property and independence and assumed a client status in relation to the powerful, not much was expected, even when they were called upon in times of necessity to broaden their master's support base. The lower one's stake in society and in the profits of conflict, the lower one's motivation as a warrior. Furthermore, as a rule, a life–long habit of servitude made for poor warriors. The more tribal societies were transformed by growing stratification and rising chiefly and 'big men's' power, the more they lost their celebrated simple and unruly, 'egalitarian', warrior prowess. On the other hand, as instruments of power, more centralized polities could compensate for that loss by more authoritative forms of mobilization and command, and by greater scale.

10

Armed Force in the Emergence of the State

The early state is a deceptively familiar phenomenon. Literacy—for which the state is a necessary (though not a sufficient) precondition—brings about a quantum leap in the quantity and quality of the information at our disposal in comparison with earlier phases of human development. But the light of history is like the proverbial lamppost that makes only the coins under it shine. In the minds of most people, the relatively 'solid' reality of the last few millennia—a mere fraction of our past—*is* our past. Furthermore, within this picture, states already figure almost full blown from the start. Their growth, which like that of any social institution was an evolutionary and gradual process, is necessarily obscured in pre- and proto-history, because, as mentioned, literacy itself came only with state society and, thus, developed after its formation. The question addressed in this chapter, then, is how states evolved and what role violent conflict played in this process.

The materials and method that I have used in approaching this question are in principle similar to those employed earlier in the book. Evidence is drawn from archaeology as well as from the written records of literate cultures that came in contact with more backward societies undergoing the transformation into statehood. Furthermore, oral traditions of the pre- and early state period, written down later in its development, become a widely available and highly significant source, which in many cases contributes to

231

making the growth of the state a proto- rather than a prehistorical process. As before, evidence from a large variety of evolving states, drawn from around the globe and across 'relative' time, is examined comparatively. As I hope to have demonstrated, the faint echoes from pre- and protohistory, which regularly leave the student of a single society with little that can be securely relied upon, can become much clearer patterns when similar evidence repeatedly re-emerges and reinforces itself across the ethnographic record. Whereas in 'unified history', the state—followed by urban and literate civilization—emerged some 5,000 years ago in Sumer and Egypt, in the relative frame used in this book, state emergence from stratified/chiefly tribal society—with all the related marks of the state period—kept occurring in different and variably connected regions of the world almost up to the present. This is not to argue that all evolving states were the same—far from it. Different states, evolving in different ecological niches and social circumstances, took somewhat different evolutionary paths. All the same, environmental constraints and human propensities were responsible for a fundamentally limited variety and significant similarities among them. Both variety and similarities are considered.

What state emerged first in absolute chronology matters, of course, to the extent that earlier states generated further state formation around them—as both internal evolution and outside influences are significant for the way that states came into being. Internally, state evolution was the almost 'necessary' culmination and fruition of processes set in motion by the transition to and growth of agriculture—at least where the right conditions were present. This is strikingly demonstrated by the fact that the four regions of the globe where states first emerged were the very same original centres of the agricultural revolution: the Near East, north China, Mesoamerica, and the Andes. In all these centres, independently and separated by thousands of years in absolute chronology, yet with remarkably similar trajectories, it took more or less five millennia for agriculture and agricultural society to evolve to the point where state structures emerged. There is scant evidence of any significant connection between the earliest centres of state emergence on the opposite sides of Asia, or between those of Central and South America. Claims of significant connections between the Old and New Worlds are even less sustainable. Thus, in these separate 'laboratories', processes of state formation were independently taking place, spontaneously activated by similar processes, but measured by separate clocks on relative time.

Internal processes of evolution within agricultural tribal societies were paramount in the emergence of all other states as well. However, to a greater or lesser degree their growth was affected by diffusion, the radiation of state influence from earlier zones of state formation. Does this make these states, often referred to as 'secondary' states, a wholly separate category from the so-called pristine states, possessing a different developmental history, as some scholars believe?[1] My view of this question is flexible: some states from other than the four 'earliest' regions of state formation were sufficiently isolated to claim pristine or almost pristine status themselves; the formation of others was heavily affected by existing states, making the process and trajectory of their growth somewhat different; still others fall in between. The designation 'secondary' lumps together all these states in too sharp a dichotomy from pristine states. Furthermore, I argue that the designation 'pristine' itself is misleading. Even in the earliest regions of state formation no state was truly 'pristine' in the accepted sense that assumes that it was created under no interaction with other states. In all the 'pristine' centres as well—Sumer, Egypt, north China, Mesoamerica (Olmec), and the Andes— states emerged as part of a local states *system* and co-evolved in interaction with the other nascent states in this system.[2] From this perspective and taking all variations into account, evidence from across space and relative time furnishes a substantial number of diverse historical instances of state formation.

What were the internal and external forces, the operation of which gave rise to the state? I excuse myself from going into many, much rehashed debates on this subject in the anthropological literature, because most of these debates have more or less exhausted themselves, and the broad trend has more recently been towards synthesis and multivariable explanations.[3] Neither elite coercion from above nor the social and economic needs of a more complex society from below would now be regarded alone as the mechanism of state formation, but rather some combination of these forces. Nor has much faith survived in any single factor—'prime mover'—that can in itself be credited with responsibility for the formation of the state: be it war, religion, irrigation agriculture, or trade. It is the combined processes of power accumulation experienced by stratified/chiefly tribal society that formed the basis for the emergence of the state power structure. These interrelated processes, described in Chapter 9, included: agricultural intensification; demographic growth; increasing economic and social stratification;

and enhanced power of 'big men' and chiefs, relying on retinues of clients and armed men, largely built on the spoils of raiding and tightening their hold on communal (and increasingly centralized) ritual, cult, and magic.

In different societies the road to power accumulation involved various blends of these factors, but hardly ever was any of these factors absent. It has been suggested, for example, that staple economy cum priestly type leadership was more prominent in the evolution of polities in some regions, and elite-led warrior groups in others.[4] In the archaeology of power this is reflected in the conspicuousness of cult structures in the former and of military construction in the latter—temples versus castles—both of which could evolve to monumental scale. However, although this distinction has a strong foundation in reality, a more intricate interrelationship is revealed wherever literary records are available to supplement purely material finds. Forms of power flow and translate into each other, or, to put it in a less reified manner, possessors of power move to expand and guard it, among other things by gaining hold and tightening their grip on the various levers of power. No effective state power can maintain control, defend its realm against outsiders, or safeguard against usurpation without a substantial underpinning of force. We have already seen all this in the discussion of chiefdoms, with the diverse Polynesian island societies serving as a prime example. In all of them, fighting was endemic. Hawaii, for example, one of the most complex and hierarchical of these societies, is a model irrigation–staple-economy cum religious chiefdom/nascent state, yet inter-polity fighting, social coercion, and violent usurpation were the rule before and during contact, even though only religious and no military construction are detectable in the archaeological remains. As we see later, the evidence reveals a no less violent picture in other archaeologically known 'priestly' polities, earlier believed by many to have experienced a peaceful existence.

Some formal criteria of what it is that makes a state are customarily put forward. It is generally agreed that, compared with pre-state society, the state employed central coercive power on a new level to command obedience, to organize society, and to mobilize resources. What made this possible was the supplementation of kin-based relations by other means of social power. A multilayered state apparatus, largely based on hierarchical power relations and benefits allocation, became dominant in the public domain. Although all this is widely accepted, it must be stressed that kin affiliations remained central to social networks, loyalties, and behaviour under the state: within the ruling elite, in social networks at large, and as a constitutive element of ethnicity. Furthermore, the new, supra-kin apparatus of state power grew from pre-state processes and structures rather than suddenly appearing in 'ideal form'. No formal criterion or 'definition' should obscure the fact that the early state did not emerge full blown and in a clear-cut form. Its formation was a process rather than a one-time event, which regularly took generations and centuries to unfold.

This process involved the accumulation and concentration of power to the point where it could be institutionalized and upgraded to a new level. This seems to have been mostly achieved by individual leaders and their followers who succeeded in gaining the ascendancy over their contenders within the elite, but sometimes in a more collective elite form. Wherever such foci of state power were emerging, an upward leap in power effectiveness was being gained, feeding on itself in a positive loop mechanism. Private retinues were turned into state household troops and a nucleus standing army. Freely assembled tribal and local militias were becoming subject to compulsory levy and call-ups. Military leadership could enforce discipline on the armed hosts. 'Gifts' and services to chiefs and 'big men' were being turned into regular taxes and corvée labour. In turn, conquered land and increasing spoils of war gained by all these means mainly flowed into the hands of rulers, further enhancing their power. In this way, independent foci of power within segmentary society could be driven to subordination, disparate tribal units within the same *ethnos* could be welded together and amalgamated, and outside tribes and *ethnies* could be assimilated. A process of 'state building' took place.

From the very beginning, this process of state growth and expansion tended to follow a pattern: in every stage, domination was initially extended through hegemonic rule, 'suzerainty', or 'overlordship', which was gradually transformed, where it did, into a more unified, direct, and bureaucratic structure. A deeply grounded causal mechanism accounts for this recurring pattern. Peripheral elites were driven into submission to a political centre by a combination of superior force and the promise of retention of their local dominance; both coercion and co-optation were involved. Equally, rule through intermediate local elites harnessed traditional legitimacy, as well as being the simplest method of central domination, requiring minimal administrative machinery. It took time for both the processes of internal integration and the development of a more elaborate central administration to reach a point where a more unified polity would form. This recurring pattern of development from hegemonic overlordship into more direct rule has not been well recognized in the scholarly literature on the early state, even though it has been widely noted in particular studies of specific polities and has been well identified with respect to the development of empires.[5] The reason for this failure, again, is that the early stages of state evolution are all too often shrouded in the mists of pre- and protohistory, taking place, as they did, before the development of writing, which could have recorded them.

Emergent, nucleus state structure acted as the main catalyst for state expansion in a tribal/chiefly environment, while also contending with other emerging state nuclei, if several such nuclei evolved more or less simultaneously in an interrelated process. Presenting a comparative overview of the fragmented evidence from quite a number of pre- and protohistorical cases, this chapter aims to reconstruct the role and characteristic features of armed forces in relation to the evolving structure of the early state, in its various types.

WARFARE IN THE MAKING OF RURAL PETTY-STATES AND STATES

State Creation in the Tribal Zone

The formation of the Zulu kingdom under Shaka in the early nineteenth century, in what was later known as Zululand and Natal in South Africa, is a popular case study of state emergence.[6] For the Zulu state formation dates very late in terms of absolute time—the latest example that is examined here—and was therefore well recorded by Europeans who arrived shortly after the event. Nevertheless, it took place in a tribal/chiefly zone before serious contact with Europeans and with little outside influence. It thus constitutes an almost pristine case, located very early in *relative* time. Furthermore, this early state formation left virtually no archaeological markers, such as monumental construction. It can thus serve as an archetype of similar, presumed but unrecorded occurrences of early state formation of a predominantly military nature in the prehistoric agricultural tribal/

236

chiefly zone. More generally, the Zulu case fully exhibits features that are familiar from many other known instances of state formation.

The Zulu state emerged within the realm of a single ethnic stock, or *ethnos*, the Nguni-speaking Bantu, who practised cattle raising and shifting agriculture. As mentioned in Chapter 9, an *ethnos* is not a political entity. Until the late eighteenth century, the Nguni were divided among many, 'politically' separate chiefdoms that incorporated separate tribes and sub-tribes. Clans were the dominant social bodies, and chiefs' retinues regularly numbered no more than a few dozen men. Violent struggles of inheritance within the chiefly families after the death of chiefs were commonplace. Frequent inter-chiefdom warfare took the familiar dual form of raids—mainly for cattle, the main property and measure of wealth—and of low-casualty spear-throwing battles, neither involving more than a few hundred warriors on each side. The chiefdoms' small kinship-based structure precluded wars of subjugation. However, at the beginning of the nineteenth century, one chieftain, Dingiswayo, succeeded in breaking away from the power constraints of kinship, into formative kingship. By force of arms coupled with moderation, he gradually extended overlordship over other chiefdoms, retaining their ruling clans in place but often substituting the former chief with a junior member of the same clan, who thus owed him his position. He also dismantled the old clan-based militia, establishing in its place permanent age-grade units from mixed localities with appointed officers at their heads. These supra-tribal warrior units, kept on the spoils of war, in turn formed the basis for further conquests and power accumulation. Some 30 different tribes came under Dingiswayo's overlordship. Although warfare paved the way for this expanding realm, domestic peace was proclaimed within it, with the supreme ruler acting as high judge.

After Dingiswayo was killed in 1817, his nascent kingdom was fought for and taken over by one of his best military commanders, Shaka of the Zulu clan, which gave the new realm its name. Shaka continued with Dingiswayo's methods, supplementing them only with proverbial cruelty and new battle tactics—the two elements being not entirely unrelated. He forced his warriors to substitute a new thrusting spear and close-in assaults for the traditional spear-throwing battles. The bloody, all-out battle, which we tend to identify with warfare in world history but which was in fact everywhere a novelty in the tribal zone, was thus initiated in Zululand, terrifying Shaka's opponents. Hosts of refugees swept through southern Africa. Shaka's armed force grew to several tens of thousand men, many of them permanently employed in raiding across the Zulu borders. They were posted in 'barracks' around the realm, away from their original tribes, so that they could not serve local tribal resistance. Shaka's kingdom expanded to perhaps as much as 200,000 square kilometres—roughly the size of England—and its population numbered in the low hundred thousands. Among the means that Shaka used to consolidate his realm was the institution of communal rituals, associated with and presided over by himself, which supplemented the traditional family ancestral worship and village cults.

In 1828, Shaka's reign of terror ended with his assassination by his half-brother, who after his own reign of terror was deposed in 1840 by a still younger half-brother. This more moderate ruler, Mpande, continued to pursue the consolidation of the kingdom. He transformed tribal domains into state territorial administrative districts, and placed his many sons from polygynous marriages in important administrative positions. At the same time, he married his daughters to distinguished people and local chiefs, while marrying their daughters, thus further tightening the ruling kin network around the crown. An increasingly stronger sense of Zulu identity and unity was being forged and gradually coming into being. Meanwhile, other African states had emerged on the borders of the Zulu state, partly under its impact. Furthermore, from the mid-1830s the Afrikaner trek from the Cape to Natal had been taking place, leading to bloody encounters with the Zulu. Coexistence of a sort prevailed during Mpande's reign, but not long after his death in 1872 the Zulu state came to the end of its independence as the British Empire established control over it. The fearsome Zulu mass charges were famously broken by western firepower.

A British official described the Zulu nation and state somewhat partially as 'a collection of tribes, more or less autonomous, and more or less discontented; a rope of sand whose only cohesive property was furnished by the presence of the Zulu ruling family and its command of a standing army.'[7] Although there was a very substantial grain of truth in this, reality was more complex. As already mentioned, armed force was instrumental in generating all features of state formation that are encountered again and again: the expansion of nucleus state power by the combined coercion and co-optation of formerly independent chiefs within a system of overlordship; the harnessing of both kinship ties within the new pan-elite and supra-kin institutions to strengthen state rule; the assumption of supreme military, judicial, and religious authority by the overlord; and, over time, the welding of the realm into an increasingly unified state through increasing bureaucratization and processes of cultural fusion and common identity formation.

All these processes are also evident in the tribal states of east Africa (in today's Uganda), another prime example of early state formation that is lit by historical and protohistorical sources while being sufficiently isolated. Europeans first arrived in the region in 1862, finding there the states of Buganda, Ankole, Bunyoro, and Toro. Although these states varied substantially in size and power, they all extended over tens of thousands of square kilometres and their populations numbered in the hundreds of thousands. Oral traditions and king lists—supported by archaeological evidence from royal graves and shrines—indicate state history in the region of some five centuries. As mentioned in Chapter 9, successive waves of pastoral immigrations from the north may have provided the states' first ruling elites. State and empire building was carried out by emergent royal clans, coercing and co-opting local chiefs who were incorporated into the state structure. The chiefs collected taxes and gifts, maintaining a delicate balance within the royal court, a balance fostered by marriage ties, benefit allocation, and the prospect of promotion as state officials. The court camp itself, with its state officials and huge royal harem, was frequently moved from place to place. The divine and sacred king presided over elaborate state ritual. Youths from all over the realm were called up for training in the vicinity of the royal court and were garrisoned in the provinces under appointed officers. Local militias were called upon in time of war, which consisted of cattle raiding, tribute taking, conquest, and the transformation of neighbouring polities into dependent satellites. Murderous struggles for succession among a deceased king's sons as well as other members of the royal clan were no less endemic.[8] As with the Zulu, force was central to every aspect of state formation in east Africa. Force capability increased with size, growing in a positive feedback process with every further expansion. In addition, force increased through the centralization and regimentation of the tribal armed forces, which made these forces far more available and subject to control under much wider circumstances determined by the state.

It is mainly in these factors that the power advantage of states over tribal societies lay. Man to man, tribal warriors were more than a match for state conscripts, and many tribal lands—although not as densely populated as the state-civilization zone—could potentially produce a large number of fighting men. Still, tribal societies were of small scale, were divided among themselves, and possessed little coercive power over their members. Although emergencies and desperate situations such as enemy invasion or tribal migration could force a general participation in warfare, such concerted efforts were hard to sustain for long, and in other circumstances self-interest and self-preservation encouraged 'defection' from the common effort. Among other things, states greatly reduced 'cheating' and worked to eliminate 'free riders' by coercing their members into co-operation, in either these members' 'genuine' interest, thus relieving them from a 'prisoner's dilemma', or the ruler's interest, or in any combination of the two.

According to the biblical protohistorical tradition, for example, this was the crucial action taken by the founder of the Israelite state, King Saul, elected to unite a disparate and shifting tribal conglomeration against increasing foreign state power on its borders. Faced with an Ammonite attack in Trans-Jordan, which earlier would have been confronted only by the locals, 'he took a yoke of oxen, and cut them in pieces, and sent them throughout all the borders of Israel by the hand of messengers, saying, whosoever cometh not forth after Saul and after Samuel, so shall it be done unto his oxen. And the dread of the Lord fell on the people, and they came out as one man' (1 *Samuel* 11.7). After his victory, in a forming state that recalls the rural tribal kingdoms of east Africa, Saul kept with him 3,000 men as a newly instituted permanent army, with which he was able to enforce his authority on tribal society and strengthen his control of the tribal militia (1 *Samuel* 13.2).

Moving to more solid historical ground, the same drawbacks from which tribal societies suffered is evident, for instance, in Julius Caesar's conquest of Gaul, whose population of some five million succumbed to a Roman army of 80,000 soldiers at most (eight legions and auxiliaries).[9] Again, it was precisely these drawbacks that Vercingetorix, the leader of the general revolt against the Romans in the later stage of Caesar's campaigning, tried to remedy. He set quotas of soldiers and arms to each tribal canton and, similar to Shaka, strove to enforce state-like disciplinary measures. As Caesar writes (*The Gallic War* 7.4):

> To the utmost care he added the utmost strictness of command, compelling waverers by severity of punishment. Indeed for the commission of a greater offence he put to death with fire and all manner of torture; for a lesser case he sent a man home with his ears cut off or one eye gouged out, to point the moral to the rest and terrify others by the severity of the penalty.

One could hardly learn from Caesar that ruthless—more regulated—disciplinary measures were fundamental to the Roman state's military system.

According to Caesar, Vercingetorix's father was himself an important chieftain who aspired to kingship in Gaul and was executed for that. As already seen, in the increasingly stratified Gallic society of the time 'the more powerful chiefs, and such as had the means to hire men, commonly endeavoured to make themselves kings' (*The Gallic Wars*, 2.1). Although Caesar may have played on the Roman aversion to kingship in attributing this motive to the barbarian leaders who opposed him, his was not mere rhetoric. Command over men in successful wars was the major avenue to kingship, because: it could enrich the successful war leader and expand his retinue and clientèle above those of his peers and contenders, the other tribal powerful; because it could win him prestige and empower him with popular support and legitimacy within the tribe, again with the same result; or, indeed, because it could attract to him a host of warriors from far afield, thus creating around him an independent power base outside his original tribe.

These variably connected intra- and extra-tribe politics of power accumulation through military leadership are, again, demonstrated by Vercingetorix, who started out his revolt against Roman rule by gathering an armed host from among his native Arverni around the flag of liberty. By this means he was able to drive out his rivals in the Arverni elite (*The Gallic War*, 7.4). Orgetorix, the Helvetti aristocrat who initiated their massive invasion of Gaul that served as the pretext for Caesar's initial intervention, was also alleged by Caesar to have been motivated by the desire for kingship over his people (1.2–4). At the same time, as Caesar entered Gaul from the south, the warrior leader Ariovistus was carving for himself a Germanic proto-kingdom in north-eastern Gaul, into which he invaded and attracted armed men and part tribes from all over western Germania (1.31 and 1.51). His nascent state building, and subjugation of the local Celt tribes, were terminated by Caesar only in a gigantic campaign and battle that drove the defeated Germans in flight back across the Rhine.

Whether or not there were other, earlier warrior kings-in-being in the expanding Germanic realm before Ariovistus, who is the first to come under historical light through Roman records, is difficult to say. The answer is obscured in prehistory.[10] Others, however, would follow, recorded by the

241

Romans, and increasingly influenced by the growing Roman presence in a way that Ariovistus's rise to power had barely been. Rising to power not long after Ariovistus, the Marcomanni's Maroboduus best exemplifies the new authority of the early Germanic warrior-king. Historian E. A. Thompson offers a keen anthropological analysis of the processes involved:

> Maroboduus, leader of the Marcomanni, was the first German known to us who transformed his position from that of a confederate chieftain dependent on the goodwill of his people into that of a monarch who could impose his will on his subjects. In one of the last years B.C. Maroboduus had withdrawn the Marcomanni in the face of the Roman advance into western Germany and had led them from the Main valley to new homes in Bohemia. . . . In Bohemia he built himself a 'palace' which lay close to, but was nevertheless distinct from, his people's stronghold. . . . [W]e do not know precisely how he won his despotic power or what role his retinue played in winning it for him.[11]

It seems, however, clear that, as in other places, a transformation of the free tribal militia—fighting in a loose formation and led merely by example in heroic fashion—was an integral part of Maroboduus's project:

> The adoption of something like a State army was only possible when something like a State organization of society in general had taken the place of the organization based on the clans. . . . This alteration in the character of the army . . . presupposes a higher degree of coercive power than existed elsewhere in Germany.[12]

As with the Zulu and east Africa, the creation of supra-kin state machinery, including its military part, made possible further external expansion, and vice versa:

> It is not accidental, then, that Maroboduus' name is also associated with another innovation in Germanic history. In general, the wars fought between themselves by the Germanic peoples . . . were fought for the possession of disputed lands, for cattle, prestige, and so on. In extreme cases they might end in the migration of the weaker side . . . or even in something like the annihilation of one of the people concerned. But from the beginning of the Christian era a new kind of war begins to make its appearance. . . . This is the war which ends in the subjugation of the beaten side and of its reduction to the status of subjects of the conquerors.[13]

Earlier, there had been 'no administrative machinery for collecting tribute, taxes, or the like'. Now, however rudimentary Maroboduus's state apparatus remained, spoils of war were kept in the 'palace and adjoining fortress'.[14] From his Bohemian formative state, Maroboduus 'engaged in a series of wars with his new neighbours . . . which left them subject to his rule; and he forced their warriors to accompany him on his campaigns and to fight for him'.[15] A snowball effect was created. 'Indeed, his empire was very large, for from his headquarters in Bohemia he even ruled over the Lombards, who are thought to have lived at this date in the lower part of the basin of the Elbe.'[16]

While Maroboduus was replaying Ariovistus's nascent-state building on a grander scale, the young Cherusci nobleman and war chief Arminius was restaging, in western Germany, Vercingetorix's general revolt cum nation and state building against the Romans with greater success, at least as concerns the first part of this project. The famous destruction of three Roman legions in an ambush at the marshy Teutoburg Forest in AD 9 effectively ended the Roman attempt during Augustus's reign to subjugate Germania. Although this result was certainly dramatic, its causes were less so. The Roman disaster was an exceptional event. In the years immediately before and after it, Roman armies operated victoriously throughout Germany. All the same, Emperor Tiberius's historic decision in AD 16 to abandon the conquest of Germany simply recognized that, in a remote, wild, and poor country, beyond the urban (oppida) line, it was difficult to keep elusive tribal people down and that the prospective gains were in any case not worth the effort. The Romans opted for indirect control and divide-and-rule policies through the tribal elite, which was swayed and manipulated by gifts, imperial honours and prestige, Roman education, and deterrence—policies that on the whole would serve the Romans well for centuries.

It is, however, Arminius's, rather than the Roman, activity within this tribal environment that is of interest to us here. During the struggle against Rome, he tried to introduce better discipline and more systematic war making among the tribal hosts, and to coerce waverers and collaborators with the enemy. Nevertheless, he continued to operate within the limits set by tribal institutions and tribal traditions and had to contend with the other tribal powerful, who often rejected his plans if they did not oppose him outright. As in Vercingetorix's case, this opposition included leading men from Arminius's own closest family, who advocated different policies and held their own ambitions. Yet, unlike Vercingetorix, Arminius did not reach for king-like powers to suppress them during the war. After it, however, he did try to emulate his contemporary and rival Maroboduus in establishing autocratic rule over his people by means of his retinue. In the end, he was killed treacherously by his own kinsmen.[17] Maroboduus, too, was finally driven out by the Marcomanni elite and people, and his nascent state disintegrated.

These echoes of early kingship in the Germanic realm help to demonstrate how frail and susceptible to disintegration the early state structure tended to be. Again, this fact has attracted little scholarly attention because in most cases it remains half-hidden in pre- and protohistory. Popular and particularly elite resistance to the loss of the old freedoms combined with weak socioeconomic infrastructure, capable of supporting a developed state apparatus, in making early states a tenuous institution. The gradual emergence and consolidation of states—the fact that they increasingly came to stay and grow to dominate both the internal and the external arenas—were intertwined with a number of continuous, mutually dependent, and mutually reinforcing processes: growing social stratification and economic complexity, which in turn eroded the primacy of kin networks as the constitutive element of society and facilitated the intensification of the state structure and apparatus; growth in states' size; and expansion of the state system as a whole. The overall historical trend of states was in these directions.[18]

From Petty-States to States: The North European Laboratory

In some cases, a single nucleus predominated in the consolidation of a state structure, which fairly rapidly and extensively expanded in a tribal/chiefly space. However, in other, perhaps most, cases, state consolidation was carried out simultaneously by several competing state nuclei, resulting in much smaller early state units. This petty-state 'missing link' constitutes yet another lacuna in the scholarly literature on early state evolution. There have been many references to 'princely states', princedoms, or principalities (Fürstentum), 'petty-states' (Kleinstaat), and even 'micro-states', as well as to petty-kings (Kleinkönig) as opposed to great kings (Grosskönig), but no systematic recognition of how prevalent the petty-state 'phase' was in the growth of states.

The reason for this lacuna is the very same problem of pre- and protohistoric obscurity. Indeed, the only type of petty-state that is widely recognized is the city-state, again, precisely because its advanced urban and literate culture puts it clearly in the light of history. The city-state is discussed in the

second part of the chapter; it was, however, only one form and one developmental path of petty-states. Some scholars have conflated the city-state with
that other form that will be termed here the rural petty-state. Others have
posited city-states and 'village', 'territorial', or 'country' states as the two
types of early state, while assuming that the latter emerged on a large geographical scale from the start.[19] In fact, more often than not, the large-scale
'territorial', 'village', or 'country' state, too, evolved gradually and from a
petty-state system. Rural petty-states rather than tribes and chiefdoms were
welded together in this process.

Let us return to the growth of Germanic kingship. Germanic societies
underwent a number of interrelated processes during the first centuries AD:
interaction with the Roman Empire increased through trading, raiding, war,
political dependence, and mercenary service; agricultural intensification,
demographic growth, and social stratification took place; larger tribal confederations, such as the Franks, Alamanni, and Saxons, were coming into
being; and 'petty-kings' became increasingly evident among some of the
Germanic peoples from the third century AD on. Among the Goths of the
fourth century, for example, both Roman records and archaeological evidence of fortified centres suggest the emergence of perhaps as many as six
independent kingly domains, ruling over separate tribal groupings of various
sorts.[20] The Alamanni during the third century alternated between small
kings/chiefs and the occasional major war-making king, mainly rising in
connection with war with the Roman Empire.[21] Among the Franks of the
fourth and fifth centuries there were simultaneously a number of petty-
kings (*reguli*), each ruling over a separate tribal grouping. In all these cases,
warrior retinues played a dominant role in the establishment and exercise of
royal power, and in all of them the line between centralized 'chiefdoms' and
nascent kingship was thin, somewhat arbitrary, or, most accurately,
evolutionary.

Indeed, 'full-scale' Germanic kingships and more solid, although
still rudimentary, state structures were formed only among some of the
Germanic ethnic formations with the great migrations into the Roman
Empire. Large-scale, successful, military leadership increased royal authority,
wealth, and power. The occupation of foreign lands and foreign peoples
weakened the invaders' old tribal kinship ties and subsumed them within
the newly created mixed societies/polities. Surviving Roman administrative
and tax-collecting systems were taken over by the new successor states. Thus

245

Visigoth, Ostrogoth, Burgundian, Vandal, and Langobard states came into being around new 'national' kings, whereas the Alamanni, for example, which had maintained tribal/chiefly institutions and had developed no unified kingly state, found themselves at a disadvantage. Among the Franks of the late fifth and early sixth centuries, King Clovis disposed of all the other Frankish 'petty-kings', having them killed brutally and treacherously, sometimes by his own hands, including many of his blood relations. He started out with a retinue that is estimated at no more than 400–500 warriors, incorporating the defeated rulers' retinues as he went.[22] Thus Clovis's successful war making, which expanded Frankish rule in northern and then into southern Gaul, strengthened his hand in intra-Frankish politics; in turn, his state and nation building made the Franks yet stronger and even more successful in their outward expansion.

The gradual, centuries-long, interrelated processes of state emergence, consolidation, and expansion took a more or less similar form in Germanic Anglo-Saxon England. Angles, Saxons, and Jutes arrived in Britain from the fifth century AD on as raiders, mercenaries, usurpers of local power, and, increasingly, immigrant settlers. The many petty-kingdoms that emerged around individual war leaders and their retinues were, over the following centuries, subject to what one historian has called 'a knock-out competition' that progressively decreased their number. The remaining petty-states known from the seventh century, when the veil of prehistory begins to lift—those of Kent, the West, South, and East Saxons, East Angles, Mercia, and Northumberland—were also occasionally welded together under the 'suzerainty' of one of their number through violence, coercion, and co-optation, only repeatedly to disintegrate into their constitutive parts after the death of the successful overlord. Only in the late eighth century did the kings of Mercia (whose estimated population of about 12,000 households typifies the size of these petty-states) manage to effect a more stable union of all the southern and some of the northern petty-kingdoms under their overlordship. The kings of Wessex established their suzerainty a century later, after Mercia had been destroyed by the Vikings. A 'unified' Anglo-Saxon kingdom was thus coming into being.[23] In Celtic Ireland and Wales as well, from the fifth to the twelfth centuries, petty-kings rose over local chiefs, forming states of perhaps some 1,500 square kilometres and constantly fighting and raiding each other in pursuit of hegemony and booty (mainly cattle). Over time, the number of these petty-states shrank, because some were being swallowed by others, with 'superior kings' (*ruiri*) and 'kings of superior kings' (*ri ruirech*) extending overlordship over continuously growing parts of the country.[24]

Whereas evidence about the British Isles' Dark Age is meagre, that which relates to Scandinavia barely exists. Still, the outline of state development there was similar. Kings emerged in Denmark around the sixth century AD—more or less by the time that they are known to have been present in Sweden—and around the late ninth century in Norway. As in other places, they were kings *in* rather than *of* these latter-day countries. How many they were and how stable their lineages proved to be are unknown. According to one, potentially instructive computation, relating to the later Viking period, more than a third of the Norwegian kings died in battle and another third were banished. At any rate, in the following centuries the rulers of these state nuclei progressively expanded their realms, eliminating rival state nuclei and extending overlordship over the local powerful. In this bloody process, they substituted earldom status for independence to those who submitted to them, or replaced them with the king's own kin and followers.[25]

In all these cases the same features are discernible. The core of kingly power was their retinue, turned into royal 'household' or rudimentary professional troops. In some cases, true mercenary units were employed, mainly but not only where foreign ethnic troops of ferocious warrior reputation were involved (for example, Vikings in Ireland). King Miesco, for instance, suddenly appears in the light of history in the tenth century at the head of a Polish state, the establishment of which followed an obscure period of consolidation from Slav tribal entities (including the eponymous Polanie) and petty-states (such as that of the 'Vistulanians' around latter-day Kracow). He commanded a paid retinue of 3,000 armed men.[26] In an onion-like or snowball model of power, the subordination of the local powerful to the emergent overlord tied them and their own semi-permanent service/warrior retinues as the second major component of the state's armed force. Finally, the overlord and provincial leaders marshalled the local militia, which were subject to a general call-up in times of emergency and to more selective recruitment in lesser cases.[27] Before their conversion to Christianity, kings in all the above-mentioned cases commonly claimed divine descent and performed a liturgical–magical function.[28]

The warrior retinues that were instrumental in the formation of states could come from outside as well as from inside the tribal/stratified societies.

The emergence of Rus, the earliest state polities in today's Russia and Ukraine from about AD 750, is a striking case in point, even if its precise details—as with all state formations—are obscure in protohistory. They must be reconstructed with the aid of archaeology from the oral traditions codified in the *Primary Chronicle* in twelfth-century Kiev. Rus is actually the Western Finnic and Estonian name for Swedes, who by the time of the western voyages of their neighbours in Norway and Denmark had sailed the eastern Baltic and down the tributaries of the rivers Volga and Dnieper, trading in furs, slaves, and silver with the eastern Roman Empire, the Islamic Caliphate, and the Turkic Kazars and Bulgars of the lower Volga. Organized similarly to their western kin in semi-egalitarian armed bands around a war leader, they opportunistically traded, raided, pirated, looted, exacted tribute, kidnapped, and raped. The evidence suggests that deadly violence and feuds among themselves were also rife. They established settlements/trading posts, some of them fortified, along the river highways, first in the north around lakes Ladoga and Ilmen (of which Novgorod would later become the most famous), and then, from the late ninth century, further south, most notably at Kiev. From these settlements they extended their rule over the surrounding area, thinly populated by loosely organized Balt- and Slav-speaking tribes, who possessed only an elementary material culture.

We have little information about the exact mechanism of this process, but 'protection' of sorts—that is, tribute for defence against the Kazar and Bulgar steppe nomads in the south and, indeed, from the Northmen themselves—was involved, as well as trade with the heads of the local clans who also gave women in marriage to the newcomers. The emergent small polities evolved from chiefdoms into petty-states of a fortified town and countryside, each headed by the former band leader–adventurer turned Khagan (chief) and then prince. The Scandinavian elite host of raiders and traders adopted the east Slavic language of the locals, and a process of pagan and shamanist syncretism was taking place before the adoption of Christianity. From the late tenth to the mid-eleventh centuries, the princes of Kiev expanded overlordship over Ukraine and the north, raiding and campaigning as far as the Balkans. Thereafter, the realm again fragmented into independent, often warring petty-states, each with its own prince surrounded by his armed retinue of a few hundred, a local militia, and, occasionally, some mercenary forces.[29]

The Scandinavia from which the 'Rus' arrived was more entrepreneurial and war-like, but only slightly more politically organized than the Balts and Slavs upon which the newcomers established their rule. However, in other cases, a foreign leader and his retinue came from a neighbouring developed state, or were even invited by a tribal–chiefly society in order to help it cope with the challenge posed by foreign state power. For example, early Rome's last three kings carry Etruscan names. Archaeology suggests that whereas the earlier *reges*/confederate war chiefs of Roman traditions had belonged to a simple rural–tribal society, the Etruscan kings' reign tallies with the growth of urbanism and statehood in both Etruria and Rome in the seventh and sixth centuries BC. Scholars once believed that Etruscan occupation was responsible for the transformation of Rome. However, no such occupation is mentioned by the Roman sources, and the Etruscan themselves were divided among antagonistic city-states and formed no unified empire. It is more likely that Etruscan war-band leader adventurers took over or were welcomed to Roman state leadership. It has been proposed, for example, that King Servius Tullius of the mid–sixth century BC, in many ways perhaps the real founder of the Roman state and army, was a figure of this nature.[30]

Indeed, although some coercion is likely to have been involved in such takeovers, a ruler from outside could be a more attractive proposition than is intuitively realized. The tribal powerful, who viciously competed with each other for leadership, power, and prestige, often preferred a foreign ruler to the election of one of their own. The Aztecs, for example, entered the Valley of Mexico in the early fourteenth century AD as a poor and backward tribal society that settled at the periphery of the region's advanced urban states and was ruthlessly dominated by them. To cope, they substituted the regular office of king (*tlacochcalcatl*) for their paramount war chief, inviting the foreign aristocratic Acamapichtli from the city-state of Colhuacan to take up the post. The new king married the daughters of each of the 20 tribal clan (*calpolli*) heads, who thus linked themselves to, and ensured their interests with, the new regime.

As a result of Roman and Church literacy, northern Europe—similar to the Zulu—offers fragmented but better–than–usual evidence for the inherently shadowy process of state formation. Clearly, however, interaction with Mediterranean civilization was decisive in the north European cases. For this reason and because of the backwardness of the north European societies, predatory warrior bands proved to be the main instrument of power accumulation on these societies' road to statehood. However, did these instances (and the Aztec) not represent a quintessential 'secondary' state formation? And in any event, as Marx and Engels and later scholarship have noted, did the 'Germanic state' and its formation not fundamentally differ from other cases, most notably the 'Asiatic state'?

To be sure, biblical traditions tell about the role of armed retinues in the formation of Israelite kingship too. An early, short-lived attempt at kingship was made by Abimelech in the central Ephraim Hill on the strength of a small warrior band hired with money provided by the people of Shechem from the local temple (*Judges* 9). Later, David at the head of 400–600 brigands and Philistine mercenaries was made king over the southern tribe of Judah (1 *Samuel* 22–30; 2 *Samuel* 2). He then used this small tribal kingdom as a power base for the creation of a unified Israelite state. His veteran group was now turned into a regular force including a 'companion hero' retinue/troop leaders (traditionally 37) and the foreign Philistine Sea Peoples' Kerethite, Pelethite, and Gittite mercenaries, numbering some 600. This force served to cement the king's hold over the tribal militias (2 *Samuel* 15, 20, 23). All the same, as the biblical tradition clearly indicates, with the ancient Hebrews, too, early state formation around 1000 BC was 'secondary' and originated as a response to military pressure from earlier neighbouring states, especially the Philistines and the newly emergent Trans-Jordanian kingdoms. If there were other, and more 'pristine', paths to statehood, what role did armed force and violence play in them? To address these questions, it is time to go further back in absolute chronology to examine the earliest states ever.

From Petty-States to States: Some of the Earliest Examples

The first states tended to emerge in environments of intensive-irrigation agriculture.[31] Contrary to the 'hydraulic' theory of state emergence, this does not mean that states could or did not emerge independently in other ecological circumstances, but merely that the processes set in motion by the agricultural revolution created conditions of demographic density and social complexity the fastest where intensification was achievable the earliest.[32] In absolute chronology, Sumer and Egypt are renowned for being the earliest of these early state centres and civilizations, already emerging as such in the centuries before 3000 BC. Although there is fragmented evidence that might indicate some Mesopotamian interaction in the Nile Valley at a very early stage, both geographical distance and archaeological cultural distinctiveness leave little doubt that Egyptian state formation was fundamentally autochthonous.

It is this unrivalled model of an early unified and huge kingdom that first calls for our attention. Everything about it seems to have been big from the very start. The accepted image of Egypt from the moment it emerges on the historical stage is dominated by the monumental royal cemeteries of the Early Dynastic kings of the unified state at Abydos and Saqqara, further evolving into the pyramid graves, symbolizing the autocratic might of the Old Kingdom's rulers. Spanning an entire millennium, roughly 3100–2100 BC, the Early Dynastic and Old Kingdom periods were also marked by relative peace. Protected by desert and sea, Egypt's defensive and imperialist initiatives towards her mainly tribal Nubian, Libyan, and (partly urban) south Levant neighbours were on the whole of limited significance for the Egyptian state.

Images, however, can be deceptive. The Egypt that comes under literate, historical light did not emerge full blown. It had to be created, 'unified', from a multiplicity of petty polities, in a protohistorical process that is only vaguely recorded in tradition and by archaeology, and in which warfare played a central role.[33] By this stage of our study, the process involved would appear surprisingly familiar. The archaeological record suggests that during the fourth millennium BC agricultural tribal/chiefly society along the Nile Valley coalesced around small regional polities. Egyptologists tend to believe that the later Egyptian administrative districts, or *nomes*—about 40 in number—preserved the original layout of these independent petty-polities, in the same way as county and province names in England and much of continental Europe, for example, do. A relief on a ceremonial palette from the late Pre-Dynastic or the beginning of the Early Dynastic period (about 3100 BC), known as the 'Towns' Palette', shows a multiplicity of fortified settlements, complete with regularly spaced wall bastions. In each fortified settlement there are symbolic animal representations both inside and outside, commonly interpreted as ruling clans' totems of the defenders and attackers. Over time, a process of unification had taken place. Archaeological evidence indicates the formation of two cultural spheres, one in the south and the other in the north, in Upper Egypt and the Delta. Of the two, the former appears to have been the more centralized and hierarchical state, with its state–religious urban walled centre at Hierakonpolis. The northern, Delta state—if that is what it was, as it would increasingly seem to be—apparently had its centre at Buto, currently under excavation.

251

The 'Towns' palette'. Animal images probably representing the besiegers of and besieged in the walled settlements. Late Pre-Dynastic to First Dynasty, c. 3100 BC

Although everything about proto-history—Egyptian included—is partly conjectural, the archaeological finds increasingly tend to confirm the general outline of later Egyptian records about the state's origins. According to these, the Nile Valley was united by Menes, King of Upper Egypt, who had conquered Lower Egypt. Archaeological evidence, most strikingly in the form of various decorated palettes, seems to reveal a process that may have taken as long as two centuries. A series of Upper Egypt warrior rulers whose symbols or names are recorded—Ka, Iryhor, Scorpion, and Narmer (Menes?)—are presented as smiting their enemies in glorifying scenes of battle, victory, and subjugation, beheading prisoner leaders and warriors. Evidence of sacrificed people has been discovered, a custom that would quickly disappear after unification. The Nile, running through the long and narrow strip of fertile flood agricultural land that is Egypt, served as the highway upon which troops were shipped in the process of unification.

One unrecognized element in this scheme of gradual state formation

King Narmer smiting his enemies. Early First Dynasty c. 3100. Hierakonpolis

needs pointing out. As already mentioned and contrary to customary assumptions, even in this 'pristine' core, the Nile Valley, the state did not evolve independently of any other state. Again, the image of the later, unified Egyptian state is misleading. In all stages of polity evolution in the Nile Valley, states co-evolved in interaction with, and in a reciprocal loop response towards, each other. This was from the outset an inter-polity and inter-state system 'within' latter-day 'Egypt', to say nothing of

253

interactions—commercial or other—outside the Nile Valley. Polity formation in one place brought about parallel developments among neighbours within the Nile Valley, which in turn led to further intensification of the process. In ostensibly 'pristine' cases, too, both internal processes and outside stimuli were involved and interacting.[34]

Once united, Egypt's unique geographical isolation helped to secure the new union from outsiders. State building and, indeed, the earliest nation building ever,[35] could run their course within a few centuries: a new capital was established at Memphis, on the former border between Upper and Lower Egypt; the symbols of power—the titles, crowns, and royal icons of the former kingdoms—were combined; religious syncretism of the earlier regional deities was initiated from above, creating a state religion with a divine king at its centre; local dialects were subsumed under an official (Upper Egypt) state language (how much of an *ethnos* the Neolithic inhabitants of the Nile Valley had been is unknown); internal peace was enforced; royal administration, taxation, economy, justice, and military systems were imposed; and monumental state construction, state art, and state literacy to record and run the extensive state affairs evolved rapidly.

The pattern of political evolution through petty-states and extended overlordship to larger political formations—a pattern that involved force as well as all the other means of power consolidation—was in many ways remarkably similar in different and unrelated geographical settings. However, it also varied a great deal, because any difference in environmental, subsistence, or social conditions meant that every culture was specifically determined in a different form. Thus state emergence in China, on the other side of the Asian landmass, can be viewed as close to the Egyptian model, while also being considerably different. As in Egypt, 'China'—in its later and well-recognized image as a huge nation-state–empire and, indeed, civilization—was not 'primordially' there as such but, rather, gradually came into being, was 'created', in a process of state and nation building by evolving state nuclei. As in Egypt, the setting of this formative evolution was the fertile alluvial floodland of a great river, the Yellow River, in today's northern China, in which millet, wheat/oats, vegetables, and livestock constituted the basis of the economy. In absolute chronology roughly 1,000 years later than the western end of Asia for both the start and fruition of the process, agricultural intensification during several millennia of the Neolithic produced developed village societies along the Yellow River by the fourth millennium BC and stratified 'chiefdoms' by the third (Lungshan culture). Traces of ditches and palisades around settlements are detectable from earlier in the Neolithic, but as slash and burn, shifting agriculture was being replaced by sedentary villages, archaeological evidence of stamped earth walls and ditches around villages and towns, destruction by fire, and mutilated skeletons become all the more evident.[36] From around 2000 BC, as protohistory begins in the Yellow River region, at least hundreds of petty-states are identified, typically built around a walled town or fortified palace, the seat of a reigning clan. However, yet again, the number of independent polities in this early state system continuously shrank, as some were being swallowed by others.[37]

Although an autochthonous system of writing appears to have evolved in the Yellow River basin with the state during the second millennium, written material has not survived as well as in comparable civilizations. Mainly done on perishable substances such as wood, bamboo, and silk, writings did not enjoy the low humidity of Egypt or the durability of the Mesopotamian clay tablets. Only from about 1200 BC have some writings made on more durable materials—mainly bronze artefacts and oracle bones and shells—survived in more considerable quantity. This written information, together with other archaeological finds, on the whole tally with the basic outline of later Chinese traditions and histories regarding Chinese state emergence. These historical traditions tell of Three Dynasties, successively, the Hsia, Shang, and Chou, the chronology of which begins in the early second millennium BC. Whereas definite archaeological identification of the Hsia has so far not been possible in spite of growing potential evidence,[38] the Shang, who ruled more or less from the eighteenth to the twelfth or eleventh centuries BC, have been clearly identified by modern archaeology through their sites, written material, and artefacts. They seem to have taken over from the Hsia, continuing and expanding the latter's system of rule.

The Shang realm extended over the Yellow River basin and beyond, finally reaching maybe as far south as future China's second great river, the rice-cultivated region of the Yangtze. Its loose structure hints at what the Shang state had come to be. This was an overlordship exercised by a king from the Shang royal clan, who reigned from a political and religious capital (seven successive ones have been identified) over and through a network of regional elite clans, each residing in a walled town at the centre of its domain. The Shang themselves are called after their native principality, from which they had risen to power. From the start their overlordship (in the Hsia's footsteps) was created by a mixture of conquest, coercion, and co-optation, and was welded together by kinship: alliance between the royal and elite regional clans was cemented by constant intermarriage in a polygynous system; vacant and new regional lordships were allocated to members of the Shang royal clan. The clan elite, with the Shang at its pinnacle, instituted state-centred ritual and established a monopoly over 'High Shamanism'. The ethnic and lingual fragmentation of the realm remains unclear. How-ever, at least the language of the elite and of much of the population was archaic Chinese, possibly arising from one of the languages and dialects of the Yellow River Neolithic expansions but, in any case, thus beginning its outward expansion as a state language, assimilating alien elements.

Although royal administration grew in significance over time, the judicial, tax, and military structures of the Shang realm remained mainly regional, with goods flowing upwards to the regional and royal centres. Compared with Egypt's rapid pace of a few centuries, 'China' took far longer to evolve fully from an overlordship into a centralized bureaucratic state. The Shang armed forces were largely structured around the household retinues of the royal and regional elite clans (*tsu*), with chiefs who in turn also marshalled and led the local peasant populace. As in Egypt and other similar societies, this populace was organized for conscript service in the form of peacetime corvée labour, regular garrison service, or more general call-ups for war. Penalties to enforce obedience and discipline could be harsh, but the system as a whole remained a loose hegemony. It depended on the immediate interests of the regional rulers and the authority of the Shang kings, who spent most of their time travelling around their realm, personally wielding power in perpetual ritualistic activity and military expeditions. Warfare was mainly small scale, with armies numbering in the low thousands—the larg-est recorded being 13,000. As in Egypt, this represented a modest share of the state's overall population, although nonetheless being a formidable force compared with the enemies. Waged against rebellious vassals, other states that were emerging on the Shang's periphery and under its impact, and tribal neighbours, warfare was a constant state occupation. It mainly took the form of raids and ravaging campaigns, which sought decision through attrition, in pursuit of power, hegemony, tribute, precious raw materials and trade, prisoners, and, on the flip side of all these, security. Together with subsistence goods, lucrative prestige goods, such as bronze, shell, jade, and silk, were highly sought. Ritualistic sacrifice of prisoners was extensively practised and was central to the activity of war.[39]

In absolute chronology, political evolution on the islands of Japan lagged more than 2,000 years behind the Chinese. Increasingly influenced at crucial junctions by developments on the mainland, Japan is generally treated as a quintessentially 'secondary' state formation. All the same, as already noted and as the Chinese case itself demonstrates, a sharp distinction between 'pristine' and 'secondary' state formation would be much exaggerated. Political evolution is everywhere taking place in reciprocal interaction with other polities within a co-evolving states system, and is thus propelled forward by mutually affecting internal and external stimuli. In Japan the foraging and rudimentary cultivation economy that had prevailed from about 7500 BC (Jamon) was transformed from around 300 BC by the introduction from the mainland of wet rice agriculture and iron production. In the following period (Yayoi), from the third century BC to the third century AD, a rapid process of agricultural intensification, demographic growth, and social stratification took place. Fortified sedentary villages appeared, as well as archaeological signs, in the form of large burial mounds, of growth in the power of chiefs. The mounds, full of weapons and prestige goods, suggest that the chiefs competed over luxury trade goods, partly imported from the continent, and engaged in both ritual–shamanistic activity and endemic warfare. Indeed, Yayoi archaeological finds are lit by rare 'snapshots' from the mainland. A Chinese chronicle from the Former Han period (second and first centuries BC) tells about some 100 polities (chiefdoms) in those southern parts of the 'Islands of Wa' with which the Chinese came in contact. Centuries later, in AD 240, a formal delegation from China's imperial court for the first time travelled to Japan, where the Yamatai polity had become the principal. Ruled at the time of the visit by a woman paramount–queen–high shaman who resided in a palace fortified with 'towers and stockades', this early state extended suzerainty over 22 'countries' in the southern part of the Japanese archipelago by a combination of armed force and shamanistic authority.

The subsequent Yamato state, from the third century on, continued the process of political 'confederation'. From its centre at the Nara–Osaka plain, its realm progressively expanded as well as being consolidated. Its self-proclaimed 'warrior' 'Great Kings' extended overlordship over the lesser rulers of the regional elite clans, retaining many of them in place and in control of their former domains, both subservient to the centre and sharing in the benefits of state. As elsewhere, most aspects of state administration, including the military, remained largely in the hands of these local chiefs. Leading their retinues and the local peasant militia, they formed the bulk of the state's army. Only from the late sixth century AD, with progressing agricultural intensification and greatly increasing Chinese influence and threat, did Chinese-modelled religions, literacy, architecture, urbanism, and centralized bureaucratic state inaugurate Japan's historical era. State armies of peasant conscripts were instituted for corvée labour, garrison service, and campaigning on the western and north-eastern frontiers, where the evolving Japanese state had been continually expanding into, and assimilating, alien tribal lands.[40]

Switching back to the other side of Asia, early Anatolia, although not a river valley civilization, resembles other features of north Chinese political evolution. From the late third millennium BC, 'chiefdoms' in the region evolved into petty-states with fortified palaces—developing into towns—as their centres (the most famous being Troy II). These petty-states are attested to by the excavations of both the sites and the first written records found in the region, made in the early second millennium BC by Assyrian merchant colonists. Rivalry among the petty-states was endemic, with some royal clans increasingly succeeding in gaining dominance over the others. From the seventeenth century BC, the dynasty centred on the palace-citadel of Hattusa, progressively extended overlordship over the others in central Anatolia, creating what is commonly referred to in modern times as the Hittite state. The name is somewhat misleading, in the sense that there was no Hittite ethnic entity or people. The rulers of Hattusa presided over an ethnically fragmented realm, where early Anatolian population, speaking Hattian, was juxtaposed with speakers of Indo-European Nesite, Luwian, and Palaic languages. Again we have all the features that we have seen before: 'Great Kings' who wielded supreme military and religious power; previous petty rulers reduced to the status of regional grandees and vassal kings through a combination of war, coercion, kin ties with the ruling family through polygynous marriage, and the benefits of state; and continuous warfare as the principal occupation of the Great King, to create, expand, and protect the realm, and extract tribute.

As the Hittite state expanded and consolidated, royal administration of military affairs became more bureaucratic. At the centre of the armed forces there was a small permanent nucleus of an elite royal household bodyguard, which according to the available evidence numbered only in the hundreds. Garrisons manned frontier strongholds, apparently drawn mainly from semi-permanent soldier colonists who received land/rations in return for service. On call-ups for the frequent campaigns, the local aristocratic warrior retinues of the Great King and his vassal rulers were assembled—in the later state period, as in the later Shang, mainly riding the newly introduced horse-drawn chariot. The mass of the country's peasant population was similarly subject to service in these campaigns, as well as to corvée work. Overall numbers are largely conjectural: a few thousand at most were probably employed in the earliest wars; and the later kingdom fielded armies of 10,000 or more in major campaigns, with the total of its armed forces at its height reaching up to a few tens of thousand infantry and a few thousand war chariots.[41]

The emergence of the Mycenaean polities and civilization in Greece, on the other side of the Aegean cultural sphere, in many ways parallels Anatolia and offers a unique insight into the earliest stages of state evolution. Made famous by the faint, remote, and distorted historical echoes preserved in oral epic traditions and codified in the Homeric work of the eighth century BC, the Mycenaean world has been archaeologically excavated since the late nineteenth century. The deciphering of the Linear B script in the 1950s has given a snapshot view of patchy administrative records of some of the Mycenaean polities at the end of their history and moment of destruction about 1200 BC, when the clay tablets in the archives were baked by conflagration. The archaeology of the sites suggests that from the late seventeenth century BC onward the Mycenaean polities had gradually developed from complex 'chiefdoms' to petty bureaucratic states. Influence from Crete and the civilizations of the eastern Mediterranean had been stimulating what was progressively becoming a thriving centralized petty-state economy of exquisite crafts, textile industry, luxury trading goods, and far-flung maritime commerce. The massive palace–citadels, such as Mycenae, Tiryns, the Athenian Acropolis, and Thebes and Gla in Boeotia, with their 'cyclopean' walls of huge stones, were built only in the later stage of Mycenaean history, in the fourteenth and thirteenth centuries BC. Other later palaces, such as Pylos, 'Nestor's palace', were apparently unfortified.

Some scholars, grappling in the darkness of prehistory, have explained this later appearance of mammoth fortifications by speculating that the

259

occasion and severity of warfare increased in this later stage of Mycenaean history, signalling a 'time of trouble' before the ultimate doom.[42] However, the material finds from the very beginning of that history suggest that this interpretation is off the mark. Pictorial representations of early Mycenaean warrior scenes are prominent in the excavated material, which itself largely consists of elite warrior graves. These are full of weaponry, from pre-metallic tusk helmets to early bronze helmets, armour corslets, spears, swords, and daggers.[43] Warfare in all probability was relatively small scale and took the familiar form of raids and elite single combats rather than of fully fledged invasions and wars of conquest. As we have already seen, livestock and women captives were the main prizes of raids in such societies. Prisoner women from raids, working in the textile industry, are recorded in the later clay tablets, whereas the difficult-to-control men were killed on the spot, as was usually the case in early civilizations.[44] The archaeological record from the beginning of the Mycenaean period shows that 'Most settlements are located around defensible hilltops. . . . Unfortunately, later construction programmes, virtually everywhere, have swept away or concealed early buildings or fortification walls'.[45] Indeed, only when the earlier chiefly rulers gave way to increasingly more powerful and richer monarchs (*wanax*), who ruled the bureaucratic petty-states familiar from the written tablets and who mastered recognizably more organized armed forces, did it become both possible and more necessary to erect the mighty palace-citadels of the later period to guard the kings' seats of power and accumulating gold treasures. As we have already seen and discuss further later on, the evolution of fortifications is a much more complex subject than may appear at first sight.

At the end, Pylos—one of the principal Mycenaean petty-states and relatively well documented by the clay tablets—had a population estimated at about 50,000 people,[46] and its area covered a few thousand square kilometres. In addition to the king, the tablets also mention various palace, administrative, and local dignitaries. These constituted the core of armed 'companions' and 'followers' around the monarch, riding war chariots during the later state period. Whereas a few hundred chariots are cited for one or two of the mightiest Mycenaean petty-states, the others apparently possessed no more than a few dozen. In addition, there seems to have been a general obligation of the peasant populace to serve on demand, and small contingents of professional, partly foreign, infantry troops are also possible

Mycenaean troops. The Warrior Crater, Mycenae, twelfth century BC

during the later period.[47] The Iliad presents the king of Mycenae as the head of the alliance against Troy, a first among equals, or even more than that. He may have held suzerainty over the polities in the vicinity of Mycenae and some sort of hegemonic power—including maritime—further afield. The excavated clay tablets of Hattusa refer to the Great King of Ahhiyawa in the west, which in the diplomatic parlance of the period was a rank equal to the Great Kings of Egypt, Babylonia, and Hatti itself. Whether or not Ahhiyawa is to be identified with the Achaeans, and their Great Kings with the rulers of Mycenae, has been the subject of a protracted debate and would seem increasingly plausible.[48] In any case, around 1200 BC, before the Mycenaean petty-states and inter-state system could evolve further in any direction, they experienced sudden and violent destruction, which would drive Greece back to a pre-state and preliterate existence in the four centuries of the Dark Ages.

Those responsible for this sudden destruction and collapse remain unknown, and, in view of the paucity of the written evidence, speculation is of limited value. The once-popular belief that Dorian invaders from outside Greece caused the destruction has lost its credibility on both archaeological and linguistic grounds. Popular uprising (rarely if ever effective in known history) or fashionable 'system collapse' and natural disaster theories are equally unconvincing.[49] On the whole, scholars are returning to the best-documented potential culprit, already discussed in Chapter 9: the massive movement in the Aegean and the whole eastern Mediterranean about 1200 BC of disparate peoples and armed hosts from the periphery of the civilized zone. Known as the 'Sea Peoples' in the Egyptian sources, their devastating sea and land raids brought simultaneous and abrupt destruction on the fortified centres of power in Greece and the Levant coast—including the Hittite capital Hattusa and the Hittite empire—looting these centres' rich treasures. In Pylos, as in Ugarit in Syria, the last written records refer to coastal watches and naval preparations.[50] The remains of a hastily built wall across the Corinthian isthmus, which connects the Peloponnese with mainland Greece, have been excavated.

Mycenaean civilization had originally been stimulated by, and after 1500 BC took control of, the so-called Minoan civilization in Crete, which had flourished from the beginning of the second millennium BC. The Mycenaean Linear B script was an adaptation to the Greek language of the Cretan Linear A. However, as the Cretan language is unknown and was apparently non-Greek, the Linear A itself remains undeciphered. The astonishingly beautiful and sophisticated Minoan palace society thus remains with no written testimony at all for most of its history, before the Mycenaean occupation. Consequently, as the Minoan palaces in their heyday were unfortified and scenes of war are generally absent in Minoan art, the romantic and idyllic imagination, envisioning a Golden Age or Lost Paradise of peace and happiness, easily took over among early researchers. Since then, however, scholarly opinion has changed. Of course, Crete is an island and thus more secure from outside invasion. All the same, the only mechanism for maintaining internal peace—as far as such peace existed in Crete—would have been some sort of hegemonic overlordship by the kings of Knossos over the lesser rulers in the smaller palaces. This power structure is in fact reflected in Greek historical memory, both with respect to Minos and in the 'Ship List' in the *Iliad* (2.645–52), where King Idomeneus is presented as head of the island's 'hundred *poleis*'. Most scholars believe that Knossos's supremacy is also suggested by the archaeological evidence. Indeed, hilltop and palace fortifications, as well as palace destruction in warfare during the early second millennium BC, suggest that intra-island warfare had taken place before the establishment of hegemonic rule in Crete. In turn, elite dominance in all its aspects was the only way by which the populace could be brought into subservience to the regimentalized luxurious palace economy and its wealthy residents.

Abroad, Minoan maritime dominance over trade and markets—or thalassocracy, the Greek for mastery of the sea—was underpinned by the powerful Minoan naval force. According to Thucydides (i:4): 'Minos is the earliest of all those known to us by tradition who acquired a navy. He made himself master of a very great part of what is now called the Hellenic Sea, and became lord of the Cyclades islands and first colonizer of most of them, driving out the Carians and establishing his own sons in them as governors.' Herodotus, too (*Histories* 1.171, also 173), refers to islanders under King Minos's rule who were obliged to man his ships upon request. Minoan colonization of the islands is now increasingly accepted by archaeologists. Fortifications on these islands are interpreted as having been erected by Minoan colonists against the local inhabitants, or the other way around, but are in any case indicative of conflict. Indeed, an exquisite wall painting discovered on the island of Thera (Santorini), in the Minoan sphere, depicts detailed scenes of galleys, warriors, and a seaborne campaign. Last but not least, the remains of sacrificed people have been excavated in several locations in Crete, casting a darker shadow on the earlier bright image of Minoan religion. The later Greek myth of Theseus, according to which the

Minoan troops with spears, swords, boar tusk helmets, and shields, sixteenth century BC. Note the galley, and the rich and elegant setting. The Procession Frieze from Akrotiri

Athenians were coerced by King Minos annually to send seven young men and maidens for sacrifice to the Minotaur, may be a faint echo of a grim reality. In the myth Theseus kills the Minotaur, which again may be evocative of historical events, because around the mid-fifteenth century Mycenaean warrior bands from the mainland took over Knossos and the lesser palaces and established their rule over Crete. This may or may not have been connected to the destruction of the Minoan palaces and ships about 1500 BC by the well-documented catastrophic volcanic eruption that blew up the entire centre of the island of Thera.[51]

In conclusion, this overview of the evidence for state formation, from tribal/stratified/chiefly society and rural petty-states through hegemonic overlordships to larger states, demonstrates that, whether in 'pristine' or more 'secondary' evolution, armed force was a major, and sometimes the major, factor, side by side and together with co-optation and all other—economic and religious—means of power accumulation. The reason for this widely observable but far from generally acknowledged fact is simple almost to the point of being self-evident and has already been mentioned earlier: without the underpinning of superior, covert or overt, coercive force, political power accumulation, with all the benefits that it entails, cannot be achieved in the teeth of opposition from others who stand to lose by it, or be secured once it has been achieved against power holders who stand to gain by its usurpation. It may be impossible, as Talleyrand piqued, to sit on bayonets; but whatever cushions are necessary, they must be supported by sharper tools. Legitimacy of all sorts is highly important, but it cannot be sustained by itself.

Japanese sacred kingship is an illuminating case in point. As we saw, the first Chinese envoy to Japan, in the mid-third century AD, found a queen–priest of the Yamatai polity engaged in shamanist activity in the seclusion of her palace–castle. It was, however, not by magical charisma alone that power was wielded in the real world. Actual power was in effect held in the hands of the queen's brother, who ruled the realm by temporal means.[52] As Japanese Heavenly Sovereigns from the seventh century AD on often tended to retreat from the follies of this world into religious meditation, the same pattern resurfaced, with a close relative holding the reins of power. Indeed, the only reason why the same Japanese dynasty of divine monarchs has more or less survived ever since is that, from the twelfth century on, it held only formal, symbolic power. Actual political–military–economic rule, and everything that it conferred, were held by 'military governors', the shoguns, whose dynasties, not surprisingly, constantly rose and fell through armed competition and deadly usurpation. Supreme religious authority was regularly a central aspect of political power and a major source of legitimacy but could never be its sole or even principal mainstay, either in chiefdoms or when these chiefdoms evolved into states. The rulers of all the rural petty-states and overlordships reviewed here wielded mixed—temporal and religious—power.

Once power was accumulated, it could serve to accumulate yet more power in a stepping-stone, 'knock-out' model, which progressively eliminated smaller contenders—whether they were tribes/chiefdoms or petty-states—bringing them under larger hegemonic state structures. Over longer periods, hegemonic state power could then generate processes of cultural and ethnic fusion or 'nation building' and develop state bureaucratic machinery to replace disparate hegemonic rule. As remains to be seen, more centralized national armies resulted.

Non-Tribal and Non-State Armed Hosts

Petty-states and states were not the sole possessors of corporate fighting forces in the evolving states system. We have already seen the dominant role played by armed retinues in the creation of states, but armed hosts continued to figure significantly outside the state structure. In the first place, the 'state structure' itself was a very loose concept, in which the local powerful retained control over their men and localities. These were more or less considered legitimate power holders. Furthermore, as the petty-states, hegemonic overlordships, and, indeed, the emergent inter-state system itself were all generally small and fragmented, there was much 'frontier land' on the periphery of, and between, states. In addition to the tribal/barbarian marches, there were also non-tribal and non-state armed hosts that formed in the inner and outer no-man's-land of state territory. They miscellaneously consisted of fugitives from justice or blood revenge, disinherited and banished illegitimate or younger sons, exiled aristocrats, debtors, escapees from bondage, or simply poor peasants who opted for the brigand and adventurous way of making a living. As petty-states were small and even larger states' power was diffused, the bigger of these hosts—numbering in the hundreds—could pose a real challenge to the authorities.

Indeed, there was arguably not that much difference between such hosts and the authorities, apart from the fact that the former were usually outcasts and often recruited their men from the bottom of society, whereas the authorities had been legitimized by time and power; the 'free companies' extracted tribute from the peasant population in return for 'protection', in much the same way that states did. Moreover, these brigands, bandits, and pirates often moved to and fro across the legitimacy line into state service, or themselves became the state. Operating in a state environment meant that there was money for hiring warrior hosts into mercenary service from either the tribal zone or the state realm itself, especially in an emergency but also on a more permanent footing. Given the opportunity, particularly in times of trouble, these hosts seized power, in petty-states and even in larger ones. In a fragmented political and ethnic landscape, they sometimes collaborated with other non-state hosts, such as aristocratic retinues and tribal bands, adding up to a force that could undermine weakening state power.

References to brigand groups go back to the earliest state system in early Mesopotamia, but not surprisingly they are particularly plentiful and significant in the records of the petty-states in the politically fragmented Levant during the second millennium BC, wherever and whenever such records have been found, from Mari in the north to Canaan in the south.[53] In Canaan these brigand groups on the periphery of society were called *habiru* or *apiru*, which early scholars tended to identify ethnically with the early Hebrews, but which are now understood as a broader generic designation, from which the forming Hebrews may have derived their ethnic name. Many forming ethnic identities are given their collective, often derogatory, names by more developed societies on their borders. A later biblical tradition tells about one such group of brigands under Jephthah, the son of a prostitute, disinherited and banished by his father's family but called by the elders of Gilead in time of trouble to save the district from the Ammonites. After his victory, he became leader of Gilead and the surrounding tribes (*Judges* 11–12). We have already mentioned the role played by another such brigand group under David during the later emergence of the Israelite state. A fugitive from King Saul's service, he and his group exacted tribute from the frontier peoples of Judah and hired their services to the Philistine Achish of Gath, before returning to take up power in Judah and later also in Israel after Saul's defeat and death in battle.

The Hebrews, of course, were only one small group in the Levant, a group whose traditions have been comparatively so well preserved only because of the later remarkable career of their tribal religion. By contrast, we know very little about the Hyksos, or 'chiefs of foreign countries' in the Egyptian records, who from the mid-seventeenth to the mid-sixteenth centuries BC took advantage of weakening central power in Egypt to establish their overlordship over the Nile Delta and most of the rest of Egypt. Their recorded personal names and other evidence indicate mostly Semitic, Canaanite–Amorite origin from the southern Levant. Contrary to a still popular image, they did not come riding the new war chariot, with which they were able to storm Egypt. The chariot's gradual spread through the ancient Near East reached Egypt only later in their reign. The Hyksos may have represented an assorted conglomeration of Asiatic chiefly forces, aristocratic retinues, mercenaries, and brigand groups, which co-operated with Semitic urban and pastoralist immigrants to the Delta in taking over Egypt.[54]

Shortly after, from the second half of the sixteenth century, Hurrian and Kassite chiefly, tribal, and brigand warrior groups from the north of the Fertile Crescent penetrated the entire Near East in search of fortune. Finally, I have already discussed the Sea Peoples of mostly Aegean and Anatolian origin, who about 1200 BC devastated the Levant coast and invaded Egypt. Although information is again very sketchy, they, too, seem to have been a disparate assortment of war bands, exiles, and migrating peoples of various ethnicities, who looted and hired their services to foreign powers (including intermittently both the Egyptian pharaohs and the Libyan chiefs who invaded that country), as well as carrying out larger military expeditions themselves. After a failed offensive on Egypt, some of them, including the biblical Philistines, were settled by the Egyptians on the coastal plain of Canaan as mercenary garrisons. When Egypt's central government again declined from the mid-twelfth century BC, they took over as lords where they had been stationed, with the Philistines—for example, establishing five allied petty-polities on the southern plain. Another sea people, the Tjekker, took over on the northern coastal plain of Canaan. The Aegean origins of these ruling warrior bands is well preserved in the archaeology of their early sites, but they soon assimilated into the local Canaanite culture and language.[55]

There is significant evidence for the operation of brigand warrior bands in the war-like environment of late-classic and post-classic Mesoamerica, from the seventh century AD on, where they again variably acted independently and as mercenary troops. These 'New World *Condottieri*', as one historian suggested they might be described, mostly came from the fringes of the great civilizations of Teotihuacan and the Maya in central Mexico and Yucatan—the Gulf coast and the north. They served the rulers of these civilizations as mercenaries, very possibly contributed to their collapses around AD 650 and 850 respectively, and played a central role in the mayhem that followed.[56] Some of them became elite warrior rulers of post-classic polities. The most famous Mesoamerican epic tradition tells about the leader of Toltec Tula, Quetzalcoatl, who lost out in the struggle for power and left east on exile with his followers. There seems to be a kernel of historical reality in the epic, for more than 1,000 kilometres east, in the lowland Maya petty-polities of the post-classic period, both tradition and archaeology testify to the appearance of Toltec war bands headed by Kukulcan (the Feathered Serpent: Quetzalcoatl in Maya), who in AD 987 took over the local Maya polities, bringing with them their unmistakable art, architecture, and religious symbols. From their capital at Chichen Itza they dominated northern Yucatan for some 200 years.

There are, of course, many additional examples from other petty-state systems. I have already mentioned the independent armed hosts and adventurer leaders operating within the Etruscan city-states system. Some 2,000 years later, the multi-national 'free companies', which formed in, and ravaged, France in the mayhem of the Hundred Years War, went on to make a particularly successful career in the politically fragmented Italian peninsula. They intermittently offered their mercenary services to the antagonistic Italian city-states and fended for themselves, preying on the population and stimulating locals to pursue a similar career in *condottieri* warrior hosts. However, these and other instances of brigand armed hosts operating in developing markets for mercenaries are better explored further in connection with my discussion of city-states.

Indeed, over time, cities evolved within the rural cum palace/temple/fortified-centre polities. Expanding scale, centralized state government and bureaucracy, and diversified, more complex state economy, tribute, and other spoils of war were all responsible for this process in the emergent states that have already been reviewed. The Egyptian and Chinese royal capitals are examples of the growth of these state-induced metropolitan centres. In Japan, too, a Chinese-style royal capital city was built at Nara in the eighth century AD by the new bureaucratic state. In the Hittite domain, a city continuously grew around the former citadel of Hattusa, as the kingdom was gaining in size, power, and wealth. Increasingly larger settlements formed around the Minoan palaces, particularly Knossos, where an esti-mated few tens of thousand people lived around the palace. Small settle-ments of a few thousand began to grow around the Mycenaean palaces/citadels, and were burnt and destroyed with them.

It should be noted that, in all these cases, while closely intertwined with state evolution and consolidation, the rise of cities followed and was largely 'secondary' to that process; the cities evolved only after the petty-state level had been transcended. In some other cases, however, city growth took place with, and was central to, state formation from the petty-state level. In view of its special features—including the military—and high historical profile, this city-state variant of the petty-state merits a separate discussion.

WARFARE IN THE RISE AND FALL OF CITY-STATES

Defence in the Formation of City-States

In its prime, the city-state variant of the petty-state—proverbially a seat of urbanity and civil life—was often literate and therefore historical. However, here as well, when one goes only a short way back from this familiar and sometimes renowned prime to the city-state's formative period, historical reality almost immediately fades into appalling ignorance, only somewhat alleviated by myth, tradition, and archaeology. Again, a compara-tive study of this scant evidence, covering a multiplicity of cases, can be a means of gaining extra insight. It reveals, for example, that city-states gener-ally emerged around a chiefly/cultic centre, which in a self-reinforcing process became the site of the local market and attracted tradesmen and artisans, while serving as a point of refuge for a larger population.

Here, too, it used to be thought and is still widely held that some of these chiefly centres were mainly religious and economic, evolving around a tem-ple complex, whereas others were 'secular' and military, growing in the shadow of a stronghold or castle. The principal example of the religious–economic type is considered to be the Sumerian city-states, the world's earliest literate civilization together with Egypt (and slightly ahead of it). Archaeologically, the Sumerian city-states are known to have evolved in the late fourth and early third millennia BC around the temple sites that had grown during the earlier Ubaid period in the fertile alluvial river basins of the lower Euphrates and Tigris, in today's southern Iraq. The title of the early kings, which survived into historical times, was *en* and, later, *ensi*, literally 'priest who laid the foundation (of a temple)', indicating their paramount religious role. The title changed to *lugal* (literally 'big man') during the Early Dynastic period (twenty-ninth to twenty-fourth centuries BC) which is thought to have brought about intensified warfare, although 'it is probable that the inhabitants were not less pugnacious in earlier times, of which little is known'.[57] For example, the excavated village of Tell es-Sawwan from about 6000–4500 BC was surrounded by a deep and wide defensive ditch and fortified wall with elaborate defended gateways. At the contemporary village of Choga Mami a similar elaborate gate fortification protected the only excavated entrance to the village.[58] Moving later in time, an excavated cylinder seal from the protohistoric Uruk period shows bound captives and smitten enemies.[59] Indeed, precisely the somewhat accidental nature of such discoveries brings me back to the inherent ambiguity of the archaeological markers for warfare in pre- and proto-state societies. The problem is difficult to overcome, but analogies can help.

The one with the most resounding moral is with the Maya of Yucatan, in today's southern Mexico, Guatemala, Honduras, Belize, and El Salvador, the city-state polities of which emerged from the third century AD around earlier and growing ceremonial/cultic centres, in a village society that had evolved from about 1500 BC. So far in this chapter I have barely dealt with the earliest states in the Americas, because they generally lacked a developed system of writing, and thus any sort of narrative history at all. They are called by the names that the Spaniards or modern archaeologists gave their prehistoric sites, because we do not even know their own self-designated names. An exception is the Maya, whose hieroglyphic script was largely deciphered from the 1950s. The decipherment marked a watershed in the scholarly picture of the Maya. Before the Maya texts could be read, it had been generally assumed that theirs had been a peaceful priestly society. The archetypal idyllic–mythical image—which together with its opposite is deeply embedded in our psyche—of happy peasant communities, willingly offering their produce to the gods through the mediation of a priestly elite, had enjoyed a free rein. All possible signs of warfare had been interpreted otherwise. However, once the Maya texts could be read, a completely

Maya battle scene. Mural on the south wall of the Upper Temple of the Jaguars, Chichen Itza

different picture emerged. High priesthood was indeed one of the major roles of the Maya kings, who presided over, and were themselves tied by, a strict ceremonial protocol and ritualistic activity—including human sacrifice—all intended to safeguard the proper functioning of the world and ensure the community's well-being. At the same time, however, the Maya kings were also the military leaders in endemic warfare that took place among the various city-state polities. It was above all the records of their alleged victories and glory in war that they chose to engrave on the temples and monuments of the cities' plaza centres. They were simultaneously secular, military, *and* religious leaders, and most scholars today hold that they had been so since the pre-state period, when the Maya chiefdoms and temple/civic centres had evolved.[60]

The evidence suggests that the same applies to every other chiefly cum temple nascent polity in the Americas. At this stage, I look only at one more example, Cahokia on the Mississippi, in today's Illinois. Although being the most advanced polity in temperate North America, it emerged in absolute chronology 2,000 years after (and was possibly influenced by) the Mesoamerican culture sphere. Growing from earlier chiefdoms and paramount chiefdoms that had evolved in the region in the preceding centuries—vying for, and replacing each other in, hegemonic rule—Cahokia emerged as a nascent state from the eleventh to the fourteenth centuries AD.[61] As the Mississippi culture had no time to evolve further before the arrival of the Europeans, no later layers of civilization were built on its sites, which thus uniquely preserve their nascent-state form. The centre of the Cahokia polity, around which a city of tens of thousands grew, was a large ceremonial plaza and seat of the polity's ruler. The site comprised huge earth mounds—everywhere the first stage in the evolution of stone or brick pyramids—upon which the shrines and altars were built. Excavations have revealed that the plaza was surrounded by a log palisade. Enclosure walls could, of course, serve many possible purposes, but the function of parapet walks on, and tower-bastions in, the wall leaves little room for ambiguity. The bastions were evenly erected every 20 metres, gates were elaborately protected, and, last but not least, plenty of arrowheads have been found around the wall.[62] Cahokia's seat of power was a defensive enclosure that was experiencing attacks.

The Indus civilization in the Indian subcontinent offers another striking case in point. One of the earliest and greatest civilizations anywhere, unearthed from total oblivion in the 1920s, it apparently evolved indigenously from agricultural communities and towns of earlier millennia into the large, sophisticated, and systematically planned cities of the second half of the third millennium BC. As the Indus (Dravidian?) language and script have not been deciphered, knowledge about this civilization, which transcends the material finds, remains extremely vague. Craft and trade were obviously dominant in the city polities, and the lack of any evidence for autocratic dominance suggests a priestly/mercantile form of government. Some early speculations about the Indus civilization's possible pacifist nature have been muted by the archaeological finds. The cities possessed fortified acropolises and were surrounded by long and massive fortification walls with bastions and fortified gates. Evidence of repeated destructions and conflagrations has also been discovered in many sites. Earlier town fortifications, dating from the fourth millennium BC, clearly show that armed conflict was an integral factor in the evolution of the Indus civilization from its beginnings.[63] The Indus civilization and cities mysteriously collapsed around 1700 BC. It remains unclear whether or not this had anything to do with the arrival into the Indian subcontinent around that time of the Indo-European Aryan pastoralists from the north-west. The war-like exploits of these newcomers—riding war chariots, fighting the dark-complexioned natives, and conquering their urban strongholds—are celebrated in the epic hymns of India's earliest known Sanskrit text, the *Rigveda*.

Thus, as already seen with respect to chiefdoms and rural petty-states, the more general conclusion to be drawn from all this is that any sharp distinction between 'religious/economic' and 'secular/military' rule is belied both by common sense and wherever sufficient empirical evidence is available. Whenever *real* religious/economic political power—that is, command of people and accumulated resources—is achieved, it is unlikely to remain immune to usurpation by force from either inside or outside, nor, indeed, likely to have been instituted in the first place without underpinning from other sources of coercive power.[64] Although avenues to political power differed, they were not that different in this fundamental respect, and, in any case, they continuously came under a strong convergence effect, because, to use the formal cliché: the medium of politics is power. As the cases we have already reviewed demonstrate, this fundamental reality applies to the chiefly/ civic/cultic centres around which city-states emerged, notwithstanding the considerable variation between them: they all incorporated mixed functions.

Our knowledge of the growth of the Greek city-states, for example, from the eighth century BC on, after the Dark Age that had followed the demise of the Mycenaean polities, is sparse in the extreme. In most cases, however, the city-states seem to have emerged around a defended enclosure—sometimes the seat of a paramount chief—which served both as a refuge stronghold for the population and their livestock and as the location of a growing and increasingly centralized sacred site of shrines and temples; indeed, the stronghold also defended the cultic centre.[65] The word itself for a city in Greek—*polis*—was derived from an Indo-European designation for a fortified enclosure (Sanskrit *pur*, Lithuanian *pilis*),[66] around which the city-state had grown and which in classical times was known because of its often elevated location as Acropolis or Upper City. The Hittite Hattusa and the other fortified centres of Anatolia, the Palatine and Capitoline Hills in Rome, and the Gallic *oppida* are some instances of the same pattern of city growth around a hilltop chiefly/royal seat cum cultic centre cum refuge stronghold. Other designations for a city, such as the Slavic *gorod* and Germanic *burgh*, carry the same meaning of a fortified enclosure, around which the future city formed. As the pioneering historian Henri Pirenne sensed and students of African urbanism suggest, the south-east African and Zulu *Kraal* of herdsmen and peasants represented a similar sort of defended chiefly and religious enclosure and nascent commercial centre.[67] The same functions are also evident in the *kibuga*, the successive fortified hilltop enclosures that served as royal capital of Buganda in east Africa.[68] Archaic references to the Sumerian city of Uruk regularly describe it as 'Uruk-the-(sheep)-enclosure', which has continuously raised questions among translators, who have found it difficult to see how this phrase could relate to the historic city's splendour. A recent translator is typical in noting: 'I prefer to translate the notion of a sage refuge for the weak as "Uruk-Haven".'[69] However, the literal meaning may very well have been the original one.

This brings us to the crux of the matter: centralized ceremonial/cultic/civil centres, marketplaces, and artisan workshops would mean little in the development of city-states were it not for the overarching imperatives of defence. What are the grounds for this sweeping assertion? The striking thing about city-states is the urban coalescence, nucleation, of much or even most of its countryside population—the process that in effect created the city-state. Some 80–90 per cent of the Sumerian city-states' population are estimated to have lived in the cities, and it was their movement there from the countryside in the late fourth and early third millennia BC that had made these cities into what they were.[70] To appreciate the significance of this extraordinary data, it should be remembered that the economy of pre-industrial societies was exactly the reverse—that is, 80–90 per cent of the population consisted of food-producing farmers. Even when some city-states became craft and long-distance trade centres that attracted workers from the countryside, the majority of their population remained agri-cultural. The urban population mostly consisted of peasants, who together with their animals walked daily to work in their fields and farms.

Although knowledge about the Indus city-states is greatly inferior, the same logic would appear to have prevailed there as well. Pre-colonial Africa is perhaps the most instructive laboratory in terms of the recent historicity of the evidence on the early city. Although they incorporated a large indus-trial sector, 'African cities and towns were basically agrarian. At least 70 percent of their male residents commuted regularly to outlying farms'.[71] Although the Yoruba of western Nigeria were 'undoubtedly the most urban of all African peoples' in the pre-colonial period, their large cities were 'based upon farming rather than industrialization'. Historians of Africa gen-erally assume that Africa was special in this, but in fact it was not. The reason for the paradox of peasants' urbanism was defensive coalescence. Historical records of the Yoruba, which become fuller in the nineteenth century, with the more permanent arrival of Europeans, tell of heavy raids by the mounted Fulani herdsmen from the north as well as of endemic intercity warfare. Archaeological evidence in the form of extensive city fortifications stretches further back for centuries.[72]

It is increasingly clear that urbanization and, indeed, the formation of the Greek *polis* itself during the Archaic period, about 750–500 BC, were a protracted and gradual process.[73] The urbanism percentage reached by the Greek *poleis* by the classical period remains a deeply confused subject.[74] As usual, the best-documented case is Athens. According to Thucydides (2.14 and 2.16), most of the population of Attica had lived in the countryside before they were evacuated into Athens at the beginning of the Pelopon-nesian War (431 BC). Archaeological estimates support this.[75] However, although Athens is the best-documented Greek *polis*, it is also (together with the second best-known *polis*—Sparta) the most unusual one. As Thucydides writes (2.15), life in the countryside was the characteristic of the Athenians more than of any other Greeks. For one crucial aspect of Athens' uniqueness was its gigantism: it possessed a vast territory in classical Greek terms, encompassing as it did the whole region of Attica. This regional size of the Athenian *polis* meant that it was in any case not possible for its peasant population to live mostly in the city itself even had the peasants so desired (which they did not), because this would have meant an impossible distance from their fields. Most of them resided in the countryside (*khora*), in villages and towns (*komai*), some of which were walled. On the other hand, as Attica was a peninsular pocket with the only exposed land side, the north, largely blocked by the city of Athens itself, Attica was virtually immune to threat, except for the large-scale Persian and Spartan invasions of the fifth century. The same circumstances did not apply to most Greek *poleis*, with a territory that was small and exposed—marked regional variation admitted.

Unfortunately, knowledge about *poleis* other than Athens is greatly inferior. One scrap of evidence relates to Plataea in Boeotia. Lying only some 13 kilometres away from its arch-rival, Thebes, it was attacked by surprise by the latter at the beginning of the Peloponnesian War. Consequently, according to Thucydides (2.5), some Plataeans and some property (*kataskeue*) were caught out in the fields (*agroi*). It seems clear from the account that most of the peasant population of this typical-size *polis* lived within the city, from which they walked to tend their fields, only a few kilometres away. Indeed, if the majority of Plataea's tiny, mostly peasant, population of about 1,000 adult male citizens (and their families) did not live in the 'city', what city was there that can fit Thucydides' description of Plataea as a walled urban residential place?[76] In attempting to demonstrate the centrality of the *polis*'s rural population, historian Victor Hanson cites Brasidas's surprise attack, during the Peloponnesian War, on the rural population residing outside Amphipolis on the Thracian coast (Thucydides 4.102–4).[77] However, not only did Amphipolis lie on the margins of mainland Greece; the city's environs constituted a naturally protected 'island', 'as the Strymon [River] flows around it on both sides'. Only Brasidas's capture of the bridge made possible his incursion. Indeed, from the fact that Thucydides finds it necessary to mention specifically that part of the people of Amphipolis lived dispersed in the countryside, one can infer that this was not the norm in other *poleis*.

Another piece of evidence on the subject in the ancient sources (Xenophon, *Hellenica* 5.2.6–8) relates to Mantinea in the Peloponnese, after the city fell before Sparta and its allies in 385 BC. According to the peace terms imposed by Sparta, 'the wall was torn down and Mantinea was divided into four separate villages, just as the people had dwelt in ancient times'. Xenophon writes that after the initial shock the landholders in fact found this arrangement convenient, because they could now reside close to their farms. All the same, once Mantinea regained its independence in 371 BC, urban coalescence, the indispensable condition of self-defence by an independent *polis*, was resumed (*Hellenica* 6.5.3–5).

The archaeological settlement surveys conducted in various areas of Greece are the principal means for generating new and highly significant information on the question of urbanism. The Kea survey has suggested that at least 75 per cent of the population, if not more, lived in the urban settlement. According to the southern Argolid survey close to 60 per cent of the population in the mid-fourth century BC lived in 'urban' settlements, whereas an estimated 36 per cent lived in villages and some 5 per cent lived in farmsteads. The ongoing survey of Boeotia barely addresses the question directly. But the authors cursorily estimate that about one-third of the population of Boeotia lived in 'cities', and the percentage of the urban population rises to about 40 per cent if the satellite 'towns' are added. As already seen with respect to Attica, the seemingly paradoxical conclusion of all this is that the smaller the *poleis* the more urban it tended to be.[78]

Why then did the peasants in these petty-polities coalesce in cities? All the city glitter could not compensate for the crowded living conditions, bad hygiene, high prevalence of epidemic disease, and hours-long walk to the fields, which were the inseparable aspects of city life. The principal motive was defence, as has been variably realized by scholars of various city-state civilizations but hardly recognized in general. City-states were so decisively and unusually urban not because of massive industrial and commercial concentration, which—as a result of the realities of food production and transportation in pre-industrial societies—existed only in a few high-profile, especially maritime, historical cases; rather, city-states were so configured because of the threat posed by the presence of *other* city-states only a few kilometres away. It is this that accounts for the highly conspicuous but barely noted fact that city-states nearly always appeared in a *cluster* of dozens and even hundreds. There were some 1,200–1,500 Greek *poleis*, hundreds of city-states in mediaeval northern Italy, 30-odd Mesopotamian city-states, and 40–50 city-states in the pre-contact Valley of Mexico. Needless to repeat, very few of the city-states in these systems possessed a highly specialized commercial economy. Fifth-century Athens was a far cry from the typical *polis*, nor was Venice, Milan, Florence, or Genoa characteristic of the average medieval Italian city-state. City-states emerged where large-scale territorial unification did not take place early in political evolution; indeed, their otherwise inexplicable massive urban nucleation occurred only *because* no large-scale political unification had taken place. Space was divided between small antagonistic political units, which meant *both* high threat levels from close-by neighbours and the ability of peasants to find refuge by living in the city while working outside it, only a few kilometres away. It is not surprising that scholars have regularly encountered problems with the concepts of 'city' and even 'urbanism' as applied to these often miniscule 'town'-polities, which could be more adequately described as densely and centrally nucleated petty-polities. Contrary to scholars' assumptions, the rural/urban *residential* split in the city-state did not overlap the agricultural/commercial-cum-manufacturing *occupational* split.

Thus it was again in interaction and co-evolution within an inter-polity system—rather than in isolation—that city-states emerged, including those of the proverbially 'pristine', earliest civilization: Mesopotamia.[79] City-states were the product of war. Indeed, where the defensive motive did not exist, as in the unified and secure kingdom of Egypt, the peasants continued to live in the countryside and around unwalled market towns, whereas large cities were few and functioned as truly metropolitan administrative and commercial centres.[80]

Riddles of Fortification

This brings us to the vexed question of early city fortifications, or their elusiveness—the cause of considerable confusion. I have already discussed the problem of fortifications with respect to horticultural tribal society, where shifting cultivation versus sedentism, and resource spacing out versus resource concentration, were some of the factors determining settlement patterns and thus the presence of fortifications. Lack of fortifications in these societies did not in itself mean the absence of warfare, as historically and ethnographically known cases demonstrate, but as many archaeologists have failed to realize. A somewhat similar problem manifests itself with respect to early city fortifications, and nowhere is it more puzzling than in relation to pre-Columbian America. The principal reason why, before the deciphering of the Maya script, scholars used to believe in the pacific nature of these polities was the apparent absence of city walls around them and the initial inconspicuousness of other sorts of fortifications. On the whole, cities throughout pre-Columbian America seemed to have lacked circuit city walls on a scale that even remotely resembled the familiar Old World pattern, although the evidence not only from the Maya but also during European contact, most prominently in the case of central Mexico, clearly showed that the local city-states were regularly at war with each other. This apparent difference between the New and Old Worlds has remained a puzzle.

In reality, however, there was little difference between the Old and New Worlds, because the pattern *everywhere* was that city fortifications evolved gradually in step with city evolution, with the familiar circuit stone walls taking shape only after centuries of evolution. Our familiarity with later developments in the Old World distorts perception of the evolutionary course that had led to them. In the case of Sumer, for example, scholars tend to associate closely the pre- and protohistorical emergence of cities during the Uruk to Early Dynastic periods with the construction of circuit city walls. However, in Sumer, too, the very large circumference of the enclosed area indicates that the walls were erected only after substantial initial city evolution had taken place. It should never be forgotten that several centuries are a considerable time even in pre- and proto-history and around 3000 BC. The renowned Uruk city walls, erected in the Early Dynastic period, are 9 kilometres long, encompassing an area of 400 hectares, with an estimated population of 40,000 at the minimum.[81] This had already been a highly developed city by any standard.

In the Indus civilization, too, the massive city walls, encompassing large, highly populated, and remarkably well-planned urban spaces, indicate a late construction, after considerable formative urban development had already taken place. In smaller sites, only the acropolis was fortified, whereas the surrounding lower city remained unwalled,[82] strongly suggesting the initial stages of development in all urban fortifications. Some 1,000 years later, as urbanism gradually revived in Early Historic India along the Ganges Valley from about 550 BC, a clear sequence of evolution is discernable from towns and earthen, mud, and timber fortifications to regularly laid-out cities surrounded by walls, some made of stone.[83]

In western Nigeria the excavated fortifications of the Yoruba cities reveal several concentric lines, erected in step with the cities' growth. All the same,

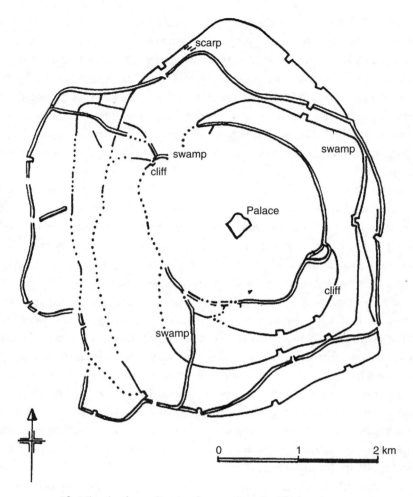

scarp

swamp

swamp

cliff

Palace

cliff

swamp

0   1   2 km

Ife, Nigeria: the earliest, and expanding, fortified perimeter

even the Yoruban Ife's earliest circuit fortifications, which have a circumference of more than 5 kilometres, indicate the pre-existence of a large city by
the time of their construction. In Benin City the circuit fortifications,
consisting of a massive earthen bank and ditch, have a circumference of
11.6 kilometres. A trend from ditches and stockades to mud ramparts and
more solid walls is universally discernible.[84]

As to the Greek city-states, it would surprise most people to learn that
they had no circuit walls until the sixth century BC in Ionia and southern
Italy and until the fifth on mainland Greece, after centuries of city growth.[85]

Athens, the largest Greek *polis*, was evacuated without resistance by its population and burnt down by the Persians in 480 BC because it still had only the Acropolis walls and possibly the beginnings of further fortifications encompassing a larger public area around the centre.[86] It acquired its celebrated circuit walls only after the Persian War and despite Spartan objection to the novelty. Only by the time of the Peloponnesian War had most Greek city-states erected circuit walls, with the unwalled Sparta remaining as an exception and reminder of earlier times. As late as the second half of the fourth century BC, Aristotle, writing that 'a citadel (or *acropolis*) is suitable to oligarchies and monarchies; a level plain suits the character of democracy', still found it meaningful to discuss the question whether or not it was good for a *polis* to have a fortification wall (*Politics* 7.11.5–12). The Italic city-states of the same period followed a similar pattern.[87] For instance, excavations show that Rome's circuit stone wall was built only after the sacking of the city in 390 or 387 BC by the Gauls, who would not have been able to take the city if it had been fully fortified. Only particularly exposed stretches of the city's perimeter appear to have been protected by discontinuous ditches and earthworks (*ager*). The Roman population took refuge in the Capitoline Hill, where some sort of fortifications probably augmented the natural stronghold.

Much the same applied to the mediaeval city-states that were beginning to grow substantially in Italy, Germany, and Flanders from about the tenth century AD, after the urban decline of the European Dark Age that had followed the Germanic migrations. The city-states emerged around castles or fortified monasteries/bishop seats that served as their point of refuge, some of them relying on old Roman fortifications (*castra*). During the eleventh century a larger civil centre encompassing the market and main public buildings was fortified around the original stronghold in many nascent cities. The residential suburb (*faubourg, suburbium, portus*) that continued to grow as an adjunct to the fortified core was defended, if at all, only by elementary timber and earthen fortifications. Full circuit walls began to be built only towards the end of that century and mostly in the twelfth, after some two centuries of city evolution.[88]

Finally, returning to pre-Columbian America, there, too, fortifications evolved in step with city evolution, including the gradual emergence over the centuries of circuit walls. Further excavations of the Maya sites have brought to light a sequence that eluded earlier researchers. The most ancient finds, first regarded as drainage systems, are now firmly identified as formid-able earth fortifications. In Los Naranjos, for example, 'an earthwork system composed of ditch and embankments, approximately 1300 m long,' stretch-ing from a swamp to a lake, defended the approaches to the main site as early as 800–400 BC, long before the state period. A second system, more than double in length, was apparently erected around AD 400–550, during the classic period. In the pre-classic site of Mirador, a 600 metre long wall has been discovered. In the massive site of Tikal, another earth and rubble system, composed of a ditch, parapet, and gates, defended the approaches to the site from the north, stretching from swamp to swamp for 9.5 kilometres. It was built 4.5 kilometres away from Tikal's Great Plaza and 4 hours' walk from its nearest large neighbour Uaxactum. The system is believed to have evolved from the early classic period and reached its zenith in the middle and late classic periods. The Edzna 'citadel' was surrounded by a water-filled moat even before the classic period. Becan is the first large-scale site pres-ently known to have been completely surrounded by a ditch and parapet from as early as the pre- or early classic period (AD 100–450). The ditch was '1.9 km in circumference with an average width of 16 m and depth of 5.3 m'. The parapet behind it was 5 metres high. Other fortified sites from various periods of the classic have been identified, although many have not yet been excavated.

By the late- and post-classic periods, circuit walls evolved around many sites, particularly in the northern lowland. Although some of these fortified sites were no more than central ceremonial/civic/refuge enclosures, others encompassed a much wider urban centre. Mayapan was the latest and largest, with a 9 kilometre long outer wall, encompassing 4.2 square kilometres, and an inner (earlier?) wall around its ceremonial–civic centre. In Tulum and Ichpaatun the walls were squarely laid out and made of stone. In some sites stone walls were topped by timber stockades. Fortifications everywhere relied extensively on the natural defences of heights, swamps, and sea. In the post-classic Maya highland, steep slopes provided the basis for formidable discontinuous defences at the approaches to urban sites.[89]

In central Mexico, the giant city-state Teotihuacan dominated the entire region during the classic period, with its influence extending throughout Mesoamerica. As the city reached its apogee, it had massive but no circuit walls, some of which were 5 metres high and 3.5 metres wide at the base. The stretches of the city's circumference that were not defended by walls

Maya fortifications: Tulum. The acropolis and perimeter walls

were protected by a maze of canals, flooded areas, and cactus vegetation, and the sheer size of the building compounds within the city would have functioned as 'natural fortresses'.[90] In any event, during its heyday Teotihuacan apparently had few serious rivals. Only after the time of the city's destruction by an unknown agent about AD 650 was the system becoming far more competitive, as a multiplicity of antagonistic city-states emerged in late- and post-classic central Mexico. Some of the leading cities in this system had a fortified acropolis, whereas others, such as Xochicalco and Cacaxtla, were evolving circuit defensive systems, which usually relied on strong natural defences. In Xochicalco, for example, the central hilltop religious–civic enclosure was surrounded by a wall, whereas the larger perimeter of the hill was defended by a discontinuous system of ramparts and ditches that closed the gaps between steep slopes. Some cities possessed circuit walls at the time the Spanish arrived, whereas in others—such as the Aztec capital Tenochtitlan, lying in the middle of a lake—a strong natural location was reinforced by man-made constructions. Further south, in the Valley of Oaxaca from the late pre-classic and during the classic (periods I to III; roughly first half of the

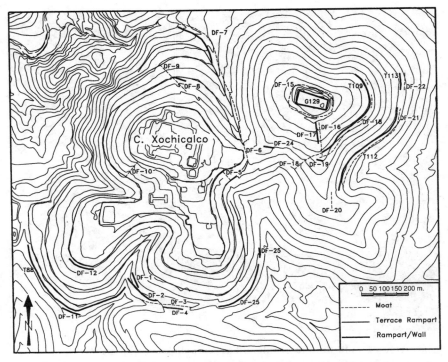

Xochicalco: discontinuous terraces, ramparts, and moats augment the city's natural defences. Such layout was common enough in many early urban sites in the Old World as well

first millennium AD), the prospering city of Monte Alban was defended by kilometres-long, discontinuous, fortification walls that augmented the site's strong hilltop position. Hilltop stronghold refuge sites abounded in the Valley.[91] To conclude my discussion so far, it would appear that only the misleading perspective of absolute chronology—where the relative one is far more appropriate—creates the optical illusion that pre-Columbian America was fundamentally different from the Old World.

All this, however, only makes the puzzle more general: if, as argued earlier, the main motive for the coalescence of the countryside population and nucleation of settlement that characterized the growth of city-states was defence—in the Old World as well as in America—why were they not fully surrounded by brick and stone circuit walls from the start? Indeed, what defensive use was there in settlement aggregation in the absence of such walls?

Underlying this puzzle are, again, the generally unfamiliar patterns of pre- and proto-state warfare, which stand in variance to our historically shaped concepts of war. Pre- and proto-state warfare consisted mainly of raids, carried out by war parties. Lives and property in scattered countryside settlements were mostly at risk. By coalescing around a central stronghold people not only could find refuge in time of emergency for life and some valuable movable possessions—chiefly livestock—but also ceased to present small, isolated, and highly vulnerable targets for raiders. As with herd animals, schools of fish, and flocks of birds, there was increased safety in numbers. On top of all defensive works, cities were protected by *size*. Substantial settlements could not be quickly eliminated in a surprise night raid. Their inhabitants would have constituted a considerable force and would have had time to wake up and resist. Indeed, taking on a city meant direct fighting of the most severe, sustained, and dangerous nature: from house to house, with every building top potentially serving as a minor stronghold. This was precisely the sort of fighting that 'voluntary' pre- and proto-state warriors tended to avoid.

This is not mere speculation; the evidence from both Archaic Greece and late pre-contact Mexico (and pre-colonial Africa) supports it. Warfare for the Archaic Greek city-states meant raiding the countryside or, if the enemy came out to defend his fields and orchards, a fierce but short face-to-face encounter. The encounter ended either in the attackers' withdrawal, as seems to have happened in most cases, or, if it was the defenders who withdrew, in a resumption of ravaging. Tellingly, the cities themselves appear to have been rarely attacked. Experts on Greek warfare have recognized that occupying another city-state by force was simply beyond the capability of a seventh- or sixth-century BC *polis*. Generally, however, this fact has been ascribed to rudimentary siege-craft before the late fifth century BC and to the short staying power of the citizen militia, both factors being valid for most of the fifth century. Curiously, however, the fact that the *poleis* of the Archaic period still had no circuit walls has somehow not sunk in.[92]

Why then were the cities so rarely conquered? The phalanx hoplite warriors are justly celebrated for their unique bravery in accepting and withstanding face-to-face encounters. However, they regularly did so on a level plain and equal terms, while avoiding attack on enemy forces that held superior positions, for example on elevated ground. Evidently, they recoiled even more from unequal out-and-out urban street fighting. It should be noted that, even after the crushing Theban victory of Leuctra in 371 BC, in a period in which sieges had already become more common, the Thebans and their allies, having invaded the Peloponnese and Laconia, recoiled on two different occasions from an attack on the still unwalled Sparta for precisely these reasons (Xenophon, *Hellenica* 6.5.27–31, 7.5.11–14.) Thus, although early Greek 'campaigns' were brief—often lasting no more than a single day or a few days—conflicts were inherently indecisive and protracted. It was people's desire for self-preservation, as well as the absence of coercive central command and organizational stamina in the early city-state, that accounted for this type of warfare, so unfamiliar to the modern mind. The notions of 'ritualized' warfare and customary restraint, routinely evoked by scholars to explain the puzzle of Archaic Greece, Mesoamerica, or, as already seen, any pre-state society, have little foundation in reality; there was very little restraint and much viciousness and cruelty in early Greek and Mesoamerican inter-city-state warfare.[93]

Indeed, among the Maya, too, aristocratic-led raids (and aristocratic single combats) were the principal form of warfare, making it inherently indecisive and protracted for most of Mayan history.[94] And despite the reputed viciousness of Aztec warfare, 'flowery wars'—a continuation of the 'ritual-ized battle'—remained dominant in it. Large-scale Aztec ravaging raids were the principal means for achieving enemy compliance. Weaker victims gave in to the pressure, and, as the Aztec hegemonic empire and armies grew, their enemies' cities and central cultic/civic strongholds became more vulnerable to storming or to the threat of it. All the same, scholars have only recently begun to come to terms with the highly conspicuous fact that, despite some 70 years of rivalry, the Aztecs never managed actually to conquer the city of their implacable arch-rival, Tlaxcalla, and its allies in the Valley of Puebla, which were protected by natural defences, supplemented by border fortifications and refuge strongholds, and yet possessed no circuit city walls.[95] Nor, for that matter, did Sparta ever manage to conquer its own main protagonist since the Archaic period, Argos. Among the Yoruba of western Nigeria, as well, intercity warfare mostly consisted of raids and skirmishes.[96]

In the exceptional case of the worse coming to the worst and the enemy forcing its way into the early city, the population would withdraw to the central ceremonial/civic stronghold. If this was a hilltop enclosure (or a small peninsula), its natural defences could be augmented by the simplest

286

forms of fortifications, such as ditches and earth-and-timber ramparts, which everywhere served as the most readily available and most easily handled materials. Brick and stone construction became more widespread only later, or in environments where stone or clay mud was plentiful whereas wood and even earth were scarce. Even in those regions, such as Mesopotamia and, to a lesser degree, the Maya lowland, where a flatter topography dictated that the ceremonial/civic centres would not possess the natural protection of commanding height, they still served as refuge strongholds, as the Mesoamerican evidence at any rate extensively shows. The monumental buildings themselves constituted the last line of defence, and they were further surrounded and connected by permanent or hastily improvised ditches and ramparts. In the prehistoric Andean civilizations of South America, too, the widespread prevalence of hilltop refuge strongholds and citadels in the mountain polities and of fortified urban ceremonial/civic centres in the coastal plain tell the same story.[97] Indeed, it was the capturing and destruction by fire of the city-state's refuge/cultic stronghold that everywhere—in both the Old and the New Worlds—signified supreme victory, not only symbolically, as some scholars have held, but also practically, for it was the main and last point of resistance for the city's population.

Moche fighting scene. Moche polities flourished in northern Peru in AD 100–800

All in all, a sequence in the evolution of city fortifications is discernible more or less worldwide (Japan is another instructive example): there is evolution from earth, rubble, and timber construction, through 'intermediate forms' such as the *morus gallicus* of the *oppida* which added stone facing, to brick and stone, and finally to pure stone; in parallel, there was evolution from defended central enclosures, often through somewhat larger fortified civic centres, to full circuit walls.[98]

What then were the factors that fuelled this evolutionary sequence and brought the familiar brick-and-stone circuit city walls into being? Again a broad interrelated process was at work, tied up with the consolidation of mass urban society/polity. The larger and more organized and resource rich the city-states had grown to be and the more capable they had become of long-term, sustained military effort in enemy territory (which in Greece, for example, happened only in the fifth century BC), the more they were capable of undertaking attacks on cities, deploying siege engines, and indeed of holding the cities after they had been occupied. At the same time, however, the very same developments that had enhanced offensive capability and threat had also increased defensive capability. Capability and necessity grew together. To give just one instance, money payment to recruits for protracted campaigning away from home—a crucial offensive upgrade—was introduced in Greece, Rome, and the medieval Italian city-states alike at roughly the same time that circuit city walls were erected. Taxes to pay for both were more or less simultaneously imposed.[99] Kilometres-long, circuit, brick-and-stone city walls now made their appearance where only ditches and earth-and-wood palisades around villages and refuge strongholds, or stone citadels at most, had existed. This was a massive construction, necessitating both investment and political co-ordination. A growth in state power, integrating earlier, loose agricultural cum nascent urban kin–tribal society, was reciprocally both a cause and a result of all these interrelated processes.[100]

In the Sumerian epic tradition, the erection of Uruk's circuit city walls was associated with the reign of a more powerful king, Gilgamesh (some time between 2700 and 2500 BC), whose power grew as a result of his resistance to the hegemonic rule of another powerful city-state king, Agga of Kish.[101] The growth in offensive, defensive, and political power was intertwined and self-reinforcing. In western Africa 'the first set of walls in Kano were begun by Sarki (king) Gijinmasu (ca. 1095–1134) and completed by his son. . . . In about 1440 Eware the Great, ruler of the Benin kingdom, constructed high walls and deep protective trenches around Benin city'.[102] Among the Maya, more elaborate defences, including stone circuit walls, evolved together with the growth of larger, regional city-state polities, mercenary service, more systematic state warfare, and wars of conquest.[103] In both Ionia (Anatolian coast) and Magna Graecia (southern Italy), the advanced peripheries of the Greek world, city fortifications came in the sixth century BC with the new autocratic power of the tyrants and the threat of great powers' professional armies: the Lydian and Persian in the east and the Carthaginian in the west.[104]

The rise in state power did not, however, always and necessarily take autocratic form. By the time Athens acquired its circuit walls, the work of a tyrant, Peisistratus, had been followed by a democratic reformer, Cleisthenes, who substituted a territorial political organization for the earlier kin-based structure of the Athenian polity. Similarly, although archaeology does not support Roman traditions that the city's walls were erected by King Servius Tullius in the mid-sixth century BC, it is interesting to note that it was to the same king that the reorganization of the Roman state from kin to territorial basis, as well as the institution of the legion army, were ascribed. Probably, as scholars tend to believe, a series of political and military reforms over two centuries of Roman state formation during the monarchy and early republic were compressed by later Roman traditions and ascribed to the proto-historical king, who may have launched the initial steps.[105] In the medieval communes, the expulsion of the local archbishop/prince and the establishment of the commune as an organized self-governing civic community coincided with the erection of circuit walls in the twelfth century.

The Rise of City-States: From Aristocratic Warriors to a Citizen Militia

City-states evolved in a stratified rural society dominated by chiefly and big men's armed retinues. Their rise was therefore inextricably tied up with a successful struggle against aristocratic warrior power. This has been fairly well recognized in the study of specific historical instances but has never been conceived in general terms. Aristocratic retinues' power was strongly associated with the horse in historically familiar cases of city-states' emergence. However, the sample is biased, because practically all the historically familiar cases are those of societies into which the horse had already been introduced. The costly horse undoubtedly reinforced the fighting power of the wealthy elite, but it would be interesting to know whether a struggle between city folk and big men's retinues had also marked the rise of city-states in pre-horse or horse-less cultures, such as early Mesopotamia and Mesoamerica. Evidence, however, is close to non-existent, and I mention the little there is later. I therefore start with the emergent city-states of

Archaic Greece, the first case with outlines that are vaguely recognizable, even though its details, too, are lost in protohistory.

Late Dark Age Greek warfare, during the ninth and eighth centuries BC, was dominated by the aristocratic heads of the big house estates (*oikoi*) and their retinues, who dominated society at large. These aristocrats rode horses; bigger horses and horseback riding had been introduced into the civilizations of the eastern Mediterranean at that time. However, principally because of Greece's rugged landscape, the mounted warriors mainly used their horses for transportation and 'strategic' mobility, and usually dismounted to fight on foot.[106] Peasants were no match for these aristocratic warriors and their retinues, who coerced them into subservience at home and preyed upon them outside. Either in their private feuds or when leading the local hosts in more general conflicts, the aristocratic warriors sometimes fought each other in the 'heroic' fashion described by Homer, which occasionally consisted of single battles and in which the throwing-spear was the principal weapon.

Scholars have pointed out that infantry hosts and mass infantry battles are prominent in the *Iliad*, and thus must have been a familiar feature of Homer's time in the late Dark Age. Some have even gone further in arguing controversially that these scenes in effect show that there were phalanx-like mass infantry armies during that period, no different in fact from those of later times.[107] This latter argument would, however, appear to misinterpret the social context and military realities of the time. An infantry host in itself does not yet make for an effective phalanx, when either operating in an open and undisciplined array or adopting a crude 'shield wall' formation, as later north European 'barbarian' societies are often reported to have done. Furthermore, whether the Dark Age infantry hosts consisted of aristocratic retinues or local peasant militia, or both, an analogy with early medieval European societies suggests that these forces were largely subservient to the aristocratic warriors, and often played a secondary role to them. However, from the seventh century BC a dramatic change was taking place. As both pictorial representations and literary fragments show,[108] the phalanx, a mass formation of citizen farmer and artisan foot soldiers in dense order, was making its appearance in the nascent Greek city-states, taking over from the mounted aristocrats and their retinues, and henceforth dominating Greek warfare. Only in the flat and politically backward Thessaly, where the *polis* did not take root, did an equestrian feudal aristocracy retain social and

The earliest known depiction of a Greek phalanx. Late seventh century BC
Corinthian vase

military supremacy on the old model down to the classical era. This close
interconnection between the 'hoplite revolution' and the rise of the *polis*,
and the popular aspect of these developments, have been emphasized by
scholars.

There is far less information about the early Greek mounted aristocratic
warriors than about the later Greek city-states' infantry mass armies,
whereas the opposite is true with respect to medieval European history. In
both societies, however, the process that took place was in many ways
remarkably parallel. The more stratified the Dark Age European societies of
the post-migrations period became, the more they were dominated by
the local aristocratic elite and their armed retinues. From the eighth century
AD in western and central Europe, this aristocratic elite was increasingly
equestrian and more formally in charge. Its military dominance in a rural
European society, in which state power was weak and often close to non-
existent, went on for centuries until European society itself was transformed
by several interrelated processes. One of these processes was the emergence
of cities and city-states. Wherever they emerged, nascent city-states—or
communes, as they were called—strove to shake off the local nobility's
dominance, and everywhere their instrument for doing so was their citizen,

predominantly infantry mass armies of artisans and farmers, organized by regions, boroughs, and guilds.

All in all, the city-states' success was overwhelming, with an unmistakable pattern revealing itself throughout Europe. In northern Italy the armies of each of the emerging city-state polities—even though they acted separately and were rivals to each other—everywhere managed to drive away the local nobles and take over their strongholds, in the city and then in the country-side. Subsequently, the combined city-states' citizen armies of the Lombard League, headed by Milan, won victory over feudal power in the form of the German Emperor Frederick Barbarossa's army in Legnano (1176). In Flanders the citizen armies of each of the communes—again acting separately from each other—achieved a similarly uniform string of successes against local aristocratic power in their respective surrounding territories. Furthermore, in the Battle of Courtrai (1302), the civic infantry militias of the allied communes, deployed in a dense, eight-deep formation, soundly defeated the King of France's knightly army. In the following decades, in what was to become Switzerland, the peasant communities of three mountain and forest cantons defeated the German nobility's attempt to subjugate them, an achievement that was, of course, facilitated by the nature of the landscape. The mountain people then allied with the city-states of the plain, and the Swiss mass infantry armies, fighting in dense formation, destroyed every knightly force that took the open field against them. In the late fifteenth and early sixteenth centuries these armies would go on to become the supreme infantry and terror of the European battlefields.[109]

To be sure, there were very substantial differences between the city-state polities in the various periods, regions, and cultures described, differences

Milanese communal troops returning after the Lombard League's victory at Legnano (1176) over Emperor Frederick Barbarossa

that are more fully explicated as discussion unfolds. One such significant difference lay in the fact that the European mediaeval communes emerged within a political environment already dominated by large, albeit segmentary and weak, feudal states, rather than in a non-state environment, as most of the other city-state systems described here are. The feudal state is discussed in Chapter 11. For the moment, however, it should be noted that, although the weakness of central power was an indispensable condition for the growth of city-states in feudal Europe, the existence of that power nevertheless variably limited the degree of autonomy that the communes were able to achieve, particularly where central state power was relatively stronger—for example, in Flanders (France) and Germany, as against Italy.[110] The existence of state power also affected the pattern of the communes' growth. It explains the widely noted phenomenon that, unlike other city-state systems, the medieval communes expanded politically from the city nucleus out. Although constantly absorbing people from the countryside as they grew, they extended their rule over that countryside and its peasant population (*contado*) only as their power increased. Thus, the artisan guilds and boroughs played a more dominant political and military role in them, although both demography and the sturdiness of the peasant soldier dictated that the peasant element would be at least partly co-opted.

All these differences notwithstanding, mass citizen infantry armies—often highly effective—were closely associated with the rise of city-states. As already mentioned, we lack evidence about warfare patterns in pre- and proto-state Mesopotamia. However, with respect to the state period itself the excavation of the Vulture Stele, commemorating a war between Lagash and Umma (about 2450 BC), has revealed to astonished modern scholars the familiar ranks and files of a six-deep phalanx-like dense formation, with locked shields and levelled spears, previously identified with the Greek *poleis* of almost 2,000 years later. Indeed, rather than being uniquely Greek, the close-order and close-quarter infantry formation has been independently invented several times over, most notably by city-states. The early Moslem armies from Arabia are a striking case in point, quite in contrast to their popular image. Although later-day Moslem armies are associated with the prestigious horse, in fact the Moslems adopted it only after they had conquered the Middle East and north Africa. In arid Arabia cavalry forces were impractical. It was the solid infantry forces raised from the townsfolk of

The Stele of Vultures, c. 2450 BC. The king of Lagash leads a phalanx-like formation.
The spears, held with both hands and protruding from the front line, indicate a
six-file formation

Mecca, Medina, and the other caravan city-states of south-west Arabia that
constituted the backbone of early Islamic armies. Allied tribesmen provided
light forces, but only in the north did they ride horses. The camel was the
main riding animal, which provided strategic mobility over long distances
and from which the riders dismounted to fight on foot. In both of the
decisive battles of Yarmuk in Trans-Jordan (AD 636) and al-Qadisiyya in
Iraq (AD 637), against the armies of the Byzantine and Persian empires
respectively, the invading Moslems took up strong defensive positions,
where their tightly packed spearmen and shield wall repulsed and ultimately
routed their enemies' cavalry charges.[111]

Returning to more widely familiar examples, in both the south and north
of medieval Europe, in Italy and Flanders, the communes' citizen infantry
armies wore at least some protective armour and wielded spears, pikes,
and crossbows. Independently of either, the most formidable medieval
phalanx-like formation, the dense and deep Swiss infantry hedgehogs,
consisted of pike-men and halberdiers in close order. Finally and remarkably, the Yoruba of western Nigeria were experiencing a similar process.
After the introduction of the horse into western Africa in the sixteenth
century, mounted chiefly retinues constituted the backbone of Old Oyo's
imperial armed forces. However, by the late eighteenth century the empire
had disintegrated, and the newly independent city-states waged their wars,
and defeated the Fulani horseman pastoralists, by means of their infantry

Ghent's communal army c. 1346

militias. These employed both long swords and bows, until firearms became increasingly widespread towards the middle of the nineteenth century.[112] What was it then that accounts for this almost universal phenomenon, starting with the preponderance everywhere of the city-states' militias over the local aristocratic, often mounted, warriors and their armed retinues, which had earlier dominated warfare?

The relative strength of the infantryman and horseman vis-à-vis each other is accorded a special comparative treatment in Chapter 11. At the moment, however, some technology-based explanations for the question at hand must be rejected as being of secondary significance at most. It has been suggested, for example, mostly by non-specialists, that it was the much cheaper and more widely available weapons of the Iron Age during the first millennium BC—as opposed to the earlier expensive bronze armament that had been confined to the elite—that broke aristocratic military dominance by making possible the armoured infantry armies of the Archaic *polis*.[113] It should be noted, however, that the bulk of the Greek hoplite's equipment during the Archaic and classical periods—his helmet, armour corslet, greaves, and the metallic parts of his shield—were still made from the easily cast bronze. Iron was mainly used for swords and spearheads. Thus the suit of armour remained as expensive as before. Indeed, the hoplite army, although

The Battle of Morat (1476), where the Swiss pikemen defeated the peak knightly
army of Charles the Bold, duke of Flanders

being far more popular in composition than the earlier aristocratic retinues,
still consisted only of the *polis*'s propertied farmers and artisans—estimated
at about a third to a half of its able-bodied adult male population (closer to
the larger estimate, in my opinion)—who could afford the armour suit.
Furthermore, the heavy defensive equipment was mainly important for the
close *infantry* battle between two opposing infantry formations, rather than

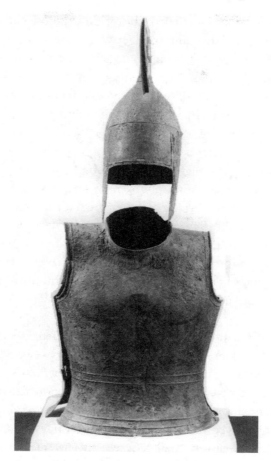

The earliest surviving hoplite bronze corslet and helmet, found in an eighth century BC
warrior grave at Argos

for the defeat of horsemen. For the latter job a solid formation of infantry,
armed with no more metal than that found in the tip of their spears, was all
that was necessary. Both the famous Macedonian phalanx and its later-day
Swiss counterpart wore no metal armour at all. Indeed, in classical Greece,
too, from the late fifth century BC, the heavy and expensive bronze body
armour was widely given up by hoplites in favour of handier hardened linen
or skin–protective closing. Metal armour was not essential to the concept of
the phalanx.

Scholarly treatment of the same question with regard to the European
Middle Ages has been conducted with little comparison to antiquity, both

because it involved a separate field of historical expertise and because it has been widely assumed that improved cavalry equipment—the successive introduction of the saddle, horseshoe, and, above all, stirrups—made horseback fighting in the Middle Ages far more effective than it had been in early antiquity. The stirrups have been credited with the preponderance of knightly equestrianism in Europe from the eighth century AD. Yet, as we have already seen, by the late Middle Ages (and before the advent of field firearms, which in the popular mind are associated with the demise of the mounted knight) this highly equipped horseman elite was being regularly and soundly defeated not only by new weapons, such as the English longbow, but also by the revived dense infantry formation, which in some cases, most notably the Swiss, was armed with the most elementary of weapons. The crux of the matter, then, was to place a dense and cohesive mass infantry formation on the field. What should have made this seemingly simple measure such a difficult undertaking? The answer had much more to do with social make-up and political evolution than with any technological factor.

As we saw in Chapter 9, 'egalitarian' tribal societies—where self- and kin-reliance, often violent, was the underlying reality—were generally conducive to the cultivation of a warrior spirit. However, these societies lacked a coercive central authority that would mobilize and organize the tribal manpower for mass organized warfare. As more intensive agriculture and a more stratified society evolved, chiefly and big men's retinues predominated, even though they were relatively small, because they were the only organized forces within society and could be checked only by other such forces. In consequence, their dominance tended to grow in a snowball process, making society increasingly more stratified. The progressively subservient populace offered no effective resistance to this process, because, being widely scattered throughout the countryside in their farms and hamlets, they found effective communication and co-operation difficult to achieve and were individually vulnerable to aggression. It was these 'objective conditions' above all that dictated that rural society everywhere was subjugated by armed elites, and indeed, explain how the many could be so harshly exploited by the few. Correspondingly, the local militias were increasingly falling in significance. In part, the elite regarded them as potentially dangerous. More importantly, subjugated and desolate peasants, who had no stake in social and political affairs and little interest in the fruits of fighting, universally made poor warriors. And the more subservient they had become, the more 'useless' they proved to be on the battlefield, even when their hosts were called up to augment the aristocratic warriors and their retinues.

The emergence of the city-state was, however, bound up with a drastic reversal in the power of its populace, which is somewhat captured by the medieval proverb that 'city air makes man free'. There was power—and decreased vulnerability—in mass, and urban aggregation made communication and political organization easy and effective. Scholars of ancient Greece maintain that the *polis* revolution consisted in the creation of a 'citizen-state' even more than of a city-state;[114] the two developments were, however, obviously connected. Again, all this was a process rather than an event, in which aristocratic retinues' power was rolled back, serfdom and other traditional forms of bondage were replaced by the obligations of tax payment and military service, autonomous city institutions were built up, urban concentration gathered momentum, and farmers and artisans grew more self-confident, increased their stake in communal affairs, and were habituated to running their own affairs. In consequence, city-state societies gave rise to the hitherto unique combination of a mass army of free citizens which was at the same time politically organized and therefore subject to at least the rudiments of central mobilization, control, and command.

Very short distances between polities, tiny territories, and brief campaigns also facilitated unprecedented levels of manpower mobilization.[115] In contrast to pre-state tribal/chiefly/stratified segmentary societies or to other sorts of polities, collective co-operation for protecting the closely lying mosaic of fields, orchards, and pastures—all in the immediate vicinity of the city—was more evidently a self-interest and could be maintained in the intimate city-state community by collective sanction that strongly discouraged 'free riding' and passive forms of 'defection'. As an enemy host was observed crossing into the city-state's territory, the city men could be called upon to take arms in very short order—with the watchful eyes of neighbours and political and military officials ensuring that individuals did not lag behind—and march out to confront the enemy and stop their ravaging.

At its best, this was a winning combination, as the classical Greeks were well aware. They attributed their victories over the Persian Empire to the fact that they were free men, fighting in their own collective interests, whereas the conscripted subjects of the Persian Empire were 'slaves', who could be brought to the battlefield but barely made to risk their lives in a serious, direct clash of arms. Indeed, the short distances between the rival city-states, their manpower concentration, more inclusive sociopolitical organization, and intensified agricultural investment in, and dependence upon, fields and orchards (as opposed to an earlier more pastoral–shifting-agriculture–foraging economy) meant that pre-state stealth tactics, which had taken place in a wild, sparsely populated and sparsely cultivated land-scape, underwent transformation. Face-to-face collective encounters in defence of immovable agricultural property, the fruit-bearing trees and crops upon which people's livelihood depended, rose in significance.[116]

As the stakes of battle grew and the indecisive encounter from a distance gave way to closer and more risky clashes of arms, the warriors in each army drew closer together, seeking increasing shock effect and mutual protection in the simple dense formation, known as a phalanx or any other name. Shock weapons—the thrusting-spear, sword, or halberd—grew to dominate the increasingly close-order, close-quarters battle, largely replacing the mis-sile weapons of the earlier stand-off battle, such as the throwing-spear and the bow. (Archery was in any case an art that could be cultivated only in a life in nature and was generally beyond the reach of city folk, at least until the introduction of the simple-to-operate crossbow.) The historically familiar, hazardous, face-to-face, close-in battle thus gained its status as the climactic and defining event of warfare. Classical historian Victor Hanson has admirably described much of this process in relation to the growth of the Greek *polis*.[117] Why the close-in infantry battle would become more characteristically associated with European, or 'western' warfare, as Hanson claims it did, is examined in Chapter 11. However, as the Sumerian phalanx, the early Moslem armies, and the Yoruba infantry militias indicate, the process had wide applicability among city-states.

It is time to make clear that reference to the 'popular', 'inclusive', 'communal', and 'self-governing' nature of the city-state and its civic militia does not imply democratic government. Fifth- and fourth-century BC democratic Athens, which in the popular image exemplifies the Greek *polis*, was in fact pretty much the exception. Nor were city-states—Athens included—socially and economically egalitarian. The popular, inclusive, and communal features that were integral in the making of city-states typically found expression less in democracy than in one of two regimes: the popular autocracy and the aristocratic–popular mixed polity or republic.

A single ruler and city folk were often allied in the struggle to curb aristocratic dominance, especially but not only during the city-state's formative period. Historical evidence regarding the early Sumerian city-states is very slim indeed. However, scholars deem to find in the epics of Gilgamesh, early king of Uruk, traces of that city's formative social institutions. Two features of these institutions have drawn attention: kingly power seems to have grown in the Early Dynastic period in comparison to that of the earlier ruler–priest *en*; but so also had the power of the popular assembly, causing scholars, who are accustomed to the later despotic regimes of the ancient Near East, to refer to the 'democratic' traits of the early Sumerian city-states. The epic tradition seems to reveal a relationship between these processes. When the king's proposal to go to war is opposed by the aristocratic Council of Elders, he brings it before and gets it approved by the popular assembly of the city's young men, in effect the city-state's warrior militia.[118]

The evidence with respect to the early Greek *poleis* is somewhat better. The rise of the *polis* in the seventh and sixth centuries BC coincided with Greece's first era of tyrants—or autocratic rulers, to differentiate them from the earlier *basilei* or chiefly leaders of more limited authority. These tyrants were abhorred by the aristocracy, above which they rose to rule, but in many cases apparently enjoyed popular support. Indeed, this was the same period in which the more popularly based phalanx formation appeared and took over from the aristocratic mounted warriors. Some evidence suggests that the advent of the phalanx may be directly linked with the seizure of power from the seventh century by tyrants such as Cypselus of Corinth, Orthagoras and Cleisthenes of Sicyon, and, perhaps more securely, Pheidon of Argos, a king who according to Aristotle (*Politics* 5.10.5–6) transgressed the traditional power limitations of the *basileus* in search of more autocratic authority. In Athens of the early sixth century BC, on the brink of a civil war between the aristocracy and the people, property–military classes, the basis of the phalanx army, were introduced in place of pure aristocratic rule by Solon. Solon was offered and declined tyranny, but, as already mentioned, his work was continued by the tyrant Peisistratus and the democratic reformer Cleisthenes. As scholars have widely noted, all these processes appear to have been closely interrelated: growing popular power associated with the rise of the *polis* combined with a successful leader in a common front against the aristocracy.[119]

In Rome, King Servius Tullius seems to have represented a similar shift in the status and power of the *reges*. He is said to have inextricably undermined the political kin basis of the powerful aristocratic clans, created the citizen phalanx army of the legion, and established the citizen hoplite assembly, the *comitia centuriata*, as the principal institution of the Roman state.[120] At the very same time, the second half of the sixth century BC, the Magonid kings of Carthage (and the failed Malchus, if he existed) apparently relied on the army and popular support to increase monarchic autocracy at the expense of the oligarchy.[121] Much the same process took place in both medieval Italy and Flanders. While rising commune power drove out the local nobility, the wealthiest merchant families themselves were becoming a patrician aristocracy that dominated communal politics. They constantly vied among themselves for power and prestige in struggles that frequently became violent and resulted in an almost endemic civil war between their armed retinues. In reaction, the city populace and citizen militia took steps to tighten state control over the great families. Furthermore, in Italy in particular, they increasingly instituted a popularly based rule by a *capitano populi* or *podesta*, to curb aristocratic power, turning the commune into a *signoria*.[122]

Autocratic rule was prone to 'excesses' and, in many early city-states, the aristocracy succeeded in abolishing it. However, wherever aristocratic power remained dominant in emergent city-state polities, it was necessary to establish some sort of a concord with the populace and form an inclusive type polity. This in effect is what Aristotle termed *politeia* and the Romans *res publica*. Not only, as already mentioned, were the people's concentrated masses a strong force that could not be ignored domestically; once popularly based mass infantry armies emerged in other, neighbouring city-states, an aristocratic-led petty-polity could hardly survive interstate conflict unless it was able to reach out and in some form or another co-opt its own populace into military service and, inevitably, into political society as well. City-state formation was thus again a self-reinforcing and expanding—'contagious'—process, in which intra- and inter-polity forces interacted. It can be assumed, for example, that in Archaic Greece the decline of the aristocratic warrior retinues was affected not only through separate domestic development in each emerging *polis*, but also through the external military pressure of more popularly based hoplite phalanxes, already established in some core area and generating an expanding, ripple wave of emulation.[123] This core area appears to have been located around Argos and Corinth in the eastern Peloponnese, as possibly indicated by the fact that the Argive shield and Corinthian helmet were the defining items of the hoplite panoply.

The unrivalled and somewhat better documented model of this sort of development was early Rome. The citizen militia phalanx formation, introduced into Italy by the Greek city-state colonies, spread rapidly. It was adopted by the evolving Etruscan city-states, where it replaced the chariot and mounted warfare of the aristocratic warrior retinues that had prevailed in the region since the Iron Age Villa Nova culture. There are indications, however, that Etruscan society remained highly stratified, and that the phalanx formation was adopted by the aristocratic retinues rather than becoming the basis of a true citizen mass army.[124] If indeed this was the case, it can help to explain the Etruscan military decline. In contrast, Rome under Servius Tullius fully embraced the civil–military reform made necessary by phalanx warfare. And when the *reges* were driven out of Rome in 510 BC, the aristocracy was able to hold on to power only by reaching a long series of compromises with the *populus*, a process that established Rome as a mixed aristocratic–popular republic. Even more than direct confrontation, the *populus*'s principal weapon in this struggle was simple: it refused to enlist for war in the phalanx-legion army, leaving the ruling patrician clans no choice but to concede.

The evidence regarding Mesoamerica is misty in the extreme. However, if it is true, as scholars believe, that aristocratic war bands remained paramount in Maya city-states' warfare whereas the post-classic city-state polities of central Mexico developed a broader, more popularly based military organization, this may explain the evidence for a Toltec take-over of the northern lowland Maya polities from around AD 1000, and possibly also a central Mexican role in the mysterious collapse of the classical Maya in the ninth century.[125] The Yoruba of western Nigeria during the nineteenth century offer additional, remarkable evidence of mixed-polity formation in relation to the rise of civic militias, evidence that recalls historically familiar early city-states from antiquity. According to a British officer's report (1861):

> . . . in order to obtain the voice of the people the chief who is selected to that position by popular voice from his warlike capacity . . . assembles the 'Obonis' or Elders and states the case . . . they then retire and having deliberated return to give him the decision at which they have arrived. . . .

> Under such a form of government there does not exist a standing army. The question of war is generally decided in public in what is called an 'Oio' or an extraordinary meeting held in the open air for the purpose of obtaining an expression of public opinion and passing certain edicts in conformity with that opinion. . . .

303

With the exception of . . . few armed retainers the remainder of the Tribe are almost without exception Farmers or engaged in peaceful occupations. They are docile, obedient to command, capable of enduring great bodily fatigue and marching with ease 40 miles a day. . . . By a system of voluntary enlistment the Abbeokutan army is raised, but often extreme measures are resorted to as in the case of the present war, where, at the 'Oio' before mentioned an edict was passed that whosoever did not proceed at once to the war should be deprived of his heart.[126]

In the mixed aristocratic–popular city-states, the old-reformed or new aristocracy that maintained a leading political, social, and economic status provided the leadership for the city-states' armies. They also held an elite, albeit much reduced, status within the fighting troops. Where the prestigious horse, which only they could afford, was present, they invariably continued to form the small mounted arm beside the infantry mass army, constituting roughly 10 per cent of its total. But even in pre-horse and horse-less societies, they reserved elite status for themselves. In central Mexico, for example, from Teotihuacan through the Toltecs to the Aztecs, the elite force within the army was the military orders of the jaguar and the eagle, which mainly consisted of the aristocratic young. Upward mobility into these orders and into the ranks of the nobility was open by merit to exceptional commoners who exhibited outstanding valour.

Mercantilism, Sea Power, Mercenary Armies, and Condottieri Rule

The city-state was a dynamic, evolving phenomenon, which continued to transform after its emergence, as intra- and inter-polity processes were constantly creating the preconditions for yet further development. The dominating image of the city-states at their zenith tends to obscure this continuous evolution. There were various interacting elements within this development, some of which—and their military aspects—are, for clarity's sake, treated here separately, in succession.

Mercantilism grew in some city-states hand in hand with their urban growth. Urban concentration was creating an embryonic nucleus of markets, artisan shops, and merchant businesses that was self-reinforcing and expanding. As already noted, the medieval communes' growth within a feudal state system that dominated the countryside explains the dominance of manufacturing and commerce within them. In most other locations, agriculture and the farmer population played the prominent role in the emergence of city-states, but crafts and trade also developed variably.[127] Thus some city-states—such as the Phoenician cities on the Levant coast and their colonies, most notably Carthage, many medieval communes, and, possibly, the largest city-states of the Indus civilization and Teotihuacan in the Valley of Mexico—appear to have grown as craft and trading centres from early on, becoming increasingly more so over time. Others—such as the Mesopotamian city-states and Greek *poleis* in Ionia, as well as Corinth and Athens in particular on the mainland, and some *poleis* of Magna Graecia in southern Italy—had craft and trade as an important aspect of their economy from very early and developed in a yet more commercial direction later on. Some of the commercial city-states, such as Teotihuacan, early Ashur, Florence, Milan, and the medieval city-states of southern Germany, were land locked. Some—such as the lower Mesopotamian city-states, many Greek *poleis*, and the communes of medieval Flanders—lay on or close to the sea and developed a mixed maritime–(river)–land orientation, as was manifest in their war-making patterns and institutions. Some, especially those that lacked a substantial agricultural hinterland because of geography or politics (or for lack of a land frontier altogether)—such as the Phoenicians, Greek *poleis* of the Aegean islands, the medieval Italian maritime communes, and those of the Hanse—were predominantly maritime.

As already noted, large-scale commercialism took place in a small number of city-states only, out of the dozens and hundreds of city-states in each city-state system. Population composition and occupational structure—as well as the war establishment—of these latter, commercial–maritime city-states in particular were largely different from those seen till now. Developing as international maritime traders, their economy was more specialized than that of most city-states. The free farmer element was smaller and weaker in them, and even the small independent artisan was losing ground relatively. The growing proletariat that these cities were creating and attracting found employment in the harbours and shipyards, on the sea, and in large-scale craft industries. In consequence, these city-states became formidable naval powers, possessing a vast mercantile fleet and dozens and even hundreds of state-controlled specialized oared warships, or galleys, for the protection and expansion of their trade routes, trading posts, and commercial interests. On the other hand, the city and maritime proletariat was ineffective for land military service, lacking the yeoman's communal cohesiveness and spirit of freedom and self-reliance that were central to the citizen phalanx army.

Thus, specialized commercial–maritime city-states tended to be less at ease about land warfare, even though some of them—such as Carthage and Venice—for various reasons turned to develop an agricultural hinterland and a continental domain after they had acquired wealth and power.

A similar process took place even in more continental city-states that were growing increasingly market oriented. Growing wealth vastly accentuated economic and social stratification. Here again, big urban industrial manufacturers and commercial enterprises, employing a large number of workers, were growing in significance in relation to the self-employed and small-employer artisans. In the countryside, too, large commercially oriented estates undermined the small freeholders, employing either slave labour or hired labourers, or both. Correspondingly, commitment to military service decreased. Members of the elite were reluctant to leave their businesses and good life behind. Free farmers and self-employed artisans were shrinking in number and significance, whereas both city and rural proletariat lacked the motivation, self-confidence, and stake in society that made for effective citizen militias.

Influx of wealth from the empire generated more or less the same effects.[128] Even in that supposedly model society, Sparta, where equality in land possession among the citizens had been grounded in the city's traditional and sacred 'Lycurgan' law, money from the empire was used by the aristocracy to accumulate land. By the fourth century BC, the number of Spartiatai freeholders who qualified for full citizenship and full-time military life had shrunk dramatically from a top figure of perhaps 5,000 to 1,500–2,000 and, later, even fewer.[129] A similar process, on an even grander scale, took place in Rome during the second century BC. The notion, first evoked by the Greeks and Romans themselves, that wealth was negatively affecting military virtue was grounded in veritable economic and social processes.

However, what commercial city-state society had lacked or lost in civic–military capacity it could partly compensate for by its purchasing power. Demand and supply rose in tandem: where there was money with which to hire troops, there were also impoverished peasants who looked for better prospects in mercenary service; and there were experienced commanders—mostly impoverished, exiled, or ambitious aristocrats turned professional generals—to lead them. As already mentioned, free bands doubling as mercenary troops had been employed as auxiliaries in early city-state systems; in the evolving market economy they had now become an increasingly significant and even the predominant military fighting force. Since the occurrence of war fluctuated within the city-states system, these mercenary hosts, similar to other service providers, moved from one place to another to meet the demand.

From the fourth century BC, mercenary troops played an increasing role in Greek warfare. Soldiers and generals who had gained experience in, and the habit of, war in the protracted Peloponnesian conflict chose to remain in the military occupation rather than return to civil life. They offered their services abroad, predominantly to the Great King of Persia but also to his domestic and foreign rivals. Greek mercenary hoplites were most sought after by both the king's satraps and the contenders to the imperial crown such as Prince Cyrus, who in 401 led the famous 10,000 Greek mercenaries as far into the empire as Babylon. From as early as the mid-seventh century BC, when, according to Herodotus (2.152–4), Pharaoh Psammetichus I hired Carian and Ionian hoplites in his revolt against Assyria, Greek mercenaries had been equally in demand in Egypt. By the fourth and third century BC, together with many other nationalities, they were also hired by Carthage, whose own citizen militia armies had been playing a decreasing role in its wars.

The Greek mercenaries' role in native Greek warfare itself grew no less significant. Athens, for example, a prospering commercialized city-state that had been proudly conducting its wars by means of its citizen armed forces only 50 years earlier, was experiencing citizen reluctance to enlist by the fourth century BC. Despite Isocrates' stricture, it relied heavily on mercenaries, as did the other *poleis*, particularly the largest and those with imperial ambitions and revenues, most notably Sparta itself.[130] By that same century, the Etruscan city-states were conducting their final struggles against Rome's rising power by means of hired, mostly Celtic, hosts. From the thirteenth century AD the Italian communes increasingly and then predominantly waged their wars with mercenary troops, or *condottieri*, as they were called after their contract (*condotte*). The citizens themselves were no longer willing to enlist.[131] As already mentioned before, foreign influx of unemployed armed bands from the Hundred Years War between England and France reinforced the trend. Despite humanists' criticism, most notably Machiavelli's, the civic citizen militia was not to be revived.

Mercenaries lacked patriotic commitment, were sometimes disloyal, and, of course, cost money, but hiring them was a means for considerably expanding the armed forces in time of war even when civil militias still constituted the bulk of the city-state's army, and for fighting wars at all where civic militias had become ineffective. This, of course, was a self-reinforcing process, because the more city-states relied on mercenary troops, the more the habit and practice of civic military service were being eroded. Mercenary professional troops generally exhibited greater tactical sophistication than inexperienced short-time militia recruits. Professional generals, too, tended to be far more consummate commanders than the non-professional and inexperienced, annually elected, civil–military magistrates who had traditionally led the city-states' armies. By the fourth century BC, the crude phalanx tactics of threshing it out in a no-nonsense, direct confrontation of two parallel lines of hoplites, who had been anxious to get back home and to work, had greatly diversified. Strategic and tactical manoeuvring, stratagems, and inter-arms co-operation among hoplites, skirmishers (*peltasts*), archers, and cavalry had increased in significance. Systematic siege-craft had developed. In all these new ways of warfare, professional generals excelled.[132] A century later, professional Greek generals such as Pyrrhus and the Spartan mercenary in the service of Carthage, Xanthippus—as well as, of course, the Punic Hannibal—demonstrated their superiority by masterminding the defeats of Roman consular armies. It was, nevertheless, the size and tenacity of its citizen militia armies that won Rome its ultimate victories in all these conflicts.

There were other major reasons besides growing commercialism for the decline of the civic militias and the rise of mercenary armies. First, however, I look at how this development affected the city-states' domestic politics, as it profoundly did. It heralded the ascendancy of a new type of upstart autocratic ruler who seized power through his command of mercenary troops. Some of these rulers cultivated and enjoyed popular support, again directed against aristocratic dominance. However, unlike early city-states' autocrats, these new autocrats were largely independent of native militia support, and many of them stayed in power by means of naked force and on foreign mercenary bayonets. Sargon of Akkad was the first and most celebrated example in a long string of autocratic military rulers who rose to power in the Mesopotamian city-states from the second half of the third millennium BC. The popular Athenian tyrant Peisistratus of the second half of the sixth century BC, having been banished by the aristocracy, seized power for a second time on the strength of a mercenary host of Thracians. A second era of tyrants began throughout the Greek world in the fourth century BC (and earlier in Syracuse), during the age of mercenaries, as mercenary generals or local leaders aided by mercenary troops seized power.[133] Even in Sparta, with a celebrated ancient constitution enacting egalitarian communalism and full-time military service among the citizens that had been long disintegrating, a tyrant, Nabis, came to power in the late third century BC on the strength of a mercenary army.[134] In late mediaeval Italy, individual *condottieri* usurped power in most of the communes, which had originally hired them to wage their foreign wars. Visconti and later Sforza in Milan are only the better-known examples.

Interestingly, the more pronouncedly maritime mercantile city-states proved the most resistant to military tyranny. The anonymous Athenian commentator, labelled the 'old oligarch' by modern scholars who have taken up his argument (and also Aristotle, *Politics*, 5.4.8, 6.7.2), claimed that the increase in Athens' maritime and commercial activities and the expansion of the city proletariat engaged in them fuelled Athens' ever-deepening process of democratization. However, in this, too, Athens was an exception. In most mercantile–maritime city-states the growing proletariat was increasingly disenfranchised, as an oligarchy of the leading merchant families was tightening its grip. To prevent commanders of mercenary troops supported by the city proletariat from taking over, this oligarchy took special precautions. In Carthage of the fourth and third centuries BC, after kingly rule had been replaced by that of two *suffetes* ('judges') and an oligarchic council, the generals were constantly suspected and kept under close surveillance by the city's government. It should be noted, however, that before and during the Second Punic War, the successful Barcid generals, Hamilcar and Hannibal, relying on both the professional army and popular support, established a practically autonomous domain in Spain, while also dominating Carthaginian politics. Venice, the most extreme case, was turned by its ruling oligarchy into a veritable totalitarian state, where state security committees and secret police employed extensive domestic espionage and the harshest measures to prevent coups.

The Expansion, Power Limitations, and End of the City-State

Growing commercialism was only one factor that transformed city-states and their armed forces. Commercialism itself was affecting and being affected by the expansion of the city-state from its petty-state form into larger political structures, because, similar to the rural petty-states' systems, city-states' systems tended to coalesce into fewer and larger political conglomerations under the gravitational forces of power politics. As the city-states grew, the larger ones tended to dominate their weaker regional neighbours, swallowing those in their immediate vicinity through direct annexation, and establishing hegemonic, 'alliance' control over their more distant periphery. Regional city-states were the result. In some cases, even larger, imperial, 'super' city-state polities followed. In a competitive political environment there was a selective advantage for size. The city-state could not compete for long in this escalating race and was thus a particularly transient phenomenon in polities' evolution. Again, its glory in its prime tends to obscure the fact that nowhere did it survive for more than a few centuries.[135] Ultimately, city-states' systems were either eliminated by one of their members or from outside.

In Sumer, the Early Dynastic period of some 30, roughly equal, independent city-states was drawing to a close towards the middle of the third millennium BC, as one dominant city at a time—Ur, Lagash, Kish, Umma-Uruk—won hegemonic overlordship over others. Then, in the twenty-fourth century BC, Sargon of Akkad for the first time unified the Land, as it was called, establishing an empire that encompassed the whole of Mesopotamia. After its collapse, regional city-state kingdoms—such as Ur of the Third Dynasty, Isin-Larsa, Hammurabi's and Kassite Babylon, Mari, Ashur, and Aleppo—dominated and even incorporated the others into their respective domains and some of them established larger empires for short periods. A similar process seems to have taken place among the city-states of the Indus Valley. With the Indus script remaining undeciphered, archaeologists can only infer from the remarkable growth of Harappa and Mohenjo-daro that these cities may have become the centres of large unified states during the later Indus civilization.[136] In early historic India of the first millennium BC, too, the numerous emergent town-and-countryside petty-states (*janapadas*) were progressively swallowed by the few that proved strongest, and that in the process turned into regional states (*maha-janapadas*) and 'super' regional states.[137] In western Nigeria, Old Oyo achieved imperial hegemony over the other Yoruba city-states during the seventeenth and eighteenth centuries.

Students of the Maya are debating whether there were some 60 Maya city-states, each covering about 2,500 square kilometres, or only about eight regional independent city-states, with an average area of 30,000 square kilometres, which maintained hegemonic overlordship over the smaller centres.[138] It would be in line with the evidence regarding Maya political evolution to suggest that, over time, by the late classic period, some of the stronger Maya city-states such as Tikal, Copan, Palenque, and Caracol expanded by force to become regional city polities. For example, the long line of fortifications defending the approaches to Tikal from Uaxactum in the north was partly demolished in the late classic period, suggesting to the excavators that one of the antagonists may have won and established a unified regional rule over both cities.[139] In any case, no Maya city-state achieved supreme domination before the lowland Maya civilization mysteriously collapsed. With respect to central Mexico, it is debated if and what system of city-states had existed before Teotihuacan achieved its wide-ranging dominance in the first centuries AD. For many centuries after Teotihuacan's collapse no other city-state achieved hegemony over the much more competitive system that ensued, although Tula seems to have gained a leading position during the tenth to twelfth centuries. However, from the fourteenth century, the newly established Aztec city-state of Tenochtitlan won hegemonic rule over the 40-odd city-states in the Valley of Mexico, and expanded further to create a hegemonic empire that encompassed the whole of central Mexico.[140]

In Greece, Athens emerges from the early Archaic period as an unusually large, regional polity, encompassing the whole of Attica. Sparta was even more unusual, maintaining military occupation over the alien helot population of Laconia and Messenia from the late eighth or seventh century BC and, in consequence, turning itself into a permanently mobilized *Herrenvolk* warrior society to prevent and suppress revolts. Through the Peloponnesian League, created in the second half of the sixth century BC, Sparta dominated regional and Greek politics. Thebes established hegemonic control over her smaller neighbouring *poleis* through the Boeotian League. From the fifth to the mid-fourth centuries BC, each of these powerful city-states in turn attempted, and succeeded in trying, to create a larger hegemonic empire around it.[141] Similarly, Syracuse became the dominant *polis* in Greek eastern Sicily. The days of hundreds of small independent *poleis* were over.

By the fourth century BC, Rome had been transforming an earlier hegemonic regional alliance with the other, smaller, Latin city-states by directly annexing some of them and establishing stricter 'alliance' hegemony over the rest. In north Africa, Spain, Sicily, and Sardinia, Carthage established hegemonic overlordship over the other dozens of Phoenician city-state colonies and acted to expand its commercial and political control in the western Mediterranean. In medieval Italy and Flanders alike, the number of independent city-states (a few hundred in Italy, scores in Flanders) was continuously and drastically shrinking in the space of two centuries. Progressively from the thirteen to fifteenth centuries AD, Florence, Milan, Venice, and Genoa more or less established their rule over most of the other north Italian city-states, each becoming a regional, super city-state polity.[142] Bruges, Ghent, and Ypres were the agents of a similar process in Flanders.

In this evolutionary race towards increased size, the city-state was almost by definition in difficulties. Growth negated its fundamental social and political features as an intimate civic community centred on a city. Where the threat came from outside in the form of large states, the only response that could preserve city-states from complete loss of civic independence was an alliance or even a confederation, the raison d'être of which was the co-ordination of foreign policy and pulling together of resources for war. In view of the city-states' very high mobilization capacity in comparison with either pre-state or state societies, these structures often proved to be very effective—especially for defence—so long as they did not succumb to internal division, domination by one of their members, or a very strong state.

The Greek city-states, for example, allied against and repulsed the Persian invasion in 480–479 BC, despite massive defection to and collaboration with the Persians and poor allied co-operation, which ultimately also frustrated their attempts to carry the war offensively into the enemy's territory. By contrast, the Greek *poleis* failed in their attempts to resist the rising Macedonian state of Philip II and Alexander, although during the third century BC the federated Aetolian and Achaean Leagues proved more successful in maintaining their independence against Macedon and were to succumb only to Rome. As already mentioned, in the twelfth century AD the communes of northern Italy, allied in the Lombard League, succeeded in defeating the German Emperor Frederick Barbarossa's attempt to bring them more firmly under his rule, whereas the Flanders' communes had a more mixed record in their struggles in the fourteenth century against their duke and against French royal power. The Swiss Confederation and north German Hanse League were established for similar purposes.

All the same, once a much stronger, increasingly unified and centralized, early modern 'national' state power began to replace the weak feudal state in Europe, the balance had changed. Even confederated city-states could not stand, to say nothing of the regional city-states of Italy, for example, which remained deeply antagonistic towards each other and were to fall divided rather than standing united against French and Spanish state power. The United Dutch Provinces, confederating the Netherlands' semi-autonomous mercantile cities, were the exception, winning and defending their freedom against Spain and France. They owed much of their success, however, to their ability to shelter behind water barriers. The Swiss mountain fortress was another successful survivor, also for geopolitical reasons. In the process, both confederations increasingly assumed a unified state form themselves.

Some city-states that turned regional also consolidated their expanding realm into a nation-state. In southern Mesopotamia these processes were more or less taking place under Ur III and Babylon, but Assyria is probably the most striking instance.[143] From the city-state of Ashur in the late third millennium BC, it grew to dominate the entire region of the upper Tigris in the early and again in the late second millennium. By the latter period Assyria had become a nation-state, and in the first millennium BC it proceeded to conquer and eliminate for good the state and regional city-state system throughout the Near East. It progressively established direct, unified bureaucratic imperial control that henceforth would become pretty much the norm in the Near East, with one imperial rule succeeding the other down to modern times.

However, in most cases where a city-state system was eliminated from within by one of its members, the perpetrator's imperial enterprise had been accomplished before it shed its city-state structure. For this process of empire building to take place, the imperial city-state had to acquire a much larger population base than the typical city-state possessed and, indeed, to expand it further in positive interaction with its imperial growth, thus progressively breaking away from the city-state's inherently limited resource base. A growing domestic manpower base could then serve to harness the fighting potential of other city-states to that of the hegemon, creating a spirally expanding imperial system.

Both Teotihuacan and the Aztec metropolis Tenochtitlan swelled into hundreds of thousands in step with the expansion of their respective hegemonic empires. The combined manpower potential of the Aztec empire probably reached a few hundred thousand warriors.[144] The average Greek *polis* was made up of maybe as few as 2,500–4,500 people. By comparison, Athens was from the start a giant, and her fifth-century BC imperial prosperity attracted to her yet more people as immigrants. Her population grew to an estimated 200,000 people, of which some 40,000 were available for military service.[145] Her allies supplied hoplites, ships, and, as Athens tightened her grip on the hegemonic alliance, increasingly sums of money. Athens' imperial power was destroyed by a counter-coalition headed by Sparta and the Peloponnesian League. However, Sparta's own reach for empire was ultimately frustrated by her closed, small, and shrinking citizen body, which even at its peak numbered fewer than 10,000 warriors. Thebes' power base in Boeotia, although respectable in Greek terms, was also too limited for an enduring empire. Carthage developed into a huge commercial metropolis of hundreds of thousands, while expanding her control over the other Phoenician city-state colonies and the tribal peoples of north Africa and the western Mediterranean. The population of the leading communes of medieval Europe grew to many tens of thousands and even crossed the 100,000 mark, as they expanded into regional polities. The population of Florence, for example—together with Milan and Venice the largest Italian commune and expanding over most of Tuscany—was about 50,000 in 1200 and grew to 120,000 by 1330, before the Black Death. That of Ghent or Bruges, the growth of which in a ducal and state environment was more constrained, is estimated at 40,000–50,000 each at their height.[146]

The most successful imperial city-state of all was, of course, ancient Rome, and its success was chiefly associated with the truly remarkable expansion of its domestic manpower base.[147] This is well recognized by scholars but barely by non-specialists. The rapidity and general ease of Rome's string of victories over all the other Mediterranean great powers in the 50 years between 218 and 168 BC (except for the Second Punic War) struck contemporary witnesses, such as the historian Polybius, but the infrastructure that had made this feat possible was forged in the preceding three centuries, as Rome had expanded its hegemonic rule over the Italian peninsula. Instances of brilliant generalship are conspicuous in their absence during that initial expansion, because the Roman political system in effect positively discouraged the growth of experienced and successful generals by limiting the tenure of the state's civil–military magistrates, the consuls, to a single annual term. The celebrated legion army can partly be credited with the success, because, over the centuries, in the protracted struggles in rugged terrain against the hill peoples of central Italy and against the Gauls, it had gradually evolved from a simple phalanx—which was suitable for fighting only on level and open ground—into a considerably more flexible and versatile tactical formation. However, above all, it was in the potential and actual *number* of the citizen legions and allied troops and, hence, in the expansion of citizenship and the structure of the hegemonic empire that the real secret of Rome's rising power lay.

The expansion of Rome's rule over central Italy increased its military manpower in three ways. In the first place, whole communities were directly annexed by being incorporated into the Roman citizen body. From early times, Rome had exhibited an unusual openness to the inclusion of foreign elements. In Latium, the incorporated Latin communities belonged to the same ethnic stock as Rome anyway. Outside Latium the Italic communities would have centuries in which to assimilate and Latinize. Second, defeated communities that were not annexed were usually obliged to cede part of their lands to Rome and its Latin allies. Roman settlement of these lands made possible a steady internal demographic increase of its citizen body. Third, all the communities that retained their separate political status were required to sign a treaty of alliance with Rome. They paid no tribute and nominally remained independent, but their foreign policy was determined by the 'alliance'—that is, by Rome—and they were obliged to supply for the 'common effort' a specified number of troops upon request. They also enjoyed a share of the booty and of the confiscated land.

As Roman power expanded further into northern and southern Italy from the mid-fourth to the late third centuries BC, the same policy was extended further. Few communities were directly annexed at this stage, but Roman and Latin colonies were systematically established on confiscated land, and all the communities in the Roman orbit joined its alliance, either after they had been defeated or of their own 'free' accord. Excellent Roman military roads allowed rapid movement over great distances and into difficult terrains. Together, the network of roads and colonies consolidated Roman rule over the entire realm. As Roman expansion over Italy took centuries, there was enough time for each concentric circle of expansion to be 'pacified', gradually lose its habit of independence, and to be integrated into the system. The local elites in particular were co-opted and had the most to lose from disloyalty. The penalty for rebellion was very harsh. Leaders

315

would be executed and the population sold to slavery. Rebellions happened repeatedly, especially during the first stages after the loss of independence. All the same, Rome's reputation of uncompromising tenacity in maintaining this policy built up the formidable deterrence of terror that kept the system in place. Formed slowly, over centuries, the Roman system proved remarkably enduring.

The most crucial and unusual element in this system was the gigantic citizen body that it created. The area of the Roman state itself and its citizen population swelled steadily. It is estimated at: 900 square kilometres and 25,000–40,000 people by 495, at the beginning of the Republic; more than 5,500 square kilometres and about 350,000 people by 338, after the Latin War; and 26,000 square kilometres and some 900,000 people by 264, at the outbreak of the First Punic War. These figures represented some 20 per cent of the land area and 30 per cent of the population of Roman Italy.[148] Roman population was about four to five times larger than that of the largest Greek *polis* by far, Athens, and than any of the largest, regional medieval Italian communes. As there was an obvious link between the size of the domestic citizen manpower and that of the dependent 'allied' population that could be harnessed by the hegemon, Rome's vast citizen body in turn made possible a hegemonic sphere that covered the entire peninsula.

In 225 BC a census of Italian manpower was carried out in preparation for a large-scale Celtic invasion. The figures, cited by Polybius, show that there were three-quarters of a million men eligible for military service in the Roman hegemonic domain, of which about a third were Roman citizens (*The Histories* 2.24). The respective figures for the 17–46 age cohorts (*juniores*), who were destined for field service, probably stood at 500,000 and 175,000. Although the exact interpretation of all these figures is debated, the regularly executed censuses of the Roman citizen body fall in the same range. As a result of both economic and logistical reasons, Rome's normal annual recruitment from this huge manpower pool was considerably smaller. During the Middle Republic it usually consisted of two consular armies of two legions each (about 5,000 citizen soldiers to a legion) and a similar or somewhat larger complement of allied forces, around 20,000 citizens and 20,000–30,000 allies in all. This has been reasonably estimated to have represented between one in six to one in four Roman citizens of active military age.[149] With this substantial but limited portion of its manpower mobilized at one time, Rome was able to maintain the war effort year after year, wearing down its enemies, and always to fall back on its enormous man-power reservoirs for further recruitment in case of military reverses or a disaster.

Here lay the material infrastructure for Rome's legendary tenacity in war. Indeed, when Rome faced the gravest crisis in its history as Hannibal invaded Italy, inflicting one disaster after another on Roman armies, and even managing to split the Roman alliance, the entire Roman manpower potential was mobilized for war. It was kept under arms for years, even though this meant economic ruin for the farmer–soldiers. Having lost some 100,000 soldiers, half of them citizens, in the calamities of the first three years of the Second Punic War (218–202 BC), Rome mobilized and deployed in the various theatres of war throughout the western Mediter-ranean armies with a total strength of up to 25 legions. Together with its allies' complement these forces must have numbered some 250,000 soldiers and sailors, half of them Roman citizens. In grinding attrition warfare over more than a decade, Hannibal and his allies were worn down. It was again Rome's gigantic manpower base, rather than the admitted advantages of the legion over the phalanx, that predominantly explains why the Hellenistic kingdoms of the eastern Mediterranean proved so unequal to Rome. The Macedonian nation-state's fully mobilized field forces consisted of no more than 30,000–40,000 soldiers. The military potential of the multi-national Seleucid Syrian–Asian empire—encompassing only the ruling Macedonian–Greek element—was about twice that number, as was that of Ptolemaic Egypt.[150] A single defeat in battle was sufficient to decide in Rome's favour each of the two wars against Macedon (200–197 and 171–168 BC) and the war against Syria (192–188 BC).

A hegemonic city-state empire that relied on the military manpower of its satellites faced the danger that their weapons would be turned against it. There was a delicate balance here that rested on several factors, some of which have already been mentioned. These included: an adequate ratio between the hegemon's own resources and those of the empire as a whole; the inherent inability of the disparate satellite polities to unite, co-operate, and co-ordinate their actions effectively—an inability that underlies all empires and, indeed, any oppressive political rule by the organized few over the disunited many; the threat of the hegemon's retaliation against defectors and rebels; and the general benefits of the empire for both elite and masses of the subject peoples. However, this delicate balance changed considerably when a successful challenger to the hegemon entered the realm. It was for this reason that imperial city-states were paradoxically most vulnerable in their own territory. Clausewitz's dictum that defence was stronger than the attack—in any case dubious as a general rule—did not apply here.[151]

Thus the Athenian empire collapsed in the conflict against Sparta and the Peloponnesian League once Athens suffered a defeat that lost it its naval supremacy. As the terror of Athens' retaliation weakened, many of the empire's satellite city-states embraced the challenger's promise of regained liberty, and a domino effect began. Sparta, too, was most vulnerable in its own territory. Earlier in the war, Athens itself had successfully established fortified strongholds on the Peloponnesian coast, which served as rallying points for fleeing and rebellious helots. Fifty years later, the Theban general Epameinondas, after defeating the Spartans on the battlefield, invaded the Peloponnese and broke Spartan power by setting the helots of Messenia free.

The most striking case is again the Second Punic War, where both Rome and Carthage proved most successful abroad and highly vulnerable at home. At the outbreak of the war in 218 BC, both sides prepared to take the offensive. The Romans planned a double attack into Spain and Africa, which was pre-empted by Hannibal's invasion of Italy. After his crushing victories in 218–216 BC and his pledge to liberate the peoples of Italy, about half of Rome's satellites changed sides, especially in southern Italy, which had been the latest to come under Roman rule. As already mentioned, this gravest threat ever to Roman power was overcome only by total mobilization of Rome's remaining manpower resources and a grinding war of attrition against Hannibal's new allies. However, the speediest and most spectacular results were achieved abroad. In Spain and later in Africa, Scipio's initial successes found Carthage's satellite peoples all too eager to break away. In the final Battle of Zama (202 BC), Hannibal, who had been recalled home, found that the best Numidian cavalry, hitherto his tactical trump card, was now on the Roman side. Millennia later, one of the main reasons for the collapse of the mighty Aztec hegemonic empire before a few hundred Spanish *conquistadors* was that its enemies (chiefly Tlaxcalla) and later some of its satellites joined the invaders in order to liberate themselves from the detested Aztec rule.[152] Of course, in most of the above cases the challenger's promises of liberty were followed by an attempt to establish its own imperial rule. In a world of larger political conglomerations, the days of the independent city-state were over.

The regional and imperial city-state polities were themselves transformed by their growth. Militarily, larger areas, longer distances, far-flung interests, and permanent occupation of alien territories and polities were necessarily affecting the city-states' way of warfare. It was no longer a matter of the citizen militia marching out after harvest for a day's, a few days', or even a few weeks' campaigning in the vicinity of their city, taking a short vacation from their farms and workshops and largely feeding off the countryside.[153] The factors that had been making possible the city-states' extraordinarily high levels of manpower mobilization were eroding. Long campaigns, protracted sieges, and garrison service—all economically ruinous for the small freeholder or artisan—were becoming the norm. Large city-states adopted various measures in order to cope with the demands of more complex commitments. Logistics, finance, and organization—all non-existent, or rudimentary, or individually taken care of by the citizen soldiers themselves during the heyday of the city-states—had now become much more complex state affairs. Daily pay for the citizen recruits was instituted, mercenaries were hired, and taxes to pay for both were introduced, unless there was an empire to pay for them. War, which earlier, as it were, had more or less taken care of itself, became by far the most expensive state activity.[154]

Rome, with a huge citizen body and holding a monopoly of power that also encompassed the paid service market, did not rely on foreign mercenaries. Faced with the vast commitments of a Mediterranean empire, it began to employ part of its own citizens on a regular, paid, long-term professional basis from the late second century BC on. These regulars came mainly from the poor rural proletariat, hitherto not recruited for legionary service and politically almost disenfranchised. As the pension system of these professional troops was never properly settled by the Republic, the legionaries were easily persuaded to follow a successful general who marched on Rome and who could promise them land upon their retirement.[155] Indeed, generalship itself inevitably changed with imperial growth. In the first place, as already mentioned, Rome's annual civil magistrates, who had led the early seasonal campaigns against poorly organized opponents on the Italian peninsula, were no match for the professional generals of more sophisticated armies that Rome encountered during later expansion. Furthermore, as with the Roman recruits themselves, there was little point in annually returning home the magistrate–generals from remote overseas theatres of war, before they had time to arrive there and get accustomed to an unfamiliar enemy and geography. From the Second Punic War, when protracted foreign campaigns against first-class generals had become the norm, the best, most experienced, and war-proven Roman military leaders were retained in command for longer periods after their year in office. By the first century BC, professional non-propertied soldiers, led by ambitious politician–professional generals, brought down the Republic.

The political transformation of imperial city-states was, of course, not confined to Rome, as we have already seen. Everywhere (except for Athens) the empire meant a decline in the power of the populace, as the resources and vast extent of the empire overshadowed the small-scale intimacy of the civic community. The metropolitan proletariat, concentrated near the seat of power, could still be a source of trouble that had to be handled with care, but its political significance shrank with its declining military role, the state's growing size, and the highly differential distribution of the empire's wealth. The aristocracy was sometimes on the benefiting, sometimes on the losing, side in this process. Autocratic power nearly always rose with empire and, the larger the empire, the more autocratic it tended to become.

The Aztecs, for example, made the change from a poor and backward ranked tribal society into city-statehood and then a mighty hegemonic empire within only 200 years, during the fourteenth and fifteenth centuries. By the time of the Spanish arrival, they still waged their wars with levied citizen armies, and popular approval was still formally necessary for a declaration of war. In reality, however, popular power had been declining, whereas that of the nobility and monarchy had risen sharply, as the spoils of war had been going disproportionately to them. The monarchy had first been established in the early fourteenth century to provide effective military leadership for coping with the competitive state environment in which the Aztecs found themselves as they immigrated into the Valley of Mexico. With the growth of the empire, the monarch (*tlacochcalcatl*), whom the Spaniards called emperor, had been growing fabulously rich and powerful, although he was still obliged to consult the heads of the nobility for important decisions. As with the Roman aristocracy, the Aztec nobility appropriated the lion's share of the conquered 'public' land, which they cultivated through clients and tenants. They increasingly differentiated themselves as an elevated caste above the commoners.[156] Where these processes would have led cannot be told, because they were interrupted by the Spanish conquest.

The Mesopotamian polities had a longer history. As we saw, the Early

Dynastic period appears to have strengthened the power of the city-state's monarch in conjunction with that of the popular assemblies. However, as empires were formed by Sargon of Akkad, the kings of the Third Dynasty of Ur, Hammurabi of Babylonia, and other rulers of regional city-states, the assemblies declined into limited municipal and judicial bodies, while the king was assuming autocratic power. Booty and tribute from war and empire went above all to the royal treasury, giving the king the resources to rise above the old city-state's institutions. The professional army—starting with Sargon's crack force of 5,400—was subordinate to him.[157] The surviving records from the north Mesopotamian city-state of Ashur, though very patchy, are better than most. They reveal that in the early second millennium BC, the city's assembly, dominated by the elders of the leading merchant families, was active and influential in Ashur, apparently constraining the power of the king, who needed their consent for important decisions. However, by the end of that millennium and in the following one, as the Assyrian military empire came into being, little is heard of the city-state's assembly. The familiar institution of the despotic oriental autocrat was in full stride.[158]

In the Indus civilization of the second half of the third millennium BC, archaeological evidence is generally interpreted as suggesting a priestly mercantile civic rule, and in the re-emergent city polities of India's historic period during the first centuries BC aristocratic republics and civic institutions are documented. However, in India, too, as larger states and empire evolved, autocratic rule took over.[159] Similarly, in the town-and-country petty-states of Rus from the eleventh to the thirteenth century, civil assemblies played a significant role in all the larger urban centres and seats of princely power. The devastating Mongolian occupation has traditionally been blamed for the loss of these freedoms in later Russian history. But whether generated from inside or imposed from outside, it was above all great size that worked against popular participation.

The logic of empire was similar in the west. The autocratic Principate that replaced the Republic in Rome preserved only the semblance of free institutions, whereas the ensuing Dominate, from the late third century AD, dispensed even with that. Reigning, rather than deceased, emperors were now proclaimed gods, as in the east. Empire in the pre-modern world—which lacked printing communication technology and government by representatives—meant autocratic rule. When created by a city-state, an empire led to the eclipse of the city-state's civic institutions and to its ultimate transformation. Indeed, by the first century BC, the process of Romanization and cultural and social integration in Italy had reached a point where the allies requested and were awarded Roman citizenship, relinquishing their former separate political identity and in effect forming a Romanized Italian people. By the beginning of the third century AD, the process had run its course throughout the empire, as all its peoples were awarded Roman citizenship and were progressively becoming members of a wider commonwealth: culturally Romanized in the west, Hellenized in the east. In this respect, too, the city-state's civic–political institutions were ill-suited to governing the emergent, large-scale, political, cultural, and, indeed, national entities that the empire had created.

11

The Eurasian Spearhead: East, West, and the Steppe

Chapter 10 dealt with the relationship between armed force and the emergence in different parts of the world of the early state. It has highlighted underlying similarities, as well as points of diversity. This chapter traces the further evolution in terms of power and complexity of the state, the inter-state system, and civilization—in their relation to war—with a focus on the world's largest landmass, Eurasia. This narrowing of the geographical focus results, rather than departs, from the evolutionary and comparative global perspective of this study. The evolution of complexity is likely to be differential within and especially between systems, and the greater the evolved complexity the larger the gaps between the less and more complex forms. The take-off of agriculture, the state, and civilization in Eurasia began earlier than in any other continent and developed a steeper trajectory. Consequently, it is primarily on the Eurasian landmass that major developments in human institutions—including warfare—beyond those reviewed in Chapter 10, took place, and were later exported to other continents, disrupting their independent or semi-independent trajectories.

The reasons why the marked lead human societies in Eurasia took over those in other continents have been brilliantly addressed in Jared Diamond's *Guns, Germs, and Steel: The fates of human societies* (1997). In the first place, the Neolithic people of Eurasia possessed the most effective farming package of all. In addition to particularly successful cereal plant domesticates, they almost exclusively possessed large domesticated beasts, providing both animal protein and work power. In turn, possession of large beasts stimulated another Eurasian exclusive—the wheel. Of the large domesticated animals, the horse—similar to the wheel, a Eurasian exclusive for thousands of years and until about AD 1500—probably had the most significant direct military impact. Furthermore, having been stimulated by their particularly successful farming package (and other factors) to embark on the transition to a sedentary way of life the earliest, Eurasian societies were the first to master the use of utility metals, such as bronze (which outside Eurasia began to appear only with the Inca, some four millennia after Eurasia) and iron (which from Eurasia penetrated only Africa). On this infrastructure, by far the world's largest and most powerful states and empires and the most advanced literate civilizations were built in Eurasia. In numbers alone, Eurasia, which comprises only about 40 per cent of the world's land surface (excluding Antarctica), was home to some 80 per cent of the world's population in AD 1500, who mostly lived on Eurasia's southern coastal shelf, along the fertile belt that stretched from Japan and China, through south-east Asia, India, and south-west Asia, to the Mediterranean and Europe.[1]

Rather than being purely accidental, these Eurasian advantages stemmed from deep-seated geographical and ecological factors. Continental landmasses mean little in themselves, unless geography is perceived from the perspective of the boundaries to ecological and cultural interactions that they create. (For example, with respect to ecological, population, and cultural diffusion, Africa north of the Sahara formed part of the Eurasian landmass via both land and the Mediterranean Sea, whereas the region's interaction with Africa south of the Sahara, 'Black Africa', was far more tenuous, on account of that formidable desert obstacle.) Eurasia was conducive to more rapid evolution, first, because of its size. Greater size (other things, such as ecological hospitability, being equal) meant a greater number of ecological niches for evolution and more intense selective competition as successful breeds from these niches diffused into neighbouring ones. Indeed, the advantage of size and enhanced competition also depends on the ease of communication through the landmass (as long as communication is not too easy, which might eradicate diversity). Here again, 'other things' were not equal, with Eurasia possessing a clear advantage. As Diamond has pointed out, Eurasia has a west–east 'axis', as opposed to the north–south 'axes' of the Americas and Africa. This made the diffusion of domesticates (and wildlife) across the continental landmass far easier in Eurasia, where the transfer could take place along similar latitudes and roughly similar climatic zones. By contrast, diffusion was almost impossible in the Americas, where biological species would have had to travel across latitudes and climatic zones. Thus, out of an extremely limited number of potential domesticates in nature (only a few hundred wild species have ever been or can be domesticated), the people of Eurasia started out with a richer variety, which once domesticated diffused more easily across the landmass. All this gave Eurasian societies a considerable head start, a more effective domesticated package, and a quicker pace of cultural evolution.

That there was a more general evolutionary pattern at work here can be seen from a remarkable parallel: not only did human cultures evolve into more potent forms in Eurasia; when in the wake of the 'European Age of Discovery', Eurasian wildlife species infiltrated the Americas, Australia, and Oceania, they almost invariably drove the local species to the margins of or into extinction. Eurasia's advantages of greater size and easier internal communication, which resulted in more intense selective competition, pro- pelled both wildlife and cultural evolution in Eurasia (although seemingly unrelated) further than in the smaller and more constrained continental systems.[2] Needless to repeat, all this implies no value preference for European over American cultures or for Eurasian wildlife mammals over Australian marsupials; it simply explains why, when these separate systems suddenly came into contact, the Eurasians prevailed.

As we progress in time, our subject becomes increasingly historical—that is, lit more or less clearly by written records. While this is obviously a tremendous benefit, I hope to avoid the 'pitfall' (often experienced in works of a general nature) of the book turning into an 'event history', charting 'one damn fact after the other' in the history of the Old World and then of the west. As shown earlier in the book, this chapter—neither denying nor reifying the contingent—strives to follow closely the empirical in order to draw out its broader patterns, main evolutionary paths, and underlying causation with respect to the further co-evolution of war and civilization. My starting point is one major contingency that will resonate throughout this chapter: as already mentioned, probably none of Eurasia's exclusives exercised such a cardinal military effect, indeed possessed such a double-edged—both productive and destructive—role in the growth of Eurasian civilizations, as the horse.

ALL THE KING'S HORSEMEN: HORSES, INFANTRY, AND POLITICAL SOCIETIES IN TIME AND SPACE

It was an ecologically constrained contingency that the horse remained extant only on the Eurasian steppe, where it would be domesticated, while becoming extinct in North America in the wake of the Ice Age and human settlement. But the consequences of this fact were fateful.

In Chapter 9 I have already overviewed the early domestication stages of the horse. Information on this subject is extremely patchy, leaving much to speculation. To re-summarize briefly, the horse was domesticated in Ukraine during the fourth millennium BC. At first, it served as just another herd animal, mainly raised for its meat and dairy products. However, scarce archaeological findings of bits and of the marks of bits suggest that horses were also ridden from very early on. All the available evidence seems to indicate that, as long as horses remained small in size, sustained horseback riding for military or other purposes remained marginal. However, around 2000 BC, the light, spoke-wheel chariot, which could be drawn by a team of horses, was apparently invented on the steppe, on the border of Europe and Asia, where the earlier ox-drawn heavy wagon and cart had already been used during the third millennium BC.

Further south, in Mesopotamia, various types of disc-wheel 'battle cars', drawn by another, locally domesticated equid, the onager, were used from the middle of the third millennium BC. They probably served mostly for elite transportation and as mobile command posts, but the warrior–dignitaries could also fight from them, either by firing missiles or after dismounting.[3] As the much swifter and more manoeuvrable horse-drawn spoke-wheel chariot made its appearance in the ancient Near East from about 1800 BC, field warfare was revolutionized, with the chariot growing to dominate it completely from the mid-seventeenth century BC. Five centuries later, by around 1200 BC, the chariot reached all the way east to China, via the steppe,

The Standard of Ur, War Panel, third millennium BC. Note the four-disc-wheel 'battle cars', harnessed to onagers

with a similar effect. Simultaneously, it also penetrated into India and Europe.

The third stage in the horse's career commenced some time in the late second millennium BC, when larger horses were bred in west Asia–south-east Europe. Making possible effective and sustained horseback riding, they inaugurated cavalry throughout the region from about 900 BC. Again it took some five centuries for the same development to reach China in the fourth century BC. From then on, a sequence of further evolutionary steps in both horse size and equestrian technology—including the development of the saddle, stirrups, and horseshoes—steadily increased the warhorse's effectiveness.

There were, of course, notable differences between horse-drawn war chariots and cavalry. I should mention only one crucial difference at this stage: although apparently invented on the steppe, the war chariot was too complex, expensive, specialized, and fragile an instrument to come into

327

its own fully among the impoverished steppe peoples, except for their wealthy elite. Mounted steppe hordes, encompassing practically the entire tribal adult manhood, could emerge only with the development of full horseback riding and the resulting nomadic–equestrian economy and life-style. Later I return to this subject. Let me start, however, by addressing both chariot and horseback warfare together, highlighting their general military characteristics and wider social and political significance. Despite major developments, these exhibit remarkable continuity from 1500 BC to AD 1500.

Perhaps the most misleading, commonly held view with respect to horsemen is that they were invariably superior to infantry militarily, or at least became so sometime in history (for example, after the introduction of the stirrups throughout Eurasia from the middle of the first millennium AD). In Chapter 10 I had occasion to show that this was not the case at all. As anybody familiar with the subject is aware and as Machiavelli acutely points out in Book II of his *On the Art of War* (1521), the horse is a sensitive and highly vulnerable animal. Consequently, horsemen were hardly able to withstand a head-on clash with infantry, provided—and these are major conditions—that the latter were massed in close order, kept their cohesion and morale, and were equipped with the necessary although simple type of weapons (mostly spears or pikes). On the other hand, the horsemen's chief advantage was their mobility, particularly on open ground. The power equations between infantry and horse were largely modulated by the different balances between these variables in a diversity of specific settings.

To put it as succinctly as possible, the horsemen's effectiveness increased vis-à-vis infantry under the following conditions:

- the flatter the terrain, where horsemen were able to operate swiftly, both tactically and strategically, unhindered by obstacles of a rugged—for example, mountainous, wooded, or swampy—landscape
- the greater the distances of military action within larger theatres of operations, where the horsemen's much greater strategic mobility could come into play
- the less densely inhabited a country, because intensive agriculture meant less pastureland for raising horses, whereas a larger number of fortified urban settlements translated into more siege warfare, for which mounted warriors were useless.

In addition to their impact on the balance of power between horsemen and infantry, these factors also affected the horsemen's own configuration: the more 'closed' the theatre of operation, the more the horsemen tended to dismount and fight on foot, using their horses largely for their superior mobility into battle, as well as for the mere convenience of transportation; also, the more 'closed' the theatre of operation, the heavier they would be equipped for close-quarter encounters (mounted or dismounted), as opposed to the light, hit-and-run missile tactics of the open country.

This was the geography and ecology of the warhorse in a nutshell. Yet, although geography and ecology meant a great deal, social, economic, and political structures were almost as significant. Stratification and elite dominance greatly developed in agricultural societies also in the absence of the horse, in both the pre-horse societies of Eurasia before the middle of the second millennium BC and in the horse-less societies of the Americas, Africa, and Oceania. However, the introduction of the horse added a new dimension to elite supremacy. It should be noted that in sedentary societies the horse possessed little economic utility value. Carts and ploughs were tracked by oxen until the breast-and-shoulder horse harnesses spread through Eurasia during the first millennium AD, replacing the inefficient throat-and-girth harness of antiquity which had the negative effect of choking the animals. On the other hand, the horse required specialized and expensive feeding. It follows that in sedentary societies the horse was the possession of the elite—because it was expensive and luxurious rather than utilitarian, and prestigious for these reasons. Thus the horse's military role—in effect, its main utilitarian function—was inextricably intertwined with the patterns of domination and power relationships that prevailed between elite and populace in each particular society. Geography, ecology, political society, and the horse were variably juxtaposed and mutually affecting across Eurasia and throughout its history.

In Chapter 10 I already noted that, the greater the social dominance of 'big men' and their retinues in sedentary 'class' societies, the more mass popular militias shrank in significance and military effectiveness. This was a two-way process: the more oppressed the populace, the more reluctant the elite was to see it possess and become accustomed to the use of arms, which might be used domestically against the socially superior; at the same time, impoverished, disenfranchised, servile, and dispirited mass peasantries, with very little stake in the society and in the fruits of war, exhibited scant martial

329

qualities. The horse reinforced this trend—domestically and hence also in foreign wars. Possessing longer and easier reach, mounted elites became more capable of dominating dispersed peasantry in the countryside. Reducing the peasantry to subservience at home, they also preyed on it outside, where the main opposition that they were likely to encounter would again come from their mounted aristocratic counterparts.

We saw this taking place, for example, in the segmentary pre- and proto-state societies of the late Greek Dark Age (roughly eighth century BC) and of contemporary Villanova culture in north Italy. As a result of the rugged topography of the Greek and Italian peninsulas and other geopolitical factors, the equestrian elites that dominated these societies would ultimately give way in the face of the politically organized infantry armies of city-states (and, later, states). Significantly, however, the exceptions to this development were found on the peninsulas' plains: in Thessaly in Greece, equestrianism, elite dominance, and political retardation in the development of the *polis* were mutually reinforcing; in Campania in central Italy, equestrian elites remained dominant in the countryside and cities. As the Yoruba case indicates, much the same ecological and political division emerged in west Africa from the fifteenth century AD, as the horse was introduced into the region from across the Sahara. Horsemen dominated the more arid and less densely populated north, but were checked further south by the infantry armies of city-states and states.[4]

Not only in pre-/proto-state stratified societies and city-states, but also in large states, the military and political roles of the horseman were modulated by the intersection between ecological geography and political society. The crux of the political factor was the most cardinal question of central authority: how was the state to be governed and financed? By what methods was it to extract resources and raise armed forces? State rulers were normally by far the largest property holders in the form of royal domain: vast estates that they owned and managed, and from which they extracted revenues, directly. To maximize central authority, state rulers would have ideally treated their whole realm in much the same manner, directly administering taxation and conscript labour.[5] Armed forces would similarly be centrally and directly either conscripted or paid for from the revenues of taxation. To accomplish such centralization of power, however, two preconditions would have had to be met. First and foremost, advanced economic, transportation, and bureaucratic infrastructures would have had to exist. Revenues in kind and money would have had to be assessed, collected, transported to the centres of power, stored, and reallocated, all managed by paid (or rationed) state's agents. Conscript and professional manpower—for both civil and military purposes—would have had to be similarly administered. The second precondition, related to the first, was that regional power holders would have had to be curbed.

These formidable preconditions for bureaucratic centralized states rarely materialized. As already seen, larger states typically emerged as overlordships, and they variably continued to rely on the regional aristocratic power holders to govern the realm, both because the central authority lacked a developed bureaucratic apparatus and because the local aristocracy was powerful enough to maintain its social and political position vis-à-vis the centre. Horsepower, to the extent that it increased the military strength of the aristocracy compared with the rest of the people and turned the aristocracy into a mounted elite force, thereby also strengthened the elite in relation to the central state authority. Only in horse societies was the aristocracy set apart from the rest of the population as a special arm. At the other extreme from central bureaucratization, power delegation to, and appropriation by, the regional leadership could result in power fragmentation and even in the virtual breakdown of central authority. Horsepower added a new dimension to this centralization–fragmentation tension.

Irrespective of the horse, large states and empires occasionally fragmented or disintegrated, as regional forces or provincial state officials usurped political power, establishing effective autonomy or even formal independence from the central authority. Depending on the geopolitical circumstances, such fragmentation or disintegration was sometimes relatively short-lived, registering in Chinese and ancient Egyptian history, for example, as 'intermediate periods' between more prolonged periods of national unity. Conversely, fragmentation and disintegration could be more prevalent, as was the case with the states that emerged on the ruins of successive Indian empires. Such political fragmentation and disintegration of larger states, where chunks of the state's civilian and military bureaucratic apparatus broke loose and reformed on a smaller scale under provincial governors or generals turned autonomous rulers, or even where local aristocratic power became paramount, should not be equated, however, as it often has been, with that particular type of regime that belongs within the fragmentation and disintegration range: feudalism. Here, more specifically, was a non-bureaucratic rule by a landed-military estate, directly emanating from the military use of the horse.

WHAT IS FEUDALISM?

The meaning and applicability of the concept of feudalism are notoriously elusive. Historians have traced, and debated, the development of feudalism in specific historical circumstances, predominantly medieval Europe. But by professional inclination, historians of this region and period have only a cursory interest in feudalism elsewhere in time and place, if they do not regard the generalized framing of the question as wholly suspect. Giants of social theory from Montesquieu to Marx and Weber have differed on the applicability and scope of the concept beyond Europe. Indeed, more recently, the claim that major features traditionally associated with European feudalism crystallized and formalized later than earlier has raised questions about the concept of feudalism even with respect to the European case itself.[6] In this mood it has almost become the vogue to hold that the concept of feudalism was untenable—indeed, that in reality there never was 'feudalism'. Whether or not they subscribed to such an extreme statement, just to be on the safe side, many scholars nowadays simply tend to avoid using the concept.

Obviously, if we venture to contribute anything to the understanding of feudalism, it is by approaching it from the broad comparative perspective and through the questions that guide this study. Scholars have addressed the subject of what feudalism is mainly by listing its social, political, economic, judicial, technological, and military features. However, a deeper, generalized understanding of the conditions that brought feudalism into being, and of how feudalism stood in relation to other historical social and military regimes, has rarely been attempted. Indeed, assuming that there was such a thing, would feudalism have been a one-time European idiosyncrasy or would it have been a broader social category, also identifiable in other societies? If the former is true, why was feudalism unique to medieval Europe? If it was not, what was the feudal phenomenon that we ought to have sought?

The first thing to bear in mind with respect to feudalism is that it was invariably a product of a state structure, and, provided that it did not lead to the state's complete disintegration, it remained a form of state structure, albeit a segmentary one. Feudalism is not to be conflated with non-state, wholly localized, kin-based chiefdoms.[7] On the contrary, it characteristically evolved in *large* states.[8] Nor, it should be noted, is feudalism to be equated with aristocratic dominance in the countryside, which was pretty much the rule in pre-modern state-societies. The more stratified these societies were, the more weight the landed aristocracy carried—socially, economically, politically, and militarily. It carried great weight because it was rich and powerful, and possessed a host of retainers and slaves in a social environment characterized by a graduated hierarchy of statuses and classes among the judicially free population. Merovingian Francia and Anglo-Saxon England are instances of such societies in early medieval Europe, but examples from across time and space abound. These societies may have had the potential to develop feudalism without being the same.[9] Similarly, although scholars have rightly emphasized the backward agrarian character of the feudal seigniorial–manorial economy, most pre-modern natural economies did not develop that peculiar form of economic, political, and judicial subjugation. What made feudalism special in the family of fragmented states dominated by the provincial aristocracy was that feudalism arose as an elite equestrian military system for military purposes, and perpetuated itself as such, usurping political power from the centre and reducing the countryside's population not merely to subservience but to servitude/serfdom.

All standard definitions of feudalism specify that it involved the supremacy of a specialized class of warriors, predominantly sustained by land allocation. All these definitions, however, ignore a crucial trait of these warriors, which is otherwise practically synonymous with feudalism—that is, that they were invariably horsemen.[10] Scholars have understandably recoiled from pinning an entire, multifaceted social regime on an animal, however important this animal may have been. They have avoided this even though European feudalism was wholly identified with military horsemanship, and has even been famously explained as such by some historians.[11] My own working definition of feudalism is the following: feudalism consisted of the gravitation of local–regional political and judicial power from the central authority to equestrian warriors and lords sustained by land allocation. Feudalism could only emerge:

- in societies that possessed the horse
- in circumstances that granted the horse preference as an instrument of war
- in large states with the most rudimentary small-scale agrarian economy, states that lacked the economic and bureaucratic infrastructure to support and administer the desired, but expensive, mounted troops by means other than land allocation in return for military service—'rent' was substituted for 'tax'.[12]

All these three prerequisites had to be present for feudalism to evolve.

The crucial but insufficiently recognized factor here is this: in all pre-modern states military expenditure constituted by far the largest item on, often the large majority of, the state budget; and horsemen were the most expensive military arm. Indeed, where the mounted arm was paramount, running a state was pretty much tantamount to the ability to raise and sustain that arm. It was this mammoth task that generated feudalism. To cope with the task, states that possessed a poor administrative apparatus and rudimentary, small-scale economy routinely resorted to decentralized outsourcing. Regional office holders and local strongmen became territorial lords, responsible for raising and leading the horsemen in their respective territories. These lords, in turn, repeated the process downwards through land allocation to subordinates. Only in the lowest tiers of this structure did the network become sufficiently small scale for the lords in some feudal systems (most notably Japan) to be able to keep their warriors with them on rations and other payments in kind rather than further allocate land to them. In most cases, however, the horsemen, too, were sustained by the granting of revenue-yielding property, overwhelmingly land. The principle had a lot to recommend itself. By directly linking warriors (and other service providers) to sources of revenue, the state was able to shortcut and discard the need to circulate revenue through the whole complex, expensive, and cumber-some intermediate medium of administrative bureaucracy. Furthermore, the benefactors served as a sort of managerial stratum of the allocated resources. It is therefore not surprising that the principle was commonly practised in pre-modern societies.

Recent historical scholarship has challenged key features traditionally regarded as fundamental to the formation of European feudalism. It is argued that during the ninth and tenth centuries much, if not most, of the

334

land allocated to dignitaries and for the purpose of sustaining mounted warriors did not entail a feudo-vassalic fief relationship. At the same time, it is claimed that military obligation to serve derived from the possession of land in general, rather than from any particular contractual duty peculiar to the fief. The formalization of the system on the basis of a feudo-vassalic contractual relationship and fief obligations appears to have crystallized only in the eleventh and twelfth centuries, as kings and territorial magnates attempted to reassert their authority over a landscape that had fragmented out of their control.[13] All the same, these important (and still debated) insights, while significantly revising traditional understanding of the feudal transformation, barely alter the principle involved, at least as suggested here.

The problem with land allocation—whatever its exact legal status—was that it placed the means of payment in the hands of the service providers rather than reserve them under central control. Thus, benefits could not be stopped at will when the state wished to terminate the relationship or if the benefactor failed to meet his obligations satisfactorily. The personal oath of allegiance became such a prominent feature of feudal systems, most notably the European from the eleventh century on, precisely because of the weakness of the other means for ensuring that service would be provided. The only significant but highly problematic guarantee of service was the balance of power between the lord and the benefactor and the ultimate threat of the fief being confiscated.[14] Sitting on the means of payment and holding the monopoly over armed force, members of the landed-equestrian elite over time were able to extract hereditary rights of possession over their estates and, indeed, appropriate for themselves political and judicial authority over the peasants in the surrounding countryside, whom they reduced to servitude/serfdom. Fortifying their places of residence and becoming *castellans* (as they are referred to in Francia), they vastly strengthened their position vis-à-vis both the higher authorities and the local population.

This was the feudal vicious circle: with the state attempting to short cut the need to collect revenues and reallocate them again through central bureaucratic–administrative machinery that it possessed, if at all, only inadequately, the horsemen were directly plugged into the sources of revenue in the countryside, only to take control over these sources and countryside, further drying up the state's income source and decreasing its ability to sustain a central administrative system.[15] And there was another, final, twist that completely overturned the logic of a system that had been

335

intended to secure a readily available force of professional warriors for the state: the increasingly empowered landed–mounted warriors were often able to impose a time restriction on their obligatory period of military service for their masters, which in feudal Europe, for example, was limited to 40 days.

To be sure, central authorities in many state societies—from early ancient Mesopotamia and ancient Egypt on—also allocated land to sustain foot warriors. However, there was no feudalism other than horse feudalism, with only landed horsemen having the potential of generating feudalism in undeveloped agricultural societies—that is, grow to control their localities, wrestling political and judicial power from the state's central authorities. The reason for this was not zoological but social–economic: sustaining a horseman—and a heavily armoured one in particular—was far more costly than sustaining a foot soldier, thus necessitating the allocation of a much more substantial landed property, or 'estate'. In societies for which records exist, horsemen universally possessed, or were allocated, at least twice and up to 15 times more land than infantrymen, with heavy, fully armoured elite cavalry, whose members required a number of replacement horses and several armed attendants, occupying the top range of this scale. Data on various societies are often obscure and interpretations vary, but the general picture is clear enough. In Solon's system of classes, horsemen possessed almost double the income of well-off farmers who owned a pair of oxen, the backbone of the hoplite army.[16] On average, Roman equestrian colonists were allocated twice as much land as infantrymen, whereas their census income during the Late Republic was allegedly 10 times greater.[17] Cavalrymen are reckoned to have been allocated 4 times more land than infantrymen in Byzantium, and the special heavy cavalrymen maybe 16 times more.[18] During the Middle Ages, property qualifications were over 10–18 hectares for infantry and 120–216 hectares for cavalry in the Carolingian realm, 2.5–4 times more property for knights than heavy infantry in Henry II's English army, and five times more property for a knight than for an archer on the eve of the Hundred Years War.[19]

Consequently, horsemen held an elevated economic and social status in their localities, quite apart from their military position. Whether originally the local rich and powerful of an agrarian society developed into an equestrian military class, or warriors were allocated equestrian estates by the state in order to sustain them as horsemen (both processes variably intermixed), the landed horsemen thereby constituted the local rich and powerful, whereas landed foot warriors did not. For this reason, only the former were capable of becoming agents of processes of feudalization in all recognized historical cases. As Max Weber, who stretches the concept of feudalism to cover all sorts of landholding warriors, admits with respect to infantry fiefs: 'The last-mentioned cases are functionally and also legally similar to the fief proper without being the same, because even privileged peasants remain, socially speaking, peasants or, at any rate, "common people".'[20]

Traditionally, scholarly opinion was more or less in agreement on the designation feudalism with respect to only three historical cases. The earliest of these in absolute chronology is China, following the introduction of the horse and war chariot (and the wheel) from the Eurasian steppe in about 1200 BC. We have already seen that the Chinese state of the time was an overlordship, where power was distributed among regional lords and their retinues, who resided in fortified lodgings or 'castle towns' and dominated the local peasantry. The war chariot further increased the power of these regional lords in relation to both the overlord and the peasantry. At first, the number of chariots was small. Archaeological evidence of the late Shang Dynasty shows that they mainly served a purpose for the king's transport and ceremonial activity. Even the Chou Dynasty from the west, whose overthrow and replacement of the Shang as overlords about 1050 BC may have been the result, at least in part, of their superiority in chariots, reportedly possessed only some 300 chariots during the conquest. However, the new overlords increasingly relied on the mounted arm to serve as a readily available force, rapidly deployable through their vast realm. The old provincial aristocracy transferred to chariots, and the Chou extensively allocated new estates and created vassal states as a means of governing new territories. The old conscript infantry militias declined in proportion to the military and social rise of the mounted aristocracy. The feudal snowball was gathering momentum. By the time of the later, eastern, Chou Dynasty (from 842 BC), the monarch's effective power was confined to the royal domain. By the so-called Spring and Autumn period (722–481 BC), the realm disintegrated into hundreds of practically autonomous polities, with rulers or 'dukes' who maintained only the semblance of vassal subservience to the Chou overlord, to whom they swore allegiance. In the resulting anarchy, the regional aristocratic chariot warriors (shi) engaged in endemic warfare among themselves, cultivating typical knightly warrior ethics.[21]

The two other, better-known cases of feudalism are the Japanese and the European; in both, the circumstances in which feudalism emerged from the eighth century AD, and its trajectory, were remarkably similar. In both the Japanese and Carolingian Frankish realms, society was small-scale agricultural, practically non-urban and non-mercantile, and overwhelmingly illiterate. Communications were also poor. In Europe, the legacy of Roman civilization in all these fields had sharply declined after the Empire's fall. In Japan, the cultural imports from the Chinese civilization, although highly significant, had nevertheless been confined to the centre and were superficial in their penetration of the countryside and society. Growing into large-scale state form only shortly earlier, both the Japanese and Carolingian states possessed underdeveloped infrastructures to contend with the administrative and military organization of their vast realms. Furthermore, both of them had until then waged their wars mainly using short-term peasant militia armies, and both found this instrument less suitable for their new, remote, frontier wars. For the endemic raiding, counter-raiding, and manhunt operations against the tribal barbarians on its north-eastern frontier, who relied heavily on horse archery, the Japanese state found standing horsemen retinues of the provincial notables and large estate owners (shoen) far more effective than the cumbersome and poorly motivated forces of peasant conscripts. The Carolingian rulers—finding as their main military challenges warfare in remote frontier zones, mounted raiding by the Moslems from Spain and the Hungarians, and maritime and river raiding from the Northmen—similarly inclined towards readily available and fast-moving cavalry as their most effective military force. Thus, both Japan and Francia gradually but increasingly relied on mounted troops sustained by land allocation, leaving their peasant infantry militias and conscript forces to decline. Conscription was officially abolished in Japan in AD 792, whereas the Carolingian rulers from around 800 on openly preferred the mobilization of horsemen who would come under the command of regional lords.

Again, in both cases the process of feudalization was to run its course during the following centuries, even though its exact trajectory remains in dispute. In Japan, where payments to the mounted warriors by the feudal lords (daimyo) were more common than in Europe, the warriors controlled a much smaller portion of the land, the oath of fealty played a less significant role, the gap between lord and knight was wider, and warrior mobility from one feudal master to another was greater.[22] All these long-noted but little explained differences between Japanese and European feudalism were closely interrelated. Land possession and political and judicial authority thus devolved lower down the feudal hierarchy in Europe than in Japan, but the principle was the same. Gradually, the regional lords and mounted warriors extracted hereditary rights over their estates, extended social, political, economic, and judicial domination over the countryside, reduced the free peasants to servitude, and became a closed chivalrous aristocracy (samurai; knights).[23] Central power was substantially diminished, in some places to near insignificance.

In both Japan and Europe, feudalism evolved not only along largely similar lines (also exhibited by the Chou Dynasty), but more or less during the same period of time. The mounted warriors sustained by land allocation in the countryside began to rise in significance in the eighth century AD, with the feudalization of the system reaching a zenith in the eleventh to twelfth centuries in western Europe and in the fourteenth to sixteenth centuries in Japan. This parallelism can be attributed not merely to similar general circumstances prevailing in both Japan and Europe, but to the simultaneous spread through Eurasia of a new invention, the stirrups, the diffusion of which was more or less simultaneously felt at both ends of the landmass. In a brilliant article, historian of technology Lynn White has argued that, by stabilizing the horseman on his mount, the stirrups made possible enhanced shock tactics with lance locked under the rider's arm, rendering cavalry that much more effective. According to White, this development laid the ground for the growth of feudalism in western Europe (and, by implication, also in other places, such as Japan).[24] Indeed, the notion that enhanced cavalry power inaugurated not only feudalism but the Middle Ages in general is well entrenched in many minds.

In actuality, however, even though the stirrups indisputably enhanced cavalry's effectiveness and contributed at least something to its ascendancy, their effect has been greatly overestimated. In contrast to popular belief, horsepower did not have that much to do with the fall of the Roman Empire, and the stirrups (only diffusing after AD 500) had none at all. The Battle of Adrianople (AD 378), where the Gothic—pre-stirrups—cavalry took the Roman army from the flank and by surprise as the legions were attacking the Gothic infantry and wagon camp, leading to the Romans' annihilation, is largely responsible for this misconception, as if the battle inaugurated the 'Age of Cavalry'.[25] In fact, quite a number of battles in antiquity had been decided by a similar cavalry 'hammer and anvil' action (Alexander's, and—involving Rome—Cannae and Zama, to mention but a few well-known instances). Furthermore, Adrianople was a traumatic but isolated episode in Rome's fall. The Goths from the Ukrainian steppe indeed possessed a strong cavalry arm, but the great majority of the Germanic peoples who invaded and dismantled the Western Empire in the fifth century AD primarily consisted of tribal foot warriors. Indeed, their reliance on cavalry was one reason for the Goths' ultimate defeat by the Frankish infantry.[26]

As for the rise of feudalism, scholars have shown that the diffusion of the stirrups in the Frankish realm was probably considerably slower than what White has suggested, proceeding gradually during the ninth and tenth centuries, after Charles Martel had initiated land allocation for cavalry towards the mid-eighth century. The adoption of the high saddle and the employment of the lance in the locked under-arm position for shock tactics

Charging heavy cavalry c. 925. Note their stirrups (not available to the opposing formation)

appeared even later, in the twelfth century.[27] In Japan, the rising horse warriors were in any case mounted archers rather than lancers. Furthermore, as we have already seen in Chapter 10 and see later, by the late European Middle Ages, the equestrian elite would be defeated by infantry armies employing the same old and simple mass tactics used in antiquity. It thus appears that, rather than being a consequence of the stirrups, Martel's measures, the ascendancy of cavalry, and the rise of feudalism were related to the particular economic, social, political, and strategic factors specified above as conducive to feudalism, factors that prevailed in both medieval Europe and medieval Japan. Indeed, it is noteworthy that across the Eurasian landmass it was only in Europe and Japan that feudalism emerged as a full-blown system. This indicates a similarity in conditions between the two regions, which also warrants the extension of the designation medieval to Japan, alone of all the other regions of the world to which this European periodization is arbitrarily applied, because their developed and urban civilizations proceeded pretty much as before.

But why, as most scholars more or less agree, did feudal regimes par excellence materialize only in two or three cases in history? According to the argument advanced here, it was the scarce combination of all of the above-mentioned necessary preconditions for the emergence of feudalism that explains its distribution and relative rarity. In all other state-societies that possessed the horse, full-blown feudalism did not evolve because:

- strategic conditions did not favour mounted troops, and/or
- the populace—rural or civic—was able to uphold its social and military status vis-à-vis the mounted elite, and/or
- the society was sufficiently developed in terms of the economy, communications, urbanism, and literacy to produce the infrastructure required by the central state authority to sustain and administer the armed forces directly, relying on its own revenues and bureaucratic system.

They were thus able to avoid the drift down the slippery slope of military and economic power outsourcing and political fragmentation, so detrimental to the central authority.

The fundamental significance of these preconditions for feudalism is demonstrated by many more cases of state-societies that incorporated feudal traits or were even 'semi-feudal', without reaching the feudal 'pure model' exhibited by Chou Dynasty China, medieval Europe, and medieval Japan.

These 'semi-feudal' societies have regularly confounded scholarly discussion about feudalism's wider applicability. Consequently, narrow and broad definitions of feudalism emerged. The narrowest, originating with Montesquieu, confined the concept to Europe. To this, Marx and most modern scholars added the one or two other cases of the 'pure model' and, reservedly, possibly a few more proximate cases.[28] Yet broader concepts of feudalism, originating with Voltaire and developed by Weber and many Marxists, employed a looser frame to incorporate wider categories of landed–military aristocratic dominance in 'semi-feudal' cases.[29] But how does this feudal 'gradualism' impinge on our understanding of the deeper causes of the feudal phenomenon?

According to the line of explanation pursued here, feudal traits and even 'semi-feudal' systems existed where the preconditions for feudalism only partly materialized. Most typically, partially feudal states relied on the landed elite—or, indeed, initiated a systematic policy of land allocation—for the maintenance of their mounted troops, because of the system's economic simplicity and/or on account of the central authority's need to compromise with and accommodate the regional power holders. However, partially feudal states presided over a more developed commercial, urban, and literate society than that characteristic of the 'pure model'. Consequently, they possessed central bureaucratic and tax-collecting systems to a degree that made it possible for the central authority also to rely on its own revenues and raise troops from sources other than the feudal. In addition, the central authority was more capable of administering the landed horsemen directly, through its own command and administrative structure, rather than being obliged to rely on a landed–feudal hierarchy. Therefore, the economic–administrative principle of land allocation for raising horsemen, with the usurpation and fragmentation of political power, which is feudalism, that it brought in its train, was not allowed to take over entirely. Instead, this principle and, hence, feudal tendencies remained balanced and constrained by other methods used for financing and raising troops. A more mixed social, political, and military equilibrium, and, thus, a more centralized state, was the result. The landed horsemen, although certainly powerful both militarily and socially, often enough so as to secure hereditary rights over their land and a degree of domination over the countryside, were less successful in appropriating political and judicial authority to the virtual fragmentation of the central state.[30]

It thus turns out that feudalism stemmed from one of the options open to large states for raising and sustaining the costly mounted arm—their most significant military, economic, and administrative task—indeed, that it was a consequence of the 'primitive' option, which, in the absence of a developed central economic–bureaucratic infrastructure, plugged the horsemen directly into the sources of revenue in the countryside. Contrary to the implication of the simple Marxist model of the Communist Manifesto, feudalism does not represent a 'higher' evolutionary stage in relation to ancient society in world history. True, in medieval Europe and Japan feudalism emerged after 'antiquity' (and may or may not have been more conducive to the subsequent growth of capitalism). But in Europe it evolved in backward Germanic state-societies only in the wake of the unrelated collapse of the advanced literate, urban, moneyed, and bureaucratic societies of classical Mediterranean antiquity centuries earlier. And in Japan feudalism gained power at the expense of a newly created large centralized state that was economically and socially more or less as underdeveloped as its feudal successor—its rudimentary, imported (Chinese) civilization notwithstanding.

Indeed, China is an instructive case in point, because there feudalism evolved in the 'right order' during the Spring and Autumn period (722–481 BC), out of an archaic imperial overlordship (Shang/Chou), similar to that in Japan and the Carolingian domain, but, as we see, *before* the centralized–bureaucratic–urban–moneyed states of classical China that would replace it.[31] Thereafter, in later Chinese history, even during periods of imperial disunity and political fragmentation and disintegration, feudalism was never to re-emerge as anything near the 'pure model'. In contrast to medieval Europe, sufficient levels of urbanism, commercialism, and literacy survived during China's periods of disunity to support bureaucratic–administrative–moneyed systems in splinter states and at the service of regional warlords.[32]

SEMI-FEUDAL AND CENTRALIZED–BUREAUCRATIC MILITARY SYSTEMS

Feudalism thus serves to highlight the more general topic of the centralization–fragmentation continuum of state structure and of the organization of armed forces, a continuum that extended to include partially feudal and more fully bureaucratic regime types. This continuum is demonstrated

343

by the civilizations of the ancient Near East, when the war chariot was introduced into them from the mid-seventeenth century BC. While effecting as sweeping a revolution in military affairs as it would in Chou China, the chariot's incorporation into the region's various polities produced a diversity of political–administrative–military regimes, depending on the particular circumstances of each case.[33]

Information is uneven and patchy. For instance, we know little about the internal structure of the powerful Mitanni–Hurrian empire in eastern Anatolia–northern Mesopotamia (late sixteenth to late fourteenth centuries BC). Its possibly Aryan equestrian elite, apparently arriving from the north, via Iran, may have comprised the force that introduced the war chariot into the ancient Near East. The evidence suggests that the kingdom's elite chariot warriors (*mariyannu*) were sustained by landed estates, and that the monarch mainly functioned as a military overlord. Still, how the landed equestrian elite stood in relation to the rest of society and to what extent the system was feudal remain in the dark.[34]

Information about the New Hittite Empire (about 1420 to about 1200 BC), which succeeded Mitanni as the predominant power in the north of the Fertile Crescent, is more abundant. In Chapter 10 we saw that the Hittite Empire had emerged as, and largely remained, an overlordship. Yet the Hittite Great Kings possessed a sufficiently developed bureaucratic apparatus and vast treasures, derived from taxation as well as from tribute and booty. They were thus able to retain their predominance over the realm and keep regional aristocratic power holders in check. The mounted arm increasingly grew in strength and significance during the New Kingdom's lifetime, expanding from hundreds of chariots to thousands, as campaigning became increasingly long distance and directed into the Syrian and north Mesopotamian plains. According to Egyptian records, 3,500 Hittite and allied chariots participated in the Battle of Kadesh (1285 or 1274 BC) against Pharaoh Ramesses II.[35] However, in addition to the mounted semi-feudal aristocratic vassals and their retinues, the king directly commanded regular armed troops in the form of a royal guard and mercenary forces paid in money and in kind (rations). He also maintained frontier garrisons, supported by either or both systems of land allocation and rations. And he was in control of the labour and militia service of the peasants, who, although socially subservient and possibly declining in military significance in view of all the above, were never reduced to servitude to the aristocracy. Semi-feudal, bureaucratic, moneyed, and conscript elements were intermixed and mutually balanced within the Hittite state structure, with the central authority retaining its ascendancy.[36]

State structure of Egypt in the New Kingdom, the third great power of the age of the chariot and, successively, Mitanni's and Hatti's rival for domination in the Levant, was yet more centralized. With her relatively homogeneous and isolated territory traversed by the Nile communication highway, her developed literate bureaucracy, and her powerful monarchy traditionally reinforcing each other to produce a highly centralized state, Egypt of the New Kingdom established a centralized chariot force. For Egypt, too, the great power struggle involved distant campaigning in the Levant, and the deployment of chariots, paid garrisons and mercenaries, and conscript peasants. Here, too, the chariot force was an elite corps, growing to thousands by the fifteenth to thirteenth centuries BC. However, in Egypt, the warriors who rode the chariots constituted a service elite, which served in state facilities and in the court. As in all agrarian societies, the granting of land was, of course, a principal means for remunerating this mounted warrior elite, but other means of payment, in cash and in kind, were also used. The mounted warrior came with his chariot, but much of the facilities were concentrated in a system of royal stables, from which firm central command was exercised.[37]

In the major 'palace'-city petty-states of the Levant and the Aegean, the chariot forces were similarly or even more centralized. Mercantile, wealthy, and territorially small, these polities were highly centralized and bureaucratically run. The mounted warrior elite in many of them (the Hurrian term 'mariyannu' was borrowed throughout the Levant) rode chariots that were owned by the state and minutely supervised by its central apparatus. As in late medieval Europe, the aristocratic–military horsemen appear to have been maintained at various statuses and by a variety of remuneration methods, including direct payments and land allocation. The petty-states' arsenals ranged from a few dozen chariots to hundreds among the most powerful and the regional hegemons, such as Ugarit and Hazor in the Levant and Mycenae and Knossos in the Aegean. Pharaoh Tuthmosis III boasted of taking 894 chariots from a Levantine coalition in the Battle of Megiddo (1468 or 1457 BC), whereas his successor Amenophis II claimed to have captured 730 and 1,092 chariots in his two Levant campaigns.[38]

The shift from chariots to horseback riding for military purposes (initially the two equestrian forms everywhere coexisted for a few centuries) barely affected the parameters of the fragmentation–centralization continuum of state structure. This continuum extended from the relatively rare cases of 'pure' feudalism for sustaining the expensive cavalry arm, to the semi-feudal, to more fully bureaucratic systems of more highly developed polities. Military horseback riding was first introduced into the civilizations of the ancient Near East during the ninth century BC, apparently from the Ukrainian–west Asian steppe to their north. It was incorporated into the armies of the Assyrian Empire, the mightiest power of the day, in a fairly centralized–bureaucratic form. In Assyria, as elsewhere, the aristocracy was mainly equestrian, riding first war chariots and later also horseback. However, despite periodical lapses, royal power was sufficiently strong to prevent the feudalization of the realm. Furthermore, as Assyria had become a huge tribute-extracting machine, much of the cavalry during the later Empire (mid-eighth to seventh centuries BC) consisted of paid professionals/mercenaries. The procurement and raising in large farms of the tens of thousands of horses that the army required became a major state industry, bureaucratically run by a highly developed state apparatus.[39]

By comparison, in politically and economically less developed states on the Assyrian marches, feudal forms were variably intermixed with state-centred means and methods for raising troops. We know far too little to be able to establish in any detail the social, political, and military structure of the wealthy Lydian empire, which dominated western Anatolia on the strength of its mounted lancers from the seventh to the mid-sixth centuries BC, when it was crushed by Cyrus the Great of Persia (Herodotus 1.79). However, knowledge about the successive Iranian great powers is somewhat richer.

The Median state was the earliest of these. It was created from six tribes and dozens of petty-states centred on citadel towns that crystallized as an overlordship in 673 BC, in response to protracted Assyrian pressure. It allied with Chaldaean Babylon finally to destroy Assyria in the late seventh century, further expanding its suzerainty over the various peoples of Iran and eastern Anatolia. As with all the powers of the region, Media had striven to emulate the Assyrian military system, combining shock and missile infantry, horsemen, and siege and engineering corps. Apparently, all free men were liable for service, and the wealth that the king collected from booty, tribute, and taxation also made it possible for him to pay for some permanent household and garrison troops. The power of the landed aristocracy and its retinues, which provided most of the cavalry and much of the military leadership, thus appears to have been checked within a 'mixed' state structure. All the same, the aristocracy remained very powerful, and perhaps even gained in strength as it accumulated great wealth with the empire. Indeed, when the Median aristocracy grew dissatisfied with the monarch Astyages, who had attempted to curb its power, it switched its allegiance to the Achaemenid Cyrus of Persia, a country neighbouring and hitherto dependent on Media, and of a close Indo-Iranian ethnicity, assisting Cyrus into the throne of a combined Persian–Median empire (550 BC).[40]

Under Cyrus and his successors, the empire expanded over the entire ancient Near East, incorporating its great centres of civilization. But with the empire now in command of fabulous wealth, the commercial and literate resources of major urban centres, and a developed road system constructed by the state, Darius I (522–486 BC) made it increasingly bureaucratic, curbing the power of the aristocracy. According to our mainly Greek sources, a central permanent army of perhaps 10,000 cavalry and 10,000 infantry was established, in addition to garrison troops positioned in key locations throughout the empire, some of them foreign mercenaries. Together with money payments, land allotment remained one of the methods for supporting semi-permanent troops of all arms, especially in the provinces. Levied troops were also called up to augment the standing army in large-scale campaigns and emergencies. The king continued to grant large estates to his favourites, and the Persian–Median landed equestrian aristocracy in general remained rich and influential. However, it took its place as a service elite within the state's apparatus, in the imperial royal palaces and capital cities or in ruling the imperial provinces.[41]

As empires periodically re-emerged in subsequent Iranian history, they exhibited much the same features as their Median and early Achaemenid predecessors. In both the Parthian and Sasanian empires (247 BC to AD 224 and AD 224–651, respectively), the great landed aristocracy and its mounted retinues constituted the state's elite fighting force, maintaining a strained balance with the central authority. The infantry mass, called up from among the free men, was secondary and subservient to the mounted aristocracy. The more these empires expanded to include important urban centres (mainly Hellenistic and Mesopotamian) beyond the Iranian upland plateau and the more the kings were able to rely on the taxation of land and trade to raise household troops and hire foreign mercenaries, the more successful they were in tilting the balance in favour of the central royal power in these semi-feudal states.[42] In the subsequent Turkic–Iranian empire of the Safavids (AD 1501–1736), the shahs undertook similar measures to curb the power of the tribal–feudal aristocracy.[43]

In the old Near Eastern centres of civilization and urbanism, the balance unsurprisingly tilted yet farther in favour of the central state authority. The fief system for sustaining cavalry was widely used, producing processes of feudalization in some periods and regions. However, states overall were in command of more developed economic and administrative infrastructures, and were thus more successful in keeping the system in check. Even the *beneficium* itself incorporated more advanced, financial means in comparison to the landed fief of the European natural economy, often consisting of income from commercial and industrial enterprises (the Byzantine *pronoia*, Arab *iqta*, and Turkish *timar*).[44]

The Byzantine Empire, for example, relied extensively on land allotment to both infantry and cavalry, with the expensive-to-maintain cavalry receiving farms that were five times larger than those of the infantry. However, the wealthy empire also paid for a strong central army (which expanded and shrank with the changing fortunes of the empire during its 1,000-year history) and for foreign mercenaries, and was highly bureaucratic. Consequently, the relatively affluent holders of cavalry fiefs never really had the space to grow into feudal strongmen.[45] In the wake of the Arab conquest in the seventh century AD, the lands of Islam were ruled by the elite tribal nomads and paid warrior contingents, centred on garrison towns. Later, however, the fief system was extensively practised, tenuously balanced by the ruler's household troops and paid mercenaries. Here and there, a decline of central power and processes of feudalization went hand in hand.[46]

The Ottoman Empire, expanding over the entire region from the second half of the fifteenth century AD, also resorted to extensive fief allocation for sustaining its mounted warriors (*sipahi*), which in its peak, in the sixteenth century, reached 100,000–120,000. But, again, the sultans possessed a strong central standing infantry force (*janissaries*), provincial garrison troops, and well-developed professional services, all maintained on the empire's enormous wealth. Furthermore, the sultans were able to draw on the human resources of the subject provinces for the creation of the administrative machinery that governed the empire. Only during the decline of the empire did the *sipahi* win hereditary rights and greater domination of their

Suleyman's army at the Zigetvar campaign, Hungary (1566), showing the *sipahi* cavalry and *janissaries* infantry

localities, which resulted in deepening processes of feudalization. They also increasingly evaded military service.[47] The structure and development of imperial polities on the Indian subcontinent was fairly similar.[48]

All this also accords with the trajectory of that model case of feudalism, the European. If it was the relative backwardness of the economic and bureaucratic infrastructure of the Frankish state that set the process of feudalization in motion once the military demand for cavalry increased, it was precisely the growth of that infrastructure in the new European monarchies that progressively rolled feudalism back. It was this rather than any particular, externally or internally induced, economic crisis within the seigniorial–manorial 'mode of production' that brought about its decline.[49] As feudalism was reaching its peak in the eleventh to twelfth centuries AD, the rise of the cities and the revival of trade began to provide rulers with both revenue sources and administrative skills. Thus, first territorial magnates and, by the late Middle Ages, monarchs were more and more able to expand their household troops, which they increasingly kept on salaries, to hire foreign mercenaries, to keep feudal levies in service for longer periods of time on cash payments, and to revive national militia infantry armies of free men, both civic and rural. They increasingly imposed taxes and expanded the administrative apparatus intended for supervision over all this, as well as employing private entrepreneurs on market principles.[50] They steadily grew in power vis-à-vis the feudal aristocracy, in a process that was as self-reinforcing as feudalization had been. Consequently, beginning from the thirteenth century, the European system no longer approximated the 'pure' feudal model, but transformed into the 'semi-feudal', estate, or corporate state; that is, it included strong feudal features and elements alongside other—civic, moneyed, and centralized–bureaucratic—methods for raising troops and ruling the country. As the process would run its course during the early modern period, the old feudal aristocracy would increasingly transform into a service aristocracy, manning the upper echelons of the state's machinery in the bureaucracy and armed forces. Thus the erosion of Europe's 'pure feudalism', similar to European feudalism itself, should not be viewed in isolation, but considered within a much wider, comparative context and in the light of the fundamental preconditions that brought feudalism into being.

Finally, there were the most centralized–bureaucratic political–military regimes. In China, for example, in a process that in many ways resembled the one that took place in late medieval Europe, the complete feudalization and fragmentation of the system during the Spring and Autumn period (722–481 BC) was reversed during the Warring States period (fifth century to 221 BC). Central states' authorities, largely drawing on the economic and human resources of emergent urbanism, consolidated the realm into a small number of increasingly centralized, bureaucratically run states. The largest of these states possessed chariot forces that numbered in the thousands (comparable to the great powers of the ancient Near East) and that were increasingly controlled by central administration. As China was united by the most centralized of these states, the Ch'in, the new empire under the Ch'in (221–206 BC) and Han (from 206 BC) Dynasties created a strongly bureaucratic type of regime. In its army of conscripts, the cavalry (which had replaced charioteers) was just another arm, and, as in Assyria, a special state bureaucracy took care of the procurement and raising in huge state farms of the army's hundreds of thousands of horses.[51]

In Rome, too, the aristocracy comprised the cavalry during much of the Republic, although, as already seen, in warfare among city-states, in rugged terrain, and over relatively short distances, the cavalry's military prowess diminished. All the same, as the Roman army was professionalized during the Late Republic and under the Empire, the cavalry, as in Imperial China, became just another arm. In both these cases of centralized bureaucratization, aristocratic social supremacy and the mounted arm would become largely disassociated from each other. Rather than consisting of knights and cavaliers of all sorts and designations, the mounted arm would become simply cavalry.

STATE-ORGANIZED INFANTRY ARMIES AND THE DECLINE OF KNIGHTLY POWER

Given the right social and political conditions and strategic demand, sufficiently powerful central state authorities were also capable of creating effective mass infantry armies. As already seen, the problem of the masses was that they were widely dispersed in the countryside. Therefore, being barely capable of co-operating against aristocratic dominance, they were easily reduced to subservience. For this reason, formidable infantry armies were mostly to be expected in small-scale and relatively egalitarian tribal societies, or in city-states, where urban concentration empowered the populace vis-à-vis the aristocracy. However, the political organization of the masses for war, achievable from below in small-scale polities, could also be achieved from above in large-scale 'country' states. In addition to their role in foreign wars, mass infantry armies raised by the central authorities of large states curbed the power of the mounted aristocracy, strengthening the first and third elements in the monarchy–aristocracy–populace dynamic power triangle.

As mentioned earlier, when operating on suitable ground and employing appropriate tactics, infantry armies were more than a match for horsemen. Furthermore, they were far cheaper to maintain and, thus, could be mobilized en masse. The highly expensive horsemen—most notably of the knightly type—necessarily comprised a small elite force. Estimates in various historical cases indicate that there was one knight for every 500–1,000 people in society (0.1–0.2 per cent of the population), with an average of two to three armed attendants accompanying each knight. Individual estimates are tenuous, but, taken together, they again tend to converge. There were about 9,000 knights to a population of perhaps 10 million (about 0.1 per cent) in the German Empire in AD 981,[52] and 5,000–6,000 knights to 2.5 million people (about 0.2 per cent) in an exceptionally centralized England in 1166.[53] France's population in 1300 of about 16 million should thus have been able to support roughly 16,000–32,000 knights, which agrees with prevailing estimates. The Crusader Kingdom of Jerusalem in the twelfth century, with a population of less than half a million, maintained some 600 knights (0.15 per cent). To these were added a similar number of knights who belonged to the military–monastic orders that drew most of their income from abroad.[54] In Japan around 1200, with a population of about 7.5 million, there were perhaps 5,000–6,000 samurai (less than 0.1 per cent).[55] Possessing a richer and probably more efficient economy than that of high feudal Europe or Japan, the Ottoman Empire around 1600, with a population of some 28 million people, sustained some 100,000–120,000 *sipahi* (0.35–0.4 per cent).[56] Similar ratios seem to have applied to chariots. Such a small elite force could become highly vulnerable when faced by effective infantry armies.

Scholars are not sure exactly what suddenly, around 1200 BC, brought down the chariot polities of the Late Bronze Age throughout the eastern

Mediterranean, such as the Mycenaean petty-states, the Hittite Empire, and the city-states of the Levant. The evidence strongly suggests that this was the making of the Sea Peoples, an assortment of tribal hosts and war bands from the Aegean and Anatolian marches of the civilized zone. The representations of these people on Egyptian reliefs show that they were foot warriors. According to one theory, the polities of the day fell victim to their increasing overdependence on their elite chariot forces, which the marauding hosts proved capable of neutralizing and destroying.[57] We know from written Egyptian records that it had been precisely as fast-moving sword and javelin-throwing skirmishers, called 'runners', accompanying the chariots into battle with the aim of disrupting the opposite chariot force, that warrior bands from these peoples excelled. They had been regularly employed in that role as mercenaries in the armies of the pharaohs. Tellingly, the only eastern Mediterranean power that survived the onslaught was Egypt herself, which may have been somewhat less dependent on the elite aristocratic chariot force, dominant in her armies as it surely was. In the two great battles, on land and in the Nile Delta, in which her army defeated the invaders, Egypt's native foot archers played a leading role and apparently proved decisive.

The Egyptian peasants were, however, far too subservient—to the state if not to the aristocracy—to constitute first-class infantrymen. It was above all

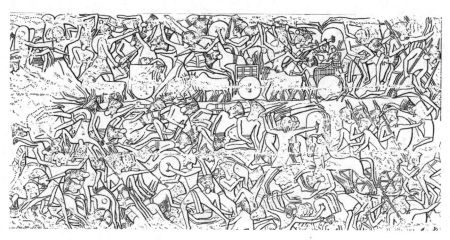

Ramesses III's land battle against the Sea Peoples, early twelfth century BC. Note the ox-drawn disc-wheeled carts, carrying the Sea Peoples' families, and the role of Egyptian infantry. Relief at Medinet Habu. (For the sea battle see p. 221)

the Assyrian monarchy that in the ensuing period succeeded in mobilizing its free population into military service. It thus created highly effective mass infantry that complemented the chariots and cavalry in a large well-organized combined-arms force, granting Assyria unprecedented ascendancy over the entire ancient Near East. This meant that the dry-farming Assyrian freeholder, although living in a highly stratified society and subject to the state's dictates, retained a higher social status than was commonly the case in other polities of the region. Only with the later empire, as professionals increasingly took over and the enormous inflow of wealth accentuated social stratification in Assyria, did her class of freeholders progressively erode and lose ground.[58]

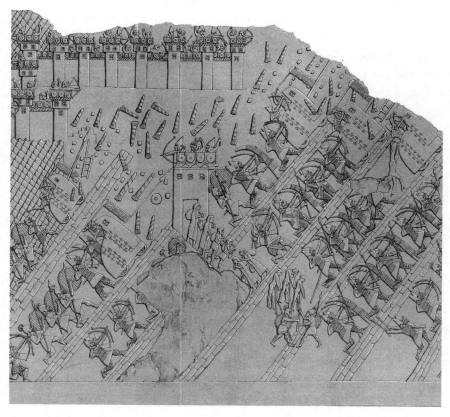

Sennacherib's army at the Siege of Lachish in Judea (701 BC). Assyrian light and heavy missile and shock infantry. Note the siege ramps and battering rams, the conquered population leaving for exile, and the impaled victims

The Eurasian Spearhead: East, West, and the Steppe

In the China of the Warring States period, the growing centralized–bureaucratic monarchies also established infantry armies of conscript peasants, organized and commanded by the state. Conjointly, the peasants were freed from their subservience to the aristocracy and were granted private possession of their land. This was a central element in the process by which feudalism was crushed and huge combined-arms state armies were created, vying with each other for supremacy, until the State of Ch'in, which pushed this process the furthest, conquered all the others and united China. Ch'in was an extremely ruthless and despotic state. But its rulers, and those of the subsequent, more moderate and enlightened Han Dynasty, took special care to safeguard the class of small peasants, which they regarded as the economic and military backbone of the state. Only during the later Han did land accumulation in large estates bring about a decline of the small peasantry, which in turn contributed to the decline of the militia armies.[59]

Ch'in's mass infantry armies (and cavalry), remarkably represented by the thousands of terracotta figures in the Xi'an grave of China's First Emperor

Macedonia, Europe's earliest nation-state, is another case in point. In a typical process of state and nation building during the fifth and first half of the fourth centuries BC, she was welded together by the Macedonian monarchy from a thinly populated tribal kingdom of shepherds and peasants on the semi-barbarian march of the Greek world. Its growth had been fostered by vassalage to Persia in the late sixth and early fifth centuries; by cultural imports and political and economic contact with the Greeks in the south,

355

including military friction on the Aegean seashore, dominated by Athens, and by endemic warfare with raiding Thracian and Illyrian tribal war hosts in the northern provinces. All these strengthened monarchic power. Traditionally, the Macedonian war host primarily consisted of the mounted tribal aristocracy and its retinues, with equestrian skills that had been highly developed in the open and sparsely cultivated Macedonia. However, by the fourth century BC, more sedentary agriculture had taken root in the southern part of the country, and towns had grown and expanded with active monarchic support. King Philip II, who had been educated at Thebes, was able to draw on these resources, raising money and creating virtually from scratch a phalanx army of peasant and city conscripts, which steadily gained in experience and confidence in the king's unceasing wars. Carefully husbanding his kingdom's modest resources, Philip expanded his realm over his tribal and Greek neighbours, acquiring new subjects and dependent allies. As his power grew, the Macedonian aristocracy was drawn closer to the court. It sent its children to be educated there and formed the state's first-rate 'companion' cavalry, which together with the new mass infantry phalanx comprised the main body of Philip's and Alexander's war machine. The freedom of the Macedonian peasant-soldiers, a vestige of the country's tribal heritage, was enhanced by, and became the cornerstone of, Macedonian power and monarchic authority. In turn, the king had to pay heed to the voice of the soldier assemblies as well as to the wishes of his aristocratic 'companions', until the imperial power and fabulous resources gained by Alexander and his successors in the east would make the Macedonian–Hellenistic monarchs more autocratic and less dependent on the wishes of either of these groups.[60]

Finally, somewhat similar processes are discernable in the rise of central royal authority in the European new monarchies of the late Middle Ages. England is perhaps the most striking case. From the time of Henry II, the kings of England reimposed the traditional obligation of militia service in the infantry on the townsmen and yeoman freeholders, who had maintained their freedom alongside the feudal system. From the late thirteenth century, in light of the experience gained in the wars in Scotland and Wales, these troops were primarily trained with the longbow. It was they, rather than the kingdom's feudal cavalry, that proved decisive in the Hundred Years War, soundly defeating, time and again, the French knightly army. During that protracted struggle, both the English feudal levies and the yeomanry militia became professionalized—that is, the state maintained them on a more permanent footing, based on money payment, booty, and predatory extortion in the conquered territories.

Correspondingly, as the French monarchy was painfully getting its own act together, King Charles VII created a national infantry militia army of 8,000 men (AD 1448), to be further expanded by Louis XI. However, this major social–military reform was allowed to degenerate within one generation. As already mentioned, militia armies of the socially subservient were both viewed as a threat by the aristocracy and of dubious military value— the vicious circle of subservience that only a strong royal action might break. Yet, having been impressed by the indomitable fighting spirit and deadly effectiveness of the Swiss infantry of free peasants, who had crushed the army and chivalrous cavalry of Charles the Bold, duke of Burgundy, the kings of France opted for the easier and supposedly superior solution, hiring the Swiss in large numbers to serve as France's main infantry.[61]

Indeed, it should be noted that, if the central authority sometimes allied with the free populace to curb aristocratic power, it engaged here in a fine balancing act, because the central authority even more routinely found itself in a common front with the aristocracy in order to keep the populace in its place. In most societies, the aristocracy was considered indispensable by the state both for its paramount military role and as the upper stratum of a social–political system based on the subservience of masses of tribute-paying agrarian producers.[62] Japan offers a particularly interesting example of the above. As in Europe, Japan's feudal system was transformed in the fifteenth and sixteenth centuries, as the large territorial lords (*daimyo*) raised strong infantry armies of commoners, armed with pikes, halberds, crossbows, and, from the 1540s, muskets. These armies increasingly dominated the battlefield, eclipsing samurai military ascendancy. However, when Japan was united by these means under the strong central government of the Tokugawa Shogunate (1600–1868), the mixed absolutist–feudal regime now established, while keeping the regional lords closely in check, also monopolized military force in the hands of the samurai, abolishing budding municipal autonomies and completely disarming the populace.[63] Isolated from the rest of the world and, in consequence, free from the external constraints of power politics that had facilitated the transformation of feudal Europe, aristocratic–warrior rule in Japan was able to survive well into modernity.

Feudal and conscript levies thus alternated and mixed with foreign mercenaries and standing professionals in the military establishments of states and empires. Having so far focused on the advent of military horsemanship in the sedentary states of Eurasia—examining the social and political dimensions of this process—I now broaden the frame to consider the wider factors shaping states' military systems.

THE GROWTH AND DECLINE OF EMPIRES

Large States, Imperial Armies

Reviewing the rise of the modern European state, sociologist Charles Tilly summarized it in terms of more general applicability: 'War made the state, and the state made war.'[64] As we have seen, the state was above all a concentration of force elevated to a commanding position over society and institutionalized, thus making possible yet greater mobilization of power and resources through the imposition of taxes, corvée labour, and military service. Furthermore, whatever other mechanisms—economic, social, or religious—contributed to the formation of state authority in relatively small and close-knit communities, military power and war were predominant in the formation of larger states, which welded together distinct and different communities, and, indeed, separate societies, ethnicities, cultures, and polities. In such expansions, the state was all the more an instrument of power, ruling through conquest, subjugation, and coercion, at least until other bonds of cohesion evolved. For, in due course, spreading state power had a unifying effect on its realm, as contact and integration increased through the binding effect of the state's apparatus, state's religion and language, improved communications, cultural diffusion, elite integration, population movement, larger-scale economy, and military service.[65] The expansion of the state thus had the effect of gradually diminishing tribal and local boundaries within the same ethnos, and of reducing the differences between separate *ethnies* in multi-ethnic states and empires, subsuming them within supra-ethnic identities, even to the point of creating new, transformed, and larger ethnic identities. Tilly's dictum is therefore matched by another: 'ethnicity made states, and states made ethnicity.'[66]

To be sure, these processes took centuries to unfold, never eradicated local diversity, and regularly relapsed, as large states and empires disintegrated into smaller political units and lower levels of integration. All the same, the general evolution of civilization over time moved in this direction. And Eurasia, where civilization grew the earliest and fastest, thereby produced both explosive cultural diversity and the largest political units, with the processes of cultural and ethnic amalgamation that these brought in their train. Language, of course, is one of the most distinctive marks of cultural diffusion. In Eurasia, lingual diversity is lower by a factor of four compared with both Africa and the Americas.[67] As we have already seen, many variables increase lingual uniformity, the most significant being: open landscape; less lush habitats; the original agricultural expansions; pastoralist expansions and elite dominance; and, now we can add, state's authority and expansion, especially where literate civilization existed. In central Mexico, the Aztec Empire's short history, hegemonic rather than unified structure, and illiteracy meant that its native Nahuatl was only one of many dialects and languages, lacking the time to develop into an imperial *lingua franca*. Things were similar in the Andes, even though the Inca Empire, while relying heavily on the local elites, assumed a more direct rule. In the politically fragmented Maya realm, some 30 languages of the Maya language family remained in existence, despite a shared culture and a shared script.

In Eurasia, by comparison, we have already mentioned the centuries and millennia long process of cultural unification in the Nile Valley through nation-state building by the Egyptian monarchy. In the vast and much more fragmented ancient Near East, a general political unification was first imposed on the peoples of the region by imperial Assyria, after over two millennia of civilization. In the process, King Tiglath-pileser III (744–727 BC) substituted direct rule by bureaucratic imperial administration for Assyria's earlier hegemonic domination of dependent, tribute-paying states. He also initiated massive deportations of conquered peoples, which greatly mixed ethnicities across the entire region.[68] As one imperial power followed another in ruling the region, with only short relapses, from Assyrian times until the twentieth century, empire-induced cultural suprastructures were being forged above the local ones. Thus, for example, Aramaic (during the Assyrian, Babylonian, and Persian empires), Greek, and Arabic, in succession, became the region's *lingua franca*, coexisting with, or replacing, the local languages and dialects. In 'China', northern Mandarin state Chinese, assumed a similar overarching status, above seven other related Chinese languages (and some

130 languages of non-Chinese minorities), still spoken after more than two millennia of imperial unification.[69] Roman rule first took a few centuries to Latinize the diverse ethnicities of Italy—who had earlier spoken dozens of separate Italic languages—creating in effect an Italic people. It then took several additional centuries to Latinize the western Mediterranean–southwestern Europe, forming a multi-ethnic but Latinized commonwealth. (After writing this I was delighted to discover that Gibbon, in *The Decline and Fall of the Roman Empire*, Chapter 2, had expressed the same view.) Only the collapse of the Roman Empire put an end to this process, although leaving behind the Latin family of languages, each evolving in its diverging course, and a classical–Christian cultural heritage. Similar and numerous smaller-scale processes of ethnic–cultural–lingual amalgamations through state and nation building took place throughout Eurasian history.

Owing to the power advantage derived from size, larger states and empires swallowed petty-states, with overlordship tending to give way to direct rule, and both popular and aristocratic power losing ground in relation to autocracy. In the pre-modern world, before the advent of printing communication and government by representatives, no large state was, indeed was capable of being, democratic or republican, as tribal societies and city-states could be (even, up to a point, when city-states turned imperial). All large states were autocratic. It should be noted, however, that although greater size translated into greater power, it also carried with it its own weaknesses, including, and reflecting on, the military.

In Chapter 10 we saw that petty-states were capable of massive mobilization of manpower for war. Their small size and the proximity of military activity to home meant that military service was brief and seasonal, and could be harmonized with the people's civilian activities, most notably with the rhythm of agricultural production. Brief campaigning close to home and after harvest made logistics equally simple, because the militiamen individually took care of a few days' provisions, while also living off the enemy's land. To what degree the petty-state's great mobilization potential was realized and how effective the mobilized host was are another matter, depending on the level of integration between state and people. In their heyday as small-scale polities, agricultural city-states in which the populace was co-opted were usually the most successful, raising cohesive militia armies that incorporated a large portion of their free adult manhood or up to a fifth of their total population.

The Eurasian Spearhead: East, West, and the Steppe

The larger the state, the less practical mass militia armies would become, in the first place because of long distances. We have already seen this with respect to imperial city-states. The mass of the population could not engage in warfare in far away theatres of war, because this would have meant an impossibly prolonged absence from their sources of livelihood. Logistics became equally complex, necessitating elaborate arrangements by state authorities, and imposing the most significant limitation on both the upper size of armies and the scope of operations.[70] Thus, although in absolute figures greater state size translated into larger active military forces and greater reserves—which gave larger states power advantage over small ones— in relative terms small states were capable of more intensive mobilization. Larger size produced lower marginal capacity for active force raising. National armies could perpetually be kept in arms and war be made to pay for itself only during spectacular, brief, and rare spates of military success and expansion, such as were characteristic during periods of rapid empire creation. Assyria, a highly developed looting and extortion machine, could support her largely professionalized conscript militia in the field for longer, and, since the days of Tiglath-pileser III, back it with fully professional standing troops. War paid for war in a perpetual, ruthless cycle. In most cases, however, after reaching the boundaries of viable expansion, empires necessarily settled down into a more peaceful existence and had to devise more economical military systems.

How then did large states go about constructing their military systems under the inherent limitations that distance placed on their mobilization capacity? One method was to call up only part of the country's manpower for active, longer militia service in time of war. If communities and extended families were requested to provide only one warrior out of five, ten, or twenty men of military age, the rest would be able to fill in for him on the farmland and in other various trades, or simply pay for his upkeep during the campaign. In large states, this method still produced a considerable number of warriors. During the Old Kingdom and thereafter, the Egyptian state assigned to the district officials quotas for the levy in times of war. Even during the New Kingdom, when more substantial professional troops were maintained, the bulk of the pharaonic armies that were sent to the distant Levant theatre of great power struggle seem to have comprised levied Egyptian troops.[71] The largest of these expeditionary armies numbered some 20,000, a very strong force in the second millennium BC but still only

361

a small fraction of Egypt's total estimated population of about three million, with her entire manhood in principle being liable for conscript service.

With some later states, the system was yet more strictly regulated and able to produce yet larger numbers in response to greater military demands. The Warring States of China (fifth century to 221 BC) were engaged in a relentless power struggle. Imposing military service on their peasant populations, they drew on this resource to raise armies of many tens of thousands and up to 100,000 warriors, out of hundreds of thousands of men eligible for service, in populations that numbered in the millions for the largest of them. In early imperial Japan, too, the laws of AD 689 and 702 prescribed that one in every three or four men in every household was liable for the draft.[72] As we have already seen, mid-Republican Rome, already an imperial city-state with military commitments throughout the Italian peninsula (and beyond it), regularly called up for service each year two consular armies, comprising together 20,000 citizens and at least as many allied soldiers. This has been reckoned to constitute about one in six to one in four of its free adult manpower eligible for field service.[73] The Carolingian empire and pre-Norman Anglo-Saxon state each called up a similar or smaller portion of their free manpower liable for militia service as 'select ban' or 'select fyrd' for distant campaigning in time of war.[74] An alternative or complementary strategy for mobilizing the militia was to call it up in whatever region happened to be closer to a particular theatre of war at a particular time. This was often done, principally for the purpose of defence. However, the habit of military service could be maintained only by regular mobilizations for, and participation in, warfare, and militias would tend to decline in regions where the habit died out.

United China under the Han Dynasty took the militia system a step further by introducing universal active conscript service for all men at the age of 23. After a year of training as infantry, cavalry, or sailors in their native regions, the conscripts moved to spend another year in garrison duty, frontier armies, or naval service. They were then discharged and called up for training every eighth month until the age of 65 (later lowered to 56).[75] The system had many advantages over the pure militia: by calling up all young men for short-term active service, it created permanent forces that were readily available for military action; it systematically trained the empire's entire manhood for war; and it decreased the disruption of economic and family life. China was the only notable power to adopt such a system before the nineteenth century. All the same, in large states and empires, including China, even advanced conscription–militia systems proved to be problematic.

Empires needed standing armies, to quell revolts and for frontier service in their vast territories. Rotating militia troops and even short-term conscription were ill-suited for this strategic requirement, for several reasons. Perpetual rotation of troops to and from their assigned posts resulted in a short period of actual service, leaving the militia conscripts little time to become familiarized with the localities and their military tasks. Furthermore, most of the army would consist of raw recruits in the course of basic training or newly trained, with very little military experience. To this was added the problem of motivation, invariably low in large, anonymous, autocratic–bureaucratic empires and with compulsory service far away from home. All these would result in troops of dubious fighting quality. Thus, at least for providing the required permanent element of the empire's war establishment, regularly rotated short-term recruits constituted an inefficient and wasteful system. For standing troops, professionals offered better value for money.

Empires thus opted for various mixes of professional, semi-professional, and militia troops. The Roman imperial army of the first three centuries AD, from Augustus to Diocletian, was unique in that it was wholly constituted of full-time paid professionals. It has barely been noticed that no other great power embraced a similar system until modern times.[76] The 25–28 legions—together with their full-time professional (non-citizen) auxiliaries, some 250,000–300,000 men in all—successfully safeguarded the empire from both internal and external threats for a very long time, although further substantial territorial expansion was practically relinquished after Augustus. It has been argued that the ending of expansion accounts for the subsequent decline of the Roman Empire, because there were no longer booty and captive slaves to fill up the imperial treasure. This makes no sense, however, because: systematic taxation of directly governed provinces was much more efficient than predatory looting; Rome remained prosperous and safe until the third century AD, two centuries after Augustus's reign. Spread out along the entire perimeter of the large Mediterranean empire, the professional army that Augustus established proved sufficient for putting down national–popular revolts within the Empire and for defending against raids from highly fragmented barbarian marches.

The Empire's real problem, which we have already seen, was that its presence was stimulating processes of larger tribal conglomeration in the marches, resulting in stronger pressures on the imperial frontiers. By the late third century AD, Emperor Diocletian found it necessary to almost double the Empire's military forces, which from then on numbered some 450,000–600,000 men. However, Augustus's quarter of a million men had not been an arbitrary figure but constituted the upper limit of what the Empire was reasonably capable of paying for. An iron rule throughout history—again, barely recognized, although already noted by Adam Smith[77]—prescribed that no more than one per cent of a state's population (and normally less) could be sustained economically on a regular basis as fully professional troops. With the population of the Roman Empire declining from its estimated peak around AD 200 of about 46 million,[78] Diocletian's sharp increase severely strained the imperial budget. Furthermore, selling their loyalty to the highest bidder from among the contenders to the imperial throne during the civil wars of the late second to third centuries AD, the professional troops succeeded in considerably raising their wages, as well as reaping other forms of subsidy. In addition to increasing taxation in order to pay for the extra expense, the emperors were obliged to adopt new military–organizational measures to supplement the old.

From the time of Diocletian's successor, Emperor Constantine I, the Roman imperial army was divided into two separate categories. The *comitatenses* comprised a central reserve or mobile field army, and were fully paid on the old principle. As the Empire found it increasingly difficult to pay for them, these troops decreased in proportion to the rest of the army, numbering about half as many as the *limitanei* or frontier troops. As the *limitanei* were intended for a more or less stationary role in their respective zones along the frontier, a principle long used by other empires was introduced for their upkeep. They were granted plots of land to cultivate, effectively turning them into part-time soldiers/part-time farmers.[79] As the military profession is economically non-productive, while mixing prolonged periods of preparedness and deterrence with only occasional spates of active military action, empires had long resorted to this principle of military colonists for sustaining garrison and frontier troops by their own farm work. In mid-Republican times, the Romans themselves had in effect resorted to this principle in establishing citizen and Latin colonies as agricultural–military strongholds in the midst of recently conquered Italian territory. Thus the late Roman Empire adopted the system of frontier colonist–soldiers not so much because of strategic reasons as such, based on considerations of concentrated–mobile versus forward–frontier defence, as some scholars have debated, but rather for economic reasons.[80] More accurately, the strategic configuration of frontier defence made possible this economic expediency in the context of a rising demand for troops, an expediency that nevertheless involved a significant compromise in terms of military effectiveness.

In the first place, the frontier soldier-farmers inevitably turned into second-rate troops, inferior to the fully professional crack forces of the former legion army and of the new mobile field army. And there was another consequence. Ever since the establishment of a fully professional army by Augustus, the Roman Empire had lacked any militia at all. Army and civilian life were completely separate, and the civilian population of the Empire entirely lost the habit of war.[81] As we see later, such pacification processes took place in all empires. As the barbarian pressure increased, the Empire, which possessed no militia and with a standing army largely tied up at the frontiers, had only about 100,000 troops in either its eastern or western mobile field armies to contend with the various threats. This was still a formidable number and may have sufficed—in fact did suffice despite everything until the fifth century AD—if it were not for the materialization of the worst case scenario, which the Empire's military forces were not able to withstand.

As mentioned earlier, large oppressive power relies on the fact that its many enemies and those under its yoke, lacking a higher authority of their own, are disunited and little capable of co-operating effectively. This was also true of the Roman frontier, because, as Tacitus saw (*Agricola* 12), the Empire's barbarian neighbours, although coalescing into larger unions, remained hopelessly divided both within and between their tribal confederations. They were thus easily manipulated, or, if it came to war with one of them, the imperial armies were able to fight and defeat the tribal enemy more or less on its own. In the same way that the 'general strike' of all the workers, which in principle looked like an assured recipe for bringing down capitalism at the turn of the twentieth century, never materialized for lack of a truly binding central authority among the workers, capable of enforcing such a grand move, the Roman barbarian neighbours never united for concerted action above the local level. They were, however, suddenly pushed into it by an exterior force.

The arrival of the Hun horse nomads from the Eurasian steppe into south-eastern and central Europe drove the terrified Germanic peoples en masse into the Empire. The Gothic crossing of the Danube frontier into the Balkans in AD 376 was to be surpassed on New Year's Eve 406 by a yet larger crossing, over the frozen Rhine into Gaul, by the Vandals, Alans, and Suevi, followed by the Burgundians. The Roman standing armies, particularly the mobile field forces, were too small to repulse these sweeping mass migrations all across the imperial frontier, and a domino effect ensued.[82] It should be borne in mind that the invading hosts still comprised no more than 15,000–25,000 warriors for each of the tribal confederations, with a combined grand population total of perhaps 1 million for all of them. These compared with a densely populated Roman Empire, the inhabitants in the western part of which alone are estimated at 16 million, and of which, in principle, millions were capable of bearing arms. This population had been thoroughly Romanized and wanted the Empire to stay. In the fifth century the emperors desperately attempted to re-activate this vast manpower reservoir, issuing edicts that mobilized the urban population in particular for manning the newly erected city walls. As the central authority was losing control, provincial generals, notables, and aristocrats organized the town and country people for local defence. All the same, pacified for so long under the *pax Romana* and disassociated from any involvement in the state, the Empire's vast population remained on the whole passive, offering little resistance to the invaders.[83] The eastern Roman or Byzantine Empire also had only its large but limited central field army (of which merely a few tens of thousands were available) to confront the fairly modest forces of Moslems from Arabia, once these had breached the *limes*. As that army was defeated (AD 636), most of the Empire's eastern provinces, with the exception of Anatolia itself, fell into the hands of the invaders, with the demilitarized civilian population again remaining mostly passive.[84]

This does not mean that other imperial military systems were superior to the Roman or more successful in escaping inherent weaknesses and dilemmas. The opposite, of course, is true. Most empires possessed a three-tier army.[85] The first tier consisted of a relatively small nucleus of fully professional troops, mainly comprising a central army/imperial guard. As already mentioned, in the Achaemenid Persian Empire this central standing force appears to have numbered some 20,000 troops, half of them horse and half foot. According to Herodotus, they were called the 'Immortals', but his source probably confused the Persian word with a similar one meaning (the king's) 'Companions', which would make much more sense. In Han China, a central standing professional army of roughly the same size as the Persian one was stationed around the capital, augmenting the masses of conscripts.

The second tier consisted of garrison troops in the provinces and on the frontier, to which empires widely applied the principle of military colonists. Although most of the land allotment in return for semi-professional military service was carried out in the frontier provinces, it was also variably practised in the Empire's heartlands, because the beneficiaries of this system proved somewhat more committed to actually fighting than ordinary imperial levied troops. The system is earliest attested to in Akkad and then in Hammurabi's Babylonia in the eighteenth century BC, as well as in the Hittite Empire. It persisted in Mesopotamia in Assyrian and Chaldaean times, was taken up by the Persian Empire, and later served the Hellenistic kingdoms for sustaining their mostly Greek and Macedonian colonist–soldiers. The same principle was widely used in China, becoming more prominent during the later Han in inverse relation to the decline of the conscript–militia forces. After a return to militia armies during the Sui and T'ang Dynasties (AD 581–907), the institution of military colonists and military families was revived by the later T'ang, together creating a mixed force pool of about 600,000. A more or less similar force structure was maintained by all subsequent Chinese dynasties, for the same reasons that had handicapped the militia in earlier times.[86] In Indian states, too, military fief holders, maybe those referred to in Kautilya's *Arthasastra* (9.2) as 'hereditary troops', augmented the royal retinue as a more trustworthy element than the assortment of hired and levied troops.[87]

Third, for large-scale campaigns and during emergencies, levied forces would be assembled and constituted the mass of the army. Native national conscripts from the Empire's core ethnicity tended to be of at least some military value, depending on the social and geo-strategic circumstances, but they nevertheless played a secondary role to the Empire's professional and semi-professional forces. Levied short-term conscripts from subject peoples in multi-ethnic empires normally proved to be of very little value. Pressed into battle, they could not be relied upon to do any serious fighting. Although examples abound from across time and space in Eurasia, the multi-national mass armies of the Achaemenid Persian Empire, 'driven into battle with lashes', went down in historical memory as typifying such hosts.

Their image has survived because the armies were recorded by Greek historians and because both the Persian Empire and its armies were indeed large, although the size of the armies was wildly exaggerated in the Greek sources. Authors invariably exaggerated the enemy's numbers in pre-modern times, because they both lacked precise information and were patriotically biased.

We have no way of ascertaining the size of Xerxes' invasion army of Greece in 480–479 BC, which numbered in the millions according to Herodotus (7.60–99), or the size of the armies assembled by Darius III against Alexander at Issus (333 BC) and Gaugamela (331 BC), again estimated at 300,000–600,000 and 200,000–1,000,000, respectively, by the Greek sources. Buckets of scholarly ink have been spilt in the effort to make sense of these untenable numbers. Demographic and logistic considerations and comparative deductions would suggest, in my view, that Xerxes' army may have numbered anything between 100,000 and 200,000 men. For reasons already explained, this imperial army was not overwhelmingly superior in numbers to the combined forces of the Greek militiamen fighting on their native soil, if only the Greek *poleis* had not been fraught with division among themselves in an all too familiar fashion, many of them allying with the invaders. Darius III's armies were probably of more or less the same size as Xerxes', including a few tens of thousand cavalry. All in all, it is not commonly recognized that there were probably more Greeks in the world than ethnic Persians. Indeed, in the huge multi-ethnic levied imperial armies, the relatively small Persian and Mede standing forces, together with the levied Iranian contingents, both horse and foot, were relied upon to shoulder most of the fighting. To these more trustworthy elements were added allied Greeks in Xerxes' army and Greek mercenaries in later Persian armies, including those of Darius III, troops who increasingly constituted the heavy infantry of the imperial armies.[88]

As we have already seen in Chapter 10, some of the professionals could be recruited from outside, from an extra-state market for troops in inter-state systems or from the marches of hegemonic powers. Particularly when hired en bloc in their own independent hosts, rather than on an individual basis into state units, these foreign professionals are generally referred to as mercenaries. Foreign troops were sometimes hired as an instrument of domestic politics and social control, being detached from society and loyal only to their paymaster. But there were also two *military* reasons for foreign recruitment.

In the first place, it made possible a rapid increase in the number of professional troops in time of war, without the need to sustain these troops in peacetime, thus making foreign recruitment economically rational. Second, even permanent employment of foreign recruits made sense when it involved ethnic troops who excelled in the use of a particular weapon or as a particular arm, and/or were ferociously war-like. With the passage of time, empires increasingly tended to incorporate them as a significant element of their standing forces. Coming from the barbarian or semi-civilized marches and from unruly and insecure tribal societies or highly antagonistic petty-state environments, these foreign troops were far more conditioned to warfare than the long pacified populations of empires.

Throughout the lands of Islam, the so-called slave soldiers, or *mamluk*, were a unique form of foreign recruitment. These elite troops were slaves only in the sense that their members had been bought as children by the state from the marches of Islam—be it Turkic, Caucasian, Balkan, or African—and were legally the property of the state. It has been suggested that the system was peculiar to Islam because of that religion's trenchant opposition to wars among the believers, which restricted the possibility of social mobilization.[89] Be that as it may, the slave troops combined the advantages of foreign recruitment with the peak of professionalism. Raised in the barracks, trained for soldiery from childhood, and infused with Islamic zeal, they became a fierce fighting force. Usually originating as part of the ruler's bodyguard/household troops, they would later expand in numbers and military role, excelling as cavalry in Mamluk Egypt and constituting the elite professional infantry, the *janissaries*, in the mostly cavalry armies of the Ottoman Empire. Lacking normal roots in society, the slave troops were supposed to be entirely loyal to the ruler. In reality, however, they regularly formed into a privileged cast, and in due course occasionally took over as rulers, particularly where the people had been completely demilitarized and politically excluded; because as we see later, empires typically underwent internal dynamics and transformation, affecting and affected by their military problems and military organization.

The Cycle of Empires

The cycle of rise and fall, or growth and decadence, of empires and dynasties is a theme that has been continuously referred to by thinkers and commentators contemplating history and politics, at least since Plato and the Roman moralists, if not earlier. It has been highlighted by Ibn Khaldun, who composed his *Prolegomena to History* (1377) in Moslem north Africa. It remains, however, on the margins of today's scholarly discussion. Suspected of deterministic grand abstractions to be the stuff of legitimate study for historians, it is also surprisingly neglected by historical sociologists, who might have translated traditional insights and moralist notions into the more modern language of empirical social, economic, and political processes.[90] These processes variably applied to both rulers and ruled, and one might sketch them out from the top down.

Almost by definition, the founders of dynasties were people of exceptional capabilities and energy, upstarts with great experience in the realities of life and a hunger for power and everything that it entailed. Their successors rarely exhibited the same qualities, and not only because of the haphazardness of biological inheritance. On the positive side, they were sometimes able to benefit from a more dedicated training for government from youth. However, in large and autocratic empires in particular (and these two features correlated closely), seriously detrimental conditioning factors were almost built into palace life. Autocrats were normally secluded from their surroundings because of their elevated, quasi-divine status—enshrined in religious custom and court protocol—to say nothing of security reasons. Having little direct contact with the outside world, they were exposed to selective information and susceptible to flattery. Furthermore, they regularly became absorbed in the pleasures of the palace and harem, from which they would not easily depart, only wishing to be left in peace. In turn, their many wives and concubines and numerous children turned the harem into a hornets' nest of intrigue, centring on the question of inheritance to the throne. This would often lead to palace assassinations and bloodbaths during succession. Where primogeniture was not the rule, and in most autocracies it was not, this also meant that the heir to the throne could not always be trained for the job in advance.[91] All these tended to weaken dynastic government, as well as making it vulnerable to usurpation.

Dynastic decadence was only part of the problem, however. During much of its history, imperial Rome, for example, adopted a non-dynastic and meritocratic system of autocratic inheritance, by which the reigning emperor chose and trained his successor from among the Empire's best generals and administrators. All the same, succession aside, the imperial administration of empires would itself over time become ever more stifling, as it tended to grow increasingly bureaucratic, centralistic, and interventionist, leaving less and less room for local and individual initiative. In the process, bureaucrats would proliferate and become more entrenched, little checked by any counterforce, not even by the autocrat. Correspondingly, the tax burden tended to fluctuate in only one direction: upward—to sustain these bureaucrats and the rulers' ostentatious consumption, to be sure, but above all in order to pay for the growing costs of the army, which in any case invariably comprised the largest element of the state's expenditure, often the majority. Calculations of Roman state income during the empire suggest that the armed forces absorbed 40–70 per cent of the expenditure, and in Rome the civilian part of the budget—financing massive public construction, and subsidized corn and circus games—was particularly high.[92] However, as we have seen, the army not only grew in numbers to contend with the increasing threats but also, holding the monopoly over armed force, often managed to extract higher wages from the state. In both the Roman Empire and T'ang China, for example, these spiralling costs and the chain reaction that they generated through the economy and society accelerated decline. The T'ang switch from militia to professional and semi-professional troops combined with escalating military wage demands to increase the costs of imperial frontier defence fivefold between 714 and 741, with a further 40–50 per cent increase between 742 and 755.[93]

All this also affected the aristocratic elite. If it did not take advantage of the weakening of central dynastic power to gain control over the provinces, fragmenting imperial power, which often happened, the aristocracy would become increasingly stripped of its traditional role in local leadership by expanding imperial bureaucracy. As trained professionals would take its place in the public service, including the military, the aristocracy would withdraw into luxurious private life, becoming progressively disassociated from the affairs of state. Consequently, as Machiavelli (*The Prince* 4) has perceived, once the state's central machinery succumbed to any other power, the empire might fall with surprising swiftness, because there would be no stratum of active, militarized, local power holders that would be able to generate further resistance. As a counterbalance to my discussion of feudalism, it should be noted that centralization did not always strengthen state power, particularly when centralization went hand in hand with autocracy.

Correspondingly, popular participation, where it existed at all, also tended to weaken under the combined pressures of aristocratic economic supremacy and autocratic centralization. Growing aristocratic estates reduced the number and status of small freeholders and increased the ranks of dependent and servile workers in the countryside and cities. Stripped of individual and communal influence over the shaping of their lives and oppressed by heavy taxation and labour services, the rural populace grew alienated from and apathetic towards the remote and anonymous imperial authorities, and in any case was habituated to passivity. The uprooted and ethnically heterogeneous population that formed the Empire's metropolises had practically no military value. As we have seen in Chapter 10, similar processes might also take place in smaller polities, but in larger states and empires they assumed much greater scale. Furthermore, the internal peace established by large empires, imperfect as it may have been, meant that the people's socialization for warfare and the motivations of booty and communal defence—both prominent in belligerent small-scale tribal and civic communities—were all but lost. By the late Roman Empire, for example, Italians almost ceased to enlist in the legions. Enlistment derived from more war-like provincials even before it became dependent on barbarians from outside the Empire.

Over time, these processes tended to transform the nature of empires' war-like activity and military forces. During their expansion, empires mainly fought other states, which they would conquer, subjugate, and in due course incorporate within a unified realm. Putting down recurring rebellions by conquered peoples that sought to regain independence—the bloody process denoted by the euphemism 'pacification'—remained for long one of the principal functions of imperial armies. Normally, however, after a few centuries of *direct* imperial rule, national revolts almost invariably died out, as practices and memories of independence faded away and both elites and masses underwent imperial acculturation and incorporation. The main security threats and challenges to the empire would now come from other sources.

Domestically, national revolts gave way to civil wars of two sorts. First, there was the danger of economically and socially rooted peasant/serf/slave uprisings in the countryside and/or urban rioting by the city proletariat, with the former in particular capable of flaring up into catastrophes of horrendous proportions. Second, there were the endemic succession and usurpation struggles. If not confined to palace and court intrigues in the capital, often involving the imperial guard, they too could engulf the entire realm. Such struggles for power could be perpetrated by members of the royal house, mostly siblings, who would vie for the crown, dividing the allegiance of the elite and army; or they were initiated by provincial governors and army generals, who succeeded in enlisting the support of their professional troops, partly through the power of their personality but mostly by the promise of reward. Civil wars, in which fighting, killing, looting, and devastation raged in the midst of the country, were famously the most destructive and lethal form of war. As far as the state structure was affected, such wars might result in the toppling of the autocrat or fall of the ruling dynasty, but could also lead to anarchy or at least temporary fragmentation of the state. Furthermore, they distracted attention and efforts from external threats. One disadvantage of the lack of dynastic legitimacy and continuity in the late Roman Empire was the endemic civil wars that raged among generals of the large professional army over the imperial throne. These wars were a major reason for the Empire's failure to get its act together in the face of the Germanic invasions. Civil wars of succession were a contributing factor also in most other cases of imperial fall before a foreign power.

Externally, empires were sometimes locked in struggle with neighbouring empires, resulting in a dynamic equilibrium or even in the fall of the one before the other. But even if no such imperial rival existed, empires were liable to fall prey to much smaller, semi-barbarian states or barbarian tribal confederations on their marches, which they had earlier dominated and terrorized.[94] At face value this seems curious, because although it appears normal for states to be defeated by the superior strength of larger states and empires and for empires to succumb to other powers from their own league, why would large empires surrender to much smaller rivals? This takes us back to the weaknesses and dynamics of empire, including the pacification of its elite and populace. Pacification did not, of course, mean that the state and its elite became less war prone or brutal. Even in the relatively rare cases, such as imperial China, where the court and ruling elite of various dynasties in time assumed a demilitarized civilian character and outlook, and increasingly viewed war with disdain as abhorrent, disruptive, and uncivilized, they still regarded it at the least as a necessary evil for the control and defence of the realm, for which the appropriate military machine had to be maintained. However, foreign recruits were increasingly relied upon to man this machine and do the job.

It should be clarified that state soldiers were by no means inherently inferior to tribal warriors, often quite the opposite. Coming from unruly, kin-based, and insecure societies, tribal warriors lacked discipline, cohesion, and staying power for the very same reasons that also conditioned them to violence and ferocity. By contrast, state troops brought with them the obedience, perseverance, and habit of co-operating in large-scale social formations that were instilled by life in more orderly societies. And yet, down the cycle of empires, the balance was changing on both sides.

Enlisting barbarian or semi-barbarian warriors from the marches was too natural an option for empires to miss. The marches provided a readily available source of war-like recruits, when motivation for service and the warrior spirit within the empire itself were declining. The arrangement worked well enough for many empires for long periods, but a snowball effect could easily be set in motion. Reliance on foreign troops would reinforce the pacification of the empire's own population. Furthermore, mercenary service in the empire would instil greater discipline and order in the barbarian recruits, which they would take back home to their native lands. This would have a partially beneficiary effect for the empire, contributing to processes whereby the marches would be tamed under the influence of civilization. But the same process would also contribute to the growth of larger and more orderly political formations on the marches, which would constitute more dangerous rivals. And it would give the foreigners and their leaders an intimate familiarity with the strengths and weaknesses of the empire, which they would then be able to exploit.

With foreign warrior recruits would also come foreign warrior leaders. These would either rise up the hierarchy of the imperial service, because the empire would experience scarcity in native command for the very same reasons that it would experience scarcity in native recruits; or they might come as leaders of their men, when an entire war host might be taken into the imperial service *in toto*. There was a slippery slope here, generating increasingly desperate measures by the empire. As imperial security declined, hiring barbarian hosts might become one form of the bribe money that empires widely used to buy off barbarian threats. Both exploiting and precipitating times of trouble, anarchy, and mayhem, independent foreign barbarian troops and their leaders, serving within the empire and even as imperial guards in the capital, could become instrumental in opening the gates of the empire and in bringing it down, or they could themselves seize power.

From earliest times empires were repeatedly taken over from the marches, in a sequence that often involved their former mercenary troops. The 'first empire', that of Sargon of Akkad (twenty-fourth to twenty-second centuries BC), was destroyed during the reign of his successors by the Gutians from Mesopotamia's north-eastern barbarian march. Later, Amorite, Kassite, and Chaldaean march tribesmen and chieftains successively gained control over Babylonia. The same was performed in Egypt, by the Asiatic Hyksos, Libyans, and Nubians (Sudanese), and was almost achieved by the Sea Peoples as well. Indeed, during most of the Late Kingdom (after 1069 BC), Egypt was ruled by foreigners. China's first recorded empire, the Shang, was taken over by the Chou, who originated in the western semi-barbarian march, and it was from the same direction that the semi-barbarian Ch'in came and succeeded in defeating all the other states and uniting China in 221 BC. After China largely incorporated its western march (excluding Tibet), it was now from her north-eastern march that she was three or four times taken over by the semi-barbarian Manchurians. Similar to Egypt of the Late Kingdom, China was ruled by foreigners during most of her history after the fall of the T'ang Dynasty in AD 906. The list of fallen empires continues with a chain of familiar cases: Germans in the Roman Empire; Bulgars, Slavs, Northmen, and Arabs in Byzantium; and Turks throughout Asia, from China to Iran, the Near East, and India.

Empires could be replaced, merely seized, or fragmented by the intruders. Replacement tended to take place when the invaders possessed a strong political and cultural base of their own, and, while taking over the imperial structure of the conquered and inevitably also some of their cultural heritage, they constituted a distinctively different identity, politically and culturally. The Greek conquest of the Persian Empire and the Arab–Moslem conquest of the Byzantine east (but not of Persia) are prominent examples of such replacements. In most cases, however, barbarian or semi-barbarian war hosts from the marches, viewing the wealth and splendour of the empire with awe, were all too eager simply to take over as its rulers, appropriating as much as they could of the existing state machinery, and largely assimilating into the conquered culture. To the imperial population at large this amounted to little more than a change of dynasty and partial replacement of the social elite. This may have barely affected the life and duties of the masses of peasantry in the countryside, although the feeling that the new rulers were foreigners was strong enough and not to be underestimated. This would be exploited to mobilize patriotic sentiments by power holders who might rise to topple the 'foreign intruders', sometimes after another cycle of dynastic imperial rule had run its course and after the foreign rulers and elite had themselves lost their barbarian vigour in the amenities of civilization and power. Finally, an empire might also be fragmented and disintegrated if the barbarian or semi-barbarian conquerors were too weak to take over and preserve the imperial structure *in toto*, as happened irreversibly to the Roman Empire and, repeatedly but only for brief periods, in China.

Although the sedentary and semi-sedentary marches posed a constant security challenge to, and constituted a source for occasional takeovers of, empires, a steppe frontier generated yet larger-scale raiding and systematic extortion of an entirely different order of magnitude. The extensive adoption of horseback riding was even more transforming in the vast Eurasian steppe than it was in the Eurasian sedentary–civilized zone, making possible, as it did, an increasingly nomadic–pastoralist–predatory way of life. With the steppe stretching along the whole length of the Eurasian heartland, its peoples affected the civilizations of both the east and the west decisively, yet differentially.

MOUNTED RAIDERS AND EMPIRES OF THE STEPPE

The sea of grassland which is the Eurasian steppe stretches along 7,000 kilometres, from Ukraine to the Mongolian plain, and across some 1,500 kilometres from north to south. Latitude and extreme, continental climatic conditions, resulting in little precipitation, dictate that in most of this huge habitat trees barely grow. Further north, the even sparser population of the forests and taiga persisted in the hunter–gatherer–fisher–trapper way of life of pre-Neolithic times. On the steppe itself, however, the Neolithic package that had arrived from the agricultural societies in the south transformed the economy and demography. In the river valleys—where rivers existed— annual cereals crops were cultivated, and somewhat denser populations developed. But the herding of sheep and cattle was of even greater significance, extending farther afield across the steppe and supplementing grain cultivation and gardening within a mixed pastoralist–agricultural, semi-nomadic semi-sedentary, economy. To this was added from early on, in the fourth millennium BC, a local domesticate, the horse.

As already seen, fully fledged, sustained, horseback riding, evidently associated with the breeding of larger, 14–15 hands (140–150 centimetres high) horses, apparently originated only in the late second millennium BC on the western part of the steppe, maybe in the region around the Caspian and Aral Seas. This may be connected to the fact that in historical times, in the early centuries BC, both the Persians and the Chinese coveted the big, 'heavenly' or Nesaen, horses of central Asia. The economic–demographic–military effects of the development of horseback riding were overwhelming. On horseback, herding could be taken into the depth of the steppe, covering far greater distances in search of pasture and water. Consequently, although populations residing along the steppe's rivers and around oases retained a semi-sedentary semi-pastoral mode of subsistence, other groups assumed a wholly mobile existence and became fully nomadic—a novelty in comparison with pre-horse pastoralists. This does not mean that these groups completely cut loose from their agricultural neighbours. On the contrary, a fully nomadic pastoral existence was inherently symbiotic, necessitating exchange with sedentary populations, from which agricultural produce—most notably grains—and other goods could be obtained. Indeed, as we have already seen with respect to horse-less pastoralists, if the necessary goods could be extracted by force rather than be paid for, so much the better.

The horse pastoralists' way of life gave them military advantages that far exceeded those of horse-less pastoralists, and even those of steppe charioteers. The chariot, which had apparently been invented on the steppe and had carried steppe tribal war hosts through Iran into conquest and domination in northern Mesopotamia (Mitanni) and north India in the second millennium BC, had nevertheless been an elite weapon. A specialized and sophisticated instrument, it was difficult and expensive to make and maintain. The chariot was possessed only by the tribal elite and, once introduced into the zone of civilization, it was even more successfully employed there, because organized sedentary societies possessed superior infrastructure for their manufacture and upkeep. By contrast, horseback riding required no specialized equipment, and the same horse that constituted the very basis of the pastoralist–nomad economy and way of life doubled as an unmatched instrument of war. The riding horse thus radically altered the balance of power between the steppe and the sown. Nomadic existence in a vast pastureland made the horse available in large numbers to all members of society, creating mounted hordes that encompassed practically all of the tribal manhood. By contrast, in the zone of sedentary civilization the horse was confined to the elite and could be kept only as a luxury.

Hordes can be a highly misleading term. Wild exaggerations by ancient authors notwithstanding, the horse pastoralists were incomparably inferior to sedentary societies in numbers, because the agricultural mode of subsistence is far more intensive and produces populations that are denser by a factor of tens. The manhood of tribal hosts numbered in the hundreds and low thousands, and even truly large tribal confederations possessed no more then a few tens of thousand mounted men. The most formidable steppe tribal conglomeration ever, the one created by Chinggis Khan, which encompassed all the tribes of Mongolia, incorporated only about 95,000 men–warriors in 1206 and 129,000 in 1227. This is recorded in the so-called *Secret History of the Mongols* and other contemporary sources, because the Mongols' conquest of sedentary literate civilizations, highly unusual among nomadic peoples, made possible internally written documentation of their history, including reliable figures.[95] China's population outnumbered Chinggis Khan's nomads by about 100 to one. All the same, comparisons of absolute population numbers between the steppe and the sown meant little, because it was the horse nomads who called the shots.

The nomadic life of long-range movement in the open and activities of herding and hunting were the closest simulation of real campaigning. Furthermore, endemic conflict existed between the nomadic tribal hosts over pastureland, water, and animal stock, making warfare a life-long habit for them. When directed against their sedentary neighbours, the herder hosts' far superior mobility made it possible for them to raid scattered agricultural settlements in the countryside, constantly shifting their operations from one place to another, easily travelling 70 kilometres a day. High mobility and shifting operations in enemy agricultural countryside also meant outstanding logistical flexibility, because both horses and men lived off the land. Counter-concentrations by agricultural societies of superior numbers of slow-moving foot warriors would have had no time to assemble and in any case would not be engaged by the horse nomads. Only cavalry could keep up with the raiders, but the limited number of cavalry that sedentary societies were able to maintain at a great expense at best enjoyed no advantage in numbers over the horse nomads, while being inferior to them militarily or, at the very least, ill-suited for fighting them. Life on horseback made the horse nomads unequalled in equestrian skills. Moreover, their principal weapon was the small and powerful composite bow, made of sinew, horn, and wood laboriously processed and glued together. Trained from childhood, they were able to shoot it with devastating speed and accuracy, in full gallop and even backwards, during flight. The cavalry of sedentary societies, more heavily armed for shock action, was barely capable of forcing them into action.

Indeed, and here is the crux of the matter, the steppe light horsemen were able to keep up that mode of warfare and eschew direct confrontation if they so wished, because there was nothing that they were forced to stand up and defend. There was no target against which the forces of sedentary societies could counterattack effectively, either to annihilate their tormentors or to deter them. The horse pastoralists' families and herds were beyond reach and almost as mobile and elusive as the nomad warriors themselves. Some of the horse nomads even gave up the heavy ox-drawn wagons that had been used by steppe pastoralists before the era of fully fledged horseback riding. The nomads' atrociousness towards their sedentary neighbours—accounting for some of the most horrendous pages in history—was a consequence of all these factors. Not only did the exponents of the two alien ways of life look down on each other, with the nomads lacking sympathy for the property and toil upon which sedentary life depended, but the nomads also had little to fear from retaliation, a major constraining force in relations between two sedentary or pastoral societies. Furthermore, they were too few in number to coerce or hold down sedentary societies by means other than sheer terror. And being mostly geared towards plunder, they were less interested than 'ordinary' invaders—who came to conquer—in sparing the land and population as a permanent spoil of war. To sum up, while comprising only a few per cent of Eurasia's total population, the horse nomads were turned by their adoption of the riding horse into a momentous force that bore decisively on the history of the landmass's sedentary societies, which greatly outnumbered them.

From the Rims of the Fertile Crescent to the Gates of China

The western part of the Eurasian steppe, from Transoxiana to Ukraine, where the larger, riding horse was first bred, was inhabited by peoples who spoke Iranian languages, most notably Scythians (shooters in Indo-European etymology; they were called Saka in the east). It took no more than a few centuries—during which the riding horse spread, a fully mobile nomadic economy evolved, and the steppe population swelled—for these peoples to make their mark southwards, bearing heavily on the civilizations of the ancient Near East. Apparently, it was from the steppe that the riding horse and cavalry were introduced into the Assyrian army in the ninth century BC, and spread throughout the region. Moreover, in the late eighth century BC and during the first half of the seventh, the Cimmerians (about whom little is known) apparently crossed from the Crimea through the Caucasus, inflicting a heavy defeat on Urartu, Assyria's northern arch-rival. They then established themselves in Anatolia, destroying the Phrygian great power. Raiding in all directions, they bore down heavily on Lydia and the Greeks of Ionia, and harassed Assyria.[96] In the early seventh century BC, the Scythians followed suit, riding down the eastern Caucasus along the Caspian shores into eastern Anatolia and the Iranian plateau. First allying with the newly emergent Mede union against Assyria, then allying with Assyria, and for a while even establishing suzerainty over Media (653–624 BC), they raided both powers and throughout the ancient Near East during the seventh century BC.[97] However, having thus become a significant factor in Near Eastern power politics for a century, the horse nomads' threat ebbed. The hot, dry, partly mountainous, and densely populated Near East offered insufficient pastureland for their horses. Access into the region from their homeland in the steppe to the north was highly constrained, blocked as it was by the Black and Caspian Seas and limited to the mountainous Caucasian corridor.

The horse nomads had easy access only to Iran, but the peoples of that country, especially in the more arid north and east, were themselves partly pastoralists and extensively adopted the riding horse. Media and, subsequently, Persia deployed strong cavalry recruited from all over Iran, including the eastern province of Bactria and from the Scythians/Saka themselves, whose tribal raids along Iran's northern steppe frontier constituted a constant nuisance to the Empire. Cyrus the Great reportedly found

First images of true cavalry, Assyrian, first half of the ninth century BC. The horsemen, riding on the animals' bare back, operate in pairs. One is holding the reins of both horses, while the other is shooting his bow: 'like a chariot team without the chariot'. Ashurnasirpal II's palace at Nimrud

his death while campaigning against the nomads in Transoxiana (Herodotus 1.214; 530 BC). Darius I was more successful in his campaign against the Saka (520–519 BC) in the east, capturing their chief/king. Yet the near futility of any serious attempt to subjugate or crush the nomads was demonstrated by the failure of his massive invasion of Scythia (Ukraine) in 514 or 512 BC. Herodotus's account of the nomads' strategy is archetypal (Herodotus 4.120, 121, 127, 128): the Scythians 'resolved not to meet their enemy in the open field . . . but rather to withdraw and drive off their herds, choking the wells and springs on their way and destroying the grass from the earth. . . . As for the wagons in which their children and wives lived, all these they sent forward, charged to drive ever northward. . . . For the Scythians have not towns or planted lands.' Avoiding direct confrontation, they followed the Persians from a distance, attacking them 'whenever they were foraging for provisions. . . . The Scythian horse ever routed the Persian horse . . . and the Scythians, once they had driven in the horse, turned about for fear of the foot. The Scythians attacked in this fashion by night as well as by day.' Finding itself deep within the country without having any significant impact, the Persian army was forced to withdraw in haste for fear of starvation and because its communications with its home base were in danger of being cut off.

The outcome of this first large-scale campaign into the steppe fore-shadowed that of countless later efforts, most notably those by China along its vast steppe frontier. But before shifting our attention to that other side of the Eurasian steppe, we might add that, after Alexander destroyed the Persian Empire and after his Seleucid successors centred themselves in Syria, no Iranian great power existed to block the Near Eastern open steppe flank. Consequently, the vacuum was quickly filled by other Iranian-speaking nomadic horse archers from the north: the Parthians, who moved south to establish their rule over the Iranian highland plateau and parts of Mesopotamia. From 247 BC to AD 224, this empire of the transitional, mixed zone between the steppe and the sown acted as a counterbalance to the Mediterranean empires, first the Seleucid and later Roman, constituting Rome's only surviving great power rival.

Significantly, however, even though originally the horse had been domes-ticated, the chariot developed, and the riding horse bred in the western part of the Eurasian steppe—which when the veil of prehistory lifted was populated by speakers of Iranian languages—it was in the east of the Eurasian steppe that the most formidable horse nomadic peoples would repeatedly emerge. Speaking Altaic—Turkic and Mongolic—languages in historical times, they evidently adopted from the west first the horse-drawn chariot and then the riding horse. Each of these imports, successively, arrived in the east across the length of the steppe about half a millennium after it had originated in the west. A remnant of this prehistoric eastward spread seems to have survived in the isolated population on China's north-western frontier, who, as late as the third quarter of the first millennium AD, wrote texts in the Indo-European language named Tocharian by scholars. Apparently to be identified with the Yüeh-chih of the Chinese records, their strikingly Caucasian features—such as red hair and blue eyes—are revealed in ancient artistic representations and by their excavated mum-mies.[98] All the same, once the Altaic populations had adopted horse nomad-ism themselves, the tide turned, and waves of migrations now invariably and repeatedly swept towards the other direction only: from the east westward across the steppe, into western Asia and eastern Europe.

Why was this so? What was the reason for the Turkic and Mongol peoples' ascendancy over the steppe and their overwhelming impact on the sedentary civilizations of Eurasia? This is a question that seems never to have been framed in such broad terms.[99] No innate aptitude was involved, of course. It was, once again, geography and ecology that made the difference. Although it was in the western part of the Eurasian steppe that fully nomadic horse pastoralism was inaugurated, not all the inhabitants of that region were pure nomads. Among the Scythians, for example, only some of the tribes—Herodotus's Royal Scythians (*Histories* 4.18–20)—were fully nomadic, whereas the rest, especially those living in the river valleys and in the rainier west, remained semi-nomadic and engaged in a combination of herding and agriculture. After all, in terms of both diet and comfort, the mixed way of life was more satisfactory. Ecological conditions that precluded agriculture were the factor that imposed the harsher, fully nomadic option of the open steppe. Significantly, however, that option brought out the military advantages of the horse peoples in their purest form. Military superiority thus rested with the harsher, more impoverished way of life. For this reason, the nomadic Scythians dominated the more sedentary Scythians. Similarly, from the third century BC on, the Sarmatians from the more arid steppe east of the Don took over Scythia.

In the eastern part of the Eurasian steppe, at the foot of the Altai Mountains, along the Gobi Desert, and on the Mongolian Plain, there was less precipitation than in the west, and fewer river valleys. Consequently, the native populations became more pastoralist–nomadic and less agricultural–sedentary, with all the military advantages that that way of life entailed. Thereby they also became far more dependent on their sedentary neighbours in China for agricultural produce and other goods. Furthermore, unlike the ancient Near East, China's northern frontier with the steppe was long and wide open, unsheltered by geographical obstacles such as vast inland seas. Finally, in contrast to Iran, which served as the nomads' main corridor into south-west Asia but also as a semi-pastoralist buffer zone against them, the transition in China from the steppe to the dense agricultural land of the Yellow River valley was far less gradual. There were mixed pastoral–agricultural zones on both flanks, particularly Manchuria in the east, but a much less significant one at the centre, opposite the heartland of Chinese civilization. It was the combination of all these factors that turned the horse nomads on China's steppe frontier into such a formidable world-historical force.

Only in the fourth century BC, four centuries after south-west Asia, did China of the Warring States period become the victim of raids by emergent horse nomads from the north, while also adopting cavalry herself.

Subsequently, as the Ch'in (221–206 BC), followed by the Han (206 BC to AD 220), united China, a parallel empire of the steppe—a huge tribal confederation known as Hsiung-nu in the Chinese sources—formed on its northern frontier. Whether it was (proto-)Turkic or (proto-)Mongolic speaking, or both, remains unknown, although it may have included Caucasian elements as well. From then on, political developments in China and the steppe were inextricably linked, as if the two lands were symbiotic Siamese twins. China's greatest imperial dynasties witnessed the emergence of equally formidable steppe empires opposite them. The Han and Hsiung-nu, after a period of disintegration, were followed by the Sui and T'ang Dynasties in China (AD 581–907) which faced the vast Turkic empires on the steppe.

As historical anthropologist Thomas Barfield has pointed out, states and empires of the steppe emerged not merely because of the usual factors—including war—that prompted state formation on the marches of civilizations, but specifically as larger extortion conglomerations, capable of taking on the sedentary empires.[100] Contrary to a commonly held impression created by the Mongol Empire of Chinggis Khan and his successors, the steppe nomads did not normally attempt to conquer and rule the sedentary–civilized zone. This would have meant commitments that they were little qualified or inclined to shoulder and a transformation, if not abandonment, of their pastoralist–steppe way of life. Rather, their aim was plunder, preferably upgraded to extortion (as well as the exacting of trading rights). Their ideal was to force the state authorities of the sedentary zone to work for them, by negotiating and raising the vast quantities of agricultural produce and luxury goods that were to be sent to the steppe as 'protection money', thus saving both sides the trouble, death, devastation, and misery of regular raiding. If the imperial authorities abrogated on the delivery of the heavy tribute, large-scale raiding would resume to force them to reconsider. In all this the steppe nomads were in fact no different from other predatory pre- and early state societies which, as we have seen, raided and extorted tribute rather than established direct rule.

But why would the mighty and proud emperors of China agree to extortion by the steppe nomads, as they did for the centuries and millennia during which China was held in the embrace of the steppe in a symbiotic, parasitic stranglehold? There was no reason, of course, other than that there was practically no definitive military solution to China's plight.

The Eurasian Spearhead: East, West, and the Steppe

Two strategies—defensive and offensive—were alternately or conjointly attempted from the very start. Defensively, the Warring States that bordered on the steppe erected Chinese-style stamped earth walls to shield their territories from nomad raiding. China's First Emperor, Shih-huang-ti (221–210 BC), integrated these fortifications into the famous Great Wall, which would repeatedly be rebuilt in later periods.[101] However, although stretching along thousands of kilometres, the Wall could not entirely block out massive raids by large and mobile mounted hordes.

The other, mobile-offensive strategy attempted by the Chinese consisted of the employment of large forces of light cavalry, which, emulating the steppe horsemen in fighting gear and tactics, sought to ambush, intercept, and track them down. This mode of action, too, was first adopted during the Warring States period by King Wu-ling from the state of Zhau (307 BC). The change also affected inter-state Chinese warfare, as chariots increasingly gave way to cavalry.[102] Two centuries later, after the Hsiung-nu's demands had grown excessively heavy, while treaties and trading with them had not completely prevented their raiding, the Han emperors revived this strategy, taking it a step further. From 129 BC on, they launched massive invasions of the steppe in an effort to track down and capture the tribal folk and herds. However, even at its most successful, this strategy proved to be of limited effectiveness, while being hugely expensive. As already mentioned, the nomadic tribes were highly elusive. On the Chinese side, raising large cavalry armies, whose hundreds of thousands of horses, bred and fed on state farms, possessed no value other than military, involved an enormous logistical and financial outlay. The high cost and logistical complexity of wide-scale campaigns into the arid steppe were equally mind boggling, contrasting sharply with the nomads' self-contained and flexible logistics. Thus the Chinese authorities throughout history could not but agonize over whether a settlement with the nomads on a reasonable tribute was not less costly and the lesser of two evils.[103]

It was this chronic and costly dilemma, in the shadow of an almost continuous nomadic menace, that China was forced to endure. She was relatively successful in dealing with the nomads only when they experienced growing internal divisions and a weakening of central authority. Chinese imperial policy was then able to exploit these developments, turning one faction against the other and enlisting allied nomadic clients by means of payment, diplomacy, and military support. Even more successful was the incorporation of part of the steppe into a joint Chinese–steppe empire, pursued in particular by imperial rulers who came from semi-nomadic–semi-sedentary Manchuria, on China's north-eastern march. Unlike the fully nomadic horse pastoralists of Mongolia, the Manchurians did attempt to seize, and occasionally succeeded in seizing, control over China or parts of it in times of dynastic decline and imperial anarchy. The most successful were the T'o-pa Wei (AD 386–556), Khitan-Liao and Jurchen-Chin (AD 907–1234), and Manchu-Ch'ing (AD 1616–1912).[104] As in Iran, the resulting hybrid pastoralist–sedentary polity was more capable of containing the steppe's horse nomads than the intensively agricultural China proper.

The only nomadic steppe empire to attempt and succeed in actually conquering China and ruling it directly was the Mongol Empire of Chinggis Khan and his successors. That fugitive son of a tribal chief managed to unite the steppe tribes in ever-widening circles under his rule by constant warfare that stretched over 20 years. In AD 1206, he was proclaimed Great Khan over all the Mongol and Turkic tribes of the Mongolian steppe, after which he brought the semi-nomadic, Sinified states on China's frontier under his suzerainty. Initially, Chinggis Khan's ambition appears not to have diverged from this traditional goal of creating a unified steppe empire, to be followed by a reimposition of tributary payments on China. His first campaigns in China in AD 1211–14 were carried out with this purpose in mind. However, external circumstances and innovations within the nomad polity itself combined to take his policy in a new direction. Externally, after fierce fighting and massive devastation, the Chin rulers of north China gave in and conceded to a treaty in 1214. However, they then moved their capital away from the steppe frontier, which Chinggis Khan interpreted as a sign of their intention to resume resistance. Simultaneously, the Mongolians were drawn into launching an unintended massive war of revenge in the west. They invaded and destroyed the powerful Khwarazm state in Transoxiana (AD 1219–20), the ruler of which, Shah Muhammad, had killed the Great Khan's envoys.

Under these circumstances, and being more centralized and orderly than earlier nomad empires of the steppe, Chinggis Khan's empire was able to apply its domestic source of strength outwards. Rather than relying on the tribal hosts, Chinggis Khan had organized his steppe army into hierarchical decimal units, consisting successively of 10, 100, 1,000, and 10,000 warriors. At the head of these units he had placed nominated commanders, appointed and promoted by merit, after they had proved their distinction in the field and loyalty to the Great Khan. The steppe horsemen's characteristic military qualities were thereby supplemented by remarkable order, discipline, and organizational unity. Although this military command system was obviously incapable of ruling complex sedentary societies by itself, it constituted a centralized and permanent state structure, through which civil government could be further delegated.

During the conquest, the Mongols initially considered 'depopulating' northern China, with the view of turning it into pastureland for their horses and flocks. A former senior Khitan administrator, Yeh-lü Ch'ü-ts'ai, now in the service of the Great Khan, allegedly averted the catastrophe by explaining to the new rulers that, if they let him run the country in peace, he would be able to raise for them annually 500,000 ounces of silver, 400,000 bags of grain, and 80,000 pieces of silk.[105] The Mongols accepted, resorting to ruling China through the old imperial bureaucratic apparatus. Furthermore, although their own forces that were carrying out the conquest of China never numbered more than 65,000 steppe horsemen, they extensively recruited native Chinese, to be mainly employed as infantry and for siege operations and other technical services. From the time of Chinggis's grandson, Kublai Khan (1260–94), the China part of the Mongol Empire became increasingly Sinified, as the Mongol ruling and military elite progressively cut loose from the steppe and assimilated into Chinese culture. Assuming the dynastic name of Yüan, the Mongols ruled China for another century, until they were driven out by the Ming Dynasty in 1368, after a period of decline and loss of control.

The armies of Chinggis Khan and his successors also swept westward. Incorporating the native steppe nomads as they progressed, they launched a two-pronged offensive: one host invaded south-west Asia, conquering Iran and destroying the Moslem caliphate in Baghdad; another invaded eastern Europe, routing and subjugating the Rus states of Ukraine and Russia, and then campaigning further west into Poland and Hungary, defeating the local rulers. The Mongol Empire and its successor states would rule the largest empire that the world had ever known, including north India.

The Gates of Europe

Chinggis Khan's armies were, however, closer to being the last, rather than the first, of a chain of Turkic–Mongolian tribal hosts that had moved westward over the preceding 1,000 years, taking over the western part of the steppe from the Iranian-speaking pastoralists and bearing heavily on the civilizations of south-west Asia and Europe. As it took about half a millennium for the fully nomadic horse-pastoralist way of life to reach the eastern steppe from the west, so it took another half a millennium for horse pastoralism to build up on the eastern steppe to a level that generated repeated waves of migration westwards. It is this time sequence—as the new way of life arrived in the Far Eastern steppe, took root, and filled it up—that explains why the first wave in a would-be continuous flow of migration, the Huns' sudden appearance in Ukraine in the early AD 370s, took place at that particular point in time rather than at any earlier moment in western history, and was from then on followed by almost regular pulses of further intrusion. A new element was introduced into western history.

As on China's frontier, the Far Eastern horse nomads radically altered the steppe–civilization balance of power in western Eurasia. They were a far more menacing and destructive force than the local, less mobile, economically more mixed, Iranian-speaking, Cimmerian, Scythian, Sarmatian, and Alan horse pastoralists had been. Similar to the Hsiung-nu on China's steppe frontier, the language of the Huns remains unknown, because it was not recorded in writing by the civilizations that they encountered. Scholars are equally unable to ascertain whether or not the Huns were a tribal group emanating from the Hsiung-nu's orbit that moved westward during the power struggles that followed the fragmentation of that empire.[106] The most reasonable assumption, however, is that they were, and that both of these tribal groups spoke Turkic languages.

Probably numbering in the low tens of thousands of warriors, the Hun tribal hosts raided and defeated the local Iranian-speaking peoples and Germanic Goths in Ukraine, driving them in terror westwards, into the Roman Empire. Raiding further west into central Europe, they pushed the terrified Germanic peoples wholesale into the western Empire. It was in this sense that the horse can be said to have brought down the western Roman Empire. It was not that cavalry suddenly proved to be superior to Roman infantry; rather, the advent of the steppe horsemen triggered a widespread chain reaction among the Germanic peoples on Rome's barbarian marches, with their migration, settlement, and predominantly *foot* armies ultimately destroying the Empire. It was the distant rise over millennia of the steppe horse-nomadic way of life that so decisively, but indirectly, affected the far west.

388

The Eurasian Spearhead: East, West, and the Steppe

The Huns' own direct action was of an entirely different sort. Contact with the Roman Empire triggered among them a process similar to what repeatedly took place on China's steppe frontier. Hun tribal society was united by Attila (AD 440s to 453) into an empire that incorporated dependent Iranian- and Germanic-speaking peoples of the steppe and central Europe. The Huns had repeatedly raided the eastern Roman Empire, as well as Sasanian Persia. Attila's power now made extortion possible on an unprecedented scale. Contrary to popular impression, he did not attempt to conquer either the eastern or the western Roman Empire. Repeatedly leading his horsemen into the Empire in massive raids of looting and destruction, particularly in the richer eastern part, he extracted fabulous sums of money as tribute from the imperial rulers.

After Attila's death, his empire disintegrated in an internal struggle of power among his successors and amid rebellion of the dependent peoples. But a chain of Turkic migrations from their Altaic homeland followed. In Europe, the Avars (possibly the Juan–Juan of China's frontier) arrived in the mid-sixth century AD, and the Bulgarians in the early seventh. Next to arrive, in the ninth century, were the Hungarian–Magyars from the Ural. These were a Finno–Ugric rather than Altaic–Turkic tribal people. Living on the northern edge of the steppe, however, they were swept into the horse-pastoralist way of life and were driven westward by their Bulgar, Khazar, and Pecheneg Turkic neighbours, who dominated north–central Asia. In south–central Asia, the Yüeh-chih (including the Caucasian 'Tocharians') moved west from China's border into Transoxiana in the first century BC and proceeded to establish the Kushan Empire in Afghanistan and north India during the first to fifth centuries AD. Kushan was destroyed by the arrival in the fourth to sixth centuries of the Hephthalites or White Huns, who raided and invaded Iran and north India. From the middle of the eighth century AD, Turkic tribals continuously arrived from the north-east into the Islamic world in Iran, Mesopotamia, and Anatolia. First serving the local rulers as mercenaries, they soon took power throughout the region, most notably the Seljuk Turks.[107]

All the same, the horse nomads' impact on western Europe, significant in various ways as it was, was less momentous than their impact on east, south-west, and south Asia, or, indeed, eastern Europe. Western Europe was never dominated, let alone conquered, by the steppe nomads. The reason for this is simple. Compared with the other regions mentioned, the closed and rugged landscape of western Europe offered no open and spacious pastureland for the nomads' horses and herds, the basis of their peculiar mode of subsistence and way of life. The Hungarian plain had always constituted the westernmost boundary of the steppe nomads' migrations, from where they were able to raid and terrorize central and western Europe. But the Hungarian plain was too small to form a homeland for truly large horse-pastoralist peoples. With respect to Attila's Huns, the Avars, and the Hungarian–Magyar alike, restricted pastureland on that plain has been discerned as a major reason for the decline of the horse nomads' threat over time. Furthermore, as the nomadic tribals became more sedentary, they increasingly relied on carts and wagons to carry away their booty, thereby maximizing their looting capacity but compromising their mobility and becoming easier to intercept and pin down. Again, this process affected and ultimately broke the military ascendancy of Attila's Huns, the Magyars, and the Crimean Tartars, each in their turn. The Ottoman Turks, for their part, increasingly adapted to rule directly the sedentary societies of western Anatolia and the Balkans, among other things creating an efficient infantry force and siege train and giving up much of their tribal–nomadic heritage.[108]

It was only on the vast south-eastern European steppe that the nomads were able to take root. The successor of Chinggis Khan's empire in that region, the Golden Horde, dominated, lived on the tribute of, and, indeed, was possible as a vast steppe imperial conglomeration only because of, the agricultural state societies that had emerged in eastern Europe since the late first millennium AD. After the disintegration of the Golden Horde in the late fifteenth century, its splinter groups, the Khanates of Crimea, Kazan, and Astrakhan would for centuries continue to raid and devastate the steppe frontier of Poland–Lithuania and Muscovite Russia, regularly carrying away loads of loot and masses of captives, to be sold into slavery in the sedentary societies of the south, chiefly the Ottoman Empire. The increasingly powerful early modern east European states reacted in an all-too-familiar manner, fortifying their frontier settlements and establishing a chain of fortresses, from which light cavalry, partly consisting of hired steppe nomads, attempted to ambush, pursue, and intercept the raiders. All the same, there was no definitive solution to the problem of the steppe frontier, where rural devastation and human misery on a vast scale were the norm until well into modernity.[109] Only then would the ground rules, established millennia earlier on China's steppe frontier be finally transformed.

WEST VERSUS EAST

The lesser impact of the pastoralists was just one consequence of western Europe's peculiar ecology and physical geography, which set it apart from the other major zones of civilization in Eurasia, making Europe or the west and Asia or the east proverbially, but also puzzlingly, different from each other. To be sure, all these designations should be read as if appearing within inverted commas, as political–cultural categories in the broadest sense. Indeed, most historians tend to be highly suspicious of such grand abstractions, which, admittedly, have all too frequently been crudely made, often disguising bigotry. Most historians are also hostile towards geographical–ecological explanations, which they criticize for being deterministic and ignoring the contingent and cultural–historical processes— whereas in fact they contextualize them. Inexplicably, in a sort of disciplinary split personality, this attitude is reversed and transformed into deep reverence in historians' attitude to the work of the historiographic school known as *Annales*. This school extensively evokes deep-seated regional geographical, climatic, and ecological factors for explanations of the particular histories of different societies over the *longue durée*. Originating in France of the twentieth century, the *Annales'* approach itself stems from deeper roots, going back to the early modern period and the Enlightenment, and culminating in Montesquieu. It was then that European exploration and expansion, together with printing technology, provided Europeans with a global perspective, steadily improving information about other societies of the world, and a better sense of these societies' characteristic features and the differences between them. From Montesquieu on, every major historical and social thinker—Voltaire, Hume, Adam Smith, Herder, Hegel, Marx, and Weber are only the giants among them—posited, and variously attempted to explain, the differences between east and west, differences that the educated public at large widely sensed, even if failing to define and account for them adequately.

In recent times, the various observations of these thinkers have been supplemented by more dedicated studies of the reasons for the so-called European miracle or 'rise of the west' in the modern age: what was it that gave Europe its unrivalled supremacy in science, technology, economy, and power from the sixteenth century on.[110] This question is typically treated separately from that of the other European 'miracle', the one associated with the ancient Greeks and the 'rise of the west' two millennia earlier. But were these two European developments unrelated to each other, or did they share something of consequence in common? And if the latter is true, what can account for the similarities: is it simply a matter of cultural continuation and transmission within Europe from antiquity to modernity; or is it to be understood with reference to infrastructural factors that underlie European history, affecting its general contours?[111]

Obviously, every region, period, and culture is unique. The histories of China, India, and south-west Asia reveal, individually, great diversity over space and time, as does Europe's, while also being no less distinctive and unique in their own ways than Europe's. The question that should be asked, then, is what the particular 'uniqueness' was that constituted the histories of east and west, respectively, distinguishing them from each other. Yet again, this question is treated here within the context of this book's general themes: in what way were war and military force modulated differently and variably, affecting and affected by specific environmental, economic, social, and political factors in the east and west? So far in this chapter I have focused on shared elements that set cultural evolution in Eurasia apart from the rest of the world, attempting a generalized treatment of war and military institutions across the landmass. Now I turn to consider some of Eurasia's major regional variations.[112]

One of the most distinctive features of European history compared with Eurasia's other three major zones of dense sedentary civilization concerns imperial unity. At both ends of Asia—the Near East and China—imperial unification on a massive scale, more or less incorporating the entire agricultural zone, was achieved early on in their histories, and thereafter became the norm, with only relatively brief relapses. Even in India, empires that encompassed most of the subcontinent, except for its southern tip—including the Maurya, Gupta, Delhi Sultanate, and Mogul—alternated with periods of greater fragmentation. (The last two empires were created by cavalry armies of Turkic and Mongol dynasties from Afghanistan and inner Asia.) By contrast, a most conspicuous but rarely noted fact about European history is that Europe—alone of all the other regions—was never united by force from within or conquered from without. Rome, the only arguable exception, was a Mediterranean, rather than a European, empire that incorporated only southern Europe, and although enduring for centuries and being highly influential, lasted for only a fraction of European history. All other attempts at imperial unification—the Carolingian, Ottonian, Habsburgian, and Napoleonic—were geographically even more confined and short-lived.

Montesquieu defined this European uniqueness the earliest and clearest, while also discerning the geographical and ecological factors that underlay it:

> In Asia one has always seen great empires; in Europe they were never able to continue to exist. This is because the Asia we know has broader plains; it is cut into larger parts by seas; and, as it is more to the south, its streams dry up more easily, its mountains are less covered with snow, and its smaller rivers form slighter barriers. Therefore, power should always be despotic in Asia. . . . In Europe, the natural divisions form many medium-size states, in which the government of laws is not incompatible with the maintenance of the state. . . . This is what has formed a genius for liberty, which makes it very difficult to subjugate each part and to put it under a foreign force.[113]

South-west and east Asia, as well as the north of the Indian subcontinent, incorporate large open plains, which facilitated rapid troop movement and imperial communications. By contrast, southern–western–central Europe is highly fragmented by mountains and sea. Sheltered behind these obstacles, while also benefiting from individual access to the sea, the multiplicity of smaller political units that emerged in this fragmented landscape were able to defend their independence with much more success than those of Asia.

Greece is paradigmatic in this respect. It was the region of Europe into which agriculture and civilization first spread in their gradual outward expansion from the ancient Near East. Being Europe's most fragmented peninsula, criss-crossed as it was by mountains and sea, Greece foreshadowed in miniature the political fragmentation of the peninsular and rugged continent as a whole. More than coincidence, memory, and cultural transmission connected the Greeks to later European history. It should be noted, however, that the same sea that sheltered and granted access to the open to the Greek and other Mediterranean polities could also serve as a communication highway—comparable to Asia's open plains—for prospective land empires that succeeded in mastering it. Rome established such mastery from the mid-third century BC, after it had completed the conquest of the Italian peninsula and clashed with Carthage. It is in this sense that we have described Rome as a Mediterranean empire, because it was the communication and logistical highway of the Mediterranean *mare nostrum* that made possible the Empire's large scale. In anticipation of criticism, I hasten to stress that all this does not mean that Europe *could not possibly* be united by force or conquered from outside, that this was somehow 'deterministically preordained'. It simply means that, rather than being wholly accidental, this fact of European history rested on physical and ecological conditions that made the consolidation of large political units on this continent that much more difficult.

I have already noted that smaller political scale was generally less conducive to the concentration of autocratic power at the expense of both the aristocracy and populace, as became the rule in Asia once vast empires formed there—the so-called Oriental despotism. As Edward Gibbon has clearly noted, the increasingly autocratic late Roman Empire demonstrates that Europe, too, was not immune to such processes.[114] And there were other geographical–ecological factors, beside fragmented landscape, that contributed to Europe's political fragmentation and greater power distribution. As already mentioned, western Europe was not exposed to a vast pastoralist steppe frontier, as China and even north India were. Nor was it internally divided into arable and more arid, pastoral strips and zones, as was the case in south-west Asia, where pastoralist raids and take-overs had been a prominent feature of civilization throughout history. In temperate Europe, where rainfall was nearly everywhere sufficient for agriculture, separate herding subsistence economies and herding societies barely existed. Rather, herding was commonly practised within mixed, agricultural–pastoral farming, with local variations, of course.

Furthermore, Europe's rainfall patterns also determined that dry rather than intensive-irrigation farming was the rule, and that settlement was more or less evenly spread out rather than being densely concentrated in river valleys. According to various calculations, this meant that the European population density was only a third of that of the river valley civilizations, and perhaps only a tenth of the population density in the river valleys themselves.[115] This subsistence-settlement pattern had political consequences. As Montesquieu, Weber, and others have seen, irrigation agriculture was more conducive to autocratic rule.[116] In the first place, large irrigation systems necessitated communal organization and construction work, whereas practitioners of dry farming were more independent. Second, irrigation cultivators were much more vulnerable to the destruction of their livelihood by a force that might disrupt the irrigation system. Third, highly intensive cultivation of small, irrigated plots left less time for other activities—including war—than was the case with dry farming. As a consequence of all of these, irrigation cultivators tended to be more servile than dry farming agriculturalists. It is probably no coincidence that the most effective infantry in the ancient Near East was produced by Assyria, with a peasant economy in northern Mesopotamia that was predominantly based on dry farming, as opposed to the irrigation agriculture of Babylonia to its south and of Egypt.

Thus, in comparison to the civilizations of Asia, geographical fragmentation and rainfall patterns contributed to making the southern–central–western European inter-state system more fragmented, and state-societies smaller, less polarized in terms of class and wealth, and less oppressive. This might be accepted with some scepticism in view of the huge social and economic gaps and massive oppression that characterized many periods and regions of pre-modern and modern Europe. All the same, studies by present-day historians and social scientists confirm what their predecessors, from Montesquieu and Adam Smith on, always sensed: in *relative* terms, Asian societies were more susceptible to imperial rule, more despotic, and socially and economically more polarized.[117]

All this closely interacted with the patterns of war making and military organization in the west, compared with the east. In the first place, as already seen, smaller size meant relatively higher mobilization levels, because campaigning was closer to home and entailed lesser economic and logistical complications. In turn, smaller and more numerous polities, campaigning close to home, and higher mobilization levels also meant far higher exposure of the men and of the population at large to warfare than was the case in large empires. It was this that gave Europe its all-time reputation as a place of incessant warfare and made it an armed camp, as opposed to the largely pacified populations of the Asian empires, or indeed, of the *pax Romana*. Furthermore, rugged terrain, limited pastureland, shorter campaigning distances, urban defensive concentration, and higher mobilization levels were responsible for the preponderance of infantry in Europe, which, in turn, increased popular bargaining power within society.

Tellingly, in Europe too, infantry declined vis-à-vis cavalry whenever these underlying conditions lost force. In the late Roman Empire—well before the stirrups—cavalry grew in significance, especially in the eastern provinces. The long Danube frontier required more mobile forces to forestall Gothic and Hunnic horse raids from the Ukrainian steppe. The long Near Eastern *limes* demanded mobile mounted troops even more badly to counter the large cavalry forces of the Sasanid Persian Empire, as well as for intercepting nomadic raiding from the desert. As already seen, equestrian warfare was in the ascendancy in western Europe from the eighth century AD, because long-range campaigning on the frontiers of the larger Frankish realm and highly mobile raiding from all quarters necessitated quick-responding, mobile, mounted troops. In a primitive and segmentary agricultural society, the mounted warriors were able to seize power and maintain their social–military preponderance during the period of high feudalism in the eleventh and twelfth centuries. Thereafter, even before firearms, infantry returned to constitute the main arm, at least militarily, as it had been throughout most of European history.

Furthermore, European infantry was of a particular sort, a phenomenon that we have already begun to see with respect to city-states. Close-quarter shock tactics were the norm throughout most of Europe's civilized history for the following, interrelated reasons: infantry played a leading rather than a supporting role in battle; settled agricultural and civic communities rather than pastoral or shifting hosts predominated and, in combination with the short distances and more evenly spread population, made stealth tactics that much less effective; and the people's integration, status, and stake in society and state were stronger, increasing its motivation to stand up and fight. Here was the structural underpinning of that distinctive 'western way in warfare', which was first revealed with the Greeks and continued to characterize European history in different regions and eras, not merely because of a habit, tradition, or cultural transference (strong as all these sometimes may have been), but because of the west's 'objective' conditions.[118]

Indeed, in Asian states and empires, where conditions were close to the opposite of those just cited for Europe, close-quarter shock infantry tactics were uncommon, whereas the stand-off missile battle was very much the rule. Even the heavy contingents of the Assyrian infantry, wearing defensive armour and battle-worthy, apparently did not fight in a phalanx-like, dense mass formation, or play the decisive role on the battlefield. In the vast open spaces of south-west Asia, the mounted arm—chariots and cavalry—predominated. The infantry mass, paramount in siege craft and other special tasks, was chiefly employed in battle for softening and disarraying the enemy with missiles, preparing the ground for the horsemen to deliver the decisive

A rare image of Assyrian spearmen in ranks on the open field. Reign of Sennacherib

blow. The main function of the foot spearman was to defend the bowman. The Achaemenid Persian armies, as described by Herodotus, were heirs to this mode of fighting.[119] Although we lack specific information, much the same also seems to have applied to the infantry armies in China of the Warring States period, and to ancient India, where war elephants increasingly played the decisive role, driving the horsemen into second place.[120]

It was the massive mobilization capacity of the Greek city-states close to home, in infantry rather than horse country, that won them victory over

Xerxes' imperial army during the 480–479 BC Persian invasion. (Naval superiority was probably no less important, of course.) As a result of their special aptitude as heavy infantry, Greeks were later hired to fill this role in the Persian army as well. When Greek shock infantry tactics were combined by the central state power of Philip II and Alexander with the shock cavalry of the more open lands further north—Macedonia, Thessaly, and Thrace—the western way in warfare was able to achieve victory in the east as well, at least for a while. Indeed, with horsemen, too, the west was more inclined towards heavy, shock tactics, as opposed to the lighter, missile tactics of the east, and for pretty much the same reasons mentioned with respect to infantry. Under conditions of closed landscapes, short campaigning distances, and settled and evenly spread habitation, which lacked shifting populations and wide open spaces, there was much less room for hit-and-run, missile, light horse tactics. Under these conditions, heavy, shock mounted troops were that much more able to force contact and crush lighter adversaries.

It would appear that as early as the age of the chariot—where operation was, of course, even more constrained than that of cavalry by Europe's rugged terrain—typical mounted action was significantly different between the east and the west. Swift tactical manoeuvring and arrow shooting from a distance, which were the rule on the plains of the ancient Near East, were far less feasible in Europe. Chariots provided strategic mobility (and easier, prestigious transportation for the elite), but on the battlefield the chariot warriors often dismounted to fight on foot with heavy arms. Homer's depiction of the Mycenaeans (Achaeans) as fighting in this manner has been criticized by some modern scholars. They have claimed that, being unfamiliar with chariot warfare, long gone by his time, Homer anachronistically projected the pattern of cavalry warfare of his day on past ages. As we, too, lack direct evidence for the pattern of Mycenaean chariot warfare, these scholars have held that the Near Eastern evidence should serve as the only adequate analogy. But as other scholars have realized, if cavalry regularly found it necessary to dismount in the Greek rugged terrain, chariot warriors must have done so even more habitually, because the chariots' dependence on plain and level ground for effective operation was incomparably greater than that of cavalry.[121] As clear differences in the style of cavalry warfare between east and west would exist throughout history, what grounds were there for assuming a uniform mode of chariot warfare?

Indeed, neglected by Homer's critics, the only clear evidence of chariot warfare in rugged European conditions is offered first hand by one of the greatest authorities ever on military affairs, Julius Caesar. Confronted by elite chariot troops during his invasion of remote and isolated Britain (54 BC), where chariots had not yet been replaced by cavalry as was the case throughout Europe, Caesar (*The Gallic War* 4.33) describes chariot warfare in terms quite akin to Homer's:

> First of all they drive in all directions and hurl missiles. . . . When they have worked their way in between the troops of cavalry, they leap down from the chariots and fight on foot. Meanwhile the charioteers retire gradually from the combat, and dispose the chariots in such fashion that, if the warriors are hard pressed by the host of the enemy, they may have a ready means of retirement to their own side. Thus they show in action the mobility of cavalry and the stability of infantry.

In the east, too, there was heavy shock cavalry, such as the fully armoured lancers (*cataphracts*) raised from among the nobility in Parthian and Sasanid Persia, whereas there were, of course, missile light horsemen in the west as well. But diverging conditions prescribed that it was heavy shock cavalry, culminating in the medieval knight, that predominated in the west, albeit playing a secondary role to heavy shock infantry throughout most of European history. On the other side, light cavalry, most notably the mounted archer, dominated in the east.

Thus the Achaemenid Persian expansion reached its limit in Greece, whereas Alexander's conquests east of the Levant shores soon reverted to the horse-dominated Iranian peoples. The Roman frontier in Mesopotamia ran even further to the west than the Seleucid. In 53 BC, in the first serious military encounter between Rome and Parthia, the Parthian army, wholly composed of 10,000 cavalry, of which 9,000 were mounted archers, annihilated the legion army under Crassus on the open battlefield of Carrhae on Syria's northern plain. The legionaries were simply unable to force their enemy into contact and had no means of responding to its stand-off fire. Rome was the stronger of the two powers and would exercise pressure on Parthia during most of the following centuries, but the borderline between the two in northern Mesopotamia would not change much. Invasions of Parthia by Mark Anthony and by a succession of Roman emperors (and, later, of Sasanian Persia) repeatedly failed, because ultimately the Iranian cavalry would not be pinned down to give battle. Indeed, as already mentioned above, the Roman Empire itself would increasingly adopt cavalry as the dominant arm in its eastern provinces, as would all later great powers of the region.

I return to examine the west's distinctive evolutionary trajectory in my discussion of modernity and war in Part 3. But, first, it is time to summarize more analytically the interrelationship between armed force and the transformation of humankind by the adoption of farming and the growth of the state and of civilization, as reviewed in Part 2. It is also time to consider how this cultural transformation related to the evolution-shaped innate human propensities pertaining to violent action that were examined in Part 1.

12

Conclusion: War, the Leviathan, and the Pleasures and Miseries of Civilization

Although humankind's gradual transition to farming and animal husbandry did not inaugurate human fighting, it radically transformed it—and human life in general—vastly accelerating cultural evolution. At base level, productivity and population grew steadily, increasing by as much as 100-fold by the eve of modernity. As population growth more or less correlated with the rise in productivity, surpluses did not increase much, and the vast majority of people continued to live as food producers precariously close to subsistence levels. However, increasingly dense and sedentary populations, stationary means of production, and accumulated property now made possible a differential concentration and appropriation of surpluses. In a process first outlined by Rousseau, existing natural differences between people were enormously magnified and objectified by accumulated resources.

As power and resource accumulation reinforced each other in a positive loop mechanism, massive social power structures emerged. Control over resources meant that a host of dependants were tied to the rich and powerful in an asymmetrical relationship. This, in turn, meant that for a highly differential share of the benefits or for fear of sanction, or both, they supported the rich and powerful as the latter further increased their wealth and power by taking advantage of economic opportunity and through the exploitation and extortion of others. Relying on these hierarchical power concentrations, the rich and powerful dominated social life, allying but at the same time also fiercely competing with each other. State emergence was the culmination of this process, when a single power nucleus won against all others in the often-violent intrasocial competition, or else power nuclei joined to regulate the competition among them. Either way, one power structure established command over a population, institutionalizing power, driving other social power nuclei into subordination, and introducing hitherto unprecedented levels of hierarchical organization, coercion, systematic resource extraction, and force mobilization, while competing with neighbouring state structures. State structure thus arose from either or both the domestic growth of 'class society' and foreign pressure by other states.

COERCIVE STRUCTURES AND EXPONENTIAL GROWTH

The evolution of these concentrations of power cum resources within and above societies was the force that fuelled the growth of civilization. Political societies grew in size, creating economies of scale, aggregating and purposefully directing resources and human activity, and regulating social life. Monumental building, literacy, high art, and all the rest were consequences of the above. Scale and coercive structuring were the keys to the whole process. The superiority of power that they accorded in competition and conflict unleashed an evolutionary race, which, despite occasional collapses and regressions, continuously spiralled upwards in a self-reinforcing process. The larger the resource base, the greater became the resource and power aggregation both within and between societies. Thus 'egalitarian' societies became increasingly stratified: segmentary societies were transformed into state societies; hierarchical apparatuses were superimposed on kinship networks; petty-states, both rural and urban (where warfare drove the peasants to seek safety in nucleated settlement), became progressively dominated by one of them and consolidated into federations, hegemonies, and larger states; states were swallowed within empires (a term that generally denotes very large states and/or multi-ethnic ones, usually with one of the peoples as supreme); and overlordship gave way to more direct rule and more unified polities. As the size of polities grew, the population of each swelled from a few thousand to tens and hundreds of thousands, to millions. The more the network of the states expanded and the complexity deepened, the less they were likely to experience complete systemic collapses, because peer interaction and co-evolution were far more pervasive than in early and more isolated civilizations.[1]

The use and threat of force were the principal means by which the continuous process of political conglomeration was achieved. Neither long-distance trade nor religious authority was even remotely as significant as force accumulation in bringing about this process in overwhelmingly agrarian, and thus fundamentally local and self-sufficient, societies. Indeed, both trade and religious authority constituted at least as much a consequence as a cause of political unification.[2] Ethnicity constituted a stronger factor in determining political expansion, although here, too, a similar interrelationship prevailed. Contrary to some fashionable theories, ethnic bonds—grounded in kin solidarity—were neither wholly 'invented' nor entirely superseded by the political power structures superimposed on them. Large-scale ethnic formations came into being before state emergence, most notably in regions of the world that had experienced the original agricultural expansions or pastoralist take-overs.[3] Such ethnic spaces and ethnic boundaries were paramount in the establishment of political boundaries. In turn, political unification by force over time eroded tribal and ethnic differences, amalgamating the realm into larger ethnic identities, and/or building supra-ethnic–cultural ties over existing ones.

Geographical and ecological niches and discontinuities were another major determinant of both ethnic and political boundaries. Indeed, the territorial expansion of political units did not continue indefinitely, because at some point the power advantage accorded by greater size was counterbalanced by ethnic, geographical, and ecological factors. Consequently, expansion stabilized at an equilibrium size, which depended, of course, on the particular conditions of the time and place. Distance in itself, as well as other constraints on accessibility, placed limits on states' size, because communication, effective control, and force concentration became ever more difficult, increasing the danger of both encroachments from outside and internal disintegration.[4]

Indeed, the struggle for power and for the benefits that power entailed took place simultaneously and inextricably (albeit somewhat differently) both within and between states. The state has all too often been perceived as the elementary and supposedly coherent unit of war, which mobilized its people and resources against other states. To be sure, a commanding position over a population and over all intrasocial concentrations of power—a commanding position that is the very essence of statehood, the cause and effect of its unique organizational and coercive strength—amounted to a quantum leap in social power. It considerably altered the rules of the game within the state's jurisdiction, in the constituted 'domestic' realm. The stronger the state, the more successful it was in regulating society, substituting internal peace for Hobbes's general anarchic insecurity, his 'warre of every man against every man'. All the same, the state did not entirely eliminate violent domestic power competition, but rather more or less bounded and suppressed it. In Max Weber's definition, the state successfully holds claim to monopoly over legitimate force.[5] However, a claim to monopoly over legitimate force, even a successful one, never actually amounted to a monopoly, not even over legitimate force. Existing around and inside the leviathan were not only countless sardines but also many sharks and barracudas.

In the first place, the state had to share power with power nuclei within society, which it partly subdued but did not eliminate: because it was beyond its power to do so; because it was obliged to co-opt these power nuclei in order to govern the realm; because they in effect constituted the state (as in aristocratic government); or because of any combination of these factors. The aristocracy as a class, and individual aristocrats, constituted a major, often the major, concentration of non-central power. The dynamic balance of power between the state and the aristocracy was maintained by benefit sharing but also through mutual deterrence. Inherently strained relations occasionally erupted into more or less limited armed confrontations. In more bureaucratic states, the local aristocracy was stripped of much of its power and was largely demilitarized, although its members often manned the upper echelons of the state's apparatus. All the same, it was now mainly by concentrations of power within this apparatus that the state was threatened. Provincial state governors utilizing local resources and army generals at the head of their men occasionally rebelled, either aiming to establish regional sovereignty or marching on the capital. They spent the country's resources on buying the support of the professional troops, who joined the highest bidder, extracting pay raises and special bonuses. The royal guard in particular, intended to protect the state rulers and strategically located around the capital, exploited its semi-monopolistic power to gain privileged access to benefits (differentially, of course, down its command system). The guard occasionally assumed the role of kingmaker, especially when struggles for power among the rulers themselves broke out, most notably during succession, which often involved rivalries between kin and siblings.

Bandits and pirates constituted other intrasocial non-state concentrations of armed, violent, and coercive force. During periods of political disintegration, they grew in power in direct relation to the weakening of state authority, sometimes to the point of obtaining the ability to seize power in the provinces and, from there, even to advance on the capital and become themselves the state. Finally, oppressed by high taxes and other forms of state exploitation and by the social elite, the rural or urban masses on occasion revolted or rioted (particularly during times of economic hardship), threatening all social power hierarchies. Furthermore, although state law and state sanction secured a much greater degree of public safety, the state's penetration of grass-root localities varied widely between states and across time. Among individuals, kin groups, and communities, self-support and mutual support remained a significant factor for deterring, withstanding, and/or instigating violent pressure, which occasionally escalated into feuds, blood revenge, and executions of private justice.

The state's internal and external power politics were thus mutually affecting. While raising troops to confront foreign rivals, the state had to consider that these troops—aristocratic, popular, or professional—might each become an agent of domestic power politics. Furthermore, the state's success or failure to master the domestic arena affected its ability to deal with foreign rivals, whereas record abroad greatly affected political standing at home. Despite all the ink spilt on this subject, it is no more possible to generalize which of these spheres—foreign or domestic politics—holds the primacy than to determine which hand is responsible for clapping. Indeed, this interdependency could purposefully be manipulated, because action in one sphere could actually be intended for its effect in the other. For example, state rulers might instigate war in order to effect a galvanizing 'rallying around the flag' that would consolidate their domestic position, whereas generals might do the same to win the resources and prestige necessary for a successful usurpation. This constituted a 'two-level game' that might involve violence on both levels.[6]

In the domestic arena, too, open violence sometimes ruptured the state's crust. Successful internal power challenges to the leviathan or a split at its head occasionally resulted in intra-state armed conflicts and at least a temporary breakdown of central authority. Many such conflicts remained small-scale court affairs, which mainly affected the limited circles of those directly involved. Others, however, had the power to engulf society. Mass popular uprisings sometimes resulted in horrendous blood baths, but even intra-elite violent struggles could exact a huge toll from society as a whole in terms of mobilization, resource extraction, economic disruption, devastation, and mass killing. Although such 'civil wars' did not result in a complete return to the 'state of nature', their closeness to home and the spread of anarchy that on occasion resulted from them sometimes degenerated into a Hobbesian 'warre', the destructiveness and lethality of which dwarfed 'normal' foreign war.

Indeed, although the prospect of violent conflict dominated state existence not only abroad but also at home, in 'normal' times statehood sharply differentiated between the two spheres, creating that gulf between murder and feud, on the one hand, and war, on the other—between 'warre' and war, as it were—a distinction that we take for granted but that is as recent a historical development as the state itself. We tend to think of the state as some five millennia old, but this age applies only to the earliest states, in Mesopotamia and Egypt. In other parts of the world—including those that are currently among the most advanced—statehood evolved much later; in both northern Europe and Japan, for example, it emerged only in the second half of the first millennium AD, whereas in some other regions of the world it is yet younger. And even 5 millennia constitute only about 5 per cent of the history of our kind, *Homo sapiens sapiens* (and the history of the genus *Homo* is 20 times longer), whereas one and half millennia constitute 1.5 per cent. Nevertheless, this tip of the iceberg, where states have existed, dominates our perception of human fighting, indeed, of humankind. Before the state, too, there was some difference between in-group and out-group killing, with the former modulated in small-scale, Palaeolithic human societies by successively extending and weakening kin circles, up to the regional group of hundreds or, at most, a few thousand. In agricultural tribal societies these onion-like kin circles grew larger, although anarchy, voluntary participation, and small numbers continued to dominate both internal and external fighting. Political organization, however, vastly magnified the difference between the two 'forms' of fighting, casting the latter—constituted as war—in the mould of the state's most characteristic attribute.

Thus coercive mobilization of people, resources, and growing scale resulted in a continuous increase in the size of the fighting hosts and in a wholly new level of regimentation: enforced discipline rendered participation obligatory rather than voluntary; armed forces grew massively from scores and a few hundred men—warriors into thousands, tens of thousands, and hundreds of thousands, with individual campaign armies increasing up to an upper limit of around 100,000 in the largest of states; warriors became soldiers; unorganized kin-based hosts gave way to orderly fighting formations (which still continued to rely widely on kin–communal–ethnic bonding); and stricter hierarchical command replaced leadership by example. With sedentary settlement and accumulated resources came fortifications, which grew progressively more monumental with the evolution of state power. In turn, the ability of states to master the resources and labour necessary for massive construction prompted and was prompted by the growth in their capacity to carry out systematic and protracted siege operations. Fortifications, much denser sedentary settlement, and greater distances spelled a decline in the significance of the raid—the predominant and most lethal, asymmetrical form of warfare in pre-state societies—because wholesale surprise of the enemy community became more difficult to achieve. The siege and the battle became almost synonymous with war.

Correspondingly, the low-casualty, 'ritualistic', stand-off battle, where the sides kept a distance from each other in order to minimize harm to themselves, was transformed. The fewer the options for evasion, the greater the stakes and the troops' motivation, and the stricter the state's coercive discipline—the more the troops accepted the anguish of face-to-face fighting and the heavier casualties that this form of battle entailed. Large-scale and long-distance campaigning, which required complex logistics, was another radical upgrade associated with state-societies. The state's organizational apparatus was called upon to support and sustain larger and more permanent armies in peacetime and in theatres of war, establishing the necessary bureaucracy, securing finance, and supervising the acquisition and requisition of provisions. Indeed, the state apparatus also made possible permanent conquest and direct government of other people(s)—that crucial novelty in the activity of war that was directly responsible for the state's continuous increase in size.

It is in view of all this that war is customarily identified with the state and politics—regarded as 'a continuation of state policy', as Carl von Clausewitz, the Prussian philosopher of war, famously defined it in his *On War* in the early nineteenth century. Large-scale 'war' is, indeed, characteristically a state-organized 'political' activity. Yet these formal concepts might be misleading if understood as representing some immutable and distinct 'essences'. Clausewitz's view was constrained by his historical horizon during the apogee of the European state system and of state-run warfare.[7] Large-scale 'war', as well as the state and 'politics', are, however, all historically shaped phenomena, which co-evolved. Indeed, what many regard as the mystery of the differences between human wars and intraspecific animal violence also dissolves once the nature and relatively recent occurrence of this co-evolution are recognized. Among social animals, as with small-scale human societies, group fighting and killing regularly take place, with most killing carried out asymmetrically so as to avoid self-injury. Only the massive growth of human groups through coercive political organization during historical times (that is, the evolution of large-scale politics, which Aristotle believed to be natural to humankind) carried with it that momentous growth in the scale and complexity of intergroup human fighting. Group fighting grew in scale with the growth in size of the human groups themselves.

Although a growing scale was an underlying trend for all this, overall violent mortality rates evidently *decreased* with the growth of the state and the transition from 'warre' to war. This has already been discussed in Chapter 6. The state's success in imposing internal peace—limited, fragile, and wavering as it was—was probably the major reason for the decrease in violent mortality. But there was another factor involved, less recognized, if not wholly at variance with commonly held intuitions. As states grew in size, their civilian populations became less exposed to fighting, and adult male participation rates in their armed forces declined (both of which compared with small-scale societies, be they segmentary or politically organized). Thus, whereas armies, wars, and killing in individual engagements all grew conspicuously larger, only particularly catastrophic spates of state warfare resulted in anything near the 25 per cent violent mortality rates among men that small-scale segmentary societies are recorded as having incurred as a matter of course in their incessant inter- and intragroup violence. Rising agricultural productivity, partly facilitated by economies of scale and the faster diffusion of technological innovation in larger political systems, was the main engine of demographic growth. However, much greater internal security and lesser exposure to killing from outside were probably no less responsible for the steady rise in population numbers in large and powerful states. Indeed, outbreaks of protracted civil war and anarchy and/or particularly severe foreign invasions punctuated this trend with occasional relapses. In such crises, mortality from actual fighting was compounded by both outbreaks of famine, caused by the disruption of agricultural life, and epidemic diseases, disseminated by the travelling armies and more virulent in their effect on populations weakened by malnutrition.

The decline in violent mortality under the leviathan—as first suggested by Hobbes—thus runs counter to the view that blames fighting on the state. The state has been aptly likened to organized crime, in the sense that it monopolized force and compulsorily extracted resources from society for its own profit in return for the promise of protection from both internal and external violence.[8] Indeed, some would further extend the analogy by arguing that the main threat of both types of violence came from the state itself—that it offered a solution to a problem of its own making. However, in view of what we have seen, at least the latter conclusion should be regarded with caution. Pre-state violence—'ordinary crime' as it were—was more rife and more lethal than state violence would become. Although violence under the state, as under organized crime, was of greater magnitude and more spectacular, it actually produced fewer casualties. Systematic 'extortion' by the state was economically less disruptive than 'warre', while the state offered more protection. Undeniably, however, 'protection money' was channelled upwards, and the larger the span of the coercive organization the more hierarchical and differential was the distribution of the rewards.

CUI BONO—WHO GAINS? THE MATERIAL ELEMENT

As already seen in Part 1, the motivations that lead to fighting are fundamentally derived from the human motivational system in general.

Fighting, to change Clausewitz, is a continuation of human aims, and the behaviour designed to achieve them, by violent means, and, now, on a progressively larger scale and with increasing organization, mainly associated with the state. But indeed, how did cultivation, accumulated resources, stratification, coercive structuring, and a growing scale—those mutually reinforcing features of the transition to agriculture and the rise of the state—affect the motivational system that led to fighting?

Territories for cultivation (and for pasture) replaced foraging and hunting territories as an object for competition. However, whereas both of the above involved competition over the right of access to nature, the real novelty brought about by cultivation was the direct exploitation of human labour. With cultivation it became possible to live off other people's work. Produce, in the form of accumulated foodstuffs, could be appropriated by looting. Highly movable livestock in particular constituted the main booty in those simple agricultural societies that possessed it. Somatic-utility objects, such as fabrics, tools, and metal (both tools and ingots), were also desirable targets. In addition to utility, objects possessed decorative, status, and prestige value, whereas the value of some was purely of that nature. Precious objects that acquired the role of money, most notably precious metals, became the most highly prized booty. Control over both natural sources of raw materials and the circulation of goods (trade) also remained a source of competition, only on a much larger scale. Furthermore, not only produce but also the producers themselves could be captured and carried back home as slaves, to labour under direct control. Initially it was mainly women and children who were thus enslaved, whereas captive men were massacred, because they were far more difficult to restrain and more likely to escape from slavery. But, as political societies and territories grew in size and campaigning and raiding were carried out across much greater distances, the enslavement of war captives became more prevalent and a goal in itself, because now slaves were less able to escape and find their way back home.

Looting could be further upgraded into tribute extraction, a more systematic appropriation of labour and resources through political subjugation, with the tribute payers either left under their own government or ruled directly. With reference to various historical cases scholars often write about empires' declining profit from war as they ceased to expand. It should be noted, however, that tribute exaction was generally a far more efficient system of exploitation than looting, because the latter was inevitably haphazard and involved great destruction, waste, and disruption of productive activity. Consequently, looting made the vanquished loss far more extensive than the victor's gain, which in effect meant that the victor extracted far less than it was potentially able to. This fundamental reality is obscured by the spectacular gains that the initial conquest could bring, as the victor took over huge treasures, accumulated and hoarded over years and generations in temples and palaces. These, however, were by nature one-time gains. Thereafter, indiscriminate enslavement and looting meant killing the goose that laid the golden egg. As with any profitable venture, efficient exploitation required careful husbanding of the resources for exploitation. To be sure, a regulated regime of tribute exaction might involve substantial overheads, as the victor assumed administrative and military responsibilities in the conquered territories. Indeed, in some circumstances, increasing overheads and extra responsibilities could prove crippling. Nevertheless, the richest empires by far were those based on regulated tribute exaction. Internally, too, a corresponding change took place, as mediated, state-run systems of benefit allocation, in the form of regular pay to the soldiers who guarded the empire, supplanted or supplemented the direct distribution of booty and conquered land among the victors.

The balance of costs and gains is the most intricate, and intriguing, point here. As shown in Part 1, hunter–gatherers, similar to all other organisms in nature, were forced by the reality of unregulated competition and conflict into investing energy and, thus, resources in the competition and conflict themselves. This investment might bring positive returns and net gains to the winners, in which case the rationale behind it seems obvious. However, alternatively it might result in a 'Red Queen effect', when arms races, fuelled by the hope of outweighing the enemy or gaining a margin of safety against him (the 'security dilemma'), merely increase the burden on the antagonists without providing any of them superiority over the others. Unregulated competition might generate this seemingly paradoxical result simply by virtue of the fact that conflict is there as an option to which any player might resort and for which, in consequence, all others must prepare. Thus the logic of unregulated competitive systems dictates that the resources 'wasted' on competition and conflict by a protagonist are worthwhile to him so long as the balance of benefits and costs *relative to the others* allows him to remain in the race. This means, for example, that all the protagonists might spend more then they gain from the competition—they might all lose—yet remain bound to the race and survive as long as their relative losses do not become crippling.

Cultivation greatly increased the material price of fighting. The costs incurred in fighting by hunter–gatherers (and animals) included the following: death; injury that might reduce somatic and reproductive prospects; energy spent on building up strength and in fighting; and reduced efficiency in somatic activity because of restrictions imposed by enemy threat and time wasted in safeguarding against it and in actual fighting. In all these, only the competitors and their productive activity were harmed, but (with minor exceptions) barely the resources themselves. Cultivation, however, added to the above the ability to inflict direct damage on the resources and on other somatic and labour-intensive hardware. Antagonists regularly ravaged crops, livestock, production implements, and settlements in order to weaken and/ or increase the cost of war incurred by the opponent. Furthermore, growing political units and technological advancement meant that fighting no longer took place close to home, during lulls in agricultural production, and with simple arms and improvised logistics. Metal weapons, fortifications, horses, ships, pay for long-term soldiers, and provisions consumed huge resources. Exact data are extremely sparse, but it is clear that military expenditure regularly constituted by far the largest item of a state's expenditure, in most cases the great majority of it. Tax revenues of states may have reached up to 10 per cent of the national product in those states in which enforcement and collection systems were the most efficient.[9] With conscription imposing an extra burden in terms of the loss in productive labour—again depending on the efficiency of the state's mobilization system—military expenditure may have devoured as much as 10 per cent of the national product, and risen to even higher levels during emergencies. In pre-modern subsistence economies, where malnutrition was the rule and starvation an ever-looming prospect, such a burden literally took bread out of people's mouths.

Resources ravaged by and invested in war thus constituted a new, massive addition to the cost side of fighting. Whereas among hunter–gatherers the struggle for resources approximated a zero-sum game, wherein resource quantity remained generally unaffected and one antagonist's gain was the other's loss, fighting now invariably decreased the sum total of resources, at least so long as the fighting went on. Only the relative distribution of these decreased resources and, moreover, the re-channelling of their future yield might result in net gains for one at the expense of the other.

But who was that 'one'? Neither humanity nor even individual societies counted as real agents or units of calculation in the competition. Unequal distribution was the rule not only between but also within rival 'sides'. Chiefs and their war hosts might accumulate wealth through raiding, whereas the rest of the tribal people suffered the consequences, in the form of enemy reprisals, counter-raiding, and ravaging. Within the raiding host itself, a differential benefit distribution developed among the chief, his lieutenants, and the warriors, growing ever more marked with greater success and greater accumulation of wealth and power. Indeed, the state itself was largely the outgrowth of such processes: power gave wealth, which, in a self-reinforcing spiral, accentuated intrasocial power relations in a way that obliged people down a progressively more hierarchical social pyramid to follow their superiors, while receiving a lesser and lesser share of the benefits. People could thus be made to fight not only for the expected benefits (including the defence of their own), but also, and even solely, through coercion—that is, for fear of punishment from their superiors that outweighed the loss that they might incur from the fighting itself. People were often coerced into participating in an activity that, in a highly differential system of benefit allocation, under-rewarded them for the risks and losses that they took. Pure coercion, with no benefits at all, was an ineffective way of getting people to fight. Nevertheless, coercion was now added in varying degrees to benefit allocation for achieving that goal.

To repeat, the salient point of all this was that cultivation, resource accumulation, and the state for the first time made predatory, 'parasitic' existence on the fruits of other people's labour possible. Whereas productivity-related competition generally increases productive efficiency, predatory–parasitic competition increases predatory–parasitic efficiency while decreasing productive efficiency. All the same, by being efficient in the predatory competition, one was able to secure the benefits of production. Indeed, once anyone in an anarchic system resorts to the option of predatory competition, he thereby obliges anyone else to choose between resource surrender and entering the violent competition themselves, at least for defensive purposes.

It is important to emphasize at this point that, despite the general overall loss of resources in war, there could be—in fact, there *were*—also 'spin-off' and long-term net productive gains from the power race. How much of a substantial independent 'spin-off' effect military innovation in metallurgy, engineering, horse breeding, naval architecture, and supply had on society is difficult to establish. But the most significant spin-off effect seems to have been the state itself. It was through violence that one power established authority over a territory or society, thereby securing increased internal peace and imposing co-ordinated collective efforts, some of which, at least, were to the common good, rescuing the people of a collective from a 'prisoner's dilemma' situation by decreasing 'free riding'. As already mentioned, large states introduced economies of scale, and, as long as they did not become monopolistically big and overburdened by overheads, they generated and accelerated innovation, largely of a civilian nature.[10] There is a long-standing debate on whether states were created from above, by an exploitative elite that imposed itself on society, or whether complex societies emerged in response to demands from below for social regulation and other social services.[11] Rather than being mutually exclusive, it would seem that both processes were variably combined.

The warriors and the population at large might share the benefits of successful war making. Furthermore, successful military expansion that was consolidated into relatively stable large states—as, for example, in Egypt, Rome, and China—considerably increased security, contributing to rising prosperity and demographic growth, for which heavy military expenditure might be considered a worthwhile premium. However, although the populace might grow in number as a result of successful wars and expansion, its prosperity per capita normally remained little improved, whereas the elite might accumulate great wealth (differentially again, down the hierarchical pyramid). Indeed, the larger the conquered realm, the greater the command span and resource base from which the elite was able to draw benefits. In line with what I have argued above about the advantages of regulated tribute extraction over looting, heavy investment in the armed forces once the realm had been consolidated did not necessarily pay off directly—that is, through the benefits of foreign war (in most cases it did not); rather, it paid off indirectly, as a defensive security premium for a huge tax-paying internal domain. Again, war was a 'two-level game', in which both external and internal power relations and external and internal benefit extraction were linked.

SEX AND HAREMS

The same logic applies to that other principal source of human competition—the sexual—considered from the perspective of male fighting. So far in this chapter I have referred to 'benefits' mainly in terms of material resources. But did sexual competition, which played such a prominent role in 'primitive warfare', decline in significance as a motive for fighting with the development of resource accumulation and orderly state societies? On the face of it this would seem to be the case. Students of war scarcely think of sexuality as a motive for fighting; it obviously did not occur to Clausewitz that sexual benefits might be included among the 'serious ends' of 'politics', for which the 'serious means' of war were employed (*On War* 1.1.23). The underlying links that connect the various elements of the human motivational system have largely been lost sight of.[12]

Silence is one reason for this blind spot. Although some aspects of sexuality are among the most celebrated in human discourse, others are among the least advertised and most concealed by all the involved sides. Nevertheless, the evidence is overwhelming and unmistakably clear, and has recently retuned to the headlines, shocking the western public with mass documentation from the wars in Bosnia, Rwanda, and the Sudan. Throughout history, widespread rape by soldiers went hand in hand with looting as an inseparable part of military operations. Heavy penalties were variably effective in restraining both raping and looting in friendly territories and in conquered ones that had already been brought under orderly occupation, as well as in postponing them during the height of fighting. Both, however, were endemic in enemy territory, normative where resistance was met, and given a free rein in the wake of fighting—most notably after defended settlements were stormed—when raping and looting were considered to be the warriors' acquired right and reward for their risk and valour. Indeed, the prospect of sexual adventure, as well as of looting, was one of the main attractions of war-like operations, which motivated men to join in. Young and beautiful captured women were a valued prize, in the choice of which—as with all other booty—the leaders enjoyed a right of priority. Although in heroic sagas of semi-barbaric societies, such as the *Iliad*, the sexual value of that prize was barely veiled, the practice was no less in force—openly or more discretely—in the armed forces of more civilized societies. There is a view that has gained much currency in contemporary discourse, according to which rape is an act of violence, humiliation, and domination, rather than of sex. However, this false dichotomy is deeply misleading, because rape is precisely violently forced sex. To the extent that the perpetrator also gives vent to a desire to dominate and humiliate his victim, be it the individual woman or the enemy in general, there is a combination rather than a contradiction of motives here.[13]

The other major reason—apart from the silence of both victors and victims—for the oversight of sexuality as one of the potential benefits of fighting was the exponential rise in large-scale civilized societies of accumulated wealth, which functioned as a universal currency that could be exchanged for most of the other good things in life. As already seen, among hunter–gatherers and horticulturalists fighting could advance reproductive success directly, as women were raped and kidnapped. Yet it could also advance reproductive success *indirectly*, as the resources and status won by fighting advanced one in the intrasocial competition for the acquisition and upkeep of women domestically—indeed, of an ever-larger number and a higher 'quality' of women. This indirect avenue for sexual success now largely overshadowed the direct one. Warfare might bring wealth and status, which among other things brought sexual success at home. Conversely, even a peaceful route to wealth and status required armed defence. Intrasocial polarization in sexual opportunity and sexual success ran parallel to the widening gaps in power distribution and property holding; indeed, it was closely related to them. By and large, power, wealth, and sexual opportunity made up overlapping and interlinked hierarchical pyramids.

In the first place, where polygyny was permitted, the rich and powerful acquired a greater number of wives and enjoyed a marked advantage in choosing young, beautiful, and otherwise worthy ones (cues for productivity and good parenthood and partnership potential). On top of or in lieu of these qualities, high-ranking status was valued in women, too, because it brought large dowries and powerful marriage alliances. In addition to wives, or where multiple marriages were not permitted, many societies sanctioned official concubines, often taken from a lower rank of society, as second-tier liaisons.[14] Where that form of official liaison was not customary, there were, of course, unofficial concubines or mistresses. Yet another avenue of sexual opportunity was the women in the household, some of whom were slave girls captured in war and raiding. It is for this reason that beautiful slave girls fetched high prices in the marketplace. Finally, there was the sex trade itself, where again the most consummate and graceful exponents of the trade could be highly expensive. In some cultures they were refined ladies, courtesans who played a prominent role in the elite's social life.

It should be noted that it was *relative* power concentration and distribution that underlay the distribution of sexual opportunity, as well as of resources. It is no coincidence that, in the west, narrower gaps in power and property within society at large and within the elite, compared with other civilizations, were associated not only with less despotic regimes but also with a more egalitarian distribution of sexual benefits. This explains the conspicuous and otherwise inexplicable fact that official monogamy became the rule in the west, eventually applying even to kings. The west's distinctive traits—relatively small state size, more pluralistic domestic power distribution, narrower property gaps, and official monogamy—were all closely interrelated. To be sure, in the west, too, the greater the power and wealth of the rulers and elite, the better was their sexual opportunity and the less they needed to pay heed to public sensitivities and keep up appearances. Not only were practices thus dependent, but so too were the very concepts of ostentatious consumption and sexual 'indulgence' or 'excesses'—that is, the norms themselves were largely social constructs that were shaped by social power distribution and, hence, by social constraints on power. In large despotic empires, effusiveness at the top was fabulous and social norms aligned with that reality.

The manner in which power, wealth, and sexual opportunity were linked is most strikingly demonstrated at the apex of the hierarchical pyramids, most notably in the figure of the so-called Oriental despot, who had his counterpart in the empires of pre-Columbian America. We have already seen that chiefs in pre-state societies, particularly in the more affluent and stratified ones, enjoyed much greater reproductive success than commoners, possessing scores of wives and siring numerous children. Presiding over yet greater power accumulation, state rulers were able to achieve even more. In all the large empires of the ancient Near East, the rulers possessed large harems. As the institution was by definition private and barred to outsiders—the word harem itself is derived from the Semitic root for the forbidden, and only women and eunuchs served in the household and as guards—inside information about harem life is scarce and almost accidental. For example, according to the Greek authors, Alexander of Macedon captured 329 of King Darius III's concubines after the Battle of Issus (333 BC). Finding it difficult to extract themselves from the pleasures of life and travelling in luxury even when on campaign, the later Achaemenid rulers were accompanied into the field by a select contingent from their harem. The women travelled in closed wagons, guarded by their eunuchs.[15] Only from a slightly later period, Kautilya's *Arthasastra* (1.20 and 1.27), that classic inside account of statecraft apparently written by an Indian high official, provides a detailed description of the construction and procedures of the harem, as well as an account of the bureaucratic apparatus that supervised over the march of prostitutes who were invited to the court.

Indeed, whereas fantasy has always filled in for the almost non-existent evidence on harem life, bureaucratic records, where they survived, constitute the most solid source, from which verified *numbers* can be derived. (The Hebrew King Solomon's 1,000 women, as with most other details about him, are fable, written centuries after his reign.) After all, the women and their children had to be maintained by the treasury. The most bureaucratic and most magnificent of empires was, of course, China. According to the state's records, the imperial harem of the Early Han (second and first centuries BC) comprised some 2,000–3,000 women, whereas that of the Later Han (first and second centuries AD) reached 5,000–6,000. The women were officially ranked and remunerated on a bureaucratic scale.[16] To be sure, affluence for some, derived from a finite resource, meant deprivation for others. Although even thousands of women in the imperial harem did not affect the ratio between eligible men and women in China, polygyny by the rich throughout society did, especially as it was compounded by widespread female infanticide, which was the norm in pre-industrial societies, including China. Inevitably, poor males suffered the most from the deficiency in the number of women. In more modern times, for which there is evidence, some fifth of the males in Chinese provinces are reckoned to have remained unmarried. Scholars have pointed out that groups of young, poor, and unmarried men, the 'bare sticks' in Chinese (*guang gun*: slang for the male sexual organ), were greatly feared by the imperial authorities, constituting the mainstay of bandit bands, which among other things perpetrated violent sexual offences.[17]

Imperial China seems to represent the ultimate in terms of harem size. A comparison can be made with the harem of the Ottoman sultans, the grand seigniors, tales and fantasies about which preoccupied Europe for centuries.

The records of the Ottoman Privy Purse indicate that, at its zenith, during the first half of the seventeenth century, the harem comprised some 400 women, with another 400 kept in a separate harem on a 'retired list' (mostly the wives and concubines of the former ruler).[18] Notably, the harem reached its zenith after imperial power had already begun to wane—in the Ottoman Empire, as in China, and everywhere else. After all, what should have motivated imperial rulers to engage in dangerous and tedious military exploits when they already possessed all the pleasures of life in which to indulge? Indeed, the imperial rulers often became semi-prisoners in the golden cage of their palace and harem, leaving the job of government to imperial bureaucrats of all sorts, who in turn did their utmost to encourage the rulers to persist in this path. Only a usurping upstart was able and likely to smash these comfortable arrangements and start the whole cyclical game afresh.

GARDENS OF PLEASURE AND CHERUBS WITH FLAMING SWORDS AT THEIR GATES

All this is not to be regarded—as it often is—as a piece of exotic piquancy, something peripheral to the real business of government. Quite the contrary. As with the other elements in the human motivational system, it was in defence of the supreme commanding position over the garden of pleasures that people reached out or fought for, killed and got killed. As Ibn Khaldun wrote: 'royal authority is a noble and enjoyable position. It comprises all the good things of the world, the pleasures of the body, and the joys of the soul. Therefore, there is, as a rule, great competition for it. It rarely is handed over (voluntarily), but may be taken away. Thus discord ensues. It leads to war and fighting.'[19] The same reality had been vividly captured by the ancient Greek tale of wisdom about the sword of Damocles. The ruler, according to this tale, was seated at a table packed full with all the world's delights and objects of desire, while a sword hung on a horse-hair above his head, liable to fall down and kill him at any moment.[20] Ruling was a high-stake–high-risk–high-gain affair.

A rigorous study of royal violent mortality rates has yet to be undertaken, and these rates obviously fluctuated across time and space. All the same, some data may illustrate the point. As already seen

> the usurpation of power, by prominent warriors and particularly by junior collaterals of a ruling chief, is a recurrent theme of Polynesian political traditions. . . . Hawaiians say, 'Every king acts as a conqueror when he is installed', for if he has not actually sacrificed the late king, he is usually presumed to have poisoned him.[21]

Another study tentatively estimates that during the later Viking period more than a third of the Norwegian kings died in battle and another third were banished.[22] Six of eight kings of Northumbria in the seventh century AD died in war.[23] Similarly, according to the biblical record, only nine of the nineteen kings of Israel died naturally (monarchic legitimacy was less established in Israel in comparison with that enjoyed by the House of David in Judea). Of the others, seven were killed by rebels, one committed suicide to escape the same fate, one fell in battle, and one was exiled by the Assyrians. Four or five of Achaemenid Persia's thirteen kings were assassinated and one was apparently killed in war.[24] During the last century of the reign of the Hellenistic Seleucids (162–163 BC), who replaced the Achaemenids in ruling south-west Asia after Alexander's conquests, virtually all of the 19 reigning monarchs became victims (after being perpetrators) of usurpation and violent death, as a merciless war raged between two branches of the ruling house.

Even during the relatively stable reign of Rome's first imperial dynasty, the Julio-Claudian, three of the six ruling members of the family—Julius Caesar himself, Caligula, and Nero—met a violent death. With respect to the other three—Augustus, Tiberius, and Claudius—rumours of a murderous end persisted (and seem to be warranted in the last-mentioned case) but cannot be verified. Nero was followed during 'the year of the four emperors' (AD 68–9) by the rapid fall and death in civil wars of the three generals who successively seized power: Galba, Otho, and Vitellius. The fourth general to seize power, Vespasian, established a stable dynasty. But his son and second successor, Domitian, was assassinated (AD 96), and the dynasty ceased. There followed the most stable period of Roman imperial government, with the five so-called enlightened emperors. However, all records were broken during the ensuing century of anarchy (AD 192–284). Of the 37 emperors who replaced each other in quick succession, 24 were assassinated, 6 killed in battle, 2 committed suicide (to avoid the first two options), 1 died in enemy captivity, and only 4 died of natural causes (3 of whom after a very short reign, thus not having the time to meet a violent death). Later on, of the 30 emperors who ruled over the Empire or its western part between AD 284 and 476, when the western Empire ceased to exist, only 12 died non-violently on the throne.[25] This meant that during the 500 years of the Roman Empire, roughly 70 per cent of its rulers died violently, not to mention the countless contenders who were killed without ever making it to the imperial crown. During the lifespan of the eastern Roman Empire or Byzantium (AD 395–1453), 64 of its 107 emperors, more than 60 per cent, were deposed and/or killed.[26]

The Ottoman Empire provides the most grisly reminder of the fact that the contenders to the crown in most states and empires were members of the reigning family, usually siblings or half-siblings from different mothers. At the Empire's height (fifteenth to sixteenth centuries AD), when it lacked a clear rule of succession and with the sultans fathering children from the many women in their harem, the son who succeeded in winning power after his father's death proceeded to kill all his brothers and brothers' sons, or at least severely mutilate (blind) them, in order to disqualify them for the throne. Father–son killings for power also took place. Only the establishment of seniority succession to the crown within the family, in the early seventeenth century, put an end to these terrifying battles for power, the ever-present effect of which on court and family daily life can only be imagined. For every son of the sultan the struggle for power simply meant a struggle for survival. If for no other motive, the 'security dilemma' in itself—pure self-defence—forced *all* of them to struggle as viciously as they could.[27]

All these are merely examples from countless similar tales of insecurity, violent struggle, and bloodbaths at the apex of political power. Violent usurpations spelled doom not only for the ruler or the contender, but also for their families and their followers, and, if the struggle turned into a fully fledged civil war, for masses of soldiers and civilians. As usurpation was an ever-present threat, rulers lived in constant anxiety and suspicion, surrounding themselves by heavy security, which curtailed their freedom of movement and much else besides. In Assyria, where regicide and violent usurpation were the rule as everywhere else, the records of the young, and later great, King Ashurbanipal (668–627 BC) give a revealing feel of the inside reality:

... there is danger to be anticipated from the bearded chiefs, the king's Companions, his own brother or the brothers of his father, the members of the royal family. He doubts the loyalty of his charioteer and of his chariot attendant, of the night watch, of his royal messengers and of his body-guard, of the officers in the palace and those on the frontier, of his cellarer and baker. He fears for what he eats and what he drinks, he fears by day and by night; in the city and without there is danger that a revolt against him will be undertaken.[28]

Kautilya's *Arthasastra* (1.20–1) offers an unmatchable, matter-of-fact, inside account of the security precautions taken to safeguard Indian monarchs. When we think about the glory of kings, we rarely contemplate these aspects. All the same, there was no shortage of candidates to take up this high-risk–high-gain game, provided that they felt that they were suitably positioned to embark on it and that they had a fair chance of success.

Why was this so? Was it 'worth it' and in what sense? As shown in Part 1, our motivational system was evolutionarily shaped by, and finely tuned to, the somatic and reproductive pressures experienced during geological time spans by people who lived in small-scale kin societies as hunter–gatherers. The evolutionary calculus of the adaptive, in terms of ultimate reproductive success, constantly trimmed human behaviour by trimming gene pools or, less abstractly, humans. But how have the expansion of human societies and the growth of wealth, hierarchy, and complexity over the last few millennia (only centuries for many societies) affected the human evolution-shaped motivational system and redefined adaptive behaviour? This, of course, is among the most intriguing questions concerning humankind's amazing natural–cultural co-evolution. Undoubtedly, cultural evolution has dramatically changed and diversified human behaviour. Yet, as already mentioned and contrary to a still widely held view, cultural evolution did not operate on a 'clean slate', nor is it capable of producing simply 'anything'. Its multifarious and diverse forms have been built on a clearly recognizable deep core of innate human propensities and predispositions, which represent evolution-shaped basic needs and the proximate emotional mechanisms 'designed' for attaining them. With cultural evolution all bets are not off; they are hedged. But, if so, have our evolution-shaped behaviours remained adaptive—in the original sense of ultimate reproductive success—in much altered, 'artificial', cultural conditions, so different from those of the 'evolutionary state of nature' where human predispositions were shaped?

To a large degree, the answer is affirmative: people in radically altered and diverse conditions have continued to give birth to children, to care for them, and to pursue the range of reproductive and somatic behaviours stemming from the above and the whole plethora of derivative activities connected to them, as outlined in Part 1. Indeed, human population has swelled by a factor of 1,000 since the Neolithic cultural take-off. All the same, although *in sum* this growth represents a staggering reproductive success, it does not mean that the whole range of specific behaviours has retained its adaptive fine-tuning in radically altered conditions. We should bear in mind that cultural take-off took place much too recently to affect human biology in any significant way through selective pressure. Biologically, we are virtually the same people as our Stone Age forefathers and are endowed with the same predispositions. People's desire for sweetness, which is now artificially produced and harmful rather than indicative of ripeness and of high nutritious value in fruits, again serves to illustrate originally adaptive propensities that have gone astray in altered cultural conditions. Obesity, when appetite that was adaptive in an environment of food scarcity is indulged in a society of plenty, is another illustration.

Indeed, rather than the evolutionary ends themselves, it is the proximate mechanisms, those behaviours that carry emotional gratifications and originally evolved as a means to attain somatic and reproductive ends, that motivate human behaviour. Where radically new conditions sever the original link between a proximate mechanism and its original evolutionary end, it is the proximate mechanism, rather than the evolutionary end, that people are tied to by powerful emotional stimuli. It is the calculus of emotional gratification rather than that of reproductive success that guides people's behaviour, even when the former more or less diverged from the latter. As another example, people continue to be constantly engaged in lovemaking for romantic and sexual gratification, even though effective contraception has made the overwhelming part of this obsessive activity irrelevant in terms of reproductive success.

So, did people who engaged in the high-gain–high-cost, intra- and inter-social, 'two-level' game of power politics improve their ultimate reproductive success, which was the evolution-shaped, original source of their desires and pursuits? The answer to this question seems very difficult to compute. On the one hand, rulers enjoyed much greater reproductive opportunities, culminating in the autocratic harem. On the other, contenders to the throne, and even incumbent rulers, played a highly risky game for both themselves and their families. Some light on the question is shed by a remarkable recent study of the Y (male) chromosome in central and eastern Asia, from China to the Caspian Sea, which demonstrates how great a ruler's reproductive advantage could be. It reveals that some 8 per cent of the population in the region (0.5 per cent of the world's population) carry the same Y chromosome, which can mean only that they are the descendants of a single man. Furthermore, the biochemical patterns indicate that this man lived in Mongolia about 1,000 years ago. It was not difficult to identify the only likely candidate, Chinggis Khan—an identification confirmed by an examination of the Y gene of his known surviving descendants. This, of course, does not mean that Chinggis Khan alone sired so many children from a huge number of women, an obvious impossibility even if he had ceased his military conquests altogether. The tremendous spread of his Y chromosome is the result of the fact that his sons succeeded him at the head of ruling houses throughout central and east Asia for centuries, all enjoying staggering sexual opportunities.[29]

To be sure, Chinggis Khan was among the greatest warlords ever, and his dynasty probably the most successful. Countless unsuccessful bidders for power, whose line ceased because of their failure, have to be figured into the other side of the equation. All the same, no overall reproductive gain needs to be assumed to explain one's behaviour in the new, 'artificial' conditions created by rapid cultural evolution, because it was the proximate mechanisms, human desires, that dominated people's behaviour and drove them into the game of power politics, whether or not it remained 'adaptive' for them.[30] The apex of the social pyramid held such a powerful attraction for people because human desires could be set loose and indulged there on a gigantic scale. Many contenders for this ultimate prize might be likened to heavy gamblers for the jackpot in lottery games. Clearly the odds for winning in any such game are against the gamblers, and for heavy gamblers the losses might be very substantial indeed. Yet there is no shortage of such heavy gamblers, either because, as cognitive psychology reveals, errors in the evaluation of probabilities are among the most common of human cognitive distortions, or because the allure of the prize can generate compulsive–addictive gambling behaviour, disrupting the functioning of our mental mechanisms that assess cost-effectiveness. This, of course, does not mean that all the contenders in lethal power struggles at the top played against 'expected utility', the concept in game theory that measures the prize against the probability of gaining it. Many of them, however, patently did. On a more modest scale, the same considerations held true further down the social hierarchy.

THE QUEST FOR POWER AND GLORY

Exponential growth and hierarchical structuring also affected all the other, 'derivative' elements in the human motivational system, reviewed in Part 1. Status, leadership, and power were sought in the evolutionary state of nature because of the advantages that they conferred in access to somatic and reproductive resources. With resource accumulation and hierarchical organization, the scope and significance of coercive social power rocketed. Furthermore, as both resources and power could now be accumulated and expanded on a hitherto unimaginable scale, while being closely intertwined and interchangeable, power, similar to money, grew into a universal currency by which most objects of desire could be secured. Power became the medium through which all else was channelled, and the quest for power thus stood for all else. Indeed, for this reason, the quest for power seemingly acquired a life of its own and was pursued for its own sake.

Not only was power positively desired; the 'security dilemma' in itself drove people and political communities to expand their power, because in a competitive race one would rather swallow than be swallowed. The acquisition of greater size and greater power was among other things a defensive measure, crucial for deterrence, bargaining, and the actual trial of force alike. At the same time, great strength built up for security purposes could also be utilized for achieving positive ends at the other's expense, putting that other at a disadvantage. As the same logic applied to all the actors, a constant struggle for power ensued, which refuelled the race, thus largely feeding on itself. Strong security pressures were associated with the formation, militarization, and expansion of some of the mightiest of empires, such as the Assyrian, Roman, and many others. Although scholars tend to be sceptical about professions of defensive motives, citing the expected benefits that drove states into expansion, security considerations intermixed rather than contrasted with the expected gains.

Similar to status and power and closely linked with them, the quest for honour and prestige was originally 'designed' to facilitate access to somatic and reproductive resources. As such, it too is stimulated by powerful emotional gratifications, which give it a seemingly independent life of its own. Again, the potential for the fulfilment of this quest increased exponentially in large-scale societies. Particularly at their apex, people have been able to indulge in this craving on a scale undreamed of in the evolutionary state of nature, where it originally took shape. Indeed, this indulgence in itself constitutes one of the main attractions of power. Glory—something that could come into being only in large-scale societies—was pursued by rulers (and others, of course) as a means of strengthening their hold on power and everything that it entailed, but also as an independent and most powerful source of emotional gratification. The stellas on which autocrats celebrated their achievements in superhuman images are interpreted by scholars as instruments of royal propaganda, but, equally, they express the quest for the ultimate fulfilment of the craving for boundless glory and absolute domination, which could now be extended to the 'four corners of the world' and 'everything under the sun', as the mightiest of imperial rulers boasted. Satisfaction, and hence motivation for action, were derived from extending one's dominance over—indeed, bringing under one's heel—as many and as much as possible, both at home and abroad, in connection with, but also independent of, the more tangible gains involved.

If the last few pages have concentrated more on the lavish potential for indulgence enjoyed by autocratic rulers, it should be stressed that all the above also applied to individuals in general and to political communities at large. Community members bathed in their collective glory and were willing to pay for its advancement and protection. This again derived from the conversion value of honour and glory in terms of power, deterrence, and inter-state bargaining. Individuals and political communities jealously guarded their honour and responded forcefully even to slight injuries, not because of the trifle matters involved, but because of the much more serious ones that might become the issue if they demonstrated weakness and became subjects to a process of victimization. To paraphrase Winston Churchill: choosing shame rather than war might very likely beget shame and then war. An injury left without adequate response invited only more and graver injuries, as one's prestige and standing deteriorated. As acute sensitivity to the above was deeply engraved in the human psyche by a long evolutionary history, honour became almost an end in itself. Furthermore, protagonists might become locked into retaliation and escalation, which thus tended to spiral even when nobody actually wished it to, pushing both sides beyond their original motives for a conflict and costing them far more than the worth of the actual bone of contention.

Finally, as already shown in Part 1, as with any other vital pursuit, the triggering and sustenance of the activity of fighting itself are underpinned by powerful emotional stimuli, which are particularly potent in the young, including: elation and exhilaration, associated with the playful competitive exercise of physical, mental, and intellectual faculties; ecstatic violent frenzy; and the thrill of high-risk–high-gain adventurism and exploration, which now also meant an escape from the constraints and dull routine of life in the local community. Among other motives, one might join the army to see the world. Thus, on top of the expected gains, people might take pleasure in the activity of fighting as such, and hence also pursue it 'purely' for its own sake.

Chinggis Khan revealingly bound together the above-mentioned elements of the human motivational system when he allegedly said: 'The greatest joy a man can know is to conquer his enemies and drive them before him. To ride their horses and take away their possessions. To see the faces of those who were dear to them bedewed with tears, and to clasp their wives and daughters in his arms.'[31] As shown above, we now have remarkable statistical evidence of what he meant by the last clause.

KINSHIP, CULTURE, IDEAS, IDEALS

All this rings true enough, but is it all? Are people interested only in these crude materialistic objectives, which even after humankind's dramatic cultural take-off can ultimately be shown to derive from evolution-shaped sources? Do not people also live and die for more lofty ideas and ideals than those expressed by a Chinggis Khan? They undoubtedly do, but, as already shown in Part 1, as a continuation rather than as negation of the above. A highly intricate interface links the natural with the cultural. Obviously, only a primary unravelling of this complex threading can be attempted here, confined to our particular subject: human fighting.

Let me start with the factor of identity. We have already seen that people exhibit a marked, evolution-shaped innate predisposition to favour kin over 'strangers'—that is, to favour those with whom they share more genes. Kinship extends—and declines—in concentric circles. The resulting arithmetic of kin altruism and competition are not repeated here. Roughly, however, it means that people in any kin circle struggle among themselves for the interests of their yet closer kin (ending in themselves and their offspring), while at the same time tending to co-operate against more distant circles. In this incessant multilevel game, internal co-operation tends to stiffen when the community is faced with an external threat, whereas inner rivalries variably diminish, although never disappearing (to the agony of patriots, who castigate them as being self-weakening to the point of self-destruction). Indeed, at the extreme end of the spectrum, in acts that widely arouse deep negative sentiments and bear a moral stigma, people might ally with outsiders in order to win struggles with their brethren. It should, of course, be added that non-kin co-operation and alliances for mutual gain— which do not diverge from kin interests—are commonplace, becoming only more so with the growth of large-scale organized society.

Although the above, highly significant limitations on kin co-operation must always be kept in mind, the range of kin affinities and kin bonds—like so much else that we have seen—expanded dramatically in large-scale state societies. The largest hunter–gatherer kin circles were made up of hundreds or, at most, a few thousand. Wherever they took place, agricultural expansions in particular created *ethnies* that often encompassed hundreds of thousands, but that were divided among separate, competing, and often hostile tribes, tribal confederations, and, later, petty-states. It must be re-emphasized that, rather than a unity, an *ethnos* was made up of a mosaic of enormous diversity. Devotion to the local tribe or polity (and to the clan within them) was the overriding attachment, creating powerful centrifugal forces and regularly throwing the various communities apart, and at each other's throats. On the other hand, it is not sufficiently recognized that above all it is within such ethnic spaces that larger states tended to emerge and expand, because people of a similar ethnicity could be more easily united and kept united, relying on shared ethnocentric traits and bonds. Indeed, it was primarily on their loyal native ethnic core that states and empires relied when they expanded beyond that core to rule over other ethnicities. Thus, contrary to a widely held view, ethnicity mattered a great deal in determining political boundaries from the very start, rather than achieving that effect only with modernity.

Since the 1980s, it has become fashionable to claim that ethnicity and nationalism are wholly 'invented' and that the deep sentiment held by most peoples that they each share a common descent or a common stock is a pure myth. Nobly reacting against the explosive and horrendous manifestations of both nationalism and racism, this view of ethnicity, as 'constructed', manipulated, and mythologized by states and elites, has made such headway because it obviously has a great deal of truth in it, and yet a partial truth, nevertheless. The exponents of this view insist that ethnicity is a cultural rather than a genetic phenomenon. This, however, is a false dichotomy that misses a far more intricate reality. In the first place, as we have already seen, studies show that in general the world's broader cultural (lingual) and genetic boundaries remarkably coincide, especially when elite take-overs and large-scale migrations that occurred in historical times are taken into account.[32] Most ethnicities far predate modern nationalism, forming the nucleus around which the latter was built.[33] Indeed, even where an ethnic formation originally brought together disparate groups, as was often the case, widespread intermarriage over sufficient time gave the new formation shared genetic markers.[34]

To be sure, it is overwhelmingly cultural features rather than genetic gradations that separate ethnicities from each other. To avoid any misunderstanding, one must hasten to add that most of the genetic differences are negligible and irrelevant to human culture. The point is entirely different, as we have already seen. As in small hunter–gatherer groups kinship and culture overlapped, not only phenotypic resemblance (similarity in physical appearance) but also shared cultural traits functioned as cues for kinship, as well as proving vital for effective co-operation. Thus, whether or not national communities are genetically related (and most of them are), they feel and function as if they were, on account of their shared cultural traits. To be blind to the sources and workings of these intricate mental mechanisms of collective identity formation inevitably means to misconceive some of the most powerful bonds that shape human history.

Indeed, it is this that explains ethnocentrism—the deep human identification with, devotion to, and willingness to sacrifice for one's people—which has a patently atavistic nature that has repeatedly perplexed and shocked modern social thinkers, historians, and commentators, proving transparent to their accepted categories of analysis. As discussed in Chapter 3, the expansion of kin altruism beyond its original boundaries in the Palaeolithic regional group of hundreds, to embrace peoples of many thousands and millions, overstretched the evolutionary rationale that had shaped this predisposition in the first place. The far larger grouping, which because of its shared physical and cultural phenotype one identifies as one's people, is not as closely related to one's self as the regional group was. Furthermore, although one's fate is closely linked to that of one's people, the ability of an individual to influence the fate of his or her people by self-sacrifice is negligible. All the same, it is again the proximate mechanism that dominates people's behaviour, despite the changes that have taken place in the original conditions that shaped this mechanism. Although balancing the interests of their people against their own and those of their close kin, individuals are deeply invested emotionally in the prosperity of their people. Although state and communal coercion are obviously major enforcers of collective action, individuals are *willingly* susceptible to recruitment on these grounds.

Independence from foreign domination has been perceived as crucial to a people's prosperity, often evoking most desperate expressions of communal devotion in its defence. Not only did foreign subjugation imply a channelling of resources into alien hands, it also posed a threat to the integrity of the community's shared culture. Indeed, this further broadens our perspective. Why do people feel such a powerful attachment to their shared culture and a sense of grave threat when it appears to be jeopardized? One reason has just been mentioned. People are highly tuned to and predisposed towards cherishing the infinite, subtle, and distinct manifestations of behaviour, outlook, and appearance that mark them as a community of kinship and mutual cooperation. A threat to a shared culture carries with it a threat to communal integrity. Moreover, once acquired in youth by a long process of socialization, cultural forms become extremely difficult to replace. Brain structure consolidates in adults, who lose most of the brain's earlier elastic ability to rearrange itself through learning. Sticking to the things that one knows best and is unlikely to supplant successfully—language, patterns of behaviour and belief, social codes—is thus largely imposed on people as their superior option. Indeed, the intimately familiar landscapes of one's native land, engraved in one's consciousness for the very same reasons, evoke great attachment and devotion, and will not be carelessly forfeited. Needless to repeat, rather than 'blind instincts', these are all deep-seated but highly modulated predispositions, with particular expressions that are largely circumstantial. Obviously, people regularly adopt foreign cultural forms, sometimes eagerly, and they might also migrate from their native land (where conditions might be harsh), provided that they consider these acts beneficial to them and that they can pull through.

This is not all, however. We know that the power of ideas is more far reaching. People everywhere kill and get killed over ideas, irrespective of kinship and across nations. Why is this so? How is this lofty sphere—often most abstract metaphysical ideas, indeed, all too often, seemingly absurd notions—connected to the practicalities of life? The key for understanding this query is our species' strong propensity for interpreting the surroundings as deep and as far as the mind's eye can probe, so as to decipher their secrets and form a mental map that would best cope with their hazards and opportunities. I use the word 'propensity' advisedly, even though it is likely to arouse disbelief in those who already suspect that propensities are all too easily evoked here to explain anything that cannot be explained otherwise. Nevertheless, my contention is precisely that *Homo sapiens sapiens* possesses an innate, omnipresent, evolution-shaped predisposition for ordering its world, which among other things extends to form the foundation of mythology, metaphysics, and science. As with all other adaptive predispositions, this human propensity to construct interpretative mental frameworks of the world expresses itself as a powerful urge, a profound emotional need, which humans simply cannot help or do without. We are compulsive meaning seekers. It is this propensity—intertwined as it is with the evolution of symbolic representation and generalized conceptual thought—that is responsible for our species' remarkable career.

The innate propensity to look for and impose structure is revealed as a prominent feature of our species both by archaeology and in extant hunter–gatherer societies.[35] As already seen in Part 1, the cosmos of these societies was permeated with meaning and intent that had to be coped with and harmonized. Carried to its furthest, this perpetual process of interpretative trial and error was responsible for technological advancement and proto-science of every sort—astronomical, metaphysical, biological, geographical, historical, and social. Barely a thin line distinguished all these from the wide array of the 'supernatural'—magic, myth, and superstition. Contrary to widely held perceptions, the latter coincided with more than diverged from the former, because in the absence of developed procedures of verification it could not be easily established which interpretative narratives and manipulative techniques were valid and which were not. By the same token, however, deeply entrenched fantasies and persistent, most cherished illusions can at least partly be explained as 'bugs' or 'viruses' in, or 'mis-activations' of, our sophisticated and highly sensitive intellectual software, which is driven but also easily disrupted by, and addicted to, our restless and insatiable need for meaning, order, control, and reassurance.[36]

Thus the array of ideas regarding the fundamental structure and working of the cosmos and the means and practices required for securing its benevolent functioning have been largely perceived as *practical* questions of the utmost significance, evoking as powerful emotions and motivation for action—including violence—as any other major practical question.[37] Indeed, they might evoke more powerful reaction than any ordinary practical question, because the supreme forces concerned might be perceived as more potent than anything else and surrounded by 'sacred horror'. Ever since the earliest and simplest societies, all this has been capable of generating conflict wherever disputes concerned the right practices to be adopted or the adequate fulfilment thereof. Later on, the dramatic expansion of society, the growth of social and economic complexity and diversity, and the concentration, institutionalization, and formalization of power were all mirrored in the public sphere of the sacred, cosmic, and spiritual.[38] Most notably, large-scale, institutionalized religions were formed.

As a matter of course, rulers moved to consolidate their hold on the spiritual as a major element of social power. Local deities, rituals, and belief systems in the unified realm were syncretized by the state, institutionalized, and imposed though the state's system of sanctions and benefits. In the process, specialized full-time clerics, maintained on institutionalized forms of resource extraction, proliferated and became more entrenched, forming vested interest groups and semi-autonomous foci of social power, which all too often conflicted with the rulers.[39] The world of beliefs and rituals constituted an arena of power politics, because control over minds formed an aspect of power, and, as such, it was inextricably linked to the attainment of all the other benefits in the human motivational system, and because, as with other major cultural differences, those of faith between communities, sects, and denominations might lead to divisions and conflict, whereas unity of faith fostered political unity.[40] Consequently, questions of faith and ritual were themselves political issues. It should be noted, however, that this was an intricate, two-way interrelationship. Manipulations of the sphere of belief and ritual were underpinned by the social fact that ideas about the deeper working of the cosmos and the practices required for controlling them mattered to people. Indeed, these ideas and practices usually also mattered to the power holders themselves, to the rulers and priests who engaged in 'manipulation'. Contrary to the view espoused by Enlightenment thinkers since the eighteenth century, these manipulative power holders were not simply cynical crooks, but more customarily were themselves emotionally and intellectually deeply invested in the world of belief. To adopt a manner of expression in the tradition of the Enlightenment, they were 'superstitious crooks', themselves addicted to the 'opium of the masses'.

In war, the gods, temples, and cults constituted at one and the same time an entity to which appeals for help could be made, a sacred part of the shared culture for the defence and glory of which people could be easily aroused, and, indeed, a semi-independent source of warfare for the satisfaction of the gods' own special requirements, such as human sacrifice. This powerful projection of the community in the supernatural sphere thus constituted as potent an instrument of and motivation for war as did other—more 'real'— tangible or symbolic factors. On the other hand, the supernatural never stood alone as an independent source of warfare, as is often claimed, for example, with respect to the Aztec war complex. The Aztec elite in fact acted as quintessential 'superstitious manipulators', whose drive to conquer, subjugate, and exact tribute became inextricably linked with the gods' thirst for human blood. Massive killing and ruthless exploitation, rather than the taking of prisoners for ritual sacrifice, were the rule in Aztec warfare.[41] In any case, in all cultures war on earth was customarily paralleled by war in and from the heavens, as rival communal and national gods were enlisted to back their respective peoples. Similar to a superior and capricious ally, the gods constantly had to be pampered, wooed, and appeased, lest in their wrath they deserted or even worked against their people's cause.

It is this pattern that one finds everywhere around the globe. Yet the further evolution of civilization in Eurasia also saw further developments in the sphere of belief and the spiritual. The advanced literate culture that materialized in Eurasia alone was probably the single most significant factor behind these developments.[42] It made possible the accumulation, storage, and transmission of a vast amount of information and ideas, all on a previously unknown level of accuracy, complexity, and detail. The literati—

433

clerics, bureaucrats, and members of the social elite, but also common people—partook of an information network based on the medium of the text, through which comprehensive world-views could now be articulated and communicated, and, indeed, exist in somewhat greater autonomy from the state.

Mushrooming across the literate civilizations of Eurasia, these new ideologies—systems of belief, ethics, and conduct—did not concern themselves solely with human relationship with the cosmic and supernatural, with the appeasement of the gods, although this remained a fundamental, often *the* fundamental, aspect of their teachings; in conjunction with this aspect, they also each promoted their particular vision of social improvement and individual salvation. As widely different from each other as these spiritual ideologies were, they all put forth an all-encompassing blueprint of how the problems of life—death, pain, and wants of all sorts—might be alleviated, resolved, or transcended. They elevated and codified into ethical systems of justice the principle of 'reciprocal altruism' and 'generalized reciprocal altruism', which, as we have already seen, constitute the basis of social co-operation in nature. Large-scale, complex, and 'alienating' societies—most notably in metropolitan and cosmopolitan cities—and a world that had lost its intimacy stimulated the articulation of such comprehensive social and spiritual solutions.[43]

For their followers, these doctrines dealt with *practical* questions of the first order, held the key to individual, communal, and cosmic salvation in this and/or other worlds, worthy of the greatest dedication and even of dying for. This perception of utmost *practical* significance to human existence warrants emphasis. It should be noted that *only* the sort of metaphysical and ethical doctrines that appealed to large numbers of people with the promise of personal and communal salvation were capable of mobilization for action. No purely academic metaphysical or scientific doctrine that failed to touch on these deep sources was ever capable of generating such an intense response.

Although such religious, and later secular, salvation-and-justice ideologies regularly emerged and sometimes remained grounded within a particular people, they often carried a universal message that transcended national boundaries. They constituted a community of faith and conduct that, similar to other non-kin collaborations, might cut across peoples. The cosmic no longer enlisted automatically (albeit capriciously) in the patriotic cause, although it often still did. Furthermore, the relationship of the new universal religious ideologies with war was complex, multifaceted, and case dependent. The obligation of a 'just war' was already evident in many of the older religions. This demonstrates that notions of justice towards the 'other', embedded in the biosocial principle of reciprocity, were felt and had to be satisfied in order to sanction war both with the domestic public and, even more, with the projected, seemingly detached gods. (The fact that this obligation was usually easily satisfied equally demonstrates how biased towards the self these notions of justice are.) With the new universal religious ideologies, the obligation of a 'just war' was reinforced, as was the ban on belligerency among the faithful.

On the other side of the same coin, some of the new salvation ideologies incorporated a strong missionary zeal that could be translated into holy belligerency against non-believers. Furthermore, militant salvation ideologies generated a terrific galvanizing effect on the holy warrior host, because: the world's salvation was dependent on the triumph of the true faith; these ideologies universally preached co-operation and altruism within the community of believers; and, indeed, they were variably able to foster such co-operation and altruism by the promise of great worldly and non-worldly rewards, possibly imagined in the eyes of external observers but often more real than anything else in the eyes of the believers.[44] Together with the other motives for fighting in the human motivational system—always in conjunction with them—the real and the imagined-but-perceived-and-functioning-as-real rewards offered by such salvation ideologies thus explain Dawkins' proclamation: 'What a weapon! Religious faith deserves a chapter to itself in the annals of war technology.'[45]

Christianity, starting as a religion of love, compassion, and non-violence, later developed a brutal militant streak towards non-believers and heretics, which awkwardly but continuously coexisted with its opposite in both doctrine and practice. Regarding the relationships among the faithful its position was more consistently pacifist. Islam incorporated the holy war against the non-believers as an integral part of its doctrine from its inception, while preaching unity and non-belligerency within its own house. The blatant fact that within both Christianity and Islam fighting went on incessantly despite religious condemnation merely indicates that, although a very potent force, religious ideology was practically powerless to eradicate the motivations and realities that generated war.

435

Indeed, the same applies to eastern Eurasia, where spiritual ideologies were even more conflict averse. Whereas in western Eurasia the two major universal religious ideologies incorporated a strong militant missionary and exclusivist streak, the universal cosmic and ethical systems of eastern Eurasia—such as Buddhism and Confucianism—although being missionary, were not exclusivist by doctrine nor did they espouse forceful conversion. The reasons for these differences between western and eastern Eurasia are not easy to explain and, in any case, are not my concern here. They obviously have much to do with monotheism, which fiercely rejected all other gods, thereby distinguishing the new religions of western Eurasia not only from the doctrines of the Far East but also from the older, polytheistic, and relatively tolerant religions of western Eurasia itself.[46] Be that as it may, the fact remains that, although in eastern Eurasia, too, spiritual ideologies constituted part of the cultural differences that set societies apart and the supernatural was regularly enlisted in the patriotic cause, war of opinion in the transcendental sense—involving systems of belief and conduct with respect to life and afterlife—was markedly less noticeable than in western Eurasia, although warfare in general was more or less as prevalent.

Some of the cosmic and ethical ideological systems of Eurasia thus infused the community of faith with a spirit of unity and ferocious zeal, fostered by the promise of individual and communal salvation and non-worldly rewards. By the same token, some of them expressed not merely a preference for peace and justice, but growing alienation from and rejection of the insatiable, Sisyphic, intrinsically frustrating pursuit of those worldly goals such as wealth, sex, honour, and all the other elements in the evolution-shaped human motivational system, the goals that among other things drove people into conflict. This streak of social sentiment, to which I return shortly, constituted merely one aspect of a more general feeling of doubt and desperation about whether the whole business of war was not a futile and senseless affair.

WAR: A SERIOUS MATTER FOR SERIOUS ENDS OR A SENSELESS AFFAIR?

Chinggis Khan's alleged pronouncement, quoted earlier, about the fruits of war as the greatest of joys, undoubtedly represented genuine human sentiments. Yet, as already mentioned, he was among the most successful warlords ever, and when one wins on such a grand scale one naturally tends to be enthusiastic about it. Few, however, were even remotely as successful. If only for this reason, misgivings about war were as prevalent as its praises.

As already seen, the potential dangers and costs of fighting deterred people (as all animals) from it as much as its potential gains attracted them, making fighting one of the most polarized of human activities in terms of the conflicting emotional mechanisms that switched it on and off. The death, mutilation, material loss, and hardship that individuals and collectives were likely to suffer caused massive pain, fear, horror, misery, anguish, weariness, and despair. Where sweeping successes were won, very few question marks were raised. But contrary to appearance, decisive victories were the exception rather than the rule in history: armed rivalries endured from generation to generation, many times with little apparent gain to either side; massive costs in life, invested resources, and ravaged wealth were seemingly swallowed into that black hole to no avail; even when success was achieved, the pendulum often swung back as the vanquished reasserted themselves to redress the balance. Although they did not conceptualize theoretical tools such as the 'prisoner's dilemma', the paradoxes of the 'Red Queen' in arms races, the traps of tit for tat, and the cycles of escalation (see Chapter 5)—in all of which antagonists in unregulated competitive systems were locked—people acutely sensed them, responding with despair and a profound feeling of helplessness. The notion that war was a curse from heaven, a scourge that devoured people against their true wishes, one of those catastrophic and alien, nature-like forces—together with famine and pestilence—that bedevilled humankind gained wider currency.

Indeed, ever since the advent of farming and accumulated property, war almost invariably meant an overall net loss of resources (which might still result in a net gain—sometimes even huge—on one side). The shorter and jollier a war could be kept, the easier the victory, and the more obvious the benefits, the easier was the enthusiasm that it sparked from sources very close to the surface of man's psyche. Defence of self, kin, property, and communal identity was similarly capable of generating tremendous feats of emotional mobilization—often more desperate than enthusiastic. Otherwise, even when war seemed to promise nothing good, people often chose to cling to it with a mixture of grimness, desperation, and bewilderment,

437

because all other options seemed to harbour still worse consequences, imminently or in the longer run.

The ancient Greeks put a sceptical and paradoxical view of the benefits of war in the mouth of the philosopher Cineas, a companion of King Pyrrhus of Epirus, the celebrated but ultimately unsuccessful general and adventurer, who fought Rome and Carthage in an effort to carve for himself a Hellenistic empire in the west (281–274 BC). Pyrrhus has been viewed as an embodiment of the compulsive gambler for the jackpot, mentioned above. The ancients acutely felt so: 'what he won by his exploits he lost by indulging in vain hopes, since through passionate desire for what he had not he always failed to establish securely what he had. For this reason Antigonus used to liken him to a player with dice who makes many fine throws but does not understand how to use them when they are made.'[47] The notion of a 'Pyrrhic victory'—a victory on the battlefield that because of the losses incurred amounts to defeat—applied to Pyrrhus not only militarily but also politically.

It was this point and also another one that Cineas sought to make in a conversation with the king. He asked Pyrrhus how he would use his victory over the Romans, if such were won. Pyrrhus replied by describing the size, richness, and importance of Italy. Cineas pressed for what they would do next. Pyrrhus replied that they would then be able to seize Sicily, with all its wealth and people. In response to further probing by the philosopher, the king said that these initial victories would make it possible for him to conquer Carthage and north Africa, and that with the strength thus accumulated he would proceed to take Macedonia and Greece. Cineas continued to ask what they would do then, to which Pyrrhus smiled and said: 'We shall be much at ease, and we'll drink bumpers, my good man, every day, and we'll gladden one another's hearts with confidential talks.' The philosopher, who had anticipated that conclusion all along, retorted that, as they already possessed all that was necessary for enjoying the leisurely activities mentioned by the king, what prevented them from the privilege of pursuing these activities right then, rather than go through all the trouble, perils, pain, and bloodshed of protracted wars.[48]

Notably, it was the philosopher rather than the king-general who expressed this view and, apart from the differences in inclinations and occupational perspectives between the two, it was obviously the latter rather than the former who was positioned to indulge in the fruits of success, if it came.

But, indeed, in view of the costs and risks of war, when did indulgence reach the point of diminishing returns? Although people's drive to attain greater access to resources is in many ways insatiable and infinite, it is also relative to what others have and is weighed against potential losses. If high status vis-à-vis one's peers is achieved, while further gain involves serious risks, people tend to pursue more conservative strategies, preferring to preserve what they already have. Furthermore, as Cineas suggested, one might aspire to achieve more and more, but above a certain level how much more can one consume, even of the most ostentatious luxuries? It is for this reason that it is mainly the lean and hungry upstarts who are willing to take the greatest risks. Much the same applies to sexual gratification. Male appetite in particular is in many ways open-ended. At the same time, above a certain (high) level it is nevertheless practically constrained. Consider the ultimate autocrats, at least in this respect, the Han emperors of China. Could they really avail themselves of all the 2,000–6,000 beautiful females in their harem? Here, too, at some point a further increase becomes far less important than preservation. And the same applies to honour and the other elements in the human motivational system.

Furthermore, as already mentioned, a yet more radical attitude with respect to human motivation revealed itself in the advanced literate civilizations and large-scale societies of Eurasia. Our system of desires has been 'imposed' on us by evolution. However, in contrast to other animals, our vastly enlarged intellectual and imaginative faculties and shared intergenerational wisdom detect the insatiable, Sisyphic, and intrinsically frustrating aspects of our worldly pursuits, the pain and suffering involved, and our ultimate death. All these breed a widespread sense of anxiety, futility, and disgust, most notably perhaps in large-scale and complex societies, where: the range of temptation but also of frustration is far greater; communities are less intimate and less supportive; the realm of texts both expresses this and creates worlds of the imagination—fictional and non-fictional—where one can concern, hide, and console oneself: 'sublimate' worldly desires.

Short of suicide, the most extreme expression of the reaction against the pains and frustrations inherent in our evolution-shaped system of motivation is the ascetic quest to cut loose of, transcend, sensual desires and all activities relating to them, to find peace of mind in sensual denial, eschewing the restless race for fulfilment.

This trend is exemplified in the tale of the young Prince Siddhartha

Gautama, the future Buddha, who supposedly lived in northern India around 500 BC. Discovering one day that all people are bound to encounter pain, illness, bodily degradation, and death, he left everything and dedicated himself to finding spiritual elevation by eschewing everything worldly and sensual. Great masses of people throughout south and east Asia identified with his teaching, while some have taken up his example in practice as Buddhist monks. Indeed, quite a number of emperors of Japan retired from the pleasures of their courts to Buddhist monasteries, some of them because they were forced to, but others of their own free will, most of them perhaps after they had passed the age of most intense passion. It was after his body had betrayed him in old age that the disenchanted biblical king Solomon, to whom myth attributes 1,000 wives and concubines as well as every other form of luxury, is fabled to have pronounced: 'Everything is meaningless' (*Ecclesiastes* 1.2).

Indeed, asceticism of various sorts emerged in western Eurasia as well. Again, in a famous fictitious tale, the Greeks opposed the greatest of the kings, generals, and conquerors, Alexander of Macedon, with a philosopher, Diogenes of the Cynic School (literally: doggish), who eschewed luxury of all sorts. Coming to see Diogenes, who lived in a barrel, Alexander offered him anything he desired, to which the philosopher retorted by asking Alexander to move away so that he would not block the light. The king, it is told, said that if he were not Alexander he would have wished to be Dio-genes.[49] Conflicting strategies about the dilemma of sensual gratification–frustration are represented by the two other major philosophical schools of the cosmopolitan, and increasingly alienated, Hellenistic and late Roman world. Although Epicureans supposedly celebrated pleasure and sensual ful-filment, the Stoics taught control of worldly desires. Asceticism permeated Christianity, and was actively practised by its hermits and monastic orders.

So how is asceticism to be understood within our general framework, and how has it affected human fighting? Rather than the normal balancing of desires against each other and against possible costs, asceticism involves an attempt at a wholesale suppression of desire and constitutes a rebellion against the evolution-shaped human motivational system. Indeed, it is for this very reason that asceticism has remained marginal in human society, because it has gone against our most deeply rooted, innate predispositions. Seriously attempted only by a very small minority, it has mostly served as an unfulfilled option, a spiritual yearning, a creed, or, at most, a disciplinary constraining factor, for those among the vast majority of people who have felt tortured by the frustrations of desire.

Let us turn now to asceticism's effect on fighting. The Buddhist analysis of the causes of conflict is remarkable, typically leading to pacifism: 'Conflict often arises from attachment to material things: pleasure, property, territory, wealth, economic dominance, or political superiority. At *M.* 1.86–7, the Buddha says that sense-pleasures leads to desire for more sense-pleasure, which leads to conflict between all kinds of people, including rulers, and thus quarrelling and war.'[50] All the same, asceticism and, even more, non-world-liness—the projection into other worlds of the hope for ultimate reward—have expressed themselves in belligerency as well as in pacifism, because, as we have already seen, the spread of a creed by force has been sanctioned by some spiritual movements, rewards greater and purer than the earthly have been promised to those who have been willing to die fighting for the cause, and sensual self-denial has often translated into extreme toughness and single-mindedness. Throughout history, ascetic zealots have been among the best warriors, among others in Christianity, Islam, Hinduism (Yogi), and even Buddhism, the warrior-monks of which have nowadays become the subject of great popular interest.[51]

Not only self-denial but denial in general had the potential to produce the above effect and to generate motivation for action far greater than that exhibited by the satiated and indulgent. It was not the rigours of asceticism but rather the amenities and other traits of sedentary civilization that eroded belligerency. While instituting discipline and the habit of sustained large-scale co-operation, orderly society and state authority also introduced relative internal peace. In comparison with tribal and other less orderly societies, people were socialized into far less violent daily behaviour—they were 'domesticated', which necessarily reflected on their war-like inclinations.[52] Furthermore, the larger the state and the more remote the external enemy, the less were people conditioned to war by an ever-present foreign threat and the less they felt that such a threat was their concern. In addition, the more oppressed, excluded, and alienated the masses, the less were they motivated and habituated to fight. At the same time, higher in the social hierarchy, the more home-generated wealth was, the poorer the marches, and the more satiated the rulers and the social elite with wealth and pleasure, the less prepared were these rulers and elite to risk and endure the ordeal of war. The state was still able to sustain large armies by virtue of its economic

441

and administrative infrastructure, but soldiering was handed over to professionals and people of the marches, who might then take over the power themselves.

For indeed, as long as both at home and abroad there was a direct link between the covert and overt use of armed force and benefit acquisition, armed force remained as essential as—more essential than—productivity for reaping benefits. Even though, because of destruction and lost productivity, fighting among sedentary societies in particular generally resulted in overall net loss to those involved, it could still lead to a substantial redistribution of benefits in favour of the victor, which meant that there were great benefits to be won by force. Let it be clear: great benefits were sometimes won by force. Consequently, there were always those who were willing to take up the game of violence—espouse the conflictual option of competition—in the hope of making gain, thereby forcing the game on those who may have been more reluctant to engage in it. For this reason, at the very least, one had to prepare for conflict. All too often this meant that all sides found themselves locked in a 'prisoner's dilemma' and experienced a 'Red Queen effect', where they continuously spent resources on war and on preparation for it without gaining the advantage over their rivals or making any gain— that is, they all lost in comparison with what they might have had in the absence of conflict. Thus, rather than being mutually exclusive, both 'realist' and 'idealist' attitudes to war have touched on deep truths: because of its very existence as an option, violent conflict has been both a 'serious means to a serious end' and shockingly absurd; both highly beneficial to some and terribly wasteful overall, sometimes even for all; both an indispensability that could not be eliminated by idealist visions and something often imposed on all the protagonists 'against their will', as if it were an alien force.

It would only be with modernity—at the very same time that the ability to generate force grew exponentially, in line with growing productivity— that the tie between force and wealth acquisition would begin to unravel.

Part 3

MODERNITY: THE DUAL FACE OF JANUS

13

Introduction: The Explosion of Wealth and Power

The take-off of modernity is customarily traced to the late fifteenth century. It took another century and a half before the notion that the world had entered a new epoch, more advanced than anything that preceded it, began to gain currency. According to Francis Bacon's famous pronouncement (1620), three novelties brought modernity in their wake: gunpowder, ocean navigation, and the printing press. And if the first of these was directly related to war, the other two affected it no less decisively.

To be sure, Bacon's trio did not stand in isolation. It stemmed in Eurasia from a broader, more general, and accumulative evolution of technological infrastructure and social organization, which, despite occasional relapses and regressions, had been steadily taking place over centuries and millennia. For pre-modern and pre-industrial civilization—'agraria', as it is sometimes termed—was far from being stagnant and changeless, frozen socially and technologically, as some scholars have judged it to be, applying the standard of modernity's vastly accelerated tempo of change.[1] Historians of technology and economy have revealed the steady improvement in agricultural technique, horse harnessing, ironwork, and mining, the advent and spread of the watermill and windmill, the compass, and the lateen, triangular sail, and advances in water damming and canal building—all resulting in a continuous growth in productivity and population throughout the landmass.

Furthermore, the above growth 'in depth'—that is, within societies—was inextricably linked to civilization's continuous outward expansion. That spatial, 'horizontal' spread bore major consequences. The incorporation of new ecological regions diversified the system with their special crop and animal breeds, technological implements, and raw materials. Indeed, as former marches that lay on the borders of and in between the old centres of civilization were drawn into its zone, hitherto separate networks of communication and exchange became connected, and the network as a whole constantly expanded, facilitating the dissemination of invention from one region to the other, across the landmass. Among other things, this 'system effect' countered regional regressions and collapses, as regional recoveries from 'dark ages' (of which the European was only one historical instance) were boosted not only by internal developments but also by powerful external stimuli.

All the same, although modernity was built upon the earlier gradual evolution of technology and social organization, it at the same time constituted the crossing of a threshold. As with the Neolithic transition/revolution to agriculture ten millennia before, a slow accumulative process reached a take-off point, from which it exploded into a sweeping transformation and vast acceleration of the pace of change. The interrelated growth, from early modernity, of a global trading system and commercial capitalism, centred in Europe, generated a chain reaction that was to spark off industrialization— all within a few centuries—unleashing an unprecedented, exponential rocketing of both wealth and power. And it is above all the interaction between, and the effects of, wealth and power, in their modern forms and magnitudes, that concern us throughout Part 3.

These introductory comments focus on only two aspects of that interaction. In the first place, productive capacity and military might now became closely related. This interrelationship is the main theme of Paul Kennedy's *The Rise and Fall of the Great Powers: Economic change and military conflict from 1500 to 2000* (1988). But, indeed, it should be realized that the interrelationship applied as directly and unequivocally as it did only *after* 1500, with the growth of modernity. It was from that time that success in war became critically dependent upon military hardware—above all firearms—that required an advanced technological infrastructure to produce and a highly organized sociopolitical infrastructure to deploy effectively. Before modernity, too, wealthy civilizations were generally able to pay for and sustain larger and better-equipped armies than their poorer neighbours on the marches. But this was an ambivalent advantage, because, as we have seen, the march people all too often compensated for their poverty by superior ferocity and by relying on improvised logistics, living off their enemy's land. They repeatedly took over the wealthiest states and empires, the power of which had waned, in a perpetual cycle of civilizations. The Mughal conquest of northern India from Afghanistan in 1526 and the conquest of China in 1644 by the Manchurians can be regarded as the last instances of such recurring take-overs from the march. In India only the invaders deployed firearms effectively, whereas in China they adopted them on their way to success. Henceforth, however, as both Edward Gibbon and Adam Smith observed, the balance between the civilized and the barbarian had changed fundamentally.[2]

Deducing from historical experience as interpreted by the wisdom of the ages, their contemporary and Smith's friend, Adam Ferguson,[3] and many others after him, down to US president Richard Nixon, feared that the growing wealth and prosperity of their civilized societies eroded civic and military virtue, bred 'softness' and decadence, and augured eventual downfall. But Smith and Gibbon saw that, as a result of their superior wealth and more advanced infrastructure, modern civilized societies had freed themselves from the spectre of a military take-over from the marches that had haunted earlier civilizations, including the invasions by horse nomads that had exercised such a decisive influence on Eurasian history. Wealth, technological advance, and military might had become inseparable. For the first time in history, only the wealthy qualified for the league of the mighty, with an almost uninterrupted positive loop mechanism between wealth and military prowess developing, where previously an ambivalent relationship, indeed a self-destructive cycle, had existed.

The second aspect of the modern forms of wealth and power to be noted here is that they both constituted extremely effective replicators, which spread incessantly, conquering everything in their way. Marx famously highlighted this as an intrinsic element in the growth and expansion of capitalism, the large-scale orientation and rationalization of economic life towards the market: by producing large volumes of low-price commodities, capitalism progressively destroyed and replaced earlier forms of economic organization, which it rendered uncompetitive. In Marx's memorable metaphor: 'The cheap prices of [capitalism's] commodities are the heavy artillery with which it batters down all Chinese walls, with which it forces the barbarians' intensely obstinate hatred of foreigners to capitulate. . . . It compels them to adopt what it calls civilization into their midst.'[4] And as the metaphor implies, modern armies and navies proved equally superior to all earlier forms of military organization, either compelling traditional armed forces to transform and adapt or pushing them into extinction. These two processes were intimately related: Chinese walls had to be battered down by the advanced armies and navies of capitalist societies before capitalist commodities were allowed in to do their work, and no effective military counterforce could be forged by the penetrated societies before they undertook domestic economic–social–political modernization. The modern forms of both wealth creation and war making swiftly expanded and evolved, each propelled by an intense competitive race, while closely reinforcing each other.

Indeed, the growing competitive edge and continuous expansion of both capitalism and modern armed forces gave the European states, where these processes most successfully unfolded, ever-increasing domination over the rest of the world. For this reason, our focus seemingly continues to narrow, this time from Eurasia to Europe and its relationship with the rest of the world—'the west and the rest'. More accurately, however, Part 3 examines how those most effective wealth- and power-inducing replicators that evolved in the west spread to replace earlier sociocultural forms on a global scale. They thereby generated a massive convergence effect that brought hitherto distinct or tenuously connected human communities into ever-closer contact, interaction, and similarity with each other. At the same time, deep differences have remained, the benefits of the explosive growth of wealth and power have been unevenly spread, the process itself has been permeated with violence and conflict, and its shockwaves resonate worldwide.

The modern period, European developments, and even the west's relationship with the rest of the world are probably the most intensively studied fields of historical and social scholarship. Nevertheless, although building upon this most valuable scholarship, the present study hopes neither to repeat a familiar story nor to produce yet another generalized historical narrative of war and military institutions in the west. Instead, while striving to remain firmly grounded in fact and tuned to diversity, Part 3, similar to Parts 1 and 2, aims to focus on war's deepest sources and its interrelationship with the cultural transformation of human life, this time as powerfully generated by modernity.

448

14

Guns and Markets: The New European States and a Global World

Modernity took off in Europe, which excelled above all others in the development of each of Bacon's three revolutionary innovations: firearms, ocean navigation, and printing (none of which originated in it). Within a few centuries Europe's remarkable transformation increasingly gave her ascendancy in, and subsequently transformed, the world. What accounts for this revolutionary outburst, the so-called European miracle and the rise of the west over all the rest? This question has attracted considerable scholarly attention that has focused on modern times. However, in some major respects the west had diverged from the other great civilizations of Eurasia long before modernity, for reasons outlined in the last section of Chapter 11.

For reasons also explained in Chapter 11, the world's most advanced historical civilizations emerged along the crescent-shaped belt that spanned eastern, southern, and western Eurasia, stretching almost continuously all the way from Japan to Europe. Along this belt temperatures were sufficiently high and water abundant enough to produce densely populated agricultural societies that, in AD 1500, comprised an estimated 70 per cent of the world's population. The fact that the belt lay on the continental rim bordering oceans and inner seas was a crucial factor. It both contributed to the favourable climatic conditions and facilitated long-range bulk transportation, which in pre-industrial societies was mainly confined to water. Among the civilizations of the Eurasian belt, those of south-west Asia, India, and China went much further back in time than Europe, which constituted a relatively new creation. European civilization emerged only in the late first millennium AD from the fusion of the previously barbarian northern Europe with the older regions of classical–Christian Mediterranean civilization, which after the barbarian invasions had themselves experienced a sharp regression in terms of urbanism, trade, economic complexity, and literacy. Indeed, by the eve of modernity the other great civilizations of Eurasia seemingly outshone Europe in imperial power and splendour, variety of produce, and fine crafts.

I write 'seemingly' because the revived-upstart European civilization, as it emerged from around the year 1000 AD, was not the small, backward, and remote appendix to a huge Eurasian landmass that it is sometimes portrayed to have been. Most of Asia in fact consisted of arid and semi-arid steppe. Thus, in both size and population, Europe (excluding Russia) was on average larger than south-west Asia, only marginally smaller than India, and about half as large as China. Endowed with a more temperate climate and more even rainfall patterns, her population was more evenly spread and apparently enjoyed greater wealth per capita from as early as 1400 AD, especially in animal stock.[1] Of course, split throughout by high mountain ranges and surrounded by seas that everywhere penetrated deep between its constitutive parts, Europe's space and population were not unified in great imperial continental blocs, like those that existed in the other main centres of civilization, but were divided into a large number of political units. Yet, as scholars have pointed out, it was precisely this political division that proved to be the source of Europe's competitive edge.

There were undoubtedly some advantages to large political blocs in terms of facilitating economic complexity and technological innovation, but these advantages were regularly counterweighed by monopolistic and despotic central authorities and by stifling imperial administrations.[2] It is no coincidence, for example, that for all of imperial China's glorious achievements and continuous growth, the bulk of that country's cultural heritage had been shaped, and her period of most rapid evolution and technological innovation had taken place, when the country was divided into the fiercely competing 'warring states' (fifth century to 221 BC). Europe's political disunity, as well as the greater internal power distribution within its various states, meant that it was more difficult in it to suppress innovation politically. Furthermore, such suppression was likely to be penalized by the adoption of the same innovation by other polities, which could thereby gain the advantage in the intense economic and military inter-polity competition that prevailed in the European system. Indeed, any relative inefficiency was likely to be penalized in the same way in such a competitive environment, a factor that greatly accelerated the pace of evolution.

THE EMERGENCE OF EUROPE'S 'WARRING STATES'

Thus, Europe's rise has commonly been associated with the progressive consolidation from the late Middle Ages of the so-called national state as her predominant form of political organization, and with the consequent formation of a European system of competing national states. This early national–'territorial'–'country' state is generally regarded as a unique European development, unprecedented in earlier history. But why this was the case—if indeed it was—has barely been asked. The circumstances that underlie the formation of the new European state have not been rigorously compared with other parts of the world, or other periods of time, including Mediterranean Europe's classical antiquity.

In fact, the national–'territorial'–'country' state did not originate with the new European civilization. Other loci of civilization merely proved geographically and ecologically more conducive to smaller or larger forms of political organization: the city petty-state and the empire. In the ancient Near East, for example, national–'territorial'–'country' states regularly emerged in formerly tribal spaces or from the unification of petty-states. As already seen, Egypt and Middle Empire Assyria constituted examples of such states, as did Urartu, Elam, Persia, and perhaps also Kassite and Chaldaean Babylonia. The Levant during the early first millennium BC saw the development of the Israelite, Ammonite, Moabite, and Edomite small national–territorial states in the south, whereas the larger Aramaic ethnos in the north remained divided among several states. Yet, by the seventh century

BC, the emerging national states, as well as all the other polity types throughout the Near East, were conquered by the Assyrian Empire, and Assyria proved to be merely the first in an almost uninterrupted succession of empires that swept through and ruled the open plains of south-west Asia up until the twentieth century, subsuming its various ethnicities under their imperial structure.[3]

By contrast, the part of Europe that is the closest to the ancient Near East and into which, consequently, agriculture and then civilization first spread was purely by chance of geography Europe's most rugged peninsula cum archipelago—Greece. And by a similar chance, the next closest geographical region, into which civilization spread from Greece, was Europe's second most rugged peninsula cum archipelago—Italy. (I exclude Norway, because this was the part of Europe most distant from the Near East, and where, as a result, civilization would reach last in its gradual north-westward advance.) As already seen, in both the Greek and the Italian peninsulas, gouged as they were by mountains and seas, a multiplicity of city-states dominated the fragmented landscape, even though at least Greece (but not Italy) was inhabited by people who regarded themselves as a single ethnos.

However, the north-westerly gradient that marks the spread of agriculture and civilization into Europe also signifies a transition into the more open plain lands that lie in between and north of the main Alpide mountain ridges. In addition, even where seas bordered on these lands, they constituted a much lesser part of their perimeter than was the case in Greece and Italy. Indeed, it has barely been noted that Europe's earliest national state did not appear in late medieval or early modern times, but was in fact ancient Macedonia. As we have already seen, it was in the more open and less fragmented landscape north of Greece and north of the Mediterranean coastline that successful state and nation building was carried out in the fifth and fourth centuries BC by the Macedonian royal house, which welded together the ethnically related Macedonian tribes, as well as some Thracians, Illyrians, Thessalians, and Greek *poleis*. By virtue of her superior size and power, Macedonia was then able to conquer and dominate (although not unite) Greece, and even go on to conquer the huge Persian Empire. Subsequently, however, Macedonia fell prey to the imperial super city-state, Rome, which later transformed into a unified empire that encompassed the whole of the Mediterranean perimeter.

All the same, later developments would show that Macedonia's course of evolution, whereby a tribal–ethnic space was consolidated into a national–country state rather than into a fragmented city-state system, did not represent an isolated case; more typically, it constituted the norm north and west of the Greek and Italian rugged peninsulas, as that vast barbarian zone was gradually drawn into contact with civilization, with the ensuing economic, social, and political transformation that this contact set in motion. Thus, for example, in the lower Danube plain contact with Rome stimulated the consolidation of the national–country state of Dacia in the first century AD. And while Rome conquered and destroyed that state, as well as disrupting other attempts at large state building on her northern barbarian frontier, her downfall signalled the mushrooming of national–country states throughout Europe. This applies not only to the Germanic successor states that formed within the former imperial frontier, such as the Visigoth and Merovingian Frankish states, which mixed conquerors with conquered in an ethnic mosaic and relied on Roman provincial infrastructure, but even more strikingly to the whole series of national–country states that sprang up in the course of the following centuries, mostly outside the old Roman frontier, such as Anglo-Saxon England, the Scandinavian states, Poland, Hungary, Moravia and Bohemia, Bulgaria, Serbia, and Scotland (with the 'empire' of the German nation as a somewhat more ambivalent case). Whether involving a brief transition through a multiplicity of rural petty-states or direct consolidation from a tribal space, the striking feature of all these cases is that in all of them substantial territorial states were predominantly built around an ethnically related population.[4]

This sweeping 'spontaneous' mushrooming of national states across the breadth of the continent—occurring, needless to say, through intensely violent processes of state building and under a combination of heavy external pressures and stimuli—can hardly be regarded as a coincidence. It indicates that the national–country state sprang 'naturally' in the sort of landscape that characterized western–central–northern Europe, particularly after human population densities increased and the forests contracted with the continuous growth of more intensive agriculture. On the other hand, although less fractured by mountains and seas than Greece and Italy, western–central–northern Europe was more fragmented geographically than the great zones of civilization in Asia. Consequently, the Carolingian attempt at a European empire quickly disintegrated, whereas later ones repeatedly failed.

Again, a comparison with other civilizations helps put the European experience of national–territorial states in perspective. Unlike the multi-ethnic empires of south-western Asia, imperial China, after unification around two large river valleys, in effect became a huge national state. Although many 'minorities' were of course incorporated into China, Han Chinese comprised the overwhelming majority of her population. At the same time, China was a national state that more or less monopolized the entire east Asian continental agricultural zone. She was a hegemon, who, apart from nomads, was surrounded only by much smaller neighbours. Although some of them, in Korea, Manchuria, and Indochina, developed into national–territorial states, no competitive state system similar to the European one existed in eastern Asia. Japan, too, united into a national state in the mid-first millennium AD, in her case of medium size. This national state periodically fragmented and was fraught with civil war. And yet, surrounded and wholly protected by the sea, Japan partook of no intensely competitive inter-state system, her occasional foreign forays notwithstanding. In Africa, national states emerged regularly from the end of the first millennium AD (the Zulu state being a late pre-colonial example). But, as we have seen, Africa's relative isolation behind the Sahara slowed her development compared with Eurasia. All this goes to show that, contrary to the widely held view, the national–territorial state was far from being an exclusive late medieval–early modern European creation. At the same time, however, it was western–central–northern Europe's special and highly contingent geographical and ecological configuration that made the multiplicity of medium-size national–territorial states its norm.

Another idiosyncratic European phenomenon that has distorted scholarly perception about the growth of the national–territorial state is feudalism. Although, as noted above, national–territorial states sprang up throughout western–central–northern Europe as soon as that region had entered the fold of civilization in the late first millennium AD, preference for heavy cavalry, when it combined with poor state infrastructure, later led to feudal disintegration of central political authority. As a result of this hiatus, the revival of royal power from around 1200 and the emergence of what again resembled functioning states have been interpreted as the beginning of something entirely new, supposedly fixing the birth of the national–country state in the thirteenth century.

The New European States and a Global World

As the national–country state was not actually a new European development, and in view of the fact that it re-emerged in Europe from around 1200, its evolution should not be attributed to later novelties of modernity such as Bacon's trio. Contrary to a popular belief, we see that it was not the cannon that destroyed the baronial castles and humbled the feudal aristocracy. French monarchs from Philip Augustus on, creators of the new French state in the thirteenth century, accomplished that long before the cannon, and similar processes had been taking place in more or less the same period in the other European new monarchies. Indeed, millennia before the advent of firearms, similar processes had taken place in China during her transition from the highly fragmented feudalism of the 'Spring and Autumn' period (722–481 BC) to the increasingly centralized–bureaucratic 'warring states' and unified state. As already seen in Chapter 11, feudalism was rolled back—in late medieval Europe as well as in other times and places—when royal central authority was able to draw on the financial and administrative resources of an increasingly commercial and urban society, which the state employed to reassert itself over the regional rural–warrior elite.

Similarly, the growth of the new European state spelled the demise of the city-state in Europe for reasons that were scarcely uniquely modern. We have already seen that after a few centuries of existence city-state systems everywhere succumbed to larger concentrations of power which developed in their midst or on their borders. They simply found themselves too small to compete successfully. Strikingly demonstrating the geopolitical logic outlined above is the fact that throughout medieval Europe it was yet again only mountainous and peninsular Italy that saw the emergence of a system of fully independent city-states, rather than of a national–territorial state. However, once the new large states emerged on their borders, the days of the Italian city-states were numbered, irrespective of their financial–commercial wealth and splendour. Again, as we see later, their fall had little to do with gun power. Instead, it was a direct consequence of the fact that even the largest and wealthiest of them, the imperial city-state of Venice, which ruled perhaps as many as one and a half million people, comprised less than a tenth of the population of France and a fifth to an eighth of that of Spain or the Spanish Empire (although Italy as a whole more than equalled Spain in population). In order of magnitude, by the sixteenth century the budgets of France and Spain had each outgrown Venice's by a factor of 10, those of the other large Italian regional city-states by a factor of

50, and those of the city communes of northern Europe by a factor of hundreds.[5] Indeed, for similar reasons the Hanse cities in northern Germany declined in proportion to the rise of Denmark and Sweden.

Only two clusters of formerly semi-autonomous urban communes retained independence, by forming a league and because they were extremely well sheltered geographically, either as a mountain fortress, in Switzerland, or behind water barriers, in the Netherlands. In the process, both the Swiss and Dutch confederations were increasingly transformed into states. Scholars have pointed out that in consequence of the intense power race that gave the advantage to size, the number of political units in Europe shrank during modernity from some 500 to 25, as the smaller units lost out and were swallowed up by their larger counterparts.[6] It should be added, however, that practically all the 'victims' in this process were semi-independent magnate domains, autonomous city communes, and independent city-states. National–territorial states, great or small, exhibited remarkable buoyancy, for reasons that are discussed later.

So far it has been argued here that the new national–territorial European states began to grow before the advent of, and for reasons unrelated to, peculiarly modern developments. All the same, it so happened that modern novelties appeared on the scene not long after the process had started, became inextricably linked with it, and affected it deeply. It is the effect on, and interaction with, war of distinctively modern innovations such as Bacon's trio that the following seeks to unravel.

WHAT CONSTITUTED THE 'MILITARY REVOLUTION'?

Europe experienced a so-called military revolution: firearms transformed both field and siege warfare; armies greatly expanded and became more permanent; they were increasingly paid for, administered, and commanded by central state authorities that grew progressively more powerful; similar processes affected navies, with which the Europeans gained mastery over the seas. All of the above are widely agreed upon. Yet the time frame of the 'revolution' and the causal relationship between its various elements remain in dispute among scholars, and the whole issue calls for a general reassessment.

The first question to address pertains to when exactly the 'military revolution' took place. Michael Roberts, who coined the phrase, was a historian of northern Europe, so it is not surprising perhaps that he traced the crucial phase of the process to that region during its period of greatness (1560–1660). A distinguished historian and a pioneer, Roberts has been treated with courtesy by subsequent scholars. But his overall reasoning, especially concerning the causes of the process, is improbable and requires little direct reference here.[7] It was historian Geoffrey Parker who took up the subject, developed it, and made it his own.

A leading student of military developments in the Spanish Empire, Europe's mightiest power in the sixteenth century, Parker has pointed out that the processes described by Roberts had in fact been well under way in the Spanish army from early on in that century. Mapping the general scope of the change, Parker has written: 'Between 1530 and 1710 there was a ten-fold increase both in the total numbers of armed forces paid by the major European states and in the total numbers involved in the major European battles.'[8] The former increased from a few tens of thousands to hundreds of thousands, whereas the latter increased from many thousands to many tens of thousands on each side; and all this in a period when Europe's population as a whole only grew about 50 per cent. The record in absolute numbers was naturally held by Europe's greatest powers. The Spanish Empire paid for 150,000 soldiers in the 1550s, 200,000 in the 1590s, and 300,000 in the 1630s. France, who succeeded Spain as Europe's mightiest power in the seventeenth century, paid for 50,000 soldiers in the 1550s, 150,000 in the 1630s, and 400,000 in the 1700s.[9] (In both cases actual numbers of men in service were somewhat lower.[10])

As Parker's reckonings show, Roberts's time frame for the 'revolution' not only starts too late but also ends too early. Whereas Parker has concentrated on pushing the beginning of the 'revolution' back in time, students of late seventeenth- and eighteenth-century Europe have called attention to the period 1660–1720, when the European armies continued to grow while also becoming yet more permanent.[11] One may add that, although France did not match her exhaustive 1700s' record during most of the eighteenth century, other armies continued to expand, because it was now not only Europe's largest army but the armies of each of the great powers that grew to hundreds of thousands in war time. Furthermore, why stop in the eighteenth century, as the debaters have done? By the last years of that century, the French Revolutionary armies comprised 750,000 men, to say nothing of the armies of millions that came after industrialization. And returning to the beginning of the process, a historian of late medieval Europe has further expanded the time frame into that period.[12] Long-serving paid troops became common during the Hundred Years War, and the foundations of permanent state armies, such as the French *compaignies d'ordonnance*, were laid down towards the end of that war.

Thus the so-called military revolution extended over quite a number of centuries. It is argued here that it paralleled and was closely related to Europe's wider, sweeping transformation during those same centuries—indeed, formed an 'aspect' of early modernization.[13] What then constituted the 'revolution' and how did it interact with Europe's general transformation? As Parker has indicated, one major element of the 'military revolution', which also contributed to the rise in the size of armies, was the revival and proliferation of infantry. Half as expensive as cavalry, infantry accounted for most of the armies' growth in absolute terms. As already explained in Part 2, here, too, the process had been in full swing well before and irrespective of the advent of infantry firearms, which entered into general use only around 1500. It was most prominently manifested in the crushing victories of both the English longbow and the Swiss pike formations over the knightly cavalry in the fourteenth and fifteenth centuries. Indeed, although the introduction of firearms into field warfare is widely believed to have caused the demise of cavalry, it actually revived it. As a result of the matchlock's slow rate of fire—about one shot per minute—arquebusiers and musketeers during the sixteenth and seventeenth centuries required the protection of spearmen. This combination of shot and pike was cumbersome, and decreased infantry's tactical flexibility, mobility, and shock effect in comparison to the earlier, irresistible Swiss phalanx. It thus contributed to infantry's growing tendency to seek protection behind field fortifications. Supplementing its shock weapons with pistols, cavalry again became the principal offensive arm in the open field, as it would remain for another two centuries, in and outside Europe. Although the cheaper and more versatile infantry proliferated and increasingly adopted firearms, cavalry's share in the army remained high, usually between a quarter and a half, sometimes more.[14]

Thus the rise of infantry can only partly account for the armies' growing size and adoption of more regular service, because, although infantry grew in number and in relative share, cavalry too increased. Armies grew overall. According to Parker, what mainly accounts for the growth is another major element of the 'military revolution'—the advent of firearm fortifications, because firearms reshaped siege warfare, as they did field warfare. The pinnacle of fortification from Neolithic Jericho and throughout historical times (varying surprisingly little in basic architecture) had been the tall curtain wall that physically blocked enemy assault. Gun power put an end to that type of fortification.

The early history of gunpowder is summarized here as succinctly as possible. Both gunpowder and the gun were evidently pioneered in China. Invented as early as the ninth century, gunpowder was introduced into military use by the eleventh, followed by the gun in the thirteenth or possibly even in the twelfth. Both spread very rapidly as the Mongols connected east and west, so that from the second or third decade of the fourteenth century the cannon is recorded in Europe, arriving in the Ottoman realm by the second half of the century and in India in the fifteenth century. By then western Europe had taken the lead in the development of the gun. Its divided and antagonistic political system stimulated that development, which also benefited from the region's abundant mining resources and burgeoning metallurgic industry. Moreover, as historian Kenneth Chase brilliantly explains in his recent book, firearms proved to be more useful for the Europeans than for those sedentary state societies that bordered on the steppe. These societies' main security problem was the horse nomads, who had no walled settlements to be breached and against whom infantry was ineffective because they could not be pinned down.[15]

By the middle of the fifteenth century, after continuous technical improvements, European wrought iron guns, using 'corned' powder and firing stone balls, became potent enough to render tall walled fortifications ineffective. At the end of the Hundred Years War, French bombards breached the English strongholds in Normandy and Guienne (1449–53). At that same time, the huge bombards of the Ottoman Sultan Mehmet II, built by a Hungarian gun master, smashed through the great walls of Constantinople, the mightiest in western Eurasia (1453). The power race between France and Burgundy in the 1470s prompted further advances. By the end of the century, the siege guns of the king of France, Charles VIII—cast from

The earliest known image of a gunpowder weapon. China, c. 1128. The earliest
representation of a European 'bombard', dated to 1327, is remarkably similar

bronze, made mobile on wheeled carriages, and shooting iron balls—easily
and sensationally opened the gates of every fortified city that the king
encountered during his 1494–5 invasion of Italy.

Thus, for a short while, the siege gun reigned supreme. Yet a process of
adaptation was taking place almost simultaneously, reaching maturity within
a few decades. In Italy, for 50 years the hapless scene of the struggle for
European supremacy between the Habsburg Empire and France, but also
the European leader in architecture, military engineers developed the

The Dardanelles Gun, Turkish, dated 1464. Cast bronze in two parts: chase and breech, weighing together 16 tonnes. Fires a stone shot weighing 300 kg to over a kilometre and a half. Probably not very different from the great bombards that had breached the walls of Constantinople in 1453

answer to siege artillery. Ramparts were built thicker and lower, presenting a smaller target for the attacker's guns. The ditch in front of the ramparts was widened to block enemy assaults that would be primarily forestalled by firepower. A new type of perturbing angular stronghold, the bastion, replaced the old square or round tower, providing a broad platform from which guns could keep the enemy at a distance and sweep the ditch with flanking crossfire. Thus artillery fortifications were developed as the answer to siege artillery. Whereas old-style fortifications could not prevent the attacker from advancing his men up to the walls, while effectively blocking them from passing through, firearm fortifications constituted a smaller physical obstacle but prevented the enemy from approaching the fortifications. The attacker was now obliged to dig his way laboriously towards the defences, so as to remain sheltered from fire. Having thus advanced very close to the fortifications, he attempted to blast a breach through them with mines and point blank artillery fire and then to storm his way in.[16]

Bombard and arquebusiers (c. 1483). Infantry firearms became practical in late fifteenth-century Europe

In the following centuries, both firearm fortifications and siege craft underwent further improvements, making them increasingly elaborate and systematic, the work of geometricians and engineers. All the same, from the 1520s–1530s the balance between besieger and besieged was restored to pretty much what it had been before the advent of the gun. Contrary to popularly held perceptions, the supremacy of the siege gun over the castle was brief and transitory. The siege again became a slow and laborious

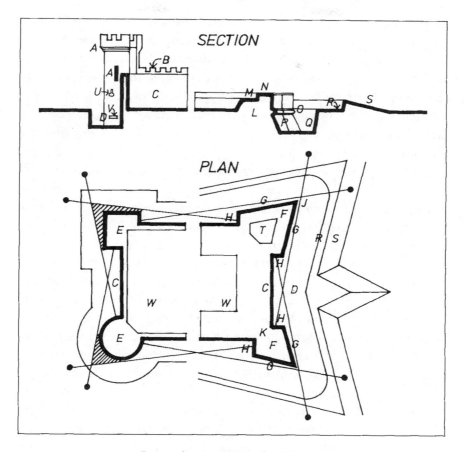

SECTION

PLAN

Pre-modern vs artillery fortification

process, as it had been throughout history. At least in Europe, where the new technologies and techniques became available to both sides in each theatre of war into which they spread, improvements of the attack and defence of fortified places pretty much cancelled each other out in a 'Red Queen effect'.

How then did the revolutionary advent of the new forms of fortification and siege craft relate to the growth of armies, as Parker believes it did? Parker has rightly pointed out that the new style of fortifications that spread from Italy to the rest of western Europe (where it was known as *trace italienne*) was so successful that it came to dominate warfare. Places fortified in the new style proliferated and became almost impregnable to gun power. Unless aided by tactical surprise or by treason, sieges spanned over many months and, in a few cases, even years.[17] Battles became rare. Armies engaged primarily in sieges and raids. All this is undisputed. However, according to Parker, the multiplication of such fortresses required more garrison troops than before. Furthermore, because the fortress grew bigger and dominated hundreds of metres around it with gunfire, larger forces were needed to surround and besiege its perimeter. This explanation for the growth of the European armies has been incorporated into many history books, yet some scholars disagree. Examining the contemporary data, John Lynn has concluded that the new fortresses did not absorb larger forces of either the defender or the attacker and, hence, this was not the reason for the growth of the European armies.[18] Indeed, one may add, the fortress obviously cannot explain the inflation in the size of *navies*, which developed parallel to the growth of the armies as an integral part of the 'military revolution'.[19]

I concur with Lynn and wish to expand the argument further. As already indicated above, I hold that, apart from the brief transition period between 1450 and 1520, the introduction of the gun into both siege craft and fortifications, although profoundly transforming them, nevertheless fundamentally changed the balance neither between them nor between siege and field warfare, compared with earlier periods. Throughout history, sieges were slow and laborious, taking many months and years to complete successfully. In regions where fortified cities and fortresses abounded, warfare pretty much revolved around sieges. Armies often concentrated on one selected prize for each annual campaign, as they would do in early modern Europe.

Examples are so much the stuff of history as to make the citing of them a little trivial. They start with the campaigns of subjugation conducted by the empires of the ancient Near East, and those of pre-unification China. Although the Roman legions are renowned for their battlefield performance, experts are well aware that siege work was just as, if not more, significant in Rome's centuries-long expansion in Italy. Similarly, Hannibal's War is remembered for its crushing battles of the Trebbia (218 BC), Trasimene (217 BC), Cannae (216 BC), and Zama (202 BC). But it was in the grinding and protracted attrition of siege warfare, year after year, that Hannibal was defeated. Concentrating on one great objective at a time, the Romans took Syracuse (212 BC) after a two-year siege, Capua (211 BC) after another two years of siege, and Tarentum (209) after the city was betrayed to them, and these were only the largest cities. Carthage itself fell to Rome in the Third Punic War, after a siege that lasted no less than three years (149–146 BC)—even though the Roman army was the master of such operations. Siege work dominated Rome's protracted 'pacification' of Spain and subjugation of all the other lands of the Mediterranean. And apart from incessant raiding and a few large-scale invasions, Rome's centuries-long conflict with Parthia and Sasanian Persia revolved around siege operations against any one of a host of fortified walled cities situated throughout their border zone in Mesopotamia and Anatolia.

It is equally well recognized that in medieval Europe itself, before the advent of the gun, warfare was dominated by the existence of a dense network of fortified strongholds, both baronial and royal, which influenced the pattern of warfare in much the same way as they would in the early modern period. Battles were rare and, apart from raiding, warfare predominantly consisted of more or less sustained efforts to take a key fortified stronghold in an annual campaign. It was this pattern that characterized the French kings' military drive to reduce the English–Angevin empire in France, the Hundred Years War, and the struggles between Christians and Moslems in both Spain and the Holy Land.[20]

All the above constituted protracted struggles of attrition—often dragging on for years, decades, and centuries—as was the case in northern Italy, the Low Countries, and the Rhineland, those regions of intense warfare in the sixteenth and seventeenth centuries, where, as a consequence, the new firearm fortifications proliferated. Parker has argued that firearm fortifications were larger in size than the older ones, but it was in fact the towns and cities themselves that greatly expanded during the late Middle Ages and early modernity, from their humble medieval beginnings. As a consequence, their fortified area expanded as well. (Indeed, it took a long time before medieval cities filled up the perimeter of their ruined Roman walls, where such existed.) Pre-artillery fortifications had been as extensive as modern ones in the large cities of the ancient Near East, classical antiquity, Byzantium, Islam, and China. Uruk's walls stretched for 9 kilometres in the mid-third millennium BC, classical Athens' long walls for 35 kilometres, Carthage's triple lines of fortifications for 34 kilometres, Syracuse's for 27 kilometres, those of the T'ang capital Chang'an for 35 kilometres, and Ming Nanking for 39 kilometres. These, of course, were the giants of cities, but pre-modern city fortifications regularly stretched for kilometres, sometimes in double and triple lines, and were as long and as elaborate as any city fortifications in the early modern period.

Thus, although Parker is correct in claiming that the perimeter of the siege had to be enlarged in the early modern period in order to distance the besiegers a few hundred metres from the fortress's ramparts and gunfire, this extension was not as significant as he reckoned, because in sieges of large pre-modern cities the besiegers already held lines that stretched for many kilometres and even tens of kilometres. In each of the great Roman sieges mentioned above, the Roman armies that numbered in tens of thousands erected long double lines of fortifications facing both the besieged city and outside relief armies. Investing Alesia, the great Gallic stronghold (52 BC), Julius Caesar's 8 legions (theoretically close to 80,000 men, including the *auxilia*) constructed an inner ring of some 17 kilometres and an outer one of 22 kilometres. Moreover, it should be noted that, even if the perimeter of the siege was enlarged as a result of firearm fortifications, this did not necessarily place a greater demand for troops on the besieger, because firearms meant that armies also adopted a shallower formation than earlier, both on the battlefield and in manning lines of investment.

In addition, Parker has claimed that the new massive fortifications were highly expensive. They allegedly consumed such great resources that, despite the continuous growth in military manpower, field armies never grew sufficiently to overcome the tangled web of fortifications. Consequently, wars dragged on and became inherently indecisive. Again Parker's claim has been echoed by many historians, who quote impressive sounding sums of money spent on individual fortifications, albeit out of context of the powers' overall military expenditure. In actuality, statistics derived from a variety of separate cases throughout Europe consistently reveal that fortifications consumed a fairly *small* portion of the total military expenditure. In Venice, which heavily fortified both its Italian Terrafirma territory and its overseas empire, fortifications comprised only about 5–10 per cent of the total defence expenditure in the sixteenth and early seventeenth centuries. The data from Spain are similar, about 5–10 per cent and closer to the lower figure. In France, when a sophisticated and exceptionally expensive fortress-building programme was carried out for Louis XIV by Marshal Vauban, the cost in the peak years (1682–3) reached only some 17 per cent of the total military expenditure, whereas the average annual cost throughout the century was far lower.[21]

In correspondence with me, Parker has argued that these relatively modest sums are misleading, because much of the cost of fortifications was borne by the local authorities and population and did not register in the state's budget. But, in fact, this was also true of other major items of military expenditure, apart from fortifications—for example: the costs of billeting and food for troops, non-stipendiary military service, corvée labour, and so on. Hence, local contributions probably did not significantly change the *share* of expenditure allocated to fortifications in the total military expenditure. Moreover, part of the cost of war, including fortifications, had *always* been paid locally. There was no fundamental change here in early modernity that can account for the Revolution. If anything, the change went in the opposite direction, as we see later.

Furthermore, in contrast to the prevailing assumption, a number of specialized studies on the subject have indicated (to little avail) that the new style of fortifications was by no means more expensive than the old one. The new broad and low-lying ramparts were erected from earth and rubble dug up from the ditches, which absorbed artillery fire better than stone or bricks. Therefore, they were built in much less time and with greater ease than the older stone fortifications. Masonry or bricks were occasionally used, but only for outer facing, to protect the earth from rapid erosion by the elements. In most cases, as in earlier times, the local population was conscripted as unskilled labour to carry out most of the construction, supplemented by a small number of paid skilled artisans.[22] The main economic problem with the new style of fortifications, unnoted by scholars, was actually the revolutionary nature of the change: older fortifications had to be built anew within a few decades or even years, concentrating the financial outlay in each region of Europe that was reached by the change to a brief period of time. All the same, while military expenditure, including that allocated to fortifications, dramatically rose *overall* during early modernity, the new fortifications apparently continued to comprise pretty much the same share of that expenditure as had pre-artillery fortifications in older times, when the 10 per cent figure seems to keep turning up in the rare surviving records.[23]

If artillery fortifications in themselves were not more expensive than earlier fortifications, however, were they not actually made more expensive by the cost of the artillery that was mounted on them, and the powder and shot that they stored? In all countries the vast majority of land guns and complementing ammunition were deployed in fortified places rather than

Naarden in the Netherlands from the air

with the field armies. Still, although widely assumed by scholars to have represented a huge financial outlay, artillery, too, is consistently shown by separate data from the various powers throughout the early modern period (including France, Venice, Spain, and Russia) to have comprised as modest a share as fortifications of the European states' overall military expenditure, probably around 4–8 per cent.[24] Nor were handheld firearms fundamentally more costly than the highly expensive defensive and offensive cold steel arms and crossbows of medieval times.

These data bear on other significant questions. For example, contrary to myth, the magnates' independent power did not decline because of the siege gun that destroyed their castles or the cost incurred in remodelling their castles according to the new style, or the cost involved in maintaining their own artillery and other firearms. Both magnates and city-states acquired artillery and constructed bastion fortifications.[25] As already mentioned, their problem—which revealed itself even before the advent of gunpowder—was not in their inability to adopt the new technologies, which they did, but in being too small to withstand the new, large, increasingly bureaucratic–financial, national–territorial states.

The price of fortifications, artillery, and other firearms is indicative of the structure of the military budgets in general: although financially significant, military hardware and capital goods constituted only a minority of the powers' overall military expenditure. Navies, the most capital-intensive armed service, is a striking demonstration of this general rule. Even in Venice, the foremost Italian maritime power, the army cost more than the navy throughout the sixteenth century, sometimes twice as much.[26] In the leading naval power of the first half of the seventeenth century, the Dutch Republic, which like Venice was also obliged to maintain a large army, the army cost more than twice as much as the navy.[27] Even in Britain, the leading naval power of the eighteenth century and an island, expenditures on the army and navy ran neck and neck.[28] More significantly, the price of the warships themselves comprised only a minor share of the navies' overall budget. Lumber, the main raw material, was inexpensive and, at least in the sixteenth century (though no longer so in the seventeenth), was still locally plentiful for use by all the powers. As for the workforce employed in naval construction, expensive as it was per capita, it was much smaller in size compared with the manpower engaged in the armed forces.[29] Around the middle of the sixteenth century, the annual upkeep of a galley, the standard oared warship of the Mediterranean that on average lasted for years if not decades, 'equaled the cost of its original construction, about 6000 ducats', with foodstuffs costing twice as much as hardware in the provisions.[30]

Indeed, it is because pay and provisions rather than the cost of ships constituted the main cost of navies that the Ottomans were able to respond to the destruction of their fleet and loss of some 200 galleys in the Battle of Lepanto (1571), against the combined fleets of Venice, Spain, the Pope, and their allies, with a massive rebuilding programme, which within less than a year recovered the lost materiel, although not the manpower.[31] (The economy of the Mediterranean galley fleets changed little through the ages: similar feats had been performed by Rome within months of her disastrous naval losses, mainly to storms, during the First Punic War, which overall cost her more than 500 large galleys [quinquereme].[32]) The expenditure on sailing warships during the seventeenth and eighteenth centuries followed the same pattern, even though each ship carried up to 100 heavy guns, more than any field army: the cost of maintaining a sailing warship for a year was roughly the same as the price of one.[33]

The Battle of Lepanto (1571), between the Ottomans and the Christian coalition. The last of the great oared ship engagements of the Mediterranean, involving more than 200 galleys on each side and perhaps 170,000 men altogether. Although adapted to carrying artillery, the galley was being eclipsed by the combination of gun and sail

The simple fact behind all these statistical data has been noted by only a few scholars: although hardware of all sorts was expensive, pay and provisions for soldiers and mariners comprised by far the largest item, indeed the large majority, of the state's military and naval expenditure.[34] As mentioned above, in the early modern period hardware became crucial for victory and required an advanced and sophisticated technological and social infrastructure to produce and deploy effectively. Nevertheless, paying and providing for the growing and increasingly more permanent manpower employed mostly in armies and, in smaller numbers, in navies constituted the principal cost of the 'military revolution'.[35] Indeed, to the extent that warfare became static and indecisive, it was not because fortifications were so expensive but, on the contrary, as earlier in history, because they were so much cheaper than troops that they constituted better value. 'It was much cheaper in the long run to invest capital in a fortress and then to maintain within it a small garrison than to meet the crippling recurrent burden of large numbers of troops.'[36]

Let us now put aside the effect of fortifications and pass on to a more general point: any explanation for the huge increase in the military manpower and expenditures of the European states during early modernity that is based on growing needs or necessities, whether caused by fortifications or by any other factor, is fundamentally misconstrued. To be sure, high levels of conflict increase resource mobilization and allocation for war. Yet when embroiled in struggles for high stakes, often the highest, and locked into arms races, antagonists typically strive to mobilize as large a force as they possibly can, often pushing the limits of their capabilities. Their reciprocal 'need' to outweigh each other is expressed in greater investment, most notably in larger armies, irrespective of whether or not fortifications play a significant role. This has been the case throughout history whenever conflict levels were high. Early modernity was not unique in this respect.[37] However, whereas needs are unbounded, resources are not. If early modern European armies, navies, and war expenditure grew continuously, it was not because of 'needs'—of whatever nature and however pressing—but because the powers were able to mobilize greater resources than before, leading to the escalation of arms races. Although supply and demand are closely related, it is chiefly on the supply side, Europe's overall resources and the states' ability to tap them, that one should concentrate.

STATES AND ARMIES

Indeed, it is widely recognized that growing resource mobilization for war and the rise of the central state in Europe were closely linked and mutually reinforcing processes.[38] 'War made the state, and the state made war.'[39] From the thirteenth century on, many European rulers increasingly succeeded in obtaining the reluctant consent of representative assemblies to the imposition of taxes that were intended to cover the high costs of state wars. For, in contrast to the endemic small-scale warfare that was salient in the politically fragmented Europe of the High Middle Ages, the real economic problem with state wars was that they had to be paid for directly. As already seen in Chapters 10 and 11, large states meant distant wars, distance meant time, and time was money. Prolonged campaigning far away from home required both special and costly logistical arrangements and pay for long-serving warriors rather than reliance on local part-timers. In sedentary states, this presupposed a system of resource extraction on a national scale (the weakness of which had led to the adoption of feudal arrangements by the early medieval state). With fortifications, too, contrary to Parker's reasoning, the truly significant change in terms of their economic burden was that they were now increasingly built by the state rather than by local barons. Although still largely constructed by local corvée labour and relying on local resources, they nevertheless involved money allocations from a central purse, which presupposed resource circulation, to and from the state. A spiralling, centuries-long process was set in motion, whereby money voted for the state to pay for troops increased central state power and gradually gave it monopoly over legitimate force, making warfare all the more a state affair and, in turn, further increasing the state's powers of taxation, administration, and command. The 'tax state' gradually superseded the feudal 'domain state',[40] whereas paid soldiers replaced feudal troop levies.

But, again, how does the European experience stand in a global perspective? How does the new, early, modern European state compare with other large-scale centralized states in history? After all, what constituted a novelty in western Europe was hardly a novelty in other regions and times. The new European state was actually *less* centralized–bureaucratic than, for example, imperial Rome and imperial China during their golden ages. While highlighting the rise of the early modern state, scholars have also become much more aware of its power limitations. The state had to compromise with local power, privileges, and institutions, with a resistance to a diminution of their independence and status that repeatedly flared up in civil wars. These compromises, which resulted in tax exemptions and an uneven tax burden, caused serious inefficiencies in the state's money-raising system. In particular, the state compromised with the aristocracy that shed some of its old privileges but gained others in return. The so-called absolutist state was actually a heterogeneous composite of territories and privileges, wherein the aristocracy was incorporated as the upper office-holding stratum of the state's structure.[41] Thus, as the state was unable to subdue local aristocratic power, the penetration of state administration was limited; and as state administration was limited, the state depended on the aristocracy to serve as an intermediate agent of government.

Although coming under increasingly tightening state control, the administration of war and the armed forces, by far the largest component of state activity and expenditure, exhibited this structural pattern as any other field. Lacking a sufficiently developed bureaucratic machinery, the state delegated the recruitment, administration, and partly even the financing of troops to other agents. During the Renaissance, *condottieri* provided states with ready-made troops in return for an agreed sum of money. Some of these *condottieri* grew into large-scale entrepreneurs and financiers, but herein also lay their danger. Being independent, they could not be relied upon if the state ran out of money. Moreover, as with other mercenaries in history they could become more powerful than states and take over as rulers. *Condottieri* regularly did so in the Italian city-states, and Albrecht von Wallenstein, the most successful *condottiero*, who raised an army of over 100,000 men for the Holy German Emperor during the Thirty Years War, became a threat even to such a powerful master.[42]

For these reasons, the state assumed supreme control over the organization and command of armies. From the second half of the seventeenth century (a century earlier in the Spanish Empire), the state managed armies directly through its developing bureaucratic apparatus. Even then, however, it continued to depend on enterprising individuals, usually local dignitaries, for the lower-level organization. Commissioned as colonels by the state, they raised, administered, and led regiments for standard lump payments, while subcontracting companies to captains.[43] In France, for example, the state took over these functions only after the Seven Year War, on the eve of the Revolution. Similar processes affected navies, which in the sixteenth century still predominantly relied on privately owned ships commissioned or requisitioned for a campaign. 'Privateers' licensed to harass enemy trade continued to play a major role up until the eighteenth century.

Let us now examine the growth of large-scale standing armies, that central element of the 'military revolution', and enquire how they stand in a comparative perspective. As already noted above, a large state's size generally favoured standing armies. The European experience presents no special case. Distance was a key factor.[44] European armies grew increasingly permanent largely because the new large states fought protracted wars in remote theatres of operations. Even though the much cheaper militias were greatly encouraged by rulers, they remained invariably insignificant, because their active employment consistently floundered on their unwillingness to serve for long periods of time and far away from their home territories.[45]

As for the size of the armies, I have already noted in Chapter 11 that historically 1 per cent of the population constituted the upper *sustainable* limit of purely professional troops. The Roman Principate's ratio, as fixed by Augustus, of some 250,000–300,000 regular soldiers to an imperial population of over 40 million exemplifies this golden rule. As the later Empire was obliged to increase that number substantially, it found itself locked in an economic–military vicious circle. In this respect, too, the new European states do not appear to have diverged much from historical standards.[46] As a result of rising agricultural productivity, especially in northern Europe, they were more densely populated than the lands of antiquity. Gibbon noted that Louis XIV of France possessed an army that was as large as that of imperial Rome, even though France (ancient Gaul) constituted only one province of the ancient Roman Empire.[47] However, at 20 million, France's population was four times larger than that of Roman Gaul and about half as large as that of the entire Roman Empire. Furthermore, Louis XIV's increase of the number of French troops to a peak of 350,000–400,000, or almost 2 per cent of the population, during his later wars around 1700, was as unsustainable as the increase in the number of Roman troops to as much as double Augustus's ratio during the wars of the triumviri, the civil wars of the third century AD, and the Late Empire. The exceptionally large French army was kept for only a few years under dire military circumstances, contributed to France's defeat through exhaustion, and was reduced to a peace establishment of around 150,000, below 1 per cent of the country's population.

Earlier, the Spanish Empire, with a European population of some 12–13 million, surpassed the 1 per cent mark in 1555 and the 2 per cent mark in the 1630s. However, even though this increase was partly financed by the flow of bullion from Spain's American possessions, which by the late sixteenth century accounted for nearly a quarter of the state's income,[48] such troop levels were unsustainable and precipitated Spain's bankruptcy and decline from power. The Dutch, with a European population of about 1.5 million, were exceptional in their ability to sustain an army of 50,000, or 3 per cent, during the 1630s (in addition to a powerful navy), but they, too, overtaxed themselves when Louis XIV's wars against them during the last three decades of the century forced them to maintain as many as 100,000 men under arms with a European population that still numbered less than 2 million. Seventeenth-century Sweden under Gustavus Adolphus and his successors, with a population of less than one and a half million in Sweden and Finland proper and perhaps double this when the 'empire' is counted, kept armies that occasionally exceeded 100,000 (a peak of 180,000, or 6 per cent). But Sweden was able to do so only by living in and off foreign territories through exceptionally effective looting and extortion of her neighbours in Germany and the Baltic, where her armies campaigned. (More normally successful armies appear to have been able to squeeze about a quarter of their cost from enemy territories by way of requisitions and indemnities.) In addition, Sweden was heavily subsidized by France during the Thirty Years War. Once she lost the military pre-eminence that made these measures possible, Sweden rapidly shrank to her natural size.[49] Eighteenth-century Prussia under Frederick II, 'the Great', who with a population of about 5 million held a 250,000 soldiers under arms during the Seven Years War (1756–63) and more than 150,000 in peacetime, or 3–5 per cent, employed similar methods.[50] In addition, Prussia, which was more efficiently run than her neighbours and was wholly dedicated to her army, revived (similar to Charles XII's Sweden) the principle of keeping some of her soldiers on a semi-professional basis by releasing them for long agricultural leaves during parts of the year (the canton system), and received heavy subsidies from her British ally during the Seven Years War. Her extreme concentration on the military elicited Count Mirabeau's famous remark that Prussia was an army that possessed a state rather than the other way around.

Britain, with a home population of 9 million at the advent of the eighteenth century (which began to grow rapidly in the later part of the century), expanded her army and navy to over 100,000 men, or 1 per cent, during her first major European involvement, the Nine Years War (1689–97). She came close to 200,000, or 2 per cent, during the Seven Years War and the American revolutionary war. However, these were peak war numbers, and Britain's peacetime establishment was less than half this. On the other hand, her navy and army were engaged globally and their provision was particularly costly. Moreover, Britain's wartime subsidies to her allies amounted to between a fifth and a quarter of her entire defence expenditure. During the Seven Years War, for example, she paid for 100,000 allied (mostly Prussian) troops. Costs and manpower figures continued to spiral upwards during the Napoleonic Wars, when Britain was able to match the French revolutionary and imperial might with the proceeds of burgeoning industrialization. In 1809, for example, Britain employed some 375,000 men in her army and navy. With a population of 12 million plus 5 million in Ireland, this figure constituted over 2 per cent. Subsidies to her Continental allies during the final campaigns (1812–15) comprised the same proportion of Britain's much larger defence expenditure as previously, this time paying for nearly 500,000 allied troops, mostly Russian, Prussian, and Austrian.[51] However, these again were peak war effort years that could not be and were not sustained indefinitely.

Thus, on the face of it, the much discussed steep rise in the size of the European armies during early modernity, although very real, barely seems to represent an increase over historical levels of mobilization of standing armies in large states. When examined in broader, comparative, terms, it was not in fact such a novelty. Indeed, here, as in general, the European case involves an optical distortion. Some changes that seem revolutionary in early modern Europe because of that civilization's peculiar ascent from very low levels of political concentration, urbanism, and commercialism within only a few centuries, were incremental in other civilizations that had maintained greater cultural and political continuity, having experienced no such severe regression as the European Dark Age.

Similarly, it is not at all clear that the early modern European powers were exceptionally war prone by historical standards, as they are widely assumed to have been. Between 1500 and 1750 each of the European great powers engaged in war more than 50 per cent of the time.[52] However, as already noted, the pluralist European political system had always been highly competitive. In antiquity, the fierce intra-polity conflict was alleviated only by the *pax Romana*. And medieval fragmentation simply bred incessant violence at the local level, so-called private war, in addition to state war. Furthermore, it is far from evident that the other great centres of civilization, in the Near East, India, China, and Japan, were less war prone than Europe, again depending on the fluctuations in the competitiveness of their respective systems and the aggressiveness of imperial hegemons, as well as on the frequency of civil wars in each of them. And while central resource mobilization certainly increased by leaps and bounds in early modern Europe from its low medieval levels, most Asian powers possessed a developed resource mobilization capacity from earlier on.

Much the same applies to the advent of firearms, with a transforming effect on society and state, in Europe as well as elsewhere in Eurasia—at least before the eighteenth century—that is often much exaggerated. As Chase has shown so well, firearms proved the most useful for the people of west–central Europe because geography dictated that pitched battles and sieges, rather than the elusive light horsemen of the steppe, constituted their main military challenge. Fighting against Europeans in the Balkans, the Ottomans adopted firearms no less successfully. All the same, other, sometimes earlier, economic, social, and political developments had been mainly responsible for the transformation of the European state system from the later Middle Ages. And in the Ottoman Empire, as well as in other civilizations of Eurasia where firearms replaced older weapons and reshaped battle tactics and siege craft, the already developed state armies otherwise exhibited few changes. Although incorporating artillery and infantry firearms, there was little fundamental change in army and state structure, organization, and social composition between the Ottomans and their Turkic and Iranian predecessors or Mamluk and Safavid contemporaries, between Mughal India and the earlier Delhi Sultanate, and between the Ming or Manchu (Ch'ing) and their predecessors in China. Nor were any of these powers inferior to Europe in military might, to say the least. The Ottomans, the only one that bordered Europe, exerted heavy military pressure on it for centuries. Thus in historical terms the much-used concept of 'gunpowder empires' has far less to it than is commonly assumed.

The introduction of firearms was undoubtedly a historical landmark. Firearms transformed field and siege warfare, and they were indispensable for keeping up militarily in wars of conquest within the sedentary zone.

477

Manchu horsemen overrunning Ming artillery and musketeers during
their conquest of China

The Battle of Nagashino (1575). Oda Nobunaga's infantry, taking cover behind prepared obstacles, employ firearms to break Takeda's cavalry in the civil wars that would end in Japan's reunification

The Mamluks who ruled Egypt and Syria succumbed to the Ottomans (1516–17) because they fell behind in the adoption of firearms. The Iranian Safavids were able to escape a similar fate only because their light horsemen adjusted their tactics and proved too mobile to pin down in the vast and arid terrain of their homeland and the frontier territories that separated them from the Ottomans. The Delhi Sultanate's fall in 1526 to Babur, founder of the Mughal Empire, owed much to the latter's superior use of firearms. After the Portuguese introduced the gun into Japan in 1543, warlord Oda Nobunaga employed muskets decisively in the Battle of Nagashino (1575), and gun power continued to rise in significance during the civil wars that led to unification. To cite Chase again, as Japan, similar to western Europe, was sheltered from the steppe nomads, firearms proved more useful in its internal wars than they did anywhere else in east Asia. How decisively they contributed to Japan's unification, which, as with the European new monarchies, had been long in the making—propelled by far deeper sociopolitical processes—is, however, another matter, at least in my judgement. In any event, the development of firearms later stagnated in Tokugawa Japan because the unified and isolated island kingdom no longer faced any serious military challenge.[53]

By the same token and to summarize this brief survey: where there was no decisive *imbalance* in the possession of firearms, the effect of firearms on military affairs and, through them, on society and state—in Europe and elsewhere—was not so revolutionary. As scholars have recognized, gunpowder exercised a far more revolutionary effect at sea, in combination with that second element of Bacon's trio of modernity—ocean navigation.[54]

MASTERY OF THE SEAS AND THE COMMERCIAL–FINANCIAL REVOLUTION

The establishment of a European trading system after 1500 which for the first time in history encompassed the entire globe, connecting the various continents via the oceans, constituted the single most important factor in the shaping of modernity and was the true engine of the 'European miracle'. It transformed European society, economy, and state. Markets grew to play an unprecedented role, granting some European states greater resources and, hence, greater power than other states, while making Europe as a whole increasingly wealthier and more powerful in relation to other parts of the world. Ultimately, the global trading system stimulated industrialization, and a quantum leap in wealth and power. Although challenged by some recent scholarship, this picture, originating with both Adam Smith and Marx, remains, in my view, broadly valid.[55]

I can only briefly address that intriguing and much-discussed question: why was it Europe, rather than any of the other civilizations of Eurasia, that connected the continuously expanding inter-regional trade systems (somewhat misleadingly referred to as 'world systems') into the first global system.[56] Again, the process that matured abruptly around 1500 had been long in the making throughout Eurasia. During the late Middle Ages, Europe itself developed dynamic trading networks that connected the Mediterranean, Atlantic, North, and Baltic Seas that surrounded it. Whereas in the ancient Roman realm around the Mediterranean low climatic and ecological diversity equalized conditions in terms of both agricultural produce and manufacture, thereby restricting exchange, far greater diversification between the north and south of Europe stimulated trade not only of luxuries but also of bulk staple goods.[57] The lateen sail, originating in the Indian Ocean, arrived in Mediterranean Europe via the Arabs in the early Middle Ages. The compass, widely used by the Chinese for navigation by the eleventh century, reached Europe in the late twelfth century.

Indeed, other regional networks were as advanced as, if not more advanced than, the European one. Arab and Moslem merchants dominated the Indian Oceans and its tributaries. Great imperial Chinese fleets comprising huge multi-mast sailing ships, larger than any that Europe would know until the seventeenth century, were led in the early fifteenth century (1405–33) in great naval expeditions by the eunuch admiral Cheng Huo, sailing as far as east Africa.[58] And yet it was the Europeans who fully mastered the world's seas and reached the east, rather than the other way around. Building on their earlier interest in the gold and slaves of west Africa and seeking to break the Venetian–Mamluk monopoly over Europe's spice trade through Egypt, the Portuguese perfected the navigational techniques and sailing ships that were necessary for circumnavigating Africa.[59] With Europe anyway located at the extreme end of Eurasia, this route meant that

Europeans had far longer to travel by sea in order to reach their desired trade partners in south and east Asia.

Asians had less reason for carrying out such long-range sea voyages because they were geographically more conveniently placed and because the poorer European markets offered little attraction for them. Europe's disadvantages thus proved to be a positive challenge. At the other end of Eurasia, China's leaders had good reason to feel that their rich and sophisticated civilization already possessed everything that they needed. After Cheng Huo returned from east Africa in 1433, the Ming decided to dismantle their advanced fleet of ocean-going junks and banned further long-range voyages. State funded, these voyages had been costly and their rewards dubious. A renewed nomadic threat from the north directed the imperial government's attention and resources elsewhere. Nor was long-range naval activity allowed to proceed in private hands and along more commercial lines, because the despotic Chinese state with its Confucian mandarin bureaucracy disliked and suspected trade, traders, and independent capital. Therefore, the Portuguese met with little effective resistance at sea when Vasco da Gama burst into the Indian Ocean (1498). And when Columbus, in the service of the Spanish monarchs, crossed the Atlantic en route to east Asia and stumbled on to America (1492), the natives could offer little effective resistance on land. An additional huge prize was thus quite unexpectedly reaped as a consequence of Europe's ocean-going capability. Within a few years the world was opened up for European exploration and profit.

The military aspects of this exploration have been thoroughly covered by scholars and can be summarized briefly here. In the Americas, the most advanced native civilizations—powerful political structures with populations in the millions and great urban centres—were nevertheless based on Stone to early Bronze Age technology and were separated from the European newcomers by millennia of technological evolution. They proved to be easy prey for the mere handfuls of Spanish *conquistadores*, armed with steel weapons, horses, and firearms, aided by the element of surprise and cultural shock, and supported by local allies. Lack of immunization to Old World epidemic diseases, which devastated the natives before and during the *conquistadores'* arrival and were to reduce the population of the Americas by perhaps as much as 90 per cent within a century, proved to be at least as, if not more, detrimental to their chances of reasserting themselves in the face of the invaders. Elsewhere on the continent, where the native population was more dispersed and lacked developed political structures, it was mass European immigration and agricultural settlement over the centuries that ultimately conquered the land, much as we have seen with respect to the original agricultural expansions.[60]

By contrast, in south and east Asia during the first two centuries of their presence, the Europeans were far too weak to challenge the mighty empires, on the margins of which they were more or less tolerated. However, these empires were decidedly continental and inward looking, showing little interest in the sea. And those local rulers and merchants in the smaller states and seaports from Oman to Malaya who engaged in maritime trading proved weaker than the Europeans. By sheer historical coincidence, guns were now making the sailing, traditional merchant ship a superior warship to the oared galley that had dominated sea warfare in the narrow seas.[61] The European sailing ships, heavily armed with guns, which from the early sixteenth century were massed along the decks, firing through gun-ports located along the ship's sides, mastered the south and east Asian seas and much of their trade.[62]

Yet, while gun power was a significant contributing factor to the

The *Mary Rose*, Henry VIII's warship (c. 1545), showing the gun-ports and general architecture of the new sailing warship

Europeans' new global success, other factors were more decisive in deciding *which* Europeans would reap the advantages of that success—economically and, consequently, also politically and militarily. For, as we have already seen, the pluralist European state system—unlike that of Asia—was highly competitive. Although pre-industrial European economy remained predominantly agrarian, mastery over markets of a global scale and a growing manufacturing sector, which prospered by virtue of that mastery, became a very significant source of wealth, of a more liquid sort than previously known. The emergence of a global trading system thus became the prime catalyst for the formation of capitalism in Europe.[63] Indeed, the sheer unprecedented scale of the global trading system transformed power relationships between and within European societies, more than any previous commercial supremacy ever had. The states that won out in the contest for domination over global trade secured the resources that made them strong in the European power struggle. And it was the traders' states that were best equipped to win the global trade contest.[64]

Whereas earlier in history power brought wealth, while wealth translated into power more equivocally, wealth and power were becoming increasingly interchangeable. No longer was there such a thing as a poor strong power. Consequently, to survive, power had to serve the interests of the producing and trading economy, and the more it did so the more power was generated. Any shackles put on social wealth creation by the state's political and military elite only undermined the power of that elite in competition with other states. For the first time in history parasitic warrior states and warrior elites were falling behind economically productive states and elites in terms of *power*. Economic performance was becoming the key to power, and the capitalist trading and manufacturing economy increasingly spearheaded economic performance.

Let us now return to the 'military revolution'. It has been argued here that in historical, comparative terms there seems to have been no *radical* novelty in the size of the new standing European armies. And yet, if armies and navies together grew somewhat larger in comparison with those of other large states and if hardware such as guns marginally increased the cost of war, there were three main sources for such possible growth. First, growth in agricultural productivity per capita since antiquity appears to have marginally increased Europe's surpluses. Second, there was the income that came from extra-European activities, such as the flow of American bullion into the Spanish treasury (a mixed blessing, which deepened Spain's economic retardation as a 'rentier state'), and earnings from global trading and prosperous manufacturing that were mostly reaped by the Dutch and English. Third, the early modern state developed deficit financing to historically unprecedented levels. These three sources were intricately intertwined, and the European states varied in the efficiency with which they tapped them and, hence, in their success in the great powers' struggle.

In the first place, the states differed in their taxing ability. The larger the state, the greater its aggregate tax revenues, yet there were also disadvantages to size in early modern Europe. As already noted, the new, territorially 'composite', and 'absolutist' European state, with its regional and class privileges, probably taxed less efficiently than, for example, the Roman Empire. The main tax burden in imperial Spain lay on Castile, and all attempts to equalize it throughout the Empire (something pursued most rigorously by chief minister Count-Duke of Olivares during the Spanish decline) met with very limited success and precipitated rebellions in the Low Countries, Catalonia, Naples, Sicily, and Portugal, which lost the first and last of these. In France, provincial privileges, defended by local assemblies, were almost equally entrenched. And in the eighteenth century, the territorially 'composite' Austrian Empire faced even greater taxing difficulties than France. Smaller and more homogeneous states, such as England, the Dutch Republic, and Prussia, were ultimately able to tax more evenly. But England, too, lost her American colonies when she tried to spread the burden of taxation on to her imperial periphery. With the exceptions of militia service in the overseas colonies themselves and, from the mid-eighteenth century, regular *sepoy* service in India, it is therefore justified to exclude the extra-European population under the European powers when calculating their ratios of standing forces.

Mastery over global trade and a prosperous manufacturing sector were two other factors that enhanced taxation efficiency in various ways. Indeed, their indirect benefits transcended their direct contributions to national wealth. A comparison of the national wealth of Britain and France during their eighteenth-century struggle indicates that, because France's population was about three times greater than Britain's and agriculture was still the largest sector of the economy, the French economy was more than double that of Britain.[65] And yet it is agreed that Britain won the naval–military contest by virtue of her superior financial capability. The more liquid financial resources of Britain's far more commercialized economy constituted the key to her success.[66]

Furthermore, the trading states excelled in the development of deficit financing, raising low-interest loans in the new financial markets and successfully servicing a large national debt. This significant expansion of states' ability to tap social resources for war supplemented earlier, more traditional means. As wars were irregularly spread over time and involved huge spending, states throughout history resorted to special measures in order to pay for them. Several options were open to them. They taxed surplus earnings more heavily in wartime, as with the 'extraordinary' taxes approved by representative assemblies in the new European states from the thirteenth century on. Moreover, in their efforts to outpace each other, antagonists throughout history were driven to exceed the surpluses of the wartime years, making use of savings and accumulated capital, both public and private. States could sell public property, most notably land, and spend money kept by the state and in temples. They could also squeeze capital from private hands, through more or less arbitrary means.

The richer and more vulnerable the potential source of money, the greater was the temptation. Merchants were everywhere an obvious source of disposable capital, although they were more defenceless in the despotic east. The Jews were a particularly easy target in medieval Europe, where states repeatedly squeezed them dry to finance wars, before deporting them. In availing themselves of money kept in religious institutions, states often acted with those institutions' consent for the purpose of national and religious salvation. But violent confiscation also took place where normal religious piety or the appearance of it was not required, or could be turned against the targeted institutions. The wealth of the aristocracy presented a far more difficult target, because the aristocracy were powerful and, indeed, constituted part of the state's ruling elite. This usually became vulnerable only in the context of civil wars, when rivals were exposed to proscriptions and confiscations, and when naked force by contending army leaders became the rule.

Yet seizure of capital had its disadvantages even where the rulers possessed despotic power and could carry it out more or less at will—for example, heavy levies imposed on merchants could kill the goose that lay the golden egg. The merchants could be brought to ruin, lose their business to foreigners, or take it elsewhere. Furthermore, where property rights offered no security against an ever-present threat of arbitrary confiscation, economic activity was inhibited and money was driven into hiding, hoarded, and thereby taken out of circulation. Thus unlimited power to dip into people's pockets proved too easy an option, precisely because it constituted an almost irresistible temptation. It was in those states where political power was limited, most notably because the rich themselves ruled the state or were powerful enough within it to safeguard property rights, that a different avenue to tap accumulated 'private' capital for public spending—predominantly on war—emerged: loans.[67]

Republican Rome offers a prime example. Massive mobilization during the protracted and ruinous First and Second Punic Wars exhausted the Roman state. To pay for the wars the state doubled and tripled the 'extraordinary' property war tax that it levied from its citizens (*tributum*), sold public land, and used the sacred emergency treasure. But, in addition, it loaned money from the wealthy citizens, most of whom probably belonged to the leading senatorial class.[68] When both antagonists became completely exhausted in the final stage of the First Punic War, it was the wealthy citizens who pushed the Roman state to carry out one more effort, lending it the money to build yet another large war fleet, with its successful appearance at sea driving Carthage to sue for peace.[69] Of course, the Roman elite were not only paid back their money but were also the direct beneficiary of the fruits of war in one of the most successful war-making states ever, with a constantly expanding wealth. Rome's wars thus constituted an excellent investment. By comparison, things were more ambivalent in the commercial republican city communes of Renaissance Italy and Germany. Financially advanced, they greatly developed the system by which the huge 'extraordinary' cost of war was spread over the peace years by means of loans and the selling of bonds that were to be paid back with interest. However, the strategy of borrowing capital (some of it compulsorily, some voluntarily) was resorted to in lieu of levying direct taxes that would have fallen mostly on the rich and which the municipal elite was reluctant to pay. This tenuous tax basis had the following interrelated consequences: public debt spiralled and annual interest payments took up a substantial part of the cities' expenditure, which the cities, in turn, found increasingly difficult to service because of tax income shortage. Therefore, they occasionally resorted to the suspension of interest payments. As the financial burden mounted owing to the cities' losing struggle against the rising territorial states, the system pretty much broke down.[70]

For borrowing, too, was a slippery road that possessed its own dangerous temptations, which the new European national states did not escape either. To finance war, the state rulers from the thirteenth century onward turned to credit, for which they had two main sources. One was again the vast capital accumulated in the great European trading cities. As the state rulers lacked despotic powers and as in any case some of these trading and banking centres lay outside their borders, they resorted to borrowing in a European-wide money market, initially dominated by the Italian (and Flemish) cities and, by the sixteenth century, centred in Augsburg, Genoa, Antwerp, and Lyons. Indeed, as with the international market for hired soldiers, resorting to international loans had the additional advantage of tapping foreign resources for war. To cover the annual interest payments and service the loans, rulers imposed a special war tax for each loan. Yet, as the lending bankers were largely foreigners or, at any rate, were separate from the state, there was a great temptation to default on the payments in difficult times, when the state's expenditure on war rocketed, rather than cut down on expenses and bear the consequences in terms of political and military losses. Thus the kings of Spain repeatedly defaulted, in 1557, 1560, 1575, 1596, 1607, 1627, 1647, 1652, 1660, and 1662, famously ruining the banking house of the Fuggers of Augsburg, the richest in the world, and many others. The French monarchy did the same in 1558, 1564, 1598, 1648, and 1661. However, defaulting on payments backfired no less, if not more, than confiscation, ruining not only the bankers but also the state's credit. Loans became scarcer and carried higher interest rates to compensate for the greater risk. A vicious spiral was created.

The early modern European state also resorted to another source of credit, raised on an individual basis from members of the wealthy elite. The state mainly tapped this resource through the sale of offices, both civil and military. Individuals' cash investment in the purchase of offices was earned back through regular state pay over the years, as well as from the opportunities for profit offered by the embezzlement of public money, such as that allocated by the state for the pay and supply of troops in the regiments and companies. Indeed, here, too, the easy temptations of credit created a vicious spiral of costs, coupled with inefficiency. Not only was the state's administrative machinery corrupted by the state's need to raise money, but the ever-increasing sale of 'venal' offices for that purpose expanded the number of office holders in France (the worst case) from around 5,000 in 1515 to some

50,000 in 1665. By 1787 the number of French army officers had swollen to 36,000, about a third of whom were in active service and all drawing pay. There were 1,171 general officers compared with Prussia's just over 80 and Austria's 350. Officers' pay consumed half of the French army's budget. Indeed, as with any credit snowball, massive repayment costs in the form of salaries ultimately swallowed up the proceeds from the system, leaving behind only its all-pervasive negative legacy.[71]

In general, credit can be profitable only if it is resorted to responsibly, if it is kept in adequate proportion to income and spending, and, most importantly, if it brings gains that ultimately exceed the cost of the borrowing. In this delicate balancing act, seventeenth-century Spain and eighteenth-century France eventually found themselves on the losing side and in increasingly desperate straits, overburdened with growing debts that they were unable to service. By contrast, in seventeenth-century Holland and eighteenth-century Britain, deficit financing formed part of a winning package. As already hinted above, flourishing trade was the key to that difference. Successively in the Netherlands and England, it created great financial wealth and a sophisticated money market, where new instruments such as stock exchanges and a national bank were used to float massive loans, reaching a wide internal and external investing public on market principles. Interest rates on state borrowing fell to as low as 2.5–4.0 per cent, roughly half those paid by France to its creditors, and perhaps a third to a sixth the average historical price of credit to states.[72] There was much more to the story, however.

MARKET REGIMES AND MILITARY PROWESS

Rich markets and sophisticated financial tools comprised only one element in a wider political–economic system. The high financial credibility of the Dutch and British states reduced the risk of default on payment and lowered interest rates, while lower interest rates in turn increased these states' credibility. But underlying that high credibility was the fact that, rather than constituting an alien body, the state served the interests of the mercantile economy and, indeed, was largely controlled by the mercantile classes who dominated its powerful representative assemblies. Not only did strong representative governments in seventeenth-century Holland and eighteenth-century Britain provide greater security against default, but also the represented elite were willing to pay higher taxes in order to finance wars that served their interests. In the Netherlands the wars initially defended independence and later fostered a trading mastery, whereas in Britain after the Glorious Revolution (1688) they were fought in defence of the new representative regime against the allies of the deposed Stuarts and, later, in support of a booming trading empire. A broader tax base and increased income in turn made it possible for the Netherlands and Britain to raise larger loans, which they were able to service and repay more easily.

As we have seen throughout history, the greater the incorporation of social groups into the state and the bigger their stake, the greater was their commitment; the more alien the state and its aims, the less voluntary support could it expect. Indeed, as Montesquieu observed in *The Spirit of the Laws* (Part 2, Book 13, especially Chapter 12), the freer the state the more taxes was it able to levy. The Netherlands and Britain were the most heavily taxed, whereas absolutist France, conceding to exemptions to the aristocracy, had lower tax revenues for its size, and the despotic Ottoman Empire was the most lightly taxed. An earlier generation of historians emphasized the greater taxing power of the new centralized absolutist state compared with feudal fragmentation. But more recently it has been recognized that the representative–inclusive state regimes were even stronger and more able to generate and harness social resources or 'infrastructural power' than the seemingly despotic absolutist states. If early modern European states variably taxed an estimated 5–15 per cent of national income, Britain's wartime taxation exceeded 20 per cent in the eighteenth century, two to three times the per capita taxation of France, and four times Britain's own taxation level before the Glorious Revolution of 1688.[73] As with the Dutch Republic, this was partly the result of Britain's superior commercial wealth. Still, no (heavy) taxation without representation turns out to have been not merely a North American Revolutionary slogan but a more general reality.

The representative institutions that emerged in the Europe of the late Middle Ages broke the rule that we have encountered in earlier history, according to which freedom could be achieved only in small polities, whereas large states were necessarily despotic.[74] Originally, representative institutions emerged in the unique circumstances of feudal Europe, where the rising monarchies that still exercised only limited authority over a fragmented political landscape required the consent of aristocrats and burghers for taxation. Indeed, as it gained strength, the monarchy in some of the states succeeded in rolling back the power of the assemblies—that is, became more despotic (although because of west–central Europe's greater social power distribution and ensuing traditions, the monarchies' arbitrary power never reached that of the Asian state). However, in some other European states the national assemblies held their own and grew to dominate. These latter states thus combined the freedoms and participation of small polities, such as the city-state, with the large size of a country-state.[75] Participation, in turn, meant that the state had to become much more attuned to the wishes and interests of the represented, rather than to serve the ambitions of autocratic rulers; the represented became effective rulers and the state's business became their own, or vice versa. The cardinal question, then, is who they were.

In Poland, for example, only the aristocracy was represented in the *seym*, whereas the burghers were excluded. In this aristocratic 'republic', where the monarchy became elective, the landed aristocracy's social dominance and regional autonomy constituted the overriding consideration. Representation thus bred extreme decentralization of power that ultimately made that once powerful country an easy prey to its neighbours. By contrast, in the United Provinces, which in effect comprised confederated city communes and their countryside, the assemblies (States) were dominated by the commercial municipal oligarchy (particularly that of Holland, and Amsterdam within it), who co-operated, not without great strain, with the princely Stadtholders of the House of Orange. Although institutionally the United Provinces constituted anything but a centralized state, their trading centres were generators of wealth and, therefore, of power, and their commercial elites shared an interest in investing heavily in the common defence and prosperity.

England is the most intriguing case, because she was dominated neither by the aristocracy nor by the merchants alone. As in other large 'territorial' states, both lords and burghers sat in its national representative assembly, the Parliament. However, these estates' interests contrasted less than was generally the case elsewhere in Europe, because it was in England that a momentous transformation took place, changing the relationship that had prevailed earlier in world history between the two main methods of wealth acquisition—forceful extraction and productive creation—of which the former had usually held the ascendancy. To be sure, the English social–political–military nobility did not give up its power but rather transformed in response to the great attraction of the vastly expanding markets. As Adam Smith has observed, this historical transformation took place from the late Middle Ages on, when feudal lords in England, rather than live off rent extracted from serf peasants (which inhibited rise in productivity), found it more profitable to produce to a burgeon manufacturing and trading urban market of a national and west European scale.[76] They then moved on to participate directly in that market as it expanded globally. As already noted, scale was the key to that process. The larger the market economy grew, the more profitable in comparison with the small-scale, fundamentally autarkic, agricultural lordship that it became, and the more it lured members of the aristocratic elite. Crossing the line that had traditionally separated aristocrats from merchants, they turned from rent extractors into fully fledged commercial enterprisers.

The English elite thus became as interested as, indeed more interested than, anyone else in the commercial prosperity of the country and ready to invest in it militarily. It was these processes that turned England into the leading European trading nation and the spearhead of modernization. As Marx has pointed out, the new economic–social–political regime was still based on massive coercion by the commercialized aristocratic–bourgeois elite, who enforced the regime on the non-represented populace through state and law. All the same, Marx maintained that the capitalist market economy differed from earlier forms of social organization in that it was geared towards production, and by the fact that its extraction mechanism was predominantly economic, rather than based on the direct use or threat of violence.

Yet, if in some European states commercial profiteering became increasingly more promising to the elite as an avenue to wealth than forceful extraction, and peaceful free trade could be safeguarded throughout the realm by the state leviathan, in the relationships *between* states violent conflict remained fully intermixed with economic competition. Throughout history traders strove to monopolize resources and markets by force if they were powerful enough to do so, rather than share them in open competition with others. Now, however, the game assumed global dimensions. Rivals were denied access to home markets by regulations and tariffs, and were directly pressurized by war with the intention of weakening them, forcing them into commercial concessions, and banishing them from colonies and foreign markets. Labelled mercantilism, this commercial–military complex became the prime driving force behind the incessant wars of the seventeenth and eighteenth centuries between the powers that lay on the shores of the Atlantic and of the North and Baltic Seas.[77] These wars took place simultaneously in Europe and overseas, most notably in south-east Asia and India, the Caribbean, and North America. The historical bottom line of these wars is familiar enough: in the seventeenth century the Netherlands took over Portugal's trading empire in the east, as well as expanding their control over bulk trade in European waters.[78] However, later in that century their trading supremacy came under heavy military and naval pressure from two much larger and stronger powers, France and England, pressure that overtaxed Dutch strength. In the eighteenth century, Britain emerged victorious from her contest with France, driving the French out of Canada and India and establishing herself as the foremost naval and trading nation.[79]

It is, however, the more general aspect of these historical developments that concerns us here. The 'military revolution' was closely associated with the European commercial and financial revolutions because the vast concentration of capital amassed by Europe's transformation into the hub of a global colonial and trading system fuelled the great powers' race towards larger standing armies and navies that were maintained in distant theatres of war year after year. As we have seen, one means to harness this massive capital accumulation for war was highly developed deficit financing. In contrast to confiscation and taxation, this method ensured that private capital would become voluntarily and easily available to the state, rather than be defended by the rich and socially powerful, driven into hiding, or taken elsewhere. It also attracted foreign resources. However, easily borrowed money was made available in the present only by mortgaging the future. It constituted a more or less prudent investment in that future, and like any 'leveraged' investment was a high-risk–high-gain one. A Darwinian race for credit grew to dominate the arms race between the powers. All of them pushed borrowing to the limit and beyond it, building up massive debts.

The Spanish debt in 1623 spiralled to ten years of royal receipts.[80] Powers such as Spain, with a credit status that had deteriorated, ultimately lost out in the race, having been caught up in a hopeless financial tangle. In the French case, such a tangle famously brought down the monarchy and the *Ancien*

Régime. France fell victim to the crisis even though in absolute terms her debt amounted to only some 60 per cent of Britain's; in relative terms her debt burden was smaller still, because it equalled just over half of France's gross national product (GNP), whereas Britain's debt was almost twice her GNP.[81] Indeed, the British national debt leapt upward with every war during the eighteenth century, rocketing to a staggering 20 times her average annual tax income after the American War of Independence. Between half and two-thirds of Britain's tax income were spent annually on (low) interest payments to service the debt, which paid for 30–40 per cent of her spending during the wars. Importantly, around 20 per cent of the debt represented foreign investment.[82] Britain was the ultimate winner in the 'leveraged' race only because victories gave her a colonial empire and commanding position over global trade, which in turn also boosted her home economy in a period of substantial economic expansion. Wealth paid for war, whereas war laid the foundation for greater wealth creation. It was the wealthy and economically more efficient that won out in that race.

The military and naval race obviously constituted a tremendous waste in terms of resources. In addition to the massive devastation and loss of productivity, war and debt servicing caused by war comprised the largest single item of state expenditure during early modernity, ranging from around 40 per cent in peacetime to 80–90 per cent during the frequent wars. And, as already noted, between 1500 and 1750 each of the European great powers engaged in war more than 50 per cent of the time.[83] Scholars have debated whether or not this 'waste' proved economically beneficial in the final analysis, owing to the spin-off effects on a developing economy of large state investment in metallurgy, mining, shipbuilding, and supply.[84] But, more significantly perhaps, war formed an integral part of a historical process in which more productive market economies triumphed over traditional economic–political regimes. The European and global penetration of the market economy was made possible and was greatly speeded up by the close interaction of economic success and military superiority. If this was the case, then early modern war carried a huge dividend in terms of economic development. Indeed, because of the strong interaction that existed between wealth and power, states were driven to make themselves economically more productive in order to stay competitive in the great powers race, no less than the other way around. For this purpose they undertook economic, social, and political reform.[85] War thus played a central role in propelling forward the process of modernization in general.

We have already cited the examples from western Europe, wherein the market economy famously went hand in hand with representative government and political liberalism. Developments in the Netherlands and England precipitated those in France, where the combination of a growing market economy and internal social evolution, on the one hand, and irresolvable war financing and debt crisis, on the other, eventually brought about the Revolution. However, one may argue that our concentration on the west European mercantilist race is geographically restricted, leading to biased conclusions in a progressivist 'Whig' vein. After all, the new great powers that emerged in central and eastern Europe during the eighteenth century—Prussia and Russia—were neither global maritime traders possessing advanced financial markets, nor representative and liberal regimes. Both these powers were autocracies that ruled despotically and often ruthlessly, imposing centralization, levying taxes, and raising large armies. Their first steps to modernization actually involved greater coercion, the suppression of assemblies, and deepening enserfment of the peasantry within an absolutist–(neo-)feudal–estate-service state.[86]

And yet in Russia and Prussia, too, economic modernization and, consequently, social and political modernization were the necessary preconditions of power. Put in somewhat simplified terms: whereas in England the agent of both economic modernization and the growth of national might was a wealth-seeking, commercialized, social elite, power-seeking autocratic state rulers were the agents of both these processes in Russia and Prussia, where a commercialized social elite was absent or weak and had to be created by the state. The 'enlightened' rulers of these states were driven to drag their respective countries to modernize—cultivating industries and other economic ventures, establishing state bureaucracies, and drawing on foreign expertise and capital—in order to create the tax base and manufacturing infrastructure that would allow them to qualify for the great powers' league. Time and again in the subsequent centuries, it was above all the spur of the great powers' struggle that would propel these states to initiate new waves of reform so as not to fall hopelessly behind. Economic and social modernization was enforced on them through the medium of war rather than being voluntarily generated from within. Indeed, growing modernization necessarily drove them into intractable domestic tensions

495

and contradictions, conflicting with and undermining the authority of the autocratic regime and traditional agrarian elite that ruled these societies. Modernization increasingly forced them to incorporate wider segments of society into the state in order to remain competitive in the economic cum military race. Market regime, then and later, was not merely an economic concept but also a social–political and, indeed, a military one.

Thus the modernizing reforms initiated by the Hohenzollerns in Prussia and by Peter the Great and his predecessors and successors in Russia were pushed further—despite deep autocratic apprehension and obstruction-ism—after Prussia's defeat by Napoleon's national mass armies (1806) and in the wake of Russia's defeat in the Crimean War (1853–6) to the industrial–military might of Britain and France. Soon after, the same processes would begin to affect China and Japan.[87] The growth of capitalist market econ-omies and national mass participation within some societies, while directly transforming other societies, would never have succeeded as sweepingly as they did, 'battering down all Chinese walls' built to block them out, without the mediation of inter-state power politics, first in Europe and then throughout the world. Market regimes in themselves could not have pre-vailed had they not also generated superior force. The two most successful replicators of modernity, the capitalist economy and advanced armed forces, proliferated in tandem, as wealth and power became interchangeable.

PRINTERS, NATIONS, AND MASS ARMIES

The unifying effect of the state's central apparatus (including its mili-tary branch), large-scale national (and international) economies, and grow-ing political participation combined with the third great invention on Bacon's list, the printing press, in generating early modern nationalism in Europe.

I emphasize *early modern* nationalism because, as repeatedly pointed out in this book and contrary to a fashionable view, nationalism was far from being an entirely new 'invention' created in Europe in the eighteenth or nine-teenth centuries, or even somewhat earlier (there are various approaches here).[88] As with other social phenomena, wherein innate human predisposi-tions interact with changing cultural–historical conditions, it evolved from earlier forms of ethnocentrism and pre-modern nationalism, and would continue to evolve throughout modernity under the impact of further changes. As already seen, it was from the beginning of history that tribal *ethnies* that came under a unifying framework of a state structure developed strong kin bonds of identity and solidarity as peoples. Failure to recognize the great potency of these sentiments in shaping political loyalties and boundaries from earliest times is one of the mysteries of more recent scholarly trends. In the special geopolitical conditions of northern Europe, peoples and states commonly converged in pre-modern national states from the start of that region's political consolidation in the Middle Ages. The advent of printing, however (in addition to the other above-mentioned factors), was a new—truly modern—prime factor that powerfully reinforced national identity.

The great impact of printing technology on European society, including the formation of modern nationalism, has been much emphasized by scholars. It created what social historian Benedict Anderson has labelled 'imagined communities': large-scale bodies of people who, although experiencing no face-to-face interaction as in small traditional communities, partook of a shared world of culture and ideas and were connected by a greatly intensified and intensifying information network, formed by the printing medium of books, pamphlets, journals, and newspapers.[89] Again, the prominence of shared culture and national bonds of solidarity beyond family and local community in pre-print peoples should not be underestimated. All the same, the much-enhanced means of cultural transmission and communication introduced by the printing press greatly reinforced both national identity and the potential for co-operation on a national scale. As no hegemonic supra-ethnic empire emerged in the west after the fall of Rome to impose its *lingua franca*, vernaculars (usually one culturally and/or politically dominant dialect in each lingual zone) gradually displaced Latin as literary languages from the late Middle Ages and with the rise of national states. In turn, this development further strengthened the national state, as lingual, cultural, and political boundaries in Europe increasingly converged.

Other civilizations, where a hegemonic empire prevailed, again offer illuminating comparisons and contrasts to Europe. Although both paper and block printing were invented in China, the absence of an alphabetical script with a small number of letters hindered the development of movable print.

Furthermore, the state rulers and Mandarin establishment in China (and the authorities in Tokugawa Japan) had no particular interest in facilitating the mass diffusion of ideas. The same applied to the world of Islam, where the Ottoman rulers banned the new technology.[90] In this, too, Europe's political fragmentation meant that obstruction of the new invention and censorship of its products could not be as comprehensive and effective as elsewhere in Eurasia. Europe underwent great intellectual ferment, the like of which was not experienced by any of the other civilizations. Martin Luther reached a wide public of the 'German nation' by using printed vernacular to spread his subversive ideas, and in other countries the Reformation was generated by similar means. The diffusion of the scientific revolution was no less intimately tied up with printing. And the climate of ideas known as the Enlightenment—subversive to both state and church—spread among Europe's literate classes through the same medium.

Indeed, it was predominantly the literate who were connected by printing into large-scale 'imagined communities' of culture, language, and information, and who were the agents of early modern nationalism in each country. Illiterate peasants remained parochial in outlook and xenophobic in their attitude towards people of relatively close dialects and localities, although they, too, distinguished them very well from distant foreigners. But country gentlemen and city and provincial town burghers were now brought up on a shared diet of classical and modern books. Moreover, they were increasingly informed about national current affairs by an ever-growing volume of pamphlets (from the sixteenth century), newsbooks (from the seventeenth), and journals and newspapers (from the eighteenth). And it was precisely these people who spearheaded the English, American, and French revolutions.[91] Wider political participation became possible in modern country-states not only by virtue of representatives who went from the country to the capital, but equally because of the much greater availability of information that travelled in the opposite direction.

Early modern nationalism formed sooner in some countries than in others. Understandably, it emerged earlier among ethnically more homogeneous peoples who were united under a single independent state. Thus a strong English national identity was evident as early as the fourteenth century and was much consolidated by the sixteenth. The same was true in Scotland, Denmark, Sweden, Poland, and Portugal by the sixteenth century, in some of them even earlier.[92] The French case is more complex, although France is widely regarded as paradigmatic in discussions on nationalism, which often distorts perspectives on the subject. The vast land over which the medieval French kings held suzerainty was a mosaic of provincial identities and Romance dialects, indeed mutually unintelligible languages between French in the north (*langues d'oïl*) and Occitan in the south (*langues d'oc*), with an addition of Breton, Basque, Catalan, German, and Flemish. As the French kings successfully tightened their control over the country from around 1200, a French national identity began to emerge in the north, becoming increasingly evident by the fifteenth century. In the following centuries the impact of the French state, together with the elevation of the dialect of the region around Paris into the status of both the official French language of government and the printed *lingua franca*, expanded French national identity throughout the realm, especially among the literate classes. Nevertheless, by the time of the Revolution most people in France still could not speak French.[93]

And yet, although French national identity spread more belatedly and imperfectly than was the case with some other, ethnically more homogeneous European national states, it was above all in France during the Revolution that the ideas of nationalism and national mass armies most strikingly manifested themselves. Why was this so? Obviously there were other factors involved besides the congruence of people and state. Both the people's inclusion in society and state and the type of wars fought by the state played important roles, because, again, as seen throughout history, the less polarized society was in terms of wealth, power, and status, and the more inclusive the state, the more the people identified the state's wars with their own interests and the more committed they were to fight under its banner. Both taxation and conscription—the two main expressions of social commitment—obeyed the same rule. Indeed, rather than constituting a purely modern novelty, national armies—that is, mass armies recruited throughout the realm of national states and infused with patriotic sentiments—were as old as the national state itself, in Europe as elsewhere. This was pretty much the sort of army that King Philip II raised in ancient Macedonia, Europe's first national state. Similar armies, of which the Frankish *ban* and the Anglo-Saxon *fyrd* were instances, prevailed throughout northern Europe in the early Middle Ages. However, as already seen, growing social polarization in those societies was later to erode mass national armies, whereas the requirements of distant campaigning promoted standing elite forces and led to feudalization.

Tellingly, England, where an estate of free farmers, or yeomen, held its own within the feudal system, was able to create a national army by the outbreak of the Hundred Years War, and a national militia infused with a strong patriotic sentiment existed under the Tudors. Yet the English crown waged its wars far away from home, a type of service for which militia armies were ill-suited. As a substitute for feudal levies, the crown increasingly resorted to market principles in order to raise professional troops for that type of engagement. In addition to native recruitment, it relied on the growing European market of hired soldiers, who were readily available and readily dismissible upon the outbreak and at the end of hostilities, respectively. From the late fifteenth to the late seventeenth centuries, England's military involvement in foreign land anyway declined sharply. Only during the Civil War in the mid-seventeenth century did recruitment on a national scale take place, which under Parliament and Cromwell created a strong national army, distinguished for its religious, civic, and patriotic zeal.

A native professional army came into being from late seventeenth-century England to serve together with foreign mercenaries in the wars of the new parliamentary regime and trading empire. Yet these again were regulars who served in distant expeditions. Furthermore, parliamentary England that incorporated the gentlemanly elite into the state remained a highly stratified society, where the populace was disenfranchised and oppressed. Consequently, although by no means lacking national sentiment and national pride, the dispirited, socially lowly, British regulars—the 'scum of the earth', as the Duke of Wellington ungraciously called the troops with which he beat Napoleon—were poorly motivated. As in the other armies of the *Ancien Régime*, harsh discipline and corporal punishment were instituted to keep them in service and in the battle line. Desertion was the scourge of armies, constituting the greatest drain on their manpower, before sickness and, only last, battle casualties. Desertion became yet more pervasive where political boundaries were diffuse, as was the case in Germany.

'Germany' was of course a loose ethnic–cultural designation, where, in contrast to France, the various 'principalities' had triumphed over the central state-empire by the late Middle Ages, leading to political disintegration. Both the multi-ethnic Habsburg–Austrian Empire that comprised Germans, Magyars, various Slavs, Flems, Valons, and Italians, and the absolutist–feudal German states could barely rely on national sentiments among their recruits, although a distinct sense of xenophobic native identity existed in the various regional states. Furthermore, Germany's loose political order made recruitment across state boundaries a common practice, widely resorted to by German and foreign powers alike from the late fifteenth century on.[94] The large-scale German troop market was extensively drawn upon by the nearby United Provinces from the beginning of their revolt in the late sixteenth century, because, although militias of various sorts participated in civic defence and garrison duty during the Netherlands' protracted wars against Spain and France, dwellers of large-scale commercial cities never constituted the most suitable material for field service, and they preferred to hire others to fight for them.[95] It should be further noted that a sense of Dutch national identity gradually developed among the disparate populations of the various provinces that had come together in the original Revolt.

The most prominent example of a national army in early modern Europe was the Swedish army that landed in Germany with Gustavus Adolphus in 1630, because not only was Sweden a distinctly defined nation, but it was also one of the least stratified societies and the most participatory state in Europe. Feudalism barely took hold in Sweden, and it was the only country where the peasants were represented in the national assembly, the Riksdag. Conscripted by quota from each local community, the Swedish troops were infused with a strong national (and religious) spirit and were highly motivated, far more than the 'volunteer' professionals of other armies. The only problem was that the Swedish population was very small and suffered decimating losses in the protracted foreign wars during Sweden's period of glory in the seventeenth century. Consequently, the monarchs had to rely increasingly on mercenaries to swell the ranks of the army, whom they again mostly hired from the German troop market.[96]

The North American British colonies present another interesting example. As their rebellion against the crown turned into a fully fledged War of Independence, a new American national identity began to form, bridging over the deep divisions that had separated the colonies from each other. A representative Continental Congress created a Continental Army commanded by George Washington, whereas militias operated locally. As war touched close to home and social involvement in what was to be a new republic was high, popular participation in the patriotic war became a significant factor in the victory. One of the symbolic figures of the rebellion was the printer, newspaper publisher, and man of the Enlightenment Benjamin Franklin. Indeed, the new press that informed the colonies' town folk about the unfolding events and debated the political issues served as a major catalyst of the forming national American identity. Furthermore, the founders of the Republic were infused with the ideology of the Enlightenment, disseminated through a shared diet of books in the same way as the religious ideologies that had animated the wars of the sixteenth and seventeenth centuries.

All of the above factors and processes climaxed in revolutionary France, because the revolutionary state recognized no source of legitimacy other than the French people, no internal boundary or privilege, no status except that of French citizens. And these principles remained in force when a popular Empire replaced the revolutionary Republic. More than Spain, the French state succeeded in subsuming diverse regional identities under the French national banner, a process that had begun under the monarchy and was greatly boosted by the Revolution. Combining a participatory civic ethos hitherto associated with city-states with the large size of a country-state, the revolutionary state was able to arouse national–patriotic energies, marshal resources, and mobilize mass citizen armies. Proclaiming *levée en masse* in 1793, it conscripted close to a million Frenchmen within a few years. Initially improvised, inexperienced, ill-equipped, and badly supplied, the revolutionary armies, shaped by the organizational genius of Lazar Carnot, were as large as the combined forces of the powers of the *Ancien Régime*. Indeed, drawn from all classes of society, they compensated for their deficiencies by superior numbers and morale.[97] They adopted more flexible and aggressive shock tactics and, less inhibited by the (still acute) problem of desertion than the armies of the *Ancien Régime*, they were able to rely on improvised logistics, with the troops foraging widely in the countryside. Furthermore, the large numbers of easily replaceable recruits translated into aggressive, battle-oriented strategy. This was the material underpinning Danton's slogan—'L'audace, et encore de l'audace, et toujours l'audace'—which would find its ultimate consummation in Napoleon's crushing strategy. The Emperor exaggerated when he once told Metternich that he could afford to lose 30,000 French troops every month. Nevertheless, paradoxically, manpower inflation made the price of casualties cheaper for the French revolutionary state than any other military hardware, cheaper than the hard-to-replace professional troops of its *Ancien Régime* adversaries. National conscription made troops easily available.

However, contrary to the widely accepted view among scholars, it should be emphasized that revolutionary France was no more able than earlier states in history to keep over 1 per cent of her population under arms for any prolonged period of time. No miracles were performed here. With a population of some 25 million, France reached a peak of 750,000 soldiers in 1794 only at a price of economic mayhem, and numbers fell to around 400,000 the year after, where they remained until the end of the decade. War was financed by the sale of land confiscated from the nobility and church, by inflationary means, and by extensive looting. As the French armies repulsed the invaders and carried the war into foreign territories, they resorted to widespread requisitioning to feed themselves and sustain the French treasury. And these arrangements were systematized under the Empire. In 1805 the French army numbered only about 300,000 men, when France's population had grown to nearly 30 million because of annexations. But war and conquest spiralled thereafter. Two million Frenchmen were drafted during the years 1800–15, with 600,000 in active service constituting the peak (1813). Furthermore, a host of satellite states supplied troops to the imperial army at their own expense, doubling its size during the Empire's zenith, as well as paying for French troops stationed on their territory. Large war indemnities were imposed on the vanquished. The whole of western–central Europe was thus harnessed to support imperial France's military might. In addition, during emergencies Napoleon resorted to loans taken from private bankers and financiers.[98]

Napoleon fell because (1) Britain and Russia, the one secured behind sea and the other by her vast space, remained beyond his reach and became the foci around which resistance to French domination crystallized; (2) he exerted such heavy pressure on the European order that the other great powers—otherwise deeply divided among themselves—were ultimately driven to co-operate and fight him to the end; and (3) those powers—most notably Prussia, which had been the most gravely crushed and humiliated—were obliged to 'fight fire with fire', initiating social reform in order to raise the mass armies and generate the popular participation in the state that had made revolutionary France strong. Again, the pressure of war played a key role in precipitating modernity.

MODERN WAR—MODERN PEACE

It is time to return to the much-debated concept of the 'military revolution' to see how it is to be understood. A definition of what its time span and constitutive elements were makes sense only by viewing it as an interacting component, an 'aspect', of the west's overall—continuous and sweeping—transformation, rather than in narrower military terms.

This transformation picked up from about 1200, as the revival and growth of urbanism, money economy, and large-scale, centralized country-states generated increasingly larger, more centralized, and more permanent state armies, with infantry playing a more prominent role. All these were greatly boosted from the late fifteenth century by the far-reaching effects of Bacon's trio that launched modernity: gunpowder, ocean navigation, and the printing press. The introduction of firearms, while transforming both siege and field warfare, quickly resulted in restored equilibria—barely different from those that had prevailed earlier—between fortifications and siege craft as between infantry and cavalry. The staggering growth in the size of the European armies, compared with mobilization levels during the earlier period of Europe's medieval fragmentation, was indeed revolutionary in European terms. However, mainly attributed to the process of state centralization in Europe, the new large permanent armies were far less revolutionary when measured in historical and comparative terms. For quite a while, the early modern European experience represented no significant increase over sustainable mobilization levels achieved by well-organized, large, bureaucratic states through history—up to 1 per cent of the population. It was only the interaction of these developments with Bacon's two other modern innovations that was to make the European experience truly path breaking—compared with the past and with the record of Asia's great civilization centres of the time.

Indeed, by the eighteenth century, the Europeans steered ahead of all the other civilizations of Eurasia in terms of power and wealth. As already mentioned, at least initially empires throughout Eurasia incorporated firearms within traditional social and institutional frameworks—in the Ottoman case hardly less thoroughly than the Europeans. As late as 1683 the Ottoman army was still capable of besieging Vienna, a century and a half after it had done so for the first time. Yet this was the swansong of Ottoman military might. Even during the heyday of the Ottoman Empire there had never been a real threat of it conquering central and western Europe. Its power could not be extended farther than the Danube plain, where its armies could be supplied by river, and where its *sipahi* feudal cavalry were able to graze its horses, enjoyed tactical superiority, and were not too far away to return home after their obligatory summer campaigning season.[99] After 1683, however, military superiority, hitherto enjoyed by the Ottomans, increasingly shifted to the Europeans, and the Ottoman frontiers in Europe began to roll back.

The unfolding effects of Bacon's trio were responsible for this change in the balance of power. First, as long as matchlock arquebusiers and musketeers needed the protection of pikemen in the face of cavalry and in hand-to-hand fighting, the tactical flexibility and offensive role of infantry were severely hindered. During the sixteenth and seventeenth centuries, cavalry continued to figure in large numbers as the main arm of manoeuvre in the European armies. However, with the development of the bayonet that was fixed to the muzzle of the musket, the pike could be abandoned. At about the same time, the flintlock replaced the matchlock, again increasing the musket's reliability and effectiveness.[100] Only now did the infantry, made up solely of musketeers, become the 'queen of the battlefield', in Europe and overseas. Because for geopolitical reasons European infantry had traditionally been superior to others, Europe was the main beneficiary of that change. Thus the Ottomans' elite *janissary* infantry now proved too small a force, whereas their large mass of cavalry—including, at last, the horse archer—became obsolescent.[101]

It was, however, Europe's mastery of the seas (aided by her naval gun power) that proved to be the decisive factor in her development, creating the first global trading system and precipitating the rise of capitalism in Europe. And whereas firearms could largely be assimilated into traditional societies, a highly developed market economy could not. By the eighteenth century, even before industrialization, Europeans had grown perhaps as much as twice as rich as their contemporaries in Asia, in per capita terms.[102] Not only did this growth provide Europe with the resources and financial institutions necessary to maintain progressively larger and more permanent armies and navies, and with a productive infrastructure with a capacity and technological sophistication that made European artillery, for example, increasingly superior to that of others; the expansion of the market

economy also transformed European society and politics. The old military–
agrarian extractory elite was gradually drawn into the market and/or had to
share power with the rising commercial bourgeoisie. Autocratic power,
which initially benefited from and reinforced these processes, sooner or later
had to become attuned everywhere to the interests of these economically
and socially powerful classes, incorporate them into the state, or hand power
over to them.

With the aid of print communications, the increasingly participatory
civic–national state thus turned into a *res publica* in the ancient Roman sense,
where state power became 'impersonal', public resources were separated
from the private wealth of leaders and subjected to closer scrutiny, and the
rule of law prevented arbitrary state action. No longer did autocratic rule,
'patrimonial' political power, constitute the main avenue to wealth.[103]
Whereas most earlier historical states were tools in the hands of their rulers
for the exercise of arbitrary power as well as for the provision of some public
services, the modern state progressively lost the former aspect, while becoming more and more identified with the latter. Hitherto subservient to extractory political power, wealth creation increasingly dominated it, thereby
generating yet greater power.

Although decreasing 'despotic power', these developments greatly
enhanced the states' 'infrastructural power', among other things by deepening social mobilization. Furthermore, as greater public legitimacy was conferred on the regime, as its social support base was greatly widened, and as
lawful and peaceful means for changing government became available,
violent usurpation decreased and domestic political stability increased.
These again reflected the old virtues of 'mixed polities', already identified by
Aristotle and his disciples and now expanded to a national scale through
representative institutions and print technology. European states increasingly freed themselves from both spectres of regicide and imbecile hereditary rulers that haunted traditional autocratic states and regularly threw
them into periods of chaos or inaction. Indeed, the cycle of decadence and
decline that characterized pre-modern power broke down in modern societies: greater productive wealth and technological advancement now
translated much more directly than earlier into greater power, and, although
luxury and comfort continued to tempt members of established elites away
from a life of action, there were always economic and political upstarts who
moved in and up to take the lead. Thus, before industrialization Europe

had already developed a marked financial and technological advantage over the other Eurasian civilizations, whereas its more effective sociopolitical structures gave it an extra edge.

Indeed, by the eighteenth century not only the Ottomans but also other Asian empires found themselves falling behind Europe in wealth and power, as well as experiencing domestic–dynastic decline. In India, the decline and disintegration of the mighty Mughal Empire in the early eighteenth century made it possible for the British East India Company, a state-like efficient capitalist organization employing upstart officials and generals, to take over as the new overlords. Utilizing its great wealth (largely derived from India herself) to hire native troops, the Company also built on the newly developed superiority of European-style musket-bayonet infantry and field artillery over the semi-feudal cavalry that constituted the mainstay of Indian social and military power. In the late eighteenth and early nineteenth centuries, Indian states responded by successfully emulating the Europeans, hiring European officers, adopting and manufacturing advanced artillery, and raising modern infantry armies. Nevertheless, all resistance attempts ultimately failed, because although the Indian *sepoy* could be made into no less effective infantry than the European serf peasant, the Indian states did not enjoy the monopoly over armed force and the degree of social cohesiveness that had been achieved in Europe by the eighteenth century.[104]

In China, decline of the Manchu Dynasty was to come only a century after the Mughal, and Europeans were powerless to make inroads into that country until well into the nineteenth century. All the same, although industrialization during that century is rightly cited as the crucial advance that made China (and Japan) impotent vis-à-vis western power, preindustrial national European armies of the Napoleonic era were already far superior to any outside Europe. The Mamluk and Ottoman forces proved to be no match for Napoleon's expeditionary army during his 1798–9 campaign in the Levant. Only China's huge size, as well as distance and the problems of power projection, sheltered China (and Japan) from European intervention for a further short time.

To recapitulate, the so-called military revolution that was to give Europe global ascendancy emanated neither from muskets and drill nor from artillery fortifications—or, indeed, from any other tactical development in itself. Rather, it constituted an element of Europe's general, centuries-long process of modernization, boosted by the unfolding and interacting effects

507

of all the three elements of Bacon's trio of modernity, which transformed European economy, society, and state, and with them—the military
and war.

Yet, if commercialism and national participation made European states
increasingly powerful and successful in war, they also worked against these
qualities, at least potentially. For if the opportunity for great wealth created
by the formation of a much expanded mercantile economy and a global
market made it domestically more profitable for both the socially powerful
and the state to release and ride on, rather than interfere with, the operation
of the market forces, the same logic should in principle have prevailed
internationally. This was the logic that increasingly gained currency during
the Enlightenment, expressed by the physiocrat economic theorists in
France, the great loser of the eighteenth-century mercantilist race, but perfected by Adam Smith, who worked in the greatest winner of that race,
Britain.[105] As Smith, the theoretician of the market economy, argued in
The Wealth of Nations (1776, 4.7–8), 'mercantilism' might give more powerful countries a *relative* economic advantage over others, but, by dividing
international trade along political lines, it decreased *overall* wealth, lessening
the *absolute* prosperity of the leading mercantilist countries themselves. It
reduced economic competitiveness and the scale of international economic
specialization and exchange, which were the true engine of greater efficiency, productivity, and innovation. Smith's doctrine of free trade was
theoretically elaborated upon by David Ricardo, espoused in the nineteenth
century by the Manchester School, and has since been championed by
economic liberals as a recipe for both prosperity and peace.

However, did this logic not again shatter against the rocks of the anarchic
reality that prevailed in the international arena? In contrast to the domestic
realm, there was no sovereign out there who monopolized power and was
able to safeguard the rules of competition, thereby releasing the players
from the 'prisoner's dilemma' by securing them against those who might
resort to the violent–conflictual option. The logic of mercantilism was that
power brought wealth and wealth brought power. So long as violence
remained an option, how does one escape this logic and relax one's vigilance? Smith himself conceded that considerations of the balance of power
may legitimately impose constrains on free trade, for 'defence . . . is of much
more importance than opulence' (4.2.23). If by monopolizing markets
we achieve Smith's 'relative advantage', how could we dare open them to

all in order to increase overall, absolute wealth, while taking the risk that others might become richer than us and then use *their* 'relative advantage' to fight us into ruin?[106]

Something of this nature would in effect be experienced by Britain herself, who in the eighteenth century had become the mercantilist economic–naval–imperial leader. By the nineteenth century, while further increasing her relative economic advantage with industrialization, Britain retracted from mercantilism, opened her markets to foreigners and foreign goods, and lifted restrictions on investment and the sale of technology abroad. In the middle of the nineteenth century Britain abolished all protectionist tariffs and the navigation laws, becoming a free trading state. Thereby she boosted her own growth while fuelling that of the rest of the world. And yet in relative terms this open policy made it easier for others—above all the USA and Germany—to catch up and eventually overtake Britain economically, and, consequently, challenge her position as the leading world power. Free trade may indeed lessen the motive to amass and use force in order to gain access to economic opportunity, but it can be exercised securely only if one is reasonably confident that the *others* will not resort to force for economic or other purposes. However, in a Hobbesian, anarchic, international system that has no superior sovereign force to regulate it, where can such confidence come from?

During the eighteenth century, Enlightenment thinkers addressed themselves to the question of how war could be eliminated, grappling with the problems of anarchy and the modern world. In his *Projet de la paix perpetuelle* (1713), St Pierre proposed an alliance of all the European rulers who would together impose a general peace by deterring and punishing those who threatened to infringe on it. He failed, however, to address the core of the problem: why would co-operation for that purpose override opportunities for some states to gain through the use of force, and their consequent mistrust of each other (the 'security dilemma')—that is, both the temptation and fear of defection. Assessing St Pierre's programme, Rousseau argued that autocratic rulers could not be trusted to carry it out because they would never forfeit part of their sovereignty or their hopes of foreign aggrandizement, even though cool consideration demonstrated that their chances of success were slim whereas the price was heavy. Only a revolution that would rob the princes of their power might give hope for such a peace project.[107]

Republican proponents of the Enlightenment, such as the Marquis de

Condorcet in France and Thomas Paine in the USA, were among those who voiced this growing trend of thought. According to Paine in his *The Rights of Man* (1791–2):

> If universal peace, civilization, and commerce are ever to be the happy lot of man, it cannot be accomplished but by a revolution in the system of governments. All the monarchical governments are military. War is their trade, plunder and revenue are their objects. While such governments continue, peace has not the absolute security of a day.[108]
>
> Why are not republics plunged into war, but because the nature of their Government does not admit of an interest distinct from that of the Nation?

Consequently,

> When all the governments of Europe shall be established on the representative system, nations will become acquainted and the animosities and prejudices fomented by the intrigue and artifice of courts, will cease.[109]

Moreover, based on plunder at home and abroad, monarchies interfere with commerce, which

> is a pacific system, operating to cordialize mankind, by rendering nations, as well as institutions useful to each other. . . . If commerce were permitted to act to the universal extent it is capable, it would extirpate the system of war.[110]

Immanuel Kant expressed very similar Enlightenment ideas in his own *Perpetual Peace* (1795). He too suggested that the project could materialize as the states developed constitutional–republican regimes. The people would tend not to vote for war, because they themselves would have to shoulder and pay the price for it. Building on this basis, constitutional–republican states should then federate in order to resolve their differences peacefully, bringing themselves out of their anarchic situation in the same way that individuals had done within societies. Although there was no sovereign force capable of guaranteeing the peace, as was the case within societies, Kant's vision was predicated on the notion that the very existence of constitutional–republican states with their internal abhorrence for war would achieve a similar effect.[111]

Kant wrote his book amid the general (short-lived) enthusiasm among Europe's intellectuals for the French Revolution. But a glance through history would have taught him (and Paine) that, contrary to the Enlightenment's view, some participatory republics were among the most bellicose and militarily successful states ever. This applied not only to direct democracies (such as ancient Athens), which Kant believed lacked constitutional restraints and exercised a tyranny of the majority, but also to other Greek and Renaissance city-state republics—indeed, above all to the mixed-republic Rome. In all of these the more the people held political power and shared in the spoils of war the more enthusiastically they supported war and imperialism, and the more tenaciously they fought. Furthermore, when Kant wrote his book, the wars of the Revolution could reasonably be viewed as defensive and imposed on France by the powers of the *Ancien Régime* who set out to nip her newly gained liberties in the bud. Soon, however, it was revolutionary France that took the offensive, and her mass citizen armies swept through Europe, subjugating it under French imperial domination.

Indeed, Smith, Paine, and Kant wrote just before the beginning of a new epoch, when fully fledged modernity would take off. In the following centuries industrialization was to generate resources and energies of Promethean magnitude and set in motion processes that radically transformed society. It thereby injected into war undreamed of forces of destruction and unleashed 'total' peoples' wars. How illusionary, then, were the above thinkers' predictions and recipes, and what links in the causal chain did they miss, if they did?

15

Unbound and Bound Prometheus: Machine Age War

 T he Industrial Revolution constituted a quantum leap in human cultural evolution, comparable only to the advent of agriculture and animal husbandry millennia earlier. As with that earlier Neolithic revolution, the change came in the wake of a longer accumulative process and took some time to unfold. Thus, for both the Neolithic and Industrial revolutions the terms 'transition' and 'industrialization', respectively, are sometimes preferred. Still, semantics aside, each of these transformations represented a staggering acceleration in comparison to earlier development. Compressed into a few millennia (the Neolithic) or centuries (industrialization), each signified a 'take-off' into a radically new level of human existence, 'punctuating' not equilibrium but a far slower, older rate of change. The economy, society—and war—rocketed upward into a new evolutionary stage. What did it consist of?

In the first place, the new stage consisted of a massive harnessing of non-animate energy—other than the limited muscle power of people and domesticated animals—to drive machines. Interestingly enough, the first (and rarely noted) major breakthrough in this direction was achieved in the military field—well before the Industrial Revolution—with the introduction of firearms that used chemical energy. It was only centuries later and with a different energy-extracting process that a revolution already pioneered in destructive power reached production, and with a far more radical sweep, that was also to revolutionize destructive power further. Famously, this revolution in production took off in late eighteenth-century Britain, the most developed market economy, leading manufacturer, and hub of European and global commerce, where, in addition, huge coal and iron deposits existed and had already come into use. The Revolution's motive power was the steam engine, developed to pump out water from mines and then harnessed to the newly developed spinning and weaving machines of the cotton industry, increasing productivity in that industry by a factor of hundreds. Indeed, the steam engine—practically the only engine in existence until the late nineteenth century—could be and was progressively adapted to propel all sorts of different machines, in a growing number of manufacturing branches, and not only in manufacturing. After the textile and metallurgic industries, it was above all transportation that was revolutionized by the steam engine. Harnessed to pull trains of wheeled carriages that ran on rail tracks, it revolutionized land transportation from the 1820s on, placing it for the first time on an equal footing with water transportation and opening up the interior of the world's great continental landmasses. Although the technological potential of the steam engine at sea was demonstrated as early as 1807, the great sailing ships, being one of the pinnacles of pre-mechanized technology, gave way to further developed steam propulsion only during the last third of the nineteenth century.

All this is not intended to summarize a much-repeated and complex story. (As a result of the inexhaustible material available with regard to modern times, references, too, are confined to the bare minimum in the remainder of this book, contrary to my practice up to this point.) My aim here is to bring out the essence of the great transformation that was launched in eighteenth-century Britain and has been unfolding since; because, as the revolution in transportation demonstrates, the Revolution was never narrowly industrial. Nor would it remain confined to mechanics— witness the development of telegraph communications from 1837, of electricity and chemicals from the late nineteenth century, and the electronics-led revolution a century later. It was the pace of technological development in general, of innovation itself, that was broken out of old bonds by the Promethean harnessing of non-animate sources of energy to man-made machines. In the process, innovation could be increasingly systematized, becoming scientific among other things. In step with an immanent tendency of evolutionary systems, cultural evolution itself accelerated; people became far better at innovation. Although I continue to use the terms 'Industrial Revolution' and 'industrialization' in this chapter as accepted shorthand, my meaning is broader.

The main change to human existence brought about by the Revolution was a steep and continuous growth in per capita production, a dramatic break away from the 'Malthusian trap' that had characterized earlier human history. As we have seen, the advent and intensification of agriculture and animal husbandry since the Neolithic transition increased human productivity by a factor in the range of 100 compared with the hunter–gatherer way of life. Yet this increase was largely absorbed by population growth of a similar proportion worldwide. Although the social elite improved its standard of living substantially—sometimes fabulously—through surplus extraction, the vast majority of people continued to live in dire poverty, precariously close to subsistence levels. Consumption per capita remained almost stagnant, as slowly growing productivity over the millennia was cancelled out in a 'Red Queen effect' by demographic growth.

From the outbreak of the industrial–technological revolution, however, all this changed. Average data on global growth since the eighteenth century are impressive enough, but are still misleading with regard to the full scope of the change, because different countries and regions were reached by the Revolution at different times. Many regions have been affected only quite recently and are still in initial or intermediate stages of transformation. Therefore, the developed countries provide the truly indicative measure of the change. In these countries, production has variably increased since pre-industrial times by a factor of 50–120, so far. Manufacturing output rose by as much as double those rates. As the population grew only by a factor of four to five on average (with great emigration from denser regions such as Europe), per capita production has increased by a factor of 15–30, more or less in the same range as the developed world's advantage over today's least developed countries (some of which are actually poorer than eighteenth-century western Europe). The gap between the richer and the poorer countries increased tenfold in comparison with pre-industrial times. Although undergoing slower and faster periods, average growth in the industrializing and industrial world became some ten times faster than in pre-industrial times, with production per capita for the first time registering substantial and sustained real growth at an average annual rate of 1.5–2.0 per cent.[1]

When algorithmic representations are not used (and even when they are), this steep growth regularly registers on diagrams as a sharp curve, which after crawling close to the bottom of the diagram for the overwhelming part of human history suddenly rocketed upward during the last two centuries.

THE TECHNOLOGICAL EXPLOSION AND THE INFRASTRUCTURE OF POWER

The explosive surge in technologically induced production translated into an explosion in military power of the same order of magnitude, as the two became virtually inextricable. Military force capability increased exponentially, with those in the lead economically opening a similar gap militarily. Consequently, as Paul Kennedy ably demonstrated, there was a clear correlation between superiority in productive capacity and military victory in the great powers' clashes of the industrial age. The stronger side industrially almost invariably won.[2] Bairoch, who provided the seminal set of comparative historical economic statistics mainly relied upon by Kennedy, noted that total gross national product (GNP) did not in itself constitute an adequate measure of a country's economic power, because tens and hundreds of millions of peasants engaged in subsistence agriculture may add up to a significant bulk without rising above subsistence levels. Nineteenth-century China and, to a lesser degree, Russia remained giants in terms of total GNP even when the backwardness of their pre-industrial economies was starkly exposed and, with it, their military weakness and plummeting status as great powers. Bairoch suggested, as a more representative measure of economic strength, the value size of countries' manufacturing output, which reflected the leading and more advanced element of the economy in the industrial age.[3] Adopted by Kennedy, this measure proved to be no less remarkably representative of the great powers' relative war-waging potential, as revealed by historical experience.

I accept most of Kennedy's historical analysis, although I differ with some of it.[4] I am also more interested in the *overall* exponential surge in infrastructural power since the beginning of industrialization than with the shifts in *relative* power among the leading countries. To outline both, the following reproduces Bairoch's measure for selected great powers at some key historical junctions during the last two centuries. While I find some other existing measures of national power more problematic, I have complemented Bairoch with my own measure, which compounds a country's total gross domestic product (GDP) and GDP per capita, the latter being the most obvious and generalized indicator of economic advance. (For problems with some other measures see the endnote.[5])

Before proceeding to examine the statistics, the customary disclaimers are in order: the data are inherently crude and inexact; they are based on more or less accurate estimates, sometimes, especially with respect to undeveloped countries—today or in the past—on little more than informed guesswork; and, not least, the data suffer from systematic distortions in comparing across boundaries and across time. Other datasets from those used here may and do yield somewhat different results. Moreover, many factors other than economic strength have played their role in determining war outcomes, such as political institutions and leadership, social cohesion, economic self-sufficiency, investment in the armed forces, military effectiveness, geography, and other material and non-material factors (some of them variably correlating with the economic indicators). Much of this is addressed later. All the same, the data about the economic infrastructure of state power in the industrial–technological age are illuminating.

Let us briefly examine the tables presented below to evaluate the surge in infrastructural power generated by the industrial–technological revolution and review the consequent shifts in the global balance of power.

On the eve of industrialization, China (already beginning to experience dynastic–political decline) still constituted by far the largest economy and probably the strongest power. However, with Europe being the hub of world trade, each of the west European powers was about twice as rich and productive as China, relative to population. In 1820, Britain, the world commercial leader and already at the beginning of industrialization, was three times as productive per capita, possessing a fourth to a fifth of China's potential power with only a twentieth of China's population; and her power was fast increasing. Britain was already the most powerful country in Europe. However, France, with 1.5 times Britain's population, was still in the same range, and Russia, with 2.5 times Britain's population, ranked not far behind and was thus able to perform as the policeman of central Europe. Neither Germany nor Italy was yet unified (data for Prussia are not provided). Although, similar to China, India already lagged behind Europe

Table 1 GDP (and world share), population, GDP per capita, infrastructural power (and percentage from the leader)[6] from 1820 to 1913

	1820	1870	1913
UK: GDP (world share)	$36,232m (5.2%)	$100,179m (9.1%)	$224,618m (8.3%)
Population/GDP per ca.	21m/$1,707	31m/$3,191	45m/$4,921
Infrastructural power (percentage from leader)	1.4/2.3 (25–20%)	5.6/7.5 (100%)	15.7/18.7 (40%)
Germany: GDP (world share)	$26,349m (5.5%)	$71,429m (6.5%)	$237,332m (8.8%)
Population/GDP per ca.	24m/$1,058	39m/$1,821	65m/$3,648
Infrastructural power (percentage from leader)	. 0.8/1.5 (15–12%)	3.0/4.6 (53–61%)	14.3/18.4 (37–40%)
France: GDP (world share)	$38,434m (5.5%)	$72,100m (6.5%)	$144,489m (5.3%)
Population/GDP per ca.	31m/$1,230	38m/$1,876	41m/$3,485
Infrastructural power (percentage from leader)	1.3/2.2 (23–19%)	3.1/4.7 (55–62%)	8.5/11.0 (19–25%)
Italy: GDP (world share)	$22,535m (3.2%)	$41,814m (3.8%)	$95,487m (3.5%)
Population/GDP per ca.	20m/$1,117	27m/$1,499	37m/$2,564
Infrastructural power (percentage from leader)	0.7/1.2 (13–10%)	1.5/2.5 (26–33%)	4.8/6.7 (12–15%)
Russia: GDP (world share)	$37,710m (5.4%)	$83,646m (7.6%)	$232,351m (8.6%)
Population/GDP per ca.	54m/$689	88m/$943	156m/$1,488
Infrastructural power (percentage from leader)	0.9/1.9 (16–15%)	2.5/4.5 (44–60%)	8.9/14.4 (23–31%)
USA: GDP (world share)	$12,548m (1.8%)	$98,374m (8.9%)	$517,383m (19.1%)
Population/GDP per ca.	10m/$1,257	40m/$2,445	97m/$5,301
Infrastructural power (percentage from leader)	0.4/0.7 (7–6%)	4.8/6.8 (85–90%)	37.6/44.1 (100%)
China: GDP (world share)	$229,237m (32.9%)	$189,349m (17.2%)	$241,084m (8.9%)
Population/GDP per ca.	382m/$600	357m/$530	436m/$552
Infrastructural power (percentage from leader)	5.6/11.3 (100%)	4.3/9.0 (76–120%)	5.6/11.7 (14–26%)
India: GDP (world share)	$111,483m (16%)		
Population/GDP per ca.	209m/$533		
Infrastructural power (percentage from leader)	2.5/5.3 (44%)		
Japan: GDP (world share)	$20,903m (3%)	$25,319m (2.3%)	$63,302m (2.3%)
Population/GDP per ca.	31m/$669	34m/$737	45m/$1,387
Infrastructural power (percentage from leader)	0.5/1.0 (9–8%)	0.6/1.3 (10–17%)	2.3/3.8 (6–8%)

1990 international $ (in purchasing power parity—PPP).

in terms of development, it was still a giant and potentially twice as powerful as Britain (having been some six to seven times more powerful than Britain at the beginning of the eighteenth century). This tends to confirm the accepted view among scholars that, if it were not for Indian disunity after

Table 2 GDP (and world share), population, GDP per capita, infrastructural power (and percentage from the leader) from 1938 to 1998

	1938	1973	1998
USA: GDP (world share)	$800,300m	$3,536,622m (22%)	$7,394,598m (21.9%)
Population/GDP per ca.	130m/$6,134	212m/$16,689	270m/$27,331
Infrastructural power (percentage from leader)	62/71 (100%)	457/402 (100%)	1,222/950 (100%)
Russia (USSR): GDP (world share)	$359,000m	$1,513,070m (9.4%)	$664,495m (3.4%)
Population/GDP per ca.	167m/$2,150	250m/$6,058	147m/$4,523
Infrastructural power (percentage from leader)	16/24 (26–34%)	117/133 (25–33%)	44/54 (3–5%)
Germany: GDP (world share)	$351,400m	$944,755m (5.9%)	$1,460,069m (4.3%)
Population/GDP per ca.	68m/$5,126	79m/$11,966 W&E	82m/$17,799
Infrastructural power (percentage from leader)	25/30 (40–42%)	103/98 (22–24%)	194/168 (15–17%)
UK: GDP (world share)	$284,200m	$675,941m (4.2%)	$1,108,568m (3.3%)
Population/GDP per ca.	47m/$5,983	56m/$12,022	59m/$18,714
Infrastructural power (percentage from leader)	22/25 (35%)	74/70 (16–17%)	151/129 (12–13%)
France: GDP (world share)	$185,600m	$683,965m (4.3%)	$1,150,080m (3.4%)
Population/GDP per ca.	42m/$4,424	52m/$13,123	58m/$19,558
Infrastructural power (percentage from leader)	12/15 (19–21%)	78/73 (17–18%)	160/135 (13–14%)
Italy: GDP (world share)	$140,800m (3.2%)	$582,713m (3.6%)	$1,022,776m (3%)
Population/GDP per ca.	43m/$3,244	54m/$10,643	57m/$17,759
Infrastructural power (percentage from leader)	8/11 (13–15%)	60/59 (13–14%)	136/117 (11–12%)
Western Europe: GDP (world share)		$4,133,780m (25.7%)	$6,960,616m (20.6%)
Population/GDP per ca.		358m/$11,534	388m/$17,921
Infrastructural power (percentage from leader)		444/428 (97–106%)	931/805 (76–84%)
China: GDP (world share)	$320,500m	$736,588m (4.6%)	$3,883,008m (11.5%)
Population/GDP per ca.	411m/$778	877m/$839	1245m/$3,117
Infrastructural power (percentage from leader)	9/17 (14–24%)	21/39 (4–10%)	266/290 (21–30%)
India: GDP (world share)		$501,780m (3.1%)	$1,688,264m (5%)
Population/GDP per ca.		588m/$853	966m/$1746
Infrastructural power (percentage from leader)		14/27 (3–6%)	70/109 (5–11%)
Japan: GDP (world share)	$169,400m	$1,232,985m (7.7%)	$2,582,000m (7.7%)
Population/GDP per ca.	72m/$2,356	107m/$11,439	126m/$20,413
Infrastructural power (percentage from leader)	8/12 (13–17%)	131/127 (28–31%)	360/308 (30–32%)

1990 international $ (in purchasing power parity—PPP).

518

Table 3 Manufacturing output (and world share)[7] from 1830 to 1973

Country	1830	1860–1880	1913	1938	1973
UK	17.5 (9.5)	45–73 (19.9–22.9)	127 (13.6)	181 (10.7)	462 (4.9)
France	9.5 (5.2)	18–25 (7.9–7.8)	57 (6.1)	74 (4.4)	328 (3.3)
Germany	6.5 (3.5)	11–27 (4.9–8.5)	137 (14.8)	214 (12.7)	550 (5.9)
Austria	5.8 (3.2)	9.5–14 (4.2–4.4)	40 (4.4)		
Italy	4.6 (2.4)	5.7–8 (2.5–2.5)	22 (2.4)	46 (2.8)	258 (2.9)
Russia	10.3 (5.6)	16–24 (7–7.6)	76 (8.2)	152 (9)	1,345 (14.4)
USA	4.6 (2.4)	16–47 (7.2–14.7)	298 (32)	528 (31.4)	3,089 (33)
China	54.9 (29.8)	44–40 (19.7–12.5)	33 (3.6)	52 (3.1)	369 (3.9)
India	32.5 (17.6)				194 (2.1)
Japan	5.2 (2.8)	5.8–7.6 (2.6–2.4)	25 (2.7)	88 (5.2)	819 (8.8)

Output as percentage: UK in 1900 = 100.

the collapse of the Mughal Empire, British rule in India may not have been achievable at the time that it was achieved. Indeed, famously, the British East India Company conquered the divided subcontinent by means of India's own financial and manpower resources.

With her power growing by a factor of three to four since 1820, Britain overtook China to become the world's most powerful state around 1860, the height of the *pax Britannica*. China's infrastructural power eroded during that period, not only in relative but also in absolute terms. Furthermore, because of China's steep dynastic decline and political enfeeblement, Britain had already been able to humiliate China as early as 1839–42, in the Opium War, and again in 1856–60. Operating along China's seashore and waterways, naval power—Britain's main arm, which most reflected western technological advantage—constituted the key to victory. Russia's fall behind western Europe in terms of industrialization was humiliatingly exposed by Britain and France in the Crimean War (1854–6). After 1870, Russia was increasingly overshadowed by the fast industrializing unified Germany. Until (but not after) 1870, Prussia and her German allies were evenly matched with France in infrastructural power, and they only won the Franco–Prussian War (1870–1) because of far superior military mobilization and a more effective military system generally. As a result of massive immigration and industrial take-off, the USA exhibited the most staggering growth. Compared with 1820, her power grew maybe fivefold by 1860 and fifteenfold by 1880. By the later date the USA caught up with Britain, having amounted to less than a third of British power in 1820. From ranking last among the powers, the USA was moving into first place within two-thirds of a century. Still somewhat weaker than Japan in 1820, the USA became three times as powerful as Japan in terms of economic infrastructure a generation later. This superiority underlay successful American coercion of Japan to open her gates in 1853–4, putting an end to Japan's isolation and setting her on the road to political reform and industrialization.

Although in the industrially more mature Britain infrastructural power increased nearly threefold between 1870 and 1913, it grew seven- to tenfold and five- to sixfold, respectively, in the fast industrializing USA and Germany (both of which also demonstrated some structural advantages over Britain). Thus the USA—which continued to absorb mass immigration—was becoming the world's superpower, more than twice as powerful as the next in line, whereas Britain was 'managing decline', sharing a second/third place with Germany but continuously losing ground. Germany had grown to match the combined power of Russia and France (although she was already becoming concerned over the start of industrial take-off in Russia). Even when British power was added against Germany in the First World War, it took years to mobilize, because Britain had no conscript army as the Continental powers did. In the meantime, Germany, although economically cut off from the rest of the world, was able to occupy the industrially significant Belgium, Luxemburg, and the north of France, and later to knock Russia out of the war and expand east. Only the entry of the USA into the war brought about Germany's defeat. Still a giant in 1870, unindustrialized China, stagnating in absolute terms, continued to contract rapidly in relative terms, with her infrastructural power slipping behind most of the European powers. This, in conjunction with her regime's total decline, made possible the 'scramble for China' and the threat of imminent dismemberment in the late 1890s. Japan, industrializing as fast as the western powers but beginning belatedly and from a lower starting point, was still inferior in strength to most of those powers. Yet she was able to hold her own against them, defeating Russia in 1904–5, because of her efficiency, tremendous resolve, and the mammoth logistical problems involved in power projection from Europe into east Asia, across continents and oceans.

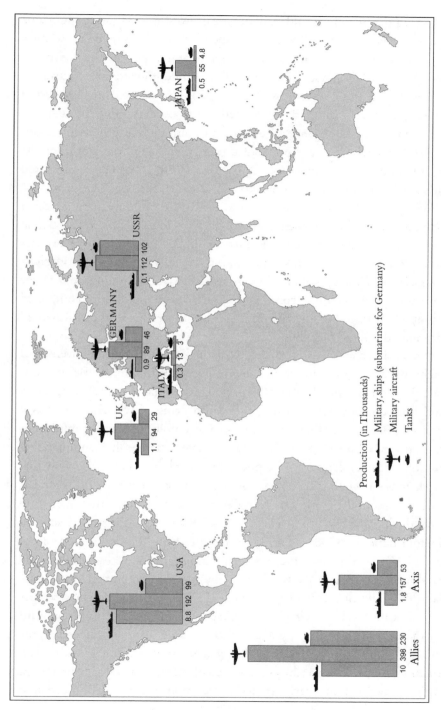

War production: the Second World War. (Source of data: Mark Harrison, *The Economics of World War II*, Cambridge University Press, 1998, pp. 15–16)

War in Human Civilization

During the Second World War, in an east–west reversal on the previous war, Germany this time defeated France before the slowly mobilizing Britain had time fully to materialize her potential power. But Germany failed to knock out Soviet Russia, which had undergone massive industrialization during the 1930s, possessed vast space to absorb the devastating German blow, and ruthlessly mobilized her resources under the regime's iron hand. All the same, only American entry into the war promised victory for the Allies, which now commanded more than half of the world's infrastructural power, as against some 20 per cent for the Axis (albeit measured within the borders of 1938 rather than 1942, when the Axis gains may have reduced the potential—although not actual—power imbalance to three to two in favour of the Allies[8]). Although her growth since 1913 was the world's fastest, Japan had only a sixth of the USA's strength (as well as lacking economic self-sufficiency), and her defeat was assured by American mobilization. China, beginning to industrialize and resuming growth for the first time in a century, continued to suffer from political instability and disunity. Italy, as in the First World War, was the weakest of the powers, and contributed little to her allies.

Obviously, as we see later, nuclear weapons greatly changed conventional equations of power, although in some respects not that much. Be that as it may, the post-Second World War period experienced the fastest growth ever, after the slowdown during the world crisis of war and depression between 1914 and 1945. Growing six- to sevenfold in terms of infrastructural power between 1938 and 1973, the USA retained her commanding position, with her share of world power unaltered since 1913. The view that this share was declining in comparison with its post-Second World War peak, when the rest of the world's industrial societies lay in ruin, misses the overall trend during the twentieth century. The Soviet Union grew seven- to ninefold between 1938 and 1973, recovering from the devastation of the Second World War and intensifying its industrialization, which had still stood at intermediate levels in 1938. In consequence, it climbed into second place, although still lagging far behind the USA. Only its regimented society and economy made it possible for the Soviet Union to keep up militarily. On the other hand, after it exhausted the process of industrialization, the Soviet Union's structural problems began to show, leaving it with lower levels of economic power than those achieved by its capitalist competitors, relative to population. Furthermore, as mass industrial production began to give way to information economy, the Soviet Union would find itself particularly cumbersome and disadvantaged. Indeed, Japan, which similar to the Soviet Union recovered from the devastation of war while intensifying industrialization from still intermediate levels in 1938, increased her infrastructural power ninefold according to one dataset or sixteenfold according to another, beginning to rival the otherwise bigger Soviet Union. Only Japan's demilitarization behind the American military umbrella prevented her from ranking as a mighty military power. Similarly, although Britain, which grew only threefold from 1938, declined sharply in relative terms, western Europe as a whole, recovering from the war and beginning to unite, far outstripped the Soviet Union in infrastructural power. It was only Europe's unwillingness to shoulder the military burden and its reliance on the USA that prevented it from becoming capable of standing up to the Soviet Union with Europe's own forces. While Chinese industrialization went on, China's infrastructural power remained modest, relative to her population. However, in contrast to the past, nobody wanted to mess with her any longer, because communist China now possessed a strong and highly mobilizing central regime, profited from the transfer of advanced Soviet military technology during the late 1940s and 1950s, and became nuclear in 1964.

Finally, a snapshot of today's world. With her infrastructural power increasing almost threefold between 1973 and 1998, the USA continues to retain her commanding position and world share. Not only did her productivity grow among the fastest in the developed world; being an immigration country with only about a quarter of the population density of the European Union, a quarter of that of China, and a tenth of that of Japan and India, the USA also continued to grow significantly in population. For these reasons the USA grew faster than the uniting Europe, and as fast as Japan. Contrary to earlier assessments during the 1980s, Japan sharply slowed down after exhausting the competitive advantages that she had enjoyed while still in the process of catching up with the developed countries in terms of industrialization. The disintegration of the Soviet bloc and the Soviet Union resulted in a plummeting of Russian power, although the data presented in Table 2 for 1998 are skewed sharply downward because of the severe economic dislocation caused by the change of system. By contrast, China has been successfully effecting a transformation into a market system. Although still far behind the USA, China is growing the fastest in the world in terms of infrastructural power—twelvefold between 1973 and 1998, and continuing —while managing to maintain political stability, *so far*. Given her huge population and still low levels of development, China's growth harbours the most radical potential for change in global power relations, as the country moves towards regaining its historical pre-eminence. Obviously, the process is extremely conducive, and vulnerable, to political upheavals, both domestic and international. Furthermore, even assuming that China's superior growth rate persists for a long while, her surpassing of the USA in terms of total GDP, were it to be achieved by the 2020s, as variously fore- cast, would still leave her with just over a third of the per capita wealth of the USA, and, hence, with considerably smaller infrastructural power (using my measure: an estimated half to three-quarters of that of the USA). Closing that far more challenging gap in high technology with the developed world assumes an extraordinarily smooth economic–political transformation in China, and, even if this assumption is validated, it would take decades more. Thus, widely quoted estimates of China's future economic and military power, based on total GDP alone, are misleading, which might adversely affect policy decisions.[9] Albeit at a slower rate than China, India, too, has begun to realize her vast potential.

All in all, since the beginning of the industrial–technological revolution two centuries ago, average infrastructural power—and war-waging poten- tial—among the leading countries increased by a factor of 120–250,[10] and even the higher figure might constitute an underestimate if indeed techno- logical advance is undervalued in calculations of growth, as critics suggest.

WEALTH, TECHNOLOGY, AND MILITARY HARDWARE

What exactly accounts for this tight association between exploding economic capacity and military force potential? In the first place, the surge in overall economic wealth obviously translated into rising capacity for military spending. Moreover, governments in wartime were now capable of extracting and spending for war purposes a larger *share* of the already increased GNP.[11]

During the eighteenth century, the state budget of Britain, the European leader in this regard, absorbed about 10 per cent of the total GNP in peace years, doubling to 20 per cent in wartime, when the large majority of the budget went to military spending. Government spending further increased to 30–40 per cent of the total British GNP during the Napoleonic wars. During the mostly peaceful nineteenth century (1815–1914), public spending again declined to just over 10 per cent of British GNP, with military spending falling to less than half that amount, more or less as had been the case during the peace years of the eighteenth century. Spending patterns in the other European great powers were roughly similar. Indeed, although registering some increase, military spending retained these modest levels even during the supposed 'arms race' between the European powers in the decade before the First World War. American military spending was much lower than in Europe, except during the Civil War. The more industrial North is estimated to have spent 18 per cent of its GNP on the war effort, whereas the estimate for the South is even higher: 25 per cent. These Civil War levels of military expenditure indicate an upward trend, in line with the increase registered by Britain earlier in the century, but are still far below the levels of the World Wars. Thus in the unsettled debate of whether or not the Civil War constituted the first 'total war', the obvious answer is that it stood half-way in that direction.[12]

Indeed, during the twentieth century, public spending in the developed countries steadily grew to around 30–50 per cent of the GNP, mainly to finance expanding social services. Military spending fluctuated widely, depending on the level of international tensions and the special circumstances of the various powers. During peace years (the vast majority of the time for all the great powers), military spending generally retained the same, surprisingly resilient, levels as in earlier centuries: over 5 per cent of the GNP for the USA during the Cold War; around 3 per cent for the European countries. Therefore, contrary to oft-voiced concerns, military spending did not 'spiral', but generally kept in line with the overall growth in GNP. However, during the two World Wars, military spending of the warring great powers leaped to some 80–90 per cent of overstretched public spending, as during wartime in the eighteenth century, only now amounting to around half of the total GNP, sometimes more. Thus, the *share* of wartime military spending out of the total GNP tripled from some 15 per cent for the leader (Britain) in the eighteenth century (already high in historical terms) to around 50 per cent in the twentieth century, over and above the fantastic surge in total GNP. Not only did the entire pie expand dramatically, but the slice of it allocated to wartime military spending also grew. Again, this amounted to an overall absolute increase in the *wartime* military expenditure of advanced powers by a factor in the range of 150–360 compared with pre-industrial times.

Partly, the state's greater extraction capability was a result of the far enhanced reach of its bureaucratic apparatus, as well as the state's greater legitimacy; and, partly, it was a function of increasing disposable surpluses above subsistence level, surpluses that far exceeded pre-industrial rates. It should be noted, however, that disposable surpluses and government extraction capacity did not grow at the same rate as per capita income. For example, even though per capita GNP in both the Soviet Union and Japan during the Second World War was only about half that of the most advanced powers, they were still able to spend the same—and greater—share of their respective GNPs on their war effort as the more advanced powers: around 50 per cent and even more. Japan's war outlay in 1944 reached three-quarters of her GNP, despite the fact that Japan lacked access to wide-scale deficit financing (which in Britain paid for over half of government spending in the peak years).[13] Not only, as was the case with the Soviet Union and Japan, are strong state authorities capable of achieving high extraction rates from societies that are accustomed to lower levels of subsistence, but higher per capita consumption in more developed economies partly pays for the larger operational costs of a more advanced and more complex system—for example, the costs of transportation and education. Furthermore, the less developed the economy, the lower the cost of manpower.

This last factor helps to explain the direction in which the fantastic surge in military spending has mostly been channelled during the industrial–technological era. Although military manpower grew significantly in absolute numbers, increase relative to the growing population (social participation rate) was more ambivalent. Here, again, there prevails the same difference between wartime and peacetime growth that we have already seen with respect to military spending in general. Peacetime armed forces continued to amount to around 1 per cent of the population or less, in line with their historical levels of sustainability, partly because manpower remained as expensive as before, as wages increased with soaring productivity. On the other hand, peak wartime mobilization levels reached up to 13 per cent of the population during the World Wars, basically incorporating all able-bodied men (and some women), although the manpower requirements of war production tended to lower the rate to about 8–9 per cent.[14] These wartime levels were much higher than those specified in Chapter 14 for early modern European states, which, however, did not have conscription. They were also much higher than the wartime mobilization levels achieved by revolutionary and Napoleonic France, which had conscription. Later in the nineteenth century Prussia and her allies in the war against France (1870–1), with a population of about 39 million, called to arms close to 1.5 million conscripts (3.8 per cent), who served at least for some time. The German armies in France never numbered more than a million at any one time.[15] The American Civil War (1861–5) was much more protracted, giving the sides time to harness their resources. Over two million men passed under the Union's flag, with a peak of about one million in active service reached in the last years of the war, or 5 per cent of the North's population. In the much less industrialized Confederacy an estimated 850,000–900,000 saw service, again with about half of these in actual service at the peak—that is, close to 5 per cent if the slave population is included, and 8 per cent if it is not.[16]

Whereas the Civil War's high mobilization rates may be cited as an indication of its increased modernity, the Confederacy's case serves as a reminder that very high mobilization rates were not unique to industrial, 'total' war. Similar record mobilization levels had been achieved in cohesive, large-scale, pre-industrial societies that possessed conscription, such as Rome during the height of the Second Punic War, or, more recently, Serbia and Montenegro in the First World War. Although among the most backward in industrial development, Serbia and Montenegro were the most intensely mobilized of all the belligerents in terms of military manpower: a sixth to a fifth of their population.[17] What constituted 'total war' and what exactly was new about it have generated extensive scholarly debate but no clear specifications and quantifiable criteria. As it would have become apparent here, modern wars were not historically unique in their high level of casualties and physical destruction (relative to population and wealth), or in collapsing the distinction between combatants and non-combatants (actually a modern distinction) and the exposure of the civilian rear, or even in high manpower mobilization levels. The world wars were uniquely 'total' chiefly in the sense that they combined high mobilization rates with far enhanced GNP extraction levels that were mostly channelled to the industrial mass production of military hardware. At first, during the First World War, this mainly meant ammunition for quick-firing and long-range artillery and, later, technologically advanced war machines.

Indeed, it was above all in mechanical–technological hardware that the exponential surge in military power took place—that, after all, was the nature of the revolution in general. Although military spending, including that on manpower, was spiralling as a consequence of the explosive economic growth, spending on hardware also increased its *share* of military spending.[18] We have seen that during the early modern period pay and provisions far outweighed the cost of military hardware, not only in the armies but also in the capital-intensive navies. However, as the armed forces became increasingly mechanized and hardware dependent, this ratio tilted in the other direction. In the navies, the first intensively mechanized service, manpower costs (including pay, provisions, and clothing) declined to about 40 per cent of the naval budgets by the last decade of the nineteenth century and to around 30 per cent by the first decade of the twentieth century. At the same time, warship construction costs grew to over one-third of the naval budgets, with nearly as much additional spending dedicated to repairs, maintenance, and ammunition. Thus materials grew to outweigh manpower costs by two to one.[19] The US navy's budgetary figures a century later, in the 2000s, remain in the same range for manpower, procurement plus research and development (R&D), and operations and maintenance, respectively, with some years after 1945 even registering manpower costs as low as 25 per cent of the naval budget.[20]

Armies were still far less mechanized than navies around 1900. Although I cannot cite data, manpower costs (direct and indirect, where conscription was involved) undoubtedly still constituted the majority of army expenditure in all the great powers. Yet this picture is misleading, because one of the major elements of military power was the railway system—for mobilization, strategic mobility, and logistics. And the overwhelmingly civilian infrastructural costs of that system (and others) did not register in military budgets. From the First World War on, however, armies increasingly mechanized. Consequently, manpower costs in the US army, for example, fell to around 40 per cent of the army's budget in the 2000s, and even to as low as a third in some years after 1945. Material costs (excluding construction) amount to about half of the budget, with operations and maintenance costing

The ships of the German High Seas Fleet. The first capital intensive arms race took
place at sea between Britain and Germany before the First World War

twice as much as new procurement and R&D.[21] Finally, whereas armies
remain the most labour-intensive armed service, air forces, only coming
into being before and during the First World War, are the most capital
intensive of all armed services. Manpower costs amount to only 20 per cent
of the US air force's budget in the 2000s, with operations and maintenance,
procurement, and R&D together taking up about three-quarters of the
budget.[22]

As with military spending in general, weapon systems' cost did not spiral
out of control with every new generation, nor did they become prohibitively
expensive—again contrary to a widely held view. With the military budget's
share in total GNP showing little change over time, the rising cost of some
weapon systems was simply compensated for by smaller numbers or by a
changing balance within military procurement, both matters of cost-
effectiveness. As already pointed out in Chapter 14, military spending does
not simply rise with a 'free-floating' cost of weapons, but is always bounded
by economic capabilities, priorities, and enemy spending, in turn bounded
by similar constraints. What is true, however, is that hardware's *share* in military spending has grown during the industrial–technological era. The challenge (and trade-off) has been how to arm the available (and ultimately
finite) manpower with more, costlier, and more *advanced* military hardware.

Of course, since the beginning the industrial–technological revolution
there has been an exponential surge not only in the *volume* of hardware

but also in its effectiveness. Weapon systems' effectiveness, while difficult to measure exactly, probably increased at the same rate as technological productivity in general during that period—that is, by a factor of hundreds. The *pace* of innovation in military technology accelerated dramatically in comparison with pre-industrial times. In historical *agraria* (and the steppe) military equipment improved slowly, over millennia, so that Iron Age armies differed little from, and would probably have been able to hold their own against, their counterparts on the eve of modernity, before gunpowder. Firearms improved at a quicker pace, as the pace of innovation in general accelerated in Europe during early modernity. Still, between each significant 'punctuation' in firearms' development, something close to a technological equilibrium often prevailed for centuries. The main infantry weapon, the musket, changed little from 1690 to 1820. However, from the beginning of the industrial–technological era, as military theorist J. F. C. Fuller saw, the pace of technological innovation became such that the best armed force of one generation would have been totally unable to confront in the open a well-equipped opponent of the next generation.

As Fuller equally saw, the advances in military technology were closely related to civilian developments, and both did not take place more or less evenly in time and across the technological front, but mainly clustered around consecutive breakthroughs in a number of sectors each time, which variably affected all the rest.[23] Taking several decades to run their course, these technological breakthroughs then gave way to other breakthroughs in different sectors. Although some oversimplification is necessarily involved, Fuller rightly identified three such major revolutionary waves of civil–military technological change during the nineteenth and twentieth centuries.

The so-called First Industrial Revolution, taking about a century to unravel, was led by the steam engine and major advances in metallurgy and machine tools. As already noted, the steam engine could be applied to many processes, revolutionizing each. In the military field, the railway increased armies' strategic mobility and logistical capability by a factor of hundreds. Although naval mobility only doubled or tripled as steam replaced sail, naval tonnage grew four- to fivefold and (iron and steel) battleship's size—and might—tenfold and more.[24] To these was added the revolution in information communications, as electric telegraph lines connected not only armies across countries but naval bases across oceans and continents in real time, where weeks, months, and years had been necessary. Simultaneously during

Battle scene around Metz, the Franco-Prussian War, 1870. Note the rail and telegraph lines, typically running parallel, that transformed strategy

the nineteenth century, the revolution in metallurgy (iron followed by steel) and machine tools generated a revolution in firearms and tactics. Rifling and breech loading were pioneered in infantry firearms during the 1840s, and in artillery during the 1850s and 1860s. Magazine-fed rifles, 'repeaters', were developed in the 1860s and 1870s, and quick-firing artillery, using a hydraulic mechanism to absorb the gun's recoil, in the 1880s and 1890s. As a consequence, range, accuracy, and rapidity of fire each increased some ten-fold within 60 years, not counting the development of the automatic machine gun from the 1880s, which multiplied firepower yet more.[25] Naval gunnery underwent similar developments, to which the torpedo was added from the 1870s.

All these, however, were lopsided revolutions, especially on land. As in the economy, so in the military, spheres of activity to which the steam engine could not be applied remained manual and unaffected by the Revolution. Thus, while armies rode trains on their way to the battlefield and were

531

easily controlled by telegraph, they fell from the pinnacle of high-tech communications back to Napoleonic if not Alexandrian times once *on* the battlefield. Their campaign and tactical mobility remained confined to human muscles, with their artillery and supply drawn by horses, of which hundreds of thousands and millions remained in each of the great powers' armies during the First World War (and in some, including the German, also during the Second World War). Field command and control, where telegraph lines could not be laid in advance, were similarly downgraded to messengers on foot or horseback. Furthermore, whereas firepower increased tenfold and above, troops, while dispersing and taking cover, still had nothing better than their skin to protect them from the storm of steel on the open field. Hence the murderous stalemate on the Western Front during the First World War, both tactical and operational, when even those puny gains made by attacking infantry at terrific cost were reversed, as decimated foot-walking troops, struggling to extend their tactical gains deeper, were pushed back by enemy reinforcements rushed up by rail.

However, from the 1880s a new revolutionary wave of industrial technology, the so-called Second Industrial Revolution, was beginning to unravel in civilian life, affecting the military field as profoundly as the First Industrial Revolution had. Chemicals, electric power, and the internal combustion engine dominated that second revolutionary wave. Although the chemical industry contributed new explosives and was soon to produce chemical warfare, and developments in electricity also had various military applications, including radio communication, it was the internal combustion engine that affected war the most decisively. Lighter and more flexible than the steam engine, the internal combustion engine made possible mobility in the open country, away from railways. Passenger and transport automobiles (as well as the tractor) evolved between 1895 and 1905, increasing cross-country mobility by a factor of tens. The First World War inaugurated the tank—an armoured and armed tractor—which introduced mechanized mobility and mechanized armoured protection into the battlefield, thereby redressing the huge imbalance created by steam. Controlled by radio, which similarly extended real-time information communication into the field, away from stationary telegraph lines, mechanized armies on tracks and wheels matured by the Second World War, some half a century after the pioneering of the technologies that had made them possible.[26]

A devastated battlefield with a ruined tank, Ypres, 1918. The great struggle of materiel that was the First World War was dominated first by artillery and small arms firepower and later by emergent mechanization in the air and on land

Simultaneously, the internal combustion engine also made possible mechanized air flight. A remarkably similar trajectory followed, with the first such flight taking place in 1903, and massive air forces quickly coming into being during the First World War and further developing by the Second World War. Ships, already steam powered and armoured, were less dramatically affected by the internal combustion engine. Nevertheless, naval warfare in general was revolutionized. Dual propulsion by the internal combustion and electric engines made possible the first workable submarine, again in 1900, whereas the aircraft were to bring about the demise of the gunned battleship. Once more, both the submarine and the aircraft at sea made their military debut during the First World War, and together they completely dominated naval warfare in the Second World War.

By the Second World War the technological potential of the internal combustion engine had matured (although the coming of jet propulsion

533

gave aircraft development a new boost). However, new technological break-throughs were now occurring in other sectors, most notably electronics, again revolutionizing both civilian life and war in the so-called Third Industrial or Information Revolution. Radar, developed in the late 1930s, deeply affected air, air–land, and sea warfare during the following decades. From around 1970, electro-optic, television, and laser guidance for missile weapon systems began to revolutionize air–land and land battle. Since then, fast-improving sensors of all sorts, in combination with electronic computation capacity that more or less doubled every 18 months, made the identification, acquisition, and destruction of most hardware targets almost a foregone conclusion, almost irrespective of range. Showing little signs of levelling off, the electronic revolution is bringing about increasing automation: the electric–robotic warfare that the pioneering Fuller predicted as early as 1928 as the third great wave after mechanization.[27]

Arms races thus gained a wholly new significance in the technological age. Particularly when one side succeeded in securing a decisive lead in the acquisition and assimilation of breakthrough weapon systems, it might thereby gain a 'force multiplier' that could produce one-sided battlefield results. Examples include the Prussian breech-loading rifle in the 1866 war against Austria, the German mechanized forces at the beginning of the Second World War, and the American electronic weapon systems during the campaigns of the 1990s and early 2000s in Iraq, the former Yugoslavia, and Afghanistan. Over time, however, there could be a cancelling out, 'Red Queen effect', as rivals caught up in the development and assimilation of new weapon systems. Technology could also be transferred—sold or given—which occasionally narrowed the gap in power between more and less advanced rivals. At sea and in the air, where fighting has been the most hardware intensive and has been carried out entirely by weapon systems (rather than by armed men), the gap between technologically more and less advanced rivals has been the widest.

What exactly does the hundredsfold increase in weapon effectiveness during the industrial–technological era measure? Destructiveness or lethal-ity may appear to be the issue, because that is what war is all about. On the other hand, as the above survey has already demonstrated, developments in military technology also exponentially increased protective power—for example, through mechanized defensive armour at sea and on land, through growing, indeed sometimes literally rocketing, swiftness and agility, and through electronic counter-warfare. All in all, contrary to widespread assumptions, studies of war lethality, measured by military and civilian casualties, show no significant increase during the nineteenth and, indeed, the twentieth centuries in comparison with earlier historical periods, relative to population. To be sure, as we see later, wars became rarer, and the intensity and lethality of those that did occur, most notably the World Wars and above all the Second World War, appear to have grown significantly in terms of mortality per time unit, even when the size of the populations involved is taken into account. Still, this increase may have had more to do with the combatants' greater manpower mobilization levels than with military technology's excess lethality over protectiveness.[28] Mortality as a percentage of the armed forces did not grow. Indeed, similar and greater rates of combat mortality—25–30 per cent of the men—had been commonplace among pre-state, small-scale societies that used the most primitive military technology. Furthermore, it is all too often forgotten that the vast majority of the non-combatants killed by Germany during the Second World War—Soviet prisoners of war, civilians, Jews (millions in each category)—fell victims to intentional starvation, disease, and mass executions, rather than to any sophisticated military technology. Instances of genocide in general during the twentieth century, as earlier in history, were carried out with the simplest of technologies.

Yet, as readers may have noticed, one—by far the most destructive—technological breakthrough has been left out of the above outline. This is the advent of nuclear power and nuclear weapons, which in a way constituted a culmination of the industrial–technological revolution in yet another quantum leap to a new, far higher level of potency. Furthermore, the overwhelming destructive power of the nuclear explosion is offset by no parallel rise in defensive power, as has been the case with many other military technologies. This was finally the ultimate weapon, a doomsday machine that gave anybody who possessed the necessary stockpile an assured ability to destroy his enemy, indeed the world, completely. I return to this subject in Chapter 16, after first moving on to explore the wider social and political transformations brought about by the industrial–technological revolution—in their relationship to war.

GREAT POWER AND NATIONAL WARS

The industrial–technological revolution, the exponential spiralling of wealth, and the radical transformation of society and politics that these developments brought in their wake also profoundly affected war in significant ways other than the staggering surge in war-making potential. In the first place, the number of wars and war years among the great powers and among economically advanced states in general—the most powerful states and most destructive inter-state wars—decreased dramatically. In the century after 1815, they declined to about a third of their frequency in the preceding century, and even lower compared with earlier times. The same lower frequency continued during the twentieth century, although the resource and manpower mobilization in the major wars that did occur, and, hence, wars' intensity and lethality per time unit, increased—again, most notably, in the two World Wars.[29] What accounts for this change? If statistics are not to lie, they must be adequately interpreted and contextualized.

Does the greater economic and human cost of the wars, their greater intensity, in and of itself explain the decline in the number of wars and war years among advanced societies? Supposedly states needed more time to recover before being able to re-engage in war. Thus, maybe a trade-off existed between the intensity and frequency of warfare: fewer larger wars replace many smaller ones. Such a trend may in fact be discernable in eighteenth-century Europe, which, while highly war-like and manifesting greater resource and manpower mobilization levels than earlier, already registered some decline in the number of years that the European great powers spent in fighting each other. This hypothesis barely holds, however, for the nineteenth century. From 1815 to 1914 (but even if the round centennial dates are chosen), although the number of wars and war years among the great powers and among advanced states in general sharply declined, the cost of wars registered little significant increase, relative to population and wealth. That no great power war occurred for 39 years after Waterloo—the longest peacetime in European history until then—is in part explained by the fact that the rulers of Europe regarded each other as allies in their struggle to suppress the rising forces of revolution within their own societies. This often forgotten aspect of the so-called Concert of Europe during the Restoration meant that inter-state power politics became subservient to Old Regime co-operation against that greater threat. However, conservative co-operation, although never disappearing, ceased to be the paramount factor after 1848–9, and cannot account for the 43 peace years among the European great powers between 1871 and 1914, a new time record.

Conversely, in the twentieth century, the mere 21 years that separated the two World Wars—the most intense and devastating wars in modern European history—do not support an inverse relationship between war intensity and frequency either. Indeed, any such relationship has been rejected by all specialized statistical studies of the subject.[30] Obviously, when great power wars did come, the antagonists were able to throw much greater resources into them. At the same time, however, they proved reluctant to embark on such wars in the first place. Finally, the World Wars were followed by a third consecutive record: 60 years of no war between economically developed countries to date. Although this 'long peace' is often attributed to the nuclear factor—a decisive factor to be sure—the trend had been evident long before the advent of nuclear weapons.

How then might the special features of the industrial–technological age account for the sharp decline in the frequency of wars waged among economically advanced societies? This question—and the principal answers to resolve it—have been around since the nineteenth century, approached with more or less scepticism, depending on the times, but never crystallizing into a satisfactory comprehensive explanation. One might just as well start again.

As we have already seen, the underlying development, and novelty, of the industrial–technological age was rapid and continuous growth in real wealth. Wealth no longer constituted a fundamentally finite quantity as it had been through the ages, when the main question about it had been how it was to be divided. Thus, wealth acquisition was progressively changing away form a zero-sum game, where one participant's gain could be achieved only at the other's expense. In advanced countries, economic activity became by far the main avenue to wealth (which poor countries became too weak to conquer). Furthermore, national economies were no longer overwhelmingly autarkic and therefore barely affected by each other—they became increasingly connected in an intensifying and spreading network of specialization and exchange, the much celebrated 'globalization' of markets and the economy. Prosperity abroad became interrelated with one's own, with foreign devastation potentially depressing the entire system and thus being detrimental to one's own well-being. The radical novelty of this state of affairs was clearly recognized by contemporaries, such as John Stuart Mill:

> . . . commerce first taught nations to see with good will the wealth and prosperity of one another. Before, the patriot, unless sufficiently advanced in culture to feel the world his country, wished all countries weak, poor, and ill-governed, but his own: he now sees in their wealth and progress a direct source of wealth and progress to his own country. It is commerce which is rapidly rendering war obsolete.[31]

To be sure, all this did not mean harmony. Economic relations remained—indeed, grew ever more—competitive. All the same, the greater the yields brought by competitive economic co-operation, the more counterproductive and less attractive conflict became. The influential social thinker Auguste Comte (echoing his mentor Saint-Simon) expressed the growing feeling in the first half of the nineteenth century when conceptualizing that warrior society had been giving way to the industrial stage of human development.[32]

This at least was the theory that nineteenth-century progressivists tended to believe, which, indeed, seemed to account for the very real decline in occurrence of war in Europe's economically advanced parts. The theory was not limited to Manchester liberals, whose doctrine of free trade dominated the mid-century until the revival of protectionism from the late 1870s. Free trade was optimal but not a necessary condition for the theory to work. No other than the famous future chief of the Prussian general staff Helmuth von Moltke wrote in 1841:

> We candidly confess our belief in the idea, on which so much ridicule has been cast, of a general European peace. Not that long and bloody wars are to cease from henceforth . . . [however,] wars will become rarer and rarer because they are growing expensive beyond measure; positively because of the actual cost; negatively because of the necessary neglect of work. Has not the population of Prussia, under a good and wise administration, increased by a fourth in twenty-five years of peace? And are not her fifteen millions of inhabitants better fed, clothed and instructed today than her eleven millions used to be? Are not such results equal to a victorious campaign or to the conquest of a province, with that great difference that they are not gained at the expense of other nations, nor with the sacrifice of the enormous number of victims that a war demands?[33]

Moltke later changed his mind and was to become the epitome of Prussian militant nationalism. Many others took a similar path by the late nineteenth and early twentieth centuries. And with the two World Wars and other cataclysms of the latter century, nineteenth-century optimistic economic pacifism lost much of its certainties. What then were the theory's flaws? Where did a generally valid economic rationale prove deficient?

We may begin by examining the great powers' wars that disturbed the nineteenth century's relative peacefulness. What were they about? Apart from the Crimean War (1854–6), waged for security reasons discussed later on, these were the War of 1859 that led to Italy's unification, the American Civil War (1861–5), and the Wars of German Unification (1864, 1866, 1870–1). Although all these wars obviously involved a variety of motives, it was above all issues of national unity, national independence, national self-determination, and national identity that constituted the deepest and most inflammable motives for these major wars. Indeed, the same held true for military conflict in general throughout Europe.[34] The hotspots of violent conflict were distinguished by recurring, more or less successful, national uprisings: in conquered and partitioned Poland, fragmented and foreign-dominated Italy, disunited Germany, the territories of the future Belgium briefly stitched to Holland, suppressed Ireland, Habsburg-incorporated Hungary, and the Ottoman-held Balkans. The pressures of disintegration in the multi-ethnic–multi-national Ottoman Empire and, indeed, also in the multi-ethnic–multi-national Habsburg Empire became the deepest source of power instability in south-east Europe. Simultaneously, the problem of Alsace-Lorraine, annexed to Germany in 1871 but retaining its affinity of national sentiment to France, remained the deepest source of tension in western Europe, preventing any possibility of a genuine Franco-German reconciliation.

So the economy was not everything. Other powerful motives determined human behaviour. The rising tide of modern nationalism that engulfed Europe during the nineteenth century overrode the logic of the new economic realities wherever problems of nationality were serious enough. Critics have already pointed this out as one of the main reasons for the failure of Marx's predictions. Indeed, a failure to grasp the deeper nature of the national phenomenon has been widespread among socialists and liberals of the universalist brand. For some of them, nationalism was wholly a product of modern historical developments such as industrialization and urbanization. For others, nationalism came equally late, but constituted little more than an artificial and manipulative 'invention' by state elites, which used new instruments, such as the universal school system and universal conscription, to instil that doctrine in the masses.[35] How could such an artificial invention succeed in evoking the most powerful, stormy emotions in populations that had always been, and largely remained, suspicious of or apathetic towards state authorities? Were not the old state elites in fact fearful of the new tide of nationalism, which they attempted to stem, with which they had to compromise, which often brought their downfall? Indeed, if nationalism was such a malleable artificial invention, why did it consistently tear apart multi-ethnic empires rather than being enlisted by the imperial authorities, 'manipulated', to turn the empires' varied populations into cohesive modern nations? Strangely enough, these questions seem not to have occurred to 'instrumentalist' theorists of nationalism.

As already indicated, nationalism has been a constant—often shocking—puzzle for many historians, social scientists, philosophers, and other literati during recent times, who have lacked the explanatory (evolutionary) framework that would account for the various human motivations and the way that they connect with each other. For, in the evolutionary calculus, kin are favoured over non-kin in expanding, weakening circles that extend from self to close family, more remote family, tribe, and people. One's compatriots are brethren in more than metaphor. Although cultural similarity often bonds together non-kin, it largely works by cuing for kinship, and in any case most ethnic groups, peoples, and nations *are* genetically related. Thus, although material well-being is of paramount significance, it is biased towards, and constitutes only one element in the overall prosperity of, those considered to be one's kin group. The real question to address, then, is in what ways older kin-based identities and forms of ethnocentrism, including pre-modern nationalism, were transformed to produce modern nationalism under the new conditions generated by modernity.

We saw earlier that this was a continuous process, successively 'punctuated' by major historical developments. National states were far more prevalent in late medieval Europe than is commonly recognized. From the early modern period, printing technology further bonded together older nationalities and other ethnic–lingual populations into 'imagined communities' of the literate. Larger centralized states, expanding capitalist economies, and greater urbanism variously facilitated that trend, within and across state boundaries. By the time of the French Revolution, well before industrialization, nationalism had become a potent force in Europe. All the same, industrialization was to become yet another, most powerful factor in the shaping of modern nationalism. The spread of railways for the first time connected rural populations that had rarely if ever left their isolated native villages. Moreover, massive population movement now took place from the countryside to the industrial cities.[36] Whereas in pre-industrial society around 80–90 per cent of the population lived in the countryside, more than half of the population became urban by about 1850 in Britain and 1890 in Germany, although only 1930 in France and most of the other developed countries. A growing share of them concentrated in metropolitan centres.[37] The masses were now crowding in the cities rather than being dispersed throughout the countryside.

The consequences of this transformation for identity were manifold. Ethnically related populations were thrown together, with much of the older local diversity in dialect and customs eradicated in the process. Gone also were the close-knit, small-scale village communities, which were replaced by the new, mobile, 'atomistic', anonymous, mass society. As *Gemeinschaft* gave way to *Gesellschaft*, intermediate foci of primary identity between the close family and the nation were either weakened or disappeared altogether. For the displaced and disoriented people, the nation thus became the principal object of kin identification beyond the nuclear family. And as the masses were now concentrated in the cities, near the centres of power and political authority, rather than being impotently dispersed throughout the countryside as earlier in history, they were well positioned to make their voice heard. Consequently, where nation and state more or less overlapped, the state, despite the deep apprehensions of the old state elites, was able to ride, and reinforce, the national tide, thereby gaining much in strength. By contrast, where national and state boundaries conflicted, the new potency of nationalism (even where the state school system did not inculcate it— indeed, struggled to suppress it) often caused ethnically composite states to disintegrate. Contrary to fashionable theories, ethnicity had mattered a great deal in multi-ethnic states and empires of pre-industrial times. Yet most people's lives had been confined to their immediate locality, and their views and sentiments had anyway counted for very little. With literacy, advanced communications, and urbanism, all this changed.

Thus, by the late nineteenth and early twentieth centuries, urban and almost universally literate mass society had come into being in north-west– central Europe and was increasingly shaping politics.[38] In nation-states, the spreading school system and compulsory military service (where it existed) reinforced the trend, serving as major agents of national socialization and promoting the national ethos. In all countries—nation-states or ethnically fragmented—people were reading the popular press that emerged to tap the new mass market, and, indeed, catered for their taste by its mostly nationalist and chauvinistic line—in support of or in opposition to the state's authorities. Matters of national honour and national aggrandizement proved to be highly emotive for these volatile masses even more than for the old state elites, creating new pressures that the latter could not ignore. As Prussian-German chief of staff Moltke declared: 'In these days, war and peace and the relations of nations are no longer cabinet questions; in many countries the people themselves govern the cabinet, and thus an element is introduced into politics which is impossible to reckon.'[39] 'The passion of the populace, the ambition of party leaders, and public opinion led astray both in speeches and by the press . . . are elements which may prove stronger than the will of those who rule.'[40] In consequence: 'The days of the cabinet wars are past, now we have only the people's war.' Once such a war broke out, Moltke famously predicted in 1890, it might rage for 7 or even 30 years.[41]

THE WARS OF EMPIRE

Nationalism contributed to the occurrence of war not only where questions of national independence, unity, and identity were directly at stake, but also as a mediating factor in other potential causes for violent conflict. Great power imperialism in the industrially undeveloped parts of the world was a major, probably *the* major, cause of conflict and mounting international tensions among the powers in the generation before the First World War, and was largely responsible for the outbreak of both World Wars. In addition, imperialism was central to relations between the industrially developed and undeveloped worlds, including a large number of colonial wars. Both aspects of imperialism—its effect on relations within the developed world and between developed and undeveloped countries, in their mutual interaction—are examined next in my quest to explain the changing pattern of war in the industrial–technological age. During the nineteenth century, but particularly in the period 1878–1920, the European powers divided Africa among themselves; together with Japan and the USA, they continued to expand in south-east and east Asia, including the carving out of China, which by the last years of the century seemed to be on the brink of partition; they also took over large parts of the Ottoman Empire, before and after demolishing that empire in the First World War. Already controlling 35 per cent of the world surface in 1800, including colonies and former colonies, Europeans increased their control to 67 per cent in 1878 and 84 per cent in 1914. The British Empire, the largest of them all, which in 1800 possessed a land area of 4 million square kilometres and a population of 20 million, expanded sevenfold in area and twentyfold in population during the following century. After the First World War, it expanded even more, encompassing 23.9 per cent of the world's land surface.[42]

What accounts for the new spate of imperial expansion that gathered momentum from the 1880s, and how did this expansion stand in relation to the economic rationale described above? This is a much debated topic that has preoccupied publicists, ideologues, and scholars ever since. Obviously, the intention here is not to summarize again a much-rehashed debate, but rather to relate it to the question of war and of war's transformation in the modern world. As with any historical phenomenon, scholars agree that a variety of factors contributed to the new wave of imperial expansion, including the 'sucking in' effect of a 'turbulent frontier', where colonial officials and metropolitan authorities found themselves increasingly involved in order to safeguard an already growing penetration by western missionaries, businessmen, and settlers. However, this and a variety of other factors are best understood within the context of the two general developments that underlie modernity (and my discussion of it): the rise of a western-dominated industrial world economy and the corresponding surge in western technological–military prowess—the explosion of wealth and power.

Indeed, although earlier students of imperialism concentrated, as we see later, on the first of these developments, a more recent study has pointed out that the second development was no less significant in generating imperialism. In his *The Tools of Empire: Technology and European imperialism in the nineteenth century* (1981), Daniel Headrick has argued that, whatever other factors were involved, to some degree imperialism took place simply because it had become so easy. Technological innovations during the nineteenth century made the penetration and military domination of

543

hitherto inaccessible territories much easier for the powers of the developed world. Steamboats were able to go up rivers into the depth of landlocked countries and continents. From the British incursion in 1841–2 on, they carried western presence into, and brought western artillery to bear upon, China's heartland: the Grand Canal connecting south and north and the capital city Beijing. River steamboats similarly paved the way for French colonial expansion in Indochina. There and in Africa, they were supplemented by the introduction of quinine, an effective medicine against the highly lethal malaria. Together the two inventions made possible European penetration of the depth of tropical Africa, which until then remained beyond their reach because of rainforests and diseases. The rifled, breech-loading, and magazine-fed infantry gun, in succession, gave westerners an unprecedented superiority in firepower over the people of the undeveloped world. The railway and the telegraph connected vast occupied territories, making them far easier to control than earlier. This was true not only for Asia and Africa but also for North America, where the conquest of the west was pretty much made possible by the last-mentioned technologies of fire-arms and communications. Thus western colonial conquest was greatly accelerated in the late nineteenth century largely because modern technology made it far easier. Natural obstacles were overcome, whereas native resistance became both more exposed and less able to withstand armed confrontation. No longer did smooth-bore musket technology constitute the standard that was more or less available to all. As the technological–industrial gap between the developed and undeveloped parts of the world opened up, so did the inequality in power, discussed earlier.

The new ease of colonial expansion and conquest accounts for a major distinction within modern wars. For only the number of wars and war years among the great powers and among economically developed countries in general declined sharply in the industrial–technological age. Wars between advanced powers and adversaries from the undeveloped world registered no such decline, and their number even increased. Taken together, then, the overall number of wars and war years barely changed, especially for colonial powers such as France and Britain, with levels of belligerency that would appear to far exceed those of Prussia–Germany and Austria. And yet these data conceal a profound transformation, all too often obscured in studies of belligerency.[43] Wars among the great powers, with a frequency that has now been sharply declining, were historically the greatest, hardest, and most destructive of inter-state wars. By contrast, the frequency of armed conflicts between developed countries and undeveloped adversaries remained unchanged (and even increased during the colonial era), precisely because such conflicts became easily won on the cheap by the developed countries—at least initially. The easier they became, the lesser were the inhibitions for the powers to be drawn into them.

This still leaves the question, why go in at all? Imperialism was of course not a new phenomenon in either universal or European history. How then did the new wave of imperial expansion during the industrial age differ, if at all, from earlier empire building? Historically throughout *agraria*, tribute— the appropriation of other people's fruits of labour in the form of booty, war indemnities, and taxation—was the principal material reward of imperial expansion. In some cases, land acquisition for agricultural settlement by one's own people constituted another significant material reward. Acquisition of trading posts and the monopolization of trade came as a distant third, figuring most prominently in the relatively few cases of trading empires created by commercial city-states.

All these material objectives—tribute extraction, agricultural colonization, and trade monopolization—continued in the period of European expansion during the early modern period. Increasingly, however, trading posts and the monopolization of trade grew in significance, as global trading became the engine of Europe's increasing wealth. In the wake of the Portuguese and Dutch trading empires, Britain won an unprecedented trading monopoly in the eighteenth century. Although the economic logic of protectionist monopolization and colonialism was rejected by Adam Smith, it was only in the industrial age that Britain embraced free trade.

Greater freedom of trade became that much more attractive to advanced economies in the industrial age for the simple reason that the overwhelming share of fast-growing and diversifying production was now intended for sale in the marketplace rather then being directly consumed by the family producers themselves as in the pre-industrial economy. Lower barriers to the flow of goods enhanced the efficiency of the exploding market economy, with an increasingly complex and deepening network of specialization and exchange that transcended political boundaries.[44] During industrialization, foreign trade of the European powers increased twice as fast as their fast-growing GNP, so that, by the late nineteenth and early twentieth centuries, exports plus imports grew to around half the GNP in Britain and

France, more than a third in Germany, and around a third in Italy (and Japan).[45] Succinctly put: greater freedom of trade was the corollary of the vast expansion of the market economy in the industrial age, as people traded rather than directly consumed most of the products of their labour. As nineteenth-century economists already grasped, there were various significant qualifications, which we see later, to this underlying rationale, which halted and even reversed trade liberalization. But it certainly held for the world industrial leader, Britain, with manufactured goods that were anyway likely to win against any competition during her mid-Victorian zenith. According to free-trade economic theory, colonies were at best irrelevant to wealth acquisition and more often detrimental to it, because of the resulting political interferences with the operation of the markets. Aggregate size of countries, and hence also imperial possessions, generally do not matter economically if free trade prevails; people's (per capita) wealth bears little relationship to their country's size.

All this, however, holds only if free trade prevails. For this reason, free trade did not eliminate imperialism but rather created 'the imperialism of free trade', as a seminal, controversial article by John Gallagher and Ronald Robinson was titled. British foreign policy during the nineteenth century strove to secure the widest possible global access to the mass-produced manufacturing of the first industrial nation that was becoming the workshop of the world. Britain's economic and military power was used to negotiate with and pressurize foreign political authorities in order to secure free trade or at least low tariff barriers for British goods. Although requesting no preference over other powers, the British were of course positioned to gain the most from the lifting of trade restrictions. Gunboat diplomacy was occasionally employed to achieve this objective around the world. Military coercion—implied or actual—thus remained part of British policy, either to open markets or to keep them open. As already seen, with wealth and power correlating in the modern and even more in the industrial age, guns were used to bring down political 'walls' that hindered the encroachment of low-price capitalist goods. According to Gallagher and Robinson, a so-called informal British empire was thereby created, in South America, the Middle East, east Asia, and parts of Africa, where a sovereign yet variably dominated periphery—economically and politically—maximized economic profit for Britain while minimizing the costs of intervention, conflict, and direct rule. The burden of direct rule was eschewed as much as possible as unnecessary.[46] This nineteenth-century British-dominated global economic–political sphere became archetypal of 'free-trade imperialism' in general, primarily associated with the USA after the Second World War.

Placing Gallagher's and Robinson's 'informal empire' within an even longer historical perspective, it should be remembered that hegemonic empire had almost universally constituted the first stage in the development of empires. Throughout history, imperial hegemons initially preferred to retain indigenous political rulers in power, so that they could collect tribute and enforce trade monopolies on the hegemon's behalf. Only when indigenous rule failed or ceased to co-operate did the imperial power develop the apparatus for, and assumed the burden of, direct rule, creating 'formal' territorial empires. This is also what happened in the age of free-trade imperialism, according to Gallagher and Robinson: formal empire figured as the last resort when informal, hegemonic imperialism had failed.

The Gallagher–Robinson thesis has been subjected to a great deal of criticism. Among other things, critics have stressed the British government's intense reluctance to get involved in the internal politics of foreign countries as well as its very limited influence on their affairs, which cast doubt on the aptness of the concepts political domination and 'informal empire'.[47] It is agreed, however, that, as Britain embraced free trade in the middle of the nineteenth century, her use of coercive power changed from what it had been during the era of monopolistic trade and monopolistic empire: 'willingness to limit the use of paramount power to establishing security for trade is the distinctive feature of the British imperialism of free trade in the nineteenth century, in contrast to the mercantilist use of power to obtain commercial supremacy and monopoly through political possession.'[48]

Moreover, one should add that the imperialism of free trade differed from the older tributary imperialism (elements of which obviously lingered on) in that its underlying rationale, at least in theory, was not extraction, but mutually beneficial trade, generating growing wealth and the whole range of attended benefits *for all*. Although historical tributary empires, too, often professed to bring peace, stability, and the blessing of civilization to their subjects, as they sometimes did, informal liberal imperialism constituted a radical departure from the past to the degree that the modern take-off itself constituted a radical departure. To be sure, the process was anything but ideal. The Opium War (1839–42), when China was forced to open up to the British import of that drug, is a glaring example of the many abuses of

547

the process. Furthermore, capitalism's 'creative destruction', in Schumpeter's phrase, involves painful transformation and dislocation as a matter of course, and all the more so for traditional, pre-industrial society. Still, connecting others to the world economy—voluntarily, by pressure, and even by force—constituted, in principle, their only road to sustained real growth and away from the material deprivation, stagnation, zero-sum competition, and high mortality of *agraria*. This has all too easily been swept aside by the rhetoric of anti-imperialism.[49] The following vision of a general progress (here applied to the Ottoman Empire) guided not only liberal theorists but liberal statesmen everywhere, from British prime minister Palmerston on to the present: A thriving trade would

> ... bring the Sultan to introduce liberal reforms which would give the subject peoples representation in government and property rights in the Courts. The productive classes were to be freed from the exactions of their quasi-feudal Moslem overlords whose rule, the British believed, had kept the country backward and poor for centuries. Once liberated, the peasant would produce more for the market, the Oriental merchant would accumulate capital and his enterprise would develop the economy in partnership with the British merchant. The flowing trade would spread liberal notions of justice and freedom.[50]

In this logic, Britain's pioneering path to modernity—although singular—would be replicated everywhere else, because the pressure of low-cost goods from the already modernized core—aided, where necessary, by superior force—would more or less automatically generate similar processes throughout the world's pre-industrial periphery.

Spreading industrial globalization indeed proved irresistible (and on the whole highly beneficial materially), and yet not quite along the lines envisaged by free-trade liberals and Whiggish notions of Progress. As it was formulated by Adam Smith and David Ricardo, the theory of free trade withstood most challenges and the vast majority of economists today embrace it; yet a few major exceptions and some nagging questions remain. The principal exception concerned those countries with a social and political infrastructure that was sufficiently developed to facilitate an industrial 'take-off'. However, as so-called national economists in these countries, from Alexander Hamilton and Friedrich List on, pointed out, their nascent industries needed the protection of tariff barriers in their home markets against the products of more established industrial economies, at least until they developed sufficiently to be able to compete successfully. For this reason, the USA, Germany, France, Russia, and Japan all adopted strong protectionist policies against British manufacturing during their period of industrial take-off in the later part of the nineteenth century. Even the self-governing, 'white' dominions of Britain's 'formal' empire—Canada, Australia, and New Zealand—adopted protective tariffs against the motherland. Contrary to liberal orthodoxy, no country in the nineteenth century—or indeed the twentieth—ever became a first-class economy without first embracing protectionism. In these developed parts of the world, there was no question of Britain exerting pressure—let alone military pressure—to enforce free trade.

The imperialism of free trade worked best in the second category of countries, where local elites could be successfully drawn into the British dominated world economy in a mutually beneficial yet asymmetrical relationship. These countries mostly exported foodstuffs and raw materials to Britain, while importing her manufactured goods. Only rarely, in times of crisis, when the local political authorities and elites that were involved in, and guaranteed the safety of, the foreign business lost control, might a short-term armed intervention be initiated to restore order and the economic interests of the hegemonic power—Britain or any other.

There was, however, a third category of countries—most notably the Islamic countries and China—where the combined pressure of low-cost goods and gunboat diplomacy met with deep-seated local resistance to change. Exposure to the western global economy and western induced modernization undermined the indigenous political–social–economic–cultural order. State authorities proved reluctant, inept, or weak, state bureaucracies stifling and corrupt. Among the prospective losers and beneficiaries from change, it was the former who held power: feudal and tribal elites were incapable and unwilling to make the transition to the market that had been uniquely achieved by the British aristocracy; the merchant class were not allowed to grow sufficiently to become significant. Cultural attitudes strongly meditated against market-oriented reform, which, furthermore, came as an alien foreign intrusion. There was, indeed, an even worse scenario. Failing to develop, native society also failed to compete economically and incurred foreign debt. National reaction against the foreigners followed, engulfing the populace which experienced only the stresses of capitalism without its benefits. Tottering collaborative indigenous political authorities could not be restored by short-term intervention. Already existing foreign interests were threatened. In these situations the hegemon was faced with the conflicting options of either withdrawal or intervention to impose direct, 'formal', imperial control. Contrary to the Gallagher and Robinson formula: 'trade with informal control if possible; trade with rule when necessary'; rarely was the last option adopted for commercial reasons in the undeveloped as in the developed parts of the world.[51]

The most notable exception was India, the 'jewel' of the British formal empire. Acquired by force in the era of monopolistic trading imperialism, it was kept in the era of free trade imperialism partly because it had already been under British rule, but also because the liberal British authorities became convinced by the mid-nineteenth century that a withdrawal of formal imperial rule would be harmful for both India and British trade. India would revert into the hands of exploitative, corrupt, and warring state rulers. Efficient administrative and honest judicial systems would be gone. Social reform and economic development would stall. Both the masses of peasantry and the urban classes would be surrendered to their social superiors. Concomitantly, British trade with a fifth to sixth of humanity living on the Indian subcontinent, now secured, would be disrupted by anarchy and trade barriers. Thus liberal morality—indeed, duty—and self-interest reinforced each other in sustaining British rule in India.[52] Humanitarian considerations—the efforts to eradicate the slave trade—were also partly responsible for the British limited expansion in west Africa before the 'scramble'. The famous missionary and explorer David Livingstone was typical in holding that only civilization, commerce, and Christianity—the three Cs *combined*—would deliver Africa from the hands of the slave traders.[53] Kipling's 'white man's burden' was not un-genuine.

China presented an opposite example to India. She did not constitute a British imperial bequest from an earlier age, whereas her susceptibility to the encroachments of free trade imperialism proved limited. The problem was not the Celestial Kingdom's strength but her weakness. Openness to British trade was imposed on China by gunboat diplomacy, but the declining dynastic rule proved little inclined to, or capable of, embracing change and reforming society and the economy. As a result, although encompassing almost a quarter of humanity, China's value as a trading partner declined compared with the developing and increasingly richer parts of the world. The growing weakening under foreign pressure of China's central government was exposed in the disastrous Tai-Ping peasant rebellion (1851–64), the greatest blood letting of the nineteenth century. Concerned about the prospect of anarchy and unwilling to saddle the burden of direct imperial rule over the huge kingdom, Britain viewed China's slow modernization and limited integration into the world economy as the least harmful of the available options.

Much the same applied to the Ottoman Empire, where market-induced social reforms and economic modernization again fell far short of liberal hopes. Nevertheless, only in Egypt did the collapse of the Khedive's regime—with a failing modernization programme and ensuing massive foreign debts that generated strong nationalist and Islamic anti-western revolutionary forces—prompted Britain to intervene (1882). And temporary intervention reluctantly turned into a permanent occupation when it became clear that withdrawal would leave behind no political power able to guarantee western interests. The British take-over proved pivotal, because it triggered the 'scramble for Africa', which in as little as two decades led to the partitioning of the entire continent among the European powers.

This eruption of massive formal imperial expansion in Africa has been viewed as puzzling, because it seemed to make no economic sense. Anarchy or hostile government in Egypt would have threatened existing western financial and commercial interests, but the potential losses in themselves would not have persuaded Gladstone's Liberal government to assume what the frustrated Gladstone termed a permanent 'Egyptian bondage' that went against all its principles. Even more the puzzle of imperial expansion concerned the vast sub-Saharan African territories—among the world's poorest, least developed, and least profitable—that promised very little for the imperial powers in return for the costs of administration, policing, and infrastructure. Gold-rich South Africa and rubber-rich Belgian Congo constituted rare exceptions where African colonies promised real rewards. The wealth of the developed world during the industrial–technological era was derived from home-based manufacturing and trade with other developed and semi-developed countries. Vast colonial empires in Africa contributed practically nothing to that wealth.

As the data for the foremost colonial empire and world's financier show, during the late nineteenth and early twentieth centuries about 40 per cent of British investment was made in Britain herself; another 45 per cent went to the USA, South America, and continental Europe; only around 15 per cent went to the formal empire. Furthermore, investment in the empire over-whelmingly concentrated in the self-governing, white dominions: Canada, Australia, and New Zealand. The empire in India came next in the volume of investment, whereas investment in the new, least developed African colonies was negligible. Contrary to the famous thesis promoted by the British economist and publicist J. M. Hobson and adopted by Lenin, nor was investment in colonial markets sought by investors in preference to diminishing returns on investment in the developed economies. The more developed the country of investment the higher were the returns, with the new African acquisitions bringing the lowest returns. Trade data for France, the second largest imperial power, were similarly distributed.[54] The new wave of imperial expansion constituted a negligible business.

This is demonstrated by the fact that the fastest growing new economic giants of the late nineteenth century were the USA and Germany, which, despite their new colonial ambitions and minor acquisitions, were the least of the colonial empires (though obviously some of the USA's meteoric growth came from its internal westward colonization within North America). Conversely, the largest and fastest growing colonial empires, Britain and France, suffered the greatest relative decline in economic status among the great powers during the era of the new imperialism. Indeed, with the close correlation of economic and military power, the empire's poor military contribution mirrored the economic one. Metropolitan Britain incurred 80 per cent of the casualties and 88 per cent of the costs of the First World War, with the remainder, the imperial share, taken mostly by the self-governing dominions.[55]

As the meagre economic, and other, benefits from Africa were recognized at the time, what brought the 'scramble'? More than Africa was at stake. In the first place, there was the British Empire in India. To secure the sea route from Europe to India, Britain had already controlled South Africa. The British intervention and stay in Egypt was prompted mostly by concern for the safety of the recently opened shorter sea route to India, through the Suez Canal. In addition to the collapse of local authority in Egypt, it was, above all, the threat to India posed by Russia's advance in central Asia and am-bitions in the eastern Mediterranean that dominated Britain's foreign and strategic policy during the nineteenth century. Thus, both of Britain's two major colonial possessions in Africa—the old and the new—were in them-selves of scant economic value and played a small economic role in Britain's system of free trade; rather, they were intended to secure that system against other powers that might threaten British trade by military force. The British concern in the Transvaal was motivated not by its newly found mineral wealth but by the fear that this wealth would lead the Boers to reassert their independence and ally with Germany, now based in south-west and east Africa. In turn, however, other powers could not but view British security-motivated actions as monopolization, as they partly were. Although India, for example, was open to trade with others, British administration in India undoubtedly gave British economic interests a preferential status. France, with her long-standing economic and political involvement in Egypt, thus regarded the British take-over of Egypt as a blow, both economically and in terms of prestige.

To a large degree the scramble for Africa can be said to have cascaded from that point.[56] Incensed by Britain's continued presence in Egypt, France moved to realize plans long entertained by her politicians and officials for huge colonial expansion across the Sahara, connecting her Algerian and west African possessions and discarding older understandings with Britain that had eschewed large-scale formal annexations in west Africa. The motive for these plans lay in the realm of national prestige rather than economics, and became more prominent in the wake of France's humiliating defeat in 1870–1. Yet the plans were now realized as leverage intended to pressurize Britain out of Egypt. In actuality, the effect achieved was the opposite. Becoming concerned that French expansion would give France control over the Sudan, the upper Nile, and, hence, Egypt's water, Britain moved to bring the entire Nile Valley under her formal control, including the Sudan, Uganda, and the east African land route to Uganda (Kenya). The process of pre-emptive land grab accelerated when Germany, which gained a favourable pivotal position in the Franco-British conflict, was given her own colonies in Africa in 1884–5. Bismarck mainly took them for domestic political reasons, because he dismissed African colonies as irrelevant and was concerned only with Europe and great power relations. The huge Congo territory was handed to the king of Belgium as his personal possession, because most of the great powers deemed this option preferable to control by any of the other great powers.

Thus the 'scramble' was a case of a defence-motivated expansion on Britain's part, which escalated after triggering the 'security dilemma' in others, reinforcing nationalist trends and setting in motion a growing fear of monopolization among all. Free-trading Britain increasingly regarded formal empire necessary not only in limited strategic areas, against security threats, but as a more general pre-emptive policy, once other, protectionist powers began to expand their own formal empires, which they would close to others. Formal empire thus became necessary for Britain to secure free trade. For protectionist powers, the pre-emptive aspect of the grab was obviously at least as compelling. Either way, the result was a runaway process.

China was, of course, an incomparably more important economic prize than Africa, yet not dissimilar inter-power dynamics developed there by the late 1890s. With the progress of her Trans-Siberian railway, Russia was for the first time reaching the brink of becoming capable of military power projection on to China's frontier. Even if Russia had no policy of territorial annexation in China, Britain was no longer able—by virtue of her naval supremacy—to guarantee China's independence as an 'open door' but British-dominated market. At the same time, other industrializing powers—Japan, Germany, France, and the USA—now made themselves increasingly present in China. China's defeat in the war with Japan (1894–5) further weakened her regime. The prospect of the country's political disintegration now appeared imminent, heightening inter-power competition, because a collapse of indigenous authority would most probably mean partition, in which no power could afford to be left behind. Although all the powers preferred a united and open Chinese market, each increased its encroachments on China's sovereignty, thereby triggering the process of partition. Regarded as an almost foregone conclusion in the closing years of the nineteenth century, partition was averted after Japan removed the threat of a Russian advance by her victory in Manchuria (1904–5). All the same, it was the powers' conflicting pressures on China to open up and for preferential rights, precipitated by and precipitating the decline of indigenous central authority, that threatened to turn China from an open-for-all trading sphere into zones of formal great power rule.

Indeed, with partition taking place in Africa and looming over China, the British-dominated free trade system was threatened by the prospect of protectionism, which was a self-reinforcing process and self-fulfilling prophecy. Britain's exports had already been suffering badly from the high tariff barriers adopted by all the other great powers, as well as from German and American surging industrial competitiveness, which progressively blunted

Britain's former lead in foreign markets.[57] Losing her position as the economic hegemon, it was now Britain that increasingly contemplated the advantages of retreating from free trade and consolidating her vast formal empire into a protectionist trade zone. Championed by colonial secretary Joseph Chamberlain at the turn of the century, and partly implemented in the wake of the First World War, this policy was finally adopted in 1932, during the Great Depression. Conversely, it was now the USA and Germany that would become increasingly interested in the removal of trade barriers to their manufacturing exports.

The USA, with her huge domestic market, was less dependent on foreign trade, yet the growth of global protectionism in the 1930s hit her exports the hardest and inhibited her recovery from the Depression. Wilhelmine Germans by the advent of the twentieth century felt that only a 'United States of Europe' free trade zone or a European common market (and at the very least an economically unified *Mitteleuropa*) would offer German industry sufficient scope to develop, comparable to the vast spaces of the USA, the British Empire, and Russia. Such a European trade zone would best be achieved by peaceful agreement, but, failing that, might also be enforced by military power and political domination. Furthermore, if the emerging global economy were to be geographically sliced among the powers rather than open to all, Germany, too, would require a large colonial empire. As Germany entered the colonial contest late, the creation of such an empire would necessitate a revision of the existing order. Germany set her eyes on a huge central African empire (*Mittelafrika*) that would weld her existing colonies, together with Portuguese Angola and Mozambique, with the resource-rich Belgian Congo, which Germans hoped would be ceded to Germany. With the First World War and, subsequently, with Germany's defeat, such designs grew more militant and extreme. For Hitler, the creation of an economically self-sufficient German Reich that would stride continental Europe and possess the capacity that Germany had lacked for sustaining a prolonged war was inseparable from his racist plans and vision of a perpetual global struggle. All the interconnected aspects of the liberal programme were replaced by their antithetical opposite.

Much the same would hold true for Japan. Lacking raw materials and heavily dependent on trade, Japan was hit hard by the erection of protectionist walls in the early 1930s by the other great powers. She increasingly regarded the establishment of her own empire as essential for her survival.

555

Her take-over of Manchuria (1931) and penetration of northern China involved Japan in an all-out war with China (1937). In turn, the necessities of that war, the lure of the French and Dutch colonial empires, with metropolitan centres that were conquered by Germany in Europe (1940), and the American embargo (1941) on critical raw materials—above all oil—drove Japan to gamble everything on a bid for a self-sufficient empire, the so-called East Asian Co-prosperity Sphere. The economic–strategic logic of an empire in a partitioned industrial–commercial world economy unravelled far beyond any initial planning by Japan.

Here lay the seeds of the two World Wars between the great powers. If the industrial–commercial world economy was to be partitioned rather than open, the pressure for territorial grab became irresistible. From this perspective, it mattered little that turn-of-the-century Africa possessed scant economic value, because it was the long-range prospects of development as part of a global colonial empire that figured most. Furthermore, the Germans, for example, viewed the spread of the English-speaking peoples and culture as an enviable model. The empire was to become the destination for German immigration, which otherwise had been 'lost' to other countries. Japan viewed her own empire in Korea and Manchuria in similar terms. Thus national considerations—always paramount—were further boosted as the free trade model of the global economy was giving way to protectionism, and consequently also to power politics. In a partitioned global economy, economic power increases national strength, whereas national strength defends and increases economic power. Rather than confining themselves to Britain's own development, the challenge that free trade critics of the British formal empire have to address is that illiberal powers—more successfully than liberal Britain—might have turned their closed empires in various regions of the world vacated by Britain into a source of strength that would, in turn, make possible yet further expansion. As we see later, such illiberal empire building—some of it highly successful—would have to be resisted by force. National size made little difference in an open international economy, but became the key to economic success in an international economy dominated by power politics. Moreover, the quest for self-sufficiency in strategic war materials became a cause as well as an effect of the drive for empire, most notably in the German and Japanese cases towards and during the Second World War.

Given this integrated complex, colonialism became a truly national project, enjoying great national–popular support. During the 1870s, British prime minister Benjamin Disraeli had already exploited the popular appeal of empire to the new mass electorate created by the expansion of the franchise. By the advent of the twentieth century, this popular appeal became a tremendous force that politicians everywhere could not ignore even if they did not share that appeal, which a growing number of them did. The 'atavistic' drive of national expansion and the rationale of a partitioned world economy reinforced each other. Nationalism and colonialism merged.

All these were aspects of a deeper change. With the coming of the twentieth century, free trade liberalism was in retreat not only because of the mutual fear of protectionism but also because it was increasingly regarded as fundamentally flawed. The market economy in general was challenged, as also was the parliamentary–liberal and progressively more democratic model of society. The market economy was losing public favour as its volatility, waste, and social costs were criticized and the virtues of planning and regulation were advocated from radically diverging quarters by progressivists, fascists, and socialists. The parliamentary–liberal model of mass society, long resisted in some countries of the developed world by conservative elites and autocratic regimes, was now confronted by new-type formidable totalitarian regimes. Indeed, the emergence of new economic and political regimes carried far-reaching consequences for both great power war and empire building.

THE TOTALITARIAN CHALLENGE AND WHY IT WAS DEFEATED

Liberal–parliamentary Britain was the first industrial nation, after already figuring among the pioneers of commercial capitalism during early modernity. There was a close connection, discussed in Chapter 14 and well recognized at the time, among all these aspects of her evolution. And during much of the nineteenth century, as Britain's epoch-making leap into modernity was transforming the world and commanding universal attention, her model constituted the paradigm against which all future development would be judged. No less than admiration and envy, this paradigm inspired deep apprehension and resistance, both within and outside the west. The disappearing virtues of traditional society were widely lamented, contrasted with the alienating rule of mammon. Traditional agrarian elites and autocratic regimes feared the inevitable loss of power. However, rejection of industrialization and its corollaries would have meant a hopeless falling behind in terms not only of wealth but also of inter-state power, as experienced by the Ottoman and Chinese Empires, the very existence of which became jeopardized. This realization was starkly expressed in the slogan of the Meiji reformers–revolutionaries who put an end to the Tokugawa regime in Japan: 'rich country and a strong army.' Thus nineteenth-century conservative–autocratic European great powers east of the Rhine, such as Germany, Austria, and Russia, as well as Japan, and many other countries— then and later—sought to embrace industrialization and carry out the necessary social and political reforms that went with it, while also preserving as much as possible their autocratic–aristocratic regimes and traditional values.

The inherent tensions, if not contradictions, within that programme were—and have since been—acutely felt by the old elites, making them variably pessimistic about the success of their 'rearguard' action. Whether or not such sociopolitical regimes could have survived and prospered in some powerful and advanced industrial societies (such as Germany, Russia, and Japan) without necessarily converging into the liberal model cannot be told, because this historical experiment was cut off by war and the rise of totalitarianism that mainly replaced autocratic–conservative regimes in their home countries. Rooted in modern developments, the new totalitarian regimes claimed to be more in line with modernity than either old conservatism or parliamentary liberalism, and were far more militant.

In either its left- or right-wing brands (the differences are addressed later), totalitarianism was a distinctly new type of regime, different from earlier historical autocracies and becoming possible only with the advent of the twentieth century. It was rooted in what contemporaries since the late nineteenth century universally and acutely felt to be the defining development of their time that we now take for granted: the emergence of mass society. Nothing compared in the social consciousness of the time with the prominence of this new reality: to repeat, the crowding of semi-educated masses—until then dispersed in the countryside out of sight and out of mind—in the metropolitan centres of power, where they could no longer be ignored. Henceforth, any regime had to be a 'popular' regime, that is, derive legitimacy from one form or another of mass consent. As a result, old liberal parliamentarism was itself transformed. Historically suspicious of the masses, apprehensive that political equality would threaten individual liberty and private property, and limiting the franchise to the propertied classes, it was now obliged to democratize. By the 1920s universal franchise had become the norm in liberal–parliamentary societies. Liberal democracy came into being, a hybrid that was almost as novel as the totalitarian regimes that emerged during that same time.

Already in the nineteenth century, more advanced communications—newspapers, the railway, and electric telegraph—gave rise to popular plebiscitean autocracy on a country scale, akin to the popular brand of tyranny that until then had been mostly limited to city-states. Pioneered by Napoleon I but exemplified by Napoleon III in France, it is labelled Bonapartism or Caesarism. By the twentieth century yet newer breakthroughs in communication technology further enhanced mass society, even in countries that lagged behind in urbanization. To the popular press were added cinema (and newsreels) and, by the 1920s, radio, with their reach into remote corners of a country. Telephone and the automobile gave police a similar reach within hours if not minutes. Controlling and harnessing mass education and mass media, and suppressing all opposition to a degree as yet not known, the new totalitarian regimes assumed unprecedented control over both public and private spheres, achieving very high levels of material and spiritual mobilization, in contrast to traditional despotism.[58]

Indeed, although massive and ruthless terror was central for achieving social mobilization and obedience, terror alone, as in the past, would never have been sufficient for generating the sort of fanatical commitment exhibited by most totalitarian societies. A sweeping popular ideological creed was indispensable for firing and motivating the masses, for eliciting the sense of participation in something that concerned them directly and deeply, without which true mobilization has never been possible. Comprehensive ideologies of virtue and salvation—secular religions of conflicting brands—now largely replaced (or supplemented) older religious ideologies. On these grounds both left- and right-wing totalitarianism, led by a vanguard of the party elite, successfully claimed to be more truly representative of the people than parliamentary liberal democracy. Both offered a sweeping alternative to liberal ideology and society.

Communism rejected both the market system, with its social inequality and antagonist social relations, and liberal parliamentarism, which it regarded, even in its democratic forms, as a thin disguise for the actual rule of capital. It projected a salvationist vision based on social ownership and social planning that would liberate people from both material want and spiritual alienation. This was a most powerful mobilizing creed; yet if only because realities in communist regimes fell so short of the ideal, all communist regimes in time of crisis successfully evoked indigenous nationalism (which they had ideologically and officially dismissed) as the supreme mobilizing agent. Nationalism was, of course, the dominating theme in right-wing totalitarianism. Although retaining capitalism, right-wing totalitarianism aimed at recasting society in a radical antithesis to liberal society. Indeed, right-wing totalitarianism, too, represented nothing less than an out-and-out reaction and revolt against what was widely regarded as the ills of the liberal model: rampant capitalism; endemic social strife; divisive party politics; erosion of communal identity and sense of common purpose; alienating individualism; shallow materialism, lack of spirituality, and the disenchantment of life; and vulgar popular culture, humanitarian weakness, and decadence. Within the right-wing totalitarian mix, capitalism was to be efficiently regulated, the poor were to be provided for and disciplined, and a cohesive national community was to be created and infused with a sense of brotherhood and purpose—domestically and against outside rivals.[59]

As liberal democracy, fascism, and communism, the three great secular ideologies that vied among themselves over the question of how the new mass industrial society should be structured, each came to rule more than one of the great powers during the twentieth century, a new ideological rivalry, much more intense than anything experienced during the nineteenth century, reinforced old great power competition. This blending of ideology and power politics in the context of specific contingent circumstances produced various combinations. Communism was ideologically committed to the destruction of the capitalist world. At the same time, however, the Soviet leaders exhibited pragmatic cautiousness, because: the Soviet bloc was inferior in power to the capitalist world; they believed that that world was heading for inevitable internal collapse as a result of its inherent contradiction; and the huge Soviet Union was economically self-sufficient and its leaders believed that they could afford to bide their time. By contrast, both Nazi Germany and radicalizing imperial Japan during the 1930s and early 1940s manifested these countries' acute sense of economic insufficiency within their narrow territorial confines, from which both regimes strove to break out once and for all by military means. In both countries, traditional warrior ethos and deep-rooted resistance to west European humanitarian liberalism now evolved into a cult of violence, belligerency, heroic sacrifice, and perpetual struggle for domination. Inextricably these were deemed both necessary for national survival and good in themselves.

The interrelationship between ideological rivalry and power politics was therefore intricate and mutually affecting. The great powers' struggles assumed global dimensions because one's span of control meant greater aggregate power—economic access and military force—which was also subtracted from or denied to the other. Obviously, as already seen with respect to the colonial race, some gains in the poorest parts of the world might actually prove to be a liability. Still, it was not always clear in advance which countries might develop into assets over time; the geography of security in terms of frontiers, troop disposition, and bases has an inherent tendency to expand; and considerations of morale and prestige militated against any loss, lest a 'domino effect' be created. Ideological antagonism, the carving out of the world economy, and the 'security dilemma' inevitably reinforced each other.

Within two decades of the Second World War, the west European liberal-democratic powers lost their vast colonial empires in Asia and Africa. I examine the reasons for that transformation more closely in Chapter 16. At the moment suffice it to say that this involved little fundamental loss for the liberal democracies in terms of power and wealth. Industrially undeveloped countries were of scant economic significance anyway; countries that successfully underwent industrialization, such as those of east Asia, were absorbed into the capitalist global economy (even though usually developing behind protectionist walls), while being shielded by western military power; and countries that possessed critical raw materials, most notably the oil-producing Persian Gulf states, were similarly shielded, while their domestic stability was fostered by the techniques of informal imperialism. It is erroneous, however, to hold, as many do on the basis of western experience, that conquest is untenable or does not pay under modern conditions. As an excellent recent study strikingly demonstrates, for non-liberal, especially totalitarian great powers in the twentieth century, wide-scale conquest proved tenable in both developed and undeveloped countries, while being highly advantageous in the former.[60] Industrially developed countries (never ruled by liberal empires) were

561

controlled by and incorporated within totalitarian empires with relative ease, once occupied. Although the conquered were mass societies imbued with a strong sense of nationalism, their complex and integrated modern economies made them highly susceptible to ruthless pressure, to the extent that occasional demonstration rather than actual application of such pressure was usually sufficient to keep them under the yoke.

The most notable case in point is the countries of north-western Europe, which Nazi Germany overran in 1940 and harnessed to her war economy almost as successfully as Germany's own national economy. Compared with 1938, Germany's economic–military power thereby increased by maybe a half by her western annexations alone.[61] Germany controlled the more agrarian and economically less valuable countries of eastern and south-eastern Europe with almost equal ease. Only in Yugoslavia and some occupied parts of the Soviet Union did resistance in difficult terrain prove more successful; yet, had Germany won the war and been able to apply more force to these troublesome spots, her genocidal and semi-genocidal methods would have most probably prevailed there too. From its inception, the Soviet Union suppressed the peoples of the old Russian Empire— Russians and non-Russians alike—with far greater brutality than its predecessor had ever done. It continued to do so more or less successfully also in the countries that it had occupied in eastern Europe during the Second World War, down to the collapse of the Soviet Union and the Soviet bloc in 1989–91 for reasons other than the national. Only in desolate Afghanistan did the invading Soviet forces fail to curb local guerrilla resistance during the Empire's wane. Imperial Japan was similarly able to develop and harness the economic potential of Taiwan (occupied in 1895), Korea (1905), and Manchuria (1931) under her rule, as she very likely would have been able to do throughout her 'East Asian Co-prosperity Sphere' had her empire survived the Second World War.

Yet it was the liberal-democratic camp that emerged victorious from all of the three gigantic great power struggles of the twentieth century. What accounts for this decisive outcome? It is tempting to look for its roots in the special traits of the opposing systems, all the more so in a structural study such as this one. Did the liberal democracies more than compensate for their inferior repression capabilities abroad with a greater ability to elicit co-operation through the bonds—and discipline—of the global market system? This is probably true with respect to the Cold War but does not seem to apply to the two World Wars. Did liberal democracies succeed because ultimately they always stuck together? Again this may have applied mostly to the Cold War, when the democratic–capitalist camp was in any case greatly superior, while also profiting from the growing antagonism within the Communist bloc between the Soviet Union and China. During the First World War, however, the ideological divide was much weaker than it would later become. The Anglo-French alliance was far from preordained, being above all a function of the balance of power rather than the fruit of liberal co-operation. Only shortly earlier, power politics had brought these bitterly antagonistic countries to the brink of war and had made Anglo-German co-operation a strong possibility. Liberal Italy's departure from the Triple Alliance and joining of the Entente despite her rivalry with France was a function of that realignment, as Italy's peninsular location precluded conflict with the leading maritime power, Britain. During the Second World War, France was quickly defeated, whereas the right-wing totalitarian powers fought on the same side. Dedicated general studies of the alliance behaviour of democracies tally with these observations.[62]

If it was not the structure of their international behaviour, was it then inherent domestic advantages that gave the liberal-democratic great powers victory in the three great struggles of the twentieth century? Did the liberal democracies, despite their strong initial reluctance to engage in war and lower levels of peacetime mobilization, ultimately prove more effective in mobilization? All the belligerents in fact proved highly effective in mobilizing their societies and economies for total war. During the First World War conservative and semi-autocratic Germany committed her resources as intensively as her liberal-parliamentary rivals. After her victories during the initial stage of the Second World War, Nazi Germany's economic mobilization proved lax and poorly co-ordinated during the critical years 1940–2. Well positioned at the time fundamentally to alter the global balance of power by destroying the Soviet Union and striding across all of continental Europe, Germany failed because her armed forces were meagrely supplied with the military hardware necessary for a task that proved to be far more demanding than expected.[63] The reasons for this fateful failure are not easy to explain, but are at least partly attributed to structural problems of competing authorities inherent in Germany's totalitarian regime. However, from 1942 on (when it became too late), Germany's highly intensified mobilization levels caught up with and surpassed those of the liberal democracies (although not, of course, their production volume—that is, that of the USA). Imperial Japan's levels of mobilization during the Second World War, and those of communist Soviet Russia, similarly grew higher than those of the liberal democracies by means of ruthless efforts. Indeed, one historian recently concluded that the totalitarian regimes demonstrated greater ability than the liberal democracies to mobilize for war, which gave them a considerable military advantage.[64]

Only during the Cold War did the Soviet communist economy exhibit deepening structural weaknesses, made all the more evident when compared with an increasingly sophisticated and globalizing market economy. Although excelling in the regimentalized techniques of military mass production during the Second World War and keeping abreast militarily during the Cold War, the Soviet system's rigidity and inherent lack of incentives proved ill-equipped for coping with the more diversified economy of the information age. Ultimately, the Communist bloc practically dismantled itself, as both Communist China and the Soviet Union, independent of each other, progressively found their system inefficient, almost irrespective of their militarized conflict with the capitalist–democratic world.

By contrast, there is no reason to suppose that right-wing, capitalist, totalitarian regimes such as Nazi Germany and imperial Japan would have proved similarly inferior. The inefficiencies that arise in such regimes from a lack of accountability and favouritism might very well have been offset by higher levels of social mobilization. Nor is there a good reason for the comforting belief that these brutal regimes (obviously Germany stands here far above Japan) would have collapsed because of their brutality, even if some future mellowing was certainly possible. Contrary to claims by some scholars, these regimes proved more inspiring than the democracies, and their soldiers, if anything, fought better. During the 1930s and early 1940s, fascism and Nazism were the exciting doctrines that generated massive popular enthusiasm, whereas the democracies stood on the defensive ideologically, appearing old and dispirited. While France collapsed like a pack of cards in 1940, Germany and Japan (and the Soviet Union) fought desperately to the last.[65] As a result of their more efficient capitalist economies, the right-wing totalitarian powers, Germany and Japan (again, particularly the former), can now be judged to have constituted a more viable challenge to the liberal democracies than the Soviet Union; Nazi Germany was so judged by the western powers before and during the Second World War. It should be noted that the liberal democracies did not even possess an inherent advantage over Germany in terms of economic and technological development, as they did in relation to their other great power rivals.

In the end, the right-wing totalitarian powers were defeated in war simply because they came against a far superior but hardly preordained economic–military coalition that combined the liberal democracies and the communist Soviet Union (with the latter taking the brunt of the war during the most critical years). In the collapse of the communist world structural factors played a much greater role: whereas the capitalist camp, which in the wake of 1945 expanded to include all the rest of the developed world, possessed much greater infrastructural power than the Communist bloc, the inherent inefficiency of the communist economies prevented that bloc from ever catching up despite its potentially vast resources. Together the Soviet Union and China were potentially larger than the democratic–capitalist camp and, had they succeeded economically, other countries would have followed. Witness also the staggering difference in development between North and South Korea.

A generalized structural explanation of the success of the liberal democracies can also be misleading because of the small number of cases involved, which may suggest heightened contingency: only three liberal-parliamentary great powers, the USA, Britain, and France (Italy during the First World War barely qualifies, particularly the status of great power); three conservative and variably autocratic great powers, Germany, Austro-Hungary, and (on the opposite side) Russia, during the First World War; two right-wing, capitalist, totalitarian great powers, Germany and Japan, during the 1930s and 1940s (Italy barely qualified, again mainly on the second count but arguably also for the totalitarian category, the application of which to the Second World War Japan also requires some stretching beyond the European models); and one communist great power, the Soviet Union (with China, more ambivalently, during the Cold War). Contingent factors may have played as significant a role as, or even a more significant role than, structural factors in causing the triumph of the capitalist liberal democracies and the demise of the totalitarian challengers. The most obvious and decisive of these contingent factors was the USA.

After all, it was little more than a chance of history that this scion of English liberalism would sprout on the other side of the Atlantic, institutionalize its liberal heritage with independence, and then expand across the most habitable territories of the Americas, thinly populated by tribal natives, while sucking in massive immigration from Europe. It was but a chance of history that by far the world's largest concentration of economic–military power was thus created. Obviously, the liberal regime and other structural traits of the USA had a lot to do with that country's economic success (consider Latin America) and even with its size, because of its attractiveness to immigrants; and yet, if the USA had not been located in a particularly fortunate and vast geographical–ecological niche, it would scarcely have achieved its great magnitude in population as well as territory, as Canada, Australia, and New Zealand demonstrate. And location, of course, although crucial, was not everything, but only one necessary condition among many for bringing about a giant and, indeed, *united* States as probably the paramount political fact of the twentieth century.

Thus, even if its liberal system was a crucial precondition for the gigantic growth of the USA, contingency was at least as responsible for the fact that it

B-24 heavy bombers are mass produced in Ford's giant factory at
Willow Run, Michigan

emerged at all in the newly discovered territories of the New World, and thereby would ultimately be there to 'save the Old'. That huge power concentration, always greater during the twentieth century than the next two great powers combined, decisively tilted the global balance of power in favour of its allies. The liberal democracies possessed greater aggregate resources than their rivals because of that crucial fact as much as because of their advanced economies (which, again, were not more advanced than Germany's). The victory of liberal democracy was anything but pre-ordained in either 1914 or 1939, although it may have been more secure in 1945; yet, if any factor gave the liberal democracies their edge, it was above all the actual being of the USA rather than any inherent advantage of liberal democracy. This 'United States factor' is widely overlooked in studies of the victory of democracy during the twentieth century.[66] Put differently, if it were not for the existence of the USA the liberal democracies would most probably have lost the great struggles of the twentieth century. This is a sobering thought, making the world created by these struggles appear much more contingent—and tenuous—than unilineal theories of development and the Whig view of history and Progress would have us believe.

CONCLUSION

I cut off my discussion of war as affected by the rise of industrial–technological society half-way at this point, leaving the more focused study of liberal democracy, as well as the nuclear factor and other weapons of mass destruction, to the next chapter, which deals with the contemporary world. First, however, a tentative summary of this chapter's main points is in order. The industrial–technological take-off signalled a revolution in human history, generating a continuous, exponential surge in wealth and power, and releasing the societies that underwent the revolution from the Malthusian trap that had dominated earlier times. It is unlikely that this radical development is not somehow connected to the sharp drop that occurred during the nineteenth and twentieth centuries in the number of wars and war years among developed countries, including great power wars that historically had been the most frequent and severe of inter-state wars. At the

The masses of American made M-4 tanks, here equipping the French Second Armoured Division during the Normandy invasion. Admittedly, American (and British) tanks lagged far behind the German and Soviet tanks in quality

same time, however, when great power wars did break out—most notably the two World Wars—the belligerents were able to mobilize far greater resources into them: a much bigger share of an already exponentially larger national product.

What then was the exact relationship between the industrial–technological revolution and the sharp drop in wars between developed countries? Did wars become costlier or peace more profitable (or both)? Although the first argument is often evoked, it is barely substantiated by the evidence. The wars of the nineteenth century were no more costly than earlier wars in history, relative to population and national wealth. Nor did the tremendous cost of the First World War prevent the Second World War from breaking out shortly after. The transformation of the economic rationale for peace may have been more decisive, and was already suggested during the nineteenth century. The new rapid and continuous growth in real wealth meant that wealth was no longer a fundamentally finite quantity, nor was wealth acquisition a zero-sum game. Economic productivity became by far the main avenue to wealth. Furthermore, national economies ceased to be overwhelmingly autarkic. Intensifying specialization and market exchange, although highly competitive, meant that both foreign growth and destruction directly affected one's own economic well-being.

Why then did wars within the developed world continue to occur, albeit much less frequently, including the World Wars that have largely discredited nineteenth-century optimism? Issues of nationality stood behind most conflicts and wars during the nineteenth century, as deep-seated kin-based identities, transformed by modernity, clashed with existing political borders. Furthermore, as the new industrial–global economy showed signs of turning in a protectionist direction, of being carved out among a number of national imperial blocs rather than remaining open, this process became a self-fulfilling prophesy with the ensuing land grab inevitably leading to heightened tensions and war among the powers.

That same process, in turn, facilitated the rise of modern totalitarian regimes in some of the great powers, in which an ideological commitment to violent struggle against the liberal model and the demands of a partitioned global economy were mutually affecting and mutually reinforcing. The liberal democracies ultimately prevailed in the mammoth struggles of the twentieth century, because of the great concentration of power that was the USA, no less than for their inherent qualities. In the process, the democratic–capitalist orbit expanded by military victory and military pressure as much as by the encroaching effect of market forces. On the other hand, possessing such an enormous infrastructural power that was sufficient to smash imperial and Nazi Germany and imperial Japan, why did the liberal democracies do so poorly in their numerous small wars against puny rivals in the industrially undeveloped world, which they had conquered so easily earlier on? In view of the unprecedented gaps in wealth that opened up between the developed and undeveloped countries, how does this part of the liberal democracies' record tally with our argument here about the close correlation created in the industrial–technological age between wealth and war-waging capability? In a world dominated, at this point in time, by affluent liberal-democratic market societies, these are pertinent questions, both theoretically and practically.

16

Affluent Liberal Democracies, Ultimate Weapons, and the World

At the advent of the twenty-first century, after the fall of fascism and communism, the world is dominated by affluent, high-technology, liberal-democratic societies. Concentrated in North America, west–central Europe, and along the Pacific rim, they incorporate less than a fifth of the world's population. Yet they are by a very wide margin the world's wealthiest societies in per capita terms (the only non-democracies among the 30 wealthiest are Singapore, Hong Kong, and a few tiny, low-tech, Arab oil principalities), accounting for more than half of the world's gross national product (GNP). By the compound measure presented in Chapter 15, they thus control among them more than 90 per cent of the world's infra-structural power.

Throughout history the most powerful states, irrespective of their regimes, were also the major belligerents, above all among themselves. Are modern liberal democracies different in this respect from earlier regime types and, if so, why? Is a world dominated by such liberal democracies significantly different from earlier international systems? The idea that this is so was first mooted during the Enlightenment, when liberalism as a doctrine and outlook emerged, weaving together several intellectual threads. Political liberalism was formulated in England by John Locke as the platform of the

Glorious Revolution (1688), emphasizing among other things the primacy of individual freedom, government constrained by law and consent, and the rule of law in general. Economic Liberalism was added almost a century later by Adam Smith, stressing the benefits of the free market and the harms of state protectionism and colonial conquest. Expressing these and other Enlightenment ideas in the wake of the American and French revolutions, Thomas Paine (rather neglected in this context) and Immanuel Kant extended the liberal vision to the international arena. In his *Perpetual Peace* (1795), Kant suggested that the spread of republican regimes, incorporating representative government, separation of powers, and individual rights guaranteed by the law, would act against the occurrence of wars. Similar to Paine, he held that the people, in contrast to autocratic rulers, would be disinclined to vote for wars that had a cost in life, misery, money, and destruction that they themselves would have to pay. Similar to Paine, Kant also mentioned the irresistible spread of the commercial spirit as inhibiting war. He believed that, as the number of republics increased over time, they would be able to develop international institutions to mediate their differences and avoid war.[1]

Liberal economic pacifism, as embodied by the Manchester School, gained much in strength in the industrial age, during the nineteenth century, but later receded with the return of protectionism and colonialism, followed by the First World War. It was because of that 'world crisis' that American president Woodrow Wilson articulated a vision of world peace, basically similar to Kant's but with some significant additions. In the first place, Wilson's peace was predicated on the spread of 'democracies' rather than 'republics'. In common with other liberals, Kant had not posited a general and equal right to vote and be elected. Indeed, similar to other liberals, he (although not Paine) had been apprehensive of democracy, which in classical times had been believed to have exhibited a tendency to degenerate into a rule of the mob incited by demagogues. Liberals had widely feared that democracy would turn into a tyranny of the majority and thereby threaten liberal rights. By the First World War, however, the franchise had steadily expanded in liberal countries so as to become practically universal in them or on the way to becoming so. A new compound, liberal democracy, had come into being, which Wilson believed was inherently peace desiring and consequently contributed to world peace as it proliferated and replaced war-like autocracies and oligarchies.[2]

Wilson's second significant addition to Kant's programme was related to the first. It addressed the factor that during the nineteenth century had become one of the major causes of conflict: frustrated nationalism. National liberation and political liberalism had been inextricably intertwined in the struggle of peoples in nineteenth-century central, southern, and eastern Europe against autocratic imperial rule. The views most prominently represented by Giuseppe Mazzini gradually penetrated liberal opinion in the powers of the free west, where self-determination had been long secured and was not automatically considered to be the universal right of all others. These others included the small nations of east and south-east Europe, with a hopeless ethnic mixture that would baffle the peacemakers of 1919;[3] and they would increasingly come to include the undeveloped parts of Asia and Africa, initially regarded as not ready for independently embracing modern civilization. In Wilson's programme for world peace, self-determination was the corollary of, and a necessary complement to, mass political participation and democracy. Alien rule should not persist against a people's will.

But did liberal-democratic countries really demonstrate greater aversion to war than other regime types, or was this merely ideological propaganda and self-delusion, a familiar manifestation of the general bias towards the self? Scepticism seemed more than justified. During the twentieth century, liberal democracies were engaged in three gigantic power struggles, largely involving on their part a traditional 'realist' competition over power and resources and pretty ruthless strategies. On the other side of these conflicts, their opponents were equally convinced that their own actions were fundamentally self-defensive, and regarded the liberal democracies as hypocritical and coercive to the point of belligerency in maintaining their unjust advantages. Imperial Germany and imperial Japan saw themselves encircled and narrowly confined by their rivals' already existing huge colonial empires. For communists, capitalist exploitation ultimately rested on violent oppression both at home and abroad, the dismantling of which was the precondition for justice, true freedom, and world peace.

Not only were these ideological arguments intricate and slippery, but the hard record seemed to support no particular peaceful inclination on the part of liberal democracies. Although liberal/democratic countries have indeed been found to have fought fewer inter-state wars, they fought more 'extra-systemic', mainly colonial, wars, against non-state rivals.[4] As a result of their

572

far-flung colonial empires and consequent 'colonial wars', old liberal/democratic powers such as France and Britain fought far more wars and war years than non-liberal great powers, such as Austria and Prussia/Germany in the nineteenth and twentieth centuries. The USA, too, after her largely forceful expansion across the North American continent during the nineteenth century, fought extensively during the twentieth century, arguably on the frontiers of her own 'informal empire'. Britain's former self-governing liberal-democratic dominions, above all Australia, but also Canada, and, to a lesser degree, New Zealand, also fought a great deal in the twentieth century, first in support of their old metropolitan centre and later as allies of the new hegemon. As we saw in Chapter 15 and see further in this chapter, there was a great difference, above all in magnitude, between inter-state and colonial wars—at least for the colonial power. Furthermore, the liberal-democratic development with respect to colonial wars was very different from that of non-liberal-democratic powers. All the same, scholars tended to be highly sceptical of a self-professed democratic aversion to war.

From the 1970s, however, a new realization dawned on scholars of international relations. Increasingly gaining in prominence, it gave a radical new twist to the whole idea of liberal/democratic pacificity. Scholars have discovered that, although liberal or democratic states (or states with a freely elected government—there were conceptual nuances here) may have not fought less than other states, they almost never or barely at all fought among themselves from their emergence in the late eighteenth and early nineteenth centuries. These findings were supported by thorough statistical–quantitative analyses. Typically, separate computerized datasets covering the nineteenth and twentieth centuries, one containing data on all inter-state wars and the other on regime types, were compared, revealing that among the thousands of war years that occurred between pairs, or 'dyads', of states during that period, none or close to none involved two democracies.[5] This was not the case with other regime types. If true, this liberal or democratic uniqueness seemed to imply, as Paine, Kant, and Wilson had suggested, that a world composed of liberal/democratic states would be peaceful.

Naturally, such a thesis and the startling findings at its base—the most significant to have emerged in the young discipline of international relations—have come under extensive scrutiny. Various criticisms have been levelled at the theoretical assumptions and data that stand at the base of the so-called democratic peace idea. The debate has generated an impressive body of scholarly literature, with the initial thesis being refined, amended, and expanded, in response to criticisms and to incorporate further contributions.[6] I hope to be excused for introducing a personal note here. When I first heard about the 'democratic peace' thesis some time around 1990, a number of major reservations and qualifications occurred to me. Now that I have actually acquainted myself with the relevant literature, I have discovered that many of those points have been addressed and largely assimilated. Some others, however, remain unnoted or unaccounted for. In what follows I seek to present my choice synthesis of findings and arguments that have emerged along the course of the debate, as well as to expand further and contextualize—indeed, redefine and reframe—them within a broader and substantially different perspective.

IS THERE A 'DEMOCRATIC PEACE'?

The first question that begs attention concerns pre-modern times. If modern liberal/democratic states have not fought each other, presumably for reasons rooted in their regime, why did the same not apply to earlier democracies, most notably those of ancient Greece? This question involves a special difficulty, which often is not quite recognized. In comparison with modernity, the information that has survived from earlier times is painfully patchy, even with respect to some of the best-documented cases, such as classical Athens and Rome. Knowledge about Greek *poleis* other than Athens (with the partial exception of Sparta) is extremely hazy. Neither for their wars nor for their regimes do we possess anything even remotely approaching a full record, as we do with respect to the nineteenth and twentieth centuries. Thus one comprehensive study has found that Greek democracies actually exhibited a somewhat *greater* propensity to fight each other than non-democracies or mixed pairs (dyads). The most dramatic case involved the famous Athenian campaign against Syracuse (415–413 BC) during the Peloponnesian War, in which the Athenian expeditionary force was ultimately annihilated, dooming the entire war for Athens. Nevertheless, the said study has left open the question of the discrepancy between the ancient and modern inter-democratic war, or lack of it, with its authors claiming that (1) democracy at the time was still very young and (2) the ancient record is badly incomplete and therefore might be distorted.[7] As the inter-democratic peace in modernity is alleged to be practically universal, this hardly constitutes a satisfactory explanation.

Given the haziness of the information about antiquity, another comprehensive study has denied that any discrepancy between ancient and modern democratic republics exists at all, asserting that the former, too, never fought each other. A few points will suffice to demonstrate the untenable nature of this claim.[8] Many of the known democracies in ancient Greece belonged to the Athenian Empire of the fifth century BC, which had developed from the Attic–Delian League headed and taken over by Athens. The empire was coercive and oppressive, with Athens forcing city-states in and preventing them from leaving by means of her overwhelming force. Rebellions were harshly put down. Athens ran the empire tyrannically, among other things preventing its members (including the democratic ones) from fighting each other. Indeed, Athens generally fostered democratic regimes among her 'allies' (whereas Sparta fostered oligarchies among hers), partly because these regimes depended on her to ward off oligarchic factions and tyrants at home, and were therefore more reliable. All the same, the allies, including democratic ones, rebelled in great numbers after Athenian power had been severely weakened during the later stage of the Peloponnesian War and was no longer able to keep them in check through force and deterrence. Thus, most of the fifth-century Greek record represents democratic imperial coercion rather than inter-democratic peace.[9] Moreover, it was consistently the Athenian *demos*, rather than the aristocratic elements in Athenian society, that pushed for aggressive imperial expansion and war.

The fourth century BC offers an even more significant test. In the first place, the number of Greek democracies had increased. Furthermore, when a second Athenian-led alliance was formed in 377 BC, against imperial Sparta, the Greek hegemon, it was based on voluntary and egalitarian principles. To weaken Sparta, Athens assisted in the restoration of independence in Thebes. Not only did Thebes become a democracy, she re-established the Boeotian League on a democratic basis. In 371 BC, the Boeotian army under the generalship of Epaminondas astounded Greece by smashing the invincible Spartans in the famous Battle of Leuctra. A dramatic change in the Greek balance of power followed. Spartan hegemony and tyrannical imperial rule were broken, while Thebes rose to prominence. Invading the

Peloponnese, Epaminondas assisted Sparta's satellites in breaking away and forming democracies and regional democratic leagues. He freed a large part of Sparta's helots, who had been subjugated for centuries and were the cause of her militarized society. And yet these noble acts, obviously advantageous to Thebes, were vigorously opposed by none other than democratic Athens, because after Leuctra it was Thebean hegemony, rather than Spartan, that Athens feared and balanced against. As David Hume has already noted, this shift serves as a striking ancient example of the operation of the balance of power.

In 369 BC, Athens joined the war against Thebes, allying herself against Greek freedom with oligarchic and oppressive Sparta and her oligarchic allies, with Greek tyrants such as Dionysius of Syracuse and the blood-thirsty Alexander of Pherae, and with foreign and autocratic Persia. For seven years the two great Greek democracies were thus engaged in a war that raged all along their imperial peripheries, where their interests collided: in central and northern Greece, the Aegean, and the Peloponnese. The war involved numerous encounters, down to the Athenian participation against Thebes in the Battle of Mantinea (362 BC), the greatest in Greek history until then, where Epaminondas again won a crushing victory but was killed. Thebean hegemony and the war thereby came to an end. As Athens attempted to reassert her own hegemony, her conduct towards her allies began to resemble her first empire, prompting a rebellion known as the Social War (357–355 BC) that broke the power of the alliance. Lest it be thought that democratic Thebes' conduct towards other democracies during her ascendancy was saintly, it should be noted that she conquered and razed to the ground her old rival, democratic Plataea (373 BC).[10]

Surprisingly, the record of republican Rome's wars in the Italian peninsula has not been examined at all in this context and, while involving similar if not greater gaps of information, it appears to be no less questionable with respect to the 'democratic peace' phenomenon. How democratic the Roman republic was remains in debate among classical scholars, with recent trends swinging in the more democratic direction.[11] Rome was classified by Polybius (*The Histories* 6.11–18) as a mixed polity, in which the people (through the assemblies and tribunes), the aristocracy (through the Senate), and individual leaders (annually elected magistrates) balanced each other's power. It should be remembered, however, that our own modern liberal democracies, too, would probably have been classified as mixed polities by the ancients, and unlike ancient republics they do not include popular assemblies of all citizenry that directly legislate and decide on important issues such as war and peace. Knowledge about the internal regimes of the Italian city-states during the time of Rome's expansion is meagre and imprecise. Still, to argue that none of the hundreds of Italic and Greek city-states that were brought under Roman rule was a republic—that Rome was in fact the only republic in Italy—is patently untenable. More-over, one may add that during the Second Punic War (218–202 BC), Rome's greatest war, her rival Carthage was judged by Polybius (6.5; following Aristotle, *Politics* 2.11 and 4.8–9) to have been a mixed polity, in which the *demos* (which supported the Barkaide war party) at that stage dominated more than it did in the Roman Republic itself. Capua and Tarentum, the two leading city-states of southern Italy that defected from Rome during the Second Punic War and were harshly crushed by her, were both demo-cratic republics at the time (Livy, 23.2–7, 24.13). Neither in these nor in any other case does the evidence with respect to public deliberations in Rome on war and peace include even a reference to the enemy's regime as an issue that merited consideration.[12]

A third line of explanation has been offered to account for the apparent inapplicability of modern peace to the classical republics. Those who emphasize liberalism above democracy as the explanation for the modern phenomenon have claimed that ancient Greek democracies did not uphold the liberal rights of the individual and other 'republican' preconditions required by Kant, such as a separation of powers (Rome's mixed polity notwithstanding).[13] Indeed, it was argued by Hegel that the Greek *polis* had been deficient on two counts: although recognizing the freedom of the individual, it still failed to distinguish him from the 'organic' city-state community; and it maintained slavery. The Roman Republic came under the same critique. However, this explanation for the discrepancy between the ancient and modern experiences is not fully satisfactory either, because in the USA slavery existed until the Civil War, long after the USA is counted as a liberal and democratic state by the proponents of the liberal/democratic peace theory. Other liberal/democratic traits were also still rela-tively weak or absent in many of the countries listed as liberal/democratic by those theorists.

Indeed, leaving the pre-modern inter-democratic war problem open for the moment, let me move on to the nineteenth century. Critics have argued that the evidence for a democratic-liberal peace in the nineteenth century is scant if not illusory. In the first place, determining what should be counted as liberal or democratic states in the nineteenth century raises serious problems. As already mentioned, can the pre-Civil War USA, where slavery existed, be regarded as liberal, or democratic? Suffrage in most nineteenth-century liberal countries was not universal. In addition to the exclusion of slaves and women, criteria of wealth and education limited the right to vote and be elected, and were only gradually relaxed. Sociologists and political scientists have adopted an expansive definition of democracy, which emphasizes regular, contested, and free elections for government by a large part of the adult population.[14] But what should be considered a large part? In the absence of universal franchise, any definition of the threshold of democracy involves somewhat arbitrary criteria. And this, in turn, raises the possibility of data manipulation, even if unintentional.

Indeed, borderline cases and possible exceptions are not few. If the USA as a whole was considered liberal and democratic before the Civil War, should not the South, also democratic for the whites while slave owning, be similarly counted, which would classify the Civil War as one between two democratic/liberal antagonists? Discounting this case as a civil rather than an inter-state war between two 'established' states, as the proponents of the democratic/liberal peace theory often do, may be too technical to carry conviction. Should the Boer republics, fighting Britain in 1899–1902, be disqualified as liberal/democratic on similar grounds? Was Britain in 1812 not liberal enough and Spain in 1898 not liberal/democratic enough to disqualify either of these countries' wars with the USA as exceptions to the rule of an inter-democratic/liberal peace? And what about the war in 1793–1802 between the arguably liberal Britain and the variably democratic and liberal revolutionary France? To say nothing about similar questions raised by the American War of Independence. Finally, did imperial Germany, a constitutional monarchy, where the rule of law prevailed and universal male suffrage existed, yet with an executive responsible to the monarch rather than to parliament, not have some claim to a democratic and liberal status by the standards of the time? Of course, this would make the First World War a fatal exception to the rule of 'democratic peace'. And if imperial Germany is suspect, what about the democratic Weimar Republic, the coal-rich Ruhr region of which was forcefully occupied by democratic France in 1923 and held for three years in order to extract the unpaid reparations imposed on Germany? Admittedly, Germany did not resist with open war, but only because she was too weak to do so. On the other hand, it can be argued that, had Germany been stronger, it is doubtful whether France would have initiated the occupation.[15]

In addition, critics have argued that in several cases during the nineteenth century liberal/democratic countries considered war and/or came close to war with each other. As the number of countries classified as liberal/democratic in the nineteenth century was relatively small, with some of them alternating in and out of the list, such 'near misses', if accidental, might seriously affect the record. The USA, for example, harboured strong designs on British-held Canada during much of the nineteenth century, going to war partly for that reason in 1812 and waiting for the right opportunity for action later on. From the other direction, the threat of war loomed during the American Civil War, when Britain objected to the Union's infringement on the right of trade with the blockaded Confederacy, with the cotton growing that made it a natural ally in Britain's international economic system. As late as 1895–6, Britain backed down from a military conflict with the USA over Venezuela. Britain and France, both liberal and parliamentary in 1830–48 and co-operating over many shared interests, nevertheless three times came close to war during those years. And, as already mentioned in Chapter 15, even more liberal and democratic Britain and France came to the brink of war over the Sudan in the Fashoda crisis (1898), whereas liberal/democratic Italy dropped out of her anti-French alliance with Germany and Austria only in the decade before the First World War.[16]

Indeed, in some of these cases traditional balance of power considerations appear to have figured more prominently than shared liberalism or democracy in averting war. By the late nineteenth century Britain was no longer powerful enough to risk war in the western hemisphere with the now gigantic USA, especially as other threats to her empire loomed globally. Equally, it was madness for France to go to war with the more powerful Britain over what was after all a peripheral interest, especially as she had already been far more seriously antagonistic with the more powerful Germany. Italy departed from the Central Powers after the Anglo-French entente had been formed (1904), because her peninsular location and trade relations ruled out war with Britain.

For all the above-cited reasons, critics have claimed that the 'democratic peace' in the nineteenth century was 'spurious'.[17] In reply, proponents of the theory have contended that, even when all factors are weighed up, democracies during that period still exhibited a far lesser tendency than the norm to go to war with each other and, indeed, to get involved in militarized international disputes.[18] It has been found that they have exhibited a lesser inclination to initiate crises, escalate from crisis to war, display force, and generally threaten each other. They have more readily submitted their disputes to mediation by others and agreed to compromise.[19] All the same, even proponents of the democratic peace theory have conceded that the evidence for the democratic peace becomes much stronger during the twentieth century, and particularly after the Second World War.[20]

However, the inter-democratic peace in the twentieth century has also been criticized as illusory, albeit on somewhat different grounds. True, there now existed a larger number of democracies, still mainly concentrated in western Europe, bordering on each other in a region that had experienced frequent wars. Yet critics have attributed the absence of wars among these democracies to the coalition effect of the alliances that they formed against joint enemies—the Axis powers in the Second World War and the Soviet bloc during the Cold War—enmities that allegedly overshadowed and suppressed conflicts and possible wars among the allied democracies.[21]

Throughout history states of similar regimes regularly fought each other. Sometimes, however, domestic politics and ideology came to the fore of conflicts. In such cases, states of similar regimes and ideologies tended to ally against their opposites, because of the issues at stake and because they could rely on one another against their enemies at home. This was the case during the Peloponnesian War, and it was also evident, for example, in the struggle in medieval Italy between Guelph and Ghibelline city-states, and during the European Wars of Religion in the early modern period. Obviously, when considerations of power politics worked against alliances of shared regime or ideology, there were major defections from them, as with democratic Athens' alliance with oligarchies and tyrants against the rising power of democratic Thebes, or Catholic France's alliance with Protestants and infidels against the preponderant power of the Catholic Habsburgs. All the same, was not the west European inter-democratic peace of the twentieth century merely an effect of such alliances? Alternatively or conjointly, was it not a result of the nuclear factor, which since 1945 has anyway deterred wars between the great powers, irrespective of their regimes? Consequently, with the end of the Cold War, should one not expect a return of armed conflict, or the establishment of nuclear deterrence, among the European countries and between them and the USA?[22] Or else, may the democratic peace in fact be unique to western Europe (and its offshoot in North America) by virtue of that region's unique historical and cultural development but not be replicable in other corners of the world, where democracies may be different and, in any case, are too few, too recent, and too dispersed to offer a true test of the theory?[23]

Indeed, the ink had not yet dried on the writings of the democratic peace theorists when the 1990s brought interesting new developments. A new wave of democratization that had been gathering momentum from the mid-1970s—in southern Europe, Latin America, and east and south Asia—intensified with the collapse of the Soviet bloc. The number and regional diversity of democracies increased greatly, providing a more extensive testing ground for the theory. On the whole, the process of democratization was carried out peacefully; yet armed conflicts, some of them serious wars, erupted here and there. A devastating war (1991–5) took place among the new states that emerged from the former Yugoslavia and were plagued by the problem of mixed ethnicities. This was followed by a full-scale military offensive by the liberal-democratic NATO countries, led by the USA, to coerce the Serbian army out of Kosovo (1999). Admittedly, the countries of the former Yugoslavia, while formally democratic, were ruled by pretty authoritarian governments. On the other hand, these were popular governments that enjoyed mass support for their war effort. Democratic Turkey and Greece came to the brink of war in 1996, exchanging threats and deploying forces around a disputed tiny and uninhabited island in the Aegean. In South America an armed conflict broke out between Ecuador and Peru—both democratic—over a mineral-rich border zone (1995), which they had been disputing for over half a century. Again, however, it has been argued that President Fujimori had assumed emergency autocratic powers in Peru and, also, that the conflict may have been too small to qualify as a war.

Perhaps the most difficult case for the inter-democratic peace theory is the conflict in Kashmir between India and Pakistan, which escalated into large-scale armed hostilities in 1999, when both countries were classified as democracies. The Indian subcontinent's record had always been central to the democratic peace theorists, being one of the very few test cases outside the modern west. They argued that during all three wars between India and

Pakistan—in 1947, 1965, and 1971—the two countries had never both been democratic (in 1947 not yet 'established' democracies). Critics claimed, however, that democracy in Pakistan had been too intermittent to make this finding statistically significant. They further claimed that since 1971 no war had occurred between the two countries irrespective of their regimes; in India, too, Prime Minister Indira Gandhi declared a state of emergency in 1975–7, suspending many civil rights. With the two countries clashing while democratic in 1999, the critics' doubts about the subcontinent's historical record have been corroborated.[24] Furthermore, as both India and Pakistan had become nuclear powers by 1998, deterrence also serves as a highly significant factor in explaining why the very tense conflict between the two countries over the inflammable Kashmir issue does not escalate into full-scale open war.

Scholarly treatment of these recent cases, as with other 'border cases' from earlier in the twentieth and nineteenth centuries, has been dominated by haggling over the question of whether or not these cases satisfy the requirements of the 'democratic peace' theory in terms of the rivals' liberalism, democracy, established statehood, and scale of hostilities. But important as this question is in each particular case, the main significance of these border cases and possible exceptions to the democratic peace thesis lies elsewhere. They should be considered together with another vexed issue raised in relation to the democratic peace theory. Moltke's statements, quoted in Chapter 15—that it was militant popular pressure rather than the wishes of reluctant governments that drove countries into war—reflected a widespread feeling during the later nineteenth century, as the masses moved to the forefront of politics and political systems underwent democratization. As we have already seen, and contrary to the logic of Paine and Kant, the *demos* was consistently the most bellicose element in ancient democratic Athens. If anything, political theorists believed that democracies and republics were militant rather than peaceful, that they exhibited, in Hume's words, 'imprudent vehemence'.[25] Not only did the masses ever since classical antiquity acquire a reputation for volatility and rashness in crisis; they proved to be easily and deeply aroused by questions of national honour and national glory. That tendency resurfaced during the wars of the French Revolution, and was later ridden on by both revolutionary and conservative leaders, such as Napoleon I, Napoleon III, and Bismarck.

However, contrary to a prevailing view, popular agitation should not be attributed one-sidedly to 'provocation' and 'manipulation' by leaders. Just as much, the leaders catered to a strong public demand. Demand was met by suppliers. Often it was the masses who swept with them cautious and peacefully inclined leaders, and all the more so in liberal/democratic countries. It was largely public pressure that drove liberal Britain into the Crimean War (1854–6). The word 'jingoism' itself, denoting a chauvinistic and bellicose public frenzy, came into currency in late nineteenth-century Britain, at a time of increasing democratization. Jingoism was widespread during the Boer War (1899–1902). The USA, another leading liberal democracy, was carried into war with Spain at the very same time (1898) on the waves of popular enthusiasm that virtually forced the government's hand. Lest it be thought that the enemy in either of these cases failed to qualify as liberal democratic, it should be noted that it was public opinion in both Britain and France that proved most bellicose, chauvinistic, and unsympathetic to the other during the Fashoda crisis (1898). It was the politicians who climbed down from war. Studies detect a change of attitude only in advanced democracies of the twentieth century, where public opinion became much more averse to war; yet new democracies in that century still exhibited greater conflictual behaviour than the more established ones.

Democratization—that is, growing responsiveness to the popular will in the new mass societies—has been claimed to promote war, at least during the transition period, also because it has been closely associated with self-determination and the assertion of hitherto suppressed ethnic identities and national aspirations, which often conflict with existing state boundaries. Thus it has been claimed that, although democracy indeed decreased the likelihood of war, the *initial* process of democratization, the democratic *transition*, had the opposite effect.[26] In a different formulation it has been shown that partly free states have been *more* war prone than non-democracies.[27] Indeed, viewed from a longer historical perspective, democratization and liberalization in general were *processes* that did not consist of a one-time transition from a non-democratic regime but continuously unfolded, often over decades and even centuries. The dichotomies of liberal/non-liberal or democratic/non-democratic, which long underlay the debate over the 'democratic peace', have been found to be crude and misleading. Much more was and is going on than can be squeezed into a simple binary split. Societies can grow more and more liberal and democratic, and have done so remarkably during modernity, affecting their attitude towards war and peace.

This insight gradually emerged among proponents of the 'democratic peace' theory. If liberal/democratic countries have grown increasingly more liberal and democratic since the late eighteenth century, this can explain why the inter-democratic peace seems to have been less secure in the nineteenth-century west and became entrenched only during the twentieth century.[28] The abolition of slavery, the long and gradual expansion of the franchise to all men and women during the nineteenth and early twentieth centuries, the extension of equal legal and social rights to women and minorities, the rise in social tolerance in general, and the increase in political transparency and accountability during the second half of the twentieth century—all these were major developments that made early liberal/parliamentary societies progressively *both* more liberal and more democratic. The standards of liberalism and democracy have continually risen, and with them the 'democratic peace' has also supposedly deepened.

As proponents of the theory have stressed, from early on in the twentieth century, the very idea of war between democracies in western Europe and North America has simply become inconceivable. No realistic considerations of the balance of power have defended Canada from the USA and prevented war between the USA and Britain, between the countries of democratic Scandinavia or, from some point, within democratic western Europe in general. No longer have the parties to peace in all these cases even been preparing, militarily or otherwise, for the *possibility* of war between them. They see no need to take precautions because they do not allow for such a possibility. Indeed, this remains so even in the post-Cold War world, when rising American–European tensions and even antagonism stand at the centre of attention at the moment that these words are being written. In the developing world, the frailness of peace between democracies has been explained by lower levels of democracy and liberalism compared with the developed west. In this respect, developing countries are more reminiscent of the nineteenth-century west.[29] There is little point in referring to centuries, or absolute time, when it is actually the relative level of democratic development that is the issue, and shows such wide divergence between different regions of the world.

The simplicity of the original democratic peace theory has been further compromised by the addition of more factors, the effect of which, too, was dynamic over time. In the first place, greater trade (relative to GNP) and greater trade openness (lower tariffs) have been demonstrated to have a diminishing effect on the likelihood of war between countries. In theory, the reason for this, as expounded by liberals from Adam Smith and the Manchester School, is clear: the fewer the obstructions to trade, the less the need to secure resources by gaining physical possession of them; and the greater the trade, the greater the ensuing economic interdependence between countries. As liberalism distanced governments from direct involvement in the economy, it thereby also much diminished the role of governmental military action in the promotion of the national economic interests.[30] However, in practice things were more complicated. Before the First World War, the volume of international trade stood at record levels, and its percentage of overall production was higher than it would be at any time up to the 1990s. Britain and Germany were each other's second largest trading partners (imports from the USA made her the first for both countries),[31] and yet war broke out between them. However, as we have seen in Chapter 15, tariffs between the major economies before the First World War were high; furthermore, it was largely expectations that the global system was retreating from open trade and moving towards monopolistic imperial blocs that vastly increased the tensions among the powers and led to war. Later, the autarkic economies of the 1930s precipitated and reinforced the political developments that led to the Second World War.[32]

With this lesson in mind, the architects of the post-war period in the west worked to decrease trade barriers multilaterally. Through the General Agreement on Tariffs and Trade (GATT), established in 1947 (from 1995, the World Trade Organization) and expanding to include most of the world's countries, average tariffs on manufactures were reduced from 40 to less than 4 per cent.[33] As during the nineteenth century and in contrast to the autarkic and stagnant period of crisis between 1914 and 1945, the volume of international trade during the post-war decades grew twice as fast as the exploding rise in GNP, fuelling the latter. And whereas GNP growth in the developed world slowed down after 1973, international trade continued to increase rapidly. With the collapse of communism and the growth in communication technology, 'globalization' was further boosted. Trade in goods tripled between 1985 and 2000, whereas trade in capital increased sixfold.[34] With free capital flow adding to the process of economic globalization, the pacifying effect of free trade has been magnified, because

585

international capital reacts to war and the threat of it by fleeing away from the danger zone, penalizing the would-be combatants.

Europe holds a special place in these post-Second World War developments. It underwent increasing economic integration through the successive establishment of the European Coal and Steel Community (1951), the Common Market (1957), and the European Union (1992). The organization envisaged by the six original members of the Treaty of Rome expanded across western Europe and into the formerly communist east, growing to 25 members in 2004. Trade liberalization, combined with joint democracy and increasing federalization, turned Europe into a region of peace and prosperity. Again critics have questioned whether it was not the Cold War alliance that produced that result. Furthermore, was the decisive factor federalization, democracy, or trade liberalization? And were not democracy and trade liberalization interrelated rather than separate factors? Expanding greatly on the initial 'democratic peace' concept, later studies have found joint democracy, mutual and open trade, and membership in international organizations—each *independently*—to have significantly reduced war. They have thus endorsed all the original elements of 'Kant's tripod for peace'.[35]

In the meantime, the Kantian framework has been expanded still more. Initially, scholars widely believed that liberal/democratic states were peaceful only towards each other, because they fought non-democratic/non-liberal states and appeared to be just as prone as those states to *initiate* such wars. However, further analyses of the data have suggested a somewhat lesser proneness on the part of liberal/democratic states to fight and initiate wars against non-democratic/non-liberal states, as partly reflected in the fact that they fought fewer inter-state wars in general. Liberal democracies have thus been suggested to be less aggressive in general and not only towards other liberal democracies.[36] Moreover, it has been argued that, when the number of casualties incurred and not only wars and war years are taken into account, the evidence shows that during the twentieth century liberal democracies have suffered much less and, hence, that they have engaged in much less severe wars. The severity of wars, not only their frequency, should be considered in judging liberal-democratic pacificity.[37]

One should note that this statistical finding is partly determined by the fact that, during the Second World War, the twentieth century's most lethal war, France and the other small democracies of western Europe were quickly conquered, thereby also leaving Britain and later the USA with no major land theatre on which to fight Germany until the summer of 1944. In contrast to the First World War, the Eastern Front thus became the main theatre of war, with Germany and the Soviet Union slashing it out in the greatest, most destructive, and lethal fighting ever (in absolute terms). However, the liberal democracies suffered fewer casualties in their wars also because they tended to possess technological superiority over colonial and other rivals from the world's undeveloped parts. Such wars with weak rivals are far less severe, at least for the more advanced power, and hence are more easily entered into and even initiated by liberal democracies.[38] Counting the American invasions of, say, Grenada or Nicaragua on equal footing with more serious wars may distort the record in some crucial respects. Finally, their constitutional and consensual nature mean that at least advanced liberal democracies during the twentieth century avoided bloody civil wars, historically the bloodiest type of war, which tended to plague old-style autocracies and oligarchies, as well as weak and semi-democracies. Here again belligerency during the process of *democratization* proved to be different in 'mature' democratic societies (consider, for example, the American and Russian civil wars, nineteenth-century Europe in general, and today's developing world). And although totalitarian regimes, too, avoided civil wars by means of ruthless repression, some of them killed their own citizens in horrific numbers as a matter of course.[39] Combining all the above, it has been claimed that liberal democracies 'kill their own people' far less than other regimes do.[40] Thus all the elements of the Paine–Kant projection, based on the inherent peacefulness of the people in constitutional and commercial republics, seem to have been vindicated.

And yet the Paine–Kant logic was incomplete and at least partly flawed. A still broader perspective is needed to account for the modern peace, to the extent that such peace has indeed been unfolding.

THE 'DEMOCRATIC PEACE' REFRAMED

The findings and insights of new research again serve to highlight the lacuna in the democratic peace theory. It has been found that economically developed democracies have been far more likely to be peaceful towards each other than poor democracies: twice as much in a study covering the years 1950–92 and consistently in a broader study covering the period since 1885. The democratic peace phenomenon between poor democracies was found to be at best weak.[41] In line with what we have already seen, economically developed democracies have also been far less prone than poorer democracies to civil war.[42] (Civil war has become the prevalent form of warfare since 1945 because the large number of the new poor developing countries that have gained independence have been particularly prone to them, whereas both nuclear deterrence and affluent liberal democracy have radically constrained inter-state war.) Indeed, what has been on the rise during the past couple of centuries, and accounts for the growth of democratic peace, has been not only liberal countries' level of democracy and liberalism, as proponents of the democratic peace theory believe, but also their wealth. Moreover, all these developments are not separate and distinct from each other but are closely intertwined. The idea that the growth of liberalism and democracy rested on the very tangible material developments of the age, such as advanced communications (both transportation and information technology), urbanization, increasing levels of literacy and education, and growing material well-being has been widely held since the nineteenth century and strongly endorsed by sociologists and political scientists.[43] Democracy on a country scale and liberal societies emerged only in the nineteenth century, rather than in any earlier time in history, and have evolved ever since, not merely because they were suddenly recognized as good ideas; their growth has been underpinned by the revolutionary changes in the socioeconomic infrastructure during modernity.

To be sure, Germany, for example, presents a significant exception in being less liberal and democratic than the other economically developed countries during the periods of the Second and, of course, the Third Reich. As we see, it is far from clear that economic development necessarily and unilinearly leads to liberal democracy. Different sociopolitical paths of development and deep-seated cultural traditions also play a decisive role. On the other hand, liberal democracies tend to be economically developed. During the past centuries, poor democracies have been found to be not only less pacific but also few in number, whereas middle-income, economically developing democracies proved to be the most vulnerable to anti-democratic regime change, as they increasingly came under the pressures of modernization.[44] True, economically developing, still predominantly agrarian, stable liberal/democratic regimes existed in the nineteenth century (most notably the USA before the middle of the century and a growing number of European and western countries later in that century), as well as in the twentieth century (most notably India). Yet not only were these cases few, but also in all of them the industrial–technological revolution had already been brewing, and its products, such as the newspaper and the railway (to which the electronic medium was added in the twentieth century), were already deeply affecting society and politics.

Furthermore, the more economically advanced a liberal/democratic society, the more liberal and democratic it becomes, with both these traits closely correlating with its pacific tendency. During the 1990s, as democracy became the sole hegemonic model after the collapse of communism, some poor countries democratized. Yet comparative studies rank poorer democracies lower on the democratic and liberal scales, leading scholars to suggest the term 'illiberal democracy' to describe some of them.[45] Democratization and liberalization, economic development, and pacific inclinations have *all* been intimately bound together in the modern transformation.

This is the missing element in Paine, Kant, and the democratic peace theory. As we have seen, Paine and Kant subscribed to the Enlightenment view that selfish autocrats were responsible for war. According to that view, once the people who carried the burden of war and incurred its costs were given the power to decide, they would recoil from war. However, as already mentioned, the *demos* was the most bellicose element in Athenian society even though it fought in the army, manned the rowing benches of the Athenian navy, and had to endure war's destruction and misery, as in the forced evacuation of Attica during the Peloponnesian War. Rome's proverbial military prowess and tenacity similarly derived specifically from her republican regime, which successfully co-opted the populace for the purpose of war. Indeed, historically, democracies proved particularly tenacious in war precisely because they were socially and politically inclusive. And, again, in pre-modern times they also did not refrain from fighting each other.

Why, then, did the citizens of Athens and Rome, for example, repeatedly vote for war, and endure devastating and protracted wars for years despite the losses, destruction, misery, and war weariness? It was not because they were less democratic than modern societies, but because, in the agrarian age in which they lived, there were great material benefits to be gained from wars. First, there was booty to be had. Furthermore, in Athens the empire meant lavish tribute that financed about half of the Athenian budget, paying for the extensive public construction and huge navy, in both of which the *demos* was employed (Plutarch, *Pericles* 12). Moreover, the empire's might boosted Athenian trade supremacy, which, in turn, increased her resources and enhanced her might, and vice versa in a military–financial virtuous circle, at least for Athens and for as long as it lasted. Finally, poor, landless Athenians were allocated farms in colonies (*cleruchies*) established on territory confiscated from defeated enemies. Although Rome did not levy tribute from her 'allies', she confiscated land from the defeated on an enormous scale throughout Italy and established on it colonies of her citizens and the Latins. Much of the land went to the senatorial class, but much was distributed among the people, making them directly interested in the Republic's wars.

To repeat the underlying rationale here: in pre-industrial times, growth in overall resources through innovation and exchange, although existing, was so slow as to make resources practically finite and the competition over them close to a zero-sum game, where one side's gain could be achieved only at the other's expense. With the expansion of European and global trade during the early modern period, a greater part of production was intended for the market (although the vast majority was still produced for self-consumption), increasing the benefits of free exchange for the parties involved. This was the process described by Adam Smith and noted by Paine and Kant. Yet only with industrialization did the balance change radically: wealth was no longer finite but rose at a staggering pace; agricultural produce, and hence territory, ceased to be the main source of wealth, and was replaced by industrial production that was best developed at home, and, later, by the service-information economy where the significance of raw materials decreased greatly; and production became overwhelmingly intended for the market, magnifying the benefits of exchange and increasing interdependence.[46] Contrary to earlier times, the enemy's economic ruin became detrimental to one's own prosperity. As John Maynard Keynes argued in his famous *The Economic Consequences of the Peace* (1920), the crippling reparations imposed on the defeated Germany in the wake of the First World War prevented her economic recovery, thereby rendering impossible a recovery of the international economy and the resumption of prosperity among the victorious Entente powers themselves. Indeed, as the economic troubles of the early 1920s appeared to bear out his point, the victors changed course, working to revive Germany's economy and political status, an effort that collapsed with the post-1929 Great Depression.

It is not the cost of war as such that has become prohibitive in modernity, as is widely claimed, not even when the costs that one incurs from the destruction of one's enemy/trade partner are figured in. Societies paid horrendous costs in wars throughout history as a matter of course, no less horrendous in relative terms than that of the total wars of the twentieth century. This was their nature-like law so long as the Malthusian logic of pre-industrial times prevailed. It has been mainly the benefits of peace, rather than the cost of war, that have risen dramatically once the Malthusian trap had been broken, tilting the overall balance between war and peace. Scholars have claimed that the Kantian 'tripod of peace' transformed the vicious circle of anarchy, mutual insecurity, and war into a virtuous circle of peace and co-operation.[47] But to the extent that such a transformation occurred, it was in fact industrialization and the escape from the Malthusian vicious circle that underlay the 'tripod'.

Indeed, the striking fact overlooked by the proponents of the democratic peace is that non-democratic countries, too, fought much less during the nineteenth and twentieth centuries, in the industrial age, than they did in earlier times. In the century after 1815, non-democratic/non-liberal great powers such as Prussia and Austria (which were not colonial powers) engaged in war not only far less frequently than Britain and France but also dramatically less in comparison with their own earlier histories: only once every eight or nine years, compared with once every two years (Austria) or three years (Prussia) in the eighteenth century, which was more or less similar to the European great powers' average during early modernity (the seventeenth century being the most war like). More significantly, after 1815 non-democratic/non-liberal great powers also shared in the general sharp decline in the frequency of the most serious inter-state wars—those waged among the great powers themselves—to about a third of their rate in early modernity.[48] Again, it should be noted that this sharp decline took place even though the wars of the nineteenth century were not as prohibitively costly as the world wars of the twentieth century are reputed to have been (and in any case, financial ruin as a result of war had been the rule in the early modern period, indeed, throughout history; there was nothing new about it in the high-stakes business of war).

The reasons why the democratic peace theorists overlooked this overall sharp decline are natural enough: since liberal and democratic countries emerged only over the last two centuries, it appeared reasonable to focus on these centuries only, which in any case seemed to be a long period of time; in addition, the most widely used database of wars covers only the period from 1815 on. In consequence, no comparison with the pre-1815 period has been carried out. Nor have the democratic peace theorists asked why liberal and democratic societies started to appear only during the last 200 years or so, and how this fact is related to the defining development of that period, the onset of the industrial–technological age. The whole question of the democratic peace has been considered out of its truly defining historical context. For this reason, both those who have found that wealth and economic growth did not affect the occurrence of war,[49] and their critics who argued that wealth was indeed very significant in reducing war but *only* in connection and in tandem with democracy,[50] have been somewhat led astray by too short a perspective: in comparison with the pre-industrial age *both* democracies and non-democracies have fought on average considerably less. It is true, however, that liberal and democratic societies have exhibited greater pacific tendencies than non-democracies during the industrial age, as mainly demonstrated by their relationships with each other and at home. Why has this been so?

The economic rationale that industrial and commercial growth radically increased the benefits of peace—as more or less captured in the above-quoted remarkably pacific prophecies made by Moltke in 1840s' Prussia—help explain the sharp decline in the number of wars fought by industrializing non-democratic and non-liberal countries, compared with pre-industrial times. Still, these countries remained less pacific than democratic-liberal countries for a number of related reasons. In many of them a militant ethos, often associated with a traditional warrior elite, was deeply imbedded in the national culture. Such elites were not always agrarian and therefore out of step with the rationale of the modern world, as Schumpeter famously suggested.[51] This was not exactly the case even in imperial Germany, where the old elite was scarcely more militant than the magnates of trade and industry, the intellectuals, and the middle class in general, all of whom enthusiastically supported imperialism. Later on, the agrarian Junkers certainly did not dominate Nazi Germany. In Japan, the transformed ruling elite that came into power after the Meiji Restoration (1868) stood for industrialization and modernization. All the same, led from above to national unification and modernization and then coming late to the imperial race, both Germany and Japan had gloriously relied in the past, and expected to rely in the future, on military force to assert their claims. Statism had been and remained central to their modern development. Conjointly, they either rejected the logic of free trade in the name of national economy and/or feared that the global liberal trade system would collapse, leaving them out in the cold. In communist countries, for their part, the total rejection of the market principle went hand in hand with their ideological commitment to its destruction by force.

All this is familiar enough, yet the implications are less so. Partly or even thoroughly repressive at home, non-liberal and non-democratic countries were little inhibited from repression abroad. Contrary to a widely held view, it has been shown that their empires could and did pay, particularly if astride more developed parts of the world.[52] Forceful extraction in industrial societies could succeed, especially, as we can now assess, in its capitalist version, as it did in the Nazi and Japanese empires. So long as the advantages and/or very viability of the liberal economic model, as opposed to the national–capitalist (and socialist) one, remained in dispute, forceful nation-centred imperialism remained a temptation, for the realization of which non-liberal and non-democratic powers were willing to go to much greater length, even if—indeed, partly because—they were latecomers to the race. This temptation sometimes counterweighed the growing benefits of peace in the industrial–commercial age, which, as already noted, significantly diminished those countries' recourse to war. Nothing except for the restraints of the balance of power stopped them from pursuing the imperialist option even more sweepingly.

By comparison, liberal-democratic countries have differed in some crucial respects. Socialized to peaceful, law-mediated relationships at home, their citizens have grown to expect and wish the same norms to apply internationally. Living in increasingly tolerant, less conformist, and less argumentative societies, they have grown more receptive to the other's point of view. Promoting freedom, legal equality, and (expanding) political participation domestically, liberal-democratic powers, although initially in possession of the greatest colonial empires, have found it increasingly difficult to justify rule over foreign people without their consent and/or without granting them full citizen and voting rights. Their original justification, shared by liberals such as J. S. Mill, was the extension of liberalism, enlightenment, and all the blessings of civilization to those so backward and inflicted by dire poverty, death, and bad government as to be incapable of embracing them by themselves.[53] Yet this justification increasingly lost legitimacy as indigenous resistance to imperial rule asserted itself. Conjointly, sanctifying life, liberty, and human rights, liberal democracies have ultimately proved to be a complete failure in forceful repression. Liberal economy, dominating despite periodical lapses, in any case rejected war and military subjugation in favour of peaceful economic growth and mutually beneficial trade. Furthermore, with the individual's life and pursuit of happiness elevated above group values, the sacrifice, let alone self-sacrifice, of life in war has increasingly lost legitimacy in liberal-democratic societies. It remains acceptable only under the gravest of imminent threats to a nation's existence and way of life (sometimes barely even then), with an endemic, never-ending controversy developing with regard to almost every conflict about whether or not those preconditions indeed materialized. As pluralism has risen, dissent gained greater legitimacy, and consensus become harder to achieve, the state has found it increasingly difficult to rally society around the flag. Indeed, democratic leaders have themselves shared the above outlook and norms or have been made by public pressure to conform to them or have been removed from office.[54]

To avoid a misconception it must be clarified that a world of steadily increasing wealth by no means ends human competition, and certainly does not bring about 'brotherly love' on earth. It is true that, when the most pressing human needs, the basic levels of what one author has described as the 'pyramid of needs', are met at a comfortable enough level—even more or less guaranteed—the impulse to use aggression to satisfy them weakens considerably. Studies indicate that people become more risk averse. Yet, as already explained in this book, human desires are open-ended, because people struggle to improve their *relative* position vis-à-vis others even in a situation of growing plenty.[55] Actually, competition can intensify with resource abundance, as tropical wildlife, for example, demonstrates. People continue to compete vigorously in liberal societies; indeed, the liberal market economy in particular has been likened to a jungle, where 'cut-throat' competition is the rule. All the same, it is precisely at their core that these metaphors are misleading. In an industrial–commercial world where peace promises increasing economic benefits, the realization of the liberal model in particular means that rule-bound co-operative competition becomes far more rewarding than conflictual competition.

For these reasons, even though non-liberal and non-democratic states, too, became much less belligerent in the industrial age, liberal democracies have proved inherently more attuned to its pacifying aspects. The notion that serious war is an unmitigated disaster and constitutes sheer madness increasingly took hold in them, as the global industrial, trading, and financial system expanded and interdependence deepened. Norman Angell's famous *The Great Illusion* (1910), the illusion that any side could gain from a modern major great power war, simply restated the traditional liberal rationale that had increasingly materialized.

It was against this background that the First World War marked such a crisis in the liberal consciousness, generating a traumatic reaction and giving rise to a powerful social aversion to war. The decline in belligerency obviously did not start with the First World War.[56] On the contrary, the war came in the wake of the relatively pacific nineteenth century, after by far the longest and second longest periods of peace in European history. The First World War was the first European great power war in 43 years and the first protracted one in 99 years. Nor was the deep trauma that developed in the aftermath of the war the result of the great losses in life and treasure *in themselves*. Again, these were not greater than the standard in massive wars throughout history, relative to population and wealth.[57] The novelty was that liberal opinion now regarded such wars as wholly out of step with the modern world. Indeed, the famous 'trauma' of the war most closely correlated with the strength of liberalism in each country rather than with a country's actual losses.

In Britain, for example, Europe's most liberal power, the retrospective reaction against the war and the mourning for the 'lost generation' were the most profound among the European powers, even though Britain's losses were the smallest. British casualties—750,000 dead—terrible as they were, amounted to no more than 12 per cent of those enlisted during the war. They were smaller in absolute terms, and even more relative to population, than France's almost million-and-a-half dead and Germany's two million. And yet the reaction against the war in Germany was far more limited than in Britain.[58] The reaction was similar only from liberal (and socialist) opinion, which was less dominant in Germany than in Britain. The most famous anti-war author was Erich Maria Remarque, a German liberal and pacifist.

In Germany, which, relative to its population, had suffered twice as many casualties as had Britain, there was certainly much war weariness and a widespread loss of enthusiasm for war. However, Germany also had strong nationalist, anti-liberal, right-wing elements that did not share, and vehemently opposed, these sentiments. Ernst Juenger's books, glorifying his experience in the trenches and exalting the qualities of war, competed with Remarque's for popularity in Germany. Similarly, powerful nostalgic evocation of soldierly trench camaraderie played a cardinal role in turning formerly liberal/democratic Italy in a fascist direction.

Perhaps the two most extreme cases in the First World War that best illustrate the correlation claimed here between the post-war 'trauma' and the level of liberalism (rather than that of material and human losses) are the USA and Serbia. The mightiest power in the world was not inflicted with heavy losses and crippling economic costs, as were the European belligerents. The USA suffered relatively light casualties in her brief involvement in the war and gained tremendously from it materially, replacing Britain as the world's leading banker, creditor, and insurer. Nevertheless, it was in the USA that the disgust with and regret over participating in the war were the most rapid and sweeping. By comparison, the small and backward Serbia suffered, relative to population, the heaviest casualties of all the warring nations and was totally ravaged by the war and occupation, but she hardly experienced the 'trauma' of, and 'disillusion' with, the war. Nor, indeed, would other traditional and developing societies that suffered hundreds of thousands and millions of casualties in the wars of the twentieth century—down to the Iran–Iraq war (1980–8)—react more traumatically than the norm among pre-industrial societies earlier in history. By contrast, as the twentieth century progressed, the smallest number of casualties has become sufficient to discredit a war in affluent liberal societies, particularly when the threat is not considered existential, imminent, and unsusceptible to effective alternative policies short of open war, or, if war occurs, when the prospects of success diminish.[59]

Moreover, to the extent that the anti-war mood that developed in post-First World War Britain can be more clearly defined, most people probably would not have denied at the time that the stakes in that war had been high and that it would have mattered if Britain had lost the war to Germany and the latter had been allowed to dominate continental Europe by force. At the same time, however, they felt that the war had conflicted with the rationale of the modern world, economic and normative, and that *everybody* had more to gain from peace, and everybody had lost from the war, even if some lost more than others. It was the powers' slide into, and then persistence in, the war, given the alternatives, that was regarded as disastrous and sheer madness. Everything possible had to be done to avoid falling into the same trap in the future. This was the fundamental notion that shaped western-liberal policy during the 1930s.[60] Ultimately, the sensible assumptions behind 'appeasement' collapsed when it turned out that the west's protagonists would not accept them. But the crucial question of whether or not the other side—even if it was not liberal democratic and/or affluent—could be co-opted into peaceful coexistence, if not co-operation, would repeatedly return to torment governments and people in affluent liberal democracies with each new rival and conflict. For the answer to this question cannot be reasoned *a priori* from cause to effect but varies in each particular case.

OTHER RELATED AND INDEPENDENT FACTORS

Additional factors might also be involved in making affluent liberal-democratic societies more pacific. It is common among international relations theorists, as among social scientists in general, to regard parsimony, the explanation of phenomena by the smallest possible number of variables, as a scientific ideal. Yet, without quarrelling with the theoretical proposition, in social phenomena a multiplicity of factors is at play, often making theoretically 'less elegant' explanations truer. Some of the additional factors suggested below are variably related to liberal democracy, whereas others are associated with economic development, which, in turn, is also variably related to liberal democracy. How and to what extent this is so has still to be determined.

Wealth and Comfort—Again

Let me return to the subject of wealth and comfort. Throughout history, rising prosperity has been associated with decreasing willingness to endure the hardship of war and military service. Freedom from manual labour and luxurious living conditions achieved by the rich in prosperous pre-modern societies conflicted with the physical hardship of campaigning and life in the field, which thereby became more alien and unappealing. There were greater amenities and less to escape from at home and fewer attractions to look for in military service. Where wealth was of a civilian nature and protected by the law, rather than based on direct forceful extraction by a warrior class, a demilitarized elite was even less habituated to violent conflict. Historically, as we have seen, this made prosperous pre-modern societies vulnerable to violent take-overs from the poor marches. Hungry wolves regularly beat satiated dogs. This relationship changed in modernity, when developed technological infrastructure, producing superior military hardware, became paramount. At the same time, however, the wealth, comfort, and other amenities formerly enjoyed only by a privileged elite spread through society as the industrial–technological age unfolded and per capita wealth in the developed countries increased by a staggering 15- to 30-fold. The bourgeois dream first appeared and then spread to encompass the greater part of society. In economically developed 'consumer societies', the average man and woman now routinely enjoy greater comfort than the aristocrat of earlier times.

Thus increasing wealth has worked to decrease war not only through the modern logic of expanding manufacturing and trading interdependence, but also through the traditional logic of the effect of affluence and comfort—now spread through society and steadily rising—on society's willingness to endure hardship. This dual rationale is reflected in *New York Times*' writer Thomas Friedman's half-whimsical rule, according to which two countries that have McDonald's fast food restaurants will never go to war against each other. Since its formulation, this rule, which made international relations theorists pause to think, has seen some exceptions, such as in the former Yugoslavia. All the same, it is based on the idea that countries that attract multinationals such as McDonald's are both sufficiently connected to the global economy *and* affluent enough to enjoy its blessings.[61] As new heights of affluence and comfort have been achieved in the developed world in the period since the Second World War, when practically all the world's affluent countries have been democracies, it is difficult to distinguish the effects of comfort from those of democracy in diminishing belligerency. Obviously, as already noted, to some degree the two factors have been interrelated. To what degree, I return to ask later on.

It is difficult for people in today's liberal, affluent, and secure societies to visualize how life was for their forefathers only a few generations ago, and largely still is in poor countries. Life is reputably hard, but it used to be much harder. Angst may have replaced fear and physical pain in modern societies, yet, without depreciating the merits of traditional society or ignoring the stresses and problems of modernity, this change has been nothing short of revolutionary. People in pre-modern societies struggled to survive in the most elementary sense. The overwhelming majority of them went through a lifetime of hard physical work to escape hunger, from which they were never secure. The tragedy of orphanage, child mortality, premature death of spouses, and early death in general was inseparable from their lives. At all ages, they were afflicted with illness, disability, and physical pain, for which no effective remedies existed. Even where state rule prevailed, violent conflict between neighbours was a regular occurrence and, therefore, an ever-present possibility, putting a premium on physical strength, toughness, and honour, and a reputation for all of these. Hardship and tragedy tended to harden people and make them fatalistic. In this context, the suffering and death of war were endured as just another nature-like affliction, together with Malthus's other grim reapers: famine and disease.

By comparison, even contrast, life in affluent–liberal societies changed dramatically. The decline of physical labour has already been mentioned. Hunger and want were replaced by societies of plenty, where food, for example, the most basic of needs, became available practically without limit, with the historically unprecedented and paradoxical result of obesity rather than starvation becoming a major problem, even, and indeed sometimes especially, among the poor. Childhood and early death became rare occurrences, with infant mortality falling to roughly a twentieth of its rate during pre-industrial times. Annual general mortality declined from around 30 to about 7–10 per 1,000 people.[62] Not only were infectious diseases, the number one killer of the past, mostly rendered non-lethal by improved hygiene, immunizations, and antibiotics, but countless bodily irritations and disabilities—deteriorating eyesight, bad teeth, skin disease, hernia—that used to be an integral part of life were alleviated by medication, medical instruments, and surgery. Anaesthetics and other drugs, from painkillers to Viagra, have dramatically improved the quality of life. People in the developed world live in well-heated and air-conditioned dwellings, equipped with mechanical–electrical appliances that perform most of the household jobs. They have indoor bathrooms and lavatories. They wash daily and change clothes as often. They drive rather than walk. They are flooded with popular entertainment through the media that occupies their spare time. They take holidays in far-away exotic places. Rising up the 'pyramid of needs', they embrace 'postmodern', 'post-materialistic' values that emphasize individual self-fulfilment. Although this may be hard for people, especially Americans, to believe, the prospect of physical violence has ceased to be an element of everyday life in developed societies (except in some particularly problematic pockets, such as America's inner cities).[63] In an orderly and comfortable society, rough conduct in social dealings decreases, whereas civility, peaceful argument, and humour become the norm. Men are more able to 'connect to their feminine side'. Whereas children and youth used to be physically disciplined by their parents and fought among themselves at school, on the playground, and in the street, they are now surrounded by a general social abhorrence of violence that habituates them against it. Social expectations and psychological sensitivity have risen as dramatically as these changes. People in affluent liberal societies expect to live, to control their lives, and to enjoy life rather than merely endure it, with war scarcely fitting into their life plan.

It is not surprising then that the 'imprudent vehemence' historically associated with republican foreign policy appears to have all but disappeared in the affluent, consumer-hedonistic, liberal-democratic societies that developed after the Second World War; moreover, this change has affected the elites and affluent middle class in these societies even more than their less affluent 'demos'. Indeed, it is no coincidence that, in the same way as the 'have-nots' within societies are more prone to violent social behaviour, so are the less affluent members of the international system.

Metropolitan Service Society

The growth of city and metropolitan life is a somewhat related phenomenon. Unlike most city-states, which, as we have seen, were actually both urban and predominantly agrarian, commercial and metropolitan cities were considered by classical military authorities as the least desirable recruiting ground. According to Vegetius, echoed by subsequent authors down to Machiavelli, sturdy farmers constituted the best recruits. In the city, artisans in professions that involved hard manual work were to be preferred, whereas people engaged in other city trades were to be avoided as being unaccustomed to the rigours of field campaigning.[64] Furthermore, typically immigrating from diverse quarters, the residents of large metropolitan centres in particular lacked traditional communal bonds of solidarity and were free from the social controls of village and small town communities. Exposed to the cities' quick dealings and temptations, they were regarded as too fickle, rootless, undisciplined, and cynical to be trusted. With modernity, urbanism and city life in large metropolises were no longer confined, as earlier, to only a few per cent of the total population, but steadily expanded to encompass the majority of the people. Correspondingly, the numbers of country folk shrank in number to as little as a few per cent. Yet the military continued to regard them as the best 'recruiting material'.

Examples abound. With the coming of the twentieth century, the German army drafted disproportionately more heavily in the countryside, and, as second best, among country–town people. It limited its recruitment from the large cities, where the masses were regarded as both militarily less suitable and politically suspect, being infected with socialism.[65] In liberal-democratic Britain, too, the world's most urban society that adopted the draft in both World Wars, country folk were regarded as the most fit for military service. Industrial workers were seen as good enough recruits but were suspected of importing into the army the insubordination and rebelliousness forged in chronically strained labour relations in the factories and mines. Office people were perceived as the least suitable for the rigours of military life. Notably, the British Empire's undisputed best troops during both world wars came from the farms of the still predominantly rural dominions: New Zealand, Australia, and Canada. Self-reliant and egalitarian freeholders throughout history had proved to be prime soldiers. Indeed, the farmer recruits from middle America who dominated the US armies during the First World War were regarded as first-class 'military material'. The American armies of the Second World War, in which city folk increased in number, still fought well enough, but did not hold the same superb reputation as their First World War predecessors. And Vietnam War draftees, especially those from the more urban states, had an even lower reputation of being endowed with 'natural' soldierly qualities. The US Army releases no statistics on the geographical breakdown of its recruitment, but an analysis of the hometown of the fallen in the Iraq War reveals that rural and small-town communities contribute nearly twice as many volunteer-recruits per population as the metropolitan centres;[66] there is a 'red'–'blue' difference here. Israel's crack units during the first decades of her existence were overwhelmingly made up of young people from a relatively small number of voluntary communal villages (*kibbutzim*) and farm communities (*moshavim*).

The far-reaching change in the occupational structure of society and the cities has to be factored in. City folk during the zenith of the industrial age consisted mainly of factory workers. Despite their above-cited short-comings, they were accustomed to physical labour, machines, and the massive scale, co-ordinated work regime, labelled 'Fordism' and 'Taylorism' after its prophets and pioneers. They lived in dense urban communities, and they were mostly literate. These qualities were major strengths for the armed forces, especially as they too were undergoing mechanization. For most purposes, the troops of industrial society, who went through the two great 'disciplining' institutions of modern society—the school and the factory—were better suited for the large-scale co-operation, quick pace, and mech-anization of modern warfare than pre-industrial, essentially pre-modern peasant armies. The free farmer element of modern societies combined the advantages of both. However, as the industrial–technological era progressed, manufacturing declined whereas the service sector rose in its share of the workforce in most advanced economies. In the USA, for example, which leads this trend, 70 per cent of the workforce is now employed in services whereas only 18 per cent work in manufacturing.[67] It can be argued with some justification that the armed forces, too, have been moving from mech-anized to information-based forces, increasingly relying on computerized data processing and accurate standoff fire to do most of the fighting. In addition, military service conditions have improved considerably, and the adventure and physical challenge of military life still appeal to many youth. All the same, adaptation to military life comes far less naturally to people from contemporary affluent societies who are accustomed to deskwork in the office and the seclusion of residential suburbia than it did to their farmer and factory worker predecessors.[68] It is not for nothing that the concepts of urbanity and urbanism derive from the same root, denoting qualities that are fundamentally non-military. Again, although high rates of industrial urbanism characterized not only liberal societies but also imperial and Nazi Germany and the Soviet Union, nearly all the advanced service economies are associated with liberal democracies, making the effect of the two factors hard to distinguish.

The Sexual Revolution

Greater sexual availability, associated with the pill, women joining the labour market outside the home, and liberalization in general, may be another factor that has dampened enthusiasm for war in advanced modern societies, especially among unmarried young men. Traditionally constituting the most aggressive element in society, largely, as we have seen, because of their unsettled status, young single males now find around them a wide range of outlets for their restlessness. Correspondingly, foreign adventure, which once lured many of them away from dull and suffocating countryside and small town communities, has lost much of its attraction, especially for city folk, whereas the sexual aspects of such adventure are severely curtailed by state military authorities. In modern imperial Japan, the troops still indulged in state-tolerated mass rape while serving abroad, some of it in the form of state-organized forced prostitution. At least two million women are estimated to have been raped by Soviet soldiers in conquered eastern Germany in 1945, many of them, possibly the majority, falling victim to multiple rape. Mass rape was a major feature of the ethnic wars in Bosnia and Rwanda during the 1990s. In the armies of the western democracies, rape is severely punished (although still occurring sporadically), but American GIs (and other Allied troops) widely availed themselves of an abundant supply of low-cost prostitution in ruined western Europe and, later, in desperately poor Vietnam.[69] All in all, however, the balance of sexual opportunity changed radically. Similar to the privileged in earlier times, young men now are more reluctant to leave behind the pleasures of life for the rigours and chastity of the field. 'Make love not war' was the slogan of the powerful anti-war youth campaign of the 1960s, which by no coincidence took off in tandem with a far-reaching liberalization of sexual norms. Once more, this liberalization mainly took place in affluent and urban liberal societies, although it is interesting to speculate how much it affected the Soviet Union in later periods and how it may affect today's China. Again, there is no need to accept fully the reasoning of Freud, Wilhelm Reich, and Michel Foucault to appreciate the significance of this factor.

To summarize all the above factors, somewhat conflicting forces are at work in modern affluent democracies. Historically, highly participatory societies tended to excel in mobilization for war, compared with autocratic and oligarchic regimes (although not with modern totalitarian ones). Yet rising affluence and city life tended to decrease citizen participation in the military. As we saw, in ancient and mediaeval city-states, citizen armies regularly gave way to professional troops recruited from the rural and urban poor and from foreigners. There were and are other reasons for the change from conscript to professional armies, yet the process as a whole cannot fail to be recognized in today's militaries in the USA, Britain, and other affluent democratic societies. Political philosophers and moralists throughout history identified luxury, city life, sexual promiscuity, cheaply available bread and circus for the masses, and a disintegration of traditional communal moral codes with 'laxness', 'softness', and 'decadence'. Indeed, the modern west and other parts of the developed world have been described as being in a state of perpetual decadence. And yet they escape social, political, and military decline, *to the extent that they do*, because of the special advantages of modern society, noted earlier in this book, such as technological superiority and highly competitive economies and political systems.

Those who lament the demise of high idealism in contemporary affluent, consumer, and hedonistic societies should recognize the flip side of the same coin: that such societies show great reluctance to get involved in serious war. This can constitute a grave problem in the face of a serious threat, yet the 'powerful pacifists' that modern affluent liberal democracies are have so far managed their balancing act reasonably well.

Fewer Young Males

In addition to changes in the circumstance and attitudes of young males, the significant decline in their relative *number* is another factor that may have decreased enthusiasm for war in contemporary developed societies.[70] In pre-modern societies, life expectancy not only at birth but also for adults was considerably lower than today. Thus the share of young adult males in the adult population was higher, even under zero demographic growth. With the onset of industrialization, as child mortality fell sharply whereas birth rates followed only slowly, the number of young adults in a fast-growing population increased not only in absolute terms but also relative to the total adult population. This was evident in the nineteenth-century west, as it was in the twentieth-century developing world. Young men were most conspicuous in the public enthusiasm for war in July–August 1914, as they were in all wars and revolutions. In today's affluent societies, however, with birth rates falling below replacement level and with increased longevity, young adults—including males—constitute a shrinking portion of an ageing population. Before the First World War, males aged 15–29 constituted 35 per cent of the adult male population in Britain, and 40 per cent in Germany; by 2000 their share dropped to 24 and 29 per cent, respectively. By comparison, for example, young men of the same age cohorts constituted 48 per cent of Iran's population in 2000. In that year, the median age in the developed parts of the world had risen to 37 (and was projected to rise to 46 by 2050), as against 24 in the less developed parts of the world, and 18 in the least developed.[71]

Again, as young males have always been the most aggressive element in society whereas older men were traditionally associated with a counsel of moderation and compromise, it has been suggested that the decline in young men's relative numbers may contribute to the pacificity of developed societies while explaining the greater belligerency of developing ones, particularly those of Islam. China's 'one-child' policy may make her more similar to a developed society; but in Islamic societies booming population growth peaked only recently, and the relative share of young men is at its height.[72] Furthermore, during the nineteenth century open borders made it possible for the young in demographically exploding Europe to emigrate in great numbers to Europe's sparsely populated overseas offshoots, whereas today the restrictive immigration policies of developed countries increase the problem of the developing world. Indeed, avoiding simplistic correlations, it is together with the lack of economic (and sexual) opportunity in traditional, stagnant, and culturally defensive societies that the restlessness of the cohorts of young men in Islam should be understood, whereas the opposite is true for the falling number of young men in affluent societies. It is always in the context of specific economic, social, and cultural conditions that people's behaviour takes place. Thus, at the height of her population growth around the middle of the nineteenth century, the share of young men in industrially booming Britain was over 40 per cent of the adult male population, not unlike today's Iran, and yet this was the period of the *pax Britannica*.

Fewer Children per Family?

Given the sharp decline in birth rate in developed societies, it has also been suggested that the far smaller number of children per family may be the cause of these societies' decreased belligerency. According to this argument, whereas in the past, too, parents obviously loved their children dearly and were very anxious to spare them from the Moloch of war, it has become that much more agonizing for them to lose a child when a typical present-day family numbers only one or two children.[73] It is doubtful, however, if this reasoning stands up to scrutiny. Historically, families with many surviving children were a transient phenomenon, limited to the period of demographic explosion experienced during early industrialization. Although birth rates had indeed been much higher in pre-modern societies, so also was infant mortality, resulting in an overall demographic equilibrium (with populations growing very slowly, in pace with the slow rise in productivity). Women gave birth to many children, but only a few survived to adulthood, keeping average numbers at about replacement rate. Thus, having raised their few surviving children to adulthood, parents in the past could no easier 'afford' to lose them than today's parents; indeed, economically speaking, they could less afford to lose their only support in old age. The real change between past and modern times is not the number of (surviving) children per family; in the past people were simply helpless to oppose the dictates of far-away and alien authorities, which did not care about their wishes, or, indeed, about their life and death. Where the people themselves ruled, as in city-state republics, the expected rewards of war—offensive and defensive—made the risk to life more acceptable. Both conditions have lost much of their validity in advanced modern liberal democracies.

Women's Franchise

Another gender-based factor may contribute to the growing social aversion to war. Although young men have always been the most aggressive element in society, men in general have always been more aggressive and belligerent than women. As seen earlier, this difference is biologically rooted, and persists across a wide variation of cultural attitudes. This is not to argue that women are inherently pacific and opposed to war—far from it. It means only that on average they are less inclined to serious physical violence and more restrained in supporting it. Obviously, men made the political decisions throughout history and, even when women found themselves in positions of power, which was rare, it was in a 'men's world' that they were obliged to operate and succeed. It is within this context of a reality where women were disenfranchised that one should understand Aristophanes' satirical play Lysistrata, written in Athens during the Peloponnesian War. Agonized by the death and misery of war, the women in Aristophanes' play declare a sex strike against their men until they agree to make peace. Having won the franchise in twentieth-century liberal democracies, women no longer need to resort to Aristophanes' fictitious ultimate weapon but have been able to influence governments' policies by electing them. Indeed, studies in the west during the past decades have shown a consistent gender gap in attitudes to the use of military force, with women being about 5–15 per cent less supportive of it.[74] As elections are often decided by a small margin and governments are necessarily responsive to their electorates, such gender differences might play a significant role in tilting the electoral balance against military ventures in modern affluent liberal democracies. The liberal/democratic and sex-related explanations for peace thereby overlap: women's vote has been suggested as a reason why liberal democracies became more pacific in the twentieth than they had been in the nineteenth century.[75] This may indeed be a significant factor, although only in addition to and together with all the other elements discussed here.

Moreover, as noted above, women are not unconditionally pacifist. In some societies and conflicts the attitudes of the sexes do not diverge significantly. For example, no such divergence has been revealed in studies of both sides of the Arab–Israeli conflict. After examining various explanations for these findings, the researchers who conducted the studies have suggested that they were most probably explained by the high 'salience' of the conflict, which generated high mobilization levels among members of both sexes.[76] Indeed, an absence of a gender gap is not peculiar to the Middle East, with the salience explanation possibly applying more generally. In the 2004 American presidential elections, for example, the so-called security moms, who feared additional mega-terror attacks at home, cast more votes for the tougher candidate George W. Bush than they did for his Democratic challenger, despite the perceived American bog-down in the controversial Iraq war. In Russia, the mothers' voice, still mute in a totalitarian system during the Soviet failed Afghan campaign (1979–88), became dominant during the first Chechnyan war (1994–6), after Russia had become liberalized. Mothers took to the streets in public demonstrations, significantly contributing to the Russian decision to withdraw. However, as with the American 'security moms', the continuation of terror attacks on Russian soil carried out by Chechen extremists after the Russian withdrawal legitimized Russian re-intervention, at least in the eyes of Russian public opinion, men and women alike.

607

Nuclear Weapons

The advent of nuclear weapons is widely regarded as the crucial factor that has prevented a great-power war since 1945. Undoubtedly, the prospect of mutual assured destruction (MAD) revolutionized the logic of war, because it eliminated the uncertainty about the outcome of war that had previously left room for protagonists to take their chances; in an all-out nuclear war all sides would be losers. Thus nuclear weapons concentrated the minds of the Cold War antagonists wonderfully. However, as already noted, the 'Long Peace' since 1945, the longest yet in the modern great power system, was preceded by the second longest peace ever between the western powers in the years 1871–1914. And this, in turn, was preceded by the third longest peace ever in the years 1815–54. Crucially, of course, nuclear weapons have all but prevented the break-up of such extended periods of peace with devastating inter-state wars as had occurred before 1945. This is a monumental change. And yet something had been changing in the relationships between industrializing/industrial great powers, and particularly between industrial liberal/democratic great powers, long before the bomb.[77]

As a leading historian of the Cold War has pointed out, it is all too often forgotten that between 1945 and 1949 the USA possessed a monopoly over nuclear weapons. Theoretically, it had every reason to pre-empt and force its way without fear of retaliation rather than adopt containment and wait for Soviet nuclearization, which, although expected to come later than it actually did, was acknowledged as ultimately inevitable.[78] Had the Soviet Union or Nazi Germany, rather than the USA, possessed a nuclear monopoly, there can be little doubt that they would have pressed for the massive production of nuclear weapons and carried out a worldwide policy of conquest and coercion. Thus, not only towards other affluent liberal democracies but also towards her Soviet arch-rival, the USA refrained from pressing its transient overwhelming advantage to the point of war. Nor, again, is there any true likelihood of today's affluent liberal democracies, whatever their possible differences, disagreements, or tensions, engaging each other in armed conflict—hot, cold, or covert—with or without nuclear deterrence, which they are similarly unlikely to deploy against each other.

The advent of nuclear weapons marks a turning point in history, wherein unlimited war between nuclear states became mutually suicidal, whether or not they were liberal democratic; yet the resulting restraint is based on arms race, deterrence, and the balance of terror, and leaves room for covert, indirect, and low-intensity forms of armed conflict. At the same time, however, and almost as independently, *any* sort of violent conflict between modern affluent–liberal democracies was becoming virtually unthinkable irrespective of the bomb. A 'positive' peace rooted in common benefit and a shared normative rejection of war, rather than a 'negative' peace based on deterrence from a full-scale open war, prevails among them. There is a big difference between the two, which does not make either of them less significant. *Both* an affluent–liberal order and nuclear weapons are genuinely epoch making. This may create a dissonance for monists. Indeed, single-factor explanations are seductively catchy. And yet here, as often occurs, multiple, more or less related, factors converged.

LIBERAL STRATEGIC POLICY: ISOLATIONISM, APPEASEMENT, CONTAINMENT, LIMITED WAR

Thus affluent liberal democracies are unprecedentedly averse to war for the reasons described, rooted in the equally unprecedented developments of the industrial–technological age and particularly in the liberal road to it. Among affluent liberal democracies—which share this aversion and its domestic and international underpinnings—a true *state* of peace appears to have developed, based on genuine mutual confidence that war between them is practically eliminated even as an option. Nothing like this had ever existed in history; but then again, modern conditions are similarly revolutionary. On further examination, scholars have become aware that (affluent) liberal democracies' aversion to war, although most clearly manifest in the 'democratic peace', extends beyond it, and has also affected the democracies' relationships with non-democracies, especially powerful ones.[79] One aspect of the liberal democracies' restraint is their tendency to eschew preventive war. Historically, they have chosen not to initiate war even when they are under threat, hold the military advantage, and are in danger of losing it.[80] The USA's avoidance of initiating war against a hostile Soviet Union when the former still held a monopoly over nuclear power has already been mentioned, but the pattern is discernible even earlier in the twentieth century.

The British reluctance to consider seriously 'Copenhagening' the German navy during the massive German naval build-up before the First World War can be cited as a case in point; the concept alludes to the destruction of the Danish navy by Lord Nelson to prevent it from joining Napoleon (1801). It is doubtful, however, that a similar action against the German navy made any political or strategic sense irrespective of Britain's sociopolitical regime, and in any case Britain was able to keep ahead of Germany in the naval construction race. It might be added, however, by way of contrast, that Germany embarked on the First World War largely as a preventive war against Russia, where massive industrial take-off, occurring at that time, was regarded by Germany as a grave threat. One may also note that, after the fall of France in 1940, the British did 'Copenhagen' the French navy of neutral Vichy in the ports of Oran and Dakar for fear that it would fall into German hands. And yet this action took place *after* the Second World War had broken out. The remarkable thing is that the western liberal democracies did not intervene by force during the mid-1930s to prevent Hitler's Germany from rearming, even though this meant that the complete military superiority that they held over Germany would be lost, making it possible for Hitler to embark on his radical expansionist policy. Until it became too late, the governments and peoples of the western democracies hoped that the worst-case scenarios would not materialize and that it would be possible to accommodate Germany peacefully or, in any case, contain her short of war. This may be seen as an instance of what Hume regarded as liberal countries' tendency for 'careless and supine . . . complaisance' towards the future.[81] On the other hand, a war not initiated might be a war averted. As already noted, there is no way of determining this in advance. The liberal democracies' strong inhibition against preventive war would move to the forefront of bitter public debate in connection with the American 'war against terror' after 11 September 2001.

The affluent liberal democracies' recoil from preventive war comprises merely one element in a wider pattern of conduct. Ultimately, the fundamental question is the following: if modern affluent–liberal democracies are recognizably different in their international conduct from other historical state-societies, as seems to be the case, is this difference also manifest in other aspects of that conduct? It is suggested here that their aversion to war has translated into a typical pattern of response to both potential and actual conflict—indeed, that affluent liberal democracies behave differently *in bello*, as well as *ad bellum*. For reasons examined earlier, the west traditionally exhibited heightened belligerency and a preference for a direct clash of forces. During the Second World War, the liberal democracies showed few scruples in wreaking total destruction from the air on Germany and Japan, most brutal enemies with which they were locked in a life-and-death struggle. Apprehension about their alleged combative 'crusading spirit' was also expressed during the early stages of the Cold War, echoing the charge of 'imprudent vehemence' long attributed to them by Hume. And yet it is argued here that with their growing aversion to war the liberal democracies also developed a new 'western way in warfare', in many ways different from the old, which, as the western model expanded, increasingly came to apply to all affluent liberal democracies.

Given these societies' fundamental attitudes, the problem of how to deal with conflict has become a tormentingly difficult issue for them. Initially, liberals, although peacefully inclined, were not pacifist, because liberalism had to be won and defended, even if by force. However, in time and as the above-described processes within affluent liberal democracies deepened, some liberals (and socialists) came to espouse more or less unilateral pacifism, which, however, could never become the dominant creed because it never explained what should be done if the other side were not similarly pacifist. More in tune with the liberal mainstream has been the effort to make the entire international system conform to the Painean–Kantian–Wilsonian model—that is, have it embrace democratic self-determination, liberalism, and free trade, link into the modern spiral of mutual prosperity, and resolve disputes through international institutions. Where the conditions for that model materialized, as they did most notably in post-Second World War western Europe, the results were truly remarkable. But most of the world proved highly resistant to the realization of that model, and much if not most of it still is. The Victorians' lesson after repeated frustrations is ever re-experienced by affluent–liberal–democratic societies: their model is far from being universally desired by other societies and cultures; the material and normative preconditions for it are often excruciatingly distant from the latter's reach; and this, in turn, makes the attainment of these preconditions, if it occurs at all, a protracted and turbulent process. The attempt to coerce others into a liberal order by direct force requires war, while proving equally

611

frustrating and all too often elusive for the same reasons. Either way, serious violent conflict may still occur against and between protagonists who live in a Hobbesian rather than a Painean–Kantian world.

If a Painean–Kantian peaceful accommodation fails to materialize because not all states are liberal (and affluent), there remains St Pierre's idea of collective security, whereby all states should combine against those who disturb peace. This idea was central to the League of Nations and the United Nations, but by and large it has failed for reasons already sensed by Rousseau: powerful states and coalitions could not be easily restrained by the threat of theoretically overwhelming collective action; this threat remained mostly theoretical, because states exhibited scant willingness to get involved in a conflict that was not their own; in the absence of coercive authority that would prevent free riding, they expected others, who were more closely involved, to do the job; they often had an even greater interest in maintaining good relationships with the 'aggressor'; and indeed, determining who the aggressor was involved value judgements, about which no consensus could be reached. All these applied to democratic as well as to non-democratic states.[82]

Thus, so long as the world has not become fully affluent and liberal democratic and collective security remains largely ineffective, liberal democracies have been obliged to address the prospect of conflict and war. I suggest that their strategic policy in facing this prospect has typically followed a pattern, progressing on an upward scale from isolationism to appeasement, to containment and cold war, to limited war, and, only most reluctantly, to fully fledged war. As with other aspects of the liberal democracies' distinctive behaviour, this pattern began to manifest itself during the later part of the nineteenth and crystallized in the twentieth century.

Liberal isolationism is a function both of a general tendency to eschew foreign conflicts that are not perceived to affect one's interests seriously and/or can be passed on to others and of the distinctive liberal aversion to war. Where isolationism could be adopted, it has been a most tempting option for liberal democracies. However, in a shrinking world of growing interdependence, it has become decreasingly tenable. And even where no significant interests are involved, the liberal commitment to universal values and human rights often makes a foreign disturbance hard to ignore.

Where a threat has been significant and could not be shut out, compromising with a rival by accommodating some of his demands and offering him economic rewards has been the liberal democracies' second most preferable option, if the price was reasonable; because this option is cheaper than war, rests on the affluent liberal democracies' strongest asset, their abundant resources, and holds the prospect of integrating the rival into a mutually beneficial economic relationship, which eventually might also lead to his liberalization. The success of such a policy of appeasement hinges on the question of whether or not the other side can become a partner to the deal offered, instead of that offer having the adverse effect of whetting his appetite and being interpreted by him as a sign of weakness. Thus appeasement must be carried out from a position of strength and entail the dangling of sticks in addition to carrots.

If appeasement fails, containment and cold war—building a deterring coalition, applying economic pressure, and engaging in covert subversion and ideological warfare—is the next step in the sequence. Finally, if an armed conflict breaks out, efforts are made to keep it limited, unless circumstances no longer make this possible. The favoured techniques have included: the provision of money and hardware to cement coalitions and strengthen local forces against adversaries; blockade; naval and aerial actions, in which developed countries possess a clear superiority; and limited operations by technologically superior strike forces. Direct large-scale warfare, especially on land, where casualties might be high, has become the least desirable option. All these, of course, are 'ideal types', which often overlap. If some of them sound quite recent, their application in fact goes back a while in time.

Thus the initial policies of both Britain and the USA during most of the nineteenth century were isolationist. Britain was the first to be drawn out of it, when external threat—mainly in the shape of the German double challenge to the continental balance of power and to Britain's naval supremacy—could no longer be contained without foreign commitments. Even then, however, Britain repeatedly sought in vain a combined naval, colonial, political, and economic deal that would bring about a *rapprochement* with Germany. And when war came, British policy was predicated on the assumption that most of the land war would be shouldered by France and Russia. Britain's contribution was assumed to be confined primarily to the naval and economic spheres, with the blockade serving as her principal weapon. Only the imminent danger of her allies' collapse gradually forced Britain into full-scale military participation.[83] The USA, for her part, was able to maintain her isolation for much longer. And even when he formally took his country to war in April 1917, President Wilson did not plan full-scale involvement in the European 'carnage'. The USA, too, was forced into full participation only by the near collapse of France and Italy and the spectre of British defeat during the U-boat campaign in the summer of 1917, the collapse and defection of Russia by the turn of the year, and the imminent disaster on the Western Front in the spring of 1918.

By the mid-1920s, the western democracies' elites increasingly felt, in the spirit of Keynes's *The Economic Consequences of the Peace* (1920), that the punitive Versailles Treaty had been a mistake. During the 'Locarno era' an attempt was made to reach accommodation with Germany by helping her to revive her economy, normalizing her international status, integrating her into international institutions, and holding before her the prospect of further peaceful settlement of her grievances. Unfortunately, this attempt collapsed with the post-1929 world economic crisis. During the 1930s, the actions of Japan, Germany, and Italy against the international status quo posed acute threats to the liberal democracies. Nevertheless, in all the liberal great powers—the USA, Britain, and France—the public's mood and the consensus in the political parties and government were unmistakably against war, even when the democracies still held the military advantage. Again their policies evolved from isolationism to appeasement, to containment and cold war, to limited action. Total war was imposed on them only by their enemies. All the liberal great powers trod that road.

Isolationism was the preferred option of those who felt themselves able to embrace it successfully: the British only toyed with the idea and then adopted a policy of partial isolationism in the shape of 'limited liability', which ruled out the commitment of substantial ground forces to continental Europe; and the USA espoused isolationism more fully and for a longer period of time. However, in view of the magnitude of the threats, isolationism in itself was deemed to be insufficient. Both countries augmented isolationism with attempts to lessen the conflict and tame the Axis powers, especially Germany, by meeting some of their grievances and offering them economic rewards and mutually beneficial trade deals. Most vigorously pursued by Neville Chamberlain, this policy of appeasement failed because ultimately Hitler's ambitions were revealed to go beyond anything that the liberal democracies were willing to accept. It should be noted, however, that even those among Chamberlain's peers who opposed his policy did not object to appeasement as such but believed that it had to be more circumspect and buttressed by force.

During the Ethiopian and Spanish crises there was still little appetite for action among the western democracies, and too small a perceived threat. All the same, consider the types of strategies that were suggested (but mostly not implemented) as a counter to the Axis's moves. Rather than direct military intervention, they included economic sanctions, the isolation of both Ethiopia and Spain by the Allies' vastly superior naval power, and the supply of armament to the Ethiopians and the Spanish Republicans. In any event, it was only the Czechoslovak crisis in the spring of 1938 that greatly alarmed western opinion. The strategic ideas then mooted in opposition to appeasement were again unmistakable. Eden, Lloyd George, Churchill, the British Labour and Liberal MPs, F. D. Roosevelt all held that Germany had to be contained by a superior coalition (incorporating the Soviet Union), capable of deterring Germany or, failing that, of strangling her economically. In 1938, before her expansion into eastern and, later, western Europe, Germany lacked the resources necessary for waging a protracted general war, as her army chiefs desperately pointed out.[84]

Roosevelt's line of thought with respect to both Europe and the Far East is typical here. In late 1937, after Japan's invasion of China and the signing of the Anti-Comintern Pact by Germany, Italy, and Japan, the president increasingly aired the notions of a co-ordinated policy of sanctions and containment against the aggressors. The idea was embodied in his famous 'quarantine speech' of 5 December 1937. Later, during the Czechoslovak crisis, Roosevelt called for a 'siege' of Germany. He suggested that the European allies close their borders with Germany, even without declaring war, and stand on the defence, relying on the economic blockade to do the job. The USA would back them economically.[85]

By the time war came in 1939, Germany had become less susceptible to economic pressure because of her domination of south-eastern Europe and her Pact with the Soviet Union. Under these circumstances the so-called twilight or phoney war which prevailed on the Western Front was not a curious aberration, as it is customarily regarded, but the most natural strategy for Britain and France. Having lost their ability to contain Germany within her old frontiers, choke her economically if she attempted to break out of them, or defeat her militarily and recover eastern Europe from her grip, Britain and France in effect opted for more or less the same strategic

615

policy that the west would adopt against the Soviet Union after the Second World War. They relied on armed coexistence, containment, economic pressure, and ideological and propaganda warfare. Militarily, Britain and France restricted themselves to peripheral and indirect action, trying to avoid escalation to fully fledged war. In all but name, this was a policy of containment and cold war. It was hoped that over time, as the western bloc formed its defences and deployed its resources, the Germans would be forced to seek an accommodation with the west. It was also hoped that the Nazi regime might mellow or lose power. As Chamberlain wrote to Roosevelt, Britain would not win the war 'by a spectacular and complete victory, but by convincing the Germans that they cannot win'. 'Hold out tight, keep up the economic pressure, push on with munitions production and military preparations with the utmost energy', but 'take no offensive unless Hitler's begins it'.[86] Unfortunately, the whole concept collapsed in May–June 1940, when the Germans succeeded in decisively defeating the Allies and overran continental western Europe.

The USA followed a similar path. In 1940–1, American policy in both Europe and the Far East encompassed all means short of open war. A crucial element in Britain's decision to keep fighting in the summer of 1940 was Churchill's belief that the USA would enter the war before long, probably after the presidential elections in November. This did not happen. Massive American economic aid in the form of Land-Lease enabled Britain to continue the fight. But the prospect of an American declaration of war remained a dubious matter throughout 1941. During the summer of that year the USA extended Land-Lease to the Soviet Union, took over the battle against the German submarines in the western half of the Atlantic, and garrisoned Iceland. Nevertheless, it became clear to the British that American entry into the war was not to be expected in the near future. The majority of Americans and members of Congress objected to the war, and Roosevelt's own intentions were unclear. He was surely not going to allow Britain to fall and probably would have used the USA's growing weight steadily to increase American influence on the course of the war. But was he waiting for more progress to be made on the USA's rearmament and was he using the time to prepare American public opinion for its eventual participation in the war? Or was he quite satisfied with the existing situation wherein Britain and the Soviet Union carried the burden of fighting with massive American political and economic support but without full

American participation? These questions remain in dispute and will probably never be answered conclusively. It is doubtful whether Roosevelt himself knew. It was only Japan's surprise attack and the subsequent German declaration of war on the USA that finally decided the issue.[87] Neither Britain nor the USA embarked on all-out war until forced into doing so by the surprising collapse of their defences, respectively in May–June 1940 in western Europe and in December 1941 in the Pacific.

Indeed, although far more powerful than Japan in all respects, the USA deployed non-military means to contain her in 1940–1. She tightened the screw of economic sanctions so strongly that her imposition of an oil embargo threatened to bring Japan to her knees.[88] Unfortunately, defensive precautions to back this policy up proved insufficient. As with Germany the year before, the policy of containment, economic coercion, and cold war floundered when the enemy did the unthinkable and in a highly successful lightning campaign broke down the walls that had been built up against him.

By the end of the Second World War the Soviet Union was taking the place of the Axis powers as the liberal democracies' potential rival. And, yet again, their response followed a path leading from appeasement to containment and cold war. As revisionist historians of the 1930s have reminded us, towards the end of the war Roosevelt and Churchill recognized Soviet control over eastern Europe for much the same reasons that Chamberlain had been prepared to see German hegemony extended over that region. Roosevelt in particular hoped to come to terms with the Soviet Union and incorporate it within a new global four-power collective security system. By 1946–7, however, American hopes were dashed, and the policy of containment and the Cold War came into being.

As already mentioned, this policy was adopted when the USA still held the monopoly over nuclear power. All the same, according to George Kennan, the intellectual architect of containment, the idea was formed in a fundamentally non-nuclear frame of mind and derived from pre-1945 experiences.[89] The atom bomb is not even mentioned in either his 'Long Telegram' from Moscow of February 1946 or his famous 'Mr X' *Foreign Affairs* article of 1947, containment's formative documents. Throughout the second half of the 1940s, Kennan insisted that the USA must refrain from using nuclear weapons as an active instrument of diplomacy and war.[90] Periods of heightened tensions and greater militarization alternated with periods of *rapprochement* and *détente* until the end of the Cold War.

After 1945 the prospect of a major great power war diminished, and it appears to have become very remote indeed since the collapse of the Soviet Union and the communist challenge. This decline in the likelihood of a great power war has resulted—separately and conjointly—from the establishment of nuclear deterrence and from the assimilation of the former right-wing authoritarian and totalitarian powers into the liberal order, followed by an ongoing incorporation of the former communist powers. By contrast, conflicts and wars between affluent liberal democracies and small, economically backward non-democracies continue to occur, with the above-described political–strategic pattern remaining very much in force in these conflicts. It has been suggested that today's world is divided between 'zones of peace', encompassing the affluent–liberal–democratic parts of the world, and 'zones of war', which continue to prevail in the world's poorer parts.[91] I now proceed to examine both more closely.

THE DEVELOPED WORLD AS A ZONE OF PEACE?

Does the liberal political and economic system hold inherent advantages under modern conditions, which explain—indeed, 'guarantee'—its triumph and, in consequence, the decline of belligerency?[92] As we saw in earlier chapters, the market economy has expanded almost irresistibly since early modernity, with the low-priced goods and the superior power that it produces working in tandem to erode and transform all other socio-economic regimes. Have political liberalism and democracy held a similar inherent advantage? Here the answer is far less clear. The triumph of the market, precipitating and reinforced by the industrial–technological revolution, has inextricably brought about the rise of the middle class, urbanization, spreading education, and the emergence of 'mass society'. But has there been an alternative to liberal democracy that could have kept in step with these modern developments? This is largely a matter of speculation, because other major historical experiments were cut short. Obviously, the old agrarian elites and the autocracies based on them could not survive under modern conditions. But was capitalist–industrial imperial Germany, for example, ultimately moving towards increasing parliamentary control and democratization, or would it have developed an authoritarian–oligarchic regime, dominated by an alliance of the officialdom, the armed forces, and industry, as imperial Japan did despite a brief liberal interlude in the 1920s? And, of course, there was the option of right-wing totalitarian dictatorship, again most ominously represented by Nazi Germany. To repeat, these authoritarian and totalitarian regimes were not defeated because of an inherent economic–military weakness vis-à-vis the liberal democracies, but mainly because of the sheer size of the democratic USA, which ultimately tilted the balance against them in both World Wars.

True, liberal economic theory prescribes that free global trade is more efficient than less open national–capitalist economies. Yet before a liberal global trade system was created in the wake of 1945, making it possible for the liberal powers to benefit from it, the world was largely divided among large political–economic blocs/empires that promised some advantages of scale, economically as well as militarily, and, in any case, left the liberal powers with no inherent advantage over their non-democratic capitalist rivals. And although in the industrial–technological world of steadily growing wealth, the rising benefits of peace and interdependence make war a less attractive option generally, greater economic autarky and strong non-liberal-democratic capitalist powers would tend to keep the potential and eventuality of war alive. It was only when the paramount capitalist–democratic power, the USA, standing at the height of her military and economic strength after the Second World War, found it a matter of both national interest and ideology to promote free trade and democratization—throwing her overwhelming weight behind them—that the liberalization of the capitalist parts of the world took place. At that particular junction, the USA both stood to gain the most from trade liberalization and was powerful enough to impose it. The contingent nature of that development is highlighted by the fact that only in the twentieth century, as her productivity edged ahead of that of all her competitors, did the USA eschew protectionism, becoming fully committed to free trade only in the 1930s.[93]

Since 1945, the enormous gravitational pull exerted by the USA and the expansion of the affluent–liberal orbit has bent patterns of development worldwide. Studies that cover this period show that democracies have been the most successful economically; at the same time, authoritarian–capitalist regimes are revealed to have been as, if not more, successful in the earlier stages of development (as 'enlightened despotism' often was in Europe's past), but tended to democratize after crossing a certain threshold in terms of economic (and hence also social) development.[94] This seems to have been a recurring pattern: in east Asia, southern Europe, and Latin America. And yet there might be something misleading about the attempt to deduce a general, unilinear pattern of historical development from these findings. As the authoritarian/totalitarian–capitalist great powers, Germany and Japan, were crushed in war and the successor states were threatened by Soviet hegemony, they lent themselves to a sweeping process of restructuring and democratization. Consequently, apart from communism, smaller countries remained with no rival model to emulate and with no powerful international players to turn to other than the liberal. Their democratization after reaching a certain level of economic development might be interpreted as the result of wholly internal processes. Equally likely, however, it was not 'necessary' but occurred under the overwhelming influence of the western-liberal hegemony— political, economic, cultural, and ideological. Currently, Singapore is the only example of a first-rate economy that still maintains a semi-authoritarian regime, but she, too, is likely to change under the influence of the liberal hegemony.

During the nineteenth century, Britain represented for others the universal model for the future, being the first industrial, and also a liberal-parliamentary, nation. Later, the hegemony of her model declined, as Britain's economic dominance waned whereas non-liberal great powers industrialized and totalitarianism offered a powerful alternative model. The communist challenge, de-colonization, and problems of development again decreased the number and relative share of democracies in the international system, which had increased in the wake of the Second World War.[95] Has the dominance of the liberal model in today's world gained such a wide-reaching hold that a threshold has been crossed and a similar relapse is unlikely? More than half of all states (and the majority the world's population) now have elective governments, and in close to half liberal rights are assessed to be sufficiently entrenched to justify their designation as fully free, and yet some observers during the 1990s anticipated a reverse wave, and this may already be occurring.[96]

Obviously, the question becomes all the more relevant with the emergence of new non-liberal giants in the system, above all the formerly communist and fast industrializing China. Russia's development, too, is an open question. (And India's ability to retain its remarkable democratic tradition while undergoing economic and social transformation is also a matter of some speculation.) Will these countries, under the dominant impact of the affluent parts of today's international system, ultimately converge into the liberal-democratic range? Or are they big enough to chart a different course and challenge the hegemonic model, creating a new non-democratic but economically developed and powerful 'second world'? Might they, for example, recreate in some form a capitalist–authoritarian regime, where officialdom, industrialists, and the military ally; which would be nationalist in orientation while participating with lesser or greater restrictions in the global economy?[97] I present these questions more as a reflection on modern historical developments than as a guide to the future, because, as anybody who has ever tried to predict the *future* can testify, such speculations, while inescapable and even necessary, have only a modest chance of piercing through its veil. So much that is unpredictable can and will occur.

Moreover, the liberal political and economic order may prove more tenuous in its current bastions in the west, undermining the foundations of the affluent–liberal–democratic peace. A crushing economic crisis affecting the global trading system in the direction of greater national and regional protectionism, a resurgence of ethnic strife in Europe, or any other unforeseen development might shake an order that presently appears to be almost irreversible, rooted, as it is, in the most fundamental developments and processes of the industrial–technological age in the west. And if the western liberal model becomes less appealing and more troubled in its core countries, how would this affect the global periphery, with a conversion to that model that is much more recent, incomplete, and insecure, and largely hinges on foreign influence? Either because of the emergence of a new, successful, non-liberal 'second world' and/or because of trouble in the liberal world, might the developing countries of the periphery not drift away from liberal democracy? Finally, what about those societies and cultures that have so far failed successfully to embark on the road to the industrial–technological age, while also finding the hegemonic liberal order alien if not repugnant? Indeed, how might new developments, especially the development and proliferation of nuclear weapons and other weapons of mass destruction, affect the old 'zone of war' and its relationship with the developed world?

621

WHERE MODERNIZED AND TRADITIONAL SOCIETIES CONFLICT

So far this chapter has examined the modernizing and modern societies—either liberal or non-liberal—that have been transformed by the industrial–technological revolution. I now turn to the parts of the world that proved more resistant to that revolution for reasons already touched on in Chapter 15. In the nineteenth-century west, liberals, Marx, and nationalists alike agreed that sooner or later these parts would necessarily be drawn into the ever-expanding orbit of modernization, the 'sucking in' and transforming pressures of which were practically irresistible. But what form this process would take remained a matter of dispute. Liberals believed that low-priced capitalist goods, sometimes aided by a measure of coercion and force, and, indeed, the liberal example (together making 'informal imperialism') would generate within pre-capitalist and pre-industrial societies processes similar to those earlier experienced by Britain. The paraphrase from Robinson and Gallagher cited on page 548 nicely captures this line of thought. Repeatedly frustrated by meagre change in the ancient civilizations of Islam and China, nineteenth-century liberals nevertheless adhered to their fundamental position while recognizing that the path to change would be a more tortuous and prolonged process than initially anticipated. They regarded even less developed parts of the world, such as sub-Saharan Africa, as economically irrelevant and socially too backward to merit serious western involvement. There the process of transformation would be even slower. Only humanitarian considerations that might necessitate direct western involvement contradicted this liberal 'hands-off' or, better, 'invisible hand' approach to the unfolding global transformation. And even on the question of humanitarian intervention liberals were divided, with Gladstone and Mill supporting it against staunch opposition by Cobden and Bright.[98] By the twentieth century, enthusiasm for humanitarian intervention would be further tempered by increasing liberal doubts about the benefits of Progress and a growing commitment to cultural pluralism. All the same, before this happened, liberals had for a time lost their hegemonic position in shaping attitudes toward foreign domination over the pre-industrialized periphery.

By the late nineteenth and early twentieth centuries, several developments had reinforced each other in causing that hegemony to slip away from liberalism. The miserable performance of many traditional societies in transforming themselves brought people in the industrial world to the view that those societies had no right to withhold their resources and commercial potential from 'development'—in the interests of the developed world and their own interests, and, indeed, for humanity's general good. In the prevailing social-Darwinist mindset, when it was in any case suspected that the peoples of less developed societies were biologically inferior, humanity's general good was interpreted by many to require that the developed west have permanent and not only temporary custody over pre-modern peoples. Even the physical displacement of these peoples by westerners was not overruled. With the intensifying competition among the industrial powers and growing expectations that the emerging global economy would be partitioned and protectionist rather than open, these attitudes gained ground in the more liberal great powers in the decades before the First World War, partly because they had grown even stronger in the non-liberal great powers. The imperialist race, the imposition of the industrial powers' rule over much of the non-industrial world, thus reached its highest point.

Yet, as that point was being reached in the aftermath of the First World War, western imperialism was already beginning to lose ground, ideologically and later politically, and the changing wind turned into a sweeping wave of de-colonization after the Second World War. What accounts for that development? Furthermore, it was sometimes accompanied by armed struggle that forced the western imperial powers out against their will. How did the poorest and weakest of societies succeed in driving out the incomparably wealthier and more powerful western imperial powers? Does this not call into question our correlation of wealth and power in the modern world?

It should again be pointed out that only the imperialism of *liberal* western countries was so undermined. German and Japanese imperialism was broken in the First and Second World Wars by defeat at the hands of other great powers, rather than by indigenous resistance in their colonies. As already noted in Chapter 15, there are no indications that such resistance would have stood a chance of succeeding in *their* cases. However, as the threat of German and Japanese colonial expansion was broken, much of the motive for formal rule by the liberal western powers disappeared. To be sure, the habit, prestige, and vested interests of imperialism, bound up as they were with protectionist economic policies, lingered on. Furthermore, communism became the new force that justified the retention of the western colonial

623

empires, because it threatened to close developing societies to the liberal powers, albeit mostly through indigenous revolutions rather than through territorial annexation by the communist powers, at least in the less developed world. All the same, with the USA determined to break up imperialism and imperial protectionism that obstructed her exports, and given the economic exhaustion of the west European imperial powers in the wake of the Second World War, imperial rule disintegrated, giving way again to the subtler encroachments of 'informal imperialism' as the liberal method of choice for dealing with the developing world.

The substitution of informal influence through the market forces and subtle coercion to formal imperialism helps to explain de-colonization. After all, liberalism rested on the tremendous power of the market forces. It should be noted, however, that 'informal imperialism' worked very imperfectly, and there was no guarantee that it would work, as many 'second world' and 'third world' countries closed themselves. But then again, imperial rule was relatively easy to give up because it mostly extended over territories of little economic significance. Wealth emanated chiefly from the developed world and from trade within that world. Thus liberal economists regard the dismantling of the empires as an unqualified economic blessing for the metropolitan countries. Notably, however, some territories, particularly the oil-producing Arab Gulf countries, possessed considerable economic value that was reluctantly forfeited and only haphazardly kept secure for the developed world through 'informal imperialism'.

Direct imperial rule was given up also because it contradicted liberal political norms that prescribed self-determination. The application of these norms became ever more pressing over time, as liberalism democratized and the franchise grew increasingly universal. Self-determination could be realized by making the indigenous populations of the colonies fully fledged citizens of the mother countries, an option toyed with but ultimately found unacceptable by both sides, particularly where their ethnic character was different. Eventually, the only alternative was colonial retreat and independence, which in some cases, most notably Algeria, was very painful because it involved the uprooting and removal of European settlers who had lived in the colonies for generations.

Indeed, despite all the above-cited liberal reasons that account for the retreat from colonial empires by countries where liberalism constituted a defining element and was growing ever stronger, imperial retreat was carried out reluctantly and often in the wake of an indigenous armed struggle against the imperial ruler. There was a military dimension to the failure of liberal empires. Moreover, liberal–democratic powers have encountered extreme difficulties in defeating indigenous resistance in far less developed societies not only in imperial settings (formal and informal), but under *any* circumstances. The powers that crushed the mightiest of challengers, such as imperial and Nazi Germany and imperial Japan, have been unable to defeat the humblest military rivals in some of the poorest and weakest of the world's societies. In the overwhelming majority of cases, they have been able to defeat any regular force that confronted them. The Battle of Omdurman (1898) in the Sudan, where the Dervish army was annihilated by the fire-power of machine guns and magazine-fed rifles of Kitchener's British forces, losing 11,000 to Britain's 140, demonstrates the huge gap that had been opening between the armies of technologically advanced powers and their rivals in less developed societies. Thereafter, the latter tended to avoid direct fighting, opting for guerrilla and other methods of irregular warfare.[99] But, indeed, it was precisely in countering that type of warfare that liberal countries proved increasingly impotent. Unable to win, withdrawal turned out to be their only option. What explains their special vulnerability?

The Battle of Omdurman, Sudan, 1898

In some cases there was a problem with the size of the troops and resources that the strong country could spare for a particular local war, given its overall commitments and the difficulties of power projection to faraway theatres. Furthermore, indigenous opponents could draw support, above all advanced arms, from outside sources.[100] Italy's first attempt to conquer Ethiopia as the era of the new imperialism unravelled constitutes a rare case wherein the developed country was actually defeated on the battlefield. At Adowa (1896) the forces of King Menelek, estimated at 80,000–123,000 men and armed with 100,000 modern rifles and modern mountain artillery, both acquired from France, defeated the Italian expeditionary army of 14,527 men.[101] But the developed countries steadily increased their technological–military advantage during the industrial–technological age. In 1935–6, employing aircraft and poison gas, Italy, under fascist rule, succeeded in her second attempt to conquer Ethiopia. During the twilight of imperialism, the Vietminh forces in Vietnam, equipped with modern Soviet arms, succeeded in besieging and conquering the isolated French outpost in Dien-Bien-Phu. But the humiliating loss of that battle meant the loss of the war for France only because of her political decision to withdraw, because the French continued to hold the overall military advantage in Vietnam, as was the case in most other counter-insurgency conflicts.

Did the developed power's limited investment and much lower breaking point then represent a lower interest and, hence, lesser motivation in the conflict than those exhibited by the indigenous force, a factor that ultimately decided the outcome? Was the developed world's greater ability to kill matched by a greater willingness to 'get killed' in undeveloped and developing societies? In the wake of the American humiliation in Vietnam, it has been suggested that the 'balance of resolve' outweighed the 'balance of capabilities' in that unequal war.[102] The awakening of modern nationalism is widely perceived in this connection as a crucial factor that galvanized indigenous resistance. However, although there is obviously much truth in these explanations, they do not explain the much greater success of non-liberal powers in subduing others, including, as we have seen, societies where nationalism was fully developed. Nominally, in terms of the number of wars and war years in which they were involved (but not their intensity), liberal powers fought considerably more during the nineteenth and twentieth centuries than non-democratic powers, if colonial wars are counted in. Indeed, as already noted, for many this record belies the claim of a greater liberal pacificity.[103] However, this record partly reflects the fact that the liberal powers, most notably Britain and France, were better positioned by virtue of their earlier possessions to embark on imperial expansion when imperial wars were still easily won; becoming the major colonial powers, they were thus later more extensively embroiled in the wars of de-colonization, which they now found so hard to win. Moreover, non-liberal powers were less involved in imperial wars of suppression precisely because they were so effective in suppression that resistance was not allowed to grow into insurgency and, indeed, was deterred before it flared up. In studies of war proneness it is often forgotten that the non-democratic imperial peace rested on successful suppression and terror. This was the case for the Soviet hegemonic sphere, as it had been for the German and Japanese. It reminds one of the problem of the 'dog that did not bark'. The liberal democracies' greater involvement in 'extra-systemic', mainly colonial, wars should be viewed in this context.

Again, there was a difference here between the liberal and non-liberal comprehensive *packages*. Inclined towards free trade, liberal countries valued formal imperial possession less than non-liberal countries; based on representation at home, they found it increasingly problematic to deny it in their foreign domains, whereas non-liberal countries encountered no such problem; committed to humanitarian values, liberal countries found the kind of suppression upon which imperial possession must ultimately rest no longer acceptable. Thus liberal empires ultimately failed as a result of a combination of liberal economic, political, *and* military factors. These factors interacted with and reinforced each other. Yet, as already noted, even when no question of foreign rule was involved, twentieth-century liberal countries still tended to lose counter-insurgency wars, as the American fiascos in Lebanon (1982–3) and Somalia (1992–4), for example, demonstrate. The reasons for this failure have been highlighted in Gil Merom's *How Democracies Lose Small Wars* (2003), which provides a brilliantly simple answer to a long elusive puzzle, while revealing yet another major dimension of the liberal-democratic peace.[104] In what follows I present Merom's key thesis, adding only a little of my own.

Throughout history, imperial 'pacification' rested on the overt threat and actual application of ruthless violence to crush any resistance in subject societies. Lacking firm control over a territory, insurgents had to rely on social collaboration—voluntary or forced—in order to maintain themselves.

However, where the people offered insurgents support and sympathy they became exposed to sweeping reprisals by the ruling power, including killing, looting, burning, and enslavement. Crops would be destroyed, causing starvation, and whole settlements might be razed to the ground and their people banished or slaughtered. Indeed, the *ultima ratio* of imperial control was the threat of genocide. All empires worked that way, including democratic/republican ones, such as ancient Athens and Rome. They could *only* work that way. During the Peloponnesian War the Athenians went back on their earlier decision to kill all the men and enslave the women and children in conquered Mytilene, which had defected from their empire (428 BC). Instead they opted 'only' for the execution of over 1,000 men held responsible for the rebellion, which, given the size of the *polis*, still amounted to a very large part of its manhood. Dismayed by this show of leniency, the Athenian leader Cleon delivered the following, highly revealing speech before the assembly:

> ... a democracy is incompetent to govern others. ... The fact is that, because your daily life is unaffected by fear and intrigue in your relations to each other, you have the same attitude towards your allies also, and you forget that whenever you ... yield out of pity, your weakness involves you in danger and does not win the gratitude of your allies. For you do not reflect that the empire you hold is a despotism imposed upon subjects who, for their part, do intrigue against you and submit to your rule against their will, who render obedience, not because of any kindness you may do them to your own hurt, but because of such superiority as you may have established by reason of your strength.[105]

Cleon's fears turned out to be unsubstantiated, as the Athenians' famous dialogue with and ultimate annihilation of the people of Melos chillingly demonstrates (416 BC; Thucydides 5.84–116). However, some time during the nineteenth century, the conduct that had sustained imperialism earlier in history became increasingly unacceptable in liberal countries.

As with the other elements of the 'liberal peace', this was a gradual process that did not immediately take effect in full force and across the board. Some mellowing of practices towards the civilian population is already discernible in west–central Europe during the age of Enlightenment in the eighteenth century, in contrast with the horrors of the seventeenth century and, indeed, any earlier period in European history. Yet in Europe's more backward parts and with respect to non-whites, practices remained very much as before. Despite sporadic British atrocities, the rebelling American colonists benefited from this mellowing of practices, intermixed as it was with the Royalist interest not to further alienate the colonial population.[106] But the people of Ireland, that 'Africa in Europe' for the British, rebelling in 1798, still bore the brunt of British suppression that had broken their backs in blood and fire during earlier uprisings in previous centuries and had crushed for ever the rebellious 'savage' Scottish highlanders after the Battle of Culloden (1746). The American treatment of the native Indians during the nineteenth century (though the great majority of them fell victim to European diseases) was similarly legitimized by their perception as savages. The French 'pacification' of Algeria and Indochina during that century was still based on the old methods. Notably, however, Marshal Bugeaud's methods in Algeria were denounced by a delegation of the Chamber of Deputies headed by Alexis de Tocqueville, which recommended the adoption of a 'continental standard of conduct'.[107] The atrocious suppression of the bloody Indian mutiny (1857) was the last that the British Empire crushed in the old ways, although in this case, too, it should be noted that the troops' retributions lacked official sanction.[108]

Indeed, if one is obliged to name a specific threshold for the change in British attitudes, what more symbolic point can be chosen than the establishment of the Liberal Party in 1859, created by a merging of the old Whig Party, free-trading Peelites who had split from the Tories and Radicals. That this was significant for various aspects of British international conduct is attested to, for example, by the British attitude towards the rebellion of the Bulgarians, supported by Russia, against their Ottoman masters (1875–8). Throughout the nineteenth century, it had been Britain's policy to back the Ottoman Empire against any Russian advance towards the Mediterranean. This fundamental British interest remained unchanged. All the same, the outrage of the British public at the Turkish atrocities in suppressing the rebellion—the mass killings, torture, and that 'worst of all evils of war, outrage on women'—fuelled by journalistic reports and by Gladstone's missionary agitation, tied the British government's hands. The Ottoman Empire was defeated by Russia and had to give up the rebellious province. 'Foreigners don't know what to make of the movement; and I am not surprised,' Lord Derby told Prime Minister Disraeli. A German observer noted that it would be almost inconceivable in any continental country.[109] No longer was British policy conducted on purely 'realist' considerations of power alone. To be sure, earlier, too, kin, religious, and cultural affinities mattered; the Greek struggle for independence from the Ottoman Empire was militarily supported by Britain (1827) on a wave of philhellenic enthusiasm. All the same, in mid- and late-Victorian Britain it was human rights that became inseparable from the public debate.

Soon enough the same attitude revealed itself with regard to Britain's own empire, first in its 'white' parts but later everywhere. The same Gladstone, as a Liberal prime minister, opened the process that was to lead the Irish within a generation, after the liberal recipe for self-determination within the United Kingdom—economic improvement, more equal citizenship, greater toler-ance, and 'Home Rule'—failed to satisfy them, to an independent Irish state. How did the country that had been kept under the British heel for centuries suddenly succeed in seceding? We have already seen that the rise of modern nationalism in Ireland cannot be the reason *in and of itself*, because national movements were successfully curbed and crushed by ruthless non-liberal powers. It was only when the demand for self-determination became hard to resist by liberals, who *also* found the old methods of forceful suppression repugnant and unacceptable, no longer compatible with what Britain had become, that Ireland was able to gain independence. Needless to say, the process was anything but easy and smooth. The Liberal Party was split over the Irish question and lost power for two decades. The Easter Uprising in Dublin in 1916 was put down by robust force, and full-scale insurgency took place in 1919–21 before Britain decided to pull out. Although British counter-insurgency tactics proved quite effective, they could never com-pletely quell the rebellion, given the restriction on ruthlessness towards civilians under which British forces operated.

Nor was Ireland an isolated case for Britain. In the Boer War in South Africa (1899–1902), Britain initially suffered humiliating defeats in regular fighting at the hand of the forces of the Free Orange and Transvaal Repub-lics. When half a million British troops were dispatched to South Africa, the course of the war was reversed and regular Boer resistance was crushed, only to give way to widespread irregular resistance. Unable to subdue that resist-ance, the British resorted to pretty draconian measures, rounding up the Boer civilian population into concentration camps, where some 30,000 people perished from various illnesses. And yet Britain was able to declare victory only by offering the Boers the most generous of peace terms that within a few years effectively surrendered to them government powers over all of the South African Federation. South Africa and Ireland were the signs of things to come in liberal countries' counter-insurgency wars.

The image of near invincibility that insurgency movements have acquired stands in stark contrast to their often low military effectiveness. They were very rarely able to defeat the regular armies of their rival by force, and they sustained far greater losses than they inflicted—sometimes crippling losses.[110] Nor is it exactly true that modern affluent liberal-democratic countries tended to lose wars against insurgency because of the democracies' inability to withstand protracted wars of attrition and the need to decide a war rapidly, as some scholars have claimed.[111] In both World Wars, grinding attrition was actually the *democracies'* strategy of choice, whereas rapid decisions by lightning campaigns were sought by their rivals—Germany and Japan. In the Cold War, too, it was the liberal democracies that outlasted the Soviets in the protracted conflict of material and endurance. Finally, the American problems in pacifying Iraq after her occupation in 2003 have been widely attributed to the commitment of too small a force, as if the deepening and failed American commitment in Vietnam had never taken place. Indeed, massive force commitment and considerable military successes ultimately failed to keep France in Algeria, the USA in Vietnam, and Israel in densely populated Palestinian territories. As suggested by Merom, liberal democracies have tended to lose protracted counter-insurgency wars against far less developed societies because their self-imposed restrictions on violence against civilian populations ultimately made their often-successful military operations futile. Only when a significant (liberal) portion of their publics realized that no 'victory' that would decisively end the war was possible under these circumstances did they turn against the continuation of these wars, most of which in any case did not involve core interests of the liberal democracies, were held in an economically unimportant periphery, and clashed with major liberal values.[112]

The liberal democracies' record of failure in counter-insurgency warfare is frequently attributed to the effects of television coverage. It should be noted, however, that Britain lost the struggle against Irish independence long before TV, as was effectively the case with the loss of her Empire in general. Similarly, the French lost the war in Vietnam before the advent of TV that would allegedly lose the war for the Americans in the same theatre. Even the French loss of the war in Algeria (1954–62) effectively

The Battle of Algiers. Though ruthless, French methods in their attempts to subdue the insurgency were not as brutal towards the civilian population as traditional imperial standards had been

predated the age of TV coverage. The transmission of the horrors and atrocities of the war into American living rooms through TV—similar to the earlier effect of mass media: the newspaper, radio, and newsreel—only reinforced a trend that had already been strongly in evidence and was getting ever stronger as liberal sensibilities steadily deepened in affluent liberal democracies.[113]

To be sure, sceptics might question the thesis pioneered by Merom on various grounds. In the first place, even during the twentieth century, liberal democracies still wielded formidable instruments of coercion and pressure in counter-insurgency wars, and their conduct was often quite brutal. Atrocities, tacitly sanctioned by political and military authorities or carried out unauthorized by the troops, have regularly been committed against both combatants and non-combatants. The massive application of violence in a life-and-death struggle conducted outside the boundaries of orderly society—which is war—makes such occurrences almost inevitable. All the same, strict restrictions on the use of violence against civilians constitute the legal and normative standard for liberal democracies. And although many, probably most, violations of this standard remain unreported, quite a number of them come to light in an open society with a free media, and are met with public condemnation and judicial procedures. All these radically limit the liberal democracies' powers of suppression, judged by historical and comparative standards.

Not only Nazi but even imperial Germany offers a telling comparative perspective. Needless to say, countless atrocities were performed in colonial settings during the late nineteenth and early twentieth centuries by all the imperial countries. Congo (Zaire), the king of Belgium's private domain, became notorious for the cruel acts of coercion employed by the king's agents to force the natives to work in milking the cauchuc trees for the rubber industry that made Leopold II fabulously rich. The French brutally suppressed local resistance during their conquest of west Africa, whereas the British were almost as ruthless in 'pacifying' Kenya, destroying crops and huts and capturing livestock to force the locals to surrender.[114] And yet, even by colonial standards, German conduct in Africa was exceptional. In German south-west Africa, today's Namibia, the Herero revolt (1904) was countered by a policy and strategy of extermination. Wells were sealed off and the population was driven out to the desert to die there or was worked to death in labour camps. Only 15,000 of 80,000 Herero survived. In German east Africa, today's Tanzania, the Maji-Maji revolt (1905–7) was similarly answered with extermination. A small force of 500 German troops destroyed settlements and crops so systematically that 250,000–300,000 natives died, mostly of starvation, more than 10 times the number of those who had risen in arms. The once populous area became a wildlife reserve.[115] These were chilling demonstrations of the effectiveness of the old techniques of imperial suppression, which ultimately rested on the threat and practice of genocide.

The same spirit extended beyond Africa. Kaiser Wilhelm II, addressing the German troops departing to participate in the suppression of the Boxer Rebellion in China (1900), called upon them to be as merciless as Attila's Huns.[116] His call attracted attention at the time not only because of the Kaiser's immature and erratic personality; it highlighted the normative gulf that had opened between the liberal countries and imperial Germany, despite the 'transgressions' from their public norms that continued to mark the liberal countries' actual practices. Indeed, German attitude and practice in western Europe itself, the core of the 'civilized world', also became increasingly reflective of that gulf. Much alarmed by French mass popular resistance and *francs tireurs* in the later part of the war of 1870–1, the Germans reacted with great severity, although hardly out of the norm as expressed by the American Civil War veteran General Philip Sheridan, who told Bismarck's entourage: 'Nothing should be left to the people but eyes to weep with.' However, harsh measures against civilian resistance were incorporated into German military manuals thereafter, while a conscious reaction against western liberalism was growing in pace with the increasing encroachments of that liberalism in Germany. In 1914, this trend expressed itself in widespread atrocities in Belgium, carried out wherever the invading German troops met or imagined civilian resistance or sabotage. And if a harsh regime, as imposed by the Germans in occupied Belgium during the First World War, was able to extract only partial co-operation from the Belgians, Nazi Germany's unbridled use of terror secured total compliance.[117]

By contrast, given liberal attitudes, not only violent insurgency, 'Mao's way', but also mass civil disobedience and demonstrations, 'Gandhi's way', were ultimately sufficient to force liberal powers out. Even though Gandhi saw very clearly that Hitlerism was supremely violent and murderous and that it possessed none of the scruples that inhibited liberal countries, he still advocated non-violence as a method against it. He advised the Jews to opt for mass disobedience against Nazi genocidal persecution, and later extended the same advice to the occupied nations of Europe, calling on Britain too to embrace civil defiance against a German invasion, in preference to armed resistance.[118] And yet this proposed application of Gandhi's approach only highlights the unique historical and geopolitical limits within which it was able to work, and succeed.

Still, sceptics might question the notion that ruthless brutality is the indispensable condition of successful counter-insurgency suppression on the grounds that it conflicted with the 'winning of hearts and minds' that has been posited as the key to such success in the recent liberal–democratic discourse. Indisputably, winning over at least the elites of conquered societies—through benefits, co-optation, and the amenities of 'soft power'—has always played a central role in imperial 'pacification', as Tacitus (*Agricola* 21) so memorably described with respect to the taming of the barbarian Britons by Rome. Yet that velvet glove always covered an iron fist that had crushed local resistance mercilessly in the first place and remained unmistakably in place as the *ultima ratio* of foreign control. The 'winning of hearts and minds' has indeed become the liberal democracies' indispensable path for the pacification of foreign societies, but only because they have practically lost the ability to crush such societies by force if the latter cannot be won over but choose to resist. This 'problem' is scarcely felt by non-liberal-democratic powers.

However, sceptics might also call into doubt the authoritarian–totalitarian supposed efficacy in suppressing and crushing insurgency. Did the Soviet Union, for example, not fail in subduing Afghanistan (1979–88) despite her brutal tactics that caused an estimated one million civilian dead and millions of wounded and refugees? And has Russia, which has been turning in a more authoritarian direction, not failed in her ruthless efforts to eradicate Chechnyan resistance? In reality, however, ruthlessness has always been a *necessary* but not a *sufficient* condition for effective suppression. Historically, defeating irregular warfare, carried out by a primitive and fanatical rival in a vast, desolate, and sparsely populated country, has always been an extremely difficult undertaking. All pre-modern empires struggled with that problem. It was largely in this context that the Soviet Union failed to win the war in Afghanistan. Yet the Soviet failure also signalled the deep problems developing within the Soviet system that would shortly thereafter lead to its collapse, including a certain loss of nerve and the Stalinist-type brutality that was essential for the survival of such a regime. Under Stalin, the Soviet Union experienced no scruples in deporting the Chechnyans en masse from their homeland, resorting to that classical technique for eradicating popular resistance. Popular resistance—armed and unarmed—in Ukraine and the Baltic countries, before and after the Second World War, was similarly crushed by the harshest of measures that occasionally escalated to a strategy of extermination. It is no coincidence that the secession of the former Soviet republics, as well as the insurgency in Chechnya, took place only *after* the breakdown of the Soviet system rather than at any time before.

Furthermore, the change from the Stalinist-type brutality to the later, somewhat more restrained Soviet practices suggests another pertinent factor. Similar to Nazi Germany (especially after the outbreak of the Second World War), wartime imperial Japan, and Mao's China, Stalin's Soviet Union cared

635

very little about opinion in the liberal west. In other times and cases, however, the power and wealth of the liberal sphere have had at least some measure of constraining effect on less brutal and less inward-looking non-liberal regimes which felt sufficiently dependent on co-operation with the liberal countries to pay some heed to their sensibilities. Thus the practices of non-liberal countries since the beginning of the nineteenth century cannot be understood purely in their own terms, because they have been working in the context of an international system in which the liberal countries and liberal public opinion carry weight and have to be taken into account, at least to some degree. Napoleonic France is an interesting early example, because it already operated within the constraints and norms of an enlightened Europe to which France had contributed so significantly and which the Empire proudly claimed to represent. Even that rare case of judicial killing under the First Consul, the abduction and execution of the duke of Enghien (1804)—which appears trifle by the standards of twentieth-century totalitarianism—was received with an outcry and condemnation both at home and abroad. Thus, despite the widespread atrocities committed by both sides during the savage war in the Iberian Peninsula (those by the French were graphically depicted by Goya),[119] Napoleon did not resort to the semi-genocidal methods that had been used by the Romans in their long struggle to 'pacify' that same difficult arena, even though the Spanish ulcer was haemorrhaging his empire. All this goes to show that as with the various circles of hell, there are degrees to brutality, and there is a hell of a difference between them. Brutal by western liberal standards as Soviet methods were in Afghanistan and Russian methods are in Chechnya, both fall far short of the genocidal methods used by a Hitler or a Stalin to curb resistance and crush insurgency.

Finally, sceptics might argue that although the Americans encountered all the familiar problems in their counter-insurgency war in Iraq (where everybody had been ruthlessly kept in check by Saddam Hussein), they proved successful in Afghanistan, where the Soviets had failed. Indeed, these recent American experiences highlight some preconditions for the success of liberal democracies in counter-insurgency wars, including: (1) the ability to apply their massive superiority in high-tech warfare, which is far more attuned to targeting hardware than people but which was more freely employed in the Afghan deserts than in Iraq's urban space; and (2) the availability of a strong enough indigenous allied force on the ground that is able to establish authority and shoulder the 'dirty work' of land warfare and occupation, a force that existed in Afghanistan but was missing in Iraq.

In any case, the American campaigns in Afghanistan and Iraq signal a major shift in the old pattern of relationships between the developed world and those societies that have failed to embrace modernity. The proliferation of weapons of mass destruction has made these societies, previously regarded as too poor and weak to be relevant, much harder to ignore.

UNCONVENTIONAL TERROR AND THE NEW WORLD DISORDER

The 11 September 2001 mega-terror attacks in New York City and Washington, DC, constitute a landmark in history and in the development of large-scale human deadly violence, not so much in and of themselves but in demonstrating an ominous potential that had been building for some time and is yet to unravel. The attacks came as a surprise, and far-reaching precautions were adopted only in their wake; yet this potential had been well recognized by experts and by government authorities from the late 1980s and particularly during the 1990s, after the end of the Cold War, even though it is still denied or misunderstood by many. It was the subject of Congressional investigations and legislation, and was highlighted by President Clinton and Defense Secretary William Cohen. A surprisingly large number of articles and books were written on the threat well before 9/11 (only a handful of which are cited here in specific reference). This is the threat of unconventional terror, employing so-called weapons of mass destruction (WMD): nuclear, biological, and chemical. In the wake of 9/11 everything has already been said about this threat and its wider global implications. It is only in relation to this book's major themes, in the context of my study of the evolution of war in general, that the significance and novelty of the new era are addressed here.

Neither terror nor WMD is entirely new. For decades the world has become accustomed to living with both of them. Terror—the targeting of civilians by small non-state groups for political purposes is probably as good a definition as any—is widely claimed to have been around throughout

The 11 September 2001 terror attack in New York City. Is unconventional terror the next step?

history.[120] More accurately, however, although the assassination of leaders is as old as humanity, terror emerged only from the late nineteenth century on the back of the modern technological and social developments that had made it possible: high explosives and, later, automatic weapons gave individuals and small groups the ability that they previously lacked to cause damage disproportionate to their number; trains and, later, cars gave them mobility across countries; and telegraph communication and popular newspapers gave their operations national publicity and resonance that vastly magnified the public 'terror' effect of what after all constituted very limited actions, thereby according them political significance. This was the material underpinning of the emergence of anarchist terrorism in Russia and the rest of Europe in the late nineteenth, followed by anti-colonial terror in the twentieth century. Again, it was mainly liberal and old-style authoritarian countries that proved most susceptible to terror. Totalitarian countries not only policed far more effectively but also denied terror the publicity that was essential for its success. From the 1960s, terror exhibited a new surge as passenger jets offered both much greater global mobility and vulnerable targets, and as TV further enhanced the terrorists' public exposure. Yet it is only the prospect of terror acquiring and using WMD that has turned it from an irritant and a media–political tool into a serious destructive threat, thereby producing the alarming twist of the new era.

The so-called weapons of mass destruction are an assortment of different technologies with widely diverging potency. As we have seen, the industrial–technological age brought about an exponential rise in destructive power that was, however, more or less paralleled by a similar increase in defensive power. Chemical weapons, pioneered in the First World War, were almost immediately countered by defensive gear, such as gas masks and special clothing, which when available sharply decreases their effectiveness. Only a few per cent of those gassed on the Western Front during the First World War died, as opposed to a lethality rate of a quarter to a third among those injured by conventional artillery and small arms.[121] For this reason, interwar military thinkers such as J. F. C. Fuller and B. H. Liddell Hart (himself gassed) actually regarded chemical weapons as humane. They argued that the ban on their use in the Geneva Protocol of 1925 (following the unsuccessful earlier prohibition of gas-filled projectiles in the Hague Convention of 1899) was irrational and unjustified.

Armed forces had little faith in the ban, which in any case covered only the *use* of chemical weapons. Development and massive acquisition of both chemical weapons and protective gear continued unabated. During the late 1930s and the Second World War, the Germans secretly developed the family of nerve gases that were far more lethal than the chemical agents then in use. All the same, the incredible happened, and even through the horrors and upheavals of the Second World War chemical weapons were not put to use. Chemical warfare's unwieldiness, mutual deterrence, and various opportunistic considerations by the warring sides caused that restraint.[122] In the handful of cases where the ban was broken and chemical weapons were used after the First World War—by Italy in Ethiopia in 1935–6, by Japan in China from 1937, by Egypt in Yemen in the mid-1960s, and by Iraq against Iran and her own Kurd people in the 1980s—the following precondition always existed: the other side was particularly vulnerable, because it possessed neither chemical weapons to retaliate and deter nor the defensive gear that would minimize its casualties. The potential use of chemical weapons by terrorists is predicated on the element of surprise, catching masses of people unprotected and therefore highly vulnerable in the open of an urban space. However, the bulk of the chemical agents needed and the problem of spreading them effectively with the means that terrorists might possess and deploy undetected make chemical weapons the least dangerous of the WMD, with lethality from a highly successful chemical terror attack estimated in the thousands.

Biological weapons pose a threat of a much greater magnitude. Also banned in the Geneva Protocol of 1925, they were nevertheless developed by the great powers from the late 1930s and during the Second World War. The strains of bacteria and viruses currently regarded as particularly potent in terms of their lethality, resistance to medication, and persistence in the environment, include: anthrax, plague, tularaemia, typhoid fever, cholera, typhus, Q fever, smallpox, and Ebola—and this is only the shortlist. Although not contagious, toxins, such as botulinum and ricin, also carry a potential for mass killing. Throughout history, the big epidemics were much greater killers than wars, with a virulent strain of influenza famously killing more people in 1918–19 (estimated at 20–40 million worldwide) than the First World War had. Since then infectious diseases have been conquered by medicine. However, with the revolutionary breakthroughs achieved during recent decades in the decipherment of the genome, in biotechnology, and in genetic engineering, new horizons have opened up in terms of lethality and accessibility. A virulent laboratory-cultivated strain of bacterium or virus, let alone a specially engineered 'superbug' against which no immunization and medication exist,[123] might bring the lethality of biological weapons within the range of nuclear attacks and result in anything between thousands to many millions of fatalities, while being far more easily available to terrorists than nuclear weapons.

Still, nuclear weapons constitute a category of their own that sets them apart from all other known weapons. Not only is their destructive power so great that a large enough nuclear stockpile is capable of destroying any rival, indeed the whole of humanity; there is also no effective defence against them that is even remotely commensurate with their destructiveness. As already noted, it is these qualities that make nuclear weapons the first ultimate weapon, which leaves no doubt as to the result of its wholesale use and nullifies any hope of gaining from a war in which they are possessed and effectively delivered by both sides. In the absence of effective defence, mutual deterrence—which had always been central to conflict, whether human or not—now came to the fore and gained almost absolute dominance, so far preventing a nuclear war and perhaps any war between nuclear states since 1945.

Herein lies the bewildering nature of the new mix that is unconventional terror, because deterrence is infinitely less effective against terrorist groups than it is against states. Not only are such groups more likely to consist of extremist zealots, who are willing to sacrifice their lives and may positively desire a general apocalypse; they are also too elusive to offer a clear enough target for retaliation, on which the whole concept of deterrence is based. If deterrence does not apply, one is left with only defensive and offensive measures, the ineffectiveness of which against WMD—particularly but not only nuclear—gave deterrence its overriding significance in the first place.

At the root of the problem is the trickling down to below state level of the technologies and materials of WMD. Chemical, biological, and nuclear facilities for both civilian and military use have vastly proliferated worldwide over the last few decades. The relatively simple technological infrastructure needed for the manufacture of chemical weapons is now available in some hundred countries,[124] and is, indeed, within the reach of non-state groups as well. The biotechnological sector in particular constitutes one of the spearheads of today's scientific–commercial revolutionary wave. This point is illustrated, for example, by the number of life science PhDs awarded in the USA, which rose by 144 per cent between 1994 and 1996 alone. By the late 1990s there were already 1,300 biotechnology companies in the USA and about 580 in Europe.[125] According to one estimate, there are some 20,000 laboratories in the world where a single person could synthesize any existing virus within the next decade. In the same laboratories, five people with US$2 million will be able to create an enhanced pathogen—a virus that could infect and kill people who have been immunized with conventional vaccines. With US$5 million, the same five people could build a laboratory from scratch, using equipment purchased online.[126] As markets and communications globalize rapidly, the materials and know-how required for WMD has become far easier to acquire and more difficult to detect and block. Much of the equipment and materials are of dual use, and can be purchased for ostensibly benign civilian purposes. Finally, the disintegration

641

of the Soviet Union left, in the debris of its advanced military infrastructure, deserted in the various republics, unemployed scientists, production facilities, unaccounted for and poorly guarded materials that can be made into weapons, and, most worrying, the weapons themselves. For these reasons, terrorists' ability to buy, steal, rob, and/or manufacture WMD has increased dramatically.

To be sure, the practical difficulties facing terrorist groups that wish to follow the unconventional path are still considerable. In 1990–5, the Aum Shinrikyo cult in Japan was the first non-state group to build production facilities for biological and chemical weapons. Immensely wealthy and including trained scientists and hundreds of engineers in its ranks, it purchased the necessary machines and materials worldwide, many of them on the open market. It produced and used botulinum toxin and anthrax, but when results proved unsatisfactory, probably as a result of poor material quality, it concentrated on nerve gases, particularly sarin. The cult struggled with acute safety problems in the production process because of the high toxicity and corrosiveness of the biological and chemical agents. Nevertheless, it went on with production and carried out quite a number of attacks—about ten biological and ten chemical. The largest of them, the sarin attack in the Tokyo subway (1995), resulted in 12 fatalities only, mainly owing to the poor quality of the sarin used and a primitive dissemination mechanism, although thousands required medical treatment. All the same, a race was taking place between the cult's developing production capacity and police detection: the cult was on course for the manufacture of more effective spraying mechanisms and 70 tonnes of sarin while also building a large biological laboratory, when the police closed in on its people and facilities.[127]

Similarly, the still unresolved anthrax attack in the USA in the wake of 9/11, delivered in envelops sent through the US postal service, killed only five people, although it created panic, contaminated entire buildings, and shut down facilities. Yet the use of aerosolized anthrax effectively sprayed can result in a disaster of an entirely different order of magnitude. According to a Congressional assessment made in 1993, a light plane flying over and spraying Washington, DC, with 100 kilograms of anthrax can fatally injure three million people. Thus, despite major difficulties and limited successes, the above two 'firsts' represent only the tip of the iceberg in terms of the future potential of chemical and biological terrorism, especially as the

'Fat Man', the nuclear bomb of the kind used against Nagasaki. Can a primitive nuclear device be assembled by terrorists?

biotechnological revolution—and its worldwide expansion—are only in their initial phases.

Nuclear weapons have not yet been used by terrorists and, in contrast to chemical and biological agents, fissile material cannot be produced by them, at least in the foreseeable future. All the same, stolen or bought radioactive materials can be used by terrorists to create a radioactive bomb, which cannot compare with nuclear weapons in destructiveness but can still contaminate entire blocks with radioactivity that is exceedingly difficult to remove. Furthermore, according to several tests carried out by scientists for the American authorities, a nuclear bomb can be built from parts available on the open market, with the fissile material bought or stolen. Indeed, nuclear weapons themselves might be stolen or bought on the black market, and not even very expensively. Abdul Qadeer Khan, the Pakistani nuclear scientist who headed his country's programme to manufacture the bomb, sold the nuclear secrets to perhaps a dozen countries—from south-east Asia to the Middle East, including North Korea, Iran, and Libya—reportedly for as little as millions and tens of millions of dollars in each case. The price of the bomb itself, bought, for example, in the republics of the former Soviet Union, possibly with the help of organized crime, may be just as cheap.

643

Earlier in this book we have seen that, during the early days of the state and throughout most of its history, non-state players, such as tribal and armed gang leaders, often challenged the state successfully. With modernity, the dominance of the state grew, because it controlled the heavy infrastructure that increasingly underlay power. Although state dominance still holds sway despite encroachments from various directions, the 'encapsulation' of destructive power in WMD, particularly the nuclear and biological, recreate a situation whereby one no longer has to be big in order to deliver a heavy punch. Scenarios of world-threatening individuals and organizations, previously reserved for fiction of the James Bond genre, suddenly become real. There emerges what *New York Times*' writer Thomas Friedman has called the 'super-empowered angry man',[128] and it does not matter what he or she is angry about. It has been claimed by some in the wake of 9/11 that it is wrong to define terror as the enemy, because terror is only a tactic, whereas the enemy is militant Islam. True, radical Islam stands behind most terrorist attacks in today's world, and dealing with it is an intricate and complex problem. Yet, although labelled a new fascist challenge, the Arab and Moslem societies from which the challenge arises are generally poor and stagnant. They represent no alternative model for the future and pose no military threat to the developed liberal-democratic world, as did the fascist powers, which were among the world's strongest and most advanced societies. Only the potential use of WMD makes the threat of militant Islam significant. Furthermore, even if the problem of militant Islam were overcome, other causes and 'super-empowered angry men' would always be present and, in contrast to the past, could now make themselves felt horrendously, because the means for this are potentially available. The Aum Shinrikyo cult, probably the yet unknown perpetrator of the anthrax attacks in the USA, and, indeed, the Christian millenarians and extreme right-wing perpetrators of the massive conventional bombing in Oklahoma City (1995) and the Atlanta Olympics bombing (1996) were not Moslem. Whereas societies in general can become pacifically inclined, as through the affluent liberal-democratic path, there will always be individuals and small groups who will embrace massive violence for some cause. Thus although Moslems are today the most likely perpetrators, unconventional terror *is* the problem.

The 'levelling' effect of nuclear weapons has been pointed out since their inception. But it was always considered with respect to relationships between states, where an otherwise weak side that possessed nuclear retaliatory capability was able to deter the strong from war. Now, however, terror groups that possess unconventional capability may benefit from a similar equalizing effect in their relationships with states, without being constrained as states are by mutual deterrence. To be sure, unconventional terror groups are still likely to be much weaker than states, among other things in terms of unconventional capability. A chemical attack that would kill thousands might be considered a trifle in comparison to the human cost of a serious inter-state war or even to the numbers killed each year in road accidents. However, biological or nuclear weapons, with a much greater killing potential, may cause a disaster on a par with the USA's most severe wars; and who now can say with any confidence that such an attack is not feasible. Indeed, and this brings us back to the root of the whole problem, because deterrence based on mutual assured destruction (MAD) does not apply to terrorists, the use of ultimate weapons is *more* likely to come from them than it is from states, even though the latter may possess far greater unconventional capability. In contrast to the habits of mind that have dominated since the onset of the nuclear age, unconventional capability acquired by terrorists is *useable*. If only because of the technical problems involved, if not for the relative paucity of terrorists who would be willing to unleash the ultimate horror, unconventional terror is likely to be used in relatively few cases; indeed, it undoubtedly will continue to constitute only a small minority of all terror cases. Yet, once the potential is available, it is difficult to see what will stop it from being realized by someone—somewhere.

Terrorists' lack of an established home base, which constitutes part of their unique threat, is of course also a source of vulnerability, which is, however, practically impossible for state authorities to exploit to the foolproof degree necessitated by the unconventional threat. Terrorist groups may work from within their target countries, smuggling in or even manufacturing unconventional weapons undetected by the authorities. The Aum Shinrikyo cult in Japan built its facilities for the manufacture of biological and chemical agents undetected in one of the world's most advanced countries. These facilities were seized by police only after the cult had carried out its chemical attacks. The whole phenomenon was home grown. The perpetrators of the 9/11 conventional mega-terror attacks trained in the USA and other western countries. In separate incidences in 2003, British and French police raided residential homes, where ricin and botulinum toxins were prepared by Islamic extremists from chemical materials ordered on the

645

open market. The notion of 'a bomb in the basement', originally coined in relation to states' undeclared development of nuclear weapons, assumes a new chilling meaning. For what chances are there that police would detect *every* unconventional terror initiative before it is consummated?

The problem is even greater with respect to countries of the developing world. Not only can terrorists find a safe haven for their activities in militant or defunct countries, but these countries are also a source for dangerous materials and weapons, because of low or barely existing security standards and high levels of corruption. Indeed, defunct states may constitute as great or even a greater problem than militant ones. The latter may be ruled by zealots and/or less than stable autocrats: the communist dictatorship in North Korea, the mullahs in Iran, the deposed Taliban regime in Afghanistan, that of Saddam Hussein in Iraq, or any other that may rise in the future. Although some such regimes, most notably the Taliban, demonstrated little concern for the massive retaliation that would follow acts of mega-terror originating from their territory, others are likely to be more susceptible to deterrence. By contrast, weak states simply do not exercise effective control over their territory and cannot be held accountable.

Contrary to a widely held view,[129] 'failed states' are not some sort of new phenomenon in the state system. States' inability to control their territory fully vis-à-vis tribal chiefs, local strongmen, independent warlords, and the leaders of armed bands, occasionally resulting in the states' falling apart in civil war and anarchy, was pretty much the norm in pre-industrial *gemeinschaft* societies. And it is mostly in such societies that states continue to 'fail' by the standards of the developed world.[130] Nothing here is new. The novelty is that in the past the mayhem in such weak or failing states only marginally if at all affected the countries of the developed world; indeed, in most cases it continues not to. However, if such states become a base for terror groups that seek unconventional capability, the picture changes radically.

The only feasible measure against unconventional terror is a co-ordinated global crackdown, which includes tightened security measures, tougher controls on the materials and facilities for the production of WMD, and a relentless pursuit of terrorists.[131] However, such a policy flounders in countries that are unable or unwilling to take part in such a crackdown, or that, indeed, may even assist terrorists in various ways, or, worse, engage themselves in the development of WMD, above all nuclear weapons. The 187 countries that have joined the Nuclear Non-Proliferation Treaty (NPT) since it was put forth for signature in 1968 have agreed not to develop nuclear weapons and have accepted an inspection regime carried out by the International Atomic Energy Agency (IAEA). The nuclear club, which in the early 1960s the US president John Kennedy apprehensively predicted would increase to 15–20 by 1975, and continue to grow thereafter, has shown only a modest rise. It now includes the five authorized members (the USA, Soviet Union/Russia, China, the UK, and France), to which India, Pakistan, Israel (undeclared), and North Korea (possibly) have been added. South Africa voluntarily disarmed herself of the nuclear capability that had been built under the regime of white supremacy. But indeed, countries determined to achieve nuclear capability have proved themselves able to do so, whether or not they signed the NPT, which is in any case formally a voluntary agreement, freely entered into by sovereign states. Other countries, such as Iraq, Libya, and Iran, tried or are trying to develop nuclear capability.[132] Precisely countries of the sort that the NPT most sought to stop—developing and unstable countries from the world's 'zone of war' that are most at odds with the existing international order and from which nuclear technology is most likely to leak—are the ones most eager to develop such weapons, in order to secure their regimes from external intervention while continuing their own internal and external activities with impunity.

A few scholars have argued that the spread of nuclear weapons should not be opposed and that it actually constitutes a good thing, because it would expand to other regions of the world the same deterrence against war that prevailed between the two blocs during the Cold War. Sceptical of any difference in political behaviour between developed and undeveloped or developing countries, they argue that the logic of MAD is so compelling that even the most militant and unstable state authorities in the world's less developed parts are unlikely to initiate the use of nuclear weapons. Nor, judging by past experience, they argue, are such states likely to compromise their control and hand over such weapons to terrorists. However, critics of this view doubt that the logic of MAD is foolproof as nuclear weapons spread into a growing number of hands in less and less stable parts of the world. Such proliferation can, indeed, result in fewer wars owing to nuclear deterrence, but also, by the same token, in the eventual use of nuclear weapons—somewhere. Furthermore, critics point out that as undeveloped countries possess far inferior technological and institutional infrastructures, the likelihood of an accidental use of nuclear weapons or of a nuclear accident is far greater in them.[133]

Indeed, with respect to terrorists, the greater threat of nuclear proliferation—more than the prospect of nuclear weapons being handed over to them by nuclear states—is the far-increased danger of leakage. Not only, as in the Pakistani case, might people and organizations with access to nuclear facilities sell or otherwise transfer nuclear materials, expertise, and even weapons to terrorists, with greater or lesser awareness by weak and segmentary states; but states in the less developed and unstable parts of the world are also ever in danger of disintegration and anarchy, which all but disappeared in the developed world. When state authority collapses and anarchy takes hold, who would guarantee a country's nuclear arsenal? The immense risks generated by the disintegration of the Soviet Union and her nuclear and other non-conventional arsenal may be the pattern of things to come if nuclear proliferation is allowed to go on unabated. The collapsed Soviet Union rather than the former nuclear superpower may be the model for future threats. The point, then, is that nuclear proliferation is unlikely to stop at the state level and, hence, with the logic of MAD. If only for this reason (and not only for this reason), nuclear proliferation should be opposed.

The concept of sovereignty, as developed in Europe from the seventeenth century, became deeply enshrined in international law for the simple reason that the strengthening states shared an interest in exercising unlimited control over their domains, while finding the internal affairs of others less important and far more difficult to influence. This book has traced the evolution of human social forms from the local and regional groups (tribes) to chiefdoms and the growth of the state. But social evolution goes on, and at an accelerated pace. In a shrinking world of fast communications and growing interdependency, state sovereignty—although still dominant and likely to remain so in the foreseeable future—is eroding with the erosion of states' self-sufficiency. The threat of WMD proliferation, heightened by the prospect of unconventional terror, contributes to this process. International norms might be undergoing change in response to a changing global reality. Inevitably, traditional liberal attitudes, too, are considered afresh.

Liberalism, like other universal creeds, has been ambivalent about the sanctity of sovereignty. Sovereignty stands in the way of the enforcement of liberal rights abroad and of forceful humanitarian intervention. On the

648

other hand, forceful foreign intervention conflicts with the affluent–liberal aversion to war that has only increased with time, particularly as such intervention concerned matters that were of little direct interest to liberal powers and proved increasingly messy, even when conducted against weak rivals. How does the potential foreshadowed by 9/11 alter these traditional liberal balance and affect affluent liberal democracies' policies? This question is presently the subject of a heated argument involving various motives and sensibilities within the liberal-democratic world, polarizing attitudes between the USA and Europe, to say nothing of the reactions in the new 'second world' and in developing countries, particularly those of Islam. Each position within the intra-liberal argument is fraught with problems that partisan opponents are quick to point out.

The European claim that the continent's experience of peaceful co-operation through supra-national institutions during the past half-century should be applied globally to deal with threats from the 'second' and 'third worlds' is beside the point, because the Europe that emerged in the wake of the Second World War had been made possible by massive force and a crushing victory that imposed liberal democracy on the continent's previously non-democratic and non-liberal countries. It was liberal-democracy that made Europe, and the west in general, into a Kantian world. Yet precisely the lack of these preconditions for a Kantian world is the issue with respect to other parts of the world that are neither liberal democratic nor affluent, and therefore live in a predominantly Hobbesian frame.[134] True, the success of the European experiment and the great benefits that joining it promised enticed dictatorial countries of southern Europe and, later, the post-communist countries of eastern Europe to adopt liberal democracy in order to qualify for admission. All the same, although proclaimed an 'idea', Europe is a geographical entity and cultural community, with fundamentally limited further expansion. Although the extension of economic benefits associated with the liberal system have been both the liberal ideal and favoured technique since the nineteenth century, it is precisely the countries and cultures that are unwilling or unable to assimilate into the liberal orbit, and that react militantly, that are the issue here. International institutions not based on a voluntary liberal consensus among affluent democracies, although not worthless, are unlikely to have a better record than the League of Nations and the UN have had, for the reasons touched upon by Rousseau in his critique of St Pierre and elaborated on above.

Opinion in the liberal democracies (again stronger in Europe but also voiced in the USA) favours various combinations of the mutually reinforcing approaches of 'informal imperialism', non-interfering coexistence, direct economic aid, appeasement, and containment for dealing with the threat of WMD proliferation in the undeveloped world. In its updated form, the first approach assumes that the march of the global market economy and the trend towards democratization, both propelled forward by the alluring model of, and economic and political pressure from, the dominant affluent–liberal-democratic core, will eventually overcome all strongholds of resistance and the most change-averse economies, cultures, societies, and states. Biding for time may thus be the most sensible policy for the liberal-democratic world, because, if threats are likely to defuse themselves in the long run, what point is there in precipitating crises. It is doubtful, however, that the processes of liberalization are unilinear or that some serious threats would not materialize before these processes are allowed to complete their course. Past experience is mixed, and not only with respect to the German and imperial Japanese cases already mentioned. China and the realm of Islam struck westerners during the late nineteenth and early twentieth centuries by their deep-seated resistance and failure to change. Max Weber, for one, believed that Confucianism was culturally antithetical to the spirit of capitalism.[135] Since then, east Asia, followed by south-east Asia and China herself, have all undergone remarkable economic modernization, which many associate with the virtues of Confucianism. However, whether or not democratic liberalization will follow economic liberalization in China remains an open question. The countries of Islam, so far painfully slow to modernize (with the Arab countries particularly troubled in this respect), might also take off in time. But given the deep-seated social, economic, and political obstacles to development and the strong cultural resistance to liberalism in that and other regions of the developing world, their transformation is likely to be a protracted and turbulent process.

Side by side with liberal expansionism, there has always existed a more cautionary school that doubted that the liberal model was universally applicable or bound to triumph. This school has favoured liberal coexistence with others for the sake of peace and stability. All the same, the proliferation of WMD in the most 'problematic' countries in terms of their militancy or governability, coupled with the threat of unconventional terror, highlights the limits of this approach, especially, one should add, as the power discrepancy between the developed world and these countries is so great as to tempt the former to act before the latter turn nuclear and therefore immune to intervention by force.

Many liberals lay stress on direct economic aid by the developed world that would help developing societies on to the path of modernization. After all, if a failure to embark on that path is largely responsible for their hostility and militancy, the answer should address the deep-seated problem, 'dry the swamp rather then try to catch the mosquitoes'. Indeed, such aid has an important contribution to make. Still, the limitations of foreign economic aid have also been revealed by experience, because, where the social, cultural, and political infrastructure for integration into the modern economy is not in place, its development is an agonizingly elusive process, which is not easily achievable by merely pouring in money. And once more, it is the countries that are most resistant to modernization that constitute the greatest risk in terms of WMD proliferation.

Appeasement, the extension of rewards, and even downright bribes to potential sources of threat in order to entice them to give up development of WMD, particularly nuclear weapons, have much to recommend themselves, if and where they can be made to work. In the most difficult cases, however, it often cannot, especially if not augmented by the threat of force. Containment, including the use of non-military, mainly economic, sanctions, is of very limited applicability to preventing WMD proliferation, because it is not sufficient to isolate prospective developers of WMD within the confines of their own realm. It is development within that realm, its possible export or leakage to other states and to terror groups, and the chain reaction of further proliferation that it may unleash in neighbouring countries that are the problem.

Thus the capability and willingness to use force—which presuppose its occasional use—appear to be indispensable for preventing WMD proliferation in unstable parts of the world's Hobbesian 'zone of war'. To the extent that this is a contentious issue within liberal-democratic societies, which currently poisons relations between the USA and Europe, there is much cause for the American chagrin. Americans blame European attitudes on a combination of naïve false consciousness, military impotence, and selfish, ungrateful, and spiteful free riding on the only power that provides the essential public service of promoting global security.[136] In this view,

651

European societies are hedonistic, ageing, and decadent, living in a fools' paradise made safe since the Second World War by American power, and hoping that the dangers from outside can be shut out, or, worse, diverted to the USA. They fail even to live up to their own professed ideals and bring themselves to intervene by force to stop genocide, as in Rwanda (1994) and Sudan (2004). Only the American involvement that shouldered the burden finally made possible military intervention to stop ethnic cleansing in Europe's own backyard, in Bosnia (1995) and Kosovo (1999).

This does not mean that the policies, currently associated with the USA, of armed intervention to impose non-proliferation, active suppression of terror, and democracy as a means for the first two do not involve intractable problems of a fundamental nature; tactical problems of application in that case or the other are not our concern here. Let us start with democratization. After the collapse of the communist challenge and as the democratic peace theory took hold in the 1990s, the Wilsonian notion that the democratization of the world should be actively pursued by the USA as a means for creating not only a just but also a peaceful world gained widespread currency. It was voiced by high-ranking officials in the Clinton administration and, in the wake of 9/11, was adopted by conservatives, who had previously been sceptical about that doctrine, which had been associated with the radical brand of liberalism. There were good reasons for such scepticism, because, although there is much validity to the democratic peace theory, it has tended to ignore some crucial factors, lending itself to simplistic understanding by political enthusiasts, who lost sight of the massive intricacies involved.[137]

In the first place, as Wilson and his successors discovered in failed efforts to establish democracy through intervention, including military intervention—in Mexico, the Dominican Republic, Haiti, Nicaragua, Costa Rica, and Guatemala—democracy is neither desired by all nor unconditionally sustainable. Contrary to a widely held view in the west, democratic freedom is not merely a neutral mechanism for best achieving any chosen value; it is itself an ideological choice, incorporating a whole set of values that many societies and cultures find to be deeply in conflict with other values that they cherish more deeply. Furthermore, as we have seen above, the adoption of democracy is not merely an act of will but has tended to occur on a country-scale in conjunction with economic and social modernization. Economic modernization, social transformation, and democratization have

652

been intimately connected. As Wilson himself came to appreciate, 'the real cause of the trouble in Mexico was not political but economic'; elections would not address 'the prime cause of all political difficulties' there, the highly unequal pattern of land distribution and, hence, of social relations. Consequently, the president grew sceptical about the ability of foreign intervention to generate real change.[138]

Indeed, the forceful democratization of Germany and Japan after the Second World War, the most successful cases of democratization in the twentieth century, had been made possible not only by the political circumstances of defeat in total war and the communist threat; although considerable cultural resistance to democracy and liberalism had to be overcome in both countries, they both possessed a modern economic and social infrastructure upon which functioning liberal democracies could be built.[139] While the attempt to bring democratization to countries—such as those of the Arab word—that lack both a liberal tradition and a modern socio-economic infrastructure, countries that are largely tribal and fraught with ethnic and religious cleavages, should persist, its limitations must be recognized. It will be a gradual process, and it can backfire under excessive pressure, threatening stability in existing moderately pluralistic and modernizing state-societies, because the opposition in most of these countries is not liberal but Islamist, and often undemocratic and radical. Not only public discussion but also much of the scholarly work seem to have lost sight of the fact that even the USA, the UK, and France became liberal and parliamentary decades, if not centuries, before turning democratic. In all these countries before modernization it was feared (and in France, for example, demonstrated in the wake of both the Great and the 1848 Revolutions) that the people's choice if given the vote would not be liberalism, or, indeed, democracy, let alone moderate and peaceful.

This brings us to the second point. The democratic peace phenomenon tends to be much weaker in the early stages of liberalization, democratization, and economic development, as already seen. Thus it is not at all clear that the democratization of Arab and Moslem states would by this very fact reduce the militancy of their societies. As in nineteenth-century Europe, and contrary to the prevailing cliché, public opinion in Arab states tends to be *more* militant than the semi-autocratic state rulers, who struggle to keep such popular pressures in check. The semi-democratic Islamic regime in Iran that replaced the autocratic Shah in a popular revolution has been highly militant, no different in this respect from revolutionary France's republican regime. Although presidential candidates in Iran must be approved by the religious authorities that disqualify those whose Islamic credentials are suspect, it is still the case that the more fundamentalist and militant candidate Ahmadinejad won a sweeping victory over the relatively moderate Rafsanjani in the 2005 popular elections. Popular support for Iran's nuclear programme transcends social and political divides. In the first democratic Algerian elections ever, held in 1992, the radical Islamic front won. The army intervened, cancelling the elections' results with the tacit approval of the west, and the ensuing civil–guerrilla war caused some 100,000 fatalities. The consequences of the victory of the Shia coalition in the January 2005, post-Saddam Hussein, free Iraqi elections are too early to determine at the time of writing. The same applies to the results of free elections in Palestinian territory, where the militant Islamic movement Hamas enjoys strong popular support. (As this book was being copy-edited in January 2006, Hamas won the Palestinian elections, seemingly validating the above observation.) Indeed, the peace treaties that both Egypt and Jordan signed with Israel are unpopular with public opinion in these Arab countries, most staunchly objected to by the urban middle classes, trade organizations, professionals, the educated, and the intellectuals. Obviously, although sharing a great deal, Arab and Moslem countries are not a monolith, and the consequences of democratization in them may diverge accordingly. Thus a more discerning approach is called for.

There exists an even more radical policy option than intervention. Historian Niall Ferguson, among others, has suggested sensationally that the USA (and the developed world) should embrace formal imperialism and assume direct rule over failed states and societies in the developing world.[140] Ferguson deserves credit for reviving the idea (which had been lost in the flood of anti-colonial rhetoric) that despite many abuses, liberal imperial rule, with the British Empire as its paradigm, brought much of the world into the fold of the new global–industrial economy, opening the door for its escape from *agraria*'s Malthusian trap of dire poverty, sickness, war, and death. Ferguson further points out that many post-colonial societies have failed to sustain modernization after gaining independence. Yet it is difficult to take seriously his suggestion that the resumption of imperial rule is desirable or practical.

One can only briefly note the flaws in Ferguson's thesis. He fails to demonstrate that the countries that went through formal imperial rule have done better than those that were merely transformed by the effects of 'informal imperialism'. He ignores the issue of national self-determination in the imperial domains, which, viewed from the other side, raises the question of whether the USA (let alone any other developed power) is prepared to grant citizenship to the populations of developing countries that would become part of a global American Empire. Indeed, it is not at all made clear what interest the USA would have in shouldering the enormous burden of direct global rule, even assuming that it could make a difference in the development of 'failed' states and societies, which in itself is very doubtful given the intractable pockets of endemic socioeconomic 'failure' that exist within her own borders. The threat of unconventional terror, which may be regarded as a possible motive, is only cursorily mentioned by Ferguson and does not tip the balance, given other options.[141] Finally, although he is well aware of, indeed, appears to be complaining about, the liberal democracies' poor record in overcoming armed resistance to their imperial rule, Ferguson fails to discuss the deep-seated reasons, examined above, for that record, which shows little signs of changing.

The fundamental restrictions on the use of violence against civilians that liberal democracies have adopted as a norm is the main *military* limitation on the American policy of forceful intervention to impose non-proliferation of WMD and remove terror-sponsoring regimes. The USA's military–technological superiority over developing countries' armed forces is greater than ever, making possible remarkable military feats. At the same time, however, the USA is scarcely able to cope successfully with popular insurgency in the absence of a strong enough indigenous central authority that is willing to co-operate. As already mentioned, the absence of effective state authorities poses no lesser, perhaps even greater, problems than hostile regimes that control their territory and can be variably coerced to co-operate. In weak and 'failed' states, covering vast and barely approachable tracts of the globe and inhabited by fragmented and unruly societies, the ability to monitor and crack down on the activity of terrorist groups is inherently limited, with or without direct involvement by American forces. The difficulties of finding a needle in a haystack pale in comparison.

All these are baffling problems, which, like most things in life, do not lend themselves to easy or clear solutions. Yet the threat foreshadowed by 9/11 is not accidental or transient but fundamental, and its gravity is likely to affect international politics profoundly. As 'encapsulated' technologies of mass destruction generated by the industrial–technological revolution proliferate and become available to non-state organizations and individuals, the prospect of them being used seem to become a matter of when rather than if, as American Defense Secretary under Clinton, William Cohen, put it even before 9/11. This threat cannot be eliminated by any means known today and will require vigorous concerted action to keep it in check. Despite much haggling and conflicts of interest, such concerted action is not utopian, because no state is immune to the threat, and therefore states share an interest in co-operating against it. Piracy was so eliminated in the nineteenth century, with the British hegemon playing the major role in naval policing and fostering co-operation; indeed, the stakes with respect to unconventional terror are much higher. International norms and practices are likely to change, as individual states, particularly the more militant and less stable ones, come under heavy pressure to give up WMD, to submit to stricter external monitoring of their facilities, and to crack down on terrorists within their territories. Various combinations of all the above-described policy options are likely to be used with varying levels of success, including political and economic sticks and carrots, but also the implied and actual use of force. How events will unfold is impossible to predict.

Some readers may be surprised that I have treated all the above as tensions between conflicting strands within liberalism, where the controversy is more commonly presented as taking place between liberals and (neo-) conservatives. Yet it is a measure of the remarkable forward march of liberalism and democracy since the eighteenth century that the liberal perspective has grown to dominate completely the public arena in the liberal democracies, gradually pushing to irrelevancy all intellectual and political opposition. So-called conservatives in the liberal democracies have long embraced the classical liberal creed—indeed, claim to be the true defenders of the liberal tenets. The great ideologies of the modern era have been described as secular religions in terms of their cognitive, ethical, and emotional functioning. This label was first applied to Marxism and fascism, but, with obvious differences, it also applies to the last major ideology that has survived to dominance in today's developed world. Offering a comprehensive interpretation of the world, a creed of justice, and a quasi-sanctified code of conduct, liberalism involves great emotional investment and evokes much zeal (albeit not necessarily a strong commitment for action and willingness to sacrifice). As with all creeds, it is susceptible to the dogmatic lure, which in pursuit of the abstract, in whatever interpretation, fails to take heed of the realities with which abstract principles have to connect. All the same, pragmatists and messianics of various persuasions, left and right, all debate within the framework of liberalism—with a capital or small l—which has become woven into the fabric of today's affluent democracies.

CONCLUSION

The point in time at which this book ends is as transient as any in the history of humankind and of human deadly violence. The temptation to regard this particular moment of the present any differently must be resisted. This is not to say that human cultural evolution is not 'punctuated' with some crucial 'take-offs' (and setbacks). The adoption of agriculture and animal husbandry was one such point, which, eventually, created the preconditions for the industrial–technological revolution that has been transforming the world over the past two centuries. It is in the context of this radical transformation that the idea of the 'democratic peace', which has been stirring the discussion in international relations theory, must be understood, and, although basically true—amended. A far more complex causal process has been at work than a simple relationship between an independent variable, liberalism/democracy, and a dependent one, the 'democratic peace'.

The emergence of the democratic peace phenomenon some time during the nineteenth century has been linked, with little further questioning, to the fact that liberal-democratic regimes began to evolve only then. But, indeed, they began to evolve on a country scale only at that point in time, rather than any earlier in history, precisely because of the modern transformation: the growth of 'imagined communities' of print; a commercial–industrial economy; 'mass', urban, society; mass literacy; the bourgeois way of life; and growing abundance. All these have been unfolding *processes* rather than one-time events, leading to *ever-growing* liberalization and democratization in *some* countries over the last centuries. The democratic peace phenomenon—the aversion of modern affluent liberal-democratic societies to war, which most strikingly manifests when both sides to a potential conflict share that aversion but which is expressed more generally in

657

liberal democracies' attitude towards conflict and war, *ad bellum* as well as *in bello*—has been intimately connected with these underlying processes and has increased with them. The democratic peace did not exist among pre-modern democratic and republican city-states not because they were not democratic or even sufficiently liberal politically, but because they were *pre-modern*, unaffected by the modern transformation. This is the piece of the puzzle that Paine and Kant lacked in their visionary tracts, if only because they themselves predated most of that transformation.

The modern transformation accounts for the fact that not only liberal/democratic countries but *all* countries, once swept by the industrial–technological age, have engaged in war far less than they previously did, a fact overlooked by the democratic peace theorists. Although the memory of the two World Wars dominates people's perception, during the nineteenth and twentieth centuries the great powers fought among themselves for only a third of the years that they had fought in earlier centuries. Rather than the cost of war becoming prohibitive (it changed little, relative to population and wealth), it was mainly the benefits of peace that increased dramatically once the Malthusian trap was broken, tilting the overall balance between war and peace for economically ever-growing, market-oriented, increasingly interdependent, industrializing and industrial societies, regardless of their regime, for which wealth acquisition ceased to be a zero-sum game. This being acknowledged, the liberal/democratic countries' path to modernity has involved a distinctly greater aversion to war than that of non-democratic and non-liberal countries, because of the political, economic, social, and normative reasons discussed above.

Other factors that have emanated from the modern transformation apply mostly to liberal-democratic countries while being only variably connected to their regime: the staggering rise in the standard of living; decrease in hardship, pain, and death; dominance of metropolitan life and the service economy—the massive expansion of classical 'urbanity'; spread of the consumer and entertainment society; sexual promiscuity, strikingly captured in the 1960s anti-war slogan 'make love not war'; women's franchise; and the shrinking ratio of young males in the population. These were long associated with 'decadence' in historical societies, which has been suspected to apply to liberal democracies by friend and foe alike during the twentieth century. And yet the liberal democracies proved highly efficient in mobilizing their advanced economies and population for the test of total war during the first half of that century, albeit only after becoming convinced that there was no way that they could escape it. They defeated the no less efficient, and militarily more efficient, imperial Germany by their greater combined weight, augmented by an alliance with autocratic Russia that was later replaced by the liberal-democratic USA, the sheer size of which dwarfed the far smaller European powers. The liberal democracies similarly defeated the right-wing totalitarian powers, Nazi Germany and imperial Japan, for much the same reasons, with the Soviet Union replacing czarist Russia and shouldering even more of the burden of war. As the right-wing authoritarian and totalitarian experiments were cut short in these wars, the liberal democracies practically monopolized the capitalist path to modernity worldwide, whereas the communist alternative proved economically ineffi-cient, especially in the more advanced stages of industrialization and the agile information age, and collapsed under its own weight. By the end of the twentieth century, the liberal democracies and the market economy dominated the globe and were again widely viewed as the way of the future. The spread of the 'democratic peace', already triumphant in North America, Europe, and, possibly, along the Pacific rim, is widely expected to follow.

A lot of things can happen to disrupt that scheme of the future, the preconditions of which are many and far from fulfilled. It is still unclear, for example, whether a fast modernizing giant such as China, as well as Russia, and some suggest that perhaps even India, are going to converge into the affluent liberal-democratic model or chart a different path, drawing on their size, special conditions, and cultural traditions. They might create a new, modern and powerful 'second world', which would be authoritarian, nationalistic, less liberal in its trade policies, and more belligerent than the liberal democracies. Smaller countries might be drawn to such new regional hegemons and emulate their model. There are also parts of the world that have so far failed to modernize successfully, some of them constituting hotbeds of militancy, simmering at either the state or social level. Democra-tization, advanced as a remedy for such societies, should be understood as part of a far more complex causal web, whereby economic and social mod-ernization are very much intertwined with successful democratization and liberalization, all of them affecting the growth of a 'democratic peace'.

Furthermore, democracy, liberalism, and economic development can help in resolving or alleviating ethnic and national conflicts only to a limited degree, if, indeed, they do not release and bring them to the fore. Ethnic and national—kin—identities are prime sources of motivation, capable of eliciting explosive violence. The liberal-democratic recipe for dealing with them—equal citizenship, inclusion, tolerance, ethno-national co-habitation, regional autonomy, or peaceful secession—as well as rising prosperity, can be affective only up to a point. Where ethnicities are inseparably mixed and hostile, creating a Balkan or Northern Ireland-type situation, the limits of that recipe become most apparent. Moreover, throughout Africa and much of Asia, ethnic and state boundaries conflict, constituting an endless source of tension. As J. S. Mill and some contemporary scholars suggested, and contrary to much of the current discourse in academia and international institutions, it is very difficult for democracy to survive in a country where deep ethnic cleavages exist; viewed from the opposite direction, ethnically divided countries tend to split once democratization allows their peoples the option of self-determination. Ethnicity and nationalism were among the major causes of conflict and war in the twentieth, as in the nineteenth, centuries.[142] To the extent that economic growth, openness, and interdependency have reduced the economic motivation for conflict, and the conflict between the great ideologies of modernity subsided, problems of ethnic–cultural identity may have become the main source of violent strife—within states even more than internationally—manifesting themselves mainly but not only in the developing world.

Militancy in the world's poorest and weakest societies would have mattered little outside their Malthusian–Hobbesian zone if not for the threat of WMD, particularly the nuclear, another transforming, Promethean, product of modernity. The prevention of open war through mutual deterrence and the logic of MAD supplemented the affluent liberal-democratic *state* of peace where the latter did not apply. States remain by far the most powerful warriors and potential users of WMD. Yet, as the technologies of 'encapsulated' mass destruction trickle down below the state level into the hands of individuals and organizations that cannot be effectively deterred, their use becomes far more likely, indeed, probably only a matter of time. A genie has been released from its bottle. Although the threat today is mainly associated with radical Islam, its true gravity lies in the fact that it can come from any 'super-empowered angry man' or group. A global crackdown on the spread of the technologies and weapons of WMD, and their likely users, is currently the only available answer to the threat.

This, at least, is how things are imperfectly viewed at the particular time of writing this book. For it is impossible to predict not only events but what new economic, social, political, and cultural forms and patterns humankind's fast, technology-driven cultural evolution will create, and how they will affect human deadly violence. Nor, needless to say, is anything guaranteed by the evolutionary process in itself, which may be set back, indeed, halted altogether, by any massive catastrophe, including one wreaked by WMD.

17

Conclusion: Unravelling the Riddle of War

The phenomenon of war has always evoked distress and puzzlement because of the killing, misery, and overall net loss in terms of destruction and wasted resources involved, which have been sensed (even if not yet clearly defined) to have often resulted in a mutually hurting 'prisoner's dilemma' situation. Equally, however, the glory and heroism of war have been celebrated through the ages—from oral epics to movies—with the activity of fighting serving as a source of excitement and exhilaration, especially for young men, because the prizes to be won or defended by war could be, and frequently were, very great indeed. Both of these contradictory but equally pervasive attitudes towards the high-stakes–high-risk–high-gain activity of fighting are rooted in inborn, evolution-shaped predispositions. Only with modernity, as the liberal outlook that emerged during the Enlightenment gradually grew to dominate the developed world, did war begin to be regarded in liberal societies as something utterly repugnant and futile, indeed, incomprehensible to the point of absurdity.

As we saw in the preceding chapters, there have been good reasons for this attitude in the wake of the industrial–technological revolution and in the context of an affluent–liberal world, wherein the Malthusian trap was broken. Abundance based on production and exchange has been increasing at a staggering pace and the balance of benefits between war and peace has radically altered as interdependent growth in real wealth replaced the zero-sum game. However, what may be true for the modern affluent–liberal world is not necessarily so with respect to the reality that preceded it, or, indeed, that may presently prevail outside the affluent–liberal orbit. As people tend to generalize from their own circumstances which they regard as 'natural', the occurrence of war has increasingly been perceived in modern liberal societies as a disturbing puzzle, a true enigma—in relation to the past as well as to the present. The view that took hold during the height of Rousseauism, from the 1960s, that widespread intraspecific killing and war are something uniquely human, or even that they are a late cultural invention, has only accentuated the puzzle.[1]

In reality, however, there is nothing special about deadly human violence and war. Fundamentally, the solution to the 'enigma of war' is that no such enigma exists. Violent competition, alias conflict—including intraspecific conflict—is the rule throughout nature, as organisms vie among themselves to survive and reproduce under ever-prevalent conditions of acute scarcity, conditions accentuated by their own process of propagation. Within this fundamental reality organisms can resort to co-operation, competition, or conflict, strategies that they variably mix, depending on each strategy's utility in a given situation and in relation to each organism's particular configuration along its evolutionary path. Evolution-shaped mechanisms embedded in organisms, from the most primitive to their highest forms, regulate the choice and combination of these behavioural strategies. As conflict is always there as an option to be taken, organisms' structural and behavioural traits (the two are obviously interlinked) are funnelled to succeed in it, variously offensively and defensively and with greater or lesser specialization. It is sufficient that some adopt this option radically to affect and change all the others in a never-ending interrelated chain reaction.

Humans are no exception in this general pattern. Contrary to the Rousseauite imagination, the evidence of historically observed hunter–gatherers and, more dimly but increasingly, that of palaeo-archaeology shows that humans have been fighting among themselves throughout the history of our species and genus, during the human 'evolutionary state of nature'. There was nothing 'ritualistic' about this fighting, nor did it take place in an environment of plenty and innocence, a Rousseauite Garden of Eden. Hobbes was much closer to the truth here, with his 'state of nature' concept made concrete by empirical data and explained by evolutionary theory. Competition for survival over scarce resources and women—with all its behavioural derivatives and myriad refractions—dominated life, often turning violent. In historically observed hunter–gatherer societies (as among primitive horticulturalists) the rate of violent death among men appears to have been in the region of 25 per cent, with the rest of them covered with scars and society as a whole overshadowed by the ever-present prospect of conflict. Such a violent mortality rate is much higher than those registered by state societies and is approximated only by the most destructive state wars; yet it corresponds to normal rates of intraspecific killing among animals in nature, which, although denied for a while during the 1960s, is scarcely regarded as purposeless or maladaptive. Indeed, the curious belief by many scholars that in the extremely competitive evolutionary state of nature human fighting (when it is admitted to have existed) occurred 'just so', to satisfy 'psychological' needs—that it was essentially non-adaptive and only began to 'pay off' with the coming of agriculture and the state—stands in stark contradiction to everything we know empirically about nature and the human state of nature, while also constituting a breathtaking negation of the evolutionary logic.

What makes 'war' *seem* different from other intraspecific deadly conflict is the same process that has transformed human existence in general over the past 10,000 years: the adoption of agriculture that led to the emergence of large-scale societies and, later, state-societies, made all human activity—including that of fighting—far larger in scale, highly co-ordinated and integrated, and coercively hierarchical. Group fighting exists among many social animals—there is nothing uniquely human about it. It was more developed among small-scale Palaeolithic human groups than among other social animals only to the degree that human intelligence and social interaction were more developed. However, as the size and complexity of human societies grew dramatically, so did human group fighting. Group fighting grew in scale with the growth in size of the human groups themselves. That 'war' is customarily defined as large-scale organized violence is merely a reflection of the fact that human societies have become large and organized.

Thus, to insist that 'true war' emerged only with the state and state politics would mean to substitute conceptual artificials for the living process of human history. More meaningfully it is the course and contours of this process that should be elucidated. To repeat: although the size of the societies that engaged in fighting and, consequently, also their armed hosts increased spectacularly, creating the false impression that state wars are particularly lethal and destructive and, therefore, that they solely merit the designation of 'true war', the death toll of human fighting actually decreased under the state. In the first place, deadly human violence now became sharply differentiated between internal and external, with non-state violence within the state's realm outlawed and more or less successfully suppressed by the state's authority. There should be no illusion here: more often than not the resulting decrease in intrasocial violent mortality was caused by the triumph of violence rather than by any peaceful arrangement. It was the triumphant rulers' violence, institutionalized into more or less effective monopoly, that enforced 'civil peace' while extracting resources from society and variably providing mafia-like 'protection' and other services.[2] All the same, the case can be made, as suggested by Hobbes and others, that even low-quality services provided by the leviathan were better than its collapse,[3] because when this happened during periods of civil war and anarchy, the 'state of nature' returned, again customarily resulting in greater destructiveness and death than inter-state wars. Civil war involved renewed large-scale fighting within society for control over it, whereas anarchy, often caused by civil war, spelt the return of small-scale but all-pervasive and highly lethal and disruptive 'banditry', 'feuding', and 'private justice'. As to 'foreign', inter-state war, it too, despite its grand scale in absolute terms, involved a lower death toll per population than pre-state fighting in all but the most severe wars, because larger societies and hence territories and distances translated into a lower social participation rate in war for the men, as well as lesser exposure of the civilian rear.

Furthermore, created and maintained above all by force of arms, state-societies were probably the most significant 'spin-off' of warfare, which in turn created the necessary preconditions for a relatively peaceful civilian existence, dense and complex orderly societies, integrated economies of scale with a developed division of labour, and literate civilizations. States' superior military power drove neighbouring tribal societies into statehood, thereby accelerating the process. Later on, modern states' superior power was central to the propelling of more traditional states into the modern fold, facilitating the exponential growth in real wealth, the breakdown of the Malthusian trap, and, ultimately, a perceivable decline in war's utility and usage. Thus warfare was not only affected by but it also affected the growth of the state and civilization, playing a decisive role in generating

665

that remarkable cultural take-off, although apparently receding where an advanced industrial–technological–liberal society developed.

To be sure, the emergence of large-scale stratified and state societies also created a differential balance of benefits and costs in war, as in all other social dealings. The benefits from war often went disproportionately to the rulers and the elite, while sharply decreasing down the social ladder, with much of the population receiving very little to compensate for their risk. Contrary to Carl von Clausewitz's idealist view that politics is the 'representative of all interests of the community', it rather represents the *ruling* interests in society, which can be more or less inclusive.[4] The more the rulers and elite were able to use their control over the machinery of the state and their socio-economic clout to coerce or sway the social body, the more it meant that it was mainly for the attainment of *their* interests that politics—and war—were geared. The imposition of military service by the state, one of the major sources of its power advantage over non-state societies, thus functioned not only to overcome the problem of 'free riding' in defence of the common good, but all too often also to coerce people to fight even where there was little positive interest for them to do so. As people sensed when the balance of risks and benefits was heavily skewed against them, armies based on coercion alone, as in the proverbial conscripted hosts of Oriental empires, proved to be close to useless militarily, especially those levied from the empire's subject peoples rather than from its core ethnicity. Real fighting could be expected only from the latter and from a militarized elite and professional troops rewarded by pay, booty, land, and other forms of economic and social benefits.

The glaring inequality in the distribution of the benefits and costs of war has contributed to the Enlightenment's belief that the occurrence of war was made possible only because of that inequality, wherein an elite minority harvested the benefits of war while leaving its risks and price to the rest of the population which did the fighting and suffered its ravaging. Yet, although obviously valid to some degree, particularly when the imbalance was most pronounced, this reasoning far from exhausted the logic of war. As in all other social activities, inequality by no means necessarily meant a negative cost–benefit balance for the populace in a war. Even under such inequality, existing universally although variably, the populace very often had considerable stakes in the war, either to protect their own against invaders—including property and family but also their people at large and communal independence—or to gain from the enemy. Furthermore, contrary to the Enlightenment's view that the differential distribution of benefits and risks was the factor that made the decision to go to war easy, it was the more egalitarian–participatory societies that proved the most formidable in mobilizing for and sustaining war—defensive and offensive—as both egalitarian tribal societies and republican city-states demonstrated. In classical Athens, for example, where the *demos* actually ruled to a degree barely matched in history, it was also the most bellicose element in society, wholly bound and committed to the preservation and expansion of the empire by force.

The differential distribution of the benefits and costs of war in integrated and hierarchical state-societies has much confused understanding of the causes and aims of war in other ways as well. Indeed, it is time to pick up again the cardinal subject of the motives for war, which I have been tracing throughout this book, from the 'state of nature' to modernity. The discipline most concerned with this subject with respect to the state level is that of international relations, wherein the so-called realist school holds a prime position. Generally, realists maintain that international politics is dominated by states with actions governed by self-interest and defined as a quest for power. Under these conditions war is an immanent and regular occurrence. Similar to the anthropological schools in the study of pre-state societies, discussed in Part 1, realist 'theory' is an analytical construct, with fundamental assumptions and insights that capture some important, albeit partial, truths about reality, without giving too much thought to the question of why its picture of reality is valid—to the extent that it is. Lacking such criteria, realism is also highly resistant to any evidence that diverges from its conceptual framework.

A small but growing number of new works in the field of international relations have taken up the evolutionary perspective, demonstrating among other things how it can validate and explain some core realist propositions. They point out, for example, the evolutionary rationale behind the realist stress of egotistic competition and conflict between states for survival and ascendancy, which is merely an extension of the same from the individual and kin-group through the tribal levels.[5] Bradley Thayer's excellent book, *Darwin and International Relations: On the evolutionary origins of war and ethnic conflict* (2004), which the author kindly sent to me, is the most comprehensive in this new literature and the only one that addresses the causes of war.

Given our shared perspective, it is not surprising that he and I agree on a great deal. Thayer suggests that evolutionary theory can resolve the disagreements that exist among realists as to the causes and aims of inter-state competition and conflict. So-called classical realists have claimed that states seek power and act to gain it even by force because the quest for power is in human nature.[6] By contrast, so-called neo- or structural realists have held that it is not human nature but rather the endemic struggle for survival in an anarchic system that *forces* states to seek power irrespective of their wishes, in self-defence, because of mutual fear and the dictates of the 'security dilemma'.[7] Yet other, 'offensive', structural realists have stressed that the constrains of the anarchic state system force states that seek to survive not merely to defend their power but ever to try to increase it actively by dominating and subduing others, again regardless of their true wishes; this has even been labelled 'the tragedy of the great powers'.[8] More ink has been spilt on such differences among realists and between realists and their critics in the discipline of international relations than in the disputes between the medieval schoolmen. One suspects, however, that the whole argument is largely misconstrued.

Critics have long suggested that realists tend to confuse ends and means. Among other things, their overall correct focusing on the quest for power has made them lose sight of the underlying reality that explains *why* the struggle for power takes place.[9] If the quest for power is rooted in human nature, *why* is it there? If, rather, it is mutual apprehension and the security dilemma in an anarchic state system that force states to act to preserve and expand their power, *why* should mutual apprehension exist in the first place, fuelling the security dilemma? Even though realists have been predisposed to stress the struggle over scarce resources, somehow this has not figured prominently in their explanation for state conduct, including war. Indeed, on the whole, the subject of the causes of war remains strangely obscure and marginal in the scholarly literature.[10]

As Thayer points out and in line with discussions earlier in this book, the underlying reality of competition over scarce resources is the ultimate cause of fighting, with the quest for power and domination being a proximate aim for the attainment of that ultimate one, as power and domination provide superior access to resources. The quest for power is indeed central to politics and is hotly pursued (as realists hold), but this is so precisely because power is the universal and vital means through which somatic and reproductive resources can be defended or won. Offensive action is regularly taken not only to achieve greater security under the security dilemma—that too—but also for potentially huge positive gains. Realists have lost contact with the purpose of the whole exercise.[11] Indeed, as already noted, it has not been clearly recognized that the security dilemma can arise only between parties that are already in a state of actual or potential competition and conflict over *something*. It is only within such a reality that one is rightly apprehensive of the other.[12] Of course, once potential or actual conflict exists, resources are sought also in order to foster power that is intended to defend and win resources—that is, there are costs to be invested in the competition itself, sometimes, although by no means always, creating a vicious circle or 'Red Queen effect', whereby all sides end up with net loss, and yet are unable to break away from their predicament.

Attempts made to find the root cause of war in the nature of the individual, the state, or the international system are fundamentally misplaced. In all these 'levels' there are necessary but insufficient causes for war, and the whole cannot be broken into pieces.[13] Indeed, as seen earlier, people's needs and desires—which may be pursued violently—as well as the resulting quest for power and state of mutual apprehension that fuels the 'security dilemma' are all moulded in human nature (some of them existing only as options, potentials, and skills in a behavioural 'tool kit'); they are so moulded because of strong evolutionary pressures that have shaped humans in their struggle for survival over geological time, when all the above literally constituted matters of life and death. The violent option of human competition has been largely curbed within states, yet occasionally it is taken up on a large scale between them because of the anarchic nature of the inter-state system. However, returning to step one, international anarchy in and of itself would not be an explanation for war were it not for the potential for violence in a fundamental state of competition over scarce resources imbedded in reality and, consequently, in human nature.

Thus, as this book claims, fundamentally wars have been fought for the attainment of the same objects of human desire that underlie the human motivational system in general—*only by violent means*, through the use of force. Politics—internal and external—of which war is, famously, a continuation, is the activity intended to achieve, at the intra- and inter-state 'levels', the very same evolution-shaped human aims that we have already seen. Some writers have felt that 'politics' does not fully encompass the causes of war. In his *History of Warfare* (1993), John Keegan rightly criticized Clausewitz for equating warfare with the state. In opposition to Clausewitz he also argued that the reasons for war are 'cultural', rather than merely 'political', in the sense that they express a far broader causal array, reflecting a society's whole way of life, identity, religion, and ideology. Thayer, who correctly argues that evolutionary theory explains ultimate human aims, nevertheless goes on to say, inconsistently, that Clausewitz needs extension because war is caused *not only* by political reasons but also by the evolutionarily rooted search for resources, as if the two were separate, with politics being somehow different and apart, falling outside evolutionary logic.[14]

What is defined as 'politics' is of course a matter of semantics, and similar to all definitions is largely arbitrary. Furthermore, culture and ideology are among the causes of state warfare, the evolutionary logic of which is not immediately apparent. Yet, as has been my contention throughout, if not attributed to divine design, organisms' immensely complex mechanisms and the behavioural propensities that emanate from them—including those of human beings—*ultimately* could have been 'engineered' only through evolution, the inherent process that replicating entities of any sort undergo. Humans have developed stupendous cultural edifices, which have taken them a dazzling distance from their original state of nature. Indeed, the larger part of this book has been concerned with this cultural development—in its interrelationship with war. And yet, although evolving through Lamarkian inheritance of learnt traits rather than through Darwinian biological evolution, cultural edifices do not take just any form. Rather (as argued in Chapter 8), they present a richly diverse but clearly constrained variety, growing from, extending, and revolving around a deep core of innate, biologically rooted desires, propensities, and skills—ultimate aims and proximate mechanisms. The challenge is to lay out how evolution-shaped human desires relate to each other in motivating war throughout history (as discussed in Chapter 12), and under modern conditions.

The desire and struggle for scarce resources—wealth of all sorts—have always been regarded as a prime aim of 'politics' and an obvious motive for war. They seem to require little further elaboration. By contrast, reproduction appears not to figure as a *direct* motive for war in large-scale societies. Appearance is often deceptive, however, because somatic and reproductive motives are the two inseparable sides of the same coin. After all, indirectly, the material means gained or protected by war enhanced reproductive success *within* societies—again differentially, down the social ladder—because they affected people's ability to provide for their families, while also feeding the social competition for more and 'better' women, as for all the other 'good things' in life. Furthermore, similar to looting, sexual adventure remained central to *individual* motivation in going to war, even if it usually failed to be registered at the level of 'state politics'. This may be demonstrated by the effects of the sexual revolution since the 1960s, which, by lessening the attraction of foreign adventure for recruits, may have contributed to advanced societies' growing aversion to war. Honour, status, glory, and dominance—both individual and collective—enhanced access to somatic and reproductive success and were thus hotly pursued and defended, even by force. The 'security dilemma' sprang from this state of actual and potential competition, in turn pouring more oil on to its fire. Power has been the universal currency through which all of the above could be obtained and/or defended, and has been sought as such, in an often escalating spiral.

Kinship—expanding from family and tribe to peoples—has always exerted an overwhelming influence on determining one's loyalty and willingness to sacrifice in the defence and promotion of a common good. Contrary to widely held views, it has always been paramount in shaping political boundaries, as well as relations within multi-ethnic polities. Shared culture is a major attribute of ethnic communities, in the defence of which people can be invested as heavily as in the community's political independence and overall prosperity. Finally, religious and secular ideologies, often converging with but sometimes cutting across kin-based identities, have been capable of stirring enormous zeal and violence. Although regularly serving, at least partly, as pious pretexts, they have been almost as commonly genuinely upheld and pursued—even violently, because grand questions of cosmic and sociopolitical order have been perceived to possess paramount *practical* significance for securing and promoting life on earth and/or, indeed, the afterlife. In the human problem-solving menus, ideologies have functioned as the most general blueprints.

Rather than separate items, a 'laundry list' of causes for war, all of the above partake in the interconnected human motivational system, *originally* shaped by the calculus of survival and reproduction, as the great majority of people until quite recently struggled through a precarious existence. People have been willing to risk and even sacrifice their lives when this calculus suggested that by the use of violence they may gain greater rewards or defend

671

against greater losses for themselves and their kin. This logic continues to guide human behaviour, mostly through its legacy of innate proximate mechanisms—human desires. This happened even where the original link between these proximate mechanisms and the original somatic and reproductive aims may have loosened or even been severed under altered conditions, especially during modernity: more wealth is desired even though above a certain level it has ceased to translate into greater reproduction; with effective contraception much the same applies to sexual success; power, status, honour, and fame—connected to the above—are still hotly pursued even though their reproductive significance has become ambivalent. It is the evolution-shaped proximate mechanisms—the web of desire—that dominate human behaviour, even where much of their original adaptive rationale has weakened.

Perceived alien threat continues to generate great alarm, suspicion, hostility, and emotional mobilization. Such an evolution-shaped response of 'better safe than sorry', involving stark stereotyping of the enemy, is often regarded—sometimes rightly so—as both harmful and much exaggerated in view of the actual risks. It is claimed to be out of proportion to our response to other risks which may be as, or perhaps even more, dangerous—such as road accidents, social problems, and natural disasters—where no intentional hostile human action is concerned. Obviously, careful control of our spontaneous responses—designed as 'short-cut' approximations—in the light of broader information is called for, to make sure that they adequately apply to the circumstances and have not diverged too far from their original rationale. At the same time, however, contrary to a common view, there is a deep rationality underlying our innate evolution-shaped responses.[15] Indeed, intentional hostile human action remains one of the gravest sources of threat, against which people understandably manifest vigilance to prevent risks from materializing.

All in all, to the extent that the industrial–technological revolution, most notably its liberal path, has fundamentally reduced the prevalence of war, the reason for this change is that the violent option for fulfilling human desires has become much less promising than the peaceful option of competitive co-operation. Furthermore, the more affluent and satiated the society and the more lavishly people's most pressing needs are met—with all the attractions available for them to indulge in, up the 'pyramid of needs'—the less their incentives to take risks that might involve the loss of life and limb.[16]

People at large in affluent–liberal societies have sensed this change very well, even when they could not always clearly conceptualize it, increasingly shrinking from the violent option and resorting to more peaceful strategies. The advent of nuclear weapons has reinforced the military arm of this pincer effect between nuclear states, but the process was and continues to be strongly in evidence where mutual nuclear deterrence does not exist.

This does not mean a millenarian era of selfless altruism. People continue to compete vigorously over scarce objects of desire. On this 'realists' are on firmer ground than radical liberals. However, liberals have been right in stressing that human reality is not static and, indeed, has been changing dramatically over the past generations, with the growth of industrial– technological affluent-liberal society going hand in hand with deepening global economic interdependency and mutual prosperity.[17] As conditions have changed dramatically *and for those for whom they have changed*, the violent option—the hammer—in the human behavioural 'tool kit' has become less practical whereas the more peaceful tools have been growing in significance. At the same time, however, most of humanity is still going through the process of modernization, struggling to catch up and charting various cultural and national paths, some of which are and may remain illiberal and undemocratic. Moreover, some societies have so far failed in their efforts to modernize and experience mostly the process's discontents. How future developments will affect the use of wide-scale violence, especially in the presence of immensely destructive ultimate weapons, the use of which is only variably constrained, is anybody's guess.

Endnotes

Chapter 1. Introduction: The 'Human State of Nature'

1. For an overview see: Paul Mellars and Chris Stringer (eds), *The Human Revolution*. Edinburgh: Edinburgh University Press, 1989; Matthew Nitecki and Doris Nitecki (eds), *The Evolution of Human Hunting*. New York: Plenum, 1987; Matthew Nitecki and Doris Nitecki (eds), *Origins of Anatomically Modern Humans*. New York: Plenum, 1994; and more popularly, Roger Lewin, *The Origins of Modern Humans*. New York: Scientific American, 1993. More up to date in incorporating the latest findings of a fast developing DNA research is: Stephen Oppenheimer, *Out of Eden: The peopling of the world*. London: Constable, 2003. The evolution and diversity of hunter–gatherers is underlined by: Robert Foley, 'Hominids, humans and hunter–gatherers: an evolutionary perspective', in T. Ingold, D. Riches, and J. Woodburn (eds), *Hunters and Gatherers: History, evolution and social change*, Vol. 1. Oxford: Berg, 1988, pp. 207–21.

2. Konrad Lorenz, *On Aggression*. London: Methuen, 1966; also the other co-founder of ethology and Nobel laureate, Niko Tinbergen, 'On war and peace in animals and man', *Science*, 1968; **160**: 1411–18; Anthony Storr, *Human Aggression*. London: Penguin, 1968, quotation from p. 9.

3. J. D. Bygott, 'Cannibalism among wild chimpanzees', *Nature*, 1972; **238**: 410–11; G. Teleki, *The Predatory Behavior of Wild Chimpanzees*. Lewisburg: Bucknell University Press, 1973; Jane Goodall, *The Chimpanzees of Gombe*. Cambridge, MA: Belknap, 1986; J. Itani, 'Intraspecific killing among non-human primates', *Journal of Social and Biological Structure*, 1982; **5**: 361–8; Frans de Waal, *Good Natured: The origins of right and wrong in humans and other animals*. Cambridge, MA: Harvard University Press, 1996; Richard Wrangham and Dale Peterson, *Demonic Males: Apes and the origins of human violence*. London: Bloomsbury, 1997.

4. Numerous studies of individual species are conveniently summarized in: C. R. Carpenter, 'Aggressive behavioral systems', in R. L. Holloway (ed.), *Primate Aggression, Territoriality and Xenophobia*. New York: Academic Press, 1974, pp. 459–96; G. Hausfater and S. B. Hrdy (eds), *Infanticide: Comparative and evolutionary perspectives*. New York: Aldine, 1984; Felicity Huntingford and Angela Turner, *Animal Conflict*. London: Chapman & Hall, 1987; I. van der Dennen

and V. Falger (eds), 'Introduction', in *Sociobiology and Conflict*. London: Chapman & Hall, 1990, pp. 1–19; J. van Hooff, 'Intergroup competition and conflict in animals and man', in I. van der Dennen and V. Falger (eds), *Sociobiology and Conflict*. London: Chapman & Hall, 1990, pp. 23–54. See also Wrangham and Peterson, *Demonic Males*, despite their exaggerated insistence on ape unique-ness. The point had already been clearly made during the heyday of Lorenz's idea by: Lionel Tiger and Robin Fox, *The Imperial Animal*. New York: Reinhart & Winston, 1971, pp. 209–10.

5. Again, this had already been argued by Tiger and Fox, *The Imperial Animal*, pp. 208–10. See especially: R. N. Johnson, *Aggression in Man and Animals*. Philadelphia, PA: Saunders, 1972; Edward Wilson, *On Human Nature*. Cambridge, MA: Harvard University Press, 1978, pp. 103–5; George Williams, cited in Daniel Dennet, *Darwin's Dangerous Idea*, New York: Simon & Schuster, 1995, p. 478.

6. R. L. Susman (ed.), *The Pygmy Chimpanzee*. New York: Plenum, 1984; T. Kano, *The Last Ape: Pygmy chimpanzee behavior and ecology*. Stanford, CA: Stanford University Press, 1992; Wrangham and Peterson, *Demonic Males*; Frans de Waal, *Bonobo: The forgotten ape*. Berkeley, CA: University of California, 1997.

Chapter 2. *Peaceful or War-Like: Did Hunter–Gatherers Fight?*

1. Margaret Mead, 'Warfare is only an invention—not a biological necessity', *Asia*, 1940; **15**: 402–5, reprinted in L. Bramson and G. Goethals (eds), *War: Studies from psychology, sociology and anthropology*. New York: Basic Books, 1968, pp. 269–74.

2. In the more general literature see, for example, Ashley Montagu, *The Nature of Human Aggression*. New York: Oxford University Press, 1976, pp. 164–80; Richard Leakey and Roger Lewin, *People of the Lake: Mankind and its beginnings*. New York: Anchor, 1978, pp. 276–80; Gwynne Dyer, *War*. London: Bodley Head, 1985; Robert O'Connell, *Ride of the Second Horseman: The birth and death of war*. New York: Oxford University Press, 1995, pp. 29–31, *passim* (this imaginative book on the evolution of warfare, equally full of insight and strange ideas, takes no account of the anthropological studies of recent hunter–gatherers and primitive agriculturalists).

3. Lawrence Keeley, *War before Civilization: The myth of the peaceful savage*. New York: Oxford University Press, 1996; ideas in the same vein were expressed in older works such as the superb book by Quincy Wright, *A Study of War*, Vol. 1. Chicago: University of Chicago, 1942, pp. 33–5, 471–8, and 527–59, 569–70 (statistics). Many scholars seem to be unaware of what is perhaps the best study ever written on the subject: Maurice R. Davie, *The Evolution of War: A study of its role in early societies*. New Haven, CT: Yale University Press, 1929. That such an old and in many ways outdated work

should be so highly rated is a sad comment on the later study of war. By contrast, Turney-High's often cited book, while also full of evidence of warfare, is much overrated: Harry Turney-High, *Primitive War*. Columbia, SC: University of South Carolina, 1949. None of the above works distinguishes between hunter–gatherers and pre-state agriculturalists. In the wake of Keeley's book and after the initial publication in article form of my work on hunter–gatherer warfare, there appeared a new work which, giving much better attention to hunter–gatherers, arrives at conclusions similar to mine: Steven LeBlanc, with Katherine Register, *Constant Battles: The myth of the peaceful noble savage*. New York: St Martin's Press, 2003.

4. Stephen Perlman, 'Group size and mobility costs', in S. Green and S. Perlman (eds), *The Archaeology of Frontiers and Boundaries*. Orlando, FL: Academic Press, 1985, pp. 33–50.

5. H. M. Wobst, 'Boundary conditions for Palaeolithic social systems: A simulation approach', *American Antiquity*, 1974; **39**: 147–78.

6. For criticism of the resulting archaeological bias see S. Vencl, 'War and warfare in archaeology', *Journal of Anthropological Archaeology*, 1984; **3**: 116–32.

7. Robert Wenke, *Patterns In Prehistory*. New York: Oxford University Press, 1990, p. 177; M. K. Roper, 'A survey of the evidence for intrahuman killing in the Pleistocene', *Current Anthropology*, 1969; **10**: 427–59; Irenaeus Eibl-Eibesfeldt, *The Biology of Peace and War: Man, animals and aggression*. New York: Viking, 1979, pp. 126–7; Martin Daly and Margo Wilson, *Homicide*. New York: Aldine, 1988, p. 144, citing E. Trinkaus and M. R. Zimmerman, 'Trauma among the Shanidar Neandertals', *American Journal of Physical Anthropology*, 1982; **57**: 61–76; Christoph Zollikoffer, Marcia Ponce de León, Bernard Vandermeersch and François Lévêque, 'Evidence of interpersonal violence in the St Césaire Neanderthal', *Proceedings of the National Academy of Science of the United States of America*, 2002; **99**: 6444–8; and a good survey in Keeley, *War before Civilization*, pp. 36–7.

8. A good updated study is: C. Irwin, 'The Inuit and the evolution of limited group conflict', in J. van der Dennen and V. Falger (eds), *Sociobiology and Conflict: Evolutionary perspectives on competition, cooperation, violence and warfare*. London: Chapman & Hall, 1990, pp. 189–226. For Greenland, see Eibl-Eibesfeldt, *The Biology of Peace and War*, pp. 131–6. As in many other instances, the point had been generally anticipated by Davie, *The Evolution of War*, pp. 46–8.

9. E. N. Wilmsen and J. R. Denbow, 'The paradigmatic history of San-speaking peoples and current attempts at revision', *Current Anthropology*, 1990; **31**: 489–525.

10. Irenaeus Eibl-Eibesfeldt, 'The myth of the aggression-free hunter and gatherer society', in Ralph Holloway (ed.), *Primate Aggression, Territoriality and Xenophobia*. New York: Academic Press, 1974, pp. 435–57; further developed in

676

Eibl-Eibesfeldt, *The Biology of Peace and War*, pp. 125–161; Bruce Knauft, 'Reconsidering violence in simple societies: Homicide among the Gebusi of New Guinea', *Current Anthropology*, 1987; **28**: 457–500; Keeley, *War before Civilization*, pp. 28–32, 132–4. Detailed battle scenes, depicting fighting both among the Bushmen and against their neighbours, from the pre-Bantu as well as post-Bantu periods, are analysed in: H. C. Woodhouse, 'Inter- and intragroup aggression illustrated in the rock painting of South Africa', *South African Journal of Ethnology*, 1987; **10**: 42–8; also C. Campbell, 'Images of war: A problem in San rock art research', *World Archaeology*, 1986; **18**: 255–67.

11. W. T. Divale, 'System population control in the Middle and Upper Palaeolithic: Inferences based on contemporary hunter-gatherers', *World Archaeology*, 1972; **4**: 222–43; Carol Ember, 'Myths about hunter-gatherers', *Ethnology*, 1978; **17**: 439–48; K. Otterbein, 'Comments on "Violence and sociality in human evolution", by B. M. Knauft', *Current Anthropology*, 1991; **32**: 414.

12. The literature on the subject is discussed in due course. In the meantime, see for the archaeology of the millennia-old evolution of bison hunting, and warfare: George Frison, 'Prehistoric, plains-mountain, large-mammal, communal hunting strategies', in M. Nitecki and D. Nitecki (eds), *The Evolution of Human Hunting*. New York: Plenum, 1987, pp. 177–223; Karl Schlesier (ed.), *Plains Indians, A.D. 500–1500: The archaeological past of historical groups*, Norman: University of Oklahoma, 1994.

13. But see Kenneth Maddock, *The Australian Aborigines*. London: Penguin, 1973, pp. 21–2.

14. Harry Lourandos, *Continent of Hunter-Gatherers: New perspectives in Australian prehistory*. Cambridge: Cambridge University Press, 1997, argues that the original native population was much larger.

15. Mead, 'Warfare is only an invention', p. 271. For the Aboriginal shield, see Baldwin Spencer and F. J. Gillen, *The Native Tribes of Central Australia*. London: Macmillan, 1899, pp. 28, 583; A. A. Abbie, *The Original Australians*. London: Frederick Muller, 1969, pp. 117–18, opposite 128. Lourandos (*Continent of Hunter-Gatherers*, p. 33) comments: 'Further aspects of competition between groups is expressed in the elaborate material culture of weaponry (shields, clubs and the like) used for display and combat.' However, typically for the current anthropological discourse, this is the only reference in his book to fighting or conflict.

16. Paul Tacon and Christopher Chippindale, 'Australia's ancient warriors: Changing depictions of fighting in the rock art of Arnhem Land, N.T.', *Cambridge Archaeological Journal*, 1994; **4**: 211–48.

17. Robert Bigelow, 'The role of competition and cooperation in human evolution', in M. Nettleship, R. D. Givens and A. Nettleship (eds), *War, Its Causes and Correlates*. The Hague: Mouton, 1975, pp. 247–8; Eibl-Eibesfeldt, *The Biology of*

Peace and War, p. 129; Edward O. Wilson, *On Human Nature*. Cambridge, MA: Harvard University Press, 1978, pp. 107–9; Timothy Anders, *The Evolution of Evil*. Chicago: Open Court, 1994, pp. 230–2.

18. R. G. Kimber, 'Hunter-gatherer demography: the recent past in central Australia', in B. Meehan and N. White (eds), *Hunter-Gatherer Demography*. Sydney: University of Sydney, 1990, p. 180; Maddock, *The Australian Aborigines*, pp. 22–3; David Harris, 'Aboriginal subsistence in a tropical rain forest environment', in M. Harris and E. Ross (eds), *Food and Evolution*. Philadelphia: Temple University Press, 1987, pp. 373–4.

19. R. Dyson-Hudson and E. Alden Smith, 'Human territoriality: An ecological reassessment', *American Anthropologist*, 1978; **80**: 21–41.

20. Gerald Wheeler, *The Tribe and Intertribal Relations in Australia*. London: John Murray, 1910, especially pp. 19–20, 29–30, 40, 62–3, 71, 118, 139, *passim*; this excellently incorporates the earliest anthropological works on the subject; Norman Tindale, *Aboriginal Tribes of Australia*. Berkeley, CA: University of California, 1974, especially pp. 10, 55–88; M. J. Meggitt, *Desert People: A study of the Walbiri Aborigines of Central Australia*. Chicago: University of Chicago, 1962, pp. 44–6, *passim*; Maddock, *The Australian Aborigines*, p. 26; Nicolas Peterson (ed.), *Tribes and Boundaries in Australia*, Canberra: Australian School of Aboriginal Studies, 1976, especially p. 20; Lourandos, *Continent of Hunter-Gatherers*, p.33; also Annette Hamilton, 'Descended from father, belonging to country: Rights to land in the Australian Western Desert', in E. Leacock and R. Lee (eds), *Politics and History in Band Societies*. New York: Cambridge University Press, 1982, pp. 85–108.

21. N. J. B. Plomley (ed.), *Friendly Mission: The Tasmanian journals and papers of George Augustus Robinson 1829–1834*. Kingsgrove: Tasmanian Historical Research Association, 1966, pp. 968–9; H. Ling Roth, *The Aborigines of Tasmania*. Halifax: King, 1899, pp. 14–15, 82; Rhys Jones, 'Tasmanian tribes', in Norman Tindale (ed.), *Aboriginal Tribes of Australia*. Berkeley, CA: University of California, 1974, p. 328; Lyndall Ryan, *The Aboriginal Tasmanians*. Vancouver: University of British Columbia, 1981, pp. 13–14.

22. Meggitt, *Desert People*, pp. 38, 42.

23. Wheeler, *The Tribe and Intertribal Relations in Australia*, pp. 118, 139.

24. W. Lloyd Warner, 'Murngin warfare', *Oceania*, 1930–1; **1**: 457–94; incorporated with some modifications into W. Lloyd Warner, *A Black Civilization: A social study of an Australian tribe*. New York: Harper, 1958(1937), pp. 155–90; references are made to the book; quotation p. 155.

25. T. G. H. Strehlow, 'Geography and the totemic landscape in Central Australia', in R. M. Berndt (ed.), *Australian Aboriginal Anthropology*. Nedlands: University of Western Australia, 1970, pp. 124–5.

26. Kimber, 'Hunter-gatherer demography: the recent past in central Australia',

p. 163. For a summary of the research on the long-range trade, see Lourandos, *Continent of Hunter-Gatherers*, pp. 40–3.

27. Arnold Pilling, cited in R. Lee and I. DeVore (eds), *Man the Hunter*. Chicago: Aldine, 1968, p. 158.

28. Warner, *A Black Civilization*, pp. 157–8.

29. John Morgan, *The Life and Adventures of William Buckley: Thirty-two years a wanderer among the Aborigines of the unexplored country round Port Philip*. Canberra: Australian National University Press, 1980(1852).

30. Generally see S. Koyama and D. Thomas (eds), *Affluent Foragers: Pacific coasts east and west*. Osaka: National Museum of Ethnology, 1979; T. Price and J. Brown (eds), *Prehistoric Hunter-Gatherers: The emergence of cultural complexity*. Orlando, FL: Academic Press, 1985; Robert Bettinger, *Hunter-Gatherers*. New York: Plenum, 1991, pp. 64–73.

31. David Yesner, 'Life in the "Garden of Eden": Causes and consequences of the adoption of marine diets by human societies', in M. Harris and E. Ross (eds), *Food and Evolution*. Philadelphia: Temple University Press, 1987, pp. 285–310.

32. P. G. Bahn and Jean Vertut, *Images of the Ice Age*. New York: Facts on File, 1988, pp. 152, 154.

33. John E. Pfeiffer, *The Creative Explosion: An inquiry into the origins of art and religion*. New York: Harper & Row, 1982, pp. 151–2.

34. Tacon and Chippindale, 'Australia's ancient warriors'.

35. Woodhouse, 'Inter- and intragroup aggression'; also Campbell, 'Images of war'.

36. John Ewers, 'Intertribal warfare as the precursor of Indian warfare on the northern Great Plains', *Western Historical Quarterly*, 1975; **6**: 399; J. D. Keyser, 'The plains Indian war complex and the rock art of writing-on-stone, Alberta, Canada', *Journal of Field Archaeology*, 1979; **6**: 41–8.

37. Keeley, *War before Civilization*, p. 38.

38. The literature on the north-west coast is extensive. A meticulous survey, concentrating on the evidence for war, is: R. Brian Ferguson (ed.), 'A reexamination of the causes of northwest coast warfare', in *Warfare, Culture and the Environment*. Orlando, FL: Academic Press, 1984, pp. 267–328, and 273, 298 (for population densities). For the northern part, see Wendel Oswalt, *Alaskan Eskimos*. San Francisco: Chandler, 1967, pp. 2–10, 113–15; Ernest S. Burch, 'Eskimo warfare in northwest Alaska', *Anthropological Papers of the University of Alaska*, 1974; **16**: 1–14; and Ernest S. Burch and T. Correll, 'Alliance and conflict: interregional relations in north Alaska', in L. Guemple (ed.), *Alliance in Eskimo Society*. Seattle: University of Washington, 1972, pp. 17–39. See also Elizabeth F. Andrews, 'Territoriality and land use among the Akulmiut of Western Alaska', in E. S. Burch and L. S. Ellanna (eds), *Key Issues in Hunter-Gatherer Research*. Oxford: Berg, 1994, pp. 65–93; Brian Hayden, 'Competition, labor,

and complex hunter-gatherers', ibid., p. 236; Leland Donald, *Aboriginal Slavery on the Northwest Coast of North America*. Berkeley, CA: University of California, 1997, p. 17.

39. Ferguson, 'A reexamination of the causes of northwest coast warfare', pp. 273–4, 278, 282, 285, 298, 312; Donald, *Aboriginal Slavery on the Northwest Coast of North America*. Examples of large-scale forceful territorial occupations are provided in: Philip Drucker, *The Northern and Central Nootkan Tribes*. Washington, DC: Smithsonian Institute, 1951, pp. 332–65; Philip Drucker, *Cultures of the North Pacific Coast*. San Francisco, CA: Chandler, 1965, pp. 75–6; Oswalt, *Alaskan Eskimos*, pp. 179–90; Burch and Correll, 'Alliance and conflict', pp. 21, 24–5, 33–4; Andrews, 'Territoriality and land use among the Akulmiut of Western Alaska', pp. 82–93.

40. In the anthropological literature these ideas are mainly developed by Brian Hayden—for example, Hayden, 'Competition, labor, and complex hunter-gatherers'.

41. Franz Boas, *Kuakiutl Ethnography*. Chicago: University of Chicago, 1966, pp. 105–19; Drucker, *The Northern and Central Nootkan Tribes*, pp. 332–65; id., *Cultures of the North Pacific Coast*, pp. 75–82; Oswalt, *Alaskan Eskimos*, pp. 178–90, 246; Burch and Correll, 'Alliance and conflict', p. 33; Burch, 'Eskimo warfare in northwest Alaska', p. 7–8; Ferguson, 'A reexamination of the causes of northwest coast warfare', p. 272; Andrews, 'Territoriality and land use among the Akulmiut of Western Alaska', p. 83; Donald, *Aboriginal Slavery on the Northwest Coast of North America*, especially p. 27.

42. Ferguson, 'A reexamination of the causes of northwest coast warfare', pp. 271, 272–4, 278, 285, 298, 312; relying on: George MacDonald, *Kitwanga Fort National Historic Site, Skeena River, British Columbia: Historical research and analysis of structural remains*. Ottawa: National Museum of Man, 1979, and other unpublished research by the latter. The 1,000-year-old antiquity of complex hunter–gatherers and warfare in southern Alaska and other areas of the northwest coast is similarly pointed out in: David R. Yesner, 'Seasonality and resource "stress" among hunter-gatherers: Archaeological signatures', in Burch and Ellanna, *Key Issues in Hunter-Gatherer Research*, p. 237; Burch and Correll, 'Alliance and conflict', p. 24; Burch, 'Eskimo warfare in northwest Alaska', p. 1; Donald, *Aboriginal Slavery on the Northwest Coast of North America*, pp. 27, 205–9.

43. Erna Gunther, *Indian Life on the Northwest Coast of North America, as Seen by the Early Explorers and Fur Traders during the Last Decades of the Eighteenth Century*. Chicago: University of Chicago, 1972, pp. 14, 43, 114, 133, 159, 187. For armour and shields among the Eskimos of the Alaskan coast see: E. W. Nelson, *The Eskimo about Bering Strait*. Washington, DC: Smithsonian Institute, 1983(1899), p. 330; Robert Spencer, *The North Alaskan Eskimo*. Washington, DC: Smithsonian Institute, 1959, p. 72; Oswalt, *Alaskan Eskimos*, pp. 186, 188; Burch, 'Eskimo warfare in northwest Alaska', p. 5. For the Plains Indians,

see, for example: F. R. Secoy, 'Changing military patterns on the Great Plains', *American Ethnological Monographs*, 1953; **21**; Ewers, 'Intertribal warfare', pp. 390, 401.

44. Jeffrey Blick, 'Genocidal warfare in tribal societies as a result of European-induced culture conflict', *Man*, 1988; **23**: 654–70 (the exception in postulating a pacific pre-contact past); R. Brian Ferguson, 'A savage encounter: Western contact and the Yanomami war complex', in R. B. Ferguson and N. Whitehead (eds), *War in the Tribal Zone*. Santa Fe, NM: School of American Research, 1992, pp. 199–227, especially 225; R. Brian Ferguson, *Yanomami Warfare*. Santa Fe, NM: School of American Research, 1995, especially p. 14; Neil Whitehead, 'The snake warriors—sons of the tiger's teeth: A descriptive analysis of Carib warfare, ca. 1500–1820', in J. Haas (ed.), *The Anthropology of War*. New York: Cambridge University Press, 1990, pp. 146–70, especially 160. They have been scathingly criticized by Keeley, *War before Civilization* (p. 20), but embraced by the Rousseauite O'Connell in his convulsed attempt to play down complex hunter–gatherer warfare: O'Connell, *Ride of the Second Horseman*, p. 49. For my critique see more fully: A. Gat 'The causes and origins of "primitive warfare"—reply to Ferguson', *Anthropological Quarterly*, 2000; **73**: 165–8.

45. For a similar conclusion see Burch, 'Eskimo warfare in northwest Alaska', p. 2. The data compiled by Keeley, *War before Civilization* (p. 202, Table 8.3), do not suggest that low population density necessarily resulted in less fighting.

Chapter 3. *Why Fighting? The Evolutionary Perspective*

1. Sigmund Freud, 'Beyond the pleasure principle', (1920) in *The Complete Psychological Works of Sigmund Freud*, Vol. 18. London: Hogarth, 1953–74, pp. 7–64; id., 'The ego and the id', (1923), ibid., Vol. 19, pp. 12–66; id., 'Civilization and its discontents', (1930), ibid., Vol. 21, pp. 57–145; id., 'New introductory lectures on psychoanalysis', (1933), ibid., Vol. 22, pp. 5–182; id., 'Why war', (1933), ibid., Vol. 22, pp. 203–215, especially 210–11. In a book reminiscent of some of Freud's other works, Barbara Ehrenreich has created another mythology to explain human fighting: *Blood Rites: Origins and history of the passions of war*. New York: Metropolitan, 1997. In her view it is an innate biological cum cultural rite of sacred ecstasy, celebrating man's transformation from prey to hunter in the species' ancient past and transferred towards other humans once hunting declined.

2. Konrad Lorenz, *On Aggression*. London: Methuen, 1966; Niko Tinbergen, 'On war and peace in animals and man', *Science*, 1968; **160**: 1411–18; Anthony Storr, *Human Aggression*. London: Penguin, 1968. Recently, Martin van Creveld appears to regard fighting as an elementary drive, with its need for expression seemingly ever present: *The Transformation of War*. New York: Free Press, 1991.

3. J. Maynard Smith and G. R. Price, 'The logic of animal conflicts', *Nature*, 1973; **246**: 15–18.

4. Bronislaw Malinovski, 'An anthropological analysis of war', *American Journal of Sociology*, 1941; **46**, reprinted in L. Bramson and G. Goethals (eds), *War: Studies from psychology, sociology, anthropology*. New York: Basic Books, 1964, pp. 245–68, especially 245–50; Ashley Montagu, *The Nature of Human Aggression*. New York: Oxford University Press, 1976; although largely obsolete, it veers in the other, Rousseauite direction; Edward O. Wilson, *On Human Nature*. Cambridge, MA: Harvard University Press, 1978, pp. 101, 106; Felicity Huntingford and Angela Turner, *Animal Conflict*. London: Chapman, 1987, pp. 86–90; R. Paul Shaw and Yuwa Wong, *Genetic Seeds of Warfare, Evolution, Nationalism and Patriotism*. Boston, MA: Unwin Hyman, 1989, p. 6; Adam Kuper, *The Chosen Primate: Human nature and cultural diversity*. Cambridge, MA: Harvard University Press, 1994, p. 145; J. Silverman and J. P. Gray (eds), *Aggression and Peacefulness in Humans and Other Primates*. New York: Oxford University Press, 1992.

5. Lionel Tiger and Robin Fox, *The Imperial Animal*. New York: Holt, 1971, pp. 149, 206; Wilson, *On Human Nature*, p. 106; Chet Lancaster, 'Commentary: The evolution of violence and aggression', in D. McGuinness (ed.), *Dominance, Aggression and War*. New York: Paragon, 1987, p. 216.

6. An older theory, assuming a simple frustration–aggression behaviour pattern, is no longer held; frustration does not always lead to, nor is it a necessary condition of, aggression. John Dollard et al., *Frustration and Aggression*. New Haven, CT: Yale University Press, 1939; Leonard Berkowitz, *A Social Psychological Analysis*. New York: McGraw-Hill, 1962; Mark May, 'War, peace, and social learning', in *A Social Psychology of War and Peace*, New Haven, CT: Yale University Press, 1943; reprinted in Bramson and Goethals, *War: Studies from psychology, sociology, anthropology*, pp. 151–8; Albert Bandura, 'The social learning theory of aggression', in R. Falk and S. Kim (eds), *The War System*. Boulder, CO: Westview, 1980, pp. 141–56; Russell Geen and Edward Donnerstein, *Aggression: Theoretical and empirical reviews*. New York: Academic Press, 1983; L. Huesmann (ed.), *Aggressive Behavior: Current perspectives*. New York: Plenum, 1994.

7. S. Howell and R. Willis (eds), *Societies at Peace*. London: Routledge; D. Fabbro, 'Peaceful societies', in R. Falk and S. Kim (eds), *The War System*. Boulder, CO: Westview, 1980, pp. 180–203; Chapters 1, 3, 5, and 6 in J. Haas (ed.), *The Anthropology of War*. New York: Cambridge University Press, 1990; J. M. G. van der Dennen, 'Primitive war and the ethnological inventory project', in J. M. G. van der Dennen and V. Falger (eds), *Sociobiology and Conflict*. London: Chapman, 1990, pp. 264–9; R. K. Dentan, 'Surrendered men: Peaceable enclaves in the post-enlightenment West', in L. E. Sponsel and T. Gregor (eds), *The Anthropology of Peace and Nonviolence*. London: Lynne Rienner, 1994, pp.

69–108; Keith F. Otterbein, *The Evolution of War*. New Haven, CT: HRAF, 1970, pp. 20–21; Maurice Davie, *The Evolution of War*. New Haven, CT: Yale University Press, 1929, pp. 46–54; Lawrence Keeley, *War before Civilization*. New York: Oxford University Press, 1996, pp. 28–32.

8. William Graham Sumner, 'War' (1911), reprinted from *War and Other Essays*, in Bramson and Goethals, *War: Studies from psychology, sociology, anthropology*, pp. 205–27. See also William Graham Sumner, *Folkways*. New York: Mentor, 1960(1906).

9. The debate broke out with the publication of the massive book: Edward O. Wilson, *Sociobiology: The new synthesis*, Cambridge MA: Harvard University Press, 1975. However, perhaps the best general presentations of the ideas and overall significance of neo-Darwinist theory are: Richard Dawkins, *The Selfish Gene*, 2nd edn. Oxford: Oxford University Press, 1989; Daniel Dennett, *Darwin's Dangerous Idea*. New York: Simon & Schuster, 1995; Jan Stewart and Jack Cohen, *Figments of Reality: The evolution of the curious mind*. Cambridge: Cambridge University Press, 1997.

10. Charles Darwin, *The Origin of Species*, in *The Origin of Species and The Descent of Man*. New York: The Modern Library, n.d., Chapter 15, p. 373.

11. Georg Simmel, *Conflict: The web of group affiliations*. Glencoe, IL: Free Press, 1955.

12. Darwin, *The Origin of Species*, Chapters 3–4, pp. 60–2, 83.

13. Lorenz, Ardrey, Morris, and the rest could find support in: V. C. Wynne-Edwards, *Animal Dispersion in Relation to Social Behaviour*. Edinburgh: Oliver & Boyd, 1962; also id., *Evolution Through Group Selection*. Oxford: Blackwell, 1986. The idea was famously rejected by: G. C. Williams, *Adaptation and Natural Selection*. Princeton, NJ: Princeton University Press, 1966; also Dawkins, *The Selfish Gene*, pp. 1–11, *passim*.

14. For the latter argument see Dawkins, *The Selfish Gene*, pp. 66–87; the former is developed as a correction by: Frans de Waal, *Good Natured: The origins of right and wrong in humans and other animals*. Cambridge, MA: Harvard University Press, 1996, p. 27; also Irenaeus Eibl-Eibesfeldt, *The Biology of Peace and War*. London: Thames & Hudson, 1979, pp. 37–40, 125, *passim*. Both arguments have been anticipated by: W. D. Hamilton, *Narrow Roads of Gene Land*. Oxford: Freeman, 1996, p. 188.

15. First suggested by Darwin, R. A. Fisher, and J. B. S. Haldane, this idea has become the cornerstone of modern evolutionary biology with: W. D. Hamilton, 'The genetical evolution of social behaviour', *Journal of Theoretical Biology*, 1964; **7**: 1–16, 17–52. For Darwin, see *The Origin of Species*, Chapter 8, and *The Descent of Man*, Chapter 5, in *The Origin of Species and The Descent of Man*, pp. 203–5, 498.

16. The basic phenomenon of so-called fraternal interest groups has also been noted by anthropologists and sociologists: H. U. E. van Velzen and W. van

Wetering, 'Residence, power groups and intra-societal aggression', *International Archives of Ethnography*, 1960; **49**: 169–200; K. F. Otterbein and C. S. Otterbein, 'An eye for an eye, a tooth for a tooth: A cross-cultural study of feuding', *American Anthropologist*, 1965; **67**: 1470–82; K. F. Otterbein, 'Internal war: a cross-cultural comparison', *American Anthropologist*, 1968; **70**: 277–89; Richard Wrangham and Dale Peterson, *Demonic Males: Apes and the origins of human violence*. London: Bloomsbury, 1997.

17. W. D. Hamilton, 'Innate social aptitudes of man: an approach from evolutionary genetics', in R. Fox (ed.), *Biosocial Anthropology*. New York: Wiley, 1975, p. 144; Irwin Silverman, 'Inclusive fitness and ethnocentrism', in V. Reynolds, V. Falger, and I. Vine (eds), *The Sociobiology of Ethnocentrism*. London: Croom Helm, 1987, p. 113.

18. Again this has been pointed out by Hamilton, 'The genetical evolution of social behaviour', p. 16 and developed by R. L. Trivers, 'Parent–offspring conflict', *American Zoologist*, 1974; **14**: 249–64. Also de Waal, *Good Natured*, pp. 212–14. For the statistics and evolutionary logic of kin killing, see Martin Daly and Margo Wilson, *Homicide*. New York: Aldine, 1988, pp. 17–35.

19. Franz Boas, *Kwakiutl Ethnography*. Chicago: University of Chicago, 1966, p. 108; also Leland Donald, *Aboriginal Slavery on the Northwest Coast of North America*. Berkeley, CA: University of California, 1997, p. 104.

20. For example, Lancaster, 'Commentary: The evolution of violence and aggression', p. 219. This well-known phenomenon may help to account for the high rates of kin homicide described in Bruce Knauft, 'Reconsidering violence in simple societies: Homicide among the Gebusi of New Guinea', *Current Anthropology*, 1987; **28**: 457–500 (see, for example, his explanation for sister killing, p. 470).

21. D. C. Fletcher and C. D. Michener (eds), *Kin Recognition in Animals*. New York: Wiley, 1987; P. Hepper (ed.), *Kin Recognition*. Cambridge: Cambridge University Press, 1991; also Scott Boorman and Paul Levitt, *The Genetics of Altruism*. New York: Academic Press, 1980, p. 16; Shaw and Wong, *Genetic Seeds of Warfare, Evolution, Nationalism and Patriotism*, pp. 38–9.

22. Colin Irwin, 'A study in the evolution of ethnocentrism', in Reynolds, Falger, and I. Vine, *The Sociobiology of Ethnocentrism*, pp. 131–56; G. R. S. Johnson, H. Ratwil, and T. J. Sawyer, 'The evocative significance of kin terms in patriotic speech', ibid., pp. 157–74.

23. Sigmund Freud, 'Group psychology and the analysis of the ego', (1921) in *The Complete Psychological Works of Sigmund Freud*, Vol. 18, pp. 101–4; id., 'Civilization and its discontents', (1930), ibid., Vol. 21, pp. 108–16.

24. The so-called Lanchester law is of course only a rough indication: Frederick Lanchester, 'Mathematics in warfare', in J. Newman (ed.), *The World of Mathematics*, Vol. 4. New York: Simon & Schuster, 1956, pp. 2138–57. More

generally see: Peter Corning, *Nature's Magic: Synergy in evolution and the fate of humankind*. New York: Cambridge University Press, 2003.

25. Mancur Olson, *The Logic of Collective Action: Public goods and the theory of groups*. Cambridge, MA: Harvard University Press, 1965.

26. Again, this key concept was developed in another classic: Robert L. Trivers, 'The evolution of reciprocal altruism', *Quarterly Review of Biology*, 1971; **46**: 35–57. It had been suggested in: Darwin, *The Descent of Man*, Chapter v, pp. 499–500.

27. Robert L. Trivers, 'The evolution of reciprocal altruism', *Quarterly Review of Biology*, 1971; **46**: 35–57. Developed by: Richard Alexander, *The Biology of Moral Systems*. New York: Aldine, 1987, pp. 77, 85, 93–4, 99–110, 117–26, *passim*; Robert Frank, *Passions within Reason: The strategic role of the emotions*. New York: Norton, 1988; Matt Ridley, *The Origins of Virtue: Human instincts and the evolution of cooperation*. New York: Viking, 1996; also James Wilson, *The Moral Sense*. New York: Free Press, 1993; de Waal, *Good Natured*.

28. Harry Lourandos, *Continent of Hunter-Gatherers: New perspectives in Australian prehistory*. Cambridge: Cambridge University Press, 1979, p. 38.

29. The leading authority on the genetic diversity of human populations in relation to humanity's lingual diversity is Cavalli-Sforza. See most notably: L. Luca Cavalli-Sforza, Paolo Menozzi, and Alberto Piazza, *The History and Geography of Human Genes*. Princeton, NJ: Princeton University Press, 1994.

30. Sumner, *Folkway*, pp. 27–9. For the biological underpinning see: Pierre van der Berghe, *The Ethnic Phenomenon*. New York: Elsevier, 1981; Reynolds, Falger, and Vine, *The Sociobiology of Ethnocentrism*; Shaw and Wong, *Genetic Seeds of Warfare, Evolution, Nationalism and Patriotism*; also Daniel Druckman, 'Social-psychological aspects of nationalism', in J. L. Comaroff and P. C. Stern (eds), *Perspectives on Nationalism and War*. Luxemburg: Gordon & Breach, 1995, pp. 47–98; Paul Stern, 'Why do people sacrifice for their nations?', in J. L. Comaroff and P. C. Stern (eds), *Perspectives on Nationalism and War*. Luxemburg: Gordon & Breach, 1995, pp. 99–121; Tatu Vanhansen, *Ethnic Conflicts Explained by Ethnic Nepotism*. Stamford, CT: JAI, 1999. Again see Darwin, *The Descent of Man*, Chapter vi, p. 492.

31. Wendel Oswalt, *Alaskan Eskimos*. San Francisco, CA: Chandler, 1967, p. xi.

32. Napoleon Chagnon, 'Yanomamo social organization and warfare', in M. Fried, M. Harris, and R. Murphy (eds), *War: The anthropology of armed conflict and aggression*. Garden City, NY: Natural History, 1968, pp. 128–9.

33. The comeback, in a greatly modified form, has been ushered in by no other than the pioneer of the 'gene-level' view of evolution: Hamilton, 'Innate social aptitudes of man'. Further, see Boorman and Levitt, *The Genetics of Altruism*; David S. Wilson, *The Natural Selection of Populations and Communities*. Cummings Menlo Park, CA: Benjamin, 1980; David S. Wilson and E. Sober,

'Reintroducing group selection to the human behavioral sciences', *Behavioral and Brain Sciences*, 1994; **17**: 585–654; id., *Unto Others: The evolution and psychology of unselfish behavior*. Cambridge, MA: Harvard University Press, 1998; also Y. Peres and M. Hopp, 'Loyalty and aggression in human groups', in J. M. G. van der Dennen and V. Falger (eds), *Sociobiology and Conflict*. London: Chapman, 1990, pp. 123–30. Darwin suggested the idea in *The Descent of Man*, Chapter v, pp. 496–500, and it was commonly held by late nineteenth- and early twentieth-century evolutionists, for example: William McDougal (1915) 'The instinct of pugnancy', reprinted in L. Bramson and G. Goethals (eds), *War: Studies from psychology, sociology, anthropology*. New York: Basic Books, 1964, pp. 37–41.

34. Hamilton, 'Innate social aptitudes of man'; Umberto Melotti, 'In-group/out-group relations and the issue of group selection', in Van der Dennen and Falger, *Sociobiology and Conflict*, p. 109; Irwin Silberman, 'Inclusive fitness and ethnocentrism', ibid., pp. 113–17. Again for the so-called fraternal interest groups: Velzen and Wetering, 'Residence, power groups and intra-societal aggression'; Otterbein and Otterbein, 'An eye for an eye, a tooth for a tooth'; Otterbein, 'Internal war: a cross-cultural comparison'; Karen Paige and Jeffery Paige, *The Politics of Reproductive Ritual*. Berkeley, CA: University of California, 1981.

35. The notion that larger and stronger grouping was of prominent significance in human evolution dominated by intergroup fighting was promoted by Herbert Spencer, and more recently it has been suggested by: R. D. Alexander and D. W. Tinkle, 'Review', *Biosense*, 1968; **18**: 245–8; R. D. Alexander, 'In search of an evolutionary philosophy of man', *Proceedings of the Royal Society of Victoria, Melbourne*, 1971; **84**: 99–120; id., *The Biology of Moral Systems*. New York: Aldine, 1987, p. 79, *passim*; it was central to: Robert Bigelow, *The Dawn Warriors: Man's evolution towards peace*. Boston, MA: Little Brown, 1969; also Hamilton, 'Innate social aptitudes of man', p. 146; Darius Baer and Donald McEachron, 'A review of selected sociobiological principles: Application to hominid evolution', *Journal of Social and Biological Structures*, 1982; **5**: 69–90, 121–39; Shaw and Wong, *Genetic Seeds of Warfare, Evolution, Nationalism and Patriotism*. None of these authors placed this development in any specific evolutionary context or prehistorical chronology, and most were not careful to differentiate between biological and cultural evolution. Only Vine mentions an idea similar to mine: Ian Vine, 'Inclusive fitness and the self-system', in Reynolds, Falger, and Vine, *The Sociobiology of Ethnocentrism*, pp. 67–8.

36. Jared Diamond, *The Rise and Fall of the Third Chimpanzee*. London: Vintage, 1992, pp. 44–8.

37. Azar Gat, 'Social organization, group conflict and the demise of the Neanderthals', *The Mankind Quarterly*, 1999; **39**: 437–54.

38. The role of evolutionary byproducts of adaptive design were famously laid out in: S. G. Gould and R. C. Lewontin, 'The spandrels of San Marco and the

panglossian program: A critique of the adaptionist programme', *Proceedings of the Royal Society of London*, 1979; **250**: 281–8.

39. This old idea was first formulated in these terms in: Dawkins, *The Selfish Gene*, pp. 189–201, 329–31; it was developed in: Pascal Boyer, *Religion Explained: The evolutionary origins of religious thought*. New York: Basic Books, 2001. A religiously based critique that, however, covers much of the relevant literature is: John Bowker, *Is God a Virus: Genes, culture and religion*. London: SPCK, 1995.

40. Dawkins, *The Selfish Gene*, p. 331. For religion as an evolutionarily useful illusion, see also Wilson, *On Human Nature*, pp. 169–93.

41. Ideas in this direction, which fail, however, even to note the effect on warfare are suggested in: H. Martin Wobst, 'Locational relationships in Paleolithic society', *Journal of Human Evolution*, 1976; **5**: 49–58; Geoff Bailey, 'Editorial', in G. Bailey (ed.), *Hunter–Gatherer Economy in Prehistory: A European perspective*. Cambridge: Cambridge University Press, 1983, pp. 187–90; and Clive Gamble, 'Culture and society in the Upper Palaeolithic of Europe', in Bailey, *Hunter-Gatherer Economy in Prehistory*, pp. 201–11. Lourandos applies this model to the Australian Aborigines without even mentioning the conflict significance of the 'alliances': Lourandos, *Continent of Hunter-Gatherers*, pp. 25–8, 38–9. After the original publication of the above in article form, there appeared an excellent specialized book on this subject, with which I am entirely in agreement: David S. Wilson, *Darwin's Cathedral: Evolution, religion, and the nature of society*. Chicago: University of Chicago, 2002; surprisingly, although perceptively pointing out the benefits of religion in fostering co-operation, Wilson overlooks the military aspect.

Chapter 4. Motivation: Food and Sex

1. See, for example, Abraham Maslow, *Motivation and Personality*. New York: Harper, 1970(1954); also J. Burton (ed.), *Conflict: Human needs theory*. London: Macmillan, 1990.

2. A survey and bibliography of the protracted 'protein controversy' by one of the chief protagonists can be found in: Marvin Harris, 'A cultural materialist theory of band and village warfare: The Yanomamo test', in R. B. Ferguson (ed.), *Warfare, Culture and Environment*. Orlando, FL: Academic Press, 1984, pp. 111–40. Also on the frustrations of the ecological/materialist approach by one of its chief proponents and authority on highland New Guinea warfare: Andrew Vayda, *War in Ecological Perspective*. New York: Plenum, 1976, pp. 1–7.

3. This is demonstrated in Harris's many remarkable books. The most systematic articulation of the theory is: Marvin Harris, *Cultural Materialism*. New York: Random House, 1979.

4. Napoleon A. Chagnon, 'Male competition, favoring close kin, and village

fissioning among the Yanomamo Indians', in N. Chagnon and W. Irons (eds), *Evolutionary Biology and Human Social Behavior*. North Scitnate, MA: Duxbury, 1979, pp. 86–132; id., 'Is reproductive success equal in egalitarian societies?' in N. Chagnon and W. Irons (eds), *Evolutionary Biology and Human Social Behavior*. North Scitnate, MA: Duxbury, 1979, pp. 374–401; id., 'Life histories, blood revenge and warfare in a tribal population', *Science*, 1988; **239**: 985–92.

5. Clark McCauley, 'Conference overview', in J. Haas (ed.), *The Anthropology of War*. New York: Cambridge University Press, 1990, p. 3.

6. Ibid.; R. Brian Ferguson, *Yanomami Warfare*. Santa Fe, NM: School of American Research, 1995, pp. 358–9.

7. For other typical misconceptions see my exchange with Ferguson: R. Brian Ferguson, 'The causes and origins of "primitive warfare": on evolved motivations for war', *Anthropological Quarterly*, 2000; **73**: 159–64; Azar Gat, 'Reply', *Anthropological Quarterly*, 2000; **73**: 165–8.

8. This point was brought home to Chagnon by: Richard Alexander, *The Biology of Moral Systems*. New York: Aldine, 1987. See Chagnon, 'Life histories, blood revenge and warfare in a tribal population'; id., 'Reproductive and somatic conflicts of interest in the genesis of violence and warfare among tribesmen', in J. Haas (ed.), *The Anthropology of War*. New York: Cambridge University Press, 1990, pp. 77–104.

9. R. Brian Ferguson, 'Introduction', in *Warfare, Culture and Environment*, pp. 38–41; id. 'Northwest coast warfare', ibid., pp. 269–71, 308–10, *passim*; id., 'Explaining war', in J. Haas (ed.), *The Anthropology of War*. New York: Cambridge: Cambridge University Press, 1990, pp. 26–55; id., *Yanomami Warfare*, pp. xii, 8–13, *passim*.

10. Ferguson, 'Explaining war', pp. 54–55; Ferguson, *Yanomami Warfare*, p. 8.

11. Perhaps the best discussion of this point is in: John Tooby and Leda Cosmides, 'The psychological foundations of culture', in L. Cosmides, J. Tooby, and J. Barkow (eds), *The Adapted Mind: Evolutionary psychology and the generation of culture*. New York: Oxford University Press, 1992.

12. William Graham Sumner, 'War' (1911), reprinted from *War and Other Essays*, in L. Bramson and G. Goethals (eds), *War: Studies from psychology, sociology, anthropology*. New York: Basic Books, 1964, p. 212; id., *Folkways*. New York: Mentor, 1960(1906), para. 22; followed by: Maurice Davie, *The Evolution of War*. New Haven, CT: Yale University Press, 1929, p. 65. See also Walter Goldschmidt, 'Inducement to military participation in tribal societies', in R. Rubinstein and M. Foster (eds), *The Social Dynamics of Peace and Conflict*. Boulder, CO: Westview, 1988, pp. 47–65.

13. Charles Darwin, *The Descent of Man*, Chapter 2, in *The Origin of Species and The Descent of Man*. New York: Modern Library, n.d., pp. 428–30.

14. In principle, this has been well noted, relying on the evolutionary rationale, by: William Durham 'Resource competition and human aggression. Part I: A

review of primitive war', *Quarterly Review of Biology*, 1976; **51**: 385–415; R. Dyson-Hudson and E. Alden Smith, 'Human territoriality: An ecological reassessment', *American Anthropologist*, 1978; **80**: 21–41; Doyne Dawson, 'The origins of war: Biological and anthropological theories', *History and Theory*, 1996; **35**: 25.

15. M. J. Meggitt, *Desert People*. Chicago: University of Chicago, 1965, p. 42.

16. For the expectation of stress as a strong promoter of war and anticipating action, see M. Ember and C. R. Ember, 'Resource unpredictability, mistrust, and war: A cross-cultural study', *Journal of Conflict Resolution*, 1992; **36**: 242–62; also W. D. Hamilton, 'Innate social aptitude of man: An approach from evolutionary genetics', in R. Fox (ed.), *Biosocial Anthropology*. New York: John Wiley, 1975, p. 146.

17. Harry Lourandos, *Continent of Hunter-Gatherers: New perspectives in Australian prehistory*. Cambridge: Cambridge University Press, 1997, p. 33.

18. Dyson-Hudson and Smith, 'Human territoriality'.

19. Again see a survey and bibliography in Harris, 'A cultural materialist theory of band and village warfare'; Napoleon Chagnon, *Yanomamo: The fierce people*, 2nd edn. New York: Holt, 1977, p. 33. Chagnon himself admits that humans, like other animals, fill up new ecological niches, rapidly approaching these niches' carrying capacity of life-sustaining material resources; in stark contradiction to his general argument, he concedes that somatic conflict is then the norm: Chagnon, 'Reproductive and somatic conflicts of interest', pp. 87–9.

20. Lawrence Keeley, *War before Civilization*. New York: Oxford University Press, 1996, pp. 109–10.

21. W. W. Newcomb, 'A re-examination of the causes of Plains warfare', *American Anthropologist*, 1950; **52**: 325; Thomas Biolsi, 'Ecological and cultural factors in Plain Indian warfare', in Ferguson *Warfare, Culture and Environment*, pp. 148–50.

22. Charles Darwin, *The Descent of Man*, Chapter 2, in *The Origin of Species and The Descent of Man*. New York: Modern Library, n.d., pp. 428–30; Konrad Lorenz, *On Aggression*. London: Methuen, 1966; Robert Ardrey, *The Territorial Imperative*. New York: Atheneum, 1966; Niko Tinbergen, 'On war and peace in animals and men', *Science*, 1968; **160**: 1411–18; Felicity Huntingford and Angela Turner, *Animal Conflict*. London: Chapman, 1987, pp. 229–30, 233–7; Charles Mueller, 'Environmental stressors and aggressive behaviour', in R. G. Geen and E. I. Donnerstein (eds), *Aggression*, Vol. ii. New York: Academic Press, 1983, pp. 63–6; Keeley, *War before Civilization*, pp. 118–19; Frans de Waal, *Good Natured: The origins of right and wrong in humans and other animals*. Cambridge, MA: Harvard University Press, 1996, pp. 194–6.

23. See, for example, Donald Symons, *The Evolution of Human Sexuality*. New York: Oxford University Press, 1979; Martin Daly and Margo Wilson, *Sex, Evolution,*

and Behavior. Boston, MA: Willard Grant, 1983; Matt Ridley, *The Red Queen: Sex and the evolution of human nature.* New York: Macmillan, 1994.

24. Chagnon, *Yanomamo: The fierce people*, pp. 123, 146 (quote); McCauley, 'Conference overview', p. 5; Ferguson, *Yanomami Warfare*, pp. 355–8, *passim*.

25. For my exchange with Ferguson, see Ferguson, 'The causes and origins of "primitive warfare" ' and Gat, 'Reply'.

26. Darwin, *The Descent of Man*, Chapter xix, p. 871.

27. John Morgan, *The Life and Adventures of William Buckley: Thirty-two years a wanderer among the Aborigines of the unexplored country round Port Philip.* Canberra: Australian National University Press, 1980(1852), citations from pp. 41, 68, but see throughout pp. 42, 59, 70, 74, 76, 81, 96.

28. Rhys Jones, 'Tasmanian tribes', in N. Tindale (ed.), *Aboriginal Tribes of Australia.* Berkeley, CA: University of California, 1974, p. 328.

29. These figures need some adjustment for age, because a few of the younger men who still had only one wife would acquire a second one or more in time. This adjustment, however, affects the overall picture only slightly. Extensive statistics can be found in: M. J. Meggitt, 'Marriage among the Walbiri of Central Australia: A statistical examination', in R. M. Berndt and C. H. Berndt (eds), *Aboriginal Man in Australia.* Sydney: Angus & Robertson, 1965, pp. 146–59; Jeremy Long, 'Polygyny, acculturation and contact: Aspects of Aboriginal marriage in Central Australia', in R. M. Berndt (ed.), *Australian Aboriginal Anthropology.* Nedland: University of Western Australia, 1970, p. 293.

30. Morgan, *The Life and Adventures of William Buckley*, p. 58; C. W. M. Hart and Arnold Pilling, *The Tiwi of North Australia.* New York: Holt, Reinhart & Winston, 1964, pp. 17, 18, 50; Meggitt, *Desert People*, p. 78; R. M. Berndt and C. H. Berndt, *The World of the First Australians.* London: Angus & Robertson, 1964, p. 172; I. Keen, 'How some Murngin men marry ten wives', *Man*, 1982; **17**: 620–42; Harry Lournados, 'Palaeopolitics: Resource intensification in Aboriginal Australia and Papua New Guinea', in T. Ingold, D. Riches, and J. Woodburn (eds), *Hunter and Gatherers*, Vol. i. New York: Berg, 1988, pp. 151–2.

31. See, for example, Meggitt, *Desert People*, pp. 80–1.

32. Daly and Wilson, *Sex, Evolution, and Behavior*, pp. 88–9, 332–3; Symons, *The Evolution of Human Sexuality*, p. 143; Chagnon, *Evolutionary Biology and Human Social Behavior*, p. 380.

33. Laura Betzig, 'Comment', *Current Anthropology*, 1991; **32**: 410.

34. Daly and Wilson, *Sex, Evolution, and Behavior*, p. 285.

35. This is ignored by Bruce Knauft, 'Violence and sociality in human evolution', *Current Anthropology*, 1991; **32**: 391–428, whose account of simple hunter–gatherers is exclusively based on the Eskimos and particularly the Kalahari Bushmen (but see the comments on his article by L. Betzig, R. K. Denton, and

L. Rodseth). As we see later, Knauft exaggerates the egalitarian nature of simple hunter–gatherers to the point of naïvety. Turning the differences of degree between simple and complex hunter–gatherers into a schism, he ties himself in strange knots: he in effect rules out any somatic or reproductive competition among simple hunter–gatherers; consequently, although fully recognizing that they too have very high violent mortality rates, he attributes them in their case to wholly expressive 'sexual frustration'. In fact, not only is polygyny practised by the few in most of these societies, but there is strong competition over the 'quality' of the wife that one can get, and constant conflict over wife stealing, adultery, and broken promises of marriage.

36. Mildred Dickemann, 'Female infanticide, reproductive strategies, and social stratification: a preliminary model', in N. Chagnon and W. Irons (eds), *Evolutionary Biology and Human Social Behavior*. North Scitnate, MA: Duxbury, 1979, p. 363; Symons, *The Evolution of Human Sexuality*, p. 152; Martin Daly and Margo Wilson, *Homicide*. New York: Aldine, 1988, p. 222 (quotation), citing A. Balikci, *The Netsilik Eskimo*. Garden City, NY: Natural History, 1970, p. 182; C. Irwin, 'The Inuit and the evolution of limited group conflict', in J. van der Dennen and V. Falger (eds), *Sociobiology and Conflict*. London: Chapman, 1990, pp. 201–2; E. W. Nelson, *The Eskimo about Bering Strait*. Washington, DC: Smithsonian, 1983(1899), pp. 292, 327–9; Wendel Oswalt, *Alaskan Eskimos*. San Francisco, CA: Chandler, 1967, pp. 178, 180, 182, 185, 187, 204; Ernest Burch and T. Correll, 'Alliance and conflict: inter-regional relations in North Alaska', in L. Guemple (ed.), *Alliance in Eskimo Society*. Seattle: University of Washington, 1972, p. 33.

37. Betzig, 'Comment', p. 410.

38. Abraham Rosman and Paula Rubel, *Feasting with the Enemy: Rank and exchange among Northwest Coast societies*. New York: Columbia University Press, 1971 pp. 16–17, 32, 110; Philip Drucker, *The Northern and Central Nootkan Tribes*. Washington, DC: Smithsonian Institute, 1951, p. 301; id., *Cultures of the North Pacific Coast*. San Francisco, CA: Chandler, 1965, p. 54; Aurel Krause, *The Tlingit Indians*. Seattle: University of Washington, 1970(1885), p. 154; Leland Donald, *Aboriginal Slavery on the Northwest Coast of North America*. Berkeley, CA: University of California, 1997, p. 73.

39. Brian Hayden, 'Competition, labor, and complex hunter-gatherers', in E. S. Burch and L. S. Ellanna (eds), *Key Issues in Hunter-Gatherer Research*. Oxford: Berg, 1994, pp. 223–42.

40. Biolsi, 'Ecological and cultural factors in Plain Indian warfare', pp. 159–60; for northern Australia see Jones, 'Tasmanian tribes', p. 328.

41. Mervin Meggitt, *Blood Is Their Argument: Warfare among the Mae Enga of the New Guinea Highlands*. Palo Alto, CA: Mayfield, 1977, pp. 182–3.

42. Ibid., p. 111; C. R. Hallpike, *Bloodshed and Vengeance in the Papuan Mountains*. Oxford: Oxford University Press, 1977, pp. 122–6, 129, 135–6.

43. Hart and Pilling, *The Tiwi of North Australia*, pp. 18, 50.

44. Oswalt, *Alaskan Eskimos*, p. 178. Also Ernest Burch, 'Eskimo warfare in North-west Alaska', *Anthropological Papers of the University of Alaska*, 1974; **16**(2): 1–14.

45. Chagnon, *Evolutionary Biology and Human Social Behavior*, pp. 385–401; Ian Keen, 'Yolngu religious property', in T. Ingold, D. Riches, and J. Woodburn (eds), *Hunter and Gatherers*. New York: Berg, 1988, p. 290.

46. Keith Otterbein, *Feuding and Warfare*. Longhorne, PA: Gordon & Breach, 1994, p. 103.

47. William Divale, 'Systemic population control in the Middle and Upper Palaeolithic: Inferences based on contemporary hunter-gatherers', *World Archaeology*, 1972; **4**: 222–43; William Divale and Marvin Harris, 'Population, warfare and the male supremacist complex', *American Anthropologist*, 1976; **78**: 521–38; Lorimer Fison and A. W. Holt, *Kamilaroi and Kurnai*. Oosterhout, The Netherlands: Anthropological Publications, 1967(1880), pp. 173, 176; Dickemann, 'Female infanticide, reproductive strategies, and social stratification', pp. 363–4; Christopher Boehm, *Blood Revenge: The anthropology of feuding in Montenegro and other tribal societies*. Lawrence: University of Kansas, 1984, p. 177.

48. Meggitt, 'Marriage among the Walbiri of Central Australia', pp. 149–50.

49. W. Lloyd Warner, 'Murngin warfare', *Oceania*, 1930–1; **1**: 479, 481.

50. Dickemann, 'Female infanticide, reproductive strategies, and social stratification', p. 364; slightly different (and inconsistent) figures in Marvin Harris, 'Primitive war', in *Cows, Pigs, Wars and Witches*. New York: Random House, 1974, p. 69.

51. Frank Livingstone, 'The effects of warfare on the biology of the human species', in M. Fried, M. Harris, and R. Murphy (eds), *War: The anthropology of armed conflict and aggression*. Garden City, NY: Natural History, 1967, p. 9.

52. Richard Lee, 'Politics, sexual and non-sexual, in egalitarian society', in R. Lee and E. Leacock (eds), *Politics and History in Band Societies*. New York: Cambridge University Press, 1982, p. 44; for the 7–15 year difference in marriage age between males and females among the Bushmen: p. 42.

53. Divale, 'Systemic population control in the Middle and Upper Palaeolithic'; Divale and Harris, 'Population, warfare and the male supremacist complex', pp. 527–30.

54. R. D. Alexander, J. L. Hoogland, R. D. Howard, K. M. Noonan, and P. W. Sherman, 'Sexual dimorphisms and breeding systems in pinnipeds, ungulates, primates, and humans', in N. Chagnon and W. Irons (eds), *Evolutionary Biology and Human Social Behavior*. North Scitnate, MA: Duxbury, 1979, pp. 414–16; Daly and Wilson, *Sex, Evolution, and Behavior*, pp. 189–95.

55. Steve Jones, *The Language of the Genes*. New York: Anchor, 1993, p. 92. Daly and Wilson, *Sex, Evolution, and Behavior*, pp. 92–7, 297–301.

56. Studies are summarized in: M. Baker (ed.), *Sex Differences in Human Performance*. Chichester: Wiley, 1987, especially pp. 109–10, 117, 127, 136–7, 180; also Symons, *The Evolution of Human Sexuality*, p. 142; Marvin Harris, *Our Kind*. New York: Harper, 1990, pp. 277–81.

57. In the psychological research this attitude dominated: S. Maccoby (ed.), *The Development of Sex Differences*. Stanford: Stanford University Press, 1966.

58. Support for this view with respect to war from a sociobiological point of view is offered in the intriguing but overdrawn book: Richard Wrangham and Dale Peterson, *Demonic Males: Apes and the origins of human violence*. London: Bloomsbury, 1997; for works in this vein see p. 284, n. 53; also the works cited in: Wendy Chapkins, 'Sexuality and militarism', in E. Isaksson (ed.), *Women and the Military Service*, New York: St Martin's Press, 1988, p. 106; Barbara Ehrenreich, *Blood Rites: Origins and history of the passions of war*. New York: Metropolitan, 1997, pp. 125–31.

59. Studies are summarized in R. M. Rose et al., 'Androgens and aggression: A review of recent findings in primates', in R. Holloway (ed.), *Primate Aggression, Territoriality, and Xenophobia*. New York: Academic Press, 1974, pp. 276–304; E. E. Maccoby and C. N. Jacklin, *The Psychology of Sex Differences*. Palo Alto, CA: Stanford University Press, 1974; Luigi Valzelli, *Psychobiology of Aggression and Violence*. New York: Raven, 1981, pp. 116–21; Anne Moir and David Jessel, *Brain Sex: The real difference between men and women*. New York: Lyle Stuart, 1991; Daly and Wilson, *Sex, Evolution, and Behavior*, pp. 258–66; Huntingford and Turner, *Animal Conflict*, pp. 95–128, 339–41; J. Herbert, 'The physiology of aggression', in J. Groebel and R. A. Hinde (eds), *Aggression and War*. Cambridge: Cambridge University Press, 1989, pp. 58–71; Marshall Segal, 'Cultural factored biology and human aggression', in J. Groebel and R. A. Hinde (eds), *Aggression and War*. Cambridge: Cambridge University Press, 1989, pp. 173–85; Ridley, *The Red Queen*, pp. 247–63; James Wilson, *The Moral Sense*. New York: Free Press, 1993, pp. 165–90.

60. Lee, 'Politics, sexual and non-sexual, in egalitarian society', p. 44.

61. Daly and Wilson, *Sex, Evolution, and Behavior*, pp. 266; Wrangham and Peterson, *Demonic Males*, pp. 113, 115; Segal, 'Cultural factored biology and human aggression', pp. 177–8; David Jones, *Women Warriors: A history*. Washington, DC: Brassey, 1997, p. 4.

62. Wrangham and Peterson, *Demonic Males*, p. 115, based on Daly and Wilson, *Homicide*, pp. 145–9. Denmark is the exception with 85 per cent for the males, but omitting infanticide the figure rises to 100 per cent.

63. Huntingford and Turner, *Animal Conflict*, pp. 332–3; K. Bjorkqvist and P. Niemela (eds), *Of Mice and Women: Aspects of female aggression*. Orlando, FL: Academic Press, 1992; Kirsti Lagerspetz and Kaj Bjorkqvist, 'Indirect aggression in boys and girls', in L. R. Huesmann (ed.), *Aggressive Behavior: Current perspectives*. New York: Plenum, 1994, pp. 131–50.

64. See especially Symons, *The Evolution of Human Sexuality*; Ridley, *The Red Queen*; de Waal, *Good Natured*, pp. 117–25. Darwin's (sharp) distinction in 'Sexual selection in relation to man' may be too Victorian for our taste: *The Descent of Man*, Chapter xix, pp. 867–73.

65. Lionel Tiger, *Men in Groups*. New York: Random House, 1969, pp. 80–92; Wrangham and Peterson, *Demonic Males*. For a few known cases of women's participation in warfare in tribal societies see Davie, *The Evolution of War*, pp. 30–6; David Adams, 'Why there are so few women warriors', *Behaviour Science Research*, 1983; **18**: 196–212; Goldschmidt, 'Inducement to military participation in tribal societies', p. 57.

66. For an even more 'egalitarian' argument in this respect, see R. Paul Shaw and Yuwa Wong, *Genetic Seeds of Warfare: Evolution, nationalism and patriotism*. Boston: Unwin Hyman, 1989, pp. 179–80.

67. Timothy Taylor, 'Thracians, Scythians, and Dacians, 800 BC–AD 300', in B. Cunliffe (ed.), *The Oxford Illustrated Prehistory of Europe*. Oxford: Oxford University Press, 1994, pp. 395–7.

68. Stanley Alpern, *Amazons of Black Sparta: The warriors of Dahomey*. New York: New York University Press, 1998.

69. See N. Goldman (ed.), *Female Soldiers—Combatants or noncombatants?* Westport, CT: Greenwood, 1982, especially pp. 5, 73, 90, 99; scholarly inferior and uneven is E. Isaksson (ed.), *Women and the Military Service*. New York: St Martin's Press, 1988, but see especially pp. 52–9, 171–7, 204–8; Jones's anecdotal and scholarly shaky *Women Warriors* (1997) throughout corroborates the traditional picture of the limits of women's participation in warfare, which he sets out to refute.

70. Alpern, *Amazons of Black Sparta*.

71. Matt Ridley, *The Origins of Virtue: Human instincts and the evolution of cooperation*. New York: Viking, 1996, p. 93.

72. Annemiek Bolscher and Ine Megens, 'The Netherlands', in Isaksson, *Women and the Military Service*, pp. 359–69; Ellen Elster, 'Norway', ibid., pp. 371–3.

73. Since the original publication of this section in article form, many more works on the subject have appeared, including, most comprehensively: Michael Ghiglieri, *The Dark Side of Man: Tracing the origins of male violence*. Cambridge, MA: Perseus, 2000; Joshua Goldstein, *War and Gender: How the gender shapes the war system and vice versa*. New York: Cambridge University Press, 2001; Martin van Creveld, *Man, Women and War*. London: Cassell, 2001. All three books present more or less the same data and arrive at similar conclusions to mine. However, Ghiglieri's is the only one that is based on the evolutionary rationale, whereas the other two recognize the biology but overlook the evolutionary process that has shaped this biology. The deeper source of the sex differences

thus remain something of a mystery, ultimately reduced in Van Creveld's book to playful male pugnacity.

Chapter 5. Motivation: The Web of Desire

1. Jane Goodall, *The Chimpanzees of Gombe*. Cambridge, MA: Belknap Press, 1986; Frans de Waal, *Good Natured: The origins of right and wrong in humans and other animals*. Cambridge, MA: Harvard University Press, 1996.

2. Elman Service, *Primitive Social Organization*. New York: Random House, 1962; Morton Fried, *The Evolution of Political Society*. New York: Random House, 1967; Allen Johnson and Timothy Earle, *The Evolution of Human Societies: From foraging group to agrarian state*. Stanford: Stanford University Press, 1987.

3. Richard Lee, 'Politics, sexual and non-sexual, in egalitarian society', in R. Lee and E. Leacock (eds), *Politics and History in Band Societies*. New York: Cambridge University Press, 1982, pp. 45–50. Knauft conveniently ignores this article, so devastating to his (and Lee's own) concept, in his naïve portrayal of simple hunter–gatherers, largely based on the !Kung: Bruce Knauft, 'Violence and sociality in human evolution', *Current Anthropology*, 1991; **32**: 391–428. For the group leaders in Tasmania (the simplest hunter–gatherers on record), all mature men and 'formidable hunters and fighters', see Rhys Jones, 'Tasmanian tribes', in N. Tindale (ed.), *Aboriginal Tribes of Australia*. Berkeley, CA: University of California, 1974, p. 327.

4. John Morgan, *The Life and Adventures of William Buckley: Thirty-two years a wanderer among the Aborigines of the unexplored country round Port Philip*. Canberra: Australian National University Press, 1980(1852), p. 72.

5. Indeed, in modern societies as well, slights to honour outweigh property as a cause of homicide: Martin Daly and Margo Wilson, *Homicide*. New York: Aldine, 1988, pp. 123–36.

6. For this widely noted theme, see especially Edward O. Wilson, *Sociobiology*. Cambridge, MA: Harvard University Press, 1975, pp. 279–97; also Donald Symons, *The Evolution of Human Sexuality*. New York: Oxford University Press, 1979, pp. 154–65; Daly and Wilson, *Homicide*, p. 135; de Waal, *Good Natured*; Robert Wright, *The Moral Animal*. New York: Vintage, 1995, pp. 248–9; Napoleon Chagnon, 'Reproductive and somatic conflicts of interest in the genesis of violence and warfare among tribesmen', in J. Haas (ed.), *The Anthropology of War*. New York: Cambridge University Press, 1990, pp. 93–5. Clark McCauley turns cause and effect on their heads: 'Conference overview', in Haas, *The Anthropology of War*, p. 20.

7. Originally see Charles Darwin, *The Descent of Man*, Chapter 3, in *The Origin of Species and The Descent of Man*. New York: Modern Library, n.d., pp. 467–8. Also, for example, Dobbi Low, 'Sexual selection and human ornamentation', in

N. Chagnon and W. Irons (eds), *Evolutionary Biology and Human Social Behavior*. North Scitnate, MA: Buxbury Press, 1979, pp. 462–87; Jared Diamond, *The Rise and Fall of the Third Chimpanzee*. London: Vintage, 1992, Chapter 9.

8. Napoleon Chagnon, 'Life histories, blood revenge and warfare in a tribal population', *Science*, 1988; **239**: 985–92. The article provoked several responses; for a bibliography of the debate see R. Brian Ferguson, *Yanomami Warfare*. Santa Fe, NM: School of American Research, 1995, pp. 359–61.

9. For this widely observed phenomenon, see especially: Lawrence Keeley, *War before Civilization*. New York: Oxford University Press, 1996, pp. 38, 99–103; Maurice Davie, *The Evolution of War*. New Haven, CT: Yale University Press, 1929, pp. 136–46; also Andrew Vayda, 'Iban headhunting', in his *War in Ecological Perspective*. New York: Plenum, 1976, pp. 43–74; Christopher Boehm, *Blood Revenge: The anthropology of feuding in Montenegro and other tribal societies*. Lawrence: University of Kansas, 1984.

10. Marian Smith, 'The war complex of the Plains Indians', *Proceedings of the American Philosophical Society*, 1938; **78**: 433, 452–3.

11. Bernard Mishkin, *Rank and Warfare among the Plains Indians*. Seattle: University of Washington, 1940, pp. 61–2; also W. W. Newcomb, 'A re-examination of the causes of Plains warfare', *American Anthropologist*, 1950; **52**: 319, 329.

12. Mishkin, *Rank and Warfare among the Plains Indians*, pp. 54–5. Goldschmidt's cross-cultural study notes the multiplicity of motives but not their interconnection: Walter Goldschmidt, 'Inducement to military participation in tribal societies', in R. Rubinstein and M. Foster (eds), *The Social Dynamics of Peace and Conflict*. Boulder, CO: Westview, 1988, pp. 47–65.

13. See Daly and Wilson, *Homicide*, pp. 221–51. Also for something along this line, see, for example: Vayda, 'Iban headhunting', p. 80; Chagnon, 'Life histories, blood revenge and warfare in a tribal population'; id., 'Reproductive and somatic conflicts of interest in the genesis of violence and warfare among tribesmen', in Haas, *The Anthropology of War*, pp. 98–101; McCauley, 'Conference overview', p. 20; de Waal, *Good Natured*, pp. 160–2. Boehm, *Blood Revenge*, especially pp. 51–5, 173, is not sufficiently aware of the interconnection between honour and deterrence, which he tends to treat separately.

14. W. D. Hamilton and Robert Axelrod, *The Evolution of Cooperation*. New York: Basic Books, 1984; in effect anticipated by: J. Maynard Smith and G. R. Price, 'The logic of animal conflicts', *Nature*, 1973; **246**: 15–18. For some modifications see endnote 17.

15. Ernest S. Burch and T. Correll, 'Alliance and conflict: Inter-regional relations in North Alaska', in L. Guemple (ed.), *Alliance in Eskimo Society*. Seattle: University of Washington, 1972, p. 34. Also E. S. Burch, 'Eskimo warfare in Northern Alaska', *Anthropological Papers of the University of Alaska*, 1974; **16**: 8, 11. For the Aborigines, see endnote 25, Chapter 2.

16. R. Brian Ferguson (ed.), 'A reexamination of the causes of northwest coast warfare', in *Warfare, Culture, and Environment*. Orlando, FL: Academic Press, 1984, p. 308.

17. For other 'adjusting' mechanisms for preventing 'tit for tat' from becoming a self-perpetuating process see: Robert Axelrod, *The Complexity of Cooperation*. Princeton, NJ: Princeton University Press, 1997, pp. 30–9; and the review in: Matt Ridley, *The Origins of Virtue: Human instincts and the evolution of cooperation*. New York: Viking, 1996, pp. 67–84.

18. M. Ember and C. R. Ember, 'Resource unpredictability, mistrust, and war: A cross-cultural study', *Journal of Conflict Resolution*, 1992; **36**: 242–62.

19. John Ewers, 'Intertribal warfare as the precursor of Indian–white warfare on the northern Great Plains', *The Western Historical Quarterly*, 1975; **6**: 397–8.

20. John Herz, 'Idealist internationalism and the security dilemma', *World Politics*, 1950; **2**: 157–80; Robert Jervis, 'Cooperation under the security dilemma', *World Politics*, 1978; **30**: 167–214.

21. R. Dawkins and J. R. Krebs, 'Arms races between and within species', *Proceedings of the Royal Society of London Bulletin*, 1979; **205**: 489–511.

22. Cited in: Edward Wilson, *On Human Nature*. Cambridge, MA: Harvard University Press, 1978, pp. 119–20.

23. This Hobbesian logic has been extensively developed with respect to anarchic state systems in: Kenneth Waltz, *Theory of International Politics*. Reading, MA: Addison, 1979.

24. The modern 'interpretative' explanation of religion is traced back to: Edward B. Tylor, *Primitive Culture*. London: John Murray, 1871; endorsed by Darwin, *The Descent of Man*, Chapter iii, pp. 468–70; also James Frazer, *The Golden Bough*. New York: Macmillan, 1922; R. Horton, 'African traditional thought and Western science', in B. Wilson (ed.), *Rationality*. Oxford: Blackwell, 1970, pp. 131–71; T. Luckmann, *The Invisible Religion*. New York: Macmillan, 1967; P. Berger, *The Social Reality of Religion*. Harmondsworth: Penguin, 1973; S. E. Guthrie, *Faces in the Clouds: A new theory of religion*. New York: Oxford University Press, 1993; Stuart Vyse, *Believing in Magic: The psychology of superstition*. New York: Oxford University Press, 1997. Emphasizing the manipulative element on top of the interpretative are: Emile Durkheim, *The Elementary Forms of Religious Life*. New York: Free Press, 1965, pp. 165ff, 476–7, 463–4; Bronislav Malinovski, *The Foundations of Faith and Morals*. London: Oxford University Press, 1936; id., *Magic, Science and Religion*. New York: Doubleday Anchor, 1954; also Terrence Deacon, *The Symbolic Species*. London: Penguin, 1997, especially pp. 416, 433–8; all in fact anticipated by Hobbes, *Leviathan*, Chapter 12. These references also apply to the next paragraph.

25. Here lies the main problem with Pascal Boyer, *Religion Explained: The*

evolutionary origins of religious thought. New York: Basic Books, 2001, as with all those who attempt to distinguish religious from scientific notions on the grounds that the latter are supposedly counterintuitive; most scientific ideas equally are.

26. See Chapter 3, pages 54–5.

27. Durkheim, *The Elementary Forms of Religious Life*; Malinovski, *The Foundations of Faith and Morals*; id., *Magic, Science and Religion*; A. R. Radcliffe-Brown, 'Religion and society', in *Structure and Function in Primitive Society*. London: Cohen & West, 1952, pp. 153–77, especially 161; Ridley, *The Origins of Virtue*, pp. 189–93.

28. For a similar idea see Johan van der Dennen, 'Ethnocentrism and in-group/out-group differentiation', in V. Reynolds, V. Falger, and I. Vine (eds), *The Sociobiology of Ethnocentrism*. London: Croom Helm, 1987, pp. 37–47.

29. Napoleon Chagnon, *Yanomamo: The fierce people*, 2nd edn. New York: Holt, 1977, p. 118.

30. Karl Heider, *The Dugum Dani*. Chicago: Aldine, 1970, pp. 130, 132.

31. Knauft, 'Violence and sociality in human evolution', p. 477.

32. M. G. Meggitt, *Desert People*. Chicago: University of Chicago, 1965, pp. 36, 43.

33. Paloa Villa et al. 'Cannibalism in the Neolithic', *Science*, 1986; **233**: 431–7; Tim White, *Prehistoric Cannibalism at Mancos*. Princeton, NJ: Princeton University Press, 1992; Alban Defleur, Tim White, Patricia Valensi, Ludovic Slimak, and Évelyne Crégut-Bonnoure, 'Neanderthal cannibalism at Moula-Guercy, Ardèche, France', *Science*, 1999; **286**: 128–31; and an excellent general survey in Keeley, *War before Civilization*, pp. 103–6.

34. P. Brown and D. Tuzin (eds), *The Ethnography of Cannibalism*. New York: The Society for Psychological Anthropology, 1983; also Peggy Reeves Sanday, *Divine Hunger: Cannibalism as a cultural system*. Cambridge: Cambridge University Press, 1986; Robert Carneiro, 'Chiefdom-level warfare as exemplified in Fiji and the Cauca Valley (Colombia)', in Haas, *The Anthropology of War*, pp. 194, 199, 202–7.

35. This was again perceptively noted in Davie's otherwise somewhat outdated treatment of cannibalism: Davie, *The Evolution of War*, pp. 65–6.

36. Morgan, *The Life and Adventures of William Buckley*, p. 190, also pp. 73, 97, 108. Thus, Meggitt's scepticism, cited above, would appear to be misplaced.

37. Marvin Harris, *Cultural Materialism*. New York: Random House, 1979, pp. 336–40; id., *Good to Eat: Riddles of food and culture*. New York: Simon & Schuster, 1985, pp. 199–234; id., *Our Kind*. New York: Harper, 1990, pp. 428–36; Michael Harner, 'The ecological basis for Aztec sacrifice', *American Ethnologist*, 1977; **4**: 117–35. The idea is not new; compare Davie, *The Evolution of War*, p. 68.

38. Compare B. Isaac, 'Aztec warfare: Goals and comportment', *Ethnology*, 1983; **22**: 121–31; Keeley, *War before Civilization*, pp. 105–6.

39. See Harris above; anticipated by Davie, *The Evolution of War*, p. 75.

40. Harris, *Our Kind*, pp. 428–30.

41. See, for example: Johan Huizinga, *Homo Ludens*. Boston: Beacon, 1955, *passim*, and with respect to war: pp. 89–104.

42. Robert Fagan, *Animal Play Behavior*. New York: Oxford University Press, 1981; also P. Smith (ed.), *Play in Animals and Humans*, Oxford: Blackwell, 1984; Felicity Huntingford and Angela Turner, *Animal Conflict*. London: Chapman, 1987, pp. 198–200.

43. Margaret Clark, 'The culture patterning of risk-seeking behavior: Implications for armed conflict', in M. Foster and R. Rubinstein (eds), *Peace and War: Cross-cultural perspectives*. New Brunswick, NJ: Transaction, 1986, pp. 79–90; this comes close to reversing the evolutionary order.

44. See endnote 22, Chapter 2 (first quotation).

45. For the use of narcotics before fighting, see, for example, Gilbert Lewis, 'Payback and ritual in war: New Guinea', in R. A. Hinde and H. E. Watson (eds), *War: A cruel necessity?* London: Tauris, 1995, pp. 34–5. Also on narcotics, dance, and ceremonies, as reinforcements: Goldschmidt, 'Inducement to military participation in tribal societies', pp. 51–2.

46. C. R. Hallpike, *The Principles of Social Evolution*. Oxford: Oxford University Press, 1986, pp. 113, 372.

47. Hallpike, *The Principles of Social Evolution*, pp. 101–13. For more on anthropologists' 'strange knots' see my exchange with Ferguson: B. Ferguson, 'The causes and origins of "primitive warfare": on evolved motivations for war', *Anthropological Quarterly*, 2000; **73**: 159–64; A. Gat, 'Reply', *Anthropological Quarterly*, 2000; **73**: 165–8.

Chapter 6. *'Primitive Warfare': How Was It Done?*

1. This has been well noted in: R. Pitt, 'Warfare and hominid brain evolution', *Journal of Theoretical Biology*, 1978; **72**: 551–75; Richard Wrangham and Dale Peterson, *Demonic Males: Apes and the origins of human violence*. London: Bloomsbury, 1997, pp. 159–62.

2. Adam Ferguson, *An Essay on the History of Civil Society*. Cambridge: Cambridge University Press, 1995(1767), p. 112. In the following, the French Colonel (drawing on the French experience against the nomads in Algeria) was probably the first to have made this pattern the cornerstone of his theory of war: C. J. J. J. Ardant du Pick, *Battle Studies*. Harrisburg, PA: The Military Service Publishing Co., 1947(1868). The concept was more or less generalized by

Quincy Wright, *A Study of War*. Chicago, University of Chicago, 1943; H. H. Turney-High, *Primitive Warfare*. Columbia, SC: University of South Carolina, 1949; Keith F. Otterbein, *The Evolution of War: A cross-cultural study*. New Haven, CT: HRAF, 1970, pp. 32, 39–40; and Christopher Boehm, *Blood Revenge: The anthropology of feuding in Montenegro and other tribal societies*. Lawrence: University of Kansas, 1984, pp. 202–27. The only good generalized account is: Lawrence Keeley, *War before Civilization*. New York: Oxford University Press, 1996, pp. 59–69.

3. Lloyd Warner, 'Murngin warfare', *Oceania*, 1930–1; **1**: 467; also in: id., *A Black Civilization*. New York: Harper, 1937.

4. Warner, 'Murngin warfare', p. 457–8.

5. See, for example, from works already cited: Gerald Wheeler, *The Tribe and Intertribal Relations in Australia*. London: John Murray, 1910, pp. 118–19, 141–5; it incorporates excellently the earliest anthropological works on the subject; M. J. Meggitt, *Desert People*. Chicago: University of Chicago, 1965, pp. 37–8, 42, 325–6; T. G. H. Strehlow, 'Totemic landscape', in R. M. Berndt (ed.), *Australian Aboriginal Anthropology*. Nedlands: University of Western Australia, 1970, pp. 124–5; A. Pilling, in R. B. Lee and I. DeVore (eds), *Man the Hunter*. Chicago: Aldine, 1968, p. 158; H. Ling Roth, *The Aborigines of Tasmania*. Halifax: F. King, 1899, p. 15.

6. John Morgan, *The Life and Adventures of William Buckley: Thirty-two years a wanderer among the aborigines of the unexplored country round Port Philip*. Canberra: Australian National University Press, 1980(1852), p. 189. For face-to-face battles see, for example, pp. 40, 41, 42, 49–50, 60, 68, 68–9, 76–7, 81, 82.

7. Aurel Krause, *The Tlingit Indians: Results of a trip to the Northwest Coast of America and the Bering Straits* (trans. Erna Gunther). Seattle: University of Washington, 1956, pp. 169–72.

8. Franz Boas, *Kwakiutl Ethnography*. Chicago: University of Chicago, 1966, pp. 108–10; see also Leland Donald, *Aboriginal Slavery on the Northwest Coast of North America*. Berkeley, CA: University of California, 1997, p. 27, and for the 'pleasing' women slaves, p. 73.

9. Philip Drucker, *The Northern and Central Nootkan Tribes*. Washington, DC: Smithsonian Institute, 1951, pp. 337–41; Philip Drucker, *Cultures of the North Pacific Coast*. San Francisco, CA: Chandler, 1965, pp. 75–81. For another brief summary of the same elements see: R. Brian Ferguson, 'Northwest Coast warfare', in id. (ed.), *Warfare Culture and the Environment*. Orlando, FL: Academic Press, 1984, p. 272.

10. E. W. Nelson, *The Eskimo about Bering Strait*. Washington, DC: Smithsonian Institute, 1983(1899), p. 327.

11. Wendell Oswalt, *Alaskan Eskimos*. San Francisco, CA: Chandler, 1967, pp. 185–8.

12. Ernest Burch, 'Eskimo warfare in Northwest Alaska', *Anthropological Papers of the University of Alaska*, 1974; **16**: especially pp. 2, 4.

13. Burch, 'Eskimo warfare in Northwest Alaska', pp. 10–11; also Nelson, *The Eskimo about Bering Strait*, pp. 328–9.

14. Robert Spencer, *The North Alaskan Eskimo*. Washington, DC: Smithsonian Institute, 1959, p. 72.

15. Marian Smith, 'The war complex of the Plains Indians', *Proceedings of the American Philosophical Society*, 1938; **78**: 436, 431.

16. Robert Mishkin, *Rank and Warfare among the Plains Indians*. Seattle: University of Washington, 1940, p. 2.

17. John Ewers, 'Intertribal warfare as the precursor of Indian–white warfare on the northern Great Plains', *The Western Historical Quarterly*, 1975; **6**: 401.

18. Frank Secoy, *Changing Military Patterns of the Great Plains Indians*. New York: Augustin, 1953, pp. 34–5. He (pp. 10–12) may have similarly erred with respect to the southern sedentary horticulturalists confronting the Spanish De Soto expedition in 1539–43. He speaks of an Indian 'massed infantry' battle of arrow fire and then shock. However, the more detailed descriptions that he himself cites, most notably those of the expedition itself, emphasize encirclement, ambush, dawn surprise attack, and the familiar line of fire rather than serious face-to-face fighting.

19. Napoleon Chagnon, *Yanomamo: The fierce people*, 2nd edn. New York: Holt, 1977, pp. 113–37; Walter Goldschmidt, 'Inducement to military participation in tribal societies', in R. Rubinstein and M. Foster (eds), *The Social Dynamics of Peace and Conflict*. Boulder, CO: Westview, 1988, pp. 49–50.

20. Chagnon, *Yanomamo: The fierce people*, p. 122.

21. Ibid., p. 40.

22. Ibid., pp. 78–9, 102–3.

23. See especially Andrew Vayda, *War in Ecological Perspective*. New York: Plenum, 1976, pp. 9–42; Ronald Berndt, *Excess and Restraint: Social conflict among a New Guinea mountain people*. Chicago: University of Chicago, 1962; Roy Rappaport, *Pigs for the Ancestors*. New Haven, CT: Yale University Press, 1967; K. Heider, *The Dugum Dani*. Chicago: Aldine, 1970; Klaus-Friedrich Koch, *War and Peace in Jalemo: The management of conflict in Highland New Guinea*. Cambridge, MA: Harvard University Press, 1974; Mervin Meggitt, *Blood is their Argument: Warfare among the Mae Enga tribesmen of the New Guinea Highlands*. Palo Alto, CA: Mayfield, 1977; C. R. Hallpike, *Bloodshed and Vengeance in the Papuan Mountains*. Oxford: Oxford University Press, 1977; Paula Brown, *Highland Peoples of New Guinea*. Cambridge: Cambridge University Press, 1978; Gilbert Lewis, 'Payback and ritual in war: New Guinea', in R. A. Hinde and H. E. Watson (eds), *War: A cruel necessity?* London: Tauris, 1995, pp. 24–36.

24. Quotations from Meggitt, *Blood is their Argument*, p. 17; Vayda, *War in Ecological Perspective*, p. 15; all authorities repeat the same words, however.

25. Vayda, *War in Ecological Perspective*, p. 23.

26. Keith Otterbein, 'Higi armed combat', in his *Feuding and Warfare*. Longhorne, PA: Gordon & Breach, 1994, pp. 75–96; Boehm, *Blood Revenge*.

27. Konrad Lorenz, *On Aggression*. London: Methuen, 1965(1963), pp. 206–9; Desmond Morris, *The Naked Ape*. London: Jonathan Cape, 1967, pp. 174–5.

28. J. Maynard Smith and G. R. Price, 'The logic of animal conflict', *Nature*, 1973; **246**: 15–18; Pitt, 'Warfare and hominid brain evolution', p. 571; Darius Baer and Donald McEachron, 'A review of selected sociobiological principles: Application to hominid evolution', *Journal of Social and Biological Structures*, 1982; **5**: 82; Matt Ridley, *The Origins of Virtue: Human instincts and the evolution of cooperation*. New York: Viking, 1996, pp. 164–5.

29. Warner, *A Black Civilization*, pp. 157–8; Pilling, in *Man the Hunter*, p. 158; R. G. Kimber, 'Hunter-gatherer demography: The recent past in Central Australia', in B. Meehan and N. White (eds), *Hunter-Gatherer Demography*. Sydney: University of Sydney, 1990, p. 163.

30. Frank Livingstone, 'The effects of warfare on the biology of the human species', in M. Fried, M. Harris, and R. Murphy (eds), *War: The anthropology of armed conflict and aggression*. Garden City, NY: Natural History, 1967, p. 9, including other relevant statistics.

31. Donald Symons, *The Evolution of Human Sexuality*. New York: Oxford University Press, 1979, p. 145; Bruce Knauft, 'Reconsidering violence in simple societies: Homicide among the Gebusi of New Guinea', *Current Anthropology*, 1987; **28**: 458; Jean Briggs, ' "Why don't you kill your baby brother?" The dynamics of peace in Canadian Inuit camps', in L. E. Sponsel and T. Gregor (eds), *The Anthropology of Peace and Nonviolence*. London: Lynne Rienner, 1994, p. 156.

32. Richard Lee, *The !Kung San*. New York: Cambridge University Press, 1979, p. 398.

33. Mildred Dickemann, 'Female infanticide, reproductive strategies, and social stratification', in N. Chagnon and W. Irons (eds), *Evolutionary Biology and Human Social Behavior*. North Scitnate, MA: Buxbury Press, 1979, p. 364; slightly different (and inconsistent) figures in: Marvin Harris (ed.), 'Primitive war', in *Cows, Pigs, Wars and Witches*. New York: Random House, 1974, p. 69.

34. J. A. Yost, 'Twenty years of contact: The mechanism of change in Wao (Auca) culture', in N. A. Whitten (ed.), *Cultural Transformation and Ethnicity in Modern Ecuador*. Urbana, IL: University of Illinois, 1981, pp. 677–704; C. A. Robarchek and C. J. Robarchek, 'Cultures of war and peace: A comparative study of Waorani and Semai', in J. Silverberg and J. P. Gray (eds), *Aggression and*

Peacefulness in Humans and Other Primates. New York: Oxford University Press, pp. 189–213.

35. Heider, *The Dugum Dani*, p. 128.

36. Meggitt, *Blood is their Argument*, pp. 13–14, 110.

37. Cited by Symons, *The Evolution of Human Sexuality*, p. 145.

38. Hallpike, *Bloodshed and Vengeance in the Papuan Mountains*, pp. 54, 202.

39. Knauft, 'Reconsidering violence in simple societies', pp. 462–3, 470, 477–8.

40. Boehm, *Blood Revenge*, p. 177.

41. Livingstone, 'The effects of warfare on the biology of the human species', p. 9.

42. G. Milner, E. Anderson, and V. Smith, 'Warfare in late prehistoric West-Central Illinois', *American Antiquity*, 1991; **56**: 583; cited by Keeley, *War before Civilization*, pp. 66–7, which includes a variety of other relevant data.

43. Meggitt, *Blood is their Argument*, p. 100.

44. See Livingstone, 'The effects of warfare on the biology of the human species'; Keeley, *War before Civilization*; M. Ember and C. R. Ember, 'Cross-cultural studies of war and peace', in S. P. Reyna and R. E. Downs (eds), *Studying War: Anthropological perspectives*. Langhorne, PA: Gordon & Breach, 1994, p. 190.

45. Peter Brunt, *Italian Manpower, 225 B.C.–A.D. 14*. Oxford: Oxford University Press, 1971, pp. 54, 63, 84, mainly addressing the calamitous years 218–216 BC.

46. Quincy Wright, *A Study of War*, Vol. i. Chicago: University of Chicago, 1942, p. 665, Table 57; these estimates appear to be very tenuous but can still serve as a rough indicator.

47. Edward O. Wilson, *On Human Nature*. Cambridge, MA: Harvard University Press, 1978, pp. 103–5; George Williams, cited in Daniel Dennet, *Darwin's Dangerous Idea*. New York: Simon & Schuster, 1995, p. 478.

Chapter 7. Conclusion: Fighting in the Evolutionary State of Nature

1. K. F. Otterbein and C. S. Otterbein, 'An eye for an eye, a tooth for a tooth: A cross-cultural study of feuding', *American Anthropologist*, 1965; **67**: 1470–82; Lionel Tiger, *Men in Groups*. New York: Random House, 1969; W. D. Hamilton, 'Innate social aptitude of men: An approach from evolutionary genetics', in R. Fox (ed.), *Biosocial Anthropology*. New York: John Wiley, 1975, p. 148; Richard Wrangham and Dale Peterson, *Demonic Males: Apes and the origins of human violence*. London: Bloomsbury, 1997.

2. J. Shepher, *Incest: The biosocial view*. New York: Academic Press, 1983.

3. Matt Ridley, *The Origins of Virtue: Human instincts and the evolution of cooperation*. New York: Viking, 1996, pp. 166–7.

4. Pierre van den Berghe, *The Ethnic Phenomenon*. New York: Elsevier, 1981; V.

Reynolds, V. Falger, and I. Vine (eds), *The Sociobiology of Ethnocentrism*. London: Croom Helm, 1987; R. Paul Shaw and Yuwa Wong, *Genetic Seeds of Warfare: Evolution, nationalism and patriotism*. Boston: Unwin Hyman, 1989; also Daniel Druckman, 'Social-psychological aspects of nationalism', in J. L. Comaroff and P. C. Stern (eds), *Perspectives on Nationalism and War*. Luxemburg: Gordon & Breach, 1995, pp. 47–98; Paul Stern, 'Why do people sacrifice for their nations', ibid., pp. 99–121; and the sources cited in: Frank K. Salter, *Emotions in Command: A naturalistic study of institutional dominance*. Oxford: Oxford University Press, 1995, pp. 8–9. See originally Charles Darwin, *The Descent of Man*, Chapter 4, in *The Origin of Species and The Descent of Man*. New York: Modern Library, n.d., p. 492.

5. The major study on this subject and on the gene–culture congruence is: L. L. Cavalli-Sforza, P. Menozzi, and A. Piazza, *The History and Geography of Human Genes*. Princeton, NJ: Princeton University Press, 1994.

6. Hamilton, 'Innate social aptitude of men', p. 148.

7. Also, again, this Hobbesian logic has been developed for the state system by: Kenneth Waltz, *Theory of International Politics*. Reading, MA: Addison, 1979.

8. Napoleon Chagnon, *Yanomamo: The fierce people*, 2nd edn. New York: Holt, 1977, pp. 162–3.

9. D. W. Rajecki, 'Animal aggression: Implications for human aggression', in R. G. Geen and E. I. Donnerstein (eds), *Aggression: Theoretical and empirical review*. New York: Academic Press, 1983, pp. 199.

10. More fully see: A. Gat, 'The causes and origins of "primitive warfare": Reply to Ferguson', *Anthropological Quarterly*, 2000; **73**: 165–8. In the meantime, the following has advanced another ecological explanation for scarcity and human conflict: Steven LeBlanc with Katherine Register, *Constant Battles: The myth of the peaceful noble savage*. New York: St Martin's Press, 2003. Although their book is much in agreement with my own findings, the authors fail to recognize the deeper, comprehensive Malthusian–Darwinian logic of their ecological insights.

11. In our subject see, for example, the criticisms by: Robert Carneiro, 'Preface', to Keith F. Otterbein, *The Evolution of War: A cross-cultural study*. New Haven, CT: HRAF, 1970. C. R. Hallpike, 'Functional interpretations of primitive warfare', *Man*, 1973; **8**: 451–70; Robert Bettinger, *Hunter-Gatherers*. New York: Plenum, 1991, pp. 178–9; Doyne Dawson, 'The origins of war: Biological and anthropological theories', *History and Theory*, 1996; **35**: 21–3. Since this section was written and published in article form, an excellent, full-scale discussion of the affinities and differences between evolutionary theory and functionalism has been independently offered by: David Wilson, *Darwin's Cathedral: Evolution, religion, and the nature of society*. Chicago: University of Chicago, 2002, Chapter 2, with which I am greatly in agreement.

12. A recent example of this approach in the study of war is found in: Robert O'Connell, *Ride of the Second Horseman*. New York: Oxford University Press, 1995.

Chapter 8. Introduction: Evolving Cultural Complexity

1. V. Gordon Childe, *Social Evolution*. Cleveland: Meridian, 1951; Leslie White, *The Science of Culture*. New York: Grove, 1949; id., *The Evolution of Culture*. New York: McGraw-Hill, 1959; J. H. Steward, *Theory of Cultural Change*. Urbana, IL: University of Illinois, 1955; Marshall Sahlins and Elman Service (eds), *Evolution and Culture*. Ann Arbor: University of Michigan, 1960; Elman Service, *Primitive Social Organization: An evolutionary perspective*. New York: Random House, 1962; id., *Origins of the State and Civilization: The process of cultural evolution*. New York: Norton, 1975; Morton Fried, *The Evolution of Political Society*. New York: Random House, 1967; Marvin Harris, *The Rise of Anthropological Theory*. New York: Crowell, 1968; R. L. Carneiro, 'Foreword', in K. Otterbein, *The Evolution of War: A cross-cultural study*. New Haven, CT: HRAF, 1970; R. L. Carneiro, 'The four faces of evolution: Unilinear, universal, multilinear and differential', in J. Honigmann (ed.), *Handbook of Social and Cultural Anthropology*. Chicago: Rand, 1973, pp. 89–110; C. Refrew, et al. (eds), *Theory and Explanation in Archaeology*. New York: Academic Press, 1982, Chapters 16 and 19; A. W. Johnson and T. Earle, *The Evolution of Human Societies: From foraging group to agrarian state*. Stanford: Stanford University Press, 1987; Tim Ingold, *Evolution and Social Life*. Cambridge: Cambridge University Press, 1986; C. R. Hallpike, *The Principles of Social Evolution*. Oxford: Oxford University Press, 1986; David Rindos, 'The evolution of the capacity for culture: Sociobiology, structuralism, and cultural selectionism', *Current Anthropology*, 1986; **27**: 315–32; Stephen Sanderson, *Social Evolutionism*. Oxford: Blackwell, 1990; id., *Social Transformations*. Oxford: Blackwell, 1995; Ernest Gellner, *Plough, Sword, and Book: The structure of human history*. Chicago: University of Chicago, 1989.

2. See especially D. T. Campbell, 'Variation and selective retention in socio-cultural evolution', in H. Barringer et al. (eds), *Social Change in Developing Areas*. Cambridge, MA: Schenkman, 1965, pp. 19–49; Richard Dawkins, *The Selfish Gene*, 2nd edn. Oxford: Oxford University Press, 1989, Chapter 11; Daniel Dennet, *Darwin's Dangerous Idea*. New York: Simon & Schuster, 1995; Dan Sperber, *Explaining Culture: A naturalistic approach*. Oxford: Blackwell, 1996; J. M. Balkin, *Cultural Software*. New Haven, CT: Yale University Press, 1998.

3. See the brilliant book: Jack Cohen and Jan Stewart, *Figments of Reality: The evolution of the curious mind*. Cambridge: Cambridge University Press, 1997. Also, earlier and anthropologically oriented: Warwick Bray, 'The biological basis of culture', in C. Renfrew (ed.), *The Explanation of Cultural Change: Models in prehistory*. London: Duckworth, 1973, pp. 73–92.

4. Noam Chomsky, *Cartesian Linguistics*. New York: Harper & Row, 1966; Steven Pinker, *The Language Instinct*. New York: Morrow, 1994; Terrence Deacon, *The Symbolic Species: The co-evolution of language and the human brain*. London: Penguin, 1997.

5. C. J. Lumsden and E. O. Wilson, *Genes, Mind and Culture*. Cambridge, MA: Harvard University Press, 1981; L. L. Cavalli-Sforza and M. W. Feldman, *Cultural Transmission and Evolution*. Princeton, NJ: Princeton University Press, 1981; Robert Boyd and P. J. Richerson, *Culture and the Evolutionary Process*. Chicago, University of Chicago, 1985; W. H. Durham, *Coevolution: Genes, culture, and human diversity*. Stanford, CA: Stanford University Press, 1991. Dawson's support for pure cultural evolution in war's later development, evolution that supposedly escaped genetic control because of its rapidity, is lopsided: Doyne Dawson, 'The origins of war: Biological and anthropological theories', *History and Theory*, 1996; **35**: 24.

6. The best here are: Cohen and Stewart, *Figments of Reality*; and earlier: id., *The Collapse of Chaos: Discovering simplicity in a complex world*. New York: Viking, 1994; as well as: John T. Bonner, *The Evolution of Complexity by Means of Natural Selection*. Princeton, NJ: Princeton University Press, 1988; Simon Morris, *Life's Solution: Inevitable humans in a lonely universe*. Cambridge: Cambridge University Press, 2003. Cruder but also useful is: Max Petterson, *Complexity and Evolution*. Cambridge: Cambridge University Press, 1996. These are more than ample rebuttals of Gould's extreme celebration of evolution as contingency in: Stephen J. Gould, *Wonderful Life*. New York: Norton, 1989.

7. In addition to the references in the previous note, see especially: Stuart Kaufman, *The Origins of Order: Self-Organization and selection in evolution*. New York: Oxford University Press, 1993. An overview is offered by: M. Mitchell Waldrop, *Complexity: The emerging science at the edge of order and chaos*. New York: Simon & Schuster, 1992. Also see Richard Dawkins, *The Blind Watchmaker*. London: Longman, 1986; John Holland, *Hidden Order: How adaptation builds complexity*. Reading, MA: Helix, 1995; Matt Ridley, *The Origins of Virtue*. New York: Viking, 1996; Philip Ball, *The Self-Made Tapestry: Pattern formation in nature*. Oxford: Oxford University Press, 1999; Peter Corning, *Nature's Magic: Synergy in evolution and the fate of humankind*. Cambridge: Cambridge University Press, 2003.

8. Cohen and Stewart *Figments of Reality*, pp. 111–12. Also Dawkins, *The Blind Watchmaker*, pp. 94–106.

9. This is well emphasized by Sanderson, *Social Evolutionism*.

10. This is rightly noted by: William McNeill, *The Rise of the West: A history of the human community*. Chicago: University of Chicago, 1963; Michael Mann, *The Sources of Social Power*, Vol. 1. Cambridge: Cambridge University Press, 1986, pp. 173, 525.

Chapter 9. *Tribal Warfare in* Agraria *and* Pastoralia

1. Useful collections of updated research are: D. Harris (ed.), *The Origins and Spread of Agriculture and Pastoralism in Eurasia.* Washington, DC: Smithsonian Institute, 1996; T. Price and A. Gebauer (eds), *Last Hunters—First Farmers.* Santa Fe, NM: School of American Research, 1992; A. Gebauer and T. Price (eds), *Transitions to Agriculture in Prehistory.* Madison, WI: Prehistory Library, 1992; C. Cowan and P. Watson (eds), *The Origins of Agriculture.* Washington, DC: Smithsonian Institute, 1992; Richard MacNeish, *The Origins of Agriculture and Settled Life.* Norman: University of Oklahoma, 1992.

2. William McNeill, *Plagues and Peoples.* Garden City, NY: Anchor, 1976, Chapters 1, 2; Mark Cohen, *Health and the Rise of Civilization.* New Haven, CT: Yale University Press, 1989.

3. Mark Cohen, *The Food Crisis in Prehistory.* New Haven, CT: Yale University Press, 1977; this gave impetus to the demographic interpretation. However, Cohen's work predates and takes no account of more recent understanding about the spread and significance of *Homo sapiens sapiens.* The lack of any particular nutritional stress among Mesolithic populations who initiated agriculture has been pointed out by: Brian Hayden, 'Models of domestication', in Gebauer and Price, *Transitions to Agriculture in Prehistory,* pp. 11–19; id., 'A new overview of domestication', in Price and Gebauer, *Last Hunters—First Farmers,* pp. 273–99; also Price and Gebauer, ibid., pp. 7, 19. On sedentism and agriculture, see David Harris, 'Settling down: An evolutionary model for the transformation of mobile bands into sedentary communities', in J. Friedman and M. Rowlands (eds), *The Evolution of Social Systems.* London: Duckworth, 1977, pp. 401–18. A good cultural–evolutionary synthesis is offered in Charles Redman, *The Rise of Civilization: From early farmers to urban society in the ancient Near East.* San Francisco, CA: Freeman, 1978; Jared Diamond, *Guns, Germs, and Steel: The fate of human societies.* New York: Norton, 1997; this is a brilliant interpretation of the problems and randomness of domestication, which resulted in different cultural trajectories in the various continents. More ideas can be found in the collections cited in endnote 1.

4. David Rindos, *The Origins of Agriculture: An evolutionary perspective.* Orlando, FL: Academic Press, 1984.

5. Martin Daly and Margo Wilson, *Sex, Evolution, and Behavior,* Boston, MA: Willard Grant, 1983, pp. 328–41; Cohen, *Health and the Rise of Civilization,* pp. 87–9, 102–3.

6. A good overview: Robert Netting, 'Population, permanent agriculture, and polities: Unpacking the evolutionary portmanteau', in S. Upham (ed.), *The Evolution of Political Systems: Sociopolitics in small-scale sedentary societies.* Cambridge: Cambridge University Press, 1990, pp. 21–61.

7. For general works, see Colin McEvedy and Richard Jones, *Atlas of World*

Population History, London: Penguin, 1978; Massimo Bacci, *A Concise History of World Population*, Oxford: Blackwell, 1997, pp. 27, 38, 41–7, for example.

8. For the whole debate and the following paragraphs see: A. J. Ammerman and L. L. Cavalli-Sforza, *The Neolithic Transition and the Genetics of Populations in Europe*. Princeton, NJ: Princeton University Press, 1984; L. L. Cavalli-Sforza et al., *The History and Geography of Human Genes*. Princeton, NJ: Princeton University Press, 1994; Colin Renfrew, *Archaeology and Language*. Cambridge: Cambridge University Press, 1987; id., 'The origins of world linguistic diversity: An archaeological perspective', in N. Jablonski and L. Aiello (eds), *The Origins and Diversification of Language*. San Francisco, CA: California Academy of Sciences, 1998, pp. 171–91; T. Price, A. Gebuer, and Lawrence Keeley, 'The spread of farming into Europe north of the Alps', in Price and Gebauer, *Last Hunters–First Farmers*, pp. 95–126; the contributions by L. L. Cavalli-Sforza, C. Renfrew, J. Thomas, M. Zvelebil, and T. Price, in D. Harris (ed.), *The Origins and Spread of Agriculture and Pastoralism in Eurasia*. Washington, DC: Smithsonian Institute, 1996; Robin Dennell, 'The hunter-gatherer/agricultural frontier in prehistoric temperate Europe', in S. Green and S. Perlman (eds), *The Archaeology of Frontiers and Boundaries*. London: Academic Press, 1985, pp. 113–39; Stephen Oppenheimer, *Out of Eden: The peopling of the world*. London: Constable, 2003, p. xxi.

9. In addition to the previous note, see the criticism in: J. P. Mallory, *In Search of the Indo-Europeans*. London: Thames & Hudson, 1989.

10. J. L. Mountain et al., 'Congruence of genetic and linguistic evolution in China', *Journal of Chinese Linguistics*, 1992; **20**: 315–31; Ian Glover and Charles Higham, 'New evidence for early rice cultivation in south, southeast and east Asia', in Harris, *The Origins and Spread of Agriculture and Pastoralism in Eurasia*, pp. 413–41; Peter Bellwood, 'The origins and spread of agriculture in the Indo-Pacific region: Gradualism and diffusion or revolution and colonization', ibid., pp. 465–98. An excellent synthesis is offered by: Jared Diamond and Peter Bellwood, 'Farmers and their languages: The first expansions', *Science*, 2003; **25**: 597–603.

11. A sophisticated analysis of the farmers' vulnerabilities is Dennell, 'The hunter-gatherer/agricultural frontier in prehistoric temperate Europe'.

12. John Iliffe, *Africans: The history of a continent*. Cambridge: Cambridge University Press, 1995, pp. 35–6, 99–100.

13. See the excellent discussion in: Lawrence Keeley, *War before Civilization*. New York: Oxford University Press, 1996, pp. 132–5.

14. Ibid., pp. 136–9; Lawrence Keeley, 'The introduction of agriculture to the Western North European Plain', in Gebauer and Price, *Transitions to Agriculture in Prehistory*, pp. 92–3; Lawrence Keeley and Daniel Cahen, 'Early Neolithic forts and villages in NE Belgium: A preliminary report', *Journal of Field*

Archaeology, 1989; **16**: 157–76; Marek Zvelebil, 'The transition to farming in the circum-Baltic region', in Harris, *The Origins and Spread of Agriculture and Pastoralism in Eurasia*, pp. 338–9; I. J. Thorpe, *The Origins of Agriculture in Europe*. London: Routledge, 1996, pp. 35–6, 39; Alasdair Whittle, 'The first farmers', in B. Cunliffe (ed.), *The Oxford Illustrated Prehistory of Europe*. Oxford: Oxford University Press, 1994, pp. 145, 150–1, 160–5; Roger Mercer, 'The earliest defences in Western Europe. Part I: Warfare in the Neolithic', *Fortress*, 1989; **2**: 16–22.

15. W. W. Hill, *Navaho Warfare*. New Haven, CT: Yale University Press, 1936; also Keeley, *War before Civilization*, pp. 135–6.

16. See again Diamond's brilliant book: *Guns, Germs, and Steel*.

17. Stuart Fiedel, *Prehistory of the Americas*. New York: Cambridge University Press, 1987, p. 209. A long awaited survey is now available in: George Milner, 'Palisaded settlements in prehistoric eastern North America', in James Tracy (ed.), *City Walls: The urban enceinte in global perspective*. Cambridge: Cambridge University Press, 2000, pp. 46–70.

18. James Mellaart, *Çatal-Hüyük*. New York: McGraw-Hill, 1967, especially pp. 68–9; also id., *Earliest Civilizations of the Near East*. New York: McGraw-Hill, 1965, pp. 81–101, especially 82–3.

19. Kathleen Kenyon, *Digging Up Jericho*. London: Ernest Benn, 1957, pp. 66–9, 75–6; Emmanuel Anati, 'Prehistoric trade and the puzzle of Jericho', *Bulletin of the American Schools of Oriental Research*, 1962; **167**: 25–31.

20. Peter Dorell, 'The uniqueness of Jericho', in R. Moorey and P. Parr (eds), *Archaeology in the Levant*. Warminster: Aris, 1978, pp. 11–18; Marilyn Roper, 'Evidence of warfare in the Near East from 10,000–4,300 BC', in M. Nettleship et al. (eds), *War: Its causes and correlates*. The Hague: Mouton, 1975, pp. 304–9; James Mellaart, *The Neolithic of the Near East*. London: Thames & Hudson, 1975, pp. 48–51. Bar-Yosef's argument that the wall and ditch were an anti-flood device and the tower a ritual construction is a well argued but unconvincing suggestion in: O. Bar-Yosef, 'The walls of Jericho', *Current Anthropology*, 1986; **27**: 157–62.

21. Hill, *Navaho Warfare*.

22. Roper, 'Evidence of warfare in the Near East from 10,000–4,300 BC', pp. 299–343; this is a specialized judicious survey, marred only by the author's assumption, based on outdated Lorenzian biology, that intraspecific killing is unnatural and, therefore, a late human invention. See also Mellaart, *The Neolithic of the Near East*, pp. 115–16, 126, 150, 152, 225.

23. Roper, 'Evidence of warfare in the Near East from 10,000–4,300 BC'; John Keegan, *A History of Warfare*. New York: Alfred Knopf, 1993, pp. 125–6.

24. This is well put by Dorell, 'The uniqueness of Jericho', and in effect also recognized by Bar Yosef, 'The walls of Jericho'.

25. Keeley, *War before Civilization*, p. 137; Whittle, 'The first farmers', pp. 145, 150–1, 160–5; Mercer, 'The earliest defences in Western Europe. Part I'.

26. Graeme Barker, *Prehistoric Farming in Europe*. Cambridge: Cambridge University Press, 1985, p. 261.

27. Polybius, *The Histories*. Cambridge, MA: Harvard University Press/Loeb, 1975, 2.17.

28. Mervin Meggitt, *Blood is Their Argument: Warfare among the Mae Enga of the New Guinea Highlands*. Palo Alto, CA, 1977: Mayfield, p. 2.

29. Irving Goldman, *Ancient Polynesian Society*. Chicago: University of Chicago Press, 1970; Patrick Kirch, *The Evolution of the Polynesian Chiefdoms*. Cambridge: Cambridge University Press, 1984, p. 195.

30. Kirch, *The Evolution of the Polynesian Chiefdoms*, p. 213.

31. My conclusions here agree with Rowlands' excellent chapter: M. Rowlands, 'Defence: A factor in the organization of settlements', in P. Ucko, R. Tringham, and G. Dimbleby, (eds), *Man, Settlement and Urbanism*. Cambridge, MA: Schenkman, 1972, pp. 447–62.

32. Morton Fried, *The Notion of the Tribe*. Menlo Park, CA: Cummings, 1975; this follows on from: id., 'On the concepts of "tribe" and "tribal society" ', in J. Helm (ed.), *Essays on the Problem of the Tribe*. Seattle: American Ethnological Society, 1968, pp. 3–20. Fried's overstatement has influenced later anthropologists. More recently see: B. Ferguson and N. Whitehead (eds), *War in the Tribal Zone: Expanding states and indigenous warfare*. Santa Fe, NM: School of American Research, 1992.

33. Dell Hymes (ed.), 'Linguistic problems in defining the concept of the tribe', in *Essays on the Problem of the Tribe*. Seattle: American Ethnological Society, 1968, pp. 23–48; this overlooks these distinctions of *ethnie*, language, and tribe. However, see, for example, Fredrick Barth (ed.), 'Introduction', in *Ethnic Groups and Boundaries*. London: George Allen, 1969, pp. 9–38.

34. Lewis Morgan, *League of the Ho-De-No Sau-Nee or Iroquois*. New Haven, CT: Human Relations Area Files, 1954(1851) is pioneering. For population estimates, see Dean Snow, *The Iroquois*. Cambridge, MA: Blackwell, 1994, pp. 1, 88, 109–11; Daniel Richter, *The Ordeal of the Longhouse: The people of the Iroquois League in the era of European colonization*. Chapel Hill: University of North Carolina, 1992, pp. 17, 293; Francis Jennings, *The Ambiguous Iroquois Empire*. New York: Norton, 1984, pp. 34–5; Bruce Trigger, 'Maintaining economic equality in opposition to complexity: An Iroquoian case study', in S. Upham (ed.), *The Evolution of Political Systems: Sociopolitics in small-scale sedentary societies*. Cambridge: Cambridge University Press, 1990, pp. 119–45; this is a good updated survey of Iroquois prehistory.

35. See the various contributions to: B. Trigger and W. Washburn (eds), *The

Cambridge History of the Native Peoples of the Americas: I. North America, Part 1. New York: Cambridge University Press, 1996, pp. 403, 408, 506.

36. Brian Fagan, *Ancient North America*. New York: Thames & Hudson, 1995, pp. 121, 141–2, 160; John Ewers, 'Intertribal warfare as the precursor of Indian-white warfare on the northern Great Plains', *The Western Historical Quarterly*, 1975; **6**: 403–7.

37. Bernard Mishkin, *Rank and Warfare among the Plains Indians*. Seattle: University of Washington, 1940, p. 25.

38. Polybius 2.17; Barry Cunliffe, *The Ancient Celts*. Oxford: Oxford University Press, 1997, pp. 72, 177.

39. For some population figures for these large post-tribal and confederate communities (some of which were probably exaggerated, as customary for enemy's numbers in antiquity) see *The Gallic War* 1.29, 2.4, and perhaps the most instructive: 7.75.

40. Barry Cunliffe, *Iron Age Communities in Britain*. London: Routledge, 1974, pp. 105, 114.

41. Malcolm Todd, *The Early Germans*. Oxford: Blackwell, 1992, p. 8.

42. Edward James, *The Franks*. Oxford: Blackwell, 1988, pp. 35–6.

43. Kristian Kristiansen, *Europe before History*. Cambridge: Cambridge University Press, 1998, p. 195.

44. Christopher Boehm, *Blood Revenge: The anthropology of feuding in Montenegro and other tribal societies*. Lawrence: University of Kansas, 1984, pp. 19, 21.

45. Kirch, *The Evolution of the Polynesian Chiefdoms*, p. 98; Marshall Sahlins, 'Poor man, rich man, big-man, chief: Political types in Melanesia and Polynesia', *Comparative Studies in Society and History*, 1963; **5**: 287.

46. Andrew Vayda, *Maori Warfare*. Wellington, New Zealand: The Polynesian Society, 1960, p. 20.

47. M. Fortes and E. Evans-Pritchard (eds), *African Political Systems*. Oxford: Oxford University Press, 1940, pp. 7, 36, 198, 239, 276–84; J. Middleton and D. Tait, *Tribes without Rulers: Studies in African segmentary systems*. London: Routledge, 1958, pp. 28, 97, 102–4, 164, 167, 203, 207.

48. This is well pointed out, much against the scholarly current, in: William Sanders and David Webster, 'Unilinealism, multilinealism, and the evolution of complex societies', in C. Redman et al. (eds), *Social Archaeology*. New York: Academic Press, 1978, pp. 249–302; Elman Service, *Origins of the State and Civilization: The process of cultural evolution*. New York: Norton, 1975.

49. See, for example, Iliffe, *Africans*, pp. 92–6, 115–17; also Elizabeth Isichei, *A History of African Societies to 1870*. Cambridge: Cambridge University Press, 1997, pp. 147, 149.

711

50. Tacitus, *Germania*. London: Loeb, 1970, sections 13, 18 (quotation), my italics; Todd, *The Early Germans*, p. 32; Gwyn Jones, *A History of the Vikings*. Oxford: Oxford University Press, 1984, p. 197.

51. Vayda suggests several forms of early land competition: Vayda, *Maori Warfare*, pp. 109–16; id., 'Expansion and warfare among Swidden agriculturalists', *American Anthropologist*, 1961; **63**: 346–58; id., *War in Ecological Perspective*. New York: Plenum, 1976.

52. The seminal theoretical formulation is Sahlins, 'Poor man, rich man, big-man, chief'; also the excellent and concise book: Marshall Sahlins, *Tribesmen*. Englewood Cliffs, NJ: Prentice-Hall, 1968.

53. For the alleged role of 'big men's' rivalry in initiating violent conflict, see Saul Sillitoe, 'Big men and war in New Guinea', *Man*, 1978; **13**: 252–71.

54. Iliffe, *Africans*, pp. 92, 94, 119; also I. Schapera, *Government and Politics in Tribal Societies*. London: Watts, 1956, *passim*.

55. T. M. Charles-Edwards, 'Irish warfare before 1100', in T. Bartlett and K. Jeffery (eds), *A Military History of Ireland*. Cambridge: Cambridge University Press, 1996, p. 26. Compare Roanal Cohen, 'The tribal, pre-state West African Sahel', in H. Claessen and P. Skalnik (eds), *The Study of the State*, The Hague: Mouton, 1981, pp. 108–9. For a general theoretical statement, see Sahlins, *Tribesmen*, p. 5.

56. Goldman, *Ancient Polynesian Society*, p. 69.

57. Keith Otterbein, 'Why the Iroquois won: An analysis of Iroquois military tactics', and id., 'Huron vs. Iroquois: A case study in inter-tribal warfare', both reprinted in Keith Otterbein, *Feuding and Warfare*. Langhorne, PA: Gordon & Breach, 1994, pp. 1–23; Richter, *The Ordeal of the Longhouse*, especially pp. 31–8, 54–74—the best, anthropologically informed, study of Iroquois society and warfare; also Snow, *The Iroquois*, pp. 30–2, 53–7, 109; Vayda, *Maori Warfare*—one of the most complete studies of tribal warfare anywhere.

58. For a general theoretical statement, in addition to the works cited in Chapter 6, see Service, *Origins of the State and Civilization*, pp. 58–9.

59. The classical depictions of the Celt warriors are strikingly summarized in Cunliffe, *The Ancient Celts*, pp. 91–105; id., *The Oxford Illustrated Prehistory of Europe*, pp. 361–4; also M. Green (ed.), *The Celtic World*. London: Routledge, 1995, pp. 26–31, 37–54. For the Germans, Tacitus, *Germania*, is an archetypal study of tribal society and tribal warfare, supported by archaeology and other sources: for example, D. H. Green, *Language and History in the Early Germanic World*. Cambridge: Cambridge University Press, 1998, pp. 21, 49–87.

60. Kristiansen, *Europe before History*, pp. 2, 314–44; Cunliffe, *The Ancient Celts*, pp. 73–5, 88–90; Mallory, *In Search of the Indo-Europeans*, pp. 63–4, 166–7.

61. Todd, *The Early Germans*, p. 189; Peter Heather, *The Goths*. Oxford: Blackwell, 1996, pp. 73, 148, 151; Herwig Wolfram, *History of the Goths*. Berkeley, CA: University of California, 1988, p. 7.

62. O. Bar-Yosef and A. Khazanov (eds), *Pastoralism in the Levant: Archeological materials in anthropological perspectives*. Madison, WI: Prehistory Press, 1992; Sheratt's papers on 'the secondary product revolution', reprinted in: Andrew Sheratt, *Economy and Society in Prehistoric Europe*. Princeton, NJ: Princeton University Press, 1997, pp. 155–248.

63. The leading work on the subject is: Anatoly Khazanov, *Nomads and the Outside World*, 2nd edn. Madison, WI: University of Wisconsin, 1994, see pp. 119–52; also Roger Cribb, *Nomads in Archaeology*. Cambridge: Cambridge University Press, 1991, pp. 45–54. A more popular, textbook overview is: Thomas Barfield, *The Nomadic Alternative*. Englewood Cliffs, NJ: Prentice Hall, 1993.

64. For some density figures, see Sahlins, *Tribesmen*, p. 34.

65. K. Fukui and D. Turton (eds), *Warfare among East African Herders*. Osaka: National Museum of Ethnology, 1977, pp. 15, 35; also John Galaty, 'Pastoral orbits and deadly jousts: Factors in the Maasai expansion', in J. Galaty and P. Bonte (eds), *Herders, Warriors, and Traders*. Boulder, CO: Westview, 1991, p. 194.

66. Elizabeth Thomas, *Warrior Herdsmen*. New York: Knopf, 1965.

67. P. Bonte, 'Non-stratified social formations among pastoral nomads', in J. Friedman and M. Rowlands (eds), *The Evolution of Social Systems*. London: Duckworth, 1977, pp. 192–4; contains important theoretical observations on pastoral tribal structure.

68. Fredrik Barth, *Nomads of South Persia*. London: Oslo University Press, 1961, pp. 1, 50–60, 119.

69. V. Müller, *En Syrie avec les Bedouin*, Paris: Ernest Leroux, 1931; M. von Oppenheim, *Die Beduinen*, Vol. 1. Leipzig: Harrassowitz, 1939.

70. Jean Kupper, *Les Nomades en Mesopotamie au temps des rois de Mari*. Paris: Société d'Edition 'Les Belles Lettres', 1957; J. T. Luke, 'Pastoralism and politics in the Mari period', doctoral dissertation, Ann Arbor, Michigan, 1965; Victor Matthews, *Pastoral Nomadism in the Mari Kingdom (ca. 1850–1760)*. Cambridge: American School of Oriental Research, 1978; Moshe Anbar, *The Amorite Tribes in Mari*. Tel Aviv: Tel Aviv University, 1985 (Hebrew; also in French 1991).

71. Israel Finkelstein, *The Archaeology of the Israelite Settlement*. Jerusalem: Israel Exploration Society, 1988, pp. 330–5.

72. D. J. Mattingly, 'War and peace in Roman North Africa: Observations and models of state-tribal interactions', in B. Ferguson and N. Whitehead (eds), *War in the Tribal Zone: Expanding states and indigenous warfare*. Santa Fe, NM: School of American Research, 1992, p. 33.

73. Khazanov, *Nomads and the Outside World*, pp. 30, 152–64; Theodore Monod (ed.), 'Introduction', in *Pastoralism in Tropical Africa*. London: Oxford University Press, 1975, pp. 114–15; Andrew Smith, *Pastoralism in Africa*. London: Hurst, 1992, p. 168; Barth, *Nomads of South Persia*, pp. 13, 16–17; Cribb, *Nomads in Archaeology*, pp. 34–5.

713

74. Thomas, *Warrior Herdsmen*, p. 152. Bonte, 'Non-stratified social formations among pastoral nomads', pp. 192–4, is again good on this interconnected complex.

75. Jacque Maquet, *The Premise of Inequality in Ruanda*. London: Oxford University Press, 1961, pp. 72–3, 82.

76. See, for example, P. T. W. Baxter, 'Boran age-sets and warfare', in K. Fukui and D. Turton (eds), *Warfare among East African Herders*. Osaka: National Museum of Ethnology, 1977, pp. 69–96; Uri Almagor, 'Raiders and elders: A confrontation of generations among the Dassanetch', ibid., pp. 119–46; also Galaty, 'Pastoral orbits and deadly jousts', especially pp. 188–92; Thomas, *Warrior Herdsmen*, pp. 3–9, 55–8.

77. See Thomas, *Warrior Herdsmen*, pp. 120–1, for a depiction of such a day raid.

78. Again, the best theoretical discussion is Khazanov, *Nomads and the Outside World*, pp. 222–7.

79. Fredrik Barth, 'A general perspective on nomad-sedentary relations in the Middle East', reprinted in id., *Process and Form in Social Life: Selected essays*, Vol. I. London: Routledge, 1981, pp. 187–97; this is a pioneering formulation of the pastoral–agricultural relationship, which focuses too narrowly on the economic cause for the pastoralists' advantage. Similarly, in reaction against earlier trends, a collection such as Monod's book, dealing with some of the most warlike societies in Africa, does not even mention conflict: Theodore Monod (ed.), *Pastoralism in Tropical Africa*. London: Oxford University Press, 1975. In stark contrast to his co-editor, Pierre Bonte's contribution to Galaty and Bonte, *Herders, Warriors, and Traders*, pp. 62–86, represents trends of the 1960s and 1970s in rejecting the notion of military domination by ethnically foreign pastoral incomers from the north as the basis for the Great Lakes' societies. Similar denials of the 'tribal'–ethnic cause were widely voiced in the west during the genocidal conflict in Rwanda in the 1990s. Here, too, there has been an overreaction to late-nineteenth and early-twentieth-century theories, best represented by: Franz Oppenheimer, *The State*, New York: Vanguard, 1926; this saw conquest by pastoralists as the general mechanism of the original state formation.

80. Ronald Oliver, 'The Nilotic contribution to Bantu Africa', *Journal of African History*, 1982; **23**: 442. For good historical and theoretical syntheses see: Service, *Origins of the State and Civilization*, pp. 117–26; Khazanov, *Nomads and the Outside World*, pp. 290–5; A. Richards (ed.), *East African Chiefs*. London: Faber, 1960; Edward Steinhart, 'Ankole: pastoral hegemony', in H. Claessen and P. Skaknik (eds), *The Early State*. The Hague: Mouton, 1978, pp. 131–50. Ronald Cohen, 'State foundations: A controlled comparison', in R. Cohen and E. Service (eds), *Origins of the State*, Philadelphia: Institute for the Study of Human Issues, 1978, p. 155; this rejects structural–functional harmonism. See

also Isichei, *A History of African Societies to 1870*, pp. 89, 139–40, 443–8; Iliffe, *Africans*, pp. 105–9. For the Tutsi–Hutu caste and patron–client systems, see Maquet, *The Premise of Inequality in Ruanda*.

81. Summaries in Mario Liverani, 'The Amorites', in D. Wiseman (ed.), *Peoples of Old Testament Times*. Oxford: Oxford University Press, 1973, pp. 100–33; Anbar, *The Amorite Tribes in Mari*, p. 179. Also, a philological–statistical analysis in: Giorgio Buccellati, *The Amorites of the Ur III Period*. Naples: Instituto Orientale, 1966.

82. The debate more or less replicates itself with respect to the Amorites in Mari and the Levant, the Aramaeans, and the Israelites. For the 'traditional' view, starting with William Albright, see: Kupper, *Les Nomades en Mesopotamie au temps des rois de Mari*; Horst Klengel, *Zwischen Zelt und Palast*. Vienna: Schroll, 1972; Kathleen Kenyon, *Amorites and Canaanites*. London: Oxford University Press, 1966. This view has been updated and balanced by: Kay Prag, 'Ancient and modern pastoral migrations in the Levant', *Levant*, 1985; **17**: 81–8; and, forcefully, by Mattanyah Zohar, 'Pastoralism and the spread of the Semitic languages', in O. Bar-Yosef and A. Khazanov (eds), *Pastoralism in the Levant: Archeological materials in anthropological perspectives*. Madison, WI: Prehistory Press, 1992, p. 172. For the 'revisionists' see: Luke, 'Pastoralism and politics in the Mari period'; Matthews, *Pastoral Nomadism in the Mari Kingdom*; M. Rowton, 'The physical environment and the problem of the nomads', in J. Kupper (ed.), *La Civilisation de Mari*. Paris: Société d'Édition 'Les Belles Lettres', 1967; M. Rowton, 'Dimorphic structure and the parasocial element', *Journal of Near Eastern Studies*, 1977; **36**: 181–98; Robert Adams, 'The Mesopotamian social landscape: A view from the frontier', in C. Moore (ed.), *Reconstructing Complex Societies*. Cambridge, MA: American Schools of Oriental Research, 1974, pp. 1–20; William Dever, 'Pastoralism and the end of the urban early Bronze Age in Palestine', in Bar-Yosef and Khazanov, *Pastoralism in the Levant: Archeological materials in anthropological perspectives*, pp. 83–92; Mario Liverani, 'The collapse of the Near Eastern regional system at the end of the Bronze Age: the case of Syria', in M. Rowlands, M. Larsen, and K. Kristiansen (eds), *Centre and Periphery in the Ancient World*. Cambridge: Cambridge University Press, 1987, pp. 66–73; Suzanne Richard, 'Toward a consensus of opinion on the end of the Early Bronze Age in Palestine–Transjordan', *Bulletin of the American Schools of Oriental Research*, 1980; **237**: 5–34; id., 'The early Bronze Age: The rise and collapse of "urbanism" ', *Biblical Archaeologist*, 1987; **50**: 22–43; Gaetano Palumbo, *The Early Bronze Age IV in the Southern Levant*. Rome: La Sapienza University Press, 1991; G. Mendenhall, 'The Hebrew conquest of Palestine', *Biblical Archaeologist*, 1962; **25**: 66–87; Finkelstein, *The Archaeology of the Israelite Settlement*; Helene Sader, 'The 12th century B.C. in Syria: The problem of the rise of the Aramaeans', in W. Ward and M. Joukowsky (eds), *The Crisis Years: The 12th century B.C. from beyond the Danube to the Tigris*. Dubuque, IO: Kendall, 1992, pp. 157–63.

83. Some steps along this line are taken by: Kathryn Kamp and Norman Yoffee, 'Ethnicity in Ancient Western Asia during the early second millennium B.C.', *Bulletin of the American Schools of Oriental Research*, 1980; **237**: 85–104.

84. Finkelstein, *The Archaeology of the Israelite Settlement*.

85. Bar-Yosef and Khazanov, 'Introduction', in *Pastoralism in the Levant*, p. 5.

86. Zohar, 'Pastoralism and the spread of the Semitic languages', p. 172. Robert O'Connell, *Ride of the Second Horseman*. New York: Oxford University Press, 1995, Chapter 6; in this O'Connell mars his perceptive views of this possibility by speculating that *horse* nomadic raiding occurred from the steppe across the Near East as early as the fourth and third millennia and by his Rousseauite approach. Gimbutas's (1970) original thesis in this vein is among her less fortunate ideas: see Marija Gimbutas, *The Kurgan Culture and the Indo-Europeanization of Europe: Selected articles from 1952 to 1993*. Washington, DC: Institute for the Study of Man, 1997, pp. 107–10.

87. For general theoretical discussions, see Talal Asad, 'The Beduin as a military force: notes on some aspects of power relations between nomads and sedentaries in historical perspective', in C. Nelson (ed.), *The Desert and the Sown: Nomads in the wider society*, Berkeley, CA: University of California, 1973, pp. 61–73; Khazanov, *Nomads and the Outside World*, pp. 212–21.

88. Rowton, 'The physical environment and the problem of the nomads', p. 120; Anbar, *The Amorite Tribes in Mari*, p. 179, relying on: Thorkild Jacobsen, 'The reign of Ibbi Suen', *Journal of Cuneiform Studies*, 1953; **vii**: 36–47.

89. This is well suggested, for example, by: Glenn Schwartz, 'The origins of the Aramaeans in Syria and Northern Mesopotamia', in O. Haex, H. Curves, and P. Akkermans (eds), *To the Euphrates and Beyond*. Rotterdam: Balkema, 1989, pp. 275–91, especially pp. 283–4; Ran Zadok, 'Elements of Aramean prehistory', in M. Cogan and I. Eph'al (eds), *Ah, Assyria: Studies in Assyrian history and ancient Near Eastern historiography*. Jerusalem: Magnes, 1991, pp. 104–17.

90. The idea that the early Semites were shepherds was widely held in the nineteenth century. More recently it has been mooted, for example, by Mellaart, *The Neolithic of the Near East*, pp. 280–2, and is interestingly developed by Zohar, 'Pastoralism and the spread of the Semitic languages'.

91. Colin Renfrew, 'Language families and the spread of farming', Harris, *The Origins and Spread of Agriculture and Pastoralism in Eurasia*, especially pp. 73–6; developing: R. Austerlitz, 'Language-family density in North America and Africa', *Ural-Altaische Jahrbücher*, 1980; **52**: 1–10; Johanna Nichols, *Language Diversity in Time and Space*. Chicago: University of Chicago, 1992.

92. Dmitriy Telegin, *Dereivka: A settlement and cemetery of copper age horse-keepers on the Middle Dnieper*. Oxford: British Archaeological Reports, 1986, with additional contributions by I. Potekhina and V. Bibikova; David Anthony and

Dorcas Brown, 'The origins of horseback riding', *Antiquity*, 1991; **65**: 22–38. Doubts regarding the marks for early domestication are cast by: Marsha Levine, 'Dereivka and the problem of horse domestication', *Antiquity*, 1990; **64**: 727–40.

93. R. Meadow and H-P. Uermpann (eds), *Equids in the Ancient World.* Wiesbaden: Ludwig Reichert, 1986(1991); Eran Ovadia, 'The domestication of the ass and pack transport by animals: a case of technological change', in Bar-Yosef and Khazanov, *Pastoralism in the Levant: Archeological materials in anthropological perspectives*, pp. 19–28; Andrew Sheratt, 'The secondary exploitation of animals in the old world', in *Economy and Society in Prehistoric Europe*, pp. 199–228. For ancient and contemporary evidence of the reindeer, including riding, see: Miklos Jankovich, *They Rode into Europe: The fruitful exchange in the arts of horsemanship between East and West.* New York: Scribner, 1971, pp. 19–22, photos after p. 24; Tim Ingold, *Hunters, Pastoralists and Ranchers: Reindeer economies and their transformations.* Cambridge: Cambridge University Press, 1980, especially pp. 104–7; Khazanov, *Nomads and the Outside World*, pp. 112–14.

94. David Anthony, 'The "Kurgan culture", Indo-European origins, and the domestication of the horse: A reconsideration', *Current Anthropology*, 1986; **27**: 291–313; Anthony and Brown, 'The origins of horseback riding'. For the more popular genre see: O'Connell, *Ride of the Second Horseman*, Chapter 6; however, Diamond carefully avoids this pitfall: Jared Diamond, *The Third Chimpanzee.* New York: Harper Collins, 1992, Chapter 15; and Keegan is exemplary: Keegan, *A History of Warfare*, pp. 155–78.

95. Gimbutas, *The Kurgan Culture and the Indo-Europeanization of Europe.*

96. Renfrew, *Archaeology and Language*, pp. 197–9; Colin Renfrew, 'All the king's horses: assessing cognitive maps in prehistoric Europe', in S. Mithen (ed.), *Creativity in Human Evolution and Prehistory.* London: Routledge, 1998, pp. 260–84.

97. For example, Renfrew, 'All the king's horses'.

98. E. E. Kuzmina, 'English summary', *Where had Indo-Aryans Come From? The material culture of the Andronovo tribes and the origins of the Indo-Iranians* (Russian). Moscow: Russian Academy of Sciences, 1994; David Anthony and Nikolai Vinogradov, 'Birth of the chariot', *Archaeology*, 1995; **48**(2): 36–41. In attempting to explain why the nomads rode chariots rather than on horseback, Anthony and Vinogradov write (p. 40) that this may have been a result of the lack of an effective mounted weapon in the shape of the composite bow, which they claim was invented only around 1500 BC. However, first, the composite bow was apparently 1,000 years older: P. R. S. Moorey, 'The emergence of the light, horse drawn chariot in the Near East c. 2000–1500 BC', *World Archaeology*, 1986; **18**: 208–210; second, its absence would also have impaired chariot warriors; third, horseback cavalry could (and would) use the simple bow, javelins, and spears.

717

99. Henri Lhote, 'Le cheval et le chameau dans les peintures et gravures rupestres du Sahara', *Bulletin de l'Institut Français d'Afrique Noire*, 1953; **15**(3).

100. Stuart Piggott, *The Earliest Wheeled Transport: From the Atlantic Coast to the Caspian Sea*. Ithaca, NY: Cornell University Press, 1983.

101. Edward Shaughnessy, 'Historical perspectives on the introduction of the chariot into China', *Harvard Journal of Asiatic Studies*, 1988; **48**: 189–237.

102. The domestication of the camel has been argued to be similarly gradual, spanning 2,000–3,000 years: Juris Zarins, 'Pastoralism in southwest Asia: The second millennium BC', in Clutton-Brock, J. (ed.), *The Walking Larder: Patterns of domestication, pastoralism, and predation*. London: Unwin, 1989, pp. 144–9. Also: Khazanov, *Nomads and the Outside World*, p. 100.

103. Lynn White, 'The origin and diffusion of the stirrup', in *Mediaeval Technology and Social Change*. Oxford: Oxford University Press, 1962, pp. 1–38.

104. Sheratt, 'The secondary exploitation of animals', pp. 217–18; Harold Barclay, *The Role of the Horse in Man's Culture*. London: J. A. Allen, 1980, pp. 28, 116–18; also Khazanov, *Nomads and the Outside World*, pp. 91–2. For the representations: P. R. S. Moorey, 'Pictorial evidence for the history of horse-riding in Iraq before the Kassites', *Iraq*, 1970; **32**: 36–50; Alan Schulman, 'Egyptian representations of horsemen and riding in the New Kingdom', *Journal of Near Eastern Studies*, 1957; **16**: 263–71; Renfrew, 'All the king's horses', p. 279.

105. For this unlikely idea, see especially: M. A. Littauer and J. H. Crouwel, *Wheeled Vehicles and Ridden Animals in the Ancient Near East*. Leiden: Brill, 1979, pp. 66–8, 96.

106. Renfrew, 'All the king's horses'.

107. Gimbutas, *The Kurgan Culture and the Indo-Europeanization of Europe*, established this idea archaeologically, even if her rigid scheme of three successive waves of expansion and her concept of Kurgan culture are no longer fully accepted.

108. Andrew Sheratt, 'The development of Neolithic and Copper Age settlement in the Great Hungarian Plain', in *Economy and Society in Prehistoric Europe*. Princeton, NJ: Princeton University Press, 1997, pp. 270–319, quotations from pp. 281–3, 309–10; also relying on I. Escedy, *The People of the Pit-Graves Kurgans in Eastern Hungary*. Budapest: Akademiai Kiado, 1979.

109. Mallory, *In Search of the Indo-Europeans*, pp. 238–40, also 261.

110. Cavalli-Sforza, in *The Origins and Spread of Agriculture and Pastoralism in Eurasia*, pp. 57–65; Cavalli-Sforza et al., *The History and Geography of Human Genes*, pp. 292–3.

111. Mallory, *In Search of the Indo-Europeans*, pp. 28, 37–8, 70. Robert Drews, *The Coming of the Greeks: Indo-European conquests in the Aegean and the Near East*.

Princeton, NJ: Princeton University Press, 1988; this has revived the thesis that favours a later, about 1600 BC, date for the arrival of the Greeks, which he suggests was an elite conquest by a small force of charioteers. Relying on a theory that the cradle of PIE is south of the Caucasus, in Armenia, Drews pushes the initial spread of the PIE speakers down to the second quarter of the second millennium and connects it with the invention of the war chariot rather than with the steppe 'proto-horse' pastoralists. His thesis leaves some obvious problems. First, if the PIE speakers came from Armenia as late as Drews suggests, how did the PIE languages spread into the south-east European steppe, presumably the springboard to their spread into central and northern Europe? Drews does not suggest a northward chariot conquest of the steppe in the mid-second millennium. Second, a small elite force of chari-oteers arriving in Greece from Anatolia (by sea!) is unlikely to have changed the autochthonous languages of the conquered country, as Drews is aware it did not in other 'takeovers' by elite war charioteers in the ancient Near East during that period, where it was the ruling warrior elite that was assimilated. Only pastoral folk migrations, as is usually suggested for the Aryan conquerors of India—still relatively small but far more substantial than a charioteer war band—were capable of affecting such a transformation. Furthermore, not only the Greek language but also the names known from the Mycenaean tablets are very different from those of the Indo-Iranians and Anatolians, who according to Drews had invaded Greece only a few centuries earlier. This, of course, still leaves the possibility of a pastoral–chariot invasion from the north by proto-Greek speakers of original *steppe* source around 1600 BC, rather than in the third millennium.

112. Mallory, *In Search of the Indo-Europeans*, pp. 66–109; Kristiansen, *Europe before History*, 190; Andrew Sheratt, 'The transformation of early agrarian Europe: The later Neolithic and copper ages 4500–2500 BC', in Cunliffe, *The Oxford Illustrated Prehistory of Europe*, pp. 190–3; id., 'The secondary exploitation of animals', pp. 218–19. The idea is also well suggested in Diamond, *The Third Chimpanzee*, pp. 271–2.

113. Khazanov, *Nomads and the Outside World*, p. 101. For the Aramaean raids, see Schwartz, 'The origins of the Aramaeans in Syria and Northern Mesopota-mia', pp. 277, 286 n. 2; also in: D. Wiseman (ed.), *Peoples of Old Testament Times*. Oxford: Oxford University Press, 1973, pp. 158, 181.

114. Again compare Diamond, *Guns, Germs, and Steel*.

115. Cited by Cunliffe, *The Ancient Celts*, pp. 93.

116. This universal relationship has been fully studied in relation to the pre-polis Greeks in: Gabriel Herman, *Ritualised Friendship and the Greek City*. Cambridge: Cambridge University Press, 1987.

117. Cunliffe, *The Ancient Celts*, pp. 73–4, 105–6.

118. Tacitus, *Germania*, 13–15. E. A. Thompson, *The Early Germans*. Oxford: Oxford University Press, 1965; this is good on the material underpinning the transformation of Germanic society.

119. M. I. Finley, *The World of Odysseus*, revised edn. London: Penguin, 1978(1954); this remains a classic. Scholarly opinion now prefers a late Dark Age date for the background described by Homer: Jan Morris, 'The use and abuse of Homer', *Classical Antiquity*, 1986; **5**: 81–138.

120. The standard archaeological study is still: Anthony Snodgrass, *The Dark Age of Greece*. Edinburgh: Edinburgh University Press, 1971.

121. D. Roussel, *Tribu et cité*. Paris: Belles Lettres, 1976, has stressed the 'invented' nature of many tribal institutions during the early *polis*, but this hardly means that tribal reality itself was invented. Instead, many of the nascent state institutions were formed on the existing framework of tribal society. For an overview of the debated kin-tribe evidence, see John Fine, *The Ancient Greeks*. Cambridge, MA: Harvard University Press, 1983, pp. 34–6, 56, 59, 183–8; Anthony Snodgrass, *Archaic Greece*. Berkeley, CA: University of California, 1980, pp. 25–6.

122. Robert Drews, *Basileus: The evidence of kingship in geometric Greece*. New Haven, CT: Yale University Press, 1983, pp. 102, 104 (for the Homeric *anax*), more appropriately entitled the *lack* of evidence, is historically exhaustive and penetrating. Also, C. G. Thomas, 'From Wanax to Basileus: Kingship in the Greek Dark Age', *Hispania Antiqua*, 1978; **6**: 187–206; Chester Starr, 'The age of chieftains', in *Individual and Community: The rise of the* Polis *800–500 BC*. New York: Oxford University Press, 1986, pp. 15–33. All these works could have become even better with the aid of some comparative anthropological insight, amply provided in: Walter Donlan, 'The social groups of Dark Age Greece', *Classical Philology*, 1985; **80**: 293–308; developed and revised in: Walter Donlan and Carol Thomas, 'The village community of Ancient Greece: Neolithic, Bronze and Dark Age', *Studi Micenei ed Egeo-Anatolici*, 1993; **31**: 61–9; and particularly Walter Donlan, 'The pre-state community in Greece', *Studi Micenei ed Egeo-Anatolici*, 1993; **31**: 5–29. Also, Oswyn Murray, *Early Greece*. Cambridge MA: Harvard University Press, 1993, p. 38; and an excellent theoretical anthropological discussion: Yale Ferguson, 'Chiefdoms to city-states: The Greek experience', in T. Earle (ed.), *Chiefdoms: Power, economy and ideology*. New York: Cambridge University Press, 1991, pp. 169–92.

123. Mallory, *In Search of the Indo-Europeans*, p. 125; D. A. Binchy, *Celtic and Anglo-Saxon Kingship*. Oxford: Oxford University Press, 1970, pp. 1–21; Wolfram, *History of the Goths*, pp. 96, 144, emphasizing the *reiks'* limited tribal-chiefly authority; as does Green, *Language and History in the Early Germanic World*, p. 133, for the early *kuning* (probably from *kuene* = kin).

124. Wolfram, *History of the Goths*, pp. 45–56; Heather, *The Goths*, pp. 40–2, 44–5.

125. Jones, *A History of the Vikings*, pp. 24–6.

126. For this and the following, see Jones, *A History of the Vikings*; Peter Foote and David Wilson, *The Viking Achievement*. New York: Praeger, 1970; David Wilson, *The Vikings and their Origins*. New York: A&W, 1980; P. H. Sawyer, *Kings and Vikings: Scandinavia and Europe AD 700–1100*. London: Methuen, 1982; also, for the military aspect: Paddy Griffith, *The Viking Art of War*. London: Greenhill Books, 1995; Karl Leyser, 'Early medieval warfare', in J. Cooper (ed.), *The Battle of Maldon*. London: Hambledon, 1993, pp. 106–7.

127. For numbers, see Sawyer, *Kings and Vikings*, pp. 80–3, 93; Jones, *A History of the Vikings*, pp. 218–19; Griffith, *The Viking Art of War*, pp. 122–6.

128. N. K. Sanders, *The Sea People: Warriors of the Ancient Mediterranean 1250–1150 BC*. London: Thames & Hudson, 1978. Whether the Shekelesh and Shardana came from Sicily and Sardinia or simply ended up there, giving these places their names, remains unclear, although the latter is more likely. Robert Drews, *The End of the Bronze Age: Changes in warfare and the catastrophe ca. 1200 BC*. Princeton, NJ: Princeton University Press, 1993; the idea suggested in Drews' stimulating book that the Sea Peoples came from no particular core area but were the local fringe people in each country of the Mediterranean world (the Philistines native to Canaan, and so on) flies in the face of all the evidence; for example, Trude Dothan, *The Philistines and their Material Culture*. New Haven, CT: Yale University Press, 1982. Similar to his book on the Indo-European roots of the Greeks, cited above, Drews' book suffers from eccentric ethnogeography.

129. For a theoretical discussion, in addition to the studies cited in the following notes, see especially Elman Service, *Primitive Social Organization*. New York: Random House, 1962; Allen Johnson and Timothy Earle, *The Evolution of Human Societies*. Stanford: Stanford University Press, 1987, Chapters 9–10; T. Earle (ed.), *Chiefdoms: Power, economy and ideology*. New York: Cambridge University Press, 1991; Robert Carneiro, 'The chiefdom: Precursor to the state', in G. Jones and R. Kautz (eds), *The Transition to Statehood in the New World*. New York: Cambridge University Press, 1981, pp. 37–79.

130. Although much has been written on the Scottish clans, a general theoretical study is surprisingly lacking; however, see Robert Dodgshon, 'Modelling chiefdoms in the Scottish Highlands and Islands prior to the "45" ', in B. Arnold and D. Gibson (eds), *Celtic Chiefdom, Celtic State*. Cambridge: Cambridge University Press, 1995, pp. 99–109, quotations from pp. 102, 106. On early Celtic chiefdom, see Binchy's excellent *Celtic and Anglo-Saxon Kingship*, pp. 1–21.

131. See Binchy's highly intelligent treatment.

132. Tellingly, Polanyi, who originally coined the phrase 'redistribution', meant this relationship as heavily one-sided—the giving of gifts to social superiors—

as opposed to *reciprocity*, which takes place among equals: Karl Polanyi, *Primitive, Archaic, and Modern Economics*. Boston, MA: Beacon, 1971.

133. Kirch, *The Evolution of the Polynesian Chiefdoms*, especially pp. 35–9, 195–7 (quotation), and 207; also Marshall Sahlins, *Social Stratification in Polynesia*. Seattle: University of Washington, 1958; this is a work of fundamental theoretical significance; Goldman, *Ancient Polynesian Society*.

134. Isichei, *A History of African Societies to 1870*, pp. 109–10, 148–9. See also Schapera, *Government and Politics in Tribal Societies, passim*.

135. Iliffe, *Africans*, pp. 70–2, 76–80.

136. Cunliffe, *Iron Age Communities in Britain*; the contributors to Cunliffe, *The Oxford Illustrated Prehistory of Europe*, pp. 244–355 Kristiansen, *Europe before History*; C. Renfrew and S. Shennan (eds), *Ranking, Resource and Exchange*. Cambridge: Cambridge University Press, 1982; D. Gibson and M. Geselowitz (eds), *Tribe and Polity in Late Prehistoric Europe*. New York: Plenum, 1988; the contributors to B. Arnold and D. Gibson (eds), *Celtic Chiefdom, Celtic State*. Cambridge: Cambridge University Press, 1995, pp. 43–63.

137. Gimbutas, *The Kurgan Culture and the Indo-Europeanization of Europe*; Mallory, *In Search of the Indo-Europeans*, pp. 218–19; Cunliffe, *The Oxford Illustrated Prehistory of Europe*, pp. 174–5; and, for an excellent general discussion of pastoralist chiefdoms, Khazanov, *Nomads and the Outside World*, pp. 164–97.

138. Milner, 'Palisaded settlements in prehistoric eastern North America', pp. 69–70.

139. For useful surveys, see Fiedel, *Prehistory of the Americas*, Chapter 6, especially pp. 243, 248, 251; Bruce Smith, 'Agricultural chiefdoms of the Eastern Woodlands', in B. Trigger and W. Washburn (eds), *The Cambridge History of the Native Peoples of the Americas: I. North America*, Part 1. New York: Cambridge University Press, 1996, 267–323, especially 281–92; R. Drennan and C. Uribe (eds), *Chiefdoms in the Americas*. Lanham, MD: University Press of America, 1987. For England, see Colin Renfrew (ed.), 'Monuments, mobilization, and social organization in Neolithic Wessex', in *The Explanation of Culture Change: Models in prehistory*. London: Duckworth, 1973, pp. 539–58.

140. Despite its subtitle this is well demonstrated in: Timothy Earle, *How Chiefs Come to Power: The political economy in prehistory*. Stanford: Stanford University Press, 1997.

141. For Anatolia and northern Syria, see Mellaart, *The Neolithic of the Near East*, pp. 124–9; Roper, 'Evidence of warfare in the Near East from 10,000–4,300 BC', pp. 323–9. For Mesopotamia: Robert Adams and Hans Nissen, *The Uruk Countryside*. Chicago: University of Chicago, 1972; Robert Adams, *Heartland of Cities*. Chicago: University of Chicago, 1981; also Gil Stein, 'The organizational dynamics of complexity in Greater Mesopotamia', in G. Stein and M. Rothman (eds), *Chiefdoms and Early States in the Near East*. Madison, WI:

Prehistory Press, 1994, pp. 11–22; id., 'Economy, ritual, and power in "Ubaid" Mesopotamia', in G. Stein and M. Rothman (eds), *Chiefdoms and Early States in the Near East*. Madison, WI: Prehistory Press, 1994, pp. 35–46.

142. See, for example, the examples cited in Thompson, *The Early Germans*, p. 55; Heather, *The Goths*, pp. 67–8; Jenny Wormald, *Lords and Men in Scotland*. Edinburgh: John Donald, 1985, p. 91; and, for Clovis: Bernard Bachrach, *Merovingian Military Organization*. Minneapolis, MI: University of Minnesota, 1972, p. 4.

143. Green, *Language and History in the Early Germanic World*, pp. 84–5, including other early European examples; Walter Donlan, 'The pre-state community in Greece', *Symbolae Osloenses*, 1989; **64**: 15–16, 22.

Chapter 10. Armed Force in the Emergence of the State

1. For the original statement, see Morton Fried, *The Evolution of Political Society*. New York: Random House, 1967, pp. 240–2.

2. I here develop Renfrew's ground-breaking idea regarding the evolution of the 'early state module' as part of a system; see Colin Renfrew, 'Trade as action at a distance: questions of integration and communication', in J. Sabloff and C. Lamberg-Karlovsky (eds), *Ancient Civilization and Trade*. Albuquerque, NM: University of New Mexico, 1975, pp. 3–59; and C. Renfrew and J. Cherry (eds), *Peer Polity Interaction and Socio-Political Change*. Cambridge: Cambridge University Press, 1986, particularly pp. 1–18.

3. See most valuably: Fried, *The Evolution of Political Society*; Elman Service, *Origins of the State and Civilization: The process of cultural evolution*. New York: Norton, 1975; R. Cohen and E. Service (eds), *Origins of the State*. Philadelphia: Institute for the Study of Human Issues, 1978; J. Friedman and M. Rowlands (eds), 'Notes towards an epigenetic model of the evolution of "civilization" ', in *The Evolution of Social Systems*. London: Duckworth, 1977, pp. 201–76; David Webster, 'Warfare and the evolution of the state: A reconsideration', *American Antiquity*, 1975; **40**: 464–70; William Sanders and David Webster, 'Unilineal-ism, multilinealism, and the evolution of complex societies', in C. Redman et al. (eds), *Social Archaeology*. New York: Academic Press, 1978, pp. 249–302; H. Claessen and P. Skalnik (eds), *The Early State*. The Hague: Mouton, 1978, especially the editors' contributions; H. Claessen and P. Skalnik (eds), *The Study of the State*. The Hague: Mouton, 1981; Jonathan Haas, *The Evolution of the Prehistoric State*. New York: Columbia University Press, 1982; J. Gledhill, B. Bender, and M. Larsen (eds), *State and Society: The emergence and development of social hierarchy and political centralization*. London: Unwin, 1988.

4. Friedman and Rowlands, 'Notes towards an epigenetic model of the evolution of "civilization" '; Kristian Kristiansen, 'Chiefdoms, states, and systems of social

evolution', in T. Earle (ed.), *Chiefdoms: Power, economy, and ideology*. New York: Cambridge University Press, 1991, pp. 16–43.

5. Edward Luttwak, *The Grand Strategy of the Roman Empire*. Baltimore, MD: Johns Hopkins University Press, 1976; Michael Mann, *The Sources of Social Power*, Vol. 1. Cambridge: Cambridge University Press, 1986, pp. 142–6.

6. Good, anthropologically informed modern treatments of the subject are: Max Gluckman, 'The kingdom of the Zulu of South Africa', in M. Fortes and E. Evans-Pritchard (eds), *African Political Systems*. Oxford: Oxford University Press, 1940, pp. 25–55; id., 'The rise of the Zulu Empire', *Scientific American*, 1960; **202**: 157–68; Keith Otterbein (1994) 'The evolution of Zulu warfare', reprinted in K. Otterbein, *Feuding and Warfare*. Longhorne, PA: Gordon & Breach, 1964, pp. 25–32; Service, *Origins of the State and Civilization*, pp. 104–16.

7. Memorandum by: Sir Theophilus Shepstone, *British Parliamentary Papers*, 12 August 1887 (about 5531), enclosed in no. 13; quoted as a motto by: John Laband, *The Rise and Fall of the Zulu Nation*. London: Arms & Armour, 1997.

8. A. Richards (ed.), *East African Chiefs*. London: Faber, 1960; in general this remains useful. Individual studies include: M. Semakula Kiwanuka, *A History of Buganda*. London: Longman, 1971 (probably the best); Christopher Wrigley, *Kingship and State: The Buganda Dynasty*. Cambridge: Cambridge University Press, 1996; Samwiri Karugirc, *A History of the Kingdom of Nkore*. Oxford: Oxford University Press, 1971; John Beattie, *The Nyoro State*. Oxford: Oxford University Press, 1971; A. Dunbar, *A History of Bunyoro-Kitara*. Nairobi: Oxford University Press, 1965; Kenneth Ingham, *The Kingdom of Toro in Uganda*. London: Methuen, 1975; Jacque Maquet, *The Premise of Inequality in Ruanda: A study of political relations in a Central African Kingdom*. London: Oxford University Press, 1961.

9. For Gaul's population see a concentration of estimates in: John Durand, *Historical Estimates of World Population: An evaluation*. Philadelphia: University of Pennsylvania, 1974, p. 29; also Colin McEvedy and Richard Jones, *Atlas of World Population History*. London: Penguin, 1978, pp. 55–60.

10. For the developed Iron Age Hallstatt (Celtic?) 'princely' seats in today's southern Germany, see Kristian Kristiansen, *Europe before History*. Cambridge: Cambridge University Press, 1998, pp. 255–73, 277.

11. E. A. Thompson, *The Early Germans*. Oxford: Oxford University Press, 1965, pp. 67–8; for the source see Tacitus, *Annals* 2.44–6, 62. Also on the authority of the kings in comparison with old-style chiefs, see J. Wallace-Hadrill, *Early Germanic Kingship: In England and on the Continent*. Oxford: Oxford University Press, 1971, p. 7.

12. Thompson, *The Early Germans*, pp. 66–7.

13. Ibid. p. 69.

14. Tacitus, *Annals* 2.62.

15. Thompson, *The Early Germans*, p. 70.

16. Ibid. p. 68.

17. Tacitus, *Annals* 1.55–60, 2.45, 88. Thompson, *The Early Germans*, pp. 72–84; this is an excellent portrayal of tribal/chiefly politics.

18. For arguments more or less along similar lines, see Robert Carneiro, 'Political expansion as an expression of the principle of competitive exclusion', in R. Cohen and E. Service (eds), *Origins of the State*. Philadelphia: Institute for the Study of Human Issues, 1978, pp. 205–23; Stephen Sanderson, *Social Transformations: A general theory of historical development*. Oxford: Blackwell, 1995, pp. 103–19; and the studies cited in each.

19. For the 'city' versus 'territorial' state, see Bruce Trigger, *Early Civilization: Ancient Egypt in context*. Cairo: The American University, 1993, pp. 8–14; less specific about the size is: Charles Maisels, *The Emergence of Civilization: From hunting and gathering to agriculture, cities and the state in the Near East*. London: Routledge, 1990, p. xvi. Justified criticism of Trigger's model of 'territorial-state' vs 'city-state' is expressed in: David Wilson, 'Early state formation on the north coast of Peru: A critique of the city-state model', in D. Nichols and T. Charlton (eds), *The Archaeology of City-States: Cross-cultural approaches*. Washington, DC: Smithsonian Institute, 1997, pp. 229–44; also in Robin Yates, 'The city-state in Ancient China', in D. Nichols and T. Charlton (eds), *The Archaeology of City-States: Cross-cultural approaches*. Washington, DC: Smithsonian Institute, 1997, pp. 71–90. However, this collection (except for Wilson) errs in the other direction by assuming that all early states were city-states, whereas many petty-states referred to in the book as city-states were in fact rural petty-states. A similar conflation of the petty-state with the city-state is found in: G. Feinman and J. Marcus (eds), 'Introduction', in *Archaic States*. Santa Fe, NM: School of American Research, 1998, pp. 8–10; Joyce Marcus, 'The peaks and valleys of ancient states: an extension of the dynamic model', ibid., p. 92. Marcus's cyclical model of political unification and disintegration (where a spiral would be closer to historical reality) also leads her to the misleading view that petty-states initially evolved from large states rather than the other way around; 'collapses' and 'regressions' to more rudimentary forms of integration can and do occur in any evolutionary system. All this demonstrates that the full implications of Renfrew's 'early state module' as being part of a petty-states system (see endnote 2) have not been assimilated.

20. Peter Heather, *The Goths*. Oxford: Blackwell, 1996, pp. 54–64.

21. Ibid., p. 64, relying on Ammianus Marcellinus 16.12.23–6; 21.4.1–6; 27.10.3–4; 28.5.8; 29.4.2ff; 30.3.

22. Bernard Bachrach, *Merovingian Military Organization*. Minneapolis, MI: University of Minnesota, 1972, pp. 3–17. Also, for a précis of Gregory of

Tours' gruesome tale, see Edward James, *The Franks*. Oxford: Blackwell, 1988, pp. 88–91.

23. Steven Bassett (ed.), *The Origins of Anglo-Saxon Kingdoms*. London: Leicester University Press, 1989; C. J. Arnold, *An Archaeology of the Early Anglo-Saxon Kingdoms*, 2nd edn. London: Routledge, 1997, especially Chapter 8; Barbara Yorke, *Kings and Kingdoms of Early Anglo-Saxon England*. London: Seaby, 1992, especially pp. 15–24, 157–72; D. P. Kirby, *The Earliest English Kings*. London: Unwin, 1991. Frank Stenton, *Anglo Saxon England*, 3rd edn. Oxford: Oxford University Press, 1971, is still a useful narrative; see p. 40 for the Mercian numbers.

24. D. A. Binchy, *Celtic and Anglo-Saxon Kingship*. Oxford: Oxford University Press, 1970, pp. 31–46; this is superb. Also excellent are Blair Gibson, 'Chiefdoms, confederacies, and statehood in early Ireland', in B. Arnold and B. Gibson (eds), *Celtic Chiefdom, Celtic State*. Cambridge: Cambridge University Press, 1995, pp. 116–28; T. Bartlett and K. Jeffery (eds), *A Military History of Ireland*. Cambridge: Cambridge University Press, 1996, Chapters 2–5.

25. For the statistics, see Paddy Griffith, *The Viking Art of War*. London: Greenhill, 1995, p. 26. On the scant evidence for Scandinavian state formation see: Gwyn Jones, *A History of the Vikings*. Oxford: Oxford University Press, 1984; P. H. Sawyer, *Kings and Vikings: Scandinavia and Europe AD 700–1100*. London: Methuen, 1982; Peter Foot and David Wilson, *The Viking Achievement*. New York: Praeger, 1970; Aron Gurevich, 'The early state in Norway', in Claessen and Skalnik, *The Early State*, pp. 403–23; Niels Lund, 'Danish military organization', in J. Cooper (ed.), *The Battle of Maldon: Fiction and Fact*. London: Hambledon, 1993, pp. 109–26.

26. Karl Leyser, 'Early medieval warfare', in Cooper, *The Battle of Maldon*, p. 108; Adenek Vana, *The World of the Ancient Slavs*. London: Orbis, 1983, pp. 193–5.

27. For example, Warren Hollister, *Anglo-Saxon Military Institutions on the Eve of the Norman Conquest*. Oxford: Oxford University Press, 1962.

28. Binchy, *Celtic and Anglo-Saxon Kingship*; William Chaney, *The Cult of Kingship in Anglo-Saxon England*. Manchester: Manchester University Press, 1970.

29. Simon Franklin and Jonathan Shepard, *The Emergence of Rus 750–1200*. London: Longman, 1996; this is excellent and covers the latest archaeological finds; see also H. R. E. Davidson, *The Viking Road to Byzantium*. London: Allen Unwin, 1976.

30. See most interestingly in: T. J. Cornell, *The Beginnings of Rome: Italy and Rome from the Bronze Age to the Punic Wars (c. 1000–264)*. London: Routledge, 1995, pp. 130–45, 151–9, 224.

31. One does not have to accept fully the 'hydraulic' theory of state emergence, originally developed by Wittfogel to recognize this. Prominent examples

include the rivers Tigris and Euphrates, Nile, Yellow River, Indus, and even the Mississippi; also the intensive irrigation systems of the Olmecs, Maya, central Mexico, Andes, Hawaii, and Sri Lanka: Karl Wittfogel, *Oriental Despotism*. New Haven, CT: Yale University Press, 1967.

32. I believe that this is a better predictor and explanatory mechanism than those offered by Carneiro's much quoted paper: Robert Carneiro, 'A theory of the origin of the state', *Science*, 1970; **169**: 733–8. Contrary to Carneiro's premise, both ecological and social circumscriptions were common among pre-state agricultural societies. It was density and complexity that counted most in state emergence.

33. For all this, see Michael Hoffman, *Egypt before the Pharaohs*, London: Routledge, 1980; Feki Hassan, 'The predynastic of Egypt', *Journal of World Prehistory*, 1988; **2**: 135–85; Michael Rice, *Egypt's Making*. London: Routledge, 1991; A. J. Spencer, *Early Egypt*. Norman: University of Oklahoma, 1995; this last contains the best pictorial representations of the archaeological finds (especially pp. 52–7). For these, see also Yigael Yadin, *The Art of Warfare in Biblical Lands in the Light of Archaeological Study*, Vol. 1. New York: McGraw-Hill, 1963, pp. 116–17.

34. Renfrew's 'early state module' as being part of a system (see endnote 2) applies here as well. Curiously, although in *Early Civilization* (p. 10) Trigger, a leading expert on Egypt, mentions that Egypt was unified from 'small states'; he entirely overlooks this fact when presenting Egypt as a model fully formed, large-scale early 'territorial state'.

35. Anthony Smith, *The Ethnic Origins of Nations*. Oxford: Basil Blackwell, 1986, pp. 43, 89.

36. Kwang-Chih Chang, *The Archaeology of Ancient China*, 4th edn. New Haven, CT: Yale University Press, 1986, pp. 242–94; this includes a comprehensive survey of fortifications and warfare.

37. Ibid. pp. 303–5.

38. Ibid. pp. 307–16.

39. Kwang-Chih Chang, *Shang Civilization*. New Haven, CT: Yale University Press, 1980, pp. 194–200 (for military force). Also, Robin Yates, 'Early China', in K. Raaflaub and N. Rosenstein (eds), *War and Society in the Ancient and Medieval Worlds*. Cambridge, MA: Harvard University Press, 1999, especially pp. 7–15; R. Bagley and D. Keightley, in M. Loewe and E. Shaughnessy (eds), *The Cambridge History of Ancient China*. Cambridge: Cambridge University Press, 1999, pp. 124–91; David Keightley (ed.), 'The late Shang state: When, where, and what?', in *The Origins of Chinese Civilization*. Berkeley, CA: University of California, 1983, pp. 523–64.

40. For all this, see especially the anthropologically and archaeologically informed: Joan Piggott, *The Emergence of Japanese Kingship*. Stanford: Stanford University

Press, 1997; Keiji Imamura, *Prehistoric Japan*. Honolulu: University of Hawaii, 1996; also the first chapters in D. Brown (ed.), *The Cambridge History of Japan*, Vol. 1. Cambridge: Cambridge University Press, 1993. Less useful is: Gina Barnes, *China, Korea and Japan: The rise of civilization in East Asia*. London: Thames & Hudson. 1993

41. Trevor Bryce, *The Kingdom of the Hittites*. Oxford: Oxford University Press, 1998; Michael Beal, *The Organization of the Hittite Military*. Heidelberg: Winter, 1992. A useful short account is: Amélie Kuhrt, *The Ancient Near East c. 3000–330 BC*, Vol. 1. London: Routledge, 1995, pp. 225–82, especially pp. 266–70.

42. For example, V. R. Desborough, *The Greek Dark Ages*. London: Ernest Benn, 1972, pp. 18–19, 22.

43. John Chadwick, *The Mycenaean World*. Cambridge: Cambridge University Press, 1976, pp. 160–72; J. T. Hooker, *Mycenaean Greece*. London: Routledge, 1977; A. M. Snodgrass, *Arms and Armour of the Greeks*. London: Thames & Hudson, 1967, pp. 15–34.

44. Chadwick, *The Mycenaean World*, pp. 79–81; M. I. Finley, *The World of Odysseus*. London: Penguin, 1979, p. 54.

45. K. A. Wardle, 'The palace civilizations of Minoan Crete and Mycenaean Greece, 2000–1200', in B. Cunliffe (ed.), *The Oxford Illustrated Prehistory of Europe*. Oxford: Oxford University Press, 1994, p. 224; compare Hooker, *Mycenaean Greece*, pp. 94, 98.

46. Chadwick, *The Mycenaean World*, p. 68.

47. Ibid. pp. 71–3, 159–60, 173. Robert Drews, *The End of the Bronze Age: Changes in warfare and the catastrophe ca. 1200 BC*. Princeton, NJ: Princeton University Press, 1993, pp. 107–8, 148–9, 155–6, 161–3; to support his argument Drews probably somewhat overestimates the number of chariots while wholly denying the existence of peasant militias, whatever their value was.

48. Hans Güterbock, 'Hittites and the Aegean world: Part 1. The Ahhiyawa problem reconsidered', *American Journal of Archaeology*, 1983; **87**: 133–8; id., 'Hittites and Akhaeans: A new look', *Proceedings of the American Philosophical Society*, 1984; **128**: 114–22; Machteld Mellink, 'The Hittites and the Aegean world: Part 2. Archaeological comments on Ahhiyawa-Achaians in Western Anatolia', *American Journal of Archaeology*, 1983; **87**: 138–41. For the most updated and authoritative account, incorporating the latest archaeological discoveries from Troy, in the Hittite archives, and from the newly found rich archive in Thebes, see: Joachim Latacz, *Troy and Homer: Toward a solution of an old mystery*. Oxford: Oxford University Press, 2004.

49. Whatever one thinks of his positive suggestions (see Chapter 9, endnote 128), Drews' critique of these theories in Part 2 of his book (Drews, *The End of the Bronze Age*) is highly effective.

50. Chadwick, *The Mycenaean World*, pp. 174–7.

51. For the above and the change in the scholarly view, see R. Haegg and N. Marinatos (eds), *The Minoan Thalassocracy: Myth and reality*. Stockholm: Paul Astroems, 1984; this includes contributions from the leading experts in the field; see especially: Chester Starr, 'Minoan flower lovers', ibid., pp. 9–12; Gerald Cadogan, 'A Minoan thalassocracy?', ibid., pp. 13–15; Steffan Hiller, 'Pax Minoica versus Minoan thalassocracy: Military aspects of Minoan culture', ibid., pp. 27–31; and Sinclair Hood, 'A Minoan Empire in the Aegean in the 16th and 15th centuries?', ibid., pp. 33–7. A nuanced and cautionary discussion of the problem of internal hegemony vs fragmentation is: John Cherry, 'Polities and palaces: Some problems in Minoan state formation', in Renfrew and Cherry, *Peer Polity Interaction and Socio-Political Change*, pp. 19–45.

52. Piggott, *The Emergence of Japanese Kingship*, p. 15; E. Kidder, in D. Brown (ed.), *The Cambridge History of Japan*, Vol. 1. Cambridge: Cambridge University Press, 1993, pp. 97–9.

53. M. B. Rowton, 'Dimorphic structure and the parasocial element', *Journal of Near Eastern Studies*, 1977; **36**: 181–98.

54. Knowledge about the Hyksos is meagre in the extreme. All the same, the study by Van Seters remains intelligent and persuasive, whereas Bietak is the authority on the latest archaeology: John van Seters, *The Hyksos*. New Haven, CT: Yale University Press, 1966; Manfred Bietak, *Avaris: The capital of the Hyksos*. London: The British Museum, 1996. The popular misconception about the Hyksos and chariotry was dispelled by T. Säve Söderbergh, 'The Hyksos rule in Egypt', *The Journal of Egyptian Archaeology*, 1951; **37**: 53–71; Alan Schulman, 'Chariots, chariotry, and the Hyksos', *Journal of the Society for the Study of Egyptian Antiquities*, 1979; **10**: 105–53.

55. Trude Dothan, *The Philistines and their Material Culture*. New Haven, CT: Yale University Press, 1982, is the authority on the archaeology. Highly interesting on the various ethnicities, although confused about their Greek or Aegean/Anatolian origin, is: Othniel Margalith, *The Sea Peoples in the Bible*. Wiesbaden: Harrassowitz, 1994.

56. Richard Adams, *Prehistoric Mesoamerica*, revised edn. Norman: University of Oklahoma, 1991, p. 263. For evidence of and further bibliography on Mexican mercenaries in the classic Maya, see Andrea Stone, 'Disconnection, foreign insignia, and political expansion: Teotihuacan and the warrior stelae of Piedras Negras', in R. Diehl and J. Berlo (eds), *Mesoamerica after the Decline of Teotihuacan AD 700–900*. Washington, DC: Dumbarton, 1989, pp. 153–72.

57. C. J. Gadd, in I. Edwards, C. Gadd, and N. Hammond, *The Cambridge Ancient History*, 3rd edn, Vol. 1, Part 2. Cambridge: Cambridge University Press, 1971, p. 121. For a 'pacifist' view, see Gil Stein, 'Economy, ritual, and power in Ubaid Mesopotamia', in G. Stein and M. Rothman (eds), *Chiefdoms and Early States in the Near East*. Madison, WI: Prehistory, 1994, pp. 35–46.

58. Joan Oats, 'The background and development of early farming communities in Mesopotamia and the Zagros', *Proceedings of the Prehistoric Society*, 1973; **39**: 147–81, especially pp. 168–9.

59. J. N. Postgate, *Early Mesopotamia*. London: Routledge, 1994, pp. 24–5; also Marc van de Mieroop, *The Ancient Mesopotamian City*. Oxford: Oxford University Press, 1997, pp. 33–4.

60. The recognition has been general, but theoretically, see most strikingly: David Webster, 'On theocracies', *American Anthropologist*, 1976; **78**: 812–28; I wholly share the conclusions of this paper.

61. Thomas Emerson, *Cahokia and the Archaeology of Power*. Tuscaloosa, AL: University of Alabama, 1997.

62. Timothy Panketat, *The Ascent of Chiefs: Cahokia and Mississippian Politics in Native North America*. Tuscaloosa, AL: University of Alabama, 1994, especially pp. 91–2; relying on W. Iseminger et al. (eds), *The Archaeology of the Cahokia Palisade: The East Palisade investigations*. Springfield, IL: Illinois Historic Preservation Agency, 1990.

63. Jonathan Kenoyer, 'Early city-states in South Asia', in D. Nichols and T. Charlton (eds), *The Archaeology of City-States: Cross-cultural approaches*. Washington, DC: Smithsonian Institute, 1997, pp. 56–62; Bridget Allchin and Raymond Allchin, *The Rise of Civilization in India and Pakistan*. Cambridge: Cambridge University Press, 1993, pp. 133–4, 146, 150, 157, 162, 171–6; Gregory Possehl, 'Sociocultural complexity without the state: The Indus civilization', in Feinman and Marcus, *Archaic States*, pp. 269–72; this presents the evidence for warfare but curiously forgets fortifications. Early notions of pacificity unfortunately found their way into important non-specialist works such as: William McNeill, *The Rise of the West: A history of the human community*. Chicago: University of Chicago, 1963, p. 86, and Service, *Origins of the State and Civilization*, p. 241, and have survived unchecked in: Robert O'Connell, *Ride of the Second Horseman: The birth and death of war*. New York: Oxford University Press, 1995, pp. 219–22.

64. For this logic with respect to early Sumer, see the classic essay by Thorkild Jacobsen, 'Early political development of Mesopotamia' (1957), in *Towards the Image of Tammuz and Other Essays on Mesopotamian History and Culture*. Cambridge, MA: Harvard University Press, 1970, pp. 142–4.

65. See, for example, A. W. Lawrence, *Greek Aims in Fortification*. Oxford: Oxford University Press, 1979, pp. 112, 132–3; Anthony Snodgrass, *Archaic Greece*. Berkeley, CA: University of California, 1980, pp. 31–3, 154–7; John Fine, *The Ancient Greeks*. Cambridge, MA: Harvard University Press, 1983, pp. 48–51; Walter Donlan and Carol Thomas, 'The village community of ancient Greece: Neolithic, Bronze and Dark Ages', *Studi Micenei ed Egeo-Anatolici*, 1993; **31**: 67–8. François de Polignac, *Cults, Territory and the Origins of the Greek City-State*.

Chicago: University of Chicago, 1995 (French original 1984), emphasizes the spread of cultic sites in the countryside and their role in the territorial formation of the *polis*, which may suggest a complementary rather than a contradictory process.

66. J. P. Mallory, *In Search of the Indo-Europeans*. London: Thames & Hudson, 1989, p. 120.

67. Henri Pirenne, *Medieval Cities*. Princeton, NJ: Princeton University Press, 1952, pp. 57–8; Richard Hull, *African Cities and Towns before the European Conquest*. New York: Norton, 1976, pp. xvii, 23–4; Max Weber, *The City*. New York: The Free Press, 1958; David Nicholas, *The Growth of the Medieval City: From late antiquity to the early fourteenth century*. London: Longman, 1997, pp. xvi, 81–8. Both Pirenne and Weber, and in effect also Hull and Nicholas, stress mixed functions in city emergence: defensive, commercial, and religious.

68. Peter Gutkind, *The Royal Capital of Buganda*. The Hague: Mouton, 1963, pp. 9–15.

69. M. Kovacs (trans.), *The Epic of Gilgamesh*. Stanford: Stanford University Press, 1985, I.10 and note.

70. The comprehensive archaeological survey of the Mesopotamian settlement patterns is Robert Adams and Hans Nissen, *The Uruk Countryside*. Chicago: University of Chicago, 1972; and Robert Adams, *Heartland of Cities*. Chicago: University of Chicago, 1981. For the urban population share see: Hans Nissen, *The Early History of the Ancient Near East 9000–2000 BC*. Chicago: University of Chicago, 1988, p. 131; Kuhrt, *The Ancient Near East c. 3000–330 BC*, pp. 31–2.

71. Hull, *African Cities and Towns before the European Conquest*, p. xiv.

72. Eva Krapf-Askari, *Yoruba Towns and Cities*. Oxford: Oxford University Press, 1969, especially pp. 3–7, 154–5; Robert Smith, *Kingdoms of the Yoruba*. London: Methuen, 1969, pp. 120–9; Hull, *African Cities and Towns before the European Conquest*, pp. 19–20; Graham Connah, *African Civilization: Precolonial cities and states in tropical Africa: An archaeological perspective*. Cambridge: Cambridge University Press, 1987, pp. 130–4; J. Peel, 'Yoruba as a city-state culture', in M. Hansen (ed.), *A Comparative Study of Thirty City-State Cultures*. Copenhagen: The Royal Danish Academy, 2000, pp. 507–18; citation from W. Bascon, 'Urbanization among the Yoruba', *The American Journal of Sociology*, 1955; **60**: 446.

73. See, for example, Chester Starr, *The Economic and Social Growth of Early Greece 800–500 BC*. New York: Oxford University Press, 1977, pp. 97–9; Anthony Snodgrass, 'Archaeology and the study of the Greek city' and Ian Morris, 'The early polis as city and state', both in J. Rich and A. Wallace Hadrill (eds), *City and Country in the Ancient World*. London: Routledge, 1991, pp. 1–58; Mogens

Hansen (ed.), 'The *polis* as citizen-state', in *The Ancient Greek City-State*. Copenhagen: The Royal Danish Academy, 1993, pp. 7–29.

74. Only lately has there been a growing awareness of this glaring lacuna, but research on the subject is still rudimentary. Most scholars who have referred to the question have erroneously assumed—either explicitly or implicitly—that the obvious dominance of food production and peasants in pre-industrial societies was directly expressed in urbanism percentages; but the two classifications were not overlapping, for example, because peasants could and did reside within the city. Examples of this confusion are: M. Finley, 'The ancient city: From Fustel de Coulanges to Max Weber', in *Economy and Society in Ancient Greece*. London: Chatto, 1981, pp. 3–23; here the problem is not even realized; Starr, *The Economic and Social Growth of Early Greece 800–500 BC*, pp. 41, 104–5, which is more cautious than: Chester Starr, *Individual and Community: The rise of the* polis *800–500 BC*. New York: Oxford University Press, 1986, pp. 6, 7, 13; the contributors to Rich and Hadrill (eds), *City and Country in the Ancient World*; Victor Hanson, *The Other Greeks: The family farm and the agrarian roots of western civilization*. New York: Free Press, 1995, p. 7, *passim*; id., *Warfare and Agriculture in Classical Greece*, revised edn. Berkeley, CA: University of California, 1998, pp. 42–9, 214–17. The following point out that Greek city-dwellers were mostly peasants, but they too offer no estimated percentage breakages: Robin Osborne, *Classical Landscape with Figures: The Ancient Greek city and its countryside*. London: George Philip, 1987; Alison Burford, *Land and Labour in the Greek World*. Baltimore, MA: Johns Hopkins University Press, 1993, pp. 10, 56–64; M. Hansen (ed.), *A Comparative Study of Thirty City-State Cultures*. Copenhagen: The Royal Danish Academy, p. 159. Only in recent years has Hansen deployed a formidable scholarly counter-argument, demonstrating—convincingly, in the present author's opinion—that the classical *polis* was indeed highly urban; see especially: Mogens Hansen, 'The *polis* as an urban centre. The literary and epigraphical evidence', in *The Polis as an Urban Centre and as a Political Community*. Copenhagen: The Royal Danish Academy, 1997, pp. 9–86.

75. M. Finley, *The Ancient Greeks*. London: Penguin, 1975, pp. 70–1, suggests between a half and a third residing in the city; Ian Morris, *Burial and Ancient Society: The rise of the Greek city-state*. Cambridge: Cambridge University Press, 1987, p. 100, tends towards the lower estimate; Osborne's important archaeological survey barely addresses the question directly: Robin Osborne, *The Discovery of Ancient Attika*, Cambridge: Cambridge University Press, 1985.

76. Contrary to Hanson's interpretation (*Warfare and Agriculture*, p. 46), both the text and context suggest a relatively small number of people working in the fields rather than living out in farms.

77. Hanson, *Warfare and Agriculture*.

78. J. Cherry, J. Davis, and E. Manzourani, *Landscape Archaeology as Long-Term History: Northern Keos in the Cycladic Islands from earliest settlement until modern times*. Los Angeles, CA: Monumenta Archaeologica 16, 1991, pp. 279–81, 337–8; Michael Jameson, Curtis Runnels, and Tjeerd van Andel, *A Greek Countryside: The Southern Argolid from prehistory to the present day*. Stanford: Stanford University Press, 1994, pp. 548–53, 561–3; J. Bintliff and A. Snodgrass, 'The Cambridge Bradford Boeotian Expedition: The first four years', *Journal of Field Archaeology*, 1985; **12**: 143. Compare Catherine Morgan and James Coulton, 'The *polis* as a physical entity', in Hansen, *The Polis as an Urban Centre and as a Political Community*, pp. 125–6. The Melos survey seems to offer no population breakage of rural versus urban residents: John Cherry and Malcolm Wagstaff, in C. Renfrew and M. Wagstaff (eds), *An Island Polity: The archaeology of exploitation in Melos*. Cambridge: Cambridge University Press, 1982, Chapters 2, 11 and 19.

79. Although Renfrew ('Trade as action at a distance', p. 32) amply stresses warfare as a central aspect of system interaction in the 'early state module', in my view he underestimates its central role in the formation of city-states.

80. Indeed, it is probably no coincidence that Egyptologists have come closest to the ideas developed here: Bruce Trigger, 'Determinants of urban growth in pre-industrial societies', in P. Ucko, R. Tringham, and G. Dimbleby (eds), *Man, Settlement, and Urbanism*. Cambridge, MA: Schenkman, 1972, pp. 575–99; id., 'The evolution of pre-industrial cities: A multilinear perspective', in F. Genus and F. Till (eds), *Mélange offerts à Jean Vercoutter*. Paris: CNRS, 1985, pp. 343–53; Fekri Hassan, 'Town and village in Ancient Egypt: Ecology, society and urbanization', in T. Shaw, P. Sinclair, B. Andah, and A. Okpoko (eds), *The Archaeology of Africa: Food, metals and towns*. London: Routledge, 1993, pp. 551–69. For Egypt, see also David O'Connor, 'Urbanism in Bronze Age Egypt and Northeast Africa', in T. Shaw et al. (eds), *The Archaeology of Africa: Food, metals and towns*. London: Routledge, 1993, pp. 570–86.

81. Postgate, *Early Mesopotamia*, pp. 74–5, 80; Charles Redman, *The Rise of Civilization: From early forms to urban society in the Ancient Near East*. San Francisco, CA: Freeman, 1978, pp. 255, 264–5.

82. Kenoyer, 'Early city-states in South Asia', p. 58.

83. A. Ghosh, *The City in Early Historical India*. Silma: Indian Institute of Advanced Study, 1973, pp. 51, 61–7; F. R. Allchin et al., *The Archaeology of Early Historic South Asia: The emergence of city and states*. Cambridge: Cambridge University Press, 1995, pp. 62, 70, 106–111, 134–6, 142–6, 202, 222–6; George Erdosy, *Urbanization in Early Historic India*. Oxford: BAR, 1988, pp. 109, 113–4.

84. J. Ajay and R. Smith, *Yoruba Warfare in the Nineteenth Century*. Cambridge: Cambridge University Press, 1964, pp. 23–8; Smith, *Kingdoms of the Yoruba*, pp. 22, 125–6; Connah, *African Civilization*, pp. 131–6; Graham Connah, 'African city walls: a neglected source?', in D. Anderson and R. Rathbone (eds), *Africa's*

Urban Past. London: Currey & Heinemann, 2000, pp. 36–51; Hull, *African Cities and Towns before the European Conquest,* p. 41.

85. F. E. Winter, *Greek Fortifications.* London: Routledge, 1971, especially pp. 54–5, 60, 101; Lawrence, *Greek Aims in Fortification,* pp. 113–14; Snodgrass, 'Archaeology and the study of the Greek city', pp. 6–10.

86. Winter, *Greek Fortifications,* pp. 61–4.

87. R. Ross Holloway *The Archaeology of Early Rome and Latium.* London: Routledge, 1994, pp. 91–102; Cornell, *The Beginnings of Rome,* pp. 198–202, 320, 331; id., 'The city-states in Latium', in Hansen, *A Comparative Study of Thirty City-State Cultures,* pp. 217–19; Christopher Smith, *Early Rome and Latium: Economy and society c. 1000 to 500 BC.* Oxford: Oxford University Press, 1996, pp. 152–4.

88. Whatever other differences they have, the following agree on this: Pirenne, *Medieval Cities,* pp. 141–3, 177–8; id., *Early Democracies in the Low Countries: Urban society and political conflict in the Middle Ages and the Renaissance.* New York: Harper, 1963, especially pp. 4, 37; Adriaan Verhulst, *The Rise of Cities in North-West Europe.* Cambridge: Cambridge University Press, 1999, pp. 70–117. Also Nicholas, *The Growth of the Medieval City,* pp. 92–5, 184. For Italy, see, for example, J. K. Hyde, *Society and Politics in Medieval Italy: The evolution of civil life 1000–1350.* London: Macmillan, 1973, p. 74 and plates 1a and b; Gordon Griffiths, 'The Italian city-states', in R. Griffeth and C. Thomas (eds), *The City-State in Five Cultures.* Santa Barbara, CA: ABC-Clio, 1981, pp. 87–8; Franek Sznura, 'Civic urbanism in medieval Florence', in A. Molho, K. Raaflaub, and J. Emlen (eds), *City-States in Classical Antiquity and Medieval Italy.* Stuttgart: Franz Steiner, 1991, pp. 403–18; Leonardo Benevolo, *The European City.* Oxford: Blackwell, 1993, pp. 34–6, 44–6, 50.

89. See especially David Webster, 'Lowland Maya fortifications', *Proceedings of the American Philosophical Society,* 1976; **120**: 361–71; id., 'Three walled sites of the northern Maya lowlands', *Journal of Field Archaeology,* 1978; **5**: 375–90; id., 'Warfare and the evolution of Maya civilization', in R. Adams (ed.), *The Origins of Maya Civilization.* Albuquerque, NM: University of New Mexico, 1977, pp. 357–9; Dennis Puleston and Donald Callender, 'Defensive earthworks at Tikal', *Expedition,* 1967; **9**(3): 40–8; an authoritative concise survey is: Adams, *Prehistoric Mesoamerica,* pp. 161–2.

90. Rene Millon, *The Teotihuacan Map,* Vol. 1, Part 1, *Text.* Austin, TX: University of Texas, 1973, pp. 39–40.

91. Pedro Amillas, 'Mesoamerican fortifications', *Antiquity,* 1951; **25**: 77–86; the various contributions to R. Diehl and J. Berlo (eds), *Mesoamerica after the Decline of Teotihuacan AD 700–900.* Washington, DC: Dumbarton, 1989, especially: Kenneth Hirth, 'Militarism and social organization at Xochicalco, Morelos', ibid., pp. 69–81, 84; Richard Blanton, *Monte Alban.* New York:

Academic Press, 1978, pp. 52–4, 75–6; Michael Lind, 'Mixtec city-states and Mixtec city-state culture', in Hansen, *A Comparative Study of Thirty City-State Cultures*, p. 572; an excellent general survey is: Ross Hassig, *War and Society in Ancient Mesoamerica*. Berkeley, CA: University of California, 1992, pp. 35–6, 41, 68, 100–9, 150.

92. Again, Hanson seems to be entirely unaware of this paradox in his otherwise admirable interpretation of hoplite warfare (which mainly deals with the early classical period): Victor Hanson, *The Western Way of Warfare: Infantry battle in classical Greece*. New York: Alfred Knopf, 1989; also Hanson, *The Other Greeks*, especially pp. 145, 251–2; id., *Warfare and Agriculture*, p. 8. Hanson (*Warfare and Agriculture*, pp. 143–4) does, however, stress the prominence of the raid in the classical period, and it was undoubtedly even more central during the Archaic period (compare Osborne, *Classical Landscape with Figures*, pp. 138–41, 145). Josia Ober, 'Hoplites and obstacles', in V. Hanson (ed.), *Hoplites: The classical Greek battle experience*. New York: Routledge, 1991, pp. 173–196, comes closer (p. 186) but still fails to factor in the absence of circuit city-walls during the Archaic period.

93. Among the Greeks there was a strong religious obligation to allow the enemy to conduct funeral processions for their dead after a battle, but otherwise mercy was not a prevalent or admired virtue. The sources tell a grim story of mass executions of prisoners and civil populations, enslavement, and destruction. For a précis, see W. Kendrick Pritchett, *The Greek State at War*, Vol. 5. Berkeley, CA: University of California, 1991, pp. 203ff.

94. For the raid as the principal form of warfare among the Maya, see David Webster, 'Warfare and the evolution of Maya civilization', in R. Adams (ed.), *The Origins of Maya Civilization*. Albuquerque, NM: University of New Mexico, 1977, pp. 357–9; Hassig, *War and Society in Ancient Mesoamerica*, pp. 74–5; Linda Schele and David Freidel, *A Forest of Kings*. New York: Morrow; 1990; this contains a lively account; Linda Schele and Peter Mathews, 'Royal visits and other intersite relationships among the Classic Maya', in T. P. Culbert (ed.), *Classic Maya Political History: Hieroglyphic and archaeological evidence*. Cambridge: Cambridge University Press, 1991, pp. 245–8; David Freidel, 'Maya warfare: An example of peer polity interaction', in Renfrew and Cherry, *Peer Polity Interaction and Socio-Political Change*, pp. 93–108.

95. See Isaac Barry, 'The Aztec "flowery war": A geopolitical explanation', *Journal of Anthropological Research*, 1983; **39**: 415–32; Ross Hassig, *Aztec Warfare*. Norman: University of Oklahoma, 1988, pp. 105–9, 129–30, 254–6; id., 'The Aztec world', in K. Raaflaub and N. Rosenstein (eds), *War and Society in the Ancient and Medieval World*. Cambridge, MA: Harvard University Press, 1999, pp. 378–80.

96. Smith, *Kingdoms of the Yoruba*, pp. 126–7.

97. See extensively in Chapters 5–7 of J. Haas, S. Pozorski, and T. Pozorski (eds),

The Origins and Development of the Andean State. Cambridge: Cambridge University Press, 1987; also, Jeffrey Parsons and Charles Hastings, 'The late intermediate period', in R. Keating (ed.), *Peruvian Prehistory*. Cambridge: Cambridge University Press, 1988, pp. 152, 204–17.

98. Weber, *The City*, pp. 75–80; this classic is insightful on this as well.

99. For the introduction of payment see W. Kendrick Pritchett, *The Greek State at War*, Vol. 1. Berkeley, CA: University of California, 1974, Chapter I (the Peloponnesian War); Cornell, *The Beginnings of Rome*, pp. 187–8 (406 BC); and Hyde, *Society and Politics in Medieval Italy*, pp. 182–4; Philip Jones, *The Italian City-State 500–1300: From commune to signoria*. Oxford: Oxford University Press, 1997, pp. 385–6; Daniel Waley, 'The army of the Florentine republic, from the twelfth to the fourteenth century', in N. Rubinstein (ed.), *Florentine Studies*. London: Faber, 1968, pp. 94–6; Nicholas, *The Growth of the Medieval City*, pp. 255–8; Philippe Contamine, *War in the Middle Ages*. Oxford: Blackwell, 1984, p. 91 (from the twelfth and mostly thirteenth centuries AD).

100. The association between royal or sovereign power and fortifications has been noted in Tracy's book, which appeared after the above had already been sent for publication in article form: James Tracy (ed.), *City Walls: The urban enceinte in global perspective*. Cambridge: Cambridge University Press, 2000, p. 6. Frederick Cooper, 'The fortifications of Epaminondas and the rise of the monumental Greek city', ibid., pp. 155–91, claims that pure stone rather than stone-faced and brick walls appeared in Greece in the fourth century BC because of the contemporaneous introduction of the catapult.

101. Andrew George, *The Epic of Gilgamesh*, London: Penguin, 1999, I.10, 17–22, and pp. 143–8; J. Pritchard (ed.), 'Gilgamesh and Agga' (trans. S. Kramer) in *Ancient Near Eastern Texts*. Princeton, NJ: Princeton University Press, 1969, pp. 44–7.

102. Hull, *African Cities and Towns*, p. 40.

103. Webster, 'Warfare and the evolution of Maya civilization'; Schele and Freidel, *A Forest of Kings*; Freidel, 'Maya warfare'.

104. For example, Herodotus 1.141, 163.

105. For a superb analysis and synthesis see Cornell, *The Beginnings of Rome*, pp. 173–96.

106. P. A. L. Greenhalgh, *Early Greek Warfare: Horsemen and chariots in the Homeric and Archaic Ages*. Cambridge: Cambridge University Press, 1973; Lesley Worley, *Hippeis: The cavalry of Ancient Greece*. Boulder, CO: Westview, 1994.

107. Joachim Latacz, *Kampfparänase, Kampfdarstellung und Kampfwirklichkeit in der Ilias, bei Kallinos und Tyrtaios*. Munich: Zetemata, 1977, p. 66; W. Kendrick Pritchett, *The Greek State at War*, vol. iv. Berkeley, CA: University of California, 1985, pp. 1–44; also Morris, *Burial and Ancient Society*, pp. 196–201; Kurt

Raaflaub, 'Soldiers, citizens, and the revolution of the early Greek *polis*', in L. Lynette and P. Rhodes (eds), *The Development of the Polis in Archaic Greece*. London: Routledge, 1997, pp. 49–59. But see Hans van Wees, 'Leaders of men? Military organization in the *Iliad*', *Classical Quarterly*, 1986; **36**: 285–303; id., 'The Homeric way of war: The *Iliad* and the Hoplite phalanx', *Greece and Rome*, 1994; **41**: I. 1–18, II. 131–55. Although van Wees's analogy in the latter article with the open and 'chaotic' New Guinea battle is illuminating and much to the point, he overlooks the later, crude, close-order, north European 'shield wall' which may constitute a closer analogy with Greece of the late Dark Age; also Snodgrass, 'Archaeology and the study of the Greek city', p. 19; Everett Wheeler, 'The general as Hoplite', in Hanson, *Hoplites: The Classical Greek battle experience*, pp. 127–8. Hugh Bowden, 'Hoplites and Homer: Warfare, hero cult, and the ideology of the polis', in J. Rich and G. Shipley (eds), *War and Society in the Greek World*. London: Routledge, 1993, pp. 45–63; this turns the tables by arguing that the *Iliad* in fact reflects the world of the early *polis* and the period 750–650 BC.

108. Snodgrass, *Arms and Armour*, pp. 49–77; id., *Archaic Greece*, pp. 100–11, and plates 11, 15, 16.

109. J. F. Verbruggen, *The Art of Warfare in Western Europe during the Middle Ages*. Woodbridge: Boydell, 1997, pp. 111–203; this is a good, socially conscious survey.

110. Compare Stephan Epstein, 'The rise and fall of Italian city-states', in Hansen, *A Comparative Study of Thirty City-State Cultures*, pp. 277–94.

111. D. Hill, 'The role of the camel and the horse in the early Arab conquests', in V. Parry and M. Yapp (eds), *War, Technology and Society in the Middle East*. London: Oxford University Press, 1975, pp. 32–43; John Jandora, *The March from Medina: A revisionist study of the Arab conquests*. Clifton, NJ: Kingston, 1990. See also Jorgen Simonsen, 'Mecca and Medina: Arab city-states or Arab caravan-cities', in Hansen, *A Comparative Study of Thirty City-State Cultures*, pp. 241–50.

112. Ajay and Smith, *Yoruba Warfare in the Nineteenth Century*, pp. 3–4, 13–22, 133–5.

113. McNeill, *The Rise of the West*, pp. 117–18; Mann, *The Sources of Social Power*, pp. 185, 188.

114. For example, Morris, *Burial and Ancient Society*; but see Hansen ('The *polis* as citizen-state') for a corrective. In the above-cited case of Mantinea, city concentration meant democracy, whereas rural dispersion meant oligarchy; Osborne (*Classical Landscapes*, p. 25) notes this very well.

115. For this latter point, compare Robert Sallares, *The Ecology of the Ancient Greek World*. London: Duckworth, 1991, p. 47.

116. Hanson, *Warfare and Agriculture*, has admirably demonstrated the considerable difficulties of causing fatal and enduring damage to agricultural plants and farmland, but even seasonal losses of crops and other damages would have been catastrophic and insufferable for the farmers.

117. Hanson, *The Western Way of Warfare* and *The Other Greeks*. The argument had been foreshadowed by Ardant du Pick, *Battle Studies: Ancient and modern battle*. Harrisburg, PA: The Military Service Publishing Co., 1947(1868). Also see: Victor Hanson, 'Hoplite technology and phalanx battle', in his *Hoplites: The classical Greek battle experience*, pp. 63–85.

118. Pritchard, 'Gilgamesh and Agga'; Jacobsen, 'Early political development of Mesopotamia'; Thorkild Jacobsen, 'Primitive democracy in Ancient Mesopotamia', in *Towards the Image of Tammuz and Other Essays on Mesopotamian History and Culture*. Cambridge, MA: Harvard University Press, 1943, pp. 157–72; I. M. Diakonoff, 'The rise of the despotic state in Ancient Mesopotamia', in Diakonoff (ed.), *Ancient Mesopotamia*. Moscow: USSR Academy of Sciences, 1969, pp. 173–203; Van de Mieroop, *The Ancient Mesopotamian City*, pp. 123–4, 132–5.

119. A. Andrewes, *The Greek Tyrants*. New York: Harper, 1963, pp. 31–49. Anthony Snodgrass, 'The Hoplite reform and history', *Journal of Hellenic Studies*, 1965; **85**: 110–22; Snodgrass's reservations on chronological and other grounds are persuasively rejected by J. Salmon, 'Political Hoplites', *Journal of Hellenic Studies*, 1977; **97**: 84–101. Snodgrass's chronological query has in the meantime lost much of its ground, because scholarly opinion now favours an earlier date— the late eighth century—for the emergence of the phalanx: Hanson, 'Hoplite technology and phalanx battle'. Also compare Hanson's general discussion in *The Other Greeks*, pp. 203–14, of the *polis*'s agricultural–hoplite regime.

120. Cornell, *The Beginnings of Rome*, pp. 148, 194–6, 238.

121. Gilbert Charles-Picard, *Carthage*. London: Sidgwick & Jackson, 1968, pp. 56–61, 80–6. The most updated scholarly book is: Maria Aubert, *The Phoenicians and the West*. Cambridge: Cambridge University Press, 1993.

122. M. V. Clarke, *The Medieval City State: An essay on tyranny and federation in the later Middle Ages*, Cambridge: Speculum Historiale, 1966(1926); Hyde, *Society and Politics in Medieval Italy*, pp. 94–118, 141–52; Daniel Waley, *The Italian City-Republics*. New York: Longman, 1988, pp. 40–5, 117–72; Griffiths, 'The Italian city-states', pp. 81–2, 93, 101–5; Nicholas, *The Growth of the Medieval City*, pp. 262–71. For Flanders, see Pirenne, *Early Democracies in the Low Countries*; David Nicholas, *Town and Countryside: Social, economic and political tensions in fourteenth century Flanders*. Bruges: Ghent University Press, 1971. Weber, *The City*, pp. 157–230; Weber's general discussion can still be read with profit.

123. This has been more or less similarly suggested by Hanson, *The Other Greeks*, p. 226.

124. This point, well noted by Weber, is developed by d'Agostino: Max Weber, *The Agrarian Sociology of Ancient Civilizations*. London: Verso, 1998(1909), pp. 261, 306, Bruno d'Agostino, 'Military organization and social structure in Archaic Etruria', in O. Murray and S. Price (eds), *The Greek City*. Oxford University Press, 1990, pp. 59–82.

125. For example, Hassig, *War and Society in Ancient Mesoamerica*, pp. 168–70; David Webster, 'Warfare and status rivalry: Lowland Maya and Polynesian comparisons', in Feinman and Marcus, *Archaic States*, pp. 332–6; David Webster, 'Ancient Maya warfare', in Raaflaub and Rosenstein, *War and Society in the Ancient and Medieval Worlds*, pp. 345–6; Schele and Freidel, *A Forest of Kings*; Freidel, 'Maya warfare'. There are some variations here: whereas Freidel believes in an almost pure elite warfare, Webster (with whom I tend to agree) sees wider popular participation under aristocratic leadership.

126. Report by Captain Arthur Jones (6 June 1861), printed in Ajay and Smith, *Yoruba Warfare in the Nineteenth Century*, pp. 132–3.

127. Weber, *The City*, pp. 68–70, differentiating between 'producer' and 'consumer' cities, was more aware than many of his disciples that this distinction did not overlap his other distinction between the 'Occidental' and 'Oriental' city.

128. For more or less the same argument with respect to the Greeks, see Hanson, *The Other Greeks*, Chapter 9.

129. Aristotle, *Politics*, 2.9.13–17; Stephen Hodkinson, 'Warfare, wealth, and the crisis of Spartiate society', in Rich and Shipley, *War and Society in the Greek World*, pp. 146–6; Paul Cartledge, *Sparta and Lakonia: A regional history 1300–362 BC*. London: Routledge, 1979, pp. 307–18; Paul Cartledge, *Agesilaos and the Crisis of Sparta*. London: Duckworth, 1987, especially pp. 37–43, 160–79; J. F. Lazenby, *The Spartan Army*. Warminster: Aris, 1985.

130. H. W. Parke, *Greek Mercenary Soldiers*. Oxford: Oxford University Press, pp. 1–32; Cartledge, *Agesila os*, pp. 314–30.

131. For the citizens' growing unwillingness to enlist see Jones, *The Italian City-State*, pp. 387–90; Contamine, *War in the Middle Ages*, pp. 157–8. Generally see Michael Mallett, *Mercenaries and Their Masters: Warfare in Renaissance Italy*. London: Bodley Head, 1974; C. C. Bayley, *War and Society in Renaissance Florence: The De Militia of Leonardo Bruni*. Toronto: University of Toronto, 1961; Caferro's excellent book focuses on the mercenaries independent raiding and emphasizing the devastating ruin and costs that they inflicted: William Caferro, *Mercenary Companies and the Decline of Siena*, Baltimore, MA: Johns Hopkins University Press, 1998; also, Kenneth Fowler, *Medieval Mercenaries*, Vol. 1, *The Great Companies*. Oxford: Blackwell, 2001.

132. J. K. Anderson, *Military Theory and Practice in the Age of Xenophon*. Berkeley, CA: University of California, 1970; W. Kendrick Pritchett, *The Greek State at War*, Vol. 2. Berkeley, CA: University of California, 1974, Chapters III,

VII–IX; Parke, *Greek Mercenary Soldiers*, pp. 73ff; Josia Ober, *Fortress Attica: Defence of the Athenian land frontier 404–322 BC*. Leiden: Brill, 1985.

133. Parke, *Greek Mercenary Soldiers*.

134. Polybius, *The Histories* 13.6–8.

135. Although this limited longevity is well noted in 'Introduction' and 'Conclusion' to Griffeth and Thomas, *The City State in Five Cultures*, pp. xix, 195–7, 201–2, it remains a puzzle to most of the individual contributors. But see with respect to the Greeks: W. Runciman, 'Doomed to extinction: The *polis* as an evolutionary dead-end', in Murray and Price *The Greek City*, pp. 347–67; and excellently in: S. E. Finer, *The History of Government from the Earliest Times*, Vol. 1. Oxford: Oxford University Press, 1997, pp. 369–84; Mann, *The Sources of Social Power*, pp. 227–8.

136. Allchin and Allchin, *The Rise of Civilization in India and Pakistan*, p. 169.

137. Ghosh, *The City in Early Historical India*, pp. 34–5; Allchin et al., *The Archaeology of Early Historic South Asia*, pp. 115–17, 334.

138. See in T. P. Culbert (ed.), *Classic Maya Political History: Hieroglyphic and archaeological evidence*, pp. 140–5, 318–25, also pp. 27–9; Adams, *Prehistoric Mesoamerica*, pp. 173–4; Simon Martin and Nikolai Grube, 'Maya superstates', *Archaeology*, 1995; **48**(6): 41–6.

139. Puleston and Callender, 'Defensive earthworks at Tikal', pp. 45–7; compare Marcus, 'The peaks and valleys of ancient states', pp. 59–94; see the following discussion and endnote 19 for my criticism of Marcus's general model.

140. Thomas Carlton and Deborah Nichols, 'Diachronic studies of city-states: Permutations on a theme—central Mexico from 1700 BC to AD 1600', and Mary Hodge, 'When is a city-state: Archaeological measures of Aztec city-states and Aztec city-state systems', both in D. Nichols and T. Charlton, *The Archaeology of City-States: Cross-cultural approaches*, pp. 209–27.

141. See, for example, Victor Ehrenberg, *The Greek State*, London: Methuen, 1969, pp. 103–31; Peter Rhodes, 'The Greek *Poleis*: Demes, cities and leagues', in Hansen, *The Ancient Greek City-State*, pp. 161–82.

142. See, for example, Giovanni Tabacco, *The Struggle for Power in Medieval Italy: Structure of political rule*, Cambridge: Cambridge University Press, 1989 (Italian original 1979), pp. 295–320; Peter Burke, 'City-states', in J. Hall (ed.), *States in History*. Oxford: Basil Blackwell, 1986, pp. 140–3. Giorgio Chittolini, 'The Italian city-state and its territory', in A. Molho, K. Raaflaub, and J. Emlen (eds), *City-States in Classical Antiquity and Medieval Italy*. Stuttgart: Franz Steiner, 1991, gets much of the following, wider European perspective of the process very well; see also Clarke (*The Medieval City-State*, pp. 147–207) for the federations discussed below.

143. Jacobsen, 'Early political development of Mesopotamia', pp. 155–6; Kuhrt, *The Ancient Near East c. 3000–330 BC*, pp. 338, 362.

144. Hassig, *Aztec Warfare*, pp. 55, 59–60; Adams, *Prehistoric Mesoamerica*, pp. 367, 389.

145. For *polis* size, see Kurt Raaflaub, 'City-state, territory and empire in classical antiquity', in Molho, Raaflaub, and Emlen, *City-States in Classical Antiquity and Medieval Italy*, pp. 565–88; Fine, *The Ancient Greeks*, p. 51; Carol Thomas, 'The Greek polis', in Griffeth and Thomas, *The City-State in Five Cultures*, pp. 43, 47.

146. Waley, *The Italian City-Republics*, pp. 21–2; Jones, *The Italian City-State 500–1300*, pp. 153, 193; Griffeth and Thomas, *The City State in Five Cultures*, pp. 87, 99, 186–7; Pirenne, *Early Democracies in the Low Countries*, pp. 104–5; Contamine, *War in the Middle Ages*, p. 117.

147. Specifically see Raaflaub, 'City-state, territory and empire in classical antiquity'. Generally see Claude Nicolet, *Rome et la conquête du monde méditerranéen 264–27*, Vol. I: *Les structures de l'Italie romaine*. Paris: Presses Universitaires de France, 1993; also the contributions by John Rich and Stephen Oakley in: J. Rich and G. Shipley (eds), *War and Society in the Roman World*. London: Routledge, 1993, pp. 1–68.

148. Cornell, *The Beginnings of Rome*, pp. 204–8, 320, 351, 380–5.

149. William Harris, *War and Imperialism in Republican Rome 327–70 BC*. Oxford: Oxford University Press, 1979, pp. 44. For all this, see Peter Brunt, *Italian Manpower*. Oxford: Oxford University Press, 1971, pp. 44–90, 416–26.

150. For the numbers see Bezalel Bar-Kochva, *The Seleucid Army*. Cambridge: Cambridge University Press, 1976; in my view Bar-Kochva's conclusion (pp. 205–6) misses the point.

151. Azar Gat, 'Clausewitz on defence and attack', *Journal of Strategic Studies*, 1988; **11**: 20–26.

152. This is well emphasized by Hassig, *Aztec Warfare*, pp. 236, 266–7.

153. For the Greeks, Hanson (*The Other Greeks*, Chapters 6–7) is very good; see also Pericles's striking strategic outline before the Athenians in Thucydides i.141–4.

154. For the heavy financial burden on the Italian communes, for example, see Hyde, *Society and Politics in Medieval Italy*, pp. 182–4.

155. Peter Brunt, 'The army and the land in the Roman revolution', *Journal of Roman Studies*, 1962; **52**: 69–84; further developed by Alexander Yakobson, *Election and Electioneering in Rome: A study in the political system of the late republic*. Stuttgart: Franz Steiner, 1999, pp. 230–1.

156. Geoffrey Conrad and Arthur Demarest, *Religion and Empire: The dynamic of Aztec and Maya expansion*. New York: Cambridge University Press, 1984, especially pp. 25–6, 33–5, much against their main argument; Hassig, *Aztec Warfare*, especially pp. 145–7; Robert Adams, *The Evolution of Urban Society: Early Mesopotamia and Prehistoric Mexico*. Chicago: Aldine, 1966, pp. 111–18.

157. Diakonoff, 'The rise of the despotic state in Ancient Mesopotamia'.

158. Morgens Larsen, *The Old Assyrian City-State and Its Colonies*. Copenhagen: Akademisk Forlag, 1976, pp. 109–91, 218–23, 366–74; also Kuhrt, *The Ancient Near East c. 3000–330 BC*, pp. 88–9, 365, 505–7.

159. Kenoyer, 'Early city-states in South Asia', pp. 65–8; Romila Thapar, *From Lineage to State: Social foundations in the mid-first millennium BC in the Ganga Valley*. Delhi: Oxford University Press, 1990; an exemplary analysis of the earlier transformation into statehood; A. Majumdar, *Concise History of Ancient India*, Vol. ii. New Delhi: Munshiram Manoharlal, 1992, pp. 32, 44, 131–44; Max Weber, *The Religion of India*. Glencoe, IL: The Free Press, 1958, pp. 87–91.

Chapter 11. The Eurasian Spearhead: East, West and the Steppe

1. Colin McEvedy and Richard Jones, *Atlas of World Population History*. London: Penguin, 1978, pp. 344–7; E. Jones, *The European Miracle: Environments, economies and geopolitics in the history of Europe and Asia*, 2nd edn. Cambridge: Cambridge University Press, 1987, pp. 3, 159.

2. See Alfred Crosby, *Ecological Imperialism: The biological expansion of Europe*. Cambridge: Cambridge University Press, 1986; Chapter 11 of this book suggests similar and additional explanations. The book foreshadowed some of the ideas later developed by Diamond.

3. M. Littauer and J. Crouwel, *Wheeled Vehicles and Ridden Animals in the Ancient Near East*. Leiden: Brill, 1979, pp. 33–6.

4. See John Thornton, *Warfare in Atlantic Africa 1500–1800*. London: University College London, 1999, especially pp. 25–8, *passim*.

5. See Weber's masterful discussion on the 'patrimonial' state: Max Weber, *Economy and Society*. New York: Bedminster, 1968, pp. 231–6, 964, 968–71, and Chapters xii–xiii.

6. Most notably: Georges Duby, *The Early Growth of the European Economy: Warriors and peasants from the seventh to the twelfth century*. London: Weidenfeld & Nicolson, 1974; Guy Bois, *The Transformation of the Year One Thousand*. Manchester: Manchester University Press, 1992; Jean-Pierre Poly and Eric Bournazel, *The Feudal Transformation, 900–1200*. New York: Holmes, 1991; Susan Reynolds, *Fiefs and Vassals: The medieval evidence reinterpreted*. Oxford: Oxford University Press, 1994; also, Marjorie Chibnall, 'Military service in Normandy before 1066', *Anglo-Saxon Studies*, 1982; **5**: 65–77. For a gradualist critique, see Dominique Barthélemy, *La Mutation de l'an mil a-t-elle eu lieu?* Paris: Fayard, 1997. Notably, contrary to their image, none of the above authorities rejects feudalism as a phenomenon and concept. A useful survey of recent trend is. Constance Brittain Bouchard, *Strong of Body, Brave and Noble: Chivalry and society in medieval France*. Ithaca: Cornell University Press, 1998.

7. Compare the foremost general treatises on feudalism: Mark Bloch, *Feudal Society*. London: Routledge, 1961, p. 446 (and Chapters 9–10); F. L. Ganshof, *Feudalism*. London: Longmans, 1964, p. xv; also, W. G. Runciman, *A Treatise on Social Theory*, Vol. 2. Cambridge: Cambridge University Press, 1989, pp. 208, 368; Kristian Kristiansen, 'Chiefdoms, states, and systems of social evolution', in T. Earle (ed.), *Chiefdoms: Power, economy, and ideology*. New York: Cambridge University Press, 1991, pp. 16–23. By contrast, standard works on political evolution conflate the two political forms: Elman Service, *Origins of the State and Civilization*. New York: Norton, 1975, pp. 81–3; Allen Johnston and Timothy Earle, *The Evolution of Human Societies: From foraging group to agrarian state*. Stanford: Stanford University Press, 1987, p. 249.

8. Well noted by Rushton Coulborn (ed.), *Feudalism in History*. Princeton, NJ: Princeton University Press, 1956, pp. 7, 186. This still valuable collection is too easily dismissed as outdated nowadays.

9. For Anglo-Saxon England, see Robin Fleming, *Kings and Lords in Conquest England*. Cambridge: Cambridge University Press, 1991.

10. Otto Hintze, 'Wesen und Verbreitung des Feudalismus' (1929), reprinted in Otto Hintze *Feudalismus—Kapitalismus*. Göttingen: Vandenhoeck, 1970, pp. 12–47, especially pp. 14, 22; Bloch, *Feudal Society*, p. 446 (although horsemanship is mentioned as somewhat almost incidental on p. 444); Ganshof, *Feudalism*, p. xv. In Weber's extensive discussions of feudalism, equestrianism is mentioned only once (p. 1077) and inconsequentially: Weber, *Economy and Society*, pp. 255–62, 1070–85; Coulborn (*Feudalism in History*, pp. 8–9) comes closest, but still refers to equestrianism outside his definition of feudalism (pp. 4–6) and as a prevalent rather than essential feature of that phenomenon. Poly and Bournazel, *The Feudal Transformation, 900–1200*, stress castles and the devolution of power to the local strongmen but not the equestrian feature of the system, which is typical of the more recent literature.

11. H. Brunner, 'Der Reiterdienst und die Anfänge des Lehnwesen', *Zeitschrift der Savigny Stiftung für Rechtgeschichte. Germanistische Abteilung*, 1887; **8**: 1–38; Lynn White, *Medieval Technology and Social Change*. Oxford: Oxford University Press, 1962, pp. 1–38. For a criticism of White's thesis, see Bernard Bachrach, *Armies and Politics in the Early Medieval West*. Aldershot: Variorum, 1993, Chapters xii, xiv, xvii.

12. This is suggested as the essence of feudalism in: Chris Wickham, 'The other transition: from the ancient world to feudalism', *Past and Present*, 1984; **103**: 3–36, which fails, however, to recognize the necessary preconditions for this change, attributing it to the strength of tax-evading aristocracy. After all, the Merovingian state was not stronger vis-à-vis its aristocracy than the Carolingian rulers who launched the process of feudalization.

13. See endnote 6.

14. Compare the thoroughly idealist interpretation of Poly and Bournazel (*The*

Feudal Transformation, 900–1200, p. 81), even though they believe that the act represented 'breathtaking realism'.

15. Again compare Ganshof, *Feudalism*, pp. 51–9.

16. Between 300 and 500 as against 200–300 measures: Aristotle, *Constitution of Athens* 7.3–4; Plutarch, *Solon* 18. For the Achaemenids, see I. Gershevitch (ed.), *The Cambridge History of Iran*, Vol. 2. Cambridge: Cambridge University Press, 1985, pp. 281, 573–6.

17. Livy 35:9, 35:45, 37:57, 45:34; Alexander Yakobson, *Elections and Electioneering in Rome*. Stuttgart: Franz Verlag, 1999, pp. 43–8.

18. Warren Treadgold, *Byzantium and Its Army 284–1081*. Stanford: Stanford University Press, 1995, especially pp. 23–5, 171–9; also John Haldon, *Warfare, State and Society in the Byzantine World 565–1204*. London: University College London, 1999, p. 128.

19. Bernard Bachrach, *Early Carolingian Warfare*. Philadelphia, PA: University of Pennsylvania, 2001, p. 55; Philippe Contamine, *War in the Middle Ages*. Oxford: Blackwell, 1986, p. 88; Charles Oman, *A History of the Art of War in the Middle Ages*, Vol. 2. New York: Burt Franklin, 1969(1924), p. 127.

20. Weber, *Economy and Society*, pp. 1071–2. Coulborn, *Feudalism in History*, and the other contributors to *Feudalism and History*, followed the same route, discussing—but ruling out—feudalism in cases of infantry 'fiefs', such as ancient Egypt and Hammurabi's Babylonia. In fifteenth- to seventeenth-century Muscovy-Russia, land allocation to sustain cavalry generated a process of feudalization and enserfment; when a new firearm infantry (*streltsy*) was created in the sixteenth century and sustained by the allocation of (much smaller) land plots, the new infantrymen never grew to become local lords; see Richard Hellie, *Enserfment and Military Change in Muscovy*. Chicago: University of Chicago, 1973.

21. Edward Shaughnessy, 'Historical perspectives on the introduction of the chariot into China', *Harvard Journal of Asiatic Studies*, 1988; **48**: 189–237; M. Loewe and E. Shaughnessy (eds), *The Cambridge History of Ancient China*. Cambridge: Cambridge University Press, 1999; Cho-Yun Hsu and Katheryn Linduff, *Western Chou Civilization*. New Haven, CT: Yale University Press, 1988; Herrlee Creel, *The Origins of Statecraft in China, I: The Western Chou Empire*. Chicago: Chicago University Press, 1970, especially Chapter 11; Li Xueqin, *Eastern Zhou and Qin Civilizations*. New Haven, CT: Yale University Press, 1985; Mark Lewis, *Sanctioned Violence in Early China*. New York: State University of New York, 1990; Derk Bodde, 'Feudalism in China', in Rushton Coulborn (ed.), *Feudalism in History*. Princeton, NJ: Princeton University Press, 1956, pp. 49–92.

22. F. Joüon Des Longrais, *L'Est et L'Ouest*. Paris: Institut de Recherches d'Histoire Étrangere, 1958; John Hall, 'Feudalism in Japan—A reassessment', in J. Hall

and M. Janssen (eds), *Studies in the Institutional History of Early Modern Japan.* Princeton, NJ: Princeton University Press, 1968, pp. 15–51; id., *Government and Local Power in Japan 500 to 1700.* Princeton, NJ: Princeton University Press, 1966; Peter Duus, *Feudalism in Japan.* New York: McGraw-Hill, 1993; Jeffrey Mass, *Warrior Government in Early Medieval Japan.* New Haven, CT: Yale University Press, 1974; id. (ed.), 'The early Bakufu and feudalism', in *Court and Bakufu in Japan.* Stanford: Stanford University Press, 1982, pp. 123–42; Ishii Ryosuke, 'Japanese feudalism', *Acta Asiatica*, 1978; **35**: 1–29; M. Jansen (ed.), *Warrior Rule in Japan*, Cambridge: Cambridge University Press, 1995 (compiled from Volumes 3 and 4 of *The Cambridge History of Japan*).

23. Whereas Japanese feudalism, more or less comparable to European feudalism, was postulated by early Japanese scholars and recognized by their western peers (for example, Hintze, Bloch, Ganshof, and Coulborn), more recent scholarship on Japan has become increasingly sceptical about the European and even feudal analogy, at the same time as European feudalism itself has come under increasing criticism. What has actually been shown, however, independently in both cases, is that in both of them the growth and formalization of feudalism were more complex and uneven than earlier held. For Europe see endnote 6. For the military aspect in Japan (in addition to the preceding note): William Farris, *Heavenly Warriors: The evolution of Japan's military, 500–1300.* Cambridge, MA: Harvard University Press, 1992; Karl Friday, *Hired Swords: The rise of private warrior power in early Japan.* Stanford: Stanford University Press, 1992. The rhetoric surrounding these generally sound observations has created the misleading impression that the new studies claim that the concept of feudalism itself was unsubstantiated. On the growing but thin veneer of the chivalrous spirit, see Georges Duby, 'The origins of knighthood', in *The Chivalrous Society.* London: Edward Arnold, 1977, pp. 158–70; Maurice Keen, *Chivalry.* New Haven, CT: Yale University Press, 1984; Matthew Strickland, *War and Chivalry.* Cambridge: Cambridge University Press, 1996. A comparative study is offered by: Stephen Morillo, '*Milites*, knights and samurai: Military technology, comparative history, and the problem of translation', in R. Ables and B. Bachrach (eds), *The Norman and their Adversaries at War.* Woodbridge: Boydell, 2001, pp. 167–84.

24. White, *Medieval Technology and Social Change*, pp. 1–38.

25. Contributing to this misconception are otherwise knowledgeable studies such as Oman, *History of the Art of War in the Middle Ages*, Vol. 1, pp. 13–14, *passim*; J. Verbruggen, *The Art of Warfare in Western Europe during the Middle Ages.* Woodbridge: Boydell, 1997, p. 5. But see, for example, White, *Medieval Technology and Social Change*, pp. 6–7; Arther Ferril, *The Fall of the Roman Empire: The military explanation.* London: Thames & Hudson, 1986, pp. 7–8, 60, *passim*.

26. Herwig Wolfram, *History of the Goths.* Berkeley, CA: University of California, 1988, pp. 127, 217.

27. Bachrach, *Armies and Politics in the Early Medieval West*, pp. xii, xiv, xvii.

28. Montesquieu, *The Spirit of the Laws*. Cambridge: Cambridge University Press, 1989, p. 30:1; Bloch, *Feudal Society*, pp. 441–7, leaving open for future research the question of the common causes of the feudal phenomenon (p. 447); Ganshof, *Feudalism* pp. xvi–xvii, allowing for a few more proximate cases.

29. Voltaire, *Fragments sur quelques révolutions dans l'Inde*, cited by Bloch, *Feudal Society*, pp. 441; Max Weber, *The Agrarian Sociology of Ancient Civilizations*. London: Verso, 1998(1909), pp. 38–9; extensively developed in Weber, *Economy and Society*, pp. 255–62, 1070–85; also Runciman, *A Treatise on Social Theory*, Vol. 2, p. 158. Runciman's awareness that the state's ability to maintain a central tax system and non-feudal troops constituted the key to resisting feudalism makes his study of particular cases more circumspect; yet he remains with a binary, feudal/non-feudal frame.

30. Hintze, 'Wesen und Verbreitung des Feudalismus', and Coulborn and the contributors to *Feudalism in History* come close to the same view.

31. Marxists have found China confusing in this respect. For a survey of Chinese and Soviet Marxist literature see: Arif Dirlik, 'The universalization of a concept: From "feudalism" to "Feudalism" in Chinese Marxist historiography', in T. Byres and H. Mukhia (eds), *Feudalism and Non-European Societies*. London: Frank Cass, 1985, pp. 197–227; Colin Jeffcott, 'The idea of feudalism in China and its application to Song Society', in E. Leach, S. Mukherjee, and J. Ward (eds), *Feudalism: Comparative Studies*. Sydney: Pathfinder, 1985, pp. 155–74; Derk Bodde, 'The state and empire of Ch'in', in D. Twitchett and M. Loewe (eds), *The Cambridge History of China*, Vol. 1. Cambridge: Cambridge University Press, 1986, pp. 22–3. For a recent Marxist example, see Li Jun, *Chinese Civilization in the Making, 1766–221 BC*. London: Macmillan, 1996.

32. This is acutely pointed out in: Chris Wickham, 'The uniqueness of the East', in T. Byres and H. Mukhia (eds), *Feudalism and Non-European Societies*. London: Frank Cass, 1985, pp. 172–5; also Bodde, 'Feudalism in China', pp. 83–92.

33. Again, Coulborn and the authors of the excellent individual case studies, *Feudalism in History* beginning with: Burr Brundage, 'Feudalism in Ancient Mesopotamia and Iran', pp. 93–119, have charted much the same way as that presented below.

34. Most of the evidence comes from the vassal state of Arrapha rather than from Mitanni itself: T. Kendall, *Warfare and Military Matters in the Nuzi Tablets*. Ann Arbor: University Microfilms, 1974. See also scepticism about the Aryan primacy in: Annelies Kammenhuber, *Hippolgia Hethitica*. Wiesbaden: Harrassowitz, 1961; id., *Die Arier im Vorderen Orient*. Heidelberg: Winter, 1968; this is countered by Manfred Mayrhofer, *Die Arier im Vorderen Orient—ein Mythos?* reprinted in Manfred Mayrhofer, *Ausgewählte kleine Schriften*. Wiesbaden: L. Reichert, 1979, pp. 48–71; Robert Drews, *The Coming of the Greeks: Indo-European conquests in the Aegean and the Near East*. Princeton, NJ:

Princeton University Press, 1988, pp. 140–7, *passim*; Gernot Wilhelm, *The Hurrians*. Warminster: Aris, 1989.

35. Alan Gardiner, *The Kadesh Inscriptions of Ramesses II*. Oxford: Oxford University Press, 1960, 80, 130–5, 150–5. Anatolian rivals of Hatti are recorded to have fielded many hundreds of chariots: Littauer and Crouwell, *Wheeled Vehicles and Ridden Animals in the Ancient Near East*, p. 94.

36. Michael Beal, *The Organization of the Hittite Military*. Heidelberg: Winter, 1992.

37. Alan Schulman, 'The Egyptian chariotry: A re-examination', *Journal of the American Research Centre in Egypt*, 1963; **2**: 75–98; id., *Military Rank, Title and Organization in the Egyptian New Kingdom*. Berlin: Hessling, 1964, especially pp. 59–62.

38. James Pritchard, *Ancient Near Eastern Texts Relating to the Old Testament*. Princeton, NJ: Princeton University Press, 1969, pp. 237, 246, 247; Kendall, *Warfare and Military Matters in the Nuzi Tablets*; Roger O'Callaghan, 'New light on the *maryannu* as chariot-warriors', *Jahrbuch für kleinasiatische Forschung*, 1950; **1**: 309–24; A. Rainey, 'The military personnel at Ugarit', *Journal of Near Eastern Studies*, 1965; **24**: 17–27; H. Reviv, 'Some comments on the maryannu', *Israel Exploration Journal*, 1972; **22**: 218–28; Michael Heltzer, *The Internal Organization of the Kingdom of Ugarit*. Wiesbaden: L. Reichert, 1982, especially Chapter 6 and pp. 111–15, 127, 192–4; Robert Drews, *The End of the Bronze Age: Changes in warfare and the catastrophe ca. 1200 BC*. Princeton, NJ: Princeton University Press, 1993, pp. 104–13, especially 112.

39. J. Postgate, *Taxation and Conscription in the Assyrian Army*. Rome: Biblical Institute, 1974, especially pp. 208–11; Stephanie Dalley, 'Foreign chariotry and cavalry in the armies of Tiglath-pileser III and Sargon II', *Iraq*, 1985; **47**: 31–48.

40. Herodotus 1.96, 98, 101, 103, 123, 127; I. Diakonoff, 'Media', in I. Gershevitch (ed.), *The Cambridge History of Iran*, Vol. 2. Cambridge: Cambridge University Press, 1985, pp. 36–148. Also, Muhammad Dandamaev and Vladimir Lukonin, *The Culture and Institutions of Ancient Iran*. Cambridge: Cambridge University Press, 1989, p. 55. For the problems and interpretation of the scant evidence, see Helen Sancisi-Weerdenburg, 'Was there ever a Median Empire', *Achaemenid History*, 1988; **3**: 197–212; her scepticism, in my view, simply amounts to the conclusion that the Median state was an overlordship.

41. J. Cook, *The Persian Empire*. London: Dent, 1983, especially pp. 53, 101–12; Dandamaev and Lukonin, *The Culture and Institutions of Ancient Iran*, especially pp. 138–52, 222–34.

42. E. Yarshater (ed.), *The Cambridge History of Iran*, Vol. 3. Cambridge: Cambridge University Press, 1985, Chapters 2, 4; Josef Wieshöfer, *Ancient Persia: From 550 BC to 650 AD*. London: Tauris, 1996.

43. The contributions by H. Roemer and R. Savory, in P. Jackson and L. Lockhart

(eds), *The Cambridge History of Iran*, Vol. 6. Cambridge: Cambridge University Press, 1986, pp. 264–6, 344, 363–7.

44. This difference between 'occidental' and 'oriental' feudalism has already been stressed by Weber, *Economy and Society*, pp. 259–62, 1073–77.

45. John Haldon (ed.), 'The feudalism debate once more: The case of Byzantium', in *State, Army and Society in Byzantium*. Aldershot: Variorum, 1995, Chapter 4; id., 'The army and the economy: The allocation and redistribution of surplus wealth in the Byzantine state', ibid., Chapter 6 (which runs close to my own thesis); id., 'Military service, military lands, and the status of soldiers: Current problems and interpretations', ibid., Chapter 7. Also, Ernst Kantorowicz, 'Feudalism in the Byzantine Empire', in Coulborn, *Feudalism in History*, pp. 151–66; Treadgold, *Byzantium and Its Army 284–108*, especially pp. 23–5, 171–9; Mark Bartuisis, *The Late Byzantine Army: Arms and Society, 1204–1453*. Philadelphia: University of Pennsylvania, 1992, especially pp. 157–60, 164–5.

46. C. Bosworth, 'Recruitment, muster, and review in medieval Islamic armies', in V. Parry and M. Yapp (eds), *War, Technology and Society in the Middle East*. London: Oxford University Press, 1975, pp. 59–77; Hugh Kennedy, 'Central government and provincial elites in the early "Abbasid Caliphate" ', *Bulletin of the School of Oriental and African Studies*, 1981; **44**: 26–38; Patricia Crone, 'The early Islamic world', in K. Raaflaub and N. Rosenstein (eds), *War and Society in the Ancient and Medieval Worlds*. Cambridge MA: Harvard University Press, 1999, pp. 309–32. Hugh Kennedy, *The Armies of the Caliphs: Military and society in the early Islamic state*. London: Routledge, 2001, pp. 59–95; in this Kennedy claims that the *iqta* was of marginal significance and not conditioned on service and that the caliphs kept their armies on payment from tax revenue; the evidence, however, is far from clear and, in any case, things changed with the decline of the caliphate.

47. Abdul Karim Rafeq, 'The local forces in Syria in the seventeenth and eighteenth centuries', in Parry and Yapp, *War, Technology and Society in the Middle East*, pp. 277–307; M. Yapp, 'The modernization of Middle Eastern armies in the nineteenth century: a comparative view', ibid., pp. 330–66, especially pp. 343–56; Rhoads Murphey, *Ottoman Warfare 1500–1700*. New Brunswick, NJ: Rutgers University Press, 1999, especially pp. 36–43. Again, my argument with respect to 'semi-feudalism' in the lands of Islam largely agrees with that of Wickham, 'The uniqueness of the East', pp. 175–82.

48. Daniel Thorner, 'Feudalism in India', in Coulborn, *Feudalism in History*, pp. 133–50; the contributors to Byres and Mukhia, *Feudalism and Non-European Societies*; and the contributors to Leach, Mukherjee, and Ward, *Feudalism: Comparative Studies*.

49. Such a crisis is advocated, for example, by Guy Bois, *The Crisis of Feudalism:*

Economy and society in Eastern Normandy c. 1300–1550. Cambridge: Cambridge University Press, 1984.

50. The literature on all this is vast. For the military aspect, see, for example, Contamine, *War in the Middle Ages*, pp. 77–101, 115–8, 150–72; Michael Prestwitch, *Armies and Warfare in the Middle Ages: The English experience.* New Haven, CT: Yale University Press, 1996; M. Keen (ed.), *Medieval Warfare.* Oxford: Oxford University Press, 1999, Chapters 6, 7, 10, 13; also Terence Wise, *Medieval Warfare.* London: Osprey, 1976; John Beeler, *Warfare in Feudal Europe 730–1200.* Ithaca: Cornell University Press, 1971.

51. Generally see Twitchett and Loewe, *The Cambridge History of China*, Vol. 1; also Hans Bielenstein, *The Bureaucracy of Han Times.* Cambridge: Cambridge University Press, 1980; for the horse bureaucracy under the T'ang: Jacques Gernet, *A History of Chinese Civilization.* Cambridge: Cambridge University Press, 1996, pp. 248–51; Denis Twitchett, 'Tibet in T'ang's grand strategy', in H. van de Ven (ed.), *Warfare in Chinese History.* Leiden: Brill, 2000, pp. 135–6; and under the Ming: Mitsutaka Tani, 'A study on horse administration in the Ming Period', *Acta Asiatica*, 1971; **21**: 73–97.

52. Contamine, *War in the Middle Ages*, p. 37; McEvedy and Jones, *Atlas of World Population History*, p. 71.

53. Contamine, *War in the Middle Ages*, p. 79; McEvedy and Jones, *Atlas of World Population History*, p. 43.

54. J. Prawer, *Histoire du royaume Latin de Jérusalem*, Vol. 1. Paris: Centre National de la Recherche Scientifique, 1975, pp. 497, 568–70.

55. Farris, *Heavenly Warriors*, pp. 341–3; McEvedy and Jones, *Atlas of World Population History*, p. 181.

56. Parry and Yapp, *War, Technology and Society in the Middle East*, pp. 282, 344; McEvedy and Jones, *Atlas of World Population History*, p. 137.

57. Drews, *The End of the Bronze Age*.

58. Ibid., pp. 139–40, 147; H. Saggs, *The Might that was Assyria.* London: Sidgwick, 1984, pp. 133ff, 243–8; Postgate, *Taxation and Conscription in the Assyrian Army*; Florence Malbran-Labat, *L'Armée et l'organisation militaire de l'Assyrie.* Geneva: Librairie Droz, 1982.

59. Lewis, *Sanctioned Violence in Early China*, pp. 61–5; Mark Lewis, 'Warring states: Political history', in Loewe and Shaughnessy, *The Cambridge History of Ancient China*, Chapter 9; Twitchett and Loewe, *The Cambridge History of China*, Vol. 1, especially pp. 27–8, 38, 162, 274, 479–82, 512–5, 616–26; Gernet, *A History of Chinese Civilization*, pp. 65–7, 80–1, 150–2.

60. N. Hammond, *The Macedonian State: Origins, institutions, and history.* Oxford: Oxford University Press, 1989, pp. 9–11, 53–65, 96–8, 100–29, 152–3, 162–4, *passim*; Eugene Borza, *In the Shadow of the Olympus: The emergence of Macedon.*

Princeton, NJ: Princeton University Press, 1990, pp. 125, 165–6, 202–5, *passim.*

61. Prestwick, *Armies and Warfare in the Middle Ages,* pp. 115–27; Contamine, *War in the Middle Ages,* pp. 88–90, 132–4, 150–1; Keen, *Medieval Warfare,* Chapters 6 and 13; Wise, *Medieval Warfare,* pp. 15–16; Jim Bradbury, *The Medieval Archer.* Woodbridge: Boydell, 1985.

62. Compare Montesquieu's classic formulation with Hall's book with respect to China: Montesquieu, *The Spirit of the Laws,* 1:4; and John Hall, *Power and Liberties: The causes and consequences of the rise of the West.* Oxford: Basil Blackwell, 1985, p. 42.

63. Duus, *Feudalism in Japan,* pp. 67ff; Hall, 'Feudalism in Japan—A reassessment'; Perry Anderson, *Lineages of the Absolutist State.* London: NLB, 1974, pp. 413–20, 435–61; Stephen Morillo, 'Guns and government: A comparative study of Europe and Japan', *Journal of World History,* 1995; **6**: 76–106; S. Eisenstadt, 'Tokugawa state and society', *Japanese Civilization: A comparative view.* Chicago: University of Chicago, 1996, pp. 184–218.

64. Charles Tilly (ed.), *The Formation of National States in Western Europe.* Princeton, NJ: Princeton University Press, 1975, p. 42.

65. Michael Mann, *The Sources of Social Power,* Vol. 1. Cambridge: Cambridge University Press, 1986, pp. 130, 142–61.

66. Best on this dialectic are: Hugh Seton-Watson, *Nations and States: An inquiry into the origins of nations and the politics of nationalism.* Boulder, CO: Westview, 1977; John Armstrong, *Nations before Nationalism.* Chapel Hill, NC: University of North Carolina, 1982; Anthony Smith, *The Ethnic Origins of Nations.* Oxford: Basil Blackwell, 1986; Walker Connor, *Ethnonationalism.* Princeton, NJ: Princeton University Press, 1994; Craig Calhoun, *Nationalism.* Buckingham: Open University, 1997.

67. The picture is complex, but see: Colin Renfrew, 'Language families and the spread of farming', in D. Harris (ed.), *The Origins and Spread of Agriculture and Pastoralism in Eurasia.* London: University College London, 1996, pp. 70–92, especially p. 73; citing R. Austerlitz, 'Language-family density in North America and Africa', *Ural-Altaische Jahrbücher,* 1980; **52**: 1–10; Johanna Nichols, 'The origins and dispersal of languages', in N. G. Jablonski and L. C. Aiello (eds), *The Origins and Diversification of Language.* San Francisco, CA: California Academy of Sciences, 1998, pp. 127–70, especially pp. 134–9; Merritt Ruhlen, *A Guide to the World's Languages.* Stanford: Stanford University Press, 1987.

68. Bustenay Oded, *Mass Deportations and Deportees in the Neo-Assyrian Empire.* Wiesbaden: Ludwig Reichert, 1979.

69. Jared Diamond, *Guns, Germs, and Steel: The fate of human societies,* New York: Norton, 1997, Chapter 16.

70. Direct evidence in the ancient sources is scarce and the subject was neglected

in modern research. Caesar's first-hand testimony is the best here. Donald Engels, *Alexander the Great and the Logistics of the Macedonian Army*. Berkeley, CA: University of California, 1978, is an exemplary study on antiquity; Martin van Creveld, *Supplying War*. Cambridge: Cambridge University Press, 1977, arrives at pretty much the same conclusions with respect to the early modern period. Also, G. Periés, 'Army provisioning, logistics and strategy in the second half of the 17th century', *Acta Historica Hungaricae*, 1970; **16**(1–2): 1–51; J. Lynn (ed.), *Feeding Mars: Logistics in Western warfare from the Middle Ages to the present*. Boulder CO: Westview, 1993. Both the following incorporate some important revisions of Van Creveld's book: John Lynn, 'The history of logistics and supplying war', in *Feeding Mars*, pp. 9–29; Derek Croxton, 'A territorial imperative? The military revolution, strategy and peacemaking in the Thirty Years War', *War in History*, 1998; **5**: 253–79.

71. R. Faulkner, 'Egyptian military organization', *Journal of Egyptian Archaeology*, 1953; **39**: 32–47.

72. Farris, *Heavenly Warriors*, p. 49.

73. See Chapter 10, endnote 149.

74. The evidence is somewhat obscure, but see Oman, *History of the Art of War in the Middle Ages*, Vol. 1, pp. 76–80; Bachrach, *Early Carolingian Warfare*, pp. 53–8; Warren Hollister, *Anglo-Saxon Military Institutions on the Eve of the Norman Conquest*. Oxford: Oxford University Press, 1962 (one man from every five-hide unit or community); Richard Abels, *Lordship and Military Obligation in Anglo-Saxon England*. London: British Museum, 1988.

75. Bielenstein, *The Bureaucracy of Han Times*, p. 114; Loewe, in Twitchett and Loewe, *The Cambridge History of China*, Vol. 1, pp. 479–82.

76. But see, perceptively, Martin van Creveld, *The Rise and Decline of the State*. Cambridge: Cambridge University Press, 1999, pp. 41–2.

77. Adam Smith, *The Wealth of Nations* 5.1.1, 1776.

78. McEvedy and Jones, *Atlas of World Population History*, pp. 21–2.

79. A. H. M. Jones, *The Later Roman Empire 284–602*. Oxford: Basil Blackwell, 1964, pp. 97–100, 607–86; Jones's magisterial book remains unsurpassed; Pat Southern and Karen Dixon, *The Late Roman Army*. London: Batsford, 1996, is a useful updated summary of the research.

80. This crucial economic aspect is not sufficiently recognized by either side of the controversy regarding the Roman *limes*: Edward Luttwak, *The Grand Strategy of the Roman Empire*. Baltimore, MD: Johns Hopkins University Press, 1976; Benjamin Isaac, *The Limits of Empire: The Roman army in the East*. Oxford, Oxford University Press, 1990. Also, Ferril, *The Fall of the Roman Empire*; Hugh Elton, *Warfare in Roman Europe, AD 350–425*. Oxford: Oxford University Press, 1996, pp. 199–214.

81. Jones, *The Later Roman Empire 284–602*, pp. 1058–64; Elton, *Warfare in Roman Europe*, pp. 102–3 (and the authorities cited); John Rich, 'Introduction', in J. Rich and G. Shipley (eds), *War and Society in the Roman World*. London: Routledge, 1993, p. 7; Dick Whittaker, 'Landlords and warlords in the later Roman Empire', in Rich and Shipley, *War and Society in the Roman World*, pp. 277–302; Bachrach, *Early Carolingian Warfare*, pp. 52–3.

82. Elton, *Warfare in Roman Europe*; E. A. Thompson, *Romans and Barbarians*. Madison, WI: Wisconsin University Press, 1982; Malcolm Todd, *The Early Germans*. Oxford: Blackwell, 1992; Thomas Burns, *Barbarians within the Gates of Rome: A study of Roman military policy and the Barbarians, ca. 375–425 AD*. Bloomington, IN: Indiana University Press, 1994.

83. Again, in my view, Jones, *The Later Roman Empire 284–602*, pp. 1025–68, makes up the best comprehensive assessment of the reasons for Rome's decline.

84. Water Kaegi, *Byzantium and the Early Islamic Conquests*. Cambridge: Cambridge University Press, 1992, p. 131, *passim*; John Jandora, *The March from Medina: A revisionist study of the Arab conquests*. Clifton, NJ: Kingston, 1990, p. 62, *passim*; also Treadgold, *Byzantium and Its Army 284–1081*.

85. Weber's discussion on 'patrimonial' armies in Weber, *Economy and Society*, pp. 1015–20, refers only to the first two of the three tiers defined here.

86. Mark Lewis, 'The Han abolition of universal military service', in H. van de Ven (ed.), *Warfare in Chinese History*. Leiden: Brill, 2000, pp. 33–76; Denis Twitchett (ed.), *The Cambridge History of China*, Vol. 3, Part 1. Cambridge: Cambridge University Press, 1979, pp. 13–14, 16, 96–103, 207–8, 362–70, 415–18; David Graff, *Medieval Chinese Warfare, 300–900*. London: Routledge, 2002; Ch'i-ch'ing Hsiao, *The Military Establishment of the Yuan Dynasty*. Cambridge MA: Harvard University Press, 1978.

87. The evidence on ancient India is extremely thin, but see: P. Chakravarti, *The Art of War in Ancient India*. Delhi: Karan Publications, 1987, pp. 4, 76.

88. Studies on the size of Persian armies are a legion, but in general see: Cook, *The Persian Empire*, pp. 53, 101–25; Dandamaev and Lukonin, *The Culture and Institutions of Ancient Iran*, pp. 147–52, 222–34.

89. Daniel Pipes, *Slaves, Soldiers and Islam: The genesis of a military system*. New Haven, CT: Yale University Press, 1981; David Ayalon, 'Preliminary remarks on the *Mamluk* Military Institution in Islam', in Parry and Yapp, *War, Technology and Society in the Middle East*, pp. 44–58.

90. Exceptions are Joseph Tainter, *The Collapse of Complex Societies*. Cambridge: Cambridge University Press, 1990; his economic explanation, which evokes declining marginal returns, is in my view too narrow; also, N. Yaffee and G. Gowgill (eds), *The Collapse of Ancient States and Civilizations*. Tuscon, AZ: University of Arizona, 1988.

91. There is no point in citing the abundant references in modern studies on the

various empires. Generally, however, Montesquieu, *The Spirit of the Laws*, 1:14, is still worth reading.

92. Data from pre-modern times are scarce and fragmentary. See Tenney Frank, *An Economic Survey of Ancient Rome*. Baltimore, MD: Johns Hopkins University Press, 1940, p. 7; Keith Hopkins, 'Taxes and trade in the Roman Empire (200 BC–AD 400)', *Journal of Roman Studies*, 1980; **70**: 101–25; J. Campbell, *The Emperor and the Roman Army*. Oxford: Oxford University Press, 1984, pp. 161–98. For the bureaucrats, see Jones, *The Later Roman Empire 284–602*, pp. 1045–58. For more general works see: S. Eisenstadt, *The Political Systems of Empires*. New York: Free Press, 1963, pp. 151–2, 318–19; John Kautsky, *The Politics of Aristocratic Empires*. Chapel Hill, NC: University of North Carolina, 1982; Michael Doyle, *Empires*. Ithaca: Cornell University Press, 1986, pp. 100–2.

93. Twitchett, *The Cambridge History of China*, Vol. 3, Part 1, p. 416.

94. William McNeill, *The Rise of the West*. Chicago: University of Chicago, 1963, pp. 50, 228; Mann, *The Sources of Social Power*, pp. 162–4; and more specifically, Bennet Bronson, 'The role of Barbarians in the fall of states', in Yaffee and Gowgill, *The Collapse of Ancient States and Civilizations*, pp. 196–218; his argument in some respects parallels mine.

95. For the first figure see Francis Cleaves (trans.), *The Secret History of the Mongols*. Cambridge, MA: Harvard University Press, 1982, x.231; for the second, in an Iranian history of the time, see H. Franke and D. Twitchett (eds), *The Cambridge History of China*, Vol. 6. Cambridge: Cambridge University Press, 1994, p. 345.

96. See especially Askold Ivantchik, *Les Cimmériens au Proche-Orient*. Friburg: Editions Universitaires, 1993; also, Anne Kristensen, *Who Were the Cimmerians and Where Did They Come From?* Copenhagen: The Royal Danish Academy, 1988; this demonstrates the difficulties of identification, even if one rejects her proposed solution.

97. R. Rolle, *The World of the Scythians*. Berkeley, CA: University of California, 1989; Diakonoff, 'Media', pp. 91–109, 117–19; Dandamaev and Lukonin, *The Culture and Institutions of Ancient Iran*, pp. 49–55; J. Harmatta, *History of Civilizations of Central Asia*, Vol. 2. Delhi: UNESCO, 1999, Chapter 1; Laszlo Torday, *Mounted Archers: The beginning of Central Asian History*. Edinburgh: Durham, 1997, pp. 274–5; Timothy Taylor, in B. Cunliffe (ed.), *The Oxford Illustrated Prehistory of Europe*. Oxford: Oxford University Press, 1994, pp. 373–410; Kristian Kristiansen, *Europe before History*. Cambridge: Cambridge University Press, 1998, pp. 185–209. Herodotus, 1.103–6 and 4, is the principal literary source, supplementing the Assyrian chronicles and archaeology.

98. A. K. Narain, 'Indo-Europeans in inner Asia', in D. Sinor (ed.), *The Cambridge History of Early Inner Asia*. Cambridge: Cambridge University Press, 1990, pp. 151–76; Harmatta, *History of Civilizations of Central Asia*, Chapter 7.

99. However, for the east, compare Owen Lattimore, 'The geographical factor in Mongol history', in *Studies in Frontier History*. Paris: Mouton, 1962, pp. 241–58, especially 257.

100. Thomas Barfield, *The Perilous Frontier: Nomadic empires and China, 221 BC to AD 1757*. Cambridge, MA: Blackwell, 1992. A counter-argument, stressing the imperial Chinese pressure on the nomads is presented in: Nicola Di Cosmo, *Ancient China and Its Enemies: The rise of nomadic power in East Asian history*. Cambridge: Cambridge University Press, 2002, especially pp. 161–205; although closely documented and well reasoned, this argument, in my view, can serve only as a limited corrective.

101. In line with his overall argument, Di Cosmo, *Ancient China and Its Enemies*, pp. 138ff, interpreted the Chinese wall building as part of an aggressive north-ward frontier expansion into the steppe, which again I find to be only partly persuasive.

102. It is this latter, inter-Chinese, aspect that is stressed by Di Cosmo, *Ancient China and Its Enemies*, pp. 134–8.

103. Ibid., pp. 29–84; Nicola Di Cosmo, in Loewe and Shaughnessy, *The Cambridge History of Ancient China*, Vol. 1, pp. 892, 962; Yü Ying-shih, in Sinor, *The Cambridge History of Early Inner Asia*, pp. 118–50; id., in Twitchett and Loewe, *The Cambridge History of China*, Vol. 1, pp. 383–405; Owen Lattimore, 'Origins of the Great Wall of China: A frontier concept in theory and practice', in *Studies in Frontier History*. Paris: Mouton, 1962, pp. 97–118.

104. For the theory see Barfield, *The Perilous Frontier*, pp. 118–19, 124–7, 145–6, 167–82, 250–77; for the history: Franke and Twitchett, *The Cambridge History of China*, Vol. 6.

105. Barfield, *The Perilous Frontier*, p. 205.

106. Otto Maenchen-Helfen, *The World of the Huns*. Berkeley, CA: University of California, 1973; E. Thompson, *The Huns*. Oxford: Blackwell, 1996(1948).

107. Best on this complex mosaic are: Golden, *An Introduction to the History of the Turkic Peoples*; *History of Civilizations of Central Asia*; Sinor, *The Cambridge History of Early Inner Asia*.

108. Rudi Linder, 'Nomadism, horses and Huns', *Past and Present*, 1981; **92**: 1–19; anticipated by Bloch, *Feudal Society*, pp. 11–14; Rudi Linder, 'What was a nomadic tribe?', *Comparative Studies in Society and History*, 1982; **24**: 689–711.

109. Two excellent works on this later stage are: L. Collins, 'The military organiza-tion and tactics of the Crimean Tatars during the sixteenth and seventeenth centuries', in Parry and Yapp, *War, Technology and Society in the Middle East*, pp. 257–76; William McNeill, *Europe's Steppe Frontier 1500–1800*. Chicago: University of Chicago, 1964; also, John Keep, *Soldiers of the Tsar: Army and society in Russia 1462–1874*. Oxford: Oxford University Press, 1985, pp. 13–20.

110. Jones, *The European Miracle*; Hall, *Power and Liberties*; also David Landes, *The Wealth and Poverty of Nations*. New York: Norton, 1999.

111. A rare broad treatment of these questions is offered by Diamond's suggestive outline in the Epilogue to his book: Diamond, *Guns, Germs, and Steel*, pp. 411–16.

112. Anthropologist Goody has pointed out that in comparison with the rest of the world Eurasian societies of east and west resembled each other as much as they differed from each other: for example, Jack Goody, *Food and Love: A cultural history of East and West*. London: Verso, 1998.

113. Montesquieu, *The Spirit of the Laws*, 17:6; also 17:4.

114. Edward Gibbon, *The Decline and Fall of the Roman Empire*, Vol. 1. London: Everyman, 1966, p. 81.

115. Jones, *The European Miracle*, pp. 5, 8.

116. Although the elaboration of this old idea by Vittfogel has been rightly criticized on various grounds, the idea remains fundamentally valid: Karl Vittfogel, *Oriental Despotism*. New Haven, CT: Yale University Press, 1967. Compare M. Finley, *The Ancient Economy*. Berkeley, CA: University of California, 1973, p. 31.

117. See endnote 110.

118. This is the broader context against which the ideas advanced by Hanson are explained: Victor Hanson, *The Western Way of War: Infantry battle in Classical Greece*. New York: Knopf, 1989. Lynn's reservations should thus be regarded as at least overstated: John Lynn, *Battle: A history of combat and culture*. Boulder, CO: Westview, 2003, Chapter 1.

119. This point has been noted by Doyne Dawson, *The Origins of Western Warfare: Militarism and morality in the ancient world*. Boulder, CO: Westview, 1996, p. 48. Most of our information derives from Assyrian royal reliefs. Fine reproductions of them can be found in: Yigael Yadin, *The Art of Warfare in Biblical Lands*, Vol. 2. New York: McGraw-Hill, 1963. For the Persians: Cook, *The Persian Empire*, p. 103; Duncan Head, *The Achaemenid Persian Army*. Stockport: Montvert, 1992.

120. 'T'ai Kung's six secret teachings', in *The Seven Military Classics of Ancient China* (trans. R. Sawyer). Boulder, CO: Westview, 1993, p. 99, 104–5; Chakravarti, *The Art of War in Ancient India*, pp. 15–57; B. Majumdar, *The Military System in Ancient India*. Calcutta: Mukhopadhyay, 1960, pp. 50–1, 70; Sarva Singh, *Ancient Indian Warfare with Special Reference to the Vedic Period*. Leiden: Brill, 1965, pp. 8–12, 22; Herodotus, 7.65.

121. A rejection of Homer's 'battlefield taxi' is expressed, for example, by Edouard Delebecque, *Le Cheval dans l'Iliade*. Paris: Klincksiek, 1951, pp. 86–109; and recently and extensively by Drews, *The End of the Bronze Age*, pp. 113–29.

Even though Greenhalgh recognizes that early Greek cavalry regularly dismounted to fight of foot, he shares this criticism, while arguing that the Mycenaeans fought mounted with lances, as he believes the Hittite also did: Peter Greenhalgh, *Early Greek Warfare: Horsemen and chariots in the Homeric and Archaic ages*. Cambridge: Cambridge University Press, 1973; id., 'The Dendra charioteer', *Antiquity*, 1980; **54**: 201–5 (for the Hittites compare Yigael Yadin, *The Art of Warfare in Biblical Lands*, Vol. 1. New York: McGraw-Hill, 1963, pp. 80, 108–9). However, Littauer and Crouwel clearly demonstrate the impossibility of mounted chariot warfare with the lance: Mary Littauer and J. Crouwel, 'Chariots in late Bronze Age Greece', *Antiquity*, 1983; **57**: 187–92. And the validity of Homer's general model is substantiated by the evidence in J. K. Anderson, 'Homeric, British and Cyrenaic chariots', *American Journal of Archaeology*, 1965; **69**: 349–52; id., 'Greek chariot-borne mounted infantry', *American Journal of Archaeology*, 1975; **79**: 175–87; Josef Wiesner, *Fahren und Reiten*. Göttingen: Vandenhoeck, 1968, p. 95; Mary Littauer, 'The military use of the chariot in the Aegean in the late Bronze Age', *American Journal of Archaeology*, 1972; **76**: 145–57; J. Crouwel, *Chariots and Other Means of Land Transportation in Bronze Age Greece*. Amsterdam: Allard Pierson Museum, 1981, pp. 121–4, 129, 145, 151; id., *Chariots and other Wheeled Vehicles in Iron Age Greece*. Amsterdam: Allard Pierson Museum, 1992, pp. 53–5.

Chapter 12. Conclusion: War, the Leviathan, and the Pleasures and Miseries of Civilization

1. As a result of the later appearance and more rudimentary development of native American civilizations, scholars studying them have postulated and unwarrantedly universalized regular collapses and cyclical patterns of evolution.

2. Compare Michael Mann, *The Sources of Social Power*, Vol. 1. Cambridge: Cambridge University Press, 1986, pp. 130, 142–61.

3. Colin Renfrew, 'Language families and the spread of farming', in D. Harris (ed.), *The Origins and Spread of Agriculture and Pastoralism in Eurasia*. London: University College London, 1996, pp. 70–92.

4. For example, Robert Gilpin, *War and Change in World Politics*. Cambridge: Cambridge University Press, 1981, especially pp. 121, 146–55.

5. Max Weber, *Economy and Society*. New York: Bedminster, 1968, pp. 54, 904.

6. The argument regarding which sphere holds 'primacy' goes back to nineteenth-century Germany, as well as to Lenin's comments on Clausewitz. For summaries, see Eckart Kehr, *Economic Interest, Militarism, and Foreign Policy*. Berkeley, CA: University of California, 1977; Azar Gat, *A History of Military Thought: From the Enlightenment to the Cold War*. Oxford: Oxford University

Press, 2001, pp. 505–7. For more recent theorizing, see: Robert Putnam, 'Diplomacy and domestic politics: The logic of two-level games', *International Organization*, 1988; **42**: 427–60; Jeffrey Knopf, 'Beyond two-level games: Domestic-international interaction in the intermediate-range nuclear forces negotiations', *International Organization*, 1993; **47**: 599–628.

7. For the above critique: Azar Gat, *The Origins of Military Thought from the Enlightenment to Clausewitz*. Oxford: Oxford University Press, 1989, incorporated in Gat, *A History of Military Thought*; Martin van Creveld, *The Transformation of War*. New York: Free Press, 1991; John Keegan, *A History of Warfare*. New York: Knopf, 1994.

8. Charles Tilly, 'War making and state making as organized crime', in P. Evans, D. Rueschemeyer, and T. Skocpol (eds), *Bringing the State Back In*. Cambridge: Cambridge University Press, 1985, pp. 169–91.

9. Whereas information about pre-modern societies is generally lacking, Rome is a better-documented case, although here, too, hard data are scarce. See an excellent example in: Tenney Frank, *An Economic Survey of Ancient Rome*, Vol. 1. Paterson, NJ: Pageant Books, 1959, pp. 146, 228, *passim*; ibid., Vol. 5, pp. 4–7, *passim*; Keith Hopkins, 'Taxes and trade in the Roman Empire (200 B.C.–A.D. 400), *Journal of Roman Studies*, 1980; **70**: 101–25. More broadly see Raymond Goldsmith, *Premodern Financial Systems: A historical comparative study*. Cambridge: Cambridge University Press, 1987, pp. 18, 31–2 (Athens), 48 (Rome), 107, 121 (Moghal India), and 142 (Tokugawa Japan); the last two represent even more tenuous estimates.

10. Compare Michael Mann, 'States, ancient and modern', in *State, War and Capitalism*. Oxford: Blackwell, 1988, pp. 64–5.

11. For summaries see R. Cohen and E. Service (eds), *Origins of the State*. Philadelphia, PA: Institute for the Study of Human Issues, 1978; Jonathan Haas, *The Evolution of the Prehistoric State*. New York: Columbia University Press, 1982.

12. There have, of course, been attempts to connect sexuality with politics, most famously Freud's disciple Reich's theorizing about the relationship between sexual oppression and repression, oppressive economic and political regimes, and human well-being: Wilhelm Reich, *The Sexual Revolution*. London: Vision, 1972(1935); id., *The Mass Psychology of Fascism*. New York: Orgone Institute, 1946(1933). Even more famous are the writings of Michel Foucault.

13. Randy Thornhill and Craig Palmer, *A Natural History of Rape: Biological bases of sexual coercion*. Cambridge, MA: Massachusetts Institute of Technology, 2000; this is finally a sound, evolution-informed study of this distressing subject; also: D. Buss and N. Malamuth (eds), *Sex, Power, Conflict: Evolutionary and feminist perspectives*. New York: Oxford University Press, 1996. Brownmiller's pioneering book represents much of the prevailing confusion on the subject while also cursorily incorporating some historical evidence: Susan Brownmiller, *Against*

757

Our Will: Men, women and rape. London: Penguin, 1976, pp. 31–113. The view that rape is an act of domination and humiliation, rather than of sex, finds expression even in Joshua Goldstein, *War and Gender: How the gender shapes the war system and vice versa*. New York: Cambridge University Press, 2001, pp. 362–9; Martin van Creveld, *Men, Women and War*. London: Cassell, 2001, p. 33.

14. See, for example, Jack Goody, *The Oriental, the Ancient and the Primitive: Systems of marriage and the family in the pre-industrial societies of Eurasia*. Cambridge: Cambridge University Press, 1990.

15. J. Cook, in I. Gershevitch (ed.), *The Cambridge History of Iran*, Vol. 2. Cambridge: Cambridge University Press, 1985, pp. 226–7; id., *The Persian Empire*. London: Dent, 1983, pp. 136–7 (both contain information concerning later Iranian empires).

16. Hans Bielenstein, *The Bureaucracy of the Han Times*. Cambridge: Cambridge University Press, 1980, pp. 73–4.

17. Elizabeth Perry, *Rebels and Revolutionaries in North China, 1845–1945*. Stanford: Stanford University Press, 1980, pp. 51–2; Matthew Sommer, *Sex, Law, and Society in Late Imperial China*. Stanford: Stanford University Press, 2000, pp. 12–15, 93–101. According to early twentieth-century statistics, the sex ratio in rural China was more than 120:100 in favour of the males, as a result of female infanticide. Although the period studied is the modern one, the same principle seems to have held true throughout Chinese history. I am grateful to Dr Neil Diamant for drawing my attention to this piece of information.

18. Leslie Peirce, *The Imperial Harem: Women and sovereignty in the Ottoman Empire*. New York: Oxford University Press, 1993, pp. 122–4.

19. Ibn Khaldun, *The Muqaddimah: An introduction to history*. New York: Pantheon, 1958, Chapter 3.1.

20. Cicero, *Tusculan Disputations* 5.20–21.

21. Patrick Kirch, *The Evolution of the Polynesian Chiefdoms*. Cambridge: Cambridge University Press, 1984, pp. 195–7.

22. Paddy Griffith, *The Viking Art of War*. London: Greenhill, 1995, p. 26.

23. Richard Abels, *Lordship and Military Obligation in Anglo-Saxon England*. Berkeley, CA: University of California, 1988, p. 12.

24. Gershevitch, *The Cambridge History of Iran*, pp. 227, 331.

25. For the data on the late Empire, see Pat Southern and Karen Dixon, *The Late Roman Army*. London: Batsford, 1996, pp. x–xii.

26. For Byzantium, see S. E. Finer, *The History of Government From the Earliest Times*. Oxford: Oxford University Press, 1997, p. 702.

27. Peirce, *The Imperial Harem*, pp. 21, 44, 99–103.

28. A. T. Olmstead, *History of Assyria*. Chicago: University of Chicago, 1960, p. 396.

29. Tatiana Zerjal, Yali Xue, Giorgio Bertorelle, et al., 'The genetic legacy of the Mongols', *American Journal of Human Genetics*, 2003; **72**: 717–21.

30. Laura Betzig, *Despotism and Differential Reproduction: A Darwinian view of history*. New York: Aldine, 1986; this overlooks both the 'downside' of power politics, in terms of ultimate reproductive success, and the dominance of the proximate mechanisms in determining behaviour in conditions that may have substantially diverged from those of the evolutionary state of nature, where these mechanisms had proved adaptive.

31. Cited in: Michael Prawdin, *The Mongol Empire*. London: George Allen, 1961, p. 60.

32. L. Luca Cavalli-Sforza, Paolo Menozzi, and Alberto Piazza, *The History and Geography of Human Genes*. Princeton, NJ: Princeton University Press, 1994; and, more popularly, L. Luca Cavalli-Sforza, *The Great Human Diasporas*. Reading, MA: Addison, 1995.

33. See Chapter 11, endnote 66.

34. This is recognized by Adrian Hastings, *The Construction of Nationhood: Ethnicity, religion and nationhood*. Cambridge: Cambridge University Press, 1997, p. 169.

35. The earliest archaeological indications of this predisposition are the subject of Steven Mithen, *The Prehistory of the Mind: The cognitive origins of art, religion and science*. London: Thames & Hudson, 1996.

36. See Chapters 3 and 5.

37. The deeply practical nature to their believers of religious questions, which supposedly pertain to the most significant factors that affect human existence, is well noted by Pascal Boyer, *Religion Explained: The evolutionary origins of religious thought*. New York: Basic Books, 2001, pp. 135–42.

38. Compare Marcel Gauchet, *The Disenchantment of the World: A political history of religion*. Princeton, NJ: Princeton University Press, 1997, Chapter 2.

39. Compare Boyer, *Religion Explained*, pp. 270–7.

40. For the last mentioned element again compare Boyer, *Religion Explained*, pp. 285–91.

41. See persuasively Barry Isaac, 'Aztec warfare: Goals and battlefield comportment', *Ethnology*, 1983; **22**: 121–31.

42. For somewhat similar ideas about the influence of advanced literacy see: Shmuel Eisenstadt, 'The axial age: The emergence of transcendental visions and the rise of the clerics', *Archives européennes de sociologie*, 1982; **23**: 294–314; Ernest Gellner, *Plough, Sword and Book: The structure of human history*. Chicago: University of Chicago, 1989; Boyer, *Religion Explained*, pp. 277–83.

43. For an excellent analysis of the effect of the alienating environment of metropolitan and cosmopolitan cities, see Rodney Stark, *The Rise of Christianity: A*

sociologist considers history. Princeton, NJ: Princeton University Press, 1996, Chapter 7.

44. For a similar argument about those who believe in non-worldly rewards, see Stark 'The martyrs: Sacrifice as rational choice', in *The Rise of Christianity*, Chapter 8; David S. Wilson, *Darwin's Cathedral: Evolution, religion, and the nature of society*. Chicago: University of Chicago, 2002. Both works overlook the military aspect.

45. Richard Dawkins, *The Selfish Gene*. Oxford: Oxford University Press, 1989, p. 331.

46. For example, Regina Schwartz, *The Curse of Cain: The violent legacy of mono-theism*. Chicago: University of Chicago, 1997. Historically naïve, this book over-states a good case, overlooking the fact that pagans also fought for common, partly religious, identity, sacred land, and the glory of the gods, as well as relying on heavenly support. Daniel Martin, *Does Christianity Cause War?* Oxford: Oxford University Press, 1997; although idiosyncratic and apologetic, this rightly claims that religion was merely one interacting element within a com-plex array of factors. Rodney Stark, *One God: Historical consequences of mono-thesim*. Princeton, NJ: Princeton University Press, 2001, Chapter 3 is the closest to the approach presented here.

47. Pyrrhus, xxvi, in *Plutarch's Lives*, Vol. ix. Cambridge, MA: Loeb, 1959.

48. Ibid., xiv.

49. Diogenes Laertius 6.32, 38.

50. Peter Harvey, *An Introduction to Buddhist Ethics*. Cambridge: Cambridge University Press, 2000, pp. 239–85 (quotation from p. 239).

51. Despite popular interest, Buddhist warrior-monks have been the subjects of very few scholarly studies. Generally see Harvey, *An Introduction to Buddhist Ethics*, and, for China, Meir Shahar, 'Ming-Period evidence of Shaolin martial practice', *Harvard Journal of Asiatic Studies*, 2001; **61**: 359–413. Whereas self-defence against banditry in troubled times was the main reason and the main justification for the cultivation of the martial arts in Buddhist monasteries contrary to the Buddhist fundamental attitude, in Japan the correct practice of these arts became integrated into the ideal of the Zen itself; see Tukuan Soho, *The Unfettered Mind: Writings of the zen master of the sword master*. Tokyo: Kodansha, 1987. I am grateful to Dr Meir Shahar for his guidance on this subject. For Hindu (Yogi) and Moslem warrior sects, see W. Orr, 'Armed religious ascetics in Northern India', in J. Gommans and D. Kolff (eds), *Warfare and Weaponry in South Asia 1000–1800*. New Delhi: Oxford University Press, 2001, pp. 185–201.

52. With respect to the modern west, this is the subject of Norbert Elias, *The Civilizing Process*. Oxford: Blackwell, 1994.

Chapter 13. Introduction: The Explosion of Wealth and Power

1. An evolutionary perspective similar to mine informs Stephen Sanderson, *Social Transformations: A general theory of historical development*. Oxford: Blackwell, 1995, Chapters 4–5.

2. Adam Smith, *The Wealth of Nations* (1776) 5.1.1.

3. Adam Ferguson, *An Essay on the History of Civil Society*, 1767, especially Parts v and vi.

4. Karl Marx and Friedrich Engels, 'Manifesto of the Communist Party', in *Economic and Philosophical Manuscripts of 1844 and the Communist Manifesto*. Amherst, New York: Prometheus, 1988, p. 213.

Chapter 14. Guns and Markets: The New European States and a Global World

1. John Durand, *Historical Estimates of World Population: An evaluation*. Philadelphia, PA: University of Pennsylvania, 1974, p. 9; Colin McEvedy and Richard Jones, *Atlas of World Population History*. London: Penguin, 1978; E. L. Jones's excellent, *The European Miracle: Environments, economies, and geopolitics in the history of Europe and Asia*. Cambridge: Cambridge University Press, 1987, pp. 3–8, 159. Kenneth Pomeranz, *The Great Divergence: China, Europe, and the making of the modern world economy*. Princeton, NJ: Princeton University Press, 2000, offers a first-rate corrective, to which I refer later on. The last word so far is Angus Maddison, *The World Economy: A millennial perspective*. Paris: OECD, 2001, pp. 42, 44, 47, 49.

2. See Chapter 11 and the authorities cited therein; also William McNeill, *The Pursuit of Power: Technology, armed forces, and society since A.D. 1000*. Chicago: University of Chicago, 1982, pp. 113–16; Paul Kennedy, *The Rise and Fall of the Great Powers*. London: Fontana, 1989, Chapter 1.

3. S. Finer, *The History of Government from the Earliest Times*. Oxford: Oxford University Press, 1997, p. 1305; this recognizes that in Asia 'country-states' were swallowed up within empires, whereas in Europe they were not, although he attempts no explanation of that difference. Eisenstadt's taxonomy and that by Giddens comprise only patrimonial or bureaucratic empires and feudal systems, but no pre-modern national states: S. Eisenstadt, *Political System of Empire*. New York: Free Press, 1963, pp. 10–11; Anthony Giddens, *The Nation-State and Violence*. Berkeley, CA: University of California, 1985, pp. 79–80. By contrast, Tilly both recognizes a broader and older category of 'national state' and attempts to explain its European ascendancy: Charles Tilly, *Coercion, Capital, and European States, AD 990–1992*. Cambridge, MA: Blackwell, 1992. He fails, however, to take into account both geography and ethnicity, and although

I largely agree with his emphasis on capital and statehood, I try to weave all the above factors together somewhat differently.

4. I am closest here to the historical discussion in Hugh Seton-Watson, *Nations and States: An inquiry into the origins of nations and the politics of nationalism.* Boulder, CO: Westview, 1977; Walker Connor, *Ethnonationalism.* Princeton, NJ: Princeton University Press, 1994, Chapter 9; Adrian Hastings, *The Construction of Nationhood: Ethnicity, religion and nationalism.* Cambridge: Cambridge University Press, 1997. While making many correct points, Patrick Geary, *The Myth of Nations: The medieval origins of Europe.* Princeton, NJ: Princeton University Press, 2002, overstates his case. Indisputably, the barbarian migrations mixed ethnic groups among the invaders, as well as among them and the conquered populations. However, Geary fails even to mention the process of national formation to the north and *outside* the old Roman realm. Furthermore, his subtitle in effect belies his fashionable main title, because, as he concedes, the roots of many modern European nations indeed go as far deep as the post-migration period, during the later part of the first millennium.

5. Roughly summarizing: Martin Körner, 'Expenditure', in R. Bonney (ed.), *Economic Systems and State Finance.* Oxford: Oxford University Press, 1995, pp. 398–401. These realities are not fully grasped by some of the contributors in: Charles Tilly and Wim Blockmans (eds), *Cities and the Rise of States in Europe, AD 1000–1800.* Boulder, CO: Westview, 1994. But see Frank Tallett, *War and Society in Early–Modern Europe, 1495–1715.* London: Routledge, 1992, pp. 205–6. Both Braudel and Blockmans note without explaining that territorial states emerged where urbanism was less developed: Fernand Braudel, *The Mediterranean and the Mediterranean World in the Age of Philip II.* London: Fontana, 1978, p. 658; Wim Blockmans, 'Conclusion', in Tilly and Blockmans, *Cities and the Rise of States in Europe*, pp. 419–23; compare with the reasoning in Chapter 10.

6. Charles Tilly (ed.), *The Formations of National States in Western Europe.* Princeton, NJ: Princeton University Press, 1975, p. 24.

7. Michael Roberts 'The military revolution, 1560–1660' (1955, 1967), reprinted in C. Rogers (ed.), *The Military Revolution Debate.* Boulder, CO: Westview, 1995, pp. 13–36. Roberts has suggested that the creation of standing armies was caused simply by tactical reasons, as the combination of shot and pike in the infantry formation necessitated more complex drilling and, consequently, longer service. He has further maintained that a more ambitious strategy made possible by tactically more flexible armies during the Thirty Years War (1618–48) called for larger forces. In a similar unilineal vein he has argued that both processes strengthened central states' authorities, with all the ensuing political and social consequences. Rather than specifically address each of these arguments, I choose to deal with them more generally in the following discussion.

8. Geoffrey Parker ' "The military revolution, 1560–1660"—A myth?' (1976, 1979), reprinted in Rogers, *The Military Revolution Debate*, pp. 37–55; see p. 43.

9. Ibid., p. 44.

10. John Hale, *War and Society in Renaissance Europe 1450–1620*. London: Fontana, 1985, pp. 61–3; David Parrott, *Richelieu's Army: War, government and society in France, 1624–1642*. Cambridge: Cambridge University Press, 2001, pp. 164–222; John Lynn, 'Recalculating French army growth during the *Grand Siècle*, 1610–1715' (1994), reprinted in Rogers, *The Military Revolution Debate*, pp. 117–48, and reproduced in J. Lynn, *Giant of the* Grand Siècle*: The French army, 1610–1715*. Cambridge: Cambridge University Press, 1997, pp. 41–64; A. Corvisier (ed.), *Histoire militaire de la France*, Vol. 1, P. Contamine (ed.), *Des Origines à 1715*. Paris: Presses Universitaires, 1992, pp. 361–6.

11. Jeremy Black, *A Military Revolution? Military change and European society 1550–1800*. London: Macmillan, 1991; id., 'A military revolution? A 1660–1792 perspective', in Rogers, *The Military Revolution Debate*, pp. 95–116.

12. Clifford Rogers, 'The military revolutions of the Hundred Years War', in Rogers, *The Military Revolution Debate*, pp. 55–94.

13. As it has been recognized that the change was in effect more protracted than originally defined, Black (*A Military Revolution?*) has suggested that it is better understood as a transition rather than a revolution. Rogers has reasonably proposed that the process corresponded to the evolutionary model of 'punctuated equilibrium', whereby periods of slower change alternated with bursts of heightened growth. In my view, once it is realized that the point at issue is in effect the massive transformation associated with 'modernity' in general in the span of a few centuries, the designation revolution or transition becomes rather semantic.

14. Parker, ' "The military revolution, 1560–1660"—A myth?', p. 44; Tallett, *War and Society in Early-Modern Europe*; M. E. Mallett and J. R. Hale, *The Military Organization of a Renaissance State: Venice c. 1400 to 1617*. Cambridge: Cambridge University Press, 1984, pp. 126, 137–8, 375. The ebbs and flows of the process are highlighted by Simon Adams, 'Tactics or politics? "The military revolution" and the Hapsburg hegemony, 1525–1648', in J. Lynn (ed.), *Tools of War: Instruments, ideas, and institutions of warfare, 1445–1871*. Urbana, IL: University of Illinois, 1990, p. 36; James Wood, *The King's Army: Warfare, soldiers, and society during the wars of religion in France, 1562–1576*. Cambridge: Cambridge University Press, 1996, especially pp. 127–33, 144–52; Parrott, *Richelieu's Army*, pp. 60–1; and Lynn, *Giant of the* Grand Siècle, pp. 527–30. In the Swedish and Russian armies of the early eighteenth century, cavalry still comprised close to a half: Carol Stevens, 'Evaluating Peter's army: The impact of internal organization', in E. Lohr and M. Poe (eds), *The Military and Society in Russia 1450–1917*. Leiden: Brill, 2002, pp. 153–4. For an explanation see Jeremy Black (ed.),

'Introduction', in *War in the Early Modern World*. London: University College London, 1999, p. 18.

15. Joseph Needham, Ho Ping-Yü, Lu Gwei-Djen, and Wang Ling, *Science and Civilization in China*, Vol. V, Part vii, *Military Technology—the gunpowder epic*. Cambridge MA: Harvard University Press, 1986, pp. 39–51, 365–9, is monumental and exhaustive; Kenneth Chase, *Firearms: A global history to 1700*. New York: Cambridge University Press, 2003, is illuminating and transforms the discussion on the subject; Thomas Allsen, 'The circulation of military technology in the Mongolian Empire', in N. Di Cosmo (ed.), *Warfare in Inner Asian History (500–1800)*. Leiden: Brill, 2002, pp. 265–93, emphasizes the Mongol role; Cipolla's pioneering work still has value: Carlo Cipolla, *Guns and Sails in the Early Phase of European Exploration 1400–1700*. London: Collins, 1965; Bert Hall, *Weapons and Warfare in Renaissance Europe: Gunpowder Technology and Tactics*. Baltimore, MD: Johns Hopkins University Press, 1997, is the most informed on the first centuries in Europe. For other regions, see: David Ayalon, *Gunpowder and Firearms in the Mamluk Kingdom*. London: Cass, 1978(1956); Djurdjica Petrovic, 'Fire-arms in the Balkans on the eve and after the Ottoman conquests of the fourteenth and fifteenth centuries', in V. Parry and M. Yapp (eds), *War, Technology and Society in the Middle East*. London: Oxford University Press, 1975, pp. 164–94; Kelly DeVries, 'Gunpowder weapons at the siege of Constantinople, 1453', in Y. Lev (ed.), *War and Society in the Eastern Mediterranean, 7th–15th Centuries*. Leiden: Brill, 1997, pp. 343–62; Iqtidar Alam Khan, 'Early use of cannon and musket in India: AD 1442–1526', in J. Gommans and D. Kolff (eds), *Warfare and Weaponry in South Asia 1000–1800*. New Delhi: Oxford University Press, 2001, pp. 321–36; Jos Gommans, *Mughal Warfare*. London: Routledge, 2002, pp. 144–62.

16. John Hale, 'The early development of the bastion: an Italian chronology, c. 1450–c. 1534', reprinted in J. Hale, *Renaissance War Studies*. London: Hambledon, 1983, pp. 1–29; Horst de la Croix, *Military Considerations in City Planning: Fortifications*. New York: Braziller, 1972, pp. 39–47; Simon Pepper and Nicholas Adams, *Firearms and Fortifications: Military architecture and siege warfare in sixteenth century Siena*. Chicago: University of Chicago, 1986; Christopher Duffy, *Siege Warfare: The fortress in the early modern world 1494–1660*. London: Routledge, 1979.

17. Geoffrey Parker, *The Army of Flanders and the Spanish Road 1567–1659*. Cambridge: Cambridge University Press, 1972, pp. 5–12; id., ' "The military revolution, 1560–1660" —A myth?'; id., *The Military Revolution: Military innovation and the rise of the West, 1500–1800*. Cambridge: Cambridge University Press, 1989, pp. 13–14; this cites a list of examples; as does Charles Oman, *A History of the Art of War in the Sixteenth Century*. London: Methuen, 1937, pp. 544–5.

18. John Lynn, 'The *trace italienne* and the growth of armies: The French case', in Rogers, *The Military Revolution Debate*, pp. 117–48.

19. As Parker himself, in fact, holds, for example, ' "The military revolution, 1560–1660"—A myth?', p. 43. Parker (*The Military Revolution*, p. 24) claims that wherever in Europe the new fortifications appeared, there was a parallel growth in the size of armies. But rather than representing cause and effect, this correlate merely demonstrates that the politically, economically, and militarily most advanced powers were ahead in applying all the elements of the 'military revolution'.

20. On this well-recognized theme, see more specifically Richard Jones, 'Fortifications and sieges in Western Europe, c. 800–1450', in M. Keen (ed.), *Medieval Warfare: A history*. Oxford: Oxford University Press, 1999, pp. 163–85; Jim Bradbury, *The Medieval Siege*. Woodbridge: Boydell, 1992. Parker (*The Military Revolution*, p. 7) himself is well aware that medieval warfare was precisely of that nature.

21. Parker, *The Army of Flanders and the Spanish Road*, pp. 5–12; id., *The Military Revolution*, p. 12. Among those who have adopted his thesis are John Hale (see below); M. S. Anderson, *War and Society in Europe of the Old Regime 1618–1789*. London: Fontana, 1988, pp. 88, 140–1; id., *The Origins of the Modern European State System, 1494–1618*. London: Longman, 1998, pp. 9–10, 22; Adams, 'Tactics or politics?', p. 36; Tallett, *War and Society in Early–Modern Europe*, pp. 10, 38, 51, 168–9; James Tracy, *Emperor Charles V, Impresario of War: Campaign strategy, international finance and domestic politics*. Cambridge: Cambridge University Press, 2002, p. 30. However, interestingly enough, all theses scholars to some degree have known otherwise. Thus, although attributing the expansion of armies and the spiralling costs of war to firearms and artillery fortifications, Hale's meticulous calculations for Venice tell a wholly different story: Mallett and Hale, *The Military Organization of a Renaissance State*, pp. 409, 432–3, 436–7, 440–1, 444–5, 468–9, 470–2, 478, 480, 483–4, 487; Hale, *War and Society in Renaissance Europe*, pp. 46–7, 234–5. For Spain see I. A. A. Thompson, *War and Government in Habsburg Spain 1560–1620*. London: Athlone, 1976, pp. 34, 69–71, 288–93; id., ' "Money, money, and yet more money!" Finance, the fiscal-state and the military revolution: Spain 1500–1650', in Rogers, *The Military Revolution Debate*, pp. 273–98, especially 276–82. G. Parker, 'In defense of *The Military Revolution*', in Rogers, *The Military Revolution Debate*, p. 253, has replied that most of the money for fortifications was spent by the Spanish Empire in Flanders, Italy, and north Africa, rather than in mainland Spain. However, the same also applied to all the other military expenses (above all troops), which probably leaves the *ratio* pretty much the same. Indeed, the above-mentioned Italian figures support Thompson's conclusions, as do the figures for France cited by Lynn, 'The *trace italienne* and the growth of armies'. Also compare the figures in Lynn, *Giant of the* Grand Siècle, p. 592, with French overall military and general expenditure in Richard Bonney, 'France, 1494–1815', in Bonney (ed.), *The*

765

Rise of the Fiscal State in Europe, c. 1200–1815. Oxford: Oxford University Press, 1999, p. 143.

22. Judith Hook, 'Fortifications and the end of the Sienese state', *History*, 1977; **62**: 372–87, accentuates earlier cursory claims that the cost of the new fortifications was prohibitive. Strangely, however, her article has close to nothing by way of figures, economic analysis, and estimated costs in relation to Siena's overall budget. Although admitting that the city was already in bad financial condition for other reasons (pp. 375, 376), she provides no evidence that the new fortifications contributed to its decline. Indeed the costs that she does cite for the fortification of Siena's dependent towns—4,000 ducats for Montalcino, 4,000 for Chiusi, 2,000 for Lucignano (pp. 379, 381)—although not insignificant, were far from prohibitive, and were partly borne by the locals. By way of comparison, the upkeep of the Spanish garrison cost Siena close to 4,000 ducats in 1551 alone (p. 375), and *one* naval galley cost 6,000 ducats to build, and the same sum to maintain *each year* (see endnote 30). Furthermore, Hook is well aware that most of the workforce was conscripted with little cost to the state (pp. 376, 377, 378, 383, 384). Indeed, frequently cited in support of the claim that the new Italian fortifications were hugely expensive, Pepper's and Adams's admirable study of Siena in fact strongly claims the opposite: Pepper and Adams, *Firearms and Fortifications*, pp. 30–4, 163, 171. Duffy, *Siege Warfare*, pp. 91–3, mainly refers to the Dutch, even lighter, earth fortifications, which were the most numerous; see also John Childs, *Armies and Warfare in Europe 1648–1789.* Manchester: Manchester University Press, 1982, p. 135. David Eltis, *The Military Revolution in Sixteenth Century Europe.* London: Tauris, 1995, p. 29 and Chapter 4, realizes but somehow does not fully assimilate the fact that the new earth fortifications were neither more expensive nor taking longer to build than their predecessors. For the cost of Venice's old-style fifteenth-century fortifications see Mallett, in Mallett and Hale, *The Military Organization of a Renaissance State*, pp. 87–94; and for the decades that old-style fortifications often took to complete, see James Tracy (ed.), *City Walls: The urban enceinte in global perspective.* Cambridge: Cambridge University Press, 2000, p. 71. Hale (*War and Society in Renaissance Europe*, pp. 207–8) rightly points out that conscript labour was not without its indirect costs. And yet much of its employment took place off-season or during leisure time, and made use of the unemployed.

23. Data for pre-modern times are extremely poor. In Athens fortifications amounted to about 10 per cent of military expenditure: Raymond Goldsmith, *Premodern Financial Systems: A historical comparative study.* Cambridge: Cambridge University Press, 1987, p. 261, n. 60. For some medieval prices see Bradbury, *The Medieval Siege*, pp. 69, 74, 131–2. During his long crusade to the Holy Land (1248–54), King Louis IX of France spent the huge sum of over one million silver livres, of which about 100,000 were spent on massive

fortifications: HF, t. 21, 512–515, cited by J. Prawer, *Histoire du Royaume Latin de Jérusalem*, Vol. 2. Paris: Centre National de la Recherche Scientifique, 1975, p. 353, n. 73.

24. Again Hale, *War and Society in Renaissance Europe*, pp. 46–7, believes that artillery and other firearms greatly increased the cost of war, but, by his own figures, in 1482 artillery comprised only 8 per cent of French military expenditure (6–8 per cent in 1500 according to Corvisier (*Histoire militaire de la France*, p. 245). Hale presumably ascribes that fairly modest share to the early date, but, given that the French army itself was still relatively small, and its artillery the most advanced in Europe and cast from expensive bronze, percentages should not be supposed to have increased in later times (when cheap cast-iron guns became the standard). Hale also cites the impressive sums of money spent on gunpowder by Venice, but according to his own figures they, too, only amounted to a few per cent of the overall defence budget: Mallett and Hale, *The Military Organization of a Renaissance State*, pp. 401–2, 461–501. Similarly, in 1538 France spent some 36,000 livres *tournois* on saltpetre, the most expensive component of gunpowder, when her overall annual defence expenditure was around one million: Corvisier, *Histoire militaire de la France*, p. 247; Bonney, *The Rise of the Fiscal State in Europe*, p. 139. All this also puts into better perspective Fernand Braudel's staggering figures for gunpowder costs in his *Civilization and Capitalism 15th–18th Century*, Vol. 1, *The Structure of Everyday Life*. Berkeley, CA: University of California, 1992 (French 1979), p. 395; his calculations of Venice's overall capital investment in gunpowder stock, even if valid, are misleading, because it is the annual replacement cost that counts. The above pattern of spending re-emerges in other countries: according to Thompson (' "Money, money, and yet more money!" ', p. 279), artillery comprised only 4–5 per cent of Spain's military expenditure in the sixteenth and early seventeenth centuries; also Thompson, *War and Government in Habsburg Spain*, pp. 290–3, 296; in mid-seventeenth century Russia, the strong but largely imported (and therefore expensive) artillery arm is calculated to have constituted less than 10 per cent of the army's budget: Richard Hellie, 'The cost of Muscovite military defense and expansion', in Lohr and Poe, *The Military and Society in Russia 1450–1917*, pp. 41–66, especially p. 65; also: J. Kotilaine, 'In defense of the realm: Russian arms trade and production in the seventeenth and early eighteenth century', ibid., pp. 67–95. The idea that artillery and gunpowder were exceedingly costly is repeated by Anderson, *War and Society in Europe of the Old Regime*, pp. 19–20, again presenting sums out of context of overall military expenditure; also Tallett, *War and Society in Early-Modern Europe*, p. 169, but see his conclusion in endnote 34.

25. Well noted by Thompson, *War and Government in Habsburg Spain*, pp. 278, 280; and forcefully, despite their inconsistencies regarding the relative cost of the new fortifications and firearms: Hale, *War and Society in Renaissance Europe*,

pp. 248–9; Tallett, *War and Society in Early-Modern Europe*, pp. 188–93, 205. For the Italian city-states' artillery, which was among the most advanced in Europe, see Mallett and Hale, *The Military Organization of a Renaissance State*, pp. 81–7; Hale, *War and Society in Renaissance Europe*, p. 156; Pepper and Adams, *Firearms and Fortifications*, pp. 12–13. *Condottieri* too possessed their own artillery. All this again contradicts Braudel, *The Structure of Everyday Life*, p. 393.

26. Hale, in Mallett and Hale, *The Military Organization of a Renaissance State*, p. 462; Jean-Claude Hocquet, 'Venice', in Bonney, *The Rise of the Fiscal State in Europe, c. 1200–1815*, p. 384.

27. Marjolein 't Hart, 'The United Provinces, 1579–1806', in Bonney, *The Rise of the Fiscal State in Europe, c. 1200–1815*, p. 312.

28. Brewer's calculations strike the balance more towards the army, whereas those presented by French suggest an average ratio of four to six in favour of the navy: John Brewer, *The Sinews of Power: War, money and the English state, 1688–1783*. London: Unwin Hyman, 1989, p. 31; David French, *The British Way in Warfare 1688–2000*. London: Unwin Hyman, 1990, p. 59.

29. Compare the calculations offered for the Venetian arsenal, one of the most developed and better documented in Europe by Robert Davis, *Shipbuilders of the Venetian Arsenal: Workers and workplace in the preindustrial city*. Baltimore, MD: Johns Hopkins University Press, 1991, p. 28, with the data in Mallett and Hale, *The Military Organization of a Renaissance State*, pp. 494–501. Also, see Frederic Lane, 'Naval action and fleet organization, 1499–1502', in J. Hale (ed.), *Renaissance Venice*. London: Faber & Faber, 1973, pp. 146–73, especially 159–62; and endnote 31 for the Ottomans.

30. Braudel, *The Mediterranean and the Mediterranean World in the Age of Philip II*, p. 841, and the documentary evidence there; also the details in Thompson, *War and Government in Habsburg Spain*, pp. 168, 171, 173, 175, 289, 294 (and notes), 300–302. Although lacking the costs of building and ammunition, the Ottoman document published by Imber appears to point in the same direction: C. H. Imber, 'The cost of naval warfare: The accounts of Hayreddin Barbarossa's Herceg Novi campaign in 1539', *Archivum Ottomanicum*, 1972; **4**: 203–16. See also the following endnote.

31. Palmira Brummett, *Ottoman Seapower and Levantine Diplomacy in the Age of Discovery*. Albany, NY: State University of New York, 1994, pp. 96, 218 n. 30; Colin Imber, 'The reconstruction of the Ottoman fleet after the Battle of Lepanto, 1571–2', in *Studies in Ottoman History and Law*. Istanbul: Isis, 1996, pp. 85–101.

32. Polybius, *The Histories* 1.20–1, 38, 59, 63. The Battle of Ecnomus (256 BC) between Rome and Carthage, waged with more than 300 quinquereme on each side and an estimated total of about 250,000 men, overshadows even Lepanto (1571), where some 200 galleys on each side and an estimated grand total of 160,000 men took part.

33. Brewer, *The Sinews of Power*, pp. 34–7.

34. Clearly noted by Childs, *Armies and Warfare in Europe*, p. 62. Having emphasized the huge expense on fortifications and artillery, Tallett, *War and Society in Early-Modern Europe*, pp. 170–1, arrives at the same conclusion, which is similarly implicit in Hale, in Mallett and Hale, *The Military Organization of a Renaissance State*, pp. 494–501, and Tracy, *Emperor Charles V, Impresario of War*, and explicit in Hellie, 'The cost of Muscovite military defense and expansion'.

35. Admittedly, it can be argued that the cost of military hardware of all sorts does not fully incorporate the general investment in manufacturing infrastructure. This may apply less to the single-purpose guns than to the price of warships that profited from the expansion of European commercial shipping and shipyards.

36. Pepper and Adams, *Firearms and Fortifications*, pp. 30–1; also Tallett, *War and Society in Early-Modern Europe*, pp. 171–2; Mallett, in Mallett and Hale, *The Military Organization of a Renaissance State*, p. 92. Hook, 'Fortifications and the end of the Sienese state', p. 387, followed by Adams, 'Tactics or politics?', p. 37, cite this as the contemporary rationale, but wrongly believes that it was erroneous. Gábor Ágoston, 'The cost of the Ottoman fortress system in Hungary in the sixteenth and seventeenth centuries', in G. Dávid and P. Fodor (eds), *Ottomans, Hungarians, and Habsburgs in Central Europe: The military confines in the era of Ottoman conquest*. Leiden: Brill, 2000, pp. 195–228, actually deals with the high cost of the troops stationed at the fortresses in this front-line province rather than with the cost of the fortresses themselves.

37. This has been noted by Eltis, *The Military Revolution in Sixteenth Century Europe*, p. 32.

38. Parker too, ' "The military revolution, 1560–1660"—A myth?', pp. 45–9, has emphasized this factor in the best and most balanced of his several formulations of the 'military revolution' thesis; and already but unilinearily in Roberts, 'The military revolution, 1560–1660', pp. 20–3.

39. Tilly, *The Formations of National States in Western Europe*, p. 42. The literature on this subject is vast, but see especially: Charles Tilly, 'War making and state making as organized crime', in P. Evans, D. Rueschemeyer, and T. Skocpol (eds), *Bringing the State Back In*. Cambridge: Cambridge University Press, 1985, pp. 169–91; Michael Mann, *States, War and Capitalism*. Oxford: Blackwell, 1988; Brian Downing, *The Military Revolution and Political Change: Origins of democracy and autocracy in early modern Europe*. Princeton, NJ: Princeton University Press, 1992; Bruce Porter, *War and the Rise of the State*. New York: Free Press, 1994; Thomas Ertman, *Birth of the Leviathan: Building states and regimes in medieval and early modern Europe*. Cambridge: Cambridge University Press, 1997; Martin van Creveld, *The Rise and Decline of the State*. Cambridge: Cambridge University Press, 1999.

40. The concepts were coined by Joseph Schumpeter, 'The crisis of the tax state', *International Economic Papers*, 1954; **4**: 5–38 (German original 1918). Bonney's two edited volumes (*Economic Systems and State Finance; The Rise of the Fiscal State in Europe*) include the most comprehensive and authoritative recent studies.

41. More or less suggested, in a Marxist vein, by Perry Anderson, *Lineages of the Absolutist State*. London: NLB, 1774; more persuasively developed by Hillay Zmora, *Monarchy, Aristocracy and the State in Europe 1300–1800*. London: Routledge, 2001.

42. Michael Mallett, *Mercenaries and their Masters*. London: Bodley, 1974; Fritz Redlich, *The German Military Enterpriser and his Work Force: A study in European economic and social history*. Wiesbaden: Franz Steiner, 1964; this remains the best study on the subject.

43. A useful outline of the changes is offered in John Lynn, 'The evolution of army styles in the modern West, 800–2000', *International History Review*, 1996; **18**: 505–35.

44. Compare Braudel, *The Mediterranean and the Mediterranean World in the Age of Philip II*, pp. 355–94; Parker, *The Army of Flanders and the Spanish Road*, p. 21, *passim*; id., *The Grand Strategy of Philip II*. New Haven, CT: Yale University Press, 1998, Chapter 2.

45. Cross-European surveys are offered in André Corvisier, *Armies and Societies in Europe 1494–1789*. Bloomington, IN: Indiana University Press, 1979, pp. 28–36, 52–60, 131–2; Childs, *Armies and Warfare in Europe*, pp. 59–60; Hale, *War and Society in Renaissance Europe*, pp. 198–208; Tallett, *War and Society in Early-Modern Europe*, pp. 83–5; Anderson, *War and Society in Europe of the Old Regime*, pp. 18–21, 90–4. For some studies of individual countries see: Mallett and Hale, *The Military Organization of a Renaissance State*, pp. 78–80, 350–66; Thompson, *War and Government in Habsburg Spain*, pp. 126–45 (by contrast, during the *Reconquista*, which had taken place close to home in the Iberian Peninsula itself, civic militias played a prominent role: Theresa Vann, 'Reconstructing a "society organized for war" ', in D. Kagay and L. Villalon (eds), *Crusaders, Condottieri, and Canon: Medieval warfare in societies around the Mediterranean*. Leiden: Brill, 2003, pp. 389–416); Lynn, *Giant of the* Grand Siècle, pp. 371–93.

46. Already noted at the time by Adam Smith, *The Wealth of Nations* 5.1.1; the low percentage has been sensed by Hale (*War and Society in Renaissance Europe*, pp. 75, 105), and, more clearly, by Tallett *War and Society in Early-Modern Europe*, pp. 217–18.

47. Edward Gibbon, *The Decline and Fall of the Roman Empire*, Vol. 1. London: Random House, 1993, Chapter 1, pp. 23–4.

48. Earl Hamilton, *American Treasure and the Price of Revolution in Spain, 1501–1650*. New York: Octagon, 1965, p. 34; Thompson, *War and Government in Habsburg*

Spain, pp. 68–9, 288; Juan Gelabert, 'Castile, 1504–1808', in Bonney, *The Rise of the Fiscal State in Europe, c. 1200–1815,* p. 213.

49. Sven Lundkvist, 'The experience of empire: Sweden as a great power', in Michael Roberts (ed.), *Sweden's Age of Greatness 1632–1718.* London: Macmillan, 1973, pp. 20–5; Sven-Erik Aström, 'The Swedish economy and Sweden's role as a great power 1632–1697', ibid., pp. 58–101; Michael Roberts, *The Swedish Imperial Experience.* Cambridge: Cambridge University Press, 1979, Chapter 2. The problem is well summarized by Porter, *War and the Rise of the State,* p. 92. Robert Frost's excellent book is currently the most comprehensive on Sweden, Poland, and Russia: *The Northern Wars: War, state and society in Northeastern Europe, 1558–1721.* Harlow: Longman, 2000.

50. Again compare Porter, *War and the Rise of the State,* p. 115.

51. Brewer, *The Sinews of Power,* pp. 30–2; Christopher Hall, *British Strategy in the Napoleonic War 1803–15.* Manchester: Manchester University Press, 1992, pp. 1, 11, 15–6; R. Bonney, 'The eighteenth century II: The struggle for great power status', in his *Economic Systems and State Finance,* pp. 380–4, 387.

52. Quincy Wright, *A Study of War.* Chicago: University of Chicago, 1942, p. 653; Evan Luard, *War in International Society.* London: Tauris, 1986, pp. 24–5, 35, 45.

53. Chase, *Firearms,* is a scholarly landmark on the causes of the differential spread of firearms in Eurasia. His chapter on Japan, which extensively utilizes Japanese sources, is particularly useful (the same is true for his chapters on China). See also Delmer Brown, 'The impact of firearms on Japanese warfare, 1543–98', *Far Eastern Quarterly,* 1948; **7**: 236–53. Noel Perrin, *Giving Up the Gun: Japan's reversion to the sword 1543–1879.* Boulder, CO: Shambhala, 1979, is criticized as scholarly dubious. I disagree with Chase's assessments on one point: although he notes (*Firearms,* pp. 175–86) that large infantry armies and increasingly larger *daimio* domains were growing to dominate Japanese warfare and politics well before the introduction of firearms, and although he concedes that firearms became widely available to all sides, he credits them with hastening unification. Parker, *The Military Revolution,* pp. 140–5, especially p. 140, who carefully avoided such a claim, later embraces it: 'In defense of *The Military Revolution*', p. 338. For my view, see also Chapter 11, endnote 63 and related text.

54. Regarding both firearms and ocean navigation, I fully agree with Braudel, *The Structure of Everyday Life,* pp. 385, 397.

55. Among the proponents of this view are: Adam Smith, *The Wealth of Nations* 4.7; Karl Marx and Friedrich Engels, 'Manifesto of the Communist Party', in *Economic and Philosophical Manuscripts of 1844 and the Communist Manifesto.* Amherst, NY: Prometheus, 1988; Karl Marx, *The Capital.* London: Penguin, 1976, Chapter 31; F. Braudel, *Civilization and Capitalism,* Vol. 2. *The Wheels of Commerce.* Berkeley, CA: University of California, 1992, p. 601; Immanuel Wallerstein, *The Modern World System I: Capitalist agriculture and the origins of*

the European world-economy in the sixteenth century. New York: Academic Press, 1974; Andre Frank, *World Accumulation 1492–1789.* New York: Monthly Review, 1978. Recent research has rightly emphasized Europe's internal economic growth, but the two developments were obviously mutually reinforcing. According to O'Brien, Europe's global commercial activities were marginal to its economic activity, constituting only 25 per cent of its trade even as late as 1790: Patrick O'Brien, 'European economic development: The contribution of the periphery', *Economic History Review*, 1982; **35**: 1–18; also (somewhat more positively), id., 'European industrialization: From the voyages of discovery to the Industrial Revolution', in H. Pohl (ed.), *The European Discovery of the World and Its Economic Effects on Pre-Industrial Society 1500–1800.* Stuttgart: Franz Steiner, 1990, pp. 154–77. However, see the decidedly positive assessment: Neils Steensgaard, 'Commodities, bullion and services in intercontinental transactions before 1750', ibid., pp. 9–23 (and the data compiled by Frank, *World Accumulation 1492–1789*, pp. 105–6, 215–9, 225, 232–3). As O'Brien himself acknowledges, it is often the marginal economic advantage that counts. Indeed, although Pomeranz, *The Great Divergence*, undermines many assumptions about the differences between western Europe and the other great civilizations of Eurasia, he emphasizes the crucial marginal advantage accorded by the Europeans' global position with great sophistication and much nuance. The same spirit and the same conclusion are found in: Janet Abu-Lughod, *Before European Hegemony: The world system A.D. 1250–1350.* New York: Oxford University Press, 1989, p. 363. Finally, Maddison, *The World Economy*, p. 93, in fact shows that, in the case of the leading British economy, extra-European trade was not marginal at all but constituted about half the country's overall trade by 1774.

56. Braudel, *The Structure of Everyday Life*, pp. 402–15, *The Wheels of Commerce*, pp. 14–37, 581–601; Wallerstein, *The Modern World System I.*

57. For Rome: Robert Lopez, *The Commercial Revolution of the Middle Ages 950–1350.* Cambridge: Cambridge University Press, 1976, p. 7.

58. Joseph Needham, Wang Ling, and Lu Gwei-Djen, *Science and Civilization in China*, Vol. 4, Part iii, *Nautical Technology.* Cambridge: Cambridge University Press, 1971, pp. 379–99; Louise Levathes, *When China Ruled the Seas: The treasure fleet of the dragon throne 1405–1433.* New York: Oxford University Press, 1994.

59. J. H. Parry, *The Discovery of the Sea.* Berkeley, CA: University of California, 1981; Bailey Diffie and George Winius, *Foundations of the Portuguese Empire, 1415–1580.* St Paul, MI: University of Minnesota, 1977.

60. A recent penetrating treatment of this much-discussed subject is: Jared Diamond, *Guns, Germs, and Steel: The fate of human societies.* New York: Norton, 1997. Noble Cook, *Born to Die: Disease and New World conquest, 1492–1650.* Cambridge: Cambridge University Press, 1998, is an updated synthesis. For

various reservations and refinements, see G. Raudzens (ed.), *Technology, Disease and Colonial Conquests, Sixteenth to Eighteenth Centuries: Essays reappraising the guns and germs theories*. Leiden: Brill, 2001.

61. For this transition in the Mediterranean, historically the classic galley arena, see John Guilmartin, *Gunpowder and Galleys: Changing technology and Mediterranean warfare at sea in the sixteenth century*. Cambridge: Cambridge University Press, 1974. R. Gardiner (ed.), *The Age of the Galley: Mediterranean oared vessels since pre-classical times*. London: Conway Maritime Press, 1995, is a comprehensive and updated survey.

62. Cipolla's pioneering *Guns and Sails in the Early Phase of European Exploration* is still of some value; R. Gardiner (ed.), *Cogs, Caravels and Galleons: The sailing ship 1000–1650*. London: Conway Maritime Press, 1994, covers the technical side; Diffie and Winius, *Foundations of the Portuguese Empire*, is a good overview; also Parker, *The Military Revolution*, Chapter 3.

63. See endnote 56.

64. This has more or less been suggested by Wallerstein, *The Modern World System I*.

65. Peter Mathias and Patrick O'Brien, 'Taxation in England and France, 1715–1810. A comparison of the social and economic incidence of taxes collected for the central governments', *Journal of European Economic History*, 1976; **5**: 601–50; Bonney, 'The eighteenth century II', pp. 336–8.

66. Brewer, *The Sinews of Power*, pp. 180–3.

67. The idea that the safeguarding of property rights by the state was the key to economic efficiency and, hence, to the ascendancy of the Netherlands and England has been advanced by: Douglas North and Robert Thomas, *The Rise of the Western World: A new economic history*. Cambridge: Cambridge University Press, 1973.

68. Tenney Frank, *An Economic Survey of Ancient Rome, I: Rome and Italy of the Republic*. Paterson, NJ: Pageant, 1959, pp. 62, 75, 79–94.

69. Polybius, *The Histories*, 1.59.

70. Jean-Claude Hocquet, 'City-state and market economy', in Bonney, *Economic Systems and State Finance*, pp. 87–100; Martin Körner, 'Expenditure' and 'Public credit', ibid., pp. 403, 407, 413, 515, 523, *passim*.

71. For the civil offices: Emmanuel le Roy Ladurie, *The Royal French State 1460–1610*. Oxford: Blackwell, 1994, pp. 17, 130; for the military: Childs, *Armies and Warfare in Europe*, pp. 81–2. Corvisier, *Armies and Societies in Europe*, pp. 101–2; Lee Kennett, *The French Armies in the Seven Years War: A study in military organization and administration*. Durham, NC: Duke University Press, 1967, pp. 65–7, 97; these give slightly different figures but draw a similar picture. For the all-pervasive corruption in the armies see: Parrott, *Richelieu's Army*, pp. 246–60, 331–65; Lynn, *Giant of the Grand Siècle*, pp. 221–47. Guy

Rowlands, *The Dynastic State and the Army under Louis XIV: Royal service and private interest, 1661–1701*. Cambridge: Cambridge University Press, 2002, is wholly dedicated to the working of the system, emphasizing the 'positive' or at least indispensable role of corruption; for the inevitable decline of income from the system, see ibid., pp. 87–8.

72. P. Dickson, *The Financial Revolution in England*. London: Macmillan, 1967, pp. 470–85, especially pp. 470–1; Bonney, 'The eighteenth century II', p. 345; Körner, 'Expenditure', pp. 507–38; Parker, *The Army of Flanders and the Spanish Road*, p. 151; and on the long-term perspective, Goldsmith, *Premodern Financial Systems*, pp. 26, 44, 139, *passim*. Although arguing that capitalist development in Asia was as intense as in Europe, Pomeranz, *The Great Divergence*, p. 178, concedes that Asian interest rates were much higher than Dutch and British rates.

73. Mathias and O'Brien, 'Taxation in England and France, 1715–1810'; Brewer, *The Sinews of Power*, pp. 89–91, *passim*; also P. Hoffman and K. Norberg (eds), *Fiscal Crises, Liberty, and Representative Government, 1450–1789*. Stanford: Stanford University Press, 1994; I. A. A. Thompson, 'Castile: Polity, fiscality, and fiscal crisis', ibid., p. 176; Phyllis Deane and W. Cole, *British Economic Growth 1688–1959*. Cambridge: Cambridge University Press, 1967, pp. 2–3; Mann, *States, War and Capitalism*; id., *The Sources of Social Power*, Vol. 2, *The Rise of Classes and Nation-States, 1760–1914*. Cambridge: Cambridge University Press, 1993, pp. 214–15, 369–70; Juan Gelabert, 'The fiscal burden', in Bonney, *Economic Systems and State Finance*, p. 560; and a useful summary of research in Ertman, *Birth of the Leviathan*, p. 220. For the older view, see, for example, F. Gilbert (ed.), *The Historical Essays of Otto Hinze*. New York: Oxford University Press, 1975.

74. See Chapters 10 and 11. Robert Dahl and Edward Tufte, *Size and Democracy*. Stanford: Stanford University Press, 1973, pp. 4, 8, first suggest (incorrectly in my view) that this relationship may have been coincidental in the ancient Greek *poleis*, but later recognizes that large-scale democracy became possible in modern times because of representation and nationalism.

75. Joseph Strayer, *On the Medieval Origins of the Modern State*. Princeton, NJ: Princeton University Press, 1970, pp. 11–12, *passim*.

76. Smith, *The Wealth of Nations* 3. This is picked up by Jones, *The European Miracle*, Chapter 5. See also Mancur Olson, *Power and Prosperity: Outgrowing communist and capitalist dictatorships*. New York: Basic Books, 2000, pp. 60–1. A somewhat similar notion (developed particularly with respect to the trading–colonial context) can be found in: Frederic Lane, *Profits from Power: Readings in protection rent and violence-controlling enterprises*. Albany, NY: State University of New York, 1979. The idea that pre-modern markets were socially 'embedded' or 'submerged' has been advanced (in Marx's footsteps) by Karl Polanyi, *Primitive, Archaic, and Modern Economies*. Boston, MA: Beacon, 1971.

77. For an attempt at a quantitative analysis, see Kalevi Holsti, *Peace and War: Armed conflicts and international order 1648–1989*. Cambridge: Cambridge University Press, 1991, especially pp. 47–51, 85–9.

78. Jonathan Israel, *Dutch Primacy in World Trade, 1585–1740*. Oxford: Oxford University Press, 1989.

79. The naval powers' ship-building effort is meticulously recorded by Jan Glete, *Navies and Nations: Warships, navies and state building in Europe and America 1500–1860*. Stockholm: Almqvist, 1993. The economic dimension is highlighted by Paul Kennedy, *The Rise and Fall of British Naval Mastery*. London: Allen Lane, 1976.

80. Geoffrey Parker, 'War and economic change: The economic costs of the Dutch revolt', in J. Winter (ed.), *War and Economic Development*. Cambridge: Cambridge University Press, 1975, p. 57.

81. Bonney, 'The eighteenth century II', 345.

82. Dickson, *The Financial Revolution in England*, pp. 10, 304–37, especially 320; Brewer, *The Sinews of Power*, pp. 30, 114–17.

83. Bonney (*Economic Systems and State Finance; The Rise of the Fiscal State in Europe*) provides the most comprehensive compilation of budgetary data. For war frequency, see Wright, *A Study of War*, p. 653.

84. Werner Sombart, *Krieg und Kapitalismus*. Munich: Duncker 1913; John Nef, *War and Human Progress: An essay on the rise of industrial civilization*. London: Routledge, 1950; and more briefly: Hale, *War and Society in Renaissance Europe*, Chapter 8; Tallett, *War and Society in Early-Modern Europe*, pp. 216–32.

85. Already noted by John Hall, 'States and societies: The miracle in comparative perspective', in J. Baechler, J. Hall, and M. Mann (eds), *Europe and the Rise of Capitalism*. Oxford: Blackwell, 1988, p. 36; Linda Weiss and John Hobson, *State and Economic Development*. Cambridge: Polity, 1995, pp. 89–90.

86. For the inability of the relatively backward Prussian economy to create a large national debt for war financing, see: Rudolf Braun, 'Taxation, socio-political structure, and state-building: Great Britain and Brandenburg-Prussia', in Tilly, *The Formations of National States in Western Europe*, pp. 243–327, especially 294–5; also Ertman, *Birth of the Leviathan*, pp. 245–63, who largely confuses cause and effect: Prussia was obliged to rely on traditionalist methods of state financing because it was poor and commercially underdeveloped, rather than the other way around. For Russian developments, see Richard Hellie, *Enserfment and Military Change in Muscovy*. Chicago: University of Chicago, 1973; John Keep, *Soldiers of the Tsar: Army and society in Russia 1462–1874*. Oxford: Oxford University Press, 1985.

87. My argument accords with that of Theda Skocpol, *States and Social Revolutions: A comparative analysis of France, Russia, and China*. Cambridge: Cambridge

University Press, 1979. By contrast, Goldstone misses the modernizing element of revolutions in early modern Europe and the modern world, as opposed to pre-modern times: Jack Goldstone, *Revolution and Rebellion in the Early Modern World*. Berkeley, CA: University of California, 1991. A rudimentary treatment of the military aspect of the process is offered by David Ralston, *Importing the European Army: The introduction of European military techniques and institutions into the extra-European world, 1600–1914*. Chicago: University of Chicago, 1990.

88. For the 'modernist' view see most notably: Elie Kedourie, *Nationalism*. London: Hutchinson, 1961; Ernest Gellner, *Nations and Nationalism*. Oxford: Blackwell, 1983; E. J. Hobsbawm, *Nations and Nationalism since 1780*. Cambridge: Cambridge University Press, 1990; Liah Greenfeld, *Nationalism: Five roads to modernity*. Cambridge, MA: Harvard University Press, 1993; id., *The Spirit of Capitalism: Nationalism and economic growth*, Cambridge, MA: Harvard University Press, 2001. For a longer view of the relationship between ethnicity and nationalism, see Brewer, *The Sinews of Power*, Chapter 11.

89. Benedict Anderson, *Imagined Communities: Reflections on the origins and spread of nationalism*. London: Verso, 1983, especially pp. 38–49. For the impact of printing in general, see Lucien Febvre and H-J. Martin, *The Coming of the Book: The impact of printing, 1450–1800*. London: Verso, 1984, especially Chapter 8; Elizabeth Eisenstein, *The Printing Press as an Agent of Change: Communication and cultural transformation in early modern Europe*. Cambridge: Cambridge University Press, 1979.

90. Bernard Lewis, *Cultures in Conflict: Christians, Muslims, and Jews in the Age of Discovery*. New York: Oxford University Press, 1995, p. 23.

91. See, for example, Joad Raymond, *The Invention of the Newspaper: English newsbooks 1641–1649*. Oxford: Oxford University Press, 1996; Bob Harris, *Politics and the Rise of the Press: Britain and France, 1620–1800*. London: Routledge, 1996.

92. The contributions by the eminent historians participating in Ranum's book, as well as Marcu, were written before more recent trends regarding the lateness of nationalism have made both titles appear like an oxymoron: O. Ranum (ed.), *National Consciousness, History, and Political Culture in Early Modern Europe*. Baltimore, MD: Johns Hopkins University Press, 1975; E. D. Marcu, *Sixteenth Century Nationalism*. New York: Abaris, 1976. In both books, however, the choice of cases (Portugal, Spain, Italy, Germany, France, England, and Russia) leaves something to be desired. Also stressing the deep historical roots of European nationalism are: Josep Llobera, *The God of Modernity: The development of nationalism in Western Europe*. Oxford: Berg, 1994; Hastings, *The Construction of Nationhood*.

93. Le Roy Ladurie, *The Royal French State 1460–1610*, pp. 26–7, 54, 278–85 (wholly convinced of the evolution of French nationalism from the late Middle Ages); William Church, 'France', in Ranum, *National Consciousness,*

History, and Political Culture in Early Modern Europe, 1975, pp. 43–66 (preferring the term 'patriotism'); Hagen Schulze, *States, Nations and Nationalism: From the Middle Ages to the present*. Oxford: Blackwell, 1996, p. 159. Military historians specify nationalism and patriotism as a motive, albeit in a limited, early modern form; see Corvisier, *Armies and Societies in Europe*, pp. 21–5; Hale, *War and Society in Renaissance Europe*, pp. 42–4; Tallett, *War and Society in Early-Modern Europe*, p. 103 (negatively). Lynn, *Giant of the* Grand Siècle, pp. 445–50, rejects these notions with respect to France. All the same, national sentiments did not emerge out of thin air with the Revolution, even if France was among the more heterogeneous countries, where nationalism developed late. Like many others, Bell emphasizes the eighteenth century: Daniel Bell, *The Cult of the Nation in France: Inventing nationalism 1680–1800*. Cambridge, MA: Harvard University Press, 2001.

94. In addition to Redlich, *The German Military Enterpriser and his Work Force*, see, for example, David Potter, 'The international mercenary market in the sixteenth century: Anglo-French competition in Germany 1543–50', *English Historical Review*, 1996; **111**: 24–58; Peter Wilson, 'The German "soldier trade" of the seventeenth and eighteenth centuries: A reassessment', *International History Review*, 1996; **18**: 757–92.

95. F. Wagenaar, 'The "waardgelder" of Den Haag', in M. van der Hoeven (ed.), *Exercise of Arms: Warfare in the Netherlands, 1568–1648*. Leiden: Brill, 1997, pp. 211–30. H. Zwitzer, 'The eighty years war', ibid., pp. 47–8; Zwitzer believes that the reason for foreign recruitment was the large size of the army in relation to the Dutch population (more than 2 per cent in 1630); although the booming Dutch economy attracted foreign manpower in many sectors, in none was foreign recruitment nearly as great as in the army.

96. Michael Roberts, *Gustavus Adolphus: A history of Sweden 1611–1632*, Vol. 1. London: Longmans, 1962, Chapter 6, especially pp. 300–1; casualties: Michael Roberts, in Geoffrey Parker et al. (eds), *The Thirty Years' War*. London: Routledge, 1984, p. 193; Jan Lindegren, 'The Swedish "military state", 1560–1720', *Scandinavian Journal of History*, 1985; **10**: 305–36, especially p. 317; Porter, *War and the Rise of the State*, pp. 88–93.

97. Jean-Paul Bertaud, *The Army of the French Revolution*. Princeton, NJ: Princeton University Press, 1988; John Lynn, *The Bayonets of the Republic: Motivation and tactics in the army of revolutionary France, 1791–94*. Urbana, IL: University of Illinois, 1984; A. Corvisier, *Histoire militaire de la France*, Vol. 2. *De 1715 à 1871* (J. Delmas, ed.). Paris: Presses Universitaires, 1992, Chapters 8–15. A corrective, warning against idealization, is S. P. Mackenzie, *Revolutionary Armies in the Modern Era: A revisionist approach*. London: Routledge, 1997, Chapter 3.

98. Bonney, 'The eighteenth century II', pp. 347–90, is an excellent synthesis; also Gilbert Bodinier, in Corvisier, *Histoire militaire de la France*, pp. 305–19.

99. See G. Veinstein, 'Some views on provisioning in the Hungarian campaigns of Suleiman the Magnificent', in *Etat et société dans l'empire Ottoman, XVIe–XVIIIe siècles*. Aldershot: Variorum, 1994, Chapter vii; Caroline Finkel, *The Administration of Warfare: The Ottoman campaign in Hungary, 1593–1606*. Vienna: VWGÖ, 1988; Rhoads Murphey, *Ottoman Warfare 1500–1700*. New Brunswick, NJ: Rutgers University Press, 1999, pp. 20–25, 65–6, 85–103, *passim*. Oman *A History of the Art of War in the Sixteenth Century*, Book VII, can still be read with profit.

100. Black, *A Military Revolution?* and 'A military revolution?'; Chase, *Firearms*.

101. Halil Inalcik, 'The socio-political effects of the diffusion of firearms in the Middle East', in Parry and Yapp, *War, Technology and Society in the Middle East*, pp. 195–217; V. Parry, 'La manière de combattre', ibid., pp. 218–56. Chase, *Firearms*. It should be noted that the Ottomans were at least partly adapting: in the seventeenth century the number of Ottoman infantry increased whereas that of the cavalry decreased: M. Yapp, 'The modernization of Middle Eastern armies in the nineteenth century: A comparative view', in Parry and Yapp, *War, Technology and Society in the Middle East*, p. 344; Murphey, *Ottoman Warfare 1500–1700*, p. 16. Ottoman use of field artillery in the seventeenth century was also more advanced than previously thought: Murphey, *Ottoman Warfare 1500–1700*, pp. 109–12; Gábor Ágoston, 'Ottoman artillery and European military technology in the fifteenth and seventeenth centuries', *Acta Orientalia Academiae Scientiarum Hungaricae*, 1994; **47**: 15–48.

102. Arguing that the east Asian civilizations did not fall behind Europe until industrialization, Pomeranz, *The Great Divergence*, does not pay sufficient attention to Bacon's trio. Paul Bairoch, 'European gross national product 1800–1975', *Journal of European Economic History*, 1976; **5**: 287, roughly estimates that European per capita product was about 20 per cent higher than Asia's in 1800. However, Maddison, *The World Economy*, pp. 28, 42, 44, 47, 49, 90, 126, 264, criticizing both Pomeranz and Bairoch, calculates that Europe overtook Asia in per capita wealth from 1400, and continuously widened its lead to twice the Asian per capita product by the eve of industrialization (three times in the Netherlands and Britain).

103. Some authors, going beyond Weber's original distinction between the 'patrimonial' and modern state, hold that only the latter deserves to be designated a state: Max Weber, *General Economic History*. Glencoe, IL: Free Press, 1950, pp. 313–14, 338ff; id., *Economy and Society*. New York: Bedminster, 1968, pp. 56, 904–10; J. Shennan, *The Origins of the Modern European State 1450–1725*. London: Hutchinson, 1974; Gianfranco Poggi, *The Development of the Modern State: A sociological introduction*. Stanford: Stanford University Press, 1978; id., *The State: Its nature, development and prospects*. Stanford: Stanford University Press, 1990, especially p. 25; Van Creveld, *The Rise and Decline of the State*. This,

of course, is a matter of semantics, but in my vocabulary states are old and the modern state is merely a new phase in a development.

104. On this I am in agreement with D. H. A. Kolff, 'The end of an ancien regime: colonial war in India, 1798–1818', in J. De Moor and H. Wesseling (eds), *Imperialism and War: Essays on colonial wars in Asia and Africa*. Leiden: Brill, 1989, pp. 22–49. Also id., *Naukar, Rajput and Sepoy: The ethnohistory of the military labour market in Hindustan 1450–1850*. Cambridge: Cambridge University Press, 1990; Jos Gommans, 'Warhorse and gunpowder in India *c.* 1000–1850', in Jeremy Black (ed.), *War in the Early Modern World*. London: University College London, 1999, pp. 105–27, especially 118–19; id., 'Indian warfare and Afghan innovation during the eighteenth century', in Gommans and Kolff, *Warfare and Weaponry in South Asia 1000–1800*, pp. 365–86; Gommans, *Mughal Warfare*, pp. 74, 166, 204; Bruce Lenman, 'The transition to European military ascendancy in India, 1600–1800', in Lynn, *Tools of War: Instruments, ideas, and institutions of warfare, 1445–1871*, pp. 100–30; John Lynn, 'Victories of the conquered: The native character of the Sepoy', in *Battle: A History of Combat and Culture*. Boulder, CO: Westview, 2003, pp. 145–77. Although failing to consider the power advantage accorded by eighteenth-century European sociopolitical organization, Pomeranz, *The Great Divide*, pp. 4, 18–20, 201–6, emphasizes the role of the European great commercial corporations and their effective use of force in alliance with their respective states.

105. For a beautiful overview see: Michael Howard, *War and the Liberal Conscience*. Oxford: Oxford University Press, 1981, Chapter 1.

106. Compare Richard Bonney, 'Early modern theories of state finance', in his *Economic Systems and State Finance*, pp. 225–6; id., 'Preface', in *The Rise of the Fiscal State in Europe, c. 1200–1815*. Oxford: Oxford University Press, 1999, p. v; and more generally Cosimo Perrotta, 'Is the mercantilist theory of the favourable balance of trade really erroneous?', *History of Political Economy*, 1991; **23**: 301–35.

107. Jean-Jacques Rousseau, 'Abstract and judgement of Saint Pierre's project for perpetual peace', in S. Hoffmann and D. Fidler (eds), *Rousseau on International Relations*. Oxford: Oxford University Press, 1991(1756), pp. 53–100.

108. In Thomas Paine, *Rights of Man, Common Sense, and Other Political Writings*. Oxford: Oxford University Press, 1995, p. 212.

109. Ibid., pp. 195–6, 321.

110. Ibid., pp. 265–6; also see pp. 128–31, 227; Howard, *War and the Liberal Conscience*, p. 29; Thomas Walker, 'The forgotten prophet: Tom Paine's cosmopolitanism and international relations', *International Studies Quarterly*, 2000; **44**: 51–72.

111. In H. Reiss (ed.), *Kant's Political Writings*. Cambridge: Cambridge University Press, 1970, pp. 93–130.

Chapter 15. Unbound and Bound Prometheus: Machine Age War

1. These are my rough calculations based on the estimated data. The most comprehensive and update estimates as of now are: Angus Maddison, *The World Economy: A millennial perspective*. Paris: OECD, 2001, pp. 28, 90, 126, 183–6, 264–5. See also Paul Bairoch, 'Europe's gross national product: 1800–1975', *Journal of European Economic History*, 1976; **5**: 301 (up to 1973); for manufacturing: id., 'International industrialization levels from 1750 to 1980', ibid., 1982; **11**: 275 (Britain), 284, 286 (Japan); W. W. Rostow, *The World Economy: History and prospect*. Austin, TX: University of Texas, 1978, pp. 4–7, 48–9. Landes' assertion that the richest states possess as much as 400 times per capita wealth than the poorest states is much exaggerated even in nominal terms, let alone in terms of purchasing power parity (PPP): David Landes, *The Wealth and Poverty of Nations*. New York: Norton, 1999, p. xx.

2. Paul Kennedy, *The Rise and Fall of the Great Powers: Economic change and military conflict from 1500 to 2000*. New York: Random House, 1987.

3. Bairoch, 'Europe's gross national product', p. 282; id., 'International industrialization levels from 1750 to 1980', *passim*.

4. Some important variations in interpretation can be found in: Niall Ferguson, *The Cash Nexus: Money and power in the modern world, 1700–2000*. New York: Basic Books, 2001.

5. Bairoch, 'Europe's gross national product', p. 282, originally searched for a similar formula, but later opted for manufacturing output for the purpose of measuring economic power. Mark Harrison (ed.), *The Economies of World War II: Six great powers in international comparison*. Cambridge: Cambridge University Press, 1998, pp. 18–19, arrives at the same conclusion as mine about the need for a measure that compounds gross domestic product (GDP) with GDP per capita, but does not offer any such measure. My own formula multiplies a state's GDP with the square or cubic root of its GDP per capita. There might be various reasons why a root value should be used, but the fact is that it seems to fit historical experience best with respect to relative power. The range between the square and cubic root values for potential power mainly correlates with the technological intensity of the type of warfare engaged—for example, naval and air warfare have tended to be more technologically intensive and therefore more dependent on level of development (thus tending towards the square root value) than land warfare (tending towards the cubic root value).

   One other existing index is the National Material Capabilities statistical set of the Correlates of War Project (on the world-wide web). This is a composite index that gives equal weight to six indicators: two industrial—iron/steel production and energy consumption; two relating to population size—general and urban; and two military—number of military personnel and military expenditure. The inclusion of the two military indicators means that the index is better at assessing existing military power and readiness at a given moment than potential power. For example, it systematically undervalues the USA, which had actual levels of peacetime military mobilization and expenditure during most of the past two centuries that tended to be low compared with those of its rivals, although its potential mobilized power was overwhelming. More importantly, although the index roughly reflects the changes in power relationships during these two centuries, its chosen indicators for technological advance create serious distortions outside the 'classic' industrial period (about 1870–1970). Energy consumption rose meteorically when steam power was introduced, much faster than the rise in military power. Thereafter it continued to grow at a far lower rate, lower than technological and military advance in general (with growing energy efficiency further offsetting some of the growth). Finally, since the 1973 oil crisis and during the information age, the growth in energy consumption has slowed even more and has even become negative in some of the most developed countries (for example, Germany, the Netherlands, and Belgium). A similar trajectory applies to iron and steel production, largely because of the obvious connection between energy consumption and heavy industry: long a central indicator for a country's economic power, iron and steel production has been declining in the developed countries during the information age and has become a mark of developing, second-rank economies. (The same applies to Bairoch's manufacturing production after 1973.) Level of urbanization, too, reaches a plateau after industrialization and ceases to grow further. To conclude, the National Material Capabilities' index is not generalized enough to take account of the changing historical conditions. The inevitable distortions are dimly sensed but not satisfactorily resolved by John Mearsheimer who selectively employs some of the index's indicators and, after 1973, gross national product (GNP) for measuring states' power in his *The Tragedy of Great Power Politics*. New York: Norton, 2001, especially pp. 63–75, 220. He, too, notes that GNP per capita best reflects the level of technological advance, but fails to see how this indicator can be combined with size.

Recognizing that GNP by itself is not a good predictor of states' power, Organski and Kugler have devised a measure that combines GNP with the government's extraction share: A. Organski and Jacek Kugler, *The War Ledger*. Chicago: University of Chicago, 1980. This is a good measure because, as we see later, both economic surplus and the state extraction capability increase with modernization. Still, as the authors themselves note (p. 209), their measure is not generalized enough. Discussions of various measures can be found in: R. Stoll and M. Ward (eds), *Power in World Politics*. Boulder, CO: Lynne Rienner, 1989.

6. My calculations of infrastructural power are based on the data from Maddison, *The World Economy*, except for 1938 (unavailable in Maddison), where the data are derived from Harrison, *The Economies of World War I*, pp. 3, 7.

7. Bairoch, 'International industrialization levels from 1750 to 1980'.

8. See endnotes 61 and 63 (and related text).

9. For China compare: Joseph Nye Jr, *The Paradox of American Power*. New York: Oxford University Press, 2002, pp. 18–40. GNP alone proves inadequate for measuring antagonists' military power also in respect of the Arab–Israeli conflict. In 1967, Egypt alone, by far the most powerful Arab state, had 1.5 times Israel's GNP, whereas in 1973 the two countries were on a par: United Nations, *Statistical Yearbook*. New York: UN, 1975, Sections 18, 185, 192. Yet when GNP per capita is compounded according to the formula proposed here, Israel emerges as up to twice as strong as Egypt in 1967 and two to three times stronger in 1973. In both cases Israel was stronger than the rival Arab coalition. Filtering out the Arabs' total surprise in 1967 and Israel's in 1973, this disparity in Israel's favour accounts for her repeated victories and continuous military preponderance in the conflict. Thus, although Israel's population is very small compared with her Arab neighbours, her relative economic prowess is a good predictor of her military success, usually explained by 'special circumstances'. Notably, Organski and Kluger, *The War Ledger*, pp. 89–94, arrive at similar results using their own measure. By contrast, the National Material Capabilities' index (see endnote 5) is entirely off the mark, suggesting that Egypt alone was 4.3 times stronger than Israel in 1967 and 2.7 times in 1973. The index is particularly distorting in this case because it incorporates only standing forces, whereas Israel has mainly a reserve army.

10. Japan, beginning from a lower starting point, grew more than double the above rate. The US growth by a factor of 1,400–3,000 is of course partly the result of a 27-fold increase in population, mainly from immigration.

11. Michael Mann, *The Sources of Social Power*, Vol. 2, *The Rise of Classes and Nation-States, 1760–1914*. Cambridge: Cambridge University Press, 1993, pp. 214–15, 365–82; this is the most comprehensive and an admirable working of the data; see also Ferguson, *The Cash Nexus*, pp. 42–7; and more specifically John Hobson, 'The military extraction gap and the wary Titan: The fiscal sociology of British defence policy, 1870–1913', *Journal of European Economic History*, 1993; **22**: 461–506; Harrison, *The Economies of World War II*, pp. 20–1, 47, 82–3, 88–9, 157–9, 257, 287.

12. Stanley Engerman and Matthew Gallman, 'The civil war economy: A modern view', in S. Förster and J. Nagler (eds), *On the Road to Total War: The American Civil War and the German wars of unification, 1861–1871*. New York: Cambridge University Press, 1997, pp. 220–1. Curiously, the contributions by Neely and McPherson, respectively, contain few figures and none for economic mobilization: Mark Neely Jr, 'Was the civil war a total war?' ibid., pp. 29–51; James McPherson, 'From limited war to total war in America', ibid., pp. 295–309. Paul Koistiner's estimate that the North spent only 10 per cent of its GNP on the war, seems too low: *Beating Plowshares into Swords: The political economy of*

American warfare, 1606–1865. Lawrence: University of Kansas Press, 1996, p. 194 (also pp. 185–6). In view of the cited figures for the Confederacy's level of economic mobilization, it is also difficult to rationalize his conclusion (pp. 265–78) that the South lost because its mobilization was low (rather than because of its overall inferiority in resources).

13. Harrison, *The Economies of World War II.* Reflecting a somewhat lower (albeit still stupendous) level of mobilization, the US peak of 41–45 per cent of gross GNP spent on the war was actually marginally smaller than that of the other major powers, even though American GNP per capita was the highest.

14. Mann, *The Sources of Social Power*, pp. 393, 804–10 (peacetime); Quincy Wright, *A Study of War.* Chicago: University of Chicago, 1965, pp. 664, 1542–3; Ferguson, *The Cash Nexus*, pp. 29–31 (wartime).

15. Alfred Kelly, 'Whose war? Whose nation? Tensions in the memory of the Franco-German war of 1870–1871', in M. Boemeke, R. Chickering, and S. Förster (eds), *Anticipating Total War: The German and American experience, 1871–1914.* New York: Cambridge University Press, 1999, pp. 287–8.

16. Engerman and Gallman, 'The civil war economy', p. 220; Koistiner, *Beating Plowshares into Swords*, pp. 172, 194, 254, 256.

17. I. Berend and G. Ránki, 'The East Central European variant of the Industrial Revolution', in B. Király and N. Dreisziger (eds), *East Central European Society in World War I.* New York: Columbia University Press, 1985, pp. 61, 74–5, 78–9; D. Zivojinovic, 'Serbia and Montenegro: The home front, 1914–18', ibid., pp. 242–3.

18. Compare Ferguson, *The Cash Nexus*, pp. 30–33; although I differ with some of his views here, our general conclusion is similar.

19. Jon Sumida, *In Defence of Naval Supremacy: Finance, technology and British naval policy.* Boston: Unwin, 1989, Tables 3–14; David Stevenson, *Armament and the Coming of War: Europe, 1904–1914.* Oxford: Oxford University Press, 1996, pp. 7–8.

20. US Department of Defense, *National Defense Budget Estimates for FY 2004.* Washington, DC: US Department of Defense, 2003, pp. 154–9, 172–7, 190–5 (on the world-wide web).

21. Ibid., pp. 148–53, 166–71, 184–9.

22. Ibid., pp. 160–5, 178–83, 196–201.

23. These ideas repeatedly occur in Fuller's voluminous writings; but see especially his books: J. F. C. Fuller, *On Future Warfare.* London: Praed, 1928; id., *Armament and History.* London: Eyre, 1946.

24. Data for Britain. See Wright, *A Study of War*, pp. 670–1 (military); B. R. Mitchell, *International Historical Statistics, Europe 1750–1988.* New York: Stockton, 1992, Tables F4 (merchant).

25. Of the many references to these developments the following two are the most expert: Dennis Showalter, *Rifles and Railroads: Soldiers, technology and the unification of Germany*. Hamden, CT: Archon, 1975 (to 1871); Daniel Headrick, *The Tools of Empire: Technology and European imperialism in the nineteenth century*. New York: Oxford University Press, 1981.

26. The subject of mechanized land warfare, especially the German, is shrouded in myth. See Azar Gat, *British Armour Theory and the Rise of the Panzer Arm: Revising the revisionists*. London: Macmillan, 2000, which is based on the documents. More or less similar ground is covered by Mary Habeck, *Storm of Steel: The development of armor doctrine in Germany and the Soviet Union*. Ithaca, NY: Cornell University Press, 2003; this is also the only comprehensive documentary study of Soviet evolution. More generally, see Azar Gat, *Fascist and Liberal Visions of War: Fuller, Liddell Hart, Douhet and other modernists*. Oxford: Oxford University Press, 1998 (incorporated in the omnibus edn: Azar Gat, *A History of Military Thought: From the Enlightenment to the Cold War*. Oxford: Oxford University Press, 2001); and id., 'Ideology, national policy, technology and strategic doctrine between the World Wars', *Journal of Strategic Studies*, 2001; **24**(3): 1–18.

27. J. F. C. Fuller, *Towards Armageddon*. London: Dickson, 1937, pp. 92, 132.

28. The general trend is more or less agreed upon by statistical studies such as: Melvin Small and David Singer, *Resort to Arms: International and civil wars, 1816–1980*. Beverly Hills, CA: Sage, 1982; Jack Levy, *War in the Modern Great Power System, 1495–1975*. Lexington: University of Kentucky Press, 1983; Evan Luard, *War in International Society*. London: Tauris, 1986. Ferguson, *The Cash Nexus*, pp. 33–6, makes the point for spiralling lethality, but he scarcely controls for population (also as a function of the geographical scope of wars) and mobilization levels, and appears to be unaware of the heightened protective aspect of improved military technology.

29. Wright's pioneering *A Study of War*, p. 653, is skewed by his inclusion of the European powers' 'small wars' against minor rivals abroad, with the result that non-colonial powers such as Austria and Prussia register a sharper decline than the other powers during the nineteenth century, to only about a third of their war years compared with earlier times. Small and Singer's *Resort to Arms*, based on their important Correlates of War database, gives no basis for comparison with earlier times. On the other hand, addressing all the states in the global system during the past two centuries, it compares 'apples with pears' by encompassing the widest range of development—in effect different worlds—in time and space. But, see Levy, *War in the Modern Great Power System*, especially pp. 112–49, which concentrates on the great powers' wars among themselves—that is, by definition, the major wars by the most advanced states. Also Luard, *War in International Society*, pp. 53, 67.

30. Small and Singer, *Resort to Arms*, pp. 156–7, 198–201; Levy, *War in the Modern*

Great Power System, pp. 136–7, 150–68; Luard, *War in International Society*, pp. 67–81; they all confirm the conclusions of earlier research by Pitirim Sorokin and by Lewis Richardson.

31. John Stuart Mill, *Principles of Political Economy*. New York: Kelley, 1961, Book III, Chapter xvii, no. 5, p. 582.

32. Auguste Comte, 'Plan of the scientific operations necessary for reorganizing society' (1822), in G. Lenzer (ed.), *Auguste Comte and Positivism: The essential writings*. Chicago: University of Chicago, 1975, p. 37; id., 'Course de philosophie positive' (1832–42), ibid., pp. 293–7.

33. Helmuth von Moltke, *Essays, Speeches and Memoirs*, Vol. i. New York: Harper, 1893, pp. 276–7.

34. Compare Kalevi Holsti, *Peace and War: Armed conflict and international order 1648–1989*. Cambridge: Cambridge University Press, 1991, pp. 139–45.

35. See the references in Chapter 14, endnote 88. Also, for the application of this fashionable view to war: Barry Posen, 'Nationalism, the mass army, and military power', *International Security*, 1993; **18**: 80–124; Jack Snyder, *From Voting to Violence: Democratization and national conflict*. New York: Norton, 2000.

36. Eugene Weber, *Peasants into Frenchmen: The modernization of rural France 1870–1914*. Stanford: Stanford University Press, 1976, is a superb historical mosaic that covers this process, but that, surprisingly, fails even to mention earlier stages in the consolidation of French nationalism, most prominently the French Revolution.

37. Jan De Vries, *European Urbanization 1500–1800*. Cambridge, MA: Harvard University Press, 1984, pp. 39, 74, 86, 239; Paul Hohenberg and Lynn Lees, *The Making of Urban Europe 1000–1950*. Cambridge, MA: Harvard University Press, 1985, pp. 84, 218–19.

38. For literacy rates, see in: C. Cipolla (ed.), *The Fontana Economic History of Europe*, Vol. 4. Glasgow: Fontana, 1973, pp. 801–2. Prussia and the northern countries were the leaders by the early to mid-nineteenth century, whereas eastern and southern Europe lagged behind, as in all other aspects of modernization.

39. *Letters of Field-Marshal Count von Moltke to his Mother and Brothers*. New York: Harper, 1892, p. 47 (letter written in 1831).

40. Helmuth von Moltke, *Essays, Speeches and Memoirs*, Vol. ii. New York: Harper, 1887, p. 133.

41. Ibid., pp. 136–7. For this much discussed topic see, for example, Stig Förster, *Der doppelte Militarismus: die deutsche Heeresrüstungspolitik zwischen Status-quo-Sicherung und Aggression, 1890–1913*. Stuttgart: Steiner, 1985.

42. Mary Townsend, *European Colonial Expansion since 1871*. Chicago: Lippincott, 1941, p. 19; D. K. Fieldhouse, *Economics and Empire 1830–1914*. Ithaca, NY: Cornell University Press, 1973, p 3; Headrick, *The Tools of Empire*, p. 3.

43. See endnote 31. However, Small and Singer, *Resort to Arms*, pp. 165–80, also contains data for the severity of the wars in terms of deaths incurred, which can be used to correct the picture. Again Levy, *War in the Modern Great Power System*, most notably p. 125, is more instructive here.

44. Although sometimes historically crude, particularly with respect to earlier periods and to the process of transformation, see Richard Rosecrance, *The Rise of the Trading State: Commerce and conquest in the modern world*. New York: Basic Books, 1986.

45. Calculated on the basis of the data in Mitchell, *International Historical Statistics*, pp. 553–62; Maddison, *The World Economy*, pp. 126, 127, 184; Simon Kuznets, *Modern Economic Growth*. New Haven: Yale University Press, 1966, pp. 306–7, 312–4.

46. John Gallagher and Ronald Robinson, 'The imperialism of free trade', *Economic History Review*, 1953; **4**: 1–15.

47. An effective criticism is D. Platt, 'The imperialism of free trade: some reservations', *Economic History Review*, 1968; **21**: 296–306; id., 'Further objections to an "imperialism of free trade", 1830–60', *Economic History Review*, 1973; **26**: 77–91.

48. Gallagher and Robinson, 'The imperialism of free trade', p. 6.

49. Compare Niall Ferguson, 'Introduction' and 'Conclusion' in *Empire: The rise and demise of the British world order and the lessons for global power*. New York: Basic Books, 2002; id., *Colossus: The price of American empire*. New York: Penguin, 2004.

50. Ronald Robinson and John Gallagher, *Africa and the Victorians*. New York: St Martin, 1961, p. 78.

51. Gallagher and Robinson, 'The imperialism of free trade', p. 13.

52. For a critique of this view and other points by the most confirmed free trader among economic historians of imperialism. see Patrick O'Brien, 'The costs and benefits of British imperialism, 1846–1914', *Past and Present*, 1988; **120**: 163–200. Also, Paul Kennedy and Patrick O'Brien, 'Debate: The costs and benefits of British imperialism, 1846–1914', *Past and Present*, 1989; **125**: 186–99.

53. Cited in Thomas Pakenham, *The Scramble for Africa 1876–1912*. New York: Random House, 1991, p. xxii.

54. Lance Davis and Robert Huttenback, *Mammon and the Pursuit of Empire: The political economy of British imperialism, 1860–1912*. Cambridge: Cambridge University Press, 1986; this invalidates Hobson: J. M. Hobson, *Imperialism: A study*. Ann Arbor, MI: University of Michigan, 1965(1902); and V. I. Lenin, *Imperialism: The highest stage of capitalism*. New York: International Publishers, 1939. See also Fieldhouse, *Economics and Empire 1830–1914*. For France: Henri Brunschwig, *French Colonialism 1871–1914: Myths and realities*. New York: Praeger, 1966, pp. 90–1, 96.

55. Patrick O'Brien, 'The imperial component in the decline of the British Economy before 1914', in M. Mann (ed.), *The Rise and Decline of the Nation State*. Oxford: Blackwell, 1990, p. 44.

56. Robinson and Gallagher, *Africa and the Victorians*.

57. For the export figures, see Rostow, *The World Economy*, pp. 70–3; Mitchell, *International Historical Statistics*, pp. 644–5.

58. Hannah Arendt, *The Origins of Totalitarianism*. Cleveland, OH: Meridian, 1958; Carl Friedrich and Zbigniew Brzezinski, *Totalitarian Dictatorship and Autocracy*. Cambridge, MA: Harvard University Press, 1965. Of these two classic studies Arendt rightly emphasizes the rise of mass society, while being less attentive to the new communication technologies stressed by Friedrich and Brzezinski.

59. For a comprehensive bibliography, see Gat, *Fascist and Liberal Visions of War*, pp. 4–6; incorporated in id., *A History of Military Thought*, pp. 522–4.

60. The following is based on Peter Liberman, *Does Conquest Pay? The exploitation of occupied industrial societies*. Princeton, NJ: Princeton University Press, 1996, which is both refreshingly original and sound.

61. Ibid. p. 43; Harrison, *The Economies of World War II*, p. 7; I apply the same compound of GNP and GNP per capita suggested previously.

62. The democratic success in war attracted considerable attention in the study of international relations and is the subject of the following: Dan Reiter and Allan Stam, *Democracies at War*. Princeton, NJ: Princeton University Press, 2002. I agree with some of this book's conclusions, among other things that alliances were not the reason for the success, while differing with quite a few of its other conclusions, as seen later. More on alliance choices: Randolph Siverson and Julian Emmons, 'Birds of a feather: Democratic political systems and alliance choices', *Journal of Conflict Resolution*, 1991; **35**: 285–306; Michael Simon and Erik Gartzke, 'Political system similarity and the choice of allies', *Journal of Conflict Resolution*, 1996; **40**: 617–35. For a summary of the literature, see Bruce Russett and John Oneal, *Triangulating Peace: Democracy, interdependence, and international organizations*. New York: Norton, 2001, pp. 59–60, 66–8.

63. At times given to hyperbolic overstatements, Overy's is the most focused presentation of this point: Richard Overy, *Why the Allies Won*. New York: Norton, 1996, Chapters 1, 6, and 7.

64. Ferguson, *The Cash Nexus*, p. 404; for the data, see also pp. 42–3, 46–8; Harrison, *The Economies of World War II*, pp. 20–1, 47, 82–3, 88–9, 157–9, 257, 287. The high mobilization rates of modern authoritarian–totalitarian regimes have also been noted by Mann, *The Sources of Social Power*, p. 60.

65. Overy's suggestion (*Why the Allies Won*, Chapter 9) that the Allies were aided by their holding of the moral high ground is belied by the telling quotation that he chose as the motto for his chapter (p. 282). Although for better and for

worse highly statistical in nature, Reiter and Stam, *Democracies at War*, conclude, curiously without providing any evidence at all, that democracies proved superior in war largely because democratic troops were better motivated and therefore fought better than their rivals. At least with respect to the World Wars, by far the most crucial for the fate of democracy, this conclusion finds little support in reality.

66. For example, this factor is not specified among the reasons for the global gains of democracy during the twentieth century in: Robert Dahl, *On Democracy*. New Haven, CT: Yale University Press, 1998, pp. 163–5. Nor is it mentioned in Ferguson, *The Cash Nexus*, Chapter 12, despite the chapter's title 'The American wave: Democracy's flow and ebb' and his vision of *future* American imperialism. Also, implicitly, Michael Doyle, *Ways of War and Peace: Realism, liberalism, and socialism*. New York: Norton, 1997, pp. 269–70, 277. More confusingly, Reiter and Stam, *Democracies at War*, p. 136, although actually recognizing that it was the participation of the USA that tilted the scales in both Europe and the Pacific, reject this as an explanation for the democracies' military success with the curious comment that one should not generalize from a single case, apparently not even if this 'single case' involves by far the greatest global power, whose participation decided the twentieth century's mightiest military conflicts and the fate of democracy. By contrast, Huntington is well aware of the international context, including the victories in the two World Wars, although he does not discuss the reasons for the democracies' victories in these wars: Samuel Huntington, *The Third Wave: Democratization in the Late Twentieth Century*. Norman, OK: University of Oklahoma, 1991. And see Tony Smith, *America's Mission: The United States and the worldwide struggle for democracy in the twentieth century*. Princeton, NJ: Princeton University Press, 1994, especially pp. 10–12, 147.

Chapter 16. *Affluent Liberal Democracies, Ultimate Weapons, and the World*

1. See excellently in Michael Doyle, *Ways of War and Peace: Realism, liberalism, and socialism*. New York: Norton, 1997; Thomas Walker, 'The forgotten prophet: Tom Paine's cosmopolitanism and international relations', *International Studies Quarterly*, 2000; **44**: 51–72, following on Michael Howard, *War and the Liberal Conscience*. Oxford: Oxford University Press, 1981, Chapter 1; and the last section of Chapter 14 above.

2. This theme was first fully stated in Wilson's declaration of war before Congress on 2 April 1917, but was kept muted in his famous Fourteen Points of 8 January 1918, which were more diplomatic, because they addressed allied Russia, where the Bolsheviks had seized power from the liberal government established in March 1917, as well as the German and Austrian enemies.

3. On this tension see beautifully: Howard, *War and the Liberal Conscience*, Chapters 2–3.

4. Melvin Small and David Singer, 'The war-proneness of democratic regimes, 1816–1965', *Jerusalem Journal of International Relations*, 1976; **1**(4): 50–69; Steve Chan, 'Mirror, mirror on the wall: Are the free countries more pacific?', *Journal of Conflict Resolution*, 1984; **28**: 617–48.

5. Dean Babst, 'A force for peace', *Industrial Research*, 1972; **14**: 55–8; although sometimes cited, this seminal article, which anticipated most of the arguments about 'democratic peace', is rarely discussed, probably because the author was not 'from the field'; for some other reason, Small and Singer ('The war-proneness of democratic regimes, 1816–1965') is often cited as a rejection of democratic uniqueness, although it remarkably covers both sides and most aspects of the problem; R. Rummel, 'Libertarianism and international violence', *Journal of Conflict Resolution*, 1983; **27**: 27–71; Michael Doyle, 'Kant, liberal legacies, and foreign affairs', *Philosophy and Public Affairs*, 1983; **12**: 205–35, 323–53; Chan, 'Mirror, mirror on the wall'; William Domke, *War and the Changing Global System*. New Haven, CT: Yale University Press, 1988; Zeev Maoz and Nasrin Abdolali, 'Regime type and international conflict 1816–1976', *Journal of Conflict Resolution*, 1989; **33**: 3–35; Bruce Russett, *Grasping the Democratic Peace*. Princeton, NJ: Princeton University Press, 1993.

6. For a general survey see: Fred Chenoff, 'The study of democratic peace and progress in international relations', *International Studies Review*, 2004; **6**: 49–77.

7. Bruce Russett and William Antholis, 'The imperfect democratic peace of Ancient Greece', reprinted in Russett, *Grasping the Democratic Peace*, Chapter 3.

8. Spencer Weart, *Never at War: Why democracies will not fight one another*. New Haven, CT: Yale University Press, 1998. Although intelligent and attractively written, this study has manoeuvred behind the veil of uncertainty, ignoring and manipulating some of the evidence and all too cleverly explaining away much of the rest. Classical scholars have disagreed with its basic contention, disputing its interpretations of various cases and citing more instances of wars between Greek democracies: see a leading expert on early Greek democracies: Eric Robinson, 'Reading and misreading the ancient evidence for democratic peace', *Journal of Peace Research*, 2001; **38**: 593–608; resulting in the following exchange: Spencer Weart, 'Remarks on the ancient evidence for democratic peace', *Journal of Peace Research*, 2001; **38**: 609–13; Eric Robinson, 'Response to Spencer Weart', *Journal of Peace Research*, 2001; **38**: 615–17. See also the leading authority on the Greek *polis* and fourth-century BC Athenian democracy: Mogens Hansen and Thomas Nielsen, *An Inventory of Archaic and Classical Poleis*. Oxford: Oxford University Press, 2004, pp. 84–5.

9. Weart postpones any mention of the first Athenian Empire to as late in his book as possible and then summarily disposes of this inconvenience (p. 246).

The problem was better acknowledged by Russett and Antholis in Russett, *Grasping the Democratic Peace*; Tobias Bachteler, 'Explaining the democratic peace: The evidence from Ancient Greece reviewed', *Journal of Peace Research*, 1997; **34**: 315–23.

10. The ancient sources for fourth-century Greece are varied and patchy. N. Hammond, *A History of Greece to 322 BC*. Oxford: Oxford University Press, 1986, can serve as a useful synthesis. David Hume, 'Of the balance of power', in *Essays: Literary, Moral and Political*, London: Routledge, 1894, p. 198. Yet Weart, *Never at War*, offers a thoroughly misleading account of that war, which clearly refutes his thesis. An example is the Battle of Mantinea (which he does not even name!), where Epaminondas deployed his famous 'oblique order', massively reinforcing his left wing while refusing his right in order decisively to crush the Spartan elite force holding the allies' right, as he had done in Leuctra. When Epaminondas was killed, the Thebans halted their pursuit, and in the general confusion the Athenians on the allies' left retreated from the battlefield, cutting to pieces some pursuing Theban troops hastily advancing on their side. Nevertheless, Weart (pp. 25–6) creates the impression that the armies of the two democracies, Athens and Thebes, tacitly chose not to fight each other. His alibi throughout is his insistence that only 200 battle casualties or more should be regarded as a criterion for war. This sounds reasonable, except that we rarely have records of casualties in antiquity, least of all reliable ones, and many of the campaigns in this war are covered with little or no detail. Furthermore, as we have seen, wars usually took the form of raids and sieges, whereas major battles were few and far between.

11. Alexander Yakobson, *Elections and Electioneering in Rome*. Stuttgart: Steiner, 1999. In conversations with me, Alex suggested a great deal of the following on Rome.

12. Weart, *Never at War*, whose unit of study is defined as republics, does not discuss Rome, the greatest of all republics, at all; and, again, this is no absent-mindedness, because he does mention Rome once, in his appendix of problematic cases (p. 297), where he lamely excuses himself from discussing her on the grounds that we lack information about Carthage. He calls Rome an oligarchic republic, even though in mid-Republican times she probably satisfied his definitions for a democratic republic (pp. 11–12) and had remarkably overcome the civil strife between the classes, another of his criteria for that status (pp. 119–24). As Weart believes that not only democratic but also oligarchic republics almost never fought each other throughout history, he labels Carthage aristocratic–anocratic (p. 404), even though no civil disorder or violence interrupted political procedure in that city during the First and Second Punic Wars. Undoubtedly, had he discussed the Roman record, he would have been forced to use similar tactics with respect to Capua and Tarentum. Whether Rome is defined as a democratic or oligarchic republic by Weart,

rivals that satisfy either definition suggest themselves. The above is sufficient to render superfluous a discussion of Weart's claims with respect to republican city-states in medieval Europe.

13. Doyle, 'Kant, liberal legacies, and foreign affairs', p. 212.

14. Joseph Schumpeter, *Capitalism, Socialism, and Democracy*. New York: Harper, 1947, pp. 269–83; Seymour Lipset, *Political Man*. New York: Anchor, 1963, p. 27; because of this loose definition, Robert Dahl, *Polyarchy*. New Haven, CT: Yale University Press, 1971, preferred this term to 'democracy' which is the more fully developed form.

15. Some of these 'difficult cases' have already been mentioned by Babst, 'A force for peace', followed by Doyle, 'Kant, liberal legacies, and foreign affairs'. For the critics, see: Christopher Layne, 'Kant or cant: The myth of the democratic peace', *International Security*, 1994; **19**(2): 5–49; David Spiro, 'The insignificance of the liberal peace', *International Security*, 1994; **19**(2): 50–86; Ido Oren, 'From democracy to demon: Changing American perceptions of Germany during World War I', *International Security*, 1995; **20**(2): 147–84. Babst, 'A force for peace', Russett, *Grasping the Democratic Peace*, pp. 16–19, and Owen attempt to explain away these cases, not always entirely persuasively: John Owen, 'How liberalism produces democratic peace', *International Security*, 1994; **19**(2): 87–125, id., *Liberal Peace, Liberal War*. Ithaca, NY: Cornell University Press, 1997. See also, James Ray, *Democracy and International Conflict: An evaluation of the democratic peace proposition*. Columbia, SC: University of South Carolina, 1995.

16. Layne, 'Kant or cant'; id., 'Lord Palmerston and the triumph of realism: Anglo-French relations, 1830–48', in M. Elman (ed.), *Path to Peace: Is democracy the answer?* Cambridge, MA: MIT Press, 1997, pp. 61–100. In addition, the critics have claimed that liberal-democratic countries did not always border on each other. As wars tend to occur more between neighbouring countries, the absence of wars between liberal-democratic countries during the nineteenth century may have had little to do with their regimes. It is questionable, however, how valid this latter claim is, because most liberal-democratic countries were actually concentrated in north-west Europe.

17. Henry Faber and Joanne Gowa, 'Politics and peace', *International Security*, 1995; **20**(2): 123–46.

18. Babst, 'A force for peace', p. 56; Zeev Maoz, 'The controversy over the democratic peace: Rearguard action or cracks in the wall?', *International Security*, 1997; **22**(1): 162–98. Proponents of the 'democratic peace' have further pointed out that at least the statistical studies of the theory have used existing and widely accepted datasets of wars and regimes, compiled neither by democratic peace theorists nor for the purpose of testing their theory.

19. Maoz and Abdolali, 'Regime type and international conflict 1816–1976'; Zeev Maoz and Bruce Russett, 'Normative and structural causes of democratic

peace 1946–1986', *American Political Science Review*, 1993; **87**: 624–38; this is incorporated in Russett, *Grasping the Democratic Peace*, Chapter 4 (and p. 21); Gregory Raymond, 'Democracies, disputes, and third-party intermediaries', *Journal of Conflict Resolution*, 1994; **38**: 24–42; William Dixon, 'Democracy and the peaceful settlement of international conflict', *American Political Science Review*, 1994; **88**: 14–32; David Rousseau, Christopher Gelpi, Dan Reiter, and Paul Huth, 'Assessing the dyadic nature of the democratic peace, 1918–1988', *American Political Science Review*, 1996; **90**: 512–33; Jean-Sebastien Rioux, 'A crisis-based evaluation of the democratic peace proposition', *Canadian Journal of Political Science*, 1998; **31**: 263–83; Michael Mousseau, 'Democracy and compromise in militarized interstate conflicts, 1816–1992', *Journal of Conflict Resolution*, 1998; **42**: 210–30.

20. Russett, *Grasping the Democratic Peace*, p. 20; Bruce Russett and John Oneal, *Triangulating Peace: Democracy, interdependence and international organizations*. New York: Norton, 2001, pp. 111–14; Maoz, 'The controversy over the democratic peace'. Also, William Thompson and Richard Tucker, 'A tale of two democratic peace critiques', *Journal of Conflict Resolution*, 1997; **41**: 428–54.

21. See Stephen Walt, *The Origins of Alliances*. Ithaca, NY: Cornell University Press, 1987, pp. 33–4; Randolph Siverson and Julian Emmons, 'Birds of a feather: Democratic political systems and alliances choices', *Journal of Conflict Resolution*, 1991; **35**: 285–306; Faber and Gowa, 'Politics and peace'; Joanne Gowa, *Battles and Bullets: The elusive democratic peace*. Princeton, NJ: Princeton University Press, 1999; Michael Simon and Erik Gartzke, 'Political system similarity and the choice of allies', *Journal of Conflict Resolution*, 1996; **40**: 617–35; Brian Lai and Dan Reiter, 'Democracy, political similarity, and international alliances, 1812–1992', *Journal of Conflict Resolution*, 2000; **44**: 203–27; Errol Henderson, *Democracy and War: The end of an illusion*. Boulder, CO: Lynne Rienner, 2002, Chapter 2. Weart's claim, *Never at War*, for an absence of war among both democratic republics and oligarchic republics, *where this claim actually has some foundation in reality*, seems to apply when the sides tended to ally along regime and ideological lines.

22. As suggested by: John Mearsheimer, 'Back to the future: Instability in Europe after the Cold War', *International Security*, 1990; **15**(1): 5–56.

23. Raymond Cohen, 'Pacific unions: A reappraisal of the theory that "Democracies do not go to war with each other"', *Review of International Studies*, 1994; **20**: 207–23.

24. See, for example, Sumit Ganguli, 'War and conflict between India and Pakistan: Revisiting the pacifying power of democracy', in M. Elman (ed.), *Path to Peace: Is democracy the answer?* Cambridge, MA: MIT Press, 1997, pp. 267–301; Himadeep Muppidi, 'State identity and interstate practices: The limits to democratic peace in South Asia', in T. Barkawi and M. Laffey (eds), *Demography, Liberalism and War: Rethinking the democratic peace debate*, Boulder,

CO: Lynne Rienner, 2001, Chapter 3; Scott Gates, Torbjorn Knutsen, and Jonathan Moses, 'Democracy and peace: A more skeptical view', *Journal of Peace Research*, 1996; **33**: 1–10; Russett and Oneal, *Triangulating Peace*, p. 48.

25. Hume, 'Of the balance of power', p. 202; Doyle, *Ways of War and Peace*, p. 265.

26. Edward Mansfield and Jack Snyder, 'Democratization and the danger of war', *International Security*, 1995; **20**(1): 5–38; Jack Snyder, *From Voting to Violence: Democratization and nationalist conflict*. New York: Norton, 2000, despite Snyder's untenable 'instrumentalist' view of nationalism: see Chapter 15, endnote 35 above. Kurt Gaubatz, *Elections and War: The electoral incentives in the democratic politics of war and peace*. Stanford: Stanford University Press, 1999, Chapter 2; Michael Mann, 'Democracy and ethnic war', in Barkawi and Laffey, *Demography, Liberalism and War*, Chapter 4; Paul Huth and Todd Allee, *The Democratic Peace and Territorial Conflict in the Twentieth Century*. New York: Cambridge University Press, 2002. Generally on nationalism and democracy as two inextricable products of popular sovereignty, see Ghia Nodia, 'Nationalism and democracy', in L. Diamond and M. Plattner (eds), *Nationalism, Ethnic Conflict, and Democracy*. Baltimore, MD: Johns Hopkins University Press, 1994, pp. 3–22. Some scholars have argued that it was in fact revolutionary regime change in general—democratic or autocratic—that is documented to have increased the likelihood of war, with a change to democracy tending to be less conducive to war than a change to autocracy. Even so, the process of democratization and a transition to democracy supposedly increased tensions and the likelihood of war, as contemporaries during the nineteenth century felt. On war as a function of political instability, see Zeev Maoz, 'Joining the club of nations: Political development and international conflict, 1816–1976', *International Studies Quarterly*, 1989; **33**: 199–231; Stephen Walt, *Revolution and War*. Ithaca, NY: Cornell University Press, 1996; Andrew Enterline, 'Driving while democratizing', *International Security*, 1996; **20**(4): 183–96; id., 'Regime changes and interstate conflict, 1816–1992', *Political Research Quarterly*, 1998; **51**: 385–409; Kristian Gleditsch and Michael Ward, 'War and peace in space and time: The role of democratization', *International Studies Quarterly*, 2000; **44**: 1–29; Michael Ward and Kristian Gleditsch, 'Democratizing for peace', *American Political Science Review*, 1988; **92**: 51–61. Contrary to others, Russett and Oneal, *Triangulating Peace*, pp. 51–2, 116–22, detect no statistical evidence for an increase in militarized dispute after a regime change, whether in the democratic or the autocratic direction, but, significantly perhaps, they examine only the period after 1886. Gaubatz, *Elections and War*, Chapter 3, detects a distinctive change of attitude towards war in twentieth-century western democracies in comparison with the nineteenth century. All the same, the statistical study by Huth and Allee, *The Democratic Peace and Territorial Conflict in the Twentieth Century*, contradicting the one by Russett and Oneal, *Triangulating Peace*, insists that new democracies remain more conflictual even during that later period.

Sara Mitchell and Brandon Prins, 'Beyond territorial contiguity: issues at stake in democratic militarized interstate disputes', *International Studies Quarterly*, 1999; **43**: 169–83, produce similar findings.

27. Maoz and Abdolali, 'Regime type and international conflict 1816–1976'; Zeev Maoz, 'Realist and cultural critiques of the democratic peace: A theoretical and empirical re-assessment', *International Interactions*, 1998; **24**: 3–89; Steve Chan, 'In search of democratic peace: Problems and promise', *Mershon International Studies Review*, 1997; **41**: 83.

28. The correlation between the *level* of democracy/liberalism and peace was first suggested by Rummel, 'Libertarianism and interstate violence', and incorporated in: R. Rummel, *Power Kills: Democracy as a method of non-violence*. New Brunswick, NJ: Transaction, 1997, p. 5 and Chapter 3; echoed by Ray, *Democracy and International Conflict*, p. 16. Both failed, however, to apply this insight historically. Historical gradualism is tentatively noted in the 1992 article by Bruce Russett and Zeev Maoz, incorporated in Russett, *Grasping the Democratic Peace*, pp. 72–3; it was more fully developed in Maoz, 'The controversy over the democratic peace'; and is integral in Russett and Oneal, *Triangulating Peace*, pp. 111–14, *passim*. By contrast, Doyle does not accept the idea of gradualism and liberal growth: M. Doyle, 'Michael Doyle on the democratic peace—again', printed in M. Brown, S. Lynn-Jones, and S. Miller (eds), *Debating the Democratic Peace*. Cambridge, MA: MIT Press, 1996, p. 370. But for the claim that Kant did, see George Cavallar, 'Kantian perspectives on democratic peace: Alternatives to Doyle', *Review of International Studies*, 2001; **27**: 229–48.

29. Russett and Maoz, in Russett, *Grasping the Democratic Peace*, p. 86. Generally regarding today's third world: Edward Friedman, 'The painful gradualness of democratization: Proceduralism as a necessary discontinuous revolution', in H. Handelman and M. Tessler (eds), *Democracy and Its Limits: Lessons from Asia, Latin America, and the Middle East*. Notre Dame, IN: University of Notre Dame, 1999, pp. 321–40; for the considerable differences in the level of democracy: Zachary Elkins, 'Gradations of democracy? Empirical tests of alternative conceptualizations', *American Journal of Political Science*, 2000; **44**: 293–300.

30. For the last point see Doyle, 'Kant, liberal legacies, and foreign affairs', pp. 231–2. For the claim that economic theoretical models are more ambivalent see Katherine Barbieri and Gerald Schneider, 'Globalization and peace: Assessing new directions in the study of trade and conflict', *Journal of Peace Research*, 1999; **36**: 387–404; but see Solomon Polachek, 'Why democracies cooperate more and fight less: The relationship between trade and international cooperation', *Review of International Economics*, 1997; **5**: 295–309.

31. B. Mitchell, *European Historical Statistics 1750–1970*. London: Macmillan, 1975, pp. 526, 573. This has been elaborated upon by Kenneth Waltz, *Theory of International Politics*. Reading, MA: Addison, 1979, pp. 212–15.

32. Edward Mansfield, *Power, Trade, and War*. Princeton, NJ: Princeton University

Press, 1994; Katherine Barbieri, 'Economic interdependence: A path to peace or a source of interstate conflict?', *Journal of Peace Research*, 1996; **33**: 29–49; this examines the period 1870–1938 and arrives at mixed results; Dale Copeland, 'Economic interdependence and war: A theory of trade expectations', *International Security*, 1996; **20**(4): 5–41; Edward Mansfield and Brian Pollins (eds), *Economic Interdependence and International Conflict*. Ann Arbor, MI: University of Michigan, 2003; building on their earlier work and studying the period 1885–1992, Russett and Oneal, *Triangulating Peace*, pp. 125–55, is the most sophisticated statistical analysis.

33. John Jackson, *The World Trading System*. Cambridge, MA: MIT Press, 1997, p. 74.

34. Richard Rosecrance, *The Rise of the Virtual State*. New York: Basic Books, 1999, p. 37; Robert Gilpin, with Jean Gilpin, *The Challenge of Global Capitalism: The world economy in the 21st century*. Princeton, NJ: Princeton University Press, 2000, pp. 20–3.

35. This was originally demonstrated by the somewhat neglected book by Domke, *War and the Changing Global System*, and impressively elaborated by Russett and Oneal, *Triangulating Peace*. By contrast, Doyle, *Ways of War and Peace*, pp. 284, 286–7, claims that all three elements together, and *only* together, are conducive to peace.

36. Both Small and Singer 'The war-proneness of democratic regimes', pp. 65–6, and Chan, 'Mirror, mirror on the wall', p. 639, pointed out that democracies initiated wars nearly as much as non-democracies. But Rummel's counter-claim that liberal countries are more peaceful in general: 'Libertarianism and interstate violence', *Journal of Conflict Resolution*, 1983; **27**: 27–71 and Rummel, *Power Kills*, is corroborated by Domke, *War and the Changing Global System*; Stuart Bremer, 'Dangerous dyads: Conditions affecting the likelihood of inter-state war, 1816–1965', *Journal of Conflict Resolution*, 1992; **36**: 309–41; Kenneth Benoit, 'Democracies really are more pacific (in general)', *Journal of Conflict Resolution*, 1996; **40**: 636–57 (restricted to 1960–80 and therefore of limited value); Rousseau et al., 'Assessing the dyadic nature of the democratic peace, 1918–1988'; David Rousseau, *Democracy and War*. Stanford: Stanford University Press, 2005; Rioux, 'A crisis-based evaluation of the democratic peace pro-position'; Russett, altering his initial position, in Russett and Oneal, *Triangulating Peace*, pp. 49–50.

37. Already noted by Small and Singer, 'The war-proneness of democratic regimes', pp. 63–4 and developed by Rummel, *Power Kills*.

38. Rousseau, *Democracy and War*.

39. Rummel, *Power Kills*; Mathew Krain and Marrissa Myers, 'Democracy and civil war: A note on the democratic peace proposition', *International Interaction*, 1997; **23**: 109–18; this finds no change over time, but fails to distinguish

between advanced and less advanced democracies; well noted, among other things, in Tanja Ellingson, 'Colorful community or ethnic witches-brew? Multiethnicity and domestic conflict during and after the Cold War', *Journal of Conflict Resolution*, 2000; **44**: 228–49; Ted Gurr, *Minorities at Risk: A global view of ethnopolitical conflicts*. Washington, DC: US Institute of Peace, 1993; Errol Henderson and David Singer, 'Civil war in the post-colonial world, 1946–92', *Journal of Peace Research*, 2000; **37**: 275–99; Henderson, *Democracy and War*, Chapter 5.

40. Rummel, *Power Kills*.

41. The best studies by far are: Michael Mousseau, 'Market prosperity, democratic consolidation, and democratic peace', *Journal of Conflict Resolution*, 2000; **44**: 472–507; id., 'The nexus of market society, liberal preferences, and democratic peace', *International Studies Quarterly*, 2003; **47**: 483–510; id., 'comparing new theory with prior beliefs: Market civilization and the democratic peace', *Conflict Management and Peace Science*, 2005; **22**: 63–77; Michael Mousseau, Håvard Hegre, and John Oneal, 'How the wealth of nations conditions the liberal peace', *European Journal of International Relations*, 2003; **9**: 277–314. Also Polachek, 'Why democracies cooperate more and fight less'; Håvard Hegre, 'Development and the liberal peace: what does it take to be a trading state?', *Journal of Peace Research*, 2000; **37**: 5–30. The correlation had already been suggested by Benoit, 'Democracies really are more pacific'.

42. Henderson and Singer, 'Civil war in the post-colonial world, 1946–92'; Henderson, *Democracy and War*, Chapter 5.

43. The seminal modern work is Lipset, *Political Man*, especially Chapters 1–2; also, Dahl, *Polyarchy*, Chapter 5; Samuel Huntington, *The Third Wave: Democratization in the late twentieth century*. Norman, OK: University of Oklahoma, 1991, pp. 59–72; Larry Diamond, 'Economic development and democracy reconsidered', in G. Marks and L. Diamond (eds), *Reexamining Democracy*. Newbury Park: Sage, 1992, pp. 93–139; Axel Hadenius, *Democracy and Development*. Cambridge: Cambridge University Press, 1992.

44. Mousseau, 'Market prosperity, democratic consolidation, and democratic peace'; Marks and Diamond, *Reexamining Democracy*. The idea had been developed by Samuel Huntington, *Political Order in Changing Societies*. New Haven, CT: Yale University Press, 1968.

45. Fareed Zakaria, 'The rise of illiberal democracy', *Foreign Affairs*, 1997; **76**(6): 22–46; Larry Diamond, *Developing Democracy*. Baltimore, MD: Johns Hopkins University Press, 1999, especially pp. 34–60, 279–80; Adrian Karatnycky, 'The decline of illiberal democracy', *Journal of Democracy*, 1999; **10**: 112–25, a summary of the Freedom House scores for that point in time, which, although open to criticisms, are the most widely accepted index of democracy and liberalism.

46. Compare Richard Rosecrance, *The Rise of the Trading State: Commerce and conquest in the modern world*. New York: Basic Books, 1986; Rosecrance, *The Rise of the Virtual State*.

47. Russett and Oneal, *Triangulating Peace*, Chapter 1.

48. See endnote 29 and related text in Chapter 15. Lars-Erik Cederman, 'Back to Kant: reinterpreting the democratic peace as a macrohistorical learning process', *American Political Science Review*, 2001; **95**(1): 15–31; this detects a decline in belligerency among non-democracies after 1945, but the main decline occurred in comparison to the pre-1815 period, which he does not examine; also, Cederman's 'learning mechanism' has no apparent motivating factor.

49. Maoz and Russett, 'Normative and structural causes of democratic peace 1946–1986'; Russett and Oneal, *Triangulating Peace*, pp. 151–3.

50. See the studies in endnote 41.

51. Joseph Schumpeter, *Imperialism. Social Classes: Two essays*. New York: World Publishing, 1972(1919), pp. 3–98.

52. Peter Liberman, *Does Conquest Pay? The exploitation of occupied industrial societies*. Princeton, NJ: Princeton University Press, 1996.

53. Generally for this theme in liberal thought, see: Beate Jahn, 'Kant, Mill, and illiberal legacies in international affairs', *International Organization*, 2005; **59**: 177–207.

54. A consensus seems to have emerged that 'structural' and 'normative' factors are intertwined in creating the 'democratic peace'.

55. On the 'pyramid of needs', see again Abraham Maslow, *Motivation and Personality*. New York: Harper, 1970(1954); I am thankful to Gil Friedman for calling my attention to the relevance of Maslow's 'pyramid' to my argument here. On absolute versus relative gain in international relations' theory, see Chapters 7, 8, and 10 in D. Baldwin (ed.), *Neorealism and Neoliberalism*. New York: Columbia University Press, 1993.

56. The impression created by John Mueller, *Retreat from Doomsday: The obsolescence of major war*. New York: Basic Books, 1989.

57. In contrast to his general claim, Mueller, *Retreat from Doomsday*, pp. 7–8, 55, recognized this.

58. Mueller, *Retreat from Doomsday*, pp. 53–68.

59. The following demonstrate that the prospects of achieving military victory have been paramount in determining the American public's casualty tolerance: Eric Larson, *Casualties and Consensus: The historical role of casualties in domestic support of US military operations*. Santa Monica, CA: Rand, 1996; Christopher Gelpi, Peter Feaver, and Jason Reifler, 'Casualty sensitivity and the war in Iraq', unpublished typescript on the world-wide web. Although this is an important corrective to the prevailing view about liberal democracies' lack of casualty

tolerance, it should be noted that non-liberal democracies are less susceptible to this constraint and that their casualty tolerance in general is much higher. Moreover, as we see later, liberal democracies' very ability to achieve victory in some types of war has been severely constrained for reasons directly linked to their norms.

60. This is the subject of Part II of Azar Gat, *Fascist and Liberal Visions of War*. Oxford: Oxford University Press, 1998; incorporated in Azar Gat, *History of Military Thought: From the Enlightenment to the Cold War*. Oxford: Oxford University Press, 2001.

61. Thomas Friedman, *The Lexus and the Olive Tree*. New York: Farrar, Straus, Giroux, 1999, Chapter 10.

62. See Mitchell, *European Historical Statistics 1750–1970*, Sections B 6 and B 7.

63. On perception versus reality here, see Martin Daly and Margo Wilson, *Homicide*. New York: Aldine, 1988, pp. 125, 276, 291.

64. Flavius Vegetius Renatus, *The Military Institutions of the Romans*. Harrisburg, PA: The Military Service Publishing, 1960, Books i.3 and i.7, pp. 14, 16; Niccolò Machiavelli, *The Art of War*. Cambridge, MA: Da Capo, 1965, Bk i, pp. 27, 33.

65. For the statistics, see Friedrich von Bernhardi, *Germany and the Next War*. New York: Longmans, 1914, pp. 243–4.

66. Bill Bishop, 'Who goes to war', *Washington Post*, 16 November 2003. Since this was written, demographic data have been released by the Pentagon, confirming the trend: Ann Scott Tyson, 'Youths in rural U.S. are drawn to military', *Washington Post*, 10 November 2005. Despite its title, this article emphasizes the recruits' poor economic background (a significant point to be sure) but not their rural roots.

67. Rosecrance, *The Rise of the Virtual State*, p. xii; also p. 26 for the other major industrial countries; Gilpin and Gilpin, *The Challenge of Global Capitalism*, p. 33.

68. This factor, as well as the exponential rise in plenty and comfort mentioned above, may not be sufficiently emphasized in works such as C. Moskos, J. Williams, and D. Segal (eds), *The Postmodern Military*. New York: Oxford University Press, 2000; although the latter trend in effect underlies Ronald Inglehart, *Cultural Shift: Advanced industrial society*. Princeton, NJ: Princeton University Press, 1990.

69. For the Soviets, see Anthony Beevor, *The Fall of Berlin 1945*. New York: Penguin, 2003, p. 410; the book is filled with chilling accounts. For the Americans and Japanese in the Second World War, see Joshua Goldstein, *War and Gender: How the gender shapes the war system and vice versa*. New York: Cambridge University Press, 2001, pp. 337, 346, respectively. Also, generally, Chapter 12, endnote 13 above.

70. Herbert Moller, 'Youth as a force in the modern world', *Comparative Studies in*

Society and History, 1967–8; **10**: 237–60; Christian Mesquida and Neil Wiener, 'Human collective aggression: A behavioral ecology perspective', *Ethology and Sociobiology*, 1996; **17**: 247–62.

71. For the data on the pre-First World War west, see Mitchell, *European Historical Statistics 1750–1970*, Section B 2, especially pp. 37 and 52; for the contemporary data: United Nations, *World Population Prospects: The 2000 revision*. New York: UN, 2001; also, The Economist, *Pocket World in Figures*: 2005 edn. London: Profile, 2005, pp. 20–1.

72. Samuel Huntington, *The Clash of Civilizations and the Remaking of World Order*. New York: Simon & Schuster, 1997, pp. 116–20.

73. Edward Luttwak, 'Blood and computers: The crisis of classical military power in advanced postindustrialist societies', in Z. Maoz and A. Gat (eds), *War in a Changing World*. Ann Arbor, MI, University of Michigan, 2001, pp. 49–75; for my critique see pp. 88–9 of this book.

74. Lisa Brandes, 'Public opinion, international security and gender: The United States and Great Britain since 1945', unpublished doctoral dissertation, 1994, Yale.

75. Bruce Russett, 'The democratic peace—and yet it moves', in Brown, Lynn-Jones, and Miller, *Debating the Democratic Peace*, p. 340; Doyle, 'Michael Doyle on the democratic peace—again', p. 372.

76. Mark Tessler and Ira Warriner, 'Gender, feminism, and attitude towards international conflict', *World Politics*, 1997; **49**: 250–81; Mark Tessler, Jodi Nachtwey, and Audra Grant, 'Further tests of the women and peace hypothesis: evidence from cross-national survey research in the Middle East', *International Studies Quarterly*, 1999; **43**: 519–31. Generally see: Virginia Sapiro, 'Theorizing gender in political psychology research', in D. Sears, L. Huddy, and R. Jervis (eds), *Oxford Handbook of Political Psychology*. Oxford: Oxford University Press, 2003, pp. 601–34.

77. I stand between the two poles represented by Mueller, *Retreat from Doomsday*; id., 'The essential irrelevance of nuclear weapons: stability in the postwar world', *International Security*, 1988; **13**(2): 55–79; and Martin van Creveld, *The Transformation of War*. New York: Free Press, 1991. In addition to their basic claims, I take issue with much of their respective reasoning. Concerning Mueller, see endnotes 56, 58, and adjunct texts. He regards the 'disillusionment' with the First World War as the reason for the decline of major war, without accounting for the deeper sources of that disillusionment, its mostly liberal character, and the decline of war in the century before 1914. Van Creveld suggests that belligerency will continue below the nuclear threshold *purely* because males are playfully pugnacious and cannot do without fighting. For a refutation, see the first section of Chapter 3.

78. John Gaddis, 'The origins of self-deterrence: The United States and the

non-use of nuclear weapons, 1945–1958', in *The Long Peace: Inquiries into the history of the Cold War*. New York: Oxford University Press, 1987, pp. 104–46.

79. See endnotes 19 and 36.

80. Randall Schweller, 'Domestic structure and preventive war: Are democracies more pacific?', *World Politic*, 1992; **44**: 235–69.

81. Hume, 'Of the balance of power', pp. 202–3; Doyle, *Ways of War and Peace*, pp. 275–7.

82. All this is insufficiently addressed in: R. Rosecrance (ed.), *The New Great Power Coalition: Toward a world concert of nations*. Lanham, MD: Rowman, 2001.

83. David French, *British Strategy and War Aims, 1914–1916*. London: Allen & Unwin, 1986.

84. Williamson Murray, *The Change in the European Balance of Power, 1938–1939*. Princeton, NJ: Princeton University Press, 1984; David Kaiser, *The Economic Diplomacy and the Origins of the Second World War*. Princeton, NJ: Princeton University Press, 1980; Mueller, *Retreat from Doomsday*, p. 69.

85. David Reynolds, *The Creation of the Anglo-American Alliance, 1937–1941*. London: Europa, 1981, especially pp. 17, 30–1, 35; Robert Dallek, *Franklin D. Roosevelt and American Foreign Policy, 1932–1945*. New York: Oxford University Press, 1979, especially pp. 163–4; Callum Macdonald, 'Deterrence diplomacy: Roosevelt and the containment of Germany, 1938–1940', in R. Boyce and E. Robertson (eds), *Paths to War*. London: Macmillan, 1989, pp. 297–329; D. C. Watt, *Succeeding John Bull: America in Britain's place, 1900–1975*. Cambridge: Cambridge University Press, 1984, pp. 82–3.

86. Richard Overy, *The Origins of the Second World War*. London: Longman, 1987, p. 77; John Charmley, *Chamberlain and the Lost Peace*. London: Hodder, 1989, p. 210; also Mueller, *Retreat from Doomsday*, p. 70.

87. J. Gwyer, *Grand Strategy: June 1941–August 1942*, Vol. 3. London: HMSO, 1964; Dallek, *Franklin D. Roosevelt and American Foreign Policy*. In recent years historians have become increasingly more sceptical about American intentions of joining the war: Reynolds, *The Creation of the Anglo-American Alliance*, especially pp. 214–19; John Charmley, *Churchill: The end of glory*. London: Harcourt, 1993, p. 332; id., *Churchill's Grand Alliance*. New York: Harcourt, 1995, pp. 16–17, 38–44, 356; John Keegan, 'Churchill's strategy', in R. Blake and W. Roger Louis (eds), *Churchill*. Oxford: Oxford University Press, 1993, pp. 338–9; Norman Rose, *Churchill*. New York: Free Press, 1994, pp. 276, 288; Gerald Weinberg, *A World at Arms: A global history of World War II*, Cambridge: Cambridge University Press, 1994, pp. 238–45 (citing recently discovered documentation).

88. That this amounted to a strategy of containment is again noted by Mueller, *Retreat from Doomsday*, pp. 75–7.

89. George Kennan, *American Diplomacy*. Chicago: University of Chicago, 1985 (1951), pp. vi–vii.

90. See the Kennan Papers at the Seeley Mudd Manuscript Library, Princeton, for example, 23 January 1947, 16/21; Memorandum to Dean Acheson, 20 January 1950, in T. Etzold and J. Gaddis (eds), *Containment: Documents on American foreign policy and strategy, 1945–1950*. New York: Columbia University Press, 1978, pp. 373–81.

91. Max Singer and Aaron Wildavsky, *The Real World Order: Zones of peace, zones of turmoil*. Chatham, NJ: Chatham, House, 1993. This excellent book has not received the attention that it deserves. Also, James Goldgeier and Michael McFaul, 'A tale of two worlds: Core and periphery in the post-Cold War era', *International Organization*, 1992; **46**: 467–91.

92. See typically, Francis Fukuyama, *The End of History and the Last Man*. New York: Free Press, 1992.

93. David Lake, *Power, Protection, and Free Trade: International sources of US commercial strategy, 1887–1933*. Ithaca, NY: Cornell University Press, 1988; Lake perceptively elaborates about this widely noted point. Also, Robert Gilpin, *Global Political Economy*. Princeton, NJ: Princeton University Press, 2001, pp. 42–3, 99–102.

94. Robert Barro, 'Determinants of economic growth: A cross-country empirical study', New York: National Bureau of Economic Research Working Paper 5698, 1996; Amartya Sen, *Development and Freedom*. New York: Knopf, 1999; this offers little by way of historical perspective. Theoretically, see Mancur Olson, *Power and Prosperity: Outgrowing communist and capitalist dictatorships*. New York: Basic Books, 2000. Niall Ferguson, *The Cash Nexus: Money and power in the modern world, 1700–2000*. New York: Basic Books, 2001, pp. 348–9, 363–9, is a good summary and analysis; also Fukuyama, *The End of History and the Last Man*, p. 123.

95. Huntington, *The Third Wave*.

96. See endnote 45.

97. For something along these lines, see John Gray, *False Dawn: The delusions of global capitalism*. London: Granta, 1998.

98. Howard, *War and the Liberal Conscience*, pp. 54–6.

99. D. Killingray, 'Colonial warfare in West Africa, 1870–1914', in J. Moor and H. Wesseling (eds), *Imperialism and War: Essays in colonial wars in Asia and Africa*. Leiden: Brill, 1989, p. 147; Martin van Creveld, *Technology and War*. New York: Free Press, 1989, pp. 229–30.

100. James Ray and Ayse Vural, 'Power disparities and paradoxical conflict outcomes', *International Interactions*, 1986; **12**: 315–42.

101. For the arms imports, see William Langer, *The Diplomacy of Imperialism*

1890–1902. New York: Knopf, 1956, pp. 273, 280; for the troop numbers, see Romain Rainero, 'The Battle of Adowa', in J. Moor and H. Wesseling (eds), *Imperialism and War: Essays in colonial wars in Asia and Africa.* Leiden: Brill, 1989, pp. 189–200.

102. Glenn Snyder, 'Crisis bargaining', in C. Hermann (ed.), *International Crises.* New York: Free Press, 1972, p. 232; Steven Rosen, 'War power and the willingness to suffer', in B. Russett (ed.), *Peace, War, and Numbers.* Beverly Hills, CA: Sage, 1972, pp. 167–83.

103. In addition to endnote 4, see the references in Doyle, *Ways of War and Peace,* p. 269; also Mann, 'Democracy and ethnic war'; Henderson, *Democracy and War,* Chapter 4.

104. Gil Merom, *How Democracies Lose Small Wars: State, society, and the failure of France in Algeria, Israel in Lebanon, and the United States in Vietnam.* New York: Cambridge University Press, 2003.

105. Thucydides, *History of the Peloponnesian War,* Vol. iii. London: Heinemann-Loeb, 1958, p. 37.

106. Harold Selesky, 'Colonial America', in M. Howard, G. Andreopoulos, and M. Shulman (eds), *The Laws of War: Constraints on warfare in the Western World.* New Haven, CT: Yale University Press, 1994, Chapter 5.

107. Merom, *How Democracies Lose Small Wars,* p. 61.

108. Andrew Ward, *Our Bones Are Scattered: The Cawnpore massacres and the Indian mutiny of 1857.* New York: Holt, 1996.

109. R. Shannon, *Gladstone and the Bulgarian Agitation 1876.* Hassocks: Harvester, 1975, quotations from pp. 26, 33; the book recognizes well the deeper significance and context of the episode, as well as the lines connecting it to Gladstone's subsequent treatment of the Irish question.

110. S. P. Mackenzie, *Revolutionary Armies in the Modern Era: A revisionist approach.* London: Routledge, 1997; this deals mainly with regular armies, but see Chapter 10 on the Vietcong; B. H. Liddell Hart, *Strategy.* New York: Praeger, 1967, pp. 373–82.

111. Dan Reiter and Allan Stam, *Democracies at War.* Princeton, NJ: Princeton University Press, 2002, Chapter 7.

112. See endnote 59.

113. For revisionist reappraisals of the alleged critical role of television in Vietnam, see: Daniel Hallin, *The 'Uncensored War': The media and Vietnam.* Berkeley, CA: University of California, 1986; William Hammond, *Reporting Vietnam: Media and military at war.* Lawrence: University of Kansas, 1998.

114. J. Lonsdale, 'The conquest state of Kenya', in J. Moor and H. Wesseling (eds), *Imperialism and War: Essays in colonial wars in Asia and Africa.* Leiden: Brill, 1989, pp. 87–120, especially p. 106 for suppression techniques and atrocities;

A. Kanya-Forstner, 'The French Marines and the conquest of the Western Sudan, 1880–1899', ibid., pp. 121–45, especially 141; and Killingray, 'Colonial warfare in West Africa', pp. 146–67, especially 157.

115. Jon Bridgman, *The Revolt of the Hereros*. Berkeley, CA: University of California, 1981; Horst Drechsler, *'Let Us Die Fighting': The struggle of the Herero and Nama against German imperialism, 1884–1915*. London: Zed, 1980; John Iliffe, *Tanganyika under German Rule 1905–1912*. Cambridge: Cambridge University Press, 1969, pp. 9–29; G. Gwassa and J. Iliffe (eds), *Record of the Maji Maji Rising*. Nairobi: East African Publishing House, 1967.

116. Langer, *The Diplomacy of Imperialism 1890–1902*, p. 699.

117. Geoffrey Best, *Humanity in Warfare*. London: Methuen, 1983, pp. 226–8, 235–7, and Chapters III–IV in general.

118. H. Jack (ed.), *The Gandhi Reader*. Bloomington, IN: Indiana University Press, 1956, pp. 317–22, 332–9, 344–7.

119. See Best, *Humanity in Warfare*, pp. 115–20.

120. This is claimed, for example, by an otherwise excellent work written even before 9/11: Walter Laqueur, *The New Terrorism: Fanaticism and the arms of mass destruction*. New York: Oxford University Press, 1999, pp. 8–12; nevertheless, in actuality he, too, begins his survey of terrorism from the late nineteenth century.

121. H. Gilchrist, *A Comparative Study of World War Casualties from Gas and Other Weapons*. Edgewood, MD: Chemical Warfare School, 1928, pp. 49ff; cited by James Hammond, *Poison Gas*. Westport, CT: Greenwood, 1999, pp. 33–6.

122. Jeffrey Legro, *Cooperation under Fire: Anglo-German restraint during World War II*. Ithaca, NY: Cornell University Press, 1995.

123. Philip Cohen, 'A terrifying power', *New Scientist*, 30 January 1999: 10; Rachel Nowak, 'Disaster in the making', *New Scientist*, 13 January 2001: 4–5; Carina Dennis, 'The bugs of war', *Nature*, 17 May 2001: 232–5.

124. Michael Moodie, 'The chemical weapons threat', in S. Drell, A. Sofaer, and G. Wilson (eds), *The New Terror: Facing the threat of biological and chemical weapons*. Stanford: Stanford University Press, Hoover Institution, 1999, p. 19.

125. Nadine Gurr and Benjamin Cole, *The New Face of Terrorism: Threats from weapons of mass destruction*. London: Tauris, 2000, p. 43.

126. Anonymous scientist cited by Anne Applebaum, 'The next plague', *The Washington Post*, 18 February 2004.

127. David Kaplan, 'Aum Shinrikyo', in J. Tucker (ed.), *Toxic Terror*. Cambridge, MA: MIT Press, 2000, Chapter 12; Gurr and Cole, *The New Face of Terrorism*, p. 51.

128. Friedman, *The Lexus and the Olive Tree*, pp. 321–9.

129. Gerald Helman and Steven Ratner, 'Saving failed states', *Foreign Policy*, 1992–3; **89**: 3–20.

130. See, for example, D. Davis and A. Pereira (eds), *Irregular Armed Forces and Their Role in Politics and State Formation*. New York: Cambridge University Press, 2003.

131. Graham Allison, *Nuclear Terrorism: The ultimate preventable catastrophe*. New York: Times, 2004; this is a proposed blueprint for such a strategy, although restricted to the nuclear threat and not always coherent or persuasive with respect to the available policy options towards proliferation in defiant and weak states. More generally: Philip Babbitt, *The Shield of Achilles: War, peace and the course of history*. London: Allen Lane, 2002.

132. Chemical weapons are covered by the Chemical Weapons Convention of 1993, which went into effect in 1997. In contrast to the 1925 Geneva Protocol, it prohibits not only the use but also the production, stockpiling, and transfer of chemical weapons and introduces verification mechanisms. The 1972 Biological and Toxin Weapons Convention included no such verification mechanisms. But, in any case, the development of chemical and biological weapons is within the reach of terrorist groups, which are able to do so without state support but can still benefit from it, as well as from state negligence and poor policing.

133. See, for example, Scott Sagan (against) and Kenneth Waltz (for) *The Spread of Nuclear Weapons*. New York: Norton, 1999; references to terrorist nuclear threat have been added in the second edition (2003) pp. 126–30, 159–66. Also (for) Martin van Creveld, *Nuclear Proliferation and the Future of Conflict*. New York: Free Press, 1993; and a good balanced treatment by Devin Hagertly, *The Consequences of Nuclear Proliferation*. Cambridge, MA: MIT Press, 1998.

134. Much of this is ably portrayed in Robert Kagan, *Of Paradise and Power: America and Europe in the new world order*. London: Atlantic, 2003. I see only two failings in this book: it does not mention the liberal-democratic ('republican') underpinning of the Kantian peace and the European Kantian experience; for the same reason it exaggerates the USA–European antagonism, with militarization being inconceivable to both sides.

135. Max Weber, *The Religion of China: Confucianism and Taoism*. Glencoe, IL: Free Press, 1951, especially Chapter VIII.

136. Again, see most pointedly Kagan, *Of Paradise and Power*.

137. Natan Sharansky, *The Case for Democracy*. New York: Public Affairs, 2004; this is reported to have particularly impressed American president George W. Bush.

138. Thomas Knock, *To End All Wars: Woodrow Wilson and the quest for a new world order*. New York: Oxford University Press, 1992, pp. 26–8; and generally, Tony Smith, *America's Mission: The United States and worldwide struggle for democracy*

in the twentieth century. Princeton, NJ: Princeton University Press, 1994, Chapter 3.

139. Compare very similar to my views: Francis Fukuyama, *State Building: Governance and World Order in the 21st Century.* Ithaca, NY: Cornell University Press, 2004, pp. 38–9, 92–3.

140. Niall Ferguson, *Colossus: The price of America's Empire.* New York: Penguin, 2004.

141. Ibid., p. 24; for a similar line and a similar failure even to mention all the difficult questions, see Sebastian Mallaby, 'The reluctant imperialist: Terrorism, failed states, and the case for American empire', *Foreign Affairs*, 2002; **81**(2): 2–7.

142. John Stuart Mill, '*Considerations on Representative Government*', in *Utilitarianism, Liberty, and Representative Government.* New York: Dutton, 1951(1861), p. 486; cited in Donald Horowitz, *Ethnic Groups in Conflict.* Berkeley, CA: University of California, 1985, p. 681; Horowitz highlights the same problem; also, Walker Connor, *Ethnonationalism.* Princeton, NJ: Princeton University Press, 1994; Tatu Vanhansen, *Ethnic Conflicts Explained by Ethnic Nepotism.* Stamford, CT: JAI, 1999. For elaboration of the Wilsonian view that democracy and self-determination go together see again: Nodia, 'Nationalism and democracy'. For the weight of nationalism as a cause of war see Kalevi Holsti, *Peace and War: Armed conflicts and international order 1648–1989.* Cambridge: Cambridge University Press, 1991, pp. 309–16, especially 312.

Chapter 17. Conclusion: Unravelling the Riddle of War

1. It is perhaps not a coincidence that a book in the field of international relations that bears the title 'The War Puzzle' holds—according to the author, in Margaret Mead's footsteps—that war is a cultural invention: John Vasquez, *The War Puzzle.* New York: Cambridge University Press, 1993.

2. Compare Charles Tilly, 'War making and state making as organized crime', in P. Evans, D. Rueschemeyer, and T. Skocpol (eds), *Bringing the State Back In.* Cambridge: Cambridge University Press, 1985, pp. 169–91.

3. For a modern version, see Mancur Olson, *Power and Prosperity: Outgrowing communist and capitalist dictatorships.* New York: Basic Books, 2000.

4. Carl von Clausewitz, *On War*, Book 8, 6B. Princeton, NJ: Princeton University Press, 1976, p. 607; other formulations to that effect, see p. 606. One does not have to be a Marxist to agree with Lenin's criticism of this view; see Azar Gat, *The Origins of Military Thought from the Enlightenment to Clausewitz.* Oxford: Oxford University Press, 1989, pp. 236–50; id., *The Development of Military Thought: The nineteenth century.* Oxford: Oxford University Press, 1992, pp. 237–8; both are incorporated in Azar Gat, *A History of Military Thought:*

From the Enlightenment to the Cold War. Oxford: Oxford University Press, 2001, pp. 238–52, 505–6.

5. W. Thompson (ed.), *Evolutionary Interpretations of World Politics.* New York: Routledge, 2001; most of the contributors consider cultural evolution, but some also biological evolution; the latter is central to Bradley Thayer, *Darwin and International Relations: On the evolutionary origins of war and ethnic conflict.* Lexington: University of Kentucky, 2004. Stephen Rosen, *War and Human Nature.* Princeton, NJ: Princeton University Press, 2005, considers mainly decision-making in the light of brain research, biological science, and evolutionary psychology.

6. Hans Morgenthau, *Politics among Nations.* New York: Knopf, 1961.

7. Kenneth Waltz, *Theory of International Politics.* Reading, MA: Addison, 1979.

8. John Mearsheimer, *The Tragedy of Great Power Politics.* New York: Norton, 2001, especially pp. 2–3, 18–21, 53–4.

9. Morgenthau is famously ambivalent about the relationship between power and other aims of foreign policy, sometimes suggesting that power is a universal means for attaining the latter, but more often claiming that all other aims are largely a disguise for the quest for power. He discusses even resources as purely a means for power and not as coveted objects. See, especially, Morgenthau, *Politics among Nations,* pp. 4–5, 27–37, 113–16, and Chapters 5–8.

10. It is an indication of the obscurity of the causes of war as a subject of the discipline of international relations that the authors of two books so entitled do not seem to be aware that they barely deal with that subject at all, but rather are concerned with various conditions that make war a more likely option and increase the frequency of its occurrence; see Geoffrey Blainey, *The Causes of War.* New York: Free Press, 1973; Stephen van Evera, *Causes of War: Power and the roots of conflict.* Ithaca, NY: Cornell University Press, 1999. R. Rotberg and T. Rabb (eds), *The Origins and Prevention of Major Wars.* New York: Cambridge University Press, 1989, brings together historians and political scientists, revealing mainly perplexity. As Jack Levy has concluded (p. 210, also p. 295): 'a clear answer is yet to be found': 'The causes of war: A review of theories and evidence', in P. Tetlock et al. (eds), *Behavior, Society and Nuclear War,* Vol. 1. New York: Oxford University Press, 1989, pp. 209–333.

11. As recently pointed out by one of them: Randall Schweller, 'Bandwagoning for profit: Bringing the revisionist state back in', *International Security,* 1994; **19**(1): 72–107. Schweller rightly makes the otherwise obvious point that states go to war not merely for security reasons but also in order to achieve 'coveted values', because they see 'opportunity for gain', 'profit', 'rewards', or 'spoils'. He does not define what these profits might be, but his list of historical examples provides an ample illustration. He points out the 'status quo bias' in much of the recent international relations literature, wherein, indeed, major theorists

seem to believe that, *inherently*, no profit can be made from aggressive action in the international arena because of the balancing effect of the coalition that would form to oppose an expansionist state; for this latter view see: Waltz, *Theory of International Politics*, pp. 108–9, 137; implicitly in Stephen Walt, *The Origins of Alliances*. Ithaca, NY: Cornell University Press, 1987; and most strongly, Jack Snyder, *Myths of Empire*. Ithaca, NY: Cornell University Press, 1991. Such reasoning is based on a very narrow interpretation of mostly modern developments discussed in Chapters 15 and 16. Snyder's defensive bias has been criticized by: Fareed Zakaria, 'Realism and domestic politics', *International Security*, 1992; **17**(1): 177–98. Mearsheimer, *The Tragedy of Great Power Politics*, p. 20, recognizes that in Waltz's 'defensive realism' there are actually no reasons for war, but he fails to see that his own 'offensive structural realism' suffers from the very same problem. Similarly based on the 'security dilemma' alone, it does not even ask what the reasons are for the existence of this dilemma.

12. But again compare: Randall Schweller, 'Neorealism's status-quo bias: What security dilemma?', *Security Studies*, 1996; **5**(3): 90–121.

13. See Hidemi Sugnami, *On the Causes of War*. Oxford: Oxford University Press, 1996; this is an excellent work of analytical philosophy that dissects Waltz's *Theory of International Politics* and his earlier book: Kenneth Waltz, *Man, the State, and War*. New York: Columbia University Press, 1959. This, more or less, is also the message in: Barry Buzan, Charles Jones, and Richard Little, *The Logic of Anarchy*. New York: Columbia University Press, 1993. Declaring his approach systemic rather than reductionist, Waltz (*Theory of International Politics*) and other so-called structural realists in effect miss the deep structural interconnections that integrate reality as an interacting whole, wherein units and system are *mutually* affected and affecting.

14. Thayer, *Darwin and International Relations*, pp. 178–9. In this he makes an error similar to Napoleon Chagnon's suggestion that 'primitive war' is caused by both material and evolutionary reasons; see Chapter 4, endnote 8 and related text.

15. For the rationality of the instincts, see Aaron Ben-Zéev, *The Subtlety of Emotions*. Cambridge, MA: MIT Press, 2000, Chapter 6; however, it insufficiently incorporates evolution.

16. See endnote 55 in Chapter 16.

17. Compare George Modelski, 'Evolutionary world politics', in Thompson, *Evolutionary Interpretations of World Politics*, p. 22; Jennifer Sterling-Folker, 'Evolutionary tendencies in realist and liberal IR theory', ibid., Chapter 4.

Index

Index

Index

Egypt (*cont.*)
480, 507; modern 551–3, 654, 782;
also see Hellenistic states
Einstein, Albert 36, 37, 72
empires, *see* imperialism
Engels, Friedrich 177, 179, 216, 250
England, *see* Britain
Epaminondas 318, 575–6
epidemic diseases 16–17, 17–18, 53,
178, 482–3, 640
Eskimos 50, 51, 74; Alaskan 15, 31,
71–2, 73, 94, 119–20; Canadian 15,
62, 71, 130; in Greenland 15, 19
ethnocentrism and nationalism 48,
50–1, 135–6, 322, 403, 428–31,
451–6, 496–503, 539–42, 572, 583,
659–60
Etruscans 216, 249, 303, 307
evolution and evolutionary theory: this
is central to chapters 3–8; and
pages 4, 422–5, 663–4, 667–73; *see
also* motivation for and causes of
war; culture vs nature, cultural
evolution
Europe, prehistoric warfare (Neolithic,
Bronze Age, and Iron Age) 167,
173–4, 225–6; *see also* Celts;
Germans
European unification and European
Union 518, 523, 586, 649, 651–2

Ferguson, Adam 116, 149, 179, 447
Ferguson, Niall 654–5
Ferguson, R. Brian 34, 59, 69, 72
feudalism 330–51, 455–6
Flanders, city communes in 292, 293,
294, 295, 302, 305, 312, 314
forms of fighting and military
organization: pre-state 114–29,
183–8; transformation under the
state 284–6, 288–9, 300, 319,
361–9, 407–8, 412; on the steppe
378–9, 385, 386–7, 390; differences

between east and west 395–400;
early modern 458; French
revolutionary 502; liberal strategic
policy 609–18; *see also* city-states;
fortifications and siege-craft;
feudalism; horse; logistics;
mobilization rates; 'military
revolution'; mechanized warfare;
guerilla; terror
fortifications and siege-craft 34, 167,
168–75, 195, 225–6, 227–8,
278–89; early-modern vs
pre-modern 459–71
Foucault, Michel 603
France: medieval 333, 335, 336, 338–40,
352, 357, 362, 455, 458, 465;
early modern 455–6, 457, 459–60,
466, 473–4, 485, 488–9, 493–4,
495, 499, 580; Revolutionary
458, 502–3, 653; modern 516–22,
541, 552, 553, 563; and liberal
democratic conduct in war
578–9, 626, 629, 631; *see also*
Franks; Gaul
Franklin, Benjamin 502
Franks 177, 178–9, 217, 245–6, 340
Frederick Barbarossa, German emperor
292, 312
Frederick II, the Great, king of Prussia
475
Freud, Sigmund 36–7, 48, 56, 142, 603
Friedman, Thomas 598, 644
Fuller, J. F. C. 530, 534, 639

Gandhi, 'mahatma' 634
Gaul 178, 211–13, 217, 240–1, 246, 274,
466, 474
gender, *see* culture vs nature; motivation
for and causes of war
geography, ecology, and demography,
effects of: on simple hunter–
gatherers 14–19; on complex
hunter–gatherers 25–6, 31–3; and

Index

Index

Index

Index

Picture Credits

Pages 20–1: B. Spencer and F. Gillen, *Across Australia*, London: Macmillan, 1912

Pages 27–9: J. Maringer and H.-G. Bandi, *Art in the Ice Age*, New York: Praeger, 1953; permission by Greenwood Publishing Group

Pages 122–3: Napoleon Chagnon, *Yanomamo*, 5th edn., New York: Harcourt College Publishers, 1997; permission by Thomson Learning

Pages 125–6: R. Gardner and K. Heider, *Gardens of War*, New York: Random House, 1968; permission by R. Gardner

Page 169: Werner Forman Archive

Page 170: James Mellaart, *The Neolithic of the Near East*; courtesy of Thames & Hudson Ltd, London

Page 171: by permission of the Council for British Research in the Levant, London

Pages 221 and 353: The Oriental Institute Museum, Chicago

Page 226: courtesy of Anthony Harding

Page 227: Dae Sasitorn/www.lastrefuge.co.uk

Pages 252 and 253: Egyptian Museum, Cairo

Page 261: by permission of the Syndics of Cambridge University Library

Page 263: The New Prehistoric Museum, Thera

Page 271: 2006 Harvard University, Peabody Museum 45–5-20/15062 T836

Page 280: courtesy of Graham Connah

Page 283: courtesy of Diego Serebrisky

Page 284: courtesy of Kenneth Hirth

Page 287: courtesy of David Wilson

Page 291: Hirmer Verlag

Page 292: Museo d'Arte Antica, castello Sforzesco, Milan

Page 294: Louvre

Page 295: The Chapel of SS John and Paul at Ghent; courtesy of the City Archives, Ghent

Page 296: Diebold Schilling, *Amtliche Chronik*; Burgerbibliothek Bern, Mss.h.h.I.3, p. 757

Page 297: École Française d'Athènes

Page 327: Copyright of The Trustees of the British Museum.

Page 340: Leiden, University Library, ms. PER F.17, f. 22r.

Page 349: Topkapi Museum, Istanbul, ms H.1524, p. 278A; Sonia Halliday

Pages 354, 381 and 397: Drawings by A. Layard, *Monument of Nineveh*, London: 1849 and 1853

Page 355: Robert Harding Picture Library

Page 460: courtesy of the Needham Institute

Picture Credits

Page 461: The Royal Armories, Tower of London

Page 462: Diebold Schilling, *Amtliche Chronik*, Burgerbibliothek Bern, Mss.h.h.I.3, p. 420

Page 463: courtesy of Simon Pepper

Page 468: Aviodrome Luchtfotografie

Page 470: The National Maritime Museum, Greenwich

Page 478: from *Thai Tsu Shih Lu Thu* (Ming +1635, revised in Chhing +1781), no. 3; by permission of the Syndics of Cambridge University Library

Page 479: The Tokugawa Art Museum

Page 483: The Pepys Library, Magdalene College, Cambridge

Page 529: courtesy of the Imperial War Museum, London: Q22375

Page 531: Musée Condé, Chantilly

Page 533: courtesy of the Imperial War Museum, London: Q10711

Page 566: The Library of Congress

Page 568: courtesy of the Imperial War Museum, London: EA32615

Page 625: from *Black and White War Album*, London 1898; courtesy of Anne S. K. Brown Military Collection, Brown University Library

Page 632: from the film La Battaglia de Algeri; the Kobal Collection

Page 638: Corbis

Page 643: courtesy of the Imperial War Museum, London: MH 6810.